# UNDERSTANDING PLAYS

*Second Edition*

❦

## Milly S. Barranger

The University of North Carolina
Chapel Hill

← I think
he has
ADD

**Allyn and Bacon**

Boston  London  Toronto  Sydney  Tokyo  Singapore

*Senior Series Editor:* Steve Hull
*Editorial Assistant:* Brenda Conaway
*Manufacturing Buyer:* Megan Cochran
*Cover Administrator:* Linda Dickinson
*Editorial-Production Service:* Colophon Production Service
*Text Design Modification:* LeGwin Associates

Copyright © 1994, 1990 by Allyn and Bacon
A Division of Simon & Schuster, Inc.
160 Gould Street
Needham Heights, Massachusetts 02194

**Library of Congress Cataloging-in-Publication Data**
Barranger, Milly S.
   Understanding plays / Milly S. Barranger. — 2nd ed.
     p.   cm.
   Includes bibliographical references and index.
   ISBN 0-205-15096-9
   1. Drama—History and criticism. I. Title.
PN1721.B37  1993
808.2—dc20
                                  93-36946
                                      CIP

Printed in the United States of America
10  9  8  7  6  5  4  3  2       98  97  96  95  94

*Part opening illustration by Alexander Farquharson.*

**CREDITS**

**The Plays**

*Credits continued on page 757, which constitutes an extension of the copyright page.*

For Heather, Lincoln, and Maggy

# Contents

❦

# Preface

Understanding the "literary" or "verbal" text of a play is the subject of this book. The book proceeds from the idea that *drama* is a special form with methods and characteristics of its own, unlike those found in poetry, fiction, and film. Drama is not literary history, biography, or a history of ideas. It is a unique form of writing for the theatre and is approached here as the playwright's literary text, having the potential for being performed by actors in the theatre. Approaches to play analysis, or to understanding drama, include Aristotle's vocabulary and perspectives found in *The Poetics*: plot, action, character, language, visual effects, and types of plays (or genres). Upon this foundation, modern approaches to understanding new types of dramatic writing and distinctly contemporary views of the world are introduced and explored in relation to dramatic texts written in our time.

This book is organized to discuss methods of play analysis with examples from seventeen principal plays written for the western theatre, ranging from the Greeks to the moderns. The book is divided into four parts with seventeen chapters. The introductory chapter deals with the distinctions between the dramatic text and the theatrical performance, and uses Sam Shepard's Pulitzer-prize-winning play from the 1970s, *Buried Child*, to provide the initial springboard into understanding plays.

Part Two, entitled "Types of Drama," addresses major types of dramatic writing, including tragedy, comedy, farce, tragicomedy, the well-made play, and such modern variations as absurdist plays, postmodernist fragments, and intercultural texts. Methods and approaches to understanding play structure, character, language, and scenography complete the essential list of playwriting techniques explored in ancient to modern texts in Part Three.

Part Four introduces modern writing styles and is based on the premise that most modern plays have their roots in realistic writing and performance styles, or in a reaction against them. The chapters on realism and realistic drama trace this writing tradition from Henrik Ibsen's *Hedda Gabler*, written in 1890, to August Wilson's *Fences*, produced in 1987. Recent writing styles that have influenced the contemporary American theatre, in particular, are represented in this book as theatricalism (expressionism and epic theatre), minimalism (absurdist plays), and eclecticism (feminist writing). The final chapters explore the intellectual background and dramatic writing labeled by today's critics as "postmodernism" and "interculturalism."

Each chapter includes one or more representative plays in support of the critical tools and methods under discussion. The representative play is prefaced by a brief biography of the playwright and an introduction. The introductions are intended to be only brief commentaries on the plays, highlighting the major characteristics and meanings of the texts themselves. While these introductions offer an approach to understanding selected plays, they are not intended to be prescriptive or comprehensive. Their purpose is to raise central questions with regard to playwriting in general and to dramaturgical techniques in particular. Each chapter summary is designed to reflect on the original subject and content of the chapter and to establish bridges into successive chapters.

If instructors want to change the order of the chapters, they will find that they can readily so do, although a representative play in a previous chapter serves as a reference point for later discussions of structure, character, language, and so forth. The book is designed in this way since many students have read few plays. Therefore, once a play, such as *Hamlet*, is established as a point of discussion, it becomes a convenient reference point for succeeding discussions. This design limits the number of plays provided for reading, while multiplying the opportunities for discussion.

Written for a basic course, this book *introduces* students to drama's characteristics, to principal types of writing for the theatre over the centuries, and to a critical vocabulary common to play analysis from Aristotle to Bertolt Brecht and others. Since many students are reading plays for the first time and discovering the similarities and differences among dramatic texts written over 2500 years ago, I have limited the number of complete play texts included here to seventeen: *Buried Child, Oedipus the King, The School for Scandal, Hamlet, Fen, The Colored Museum, The Little Foxes, The Glass Menagerie, The Cherry Orchard, On The Verge or The Geography of Yearning, Hedda Gabler, Fences, Galileo, Footfalls, The Conduct of Life, Hamletmachine,* and *Broken Eggs*. In special ways, the seventeen playwrights represented here have shifted the boundaries of writing for the western theatre and have influenced other play-

wrights as well. The playwrights are Sam Shepard, Sophocles, Richard Brinsley Sheridan, William Shakespeare, George C. Wolfe, Caryl Churchill, Lillian Hellman, Tennessee Williams, Anton Chekhov, Eric Overmyer, Henrik Ibsen, August Wilson, Bertolt Brecht, Samuel Beckett, Maria Irene Fornes, Heiner Müller, and Eduardo Machado.

Finally, while this book attempts to provide comprehensive tools for understanding the drama's characteristics, the playwrights' methods, and the critics' terms, it is neither a definitive treatment of dramatic literature nor a survey of drama's history through the ages. Rather, it is an attempt to put students in touch with their western heritage of writing for the theatre and with major plays and dramaturgical methods from the Greeks to the moderns. It is my hope, then, that students will go on to discover the rich heritage of non-western theatre and its correspondences to western writing and performance styles.

My thanks to my colleagues for their encouragement and assistance in the preparation of this revised edition of *Understanding Plays*. Those who advised and assisted on the manuscript at various stages were Gayle Austin, Georgia State University; Adam Versenyi and Anthony Fichera, University of North Carolina at Chapel Hill; William G. Biddy, Mississippi University for Women; J. Paul Marcoux, Boston College; Joy Reilly, Ohio State University; Roger Schultz, Texas A&M University; Ed Shockley, Temple University; and Joseph Whited, Kent State University. My special appreciation goes to Phyllis Ryan and Betty Futrell for their guidance in the completion of this book, and also to Annette Uhlenberg and Constance Zaytoun for their efforts.

*Milly S. Barranger*
The University of North Carolina
Chapel Hill

# PART ONE

# INTRODUCTION

# CHAPTER 1

# From Text to Performance

A scene from Arena Stage's production of *Buried Child*, directed by Gilbert Moses, with Stanley Anderson as Dodge and Kevin Tighe as Tilden. (*Photo by Joan Marcus, courtesy of Arena Stage*, Washington, D.C.)

*The manuscript, the words on the page, was what you started with and what you have left. The production is of great importance, has given the play the life it will know, but it is gone, in the end, and the pages are the only wall against which to throw the future or measure the past.*

—Lillian Hellman[1]

## DRAMA AND PERFORMANCE

We are bombarded daily with television, videos, newsprint, films, and dramatic events. Terrorists threaten the lives of airline passengers, battles are fought in faraway places, nations negotiate peace treaties, nuclear accidents threaten lives, and a famous boxer divorces his glamorous actress-wife. All are subjects for novels, films, miniseries, and plays. The larger subject is human experience (real or imagined), but the means of representing experience in artistic forms differ with the artist and with the medium. A play, or the dramatic text, is one of the theatre's principal media. It is at once a text to be read and a script to be performed.

Plays are read daily by individuals as diverse as stage directors, designers, actors, technicians, teachers, students, critics, scholars, and the general public. In contrast to novels and poetry, a play is often the most difficult type of prose or poetry to read because it is written not only to be read, but also to be performed by actors before audiences. Like a screenplay, a play is also given life by actors although the medium and technology are significantly different. Kevin Kline acts Shakespeare's Hamlet or Derek Jacobi performs Richard II on a stage before audiences for the time of the performance. In contrast, their film performances in *The Big Chill* and *I, Claudius*, respectively, are contained, unchanging, on videotape for all time.

Reading plays is a unique challenge. As readers, we must visualize all of the elements the playwright has placed on the page to convey a story to us: its characters in action and conflict, its happening in time and space, and, at the end, the completed meaning of all that has happened.

Plays have been formally analyzed since the days of classical Greece. Aristotle's *Poetics* (c. 330 B.C.) is our first record of a critical assessment of plays presented in the ancient Greek festivals. Since Aristotle, there have been many approaches to "understanding" plays. For our purposes, we will approach the analysis of plays from the viewpoint and techniques of the playwright who creates the dramatic text. As Lillian Hellman said, the words on the page are the playwright's measure, after all is said and done, of the future and the past: "The manuscript, the words on the page, was what you started with and what you have left."[2]

Although we call the playwright's words on the printed page "drama," we also use the words "drama" and "dramatic" to describe many events ranging from riots to parades, from sports events to political speeches. That these current events are "real" rather than "fiction" is the essential distinction between life's "dramas" and dramatic "texts." Martin Esslin wrote that "a dramatic text, unperformed, is literature."[3] Like a novel or poem, drama, as written words, is considered a literary text. The chief ingredient that distinguishes drama from other types of literature is, precisely, its potential for being performed or enacted. The very origin of the word "drama" implies its potential for becoming a performable script. We use the words "text" or "script" to describe this written form that becomes the basis for theatrical performance.

Drama comes from the Greek *dran*, meaning "to do" or "to act." Since the word is rooted in "doing" or "enacting," we have come to understand drama as a special way of imitating human behavior and human events. Drama is like narrative in that it tells a story; but unlike narrative, or story telling, it requires enactment before an audience. The story's events must be represented in drama, not merely told or narrated as in epic poetry. The word *"theatre"* has its roots in the Greek word, *theatron,* meaning "a place for seeing," or that special place where actors and audiences come together to experience a performance of the playwright's raw materials—the drama. The dramatic text is not wholly realized until the theatre's artists complete for audiences what the playwright began. As Hamlet, Kenneth Branaugh must breathe life into Shakespeare's character for the text to come alive in the imagined world of Elsinore Castle.

All dramatic texts are constructs. They have in common the fact that they set forth events taking place in an imagined or fictional world, whether it be ancient Thebes or contemporary Manhattan. The dramatic text is the playwright's blueprint for setting forth physical and psychological experience—to give shape and meaning to the world as the playwright sees and understands it. Over the centuries, these blueprints have related a variety of stories not as narrations, but as imitations of imaginary actions. Sophocles wrote of a king confronted by a plague-ridden kingdom (*Oedipus the King*), Sam Shepard depicted American midwesterners confronting their lost connections with the land and with one another (*Buried Child*), and Samuel Beckett presented worlds in which human beings "wait out" lifetimes (*Footfalls*).

Drama, then, is a special written way of imitating human experience. It is both a literary and a performance text. The fictional character, Hamlet, is played by the living actor Kevin Kline. It is our purpose here to learn to *read* plays, to understand the how and why of the dramatic text, without ignoring the fact that the playwright's words have the potential to be performed in the theatre. We must learn to analyze the pattern of words and conventions that have the potential for "becoming" living words and actions. The playwright provides us with dialogue—words arranged in a meaningful sequence—intended to be spoken aloud and enacted by actors before audiences. Often the playwright includes descriptions of scenes, characters, and activities in stage directions and dialogue. However, the actor remains the playwright's essential intermediary in that complex relationship between the drama and the performance.

## DRAMATURGY

In its original Greek meaning, a *dramaturg* was simply a playwright. The word "dramaturgy" defines the playwright's craft. It involves the elements, conventions, and techniques the playwright uses to delineate general and particular truths about the human condition. Those elements involve plot, action, character, meaning, language, spectacle, space, and time. We must develop skills for understanding a writer's dramaturgical skills, which deal with plot, character, language, and so forth, so that we can read plays from all periods of theatrical, cultural, and social history. Styles, conventions, language, and techniques differ among playwrights depending on the physical theatre, the writing conventions of the historical period, and the society or universe mirrored in the writer's work. Also applicable are the ever-changing cultural, social, and technological conditions under which plays have been written, produced, and performed in western society for 2500 years.

## DRAMATIC SPACE

Drama is unique among the arts in that it imitates reality through representation rather than narration. The playwright creates a fictional universe with human beings, familiar objects, and recognizable environments. Beckett's characters' feet hurt; August Wilson's hero idolizes his baseball bat; Shepard's Dodge lives out his last days on a frayed green sofa surrounded by pills and whiskey bottles. Like Beckett, Wilson, and Shepard, playwrights use "real" human beings in particular spaces and times to create the illusion of fictional worlds in which recognizable events take place in time and space. We distinguish between the *performance space* (the stage) and the *dramatic space* (the playwright's fictional locale). Dramatic space—or the play's environment—is usually described in dialogue or in stage directions found in modern texts. What is exhibited in the performance space is an interpretation, or staging, of the play's physical requirements set forth in those directions.

Dramatic space has essentially two characteristics. First, it is a "fictional" space—the characters' environment—described by playwrights in dialogue and stage directions. The fictional space may be the palace of Thebes (*Oedipus the King*), an eighteenth-century drawing room (*The School for Scandal*), or the neglected living room of a modern midwestern family (*Buried Child*). The fictional space may encompass simultaneously more than one space, such as palaces and battlefields or apartments and streets. Shakespeare's plays require locations that are miles apart, but the characters must appear in those locales within seconds. Hamlet moves from battlements, to chambers, to graveyards. Dramatic space is magical in its ability to present several locales simultaneously. Bertolt Brecht's Galileo travels many miles and journeys to many cities in his pursuit of truth and reason.

Second, dramatic space always assumes the presence of a stage and an audience and a relationship between the two. As we read plays, we are aware that they are written to be performed. While the stage where a play is produced may be almost any type—proscenium, arena, thrust, environmental—the characters may or may not be aware of the audience. In modern realistic plays, the characters are not aware that an audience is present. The pretense, or stage convention, is that a "fourth wall" exists through which the actors-as-characters cannot see, although audiences can. No character in Henrik lbsen's *Hedda Gabler* ever acknowledges the audience. In other plays, characters directly address the audience, establishing an invisible flow of space between actor and audience. Sheridan's *The School for Scandal* has many asides where characters speak directly to the audience to comment briefly on some situation. As readers, we need to be sensitive to the "look" of the characters' environment and to the intended relationship of the dramatic space to the audience.

## DRAMATIC TIME

Dramatic time is a phenomenon of the text. Jan Kott wrote that "theatre is a place where time is always present."[4] Once begun, the time of a performance is one-directional. It follows a linear path for the two or more hours of its duration. Dramatic time, in contrast to performance time, is free of such constraints.

Within the fictional world of the play, time can be expanded or compressed. Unlike the film editor's manipulation of images in films, the playwright does not have the advantage of editing and splicing film to carry us forward or backward in time. Rather, dramatic time can be accelerated by using gaps of days, months, and even years; or, it can be slowed down by using soliloquies and flashbacks. Whereas real or performance time moves in one direction (present to future) and the past can never be recaptured, dramatic time can violate the relentless forward motion of performance time measured by the clock. For example, events may be shown out of their chronological sequence, or they may be foreshortened so they occur more swiftly than they would in nature. Shakespeare's battles, requiring only a few minutes of swordplay on stage, would ordinarily require days or even months in real time. In Samuel Beckett's plays, characters experience the relentless passage of time because there are no major events or crises. An unchanging sameness characterizes their lives. In Samuel Beckett's *Waiting for Godot*, Vladimir and Estragon wait for Godot's arrival which is always postponed by the messenger's announcement that "Mr. Godot told me to tell you he won't come this evening but surely tomorrow." In Beckett's plays the experience of dramatic time is cyclical—day becomes night and night becomes day— while his characters wait out their uneventful lives in patterns that are repetitive and are experienced as "waiting." In his plays, nothing happens in the traditional sense, but time erodes lives in a relentless journey toward death.

Time and space in the fictional universe of drama are highly malleable and unlike the actual time we experience in our daily lives. Consideration of dramatic time and space has always played a large part in the different theories and rules of drama. In his *Poetics*, Aristotle briefly suggested that the amount of time it takes the actors to tell the story should ideally be concurrent with the actual time it takes to perform the play. This attention to a *unity of time*, as it was later called, is still found in modern realistic plays. However, in the many words written about drama over the centuries, the most attention has been given to the playwright's meanings and messages.

## DRAMA'S MEANINGS AND MESSAGES

The reader's greatest temptation is to concentrate on the general meaning of the literary work—the novel, poem, or play—overlooking the fact that meaning is generated as the work is experienced. A play's complete meaning does not emerge in the early pages of a text or in the first moments of a performance, but quite often the seeds of the message can be found there. Shepard's statement about the decay of American family values is evident in the first moments of *Buried Child*.

In creating the dramatic text, the playwright connects the reader (and audiences) with a common humanity through the progression of the play's events. Great plays confront us with life's verities, conveying the hope, courage, despair, compassion, violence, love, hate, exploitation, and generosity experienced by all humankind. They show us the possibilities of losing our families and property through accidents, catastrophes of war, or tyranny. Plays show us ways of fulfilling ourselves in relationships or confronting despair and death. August Wilson's characters struggle to show love and affection to one another. The most enduring plays explore what it means to be human beings in special circumstances. These circumstances may be unfamiliar, like the prince dispossessed of his rightful heritage through murder, marriage, and calumny (*Hamlet*); or bizarre, like the family that has literally buried its family skeleton in the back yard (*Buried Child*); or familiar, like the ambitions of a mother for her children (*The Glass Menagerie*).

Drama's most enduring achievements, like the representative plays contained in this book, serve as reflections of ourselves, or what potentially could be ourselves in different times and circumstances. Drama's best moments lead us to discoveries and reflections about our personalities, circumstances, desires, anxieties, hopes, and dreams. Playwrights also move beyond personal concerns to discuss social and political issues that are of a certain time, yet transcend specific historical periods. Playwrights stimulate social awareness and put us in touch with our thoughts and feelings about issues. The aim of great playwrights is to expand our consciousness on old and new social and personal issues, and to endow us with *new perspectives* on our humanity and the human condition.

Plays are written as a process of unfolding and discovery. To read plays successfully is to understand essentially "how" the playwright generates meaning. Scene follows scene in meaningful patterns; dialogue communicates feelings and ideas; characters display motives and emotions; locales give social and economic contexts. "What" a play means involves the completed action, that is, all that has gone before in organized, meaningful segments that, when taken in their totality, express the writer's vision or conviction about the world. As readers, we share that unfolding—those discoveries—with audiences. We also learn to experience the developing actions, events, and relationships which, in turn, produce a coherent statement about individuals, societies, and the universe. We learn to follow the playwright's ways and means of organizing the dramatic material into a coherent whole and to discover the writer's methods for developing the psychological and physical currents of human endeavor that result in visible (and meaningful) behavior.

The same process is at work in our personal experiences. In our daily lives, we are not instantly aware that some actions have repercussions far beyond our expectations. As we begin a trip, we cannot know the full extent of our experiences. With time, we come to understand the meaning of our experiences, feelings, and actions, as well as the motives and actions of others. In some instances, meanings are elusive—sometimes impossible to pin down. The same is true in understanding the how and the why of the dramatic text. When Tom Wingfield brings the "gentleman caller" to dine with his sister Laura in Tennessee Williams' *The Glass Menagerie*, he is not aware, nor are we as readers and audiences, of the psychological damage he is imposing on Laura's fragile emotional life.

All art condenses, clarifies, and orders the chaos, disorder, and inconsequential happenings of life. The poet William Wordsworth gives shape to girlhood innocence in his "Lucy Gray" poems. Tennessee Williams organizes Tom Wingfield's memories of his chaotic and unhappy life in his mother's home. However, great plays confront life's complexities in such a way that they cannot be reduced to a single meaning. Since there is usually no author's voice in drama, as there is in the novel where the writer can speak directly to the reader, we are left with layers of possible meaning based on the play's events. We can usually agree that Hamlet was given the task of avenging his father's murder, that he hesitated and ultimately achieved his objective at the cost of his life. What remains open to interpretation is the ultimate meaning or significance of the play—"what it was all about." For that reason, we can read and see *Hamlet* any number of times and continue to discover new meanings in this complex text. We want to learn to identify *how* playwrights order, clarify, and distill their imitations of real life in the dramatic text and what higher meanings emerge from these efforts.

Sam Shepard's Pulitzer-Prize-winning *Buried Child* (1978) is an interesting contemporary play with which to begin our process of understanding plays. Along with a post-Vietnam wave of American writers that includes David Mamet, Marsha Norman, Lanford Wilson, August Wilson, and many others, Shepard takes us into the inner workings of modern American family life which are both commonplace and bizarre. He writes about characters searching out their family histories in an effort to explain who they are and how they came to be that way. Similar to *Oedipus the King* and *Hamlet*, the central action of *Buried Child* is the individual's quest for roots and identity. Shepard's means of organizing and unfolding a family's history provide our initial introduction to play analysis. Let us begin this journey into the process of understanding plays with *Buried Child*.

# Buried Child

## SAM SHEPARD

*Sam Shepard (1943– ) was born in the Midwest, grew up in California, and began his theatrical career as a bit actor. Since 1964, he has been part of avant garde theatre in New York and London, exploring modern American myths and culture in such diverse plays as* Tooth of Crime *(1972) and* Buried Child *(1978). Recipient of the* Village Voice Off Off Broadway *(Obie) Award for distinguished playwriting on eight separate occasions, Shepard was awarded the 1979 Pulitzer Prize for* Buried Child. *Among his well-known plays are* Cowboys *(1964),* Chicago *(1965),* Red Cross *and* La Turista *(1967),* Operation Sidewinder *(1970),* The Tooth of Crime *(1972),* Angel City *and* Curse of the Starving Class *(1976),* True West *(1980),* Fool for Love *(1982),* A Lie of the Mind *(1986), and* States of Shock *(1991). Shepard has also acted in such films as* Days of Heaven, The Right Stuff, Crimes of the Heart, Steel Magnolias, Thunderhart, *and* Voyager. *He wrote the screenplay* Far North *(1988) and won the 1984 Cannes Film Festival award for best film with* Paris, Texas.

## INTRODUCTION

Written in three acts for a small proscenium stage and originally produced at the Magic Theatre in San Francisco, *Buried Child* takes place in the midwestern living room of Dodge and Halie's rural home. Shepard observes a unity of space, time, and action. The physical appearance of the single interior is set down in lengthy stage directions that describe the frayed carpet, worn green sofa, medicine bottles, faded lampshades, and an imageless and soundless television set. The opening scene contains visual clues as to the decay of personal and familial values: the neglected room, the ill father, and the "invisible" family.

The family is made up of Dodge, the dying father; Halie, the adulterous mother; two sons—Tilden, a functional illiterate, and Bradley, an amputee; and the grandson, Vincent (Tilden's son), who returns to his childhood home with his girlfriend, Shelly.

The play's central action is Vincent's *quest* for his roots (and identity). The grandson returns to his family and discovers who he is, along with the family's buried secrets, in the play's harrowing climax. What Vincent discovers about his origins are bigotry (one son, Ansel—Vincent's uncle—married into "the Catholics" and was murdered in a gangland-style killing), adultery (his grandmother's affair with the "Protestant" minister), absence of the work ethic (Dodge's farm hasn't been worked by father or sons for thirty years), incest and child murder (a baby's corpse, another male child, is secretly buried in the field behind the house).

Shepard's play is structured on the gradual revelation of the family's terrible secret. For years, they have been engaged in covering up murder and incest. The revelations of the secret crimes cleanse the spiritual life of the family. At the moment of Dodge's confession of murder followed by his quiet death of natural causes, the family's guilt is exorcised. Halie can "see" what was not visible to her before—the abundance of vegetables growing in the mysterious field behind the house. In the play's beginning, only Tilden can see and literally gather the abundant crops because he acknowledges the family's terrible history. At the end, he unearths the child's corpse and carries the skeleton upstairs to Halie's bedroom where, presumably, it was conceived. This fantastic field is Shepard's unique symbol for the family's survival once the bitter hidden truths are unearthed and confronted. Other playwrights have used various dramaturgical signs and symbols, such as a plague-ridden city, a cherry orchard, fences, and wars, to demonstrate changing spiritual and ethical values within individuals and societies.

Sam Shepard's scene in *Buried Child* is one of illness, incest, adultery, personal violation, and spiritual emptiness. Shepard "imitates" these realities by showing the absence of the normal touchstones of love, family, and fidelity. The unexpected appearance of the grandson unlocks the long-buried secrets and lost dreams. Before Vince's arrival, the family was bound together in a situation rife with betrayal, murder, violence, and guilt. Shepard reinforces ceremonially the fact that Dodge, the patriarch, is a mere shadow, or husk, of his former self. Tilden brings on stage an armful of unshucked corn from the mysterious field. He shucks the corn and spreads the husks across his father's sleeping body. The symbolism is vivid and literal. Dodge is a husk of his former self divested by age, sickness, and guilt of his potency and humanity. His illness is at once physical and spiritual.

Shepard's vision of America's myths and rituals, of family love and ethical values, is sharply projected in the action of *Buried Child*. Shepard's midwesterners of the 1970s are out of touch with the soil, once the quintessential sign of America's work ethic and psychic and spiritual vitality. The American dreams of familial love and individual success achieved by hard work have been replaced by realities of disease, loss, betrayal, violence, murder, and death. All of these conditions are contained in the play's events and actions. Nevertheless, Shepard admits the possibility of reviving those lost dreams and values symbolized by the abundance of vegetables at the play's end. These life-sustaining crops arise mystically from the soil where the buried child of the play's title is both sign and symbol of the decay of the modern American family. As the crime is literally unearthed from the soil where it has been concealed for years, the family is likewise released from the guilt that resulted in further betrayal and violence. At this point, Shepard's dramaturgy, including scene, action, message, metaphors, and play title, becomes clear: The grandson's search for his roots unearths a terrible crime that has affected the family's character, ethics, and relationships for many years. His discovery, in turn, changes their lives.

# Buried Child

*While the rain of your fingertips falls,*
*while the rain of your bones falls,*
*and your laughter and marrow fall down,*
*you come flying.*

—Pablo Neruda

## CHARACTERS

**DODGE**   In his seventies.
**HALIE**   His wife. Mid-sixties.
**TILDEN**   Their oldest son.
**BRADLEY**   Their next oldest son, an amputee.
**VINCE**   Tilden's son.
**SHELLY**   Vince's girlfriend.
**FATHER DEWIS**   A Protestant minister.

# ACT 1

## SCENE

*Day. Old wooden staircase down left with pale, frayed carpet laid down on the steps. The stairs lead off stage left up into the wings with no landing. Up right is an old, dark green sofa with the stuffing coming out in spots. Stage right of the sofa is an upright lamp with a faded yellow shade and a small night table with several small bottles of pills on it. Down right of the sofa, with the screen facing the sofa, is a large, old-fashioned brown T.V. A flickering blue light comes from the screen, but no image, no sound. In the dark, the light of the lamp and the T.V. slowly brighten in the black space. The space behind the sofa, upstage, is a large, screened-in porch with a board floor. A solid interior door to stage right of the sofa, leading into the room on stage; and another screen door up left, leading from the porch to the outside. Beyond that are the shapes of dark elm trees.*

*Gradually the form of* **DODGE** *is made out, sitting on the couch, facing the T.V., the blue light flickering on his face. He wears a well-worn T-shirt, suspenders, khaki work pants and brown slippers. He's covered himself in an old brown blanket. He's very thin and sickly looking, in his late seventies. He just stares at the*

*T.V. More light fills the stage softly. The sound of light rain.* **DODGE** *slowly tilts his head back and stares at the ceiling for a while, listening to the rain. He lowers his head again and stares at the T.V. He turns his head slowly to the left and stares at the cushion of the sofa next to the one he's sitting on. He pulls his left arm out from under the blanket, slides his hand under the cushion, and pulls out a bottle of whiskey. He looks down left toward the staircase, listens, then uncaps the bottle, takes a long swig and caps it again. He puts the bottle back under the cushion and stares at the T.V. He starts to cough slowly and softly. The coughing gradually builds. He holds one hand to his mouth and tries to stifle it. The coughing gets louder, then suddenly stops when he hears the sound of his wife's voice coming from the top of the staircase.*

**HALIE'S VOICE:**  Dodge?
   **DODGE** *just stares at the T.V. Long pause. He stifles two short coughs.*
**HALIE'S VOICE:**  Dodge! You want a pill, Dodge?
   *He doesn't answer. Takes the bottle out again and takes another long swig. Puts the bottle back, stares at T.V., pulls blanket up around his neck.*
**HALIE'S VOICE:**  You know what it is, don't you? It's the rain! Weather. That's it. Every time. Every time you get like this, it's the rain. No sooner does the rain start then you start. *(pause)* Dodge?
   *He makes no reply. Pulls a pack of cigarettes out from his sweater and lights one. Stares at T.V. Pause.*

HALIE'S VOICE: You should see it coming down up here. Just coming down in sheets. Blue sheets. The bridge is pretty near flooded. What's it like down there? Dodge?

DODGE *turns his head back over his left shoulder and takes a look out through the porch. He turns back to the T.V.*

DODGE: (*to himself*) Catastrophic.

HALIE'S VOICE: What? What'd you say, Dodge?

DODGE: (*louder*) It looks like rain to me! Plain old rain!

HALIE'S VOICE: Rain? Of course it's rain! Are you having a seizure or something! Dodge? (*pause*) I'm coming down there in about five minutes if you don't answer me!

DODGE: Don't come down.

HALIE'S VOICE: What!

DODGE: (*louder*) Don't come down!

*He has another coughing attack. Stops.*

HALIE'S VOICE: You should take a pill for that! I don't see why you just don't take a pill. Be done with it once and for all. Put a stop to it.

*He takes bottle out again. Another swig. Returns bottle.*

HALIE'S VOICE: It's not Christian, but it works. It's not necessarily Christian, that is. We don't know. There's some things the ministers can't even answer. I, personally, can't see anything wrong with it. Pain is pain. Pure and simple. Suffering is a different matter. That's entirely different. A pill seems as good an answer as any. Dodge? (*pause*) Dodge, are you watching baseball?

DODGE: No.

HALIE'S VOICE: What?

DODGE: (*louder*) No!

HALIE'S VOICE: What're you watching? You shouldn't be watching anything that'll get you excited. No horse racing!

DODGE: They don't race on Sundays.

HALIE'S VOICE: What?

DODGE: (*louder*) They don't race on Sundays!

HALIE'S VOICE: Well they shouldn't race on Sundays.

DODGE: Well they don't!

HALIE'S VOICE: Good. I'm amazed they still have that kind of legislation. That's amazing.

DODGE: Yeah, it's amazing.

HALIE'S VOICE: What?

DODGE: (*louder*) It is amazing!

HALIE'S VOICE: It is. It truly is. I would've thought these days they'd be racing on Christmas even. A big flashing Christmas tree right down at the finish line.

DODGE: (*shakes his head*) No.

HALIE'S VOICE: They used to race on New Year's! I remember that.

DODGE: They never raced on New Year's!

HALIE'S VOICE: Sometimes they did.

DODGE: They never did!

HALIE'S VOICE: Before we were married they did!

DODGE *waves his hand in disgust at the staircase. Leans back in sofa. Stares at T.V.*

HALIE'S VOICE: I went once. With a man.

DODGE: (*mimicking her*) Oh, a "man."

HALIE'S VOICE: What?

DODGE: Nothing!

HALIE'S VOICE: A wonderful man. A breeder.

DODGE: A what?

HALIE'S VOICE: A breeder! A horse breeder! Thoroughbreds.

DODGE: Oh, thoroughbreds. Wonderful!

HALIE'S VOICE: That's right. He knew everything there was to know.

DODGE: I bet he taught you a thing or two huh? Gave you a good turn around the old stable?

HALIE'S VOICE: Knew everything there was to know about horses. We won bookoos of money that day.

DODGE: What?

HALIE'S VOICE: Money! We won every race I think.

DODGE: Bookoos?

HALIE'S VOICE: Every single race.

DODGE: Bookoos of money?

HALIE'S VOICE: It was one of those kind of days.

DODGE: New Year's!

HALIE'S VOICE: Yes! It might've been Florida. Or California! One of those two.

DODGE: Can I take my pick?

HALIE'S VOICE: It was Florida!

DODGE: Aha!

HALIE'S VOICE: Wonderful! Absolutely wonderful! The sun was just gleaming. Flamingos. Bougainvilleas. Palm trees.

DODGE: (to himself, mimicking her) Bougainvilleas. Palm trees.

HALIE'S VOICE: Everything was dancing with life! There were all kinds of people from everywhere. Everyone was dressed to the nines. Not like today. Not like they dress today.

DODGE: When was this anyway?

HALIE'S VOICE: This was long before I knew you.

DODGE: Must've been.

HALIE'S VOICE: Long before. I was escorted.

DODGE: To Florida?

HALIE'S VOICE: Yes. Or it might've been California. I'm not sure which.

DODGE: All that way you were escorted?

HALIE'S VOICE: Yes.

DODGE: And he never laid a finger on you I suppose? (long silence) Halie?
*No answer. Long pause.*

HALIE'S VOICE: Are you going out today?

DODGE: (gesturing toward rain) In this?

HALIE'S VOICE: I'm just asking a simple question.

DODGE: I rarely go out in the bright sunshine, why would I go out in this?

HALIE'S VOICE: I'm just asking because I'm not doing any shopping today. And if you need anything you should ask Tilden.

DODGE: Tilden's not here!

HALIE'S VOICE: He's in the kitchen.
*DODGE looks toward stage left, then back toward T.V.*

DODGE: All right.

HALIE'S VOICE: What?

DODGE: (louder) All right!

HALIE'S VOICE: Don't scream. It'll only get your coughing started.

DODGE: All right.

HALIE'S VOICE: Just tell Tilden what you want and he'll get it. (pause) Bradley should be over later.

DODGE: Bradley?

HALIE'S VOICE: Yes. To cut your hair.

DODGE: My hair? I don't need my hair cut!

HALIE'S VOICE: It won't hurt!

DODGE: I don't need it!

HALIE'S VOICE: It's been more than two weeks, Dodge.

DODGE: I don't need it!

HALIE'S VOICE: I have to meet Father Dewis for lunch.

DODGE: You tell Bradley that if he shows up here with those clippers, I'll kill him!

HALIE'S VOICE: I won't be very late. No later than four at the very latest.

DODGE: You tell him! Last time he left me almost bald! And I wasn't even awake! I was sleeping! I woke up and he'd already left!

HALIE'S VOICE: That's not my fault!

DODGE: You put him up to it!

HALIE'S VOICE: I never did!

DODGE: You did too! You had some fancy, stupid meeting planned! Time to dress up the corpse for company! Lower the ears a little! Put up a little front! Surprised you didn't tape a pipe to my mouth while you were at it! That woulda' looked nice! Huh? A pipe? Maybe a bowler hat! Maybe a copy of the *Wall Street Journal* casually placed on my lap!

HALIE'S VOICE: You always imagine the worst things of people!

DODGE: That's not the worst! That's the least of the worst!

HALIE'S VOICE: I don't need to hear it! All day long I hear things like that and I don't need to hear more.

DODGE: You better tell him!

HALIE'S VOICE: You tell him yourself! He's your own son. You should be able to talk to your own son.

DODGE: Not while I'm sleeping! He cut my hair while I was sleeping!

HALIE'S VOICE: Well he won't do it again.

DODGE: There's no guarantee.

HALIE'S VOICE: I promise he won't do it without your consent.

DODGE: (after pause) There's no reason for him to even come over here.

HALIE'S VOICE: He feels responsible.

DODGE: For my hair?

HALIE'S VOICE: For your appearance.

DODGE: My appearance is out of his domain! It's even out of mine! In fact, it's disappeared! I'm an invisible man!

HALIE'S VOICE: Don't be ridiculous.

DODGE: He better not try it. That's all I've got to say.

HALIE'S VOICE: Tilden will watch out for you.

DODGE: Tilden won't protect me from Bradley!

HALIE'S VOICE: Tilden's the oldest. He'll protect you.

DODGE: Tilden can't even protect himself!

HALIE'S VOICE: Not so loud! He'll hear you. He's right in the kitchen.

DODGE: (yelling off left) Tilden!

HALIE'S VOICE: Dodge, what are you trying to do?

DODGE: (yelling off left) Tilden, get in here!

HALIE'S VOICE: Why do you enjoy stirring things up?

DODGE: I don't enjoy anything!

HALIE'S VOICE: That's a terrible thing to say.

DODGE: Tilden!

HALIE'S VOICE: That's the kind of statement that leads people right to the end of their rope.

DODGE: Tilden!

HALIE'S VOICE: It's no wonder people turn to Christ!

DODGE: TILDEN!!

HALIE'S VOICE: It's no wonder the messengers of God's word are shouted down in public places!

DODGE: TILDEN!!!!

DODGE *goes into a violent, spasmodic coughing attack as* TILDEN *enters from stage left, his arms loaded with fresh ears of corn.* TILDEN *is* DODGE'S *oldest son, late forties, wears heavy construction boots, covered with mud, dark green work pants, a plaid shirt and a faded brown windbreaker. He has a butch haircut, wet from the rain. Something about him is profoundly burned out and displaced. He stops center stage with the ears of corn in his arms and just stares at* DODGE *until he slowly finishes his coughing attack.* DODGE *looks up at him slowly. He stares at the corn. Long pause as they watch each other.*

HALIE'S VOICE: Dodge, if you don't take that pill nobody's going to force you.

*The two men ignore the voice.*

DODGE: (to TILDEN) Where'd you get that?

TILDEN: Picked it.

DODGE: You picked all that?

TILDEN *nods.*

DODGE: You expecting company?

TILDEN: No.

DODGE: Where'd you pick it from?

TILDEN: Right out back.

DODGE: Out back where!

TILDEN: Right out in back.

DODGE: There's nothing out there!

TILDEN: There's corn.

DODGE: There hasn't been corn out there since about nineteen thirty five! That's the last time I planted corn out there!

TILDEN: It's out there now.

DODGE: (yelling at stairs) Halie!

HALIE'S VOICE: Yes dear!

DODGE: Tilden's brought a whole bunch of corn in here! There's no corn out in back is there?

TILDEN: (*to himself*) There's tons of corn.

HALIE'S VOICE: Not that I know of!

DODGE: That's what I thought.

HALIE'S VOICE: Not since about nineteen thirty five!

DODGE: (*to* TILDEN) That's right. Nineteen thirty five.

TILDEN: It's out there now.

DODGE: You go and take that corn back to wherever you got it from!

TILDEN: (*After pause, staring at* DODGE) It's picked. I picked it all in the rain. Once it's picked you can't put it back.

DODGE: I haven't had trouble with neighbors here for fifty-seven years. I don't even know who the neighbors are! And I don't wanna know! Now go put that corn back where it came from!

> TILDEN *stares at* DODGE *then walks slowly over to him and dumps all the corn on* DODGE'S *lap and steps back.* DODGE *stares at the corn then back to* TILDEN. *Long pause.*

DODGE: Are you having trouble here, Tilden? Are you in some kind of trouble?

TILDEN: I'm not in any trouble.

DODGE: You can tell me if you are. I'm still your father.

TILDEN: I know you're still my father.

DODGE: I know you had a little trouble back in New Mexico. That's why you came out here.

TILDEN: I never had any trouble.

DODGE: Tilden, your mother told me all about it.

TILDEN: What'd she tell you?

> TILDEN *pulls some chewing tobacco out of his jacket and bites off a plug.*

DODGE: I don't have to repeat what she told me! She told me all about it!

TILDEN: Can I bring my chair in from the kitchen?

DODGE: What?

TILDEN: Can I bring in my chair from the kitchen?

DODGE: Sure. Bring your chair in.

> TILDEN *exits left.* DODGE *pushes all the corn off his lap onto the floor. He pulls the blanket off angrily and tosses it at one end of the sofa, pulls out the bottle and takes another swig.* TILDEN *enters again from left with a milking stool and a pail.* DODGE *hides the bottle quickly under the cushion before* TILDEN *sees it.* TILDEN *sets the stool down by the sofa, sits on it, puts the pail in front of him on the floor.* TILDEN *starts picking up the ears of corn one at a time and husking them. He throws the husks and silk in the center of the stage and drops the ears into the pail each time he cleans one. He repeats this process as they talk.*

DODGE: (*after pause*) Sure is nice looking corn.

TILDEN: It's the best.

DODGE: Hybrid?

TILDEN: What?

DODGE: Some kinda fancy hybrid?

TILDEN: You planted it. I don't know what it is.

DODGE: (*pause*) Tilden, look, you can't stay here . . . ever. You know that, don't you?

TILDEN: (*spits in spittoon*) I'm not.

DODGE: I know you're not. I'm not worried about that. That's not the reason I brought it up.

TILDEN: What's the reason?

DODGE: The reason is I'm wondering what you're gonna do.

TILDEN: You're not worried about me, are you?

DODGE: I'm not worried about you.

TILDEN: You weren't worried about me when I wasn't here. When I was in New Mexico.

DODGE: No, I wasn't worried about you then either.

TILDEN: You shoulda worried about me then.

DODGE: Why's that? You didn't do anything down there, did you?

TILDEN: I didn't do anything.

DODGE: Then why should I have worried about you?

TILDEN: Because I was lonely.

DODGE: Because you were lonely?

TILDEN: Yeah. I was more lonely than I've ever been before.

DODGE: Why was that?

TILDEN: (*pause*) Could I have some of that whiskey you've got?

DODGE: What whiskey? I haven't got any whiskey.

TILDEN: You've got some under the sofa.

DODGE: I haven't got anything under the sofa! Now mind your own damn business! Jesus God, you come into the house outa the middle of nowhere, haven't heard or seen you in twenty years and suddenly you're making accusations.

TILDEN: I'm not making accusations.

DODGE: You're accusing me of hoarding whiskey under the sofa!

TILDEN: I'm not accusing you.

DODGE: You just got through telling me I had whiskey under the sofa!

HALIE'S VOICE: Dodge?

DODGE: (*to* TILDEN) Now she knows about it!

TILDEN: She doesn't know about it!

HALIE'S VOICE: Dodge, are you talking to yourself down there?

DODGE: I'm talking to Tilden!

HALIE'S VOICE: Tilden's down there?

DODGE: He's right here!

HALIE'S VOICE: What?

DODGE: (*louder*) He's right here!

HALIE'S VOICE: What's he doing?

DODGE: (*to* TILDEN) Don't answer her.

TILDEN: (*to* DODGE) I'm not doing anything wrong.

DODGE: I know you're not.

HALIE'S VOICE: What's he doing down there!

DODGE: (*to* TILDEN) Don't answer.

TILDEN: I'm not.

HALIE'S VOICE: Dodge!

*The men sit in silence.* DODGE *lights a cigarette.* TILDEN *keeps husking corn, spits tobacco now and then in spittoon.*

HALIE'S VOICE: Dodge! He's not drinking anything, is he? You see to it that he doesn't drink anything! You've gotta watch out for him. It's our responsibility. He can't look after himself anymore, so we have to do it. Nobody else will do it. We can't just send him away somewhere. If we had lots of money we could send him away. But we don't. We never will. That's why we have to stay healthy. You and me. Nobody's going to look after us. Bradley can't look after us. Bradley can hardly look after himself. I was always hoping that Tilden would look out for Bradley when they got older. After Bradley lost his leg. Tilden's the oldest. I always thought he'd be the one to take responsibility. I had no idea in the world that Tilden would be so much trouble. Who would've dreamed. Tilden was an All-American, don't forget. Don't forget that. Fullback. Or quarterback. I forget which.

TILDEN: (*to himself*) Fullback. (*still husking*)

HALIE'S VOICE: Then when Tilden turned out to be so much trouble, I put all my hopes on Ansel. Of course Ansel wasn't as handsome, but he was smart. He was the smartest probably. I think he probably was. Smarter than Bradley, that's for sure. Didn't go and chop his leg off with a chain saw. Smart enough not to go and do that. I think he was smarter than Tilden too. Especially after Tilden got in all that trouble. Doesn't take brains to go to jail. Anybody knows that. Course then when Ansel died that left us all alone. Same as being alone. No different. Same as if they'd all died. He was the smartest. He could've earned lots of money. Lots and lots of money.

HALIE *enters slowly from the top of the staircase as she continues talking. Just her feet are seen at first as she makes her way down the stairs, a step at a time. She appears dressed completely in black, as though in mourning.*

*Black handbag, hat with a veil, and pulling on elbow length black gloves. She is about sixty-five with pure white hair. She remains absorbed in what she's saying as she descends the stairs and doesn't really notice the two men who continue sitting there as they were before she came down, smoking and husking.*

HALIE:  He would've took care of us, too. He would've seen to it that we were repaid. He was like that. He was a hero. Don't forget that. A genuine hero. Brave. Strong. And very intelligent. Ansel could've been a great man. One of the greatest. I only regret that he didn't die in action. It's not fitting for a man like that to die in a motel room. A soldier. He could've won a medal. He could've been decorated for valor. I've talked to Father Dewis about putting up a plaque for Ansel. He thinks it's a good idea. He agrees. He knew Ansel when he used to play basketball. Went to every game. Ansel was his favorite player. He even recommended to the City Council that they put up a statue of Ansel. A big, tall statue with a basketball in one hand and a rifle in the other. That's how much he thinks of Ansel.

HALIE *reaches the stage and begins to wander around, still absorbed in pulling on her gloves, brushing lint off her dress and continuously talking to herself as the men just sit.*

HALIE:  Of course, he'd still be alive today if he hadn't married into the Catholics. The Mob. How in the world he never opened his eyes to that is beyond me. Just beyond me. Everyone around him could see the truth. Even Tilden. Tilden told him time and again. Catholic women are the Devil incarnate. He wouldn't listen. He was blind with love. Blind. I knew. Everyone knew. The wedding was more like a funeral. You remember? All those Italians. All that horrible black, greasy hair. The smell of cheap cologne. I think even the priest was wearing a pistol. When he gave her the ring I knew he was a dead man. I knew it. As soon as he gave her the ring. But then it was the honeymoon that killed him. The honeymoon. I knew he'd never come back from the honeymoon. I kissed him and he felt like a corpse. All white. Cold. Icy blue lips. He never used to kiss like that. Never before. I knew then that she'd cursed him. Taken his soul. I saw it in her eyes. She smiled at me with that Catholic sneer of hers. She told me with her eyes that she'd murder him in his bed. Murder my son. She told me. And there was nothing I could do. Absolutely nothing. He was going with her, thinking he was free. Thinking it was love. What could I do? I couldn't tell him she was a witch. I couldn't tell him that. He'd have turned on me. Hated me. I couldn't stand him hating me and then dying before he ever saw me again. Hating me in his death bed. Hating me and loving her! How could I do that? I had to let him go. I had to. I watched him leave. I watched him throw gardenias as he helped her into the limousine. I watched his face disappear behind the glass.

*She stops abruptly and stares at the corn husks. She looks around the space as though just waking up. She turns and looks hard at* TILDEN *and* DODGE *who continue sitting calmly. She looks again at the corn husks.*

HALIE:  (*pointing to the husks*) What's this in my house! (*kicks husks*) What's all this!

TILDEN *stops husking and stares at her.*

HALIE:  (*to* DODGE) And you encourage him!

DODGE *pulls blanket over him again.*

DODGE:  You're going out in the rain?

HALIE:  It's not raining.

TILDEN *starts husking again.*

DODGE:  Not in Florida it's not.

HALIE:  We're not in Florida!

DODGE:  It's not raining at the race track.

HALIE: Have you been taking those pills? Those pills always make you talk crazy. Tilden, has he been taking those pills?

TILDEN: He hasn't took anything.

HALIE: (to DODGE) What've you been taking?

DODGE: It's not raining in California or Florida or the race track. Only in Illinois. This is the only place it's raining. All over the rest of the world it's bright golden sunshine.

HALIE *goes to the night table next to the sofa and checks the bottle of pills.*

HALIE: Which ones did you take? Tilden, you must've seen him take something.

TILDEN: He never took a thing.

HALIE: Then why's he talking crazy?

TILDEN: I've been here the whole time.

HALIE: Then you've both been taking something!

TILDEN: I've just been husking the corn.

HALIE: Where'd you get that corn anyway? Why is the house suddenly full of corn?

DODGE: Bumper crop!

HALIE: (*moving center*) We haven't had corn here for over thirty years.

TILDEN: The whole back lot's full of corn. Far as the eye can see.

DODGE: (to HALIE) Things keep happening while you're upstairs, ya know. The world doesn't stop just because you're upstairs. Corn keeps growing. Rain keeps raining.

HALIE: I'm not unaware of the world around me! Thank you very much. It so happens that I have an over-all view from the upstairs. The back yard's in plain view of my window. And there's no corn to speak of. Absolutely none!

DODGE: Tilden wouldn't lie. If he says there's corn, there's corn.

HALIE: What's the meaning of this corn Tilden!

TILDEN: It's a mystery to me. I was out in back there. And the rain was coming down. And I didn't feel like coming back

inside. I didn't feel the cold so much. I didn't mind the wet. So I was just walking. I was muddy but I didn't mind the mud so much. And I looked up. And I saw this stand of corn. In fact I was standing in it. So, I was standing in it.

HALIE: There isn't any corn outside, Tilden! There's no corn! Now, you must've either stolen this corn or you bought it.

DODGE: He doesn't have any money.

HALIE: (to TILDEN) So you stole it!

TILDEN: I didn't steal it. I don't want to get kicked out of Illinois. I was kicked out of New Mexico and I don't want to get kicked out of Illinois.

HALIE: You're going to get kicked out of this house, Tilden, if you don't tell me where you got that corn!

TILDEN *starts crying softly to himself but keeps husking corn. Pause.*

DODGE: (to HALIE) Why'd you have to tell him that? Who cares where he got the corn? Why'd you have to go and tell him that?

HALIE: (to DODGE) It's your fault you know! You're the one that's behind all this! I suppose you thought it'd be funny! Some joke! Cover this house with corn husks. You better get this cleaned up before Bradley sees it.

DODGE: Bradley's not getting in the front door!

HALIE: (*kicking husks, striding back and forth*) Bradley's going to be very upset when he sees this. He doesn't like to see the house in disarray. He can't stand it when one thing is out of place. The slightest thing. You know how he gets.

DODGE: Bradley doesn't even live here!

HALIE: It's his home as much as ours. He was born in this house!

DODGE: He was born in a hog wallow.

HALIE: Don't you say that! Don't you ever say that!

DODGE: He was born in a goddamn hog wallow! That's where he was born and that's where he belongs! He doesn't belong in this house!

HALIE: (*she stops*) I don't know what's come over you, Dodge. I don't know what in the world's come over you. You've become an evil man. You used to be a good man.

DODGE: Six of one, a half dozen of another.

HALIE: You sit here day and night, festering away! Decomposing! Smelling up the house with your putrid body! Hacking your head off til all hours of the morning! Thinking up mean, evil, stupid things to say about your own flesh and blood!

DODGE: He's not my flesh and blood! My flesh and blood's buried in the back yard!

*They freeze. Long pause. The men stare at her.*

HALIE: (*quietly*) That's enough, Dodge. That's quite enough. I'm going out now. I'm going to have lunch with Father Dewis. I'm going to ask him about a monument. A statue. At least a plaque.

*She crosses to the door up right. She stops.*

HALIE: If you need anything, ask Tilden. He's the oldest. I've left some money on the kitchen table.

DODGE: I don't need anything.

HALIE: No, I suppose not. (*she opens the door and looks out through porch*) Still raining. I love the smell just after it stops. The ground. I won't be too late.

*She goes out door and closes it. She's still visible on the porch as she crosses toward stage left screen door. She stops in the middle of the porch, speaks to DODGE but doesn't turn to him.*

HALIE: Dodge, tell Tilden not to go out in the back lot anymore. I don't want him back there in the rain.

DODGE: You tell him. He's sitting right here.

HALIE: He never listens to me Dodge. He's never listened to me in the past.

DODGE: I'll tell him.

HALIE: We have to watch him just like we used to now. Just like we always have. He's still a child.

DODGE: I'll watch him.

HALIE: Good.

*She crosses to screen door, left, takes an umbrella off a hook and goes out the door. The door slams behind her. Long pause. TILDEN husks corn, stares at pail. DODGE lights a cigarette, stares at T.V.*

TILDEN: (*still husking*) You shouldn't a told her that.

DODGE: (*staring at T.V.*) What?

TILDEN: What you told her. You know.

DODGE: What do you know about it?

TILDEN: I know. I know all about it. We all know.

DODGE: So what difference does it make? Everybody knows, everybody's forgot.

TILDEN: She hasn't forgot.

DODGE: She should've forgot.

TILDEN: It's different for a woman. She couldn't forget that. How could she forget that?

DODGE: I don't want to talk about it!

TILDEN: What do you want to talk about?

DODGE: I don't want to talk about anything! I don't want to talk about troubles or what happened fifty years ago or thirty years ago or the race track or Florida or the last time I seeded the corn! I don't want to talk!

TILDEN: You don't wanna die do you?

DODGE: No, I don't wanna die either.

TILDEN: Well, you gotta talk or you'll die.

DODGE: Who told you that?

TILDEN: That's what I know. I found that out in New Mexico. I thought I was dying but I just lost my voice.

DODGE: Were you with somebody?

TILDEN: I was alone. I thought I was dead.

DODGE: Might as well have been. What'd you come back here for?

TILDEN: I didn't know where to go.

DODGE: You're a grown man. You shouldn't be needing your parents at your age. It's unnatural. There's nothing we can do for you now anyway. Couldn't you make a living down there? Couldn't you find some way to make a living? Support yourself? What'd'ya come back here for? You expect us to feed you forever?

TILDEN: I didn't know where else to go.

DODGE: I never went back to my parents. Never. Never even had the urge. I was independent. Always independent. Always found a way.

TILDEN: I didn't know what to do. I couldn't figure anything out.

DODGE: There's nothing to figure out. You just forge ahead. What's there to figure out?

TILDEN *stands.*

TILDEN: I don't know.

DODGE: Where are you going?

TILDEN: Out back.

DODGE: You're not supposed to go out there. You heard what she said. Don't play deaf with me!

TILDEN: I like it out there.

DODGE: In the rain?

TILDEN: Especially in the rain. I like the feeling of it. Feels like it always did.

DODGE: You're supposed to watch out for me. Get me things when I need them.

TILDEN: What do you need?

DODGE: I don't need anything! But I might. I might need something any second. Any second now. I can't be left alone for a minute!

DODGE *starts to cough.*

TILDEN: I'll be right outside. You can just yell.

DODGE: (*between coughs*) No! It's too far! You can't go out there! It's too far! You might not ever hear me!

TILDEN: (*moving to pills*) Why don't you take a pill? You want a pill?

DODGE *coughs more violently, throws himself back against sofa, clutches his throat.* TILDEN *stands by helplessly.*

DODGE: Water! Get me some water!

TILDEN *rushes off left.* DODGE *reaches out for the pills, knocking some bottles to the floor, coughing in spasms. He grabs a small bottle, takes out pills and swallows them.* TILDEN *rushes back on with a glass of water.* DODGE *takes it and drinks, his coughing subsides.*

TILDEN: You all right now?

DODGE *nods. Drinks more water.* TILDEN *moves in closer to him.* DODGE *sets glass of water on the night table. His coughing is almost gone.*

TILDEN: Why don't you lay down for a while? Just rest a little.

TILDEN *helps* DODGE *lay down on the sofa. Covers him with blanket.*

DODGE: You're not going outside are you?

TILDEN: No.

DODGE: I don't want to wake up and find you not here.

TILDEN: I'll be here.

TILDEN *tucks blanket around* DODGE.

DODGE: You'll stay right here?

TILDEN: I'll stay in my chair.

DODGE: That's not a chair. That's my old milking stool.

TILDEN: I know.

DODGE: Don't call it a chair.

TILDEN: I won't.

TILDEN *tries to take* DODGE'S *baseball cap off.*

DODGE: What're you doing! Leave that on me! Don't take that offa me! That's my cap!

TILDEN *leaves the cap on* DODGE.

TILDEN: I know.

DODGE: Bradley'll shave my head if I don't have that on. That's my cap!

TILDEN: I know it is.

DODGE: Don't take my cap off.

TILDEN: I won't.

DODGE: You stay right here now.

TILDEN: (*sits on stool*) I will.

DODGE: Don't go outside. There's nothing out there.

TILDEN: I won't.

DODGE: Everything's in here. Everything you need. Money's on the table. T.V. Is the T.V. on?

TILDEN: Yeah.

DODGE: Turn it off! Turn the damn thing off! What's it doing on?

TILDEN: (*shuts off T.V., light goes out*) You left it on.

DODGE: Well turn it off.

TILDEN: (*sits on stool again*) It's off.

DODGE: Leave it off.

TILDEN: I will.

DODGE: When I fall asleep you can turn it on.

TILDEN: Okay.

DODGE: You can watch the ball game. Red Sox. You like the Red Sox don't you?

TILDEN: Yeah.

DODGE: You can watch the Red Sox. Pee Wee Reese. Pee Wee Reese. You remember Pee Wee Reese?

TILDEN: No.

DODGE: Was he with the Red Sox?

TILDEN: I don't know.

DODGE: Pee Wee Reese. (*falling asleep*) You can watch the Cardinals. You remember Stan Musial.

TILDEN: No.

DODGE: Stan Musial. (*falling into sleep*) Bases loaded. Top a' the sixth. Bases loaded. Runner on first and third. Big fat knuckle ball. Floater. Big as a blimp. Cracko! Ball just took off like a rocket. Just pulverized. I marked it. Marked it with my eyes. Straight between the clock and the Burma Shave ad. I was the first kid out there. First kid. I had to fight hard for that ball. I wouldn't give it up. They almost tore the ears right off me. But I wouldn't give it up.

*DODGE falls into deep sleep. TILDEN just sits staring at him for a while. Slowly he leans toward the sofa, checking to see if DODGE is well asleep. He reaches slowly under the cushion and pulls out the bottle of booze. DODGE sleeps soundly. TILDEN stands quietly, staring at DODGE as he uncaps the bottle and takes a long drink. He caps the bottle and sticks it in his hip pocket. He looks around at the husks on the floor and then back to DODGE. He moves center stage and gathers an armload of corn husks then crosses back to the sofa. He stands holding the husks over DODGE and looking down at him he gently spreads the corn husks over the whole length of DODGE'S body. He stands back and looks at DODGE. Pulls out bottle, takes another drink, returns bottle to his hip pocket. He gathers more husks and repeats the procedure until the floor is clean of corn husks and DODGE is completely covered in them except for his head. TILDEN takes another long drink, stares at DODGE sleeping then quietly exits stage left. Long pause as the sound of rain continues. DODGE sleeps on. The figure of BRADLEY appears up left, outside the screen porch door. He holds a wet newspaper over his head as a protection from the rain. He seems to be struggling with the door then slips and almost falls to the ground. DODGE sleeps on, undisturbed.*

BRADLEY: Sonuvabitch! Sonuvagoddamnbitch!

*BRADLEY recovers his footing and makes it through the screen door onto the porch. He throws the newspaper down, shakes the water out of his hair, and brushes the rain off of his shoulders. He is a big man dressed in a grey sweat shirt, black suspenders, baggy dark blue pants and black janitor's shoes. His left leg is wooden, having been amputated above the knee. He moves with an exaggerated, almost mechanical limp. The squeaking sounds of leather and metal accompany his walk coming from the harness and hinges of the false leg. His arms and shoulders are extremely powerful and muscular due to a lifetime dependency on the upper torso doing all the work for the legs. He is about five years younger than TILDEN. He moves laboriously to the stage right door and enters, closing the door behind him. He doesn't notice DODGE at first. He moves toward the staircase.*

BRADLEY: (*calling to upstairs*) Mom!

*He stops and listens. Turns upstage and sees* **DODGE** *sleeping. Notices corn husks. He moves slowly toward sofa. Stops next to pail and looks into it. Looks at husks.* **DODGE** *stays asleep. Talks to himself.*

BRADLEY: What in the hell is this?

*He looks at* **DODGE'S** *sleeping face and shakes his head in disgust. He pulls out a pair of black electric hair clippers from his pocket. Unwinds the cord and crosses to the lamp. He jabs his wooden leg behind the knee, causing it to bend at the joint and awkwardly kneels to plug the cord into a floor outlet. He pulls himself to his feet again by using the sofa as leverage. He moves to* **DODGE'S** *head and again jabs his false leg. Goes down on one knee. He violently knocks away some of the corn husks then jerks off* **DODGE'S** *baseball cap and throws it down center stage.* **DODGE** *stays asleep.* **BRADLEY** *switches on the clippers. Lights start dimming.* **BRADLEY** *cuts* **DODGE'S** *hair while he sleeps. Lights dim slowly to black with the sound of clippers and rain.*

# ACT 2

**SCENE**

*Same set as Act 1. Night. Sound of rain.* **DODGE** *still asleep on sofa. His hair is cut extremely short and in places the scalp is cut and bleeding. His cap is still center stage. All the corn husks, pail and milking stool have been cleared away. The lights come up to the sound of a young girl laughing off stage left.* **DODGE** *remains asleep.* **SHELLY** *and* **VINCE** *appear up left outside the screen porch door sharing the shelter of* **VINCE'S** *overcoat above their heads.* **SHELLY** *is about nineteen, black hair, very beautiful. She wears tight jeans, high heels, purple T-shirt and a short rabbit fur coat. Her makeup is exaggerated and her hair has been curled.* **VINCE** *is* **TILDEN'S** *son, about twenty-two, wears a plaid shirt, jeans, dark glasses, cowboy boots and carries a black saxophone case. They shake the rain off themselves as they enter the porch through the screen door.*

SHELLY: (*laughing, gesturing to house*) This is it? I don't believe this is it!

VINCE: This is it.

SHELLY: This is the house?

VINCE: This is the house.

SHELLY: I don't believe it!

VINCE: How come?

SHELLY: It's like a Norman Rockwell cover or something.

VINCE: What's a' matter with that? It's American.

SHELLY: Where's the milkman and the little dog? What's the little dog's name? Spot. Spot and Jane. Dick and Jane and Spot.

VINCE: Knock it off.

SHELLY: Dick and Jane and Spot and Mom and Dad and Junior and Sissy!

*She laughs. Slaps her knee.*

VINCE: Come on! It's my heritage. What dya' expect?

*She laughs more hysterically, out of control.*

SHELLY: "And Tuffy and Toto and Dooda and Bonzo all went down one day to the corner grocery store to buy a big bag of licorice for Mr. Marshall's pussy cat!"

*She laughs so hard she falls to her knees holding her stomach.* **VINCE** *stands there looking at her.*

VINCE: Shelly will you get up!

*She keeps laughing. Staggers to her feet. Turning in circles holding her stomach.*

SHELLY: (*continuing her story in kid's voice*) "Mr. Marshall was on vacation. He had no idea that the four little boys had taken such a liking to his little kitty cat."

VINCE: Have some respect would ya'!

SHELLY: (*trying to control herself*) I'm sorry.

VINCE: Pull yourself together.

SHELLY: (*salutes him*) Yes sir.

*She giggles.*

VINCE: Jesus Christ, Shelly.

SHELLY: (*pause, smiling*) And Mr. Marshall—

VINCE: Cut it out.

*She stops. Stands there staring at him. Stifles a giggle.*

VINCE: (*after pause*) Are you finished?

SHELLY: Oh brother!

VINCE: I don't wanna go in there with you acting like an idiot.

SHELLY: Thanks.

VINCE: Well, I don't.

SHELLY: I won't embarrass you. Don't worry.

VINCE: I'm not worried.

SHELLY: You are too.

VINCE: Shelly look, I just don't wanna go in there with you giggling your head off. They might think something's wrong with you.

SHELLY: There is.

VINCE: There is not!

SHELLY: Something's definitely wrong with me.

VINCE: There is not!

SHELLY: There's something wrong with you too.

VINCE: There's nothing wrong with me either!

SHELLY: You wanna know what's wrong with you?

VINCE: What?

SHELLY *laughs.*

VINCE: (*crosses back left toward screen door*) I'm leaving!

SHELLY: (*stops laughing*) Wait! Stop. Stop! (VINCE *stops*) What's wrong with you is that you take the situation too seriously.

VINCE: I just don't want to have them think that I've suddenly arrived out of the middle of nowhere completely deranged.

SHELLY: What do you want them to think then?

VINCE: (*pause*) Nothing. Let's go in.

*He crosses porch toward stage right interior door.* SHELLY *follows him. The stage right door opens slowly.* VINCE *sticks his head in, doesn't notice* DODGE *sleeping. Calls out toward staircase.*

VINCE: Grandma!

SHELLY *breaks into laughter, unseen behind* VINCE. VINCE *pulls his head back outside*

*and pulls door shut. We hear their voices again without seeing them.*

SHELLY'S VOICE: (*stops laughing*) I'm sorry. I'm sorry Vince. I really am. I really am sorry. I won't do it again. I couldn't help it.

VINCE'S VOICE: It's not all that funny.

SHELLY'S VOICE: I know it's not. I'm sorry.

VINCE'S VOICE: I mean this is a tense situation for me! I haven't seen them for over six years. I don't know what to expect.

SHELLY'S VOICE: I know. I won't do it again.

VINCE'S VOICE: Can't you bite your tongue or something?

SHELLY'S VOICE: Just don't say "Grandma," okay? (*she giggles, stops*) I mean if you say "Grandma" I don't know if I can stop myself.

VINCE'S VOICE: Well try!

SHELLY'S VOICE: Okay. Sorry.

*Door opens again.* VINCE *sticks his head in, then enters.* SHELLY *follows behind him.* VINCE *crosses to staircase, sets down saxophone case and overcoat, looks up staircase.* SHELLY *notices* DODGE'S *baseball cap. Crosses to it. Picks it up and puts it on her head.* VINCE *goes up the stairs and disappears at the top.* SHELLY *watches him then turns and sees* DODGE *on the sofa. She takes off the baseball cap.*

VINCE'S VOICE: (*from above stairs*) Grandma!

SHELLY *crosses over to* DODGE *slowly and stands next to him. She stands at his head, reaches out slowly and touches one of the cuts. The second she touches his head,* DODGE *jerks up to a sitting position on the sofa, eyes open.* SHELLY *gasps.* DODGE *looks at her, sees his cap in her hands, quickly puts his hand to his bare head. He glares at* SHELLY *then whips the cap out of her hands and puts it on.* SHELLY *backs away from him.* DODGE *stares at her.*

SHELLY: I'm uh- with Vince.

DODGE *just glares at her.*

SHELLY: He's upstairs.

DODGE *looks at the staircase then back to* SHELLY.

SHELLY: (*calling upstairs*) Vince!

VINCE'S VOICE: Just a second!

SHELLY: You better get down here!

VINCE'S VOICE: Just a minute! I'm looking at the pictures.

DODGE *keeps staring at her.*

SHELLY: (*to* DODGE) We just got here. Pouring rain on the freeway so we thought we'd stop by. I mean Vince was planning on stopping anyway. He wanted to see you. He said he hadn't seen you in a long time.

*Pause.* DODGE *just keeps staring at her.*

SHELLY: We were going all the way through to New Mexico. To see his father. I guess his father lives out there. We thought we'd stop by and see you on the way. Kill two birds with one stone, you know? (*she laughs,* DODGE *stares, she stops laughing*) I mean Vince has this thing about his family now. I guess it's a new thing with him. I kind of find it hard to relate to. But he feels it's important. You know. I mean he feels he wants to get to know you all again. After all this time.

*Pause.* DODGE *just stares at her. She moves nervously to staircase and yells up to* VINCE.

SHELLY: Vince will you come down here please!

VINCE *comes half way down the stairs.*

VINCE: I guess they went out for a while.

SHELLY *points to sofa and* DODGE. VINCE *turns and sees* DODGE. *He comes all the way down staircase and crosses to* DODGE. SHELLY *stays behind near staircase, keeping her distance.*

VINCE: Grandpa?

DODGE *looks up at him, not recognizing him.*

DODGE: Did you bring the whiskey?

VINCE *looks back at* SHELLY, *then back to* DODGE.

VINCE: Grandpa, it's Vince. I'm Vince. Tilden's son. You remember?

DODGE *stares at him.*

DODGE: You didn't do what you told me. You didn't stay here with me.

VINCE: Grandpa, I haven't been here until just now. I just got here.

DODGE: You left. You went outside like we told you not to do. You went out there in back. In the rain.

VINCE *looks back at* SHELLY. *She moves slowly toward sofa.*

SHELLY: Is he okay?

VINCE: I don't know. (takes off his shades) Look, Grandpa, don't you remember me? Vince. Your Grandson.

DODGE *stares at him then takes off his baseball cap.*

DODGE: (*points to his head*) See what happens when you leave me alone? See that? That's what happens.

VINCE *looks at his head.* VINCE *reaches out to touch his head.* DODGE *slaps his hand away with the cap and puts it back on his head.*

VINCE: What's going on Grandpa? Where's Halie?

DODGE: Don't worry about her. She won't be back for days. She says she'll be back but she won't be. (*he starts laughing*) There's life in the old girl yet! (*stops laughing*)

VINCE: How did you do that to your head?

DODGE: I didn't do it! Don't be ridiculous!

VINCE: Well who did then?

*Pause.* DODGE *stares at* VINCE.

DODGE: Who do you think did it? Who do you think?

SHELLY *moves toward* VINCE.

SHELLY: Vince, maybe we oughta' go. I don't like this. I mean this isn't my idea of a good time.

VINCE: (*to* SHELLY) Just a second. (*to* DODGE) Grandpa, look, I just got here. I just now got here. I haven't been here for six years. I don't know anything that's happened.

*Pause.* DODGE *stares at him.*

DODGE: You don't know anything?

VINCE: No.

DODGE: Well that's good. That's good. It's much better not to know anything. Much, much, better.

VINCE: Isn't there anybody here with you?

DODGE *turns slowly and looks off to stage left.*

DODGE: Tilden's here.

VINCE: No, Grandpa, Tilden's in New Mexico. That's where I was going. I'm going out there to see him.

DODGE *turns slowly back to* VINCE.

DODGE: Tilden's here.

VINCE *backs away and joins* SHELLY. DODGE *stares at them.*

SHELLY: Vince, why don't we spend the night in a motel and come back in the morning? We could have breakfast. Maybe everything would be different.

VINCE: Don't be scared. There's nothing to be scared of. He's just old.

SHELLY: I'm not scared!

DODGE: You two are not my idea of the perfect couple!

SHELLY: (*after pause*) Oh really? Why's that?

VINCE: Shh! Don't aggravate him.

DODGE: There's something wrong between the two of you. Something not compatible.

VINCE: Grandpa, where did Halie go? Maybe we should call her.

DODGE: What are you talking about? Do you know what you're talking about? Are you just talking for the sake of talking? Lubricating the gums?

VINCE: I'm trying to figure out what's going on here!

DODGE: Is that it?

VINCE: Yes. I mean I expected everything to be different.

DODGE: Who are you to expect anything? Who are you supposed to be?

VINCE: I'm Vince! Your Grandson!

DODGE: Vince. My Grandson.

VINCE: Tilden's son.

DODGE: Tilden's son, Vince.

VINCE: You haven't seen me for a long time.

DODGE: When was the last time?

VINCE: I don't remember.

DODGE: You don't remember?

VINCE: No.

DODGE: You don't remember. How am I supposed to remember if you don't remember?

SHELLY: Vince, come on. This isn't going to work out.

VINCE: (*to* SHELLY) Just take it easy.

SHELLY: I'm taking it easy! He doesn't even know who you are!

VINCE: (*crossing toward* DODGE) Grandpa, look—

DODGE: Stay where you are! Keep your distance!

VINCE *stops. Looks back at* SHELLY *then to* DODGE.

SHELLY: Vince, this is really making me nervous. I mean he doesn't even want us here. He doesn't even like us.

DODGE: She's a beautiful girl.

VINCE: Thanks.

DODGE: Very Beautiful Girl.

SHELLY: Oh my God.

DODGE: (*to* SHELLY) What's your name?

SHELLY: Shelly.

DODGE: Shelly. That's a man's name isn't it?

SHELLY: Not in this case.

DODGE: (*to* VINCE) She's a smart-ass, too.

SHELLY: Vince! Can we go?

DODGE: She wants to go. She just got here and she wants to go.

VINCE: This is kind of strange for her.

DODGE: (*to* VINCE) She'll get used to it. (*to* SHELLY) What part of the country do you come from?

SHELLY: Originally?

DODGE: That's right. Originally. At the very start.

SHELLY: L.A.

DODGE: L.A. Stupid country.

SHELLY: I can't stand this Vince! This is really unbelievable!

DODGE: It's stupid! L.A. is stupid! So is Florida! All those Sunshine States. They're

all stupid! Do you know why they're stupid?

SHELLY: Illuminate me.

DODGE: I'll tell you why. Because they're
full of smart-asses! That's why.

SHELLY *turns her back to* DODGE, *crosses to
staircase and sits on bottom step.*

DODGE: (*to* VINCE) Now she's insulted.

VINCE: Well you weren't very polite.

DODGE: She's insulted! Look at her! In my
house she's insulted! She's over there
sulking because I insulted her!

SHELLY: (*to* VINCE) This is really terrific. This
is wonderful. And you were worried
about me making the right first impression!

DODGE: (*to* VINCE) She's a fireball isn't she?
Regular fireball. I had some a' them in
my day. Temporary stuff. Never lasted
more than a week.

VINCE: Grandpa—

DODGE: Stop calling me Grandpa will ya'!
It's sickening. "Grandpa." I'm nobody's
Grandpa!

DODGE *starts feeling around under the
cushion for the bottle of whiskey.* SHELLY
*gets up from the staircase.*

SHELLY: (*to* VINCE) Maybe you've got the
wrong house. Did you ever think of that?
Maybe this is the wrong address!

VINCE: It's not the wrong address! I recognize the yard.

SHELLY: Yeah but do you recognize the
people? He says he's not your Grandfather.

DODGE: (*digging for the bottle*) Where's that
bottle!

VINCE: He's just sick or something. I don't
know what's happened to him.

DODGE: Where's my goddamn bottle!

DODGE *gets up from sofa and starts tearing
the cushions off it and throwing them downstage, looking for the whiskey.*

SHELLY: Can't we just drive on to New Mexico? This is terrible, Vince! I don't want
to stay here. In this house. I thought it

was going to be turkey dinners and apple pie and all that kinda stuff.

VINCE: Well I hate to disappoint you!

SHELLY: I'm not disappointed! I'm fuckin'
terrified! I wanna' go!

DODGE *yells toward stage left.*

DODGE: Tilden! Tilden!

DODGE *keeps ripping away at the sofa looking
for his bottle, he knocks over the night stand
with the bottles.* VINCE *and* SHELLY *watch as
he starts ripping the stuffing out of the sofa.*

VINCE: (*to* SHELLY) He's lost his mind or
something! I've got to try to help him.

SHELLY: You help him! I'm leaving!

SHELLY *starts to leave.* VINCE *grabs her.
They struggle as* DODGE *keeps ripping away
at the sofa and yelling.*

DODGE: Tilden! Tilden get your ass in here!
Tilden!

SHELLY: Let go of me!

VINCE: You're not going anywhere! You're
going to stay right here!

SHELLY: Let go of me you sonuvabitch! I'm
not your property!

*Suddenly* TILDEN *walks on from stage left
just as he did before. This time his arms are
full of carrots.* DODGE, VINCE *and* SHELLY
*stop suddenly when they see him. They all
stare at* TILDEN *as he crosses slowly center
stage with the carrots and stops.* DODGE *sits
on sofa, exhausted.*

DODGE: (*panting, to* TILDEN) Where in the
hell have you been?

TILDEN: Out back.

DODGE: Where's my bottle?

TILDEN: Gone.

TILDEN *and* VINCE *stare at each other.*
SHELLY *backs away.*

DODGE: (*to* TILDEN) You stole my bottle!

VINCE: (*to* TILDEN) Dad?

TILDEN *just stares at* VINCE.

DODGE: You had no right to steal my bottle!
No right at all.

VINCE: (*to* TILDEN) It's Vince. I'm Vince.

TILDEN *stares at* VINCE *then looks at*
DODGE *then turns to* SHELLY.

TILDEN: (*after pause*) I picked these carrots. If anybody wants any carrots, I picked em.

SHELLY: (*to* VINCE) This is your father?

VINCE: (*to* TILDEN) Dad, what're you doing here?

*TILDEN just stares at* VINCE, *holding carrots.* DODGE *pulls the blanket back over himself.*

DODGE: (*to* TILDEN) You're going to have to get me another bottle! You gotta get me a bottle before Halie comes back! There's money on the table. (*points to stage left kitchen*)

TILDEN: (*shaking his head*) I'm not going down there. Into town.

*SHELLY crosses to* TILDEN. *TILDEN stares at her.*

SHELLY: (*to* TILDEN) Are you Vince's father?

TILDEN: (*to* SHELLY) Vince?

SHELLY: (*pointing to* VINCE) This is supposed to be your son! Is he your son? Do you recognize him? I'm just along for the ride here. I thought everybody knew each other!

*TILDEN stares at* VINCE. DODGE *wraps himself up in the blanket and sits on sofa staring at the floor.*

TILDEN: I had a son once but we buried him. DODGE *quickly looks at* TILDEN. SHELLY *looks to* VINCE.

DODGE: You shut up about that! You don't know anything about that!

VINCE: Dad, I thought you were in New Mexico. We were going to drive down there and see you.

TILDEN: Long way to drive.

DODGE: (*to* TILDEN) You don't know anything about that! That happened before you were born! Long before!

VINCE: What's happened, Dad? What's going on here? I thought everything was all right. What's happened to Halie?

TILDEN: She left.

SHELLY: (*to* TILDEN) Do you want me to take those carrots for you?

*TILDEN stares at her. She moves in close to*

him. *Holds out her arms.* TILDEN *stares at her arms then slowly dumps the carrots into her arms.* SHELLY *stands there holding the carrots.*

TILDEN: (*to* SHELLY) You like carrots?

SHELLY: Sure. I like all kinds of vegetables.

DODGE: (*to* TILDEN) You gotta get me a bottle before Halie comes back!

DODGE *hits sofa with his fist.* VINCE *crosses up to* DODGE *and tries to console him.* SHELLY *and* TILDEN *stay facing each other.*

TILDEN: (*to* SHELLY) Back yard's full of carrots. Corn. Potatoes.

SHELLY: You're Vince's father, right?

TILDEN: All kinds of vegetables. You like vegetables?

SHELLY: (*laughs*) Yeah. I love vegetables.

TILDEN: We could cook these carrots ya' know. You could cut 'em up and we could cook 'em.

SHELLY: All right.

TILDEN: I'll get you a pail and a knife.

SHELLY: Okay.

TILDEN: I'll be right back. Don't go.

*TILDEN exits off stage left.* SHELLY *stands center, arms full of carrots.* VINCE *stands next to* DODGE. SHELLY *looks toward* VINCE *then down at the carrots.*

DODGE: (*to* VINCE) You could get me a bottle. (*pointing off left*) There's money on the table.

VINCE: Grandpa why don't you lay down for a while?

DODGE: I don't wanna lay down for a while! Every time I lay down something happens! (*whips off his cap, points at his head*) Look what happens! That's what happens! (*pulls his cap back on*) You go lie down and see what happens to you! See how you like it! They'll steal your bottle! They'll cut your hair! They'll murder your children! That's what'll happen.

VINCE: Just relax for a while.

DODGE: (*pause*) You could get me a bottle ya' know. There's nothing stopping you from getting me a bottle.

SHELLY: Why don't you get him a bottle Vince? Maybe it would help everybody identify each other.

DODGE: (*pointing to* SHELLY) There, see? She thinks you should get me a bottle.

VINCE *crosses to* SHELLY.

VINCE: What're you doing with those carrots?

SHELLY: I'm waiting for your father.

DODGE: She thinks you should get me a bottle!

VINCE: Shelly put the carrots down will ya'! We gotta deal with the situation here! I'm gonna need your help.

SHELLY: I'm helping.

VINCE: You're only adding to the problem! You're making things worse! Put the carrots down!

VINCE *tries to knock the carrots out of her arms. She turns away from him, protecting the carrots.*

SHELLY: Get away from me! Stop it!

VINCE *stands back from her. She turns to him still holding the carrots.*

VINCE: (*to* SHELLY) Why are you doing this! Are you trying to make fun of me? This is my family you know!

SHELLY: You coulda' fooled me! I'd just as soon not be here myself. I'd just as soon be a thousand miles from here. I'd rather be anywhere but here. You're the one who wants to stay. So I'll stay. I'll stay and I'll cut the carrots. And I'll cook the carrots. And I'll do whatever I have to do to survive. Just to make it through this.

VINCE: Put the carrots down Shelly.

TILDEN *enters from left with pail, milking stool and a knife. He sets the stool and pail center stage for* SHELLY. SHELLY *looks at* VINCE *then sits down on stool, sets the carrots on the floor and takes the knife from* TILDEN. *She looks at* VINCE *again then picks up a carrot, cuts the ends off, scrapes it and drops it in pail. She repeats this.* VINCE *glares at her. She smiles.*

DODGE: She could get me a bottle. She's the type a' girl that could get me a bottle. Easy. She'd go down there. Slink up to the counter. They'll probably give her two bottles for the price of one. She could do that.

SHELLY *laughs. Keeps cutting carrots.* VINCE *crosses up to* DODGE, *looks at him.* TILDEN *watches* SHELLY'S *hands. Long pause.*

VINCE: (*to* DODGE) I haven't changed that much. I mean physically. Physically I'm just about the same. Same size. Same weight. Everything's the same.

DODGE *keeps staring at* SHELLY *while* VINCE *talks to him.*

DODGE: She's a beautiful girl. Exceptional.

VINCE *moves in front of* DODGE *to block his view of* SHELLY. DODGE *keeps craning his head around to see her as* VINCE *demonstrates tricks from his past.*

VINCE: Look. Look at this. Do you remember this? I used to bend my thumb behind my knuckles. You remember? I used to do it at the dinner table.

VINCE *bends a thumb behind his knuckles for* DODGE *and holds it out to him.* DODGE *takes a short glance then looks back at* SHELLY. VINCE *shifts position and shows him something else.*

VINCE: What about this?

VINCE *curls his lips back and starts drumming on his teeth with his fingernails making little tapping sounds.* DODGE *watches a while.* TILDEN *turns toward the sound.* VINCE *keeps it up. He sees* TILDEN *taking notice and crosses to* TILDEN *as he drums on his teeth.* DODGE *turns T.V. on. Watches it.*

VINCE: You remember this Dad?

VINCE *keeps on drumming for* TILDEN. TILDEN *watches a while, fascinated, then turns back to* SHELLY. VINCE *keeps up the drumming on his teeth, crosses back to* DODGE *doing it.* SHELLY *keeps working on carrots, talking to* TILDEN.

SHELLY:  (*to* TILDEN) He drives me crazy with that sometimes.

VINCE:  (*to* DODGE) I know! Here's one you'll remember. You used to kick me out of the house for this one.

VINCE *pulls his shirt out of his belt and holds it tucked under his chin with his stomach exposed. He grabs the flesh on either side of his belly button and pushes it in and out to make it look like a mouth talking. He watches his belly button and makes a deep sounding cartoon voice to synchronize with the movement. He demonstrates it to* DODGE *then crosses down to* TILDEN *doing it. Both* DODGE *and* TILDEN *take short, uninterested glances then ignore him.*

VINCE:  (*deep cartoon voice*) "Hello. How are you? I'm fine. Thank you very much. It's so good to see you looking well this fine Sunday morning. I was going down to the hardware store to fetch a pail of water."

SHELLY:  Vince, don't be pathetic will ya'!

VINCE *stops. Tucks his shirt back in.*

SHELLY:  Jesus Christ. They're not gonna play. Can't you see that?

SHELLY *keeps cutting carrots.* VINCE *slowly moves toward* TILDEN. TILDEN *keeps watching* SHELLY. DODGE *watches T.V.*

VINCE:  (*to* SHELLY) I don't get it. I really don't get it. Maybe it's me. Maybe I forgot something.

DODGE:  (*from sofa*) You forgot to get me a bottle! That's what you forgot. Anybody in this house could get me a bottle. Anybody! But nobody will. Nobody understands the urgency! Peelin' carrots is more important. Playin' piano on your teeth! Well I hope you all remember this when you get up in years. When you find yourself immobilized. Dependent on the whims of others.

VINCE *moves up toward* DODGE. *Pause as he looks at him.*

VINCE:  I'll get you a bottle.

DODGE:  You will?

VINCE:  Sure.

SHELLY *stands holding knife and carrot.*

SHELLY:  You're not going to leave me here are you?

VINCE:  (*moving to her*) You suggested it! You said, "why don't I go get him a bottle." So I'll go get him a bottle!

SHELLY:  But I can't stay here.

VINCE:  What is going on! A minute ago you were ready to cut carrots all night!

SHELLY:  That was only if you stayed. Something to keep me busy, so I wouldn't be so nervous. I don't want to stay here alone.

DODGE:  Don't let her talk you out of it! She's a bad influence. I could see it the minute she stepped in here.

SHELLY:  (*to* DODGE) You were asleep!

TILDEN:  (*to* SHELLY) Don't you want to cut carrots anymore?

SHELLY:  Sure. Sure I do.

SHELLY *sits back down on stool and continues cutting carrots. Pause.* VINCE *moves around, stroking his hair, staring at* DODGE *and* TILDEN. VINCE *and* SHELLY *exchange glances.* DODGE *watches T.V.*

VINCE:  Boy! This is amazing. This is truly amazing. (*keeps moving around*) What is this anyway? Am I in a time warp or something? Have I committed an unpardonable offense? It's true, I'm not married. (SHELLY *looks at him, then back to carrots*) But I'm also not divorced. I have been known to plunge into sinful infatuation with the Alto Saxophone. Sucking on number 5 reeds deep into the wee wee hours.

SHELLY:  Vince, what are you doing that for? They don't care about any of that. They just don't recognize you, that's all.

VINCE:  How could they not recognize me! How in the hell could they not recognize me! I'm their son!

DODGE:  (*watching T.V.*) You're no son of mine. I've had sons in my time and you're not one of 'em.

*Long pause.* **VINCE** *stares at* **DODGE** *then looks at* **TILDEN**. *He turns to* **SHELLY**.

**VINCE:** Shelly, I gotta go out for a while. I just gotta go out. I'll get a bottle and I'll come right back. You'll be o.k. here. Really.

**SHELLY:** I don't know if I can handle this Vince.

**VINCE:** I just gotta think or something. I don't know. I gotta put this all together.

**SHELLY:** Can't we just go?

**VINCE:** No! I gotta find out what's going on.

**SHELLY:** Look, you think you're bad off, what about me? Not only don't they recognize me but I've never seen them before in my life. I don't know who these guys are. They could be anybody!

**VINCE:** They're not anybody!

**SHELLY:** That's what you say.

**VINCE:** They're my family for Christ's sake! I should know who my own family is! Now give me a break. It won't take that long. I'll just go out and I'll come right back. Nothing'll happen. I promise.

**SHELLY** *stares at him. Pause.*

**SHELLY:** All right.

**VINCE:** Thanks. (*he crosses up to* **DODGE**) I'm gonna go out now, Grandpa, and I'll pick you up a bottle. Okay?

**DODGE:** Change of heart huh? (*pointing off left*) Money's on the table. In the kitchen.

**VINCE** *moves toward* **SHELLY**.

**VINCE:** (*to* **SHELLY**) You be all right?

**SHELLY:** (*cutting carrots*) Sure. I'm fine. I'll just keep real busy while you're gone.

**VINCE** *looks at* **TILDEN** *who keeps staring down at* **SHELLY'S** *hands.*

**DODGE:** Persistence see? That's what it takes. Persistence. Persistence, fortitude and determination. Those are the three virtues. You stick with those three and you can't go wrong.

**VINCE:** (*to* **TILDEN**) You want anything, Dad?

**TILDEN:** (*looks up at* **VINCE**) Me?

**VINCE:** From the store? I'm gonna get Grandpa a bottle.

**TILDEN:** He's not supposed to drink. Halie wouldn't like it.

**VINCE:** He wants a bottle.

**TILDEN:** He's not supposed to drink.

**DODGE:** (*to* **VINCE**) Don't negotiate with him! Don't make any transactions until you've spoken to me first! He'll steal you blind!

**VINCE:** (*to* **DODGE**) Tilden says you're not supposed to drink.

**DODGE:** Tilden's lost his marbles! Look at him! He's around the bend. Take a look at him.

**VINCE** *stares at* **TILDEN**. **TILDEN** *watches* **SHELLY'S** *hands as she keeps cutting carrots.*

**DODGE:** Now look at me. Look here at me!

**VINCE** *looks back to* **DODGE**.

**DODGE:** Now between the two of us, who do you think is more trustworthy? Him or me? Can you trust a man who keeps bringing in vegetables from out of nowhere? Take a look at him.

**VINCE** *looks back at* **TILDEN**.

**SHELLY:** Go get the bottle Vince.

**VINCE:** (*to* **SHELLY**) You sure you'll be all right?

**SHELLY:** I'll be fine. I feel right at home now.

**VINCE:** You do?

**SHELLY:** I'm fine. Now that I've got the carrots everything is all right.

**VINCE:** I'll be right back.

**VINCE** *crosses stage left.*

**DODGE:** Where are you going?

**VINCE:** I'm going to get the money.

**DODGE:** Then where are you going?

**VINCE:** Liquor store.

**DODGE:** Don't go anyplace else. Don't go off some place and drink. Come right back here.

**VINCE:** I will.

**VINCE** *exits stage left.*

**DODGE:** (*calling after* **VINCE**) You've got responsibility now! And don't go out the back way either! Come out through this way! I wanna' see you when you leave! Don't go out the back!

VINCE'S VOICE: (*off left*) I won't!

DODGE *turns and looks at* TILDEN *and* SHELLY.

DODGE: Untrustworthy. Probably drown himself if he went out the back. Fall right in a hole. I'd never get my bottle.

SHELLY: I wouldn't worry about Vince. He can take care of himself.

DODGE: Oh he can, huh? Independent.

VINCE *comes on again from stage left with two dollars in his hand. He crosses stage right past* DODGE.

DODGE: (*to* VINCE) You got the money?

VINCE: Yeah. Two bucks.

DODGE: Two bucks. Two bucks is two bucks. Don't sneer.

VINCE: What kind do you want?

DODGE: Whiskey! Gold Star Sour Mash. Use your own discretion.

VINCE: Okay.

VINCE *crosses to stage right door. Opens it. Stops when he hears* TILDEN.

TILDEN: (*to* VINCE) You drove all the way from New Mexico?

VINCE *turns and looks at* TILDEN. *They stare at each other.* VINCE *shakes his head, goes out the door, crosses porch and exits out screen door.* TILDEN *watches him go. Pause.*

SHELLY: You really don't recognize him? Either one of you?

TILDEN *turns again and stares at* SHELLY'S *hands as she cuts carrots.*

DODGE: (*watching T.V.*) Recognize who?

SHELLY: Vince.

DODGE: What's to recognize?

DODGE *lights a cigarette, coughs slightly and stares at T.V.*

SHELLY: It'd be cruel if you recognized him and didn't tell him. Wouldn't be fair.

DODGE *just stares at T.V., smoking.*

TILDEN: I thought I recognized him. I thought I recognized something about him.

SHELLY: You did?

TILDEN: I thought I saw a face inside his face.

SHELLY: Well it was probably that you saw what he used to look like. You haven't seen him for six years.

TILDEN: I haven't?

SHELLY: That's what he says.

TILDEN *moves around in front of her as she continues with carrots.*

TILDEN: Where was it I saw him last?

SHELLY: I don't know. I've only known him for a few months. He doesn't tell me everything.

TILDEN: He doesn't?

SHELLY: Not stuff like that.

TILDEN: What does he tell you?

SHELLY: You mean in general?

TILDEN: Yeah.

TILDEN *moves around behind her.*

SHELLY: Well he tells me all kinds of things.

TILDEN: Like what?

SHELLY: I don't know! I mean I can't just come right out and tell you how he feels.

TILDEN: How come?

TILDEN *keeps moving around her slowly in a circle.*

SHELLY: Because it's stuff he told me privately!

TILDEN: And you can't tell me?

SHELLY: I don't even know you!

DODGE: Tilden, go out in the kitchen and make me some coffee! Leave the girl alone.

SHELLY: (*to* DODGE) He's all right.

TILDEN *ignores* DODGE, *keeps moving around* SHELLY. *He stares at her hair and coat.* DODGE *stares at T.V.*

TILDEN: You mean you can't tell me anything?

SHELLY: I can tell you some things. I mean we can have a conversation.

TILDEN: We can?

SHELLY: Sure. We're having a conversation right now.

TILDEN: We are?

SHELLY: Yes. That's what we're doing.

TILDEN: But there's certain things you can't tell me, right?

SHELLY: Right.

TILDEN: There's certain things I can't tell you either.

SHELLY: How come?

TILDEN: I don't know. Nobody's supposed to hear it.

SHELLY: Well, you can tell me anything you want to.

TILDEN: I can?

SHELLY: Sure.

TILDEN: It might not be very nice.

SHELLY: That's all right. I've been around.

TILDEN: It might be awful.

SHELLY: Well, can't you tell me anything nice?

*TILDEN stops in front of her and stares at her coat.* SHELLY *looks back at him. Long pause.*

TILDEN: (*after pause*) Can I touch your coat?

SHELLY: My coat? (*she looks at her coat then back to* TILDEN) Sure.

TILDEN: You don't mind?

SHELLY: No. Go ahead.

SHELLY *holds her arm out for* TILDEN *to touch.* DODGE *stays fixed on T.V.* TILDEN *moves in slowly toward* SHELLY, *staring at her arm. He reaches out very slowly and touches her arm, feels the fur gently then draws his hand back.* SHELLY *keeps her arm out.*

SHELLY: It's rabbit.

TILDEN: Rabbit.

*He reaches out again very slowly and touches the fur on her arm then pulls back his hand again.* SHELLY *drops her arm.*

SHELLY: My arm was getting tired.

TILDEN: Can I hold it?

SHELLY: (*pause*) The coat? Sure.

SHELLY *takes off her coat and hands it to* TILDEN. TILDEN *takes it slowly, feels the fur then puts it on.* SHELLY *watches as* TILDEN *strokes the fur slowly. He smiles at her. She goes back to cutting carrots.*

SHELLY: You can have it if you want.

TILDEN: I can?

SHELLY: Yeah. I've got a raincoat in the car. That's all I need.

TILDEN: You've got a car?

SHELLY: Vince does.

TILDEN *walks around stroking the fur and smiling at the coat.* SHELLY *watches him when he's not looking.* DODGE *sticks with T.V., stretches out on sofa wrapped in blanket.*

TILDEN: (*as he walks around*) I had a car once! I had a white car! I drove. I went everywhere. I went to the mountains. I drove in the snow.

SHELLY: That must've been fun.

TILDEN: (*still moving, feeling coat*) I drove all day long sometimes. Across the desert. Way out across the desert. I drove past towns. Anywhere. Past palm trees. Lightning. Anything. I would drive through it. I would drive through it and I would stop and I would look around and I would drive on. I would get back in and drive! I loved to drive. There was nothing I loved more. Nothing I dreamed of was better than driving.

DODGE: (*eyes on T.V.*) Pipe down would ya'!

TILDEN *stops. Stares at* SHELLY.

SHELLY: Do you do much driving now?

TILDEN: Now? Now? I don't drive now.

SHELLY: How come?

TILDEN: I'm grown up now.

SHELLY: Grown up?

TILDEN: I'm not a kid.

SHELLY: You don't have to be a kid to drive.

TILDEN: It wasn't driving then.

SHELLY: What was it?

TILDEN: Adventure. I went everywhere.

SHELLY: Well you can still do that.

TILDEN: Not now.

SHELLY: Why not?

TILDEN: I just told you. You don't understand anything. If I told you something you wouldn't understand it.

SHELLY: Told me what?

TILDEN: Told you something that's true.

SHELLY: Like what?

TILDEN: Like a baby. Like a little tiny baby.

SHELLY: Like when you were little?

TILDEN: If I told you you'd make me give your coat back.

SHELLY: I won't. I promise. Tell me.

TILDEN: I can't. Dodge won't let me.

SHELLY: He won't hear you. It's okay.

*Pause.* TILDEN *stares at her. Moves slightly toward her.*

TILDEN: We had a baby. (*motioning to* DODGE) He did. Dodge did. Could pick it up with one hand. Put it in the other. Little baby. Dodge killed it.

SHELLY *stands.*

TILDEN: Don't stand up. Don't stand up!

SHELLY *sits again.* DODGE *sits up on sofa and looks at them.*

TILDEN: Dodge drowned it.

SHELLY: Don't tell me anymore! Okay?

TILDEN *moves closer to her.* DODGE *takes more interest.*

DODGE: Tilden! You leave that girl alone!

TILDEN: (*pays no attention*) Never told Halie. Never told anybody. Just drowned it.

DODGE: (*shuts off T.V.*) Tilden!

TILDEN: Nobody could find it. Just disappeared. Cops looked for it. Neighbors. Nobody could find it.

DODGE *struggles to get up from sofa.*

DODGE: Tilden, what're you telling her! Tilden!

DODGE *keeps struggling until he's standing.*

TILDEN: Finally everybody just gave up. Just stopped looking. Everybody had a different answer. Kidnap. Murder. Accident. Some kind of accident.

DODGE *struggles to walk toward* TILDEN *and falls.* TILDEN *ignores him.*

DODGE: Tilden you shut up! You shut up about it!

DODGE *starts coughing on the floor.* SHELLY *watches him from the stool.*

TILDEN: Little tiny baby just disappeared. It's not hard. It's so small. Almost invisible.

SHELLY *makes a move to help* DODGE. TILDEN *firmly pushes her back down on the stool.* DODGE *keeps coughing.*

TILDEN: He said he had his reasons. Said it went a long way back. But he wouldn't tell anybody.

DODGE: Tilden! Don't tell her anything! Don't tell her!

TILDEN: He's the only one who knows where it's buried. The only one. Like a secret buried treasure. Won't tell any of us. Won't tell me or mother or even Bradley. Especially Bradley. Bradley tried to force it out of him but he wouldn't tell. Wouldn't even tell why he did it. One night he just did it.

DODGE'S *coughing subsides.* SHELLY *stays on stool staring at* DODGE. TILDEN *slowly takes* SHELLY'S *coat off and holds it out to her. Long pause.* SHELLY *sits there trembling.*

TILDEN: You probably want your coat back now.

SHELLY *stares at coat but doesn't move to take it. The sound of* BRADLEY'S *leg squeaking is heard off left. The others on stage remain still.* BRADLEY *appears up left outside the screen door wearing a yellow rain slicker. He enters through screen door, crosses porch to stage right door and enters stage. Closes door. Takes off rain slicker and shakes it out. He sees all the others and stops.* TILDEN *turns to him.* BRADLEY *stares at* SHELLY. DODGE *remains on floor.*

BRADLEY: What's going on here? (*motioning to* SHELLY) Who's that?

SHELLY *stands, moves back away from* BRADLEY *as he crosses toward her. He stops next to* TILDEN. *He sees coat in* TILDEN'S *hand and grabs it away from him.*

BRADLEY: Who's she supposed to be?

TILDEN: She's driving to New Mexico.

BRADLEY *stares at her.* SHELLY *is frozen.* BRADLEY *limps over to her with the coat in his fist. He stops in front of her.*

BRADLEY: (*to* SHELLY, *after pause*) Vacation?

SHELLY *shakes her head "no," trembling.*

BRADLEY: (*to* SHELLY, *motioning to* TILDEN) You taking him with you?

SHELLY *shakes her head "no."* BRADLEY *crosses back to* TILDEN.

BRADLEY: You oughta'. No use leaving him here. Doesn't do a lick a' work. Doesn't raise a finger. (*stopping, to* TILDEN) Do ya'? (*to* SHELLY) 'Course he used to be an All American. Quarterback or Fullback or somethin'. He tell you that?

SHELLY *shakes her head "no."*

BRADLEY: Yeah, he used to be a big deal. Wore lettermen's sweaters. Had medals hanging all around his neck. Real purty. Big deal. (*he laughs to himself, notices* DODGE *on floor, crosses to him, stops*) This one too. (*to* SHELLY) You'd never think it to look at him would ya'? All bony and wasted away.

SHELLY *shakes her head again.* BRADLEY *stares at her, crosses back to her, clenching the coat in his fist. He stops in front of* SHELLY.

BRADLEY: Women like that kinda' thing don't they?

SHELLY: What?

BRADLEY: Importance. Importance in a man?

SHELLY: I don't know.

BRADLEY: Yeah. You know, you know. Don't give me that. (*moves closer to* SHELLY) You're with Tilden?

SHELLY: No.

BRADLEY: (*turning to* TILDEN) Tilden! She with you?

TILDEN *doesn't answer. Stares at floor.*

BRADLEY: Tilden!

TILDEN *suddenly bolts and runs off up stage left.* BRADLEY *laughs. Talks to* SHELLY. DODGE *starts moving his lips silently as though talking to someone invisible on the floor.*

BRADLEY: (*laughing*) Scared to death! He was always scared!

BRADLEY *stops laughing. Stares at* SHELLY.

BRADLEY: You're scared too, right? (*laughs again*) You're scared and you don't even know me. (*stops laughing*) You don't

gotta be scared.

SHELLY *looks at* DODGE *on the floor.*

SHELLY: Can't we do something for him?

BRADLEY: (*looking at* DODGE) We could shoot him. (*laughs*) We could drown him! What about drowning him?

SHELLY: Shut up!

BRADLEY *stops laughing. Moves in closer to* SHELLY. *She freezes.* BRADLEY *speaks slowly and deliberately.*

BRADLEY: Hey! Missus. Don't talk to me like that. Don't talk to me in that tone a' voice. There was a time when I had to take that tone a' voice from pretty near everyone. (*motioning to* DODGE) Him, for one! Him and that half brain that just ran outa' here. They don't talk to me like that now. Not any more. Everything's turned around now. Full circle. Isn't that funny?

SHELLY: I'm sorry.

BRADLEY: Open your mouth.

SHELLY: What?

BRADLEY: (*motioning for her to open her mouth*) Open up.

*She opens her mouth slightly.*

BRADLEY: Wider.

*She opens her mouth wider.*

BRADLEY: Keep it like that.

*She does. Stares at* BRADLEY. *With his free hand he puts his fingers into her mouth. She tries to pull away.*

BRADLEY: Just stay put!

*She freezes. He keeps his fingers in her mouth. Stares at her. Pause. He pulls his hand out. She closes her mouth, keeps her eyes on him.* BRADLEY *smiles. He looks at* DODGE *on the floor and crosses over to him.* SHELLY *watches him closely.* BRADLEY *stands over* DODGE *and smiles at* SHELLY. *He holds her coat up in both hands over* DODGE, *keeps smiling at* SHELLY. *He looks down at* DODGE *then drops the coat so that it lands on* DODGE *and covers his head.* BRADLEY *keeps his hands up in the position of holding the coat, looks over at* SHELLY *and smiles. The lights black out.*

# ACT 3

## SCENE

*Same set. Morning. Bright sun. No sound of rain. Everything has been cleared up again. No sign of carrots. No pail. No stool. VINCE'S saxophone case and overcoat are still at the foot of the staircase. BRADLEY is asleep on the sofa under DODGE'S blanket. His head toward stage left. BRADLEY'S wooden leg is leaning against the sofa right by his head. The shoe is left on it. The harness hangs down. DODGE is sitting on the floor, propped up against the T.V. set facing stage left wearing his baseball cap. SHELLY'S rabbit fur coat covers his chest and shoulders. He stares off toward stage left. He seems weaker and more disoriented. The lights rise slowly to the sound of birds and remain for a while in silence on the two men. BRADLEY sleeps very soundly. DODGE hardly moves. SHELLY appears from stage left with a big smile, slowly crossing toward DODGE balancing a steaming cup of broth in a saucer. DODGE just stares at her as she gets close to him.*

SHELLY: (*as she crosses*) This is going to make all the difference in the world, Grandpa. You don't mind me calling you Grandpa do you? I mean I know you minded when Vince called you that but you don't even know him.

DODGE: He skipped town with my money ya' know. I'm gonna hold you as collateral.

SHELLY: He'll be back. Don't you worry.
*She kneels down next to DODGE and puts the cup and saucer in his lap.*

DODGE: It's morning already! Not only didn't I get my bottle but he's got my two bucks!

SHELLY: Try to drink this, okay? Don't spill it.

DODGE: What is it?

SHELLY: Beef bouillon. It'll warm you up.

DODGE: Bouillon! I don't want any goddamn bouillon! Get that stuff away from me!

SHELLY: I just got through making it.

DODGE: I don't care if you just spent all week making it! I ain't drinking it!

SHELLY: Well, what am I supposed to do with it then? I'm trying to help you out. Besides, it's good for you.

DODGE: Get it away from me!
*SHELLY stands up with cup and saucer.*

DODGE: What do you know what's good for me, anyway?
*She looks at DODGE then turns away from him, crossing to staircase, sits on bottom step and drinks the bouillon. DODGE stares at her.*

DODGE: You know what'd be good for me?

SHELLY: What?

DODGE: A little massage. A little contact.

SHELLY: Oh no. I've had enough contact for a while. Thanks anyway.
*She keeps sipping bouillon, stays sitting. Pause as DODGE stares at her.*

DODGE: Why not? You got nothing better to do. That fella's not gonna be back here. You're not expecting him to show up again are you?

SHELLY: Sure. He'll show up. He left his horn here.

DODGE: His horn? (*laughs*) You're his horn?

SHELLY: Very funny.

DODGE: He's run off with my money! He's not coming back here.

SHELLY: He'll be back.

DODGE: You're a funny chicken, you know that?

SHELLY: Thanks.

DODGE: Full of faith. Hope. Faith and hope. You're all alike you hopers. If it's not God then it's a man. If it's not a man then it's a woman. If it's not a woman then it's the land or the future of some kind. Some kind of future.
*Pause.*

SHELLY: (*looking toward porch*) I'm glad it stopped raining.

DODGE: (*looks toward porch then back to her*) That's what I mean. See, you're glad it stopped raining. Now you think everything's gonna be different. Just 'cause the sun comes out.

SHELLY: It's already different. Last night I was scared.

DODGE: Scared a' what?

SHELLY: Just scared.

DODGE: Bradley? (*looks at* BRADLEY) He's a push-over. 'Specially now. All ya' gotta' do is take his leg and throw it out the back door. Helpless. Totally helpless.

SHELLY *turns and stares at* BRADLEY'S *wooden leg then looks at* DODGE. *She sips bouillon.*

SHELLY: You'd do that?

DODGE: Me? I've hardly got the strength to breathe.

SHELLY: But you'd actually do it if you could?

DODGE: Don't be so easily shocked, girlie. There's nothing a man can't do. You dream it up and he can do it. Anything.

SHELLY: You've tried I guess.

DODGE: Don't sit there sippin' your bouillon and judging me! This is my house!

SHELLY: I forgot.

DODGE: You forgot? Whose house did you think it was?

SHELLY: Mine.

DODGE *just stares at her. Long pause. She sips from cup.*

SHELLY: I know it's not mine but I had that feeling.

DODGE: What feeling?

SHELLY: The feeling that nobody lives here but me. I mean everybody's gone. You're here, but it doesn't seem like you're supposed to be. (*pointing to* BRADLEY) Doesn't seem like he's supposed to be here either. I don't know what it is. It's the house or something. Something familiar. Like I know my way around here. Did you ever get that feeling?

DODGE *stares at her in silence. Pause.*

DODGE: No. No, I never did.

SHELLY *gets up. Moves around space holding cup.*

SHELLY: Last night I went to sleep up there in that room.

DODGE: What room?

SHELLY: The room up there with all the pictures. All the crosses on the wall.

DODGE: Halie's room?

SHELLY: Yeah. Whoever "Halie" is.

DODGE: She's my wife.

SHELLY: So you remember her?

DODGE: What'ya mean! 'Course I remember her! She's only been gone for a day—half a day. However long it's been.

SHELLY: Do you remember her when her hair was bright red? Standing in front of an apple tree?

DODGE: What is this, the third degree or something? Who're you to be askin' me personal questions about my wife!

SHELLY: You never look at those pictures up there?

DODGE: What pictures?

SHELLY: Your whole life's up there hanging on the wall. Somebody who looks just like you. Somebody who looks just like you used to look.

DODGE: That isn't me! That never was me! This is me. Right here. This is it. The whole shootin' match, sittin' right in front of you.

SHELLY: So the past never happened as far as you're concerned?

DODGE: The past? Jesus Christ. The past. What do you know about the past?

SHELLY: Not much. I know there was a farm. *Pause*

DODGE: A farm?

SHELLY: There's a picture of a farm. A big farm. A bull. Wheat. Corn.

DODGE: Corn?

SHELLY: All the kids are standing out in the corn. They're all waving these big straw hats. One of them doesn't have a hat.

DODGE: Which one was that?

SHELLY: There's a baby. A baby in a woman's arms. The same woman with the red hair. She looks lost standing out there. Like she doesn't know how she got there.

DODGE: She knows! I told her a hundred times it wasn't gonna' be the city! I gave her plenty a' warning.

SHELLY: She's looking down at the baby like it was somebody else's. Like it didn't even belong to her.

DODGE: That's about enough outa' you! You got some funny ideas. Some damn funny ideas. You think just because people propagate they have to love their off-spring? You never seen a bitch eat her puppies? Where are you from anyway?

SHELLY: L.A. We already went through that.

DODGE: That's right, L.A. I remember.

SHELLY: Stupid country.

DODGE: That's right! No wonder.
*Pause.*

SHELLY: What's happened to this family anyway?

DODGE: You're in no position to ask! What do you care? You some kinda' Social Worker?

SHELLY: I'm Vince's friend.

DODGE: Vince's friend! That's rich. That's really rich. "Vince"! "Mr. Vince"! "Mr. Thief" is more like it! His name doesn't mean a hoot in hell to me. Not a tinkle in the well. You know how many kids I've spawned? Not to mention Grand kids and Great Grand kids and Great Great Grand kids after them?

SHELLY: And you don't remember any of them?

DODGE: What's to remember? Halie's the one with the family album. She's the one you should talk to. She'll set you straight on the heritage if that's what you're in-terested in. She's traced it all the way back to the grave.

SHELLY: What do you mean?

DODGE: What do you think I mean? How far back can you go? A long line of corpses! There's not a living soul behind me. Not a one. Who's holding me in their mem-ory? Who gives a damn about bones in the ground?

SHELLY: Was Tilden telling the truth?
*DODGE stops short. Stares at SHELLY. Shakes his head. He looks off stage left.*

SHELLY: Was he?
*DODGE'S tone changes drastically.*

DODGE: Tilden? (*turns to SHELLY calmly*) Where is Tilden?

SHELLY: Last night. Was he telling the truth about the baby?
*Pause.*

DODGE: (*turns toward stage left*) What's hap-pened to Tilden? Why isn't Tilden here?

SHELLY: Bradley chased him out.

DODGE: (*looking at BRADLEY asleep*) Bradley? Why is he on my sofa? (*turns back to SHELLY*) Have I been here all night? On the floor?

SHELLY: He wouldn't leave. I hid outside until he fell asleep.

DODGE: Outside? Is Tilden outside? He shouldn't be out there in the rain. He'll get himself into trouble. He doesn't know his way around here anymore. Not like he used to. He went out West and got himself into trouble. Got himself into bad trouble. We don't want any of that around here.

SHELLY: What did he do?
*Pause.*

DODGE: (*quietly stares at SHELLY*) Tilden? He got mixed up. That's what he did. We can't afford to leave him alone. Not now.
*Sound of HALIE laughing comes from off left. SHELLY stands, looking in direction of voice, holding cup and saucer, doesn't know whether to stay or run.*

DODGE: (*motioning to SHELLY*) Sit down! Sit back down!
*SHELLY sits. Sound of HALIE'S laughter again.*

DODGE: (*to SHELLY in a heavy whisper, pulling coat up around him*) Don't leave me alone now! Promise me? Don't go off and leave me alone. I need somebody here with

me. Tilden's gone now and I need someone. Don't leave me! Promise!

SHELLY: (*sitting*) I won't.

> HALIE *appears outside the screen porch door,
> up left with* FATHER DEWIS. *She is wearing
> a bright yellow dress, no hat, white gloves
> and her arms are full of yellow roses.* FATHER
> DEWIS *is dressed in traditional black suit,
> white clerical collar and shirt. He is a very
> distinguished grey haired man in his sixties.
> They are both slightly drunk and feeling
> giddy. As they enter the porch through the
> screen door,* DODGE *pulls the rabbit fur coat
> over his head and hides.* SHELLY *stands
> again.* DODGE *drops the coat and whispers
> intensely to* SHELLY. *Neither* HALIE *nor* FA-
> THER DEWIS *are aware of the people inside
> the house.*

DODGE: (*to* SHELLY *in a strong whisper*) You
promised!

> SHELLY *sits on stairs again.* DODGE *pulls
> coat back over his head.* HALIE *and* FATHER
> DEWIS *talk on the porch as they cross toward
> stage right interior door.*

HALIE: Oh Father! That's terrible! That's absolutely terrible. Aren't you afraid of being punished?

> *She giggles.*

DEWIS: Not by the Italians. They're too busy
punishing each other.

> *They both break out in giggles.*

HALIE: What about God?

DEWIS: Well, prayerfully, God only hears
what he wants to. That's just between
you and me of course. In our heart of
hearts we know we're every bit as
wicked as the Catholics.

> *They giggle again and reach the stage right
> door.*

HALIE: Father, I never heard you talk like
this in Sunday sermon.

DEWIS: Well, I save all my best jokes for private company. Pearls before swine you
know.

> *They enter the room laughing and stop when
> they see* SHELLY. SHELLY *stands.* HALIE

*closes the door behind* FATHER DEWIS.
DODGE'S *voice is heard under the coat, talking to* SHELLY.

DODGE: (*under coat, to* SHELLY) Sit down, sit
down! Don't let 'em buffalo you!

> SHELLY *sits on stair again.* HALIE *looks at*
> DODGE *on the floor then looks at* BRADLEY
> *asleep on sofa and sees his wooden leg. She
> lets out a shriek of embarrassment for* FA-
> THER DEWIS.

HALIE: On my gracious! What in the name of
Judas Priest is going on in this house!

> *She hands over the roses to* FATHER DEWIS.

HALIE: Excuse me Father.

> HALIE *crosses to* DODGE, *whips the coat off
> him and covers the wooden leg with it.*
> BRADLEY *stays asleep.*

HALIE: You can't leave this house for a second without the Devil blowing in
through the front door!

DODGE: Gimme back that coat! Gimme back
that goddamn coat before I freeze to
death!

HALIE: You're not going to freeze! The sun's
out in case you hadn't noticed!

DODGE: Gimme back that coat! That coat's
for live flesh not dead wood!

> HALIE *whips the blanket off* BRADLEY *and
> throws it on* DODGE. DODGE *covers his head
> again with blanket.* BRADLEY'S *amputated
> leg can be faked by having half of it under a
> cushion of the sofa. He's fully clothed.*
> BRADLEY *sits up with a jerk when the blan-
> ket comes off him.*

HALIE: (*as she tosses blanket*) Here! Use this!
It's yours anyway! Can't you take care of
yourself for once!

BRADLEY: (*yelling at* HALIE) Gimme that
blanket! Gimme back that blanket!
That's my blanket!

> HALIE *crosses back toward* FATHER DEWIS
> *who just stands there with the roses.*
> BRADLEY *thrashes helplessly on the sofa try-
> ing to reach blanket.* DODGE *hides himself
> deeper in blanket.* SHELLY *looks on from
> staircase, still holding cup and saucer.*

HALIE: Believe me, Father, this is not what I had in mind when I invited you in.

DEWIS: On, no apologies please. I wouldn't be in the ministry if I couldn't face real life.

*He laughs self-consciously.* HALIE *notices* SHELLY *again and crosses over to her.* SHELLY *stays sitting.* HALIE *stops and stares at her.*

BRADLEY: I want my blanket back! Gimme my blanket!

HALIE *turns toward* BRADLEY *and silences him.*

HALIE: Shut up Bradley! Right this minute! I've had enough!

BRADLEY *slowly recoils, lies back down on sofa, turns his back toward* HALIE *and whimpers softly.* HALIE *directs her attention to* SHELLY *again. Pause.*

HALIE: (*to* SHELLY) What're you doing with my cup and saucer?

SHELLY: (*looking at cup, back to* HALIE) I made some bouillon for Dodge.

HALIE: For Dodge?

SHELLY: Yeah.

HALIE: Well, did he drink it?

SHELLY: No.

HALIE: Did you drink it?

SHELLY: Yes.

HALIE *stares at her. Long pause. She turns abruptly away from* SHELLY *and crosses back to* FATHER DEWIS.

HALIE: Father, there's a stranger in my house. What would you advise? What would be the Christian thing?

DEWIS: (*squirming*) Oh, well. . . . I. . . . I really—

HALIE: We still have some whiskey, don't we?

DODGE *slowly pulls the blanket down off his head and looks toward* FATHER DEWIS. SHELLY *stands.*

SHELLY: Listen, I don't drink or anything. I just—

HALIE *turns toward* SHELLY *viciously.*

HALIE: You sit back down!

SHELLY *sits again on stair.* HALIE *turns again to* DEWIS.

HALIE: I think we have plenty of whiskey left! Don't we Father?

DEWIS: Well, yes. I think so. You'll have to get it. My hands are full.

HALIE *giggles. Reaches into* DEWIS'S *pockets, searching for bottle. She smells the roses as she searches.* DEWIS *stands stiffly.* DODGE *watches* HALIE *closely as she looks for bottle.*

HALIE: The most incredible things, roses! Aren't they incredible, Father?

DEWIS: Yes. Yes they are.

HALIE: They almost cover the stench of sin in this house. Just magnificent! The smell. We'll have to put some at the foot of Ansel's statue. On the day of the unveiling.

HALIE *finds a silver flask of whiskey in* DEWIS'S *vest pocket. She pulls it out.* DODGE *looks on eagerly.* HALIE *crosses to* DODGE, *opens the flask and takes a sip.*

HALIE: (*to* DODGE) Ansel's getting a statue, Dodge. Did you know that? Not a plaque but a real live statue. A full bronze. Tip to toe. A basketball in one hand and a rifle in the other.

BRADLEY: (*his back to* HALIE) He never played basketball!

HALIE: You shut up, Bradley! You shut up about Ansel! Ansel played basketball better than anyone! And you know it! He was an All American! There's no reason to take the glory away from others.

HALIE *turns away from* BRADLEY, *crosses back toward* DEWIS *sipping on the flask and smiling.*

HALIE: (*to* DEWIS) Ansel was a great basketball player. One of the greatest.

DEWIS: I remember Ansel.

HALIE: Of course! You remember. You remember how he could play. (*she turns toward* SHELLY) Of course, nowadays they play a different brand of basketball. More vicious. Isn't that right, dear?

SHELLY: I don't know.

*.IALIE crosses to* SHELLY, *sipping on flask. She stops in front of* SHELLY.

HALIE: Much, much more vicious. They smash into each other. They knock each other's teeth out. There's blood all over the court. Savages.

HALIE *takes the cup from* SHELLY *and pours whiskey into it.*

HALIE: They don't train like they used to. Not at all. They allow themselves to run amuck. Drugs and women. Women mostly.

HALIE *hands the cup of whiskey back to* SHELLY *slowly.* SHELLY *takes it.*

HALIE: Mostly women. Girls. Sad, pathetic little girls. (*she crosses back to* FATHER DEWIS) It's just a reflection of the times, don't you think Father? An indication of where we stand?

DEWIS: I suppose so, yes.

HALIE: Yes. A sort of a bad omen. Our youth becoming monsters.

DEWIS: Well, I uh—

HALIE: Oh you can disagree with me if you want to, Father. I'm open to debate. I think argument only enriches both sides of the question don't you? (*she moves toward* DODGE) I suppose, in the long run, it doesn't matter. When you see the way things deteriorate before your very eyes. Everything running down hill. It's kind of silly to even think about youth.

DEWIS: No, I don't think so. I think it's important to believe in certain things.

HALIE: Yes. Yes, I know what you mean. I think that's right. I think that's true. (*she looks at* DODGE) Certain basic things. We can't shake certain basic things. We might end up crazy. Like my husband. You can see it in his eyes. You can see how mad he is.

DODGE *covers his head with the blanket*

*again.* HALIE *takes a single rose from* DEWIS *and moves slowly over to* DODGE.

HALIE: We can't not believe in something. We can't stop believing. We just end up dying if we stop. Just end up dead.

HALIE *throws the rose gently onto* DODGE'S *blanket. It lands between his knees and stays there. Long pause as* HALIE *stares at the rose.* SHELLY *stands suddenly.* HALIE *doesn't turn to her but keeps staring at rose.*

SHELLY: (*to* HALIE) Don't you wanna' know who I am? Don't you wanna know what I'm doing here? I'm not dead!

SHELLY *crosses toward* HALIE. HALIE *turns slowly toward her.*

HALIE: Did you drink your whiskey?

SHELLY: No! And I'm not going to either!

HALIE: Well that's a firm stand. It's good to have a firm stand.

SHELLY: I don't have any stand at all. I'm just trying to put all this together.

HALIE *laughs and crosses back to* DEWIS.

HALIE: (*to* DEWIS) Surprises, surprises! Did you have any idea we'd be returning to this?

SHELLY: I came here with your Grandson for a little visit! A little innocent friendly visit.

HALIE: My Grandson?

SHELLY: Yes! That's right. The one no one remembers.

HALIE: (*to* DEWIS) This is getting a little far fetched.

SHELLY: I told him it was stupid to come back here. To try to pick up from where he left off.

HALIE: Where was that?

SHELLY: Wherever he was when he left here! Six years ago! Ten years ago! Whenever it was. I told him nobody cares.

HALIE: Didn't he listen?

SHELLY: No! No he didn't. We had to stop off at every tiny little meatball town that he remembered from his boyhood! Every stupid little donut shop he ever kissed a girl in. Every Drive-In. Every Drag Strip. Every football field he ever broke a bone on.

HALIE: (*suddenly alarmed, to* DODGE) Where's Tilden?

SHELLY: Don't ignore me!

HALIE: Dodge! Where's Tilden gone?

SHELLY *moves violently toward* HALIE.

SHELLY: (*to* HALIE) I'm talking to you!

BRADLEY *sits up fast on the sofa,* SHELLY *backs away.*

BRADLEY: (*to* SHELLY) Don't you yell at my mother!

HALIE: Dodge! (*she kicks* DODGE) I told you not to let Tilden out of your sight! Where's he gone to?

DODGE: Gimme a drink and I'll tell ya'.

DEWIS: Halie, maybe this isn't the right time for a visit.

HALIE *crosses back to* DEWIS.

HALIE: (*to* DEWIS) I never should've left. I never, never should've left! Tilden could be anywhere by now! Anywhere! He's not in control of his faculties. Dodge knew that. I told him when I left here. I told him specifically to watch out for Tilden.

BRADLEY *reaches down, grabs* DODGE'S *blanket and yanks it off him. He lays down on sofa and pulls the blanket over his head.*

DODGE: He's got my blanket again! He's got my blanket!

HALIE: (*turning to* BRADLEY) Bradley! Bradley, put that blanket back!

HALIE *moves toward* BRADLEY. SHELLY *suddenly throws the cup and saucer against the stage right door.* DEWIS *ducks. The cup and saucer smash into pieces.* HALIE *stops, turns toward* SHELLY. *Everyone freezes.* BRADLEY *slowly pulls his head out from under blanket, looks toward stage right door, then to* SHELLY. SHELLY *stares at* HALIE. DEWIS *cowers with roses.* SHELLY *moves slowly toward* HALIE. *Long pause.* SHELLY *speaks softly.*

SHELLY: (*to* HALIE) I don't like being ignored. I don't like being treated like I'm not here. I didn't like it when I was a kid and I still don't like it.

BRADLEY: (*sitting up on sofa*) We don't have to tell you anything, girl. Not a thing. You're not the police are you? You're not the government. You're just some prostitute that Tilden brought in here.

HALIE: Language! I won't have that language in my house!

SHELLY: (*to* BRADLEY) You stuck your hand in my mouth and you call me a prostitute!

HALIE: Bradley! Did you put your hand in her mouth? I'm ashamed of you. I can't leave you alone for a minute.

BRADLEY: I never did. She's lying!

DEWIS: Halie, I think I'll be running along now. I'll just put the roses in the kitchen. DEWIS *moves toward stage left.* HALIE *stops him.*

HALIE: Don't go now, Father! Not now.

BRADLEY: I never did anything, mom! I never touched her! She propositioned me! And I turned her down. I turned her down flat!

SHELLY *suddenly grabs her coat off the wooden leg and takes both the leg and coat down stage, away from* BRADLEY.

BRADLEY: Mom! Mom! She's got my leg! She's taken my leg! I never did anything to her! She's stolen my leg!

BRADLEY *reaches pathetically in the air for his leg.* SHELLY *sets it down for a second, puts on her coat fast and picks the leg up again.* DODGE *starts coughing softly.*

HALIE: (*to* SHELLY) I think we've had about enough of you, young lady. Just about enough. I don't know where you came from or what you're doing here but you're no longer welcome in this house.

SHELLY: (*laughs, holds leg*) No longer welcome!

BRADLEY: Mom! That's my leg! Get my leg back! I can't do anything without my leg.

BRADLEY *keeps making whimpering sounds and reaching for his leg.*

HALIE: Give my son back his leg. Right this very minute!

DODGE *starts laughing softly to himself in between coughs.*

HALIE: (*to* DEWIS) Father, do something about this would you! I'm not about to be terrorized in my own house!

BRADLEY: Gimme back my leg!

HALIE: Oh, shut up Bradley! Just shut up! You don't need your leg now! Just lay down and shut up!

BRADLEY *whimpers. Lays down and pulls blanket around him. He keeps one arm outside blanket, reaching out toward his wooden leg.* DEWIS *cautiously approaches* SHELLY *with the roses in his arms.* SHELLY *clutches the wooden leg to her chest as though she's kidnapped it.*

DEWIS: (*to* SHELLY) Now, honestly dear, wouldn't it be better to try to talk things out? To try to use some reason?

SHELLY: There isn't any reason here! I can't find a reason for anything.

DEWIS: There's nothing to be afraid of. These are all good people. All righteous people.

SHELLY: I'm not afraid!

DEWIS: But this isn't your house. You have to have some respect.

SHELLY: You're the strangers here, not me.

HALIE: This has gone far enough!

DEWIS: Halie, please. Let me handle this.

SHELLY: Don't come near me! Don't anyone come near me. I don't need any words from you. I'm not threatening anybody. I don't even know what I'm doing here. You all say you don't remember Vince, okay, maybe you don't. Maybe it's Vince that's crazy. Maybe he's made this whole family thing up. I don't even care any more. I was just coming along for the ride. I thought it'd be a nice gesture. Besides, I was curious. He made all of you sound familiar to me. Every one of you. For every name, I had an image. Every time he'd tell me a name, I'd see the person. In fact, each of you was so clear in my mind that I actually believed it was you. I really believed when I walked through that door that the people who lived here would turn out to be the same people in my imagination. But I don't recognize any of you. Not one. Not even the slightest resemblance.

DEWIS: Well you can hardly blame others for not fulfilling your hallucination.

SHELLY: It was no hallucination! It was more like a prophecy. You believe in prophecy, don't you?

HALIE: Father, there's no point in talking to her any further. We're just going to have to call the police.

BRADLEY: No! Don't get the police in here. We don't want the police in here. This is our home.

SHELLY: That's right. Bradley's right. Don't you usually settle your affairs in private? Don't you usually take them out in the dark? Out in the back?

BRADLEY: You stay out of our lives! You have no business interfering!

SHELLY: I don't have any business period. I got nothing to lose.

*She moves around, staring at each of them.*

BRADLEY: You don't know what we've been through. You don't know anything!

SHELLY: I know you've got a secret. You've all got a secret. It's so secret in fact, you're all convinced it never happened.

HALIE *moves to* DEWIS

HALIE: Oh, my God, Father!

DODGE: (*laughing to himself*) She thinks she's going to get it out of us. She thinks she's going to uncover the truth of the matter. Like a detective or something.

BRADLEY: I'm not telling her anything! Nothing's wrong here! Nothing's ever been wrong! Everything's the way it's supposed to be! Nothing ever happened that's bad! Everything is all right here! We're all good people!

DODGE: She thinks she's gonna suddenly bring everything out into the open after all these years.

DEWIS: (*to* SHELLY) Can't you see that these people want to be left in peace? Don't you have any mercy? They haven't done anything to you.

DODGE: She wants to get to the bottom of it. (*to* SHELLY) That's it, isn't it? You'd like to get right down to bedrock? You want me to tell ya'? You want me to tell ya' what happened? I'll tell ya'. I might as well.

BRADLEY: No! Don't listen to him. He doesn't remember anything!

DODGE: I remember the whole thing from start to finish. I remember the day he was born.
*Pause.*

HALIE: Dodge, if you tell this thing—if you tell this, you'll be dead to me. You'll be just as good as dead.

DODGE: That won't be such a big change, Halie. See this girl, this girl here, she wants to know. She wants to know something more. And I got this feeling that it doesn't make a bit a' difference. I'd sooner tell it to a stranger than anybody else.

BRADLEY: (*to* DODGE) We made a pact! We made a pact between us! You can't break that now!

DODGE: I don't remember any pact.

BRADLEY: (*to* SHELLY) See, he doesn't remember anything. I'm the only one in the family who remembers. The only one. And I'll never tell you!

SHELLY: I'm not so sure I want to find out now.

DODGE: (*laughing to himself*) Listen to her! Now she's runnin' scared!

SHELLY: I'm not scared!
DODGE *stops laughing, long pause.* DODGE *stares at her.*

DODGE: You're not, huh? Well, that's good. Because I'm not either. See, we were a well established family once. Well established. All the boys were grown. The farm was producing enough milk to fill Lake Michigan twice over. Me and Halie here were pointed toward what looked like the middle part of our life. Everything was settled with us. All we had to do was ride it out. Then Halie got pregnant again. Outa' the middle a' nowhere she got pregnant. We weren't planning on havin' any more boys. We had enough boys already. In fact, we hadn't been sleepin' in the same bed for about six years.

HALIE: (*moving toward stairs*) I'm not listenin' to this! I don't have to listen to this!

DODGE: (*stops* HALIE) Where are you going? Upstairs? You'll just be listenin' to it upstairs! You go outside, you'll be listenin' to it outside. Might as well stay here and listen to it.
HALIE *stays by stairs.*

BRADLEY: If I had my leg you wouldn't be saying this. You'd never get away with it if I had my leg.

DODGE: (*pointing to* SHELLY) She's got your leg. (*laughs*) She's gonna keep your leg too. (*to* SHELLY) She wants to hear this. Don't you?

SHELLY: I don't know.

DODGE: Well even if ya' don't I'm gonna' tell ya'. (*pause*) Halie had this kid. This baby boy. She had it. I let her have it on her own. All the other boys I had had the best doctors, best nurses, everything. This one I let her have by herself. This one hurt real bad. Almost killed her, but she had it anyway. It lived, see. It lived. It wanted to grow up in this family. It wanted to be just like us. It wanted to be a part of us. It wanted to pretend that I was its father. She wanted me to believe in it. Even when everyone around us knew. Everyone. All our boys knew. Tilden knew.

HALIE: You shut up! Bradley, make him shut up!

BRADLEY: I can't.

DODGE: Tilden was the one who knew. Better than any of us. He'd walk for miles with that kid in his arms. Halie let him take it. All night sometimes. He'd walk all night out there in the pasture with it. Talkin' to it. Singin' to it. Used to hear him singin' to it. He'd make up stories. He'd tell that kid all kinds a' stories. Even when he knew it couldn't understand him. Couldn't understand a word he was sayin'. Never would understand him. We couldn't let a thing like that continue. We couldn't allow that to grow up right in the middle of our lives. It made everything we'd accomplished look like it was nothin'. Everything was cancelled out by this one mistake. This one weakness.

SHELLY: So you killed him?

DODGE: I killed it. I drowned it. Just like the runt of a litter. Just drowned it.

HALIE *moves toward* BRADLEY.

HALIE: (*to* BRADLEY) Ansel would've stopped him! Ansel would've stopped him from telling these lies! He was a hero! A man! A whole man! What's happened to the men in this family! Where are the men!

*Suddenly* VINCE *comes crashing through the screen porch door up left, tearing it off its hinges. Everyone but* DODGE *and* BRADLEY *back away from the porch and stare at* VINCE *who has landed on his stomach on the porch in a drunken stupor. He is singing loudly to himself and hauls himself slowly to his feet. He has a paper shopping bag full of empty booze bottles. He takes them out one at a time as he sings and smashes them at the opposite end of the porch, behind the solid interior door, stage right.* SHELLY *moves slowly toward stage right, holding wooden leg and watching* VINCE.

VINCE: (*singing loudly as he hurls bottles*) "From the Halls of Montezuma to the Shores of Tripoli. We will fight our coun-

try's battles on the land and on the sea." *He punctuates the words "Montezuma," "Tripoli," "battles" and "sea" with a smashed bottle each. He stops throwing for a second, stares toward stage right of the porch, shades his eyes with his hand as though looking across to a battle field, then cups his hands around his mouth and yells across the space of the porch to an imaginary army. The others watch in terror and expectation.*

VINCE: (*to imagined Army*) Have you had enough over there? 'Cause there's a lot more here where that came from! (*pointing to paper bag full of bottles*) A helluva lot more! We got enough over here to blow ya' from here to Kingdomcome!

*He takes another bottle, makes high whistling sound of a bomb and throws it toward stage right porch. Sound of bottle smashing against wall. This should be the actual smashing of bottles and not tape sound. He keeps yelling and heaving bottles one after another.* VINCE *stops for a while, breathing heavily from exhaustion. Long silence as the others watch him.* SHELLY *approaches tentatively in* VINCE'S *direction, still holding* BRADLEY'S *wooden leg.*

SHELLY: (*after silence*) Vince?

VINCE *turns toward her. Peers through screen.*

VINCE: Who? What? Vince who? Who's that in there?

VINCE *pushes his face against the screen from the porch and stares in at everyone.*

DODGE: Where's my goddamn bottle!

VINCE: (*looking in at* DODGE) What? Who is that?

DODGE: It's me! Your Grandfather! Don't play stupid with me! Where's my two bucks!

VINCE: Your two bucks?

HALIE *moves away from* DEWIS, *upstage, peers out at* VINCE, *trying to recognize him.*

HALIE: Vincent? Is that you, Vincent?

SHELLY *stares at* HALIE *then looks out at* VINCE.

VINCE: (*from porch*) Vincent who? What is this! Who are you people?

SHELLY: (*to* HALIE) Hey, wait a minute. Wait a minute! What's going on?

HALIE: (*moving closer to porch screen*) We thought you were a murderer or something. Barging in through the door like that.

VINCE: I am a murderer! Don't underestimate me for a minute! I'm the Midnight Strangler! I devour whole families in a single gulp!

*VINCE grabs another bottle and smashes it on the porch.* HALIE *backs away.*

SHELLY: (*approaching* HALIE) You mean you know who he is?

HALIE: Of course I know who he is! That's more than I can say for you.

BRADLEY: (*sitting up on sofa*) You get off our front porch you creep! What're you doing out there breaking bottles? Who are these foreigners anyway! Where did they come from?

VINCE: Maybe I should come in there and break them!

HALIE: (*moving toward porch*) Don't you dare! Vincent, what's got into you! Why are you acting like this?

VINCE: Maybe I should come in there and usurp your territory!

HALIE *turns back toward* DEWIS *and crosses to him.*

HALIE: (*to* DEWIS) Father, why are you just standing around here when everything's falling apart? Can't you rectify this situation?

DODGE *laughs, coughs.*

DEWIS: I'm just a guest here, Halie. I don't know what my position is exactly. This is outside my parish anyway.

VINCE *starts throwing more bottles as things continue.*

BRADLEY: If I had my leg I'd rectify it! I'd rectify him all over the goddamn highway! I'd pull his ears out if I could reach him!

BRADLEY *sticks his fist through the screening of the porch and reaches out for* VINCE, *grabbing at him and missing.* VINCE *jumps away from* BRADLEY'S *hand.*

VINCE: Aaaah! Our lines have been penetrated! Tentacled animals! Beasts from the deep!

VINCE *strikes out at* BRADLEY'S *hand with a bottle.* BRADLEY *pulls his hand back inside.*

SHELLY: Vince! Knock it off will ya'! I want to get out of here!

VINCE *pushes his face against screen, looks in at* SHELLY.

VINCE: (*to* SHELLY) Have they got you prisoner in there, dear? Such a sweet young thing too. All her life in front of her. Nipped in the bud.

SHELLY: I'm coming out there, Vince! I'm coming out there and I want us to get in the car and drive away from here. Anywhere. Just away from here.

SHELLY *moves toward* VINCE'S *saxophone case and overcoat. She sets down the wooden leg downstage left, and picks up the saxophone case and overcoat.* VINCE *watches her through the screen.*

VINCE: (*to* SHELLY) We'll have to negotiate. Make some kind of a deal. Prisoner exchange or something. A few of theirs for one of ours. Small price to pay if you ask me.

SHELLY *crosses toward stage right door with overcoat and case.*

SHELLY: Just go and get the car! I'm coming out there now. We're going to leave.

VINCE: Don't come out here! Don't you dare come out here!

SHELLY *stops short of the door, stage right.*

SHELLY: How come?

VINCE: Off limits! Verboten! This is taboo territory. No man or woman has ever crossed the line and lived to tell the tale!

SHELLY: I'll take my chances.

SHELLY *moves to stage right door and opens it.* VINCE *pulls out a big folding hunting knife and pulls open the blade. He jabs the blade into the screen and starts cutting a hole big enough to climb through.* **BRADLEY** *cowers in a corner of the sofa as* **VINCE** *rips at the screen.*

**VINCE:** (*as he cuts screen*) Don't come out here! I'm warning you. You'll disintegrate!

**DEWIS** *takes* **HALIE** *by the arm and pulls her toward staircase.*

**DEWIS:** Halie, maybe we should go upstairs until this blows over.

**HALIE:** I don't understand it. I just don't understand it. He was the sweetest little boy!

**DEWIS** *drops the roses beside the wooden leg at the foot of the staircase then escorts* **HALIE** *quickly up the stairs.* **HALIE** *keeps looking back at* **VINCE** *as they climb the stairs.*

**HALIE:** There wasn't a mean bone in his body. Everyone loved Vincent. Everyone. He was the perfect baby.

**DEWIS:** He'll be all right after a while. He's just had a few too many that's all.

**HALIE:** He used to sing in his sleep. He'd sing. In the middle of the night. The sweetest voice. Like an angel. (*she stops for a moment*) I used to lie awake listening to it. I used to lie awake thinking it was all right if I died. Because Vincent was an angel. A guardian angel. He'd watch over us. He'd watch over all of us.

**DEWIS** *takes her all the way up the stairs. They disappear above.* **VINCE** *is now climbing through the porch screen onto the sofa.* **BRADLEY** *crashes off the sofa, holding tight to his blanket, keeping it wrapped around him.* **SHELLY** *is outside on the porch.* **VINCE** *holds the knife in his teeth once he gets the hole wide enough to climb through.* **BRADLEY** *starts crawling slowly toward his wooden leg, reaching out for it.*

**DODGE:** (*to* **VINCE**) Go ahead! Take over the house! Take over the whole goddamn house! You can have it! It's yours. It's been a pain in the neck ever since the very first mortgage. I'm gonna die any second now. Any second. You won't even notice. So I'll settle my affairs once and for all.

*As* **DODGE** *proclaims his last will and testament,* **VINCE** *climbs into the room, knife in mouth and strides slowly around the space, inspecting his inheritance. He casually notices* **BRADLEY** *as he crawls toward his leg.* **VINCE** *moves to the leg and keeps pushing it with his foot so that it's out of* **BRADLEY'S** *reach then goes on with his inspection. He picks up the roses and carries them around smelling them.* **SHELLY** *can be seen outside on the porch, moving slowly center and staring in at* **VINCE**. **VINCE** *ignores her.*

**DODGE:** The house goes to my Grandson, Vincent. All the furnishings, accoutrements and paraphernalia therein. Everything tacked to the walls or otherwise resting under this roof. My tools—namely my band saw, my skill saw, my drill press, my chain saw, my lathe, my electric sander, all go to my eldest son, Tilden. That is, if he ever shows up again. My shed and gasoline powered equipment, namely my tractor, my dozer, my hand tiller plus all the attachments and riggings for the above mentioned machinery, namely my spring tooth harrow, my deep plows, my disk plows, my automatic fertilizing equipment, my reaper, my swathe, my seeder, my John Deere Harvester, my post hole digger, my jackhammer, my lathe—(*to himself*) Did I mention my lathe? I already mentioned my lathe—my Bennie Goodman records, my harnesses, my bits, my halters, my brace, my rough rasp, my forge, my welding equipment, my shoeing nails, my levels and bevels, my milking stool—no, not my milking stool—my hammers and chisels, my hinges, my cattle gates, my barbed wire, self-tapping augers, my horse hair ropes and all related materials are to be pushed into a gigantic heap and set ablaze in the very center of my fields. When the blaze is at its highest, preferably on a cold, windless night, my body is to be pitched into the middle of it and burned til nothing remains but ash.

*Pause.* VINCE *takes the knife out of his mouth and smells the roses. He's facing toward audience and doesn't turn around to* SHELLY. *He folds up knife and pockets it.*

SHELLY: (*from porch*) I'm leaving, Vince. Whether you come or not, I'm leaving.

VINCE: (*smelling roses*) Just put my horn on the couch there before you take off.

SHELLY: (*moving toward hole in screen*) You're not coming?

VINCE *stays downstage, turns and looks at her.*

VINCE: I just inherited a house.

SHELLY: (*through hole, from porch*) You want to stay here?

VINCE: (*as he pushes* BRADLEY'S *leg out of reach*) I've gotta carry on the line. I've gotta see to it that things keep rolling.

BRADLEY *looks up at him from floor, keeps pulling himself toward his leg.* VINCE *keeps moving it.*

SHELLY: What happened to you Vince? You just disappeared.

VINCE: (*pauses, delivers speech front*) I was gonna run last night. I was gonna run and keep right on running. I drove all night. Clear to the Iowa border. The old man's two bucks sitting right on the seat beside me. It never stopped raining the whole time. Never stopped once. I could see myself in the windshield. My face. My eyes. I studied my face. Studied everything about it. As though I was looking at another man. As though I could see his whole race behind him. Like a mummy's face. I saw him dead and alive at the same time. In the same breath. In the windshield, I watched him breathe as though he was frozen in time. And every breath marked him. Marked him forever without him knowing. And

then his face changed. His face became his father's face. Same bones. Same eyes. Same nose. Same breath. And his father's face changed to his Grandfather's face. And it went on like that. Changing. Clear on back to faces I'd never seen before but still recognized. Still recognized the bones underneath. The eyes. The breath. The mouth. I followed my family clear into Iowa. Every last one. Straight into the Corn Belt and further. Straight back as far as they'd take me. Then it all dissolved. Everything dissolved.

SHELLY *stares at him for a while then reaches through the hole in the screen and sets the saxophone case and* VINCE'S *overcoat on the sofa. She looks at* VINCE *again.*

SHELLY: Bye Vince.

*She exits left off the porch.* VINCE *watches her go.* BRADLEY *tries to make a lunge for his wooden leg.* VINCE *quickly picks it up and dangles it over* BRADLEY'S *head like a carrot.* BRADLEY *keeps making desperate grabs at the leg.* DEWIS *comes down the staircase and stops half way, staring at* VINCE *and* BRADLEY. VINCE *looks up at* DEWIS *and smiles. He keeps moving backwards with the leg toward upstage left as* BRADLEY *crawls after him.*

VINCE: (*to* DEWIS *as he continues torturing* BRADLEY) Oh, excuse me Father. Just getting rid of some of the vermin in the house. This is my house now, ya' know? All mine. Everything. Except for the power tools and stuff. I'm gonna get all new equipment anyway. New plows, new tractor, everything. All brand new. (VINCE *teases* BRADLEY *closer to the up left corner of the stage*) Start right off on the ground floor.

VINCE *throws* BRADLEY'S *wooden leg far off stage left.* BRADLEY *follows his leg off stage, pulling himself along on the ground, whimpering. As* BRADLEY *exits* VINCE *pulls the blanket off him and throws it over his own shoulder. He crosses toward* DEWIS *with the blanket and smells the roses.* DEWIS *comes to the bottom of the stairs.*

DEWIS: You'd better go up and see your Grandmother.

VINCE: (*looking up stairs, back to* DEWIS) My Grandmother? There's nobody else in this house. Except for you. And you're leaving aren't you?

DEWIS *crosses toward stage right door. He turns back to* VINCE.

DEWIS: She's going to need someone. I can't help her. I don't know what to do. I don't know what my position is. I just came in for tea. I had no idea there was any trouble. No idea at all.

VINCE *just stares at him.* DEWIS *goes out the door, crosses porch and exits left.* VINCE *listens to him leaving. He smells roses, looks up the staircase then smells roses again. He turns and looks upstage at* DODGE. *He crosses up to him and bends over looking at* DODGE'S *open eyes.* DODGE *is dead. His death should have come completely unnoticed by the audience.* VINCE *covers* DODGE'S *body with the blanket, then covers his head. He sits on the sofa, smelling roses and staring at* DODGE'S *body. Long pause.* VINCE *places the roses on* DODGE'S *chest then lays down on the sofa, arms folded behind his head, staring at the ceiling. His body is in the same relationship to* DODGE'S. *After a while* HALIE'S *voice is heard coming from above the staircase. The lights start to dim almost imperceptively as* HALIE *speaks.* VINCE *keeps staring at the ceiling.*

HALIE'S VOICE: Dodge? Is that you Dodge? Tilden was right about the corn you know. I've never seen such corn. Have you taken a look at it lately? Tall as a man already. This early in the year. Carrots too. Potatoes. Peas. It's like a paradise out there, Dodge. You oughta' take a look. A miracle. I've never seen it like this. Maybe the rain did something. Maybe it was the rain.

*As* HALIE *keeps talking off stage,* TILDEN *appears from stage left dripping with mud from the knees down. His arms and hands are covered with mud. In his hands he carries the corpse of a small child at chest level, staring down at it. The corpse mainly consists of bones wrapped in muddy, rotten cloth. He moves slowly downstage toward the staircase, ignoring* VINCE *on the sofa.* VINCE *keeps staring at the ceiling as though* TILDEN *wasn't there. As* HALIE'S VOICE *continues,* TILDEN *slowly makes his way up the stairs. His eyes never leave the corpse of the child. The lights keep fading.*

HALIE'S VOICE: Good hard rain. Takes everything straight down deep to the roots. The rest takes care of itself. You can't force a thing to grow. You can't interfere with it. It's all hidden. It's all unseen. You just gotta wait til it pops up out of the ground. Tiny little shoot. Tiny little white shoot. All hairy and fragile. Strong though. Strong enough to break the earth even. It's a miracle, Dodge. I've never seen a crop like this in my whole life. Maybe it's the sun. Maybe that's it. Maybe it's the sun.

TILDEN *disappears above. Silence. Lights go to black.*

## SUMMARY

As we have discovered, a play is at once a literary text and a performance text. Written in prose or verse, the literary text is described as *drama*, emphasizing its potential for being enacted or performed. It is the playwright's special literary form for "imitating" human behavior and events.

All dramatic texts have in common their imitation of imagined events and fictional worlds. For 2500 years, the dramatic text has been the playwright's blueprint for giving shape, order, and meaning to human experience as the writer sees and understands it. Playwrights create meaningful patterns of events, words, gestures, and actions to convey to readers and to audiences what it means to be human beings caught up in special circumstances, such as wars, plagues, sexual intrigues, and domestic quarrels. Since dramatic texts are written to be performed in the space and time of the theatre, there is a doubleness about our experience of a play. In the theatre, plays are experienced in the present time and in the stage space. Dramatic texts also contain their own versions of space and time which become the bases for imagined human actions in fictional worlds. Dramatic space is highly malleable and can portray locations that are miles apart; characters can move from locale to locale without violating our sense of the logical progression of events. One play may take place wholly in a living room (*Buried Child*); another may require battlefields, palaces, and graveyards (*Hamlet*). Dramatic time, also a condition of the text, is likewise flexible. Within a play's fictional world, time can be compressed or expanded to reflect hours or years.

In reading a play, we progress from "what is happening next" in terms of storytelling to "what it all means." This is our final concern because plays, like the lives or realities they imitate, progress through action and events to a discovery that those happenings have special meanings. What a play finally means to the reader and to the viewer involves the completed action—all that has gone before in organized, meaningful episodes. Upon reflection, we realize that we have followed (and experienced) the psychological and physical currents of human endeavor as the playwright has presented them to us in the text. However, the playwright's final meanings in great plays, like *Oedipus the King, Hamlet,* or *The Cherry Orchard,* are always open to many interpretations. "What it is all about" remains open to reinterpretation and to restaging because, like life, the complexities and subtleties of dramatic events and characters cannot be reduced to neat meanings. For example, Sam Shepard's contemporary play, *Buried Child*, presents a grandson's quest for personal identity and familial roots. His determined search and harrowing discovery, involving the proverbial "family skeleton," are Shepard's means of imitating shattered American myths about family togetherness, familial love, and personal achievement. Instead, we experience disconnections, misplaced values, and degeneration involving the most heinous of a society's taboos: incest and murder. However, Shepard is an optimistic writer and the play does not end with death but with the possibility of personal and familial renewal manifested in the mystical crops.

While Shepard's methods and meanings can be described and interpreted, there are events, relationships, and motives in *Buried Child* that cannot be fully explained away. Some examples are the bizarreness of the family members, the mystical field, the circumstances surrounding the dead child's conception and birth, the sons' and grandson's histories, the denial of the existence of the buried child, and so on. Shepard perhaps best expressed the elusive quality of a play's meaning when he told an interviewer, "I feel like there are territories within us that are totally unknown. Huge, mysterious, and dangerous territories. We think we know ourselves, when we really only know this little bitty part. We have this social person that we present to each other. We have all these galaxies inside of us. And if we don't enter those in art . . . then I don't understand the point in doing anything."[5] *Buried Child* contains galaxies of the mysterious which, like life, defy complete explanations. Therefore, in play analysis we concentrate on "how a play means" through the workings of plot, action, character, dialogue, visual effects, and so on.

*Buried Child* challenges our skills to understand the playwright's craft and intentions. Let us turn next to older plays and conventions. The efforts of playwrights to imitate extremes of human experience have resulted in two major types of writing for the theatre—tragedy and comedy.

## NOTES

1. Lillian Hellman, *Pentimento: A Book of Portraits* (Boston: Little, Brown, 1973): 151–152.
2. Hellman 151–152.
3. Martin Esslin, *The Field of Drama: How the Signs of Drama Create Meaning on Stage and Screen* (London: Methuen, 1987): 24.
4. Jan Kott, *The Theater of Essence and Other Essays* (Evanston, Ill.: Northwestern University Press, 1984): 211.
5. Amy Lippman, "Rhythm & Truths: An Interview with Sam Shepard," *American Theater*, 1, No. 1 (April 1984): 9.

# PART TWO

# TYPES OF DRAMA

twelve or fifteen. The chorus moved in slow and stately measures accompanied by the flute, chanting odes usually reflecting on the events immediately preceding or giving background on the myth in general. In dialogue passages, the choral leader (*coryphaeus*) probably spoke for the entire chorus. The odes were divided into stanzas, called *strophes* and *antistrophes*, delivered as the chorus moved first in one direction and then in the opposite. The odes alternated with *episodes* in which several actors told the story and moved the plot forward. The first episode was called the *prologos* and the last the *exodos;* there were typically five episodes in a tragedy. The odes separated the episodes, adding dimensions of myth, memory, emotion, and background information.

The physical theatre and its conventions, for which Sophocles wrote, were to a large degree inflexible. We must remember that the physical theatre always influences the playwright's work, resulting in peculiarities of writing throughout the centuries. We know some facts about the Theatre of Dionysus during the age of Aeschylus, Sophocles, and Euripides. The theatre was located at the base of a hillside. The audience—perhaps as large as 15,000—sat on benches rising in half circles on the southern slope of the Acropolis. The plays were performed before a long, low wooden building (*skene*) that served as background for the action and as a dressing room for the actors. In front of the scene building was the main circular acting area, called the *orchestra* or dancing circle, with an altar for Dionysus in the center. Whether or not there was a low, raised stage in front of the building and separating the main action from the choral action, we do not know. Most historians think it was an unlikely feature in the fifth century B.C. The platform stage became a known feature in later stage architecture but its existence was debatable at the time of Sophocles. Both actors and chorus wore masks to indicate age, tempera-

ment, and sex. Since men played women's parts and actors often played several parts, masks also had a practical function. The actors wore ankle-length, colorful robes (*chitons*), resembling garments worn by well-dressed Athenians. The playwright had to take into account the number of speaking actors available to him at any given time, although there could be actors in nonspeaking roles, like palace guards. The actors had to be highly trained professionals because the performance of several plays, lasting most of the daylight hours, made great demands on their voices and physical stamina.

In Sophocles' time, playwrights usually dramatized a traditional story (for example, the legend surrounding the House of Thebes). In Sophocles' treatment the old Theban myth of humanity's vain effort to circumvent divine will is a suspenseful revelation of the fateful continuity of the past into the present. There is the pathos of innocent ignorance and impotence which affects aristocrat and shepherd alike. Oedipus is ignorant of who he is and what he has done in all innocence. The structure of the story is *retrospective:* The gradual revelation of past events creates the present. Every step Oedipus takes to solve the old murder mystery of who killed Laius, every one of the chance disclosures, brings him closer both to the solution he seeks and to the self-discovery he does not expect. When the last piece falls into place, the detective has become the criminal, his success has become his doom, and his ignorance has become tragic knowledge.

The plot is heavily ironic, introducing the technique of *dramatic irony* of which Sophocles was a master. Dramatic irony operates whenever there are circumstances in plot or character of which the speaker is ignorant or misunderstands. The more unfortunate the significance of the character's ignorance, the more poignant the tragic irony. Oedipus' early words to the Theban citizens are, "There is not one of you who knows my pain." On the surface we hear the king's concern for his stricken people and his involvement in the city's fate, but, because we know the Theban myth, we also perceive the dreadful accuracy of his description of himself. The knowledgeable reader is alert to the persistent ironies in Oedipus' story: He curses Laius's murderer, promising to take revenge for the dead king, "As I would for my own father"; his berating of Teiresias, the blind seer, for his arrogance and complicity in Laius's murder hints at his own blindness; his accusation that Jocasta does not want the truth of Oedipus' identity revealed because she fears she has married a peasant hints at their true relationship; and Jocasta's painful farewell is delivered in full knowledge that she confronts husband and son in the same individual. She says, "Accursed! Accursed! I have no other name/To call you."

Sophocles' irony builds suspense and engages our interest in the unfolding story of the frailty of human defenses, the folly of our feelings of security and power, and the strange inevitability of human fate or destiny. The Greeks used other techniques to build suspense and to forward the plot in the episodes. They used the debate (or *agon*) as a means of putting two opposing points of view before the chorus and audience; the debate also demonstrated conflict between characters—Oedipus versus Teiresias, Oedipus versus Creon, Oedipus versus Jocasta. In debates, characters often exchanged a brisk staccato of one-liners (called *stichomythia*) for up to a hundred lines at a time. The effect was like a tennis match where words and emotions were volleyed back and forth between two opponents. In these debates, the turbulence of human emotions burst through the formal rhetoric in the outcries of suffering and rage. In addition, Greek writers used the convention of a messenger to report events such as carnage and death. These descriptive reports prepared the audience for the spectacle of the hero's suffering.

One such report is the messenger's account of how Oedipus, realizing the enormity of his crimes, attempts to kill Jocasta but, finding her dead, then puts out his eyes.

The logical and methodical unraveling of the past through techniques of debate, report, and irony creates suspense and demonstrates how, with the best of intentions, we can prove inadequate to control our present situation and determine our future happiness. *Irony* is a literary device for holding different and opposite truths in suspension, for focusing on the discrepancy between what seems to be and what is. It is an appropriate device to be used in a tragedy about a man's self-ignorance. At the play's beginning, Oedipus has a clear and single purpose: to find Laius's murderer. The first quest turns into a second pursuit: to learn Oedipus' true parentage and identity. The two pursuits are ironically one: The answer to the question of whose son he is also answers the question of who killed Laius. Oedipus undertakes both quests in full confidence and pride in his abilities for, after all, he solved the riddle of the Sphinx ("Who moves on four in the morning, on two at noon, and on three in the evening?") and became the city's savior. The answer was "Man." Yet, Oedipus, the man, has never known himself. The terrible recognition scene imparts the knowledge of his true identity but also the Sophoclean understanding that wisdom is achieved through suffering. His is a bitter variant of the Greek dictum, "know thyself," for the Greeks believed that knowledge was a pathway to virtue and the good life. Nevertheless, many like Sophocles believed that ultimate self-knowledge is achieved only through pain and suffering.

The troublesome question for moderns is: Does Oedipus deserve his suffering? Let us consider the facts. He has committed parricide and incest, thereby violating society's most sacred taboos. (Sigmund Freud applied his name to the most primary of sexual conflicts: the male child's jealousy of the father.) How can Oedipus be held accountable for crimes committed in ignorance? How can Oedipus be held responsible for a destiny predicted for him before his birth and for the turn of events that fulfill that destiny? Why should he have to pay, years later, for his parents' efforts to circumvent the god's will?

Before we cry out that Oedipus is no more than a puppet dangled from a supernatural string, we must distinguish between the gods' *knowledge* and their *prediction*. The god in his wisdom, knowing the kind of man Oedipus was to become, could know and predict his destiny. Nevertheless, Oedipus is the maker of his destiny, not the god. He runs away from Corinth toward Thebes, thus encountering in his anger and pride Laius, the Sphinx, and all that follows. Given all of his vulnerabilities of mind and temperament (his *hamartia*), Oedipus is victim both of circumstances he creates and of his own nature.

Oedipus is one of drama's greatest tragic heroes because he accepts responsibility for his shame as the incestuous child, his guilt as Laius's murderer, and his dishonor as The-bes' pollution. The tragic paradox is that for a second time he saves Thebes. In all of this, we are aware of the workings of a supernatural order that is ruthless but not arbitrary or malevolent. The will of the gods is inscrutable, but it must be obeyed. In Sophocles' universe, the Oedipus story affirms the workings of divine justice as inexorable, methodical, and rational. Before the absolute, human virtues—intellect, integrity, power, and will—are helpless. The chorus has the final word on the meaning of the Oedipus story for Sophocles. Before the spectacle of human suffering, the chorus is grief-stricken, awed, and bewildered. They conclude:

> . . . *behold this Oedipus,—*
> *him who knew the famous riddles and was a man most masterful;*
> *not a citizen who did not look with envy on his lot—*
> *see him now and see the breakers of misfortune swallow him!*
> *Look upon that last day always. Count no mortal happy till*
> *he has passed the final limit of his life secure from pain.*

# Oedipus the King

TRANSLATED BY DAVID GRENE

**CHARACTERS**
**OEDIPUS** King of Thebes
**JOCASTA** His Wife
**CREON** His Brother-in-Law
**TEIRESIAS** An Old Blind Prophet
**A PRIEST**
**FIRST MESSENGER**
**SECOND MESSENGER**
**A HERDSMAN**
**A CHORUS OF OLD MEN OF THEBES**

**SCENE**
*In front of the palace of Oedipus at Thebes. To the right of the stage near the altar stands the* **PRIEST** *with a crowd of children.* **OEDIPUS** *emerges from the central door.*

    OEDIPUS
Children, young sons and daughters of old
    Cadmus,
why do you sit here with your suppliant crowns?
The town is heavy with a mingled burden
of sounds and smells, of groans and hymns and
    incense;
I did not think it fit that I should hear
of this from messengers but came myself,—
I Oedipus whom all men call the Great.
(*He turns to the* **PRIEST**)
You're old and they are young; come, speak for
    them.
What do you fear or want, that you sit here
suppliant? Indeed I'm willing to give all
that you may need; I would be very hard
should I not pity suppliants like these.
    PRIEST
O ruler of my country, Oedipus,
you see our company around the altar;

you see our ages; some of us, like these,
who cannot yet fly far, and some of us
heavy with age; these children are the chosen
among the young, and I the priest of Zeus.
Within the market place sit others crowned
with suppliant garlands, at the double shrine
of Pallas and the temple where Ismenus
gives oracles by fire. King, you yourself
have seen our city reeling like a wreck
already; it can scarcely lift its prow
out of the depths, out of the bloody surf.
A blight is on the fruitful plants of the earth,
A blight is on the cattle in the fields,
a blight is on our women that no children
are born to them; a God that carries fire,
a deadly pestilence, is on our town,
strikes us and spares not, and the house of
    Cadmus
is emptied of its people while black Death
grows rich in groaning and in lamentation.
We have not come as suppliants to this altar
because we thought of you as of a God,
but rather judging you the first of men
in all the chances of this life and when
we mortals have to do with more than man.
You came and by your coming saved our city,
freed us from tribute which we paid of old
to the Sphinx, cruel singer. This you did
in virtue of no knowledge we could give you,
in virtue of no teaching; it was God
that aided you, men say, and you are held
with God's assistance to have saved our lives.
Now Oedipus, Greatest in all men's eyes,
here falling at your feet we all entreat you,
find us some strength for rescue.
Perhaps you'll hear a wise word from some God,
perhaps you will learn something from a man
(for I have seen that for the skilled of practice

the outcome of their counsels live the most).
Noblest of men, go, and raise up our city,
go,—and give heed. For now this land of ours
calls you its savior since you saved it once.
So, let us never speak about your reign
as of a time when first our feet were set
secure on high, but later fell to ruin.
Raise up our city, save it and raise it up.
Once you have brought us luck with happy
      omen;
be no less now in fortune.
If you will rule this land, as now you rule it,
better to rule it full of men than empty.
For neither tower nor ship is anything
when empty, and none live in it together.

OEDIPUS

I pity you, children. You have come full of
      longing,
but I have known the story before you told it
only too well. I know you are all sick,
yet there is not one of you, sick though you are,
that is as sick as I myself.
Your several sorrows each have single scope
and touch but one of you. My spirit groans
for city and myself and you at once.
You have not roused me like a man from sleep;
know that I have given many tears to this,
gone many ways wandering in thought,
but as I thought I found only one remedy
and that I took. I send Menoeceus' son
Creon, Jocasta's brother, to Apollo,
to his Pythian temple,
that he might learn there by what act or word
I could save this city. As I count the days,
it vexes me what ails him; he is gone
far longer than he needed for the journey.
But when he comes, then, may I prove a villain,
if I shall not do all the God commands.

PRIEST

Thanks for your gracious words. Your servants
      here
signal that Creon is this moment coming.

OEDIPUS

His face is bright. O holy Lord Apollo,
grant that his news too may be bright for us
and bring us safety.

PRIEST

It is happy news,
I think, for else his head would not be crowned
with sprigs of fruitful laurel.

OEDIPUS

                              We will know soon,
he's within hail. Lord Creon, my good brother,
what is the word you bring us from the God?
(CREON enters.)

CREON

A good word,—for things hard to bear
      themselves
if in the final issue all is well
I count complete good fortune.

OEDIPUS

                              What do you mean?
What you have said so far
leaves me uncertain whether to trust or fear.

CREON

If you will hear my news before these others
I am ready to speak, or else to go within.

OEDIPUS

Speak it to all;
the grief I bear, I bear it more for these
than for my own heart.

CREON

                              I will tell you, then,
what I heard from the God.
King Phoebus in plain words commanded us
to drive out a pollution from our land,
pollution grown ingrained within the land;
drive it out, said the God, not cherish it,
till it's past cure.

OEDIPUS

                              What is the rite
of purification? How shall it be done?

CREON

By banishing a man, or expiation
of blood by blood, since it is murder guilt
which holds our city in this destroying storm.

OEDIPUS

Who is this man whose fate the God pronounces?

CREON

My Lord, before you piloted the state
we had a king called Laius.

OEDIPUS

I know of him by hearsay. I have not seen him.

CREON

The God commanded clearly: let some one
punish with force this dead man's murderers.

OEDIPUS

Where are they in the world? Where would a trace
of this old crime be found? It would be hard
to guess where.

CREON

The clue is in this land;
that which is sought is found;
the unheeded thing escapes:
so said the God.

OEDIPUS

Was it at home,
or in the country that death came upon him,
or in another country travelling?

CREON

He went, he said himself, upon an embassy,
but never returned when he set out from home.

OEDIPUS

Was there no messenger, no fellow traveller
who knew what happened? Such a one might tell
something of use.

CREON

They were all killed save one. He fled in terror
and he could tell us nothing in clear terms
of what he knew, nothing, but one thing only.

OEDIPUS

What was it?
If we could even find a slim beginning
in which to hope, we might discover much.

CREON

This man said that the robbers they encountered
were many and the hands that did the murder
were many; it was no man's single power.

OEDIPUS

How could a robber dare a deed like this
were he not helped with money from the city,
money and treachery?

CREON

That indeed was thought.
But Laius was dead and in our trouble
there was none to help.

OEDIPUS

What trouble was so great to hinder you
inquiring out the murder of your king?

CREON

The riddling Sphinx induced us to neglect
mysterious crimes and rather seek solution
of troubles at our feet.

OEDIPUS

I will bring this to light again. King Phoebus
fittingly took this care about the dead,
and you too fittingly
And justly you will see in me an ally,
a champion of my country and the God.
For when I drive pollution from the land

I will not serve a distant friend's advantage,
but act in my own interest. Whoever
he was that killed the king may readily
wish to dispatch me with his murderous hand;
so helping the dead king I help myself.
Come, children, take your suppliant boughs and
go;
up from the altars now. Call the assembly
and let it meet upon the understanding
that I'll do everything. God will decide
whether we prosper or remain in sorrow.

PRIEST

Rise, children—it was this we came to seek,
which of himself the king now offers us.
May Phoebus who gave us the oracle
come to our rescue and stay the plague.

(*Exeunt all but the* **CHORUS.**)

CHORUS

*Strophe*

What is the sweet spoken word of God from the
shrine of Pytho rich in gold
that has come to glorious Thebes?
I am stretched on the rack of doubt, and terror
and trembling hold
my heart, O Delian Healer, and I worship full of
fears
for what doom you will bring to pass, new or
renewed in the revolving years.
Speak to me, immortal voice,
child of golden Hope.

*Antistrophe*

First I call on you, Athene, deathless daughter of
Zeus,
and Artemis, Earth Upholder,
who sits in the midst of the market place in the
throne which men call Fame,
and Phoebus, the Far Shooter, three averters of
Fate,
come to us now, if ever before, when ruin rushed
upon the state,
you drove destruction's flame away
out of our land.

*Strophe*

Our sorrows defy number;
all the ship's timbers are rotten;
taking of thought is no spear for the driving away
of the plague.
There are no growing children in this famous land;
there are no women bearing the pangs of
childbirth.

You may see them one with another, like birds
    swift on the wing,
quicker than fire unmastered,
speeding away to the coast of the Western God.
    *Antistrophe*
In the unnumbered deaths
of its people the city dies;
those children that are born lie dead on the naked
    earth
unpitied, spreading contagion of death; and grey
    haired mothers and wives
everywhere stand at the altar's edge, suppliant,
    moaning;
the hymn to the healing God rings out but with it
    the wailing voices are blended.
From these our sufferings grant us, O golden
    Daughter of Zeus,
glad-faced deliverance.
    *Strophe*
There is no clash of brazen shields but our fight is
    with the War God,
a War God ringed with the cries of men, a savage
    God who burns us;
grant that he turn in racing course backwards out
    of our country's bounds
to the great palace of Amphitrite or where the
    waves of the Thracian sea
deny the stranger safe anchorage.
Whatsoever escapes the night
at last the light of day revisits;
so smite the War God, Father Zeus,
beneath your thunderbolt,
for you are the Lord of lightning, the lightning
    that carries fire.
    *Antistrophe*
And your unconquered arrow shafts, winged by
    the golden corded bow,
Lycean King, I beg to be at our side for help;
and the gleaming torches of Artemis with which
    she scours the Lycean hills,
and I call on the God with the turban of gold,
    who gave his name to this country of ours,
the Bacchic God with the wind flushed face,
Evian One, who travel
with the Maenad company,
combat the God that burns us
with your torch of pine;
for the God that is our enemy is a God
    unhonoured among the Gods.
(**OEDIPUS** *returns.*)

**OEDIPUS**
For what you ask me—if you will hear my words,
and hearing welcome them and fight the plague,
you will find strength and lightening of your load.
Hark to me; what I say to you, I say
as one that is a stranger to the story
as stranger to the deed. For I would not
be far upon the track if I alone
were tracing it without a clue. But now,
since after all was finished, I became
a citizen among you, citizens—
now I proclaim to all the men of Thebes:
who so among you knows the murderer
by whose hand Laius, son of Labdacus,
died—I command him to tell everything
to me,—yes, though he fears himself to take the
    blame
on his own head; for bitter punishment
he shall have none, but leave this land unharmed.
Or if he knows the murderer, another,
a foreigner, still let him speak the truth.
For I will pay him and be grateful, too.
But if you shall keep silence, if perhaps
some one of you, to shield a guilty friend,
or for his own sake shall reject my words—
hear what I shall do then:
I forbid that man, whoever he be, my land,
my land where I hold sovereignty and throne;
and I forbid any to welcome him
or cry him greeting or make him a sharer
in sacrifice or offering to the Gods,
or give him water for his hands to wash.
I command all to drive him from their homes,
since he is our pollution, as the oracle
of Pytho's God proclaimed him now to me.
So I stand forth a champion of the God
and of the man who died.
Upon the murderer I invoke this curse—
whether he is one man and all unknown,
or one of many—may he wear out his life
in misery to miserable doom!
If with my knowledge he lives at my hearth
I pray that I myself may feel my curse.
On you I lay my charge to fulfill all this
for me, for the God, and for this land of ours
destroyed and blighted, by the God forsaken.
Even were this no matter of God's ordinance
it would not fit you so to leave it lie,
unpurified, since a good man is dead
and one that was a king. Search it out.

Since I am now the holder of his office,
and have his bed and wife that once was his,
and had his line not been unfortunate
we would have common children—(fortune
      leaped
upon his head)—because of all these things,
I fight in his defense as for my father,
and I shall try all means to take the murderer
of Laius the son of Labdacus
the son of Polydorus and before him
of Cadmus and before him of Agenor.
Those who do not obey me, may the Gods
grant no crops springing from the ground they
      plough
nor children to their women! May a fate
like this, or one still worse than this consume
      them!
For you whom these words please, the other
      Thebans,
may Justice as your ally and all the Gods
live with you, blessing you now and for ever!

CHORUS
As you have held me to my oath, I speak:
I neither killed the king nor can declare
the killer; but since Phoebus set the quest
it is his part to tell who the man is.

OEDIPUS
Right; but to put compulsion on the Gods
against their will—no man can do that.

CHORUS
May I then say what I think second best?

OEDIPUS
If there's a third best, too, spare not to tell it.

CHORUS
I know that what the Lord Teiresias
sees, is most often what the Lord Apollo
sees. If you should inquire of this from him
you might find out most clearly.

OEDIPUS
Even in this my actions have not been
      sluggard.
On Creon's word I have sent two messengers
and why the prophet is not here already
I have been wondering.

CHORUS
                                        His skill apart
there is besides only an old faint story.

OEDIPUS
What is it?
I look at every story.

CHORUS
                                        It was said
that he was killed by certain wayfarers.

OEDIPUS
I heard that, too, but no one saw the killer.

CHORUS
Yet if he has a share of fear at all,
his courage will not stand firm, hearing your
      curse.

OEDIPUS
The man who in the doing did not shrink
will fear no word.

CHORUS
                                Here comes his prosecutor:
led by your men the godly prophet comes
in whom alone of mankind truth is native
(*Enter* **TEIRESIAS,** *led by a little boy.*)

OEDIPUS
Teiresias, you are versed in everything,
things teachable and things not to be spoken,
things of the heaven and earth-creeping things.
You have no eyes but in your mind you know
with what a plague our city is afflicted.
My lord, in you alone we find a champion,
in you alone one that can rescue us.
Perhaps you have not heard the messengers,
but Phoebus sent in answer to our sending
an oracle declaring that our freedom
from this disease would only come when we
should learn the names of those who killed King
      Laius,
and kill them or expel from our country.
Do not begrudge us oracles from birds,
or any other way of prophecy
within your skill; save yourself and the city,
save me; redeem the debt of our pollution
that lies on us because of this dead man.
We are in your hands; pains are most nobly taken
to help another when you have means and power.

TEIRESIAS
Alas, how terrible is wisdom when
it brings no profit to the man that's wise!
This I knew well, but had forgotten it,
else I would not have come here.

OEDIPUS
                                                What is this?
How sad you are now you have come!

TEIRESIAS
                                                        Let me
go home. It will be easiest for us both

to bear our several destinies to the end
if you will follow my advice.

OEDIPUS

You'd rob us
of this your gift of prophecy? You talk
as one who had no care for law nor love
for Thebes who reared you.

TEIRESIAS

Yes, but I see that even your own words
miss the mark; therefore I must fear for mine.

OEDIPUS

For God's sake if you know of anything,
do not turn from us; all of us kneel to you,
all of us here, your suppliants.

TEIRESIAS

All of you here know nothing. I will not
bring to the light of day my troubles, mine—
rather than call them yours.

OEDIPUS

What do you mean?
You know of something but refuse to speak.
Would you betray us and destroy the city?

TEIRESIAS

I will not bring this pain upon us both,
neither on you nor on myself. Why is it
you question me and waste your labour? I
will tell you nothing.

OEDIPUS

You would provoke a stone! Tell us, you villain,
tell us, and do not stand there quietly
unmoved and balking at the issue.

TEIRESIAS

You blame my temper but you do not see
your own that lives within you; it is me
you chide.

OEDIPUS

Who would not feel his temper rise
at words like these with which you shame our
  city?

TEIRESIAS

Of themselves things will come, although I hide
  them
and breathe no word of them.

OEDIPUS

Since they will come
tell them to me.

TEIRESIAS

I will say nothing further.
Against this answer let your temper rage
as wildly as you will.

OEDIPUS

Indeed I am
so angry I shall not hold back a jot
of what I think. For I would have you know
I think you were complotter of the deed
and doer of the deed save in so far
as for the actual killing. Had you had eyes
I would have said alone you murdered him.

TEIRESIAS

Yes? Then I warn you faithfully to keep
the letter of your proclamation and
from this day forth to speak no word of greeting
to these nor me; you are the land's pollution.

OEDIPUS

How shamelessly you started up this taunt!
How do you think you will escape?

TEIRESIAS

I have.
I have escaped; the truth is what I cherish
and that's my strength.

OEDIPUS

And who has taught you truth?
Not your profession surely!

TEIRESIAS

You have taught me,
for you have made me speak against my will.

OEDIPUS

Speak what? Tell me again that I may learn it
  better.

TEIRESIAS

Did you not understand before or would you
provoke me into speaking?

OEDIPUS

I did not grasp it,
not so to call it known. Say it again.

TEIRESIAS

I say you are the murderer of the king
whose murderer you seek.

OEDIPUS

Not twice you shall
say calumnies like this and stay unpunished.

TEIRESIAS

Shall I say more to tempt your anger more?

OEDIPUS

As much as you desire; it will be said
in vain.

TEIRESIAS

I say that with those you love best
you live in foulest shame unconsciously
and do not see where you are in calamity.

OEDIPUS

Do you imagine you can always talk
like this, and live to laugh at it hereafter?

TEIRESIAS

Yes, if the truth has anything of strength.

OEDIPUS

It has, but not for you; it has no strength
for you because you are blind in mind and ears
as well as in your eyes.

TEIRESIAS

                        You are a poor wretch
to taunt me with the very insults which
every one soon will heap upon yourself.

OEDIPUS

Your life is one long night so that you cannot
hurt me or any other who sees the light.

TEIRESIAS

It is not fate that I should be your ruin,
Apollo is enough; it is his care
to work this out.

OEDIPUS

                        Was this your own design
or Creon's?

TEIRESIAS

                        Creon is no hurt to you,
but you are to yourself.

OEDIPUS

Wealth, sovereignty and skill outmatching skill
for the contrivance of an envied life!
Great store of jealousy fill your treasury chests,
if my friend Creon, friend from the first and loyal,
thus secretly attacks me, secretly
desires to drive me out and secretly
suborns this juggling, trick devising quack,
this wily beggar who has only eyes
for his own gains, but blindness in his skill.
For, tell me, where have you seen clear, Teiresias,
with your prophetic eyes? When the dark singer,
the sphinx, was in your country, did you speak
word of deliverance to its citizens?
And yet the riddle's answer was not the province
of a chance comer. It was a prophet's task
and plainly you had no such gift of prophecy
from birds nor otherwise from any God
to glean a word of knowledge. But I came,
Oedipus, who knew nothing, and I stopped her.
I solved the riddle by my wit alone.
Mine was no knowledge got from birds. And now
you would expel me,
because you think that you will find a place

by Creon's throne. I think you will be sorry,
both you and your accomplice, for your plot
to drive me out. And did I not regard you
as an old man, some suffering would have taught
    you
that what was in your heart was treason.

CHORUS

We look at this man's words and yours, my
    king
and we find both have spoken them in anger.
We need no angry words but only thought
how we may best hit the God's meaning for us.

TEIRESIAS

If you are king, at least I have the right
no less to speak in my defence against you.
Of that much I am master. I am no slave
of yours, but Loxias', and so I shall not
enroll myself with Creon for my patron.
Since you have taunted me with being blind,
here is my word for you.
You have your eyes but see not where you are
in sin, nor where you live, nor whom you live
    with.
Do you know who your parents are? Unknowing
you are an enemy to kith and kin
in death, beneath the earth, and in this life.
A deadly footed, double striking curse,
from father and mother both, shall drive you forth
out of this land, with darkness on your eyes,
that now have such straight vision. Shall there be
a place will not be harbour to your cries,
a corner of Cithaeron will not ring
in echo to your cries, soon, soon,—
when you shall learn the secret of your marriage,
which steered you to a haven in this house,—
haven no haven, after lucky voyage?
And of the multitude of other evils
establishing a grim equality
between you and your children, you know
    nothing.
So, muddy with contempt my words and Creon's!
Misery shall grind no man as it will you.

OEDIPUS

Is it endurable that I should hear
such words from him? Go and a curse go with
    You!
Quick, home with you! Out of my house at once!

TEIRESIAS

I would not have come either had you not called
    me.

**OEDIPUS**
I did not know then you would talk like a fool—
would have been long before I called you.
    **TEIRESIAS**
I am a fool then, as it seems to you—
but to the parents who have bred you, wise.
    **OEDIPUS**
What parents? Stop! Who are they of all the world?
    **TEIRESIAS**
This day will show your birth and will destroy you.
    **OEDIPUS**
How needlessly your riddles darken everything.
    **TEIRESIAS**
But it's in riddle answering you are strongest.
    **OEDIPUS**
Yes. Taunt me where you will find me great.
    **TEIRESIAS**
It is this very luck that has destroyed you.
    **OEDIPUS**
I do not care, if it has saved this city.
    **TEIRESIAS**
Well, I will go. Come, boy, lead me away.
    **OEDIPUS**
Yes, lead him off. So long as you are here,
you'll be a stumbling block and a vexation;
once gone, you will not trouble me again.
    **TEIRESIAS**
                  I have said
what I came here to say not fearing your
countenance: there is no way you can hurt me.
I tell you, king, this man, this murderer
(whom you have long declared you are in search
    of,
indicting him in threatening proclamation
as murderer of Laius)—he is here.
In name he is a stranger among citizens
but soon he will be shown to be a citizen
true native Theban, and he'll have no joy
of the discovery: blindness for sight
and beggary for riches his exchange,
he shall go journeying to a foreign country
tapping his way before him with a stick.
He shall be proved father and brother both
to his own children in his house; to her
that gave him birth, a son and husband both;
a fellow sower in his father's bed
with that same father that he murdered.
Go within, reckon that out, and if you find me
mistaken, say I have no skill in prophecy.
(*Exeunt separately* **TEIRESIAS** *and* **OEDIPUS**.)

**CHORUS**
*Strophe*
Who is the man proclaimed
by Delphi's prophetic rock
as the bloody handed murderer,
the doer of deeds that none dare name?
Now is the time for him to run
with a stronger foot
than Pegasus
for the child of Zeus leaps in arms upon
    him
with fire and the lightning bolt,
and terribly close on his heels
are the Fates that never miss.
*Antistrophe*
Lately from snowy Parnassus
clearly the voice flashed forth,
bidding each Theban track him down,
the unknown murderer.
In the savage forests he lurks and in
the caverns like the mountain bull.
He is sad and lonely, and lonely his feet
that carry him far from the navel of earth;
but its prophecies, ever living,
flutter around his head.
*Strophe*
The augur has spread confusion,
terrible confusion;
I do not approve what was said
nor can I deny it.
I do not know what to say;
I am in a flutter of foreboding;
I never heard in the present
nor past of a quarrel between
the sons of Labdacus and Polybus,
that I might bring as proof
in attacking the popular fame
of Oedipus, seeking
to take vengeance for undiscovered
death in the line of Labdacus.
*Antistrophe*
Truly Zeus and Apollo are wise
and in human things all knowing;
but amongst men there is no
distinct judgment, between the prophet
and me—which of us is right.
One man may pass another in wisdom
but I would never agree
with those that find fault with the king
till I should see the word

proved right beyond doubt. For once
in visible form the Sphinx
came on him and all of us
saw his wisdom and in that test
he saved the city. So he will not be condemned by
    my mind.

(*Enter* **CREON**.)

    CREON

Citizens, I have come because I heard
deadly words spread about me, that the king
accuses me. I cannot take that from him.
If he believes that in these present troubles
he has been wronged by me in word or deed
I do not want to live on with the burden
of such a scandal on me. The report
injures me doubly and most vitally—
for I'll be called a traitor to my city
and traitor also to my friends and you.

    CHORUS

Perhaps it was a sudden gust of anger
that forced that insult from him, and no judgment.

    CREON

But did he say that it was in compliance
with schemes of mine that the seer told him lies?

    CHORUS

Yes, he said that, but why, I do not know.

    CREON

Were his eyes straight in his head? Was his mind
    right
when he accused me in this fashion?

    CHORUS

I do not know; I have no eyes to see
what princes do. Here comes the king himself.

(*Enter* **OEDIPUS**.)

    OEDIPUS

You, sir, how is it you come here? Have you so
    much
brazen-faced daring that you venture in
my house although you are proved manifestly
the murderer of that man, and though you tried,
openly, highway robbery of my crown?
For God's sake, tell me what you saw in me,
what cowardice or what stupidity,
that made you lay a plot like this against me?
Did you imagine I should not observe
the crafty scheme that stole upon me or
seeing it, take no means to counter it?
Was it not stupid of you to make the attempt,
to try to hunt down royal power without
the people at your back or friends? For only

with the people at your back or money can
the hunt end in the capture of a crown.

    CREON

Do you know what you're doing? Will you listen
to words to answer yours, and then pass
    judgment?

    OEDIPUS

You're quick to speak, but I am slow to grasp you,
for I have found you dangerous,—and my foe.

    CREON

First of all hear what I shall say to that.

    OEDIPUS

At least don't tell me that you are not guilty.

    CREON

If you think obstinacy without wisdom
a valuable possession, you are wrong.

    OEDIPUS

And you are wrong if you believe that one,
a criminal, will not be punished only
because he is my kinsman.

    CREON

                    This is but just—
but tell me, then, of what offense I'm guilty?

    OEDIPUS

Did you or did you not urge me to send
to this prophetic mumbler?

    CREON

                    I did indeed,
and I shall stand by what I told you.

    OEDIPUS

How long ago is it since Laius. . . .

    CREON

What about Laius? I don't understand.

    OEDIPUS

Vanished—died—was murdered?

    CREON

                    It is long,
a long, long time to reckon.

    OEDIPUS

                  Was this prophet
in the profession then?

    CREON

                  He was, and honoured
as highly as he is today.

    OEDIPUS

At that time did he say a word about me?

    CREON

Never, at least when I was near him.

    OEDIPUS

You never made a search for the dead man?

CREON

We searched, indeed, but never learned of
   anything.

OEDIPUS

Why did our wise old friend not say this then?

CREON

I don't know; and when I know nothing, I
usually hold my tongue.

OEDIPUS

You know this much,
and can declare this much if you are loyal.

CREON

What is it? If I know, I'll not deny it.

OEDIPUS

That he would not have said that I killed Laius
had he not met you first.

CREON

You know yourself
whether he said this, but I demand that I
should hear as much from you as you from me.

OEDIPUS

Then hear,—I'll not be proved a murderer.

CREON

Well, then. You're married to my sister.

OEDIPUS

Yes,
that I am not disposed to deny.

CREON

You rule
this country giving her an equal share
in the government?

OEDIPUS

Yes, everything she wants
she has from me.

CREON

And I, as thirdsman to you,
am rated as the equal of you two?

OEDIPUS

Yes, and it's there you've proved yourself false
   friend.

CREON

Not if you will reflect on it as I do.
Consider, first, if you think any one
would choose to rule and fear rather than rule
and sleep untroubled by a fear if power
were equal in both cases. I, at least,
I was not born with such a frantic yearning
to be a king—but to do what kings do.
And so it is with every one who has learned
wisdom and self-control. As it stands now,
the prizes are all mine—and without fear.
But if I were the king myself, I must
do much that went against the grain.
How should despotic rule seem sweeter to me
than painless power and an assured authority?
I am not so besotted yet that I
want other honours than those that come with
   profit.
Now every man's my pleasure; every man greets
   me;
now those who are your suitors fawn on me,—
success for them depends upon my favour.
Why should I let all this go to win that?
My mind would not be traitor if it's wise;
I am no treason lover, of my nature,
nor would I ever dare to join a plot.
Prove what I say. Go to the oracle
at Pytho and inquire about the answers,
if they are as I told you. For the rest,
if you discover I laid any plot
together with the seer, kill me, I say,
not only by your vote but by my own.
But do not charge me on obscure opinion
without some proof to back it. It's not just
lightly to count your knaves as honest men,
nor honest men as knaves. To throw away
an honest friend is, as it were, to throw
your life away, which a man loves the best.
In time you will know all with certainty;
time is the only test of honest men,
one day is space enough to know a rogue.

CHORUS

His words are wise, king, if one fears to fall.
Those who are quick of temper are not safe.

OEDIPUS

When he that plots against me secretly
moves quickly, I must quickly counterplot.
If I wait taking no decisive measure
his business will be done, and mine be spoiled.

CREON

What do you want to do then? Banish me?

OEDIPUS

No, certainly; kill you, not banish you.[1]

---

[1]Two lines omitted here owing to the confusion in the
dialogue consequent on the loss of a third line. The lines as
they stand in Jebb's edition (1902) are:
OED.: That you may show what manner of thing is envy.
CREON: You speak as one that will not yield or trust.
[OED. lost line.]

CREON

I do not think that you've your wits about you.

OEDIPUS

For my own interests, yes.

CREON

But for mine, too,
you should think equally.

OEDIPUS

You are a rogue.

CREON

Suppose you do not understand?

OEDIPUS

But yet
I must be ruler.

CREON

Not if you rule badly.

OEDIPUS

O, city, city!

CREON

I too have some share
in the city; it is not yours alone.

CHORUS

Stop, my lords! Here—and in the nick of time
I see Jocasta coming from the house;
with her help lay the quarrel that now stirs you.
(*Enter* JOCASTA.)

JOCASTA

For shame! Why have you raised this foolish
squabbling
brawl? Are you not ashamed to air your private
griefs when the country's sick? Go in, you,
Oedipus,
And you, too, Creon, into the house. Don't
magnify
your nothing troubles.

CREON

Sister, Oedipus,
your husband, thinks he has the right to do
terrible wrongs—he has but to choose between
two terrors: banishing or killing me.

OEDIPUS

He's right, Jocasta; for I find him plotting
with knavish tricks against my person.

CREON

That God may never bless me! May I die
accursed, if I have been guilty of
one tittle of the charge you bring against me!

JOCASTA

I beg you, Oedipus, trust him in this,
spare him for the sake of this his oath to God,
for my sake, and the sake of those who stand here.

CHORUS

Be gracious, be merciful,
we beg of you.

OEDIPUS

In what would you have me yield?

CHORUS

He has been no silly child in the past.
He is strong in his oath now.
Spare him.

OEDIPUS

Do you know what you ask?

CHORUS

Yes.

OEDIPUS

Tell me then.

CHORUS

He has been your friend before all men's eyes; do
not cast him
away dishonoured on an obscure conjecture.

OEDIPUS

I would have you know that this request of yours
really requests my death or banishment.

CHORUS

May the Sun God, king of Gods, forbid! May I die
without God's
blessing, without friends' help, if I had any such
thought. But my
spirit is broken by my unhappiness for my
wasting country; and
this would but add troubles amongst ourselves to
the other
troubles.

OEDIPUS

Well, let him go then—if I must die ten times for it,
or be sent out dishonoured into exile.
It is your lips that prayed for him I pitied,
not his; wherever he is, I shall hate him.

CREON

I see you sulk in yielding and you're dangerous
when you are out of temper; natures like yours
are justly heaviest for themselves to bear.

OEDIPUS

Leave me alone! Take yourself off, I tell you.

CREON

I'll go, you have not known me, but they have,
and they have known my innocence.
(*Exit*)

CHORUS

Won't you take him inside, lady?

JOCASTA

Yes, when I've found out what was the matter.

CHORUS
There was some misconceived suspicion of a
    story, and on the
other side the sting of injustice.

JOCASTA
So, on both sides?

CHORUS
Yes.

JOCASTA
What was the story?

CHORUS
I think it best, in the interests of the country, to
    leave it
where it ended.

OEDIPUS
You see where you have ended, straight of
    judgment
although you are, by softening my anger.

CHORUS
Sir, I have said before and I say again—be sure
    that I would have
been proved a madman, bankrupt in sane council,
    if I should put
you away, you who steered the country I love
    safely when she
was crazed with troubles. God grant that now,
    too, you may
prove a fortunate guide for us.

JOCASTA
Tell me, my lord, I beg of you, what was it
that roused your anger so?

OEDIPUS
                            Yes, I will tell you.
I honour you more than I honour them.
It was Creon and the plots he laid against me.

JOCASTA
Tell me—if you can clearly tell the quarrel—

OEDIPUS
                            Creon says
that I'm the murderer of Laius.

JOCASTA
Of his own knowledge or on information?

OEDIPUS
He sent this rascal prophet to me, since
he keeps his own mouth clean of any guilt.

JOCASTA
Do not concern yourself about this matter;
listen to me and learn that human beings
have no part in the craft of prophecy.
Of that I'll show you a short proof.
There was an oracle once that came to Laius,—

I will not say that it was Phoebus' own,
but it was from his servants—and it told him
that it was fate that he should die a victim
at the hands of his own son, a son to be born
of Laius and me. But, see now, he,
the king, was killed by foreign highway robbers
at a place where three roads meet—so goes the
    story;
and for the son—before three days were out
after his birth King Laius pierced his ankles
and by the hands of others cast him forth
upon a pathless hillside. So Apollo
failed to fulfill his oracle to the son,
that he should kill his father, and to Laius
also proved false in that the thing he feared,
death at his son's hands, never came to pass.
So clear in this case were the oracles,
so clear and false. Give them no heed, I say;
what God discovers need of, easily
he shows to us himself.

OEDIPUS
                        O dear Jocasta,
as I hear this from you, there comes upon me
a wandering of the soul—I could run mad.

JOCASTA
What trouble is it, that you turn again
and speak like this?

OEDIPUS
                    I thought I heard you say
that Laius was killed at a crossroads.

JOCASTA
Yes, that was how the story went and still
that word goes round.

OEDIPUS
                        Where is this place, Jocasta,
where he was murdered?

JOCASTA
                            Phocis is the country
and the road splits there, one of two roads from
    Delphi,
another comes from Daulia.

OEDIPUS
How long ago is this?

JOCASTA
The news came to the city just before
you became king and all men's eyes looked to
    you.
What is it, Oedipus, that's in your mind?

OEDIPUS
What have you designed, O Zeus, to do with
    me?

JOCASTA

What is the thought that troubles your heart?

OEDIPUS

Don't ask me yet—tell me of Laius—
How did he look? How old or young was he?

JOCASTA

He was a tall man and his hair was grizzled
already—nearly white—and in his form
not unlike you.

OEDIPUS

O God, I think I have
called curses on myself in ignorance.

JOCASTA

What do you mean? I am terrified
when I look at you.

OEDIPUS

I have a deadly fear
that the old seer had eyes. You'll show me more
if you can tell me one more thing.

JOCASTA

I will.
I'm frightened,—but if I can understand,
I'll tell you all you ask.

OEDIPUS

How was his company?
Had he few with him when he went this journey,
or many servants, as would suit a prince?

JOCASTA

In all there were but five, and among them
a herald; and one carriage for the king.

OEDIPUS

It's plain—its plain—who was it told you this?

JOCASTA

The only servant that escaped safe home.

OEDIPUS

Is he at home now?

JOCASTA

No, when he came home again
and saw you king and Laius was dead,
he came to me and touched my hand and begged
that I should send him to the fields to be
my shepherd and so he might see the city
as far off as he might. So I
sent him away. He was an honest man,
as slaves go, and was worthy of far more
than what he asked of me.

OEDIPUS

O, how I wish that he could come back quickly!

JOCASTA

He can. Why is your heart so set on this?

OEDIPUS

O dear Jocasta, I am full of fears
that I have spoken far too much; and therefore
I wish to see this shepherd.

JOCASTA

He will come;
but, Oedipus, I think I'm worthy too
to know what it is that disquiets you.

OEDIPUS

It shall not be kept from you, since my mind
has gone so far with its forebodings. Whom
should I confide in rather than you, who is there
of more importance to me who have passed
through such a fortune?
Polybus was my father, king of Corinth,
and Merope, the Dorian, my mother.
I was held greatest of the citizens
in Corinth till a curious chance befell me
as I shall tell you—curious, indeed,
but hardly worth the store I set upon it.
There was a dinner and at it a man,
a drunken man, accused me in his drink
of being bastard. I was furious
but held my temper under for that day.
Next day I went and taxed my parents with it;
they took the insult very ill from him,
the drunken fellow who had uttered it.
So I was comforted for their part, but
still this thing rankled always, for the story
crept about widely. And I went at last
to Pytho, though my parents did not know.
But Phoebus sent me home again unhonoured
in what I came to learn, but he foretold
other and desperate horrors to befall me,
that I was fated to lie with my mother,
and show to daylight an accursed breed
which men would not endure, and I was doomed
to be murderer of the father that begot me.
When I heard this I fled, and in the days
that followed I would measure from the stars
the whereabouts of Corinth—yes, I fled
to somewhere where I should not see fulfilled
the infamies told in that dreadful oracle.
And as I journeyed I came to the place
where, as you say, this king met with his death.
Jocasta, I will tell you the whole truth.
When I was near the branching of the crossroads,
going on foot, I was encountered by
a herald and a carriage with a man in it,
just as you tell me. He that led the way

and the old man himself wanted to thrust me
out of the road by force. I became angry
and struck the coachman who was pushing me.
When the old man saw this he watched his
    moment,
and as I passed he struck me from his carriage,
full on the head with his two pointed goad.
But he was paid in full and presently
my stick had struck him backwards from the car
and he rolled out of it. And then I killed them
all. If it happened there was any tie
of kinship twixt this man and Laius,
who is then now more miserable than I,
what man on earth so hated by the Gods,
since neither citizen nor foreigner
may welcome me at home or even greet me,
but drive me out of doors? And it is I,
I and no other have so cursed myself.
And I pollute the bed of him I killed
by the hands that killed him. Was I not born evil?
Am I not utterly unclean? I had to fly
and in my banishment not even see
my kindred nor set foot in my own country,
or otherwise my fate was to be yoked
in marriage with my mother and kill my father,
Polybus who begot me and had reared me.
Would not one rightly judge and say that on me
these things were sent by some malignant God?
O no, no, no—O holy majesty
of God on high, may I not see that day!
May I be gone out of men's sight before
I see the deadly taint of this disaster
come upon me.

    CHORUS

Sir, we too fear these things. But until you see this
man face to face and hear his story, hope.

    OEDIPUS

Yes, I have just this much of hope—to wait until
the herdsman comes.

    JOCASTA

And when he comes, what do you want with him?

    OEDIPUS

I'll tell you; if I find that his story is the same as
yours, I at least will be clear of this guilt.

    JOCASTA

Why what so particularly did you learn from my
story?

    OEDIPUS

You said that he spoke of highway *robbers* who
killed Laius. Now if he uses the same number, it

was not I who killed him. One man cannot be the
same as many. But if he speaks of a man
travelling alone, then clearly the burden of the
guilt inclines towards me.

    JOCASTA

Be sure, at least, that this was how he told the
story. He cannot unsay it now, for every one in
the city heard it—not I alone. But, Oedipus, even
if he diverges from what he said then, he shall
never prove that the murder of Laius squares
rightly with the prophecy—for Loxias declared
that the king should be killed by his own son.
And that poor creature did not kill him
surely,—for he died himself first. So as far as
prophecy goes, henceforward I shall not look to
the right hand or the left.

    OEDIPUS

Right. But yet, send some one for the peasant to
bring him here; do not neglect it.

    JOCASTA

I will send quickly. Now let me go indoors. I will
do nothing except what pleases you.
(*Exeunt.*)

    CHORUS
    *Strophe*

May destiny ever find me
pious in word and deed
prescribed by the laws that live on high:
laws begotten in the clear air of heaven,
whose only father is Olympus;
no mortal nature brought them to birth,
no forgetfulness shall lull them to sleep;
for God is great in them and grows not old.
    *Antistrophe*
Insolence breeds the tyrant, insolence
if it is glutted with a surfeit, unseasonable,
    unprofitable,
climbs to the roof-top and plunges
sheer down to the ruin that must be,
and there its feet are no service.
But I pray that the God may never
abolish the eager ambition that profits the state.
For I shall never cease to hold the God as our
    protector.
    *Strophe*
If a man walks with haughtiness
of hand or word and gives no heed
to Justice and the shrines of Gods
despises—may an evil doom
smite him for his ill-starred pride of heart!—

if he reaps gains without justice
and will not hold from impiety
and his fingers itch for untouchable things.
When such things are done, what man shall
    contrive
to shield his soil from the shafts of the God?
When such deeds are held in honour,
why should I honour the Gods in the dance?
    *Antistrophe*
No longer to the holy place,
to the navel of earth I'll go
to worship, nor to Abae
nor to Olympia,
unless the oracles are proved to fit,
for all men's hands to point at.
O Zeus, if you are rightly called
the sovereign lord, all-mastering,
let this not escape you nor your ever-living power!
The oracles concerning Laius
are old and dim and men regard them not.
Apollo is nowhere clear in honour; God's service
    perishes.
(*Enter* **JOCASTA** *carrying garlands.*)

**JOCASTA**
Princes of the land, I have had the thought to go
to the Gods' temples, bringing in my hand
garlands and gifts of incense, as you see.
For Oedipus excites himself too much
at every sort of trouble, not conjecturing,
like a man of sense, what will be from what was,
but he is always at the speaker's mercy,
when he speaks terrors. I can do no good
by my advice, and so I came as suppliant
to you, Lycaean Apollo, who are nearest.
These are the symbols of my prayer and this
my prayer: grant us escape free of the curse.
Now when we look to him we are all afraid;
he's pilot of our ship and he is frightened.
(*Enter* **MESSENGER**.)

**MESSENGER**
Might I learn from you, sirs, where is the house of
Oedipus? Or best of all, if you know, where is the
king himself?

**CHORUS**
This is his house and he is within doors. This lady
is his wife and mother of his children.

**MESSENGER**
God bless you, lady, and God bless your
household! God bless Oedipus' noble wife!

**JOCASTA**
God bless you, sir, for your kind greeting! What
do you want of us that you have come here?
What have you to tell us?

**MESSENGER**
Good news, lady. Good for your house and for
your husband.

**JOCASTA**
What is your news? Who sent you to us?

**MESSENGER**
I come from Corinth and the news I bring will
give you pleasure. Perhaps a little pain too.

**JOCASTA**
What is this news of double meaning?

**MESSENGER**
The people of the Isthmus will choose Oedipus to
be their king. That is the rumour there.

**JOCASTA**
But isn't their king still old Polybus?

**MESSENGER**
No. He is in his grave. Death has got him.

**JOCASTA**
Is that the truth? Is Oedipus' father dead?

**MESSENGER**
May I die myself if it be otherwise!

**JOCASTA** (*to a servant*)
Be quick and run to the King with the news! O
oracles of the Gods, where are you now? It was
from this man Oedipus fled, lest he should be his
murderer! And now he is dead, in the course of
nature, and not killed by Oedipus.
(*Enter* **OEDIPUS**.)

**OEDIPUS**
Dearest Jocasta, why have you sent for me?

**JOCASTA**
Listen to this man and when you hear reflect
what is the outcome of the holy oracles of the
Gods.

**OEDIPUS**
Who is he? What is his message for me?

**JOCASTA**
He is from Corinth and he tells us that your father
Polybus is dead and gone.

**OEDIPUS**
What's this you say, sir? Tell me yourself.

**MESSENGER**
Since this is the first matter you want clearly told:
Polybus has gone down to death. You may be
sure of it.

OEDIPUS
By treachery or sickness?
MESSENGER
A small thing will put old bodies asleep.
OEDIPUS
So he died of sickness, it seems,—poor old man!
MESSENGER
Yes, and of age—the long years he had measured.
OEDIPUS
Ha! Ha! O dear Jocasta, why should one
look to the Pythian hearth? Why should one look
to the birds screaming overhead? They prophesied
that I should kill my father! But he's dead,
and hidden deep in earth, and I stand here
who never laid a hand on spear against him,—
unless perhaps he died of longing for me,
and thus I am his murderer. But they,
the oracles, as they stand—he's taken them
away with him, they're dead as he himself is,
and worthless.
JOCASTA
That I told you before now.
OEDIPUS
You did, but I was misled by my fear.
JOCASTA
Then lay no more of them to heart, not one.
OEDIPUS
But surely I must fear my mother's bed?
JOCASTA
Why should man fear since chance is all in all
for him, and he can clearly foreknow nothing?
Best to live lightly, as one can, unthinkingly.
As to your mother's marriage bed,—don't fear it.
Before this, in dreams too, as well as oracles,
many a man has lain with his own mother.
But he to whom such things are nothing bears
his life most easily.
OEDIPUS
All that you say would be said perfectly
if she were dead; but since she lives I must
still fear, although you talk so well, Jocasta.
JOCASTA
Still in your father's death there's light of comfort?
OEDIPUS
Great light of comfort; but I fear the living.
MESSENGER
Who is the woman that makes you afraid?
OEDIPUS
Merope, old man, Polybus' wife.

MESSENGER
What about her frightens the queen and you?
OEDIPUS
A terrible oracle, stranger, from the Gods.
MESSENGER
Can it be told? Or does the sacred law
forbid another to have knowledge of it?
OEDIPUS
O no! Once on a time Loxias said
that I should lie with my own mother and
take on my hands the blood of my own father.
And so for these long years I've lived away
from Corinth; it has been to my great happiness;
but yet it's sweet to see the face of parents.
MESSENGER
This was the fear which drove you out of Corinth?
OEDIPUS
Old man, I did not wish to kill my father.
MESSENGER
Why should I not free you from this fear, sir,
since I have come to you in all goodwill?
OEDIPUS
You would not find me thankless if you did.
MESSENGER
Why, it was just for this I brought the news,—
to earn your thanks when you had come safe home.
OEDIPUS
No, I will never come near my parents.
MESSENGER
Son,
it's very plain you don't know what you're doing.
OEDIPUS
What do you mean, old man? For God's sake, tell
me.
MESSENGER
If your homecoming is checked by fears like these.
OEDIPUS
Yes, I'm afraid that Phoebus may prove right.
MESSENGER
The murder and the incest?
OEDIPUS
Yes, old man;
that is my constant terror.
MESSENGER
Do you know
that all your fears are empty?
OEDIPUS
How is that,
if they are father and mother and I their son?

MESSENGER
Because Polybus was no kin to you in blood.
OEDIPUS: What, was not Polybus my father?
MESSENGER
No more than I but just so much.
OEDIPUS
                                        How can
my father be my father as much as one
that's nothing to me?
MESSENGER
                            Neither he nor I
begat you.
OEDIPUS
                    Why then did he call me son?
MESSENGER
A gift he took you from these hands of mine.
OEDIPUS
Did he love so much what he took from another's
        hand?
MESSENGER
His childlessness before persuaded him.
OEDIPUS
Was I a child you bought or found when I
was given to him?
MESSENGER
                                On Cithaeron's slopes
in the twisting thickets you were found.
OEDIPUS
                                And why
were you a traveller in those parts?
MESSENGER
                                            I was
in charge of mountain flocks.
OEDIPUS
                                You were a shepherd?
A hireling vagrant?
MESSENGER
                            Yes, but at least at that time
the man that saved your life, son.
OEDIPUS
What ailed me when you took me in your arms?
MESSENGER
In that your ankles should be witnesses.
OEDIPUS
Why do you speak of that old pain?
MESSENGER
                                        I loosed you;
the tendons of your feet were pierced and
        fettered,—

OEDIPUS
My swaddling clothes brought me a rare disgrace.
MESSENGER
So that from this you're called your present name.
OEDIPUS
Was this my father's doing or my mother's?
For God's sake, tell me.
MESSENGER
                                I don't know, but he
who gave you to me has more knowledge than I.
OEDIPUS
You yourself did not find me then? You took
        me
from someone else?
MESSENGER
                                Yes, from another shepherd.
OEDIPUS
Who was he? Do you know him well enough
to tell?
MESSENGER
                                He was called Laius' man.
OEDIPUS
You mean the king who reigned here in the old
        days?
MESSENGER
Yes, he wa    at man's shepherd.
OEDIPUS
                                            Is he alive
still, so that I could see him?
MESSENGER
                                    You who live here
would know that best.
OEDIPUS
                                Do any of you here
know of this s. epherd whom he speaks about
in town or in t..e fields? Tell me. It's time
that this was found out once for all.
CHORUS
I think he is none other than the peasant
whom you have sought to see already; but
Jocasta here can tell us best of that.
OEDIPUS
Jocasta, do you know about this man
whom we have sent for? Is he the man he
        mentions?
JOCASTA
Why ask of whom he spoke? Don't give it heed;
nor try to keep in mind what has been said.
It will be wasted labour.

OEDIPUS

                               With such clues
I could not fail to bring my birth to light.

JOCASTA

I beg you—do not hunt this out—I beg you,
if you have any care for your own life.
What I am suffering is enough.

OEDIPUS

                                     Keep up
your heart, Jocasta. Though I'm proved a slave,
thrice slave, and though my mother is thrice
    slave,
you'll not be shown to be of lowly lineage.

JOCASTA

O be persuaded by me, I entreat you;
do not do this.

OEDIPUS

I will not be persuaded to let be
the chance of finding out the whole thing clearly.

JOCASTA

It is because I wish you well that I
give you this counsel—and it's the best counsel.

OEDIPUS

Then the best counsel vexes me, and has
for some while since.

JOCASTA

                        O Oedipus, God help you!
God keep you from the knowledge of who you
    are!

OEDIPUS

Here, some one, go and fetch the shepherd for me;
and let her find her joy in her rich family!

JOCASTA

O Oedipus, unhappy Oedipus!
that is all I can call you, and the last thing
that I shall ever call you. (*Exit.*)

CHORUS

Why has the queen gone, Oedipus, in wild
grief rushing from us? I am afraid that trouble
will break out of this silence.

OEDIPUS

Break out what will! I at least shall be
willing to see my ancestry, though humble.
Perhaps she is ashamed of my low birth,
for she has all a woman's high-flown pride.
But I account myself a child of Fortune,
beneficent Fortune, and I shall not be
dishonoured. She's the mother from whom I
    spring;

the months, my brothers, marked me, now as
    small,
and now again as mighty. Such is my breeding,
and I shall never prove so false to it,
as not to find the secret of my birth.

CHORUS

*Strophe*

If I am a prophet and wise of heart
you shall not fail, Cithaeron,
by the limitless sky, you shall not!—
to know at tomorrow's full moon
that Oedipus honours you,
as native to him and mother and nurse at once;
and that you are honoured in dancing by us, as
    finding favour in sight of our king.
Apollo, to whom we cry, find these things
    pleasing!

*Antistrophe*

Who was it bore you, child? One of
the long-lived nymphs who lay with Pan—
the father who treads the hills?
Or was she a bride of Loxias, your mother? The
    grassy slopes
are all of them dear to him. Or perhaps Cyllene's
    king
or the Bacchants' God that lives on the tops
of the hills received you a gift from some
one of the Helicon Nymphs, with whom he
    mostly plays?

(*Enter an old man, led by* OEDIPUS' *servants.*)

OEDIPUS

If some one like myself who never met him
may make a guess,—I think this is the herdsman,
whom we were seeking. His old age is consonant
with the other. And besides, the men who bring
    him
I recognize as my own servants. You
perhaps may better me in knowledge since
you've seen the man before.

CHORUS

                          You can be sure
I recognize him. For if Laius
had ever an honest shepherd, this was he.

OEDIPUS

You, sir, from Corinth, I must ask you first,
is this the man you spoke of?

MESSENGER

                           This is he
before your eyes.

**OEDIPUS**

Old man, look here at me
and tell me what I ask you. Were you ever
a servant of King Laius?

**HERDSMAN**

I was,—
no slave he bought but reared in his own house.

**OEDIPUS**

What did you do as work? How did you live?

**HERDSMAN**

Most of my life was spent among the flocks.

**OEDIPUS**

In what part of the country did you live?

**HERDSMAN**

Cithaeron and the places near to it.

**OEDIPUS**

And somewhere there perhaps you knew this
man?

**HERDSMAN**

What was his occupation? Who?

**OEDIPUS**

This man here,
have you had any dealings with him?

**HERDSMAN**

No—
not such that I can quickly call to mind.

**MESSENGER**

That is no wonder, master. But I'll make him
remember what he does not know. For I know,
that he well knows the country of Cithaeron, how
he with two flocks, I with one kept company for
three years—each year half a year—from spring
till autumn time and then when winter came I
drove my flocks to our fold home again and he to
Laius' steadings. Well—am I right or not in what I
said we did?

**HERDSMAN**

You're right—although it's a long time ago.

**MESSENGER**

Do you remember giving me a child
to bring up as my foster child?

**HERDSMAN**

What's this?
Why do you ask this question?

**MESSENGER**

Look old man,
here he is—here's the man who was that child!

**HERDSMAN**

Death take you! Won't you hold your tongue?

**OEDIPUS**

No, no,
do not find fault with him, old man. Your words
are more at fault than his.

**HERDSMAN**

O best of masters,
how do I give offense?

**OEDIPUS**

When you refuse
to speak about the child of whom he asks you.

**HERDSMAN**

He speaks out of his ignorance, without meaning.

**OEDIPUS**

If you'll not talk to gratify me, you
will talk with pain to urge you.

**HERDSMAN**

O please, sir,
don't hurt an old man, sir.

**OEDIPUS**

(to the servants)

Here, one of you,
twist his hands behind him.

**HERDSMAN**

Why, God help me, why?
What do you want to know?

**OEDIPUS**

You gave a child
to him,—the child he asked you of?

**HERDSMAN**

I did.
I wish I'd died the day I did.

**OEDIPUS**

You will
unless you tell me truly.

**HERDSMAN**

And I'll die
far worse if I should tell you.

**OEDIPUS**

This fellow
is bent on more delays, as it would seem.

**HERDSMAN**

O no, no! I have told you that I gave it.

**OEDIPUS**

Where did you get this child from? Was it your
own or did you
get it from another?

**HERDSMAN**

Not
my own at all; I had it from some one.

**OEDIPUS**
One of these citizens? or from what house?

**HERDSMAN**
O master, please—I beg you, master, please don't ask me more.

**OEDIPUS**
You're a dead man if I ask you again.

**HERDSMAN**
It was one of the children of Laius.

**OEDIPUS**
A slave? Or born in wedlock?

**HERDSMAN**
O God, I am on the brink of frightful speech.

**OEDIPUS**
And I of frightful hearing. But I must hear.

**HERDSMAN**
The child was called his child; but she within, your wife would tell you best how all this was.

**OEDIPUS**
*She* gave it to you?

**HERDSMAN**
Yes, she did, my lord.

**OEDIPUS**
To do what with it?

**HERDSMAN**
Make away with it.

**OEDIPUS**
She was so hard—its mother?

**HERDSMAN**
Aye, through fear of evil oracles.

**OEDIPUS**
Which?

**HERDSMAN**
They said that he should kill his parents.

**OEDIPUS**
How was it that you gave it away to this old man?

**HERDSMAN**
O master, I pitied it, and thought that I could send it off to another country and this man was from another country. But he saved it for the most terrible troubles. If you are the man he says you are, you're bred to
    misery.

**OEDIPUS**
O, O, O, they will all come,
all come out clearly! Light of the sun, let me
look upon you no more after today!
I who first saw the light bred of a match
accursed, and accursed in my living
with them I lived with, cursed in my killing.
(*Exeunt all but the* **CHORUS.**)

**CHORUS**
*Strophe*
O generation of men, how I
count you as equal with those who live
not at all!
What man, what man on earth wins more
of happiness than a seeming
and after that turning away?
Oedipus, you are my pattern of this,
Oedipus, you and your fate!
Luckless Oedipus, whom of all men
I envy not at all.

*Antistrophe*
In as much as he shot his bolt
beyond the others and won the prize
of happiness complete—
O Zeus—and killed and reduced to nought
the hooked taloned maid of the riddling speech,
standing a tower against death for my land:
hence he was called my king and hence
was honoured the highest of all
honours; and hence he ruled
in the great city of Thebes.

*Strophe*
But now whose tale is more miserable?
Who is there lives with a savager fate?
Whose troubles so reverse his life as his?
O Oedipus, the famous prince
for whom a great haven
the same both as father and son
sufficed for generation,
how, O how, have the furrows ploughed
by your father endured to bear you, poor wretch,
and hold their peace so long?

*Antistrophe*
Time who sees all has found you out
against your will; judges your marriage
    accursed,
begetter and begot at one in it.
O child of Laius,
would I had never seen you.

I weep for you and cry
a dirge of lamentation.
To speak directly, I drew my breath
from you at the first and so now I lull
my mouth to sleep with your name.
(Enter a SECOND MESSENGER.)

SECOND MESSENGER
O Princes always honoured by our country,
what deeds you'll hear of and what horrors see,
what grief you'll feel, if you as true born Thebans
care for the house of Labdacus's sons.
Phasis nor Ister cannot purge this house,
I think, with all their streams, such things
it hides, such evils shortly will bring forth
into the light, whether they will or not;
and troubles hurt the most
when they prove self-inflicted.

CHORUS
What we had known before did not fall short
of bitter groaning's worth; what's more to tell?

SECOND MESSENGER
Shortest to hear and tell—our glorious queen
Jocasta's dead.

CHORUS
                              Unhappy woman! How?

SECOND MESSENGER
By her own hand. The worst of what was done
you cannot know. You did not see the sight.
Yet in so far as I remember it
you'll hear the end of our unlucky queen.
When she came raging into the house she went
straight to her marriage bed, tearing her hair
with both her hands, and crying upon Laius
long dead—Do you remember, Laius,
that night long past which bred a child for us
to send you to your death and leave
a mother making children with her son?
And then she groaned and cursed the bed in
     which
she brought forth husband by her husband,
     children
by her own child, an infamous double bond.
How after that she died I do not know,—
for Oedipus distracted us from seeing.
He burst upon us shouting and we looked
to him as he paced frantically around,
begging us always: Give me a sword, I say,
to find this wife no wife, this mother's womb,
this field of double sowing whence I sprang

and where I sowed my children! As he raved
some god showed him the way—none of us there.
Bellowing terribly and led by some
invisible guide he rushed on the two doors,—
wrenching the hollow bolts out of their sockets,
he charged inside. There, there, we saw his wife
hanging, the twisted rope around her neck.
When he saw her, he cried out fearfully
and cut the dangling noose. Then, as she lay,
poor woman, on the ground, what happened
     after,
was terrible to see. He tore the brooches—
the gold chased brooches fastening her robe—
away from her and lifting them up high
dashed them on his own eyeballs, shrieking out
such things as: they will never see the crime
I have committed or had done upon me!
Dark eyes, now in the days to come look on
forbidden faces, do not recognize
those whom you long for—with such
     imprecations
he struck his eyes again and yet again
with the brooches. And the bleeding eyeballs
     gushed
and stained his beard—no sluggish oozing drops
but a black rain and bloody hail poured down.
So it has broken—and not on one head
but troubles mixed for husband and for wife.
The fortune of the days gone by was true
good fortune—but today groans and destruction
and death and shame—of all ills can be named
not one is missing.

CHORUS
Is he now in any ease from pain?

SECOND MESSENGER
                                        He shouts
for some one to unbar the doors and show him
to all the men of Thebes, his father's killer,
his mother's—no I cannot say the word,
it is unholy—for he'll cast himself,
out of the land, he says, and not remain
to bring a curse upon his house, the curse
he called upon it in his proclamation. But
he wants for strength, aye, and some one to guide
     him;
his sickness is too great to bear. You, too,
will be shown that. The bolts are opening.
Soon you will see a sight to waken pity
even in the horror of it.

(*Enter the blinded* **OEDIPUS**.)

**CHORUS**

This is a terrible sight for men to see!
I never found a worse!
Poor wretch, what madness came upon you!
What evil spirit leaped upon your life
to your ill-luck—a leap beyond man's strength!
Indeed I pity you, but I cannot
look at you, though there's much I want to ask
and much to learn and much to see.
I shudder at the sight of you.

**OEDIPUS**

O, O,
where am I going? Where is my voice
borne on the wind to and fro?
Spirit, how far have you sprung?

**CHORUS**

To a terrible place whereof men's ears
may not hear, nor their eyes behold it.

**OEDIPUS**

Darkness!
Horror of darkness enfolding, resistless,
    unspeakable visitant sped by an ill wind in
    haste!
madness and stabbing pain and memory
of evil deeds I have done!

**CHORUS**

In such misfortunes it's no wonder
if double weighs the burden of your grief.

**OEDIPUS**

My friend,
you are the only one steadfast, the only one that
    attends on me;
you still stay nursing the blind man.
Your care is not unnoticed. I can know
your voice, although this darkness is my
    world.

**CHORUS**

Doer of dreadful deeds, how did you dare
so far to do despite to your own eyes?
what spirit urged you to it?

**OEDIPUS**

It was Apollo, friends, Apollo,
that brought this bitter bitterness, my sorrows to
    completion.
But the hand that struck me
was none but my own.
Why should I see
whose vision showed me nothing sweet to see?

**CHORUS**

These things are as you say.

**OEDIPUS**

What can I see to love?
What greeting can touch my ears with joy?
Take me away, and haste—to a place out of the
    way!
Take me away, my friends, the greatly miserable,
the most accursed, whom God too hates
above all men on earth!

**CHORUS**

Unhappy in your mind and your misfortune,
would I had never known you!

**OEDIPUS**

Curse on the man who took
the cruel bonds from off my legs, as I lay in the
    field.
He stole me from death and saved me,
no kindly service.
Had I died then
I would not be so burdensome to friends.

**CHORUS**

I, too, could have wished it had been so.

**OEDIPUS**

Then I would not have come
to kill my father and marry my mother
    infamously.
Now I am godless and child of impurity,
begetter in the same seed that created my
    wretched self.
If there is any ill worse than ill,
that is the lot of Oedipus.

**CHORUS**

I cannot say your remedy was good;
you would be better dead than blind and living.

**OEDIPUS**

What I have done here was best done; don't tell
    me
otherwise, do not give me further counsel.
I do not know with what eyes I could look
upon my father when I die and go
under the earth, nor yet my wretched mother—
those two to whom I have done things deserving
worse punishment than hanging. Would the sight
of children, bred as mine are, gladden me?
No, not these eyes, never. And my city,
its towers and sacred places of the Gods,
of these I robbed my miserable self
when I commanded all to drive *him* out,

the criminal since proved by God impure
and of the race of Laius.
To this guilt I bore witness against myself—
with what eyes shall I look upon my people?
No. If there were a means to choke the fountain
of hearing I would not have stayed my hand
from locking up my miserable carcase,
seeing and hearing nothing; it is sweet
to keep our thoughts out of the range of hurt.
Cithaeron, why did you receive me? why
having received me did you not kill me straight?
And so I had not shown to men my birth.
O Polybus and Corinth and the house,
the old house that I used to call my father's—
what fairness you were nurse to, and what
    foulness
festered beneath! Now I am found to be
a sinner and a son of sinners. Crossroads,
and hidden glade, oak and the narrow way
at the crossroads, that drank my father's blood
offered you by my hands, do you remember
still what I did as you looked on, and what
I did when I came here? O marriage, marriage!
you bred me and again when you had bred
bred children of your child and showed to men
brides, wives and mothers and the foulest deeds
that can be in this world of ours.
Come—it's unfit to say what is unfit
to do.—I beg of you in God's name hide me
somewhere outside your country, yes, or kill me,
or throw me into the sea, to be forever
out of your sight. Approach and deign to touch
    me
for all my wretchedness, and do not fear.
No man but I can bear my evil doom.

    CHORUS

Here Creon comes in fit time to perform
or give advice in what you ask of us.
Creon is left sole ruler in your stead.

    OEDIPUS

Creon! Creon! What shall I say to him?
How can I justly hope that he will trust me?
In what is past I have been proved towards him
an utter liar.

(*Enter* **CREON**.)

    CREON

                    Oedipus, I've come
not so that I might laugh at you nor taunt you
with evil of the past. But if you still
are without shame before the face of men

reverence at least the flame that gives all life,
our Lord the Sun, and do not show unveiled
to him pollution such that neither land
nor holy rain nor light of day can welcome.

(*To a* **SERVANT**.)

Be quick and take him in. It is most decent
that only kin should see and hear the troubles
of kin.

    OEDIPUS

                I beg you, since you've torn me from
my dreadful expectations and have come
in a most noble spirit to a man
that has used you vilely—do a thing for me.
I shall speak for your own good, not for my own.

    CREON

What do you need that you would ask of me?

    OEDIPUS

Drive me from here with all the speed you can
to where I may not hear a human voice.

    CREON

Be sure, I would have done this had not I
wished first of all to learn from the God the course
of action I should follow.

    OEDIPUS

                      But his word
has been quite clear to let the parricide,
the sinner, die.

    CREON

                Yes, that indeed was said.
But in the present need we had best discover
what we should do.

    OEDIPUS

                And will you ask about
a man so wretched?

    CREON

                Now even you will trust
the God.

    OEDIPUS

    So. I command you—and will beseech you—
to her that lies inside that house give burial
as you would have it; she is yours and rightly
you will perform the rites for her. For me—
never let this my father's city have me
living a dweller in it. Leave me live
in the mountains where Cithaeron is, that's called
*my* mountain, which my mother and my father
while they were living would have made my
    tomb.
So I may die by their decree who sought
indeed to kill me. Yet I know this much:

no sickness and no other thing will kill me.
I would not have been saved from death if not
for some strange evil fate. Well, let my fate
go where it will.

                  Creon, you need not care
about my sons; they're men and so wherever
they are, they will not lack a livelihood.
But my two girls—so sad and pitiful—
whose table never stood apart from mine,
and everything I touched they always shared—
Creon, have a thought for them! And most
I wish that you might suffer me to touch them
and sorrow with them.

(*Enter* **ANTIGONE** *and* **ISMENE**, **OEDIPUS**' *two
    daughters.*)

O my lord! O true noble Creon! Can I
really be touching them, as when I saw?
What shall I say?
Yes, I can hear them sobbing—my two darlings!
and Creon has had pity and has sent me
what I loved most?
Am I right?

    CREON

You're right: it was I gave you this
because I knew from old days how you loved them
as I see now.

    OEDIPUS

                God bless you for it, Creon,
and may God guard you better on your road
than he did me!

                     O children,
where are you? Come here, come to my hands,
a brother's hands which turned your father's eyes,
those bright eyes you knew once, to what you see,
a father seeing nothing, knowing nothing,
begetting you from his own source of life.
I weep for you—I cannot see your faces—
I weep when I think of the bitterness
there will be in your lives, how you must live
before the world. At what assemblages
of citizens will you make one? to what
gay company will you go and not come home
in tears instead of sharing in the holiday?
And when you're ripe for marriage, who will he
    be;
the man who'll risk to take such infamy
as shall cling to my children, to bring hurt
on them and those that marry with them? What
curse is not there? "Your father killed his father
and sowed the seed where he had sprung himself

and begot you out of the womb that held him."
These insults you will hear. Then who will marry
    you?
No one, my children; clearly you are doomed
to waste away in barrenness unmarried.
Son of Menocceus, since you are all the father
left these two girls, and we, their parents, both
are dead to them—do not allow them wander
like beggars, poor and husbandless.
They are of your own blood.
And do not make them equal with myself
in wretchedness; for you can see them now
so young, so utterly alone, save for you only.
Touch my hand, noble Creon, and say yes.
If you were older, children, and were wiser,
there's much advice I'd give you. But as it is,
let this be what you pray: give me a life
wherever there is opportunity
to live, and better life than was my father's.

    CREON

Your tears have had enough of scope; now go
    within the house.

    OEDIPUS

I must obey, though bitter of heart.

    CREON

In season, all is good.

    OEDIPUS

Do you know on what conditions I obey?

    CREON

                     You tell me them,
and I shall know them when I hear.

    OEDIPUS

                That you shall send me out
to live away from Thebes.

    CREON

            That gift you must ask of the God.

    OEDIPUS

But I'm now hated by the Gods.

    CREON

          So quickly you'll obtain your prayer.

    OEDIPUS

You consent then?

    CREON

        What I do not mean, I do not use to say.

    OEDIPUS

Now lead me away from here.

    CREON

          Let go the children, then, and come.

    OEDIPUS

Do not take them from me.

CREON
        Do not seek to be master in everything,
for the things you mastered did not follow you
        throughout your life.

(*As* **CREON** *and* **OEDIPUS** *go out.*)

CHORUS
You that live in my ancestral Thebes, behold this
        Oedipus,—
him who knew the famous riddles and was a man
        most masterful;
not a citizen who did not look with envy on his
        lot—
see him now and see the breakers of misfortune
        swallow him!
Look upon that last day always. Count no mortal
        happy till
he has passed the final limit of his life secure from
        pain.

## SUMMARY

Play analysis begins with the earliest surviving texts from the classical Greek theatre of the fifth century B.C. Aristotle's *Poetics*, a treatise on poetry and drama, is our earliest analytical model for understanding dramatic texts. From Aristotle's methods and the Greek playwrights' practices we have progressed over the centuries to develop critical tools and vocabularies for understanding plays. Aristotle is our first dramatic critic and his methods have proved insightful and useful through the centuries, although in modern times, other methods of analysis have emerged as playwriting and theories of drama have changed.

Aristotle's approach defines drama as an "imitation (mimetic) of an action" and sets forth elements ranging from plot and character to universal meanings, visual effects, music, and song. Moreover, he identified for all times two types of writing that imitate the antipodes of human experience: tragedy and comedy. Sophocles' *Oedipus the King* is our exemplary play for understanding the conventions of the classical Greek theatre and Sophocles' plotting of Oedipus' story prior to his self-punishment. *Oedipus the King* illustrates drama's basic elements: plot, imitative action, character, thought, language (dialogue and choral odes), and spectacle or visual effects. In addition, we are given a vocabulary for analyzing plot with its complications, crises, reversals, and resolutions. Finally, as one of the great tragedies of western dramatic writing, *Oedipus the King* introduces us to one of the two earliest types of writing about the extremes of human experience: tragedy. The next chapter deals with the second type: comedy.

## NOTES

1. David Mamet, *Writing in Restaurants* (New York: Viking Penguin, Inc., 1986): 8.

2. Francis Fergusson, *The Idea of a Theater: The Art of Drama in Changing Perspective* (New Jersey: Princeton University Press, 1949): 255.

# The School for Scandal

## RICHARD BRINSLEY SHERIDAN

*Richard Brinsley Sheridan (1751–1816), born in Dublin, became a playwright and theatre manager. At twenty-three, he wrote* The Rivals *which is famous for the comic character Mrs. Malaprop. Two years later (in 1776), Sheridan replaced the famous actor-manager David Garrick as manager of Drury Lane Theatre and thereafter had his own stage at his disposal. As author-manager, Sheridan triumphed in 1777 with* The School for Scandal, *a comedy of fashionable society and manners, superb wit, and upper-class foibles. In 1779, he staged his minor masterpiece,* The Critic; or, A Tragedy Rehearsed, *a burlesque of the theatre of his day. Within a half-decade, from* The Rivals *to* The Critic, *Sheridan ruled the London theatre scene as foremost dramatist and manager before his management career ended in financial ruin and the destruction of his theatre by fire. He then turned to a political career.*

*Of the three plays that stand as enduring contributions to eighteenth-century comedy—*She Stoops to Conquer, The Rivals, *and* The School for Scandal—*two are by Sheridan.*

## INTRODUCTION

*The School for Scandal,* one of the most famous comedies of manners in the English language, satirizes the upper-class foibles of gossips, along with the ways of fashionable London society where money and marriage for social gain are tempered by traditional comedic concerns for generosity of spirit.

The play's action combines two stories: the Teazle story concerns a wealthy, elderly man who has married a young, uninformed wife. After marriage, she learns about fashionable society from the scandalmongers whose "president" is Lady Sneerwell. The Surface story concerns two brothers—one a mean-spirited hypocrite and the other a good-natured spendthrift—whose true spirits are tested by their wealthy uncle whose benevolence triumphs over the comic villains in both plots. The theme of the good and bad brother is literally the oldest in the world, for it turns up first in the Biblical story of Cain and Abel.

Although the play flashes with witty thought and polished dialogue, the general tone is benevolent. Sheridan exposes hypocrisy, meanness, and heartlessness in Joseph Surface and the scandalmongers. He examines the loving foolishness of an aging husband who possesses a free-spirited young wife and the generous nature of a high-living young bachelor who triumphs over his brother's malicious intrigues. The comic dupes and the mean-spirited are measured against the paragons of virtue and common sense, Maria and Old Rowley. Although sentimental comedy—a popular type of play exploiting unnaturally "good" characters, pathetic situations, virtue in distress, and villains reformed—was the fashion of Sheridan's day, he makes few concessions to "sentiment" and delights in satirizing the soulful statements of the man of sentiment, Joseph Surface. There is certainly a measure of sentimentality in the play in the reconciliation of the Teazles and the triumph of good nature and tolerance (Sir Oliver, Charles, Maria, and Old Rowley) over the mean spirited and vicious (the scandalmongers). But Joseph Surface, as a satire of the "man of sentiment" so much in fashion on the stage in Sheridan's day, is revealed as an unreformed hypocrite who loses fortune and heroine in the play's resolution.

The play is structured so that for three acts scandal impels the study of manners, but yields to a comedy of sentiment and situation in the fourth and fifth acts. The scandal plot links to the Surface/Teazle intrigues in the famous screen scene (4.3) where the discoveries are made regarding Lady Teazle's indiscretions, Joseph's villainy, Charles's honesty, and Sir Peter's forgiving nature. The scandal characters furnish a necessary background to motivate Lady Teazle's behavior, to reduce the play's sentimentality, and to justify Sir Oliver's deceptions in testing his nephews. A world afflicted by scandalmongering is impelled by intrigue, gossip, and machinations of all sorts. Thus, we have sexual intrigues in both plots as well as maneuvers for fortune. The champions are the reconciled marital couple (the Teazles), the young lovers (Charles and Maria), and the benevolent truth-seekers (Sir Oliver and Old Rowley). Those that quit the field to play another day are the scandalmakers, including Joseph Surface.

Sheridan's characters are in the age-old tradition of comic villains and heroes. Among the former are the jealous, the shrewish, the hypocritical, the extravagant, and the treacherous. Among the latter are the virtuous, the faithful, the moderate, and the benevolent. Likewise the comic situations turn on familiar conventions: disguised persons, mistaken identities, and hiding scenes. Just as there are two plots, so, too, there are two discovery scenes resulting in comic recognition. The auction or portrait scene (3.3) in which Charles Surface strikes a deal with Mr. Premium (the unrecognized Sir Oliver) to borrow money to pay for his extravagances parallels the screen scene (4.3).

In the screen scene, Lady Teazle is briefly compromised by her indiscretion, Sir Peter is humiliated, and Joseph is revealed as a villain. Both scenes contribute to the resolution during which Joseph disappears into the scandal school, Lady Teazle and Sir Peter are reconciled, Sir Oliver and Old Rowley are confirmed in their belief in Charles's good nature, and Charles and Maria are betrothed. The screen scene is pivotal to Sheridan's technique and comic statement. The characters' motives are revealed in a single climactic moment: Joseph's hypocrisy and the artificial nature of his "sentiment," Charles's openness and natural spontaneity, Sir Peter's blindness to Joseph's hypocrisy, and Lady Teazle's inability to distinguish her husband's true devotion from Joseph's false declarations.

In the play's resolution, the comic world is returned to a social norm. Sheridan allows Lady Sneerwell to storm off to gossip another day; Joseph Surface, unreformed, follows to "protect" Charles from the scandal college's malice; Sir Peter forgives Lady Teazle; Maria accepts Charles's proposal of marriage and a wedding is forthcoming. True benevolence triumphs in every way. Those individuals who have remained in control of feelings and events (or who have learned control, such as the Teazles) are in authority. Sheridan's new society affirms that people must discipline themselves against the art of malice; avoid villainy derived from hypocrisy, false sentiment, wicked insinuation, and lack of charity; and exhibit virtues of generosity, directness, and honesty.

All in all, *The School for Scandal*, with its emphasis on a social world, sustained humor, characters reformed and unreformed, and the partial return of the scandal-ridden world to a fertile and charitable normalcy, is a choice example of the structure of comedy described by Northrop Frye. In the comic action, Sheridan reveals the selfishness, envy, and hypocrisy of a brittle society with remarkable skill and theatrical effect. His world of scandal is the chief device for illustrating fashionable society's manners and foibles. "Scandal," wrote Louis Kronenberger, "is a kind of amusement tax that virtue exacts of indecorum."[2]

*The School for Scandal* is possibly the most brilliant comedy written in the eighteenth century, for in Sheridan's treatment, scandal is a way of showing the humanly fallible and the socially culpable while affirming humanity's benevolence and society's continuity.

# The School for Scandal

## PROLOGUE

SPOKEN BY MR. KING[1]

WRITTEN BY D. GARRICK, ESQ.

A School for Scandal! tell me, I beseech you,
 Needs there a school this modish art to
 teach you?
 No need of lessons now, the knowing
 think—
 We might as well be taught to eat and
 drink.
 Caused by a dearth of scandal, should
 the vapors
 Distress our fair ones—let 'em read the
 papers;
 Their pow'rful mixtures such disorders
 hit;
 Crave what they will, there's *quantum
 sufficit.*[2]
  'Lord!' cries my Lady Wormwood
 (who loves tattle,
 And puts much salt and pepper in her
 prattle),
 Just ris'n at noon, all night at cards when
 threshing
 Strong tea and scandal—'Bless me, how
 refreshing!
 Give me the papers, Lisp—how bold and
 free! (*Sips.*)
 *Last night Lord L——(sips) was caught with
Lady D——*
 For aching heads what charming sal
 volatile! (*Sips.*)
 *If Mrs. B.——will still continue flirting,*
 *We hope she'll* DRAW, *or we'll* UNDRAW *the
 curtain.*
 Fine satire, poz[3]—in public all abuse it,
 But, by ourselves (*sips*), our praise we
 can't refuse it.
 Now, Lisp, read *you*—there, at that dash
 and star.'[4]
  'Yes, ma'am.—*A certain Lord had best
beware,*
 *Who lives not twenty miles from Grosv'nor
 Square;*
 *For should he Lady W—find willing,*
 WORMWOOD *is bitter'*—'Oh! that's me! the
 villain!
 Throw it behind the fire, and never more
 Let that vile paper come within my
 door.'—

> *Thus at our friends we laugh, who
> feel the dart;*
> *To reach our feelings, we ourselves
> must smart.*
> *Is our young bard so young, to think
> that he*
> *Can stop the full spring-tide of
> calumny?*
> *Knows he the world so little, and its*

---

[1] **Mr. King** Thomas King, who had the role of Sir Peter Teazle   [2] **quantum sufficit** as much as suffices

[3] **poz** positively   [4] **dash and star** referring to the practice of partly obscuring names in publishing reports of scandal

*trade?*
*Alas! the devil is sooner raised than*
*laid.*
*So strong, so swift, the monster*
*there's no gagging:*
*Cut Scandal's head off—still the*
*tongue is wagging.*
*Proud of your smiles once lavishly*
*bestow'd,*
*Again your young Don Quixote*
*takes the road:*
*To show his gratitude, he draws his*
*pen,*
*And seeks this hydra, Scandal, in his*
*den.*
*For your applause all perils he*
*would through—*
*He'll fight—that's write—a cavalliero*
*true,*
*Till every drop of blood—that's ink—*
*is spilt for you.*

## DRAMATIS PERSONAE

*Men*
SIR PETER TEAZLE  Mr. King
SIR OLIVER SURFACE  Mr. Yates
JOSEPH SURFACE  Mr. Palmer
CHARLES SURFACE  Mr. Smith
CRABTREE  Mr. Parsons
SIR BENJAMIN BACKBITE  Mr. Dodd
ROWLEY  Mr. Aickin
TRIP  Mr. LaMash
MOSES  Mr. Baddeley
SNAKE  Mr. Packer
CARELESS  Mr. Farren
*and other Companions to* CHARLES (SURFACE),
    *Servants, etc.*

*Women*
LADY TEAZLE  Mrs. Abington
MARIA  Miss P. Hopkins
LADY SNEERWELL  Miss Sherry
MRS. CANDOUR  Miss Pope
**Scene—London**

# ACT I

## SCENE I
LADY SNEERWELL's *house.*
    LADY SNEERWELL *at the dressing-table—*
    SNAKE *drinking chocolate.*
LADY SNEER:  The paragraphs, you say, Mr. Snake, were all inserted?
SNAKE:  They were, madam, and as I copied them myself in a feigned hand, there can be no suspicion whence they came.
LADY SNEER:  Did you circulate the reports of Lady *Brittle's* intrigue with Captain *Boastall?*
SNAKE:  That is in as fine a train as your ladyship could wish,—in the common course of things, I think it must reach Mrs. *Clackit's* ears within four-and-twenty-hours; and then, you know, the business is as good as done.
LADY SNEER:  Why, truly, Mrs. *Clackit* has a very pretty talent, and a great deal of industry.
SNAKE:  True, madam, and has been tolerably successful in her day:—to my knowledge, she has been the cause of six matches being broken off, and three sons being disinherited, of four forced elopements, as many close confinements, nine separate maintenances, and two divorces;—nay, I have more than once traced her causing a *Tête-à-Tête* in the *Town and Country Magazine,*[1] when the parties perhaps had never seen each other's faces before in the course of their lives.
LADY SNEER:  She certainly has talents, but her manner is gross.
SNAKE:  'Tis very true,—she generally designs well, has a free tongue, and a bold invention; but her coloring is too dark, and her outline often extravagant. She

I. [1] the **Town and Country Magazine** reported the intrigues of prominent persons

wants that *delicacy* of *hint*, and *mellowness* of *sneer*, which distinguish your ladyship's scandal.

**LADY SNEER:** Ah! you are partial, Snake.

**SNAKE:** Not in the least; everybody allows that Lady *Sneerwell* can do more with a *word* or a *look* than many can with the most labored detail, even when they happen to have a little truth on their side to support it.

**LADY SNEER:** Yes, my dear Snake; and I am no hypocrite to deny the satisfaction I reap from the success of my efforts. Wounded myself, in the early part of my life, by the envenomed tongue of slander, I confess I have since known no pleasure equal to the reducing others to the level of my own injured reputation.

**SNAKE:** Nothing can be more natural. But, Lady Sneerwell, there is one affair in which you have lately employed me, wherein, I confess, I am at a loss to guess your motives.

**LADY SNEER:** I conceive you mean with respect to my neighbor, Sir Peter Teazle, and his family?

**SNAKE:** I do; here are two young men, to whom Sir Peter has acted as a kind of guardian since their father's death; the elder possessing the most amiable character, and universally well spoken of; the youngest, the most dissipated and extravagant young fellow in the kingdom, without friends or character,—the former an avowed admirer of your ladyship, and apparently your favorite; the latter attached to Maria, Sir Peter's ward, and confessedly beloved by her. Now, on the face of these circumstances, it is utterly unaccountable to me, why you, the widow of a city knight, with a good jointure, should not close with the passion of a man of such character and expectations as Mr. *Surface*; and more so why you should be so uncommonly earnest to destroy the mutual attachment subsisting between his brother *Charles* and *Maria*.

**LADY SNEER:** Then, at once to unravel this mystery, I must inform you that love has no share whatever in the intercourse between Mr. *Surface* and me.

**SNAKE:** No!

**LADY SNEER:** His real attachment is to *Maria*, or her fortune; but, finding in his brother a favored rival, he has been obliged to mask his pretensions, and profit by my assistance.

**SNAKE:** Yet still I am more puzzled why you should interest yourself in his success.

**LADY SNEER:** Heav'ns! how dull you are! Cannot you surmise the weakness which I hitherto, through shame, have concealed even from *you*? Must I confess that *Charles*—that libertine, that extravagant, that bankrupt in fortune and reputation—that he it is for whom I am thus anxious and malicious, and to gain whom I would sacrifice everything?

**SNAKE:** Now, indeed, your conduct appears consistent; but how came you and Mr. *Surface* so confidential?

**LADY SNEER:** For our mutual interest. I have found him out a long time since—I know him to be artful, selfish, and malicious—in short, a sentimental knave.

**SNAKE:** Yet, Sir Peter vows he has not his equal in England—and, above all, he praises him as a man of sentiment.

**LADY SNEER:** True; and with the assistance of his sentiment and hypocrisy he has brought him [Sir Peter] entirely into his interest with regard to *Maria*.
*Enter Servant.*

**SERV:** Mr. Surface.

**LADY SNEER:** Show him up. (*Exit Servant.*) He generally calls about this time. I don't wonder at people's giving him to me for a lover.
*Enter **JOSEPH SURFACE**.*

JOS. SURF: My dear Lady Sneerwell, how do you do to-day? Mr. Snake, your most obedient.

LADY SNEER: Snake has just been arraigning me on our mutual attachment, but I have informed him of our real views; you know how useful he has been to us; and, believe me, the confidence is not ill placed.

JOS. SURF: Madam, it is impossible for me to suspect a man of Mr. *Snake's* sensibility and discernment.

LADY SNEER: Well, well, no compliments now;—but tell me when you saw your mistress, *Maria*—or, what is more material to me, your brother.

JOS. SURF: I have not seen either since I left you; but I can inform you that they never meet. Some of your stories have taken a good effect on Maria.

LADY SNEER: Ah, my dear Snake! the merit of this belongs to you. But do your brother's distresses increase?

JOS. SURF: Every hour;—I am told he has had another execution in the house yesterday; in short, his dissipation and extravagance exceed any thing I ever heard of.

LADY SNEER: Poor Charles!

JOS. SURF: True, madam;—notwithstanding his vices, one can't help feeling for him.—Aye, poor Charles! I'm sure I wish it was in *my* power to be of any essential service to him.—For the man who does not share in the distresses of a brother, even though merited by his own misconduct, deserves—

LADY SNEER: O lud! you are going to be moral, and forget that you are among friends.

JOS. SURF: Egad, that's true!—I'll keep that sentiment till I see Sir Peter. However, it is certainly a charity to rescue Maria from such a libertine, who, if he is to be reclaimed, can be so only by a person of your ladyship's superior accomplishments and understanding.

SNAKE: I believe, Lady Sneerwell, here's company coming,—I'll go and copy the letter I mentioned to you.—Mr. Surface, your most obedient. (*Exit* SNAKE.)

JOS. SURF: Sir, your very devoted.—Lady Sneerwell, I am very sorry you have put any further confidence in that fellow.

LADY SNEER: Why so?

JOS. SURF: I have lately detected him in frequent conference with old *Rowley*, who was formerly my father's steward, and has never, you know, been a friend of mine.

LADY SNEER: And do you think he would betray us?

JOS. SURF: Nothing more likely: take my word for't, Lady Sneerwell, that fellow hasn't virtue enough to be faithful even to his own villainy.—Hah! Maria!

*Enter* MARIA.

LADY SNEER: Maria, my dear, how do you do?—What's the matter?

MARIA: Oh! there is that disagreeable lover of mine, Sir *Benjamin Backbite*, has just called at my guardian's, with his odious uncle, *Crabtree*; so I slipped out, and run hither to avoid them.

LADY SNEER: Is that all?

JOS. SURF: If my brother *Charles* has been of the party, ma'am, perhaps you would not have been so much alarmed.

LADY SNEER: Nay, now you are severe; for I dare swear the truth of the matter is, Maria heard *you* were here;—but, my dear, what has Sir Benjamin done, that you should avoid him so?

MARIA: Oh, he has done nothing—but 'tis for what he has said,—his conversation is a perpetual libel on all his acquaintance.

JOS. SURF: Aye, and the worst of it is, there is no advantage in not knowing him; for he'll abuse a stranger just as soon as his best friend—and his uncle's as bad.

LADY SNEER: Nay, but we should make allowance; Sir Benjamin is a wit and a poet.

MARIA: For my part, I own, madam, wit loses its respect with me, when I see it in company with malice.—What do you think, Mr. Surface?

JOS. SURF: Certainly, madam; to smile at the jest which plants a thorn in another's breast is to become a principal in the mischief.

LADY SNEER: Pshaw! there's no possibility of being witty without a little ill nature: the malice of a good thing is the barb that makes it stick.—What's your opinion, Mr. Surface?

JOS. SURF: To be sure, madam, that conversation, where the spirit of raillery is suppressed, will ever appear tedious and insipid.

MARIA: Well, I'll not debate how far scandal may be allowable; but in a man, I am sure, it is always contemptible.—We have pride, envy, rivalship, and a thousand motives to depreciate each other; but the male slanderer must have the cowardice of a woman before he can traduce one.

*Enter Servant.*

SERV: Madam, Mrs. *Candour* is below, and, if your ladyship's at leisure, will leave her carriage.

LADY SNEER: Beg her to walk in. (*Exit Servant.*) Now Maria, however here is a character to your taste; for, though Mrs. Candour is a little talkative, everybody allows her to be the best-natured and best sort of woman.

MARIA: Yes, with a very gross affectation of good nature and benevolence, she does more mischief than the direct malice of old Crabtree.

JOS. SURF: I'faith 'tis very true, Lady Sneerwell; whenever I hear the current running against the characters of my friends, I never think them in such danger as when Candour undertakes their defence.

LADY SNEER: Hush!—here she is!

*Enter* MRS. CANDOUR.

MRS. CAN: My dear Lady Sneerwell, how have you been this century?—Mr. Surface, what news do you hear?—though indeed it is no matter, for I think one hears nothing else but scandal.

JOS. SURF: Just so, indeed, madam.

MRS. CAN: Ah, Maria! child,—what, is the whole affair off between you and Charles? His extravagance, I presume—the town talks of nothing else.

MARIA: I am very sorry, ma'am, the town has so little to do.

MRS. CAN: True, true, child: but there is no stopping people's tongues.—I own I was hurt to hear it, as indeed I was to learn, from the same quarter, that your guardian, Sir Peter, and Lady Teazle have not agreed lately so well as could be wished.

MARIA: 'Tis strangely impertinent for people to busy themselves so.

MRS. CAN: Very true, child, but what's to be done? People will talk—there's no preventing it.—Why, it was but yesterday I was told that Miss Gadabout had eloped with Sir Filigree Flirt.—But, Lord! there's no minding what one hears—though, to be sure, I had this from very good authority.

MARIA: Such reports are highly scandalous.

MRS. CAN: So they are, child—shameful, shameful! But the world is so censorious, no character escapes.—Lord, now who would have suspected your friend, Miss Prim, of an indiscretion? Yet such is the ill-nature of people, that they say her uncle stopped her last week, just as she was stepping into the York Diligence with her dancing-master.

MARIA: I'll answer for't there are no grounds for the report.

MRS. CAN: Oh, no foundation in the world, I dare swear; no more, probably, than for the story circulated last month, of Mrs. Festino's affair with Colonel Cassino;—though, to be sure, that matter was never rightly cleared up.

JOS. SURF: The license of invention some people take is monstrous indeed.

MARIA: 'Tis so.—But, in my opinion, those who report such things are equally culpable.

MRS. CAN: To be sure they are; tale-bearers are as bad as the tale-makers—'tis an old observation, and a very true one—but what's to be done, as I said before? how will you prevent people from talking?—To-day, Mrs. Clackit assured me Mr. and Mrs. Honeymoon were at last become mere man and wife, like the rest of their acquaintances.—She likewise hinted that a certain widow, in the next street, had got rid of her dropsy and recovered her shape in a most surprising manner. And at the same time Miss Tattle, who was by, affirmed that Lord Buffalo had discovered his lady at a house of no extraordinary fame—and that Sir Harry Bouquet and Tom Saunter were to measure swords on a similar provocation. But, Lord, do you think I would report these things! No, no! tale bearers, as I said before, are just as bad as tale-makers.

JOS. SURF: Ah! Mrs. Candour, if everybody had your forbearance and good nature!

MRS. CAN: I confess, Mr. Surface, I cannot bear to hear people attacked behind their backs, and when ugly circumstances come out against one's acquaintance I own I always love to think the best.—By the bye, I hope it is not true that your brother is absolutely ruined?

JOS. SURF: I am afraid his circumstances are very bad indeed, ma'am.

MRS. CAN: Ah!—I heard so—but you must tell him to keep up his spirits—everybody almost is in the same way! Lord Spindle, Sir Thomas Splint, Captain Quinze, and Mr. Nickit—all up, I hear, within this week; so, if Charles is undone, he'll find half his acquaintances ruined too—and that, you know, is a consolation.

JOS. SURF: Doubtless, ma'am—a very great one.

*Enter Servant.*

SERV: Mr. Crabtree and Sir Benjamin Backbite.

*Exit Servant.*

LADY SNEER: So, Maria, you see your lover pursues you; positively you shan't escape.

*Enter CRABTREE and SIR BENJAMIN BACKBITE.*

CRAB: Lady Sneerwell, I kiss your hands. Mrs. Candour, I don't believe you are acquainted with my nephew, Sir Benjamin Backbite? Egad, Ma'am, he has a pretty wit, and is a pretty poet too; isn't he, Lady Sneerwell?

SIR BEN: O fie, uncle!

CRAB: Nay, egad it's true—I'll back him at a rebus or a charade against the best rhymer in the kingdom. Has your ladyship heard the epigram he wrote last week on Lady Frizzle's feather catching fire?—Do, Benjamin, repeat it—or the charade you made last night extempore at Mrs. Drowzie's conversazione.—Come now; your *first* is the name of a fish, your *second* a great naval commander, and——

SIR BEN: Uncle, now—prithee——

CRAB: I'faith, ma'am, 'twould surprise you to hear how ready he is at these things.

LADY SNEER: I wonder, Sir Benjamin, you never publish anything.

SIR BEN: To say truth, ma'am, 'tis very vulgar to print; and, as my little productions are mostly satires and lampoons on particular people, I find they circulate more by giving copies in confidence to the friends of the parties—however, I have some love elegies, which, when favored with this lady's smiles, I mean to give to the public.

CRAB: 'Fore heav'n, ma'am, they'll immortalize you!—you'll be handed down to posterity like Petrarch's Laura, or Waller's Sacharissa.

**SIR BEN:** Yes, madam, I think you will like them, when you shall see them on a beautiful quarto page, where a neat rivulet of text shall murmur through a meadow of margin. 'Fore gad, they will be the most elegant things of their kind!

**CRAB:** But, ladies, that's true—have you heard the news?

**MRS. CAN:** What, sir, do you mean the report of—

**CRAB:** No, ma'am, that's not it.—Miss Nicely is going to be married to her own footman.

**MRS. CAN:** Impossible!

**CRAB:** Ask Sir Benjamin.

**SIR BEN:** 'Tis very true, ma'am—everything is fixed, and the wedding liveries bespoke.

**CRAB:** Yes—and they *do* say there were pressing reasons for it.

**LADY SNEER:** Why, I *have* heard something of this before.

**MRS. CAN:** It can't be—and I wonder any one should believe such a story of so prudent a lady as Miss Nicely.

**SIR BEN:** O lud! ma'am, that's the very reason 'twas believed at once. She has always been so *cautious* and so *reserved,* that everybody was sure there was some reason for it at bottom.

**MRS. CAN:** Why, to be sure, a tale of scandal is as fatal to the credit of a prudent lady of her stamp as a fever is generally to those of the strongest constitutions; but there is a sort of puny, sickly reputation that is always ailing, yet will outlive the robuster characters of a hundred prudes.

**SIR BEN:** True, madam, there are valetudinarians in reputation as well as constitution, who, being conscious of their weak part, avoid the least breath of air, and supply their want of stamina by care and circumspection.

**MRS. CAN:** Well, but this may be all a mistake. You know, Sir Benjamin, very trifling circumstances often give rise to the most injurious tales.

**CRAB:** That they do, I'll be sworn, ma'am. Did you ever hear how Miss Piper came to lose her lover and her character last summer at Tunbridge?—Sir Benjamin, you remember it?

**SIR BEN:** Oh, to be sure!—the most whimsical circumstance—

**LADY SNEER:** How was it, pray?

**CRAB:** Why, one evening, at Mrs. Ponto's assembly, the conversation happened to turn on the difficulty of breeding Nova Scotia sheep in this country. Says a young lady in company, 'I have known instances of it; for Miss Letitia Piper, a first cousin of mine, had a Nova Scotia sheep that produced her twins.' 'What!' cries the old Dowager Lady Dundizzy (who you know is as deaf as a post), 'has Miss Piper had twins?' This mistake, as you may imagine, threw the whole company into a fit of laughing. However, 'twas the next morning everywhere reported, and in a few days believed by the whole town, that Miss Letitia Piper had actually been brought to bed of a fine boy and a girl—and in less than a week there were people who could name the father, and the farm-house where the babies were put out to nurse!

**LADY SNEER:** Strange, indeed!

**CRAB:** Matter of fact, I assure you.—O lud! Mr. Surface, pray is it true that your uncle, Sir Oliver, is coming home?

**JOS. SURF:** Not that I know of, indeed, sir.

**CRAB:** He has been in the East Indias a long time. You can scarcely remember him, I believe.—Sad comfort, whenever he returns, to hear how your brother has gone on!

**JOS. SURF:** Charles has been imprudent, sir, to be sure; but I hope no busy people have already prejudiced Sir Oliver against him,—he may reform.

SIR BEN: To be sure he may—for my part I never believed him to be so utterly void of principle as people say—and though he has lost all his friends, I am told nobody is better spoken of by the Jews.

CRAB: That's true, egad, nephew. If the old Jewry were a ward, I believe Charles would be an alderman; no man more popular there, 'fore gad! I hear he pays as many annuities as the Irish tontine;[2] and that, whenever he's sick, they have prayers for the recovery of his health in the Synagogue.

SIR BEN: Yet no man lives in greater splendor.—They tell me, when he entertains his friends, he can sit down to dinner with a dozen of his own securities; have a score [of] tradesmen waiting in the antechamber, and an officer behind every guest's chair.

JOS. SURF: This may be entertainment to you, gentlemen, but you pay very little regard to the feelings of a brother.

MARIA: (*Aside.*) Their malice is intolerable!—Lady Sneerwell, I must wish you a good morning—I'm not very well. (*Exit* MARIA.)

MRS. CAN: O dear! she changes color very much!

LADY SNEER: Do, Mrs. Candour, follow her—she may want assistance.

MRS. CAN: That I will, with all my soul, ma'am.—Poor dear girl! who knows what her situation may be!
*Exit* MRS. CANDOUR.

LADY SNEER: 'Twas nothing but that she could not bear to hear Charles reflected on, notwithstanding their difference.

SIR BEN: The young lady's *penchant* is obvious.

CRAB: But, Benjamin, you mustn't give up the pursuit for that; follow her, and put her into good humor. Repeat her some of your own verses.—Come, I'll assist you.

SIR BEN: Mr. Surface, I did not mean to hurt you; but depend upon't your brother is utterly undone. (*Going.*)

CRAB: O lud, aye! undone as ever man was—can't raise a guinea. (*Going.*)

SIR BEN: And everything sold, I'm told, that was movable. (*Going.*)

CRAB: I have seen one that was at his house—not a thing left but some empty bottles that were overlooked, and the family pictures, which I believe are framed in the wainscot. (*Going.*)

SIR BEN: And I am very sorry to hear also some bad stories against him. (*Going.*)

CRAB: Oh, he has done many mean things, that's certain. (*Going.*)

SIR BEN: But, however, as he's your brother—(*Going.*)

CRAB: We'll tell you all, another opportunity.
*Exeunt* CRABTREE *and* SIR BENJAMIN.

LADY SNEER: Ha, ha! ha! 'tis very hard for them to leave a subject they have not quite run down.

JOS. SURF: And I believe the abuse was no more acceptable to your ladyship than to Maria.

LADY SNEER: I doubt[3] her affections are farther engaged than we imagined; but the family are to be here this evening, so you may as well dine where you are, and we shall have an opportunity of observing farther;—in the meantime, I'll go and plot mischief, and you shall study sentiments. (*Exeunt.*)

## SCENE II
SIR PETER TEAZLE's *house.*
*Enter* SIR PETER.

SIR PETER: When an old bachelor takes a young wife, what is he to expect?—'Tis now six months since Lady Teazle made

---

[2] **Irish tontine** a life annuity scheme sponsored by the Irish parliament

[3] **doubt** fear

me the happiest of men—and I have been the miserablest dog ever since that ever committed wedlock! We tift a little going to church, and came to a quarrel before the bells were done ringing. I was more than once nearly choked with gall during the honeymoon, and had lost all comfort in life before my friends had done wishing me joy! Yet I chose with caution—a girl bred wholly in the country, who never knew luxury beyond one silk gown, nor dissipation above the annual gala of a race ball. Yet now she plays her part in all the extravagant fopperies of the fashion and the town, with as ready a grace as if she had never seen a bush nor a grass-plat out of Grosvenor Square! I am sneered at by my old acquaintance—paragraphed in the newspapers. She dissipates my fortune, and contradicts all my humors; yet the worst of it is, I doubt I love her, or I should never bear all this. However, I'll never be weak enough to own it.

*Enter* ROWLEY.

ROW: Oh! Sir Peter, your servant,—how is it with you, sir?

SIR PET: Very bad, Master Rowley, very bad;—I meet with nothing but crosses and vexations.

ROW: What can have happened to trouble you since yesterday?

SIR PET: A good question to a married man!

ROW: Nay, I'm sure your lady, Sir Peter, can't be the cause of your uneasiness.

SIR PET: Why, has anyone told you she was dead?

ROW: Come, come, Sir Peter, you love her, notwithstanding your tempers don't exactly agree.

SIR PET: But the fault is entirely hers, Master Rowley. I am, myself, the sweetest-tempered man alive, and hate a teasing temper—and so I tell her a hundred times a day.

ROW: Indeed!

SIR PET: Aye; and what is very extraordinary, in all our disputes she is always in the wrong! But Lady Sneerwell, and the set she meets at her house, encourage the perverseness of her disposition. Then, to complete my vexations, Maria, my ward, whom I ought to have the power of a father over, is determined to turn rebel too, and absolutely refuses the man whom I have long resolved on for her husband;—meaning, I suppose, to bestow herself on his profligate brother.

ROW: You know, Sir Peter, I have always taken the liberty to differ with you on the subject of these two young gentlemen. I only wish you may not be deceived in your opinion of the elder. For Charles, my life on't! he will retrieve his errors yet. Their worthy father, once my honored master, was, at his years, nearly as wild a spark; yet, when he died, he did not leave a more benevolent heart to lament his loss.

SIR PET: You are wrong, Master Rowley. On their father's death, you know, I acted as a kind of guardian to them both, till their uncle Sir Oliver's Eastern liberality gave them an early independence; of course, no person could have more opportunities of judging of their hearts, and I was never mistaken in my life. Joseph is indeed a model for the young men of the age. He is a man of sentiment, and acts up to the sentiments he professes; but, for the other, take my word fort, if he had any grains of virtue by descent, he has dissipated them with the rest of his inheritance. Ah! my old friend, Sir Oliver, will be deeply mortified when he finds how part of his bounty has been misapplied.

ROW: I am sorry to find you so violent against the young man, because this may be the most critical period of his fortune.

I came hither with news that will surprise you.

SIR PET: What! let me hear.

ROW: Sir Oliver *is* arrived, and at this moment in town.

SIR PET: How! you astonish me! I thought you did not expect him this month.

ROW: I did not; but his passage has been remarkably quick.

SIR PET: Egad, I shall rejoice to see my old friend,—'tis sixteen years since we met—we have had many a day together; but does he still enjoin us not to inform his nephews of his arrival?

ROW: Most strictly. He means, before it is known, to make some trial of their dispositions.

SIR PET: Ah! There needs no art to discover their merits—however, he shall have his way; but, pray, does he know I am married?

ROW: Yes, and will soon wish you joy.

SIR PET: What, as we drink health to a friend in a consumption! Ah, Oliver will laugh at me—we used to rail at matrimony together—but he has been steady to his text. Well, he must be at my house, though—I'll instantly give orders for his reception. But, Master Rowley, don't drop a word that Lady Teazle and I ever disagree.

ROW: By no means.

SIR PET: For I should never be able to stand Noll's jokes; so I'd have him think, Lord forgive me! that we are a very happy couple.

ROW: I understand you—but then you must be very careful not to differ while he's in the house with you.

SIR PET: Egad, and so we must—and that's impossible. Ah! Master Rowley, when an old bachelor marries a young wife, he deserves—no—the crime carries the punishment along with it. (*Exeunt.*)
*End of Act 1st.*

# ACT II

SCENE I

SIR PETER TEAZLE'S *house.*

*Enter* SIR PETER *and* LADY TEAZLE.

SIR PET: Lady Teazle, Lady Teazle, I'll not bear it!

LADY TEAZ: Sir Peter, Sir Peter, you may bear it or not, as you please; but I ought to have my own way in everything, and what's more, I *will* too.—What! though I was educated in the country, I know very well that women of fashion in London are accountable to nobody after they are married.

SIR PET: Very well, ma'am, very well,—so a husband is to have no influence, no authority?

LADY TEAZ: Authority! No, to be sure—if you wanted authority over me, you should have adopted me, and not married me; I am sure you were old enough.

SIR PET: Old enough!—aye, there it is!—Well, well, Lady Teazle, though my life may be made unhappy by your temper, I'll not be ruined by your extravagance.

LADY TEAZ: My extravagance! I'm sure I'm not more extravagant than a woman of fashion ought to be.

SIR PET: No, no, madam, you shall throw away no more sums on such unmeaning luxury. 'Slife! to spend as much to furnish your dressing-room with flowers in winter as would suffice to turn the Pantheon[1] into a greenhouse, and give a *fête champêtre*[2] at Christmas!

LADY TEAZ: Lord, Sir Peter, am I to blame because flowers are dear in cold weather? You should find fault with the climate, and not with me. For my part, I

---

II. [1] **The Pantheon** a large concert hall in London, so called because it had a dome like that of the Pantheon in Rome  [2] **fête champêtre** outdoor entertainment

am sure I wish it was spring all the year round, and that roses grew under one's feet!

SIR PET: Oons! madam—if you had been born to this, I shouldn't wonder at your talking thus.—But you forget what your situation was when I married you.

LADY TEAZ: No, no, I don't; 'twas a very disagreeable one, or I should never have married *you*.

SIR PET: Yes, yes, madam, you were then in somewhat an humbler style—the daughter of a plain country squire. Recollect, Lady Teazle, when I saw you first, sitting at your tambour,[3] in a pretty figured linen gown, with a bunch of keys by your side, your hair combed smooth over a roll, and your apartment hung round with fruits in worsted, of your own working.

LADY TEAZ: O, yes! I remember it very well, and a curious life I led—my daily occupation to inspect the dairy, superintend the poultry, make extracts from the family receipt-book, and comb my aunt Deborah's lapdog.

SIR PET: Yes, yes, ma'am, 'twas so indeed.

LADY TEAZ: And then, you know, my evening amusements! To draw patterns for ruffles, which I had not the materials to make; to play Pope Joan[4] with the curate; to read a novel to my aunt; or to be stuck down to an old spinet to strum my father to sleep after a fox-chase.

SIR PET: I am glad you have so good a memory. Yes, madam, these were the recreations I took you from; but now you must have your coach—*vis-à-vis*—and three powdered footmen before your chair and, in summer, a pair of white cats[5] to draw you to Kensington Gardens.—No recollection, I suppose, when you were

content to ride double, behind the butler, on a docked coach-horse?

LADY TEAZ: No—I swear I never did that—I deny the butler and the coach-horse.

SIR PET: This, madam, was your situation—and what have I not done for you? I have made you a woman of fashion, of fortune, of rank—in short, I have made you my wife.

LADY TEAZ: Well, then, and there is but one thing more you can make me to add to the obligation—and that is—

SIR PET: My widow, I suppose?

LADY TEAZ: Hem! hem!

SIR PET: Thank you, madam—but don't flatter yourself; for though your ill-conduct may disturb my peace, it shall never break my heart, I promise you: however, I am equally obliged to you for the hint.

LADY TEAZ: Then why will you endeavor to make yourself so disagreeable to me, and thwart me in every little elegant expense?

SIR PET: 'Slife, madam, I say, had you any of these elegant expenses when you married me?

LADY TEAZ: Lud, Sir Peter! would you have me be out of the fashion?

SIR PET: The fashion, indeed! what had you to do with the fashion before you married me?

LADY TEAZ: For my part, I should think you would like to have your wife thought a woman of taste.

SIR PET: Aye—there again—taste! Zounds! madam, you had no taste when you married *me*!

LADY TEAZ: That's very true, indeed, Sir Peter! and, *after* having married you, I am sure I should never pretend to taste again! But now, Sir Peter, if we have finished our daily jangle, I presume I may go to my engagement of [at] Lady Sneerwell's?

---

[3] **tambour** a circular frame used for embroidering
[4] **Pope Joan** a card game   [5] **cats** horses

SIR PET: Aye—there's another precious circumstance!—a charming set of acquaintance you have made there!

LADY TEAZ: Nay, Sir Peter, they are people of rank and fortune, and remarkably tenacious of reputation.

SIR PET: Yes, egad, they are tenacious of reputation with a vengeance; for they don't choose anybody should have a character but themselves! Such a crew! Ah! many a wretch has rid on a hurdle[6] who has done less mischief than those utterers of forged tales, coiners of scandal,—and clippers of reputation.

LADY TEAZ: What! would you restrain the freedom of speech?

SIR PET: Oh! they have made you just as bad as any one of the society.

LADY TEAZ: Why, I believe I do bear a part with a tolerable grace. But I vow I have no malice against the people I abuse; when I say an ill-natured thing, 'tis out of pure good humor—and I take it for granted they deal exactly in the same manner with me. But, Sir Peter, you know you promised to come to Lady Sneerwell's too.

SIR PET: Well, well, I'll call in just to look after my own character.

LADY TEAZ: Then, indeed, you must make haste after me or you'll be too late.—So good-bye to ye.

*Exit* LADY TEAZLE.

SIR PET: So—I have gained much by my intended expostulations! Yet with what a charming air she contradicts everything I say, and how pleasingly she shows her contempt of my authority. Well, though I can't make her love me, there is a great satisfaction in quarreling with her; and I think she never appears to such advantage as when she's doing everything in her power to plague me.

(*Exit.*)

SCENE II

LADY SNEERWELL'S.

LADY SNEERWELL, MRS. CANDOUR, CRABTREE, SIR BENJAMIN BACKBITE, *and* JOSEPH SURFACE.

LADY SNEER: Nay, positively, we will hear it.

JOS. SURF: Yes, yes, the epigram, by all means.

SIR BEN: Plague on't, uncle! 'tis mere nonsense.

CRAB: No, no; 'fore gad, very clever for an extempore!

SIR BEN: But, ladies, you should be acquainted with the circumstance,—you must know, that one day last week, as Lady Betty Curricle was taking the dust in Hyde Park, in a sort of duodecimo[7] phaëton, she desired me to write some verses on her ponies; upon which, I took out my pocket-book, and in one moment produced the following:

'Sure never were seen two such beautiful ponies!
Other horses are clowns, and these macaronies!
Nay, to give 'em this title I'm sure isn't wrong—
Their legs are so slim, and their tails are so long.'

CRAB: There, ladies—done in the smack of a whip, and on horseback too!

JOS. SURF: A very Phœbus, mounted—indeed, Sir Benjamin.

SIR BEN: O dear sir—trifles—trifles.

*Enter* LADY TEAZLE *and* MARIA.

MRS. CAN: I must have a copy.

LADY SNEER: Lady Teazle, I hope we shall see Sir Peter.

---

[6] **hurdle** sledge on which traitors were taken to the place of execution

[7] **duodecimo** very small

**LADY TEAZ:** I believe he'll wait on your lady-ship presently.

**LADY SNEER:** Maria, my love, you look grave. Come, you shall sit down to cards with Mr. Surface.

**MARIA:** I take very little pleasure in cards—however, I'll do as your ladyship pleases.

**LADY TEAZ:** (*Aside*) I am surprised Mr. Surface should sit down with *her*.—I thought he would have embraced this opportunity of speaking to me before Sir Peter came.

**MRS. CAN:** Now, I'll die but you are so scandalous, I'll forswear your society.

**LADY TEAZ:** What's the matter, Mrs. Candour?

**MRS. CAN:** They'll not allow our friend Miss Vermilion to be handsome.

**LADY SNEER:** Oh, surely, she's a pretty woman.

**CRAB:** I am very glad you think so, ma'am.

**MRS. CAN:** She has a charming fresh color.

**LADY TEAZ:** Yes, when it is fresh put on.

**MRS. CAN:** O fie! I'll swear her color is natural—I have seen it come and go.

**LADY TEAZ:** I dare swear you have, ma'am—it goes of a night, and comes again in the morning.

**MRS. CAN:** Ha! ha! ha! how I hate to hear you talk so! But surely, now, her sister *is*, or *was*, very handsome.

**CRAB:** Who? Mrs. Evergreen?—O Lord! she's six-and-fifty if she's an hour!

**MRS. CAN:** Now positively you wrong her; fifty-two or fifty-three is the utmost—and I don't think she look more.

**SIR BEN:** Ah! there is no judging by her looks, unless one could see her face.

**LADY SNEER:** Well, well, if Mrs. Evergreen *does* take some pains to repair the ravages of time, you must allow she effects it with great ingenuity; and surely that's better than the careless manner in which the widow Ochre caulks her wrinkles.

**SIR BEN:** Nay, now, Lady Sneerwell, you are severe upon the widow. Come, come, it is not that she paints so ill—but, when she has finished her face, she joins it on so badly to her neck, that she looks like a mended statue, in which the connoisseur may see at once that the head's modern, though the trunk's antique!

**CRAB:** Ha! ha! ha! Well said, nephew!

**MRS. CAN:** Ha! ha! ha! Well, you make me laugh, but I vow I hate you for't.—What do you think of Miss Simper?

**SIR BEN:** Why, she has very pretty teeth.

**LADY TEAZ:** Yes; and on that account, when she is neither speaking nor laughing (which very seldom happens), she never absolutely shuts her mouth, but leaves it always on a jar, as it were.

**MRS. CAN:** How can you be so ill-natured?

**LADY TEAZ:** Nay, I allow even that's better than the pains Mrs. Prim takes to conceal her losses in front. She draws her mouth till it positively resembles the aperture of a poor's-box, and all her words appear to slide out edgeways.

**LADY SNEER:** Very well, Lady Teazle; I see you can be a little severe.

**LADY TEAZ:** In defence of a friend it is but justice;—but here comes Sir Peter to spoil our pleasantry.

*Enter* **SIR PETER TEAZLE**.

**SIR PET:** Ladies, your most obedient—Mercy on me, here is the whole set! a character dead at every word, I suppose. (*Aside.*)

**MRS. CAN:** I am rejoiced you are come, Sir Peter. They have been *so* censorious. They will allow good qualities to nobody—not even good nature to our friend Mrs. Pursy.

**LADY TEAZ:** What, the fat dowager who was at Mrs. Codille's last night?

**MRS. CAN:** Nay, her bulk is her misfortune; and, when she takes such pains to get rid of it, you ought not to reflect on her.

**LADY SNEER:** That's very true, indeed.

LADY TEAZ:  Yes, I know she almost lives on acids and small whey; laces herself by pulleys; and often, in the hottest noon of summer, you may see her on a little squat pony, with her hair platted up behind like a drummer's, and puffing round the Ring[8] on a full trot.

MRS. CAN:  I thank you, Lady Teazle, for defending her.

SIR PET:  Yes, a good defence, truly.

MRS. CAN:  But Sir Benjamin is as censorious as Miss Sallow.

CRAB:  Yes, and she is a curious being to pretend to be censorious—an awkward gawky, without any one good point under heaven.

MRS. CAN:  Positively you shall not be so very severe. Miss Sallow is a relation of mine by marriage, and, as for her person, great allowance is to be made; for, let me tell you, a woman labors under many disadvantages who tries to pass for a girl at six-and-thirty.

LADY SNEER:  Though, surely, she is handsome still—and for the weakness in her eyes, considering how much she reads by candle-light, it is not to be wondered at.

MRS. CAN:  True; and then as to her manner, upon my word I think it is particularly graceful, considering she never had the least education; for you know her mother was a Welch milliner, and her father a sugar-baker at Bristol.

SIR BEN:  Ah! you are both of you too good-natured!

SIR PET:  Yes, damned good-natured! This their own relation! mercy on me! (Aside.)

SIR BEN:  And Mrs. Candour is of so moral a turn she can sit for an hour to hear Lady Stucco talk sentiment.

LADY TEAZ:  Nay, I vow Lady Stucco is very well with the dessert after dinner; for she's just like the French fruit one cracks for mottoes—made up of paint and proverb.

MRS. CAN:  Well, I never will join in ridiculing a friend; and so I constantly tell my cousin Ogle, and you all know what pretensions she has to be critical in beauty.

CRAB:  Oh, to be sure! she has herself the oddest countenance that ever was seen; 'tis a collection of features from all the different countries of the globe.

SIR BEN:  So she has, indeed—an Irish front!

CRAB:  Caledonian locks!

SIR BEN:  Dutch nose!

CRAB:  Austrian lip!

SIR BEN:  Complexion of a Spaniard!

CRAB:  And teeth à la Chinoise!

SIR BEN:  In short, her face resembles a table d'hôte at Spa—where no two guests are of a nation—

CRAB:  Or a congress at the close of a general war—wherein all the members, even to her eyes, appear to have a different interest, and her nose and chin are the only parties likely to join issue.

MRS. CAN:  Ha! ha! ha!

SIR PET:  Mercy on my life!—a person they dine with twice a week! (Aside.)

[LADY SNEER:  Go—go—you are a couple of provoking toads.]

MRS. CAN:  Nay, but I vow you shall not carry the laugh off so—forgive me leave to say, that Mrs. Ogle—

SIR PET:  Madam, madam, I beg your pardon—there's no stopping these good gentlemen's tongues. But when I tell you, Mrs. Candour, that the lady they are abusing is a particular friend of mine—I hope you'll not take her part.

LADY SNEER:  Well said, Sir Peter! but you are a cruel creature—too phlegmatic yourself for a jest, and too peevish to allow wit on others.

SIR PET:  Ah, madam, true wit is more nearly allied to good nature than your ladyship is aware of.

---

[8] **Ring** a drive and promenade in Hyde Park

LADY TEAZ: True, Sir Peter; I believe they are so near akin that they can never be united.

SIR BEN: Or rather, madam, suppose them man and wife, because one so seldom sees them together.

LADY TEAZ: But Sir Peter is such an enemy to scandal, I believe he would have it put down by parliament.

SIR PET: 'Fore heaven, madam, if they were to consider the sporting with reputation of as much importance as poaching on manors, and pass *An Act for the Preservation of Fame*, I believe many would thank them for the bill.

LADY SNEER: O lud! Sir Peter; would you deprive us of our privileges?

SIR PET: Aye, madam; and then no person should be permitted to kill characters or run down reputations, but qualified old maids and disappointed widows.

LADY SNEER: Go, you monster!

MRS. CAN: But sure you would not be quite so severe on those who only report what they hear.

SIR PET: Yes, madam, I would have law merchant[9] for them too; and in all cases of slander currency, whenever the drawer of the lie was not to be found, the injured parties should have a right to come on any of the indorsers.

CRAB: Well, for my part, I believe there never was a scandalous tale without some foundation.

LADY SNEER: Come, ladies, shall we sit down to cards in the next room?
*Enter Servant and whispers* SIR PETER.

SIR PET: I'll be with them directly.—(*Exit Servant.*) I'll get away unperceived. (*Aside.*)

LADY SNEER: Sir Peter, you are not leaving us?

SIR PET: Your ladyship must excuse me; I'm called away by particular business—but I leave my character behind me.
*Exit* SIR PETER.

SIR BEN: Well certainly, Lady Teazle, that lord of yours is a strange being; I could tell you some stories of him would make you laugh heartily, if he wasn't your husband.

LADY TEAZ: O pray don't mind that—come, do let's hear them.
*They join the rest of the company, all talking as they are going into the next room.*

JOS. SURF: (*Rising with* MARIA.) Maria, I see you have no satisfaction in this society.

MARIA: How is it possible I should? If to raise malicious smiles at the infirmities and misfortunes of those who have never injured us be the province of wit or humor, heaven grant me a double portion of dulness!

JOS. SURF: Yet they appear more ill-natured than they are; they have no malice at heart.

MARIA: Then is their conduct still more contemptible; for, in my opinion, nothing could excuse the intemperance of their tongues but a natural and ungovernable bitterness of mind.

JOS. SURF: But can you, Maria, feel thus for others, and be unkind to me alone? Is hope to be denied the tenderest passion?

MARIA: Why will you distress me by renewing this subject?

JOS. SURF: Ah, Maria! you would not treat me thus, and oppose your guardian, Sir Peter's will, but that I see that profligate *Charles* is still a favored rival.

MARIA: Ungenerously urged! But, whatever my sentiments of that unfortunate young man are, be assured I shall not feel more bound to give him up, because his distresses have lost him the regard even of a brother.
**LADY TEAZLE** *returns.*

---

[9] **law merchant** system of laws for the regulation of commerce

JOS. SURF: Nay, but, Maria, do not leave me with a frown—by all that's honest, I swear—Gad's life, here's Lady Teazle. (*Aside.*)—You must not—no, you shall not—for, though I have the greatest regard for Lady Teazle—

MARIA: Lady Teazle!

JOS. SURF: Yet were Sir Peter to suspect—

LADY TEAZ: (*Coming forward.*) What's this, pray? Do you take her for me?—Child, you are wanted in the next room.— (*Exit* MARIA.) What is all this, pray?

JOS. SURF: Oh, the most unlucky circumstance in nature! Maria has somehow suspected the tender concern I have for your happiness, and threatened to acquaint Sir Peter with her suspicions, and I was just endeavoring to reason with her when you came.

LADY TEAZ: Indeed! but you seemed to adopt a very tender mode of reasoning—do you *usually* argue on your knees?

JOS. SURF: Oh, she's a child—and I thought a little bombast—but, Lady Teazle, when are you to give me your judgment on my library, as you promised?

LADY TEAZ: No, no,—I begin to think it would be imprudent, and you know I admit you as a lover no further than *fashion* requires.

JOS. SURF: True—a mere Platonic cicisbeo,[10] what every London wife is *entitled* to.

LADY TEAZ: Certainly, one must not be out of the fashion; however, I have so many of my country prejudices left, that, though Sir Peter's ill humor may vex me ever so, it never shall provoke me to—

JOS. SURF: The only revenge in your power. Well, I applaud your moderation.

LADY TEAZ: Go—you are an insinuating wretch! But we shall be missed—let us join the company.

JOS. SURF: But we had best not return together.

LADY TEAZ: Well, don't stay—for Maria shan't come to hear any more of your reasoning, I promise you.
*Exit* LADY TEAZLE.

JOS. SURF: A curious dilemma, truly, my politics have run me into! I wanted, at first, only to ingratiate myself with Lady Teazle, that she might not be my enemy with Maria; and I have, I don't know how, become her serious lover. Sincerely I begin to wish I had never made such a point of gaining so *very good* a character, for it has led me into so many cursed rogueries that I doubt I shall be exposed at last. *Exit.*

### SCENE III
SIR PETER'S.

*Enter* SIR OLIVER SURFACE *and* ROWLEY.

SIR OLIV: Ha! ha! ha! and so my old friend is married, hey?—a young wife out of the country.—Ha! ha! ha!—that he should have stood bluff[11] to old bachelor so long, and sink into a husband at last!

ROW: But you must not rally him on the subject, Sir Oliver; 'tis a tender point, I assure you, though he has been married only seven months.

SIR OLIV: Then he has been just half a year on the stool of repentance!—Poor Peter! But you say he has entirely given up Charles—never sees him, hey?

ROW: His prejudice against him is astonishing, and I am sure greatly increased by a jealousy of him with Lady Teazle, which he has been industriously led into by a scandalous society in the neighborhood, who have contributed not a little to Charles's ill name; whereas the truth is, I believe, if the lady is partial

---

[10] **cicisbeo** recognized gallant of a married woman

[11] **bluff** firm

to either of them, his brother is the favorite.

SIR OLIV: Aye,—I know there are a set of malicious, prating, prudent gossips, both male and female, who murder characters to kill time, and will rob a young fellow of his good name before he has years to know the value of it,—but I am not to be prejudiced against my nephew by such, I promise you! No, no;—if Charles has done nothing false or mean, I shall compound for his extravagance.

ROW: Then, my life on't, you will reclaim him.—Ah, sir, it gives me new life to find that *your* heart is not turned against him, and that the son of my good old master has one friend, however, left.

SIR OLIV: What! shall I forget, Master Rowley, when I was at his years myself? Egad, my brother and I were neither of us very *prudent* youths—and yet, I believe, you have not seen many better men than your old master was?

ROW: Sir, 'tis this reflection gives me assurance that Charles may yet be a credit to his family.—But here comes Sir Peter.

SIR OLIV: Egad, so he does!—Mercy on me, he's greatly altered, and seems to have a settled married look! One may read husband in his face at this distance!

*Enter* SIR PETER TEAZLE.

SIR PET: Hah! Sir Oliver—my old friend! Welcome to England a thousand times!

SIR OLIV: Thank you, thank you, Sir Peter! and i'faith I am glad to find you well, believe me!

SIR PET: Ah! 'tis a long time since we met—sixteen years, I doubt, Sir Oliver, and many a cross accident in the time.

SIR OLIV: Aye, I have had my share—but, what! I find you are married, hey, my old boy?—Well, well, it can't be helped—and so I wish you joy with all my heart!

SIR PET: Thank you, thank you, Sir Oliver.—Yes, I have entered into the happy state—but we'll not talk of that now.

SIR OLIV: True, true, Sir Peter; old friends should not begin on grievances at first meeting. No, no, no.

ROW: (*to* SIR OLIVER.) Take care, pray, sir.

SIR OLIV: Well, so one of my nephews is a wild rogue, hey?

SIR PET: Wild! Ah! my old friend, I grieve for your disappointment there—he's a lost young man, indeed; however, his brother will make you amends; *Joseph* is, indeed, what a youth should be—everybody in the world speaks well of him.

SIR OLIV: I am sorry to hear it—he has too good a character to be an honest fellow.—Everybody speaks well of him! Psha! then he has bowed as low to knaves and fools as to the honest dignity of genius or virtue.

SIR PET: What, Sir Oliver! do you blame him for not making enemies?

SIR OLIV: Yes, if he has merit enough to deserve them.

SIR PET: Well, well—you'll be convinced when you know him. 'Tis edification to hear him converse—he professes the noblest sentiments.

SIR OLIV: Ah, plague of his sentiments! If he salutes me with a scrap of morality in his mouth, I shall be sick directly. But, however, don't mistake me, Sir Peter; I don't mean to defend Charles's errors—but, before I form my judgment of either of them, I intend to make a trial of their hearts—and my friend Rowley and I have planned something for the purpose.

ROW: And Sir Peter shall own for once he has been mistaken.

SIR PET: Oh, my life on Joseph's honor!

SIR OLIV: Well, come, give us a bottle of good wine, and we'll drink the lad's health, and tell you our scheme.

SIR PET: *Allons*, then!

SIR OLIV: And don't, Sir Peter, be so severe against your old friend's son. Odds my life! I am not sorry that he has run out of the course a little; for my part, I hate to see prudence clinging to the green succors of youth; 'tis like ivy round a sapling, and spoils the growth of the tree. (*Exeunt.*)

*End of Act the Second.*

# ACT III

SCENE I
SIR PETER'S.

SIR PETER TEAZLE, SIR OLIVER SURFACE, *and* ROWLEY.

SIR PET: Well, then—we will see this fellow first, and have our wine afterwards. But how is this, Master Rowley? I don't see the jet[1] of your scheme.

ROW: Why, sir, this Mr. Stanley, whom I was speaking of, is nearly related to them, by their mother; he was once a merchant in Dublin, but has been ruined by a series of undeserved misfortunes. He has applied, by letter, since his confinement, both to Mr. *Surface* and *Charles*—from the former he has received nothing but evasive promises of future service, while Charles has done all that his extravagance has left him power to do; and he is, at this time, endeavoring to raise a sum of money, part of which, in the midst of his own distresses, I know he intends for the service of poor Stanley.

SIR OLIV: Ah! he is my brother's son.

SIR PET: Well, but how is Sir Oliver personally to—

ROW: Why, sir, I will inform Charles and his brother that Stanley has obtained permission to apply in person to his friends, and, as they have neither of them ever seen him, let Sir Oliver assume his character, and he will have a fair opportunity of judging at least of the benevolence of their dispositions; and believe me, sir, you will find in the youngest brother one who, in the midst of folly and dissipation, has still, as our immortal bard expresses it,—

'a tear for pity, and a hand
Open as day, for melting charity.'[2]

SIR PET: Psha! What signifies his having an open hand or purse either, when he has nothing left to give? Well, well, make the trial, if you please; but where is the fellow whom you brought for Sir Oliver to examine, relative to Charles's affairs?

ROW: Below, waiting his commands, and no one can give him better intelligence.— This, Sir Oliver, is a friendly Jew, who, to do him justice, has done everything in his power to bring your nephew to a proper sense of his extravagance.

SIR PET: Pray let us have him in.

ROW: Desire Mr. Moses to walk upstairs.

SIR PET: By why should you suppose he will speak the truth?

ROW: Oh, I have convinced him that he has no chance of recovering certain sums advanced to Charles but through the bounty of Sir Oliver, who he knows is arrived; so that you may depend on his fidelity to his [own] interest. I have also another evidence in my power, one Snake, whom I have detected in a matter little short of forgery, and shall shortly produce to remove some of *your* prejudices, Sir Peter, relative to Charles and Lady Teazle.

SIR PET: I have heard too much on that subject.

ROW: Here comes the honest Israelite.
*Enter* MOSES.
—This is Sir Oliver.

SIR OLIV: Sir, I understand you have lately had great dealings with my nephew Charles.

MOS: Yes, Sir Oliver—I have done all I could for him, but he was ruined before he came to me for assistance.

---

III. [1] **jet** point

[2] '**a tear . . . charity.**' *Henry IV, Part II,* IV.iv.31–32

**SIR OLIV:** That was unlucky, truly—for you have had no opportunity of showing your talents.

**MOS:** None at all—I hadn't the pleasure of knowing his distresses—till he was some thousands worse than nothing.

**SIR OLIV:** Unfortunate, indeed! But I suppose you have done all in your power for him, honest Moses?

**MOS:** Yes, he knows that. This very evening I was to have brought him a gentleman from the city, who doesn't know him, and will, I believe, advance him some money.

**SIR PET:** What, one Charles has never had money from before?

**MOS:** Yes; Mr. Premium, of Crutched Friars[3]—formerly a broker.

**SIR PET:** Egad, Sir Oliver, a thought strikes me!—Charles, you say, doesn't know Mr. Premium?

**MOS:** Not at all.

**SIR PET:** Now then, Sir Oliver, you may have a better opportunity of satisfying yourself than by an old romancing tale of a poor relation;—go with my friend Moses, and represent Mr. *Premium,* and then, I'll answer for't, you will see your nephew in all his glory.

**SIR OLIV:** Egad, I like this idea better than the other, and I may visit *Joseph* afterwards, as old *Stanley.*

**SIR PET:** True—so you may.

**ROW:** Well, this is taking Charles rather at a disadvantage, to be sure. However, Moses—you understand Sir Peter, and will be faithful?

**MOS:** You may depend upon me,—this is near the time I was to have gone.

**SIR OLIV:** I'll accompany you as soon as you please, Moses; but hold! I have forgot one thing—how the plague shall I be able to pass for a Jew?

**MOS:** There's no need—the principal is Christian.

**SIR OLIV:** Is he?—I'm sorry to hear it—but, then again, an't I rather too smartly dressed to look like a money-lender?

**SIR PET:** Not at all; 'twould not be out of character, if you went in your own carriage—would it, Moses?

**MOS:** Not in the least.

**SIR OLIV:** Well, but how must I talk? there's certainly some cant of usury, and mode of treating, that I ought to know.

**SIR PET:** Oh, there's not much to learn—the great point, as I take it, is to be exorbitant enough in your demands—hey, Moses?

**MOS:** Yes, that's a very great point.

**SIR OLIV:** I'll answer for't I'll not be wanting in that. I'll ask him eight or ten per cent on the loan, at least.

**MOS:** If you ask him no more than that, you'll be discovered immediately.

**SIR OLIV:** Hey! what the plague! how much then?

**MOS:** That depends upon the circumstances. If he appears not very anxious for the supply, you should require only forty or fifty per cent; but if you find him in great distress, and want the moneys very bad—you may ask double.

**SIR PET:** A good honest trade you're learning, Sir Oliver!

**SIR OLIV:** Truly I think so—and not unprofitable.

**MOS:** Then, you know, you haven't the moneys yourself, but are forced to borrow them for him of a friend.

**SIR OLIV:** Oh! I borrow it of a friend, do I?

**MOS:** Yes, and your friend is an unconscionable dog, but you can't help it.

**SIR OLIV:** My friend is an unconscionable dog, is he?

**MOS:** Yes, and he himself has not the moneys by him—but is forced to sell stock at a great loss.

**SIR OLIV:** He is forced to sell stock, is he, at a great loss, is he? Well, that's very kind of him.

---

[3] **Crutched Friars** street near the Tower of London

SIR PET: I'faith, Sir Oliver—Mr. Premium, I mean—you'll soon be master of the trade. But, Moses! wouldn't you have him run out a little against the Annuity Bill?[4] That would be in character, I should think.

MOS: Very much.

ROW: And lament that a young man now must be at years of discretion before he is suffered to ruin himself?

MOS: Aye, great pity!

SIR PET: And abuse the public for allowing merit to an act whose only object is to snatch misfortune and imprudence from the rapacious relief of usury, and give the minor a chance of inheriting his estate without being undone by coming into possession.

SIR OLIV: So, so—Moses shall give me further instructions as we go together.

SIR PET: You will not have much time, for your nephew lives hard by.

SIR OLIV: Oh, never fear! my tutor appears so able, that though Charles lived in the next street, it must be my own fault if I am not a complete rogue before I turn the corner. (*Exeunt* SIR OLIVER *and* MOSES.)

SIR PET: So now I think Sir Oliver will be convinced;—you are partial, Rowley, and would have prepared Charles for the other plot.

ROW: No, upon my word, Sir Peter.

SIR PET: Well, go bring me this Snake, and I'll hear what he has to say presently.—I see Maria, and want to speak with her.— (*Exit* ROWLEY.) I should be glad to be convinced my suspicions of Lady Teazle and Charles were unjust. I have never yet opened my mind on this subject to my friend *Joseph*—I'm determined I will do it—*he* will give me his opinion sincerely.

*Enter* MARIA.

So, child, has Mr. Surface returned with you?

MARIA: No, sir—he was engaged.

SIR PET: Well, Maria, do you not reflect, the more you converse with that amiable young man, what return his partiality for you deserves?

MARIA: Indeed, Sir Peter, your frequent importunity on this subject distresses me extremely—you compel me to declare, that I know no man who has ever paid me a particular attention whom I would not prefer to Mr. Surface.

SIR PET: So—here's perverseness! No, no, Maria, 'tis Charles only whom you would prefer—'tis evident his vices and follies have won your heart.

MARIA: This is unkind, sir—you know I have obeyed you in neither seeing nor corresponding with him; I have heard enough to convince me that he is unworthy my regard. Yet I cannot think it culpable, if, while my understanding severely condemns his vices, my heart suggests some pity for his distresses.

SIR PET: Well, well, pity him as much as you please, but give your heart and hand to a worthier object.

MARIA: Never to his brother!

SIR PET: Go, perverse and obstinate! But take care, madam; you have never yet known what the authority of a guardian is— don't compel me to inform you of it.

MARIA: I can only say, you shall not have *just* reason. 'Tis true, by my father's will, I am for a short period bound to regard you as his substitute, but must cease to think you so, when you would compel me to be miserable. (*Exit* MARIA.)

SIR PET: Was ever man so crossed as I am! everything conspiring to fret me!—l had not been involved in matrimony a fortnight, before her father, a hale and hearty man, died—on purpose, I believe, for the pleasure of plaguing me with the

---

[4] **Annuity Bill** measure to protect the estates of minors which became law during the initial run of the play

care of his daughter. But here comes my helpmate! She appears in great good humor. How happy I should be if I could tease her into loving me, though but a little!

*Enter* LADY TEAZLE.

LADY TEAZ: Lud! Sir Peter, I hope you haven't been quarreling with Maria—it isn't using me well to be ill humored when I am not by.

SIR PET: Ah, Lady Teazle, you might have the power to make me good humored at all times.

LADY TEAZ: I am sure I wish I had—for I want you to be in charming sweet temper at this moment. Do be good humored now, and let me have two hundred pounds, will you?

SIR PET: Two hundred pounds! what, an't I to be in a good humor without paying for it! But speak to me thus, and i'faith there's nothing I could refuse you. You shall have it; but seal me a bond for the repayment.

LADY TEAZ: O, no—there—my note of hand will do as well.

SIR PET: (*Kissing her hand.*) And you shall no longer reproach me with not giving you an independent settlement,—I mean shortly to surprise you; but shall we always live thus, hey?

LADY TEAZ: If you please. I'm sure I don't care how soon we leave off quarrelling, provided you'll own *you* were tired first.

SIR PET: Well—then let our future contest be, who shall be most obliging.

LADY TEAZ: I assure you, Sir Peter, good nature becomes you. You look now as you did before we were married!—when you used to walk with me under the elms, and tell me stories of what a gallant you were in your youth, and chuck me under the chin, you would, and ask me if I thought I could love all old fellow, who would deny me nothing—didn't you?

SIR PET: Yes, yes, and you were as kind and attentive.

LADY TEAZ: Aye, so I was, and would always take your part, when my acquaintance used to abuse you, and turn you into ridicule.

SIR PET: Indeed!

LADY TEAZ: Aye, and when my cousin Sophy has called you a stiff, peevish old bachelor, and laughed at me for thinking of marrying one who might be my father, I have always defended you—and said, I didn't think you so ugly by any means, and that I dared say you'd make a very good sort of a husband.

SIR PET: And you prophesied right—and we shall certainly now be the happiest couple——

LADY TEAZ: And never differ again!

SIR PET: No, never!—though at the same time, indeed, my dear Lady Teazle, you must watch your temper very narrowly; for in all our little quarrels, my dear, if you recollect, my love, you always began first.

LADY TEAZ: I beg your pardon, my dear Sir Peter: indeed, you always gave the provocation.

SIR PET: Now, see, my angel! take care—*contradicting* isn't the way to keep friends.

LADY TEAZ: Then, don't *you* begin it, my love!

SIR PET: There, now! you—you are going on—you don't perceive, my life, that you are just doing the very thing which you know always makes me angry.

LADY TEAZ: Nay, you know if you will be angry without any reason——

SIR PET: There now! you want to quarrel again.

LADY TEAZ: No, I am sure I don't—but, if you will be so peevish——

SIR PET: There now! who begins first?

LADY TEAZ: Why, you, to be sure. I said nothing—but there's no bearing your temper.

**SIR PET:** No, no, madam, the fault's in your own temper.

**LADY TEAZ:** Aye, you are just what my cousin Sophy said you would be.

**SIR PET:** Your cousin Sophy is a forward, impertinent gipsy.

**LADY TEAZ:** You are a great bear, I'm sure, to abuse my relations.

**SIR PET:** Now may all the plagues of marriage be doubled on me, if ever I try to be friends with you any more!

**LADY TEAZ:** So much the better.

**SIR PET:** No, no, madam; 'tis evident you never cared a pin for me, and I was a madman to marry you—a pert, rural coquette, that had refused half the honest squires in the neighborhood!

**LADY TEAZ:** And I am sure I was a fool to marry you—an old dangling bachelor, who was single at fifty, only because he never could meet with any one who would have him.

**SIR PET:** Aye, aye, madam; but you were pleased enough to listen to me—*you* never had such an offer before.

**LADY TEAZ:** No! didn't I refuse Sir Twivy Tarrier, who everybody said would have been a better match—for his estate is just as good as yours—and he has broke his neck since we have been married.

**SIR PET:** I have done with you, madam! You are an unfeeling, ungrateful—but there's an end of everything. I believe you capable of anything that's bad. Yes, madam, I now believe the reports relative to you and Charles, madam—yes, madam, you and Charles—are not without grounds—

**LADY TEAZ:** Take care, Sir Peter! you had better not insinuate any such thing! I'll not be suspected with*out cause,* I promise you.

**SIR PET:** Very well, madam! very well! a separate maintenance as soon as you please. Yes, madam, or a divorce! I'll make an example of myself for the benefit of all old bachelors. Let us separate, madam.

**LADY TEAZ:** Agreed! agreed! And now, my dear Sir Peter, we are of a mind once more, we may be the *happiest couple,* and *never differ again,* you know: ha! ha! Well, you are going to be in a passion, I see, and I shall only interrupt you—so, bye! bye! *Exit.*

**SIR PET:** Plagues and tortures! can't I make her angry neither? Oh, I am the miserablest fellow! But I'll not bear her presuming to keep her temper—no! she may break my heart, but she shan't keep her temper.
*Exit.*

**SCENE II**
**CHARLES'S** *house.*

*Enter* **TRIP, MOSES,** *and* **SIR OLIVER SURFACE.**

**TRIP:** Here, Master Moses! if you'll stay a moment, I'll try whether—what's the gentleman's name?

**SIR OLIV:** Mr. Moses, what *is* my name? (*Aside.*)

**MOS:** Mr. Premium.

**TRIP:** Premium—very well. *Exit* **TRIP,** *taking snuff.*

**SIR OLIV:** To judge by the servants one wouldn't believe the master was ruined. But what!—sure, this was my brother's house?

**MOS:** Yes, sir; Mr. Charles bought it of Mr. Joseph, with the furniture, pictures, &c., just as the old gentleman left it—Sir Peter thought it a great piece of extravagance in him.

**SIR OLIV:** In my mind, the other's economy in *selling* it to him was more reprehensible by half.
*Re-enter* **TRIP.**

**TRIP:** My master says you must wait, gentlemen; he has company, and can't speak with you yet.

SIR OLIV: If he knew *who* it was wanted to see him, perhaps he wouldn't have sent such a message?

TRIP: Yes, yes, sir; he knows *you* are here—I didn't forget little Premium—no, no, no.

SIR OLIV: Very well—and I pray, sir, what may be your name?

TRIP: Trip, sir—my name is Trip, at your service.

SIR OLIV: Well, then, Mr. Trip, you have a pleasant sort of a place here, I guess.

TRIP: Why, yes—here are three or four of us pass our time agreeably enough; but then our wages are sometimes a little in arrear—and not very great either—but fifty pounds a year, and find our own bags and bouquets.[5]

SIR OLIV: [*Aside.*] Bags and bouquets! halters and bastinadoes!

TRIP: But *à propos*, Moses, have you been able to get me that little bill discounted?

SIR OLIV: [*Aside.*] Wants to raise money, too!—mercy on me! Has his distresses, I warrant, like a lord,—and affects creditors and duns.

MOS: 'Twas not to be done, indeed, Mr. Trip. (*Gives the note.*)

TRIP: Good lack, you surprise me! My friend *Brush* has indorsed it, and I thought when he put his mark on the back of a bill 'twas as good as cash.

MOS: No, 'twouldn't do.

TRIP: A small sum—but twenty pounds. Hark'ee, Moses, do you think you couldn't get it me by way of annuity?

SIR OLIV: (*Aside.*) An annuity! ha! ha! ha! a footman raise money by way of annuity! Well done, luxury, egad!

MOS: But you must insure your place.

TRIP: Oh, with all my heart! I'll insure my place, and my life too, if you please.

SIR OLIV: (*Aside.*) It's more than I would your neck.

TRIP: But then, Moses, it must be done before this d—d register[6] takes place—one wouldn't like to have one's name made public, you know.

MOS: No, certainly. But is there nothing you could deposit?

TRIP: Why, nothing capital of my master's wardrobe has dropped lately; but I could give you a mortgage on some of his winter clothes, with equity of redemption before November—or you shall have the reversion of the French velvet, or a post-obit[7] on the blue and silver;—these, I should think, Moses, with a few pair of point ruffles, as a collateral security—hey, my little fellow?

MOS: Well, well. (*Bell rings.*)

TRIP: Gad, I heard the bell! I believe, gentlemen, I can now introduce you. Don't forget the annuity, little Moses! This way, gentlemen, insure my place, you know.

SIR OLIV: [*Aside.*] If the man be a shadow of his master, this is the temple of dissipation indeed!

*Exeunt.*

## SCENE III

CHARLES (SURFACE), CARELESS, &c., &c. *at a table with wine, &c.*

CHAS. SURF: 'Fore heaven, 'tis true!—there's the great degeneracy of the age. Many of our acquaintance have taste, spirit, and politeness; but, plague on't, they won't drink.

CARE: It is so, indeed, Charles! they give in to all the substantial luxuries of the table, and abstain from nothing but wine and wit.

CHAS. SURF: Oh, certainly society suffers by it intolerably! for now, instead of the social spirit of railery that used to mantle over a glass of bright Burgundy, their conversation is become just like the Spa-

---

[5] **bags and bouquets** referring to the dress of footmen

[6] **d—d register** referring to the provision in the Annuity Bill for registering life annuities   [7] **post-obit** claim to be satisfied after the death of the original owner

water they drink, which has all the pertness and flatulence of champagne, without its spirit or flavor.

**1 GENT:**  But what are *they* to do who love play better than wine?

**CARE:**  True! there's Harry diets himself for gaming, and is now under a hazard regimen.

**CHAS. SURF:**  Then he'll have the worst of it. What! you wouldn't train a horse for the course by keeping him from corn! For my part, egad, I am now never so successful as when I am a little merry—let me throw on a bottle of champagne, and I never lose—at least I never feel my losses, which is exactly the same thing.

**2 GENT:**  Aye, that I believe.

**CHAS. SURF:**  And, then, what man can pretend to be a believer in love, who is an abjurer of wine? 'Tis the test by which the lover knows his own heart. Fill a dozen bumpers to a dozen beauties, and she that floats at top is the maid that has bewitched you.

**CARE:**  Now then, Charles, be honest, and give us your real favorite.

**CHAS. SURF:**  Why, I have withheld her only in compassion to you. If I toast her, you must give a round of her peers—which is impossible—on earth.

**CARE:**  Oh, then we'll find some canonised vestals or heathen goddesses that will do, I warrant!

**CHAS. SURF:**  Here then, bumpers, you rogues! bumpers! Maria! Maria—(*Drink.*)

**1 GENT:**  Maria who?

**CHAS. SURF:**  O, damn the surname!—'tis too formal to be registered in Love's calendar—but now, Sir Toby Bumper, beware—we must have beauty superlative.

**CARE:**  Nay, never study, Sir Toby: we'll stand to the toast, though your mistress should want an eye—and you know you have a song will excuse you.

**SIR TOBY:**  Egad, so I have! and I'll give him the song instead of the lady. (*Sings.*)

**SONG AND CHORUS**

Here's to the maiden of bashful fifteen;
  Here's to the widow of fifty;
Here's to the flaunting extravagant queen,
  And here's to the housewife that's thrifty.
*Chorus.*      Let the toast pass—
        Drink to the lass—
I'll warrant she'll prove an excuse for the glass

Here's to the charmer whose dimples we prize;
  Now to the maid who has none, sir;
Here's to the girl with a pair of blue eyes,
  And here's to the nymph with but one, sir.
*Chorus.*      Let the toast pass, &c.

Here's to the maid with a bosom of snow:
  Now to *her* that's as brown as a berry:
Here's to the wife with a face full of woe,
  And now for the damsel that's merry.
*Chorus.*      Let the toast pass, &c.

For let 'em be clumsy, or let 'em be slim,
  Young or ancient, I care not a feather:
So fill a pint bumper quite up to the brim,
  —And let us e'en toast 'em together.
*Chorus.*      Let the toast pass, &c.

All. Bravo! Bravo!

*Enter* **TRIP,** *and whispers* **CHARLES SURFACE.**

**CHAS. SURF:**  Gentlemen, you must excuse me a little.—Careless, take the chair, will you?

**CARE:**  Nay, prithee, Charles, what now? This is one of your peerless beauties, I suppose, has dropped in by chance?

**CHAS. SURF:**  No, faith! To tell you the truth, 'tis a Jew and a broker, who are come by appointment.

**CARE:**  Oh, damn it! let's have the Jew in—

1 GENT: Aye, and the broker too, by all means.

2 GENT: Yes, yes, the Jew and the broker.

CHAS. SURF: Egad, with all my heart!—Trip, bid the gentlemen walk in.—(*Exit* TRIP.) Though there's one of them a stranger, I can tell you.

CARE: Charles, let us give them some generous Burgundy, and perhaps they'll grow conscientious.

CHAS. SURF: Oh, hang 'em, no! wine does but draw forth a man's *natural* qualities; and to make *them* drink would only be to whet their knavery.

*Enter* TRIP, **SIR OLIVER SURFACE**, *and* **MOSES**.

CHAS. SURF: So, honest Moses; walk in, pray, Mr. Premium—that's the gentleman's name, isn't it, Moses?

MOS: Yes, sir.

CHAS. SURF: Set chairs, Trip.—Sit down, Mr. Premium.—Glasses, Trip.—Sit down, Moses.—Come, Mr. Premium, I'll give you a sentiment; here's 'Success to usury!'—Moses, fill the gentleman a bumper.

MOS: Success to usury!

CARE: Right, Moses—usury is prudence and industry, and deserves to succeed.

SIR OLIV: Then here's—All the success it deserves!

CARE: No, no, that won't do! Mr. Premium, you have demurred to the toast, and must drink it in a pint bumper.

1 GENT: A pint bumper, at least.

MOS: Oh, pray, sir, consider—Mr. Premium's a gentleman.

CARE: And therefore loves good wine.

2 GENT: Give Moses a quart glass—this is mutiny, and a high contempt of the chair.

CARE: Here, now for't! I'll see justice done, to the last drop of my bottle.

SIR OLIV: Nay, pray, gentlemen—I did not expect this usage.

CHAS. SURF: No, hang it, Careless, you shan't; Mr. Premium's a stranger.

SIR OLIV: [*Aside.*] Odd! I wish I was well out of this company.

CARE: Plague on 'em then! if they won't drink, we'll not sit down with 'em. Come, Harry, the dice are in the next room.—Charles, you'll join us—when you have finished your business with these gentlemen?

CHAS. SURF: I will! I will!—(*Exeunt Gentlemen*). Careless!

CARE: Well!

CHAS. SURF: Perhaps I may want *you*.

CARE: Oh, you know I am always ready—word, note, or bond, 'tis all the same to me. (*Exit.*)

MOS: Sir, this is Mr. Premium, a gentleman of the strictest honor and secrecy; and always performs what he undertakes. Mr. Premium, this is—

CHAS. SURF: Pshaw! have done! Sir, my friend Moses is a very honest fellow, but a little slow at expression; he'll be an hour giving us our titles. Mr. Premium, the plain state of the matter is this—I am an extravagant young fellow who want[s] money to borrow; you I take to be a prudent old fellow, who ha[s] got money to lend. I am blockhead enough to give fifty per cent sooner than not have it; and you, I presume, are rogue enough to take a hundred if you could get it. Now, sir, you see we are acquainted at once, and may proceed to business without farther ceremony.

SIR OLIV: Exceeding frank, upon my word. I see, sir, you are not a man of many compliments.

CHAS. SURF: Oh, no, sir! plain dealing in business I always think best.

SIR OLIV: Sir, I like you the better for't. However, you are mistaken in one thing—I have no money to lend, but I believe I could procure some of a friend; but then he's an unconscionable dog—isn't he, Moses? And must sell stock to accommodate you—mustn't he, Moses?

MOS:  Yes, indeed! You know I always speak the truth, and scorn to tell a lie!

CHAS. SURF:  Right! People that expect truth generally do. But these are trifles, Mr. Premium. What! I know money isn't to be bought without paying for't!

SIR OLIV:  Well, but what security could you give? You have no land, I suppose?

CHAS. SURF:  Not a mole-hill, nor a twig, but what's in beau-pots[8] out at the window!

SIR OLIV:  Nor any stock, I presume?

CHAS. SURF:  Nothing but live stock—and that's only a few pointers and ponies. But pray, Mr. Premium, are you acquainted at all with any of my connections?

SIR OLIV:  Why, to say truth, I am.

CHAS. SURF:  Then you must know that I have a devilish rich uncle in the East Indies, Sir *Oliver Surface*, from whom I have the greatest expectations.

SIR OLIV:  That you have a wealthy uncle, I have heard—but how your expectations will turn out is more, I believe, than you can tell.

CHAS. SURF:  Oh, no!—there can be no doubt—they tell me I'm a prodigious favorite—and that he talks of leaving me everything.

SIR OLIV:  Indeed! this is the first I've heard on't.

CHAS. SURF:  Yes, yes, 'tis just so.—Moses knows 'tis true; don't you, Moses?

MOS:  Oh, yes! I'll swear to't.

SIR OLIV:  (*Aside.*) Egad, they'll persuade me presently I'm at Bengal.

CHAS. SURF:  Now I propose, Mr. Premium, if it's agreeable to you, a post-obit on Sir Oliver's life; though at the same time the old fellow has been so liberal to me that I give you my word I should be very sorry to hear anything had happened to him.

SIR OLIV:  Not more than *I* should, I assure you. But the bond you mention happens to be just the worst security you could offer me—for I might live to a hundred and never recover the principal.

CHAS. SURF:  Oh, yes, you would!—the moment Sir Oliver dies, you know, you'd come on me for the money.

SIR OLIV:  Then I believe I should be the most unwelcome dun you ever had in your life.

CHAS. SURF:  What! I suppose you are afraid now that Sir Oliver is too good a life?

SIR OLIV:  No, indeed I am not—though I have heard he is as hale and healthy as any man of his years in Christendom.

CHAS. SURF:  There again you are misinformed. No, no, the climate has hurt him considerably, poor uncle Oliver. Yes, he breaks apace, I'm told—and so much altered lately that his nearest relations don't know him.

SIR OLIV:  No! Ha! ha! ha! so much altered lately that his relations don't know him! Ha! ha! ha! that's droll, egad—ha! ha! ha!

CHAS. SURF:  Ha! ha!—you're glad to hear that, little Premium.

SIR OLIV:  No, no, I'm not.

CHAS. SURF:  Yes, yes, you are—ha! ha! ha!—you know that mends your chance.

SIR OLIV:  But I'm told Sir Oliver is coming over—nay, some say he is actually arrived.

CHAS. SURF:  Pshaw! sure I must know better than you whether he's come or not. No, no, rely on't, he is at this moment at Calcutta, isn't he, Moses?

MOS:  Oh, yes, certainly.

SIR OLIV:  Very true, as you say, you must know better than I, though I have it from pretty good authority—haven't I, Moses?

MOS:  Yes, most undoubted!

SIR OLIV:  But, sir, as I understand you want a few hundreds immediately, is there nothing you would dispose of?

CHAS. SURF:  How do you mean?

SIR OLIV:  For instance, now—I have heard—that your father left behind him a great quantity of massy old plate.

---

[8] **beau-pots** ornamental vases for flowers

**CHAS. SURF:** O lud! that's gone long ago—Moses can tell you how better than I can.

**SIR OLIV:** Good lack! all the family race-cups and corporation-bowls! (*Aside.*)—Then it was also supposed that his library was one of the most valuable and complete.

**CHAS. SURF:** Yes, yes, so it was—vastly too much so for a private gentleman—for my part, I was always of a communicative disposition, so I thought it a shame to keep so much knowledge to myself.

**SIR OLIV:** (*Aside.*) Mercy on me! learning that had run in the family like an heirloom!—(*Aloud.*) Pray, what are become of the books?

**CHAS. SURF:** You must inquire of the auctioneer, Master Premium, for I don't believe even Moses can direct you there.

**MOS:** I never meddle with books.

**SIR OLIV:** So, so, nothing of the family property left, I suppose?

**CHAS. SURF:** Not much, indeed; unless you have a mind to the family pictures. I have got a room full of ancestors above—and if you have a taste for old paintings, egad, you shall have 'em a bargain!

**SIR OLIV:** Hey! and the devil! sure, you wouldn't sell your forefathers, would you?

**CHAS. SURF:** Every man of 'em, to the best bidder.

**SIR OLIV:** What! your great-uncles and aunts?

**CHAS. SURF:** Aye, and my great-grandfathers and grandmothers too.

**SIR OLIV:** Now I give him up!—(*Aside.*)—What the plague, have you no bowels for your own kindred? Odd's life! do you take me for Shylock in the play, that you would raise money of me on your own flesh and blood?

**CHAS. SURF:** Nay, my little broker, don't be angry: what need *you* care, if you have your money's worth?

**SIR OLIV:** Well, I'll be the purchaser—I think I can dispose of the family.—(*Aside.*) Oh,

I'll never forgive him this! never!

*Enter* CARELESS.

**CARE:** Come, Charles, what keeps you?

**CHAS. SURF:** I can't come yet. I'faith! we are going to have a sale above—here's little Premium will buy all my ancestors!

**CARE:** Oh, burn your ancestors!

**CHAS. SURF:** No, he may do that afterwards, if he pleases. Stay, Careless, we want you; egad, you shall be auctioneer—so come along with us.

**CARE:** Oh, have with you, if that's the case.—I can handle a hammer as well as a dice box!

**SIR OLIV:** (*Aside.*) Oh, the profligates!

**CHAS. SURF:** Come, Moses, you shall be appraiser, if we want one.—Gad's life, little Premium, you don't seem to like the business.

**SIR OLIV:** Oh, yes, I do, vastly! Ha! ha! yes, yes, I think it a rare joke to sell one's family by auction—ha! ha!—(*Aside.*) Oh, the prodigal!

**CHAS. SURF:** To be sure! when a man wants money, where the plague should he get assistance, if he can't make free with his own relations? (*Exeunt.*)

*End of the third Act.*

# ACT IV

**SCENE I**

*Picture-room at* CHARLES'S.

*Enter* CHARLES SURFACE, SIR OLIVER SURFACE, MOSES, *and* CARELESS.

**CHAS. SURF:** Walk in, gentlemen, pray walk in!—here they are, the family of the Surfaces, up to the Conquest.

**SIR OLIV:** And, in my opinion, a goodly collection.

**CHAS. SURF:** Aye, aye, these are done in true spirit of portrait-painting—no volunteer grace or expression—not like the works of your modern Raphael, who gives you the strongest resemblance, yet contrives to make your own portrait independent of you; so that you may sink the original and not hurt the picture. No, no; the merit of these is the inveterate likeness—all stiff and awkward as the originals, and like nothing in human nature beside!

SIR OLIV: Ah! we shall never see such figures of men again.

CHAS. SURF: I hope not. Well, you see, Master Premium, what a domestic character I am—here I sit of an evening surrounded by my family. But come, get to your pulpit, Mr. Auctioneer—here's an old gouty chair of my grandfather's will answer the purpose.

CARE: Aye, aye, this will do. But, Charles, I have ne'er a hammer; and what's an auctioneer without his hammer?

CHAS. SURF: Egad, that's true. What parchment have we here? (*Takes down a roll.*) '*Richard, heir to Thomas*'—our genealogy in full. Here, Careless, you shall have no common bit of mahogany—here's the family tree for you, you rogue—this shall be your hammer, and now you may knock down my ancestors with their own pedigree.

SIR OLIV: (*Aside.*) What an unnatural rogue!—an *ex post facto* parricide!

CARE: Yes, yes, here's a list of your generation indeed;—faith, Charles, this is the most convenient thing you could have found for the business, for 'twill serve not only as a hammer, but a catalogue into the bargain.—But come, begin—A-going, a-going, a-going!

CHAS. SURF: Bravo, Careless! Well, here's my great uncle, Sir Richard Raviline, a marvelous good general in his day, I assure you. He served in all the Duke of Marlborough's wars, and got that cut over his eye at the battle of Malplaquet.[1] What say you, Mr. Premium? look at

him—there's a hero for you! not cut out of his feathers, as your modern clipped captains are, but enveloped in wig and regimentals, as a general should be. What do you bid?

MOS: Mr. Premium would have you speak.

CHAS. SURF: Why, then, he shall have him for ten pounds, and I am sure that's not dear for a staff-officer.

SIR OLIV: (*Aside.*) Heaven deliver me! his famous uncle Richard for ten pounds!—Very well, sir, I take him at that.

CHAS. SURF: Careless, knock down my uncle Richard.—Here, now, is a maiden sister of his, my great-aunt Deborah, done by Kneller,[2] thought to be in his best manner, and a very formidable likeness. There she is, you see, a shepherdess feeding her flock. You shall have her for five pounds ten—the sheep are worth the money.

SIR OLIV: (*Aside.*) Ah! poor Deborah! a woman who set such a value on herself! Five pound ten—she's mine.

CHAS. SURF: Knock down my aunt Deborah! Here, now, are two that were a sort of cousins of theirs.—You see, Moses, these pictures were done some time ago, when beaux wore wigs, and the ladies wore their own hair.

SIR OLIV: Yes, truly, head-dresses appear to have been a little lower in those days.

CHAS. SURF: Well, take that couple for the same.

MOS: 'Tis [a] good bargain.

CHAS. SURF: Careless!—This, now, is a grandfather of my mother's, a learned judge, well known on the western circuit.—What do you rate him at, Moses?

MOS: Four guineas.

CHAS. SURF: Four guineas! Gad's life, you don't bid me the price of his wig.—Mr. Premium, *you* have more respect for the

---

**IV.** [1] **battle of Malplaquet** victory over the French, September 11, 1709

[2] **Kneller** Sir Godfrey Kneller (1646–1723), a famous portrait painter

woolsack;[3] do let us knock his lordship down at fifteen.

SIR OLIV: By all means.

CARE: Gone!

CHAS. SURF: And there are two brothers of his, William and Walter Blunt, Esquires, both members of Parliament, and noted speakers; and, what's very extraordinary, I believe this is the first time they were ever bought and sold.

SIR OLIV: That's very extraordinary, indeed! I'll take them at your own price, for the honor of Parliament.

CARE: Well said, little Premium! I'll knock 'em down at forty.

CHAS. SURF: Here's a jolly fellow—I don't know what relation, but he was mayor of Manchester; take him at eight pounds.

SIR OLIV: No, no—six will do for the mayor.

CHAS. SURF: Come, make it guineas, and I'll throw you the two aldermen there into the bargan.

SIR OLIV: They're mine.

CHAS. SURF: Careless, knock down the mayor and aldermen. But, plague on't! we shall be all day retailing in this manner; do let us deal wholesale—what say you, little Premium? Give me three hundred pounds for the rest of the family in the lump.

CARE: Aye, aye, that will be the best way.

SIR OLIV: Well, well, anything to accommodate you; they are mine. But there is one portrait which you have always passed over.

CARE: What, that ill-looking little fellow over the settee?

SIR OLIV: Yes, sir, I mean that; though I don't think him so ill-looking a little fellow, by any means.

CHAS. SURF: What, that? Oh, that's my uncle Oliver! 'Twas done before he went to India.

CARE: Your uncle Oliver! Gad, then you'll never be friends, Charles. That, now, to me, is as stern a looking rogue as ever I saw—an unforgiving eye, and a damned disinheriting countenance! an inveterate knave, depend on't. Don't you think so, little Premium?

SIR OLIV: Upon my soul, sir, I do not; I think it is as honest a looking face as any in the room, dead or alive. But I suppose your uncle Oliver goes with the rest of the lumber?

CHAS. SURF: No, hang it! I'll not part with poor Noll. The old fellow has been very good to me, and, egad, I'll keep his picture while I've a room to put it in.

SIR OLIV: The rogue's my nephew after all! (*Aside.*)—But, sir, I have somehow taken a fancy to that picture.

CHAS. SURF: I'm sorry for't, for you certainly will not have it. Oons! haven't you got enough of 'em?

SIR OLIV: I forgive him everything! (*Aside.*) —But, sir, when I take a whim in my head, I don't value money. I'll give you as much for that as for all the rest.

CHAS. SURF: Don't tease me, master broker; I tell you I'll not part with it, and there's an end on't.

SIR OLIV: How like his father the dog is!— (*Aloud.*) Well, well, I have done.—I did not perceive it before, but I think I never saw such a resemblance.—Well, sir— here is a draught for your sum.

CHAS. SURF: Why, 'tis for eight hundred pounds!

SIR OLIV: You will not let Sir Oliver go?

CHAS. SURF: Zounds! no! I tell you, once more.

SIR OLIV: Then never mind the difference; we'll balance another time. But give me your hand on the bargain; you are an honest fellow, Charles—I beg pardon, sir, for being so free.—Come, Moses.

---

[3] **respect for the woolsack** respect for judges (who sat on scats made of bags of wool when they attended the House of Lords)

CHAS. SURF: Egad, this is a whimsical old fellow!—but hark'ee, Premium, you'll prepare lodgings for these gentlemen.

SIR OLIV: Yes, yes, I'll send for them in a day or two.

CHAS. SURF: But hold—do now—send a genteel conveyance for them, for, I assure you, they were most of them used to ride in their own carriages.

SIR OLIV: I will, I will, for all but—Oliver.

CHAS. SURF: Aye, all but the little honest nabob.

SIR OLIV: You're fixed on that?

CHAS. SURF: Peremptorily.

SIR OLIV: A dear extravagant rogue!—Good day!—Come, Moses,—Let me hear now who dares call him profligate! (*Exeunt* SIR OLIVER *and* MOSES.)

CARE: Why, this is the oddest genius of the sort I ever saw!

CHAS. SURF: Egad, he's the prince of brokers, I think. I wonder how the devil Moses got acquainted with so honest a fellow. —Ha! here's Rowley.—Do, Careless, say I'll join the company in a moment.

CARE: I will—but don't let that old blockhead persuade you to squander any of that money on old musty debts, or any such nonsense; for tradesmen, Charles, are the most exorbitant fellows!

CHAS. SURF: Very true, and paying them is only encouraging them.

CARE: Nothing else.

CHAS. SURF: Aye, aye, never fear.—(*Exit* CARELESS.) So! this was an odd old fellow, indeed! Let me see, two-thirds of this is mine by right—five hundred and thirty pounds. 'Fore heaven! I find one's ancestors are more valuable relations than I took 'em for!—Ladies and gentlemen, your most obedient and very grateful humble servant.

*Enter* ROWLEY.

Ha! old Rowley! egad, you are just come in time to take leave of your old acquaintance.

ROW: Yes, I heard they were going. But I wonder you can have such spirits under so many distresses.

CHAS. SURF: Why, there's the point—my distresses are so many, that I can't afford to part with my spirits; but I shall be rich and splenetic, all in good time. However, I suppose you are surprised that I am not more sorrowful at parting with so many near relations; to be sure, 'tis very affecting; but, rot 'em, you see they never move a muscle, so why should I?

ROW: There's no making you serious a moment.

CHAS. SURF: Yes, faith: I am so now. Here, my honest Rowley, here, get me this changed, and take a hundred pounds of it immediately to old Stanley.

ROW: A hundred pounds! Consider only—

CHAS.SURF: Gad's life, don't talk about it! poor Stanley's wants are pressing, and, if you don't make haste, we shall have some one call that has a better right to the money.

ROW: Ah! there's the point! I never will cease dunning you with the old proverb—

CHAS. SURF: 'Be *just* before you're *generous*,' hey!—Why, so I would if I could; but Justice is an old lame hobbling beldame, and I can't get her to keep pace with Generosity, for the soul of me.

ROW: Yet, Charles, believe me, one hour's reflection—

CHAS. SURF: Aye, aye, it's all very true; but, hark'ee, Rowley, while I have, by heaven I'll give—so, damn your economy! and now for hazard. (*Exit.*)

## SCENE II
*The Parlor.*

*Enter* SIR OLIVER SURFACE *and* MOSES.

MOS: Well, sir, I think, as Sir Peter said, you have seen Mr. Charles in high glory; 'tis great pity he's so extravagant.

SIR OLIV: True, but he wouldn't sell my picture.

MOS: And loves wine and women so much.

SIR OLIV: But he wouldn't sell my picture!

MOS: And game[s] so deep.

SIR OLIV: But he wouldn't sell my picture. Oh, here's Rowley.

*Enter* ROWLEY.

ROW: So, Sir Oliver, I find you have made a purchase—

SIR OLIV: Yes, yes, our young rake has parted with his ancestors like old tapestry.

ROW: And here has he commissioned me to redeliver you part of the purchase money—I mean, though, in your necessitous character of old *Stanley.*

MOS: Ah! there is the pity of all: he is so damned charitable.

ROW: And I left a hosier and two tailors in the hall, who, I'm sure, won't be paid, and this hundred would satisfy 'em.

SIR OLIV: Well, well, I'll pay his debts—and his benevolence too; but now I am no more a broker, and you shall introduce me to the elder brother as old Stanley.

ROW: Now yet awhile; Sir Peter, I know, means to call there about this time.

*Enter* TRIP.

TRIP: O gentlemen, I beg pardon for not showing you out; this way—Moses, a word.

*Exeunt* TRIP *and* MOSES.

SIR OLIV: There's a fellow for you! Would you believe it, that puppy intercepted the Jew on our coming, and wanted to raise money before he got to his master!

ROW: Indeed!

SIR OLIV: Yes, they are now planning an annuity business. Ah, Master Rowley, in my days, servants were content with the follies of their masters, when they were worn a little threadbare—but now they have their vices, like their birthday clothes,[4] with the gloss on. (*Exeunt.*)

SCENE III

*A library* [*in* JOSEPH SURFACE'S *house.*] JOSEPH SURFACE *and Servant.*

JOS. SURF: No letter from Lady Teazle?

SERV: No, sir.

JOS. SURF: [*Aside.*] I am surprised she hasn't sent, if she is prevented from coming. Sir Peter certainly does not suspect me. Yet I wish I may not lose the heiress, through the scrape I have drawn myself in with the wife; however, Charles's imprudence and bad character are great points in my favor. (*Knocking.*)

SERV: Sir, I believe that must be Lady Teazle.

JOS. SURF: Hold! See whether it is or not, before you go to the door—I have a particular message for you, if it should be my brother.

SERV: 'Tis her ladyship, sir; she always leaves her chair at the milliner's in the next street.

JOS. SURF: Stay, stay—draw that screen before the window—that will do;—my opposite neighbor is a maiden lady of so curious a temper.—(*Servant draws the screen, and exit.*) I have a difficult hand to play in this affair. Lady Teazle has lately suspected my views on Maria; but she must by no means be let into that secret,—at least, not till I have her more in my power.

*Enter* LADY TEAZLE.

LADY TEAZ: What, sentiment in soliloquy! Have you been very impatient now? O lud! don't pretend to look grave. I vow I couldn't come before.

JOS. SURF: O madam, punctuality is a species of constancy, a very unfashionable quality in a lady.

LADY TEAZ: Upon my word, you ought to pity me. Do you know that Sir Peter is grown so ill-tempered to me of late, and so jealous of *Charles* too—that's the best of the story, isn't it?

JOS. SURF: (*Aside.*) I am glad my scandalous friends keep that up.

[4] **birthday clothes** worn on the king's birthday

LADY TEAZ: I am sure I wish he would let Maria marry him, and then perhaps he would be convinced; don't you, Mr. Surface?

JOS. SURF: (*Aside.*) Indeed I do not.—Oh, certainly I do! for then my dear Lady Teazle would also be convinced how wrong her suspicions were of my having any design on the silly girl.

LADY TEAZ: Well, well, I'm inclined to believe you. But isn't it provoking, to have the most ill-natured things said to one? And there's my friend Lady Sneerwell has circulated I don't know how many scandalous tales of me! and all without any foundation, too—that's what vexes me.

JOS. SURF: Aye, madam, to be sure, that *is* the provoking circumstance—without foundation! yes, yes, there's the mortification, indeed; for, when a scandalous story is believed against one, there certainly is no comfort like the consciousness of having deserved it.

LADY TEAZ: No, to be sure—then I'd forgive their malice; but to attack me, who am really so innocent, and who never say an ill-natured thing of anybody—that is, of any friend—and then Sir Peter, too, to have him so peevish, and so suspicious, when I know the integrity of my own heart—indeed 'tis monstrous!

JOS. SURF: But, my dear Lady Teazle, 'tis your own fault if you suffer it. When a husband entertains a groundless suspicion of his wife, and withdraws his confidence from her, the original compact is broke, and she owes it to the honor of her sex to endeavor to outwit him.

LADY TEAZ: Indeed! So that, if he suspects me without cause, it follows that the best way of curing his jealousy is to give him reason for't?

JOS. SURF: Undoubtedly—for your husband should never be deceived in you: and in that case it becomes *you* to be frail in compliment to *his* discernment.

LADY TEAZ: To be sure, what you say is very reasonable, and when the consciousness of my own innocence—

JOS. SURF: Ah, my dear madam, there is the great mistake; 'tis this very conscious innocence that is of the greatest prejudice to you. What is it makes you negligent of forms, and careless of the world's opinion? why, the *consciousness* of your innocence. What makes you thoughtless in your conduct, and apt to run into a thousand little imprudences? why, the *consciousness* of your innocence. What makes you impatient of Sir Peter's temper and outrageous at his suspicions? why, the *consciousness* of your own innocence!

LADY TEAZ: 'Tis very true!

JOS. SURF: Now, my dear Lady Teazle, if you would but once make a trifling *faux pas,* you can't conceive how cautious you would grow—and how ready to humor and agree with your husband.

LADY TEAZ: Do you think so?

JOS. SURF: Oh, I'm sure on't; and then you would find all scandal would cease at once, for—in short, your character at present is like a person in a plethora, absolutely dying of too much health.

LADY TEAZ: So, so; then I perceive your prescription is, that I must sin in my own defence, and part with my virtue to preserve my reputation?

JOS. SURF: Exactly so, upon my credit, ma'am.

LADY TEAZ: Well, certainly this is the oddest doctrine, and the newest receipt for avoiding calumny?

JOS. SURF: An infallible one, believe me. *Prudence,* like *experience,* must be paid for.

LADY TEAZ: Why, if my understanding were once convinced—

JOS. SURF: Oh, certainly, madam, your understanding *should* be convinced. Yes, yes—heaven forbid I should persuade you to do anything you *thought* wrong.

No, no, I have too much honor to desire it.

LADY TEAZ: Don't you think we may as well leave honor out of the argument?

JOS. SURF: Ah, the ill effects of your country education, I see, still remain with you.

LADY TEAZ: I doubt they do, indeed; and I will fairly own to you, that if I could be persuaded to do wrong, it would be by Sir Peter's ill-usage sooner than your honorable logic, after all.

JOS. SURF: Then, by this hand, which he is unworthy of— (*Taking her hand.*)
*Re-enter Servant.*
'Sdeath, you blockhead—what do you want?

SERV: I beg pardon, sir, but I thought you wouldn't choose Sir Peter to come up without announcing him.

JOS. SURF: Sir Peter!—Oons—the devil!

LADY TEAZ: Sir Peter! O lud! I'm ruined! I'm ruined!

SERV: Sir, 'twasn't I let him in.

LADY TEAZ: Oh! I'm undone! What will become of me, now, Mr. Logic?—Oh! mercy, he's on the stairs—I'll get behind here—and if ever I'm so imprudent again—(*Goes behind the screen.*)

JOS. SURF: Give me that book. (*Sits down. Servant pretends to adjust his hair.*) *Enter* SIR PETER TEAZLE.

SIR PET: Aye, ever improving himself!—Mr. Surface, Mr. Surface—

JOS. SURF: Oh, my dear Sir Peter, I beg your pardon. (*Gaping, and throws away the book.*) I have been dozing over a stupid book. Well, I am much obliged to you for this call. You haven't been here, I believe, since I fitted up this room. Books, you know, are the only things I am a coxcomb in.

SIR PET: 'Tis very neat indeed. Well, well, that's proper; and you make even your screen a source of knowledge—hung, I perceive, with maps.

JOS. SURF: Oh, yes, I find great use in that screen.

SIR PET: I dare say you must—certainly—when you want to find anything in a hurry.

JOS. SURF: (*Aside.*) Aye, or to hide anything in a hurry either.

SIR PET: Well, I have a little private business—

JOS. SURF: You needn't stay. (*To Servant.*)

SERV: No, sir. (*Exit.*)

JOS. SURF: Here's a chair, Sir Peter—I beg—

SIR PET: Well, now we are alone, there is a subject, my dear friend, on which I wish to unburden my mind to you—a point of the greatest moment to my peace: in short, my good friend, Lady Teazle's conduct of late has made me extremely unhappy.

JOS. SURF: Indeed! I am very sorry to hear it.

SIR PET: Yes, 'tis but too plain she has not the least regard for me; but, what's worse, I have pretty good authority to suspect she must have formed an attachment to another.

JOS. SURF: You astonish me!

SIR PET: Yes! and, between ourselves, I think I have discovered the person.

JOS. SURF: How! you alarm me exceedingly.

SIR PET: Aye, my dear friend, I knew you would sympathize with me!

JOS. SURF: Yes, believe me, Sir Peter, such a discovery would hurt me just as much as it would you.

SIR PET: I am convinced of it.—Ah! it is a happiness to have a friend whom one can trust even with one's family secrets. But have you no guess who I mean?

JOS. SURF: I haven't the most distant idea. It can't be Sir Benjamin Backbite!

SIR PET: O, no! What say you to Charles?

JOS. SURF: My brother! impossible!

SIR PET: Ah, my dear friend, the goodness of your own heart misleads you—you judge of others by yourself.

JOS. SURF: Certainly, Sir Peter, the heart that is conscious of its own integrity is ever slow to credit another's treachery.

SIR PET: True; but your brother has no sentiment—you never hear him talk so.

JOS. SURF: Yet I can't but think Lady Teazle herself has too much principle—

SIR PET: Aye; but what's her principle against the flattery of a handsome, lively young fellow?

JOS. SURF: That's very true.

SIR PET: And then, you know, the difference of our ages makes it very improbable that she should have any great affection for me; and if she were to be frail, and I were to make it public, why the town would only laugh at me, the foolish old bachelor who had married a girl.

JOS. SURF: That's true, to be sure—they *would* laugh.

SIR PET: Laugh! aye, and make ballads, and paragraphs, and the devil knows what of me.

JOS. SURF: No, you must never make it public.

SIR PET: But then again—that the nephew of my old friend, Sir Oliver, should be the person to attempt such a wrong, hurts me more nearly.

JOS. SURF: Aye, there's the point. When ingratitude barbs the dart of injury, the wound has double danger in it.

SIR PET: Aye—I, that was, in a manner, left his guardian—in whose house he had been so often entertained—who never in my life denied him—my advice!

JOS. SURF: Oh, 'tis not to be credited! There *may* be a man capable of such baseness, to be sure; but, for my part, till you can give me positive proofs, I cannot but doubt it. However, if it should be proved on him, he is no longer a brother of mine! I disclaim kindred with him—for the man who can break through the laws of hospitality, and attempt the wife of his friend, deserves to be branded as the pest of society.

SIR PET: What a difference there is between you! What noble sentiments!

JOS. SURF: Yet I cannot suspect Lady Teazle's honor.

SIR PET: I am sure I wish to think well of her, and to remove all ground of quarrel between us. She has lately reproached me more than once with having made no settlement on her; and, in our last quarrel, she almost hinted that she should not break her heart if I was dead. Now, as we seem to differ in our ideas of expense, I have resolved she shall be her own mistress in that respect for the future; and, if I *were* to die, she shall find that I have not been inattentive to her interest while living. Here, my friend, are the drafts of two deeds, which I wish to have your opinion on. By one, she will enjoy eight hundred a year independent while I live; and, by the other, the bulk of my fortune after my death.

JOS. SURF: This conduct, Sir Peter, is indeed truly generous.— (*Aside.*) I wish it may not corrupt my pupil.

SIR PET: Yes, I am determined she shall have no cause to complain, though I would not have her acquainted with the latter instance of my affection yet awhile.

JOS. SURF: Nor I, if I could help it. (*Aside.*)

SIR PET: And now, my dear friend, if you please, we will talk over the situation of your hopes with *Maria*.

JOS. SURF: (*Softly.*) No, no, Sir Peter; another time, if you please.

SIR PET: I am sensibly chagrined at the little progress you seem to make in her affection.

JOS. SURF: I beg you will not mention it. What are my disappointments when your happiness is in debate! (*Softly.*)— 'Sdeath, I shall be ruined every way! (*Aside.*)

SIR PET: And though you are so averse to my acquainting Lady Teazle with your passion, I am sure she's not your enemy in the affair.

JOS. SURF: Pray, Sir Peter, now oblige me. I am really too much affected by the subject we have been speaking on to bestow a thought on my own concerns. The man who is entrusted with his friend's distresses can never—

*Enter Servant.*

Well, sir?

SERV: Your brother, sir, is speaking to a gentleman in the street, and says he knows you are within.

JOS. SURF: 'Sdeath, blockhead—I'm not within—I'm out for the day.

SIR PET: Stay—hold—a thought has struck me—you shall be at home.

JOS. SURF: Well, well, let him up.—(*Exit Servant.*) He'll interrupt Sir Peter—however—

SIR PET: Now, my good friend, oblige me, I entreat you. Before Charles comes, let me conceal myself somewhere; then do you tax him on the point we have been talking on, and his answers may satisfy me at once.

JOS. SURF: O, fie, Sir Peter! would you have me join in so mean a trick?—to trepan my brother too?

SIR PET: Nay, you tell me you are *sure* he is innocent; if so, you do him the greatest service by giving him an opportunity to clear himself, and you will set my heart at rest. Come, you shall not refuse me; here, behind the screen will be. (*Goes to the screen.*)—Hey! what the devil! there seems to be *one* listener here already—I'll swear I saw a petticoat!

JOS. SURF: Ha! ha! ha! Well, this is ridiculous enough. I'll tell you, Sir Peter, though I hold a man of intrigue to be a most despicable character, yet you know, it doesn't follow that one is to be an absolute Joseph either! Hark'ee! 'tis a little

French milliner, a silly rogue that plagues me—and having some character—on your coming, she ran behind the screen.

SIR PET: Ah, you rogue!—But, egad, she has overheard all I have been saying of my wife.

JOS. SURF: Oh, 'twill never go any further, you may depend on't!

SIR PET: No! then, i'faith, let her hear it out.—Here's a closet will do as well.

JOS. SURF: Well, go in then.

SIR PET: Sly rogue! sly rogue!

(*Goes into the closet.*)

JOS. SURF: A very narrow escape, indeed! and a curious situation I'm in, to part man and wife in this manner.

LADY TEAZ: (*Peeping from the screen.*) Couldn't I steal off?

JOS. SURF: Keep close, my angel!

SIR PET: (*Peeping out.*) Joseph, tax him home.

JOS. SURF: Back, my dear friend!

LADY TEAZ: (*Peeping.*) Couldn't you lock Sir Peter in?

JOS. SURF: Be still, my life!

SIR PET: (*Peeping.*) You're sure the little milliner won't blab?

JOS. SURF: In, in, my dear Sir Peter!—'Fore gad, I wish I had a key to the door.

*Enter* CHARLES SURFACE.

CHAS. SURF: Hollo! brother, what has been the matter? Your fellow would not let me up at first. What! have you had a Jew or a wench with you?

JOS. SURF: Neither, brother, I assure you.

CHAS. SURF: But what has made Sir Peter steal off? I thought he had been with you.

JOS. SURF: He was, brother; but, hearing *you* were coming, he did not choose to stay.

CHAS. SURF: What! was the old gentleman afraid I wanted to borrow money of him!

JOS. SURF: No, sir, but I am sorry to find, Charles, that you have lately given that worthy man grounds for great uneasiness.

CHAS. SURF: Yes, they tell me I do that to a great many worthy men. But how so, pray?

JOS. SURF: To be plain with you, brother, he thinks you are endeavoring to gain Lady Teazle's affections from him.

CHAS. SURF: Who, I? O lud! not I, upon my word.—Ha! ha! ha! so the old fellow has found out that he has got a young wife, has he?—or, what's worse, has her ladyship discovered that she has an old husband?

JOS. SURF: This is no subject to jest on, brother.—He who can laugh—

CHAS. SURF: True, true, as you were going to say—then, seriously, I never had the least idea of what you charge me with, upon my honor.

JOS. SURF: Well, it will give Sir Peter great satisfaction to hear this. (Aloud.)

CHAS. SURF: To be sure, I once thought the lady seemed to have taken a fancy to me; but, upon my soul, I never gave her the least encouragement. Besides, you know my attachment to Maria.

JOS. SURF: But sure, brother, even if Lady Teazle had betrayed the fondest partiality for you—

CHAS. SURF: Why, look'ee, Joseph, I hope I shall never deliberately do a dishonorable action—but if a pretty woman were purposely to throw herself in my way—and that pretty woman married to a man old enough to be her father—

JOS. SURF: Well!

CHAS. SURF: Why, I believe I should be obliged to borrow a little of your morality, that's all.—But, brother, do you know now that you surprise me exceedingly, by naming me with Lady Teazle; for, faith, I alway[s] understood you were her favorite.

JOS. SURF: Oh, for shame, Charles! This retort is foolish.

CHAS. SURF: Nay, I swear I have seen you exchange such significant glances——

JOS. SURF: Nay, nay, sir, this is no jest——

CHAS. SURF: Egad, I'm serious! Don't you remember—one day, when I called here——

JOS. SURF: Nay, prithee, Charles——

CHAS. SURF: And found you together——

JOS. SURF: Zounds, sir, I insist——

CHAS. SURF: And another time, when your servant——

JOS. SURF: Brother, brother, a word with you!—(Aside.) Gad, I must stop him.

CHAS. SURF: Informed me, I say, that——

JOS. SURF: Hush! I beg your pardon, but Sir Peter has overheard all we have been saying—I knew you would clear yourself, or I should not have consented.

CHAS. SURF: How, Sir Peter! Where is he?

JOS. SURF: Softly, there! (Points to the closet.)

CHAS. SURF: Oh, 'fore heaven, I'll have him out.—Sir Peter, come forth!

JOS. SURF: No, no—

CHAS. SURF: I say, Sir Peter, come into court.—(Pulls in SIR PETER.) What! my old guardian!—What—turn inquisitor, and take evidence, incog.?

SIR PET: Give me your hand, Charles—I believe I have suspected you wrongfully—but you mustn't be angry with Joseph—'twas my plan!

CHAS. SURF: Indeed!

SIR PET: But I acquit you. I promise you I don't think near so ill of you as I did. What I have heard has given me great satisfaction.

CHAS. SURF: Egad, then, 'twas lucky you didn't hear any more. Wasn't it, Joseph? (Half aside.)

SIR PET: Ah! you would have retorted on him.

CHAS. SURF: Aye, aye, that was a joke.

SIR PET: Yes, yes, I know his honor too well.

CHAS. SURF: But you might as well have suspected him as me in this matter, for all that. Mightn't he, Joseph? (Half aside.)

SIR PET: Well, well, I believe you.

JOS. SURF: (Aside.) Would they were both out of the room!

SIR PET: And in future, perhaps, we may not be such strangers.

*Enter Servant who whispers* JOSEPH SURFACE.

JOS. SURF: Lady Sneerwell!—stop her by all means—(*Exit Servant.*) Gentlemen—I beg pardon—I must wait on you downstairs—here's a person come on particular business.

CHAS. SURF: Well, you can see him in another room. Sir Peter and I haven't met a long time, and I have something to say to him.

JOS. SURF: They must not be left together.—I'll send Lady Sneerwell away, and return directly.—(*Aside.*) Sir Peter, not a word of the French milliner.
*Exit* JOSEPH SURFACE.

SIR PET: Oh, not for the world!—Ah, Charles, if you associated more with your brother, one might indeed hope for your reformation. He is a man of sentiment.—Well, there is nothing in the world so noble as a man of sentiment!

CHAS. SURF: Pshaw! he is too moral by half, and so apprehensive of his good name, as he calls it, that I suppose he would as soon let a priest into his house as a girl.

SIR PET: No, no,—come, come,—you wrong him. No, no, Joseph is no rake, but he is not such a saint in that respect either,—I have a great mind to tell him—we should have a laugh! (*Aside.*)

CHAS. SURF: Oh, hang him! he's a very anchorite, a young hermit!

SIR PET: Hark'ee—you must not abuse him; he may chance to hear of it again, I promise you.

CHAS. SURF: Why, you won't tell him?

SIR PET: No—but—this way.—[*Aside.*] Egad, I'll tell him.—Hark'ee, have you a mind to have a good laugh at Joseph?

CHAS. SURF: I should like it of all things.

SIR PET: Then, i'faith, we will!—I'll be quit with him for discovering me. (*Aside.*)He had a girl with him when I called.

CHAS. SURF: What! Joseph? you jest.

SIR PET: Hush!—a little—French milliner—and the best of the jest is—she's in the room now.

CHAS. SURF: The devil she is!

SIR PET: Hush! I tell you. (*Points* [*to the screen*].)

CHAS. SURF: Behind the screen! 'Slife, let's unveil her!

SIR PET: No, no, he's coming:—you shan't, indeed!

CHAS. SURF: Oh, egad, we'll have a peep at the little milliner!

SIR PET: Not for the world!—Joseph will never forgive me.

CHAS. SURF: I'll stand by you——

SIR PET: (*Struggling with Charles.*) Odds, here he is!

JOSEPH SURFACE *enters just as* CHARLES *throws down the screen.*

CHAS. SURF: Lady Teazle, by all that's wonderful!

SIR PET: Lady Teazle, by all that's horrible!

CHAS. SURF: Sir Peter, this is one of the smartest French milliners I ever saw. Egad, you seem all to have been diverting yourselves here at hide and seek—and I don't see who is out of the secret. Shall I beg your ladyship to inform me?—Not a word!—Brother, will you please to explain this matter? What! Morality dumb too!—Sir Peter, though I *found* you in the dark, perhaps you are not so now! All mute! Well—though I can make nothing of the affair, I suppose you perfectly understand one another; so I'll leave you to yourselves.—(*Going.*) Brother, I'm sorry to find you *have given that worthy man so much uneasiness,*—Sir Peter! there's nothing *in the world so noble as a man of sentiment!*
*Exit* CHARLES.

([*They*] *stand for some time looking at each other.*)

JOS. SURF: Sir Peter—notwithstanding I confess that appearances are against me—if you will afford me your patience—I make no doubt but I shall explain everything to your satisfaction.

SIR PET: If you please—

JOS. SURF: The fact is, sir, Lady Teazle, knowing my pretensions to your ward

Maria—I say, sir, Lady Teazle, being apprehensive of the jealousy of your temper—and knowing my friendship to the family—she, sir, I say—called here—in order that—I might explain those pretensions—but on your coming—being apprehensive—as I said—of your jealousy—she withdrew—and this, you may depend on't is the whole truth of the matter.

SIR PET: A very clear account, upon my word; and I dare swear the lady will vouch for every article of it.

LADY TEAZ: (*Coming forward.*) For not one word of it, Sir Peter!

SIR PET: How! don't you think it worth while to agree in the lie?

LADY TEAZ: There is not one syllable of truth in what that gentleman has told you.

SIR PET: I believe you, upon my soul, ma'am!

JOS. SURF: (*Aside.*) 'Sdeath, madam, will you betray me?

LADY TEAZ: Good Mr. Hypocrite, by your leave, I will speak for myself.

SIR PET: Aye, let her alone, sir; you'll find she'll make out a better story than *you*, without prompting.

LADY TEAZ: Hear me, Sir Peter!—I came here on no matter relating to your ward, and even ignorant of this gentleman's pretensions to her—but I came, seduced by his insidious arguments, at least to listen to his pretended passion, if not to sacrifice *your* honor to his baseness.

SIR PET: Now, I believe, the truth *is* coming, indeed!

JOS. SURF: The woman's mad!

LADY TEAZ: No, sir; she has recovered her senses, and your own arts have furnished her with the means.—Sir Peter, I do not expect you to credit me—but the tenderness you expressed for me, when I am sure you could not think I was a witness to it, has penetrated to my heart, and had I left the place without the shame of this discovery, my future life should have spoke[n] the sincerity of my gratitude. As for that smooth-tongue hypocrite, who would have seduced the wife of his too credulous friend, while he affected honorable addresses to his ward—I behold him now in a light so truly despicable, that I shall never again respect myself for having listened to him. (*Exit.*)

JOS. SURF: Notwithstanding all this, Sir Peter, heaven knows—

SIR PET: That you are a villain!—and so I leave you to your conscience.

JOS. SURF: You are too rash, Sir Peter; you shall hear me. The man who shuts out conviction by refusing to—

SIR PET: Oh!—

*Exeunt,* JOSEPH SURFACE *following and speaking.*
*End of Act 4th.*

# ACT V

## SCENE I

*The library [in* JOSEPH SURFACE'S *house.]*
*Enter* JOSEPH SURFACE *and Servant.*

JOS. SURF: Mr. Stanley! why should you think I would see him? you *must* know he comes to ask something.

SERV: Sir, I should not have let him in, but that Mr. Rowley came to the door with him.

JOS. SURF: Pshaw! blockhead! to suppose that I should *now* be in a temper to receive visits from poor relations!—Well, why don't you show the fellow up?

SERV: I will, sir.—Why, sir, it was not my fault that Sir Peter discovered my lady—

JOS. SURF: Go, fool! (*Exit Servant.*) Sure, Fortune never played a man of my policy such a trick before! My character with Sir Peter, my hopes with Maria, destroyed in a moment! I'm in a rare humor to listen to other people's distresses! I shan't be able to bestow even a benevolent sentiment on Stanley.—So! here he comes, and Rowley with him. I must try to recover myself—and put a little charity into my face, however. (*Exit.*)

*Enter* SIR OLIVER SURFACE *and* ROWLEY.

SIR OLIV: What! does he avoid us? That was he, was it not?

ROW: It was, sir—but I doubt you are come a little too abruptly—his nerves are so weak, that the sight of a poor relation may be too much for him.—I should have gone first to break you to him.

SIR OLIV: A plague of his nerves!—Yet this is he whom Sir Peter extols as a man of the most benevolent way of thinking!

ROW: As to his way of thinking, I cannot pretend to decide; for, to do him justice, he appears to have as much speculative benevolence as any private gentleman in the kingdom, though he is seldom so sensual as to indulge himself in the exercise of it.

SIR OLIV: Yet has a string of charitable sentiments, I suppose, at his fingers' ends!

ROW: Or, rather, at his tongue's end, Sir Oliver; for I believe there is no sentiment he has more faith in than that 'Charity begins at home.'

SIR OLIV: And his, I presume, is of that domestic sort which never stirs abroad at all.

ROW: I doubt you'll find it so;—but he's coming—I mustn't seem to interrupt you; and you know, immediately as you leave him, I come in to announce your arrival in your real character.

SIR OLIV: True; and afterwards you'll meet me at Sir Peter's.

ROW: Without losing a moment. (*Exit* ROWLEY.)

SIR OLIV: So! I don't like the complaisance of his features.

*Re-enter* JOSEPH SURFACE.

JOS. SURF: Sir, I beg you ten thousand pardons for keeping you a moment waiting—Mr. Stanley, I presume.

SIR OLIV: At your service.

JOS. SURF: Sir, I beg you will do me the honor to sit down—I entreat you, sir.

SIR OLIV: Dear sir—there's no occasion.—Too civil by half! (*Aside.*)

JOS. SURF: I have not the pleasure of knowing you, Mr. Stanley; but I am extremely happy to see you look so well. You were nearly related to my mother, I think, Mr. Stanley?

SIR OLIV: I was, sir—so nearly that my present poverty, I fear, may do discredit to her wealthy children—else I should not have presumed to trouble you.

JOS. SURF: Dear sir, there needs no apology: he that is in distress, though a stranger, has a right to claim kindred with the wealthy;—I am sure I wish I was one of that class, and had it in my power to offer you even a small relief.

SIR OLIV: If your uncle, Sir Oliver, were here, I should have a friend.

JOS. SURF: I wish he were, sir, with all my heart: you should not want an advocate with him, believe me, sir.

SIR OLIV: I should not *need* one—my distresses would recommend me; but I imagined his bounty had enabled *you* to become the agent of his charity.

JOS. SURF: My dear sir, you were strangely misinformed. Sir Oliver is a worthy man, a very worthy sort of man; but—avarice, Mr. Stanley, is the vice of age. I will tell you, my good sir, in confidence, what he has done for me has been a mere nothing; though people, I know, have thought otherwise, and, for my part, I never chose to contradict the report.

SIR OLIV: What! has he never transmitted you bullion! rupees![1] pagodas![2]

JOS. SURF: O dear sir, nothing of the kind! No, no; a few presents now and then—

V. [1] **rupees** Indian coins, then worth about two shillings
[2] **pagodas** Indian coins, then worth about eight shillings

china—shawls—Congo tea—avadavats[3] and India[n] crackers[4]—little more, believe me.

SIR OLIV: (*Aside.*) Here's gratitude for twelve thousand pounds!—Avadavats and Indian crackers!

JOS. SURF: Then, my dear sir, you have heard, I doubt not, of the extravagance of my brother; there are very few would credit what I have done for that unfortunate young man.

SIR OLIV: Not I, for one! (*Aside.*)

JOS. SURF: The sums I have lent him! Indeed I have been exceedingly to blame—it was an amiable weakness: however, I don't pretend to defend it—and now I feel it doubly culpable, since it has deprived me of the pleasure of serving *you*, Mr. Stanley, as my heart dictates.

SIR OLIV: (*Aside.*) Dissembler!—Then, sir, you cannot assist me?

JOS. SURF: At present, it grieves me to say, I cannot; but, whenever I have the ability, you may depend upon hearing from me.

SIR OLIV: I am extremely sorry——

JOS. SURF: Not more than I am, believe me; to pity, without the power to relieve, is still more painful than to ask and be denied.

SIR OLIV: Kind sir, your most obedient humble servant.

JOS. SURF: You leave me deeply affected, Mr. Stanley.—William, be ready to open the door.

SIR OLIV: O dear sir, no ceremony.

JOS. SURF: Your very obedient.

SIR OLIV: Sir, your most obsequious.

JOS. SURF: You may depend upon hearing from me, whenever I can be of service.

SIR OLIV: Sweet sir, you are too good.

JOS. SURF: In the meantime I wish you health and spirits.

SIR OLIV: Your ever grateful and perpetual humble servant.

JOS. SURF: Sir, yours as sincerely.

SIR OLIV: Now I am satisfied! (*Exit.*)

JOS. SURF: (*Solus.*) This is one bad effect of a good character; it invites applications from the unfortunate, and there needs no small degree of address to gain the reputation of benevolence without incurring the expense. The silver ore of pure charity is an expensive article in the catalogue of a man's good qualities; whereas the sentimental French plate I use instead of it makes just as good a show, and pays no tax.

*Enter* ROWLEY.

ROW: Mr. Surface, your servant—I was apprehensive of interrupting you—though my business demands immediate attention—as this note will inform you.

JOS. SURF: Always happy to see Mr. Rowley.—(*Reads.*) How! *'Oliver—Surface!'*—My uncle arrived!

ROW: He is, indeed—we have just parted—quite well, after a speedy voyage, and impatient to embrace his worthy nephew.

JOS. SURF: I am astonished!—William! stop Mr. Stanley, if he's not gone.

ROW: Oh! he's out of reach, I believe.

JOS. SURF: Why didn't you let me know this when you came in together?

ROW: I thought you had particular business. But I must be gone to inform your brother, and appoint him here to meet his uncle. He will be with you in a quarter of an hour.

JOS. SURF: So he says. Well, I am strangely overjoyed at his coming—(*Aside.*) Never, to be sure, was anything so damned unlucky!

ROW: You will be delighted to see how well he looks.

JOS. SURF: Oh! I'm rejoiced to hear it.—(*Aside.*) Just at this time!

ROW: I'll tell him how impatiently you expect him.

JOS. SURF: Do, do; pray give my best duty and affection. Indeed, I cannot express

---

[3] **avadavats** very small Indian songbirds    [4] **India crackers** fire crackers

the sensations I feel at the thought of seeing him.—(*Exit* ROWLEY.) Certainly his coming just at this time is the cruellest piece of ill fortune. (*Exit.*)

**SCENE II**
*At* SIR PETER'S.
*Enter* MRS. CANDOUR *and Maid.*

MAID: Indeed, ma'am, my lady will see nobody at present.

MRS. CAN: Did you tell her it was her friend Mrs. Candour?

MAID: Yes, madam; but she begs you will excuse her.

MRS. CAN: Do go again; I shall be glad to see her, if it be only for a moment, for I am sure she must be in great distress.— (*Exit Maid.*) Dear heart, how provoking; I'm not mistress of half the circumstances! We shall have the whole affair in the newspapers, with the names of the parties at length, before I have dropped the story at a dozen houses.
*Enter* SIR BENJAMIN BACKBITE.
O dear Sir Benjamin! you have heard, I suppose——

SIR BEN: Of Lady Teazle and Mr. Surface——

MRS. CAN: And Sir Peter's discovery——

SIR BEN: Oh, the strangest piece of business, to be sure!

MRS. CAN: Well, I never was so surprised in my life. I am so sorry for all parties, indeed I am.

SIR BEN: Now, I don't pity Sir Peter at all—he was so extravagantly partial to Mr. Surface.

MRS. CAN: Mr. Surface! Why, 'twas with Charles Lady Teazle was detected.

SIR BEN: No such thing—Mr. Surface is the gallant.

MRS. CAN: No, no—Charles is the man. 'Twas Mr. Surface brought Sir Peter on purpose to discover them.

SIR BEN: I tell you I have it from one——

MRS. CAN: And I have it from one——

SIR BEN: Who had it from one, who had it——

MRS. CAN: From one immediately—But here's Lady Sneerwell; perhaps she knows the whole affair.
*Enter* LADY SNEERWELL.

LADY SNEER: So, my dear Mrs. Candour, here's a sad affair of our friend Lady Teazle!

MRS. CAN: Aye, my dear friend, who could have thought it——

LADY SNEER: Well, there's no trusting appearances; though, indeed, she was always too lively for me.

MRS. CAN: To be sure, her manners were a little too free—but she was very young!

LADY SNEER: And had, indeed, some good qualities.

MRS. CAN: So she had, indeed. But have you heard the particulars?

LADY SNEER: No; but everybody says that Mr. Surface——

SIR BEN: Aye, there, I told you—Mr. Surface was the man.

MRS. CAN: No, no, indeed—the assignation was with Charles.

LADY SNEER: With Charles! You alarm me, Mrs. Candour.

MRS. CAN: Yes, yes, he was the lover. Mr. Surface—do him justice—was only the informer.

SIR BEN: Well, I'll not dispute with you, Mrs. Candour; but, be it which it may, I hope that Sir Peter's wound will not——

MRS. CAN: Sir Peter's wound! Oh, mercy! I didn't hear a word of their fighting.

LADY SNEER: Nor I, a syllable.

SIR BEN: No! what, no mention of the duel?

MRS. CAN: Not a word.

SIR BEN: O Lord—yes, yes—they fought before they left the room.

LADY SNEER: Pray let us hear.

MRS. CAN: Aye, do oblige us with the duel.

SIR BEN: 'Sir,' says Sir Peter—immediately after the discovery—'you are a most ungrateful fellow.'

MRS. CAN: Aye, to Charles——

SIR BEN: No, no—to Mr. Surface—'a most ungrateful fellow; and old as I am, sir,' says he, 'I insist on immediate satisfaction.'

MRS. CAN: Aye, that must have been to Charles; for 'tis very unlikely Mr. Surface should go to fight in his house.

SIR BEN: 'Gad's life, ma'am, not at all—'giving me immediate satisfaction.'—On this, madam, Lady Teazle, seeing Sir Peter in such danger, ran out of the room in strong hysterics, and Charles after her, calling out for hartshorn and water! Then, madam, they began to fight with swords——

*Enter* CRABTREE.

CRAB: With pistols, nephew—I have it from undoubted authority.

MRS. CAN: O Mr. Crabtree, then it is all true!

CRAB: Too true, indeed, ma'am, and Sir Peter's dangerously wounded—

SIR BEN: By a thrust of *in seconde*[5] quite through his left side——

CRAB: By a bullet lodged in the thorax.

MRS. CAN: Mercy on me! Poor Sir Peter!

CRAB: Yes, ma'am—though Charles would have avoided the matter, if he could.

MRS. CAN: I knew Charles was the person.

SIR BEN: Oh, my uncle, I see, knows nothing of the matter.

CRAB: But Sir Peter taxed him with the basest ingratitude——

SIR BEN: That I told you, you know.

CRAB: Do, nephew, let me speak!—and insisted on an immediate——

SIR BEN: Just as I said.

CRAB: Odds life, nephew, allow others to know something too! A pair of pistols lay on the bureau (for Mr. Surface, it seems, had come the night before late from Salt-Hill, where he had been to see the Montem[6] with a friend, who has a

son at Eton), so, unluckily, the pistols were left charged.

SIR BEN: I heard nothing of this.

CRAB: Sir Peter forced Charles to take one, and they fired, it seems, pretty nearly together. Charles's shot took place, as I told you, and Sir Peter's missed; but, what is very extraordinary, the ball struck against a little bronze Pliny that stood over the chimney-piece, grazed out of the window at a right angle, and wounded the postman, who was just coming to the door with a double letter from Northamptonshire.

SIR BEN: My uncle's account is more circumstantial, I must confess; but I believe mine is the true one, for all that.

LADY SNEER: (*Aside.*) I am more interested in this affair than they imagine, and must have better information. (*Exit* LADY SNEERWELL.)

SIR BEN: (*After a pause looking at each other.*) Ah! Lady Sneerwell's alarm is very easily accounted for.

CRAB: Yes, yes, they certainly *do* say—but that's neither here nor there.

MRS. CAN: But, pray, where is Sir Peter at present?

CRAB: Oh! they brought him home, and he is now in the house, though the servants are ordered to deny it.

MRS. CAN: I believe so, and Lady Teazle, I suppose, attending him.

CRAB: Yes, yes; I saw one of the faculty enter just before me.

SIR BEN: Hey! who comes here?

CRAB: Oh, this is he—the physician, depend on't.

MRS. CAN: Oh, certainly! it must be the physician; and now we shall know.

*Enter* SIR OLIVER SURFACE.

CRAB: Well, doctor, what hopes?

MRS. CAN: Aye, doctor, how's your patient?

SIR BEN: Now, doctor, isn't it a wound with a small-sword?

---

[5] *in seconde* a fencing term  [6] **Montem** a festival celebrated by the students of Eton at Salt Hill

CRAB: A bullet lodged in the thorax, for a hundred!

SIR OLIV: Doctor! a wound with a small-sword! and a bullet in the thorax?—Oons! are you mad, good people?

SIR BEN: Perhaps, sir, you are not a doctor?

SIR OLIV: Truly, I am to thank you for my degree, if I am.

CRAB: Only a friend of Sir Peter's, then, I presume. But, sir, you must have heard of this accident?

SIR OLIV: Not a word!

CRAB: Not of his being dangerously wounded?

SIR OLIV: The devil he is!

SIR BEN: Run through the body——

CRAB: Shot in the breast——

SIR BEN: By one Mr. Surface——

CRAB: Aye, the younger.

SIR OLIV: Hey! what the plague! you seem to differ strangely in your accounts——however, you agree that Sir Peter is dangerously wounded.

SIR BEN: Oh, yes, we agree there.

CRAB: Yes, yes, I believe there can be no doubt of that.

SIR OLIV: Then, upon my word, for a person in that situation, he is the most imprudent man alive—for here he comes, walking as if nothing at all were the matter.

*Enter* SIR PETER TEAZLE.

Odds heart, Sir Peter! you are come in good time, I promise you; for we had just *given you over*.

SIR BEN: Egad, uncle, this is the most sudden recovery!

SIR OLIV: Why, man! what do you do out of bed with a small-sword through your body, and a bullet lodged in your thorax?

SIR PET: A small-sword and a bullet?

SIR OLIV: Aye; these gentlemen would have killed you without law or physic, and wanted to dub me a doctor—to make me an accomplice.

SIR PET: Why, what is all this?

SIR BEN: We rejoice, Sir Peter, that the story of the duel is not true, and are sincerely sorry for your other misfortunes.

SIR PET: So, so; all over the town already. (*Aside.*)

CRAB: Though, Sir Peter, you were certainly vastly to blame to marry at all, at your years.

SIR PET: Sir, what business is that of yours?

MRS. CAN: Though, indeed, as Sir Peter made so good a husband, he's very much to be pitied.

SIR PET: Plague on your pity, ma'am! I desire none of it.

SIR BEN: However, Sir Peter, you must not mind the laughing and jests you will meet with on this occasion.

SIR PET: Sir, I desire to be master in my own house.

CRAB: 'Tis no uncommon case, that's one comfort.

SIR PET: I insist on being left to myself: without ceremony, I insist on your leaving my house directly!

MRS. CAN: Well, well, we are going; and depend on't, we'll make the best report of you we can.

SIR PET: Leave my house!

CRAB: And tell how hardly you have been treated.

SIR PET: Leave my house!

SIR BEN: And how patiently you bear it.

SIR PET: Fiends! vipers! furies! Oh! that their own venom would choke them!

*Exeunt* MRS. CANDOUR, SIR BENJAMIN BACKBITE, CRABTREE, &c.

SIR OLIV: They are very provoking indeed, Sir Peter.

*Enter* ROWLEY.

ROW: I heard high words—what has ruffled you, Sir Peter?

SIR PET: Pshaw! what signifies asking? Do I ever pass a day without my vexations?

SIR OLIV: Well, I'm not inquisitive—I come only to tell you that I have seen both my nephews in the manner we proposed.

SIR PET:  A precious couple they are!

ROW:  Yes, and Sir Oliver is convinced that your judgment was right, Sir Peter.

SIR OLIV:  Yes, I find *Joseph* is indeed the man, after all.

ROW:  Yes, as Sir Peter says, he's a man of sentiment.

SIR OLIV:  And acts up to the sentiments he professes.

ROW:  It certainly is edification to hear him talk.

SIR OLIV:  Oh, he's a model for the young men of the age! But how's this, Sir Peter? you don't join in your friend Joseph's praise, as I expected.

SIR PET:  Sir Oliver, we live in a damned wicked world, and the fewer we praise the better.

ROW:  What! do *you* say so, Sir Peter, who were never mistaken in your life?

SIR PET:  Pshaw! plague on you both! I see by your sneering you have heard the whole affair. I shall go mad among you!

ROW:  Then, to fret you no longer, Sir Peter, we are indeed acquainted with it all. I met Lady Teazle coming from Mr. Surface's, so humbled that she deigned to request me to be her advocate with you.

SIR PET:  And does Sir Oliver know all too?

SIR OLIV:  Every circumstance.

SIR PET:  What, of the closet—and the screen, hey?

SIR OLIV:  Yes, yes, and the little French milliner. Oh, I have been vastly diverted with the story! ha! ha!

SIR PET:  'Twas very pleasant.

SIR OLIV:  I never laughed more in my life, I assure you: ha! ha!

SIR PET:  O, vastly diverting! ha! ha!

ROW:  To be sure, Joseph with his sentiments! ha! ha!

SIR PET:  Yes, yes, his sentiments! ha! ha! A hypocritical villain!

SIR OLIV:  Aye, and that rogue Charles to pull Sir Peter out of the closet: ha! ha!

SIR PET:  Ha! ha! 'twas devilish entertaining, to be sure!

SIR OLIV:  Ha! ha! Egad, Sir Peter, I should like to have seen your face when the screen was thrown down: ha! ha!

SIR PET:  Yes, yes, my face when the screen was thrown down: ha! ha! Oh, I must never show my head again!

SIR OLIV:  But come, come, it isn't fair to laugh at you neither, my old friend—though, upon my soul, I can't help it.

SIR PET:  Oh, pray don't restrain your mirth on my account—it does not hurt me at all! I laugh at the whole affair myself. Yes, yes, I think being a standing jest for all one's acquaintances a very happy situation. O yes, and then of a morning to read the paragraphs about Mr. S—, Lady T—, and Sir P—, will be so entertaining!

ROW:  Without affectation, Sir Peter, you may despise the ridicule of fools. But I see Lady Teazle going towards the next room; I am sure you must desire a reconciliation as earnestly as she does.

SIR OLIV:  Perhaps my being here prevents her coming to you. Well, I'll leave honest Rowley to mediate between you; but he must bring you all presently to Mr. Surface's, where I am now returning, if not to reclaim a libertine, at least to expose hypocrisy.

SIR PET:  Ah! I'll be present at your discovering yourself there with all my heart—though 'tis a vile unlucky place for discoveries!

ROW:  We'll follow. (*Exit* SIR OLIVER SURFACE.)

SIR PET:  She is not coming here, you see, Rowley.

ROW:  No, but she has left the door of that room open, you perceive. See, she is in tears!

SIR PET:  Certainly a little mortification appears very becoming in a wife! Don't you think it will do her good to let her pine a little?

ROW: Oh, this is ungenerous in you!

SIR PET: Well, I know not what to think. You remember, Rowley, the letter I found of hers, evidently intended for Charles!

ROW: A mere forgery, Sir Peter! laid in your way on purpose. This is one of the points which I intend *Snake* shall give you conviction on.

SIR PET: I wish I were once satisfied of that. She looks this way. What a remarkably elegant turn of the head she has! Rowley, I'll go to her.

ROW: Certainly.

SIR PET: Though, when it is known that we are reconciled, people will laugh at me ten times more!

ROW: Let them laugh, and retort their malice only by showing them you are happy in spite of it.

SIR PET: I'faith, so I will! and, if I'm not mistaken, we may yet be the happiest couple in the country.

ROW: Nay, Sir Peter—he who once lays aside suspicion——

SIR PET: Hold, my dear Rowley! if you have any regard for me, never let me hear you utter anything like a sentiment—I have had enough of them to serve me the rest of my life. (*Exeunt.*)

## SCENE III

*The library (in* JOSEPH SURFACE's *house.*)

JOSEPH SURFACE *and* LADY SNEERWELL.

LADY SNEER: Impossible! Will not Sir Peter immediately be reconciled to Charles, and of consequence no longer oppose his union with Maria? The thought is distraction to me!

JOS. SURF: Can passion furnish a remedy?

LADY SNEER: No, nor cunning either. Oh, I was a fool, an idiot, to league with such a blunderer!

JOS. SURF: Sure, Lady Sneerwell, *I* am the greatest sufferer; yet you see I bear the accident with calmness.

LADY SNEER: Because the disappointment doesn't reach your *heart;* your *interest* only attached you to Maria. Had you felt for *her* what *I* have for that ungrateful libertine, neither your temper nor hypocrisy could prevent your showing the sharpness of your vexation.

JOS. SURF: But why should your reproaches fall on *me* for this disappointment?

LADY SNEER: Are you not the cause of it? What had you to do to bate in your pursuit of Maria to pervert Lady Teazle by the way? Had you not a sufficient field for your roguery in blinding Sir Peter, and supplanting your brother? I hate such an avarice of crimes; 'tis an unfair monopoly, and never prospers.

JOS. SURF: Well, I admit I have been to blame. I confess I deviated from the direct road of wrong, but I don't think we're so totally defeated neither.

LADY SNEER: No!

JOS. SURF: You tell me you have made a trial of Snake since we met, and that you still believe him faithful to us—

LADY SNEER: I do believe so.

JOS. SURF: And that he has undertaken, should it be necessary, to swear and prove that Charles is at this time contracted by vows and honor to your ladyship—which some of his former letters to you will serve to support?

LADY SNEER: This, indeed, might have assisted.

JOS. SURF: Come, come; it is not too late yet.—[*Knocking at the door.*] But hark! this is probably my uncle, Sir Oliver: retire to that room; we'll consult farther when he's gone.

LADY SNEER: Well! but if *he* should find you out too—

JOS. SURF: Oh, I have no fear of that. Sir Peter will hold his tongue for his own credit['s] sake—and you may depend on't I shall soon discover Sir Oliver's weak side!

LADY SNEER: I have no diffidence of your abilities—only be constant to one roguery at a time. (*Exit.*)

JOS. SURF: I will, I will! So! 'tis confounded hard, after such bad fortune, to be baited by one's confederate in evil. Well, at all events, my character is so much better than Charles's, that I certainly—hey!—what!—this is not *Sir Oliver*, but old *Stanley* again! Plague on't! that he should return to tease me just now! We shall have Sir Oliver come and find him here—and——

*Enter* SIR OLIVER SURFACE.

Gad's life, Mr. Stanley, why have you come back to plague me just at this time? You must not stay now, upon my word.

SIR OLIV: Sir, I hear your uncle Oliver is expected here, and though he has been so penurious to *you*, I'll try what he'll do for *me*.

JOS. SURF: Sir, 'tis impossible for you to stay now, so I must beg—Come any other time, and I promise you, you shall be assisted.

SIR OLIV: No: Sir Oliver and I must be acquainted.

JOS. SURF: Zounds, sir! then I insist on your quitting the room directly.

SIR OLIV: Nay, sir!

JOS. SURF: Sir, I insist on't!—Here, William! show this gentleman out. Since you compel me, sir—not one moment—this is such insolence! (*Going to push him out.*)

*Enter* CHARLES SURFACE.

CHAS. SURF: Heyday! what's the matter now? What the devil, have you got hold of my little broker here? Zounds, brother, don't hurt little Premium. What's the matter, my little fellow?

JOS. SURF: So! he has been with you, too, has he?

CHAS. SURF: To be sure he has! Why, 'tis as honest a little—But sure, Joseph, you have not been borrowing money too, have you?

JOS. SURF: Borrowing! no! But, brother, you know here we expect Sir Oliver every—

CHAS. SURF: O gad, that's true! Noll mustn't find the little broker here, to be sure.

JOS. SURF: Yet, Mr. *Stanley* insists——

CHAS. SURF: Stanley! why his name is *Premium*.

JOS. SURF: No, no, *Stanley*.

CHAS. SURF: No, no, *Premium*.

JOS. SURF: Well, no matter which—but——

CHAS. SURF: Aye, aye, Stanley or Premium, 'tis the same thing, as you say; for I suppose he goes by half [a] hundred names, besides A.B.'s at the coffee-houses.

JOS. SURF: Death! here's Sir Oliver at the door. (*Knocking again.*) Now I beg, Mr. Stanley——

CHAS. SURF: Aye, and I beg, Mr. Premium——

SIR OLIV: Gentlemen——

JOS. SURF: Sir, by heaven you shall go!

CHAS. SURF: Aye, out with him, certainly.

SIR OLIV: This violence——

JOS. SURF: 'Tis your own fault.

CHAS. SURF: Out with him, to be sure. (*Both forcing* SIR OLIVER *out.*)

*Enter* SIR PETER *and* LADY TEAZLE, MARIA, *and* ROWLEY.

SIR PET: My old friend, Sir Oliver—hey! What in the name of wonder!—Here are dutiful nephews!—assault their uncle at the first visit!

LADY TEAZ: Indeed, Sir Oliver, 'twas well we came in to rescue you.

ROW: Truly it was; for I perceive, Sir Oliver, the character of old Stanley was no protection to you.

SIR OLIV: Nor of Premium either: the necessities of the *former* could not extort a shilling from *that* benevolent gentleman; and now, egad, I stood a chance of faring worse than my ancestors, and being knocked down without being bid for. (*After a pause,* JOSEPH *and* CHARLES *turning to each other.*)

JOS. SURF: Charles!

CHAS. SURF: Joseph!

**JOS. SURF:** 'Tis now complete!

**CHAS. SURF:** Very!

**SIR OLIV:** Sir Peter, my friend, and Rowley too—look on that elder nephew of mine. You know what he has already received from my bounty; and you know also how gladly I would have regarded half my fortune as held in trust for him—judge, then, my disappointment in discovering him to be destitute of truth—charity—and gratitude!

**SIR PET:** Sir Oliver, I should be more surprised at this declaration, if I had not myself found him selfish, treacherous, and hypocritical!

**LADY TEAZ:** And if the gentleman pleads not guilty to these, pray let him call *me* to his character.

**SIR PET:** Then, I believe, we need add no more.—If he knows himself, he will consider it as the most perfect punishment that he is known to the world.

**CHAS. SURF:** (*Aside.*) If they talk this way to *Honesty*, what will they say to *me*, by and by?

(**SIR PETER, LADY TEAZLE,** *and* **MARIA** *retire.*)

**SIR OLIV:** As for that prodigal, his brother, there——

**CHAS. SURF:** (*Aside.*) Aye, now comes my turn: the damned family pictures will ruin me!

**JOS. SURF:** Sir Oliver!—uncle!—will you honor me with a hearing?

**CHAS. SURF:** (*Aside.*) Now if Joseph would make one of his long speeches, I might recollect myself a little.

**SIR OLIV:** (*to* **JOSEPH SURFACE**). I suppose you would undertake to justify yourself entirely?

**JOS. SURF:** I trust I could.

**SIR OLIV:** Pshaw!—Well, sir! and *you* (*to* **CHARLES**) could justify yourself too, I suppose?

**CHAS. SURF:** Not that I know of, Sir Oliver.

**SIR OLIV:** What!—Little Premium has been let too much into the secret, I presume?

**CHAS. SURF:** True, sir; but they were family secrets, and should never be mentioned again, you know.

**ROW:** Come, Sir Oliver, I know you cannot speak of Charles's follies with anger.

**SIR OLIV:** Odd's heart, no more I can—nor with gravity either. Sir Peter, do you know the rogue bargained with me for all his ancestors—sold me judges and generals by the foot—and maiden aunts as cheap as broken china.

**CHAS. SURF:** To be sure, Sir Oliver, I did make a little free with the family canvas, that's the truth on't. My ancestors may certainly rise in evidence against me, there's no denying it; but believe me sincere when I tell you—and upon my soul I would not say it if I was not—that if I do not appear mortified at the exposure of my follies, it is because I feel at this moment the warmest satisfaction in seeing you, my liberal benefactor.

**SIR OLIV:** Charles, I believe you. Give me your hand again; the ill-looking little fellow over the settee has made your peace.

**CHAS. SURF:** Then, sir, my gratitude to the original is still increased.

**LADY TEAZ:** (*Pointing to* **MARIA.**) Yet, I believe, Sir Oliver, here is one whom Charles is still more anxious to be reconciled to.

**SIR OLIV:** Oh, I have heard of his attachment there; and, with the young lady's pardon, if I construe right—that blush—

**SIR PET:** Well, child, speak your sentiments.

**MARIA:** Sir, I have little to say, but that I shall rejoice to hear that he is happy; for me, whatever claim I had to his affection, I willingly resign it to one who has a better title.

**CHAS. SURF:** How, Maria!

**SIR PET:** Heyday! what's the mystery now? While he appeared an incorrigible rake, you would give your hand to no one else; and now that he is likely to reform, I warrant you won't have him.

**MARIA:** His own heart—and Lady Sneerwell know the cause.

**CHAS. SURF:** Lady Sneerwell!

**JOS. SURF:** Brother, it is with great concern I am obliged to speak on this point, but my regard to justice compels me, and Lady Sneerwell's injuries can no longer be concealed. (*Goes to the door.*)

*Enter* LADY SNEERWELL.

**SIR PET:** So! another French milliner!—Egad, he has one in every room in the house, I suppose!

**LADY SNEER:** Ungrateful Charles! Well may you be surprised, and feel for the indelicate situation which your perfidy has forced me into.

**CHAS. SURF:** Pray, uncle, is this another plot of yours? For, as I have life, I don't understand it.

**JOS. SURF:** I believe, sir, there is but the evidence of one person more necessary to make it extremely clear.

**SIR PET:** And that person, I imagine, is Mr. Snake.—Rowley, you were perfectly right to bring him with us, and pray let him appear.

**ROW:** Walk in, Mr. Snake.

*Enter* SNAKE.

I thought his testimony might be wanted; however, it happens unluckily, that he comes to confront Lady Sneerwell, and not to support her.

**LADY SNEER:** Villain! Treacherous to me at last! (*Aside.*)—Speak, fellow, have *you* too conspired against me?

**SNAKE:** I beg your ladyship ten thousand pardons: you paid me extremely liberally for the lie in question; but I have unfortunately been offered double to speak the truth.

**SIR PET:** Plot and counterplot, egad—I wish your ladyship joy of the success of your negotiation.

**LADY SNEER:** The torments of shame and disappointment on you all!

**LADY TEAZ:** Hold, Lady Sneerwell—before you go, let me thank you for the trouble you and that gentleman have taken, in writing letters to me from Charles, and answering them yourself; and let me also request you to make my respects to the Scandalous College, of which you are president, and inform them, that Lady Teazle, licentiate, begs leave to return the diploma they granted her, as she leaves off practice, and kills characters no longer.

**LADY SNEER:** You too, madam!—provoking—insolent! May your husband live these fifty years! (*Exit.*)

**SIR PET:** Oons! what a fury!

**LADY TEAZ:** A malicious creature, indeed!

**SIR PET:** Hey! not for her last wish?

**LADY TEAZ:** Oh, no!

**SIR OLIV:** Well, sir, and what have you to say now?

**JOS. SURF:** Sir, I am so confounded, to find that Lady *Sneerwell* could be guilty of suborning Mr. *Snake* in this manner, to impose on us all, that I know not what to say; however, lest her revengeful spirit should prompt her to injure my brother, I had certainly better follow her directly. (*Exit.*)

**SIR PET:** Moral to the last drop!

**SIR OLIV:** Aye, and marry her, Joseph, if you can.—Oil and vinegar, egad! you'll do very well together.

**ROW:** I believe we have no more occasion for Mr. Snake at present.

**SNAKE:** Before I go, I beg pardon once for all, for whatever uneasiness I have been the humble instrument of causing to the parties present.

**SIR PET:** Well, well, you have made atonement by a good deed at last.

**SNAKE:** But I must request of the company, that it shall never be known.

SIR PET: Hey! what the plague! are you ashamed of having done a right thing once in your life?

SNAKE: Ah, sir,—consider I live by the badness of my character—I have nothing but my infamy to depend on! and, if it were once known that I had been betrayed into an honest action, I should lose every friend I have in the world.

SIR OLIV: Well, well—we'll not traduce you by saying anything in your praise, never fear. (*Exit* SNAKE.)

SIR PET: There's a precious rogue! yet that fellow is a writer and a critic!

LADY TEAZ: See, Sir Oliver, there needs no persuasion now to reconcile your nephew and Maria.

CHARLES *and* MARIA *apart.*

SIR OLIV: Aye, aye, that's as it should be, and, egad, we'll have the wedding tomorrow morning.

CHAS. SURF: Thank you, my dear uncle.

SIR PET: What, you rogue! don't you ask the girl's consent first?

CHAS. SURF: Oh, I have done that a long time—above a minute ago—and she has looked yes.

MARIA: For shame, Charles!—I protest, Sir Peter, there has not been a word—

SIR OLIV: Well, then, the fewer the better—may your love for each other never know abatement.

SIR PET: And may you live as happily together as Lady Teazle and I—intend to do!

CHAS. SURF: Rowley, my old friend, I am sure you congratulate me; and I suspect that I owe you much.

SIR OLIV: You do, indeed, Charles.

ROW: If my efforts to serve you had not succeeded you would have been in my debt for the attempt—but deserve to be happy—and you overpay me.

SIR PET: Aye, honest Rowley always said you would reform.

CHAS. SURF: Why as to reforming, Sir Peter, I'll make no promises, and that I take to be a proof that I intend to set about it.—But here shall be my monitor—my gentle guide.—Ah! can I leave the virtuous path those eyes illumine?

*Though thou, dear maid, shouldst wa[i]ve thy beauty's sway,*
*Thou still must rule, because I will obey:*
*An humbled fugitive from Folly view,*
*No sanctuary near but Love and—You;*

(*To the audience.*)

*You can, indeed, each anxious fear remove,*
*For even Scandal dies, if you approve.*

*Finis.*

# EPILOGUE

WRITTEN BY G. COLMAN, ESQ.[1]

SPOKEN BY MRS. ABINGTON[2]

I, who was late so volatile and gay,
Like a trade-wind must now blow all one way,
Bend all my cares, my studies, and my vows,
To one old rusty weathercock—my spouse!
So wills our virtuous bard—the motley Bayes[3]
Of crying epilogues and laughing plays!
 Old bachelors, who marry smart young wives,
Learn from our play to regulate your lives:
Each bring his dear to town, all faults upon her—
London will prove the very source of honor.
Plunged fairly in, like a cold bath it serves,

EP. [1] **G. Colman, Esq.** the dramatist, George Colman the elder (1732-1794) [2] **Mrs. Abington** Frances Abington, who had the role of Lady Teazle [3] **Bayes** alluding to the dramatist burlesqued in the Duke of Buckingham's *The Rehearsal*

When principles relax, to brace the nerves.
  Such is my case;—and yet I might deplore
That the gay dream of dissipation's o'er;
And say, ye fair, was ever lively wife,
Born with a genius for the highest life,
Like me untimely blasted in her bloom,
Like me condemned to such a dismal doom?
Save money—when I just knew how to waste it!
Leave London—just as I began to taste it!
Must I then watch the early crowing cock,
The melancholy ticking of a clock;
In the lone rustic hall for ever pounded,
With dogs, cats, rats, and squalling brats surrounded?
With humble curates can I now retire,
(While good Sir Peter boozes with the squire,)
And at backgammon mortify my soul,
That pants for loo,[4] or flutters at a vole?[5]
Seven's the main![6] Dear sound!—that must expire,
Lost at hot cockles,[7] round a Christmas fire!
The transient hour of fashion too soon spent,
Farewell the tranquil mind, farewell content![8]
Farewell the plumèd head, the cushioned tête,
That takes the cushion from its proper seat!
That spirit-stirring drum![9]—card drums I mean,
Spadille[10]—odd trick—pam[11]—basto[12]—king and queen!
And you, ye knockers, that, with brazen throat,
The welcome visitors' approach denote;

Farewell! all quality of high renown,
Pride, pomp, and circumstance of glorious town!
Farewell! your revels I partake no more,
And Lady Teazle's occupation's o'er!
All this I told our bard—he smiled, and said 'twas clear,
I ought to play deep tragedy next year.
Meanwhile he drew wise morals from his play,
And in these solemn periods stalked away:—
'Blest were the fair like you; her faults who stopped,
And closed her follies when the curtain dropped!
No more in vice or error to engage,
Or play the fool at large on life's great stage.'

## SUMMARY

Comedy apparently emerged in early societies out of the need to confront the ludicrous in human nature. As one of two principal dramatic forms found throughout the ages, comedy has exposed human folly and celebrated human survival. Comic playwrights have focused on the social world and its values of moderation and good humor in all things. Therefore, the heroes of comedy have largely been those fools, rogues, and pranksters who have defied society's norms, been exposed as aberrations, and reformed of their waywardness by humanity's common sense. As a form of dramatic writing, comedy represents the aspect of human experience that affirms moderation, compassion, love, common sense, and good nature.

Sheridan's *The School for Scandal* has provided an example of traditional comic writing whose development from complication to resolution is not unlike that of tragedy, but whose ending differs significantly.

The next two chapters on farce and tragicomedy discuss forms that emphasize other comedic facets of human experience.

---

[4] **loo** a card game    [5] **vole** the winning of all the tricks
[6] **Seven's the main** a term in the game of hazard    [7] **hot cockles** a country game    [8] **Farewell ... occupation's o'er!** these lines parody a soliloquy of Othello, III.iii.347–357    [9] **drum** an evening party at a private house    [10] **Spadille** ace of spades    [11] **pam** jack of clubs    [12] **basto** ace of clubs

## NOTES

1. Northrop Frye, "The Mythos of Spring: Comedy," *The Anatomy of Criticism* (New Jersey: Princeton University Press, 1957): 163.

2. Louis Kronenberger, *The Thread of Laughter: Chapters on English Stage Comedy from Jonson to Maugham* (New York: Alfred A. Knopf, 1952): 196.

# The Colored Museum

## GEORGE C. WOLFE

George C. Wolfe (1954– ), author of The Colored Museum, Jelly's Last Jam, and Spunk, grew up in Frankfurt, Kentucky. His father worked for the state's department of corrections and his mother was the principal of a black private school attended by the four Wolfe children. Just as his father and siblings, Wolfe attended Kentucky State University, but only for a year. He transferred to Pomona College in California and majored in theatre, where he began writing and staging plays. Following graduation, he worked at the Innercity Cultural Center in Los Angeles, where he taught and directed. In 1979 Wolfe moved to New York and taught acting at the City College of New York before enrolling in the musical theatre program at New York University, where he received the Master of Fine Arts degree. There, he made contact with Stephen Sondheim, Arthur Laurents, and Richard Maltby, who became early champions of his work.

Wolfe's first big break came when Playwrights Horizons produced Paradise, his wacky view of colonialization, which failed, but his next venture was The Colored Museum, which took familiar African-American stereotypes and turned them inside out and upside down. This popular production opened at the Crossroads Theatre, New Jersey, in 1986, transferred to The New York Shakespeare Festival Public Theatre, and established Wolfe as a new, distinctive presence in the American theatre. Named one of three Artistic Associates at the New York Shakespeare Festival, he scored another success with Spunk, an adaptation of three stories by Harlem Renaissance writer Zora Neale Hurston.

In 1987, he was librettist for Duke Ellington's opera, Queenie Pie, which premiered at The American Music Theatre Festival and at The John F. Kennedy Center in Washington, D. C. In 1992 Wolfe wrote the book for and directed Jelly's Last Jam, the life of Jelly Roll Morton, for Broadway. In 1993, he staged Tony Kushner's Angels in America: Millenium Approaches for Broadway and was named Producer of the New York Shakespeare Festival. He won the Village Voice "Obie" award for The Colored Museum and Antoinette Perry "Tony" awards for direction of Jelly's Last Jam and Angels in America.

"The major influence in my work is the culture I come from," he said. "The storytelling, the language, the energies of defying. . . . I no longer view myself as being a subculture [in America], a minority, an alternative. I am the party. I am the Jam."[7]

## INTRODUCTION

George C. Wolfe's The Colored Museum takes its structure from the musical revue (there are eleven vignettes) and its outrageous treatment of stereotypes and social icons from farce. With uncompromising wit and a frenetic style, Wolfe says the unthinkable about the history and present-day contradictions of African-Americans in the United States. He leaves society's sacred taboos in ruins for both blacks and whites at the play's end.

The setting (and situation) is an antiseptic modern museum displaying exhibits of "colored" history, beginning with the slave trade and ending with contemporary Harlem. Wolfe's strategy is not to present a museum-quality display of black history in the United States, but as a farceur and satirist, he sets about to annihilate the audience's politically correct responses and attitudes. For example, the opening sketch presents an airline stewardess, dressed in a hot-pink outfit, welcoming her Savannah-bound passengers to "celebrity slaveship" where they are expected to obey a "Fasten Shackles" seat-belt sign and are warned that they are about to "suffer a few hundred years" in exchange for receiving a "complex culture." Thus, Wolfe establishes the outrageous playfulness of traditional farce with a personal seriousness that theatre is a place for ideas and truths about society and the human condition.

The other exhibits (displayed on a revolving stage that brings them into view without interruption) comprise displays of contemporary African-Americans torn between their cultural legacy of oppression and revolt and the exigencies of living in the present. A Josephine Baker–like chanteuse, named Lala, finds her carefully created Gallicized show-business image haunted by the "little girl" she thought she had left for dead in the backwoods of Mississippi. A woman dressing for a date is traumatized when her two wigs atop her makeup table (one is a sixties' "Afro"; the other is a "Barbie Doll dipped in chocolate") come alive to debate the identity conflict they have represented in their owner's life for twenty years. A glamorous couple who admittedly cannot live "inside yesterday's pain" resolve to retreat from their past into a world of narcissistic glamor and choose to live with the beautiful people reflected in *Ebony Magazine*. They discover only the "kind of pain that comes from feeling no pain at all." A corporate type tries to throw the icons of his childhood (carried in a "Saks Fifth Avenue" shopping bag) into a trash can along with his inner adolescent self dressed in late-sixties' street style. As he attempts to eradicate his past, he discards his Afro-comb, Eldridge Cleaver's book, *Soul on Ice*, political campaign buttons of Angela Davis, and albums by Jimi Hendrix, The Jackson Five, and The Temptations. Finally, he strangles The Kid in an effort "to kill his own rage." He announces, "I have no history. I have no past," but the adolescent experience within rises again from the depths where he has been temporarily left for dead

with the other detritus of the corporate executive's life.

The central exhibit of *The Colored Museum* is "The Last Mama-on-the-Couch Play," a play-within-the-play, in which Wolfe shatters the pretensions of black acting styles along with the generational conflicts of 1950s' black-American drama in which families are preoccupied with middle-class aspirations. The target is Lorraine Hansberry's award-winning drama, *A Raisin in the Sun*, along with the performances of Claudia McNeil, Sidney Poitier, and Sandra Dee in the 1959 Broadway production. An elegant announcer, dressed in black-tie, promises a "searing, domestic drama that tears at the very fabric of racist America." Wolfe's scene satirizes a pretentious, latter-day form of black theatre (blamed on The Juilliard School of Drama) that turns into an all-black Broadway musical that spirals into an indictment of the white audience's eternal relationship to the black performer. With farcical style and satirical wit, Wolfe has torn at the fabric of racist America by revealing the cultural blind spots of blacks and whites alike: the black millionaire basketball player, soul food, sensitive family dramas, and performers (especially tap dancers and blues singers).

The playwright's themes are resolved in the final monologue, which belongs to Topsy Washington (named for the character in *Uncle Tom's Cabin* and the seat of government) who imagines a gigantic Manhattan party "somewhere between 125th Street and infinity" where Nat Turner sips champagne out of Eartha Kitt's slipper, Angela Davis and Aunt Jemima share a plate of "greens" while they talk about South Africa, and Bert Williams and Malcolm X discuss existentialism "as it relates to the shuffle-ball-change." As this fantasy merges present and past, it snowballs into a "defying logic." Topsy decides to put her rage about the past behind her so she can "go about the business of being me" and celebrate her own "madness and colored contradictions." As music, other characters, and projected images rise up from history around Topsy, it becomes clear that while the baggage of slavery cannot really be banished, the shackles of the past have been liberated by Wolfe's fearless and sustained Freudian joke that has bypassed social taboos and cultural censors. The exhibits in Wolfe's "colored museum" stress that we are our past, but our present-day awareness liberates us into a vital selfhood.

The vulnerability of black identity and African-American pride to exploitation and even destruction by the majority culture is the basic statement of *The Colored Museum*. To the charge that he has fostered stereotypes and not smashed them, Wolfe responded, "That's a manifestation of a slave mentality. Because you're still obsessing about how the dominant culture is going to judge you and I refuse to give anybody that kind of power over my thought process and creativity." He continued,

> The culture I come from is very specific and very exact and what I choose to write about is specifically about that. But what it's really, ultimately dealing with is the human condition.[8]

# The Colored Museum

**THE CAST:** An ensemble of five, two men and three women, all black, who perform all the characters that inhabit the exhibits.*

**THE STAGE:** White walls and recessed lighting. A starkness befitting a museum where the myths and madness of black/Negro/colored Americans are stored.

Built into the walls are a series of small panels, doors, revolving walls, and compartments from which actors can retrieve key props and make quick entrances.

A revolve is used, which allows for quick transitions from one exhibit to the next.

**MUSIC:** All of the music for the show should be prerecorded. Only the drummer, who is used in *Git on Board*, and then later in *Permutations* and *The Party*, is live.

THERE IS NO INTERMISSION

## THE EXHIBITS

Git on Board
Cookin' with Aunt Ethel
The Photo Session
Soldier with a Secret
The Gospel According to Miss Roj
The Hairpiece
The Last Mama-on-the-Couch Play
Symbiosis
Lala's Opening
Permutations
The Party

## THE CHARACTERS

Git on Board
    **MISS PAT**

Cookin' with Aunt Ethel
    **AUNT ETHEL**

The Photo Session
    **GIRL**
    **GUY**

Soldier with a Secret
    **JUNIE ROBINSON**

The Gospel According to Miss Roj
    **MISS ROJ**
    **WAITER**

The Hairpiece
    **THE WOMAN**
    **JANINE**
    **LAWANDA**

The Last Mama-on-the-Couch Play
    **NARRATOR**
    **MAMA**
    **WALTER-LEE-BEAU-WILLIE-JONES**
    **LADY IN PLAID**
    **MEDEA JONES**

Symbiosis
    **THE MAN**
    **THE KID**

Lala's Opening
    **LALA LAMAZING GRACE**
    **ADMONIA**
    **FLO'RANCE**
    **THE LITTLE GIRL**

*A Little Girl, seven to twelve years old, is needed for a walk-on part in *Lala's Opening*.

154

Permutations
  NORMAL JEAN REYNOLDS
The Party
  TOPSY WASHINGTON
  MISS PAT
  MISS ROJ
  LALA LAMAZING GRACE
  THE MAN (*from Symbiosis*)

## GIT ON BOARD

(*Blackness. Cut by drums pounding. Then slides, rapidly flashing before us. Images we've all seen before, of African slaves being captured, loaded onto ships, tortured. The images flash, flash, flash. The drums crescendo. Blackout. And then lights reveal* MISS PAT, *frozen. She is black, pert, and cute. She has a flip to her hair and wears a hot pink mini-skirt stewardess uniform.*)

(*She stands in front of a curtain which separates her from an offstage cockpit.*)

(*An electronic bell goes "ding" and* MISS PAT *comes to life, presenting herself in a friendly but rehearsed manner, smiling and speaking as she has done so many times before.*)

MISS PAT:  Welcome aboard Celebrity Slaveship, departing the Gold Coast and making short stops at Bahia, Port Au Prince, and Havana, before our final destination of Savannah.

Hi. I'm Miss Pat and I'll be serving you here in Cabin A. We will be crossing the Atlantic at an altitude that's pretty high, so you must wear your shackles at all times.

(*She removes a shackle from the overhead compartment and demonstrates.*)

To put on your shackle, take the right hand and close the metal ring around your left hand like so. Repeat the action using your left hand to secure the right. If you have any trouble bonding yourself, I'd be more than glad to assist.

Once we reach the desired altitude, the Captain will turn off the "Fasten Your Shackle" sign . . . (*She efficiently points out the "FASTEN YOUR SHACKLE" signs on either side of her, which light up.*) . . . allowing you a chance to stretch and dance in the aisles a bit. But otherwise, shackles must be worn at all times.
(*The "Fasten Your Shackles" signs go off.*)

MISS PAT:  Also, we ask that you please refrain from call-and-response singing between cabins as that sort of thing can lead to rebellion. And, of course, no drums are allowed on board. Can you repeat after me, "No drums." (*She gets the audience to repeat.*) With a little more enthusiasm, please. "No drums." (*After the audience repeats it.*) That was great!

Once we're airborn, I'll be by with magazines, and earphones can be purchased for the price of your first-born male.

If there's anything I can do to make this middle passage more pleasant, press the little button overhead and I'll be with you faster than you can say, "Go down, Moses." (*She laughs at her "little joke".*) Thanks for flying Celebrity and here's hoping you have a pleasant take off.
(*The engines surge, the "Fasten Your Shackle" signs go on, and over-articulate Muzak voices are heard singing as* MISS PAT *pulls down a bucket seat and "shackles-up" for takeoff.*)

VOICES:
  GET ON BOARD CELEBRITY SLAVESHIP
  GET ON BOARD CELEBRITY SLAVESHIP
  GET ON BOARD CELEBRITY SLAVESHIP
  THERE'S ROOM FOR MANY A MORE
  (*The engines reach an even, steady hum. Just as* MISS PAT *rises and replaces the shackles in the overhead compartment, the faint sound of African drumming is heard.*)

MISS PAT:  Hi. Miss Pat again. I'm sorry to disturb you, but someone is playing drums. And what did we just say . . .

"No drums." It must be someone in Coach. But we here in Cabin A are not going to respond to those drums. As a matter of fact, we don't even hear them. Repeat after me. "I don't hear any drums." (*The audience repeats.*) And "I will not rebel."
(*The audience repeats. The drumming grows.*)

MISS PAT: (*Placating*) OK, now I realize some of us are a bit edgy after hearing about the tragedy on board The Laughing Mary, but let me assure you Celebrity has no intention of throwing you overboard and collecting the insurance. We value you!
(*She proceeds to single out individual passengers/audience members.*)

Why, the songs *you* are going to sing in the cotton fields, under the burning heat and stinging lash, will metamorphose and give birth to the likes of James Brown and the Fabulous Flames. And you, yes *you*, are going to come up with some of the best dances. The best dances! The Watusi! The Funky Chicken! And just think of what *you* are going to mean to William Faulkner.

All right, so you're gonna have to suffer for a few hundred years, but from your pain will come a culture so complex. *And*, with this little item here . . . (*She removes a basketball from the overhead compartment.*) . . . you'll become millionaires!
(*There is a roar of thunder. The lights quiver and the "Fasten Your Shackle" signs begin to flash.* MISS PAT *quickly replaces the basketball in the overhead compartment and speaks very reassuringly.*)

MISS PAT: No, don't panic. I'm here to take care of you. We're just flying through a little thunder storm. Now the only way you're going to make it through this one is if you abandon your God and worship a new one. So, on the count of three, let's all sing. One, two, three . . .

NOBODY KNOWS DE TROUBLE I SEEN

Oh, I forgot to mention, when singing, omit the T-H sound. "The" becomes "de". "They" becomes "dey". Got it? Good!

NOBODY KNOWS . . .
NOBODY KNOWS . . .

Oh, so you don't like that one? Well then let's try another—

SUMMER TIME
AND DE LIVIN' IS EASY

Gershwin. He comes from another oppressed people so he understands.

FISH ARE JUMPIN' . . . come on.
AND DE COTTON IS HIGH.

Sing, damnit!
(*Lights begin to flash, the engines surge, and there is wild drumming.* MISS PAT *sticks her head through the curtain and speaks with an offstage* CAPTAIN.)
MISS PAT: What?
VOICE OF CAPTAIN (*O.S.*): Time warp!
MISS PAT: Time warp! (*She turns to the audience and puts on a pleasant face.*) The Captain has assured me everything is fine. We're just caught in a little time warp. (*Trying to fight her growing hysteria.*) On your right you will see the American Revolution, which will give the U.S. of A exclusive rights to your life. And on your left, the Civil War, which means you will vote Republican until F.D.R. comes along. And now we're passing over the Great Depression, which means everybody gets to live the way you've been living. (*There is a blinding flash of light, and an explosion. She screams.*) Ahhhhhhhhh! That was World War I, which is not to be confused with World War II . . . (*There is a larger flash of light, and another explosion.*) . . . Ahhhhh! Which is not to be confused

with the Korean War or the Vietnam War, all of which you will play a major role in.

Oh, look, now we're passing over the sixties. Martha and Vandellas . . . Malcolm X. (*There is a gun shot.*) . . . "Julia" with Miss Diahann Carroll . . . and five little girls in Sunday school . . . (*There is an explosion.*) Martin Luther King . . . (*A gun shot*) Oh no! The Supremes just broke up! (*The drumming intensifies.*) Stop playing those drums. I said, stop playing those damn drums. You can't stop history! You can't stop time! Those drums will be confiscated once we reach Savannah. Repeat after me. I don't hear any drums and I will not rebel. I will not rebel! I will not re—

(*The lights go out, she screams, and the sound of a plane landing and screeching to a halt is heard. After a beat, lights reveal a wasted, disheveled* MISS PAT, *but perky nonetheless.*)

MISS PAT: Hi. Miss Pat here. Things got a bit jumpy back there, but the Captain has just informed me we have safely landed in Savannah. Please check the overhead before exiting as any baggage you don't claim, we trash.

It's been fun, and we hope the next time you consider travel, it's with Celebrity. (*Luggage begins to revolve onstage from offstage left, going past* MISS PAT *and revolving offstage right. Mixed in with the luggage are two male slaves and a woman slave, complete with luggage and I.D. tags around their necks.*)

MISS PAT: (*With routine, rehearsed pleasantness.*)
Have a nice day. Bye bye.
Button up that coat, it's kind of chilly.
Have a nice day. Bye bye.
You take care now.
See you.
Have a nice day.

Have a nice day.
Have a nice day.

## COOKIN' WITH AUNT ETHEL

(*As the slaves begin to revolve off, a low-down gut-bucket blues is heard.* AUNT ETHEL, *a down-home black woman with a bandana on her head, revolves to center stage. She stands behind a big black pot and wears a reassuring grin.*)

AUNT ETHEL: Welcome to "Aunt Ethel's Down-Home Cookin' Show," where we explores the magic and mysteries of colored cuisine.

Today, we gonna be servin' ourselves up some . . . (*She laughs.*) I'm not gonna tell you. That's right! I'm not gonna tell you what it is till after you done cooked it. Child, on "The Aunt Ethel Show" we loves to have ourselves some fun. Well, are you ready? Here goes.
(*She belts out a hard-drivin' blues and throws invisible ingredients into the big, black pot.*)

FIRST YA ADD A PINCH OF STYLE
AND THEN A DASH OF FLAIR
NOW YA STIR IN SOME PREOCCUPA-TION
WITH THE TEXTURE OF YOUR HAIR

NEXT YA ADD ALL KINDS OF RHYTHMS
LOTS OF FEELINGS AND PIZZAZ
THEN HUNNY THROW IN SOME RAGE
TILL IT CONGEALS AND TURNS TO JAZZ

NOW YOU COOKIN'
COOKIN' WITH AUNT ETHEL
YOU REALLY COOKIN'
COOKIN' WITH AUNT ETHEL, OH YEAH

NOW YA ADD A HEAP OF SURVIVAL
AND HUMILITY, JUST A TOUCH
ADD SOME ATTITUDE
OPPS! I PUT TOO MUCH

AND NOW A WHOLE LOT OF HUMOR
SALTY LANGUAGE, MIXED WITH
SADNESS
THEN THROW IN A BOX OF BLUES
AND SIMMER TO MADNESS

NOW YOU COOKIN'
COOKIN' WITH AUNT ETHEL, OH
YEAH!

NOW YOU BEAT IT—REALLY WORK
IT
DISCARD AND DISOWN
AND IN A FEW HUNDRED YEARS
ONCE IT'S AGED AND FULLY
GROWN
YA PUT IT IN THE OVEN
TILL IT'S BLACK
AND HAS A SHEEN
OR TILL IT'S NICE AND YELLA
OR ANY SHADE IN BETWEEN

NEXT YA TAKE 'EM OUT AND COOL
'EM
'CAUSE THEY NO FUN WHEN THEY
HOT
AND WON'T YOU BE SURPRISED
AT THE CONCOCTION YOU GOT

YOU HAVE BAKED
BAKED YOURSELF A BATCH OF NE-
GROES
YES YOU HAVE BAKED YOURSELF
BAKED YOURSELF A BATCH OF NE-
GROES
(*She pulls from the pot a handful of Negroes,*
*black dolls.*)

But don't ask me what to do with 'em
now that you got 'em, 'cause child, that's
your problem. (*She throws the dolls back*
*into the pot.*) But in any case, yaw be sure
to join Aunt Ethel next week, when we
gonna be servin' ourselves up some
chitlin   quiche ... some   grits-under-
glass,

AND A SWEET POTATO PIE
AND YOU'LL BE COOKIN'

COOKIN' WITH AUNT ETHEL
OH YEAH!
(*On* AUNT ETHEL'S *final rift, lights reveal* ...)

## THE PHOTO SESSION

(... *a very glamorous, gorgeous, black couple,*
*wearing the best of everything and perfect smiles.*
*The stage is bathed in color and bright white*
*light. Disco music with the chant: "We're fabu-*
*lous" plays in the background. As they pose,*
*larger-than-life images of their perfection are pro-*
*jected on the museum walls. The music quiets and*
*the images fade away as they begin to speak and*
*pose.*)

GIRL: The world was becoming too much
for us.
GUY: We couldn't resolve the contradictions
of our existence.
GIRL: And we couldn't resolve yesterday's
pain.
GUY: So we gave away our life and we now
live inside *Ebony Magazine.*
GIRL: Yes, we live inside a world where eve-
ryone is beautiful, and wears fabulous
clothes.
GUY: And no one says anything profound.
GIRL: Or meaningful.
GUY: Or contradictory.
GIRL: Because no one talks. Everyone just
smiles and shows off their cheekbones.
(*They adopt a profile pose.*)
Last month I was black and fabulous
while holding up a bottle of vodka.
GIRL: This month we get to be black and
fabulous together.
(*They dance/pose. The "We're fabulous"*
*chant builds and then fades as they start to*
*speak again.*)
GIRL: There are of course setbacks.
GUY: We have to smile like this for a whole
month.
GIRL: And we have no social life.
GUY: And no sex.
GIRL: And at times it feels like we're suffo-
cating, like we're not human anymore.

GUY: And everything is rehearsed, including this other kind of pain we're starting to feel.

GIRL: The kind of pain that comes from feeling no pain at all.

(*They then speak and pose with a sudden burst of energy.*)

GUY: But one can't have everything.

GIRL: Can one?

GUY: So if the world is becoming too much for you, do like we did.

GIRL: Give away your life and come be beautiful with us.

GUY: We guarantee, no contradictions.

GIRL/GUY: Smile/click, smile/click, smile/click.

GIRL: And no pain.

(*They adopt a final pose and revolve off as the "We're fabulous" chant plays and fades into the background.*)

## A SOLDIER WITH A SECRET

(*Projected onto the museum walls are the faces of black soldiers—from the Spanish-American thru to the Vietnam War. Lights slowly reveal* JUNIE ROBINSON, *a black combat soldier, posed on an onyx plinth. He comes to life and smiles at the audience. Somewhat dim-witted, he has an easy-going charm about him.*)

JUNIE: Pst. Pst. I know the secret. The secret to your pain. 'Course, I didn't always know. First I had to die, then come back to life, 'fore I had the gift.

Ya see the Cappin sent me off up ahead to scout for screamin' yella bastards. 'Course, for the life of me I couldn't understand why they'd be screamin', seein' as how we was tryin' to kill them and they us.

But anyway, I'm off lookin', when all of a sudden I find myself caught smack dead in the middle of this explosion. This blindin', burnin', scaldin' explosion. Musta been a booby trap or something, 'cause all around me is fire. Hell, I'm on fire. Like a piece of chicken dropped in a skillet of cracklin' grease. Why, my flesh was justa peelin' off of my bones.

But then I says to myself, "Junie, if yo' flesh is on fire, how come you don't feel no pain!" And I didn't. I swear as I'm standin' here, I felt nuthin. That's when I sort of put two and two together and realized I didn't feel no whole lot of hurtin' cause I done died.

Well I just picked myself up and walked right on out of that explosion. Hell, once you know you dead, why keep on dyin', ya know?

So, like I say, I walk right outta that explosion, fully expectin' to see white clouds, Jesus, and my Mama, only all I saw was more war. Shootin' goin' on way off in this direction and that direction. And there, standin' around, was all the guys. Hubert, J.F., the Cappin. I guess the sound of the explosion must of attracted 'em, and they all starin' at me like I'm some kind of ghost.

So I yells to 'em, "Hey there Hubert! Hey there Cappin!" But they just stare. So I tells 'em how I'd died and how I guess it wasn't my time cause here I am, "Fully in the flesh and not a scratch to my bones." And they still just stare. So I took to starin' back.

(*The expression on* JUNIE'S *face slowly turns to horror and disbelief.*)

Only what I saw . . . well I can't exactly to this day describe it. But I swear, as sure as they was wearin' green and holdin' guns, they was each wearin' a piece of the future on their faces.

Yeah. All the hurt that was gonna get done to them and they was gonna do to folks was right there clear as day.

I saw how J.F., once he got back to Chicago, was gonna get shot dead by this po-lice, and I saw how Hubert was gonna start beatin' up on his old lady which I didn't understand, 'cause all he could do was talk on and on about how much he loved her. Each and every one of 'em had pain in his future and blood on his path. And God or the Devil one spoke to me and said, "Junie, these colored boys ain't gonna be the same after this war. They ain't gonn have no kind of happiness."

Well right then and there it come to me. The secret to their pain.

Late that night, after the medics done checked me over and found me fit for fightin', after everybody done settle down for the night, I sneaked over to where Hubert was sleepin', and with a needle I stole from the medics . . . pst, pst . . . I shot a little air into his veins. The second he died, all the hurtin-to-come just left his face.

Two weeks later I got J.F. and after that Woodrow . . . Jimmy Joe . . . I even spent all night waitin' by the latrine 'cause I knew the Cappin always made a late night visit and pst . . . pst . . . I got him.

(*Smiling, quite proud of himself.*) That's how come I died and come back to life. 'Cause just like Jesus went around healin' the sick, I'm supposed to go around healin' the hurtin' all these colored boys wearin' from the war.

Pst, pst. I know the secret. The secret to your pain. The secret to yours, and yours. Pst. Pst. Pst. Pst.
(*The lights slowly fade.*)

## THE GOSPEL ACCORDING TO MISS ROJ

(*The darkness is cut by electronic music. Cold, pounding, unretenting. A neon sign which spells out* THE BOTTOMLESS PIT *clicks on. There is a lone bar stool. Lights flash on and off, pulsating to the beat. There is a blast of smoke and, from the haze,* MISS ROJ *appears. He is dressed in striped patio pants, white go-go boots, a halter, and cat-shaped sunglasses. What would seem ridiculous on anyone else,* MISS ROJ *wears as if it were high fashion. He carries himself with total elegance and absolute arrogance.*)

MISS ROJ: God created black people and black people created style. The name's Miss Roj . . . that's R.O.J. thank you and you can find me every Wednesday, Friday and Saturday nights at "The Bottomless Pit," the watering hole for the wild and weary which asks the question, "Is there life after Jherri-curl?"
(*A waiter enters, hands* MISS ROJ *a drink, and then exits.*)

Thanks, doll. *Yes*, if they be black and swish, the B.P. has seen them, which is not to suggest the Pit is lacking in cultural diversity. Oh no. There are your dinge queens, white men who like their chicken legs dark. (*He winks/flirts with a man in the audience.*) And let's not forget, "Los Muchachos de la Neighborhood." But the speciality of the house is The Snap Queens. (*He snaps his fingers.*) We are a rare breed.

For, you see, when something strikes our fancy, when the truth comes piercing through the dark, well you just can't let it pass unnoticed. No darling. You must pronounce it with a snap. (*He snaps.*)

Snapping comes from another galaxy, as do all snap queens. That's right. I ain't just your regular oppressed American Negro. No-no-no! I am an extraterrestial. And I ain't talkin' none of that shit you seen in the movies! I have real power.
(*The waiter enters.* MISS ROJ *stops him.*)

Speaking of no power, will you please tell Miss Stingy-with-the-rum, that if

Miss Roj had wanted to remain sober, she could have stayed home and drank Kool-aid. (*He snaps.*) Thank you.
(*The waiter exits.* MISS ROJ *crosses and sits on bar stool.*)

Yes, I was placed here on Earth to study the life habits of a deteriorating society, and child when we talkin' New York City, we are discussing the Queen of Deterioration. Miss New York is doing a slow dance with death, and I am here to warn you all, but before I do, I must know . . . don't you just love my patio pants? Annette Funicello immortalized them in "Beach Blanket Bingo," and I have continued the legacy. And my go-gos? I realize white after Labor Day is very gauche, but as the saying goes, if you've got it flaunt it, if you don't, front it and snap to death any bastard who dares to defy you. (*Laughing*) Oh ho! My demons are showing. Yes, my demons live at the bottom of my Bacardi and Coke.

Let's just hope for all concerned I dance my demons out before I drink them out 'cause child, dancing demons take you on a ride, but those drinkin' demons just take you, and you find yourself doing the strangest things. Like the time I locked my father in the broom closet. Seems the liquor made his tongue real liberal and he decided he was gonna baptize me with the word "faggot" over and over. Well, he's just going on and on with "faggot this" and "faggot that," all the while walking toward the broom closet to piss. Poor drunk bastard was just all turned around. So the demons just took hold of my wedges and forced me to kick the drunk son-of-a-bitch into the closet and lock the door. (*Laughter*) Three days later I remembered he was there. (*He snaps.*)
(*The waiter enters.* MISS ROJ *takes a drink and downs it.*)

Another!
(*The waiter exits.*)

(*Dancing about.*) Oh yes-yes-yes! Miss Roj is quintessential style. I corn row the hairs on my legs so that they spell out M.I.S.S. R.O.J. And I dare any bastard to fuck with me because I will snap your ass into oblivion.

I have the power, you know. Everytime I snap, I steal one beat of your heart. So if you find yourself gasping for air in the middle of the night, chances are you fucked with Miss Roj and she didn't like it.

Like the time this asshole at Jones Beach decided to take issue with my coulotte-sailor ensemble. This child, this muscle-bound Brooklyn thug in a skin-tight bikini, very skin-tight so the whole world can see that instead of a brain, God gave him an extra thick piece of sausage. You know the kind who beat up on their wives for breakfast. Well, he decided to blurt out when I walked by, "Hey look at da monkey coon in da faggit suit." Well, I walked up to the poor dear, very calmly lifted my hand, and. . . . (*He snaps in rapid succession.*) A heart attack, right there on the beach. (*He singles out someone in the audience.*) You don't believe it? Cross me! Come on! Come on! (*The waiter enters, hands* MISS ROJ *a drink.* MISS ROJ *downs it. The waiter exits.*)

(*Looking around.*) If this place is the answer, we're asking all the wrong questions. The only reason I come here is to communicate with my origins. The flashing lights are signals from my planet way out there. Yes, girl, even further than Flatbush. We're talking another galaxy. The flashing lights tell me how much time is left before the end.

(*Very drunk and loud by now.*) I hate the people here. I hate the drinks. But most of all I hate this goddamn music. That ain't music. Give me Aretha Franklin any day. (*Singing*) "Just a little respect. R.E.S.P.E.C.T." Yeah! Yeah!

Come on and dance your last dance with Miss Roj. Last call is but a drink away and each snap puts you one step closer to the end.

A high-rise goes up. You can't get no job. Come on everybody and dance. A whole race of people gets trashed and debased. Snap those fingers and dance. Some sick bitch throws her baby out the window 'cause she thinks it's the Devil. Everybody snap! *The New York Post*. Snap!

Snap for every time you walk past someone lying in the street, smelling like frozen piss and shit and you don't see it. Snap for every crazed bastard who kills himself so as to get the jump on being killed. And snap for every sick muthafucker who, bored with carrying around his fear, takes to shooting up other people.

Yeah, snap your fingers and dance with Miss Roj. But don't be fooled by the banners and balloons 'cause, child, this ain't no party going on. Hell no! It's a wake. And the casket's made out of stone, steel, and glass and the people are racing all over the pavement like maggots on a dead piece of meat.

Yeah, dance! But don't be surprised if there ain't no beat holding you together 'cause we traded in our drums for respectability. So now it's just words. Words rappin'. Words screechin'. Words flowin' instead of blood 'cause you know that don't work. Words cracklin' instead of fire 'cause by the time a match is struck on 125th Street and you run to midtown, the flame has been blown away.

So come on and dance with Miss Roj and her demons. We don't ask for accep-

tance. We don't ask for approval. We know who we are and we move on it!

I guarantee you will never hear two fingers put together in a snap and not think of Miss Roj. That's power, baby. Patio pants and all.
(*The lights begin to flash in rapid succession.*)

So let's dance! And snap! And dance! And snap!
(**MISS ROJ** *begins to dance as if driven by his demons. There is a blast of smoke and when the haze settles,* **MISS ROJ** *has revolved off and in place of him is a recording of Aretha Franklin singing, "Respect."*)

## THE HAIRPIECE

(*As "Respect" fades into the background, a vanity revolves to center stage. On this vanity are two wigs, an Afro wig, circa 1968, and a long, flowing wig, both resting on wig stands. A black* **WOMAN** *enters, her head and body wrapped in towels. She picks up a framed picture and after a few moments of hesitation, throws it into a small trash can. She then removes one of her towels to reveal a totally bald head. Looking into a mirror on the "fourth wall," she begins applying makeup.*)

(*The wig stand holding the Afro wig opens her eyes. Her name is* **JANINE**. *She stares in disbelief at the bald woman.*)

JANINE: (*Calling to the other wig stand.*) LaWanda. LaWanda girl, wake up.
(*The other wig stand, the one with the long, flowing wig, opens her eyes. Her name is* **LAWANDA**.)
LAWANDA: What? What is it?
JANINE: Check out girlfriend.
LAWANDA: Oh, girl, I don't believe it.
JANINE: (*Laughing*) Just look at the poor thing, trying to paint some life onto that face of hers. You'd think by now she'd realize it's the hair. It's all about the hair.

LAWANDA: What hair! She ain't go no hair! She done fried, dyed, de-chemicalized her shit to death.

JANINE: And all that's left is that buck-naked scalp of hers, sittin' up there apologizin' for being odd-shaped and ugly.

LAWANDA: (*Laughing with* JANINE.) Girl, stop!

JANINE: I ain't sayin' nuthin' but the truth.

LAWANDA/JANINE: The bitch is bald! (*They laugh.*)

JANINE: And all over some man.

LAWANDA: I tell ya, girl, I just don't understand it. I mean, look at her. She's got a right nice face, a good head on her shoulders. A good job even. And she's got to go fall in love with that fool.

JANINE: That political quick-change artist. Everytime the nigga went and changed his ideology, she went and changed her hair to fit the occasion.

LAWANDA: Well at least she's breaking up with him.

JANINE: Hunny, no!

LAWANDA: Yes child.

JANINE: Oh, girl, dish me the dirt!

LAWANDA: Well, you see, I heard her on the phone, talking to one of her girlfriends, and she's meeting him for lunch today to give him the ax.

JANINE: Well it's about time.

LAWANDA: I hear ya. But don't you worry 'bout a thing, girlfriend. I'm gonna tell you all about it.

JANINE: Hunny, you won't have to tell me a damn thing 'cause I'm gonna be there, front row, center.

LAWANDA: You?

JANINE: Yes, child, she's wearing me to lunch.

LAWANDA: (*Outraged*) I don't think so!

JANINE: (*With an attitude*) What do you mean, you don't think so?

LAWANDA: Exactly what I said, "I don't think so." Damn, Janine, get real. How the hell she gonna wear both of us?

JANINE: She ain't wearing both of us. She's wearing me.

LAWANDA: Says who?

JANINE: Says me! Says her! Ain't that right, girlfriend?

(*The* WOMAN *stops putting on makeup, looks around, sees no one, and goes back to her makeup.*)

JANINE: I said, ain't that right!

(*The* WOMAN *picks up the phone.*)

WOMAN: Hello . . . hello . . .

JANINE: Did you hear the damn phone ring?

WOMAN: No.

JANINE: Then put the damn phone down and talk to me.

WOMAN: I ah . . . don't understand.

JANINE: It ain't deep so don't panic. Now, you're having lunch with your boyfriend, right?

WOMAN: (*Breaking into tears.*) I think I'm having a nervous breakdown.

JANINE: (*Impatient*) I said you're having lunch with your boyfriend, right!

WOMAN: (*Scared, pulling herself together.*) Yes, right . . . right.

JANINE: To break up with him.

WOMAN: How did you know that?

LAWANDA: I told her.

WOMAN: (*Stands and screams.*) Help! Help!

JANINE: Sit down. I said sit your ass down! (*The* WOMAN *does.*)

JANINE: Now set her straight and tell her you're wearing me.

LAWANDA: She's the one that needs to be set straight, so go on and tell her you're wearing me.

JANINE: No, tell her you're wearing me. (*There is a pause.*)

LAWANDA: Well?

JANINE: Well?

WOMAN: I ah . . . actually hadn't made up my mind.

JANINE: (*Going off*) What do you mean you ain't made up you mind! After all that fool has put you through, you gonna need all the attitude you can get and there is nothing like attitude and a healthy head of kinks to make his shit shrivel like it should!

That's right! When you wearin' me, you lettin' him know he ain't gonna get no sweet-talkin' comb through your love without some serious resistance. No-no! The kink of my head is like the kink of your heart and neither is about to be hot-pressed into surrender.

LAWANDA: That shit is so tired. The last time attitude worked on anybody was 1968. Janine girl, you need to get over it and get on with it. (*To the* WOMAN.) And you need to give the nigga a goodbye he will never forget.

I say give him hysteria! Give him emotion! Give him rage! And there is nothing like a toss of the tresses to make your emotional outburst shine with emotional flair.

You can toss me back, shake me from side to side, all the while screaming, "I want you out of my life forever!!!" And not only will I come bouncing back for more, but you just might win an Academy Award for best performance by a head of hair in a dramatic role.

JANINE: Miss hunny, please! She don't need no Barbie doll dipped in chocolate telling her what to do. She needs a head of hair that's coming from a fo' real place.

LAWANDA: Don't you dare talk about nobody coming from a "fo' real place," Miss Made-in-Taiwan!

JANINE: Hey! I ain't ashamed of where I come from. Besides, it don't matter where you come from as long as you end up in the right place.

LAWANDA: And it don't matter the grade as long as the point gets made. So go on and tell her you're wearing me.

JANINE: No, tell her you're wearing me.

(*The* WOMAN, *unable to take it, begins to bite off her fake nails, as* LAWANDA *and* JANINE *go at each other.*)

LAWANDA:
Set the bitch straight. Let her know there is no way she could even begin to compete with me. I am quality. She is kink. I am exotic. She is common. I am class and she is trash. That's right. T.R.A.S.H. We're talking three strikes and you're out. So go on and tell her you're wearing me. Go on, tell her! Tell her! Tell her!

JANINE:
Who you callin' a bitch? Why, if I had hands I'd knock you clear into next week. You think you cute. She thinks she's cute just 'cause that synthetic mop of hers blows in the wind. She looks like a fool and you look like an even bigger fool when you wear her, so go on and tell her you're wearing me. Go on, tell her! Tell her! Tell her!

(*The* WOMAN *screams and pulls the two wigs off the wig stands as the lights go to black on three bald heads.*)

## THE LAST MAMA-ON-THE-COUCH PLAY

(*A* NARRATOR, *dressed in a black tuxedo, enters through the audience and stands center stage. He is totally solemn.*)

NARRATOR: We are pleased to bring you yet another Mama-on-the-Couch play. A searing domestic drama that tears at the very fabric of racist America. (*He crosses upstage center and sits on a stool and reads from a playscript.*) Act One. Scene One.
(MAMA *revolves on stage left, sitting on a couch reading a large, oversized Bible. A window is placed stage right.* MAMA'S *dress, the couch, and drapes are made from the same material. A doormat lays down center.*)

NARRATOR: Lights up on a dreary, depressing, but with middle-class aspirations tenement slum. There is a couch, with a Mama on it. Both are well worn. There is a picture of Jesus on the wall . . . (*A picture of Jesus is instantly revealed.*) . . . and a window which looks onto an abandoned tenement. It is late spring.

Enter Walter-Lee-Beau-Willie-Jones. (SON *enters through the audience.*) He is Mama's thirty-year-old son. His brow is heavy from three hundred years of oppression.

MAMA: (*Looking up from her Bible, speaking in a slow manner.*) Son, did you wipe your feet?

SON: (*An ever-erupting volcano.*) No, Mama, I didn't wipe me feet! Out there, every day, Mama, is the Man. The Man, Mama. Mr. Charlie! Mr. Bossman! And he's wipin' his feet on me. On me, Mama, every damn day of my life. Ain't that enough for me to deal with? Ain't that enough?

MAMA: Son, wipe your feet.

SON: I wanna dream. I wanna be somebody. I wanna take charge of my life.

MAMA: You can do all of that, but first you got to wipe your feet.

SON: (*As he crosses to the mat, mumbling and wiping his feet.*) Wipe my feet . . . wipe my feet . . . wipe my feet . . .

MAMA: That's a good boy.

SON: (*Exploding*) Boy! Boy! I don't wanna be nobody's good boy, Mama. I wanna be my own man!

MAMA: I know son, I know. God will show the way.

SON: God, Mama! Since when did your God ever do a damn thing for the black man. Huh, Mama, huh? You tell me. When did your God ever help me.

MAMA: (*Removing her wire-rim glasses.*) Son, come here.

(SON *crosses to* MAMA, *who slowly stands and in a exaggerated stage slap, backhands* SON *clear across the stage. The* NARRATOR *claps his hands to create the sound for the slap.* MAMA *then lifts her clenched fists to the heavens.*)

MAMA: Not in my house, my house, will you ever talk that way again!

(*The* NARRATOR, *so moved by her performance, erupts in applause and encourages the audience to do so.*)

NARRATOR: Beautiful. Just stunning.

(*He reaches into one of the secret compartments of the set and gets an award which he ceremoniously gives to* MAMA *for her performance. She bows and then returns to the couch.*)

NARRATOR: Enter Walter-Lee-Beau-Willie's wife, The Lady in Plaid.

(*Music from nowhere is heard, a jazzy pseudo-abstract intro as the* LADY IN PLAID *dances in through the audience, wipes her feet, and then twirls about.*)

LADY:
She was a creature of regal beauty
who in ancient time graced the temples of the Nile
with her womanliness
But here she was, stuck being colored
and a woman in a world that valued neither.

SON: You cooked my dinner?

LADY: (*Oblivious to* SON.)
Feet flat, back broke,
she looked at the man who, though he be thirty,
still ain't got his own apartment.
Yeah, he's still livin' with his Mama!
And she asked herself, was this the life
for a Princess Colored, who by the translucence of her skin, knew the universe was her sister.

(*The* LADY IN PLAID *twirls and dances.*)

SON: (*Becoming irate.*) I've had a hard day of dealin' with the Man. Where's my damn dinner? Woman, stand still when I'm talkin' to you!

LADY: And she cried for her sisters in Detroit
Who knew, as she, that their souls belonged
in ancient temples on the Nile.
And she cried for her sisters in Chicago
who, like her, their life has become
one colored hell.

SON: There's only one thing gonna get through to you.

LADY: And she cried for her sisters in New Orleans
And her sisters in Trenton and Birmingham,

and
Poughkeepsie and Orlando and Miami
Beach
and
Las Vegas, Palm Springs.
(*As she continues to call out cities, he crosses offstage and returns with two black dolls and then crosses to the window.*)

SON:  Now are you gonna cook me dinner?

LADY:  Walter-Lee-Beau-Willie-Jones,     No! Not my babies.
(SON *throws them out the window. The* LADY IN PLAID *then lets out a primal scream.*)

LADY:  He dropped them!!!!
(*The* NARRATOR *breaks into applause.*)

NARRATOR:  Just splendid. Shattering.
(*He then crosses and after an intense struggle with* MAMA, *he takes the award from her and gives it to the* LADY IN PLAID, *who is still suffering primal pain.*)

LADY:  Not my babies . . . not my . . . (*Upon receiving the award, she instantly recovers.*) Help me up, sugar. (*She then bows and crosses and stands behind the couch.*)

NARRATOR:  Enter Medea Jones, Walter-Lee-Beau-Willie's sister.
(MEDEA *moves very ceremoniously, wiping her feet and then speaking and gesturing as if she just escaped from a Greek tragedy.*)

MEDEA:

Ah, see how the sun kneels to speak
her evening vespers, exaulting all
in her vision, even lowly tenement
long abandoned.

Mother, wife of brother, I trust
the approaching darkness finds you
safe in Hestia's busom.

Brother, why wear the face of a man
in anguish. Can the garment of thine
feelings cause the shape of your
countenance to disfigure so?

SON:  (*At the end of his rope.*) Leave me alone, Medea.

MEDEA:  (*To* MAMA)
Is good brother still going on and on

and on
about He and The Man.

MAMA/LADY:  What else?

MEDEA:  Ah brother, if with our thoughts and words we could cast thine oppressors into the lowest bowels of wretched hell, would that make us more like the gods or more like our oppressors.

No, brother, no, do not let thy rage
choke the blood which anoints thy
heart with love. Forgo thine darkened
humor and let love shine on your
soul, like a jewel on a young maiden's
hand.
(*Dropping to her knees.*)

I beseech thee, forgo thine
anger and leave wrath to the gods!

SON:  Girl, what has gotten into you.

MEDEA:  Julliard, good brother. For I am no longer bound by rhythms of race or region. Oh, no. My speech, like my pain and suffering, have become classical and therefore universal.

LADY:  I didn't understand a damn thing she said, but girl you usin' them words.
(LADY IN PLAID *crosses and gives* MEDEA *the award and everyone applauds.*)

SON:  (*Trying to stop the applause.*) Wait one damn minute! This my play. It's about me and the Man. It ain't got nuthin' to do with no ancient temples on the Nile and it ain't got nuthin' to do with Hestia's busom. And it ain't got nuthin' to do with you slappin' me across no room. (*His gut-wrenching best.*) It's about me. Me and my pain! My pain!

THE VOICE OF THE MAN:  Walter-Lee-Beau-Willie, this is the Man. You have been convicted of overacting. Come out with your hands up.
(SON *starts to cross to the window.*)

SON:  Well now that does it.

MAMA:  Son, no, don't go near that window. Son, no!
(*Gun shots ring out and* SON *falls dead.*)

MAMA: (*Crossing to the body, too emotional for words.*) My son, he was a good boy. Confused. Angry. Just like his father. And his father's father. And his father's father's father. And now he's dead.
(*Seeing she's about to drop to her knees, the* NARRATOR *rushes and places a pillow underneath her just in time.*)

If only he had been born into a world better than this. A world where there are no well-worn couches and no well-worn Mamas and nobody over emotes.

If only he had been born into an all-black musical.
(*A song intro begins.*)

Nobody ever dies in an all-black musical.
(MEDEA *and* LADY IN PLAID *pull out church fans and begin to fan themselves.*)

MAMA: (*Singing a soul-stirring gospel.*)
OH WHY COULDN'T HE
BE BORN
INTO A SHOW WITH LOTS OF
SINGING
AND DANCING

I SAY WHY
COULDN'T HE
BE BORN

LADY: Go ahead hunny. Take your time.

MAMA:
INTO A SHOW WHERE EVERYBODY
IS HAPPY

NARRATOR/MEDEA: Preach! Preach!

MAMA:
OH WHY COULDN'T HE BE BORN
WITH THE CHANCE
TO SMILE A LOT AND SING AND
DANCE
OH WHY
OH WHY

OH WHY
COULDN'T HE
BE BORN
INTO AN ALL-BLACK SHOW
WOAH-WOAH

(*The* CAST *joins in, singing do-wop gospel background to* MAMA'S *lament.*)

OH WHY
COULDN'T HE
BE BORN
(HE BE BORN)
INTO A SHOW WHERE EVERBODY
IS HAPPY

WHY COULDN'T HE BE BORN WITH
THE CHANCE
TO SMILE A LOT AND SING AND
DANCE
WANNA KNOW WHY
WANNA KNOW WHY

OH WHY
COULDN'T HE
BE BORN
INTO AN ALL-BLACK SHOW
AMEN

(*A singing/dancing, spirit-raising revival begins.*)

OH, SON, GET UP
GET UP AND DANCE
WE SAY GET UP
THIS IS YOUR SECOND CHANCE

DON'T SHAKE A FIST
JUST SHAKE A LEG
AND DO THE TWIST
DON'T SCREAM AND BEG
SON SON SON
GET UP AND DANCE

GET
GET UP
GET UP AND
GET UP AND DANCE—ALL RIGHT!
GET UP AND DANCE—ALL RIGHT!
GET UP AND DANCE!

(WALTER-LEE-BEAU-WILLIE *springs to life and joins in the dancing. A foot-stomping, hand-clapping production number takes off, which encompasses a myriad of black-Broadwayesque dancing styles—shifting speeds and styles with exuberant abandonment.*)

MAMA: (*Bluesy*)
> WHY COULDN'T HE BE BORN INTO
> AN ALL-BLACK SHOW

CAST:
> WITH SINGING AND DANCING

MAMA: BLACK SHOW
(MAMA *scats and the dancing becomes manic and just a little too desperate too please.*)

CAST:
> WE GOTTA DANCE
> WE GOTTA DANCE
> GET UP GET UP GET UP AND DANCE
> WE GOTTA DANCE
> WE GOTTA DANCE
> GOTTA DANCE!

(*Just at the point the dancing is about to become violent, the cast freezes and pointedly, simply sings:*)

> IF WE WANT TO LIVE
> WE HAVE GOT TO
> WE HAVE GOT TO
> DANCE . . . AND DANCE . . . AND
> DANCE . . .

(*As they continue to dance with zombie-like frozen smiles and faces, around them images of coon performers flash as the lights slowly fade.*)

## SYMBIOSIS

(*The Temptations singing "My Girl" are heard as lights reveal a* BLACK MAN *in corporate dress standing before a large trash can throwing objects from a Saks Fifth Avenue bag into it. Circling around him with his every emotion on his face is* THE KID, *who is dressed in a late-sixties street style. His moves are slightly heightened. As the scene begins the music fades.*)

MAN: (*With contained emotions.*)
> My first pair of Converse All-stars. Gone.
> My first Afro-comb. Gone.
> My first dashiki. Gone.
> My autographed pictures of Stokley Carmichael, Jomo Kenyatta and Donna Summer. Gone.

KID: (*Near tears, totally upset.*) This shit's not fair, man. Damn! Hell! Shit! Shit! It's not fair!

MAN:
> My first jar of Murray's Pomade.
> My first can of Afro-sheen.
> My first box of curl relaxer. Gone! Gone! Gone!
> Eldridge Cleaver's *Soul on Ice.*

KID: Not *Soul on Ice!*

MAN: It's been replaced on my bookshelf by *The Color Purple.*

KID: (*Horrified*) No!

MAN: Gone!

KID: But—

MAN:
> Jimi Hendrix's "Purple Haze." Gone.
> Sly Stone's "There's A Riot Goin' On." Gone.
> The Jackson Five's "I Want You Back."

KID: Man, you can't throw that away. It's living proof Michael had a black nose.

MAN: It's all going. Anything and everything that connects me to you, to who I was, to what we were, is out of my life.

KID: You've got to give me another chance.

MAN: *Fingertips Part 2.*

KID: Man, how can you do that? That's vintage Stevie Wonder.

MAN: You want to know how, Kid? You want to know how? Because my survival depends on it. Whether you know it or not, the Ice Age is upon us.

KID: (*Jokingly*) Man, what the hell you talkin' about. It's 95 damn degrees.

MAN: The climate is changing, Kid, and either you adjust or you end up extinct. A sociological dinosaur. Do you understand what I'm trying to tell you? King Kong would have made it to the top if only he had taken the elevator. Instead he brought attention to his struggle and ended up dead.

KID: (*Pleading*) I'll change. I swear I'll change. I'll maintain a low profile. You won't even know I'm around.

**MAN:**  If I'm to become what I'm to become then you've got to go. . . . I have no history. I have no past.

**KID:**  Just like that?

**MAN:**  (*Throwing away a series of buttons.*) Free Angela! Free Bobby! Free Huey, Duey, and Louie! U.S. out of Viet Nam. U.S. out of Cambodia. U.S. out of Harlem, Detroit, and Newark. Gone! . . . The Temptations Greatest Hits!

**KID:**  (*Grabbing the album.*) No!!!

**MAN:**  Give it back, Kid.

**KID:**  No.

**MAN:**  I said give it back!

**KID:**  No. I can't let you trash this. Johnny man, it contains fourteen classic cuts by the tempting Temptations. We're talking, "Ain't Too Proud to Beg," "Papa Was a Rolling Stone," "My Girl."

**MAN:**  (*Warning*) I don't have all day.

**KID:**  For God's sake, Johnny man, "My Girl" is the jam to end all jams. It's what we are. Who we are. It's a way of life. Come on, man, for old times sake. (*Singing*)

I GOT SUNSHINE ON A CLOUDY DAY
DUM-DA-DUM-DA-DUM-DA-DUM
AND WHEN IT'S COLD OUTSIDE

Come on, Johnny man, sing.

I GOT THE MONTH OF MAY

Here comes your favorite part. Come on, Johnny man, sing.

I GUESS YOU SAY
WHAT CAN MAKE ME FEEL THIS WAY
MY GIRL, MY GIRL, MY GIRL
TALKIN' 'BOUT

**MAN:**  (*Exploding*) I said give it back!

**KID:**  (*Angry*) I ain't givin' you a muthafuckin' thing!

**MAN:**  Now you listen to me!

**KID:**  No, you listen to me. This is the kid you're dealin' with, so don't fuck with me! (*He hits his fist into his hand, and* **THE MAN** *grabs for his heart.* **THE KID** *repeats with two*

more hits, which causes the man to drop to the ground, grabbing his heart.)

**KID:**  Jai! Jai! Jai!

**MAN:**  Kid, please.

**KID:**  Yeah. Yeah. Now who's begging who. . . . Well, well, well, look at Mr. Cream-of-the-Crop, Mr. Colored-Man-on-Top. Now that he's making it, he no longer wants anything to do with the Kid. Well, you may put all kinds of silk ties 'round your neck and white lines up your nose, but the Kid is here to stay. You may change your women as often as you change your underwear, but the Kid is here to stay. And regardless of how much of your past that you trash, I ain't goin' no damn where. Is that clear? Is that clear?

**MAN:**  (*Regaining his strength, beginning to stand.*) Yeah.

**KID:**  Good. (*After a beat.*) You all right man? You all right? I don't want to hurt you, but when you start all that talk about getting rid of me, well, it gets me kind of crazy. We need each other. We are one . . . (*Before* **THE KID** *can complete his sentence,* **THE MAN** *grabs him around his neck and starts to choke him violently.*)

**MAN:**  (*As he strangles him.*) The . . . Ice . . . Age . . . is . . . upon us . . . and either we adjust . . . or we end up . . . extinct. (**THE KID** *hangs limp in* **THE MAN'S** *arms.*)

**MAN:**  (*Laughing*) Man kills his own rage. Film at eleven. (*He then dumps* **THE KID** *into the trash can, and closes the lid. He speaks in a contained voice.*) I have no history. I have no past. I can't. It's too much. It's much too much. I must be able to smile on cue. And watch the news with an impersonal eye. I have no stake in the madness.

Being black is too emotionally taxing; therefore I will be black only on weekends and holidays. (*He then turns to go, but sees the Temptations album lying on the ground. He picks it up and sings quietly to himself.*)

I GUESS YOU SAY
WHAT CAN MAKE ME FEEL THIS
WAY
(*He pauses, but then crosses to the trash can, lifts the lid, and just as he is about to toss the album in, a hand reaches from inside the can and grabs hold of* THE MAN'S *arm.* THE KID *then emerges from the can with a death grip on* THE MAN'S *arm.*)

KID: (*Smiling*) What's happenin'?
*BLACKOUT*

## LALA'S OPENING

(*Roving follow spots. A timpani drum roll. As we hear the voice of the* ANNOUNCER, *outrageously glamorous images of* LALA *are projected onto the museum walls.*)

VOICE OF ANNOUNCER: From Rome to Rangoon! Paris to Prague! We are pleased to present the American debut of the one! The only! The breathtaking! The astounding! The stupendous! The incredible! The magnificient! Lala Lamazing Grace!
(*Thunderous applause as* LALA *struts on, the definitive black diva. She has long, flowing hair, an outrageous lamé dress, and an affected French accent which she loses when she's upset.*)

LALA:
EVERYBODY LOVES LALA
EVERYBODY LOVES ME
PARIS! BELIN! LONDON! ROME!
NO MATTER WHERE I GO
I ALWAYS FEEL AT HOME

OHHHH
EVERYBODY LOVES LALA
EVERYBODY LOVES ME
I'M TRES MAGNIFIQUE
AND OH SO UNIQUE
AND WHEN IT COMES TO GLAMOUR
I'M CHIC-ER THAN CHIC
(*She giggles.*)

THAT'S WHY EVERYBODY
EVERYBODY

EVERYBODY-EVERYBODY-EVERYBODY
LOVES ME
(*She begins to vocally reach for higher and higher notes, until she has to point to her final note. She ends the number with a grand flourish and bows to thunderous applause.*)

LALA: I-love-it-l-love-it-l-love-it!

Yes, it's me! Lala Lamazing Grace and I have come home. Home to the home I never knew as home. Home to you, my people, my blood, my guts.

My story is a simple one, full of fire, passion, magique. You may ask how did I, a humble girl from the backwoods of Mississippi, come to be the ninth wonder of the modern world. Well, I can't take all of the credit. Part of it goes to him. (*She points toward the heavens.*)

No, not the light man, darling, but God. For, you see, Lala is a star. A very big star. Let us not mince words, I'm a fucking meteorite. (*She laughs.*) But He is the universe and just like my sister, Aretha la Franklin, Lala's roots are in the black church. (*She sings in a showy gospel style:*)

THAT'S WHY EVERYBODY LOVES
SWING LOW SWEET CHARIOT
THAT'S WHY EVERYBODY LOVES
GO DOWN MOSES WAY DOWN IN
EGYPT LAND
THAT'S WHY EVERYBODY EVERY-
BODY LOVES ME!!!
(*Once again she points to her final note and then basks in applause.*)

Thank you. Thank you.

Now, before I dazzle you with more of my limitless talent, tell me something, America. (*Musical underscoring*) Why has it taken you so long to recognize my artistry? Mother France opened her loving arms and Lala came running. All over the world Lala was embraced. But here, ha! You spat at Lala. Was I too exotic? Too much woman, or what?

Diana Ross you embrace. A two-bit no-body from Detroit, of all places. Now, I'm not knocking la Ross. She does the best she can with the little she has. (*She laughs.*) But the Paul la Robesons, the James la Baldwins, the Josephine la Baker's, who was my godmother you know. The Lala Lamazing Grace's you kick out. You drive . . .

AWAY
I AM GOING AWAY
HOPING TO FIND A BETTER DAY
WHAT DO YOU SAY
HEY HEY
I AM GOING AWAY
AWAY

(**LALA**, *caught up in the drama of the song, doesn't see* **ADMONIA**, *her maid, stick her head out from offstage.*)

(*Once she is sure* **LALA** *isn't looking, she wheels onto stage right* **FLO'RANCE**, **LALA'S** *lover, who wears a white mask/blonde hair. He is gagged and tied to a chair.* **ADMONIA** *places him on stage and then quickly exits.*)

**LALA:**

AU REVOIR—JE VAIS PARTIER
MAINTENANT
JE VEUX DIRE MAINTENANT
AU REVOIR
AU REVOIR
AU REVOIR
AU REVOIR
A-MA-VIE

(*On her last note, she sees* **FLO'RANCE** *and, in total shock, crosses to him.*)

**LALA:** Flo'rance, what the hell are you doing out here, looking like that. I haven't seen you for three days and you decide to show up now?
(*He mumbles.*)

I don't want to hear it!
(*He mumbles.*)

I said shut up!
(**ADMONIA** *enters from stage right and has a letter opener on a silver tray.*)

**ADMONIA:** Pst!
(**LALA**, *embarrassed by the presence of* **AD-MONIA** *on stage, smiles apologetically at the audience.*)

**LALA:** Un momento.
(*She then pulls* **ADMONIA** *to the side.*)

**LALA:** Darling, have you lost your mind coming on-stage while I'm performing. And what have you done to Flo'rance? When I asked you to keep him tied up, I didn't mean to tie him up.
(**ADMONIA** *gives her the letter opener.*)

**LALA:** Why are you giving me this? I have no letters to open. I'm in the middle of my American debut. Admonia, take Flo'rance off this stage with you! Admonia!
(**ADMONIA** *is gone.* **LALA** *turns to the audience and tries to make the best of it.*)

**LALA:** That was Admonia, my slightly over-weight black maid, and this is Flo'rance, my amour. I remember how we met, don't you Flo'rance. I was sitting in a café on the Left Bank, when I looked up and saw the most beautiful man staring down at me.

"Who are you," he asked. I told him my name . . . whatever my name was back then. Yes, I told him my name and he said, "No, that cannot be your name. Your name should dance the way your eyes dance and your lips dance. Your name should fly, like Lala." And the rest is la history.

Flo'rance molded me into the woman I am today. He is my Svengali, my reality, my all. And I thought I was all to him, until we came here to America, and he fucked that bitch. Yeah, you fucked 'em all. Anything black and breathing. And all this time, I thought you loved me for being me. (*She holds the letter opener to his neck.*)

Well, you may think you made me, but I'll have you know I was who I was, whoever that was, long before you made me what I am. So there! (*She stabs him and breaks into song.*)

OH, LOVE CAN DRIVE A WOMAN TO
MADNESS
TO PAIN AND SADNESS
I KNOW
BELIEVE ME I KNOW
I KNOW
I KNOW

(LALA *sees what she's done and is about to scream but catches herself and tries to play it off.*)

LALA: Moving right along.

(ADMONIA *enters with a telegram on a tray.*)

ADMONIA: Pst.

LALA: (*Anxious/hostile*) What is it now?

(ADMONIA *hands* LALA *a telegram.*)

LALA: (*Excited*) Oh, la telegram from one of my fans and the concert isn't even over yet. Get me the letter opener. It's in Flo'rance.

(ADMONIA *hands* LALA *the letter opener.*)

LALA: Next I am going to do for you my immortal hit song, "The Girl Inside." But first we open the telegram. (*She quickly reads it and is outraged.*) What! Which pig in la audience wrote this trash? (*Reading*) "Dear Sadie, I'm so proud. The show's wonderful, but talk less and sing more. Love, Mama."

First off, no one calls me Sadie. Sadie died the day Lala was born. And secondly, my Mama's dead. Anyone who knows anything about Lala Lamazing Grace knows that my mother and Josephine Baker were French patriots together. They infiltrated a carnival rumored to be the center of Nazi intelligence, disguised as Hottentot Siamese twins. You may laugh but it's true.

Mama died a heroine. It's all in my autobiography, "Voilá Lala!" So whoever sent this telegram is a liar!

(ADMONIA *promptly presents her with another telegram.*)

LALA: No doubt an apology. (*Reading*) "Dear Sadie, I'm not dead. P.S. Your child misses you." What? (*She squares off at the audience.*) Well, now, that does it! If you are my mother, which you are not. And this alleged child is my child, then that would mean I am a mother and I have never given birth. I don't know nothin' 'bout birthin' no babies! (*She laughs.*) Lala made a funny.

So whoever sent this, show me the child! Show me!

(ADMONIA *offers another telegram.*)

LALA: (*To* ADMONIA) You know you're gonna get fired! (*She reluctantly opens it.*) "The child is in the closet." What closet?

ADMONIA: Pst.

(ADMONIA *pushes a button and the center wall unit revolves around to reveal a large black door.* ADMONIA *exits, taking* FLO'RANCE *with her, leaving* LALA *alone.*)

LALA: (*Laughing*) I get it. It's a plot, isn't it. A nasty little CIA, FBI kind of plot. Well let me tell you muthafuckers one thing, there is nothing in that closet, real or manufactured, that will be a dimmer to the glimmer of Lamé the star. You may have gotten Billie and Bessie and a little piece of everyone else who's come along since, but you won't get Lala. My clothes are too fabulous! My hair is too long! My accent too French. That's why I came home to America. To prove you ain't got nothing on me!

(*The music for her next song starts, but* LALA *is caught up in her tirade, and talks/screams over the music.*)

My mother and Josephine Baker were French patriots together! I've had

brunch with the Pope! I've dined with the Queen! Everywhere I go I cause riots! Hunny, I am a star! I have transcended pain! So there! (*Yelling*) Stop the music! Stop that goddamn music.
(*The music stops.* LALA *slowly walks downstage and singles out someone in the audience.*)

Darling, you're not looking at me. You're staring at that damn door. Did you pay to stare at some fucking door or be mesmerized by my talent?
(*To the whole audience:*)

Very well! I guess I am going to have to go to the closet door, fling it open, in order to dispell all the nasty little thoughts these nasty little telegrams have planted in your nasty little minds. (*Speaking directly to someone in the audience.*) Do you want me to open the closet door? Speak up, darling, this is live. (*Once she gets the person to say "yes."*) I will open the door, but before I do, let me tell you bastards one last thing. To hell with coming home and to hell with lies and insinuations!
(LALA *goes into the closet and after a short pause comes running out, ready to scream, and slams the door. Traumatized to the point of no return, she tells the following story as if it were a jazz solo of rushing, shifting emotions.*)

LALA: I must tell you this dream I had last night. Simply magnifique. In this dream, I'm running naked in Sammy Davis Junior's hair. (*Crazed laughter*)

Yes! I'm caught in this larger than life, deep, dark forest of savage, nappy-nappy hair. The kinky-kinks are choking me, wrapped around my naked arms, thighs, breast, face. I can't breath. And there was nothing in that closet!

And I'm thinking if only I has a machete, I could cut away the kinks. Remove once and for all the roughness. But then I look up and it's coming toward me. Flowing like lava. It's pomade! Ohhh, Sammy!

Yes, cakes and cakes of pomade. Making everything nice and white and smooth and shiny, like my black/white/black/white/black behiney.

Mama no!

And then spikes start cutting through the pomade. Combing the coated kink. Cutting through the kink, into me. There are bloodlines on my back. On my thighs.

It's all over. All over . . . all over me. All over for me.
(LALA *accidentially pulls off her wig to reveal her real hair. Stripped of her "disguise" she recoils like a scared little girl and sings.*)

MOMMY AND DADDY
MEET AND MATE
THE CHILD THAT'S BORN
IS TORN WITH LOVE AND WITH HATE
SHE RUNS AWAY TO FIND HER OWN
AND TRIES TO DENY
WHAT SHE'S ALWAYS KNOWN
THE GIRL INSIDE
(*The closet door opens.* LALA *runs away, and a* LITTLE BLACK GIRL *emerges from the closet. Standing behind her is* ADMONIA.)

(*The* LITTLE GIRL *and* LALA *are in two isolated pools of light, and mirror each other's moves until* LALA *reaches past her reflection and the* LITTLE GIRL *comes to* LALA *and they hug.* ADMONIA *then joins them as* LALA *sings. Music underscored.*)

LALA:
WHAT'S LEFT IS THE GIRL INSIDE
THE GIRL WHO DIED
SO A NEW GIRL COULD BE BORN
*SLOW FADE TO BLACK*

# PERMUTATIONS

(*Lights up on* NORMAL JEAN REYNOLDS. *She is very Southern/country and very young. She wears a simple faded print dress and her hair, slightly mussed, is in plaits. She sits, her dress covering a large oval object.*)

NORMAL: My mama used to say, God made the exceptional, then God made the special and when God got bored, he made me. 'Course she don't say too much of nuthin' no more, not since I lay me this egg.
(*She lifts her dress to uncover a large, white egg laying between her legs.*)

Ya see it all got started when I had me sexual relations with the garbage man. Ooowee, did he smell.

No, not bad. No! He smelled of all the good things folks never shoulda thrown away. His sweat was like cantaloupe juice. His neck was like a ripe-red strawberry. And the water that fell from his eyes was like a deep, dark, juicy-juicy grape. I tell ya, it was like fuckin' a fruit salad, only I didn't spit out the seeds. I kept them here, deep inside. And three days later, my belly commence to swell, real big like.

Well my mama locked me off in some dark room, refusin' to let me see light of day 'cause, "What would the neighbors think." At first I cried a lot, but then I grew used to livin' my days in the dark, and my nights in the dark. . . . (*She hums.*) And then it wasn't but a week or so later, my mama off at church, that I got this hurtin' feelin' down here. Worse than anything I'd ever known. And then I started bleedin', real bad. I mean there was blood everywhere. And the pain had me howlin' like a near-dead dog. I tell ya, I was yellin' so loud, I couldn't even hear myself. Noooooooo! Noooooo! Carrying on something like that.

And I guess it was just too much for the body to take, 'cause the next thing I remember . . . is me coming to and there's this big white egg layin' 'tween my legs. First I thought somebody musta put it there as some kind of joke. But then I noticed that all 'round this egg were thin lines of blood that I could trace to back between my legs.

(*Laughing*) Well, when my mama come home from church she just about died. "Normal Jean, what's that thing 'tween your legs? Normal Jean, you answer me, girl!" It's not a thing, Mama. It's an egg. And I laid it.

She tried separatin' me from it, but I wasn't havin' it. I stayed in that dark room, huggin', holdin' onto it.

And then I heard it. It wasn't anything that coulda been heard 'round the world, or even in the next room. It was kinda like layin' back in the bath tub, ya know, the water just coverin' your ears . . . and if you lay real still and listen real close, you can hear the sound of your heart movin' the water. You ever done that? Well that's what it sounded like. A heart movin' water. And it was happenin' inside here.

Why, I'm the only person I know who ever lay themselves an egg before so that makes me special. You hear that, Mama? I'm special and so's my egg! And special things supposed to be treated like they matter. That's why everynight I count to it, so it knows nuthin' never really ends. And I sing it every song I know so that when it comes out, it's full of all kinds of feelings. And I tell it secrets and laugh with it and . . .
(*She suddenly stops and puts her ear to the egg and listens intently.*)

Oh! I don't believe it! I thought I heard . . . yes! (*Excited*) Can you hear it? Instead of one heart, there's two. Two little hearts just pattering away. Boom-boom-boom. Boom-boom-boom. Talkin' to each other like old friends. Racin' toward the beginnin' of their lives.

(*Listening*) Oh, no, now there's three . . . four . . . five, six. More hearts than I can count. And they're all alive, beatin' out life inside my egg.
(*We begin to hear the heartbeats, drums, alive inside* NORMAL'S *egg.*)

Any day now, this egg is gonna crack open and what's gonna come out a be the likes of which nobody has ever seen. My babies! And their skin is gonna turn all kinds of shades in the sun and their hair a be growin' every which-a-way. And it won't matter and they won't care 'cause they know they are so rare and so special 'cause it's not everyday a bunch of babies break outta a white egg and start to live.

And nobody better not try and hurt my babies 'cause if they do, they gonna have to deal with me.

Yes, any day now, this shell's gonna crack and my babies are gonna fly. Fly! Fly!
(*She laughs at the thought, but then stops and says the word as if it's the most natural thing in the world.*)

Fly.

*BLACKOUT*

## THE PARTY

(*Before we know what's hit us, a hurricane of energy comes bounding into the space. It is* TOPSY WASHINGTON. *Her hair and dress are a series of stylistic contradictions which are hip, black, and unencumbered.*)

(*Music, spiritual and funky, underscores.*)

TOPSY: (*Dancing about.*) Yoho! Party! Party! Turn up the music! Turn up the music!

Have yaw ever been to a party where there was one fool in the middle of the room, dancing harder and yelling louder than everybody in the entire place. Well, hunny, that fool was me!

Yes, child! The name is Topsy Washington and I love to party. As a matter of fact, when God created the world, on the seventh day, he didn't rest. No child, he partied. Yo-ho! Party! Yeah! Yeah!

But now let me tell you 'bout this function I went to the other night, way uptown. And baby when I say way uptown, I mean way-way-way-way-way-way-way-way uptown. Somewhere's between 125th Street and infinity.

Inside was the largest gathering of black/Negro/colored Americans you'd ever want to see. Over in one corner you got Nat Turner sippin' champagne out of Eartha Kitt's slipper. And over in another corner, Bert Williams and Malcom X was discussing existentialism as it relates to the shuffle-ball-change. Girl, Aunt Jemima and Angela Davis was in the kitchen sharing a plate of greens and just goin' off about South Africa.

And then Fats sat down and started to work them eighty-eights. And then Stevie joined in. And then Miles and Duke and Ella and Jimi and Charlie and Sly and Lightin' and Count and Louie!

And then everybody joined in. I tell you all the children was just all up in there, dancing to the rhythm of one beat. Dancing to the rhythm of their own definition. Celebrating in their cultural madness.

And then the floor started to shake. And the walls started to move. And before anybody knew what was happening, the entire room lifted up off the ground. The whole place just took off and went flying through space—defying logic and limitations. Just a spinning and a spinning and a spinning until it disappeared inside of my head.

(TOPSY *stops dancing and regains her balance and begins to listen to the music in her head. Slowly we begin to hear it, too.*)

That's right, girl, there's a party goin' on inside of here. That's why when I walk down the street my hips just sashay all over the place. 'Cause I'm dancing to the music of the madness in me.

And whereas I used to jump into a rage anytime anybody tried to deny who I was, now all I got to do is give attitude, quicker than light, and then go on about the business of being me. 'Cause I'm dancing to the music of the madness in me.

(*As* TOPSY *continues to speak,* MISS ROJ, LALA, MISS PAT, *and* THE MAN *from SYMBIOSIS revolve on, frozen like soft sculptures.*)

TOPSY: And here, all this time I been thinking we gave up our drums. But, naw, we still got 'em. I know I got mine. They're here, in my speech, my walk, my hair, my God, my style, my smile, and my eyes. And everything I need to get over in this world, is inside here, connecting me to everybody and everything that's ever been.

So, hunny, don't waste your time trying to label or define me.

(*The sculptures slowly begin to come to "life" and they mirror/echo* TOPSY'S *words.*)

TOPSY/EVERYBODY: . . . 'cause I'm not what I was ten years ago or ten minutes ago. I'm all of that and then some. And whereas I can't live inside yesterday's pain, I can't live without it.

(*All of a sudden, madness erupts on the stage. The sculptures begin to speak all at once. Images of black/Negro/colored Americans begin to flash—images of them dancing past the madness, caught up in the madness, being lynched, rioting, partying, surviving. Mixed in with these images are all the characters from the exhibits. Through all of this* TOPSY *sings. It is a vocal and visual cacophony which builds and builds.*)

LALA: I must tell you about this dream I had last night. Simply magnifique. In this dream I'm running naked in Sammy Davis Junior's hair. Yes. I'm caught in this larger-than-life, deep, dark tangled forest of savage, nappy-nappy hair. Yes, the kinky kinks are choking me, are wrapped around my naked arms, my naked thighs, breast, and face, and I can't breath and there was nothing in that closet.

MISS ROJ: Snap for every time you walk past someone lying in the street smelling like frozen piss and shit and you don't see it, Snap for every crazed bastard who kills himself so as to get the jump on being killed. And snap for every sick muthafucker who, bored with carrying about his fear, takes to shooting up other people.

THE MAN: I have no history. I have no past. I can't. It's too much. It's much too much. I must be able to smile on cue and watch the news with an impersonal eye. I have no stake in the madness. Being black is too emotionally taxing, therefore I will be black only on weekends and holidays.

MISS PAT: Stop playing those drums. I said stop playing those damn drums. You can't stop history. You can't stop time. Those drums will be confiscated once we reach Savannah, so give them up now. Repeat after me: I don't hear any drums and I will not rebel. I will not rebel.

TOPSY: (*Singing*)
THERE'S MADNESS IN ME
AND THAT MADNESS SETS ME FREE
THERE'S MADNESS IN ME

AND THAT MADNESS SETS ME FREE
THERE'S MADNESS IN ME
AND THAT MADNESS SETS ME FREE
THERE'S MADNESS IN ME
AND THAT MADNESS SETS ME FREE
THERE'S MADNESS IN ME
AND THAT MADNESS SETS ME FREE

**TOPSY:**  My power is in my . . .

**EVERYBODY:**  Madness!

**TOPSY:**  And my colored contradictions.

*(The sculptures freeze with a smile on their faces as we hear the voice of* **MISS PAT**.*)*

**VOICE OF MISS PAT:**  Before exiting, check the overhead as any baggage you don't claim, we trash.

*BLACKOUT*

## SUMMARY

Farce, a subform of comedy, is a clever, physical variation on humorous activities growing out of social situations. Just as with comedy, it has its serious element. Farce expresses our darkest secrets and fantasies (whether personal or social), such as the license to insult our mother-in-law or defeat the schoolyard bully by acquiring a magical prowess or to assimilate into other cultures or to acquire separate identities. Wolfe states his contradictions in *The Colored Museum* as Topsy sings optimistically of the "power in her madness and in her colored contradictions."

In modern times, farce has achieved an unlooked-for complexity. As a dramatic form, it has expressed the endless variations on an absurd existence without purpose or meaning, or it has taken on the absurdities of the historical process, or it has taken on the icons of the dominant popular culture to test ideas within a theatrical form that permits variations on social history.

Tragicomedy, as discussed in the next chapter, further blends ideas, moods, and dramatic forms in the creation of a dominant writing mode for the second half of the twentieth century.

## NOTES

1. John Mortimer, *Georges Feydeau Three Boulevard Farces* (New York: Viking Penguin, Inc., 1985): 9.
2. Eric Bentley, "Farce," *The Life of the Drama* (New York: Atheneum, 1964): 219–256.
3. Eric Bentley, "The Psychology of Farce," *Let's Get a Divorce! and Other Modern Plays* (New York: Hill and Wang, 1958): vii–xx.
4. Sigmund Freud, *Jokes and Their Relation to the Unconscious*, trans. James Strachey (New York: W. W. Norton, 1963): 170–173.
5. Jessica Milner Davis, *Farce* (London: Methuen & Company, 1978): 97.
6. Eugene Ionesco, *Notes and Counter Notes*, trans. Donald Watson (London: John Calder Publishers, 1964): 26.
7. Janice C. Simpson, "A Jam Session with George C. Wolfe," *TheaterWeek* (October 26, 1992): 18–20.
8. *TheaterWeek* 20–21.

# Fen

## CARYL CHURCHILL

*Caryl Churchill (1938– ), born in London and gradu-
ated from Oxford University, began her career writing
radio plays. Her first theatrical play was produced in
1972 by the Royal Court Theatre in London. Since
then, she has written thirteen plays and is best known
in the United States for* Cloud 9 *(1979),* Top Girls
*(1982),* Fen *(1983),* Serious Money *(1987), and* Mad
Forest *(1990), produced Off-Broadway to critical ac-
claim. She is associated in London with the Joint Stock
Theatre Company, the Royal Court Theatre, and the
Royal Shakespeare Company. She is a 1984 winner of
the Susan Smith Blackburn Prize (for* Fen*).*

*As a writer, Churchill holds a Marxist view of
historical materialism in the creation of plays about the
possibility of change within social structures of priva-
tion and oppression.*

## INTRODUCTION

*Fen*, first performed by the Joint Stock Theatre Group at the University of Essex, England, in 1983, combines Caryl Churchill's
left-wing political views with a darkly funny
theatrical imagination.

*Fen* deals with the punishing effects of
poverty on tenant farmworkers, mostly
women, who labor in the fields of East Anglia and examines their social and economic
oppression and their endurance as well. The
play's origins reflect the methods of the theatre collective with which Churchill had
worked earlier in the creation of *Cloud 9*. In
1982, following a reading of Mary Chamberlain's *Fenwomen*, the playwright, along with
several members of the Joint Stock Theatre
Group, went to a small village in East Anglia
some 100 miles north of London to explore
the lives of these isolated laborers, mostly

women. They spent two weeks living in a
cottage in the Fens where they picked fruit
and vegetables, visited cottages and farms,
listened to the life stories of the villagers, and
talked about ideas for shaping a play. Describing the process, Churchill said,

> *We talked about anger and deference—anger and
> violence, caused by hard conditions of work,
> turned inward to self-mutilation or deflected on to
> people who weren't responsible for it. We also
> talked of women's endurance, and their pride in
> hard work. . . . We wanted to show women con-
> stantly working.*[3]

Slowly, there emerged a 90-minute script in
eleven scenes depicting the lives of twenty
villagers, a Japanese businessman, and two
ghosts. All parts were written to be played
by a cast of five women and one man.

*Fen*—Churchill's original title was *Strong
Girls Always Hoeing*—is named for the once
watery swampland of East Anglia where
centuries ago villagers came on stilts to catch
the eels that swam in the water. Then, during
the time of King Charles II, the land was
drained and the villagers had to learn to sow
and harvest for absentee landowners. Churchill's fen dwellers are descendants of these
first villagers.

*Fen* opens with a fog-shrouded barefoot
boy "from the last century" scaring crows
from the fields, followed by a bitter homage
to British economic policies in 1983 shortly
after the victorious Falklands war that returned Prime Minister Margaret Thatcher's
government to power with a landslide majority vote. A Japanese businessman praises
the "beautiful English countryside," the

"beautiful black earth" of the fens, along with all the multinational conglomerates to which the land now belongs—Esso, Imperial Tobacco, Equitable Life, etc. The executive's discourse on multinational financing is ironically juxtaposed with the conversation of fen women *"working in a row, potato picking down in a field."* This timeless image of peasant labor delineates the economic subjugation and female oppression that has been their way of life for centuries. In this bleak pastoral setting, the characters rely on religion, sex, drink, abusive behavior, or Valium to ease their inability to change their lives from one generation to the next. Fatalism becomes a drug in which the villagers find peace and contentment. Those who try to resist are jeered at as seeking the elusive "bluebird of happiness." Nell, who voices her objections to the exploitative conditions under which the women labor in the onion fields, is called a "witch" and a "morphrodite."

At the play's mid-point (scene 10), Nell narrates a long story about a runaway boy (her grandfather), a living corpse, and a vengeful farmer who skewers an adulterous couple with a pitch fork as they lie naked together in bed, and then axes them to death. The details of the gruesome story strike Nell as "funny" ("Makes me laugh," she says) in an oblique comment upon her own grim existence.

This narrative interweaves the past and the present. The historical context of violence and deprivation for three centuries is repeated in the present-day struggles of Val and Frank, Angela and Becky, Shirley and Susan, and so on. The central story of the play engages Val and Frank. Val leaves her husband and children to live with Frank, but misses the children so much that she returns to them. Unable to bear life without Frank, she leaves the children again but is haunted by thoughts of them. Caught up in a cycle of longing and grief, the couple succumbs to despair. They refuse to adjust to "how things

are," but they cannot escape to London. Val encourages Frank to kill her and he finally does so in a moment of desperation. Then he puts her body in a wardrobe and sits with his back against the door. The ghost of Val enters immediately from the other side of the wardrobe. Val re-enters the play not as a prophetic ghost but as an extended consciousness. In death, she becomes the means by which previously unexpressed hopes and desires are given form. She becomes a storyteller, first for the dead and then for the dreams of the living. She imbues the villagers' lives with hope that extends beyond the present pain and confusion of their economic oppression with all of its attendant problems, such as ignorance, superstition, substance abuse, routine, habituation, violence, hard labor, and unchanging conditions. A nameless female "ghost" (scene 9), who is witness to 150 years of working women's suffering, reproaches the landowner Tewson with the hard life the laborers have had for a century or more. Tewson reproaches himself for selling 150 acres to a conglomerate in order to finance the purchase of new farm machinery. The villagers sing in unison (scene 16) an excerpt from Rainer Maria Rilke's *Duino Elegies*, thereby giving articulate eloquence to their pain:

> *Who if I cried, would hear me among the angelic orders? And even if one of them suddenly pressed me against his heart, I should fade in the strength of his stronger existence. . . .*

With Val's ghost comes a broadening perspective on the possibilities for change in the characters' lives and also a change in the tone of the play. In her dreams, Becky frees herself from her stepmother's abuse. The elderly Nell, like a visual echo of the seventeenth-century fen dwellers who used stilts to cross the watery earth, crosses the stage on stilts, challenging the sun's earthly cycle: "The sun spoke to me. It said, 'Turn back, turn back.' I said, 'I won't turn back for you or anyone' " (scene 21). Different moments from many lives, past and present, come together in single moments of stage time. The transformations from present to past, from waking to dreaming, are characteristic of Churchill's dramatic techniques that stress human continuity in time.

In scene 21, which depicts the death and rebirth of Val, Churchill manipulates the play's tragic content into a more hopeful statement: human beings, as historical agents, can change. Val's ghost is the playwright's catalyst. The vivid longings the characters suppress in their bitter, waking lives find expression in the fantastic flow of dreams from this point on in the play. Becky's nightmare has a happy ending, Nell achieves an unlooked-for mobility in her situation, an old woman's voice is freed for self-expression, and Frank expresses his pain at having killed the only person he loved. Val's ghost assures him that he did what she wanted, but he responds in a new way: "You should have wanted something else." And, following Val's announcement that her "mother [May] wanted to be a singer. That's why she'd never sing," suddenly, *May is there. She sings.*"

In reversing the play out of its tragic context, Churchill emphasizes the women's grim awareness of the conditions that prevent their singing, leaving, and breaking free from abuse. In this context, awareness and a deep sense of personal history are the first steps in freeing oneself from the shackles of economic and social oppression. In *Fen*, Churchill emphasizes the victimization of women and men in a socially and economically deprived class system. Val's ghost is the transforming agent by means of which the villagers' dreams and submerged longings are magically given life.[4] Churchill projects for the audience the emerging awareness that promises to lift the dreamers out of their centuries-old conditions of deprivation, violence, and oppression.

Writing in what is recognized as an especially British tradition of modern tragicomedy, Caryl Churchill, along with such contemporaries as Peter Barnes, Edward Bond, and Howard Brenton, blends a social and political context with hope for the future in plays that are at once realistic and fantastic.

# Fen

As the audience comes in, a **BOY**, alone in a field, is scaring crows with a rattle. There is a thick fog. As time passes he gets weaker. It gets dark.

## SCENE ONE

A fen. A fog. **JAPANESE BUSINESSMAN**.

**JAPANESE BUSINESSMAN:** Mr. Takai, Tokyo Company, welcomes you to the fen. Most expensive earth in England. Two thousand pounds acre. Long time ago, under water. Fishes and eels swimming here. Not true people had webbed feet but did walk on stilts. Wild people, fen tigers. In 1630 rich lords planned to drain fen, change swamp into grazing land, far thinking men, brave investors. Fen people wanted to keep fishes and eels to live on, no vision. Refuse work on drainage, smash dykes, broke sluices. Many problems. But in the end we have this beautiful earth. Very efficient, flat land, plough right up to edge, no waste. This farm, one of our twenty-five farms, very good investment. Belongs to Baxter Nolesford Ltd. which belongs to Reindorp Smith Farm Land trust, which belongs 65% to our company. We now among many illustrious landowners, Esso, Gallagher, Imperial Tobacco, Equitable Life, all love this excellent earth. How beautiful English countryside. Now I find teashop, warm fire, old countryman to tell old tales.

## SCENE TWO

WOMEN and a BOY working in a row, potato picking down a field. **VAL** thirty, **ANGELA** twenty-eight, **SHIRLEY** fifty, **NELL** forty, **WILSON** sixteen. **MRS. HASSETT** forty-five, gangmaster, stands at one end of the field watching them. **SHIRLEY** sings the fireman's song from children's TV programme Trumpton.

**SHIRLEY:** (sings):
Pugh, Pugh, Barney McGrew,
Cuthbert, Dibble, Grub.
Da da diddidi da
Diddidi diddidi diddidi da
Da da diddidi da
Diddidi diddidi da, pom.
(**ANGELA** joins in and sings with her. **NELL** joins in. **VAL** stops and stands staring.)

**NELL:** You all right, girl?
(**NELL** doesn't stop working. **VAL** goes down the field to the end where **MRS. HASSETT** is.)

**MRS. HASSETT:** What's the matter, Val? Took short?

**VAL:** I've got to leave now.

**MRS. HASSETT:** What do you mean, got to leave? It ent three o'clock.

**VAL:** I know, but I'm going.

**MRS. HASSETT:** Who's going to do your work then? Mr. Coleman wants this done today. How does it make me look?

**VAL:** Sorry, I can't help it.

**MRS. HASSETT:** You think twice before you ask me for work again because I'll think twice an' all. So where you off to so fast?

**VAL:** Just back home.

**MRS. HASSETT:** What's waiting there then?

**VAL:** I've got to. I've gone. Never mind.

**MRS. HASSETT:** Wait then, I'll give you a lift halfway.

**VAL:** I've got to go now.

MRS. HASSETT: You'll be quicker waiting. I don't owe you nothing for today.

VAL: You do.

MRS. HASSETT: Not with you messing me about like this, not if you want another chance.

VAL: I'll start walking and you pick me up. (VAL *goes. The others arrive at the end of the field.* WILSON *is first.*)

MRS. HASSETT: What's your name? Wilson? The idea's to get the work done properly, not win the Derby. Want to come again?

WILSON: Yes, Mrs. Hassett.

MRS. HASSETT: Because if you work regular with me it's done proper with stamps. I don't want you signing on at the same time because that makes trouble for me, never mind you. And if I catch you with them moonlighting gangs out of town you don't work for me again. Work for peanuts them buggers, spoil it for the rest of you, so keep well clear.

NELL: Spoil it for you, Mrs. Hassett.

MRS. HASSETT: Spoil it for all of us, Nell.

ANGELA: What's up with Val?

NELL: You've got two colour tellies to spoil.

MRS. HASSETT: Think you'd get a better deal by yourself? Think you'd get a job at all?

ANGELA: Where's she gone? Ent she well?

MRS. HASSETT: She don't say she's ill. She don't say what.

NELL: You paying her what she's done?

MRS. HASSETT: Will you mind your own business or she won't be the only one don't get picked up tomorrow morning.

NELL: It is my business. You'd treat me the same.

ANGELA: Nell, do give over.

SHIRLEY: Come on, Nell, let's get on with it.

NELL: She treat you the same.

WILSON: If I do hers, do I get her money?

MRS. HASSETT: You'll have enough to do to finish your own.

WILSON: Can I try?

MRS. HASSETT: If you do it careful.

NELL: Am I crazy? Am I crazy? Am I crazy?

MRS. HASSETT: I'm off now, ladies and gent. Can't stand about in this wind. I should get a move on, you've plenty to do.

ANGELA: Nell, you're just embarrassing.

(MRS. HASSETT *goes.* SHIRLEY *and* WILSON *have already started work.* ANGELA *starts.* NELL *starts.*)

# SCENE THREE

FRANK *thirty, driving a tractor. Earphones. We can hear the music he's listening to. The music fades down, we hear him talking to himself.*

FRANK: Mr. Tewson, can I have a word with you?

Yes, Frank, what can I do for you lad?

I'm finding things a bit difficult.

So am I, Frank. Hard times.

Fellow come round from the union last week.

Little fellow with a squint?

I don't hold with strikes myself, Mr. Tewson.

I'm not against the union, Frank. I can see the sense of it for your big newfangle farms. Not when people are friends.

Fact is, Mr. Tewson, living separate from the wife and kids I can't seem to manage. It's lucky I'm able to let them stay on in the cottage. The council housing's not up to much eh?

I'm very grateful. But Mr. Tewson I can't live on the money.

You'd get half as much again in a factory, Frank. I wouldn't blame you. But I remember when your dad worked for my dad and you and your brother played about the yard. Your poor old brother, eh Frank? It was great we got him into that home when your mum died. We're like family. We'd both put up with a lot to go on living this good old life here.

I hate you, you old bugger.

(FRANK *hits* MR. TEWSON, *that is he hits himself across the face.* VAL *arrives with* DEB *nine and* SHONA *six. They have a suitcase. She leaves them at the side of the field with the suitcase and goes to speak to* FRANK.)

VAL: (*shouting*) Frank!

FRANK: (*stopping the tractor and taking off his earphones*) What happened?

VAL: Suddenly came to me.

FRANK: What's wrong?

VAL: I'm leaving him. I'm going to London on the train, I'm taking the girls, I've left him a note and that's it. You follow us soon as you can. It's the only thing. New life.

FRANK: Where are you going to live?

VAL: We'll find somewhere together.

FRANK: How much money you got?

VAL: Fifty-six pounds. I'll get a job. I just want to be with you.

FRANK: I want to be with you, Val.

VAL: All right then.

FRANK: What am I supposed to do in London?

VAL: Where do you want to go? You say. I don't mind. You don't like it here. You're always grumbling about Mr. Tewson.

FRANK: He's not a bad old boy.

VAL: He don't pay what he should.

FRANK: He was good to my brother.

VAL: I'm in a panic.

FRANK: Shall I see you tonight?

VAL: In London?

FRANK: Here.

VAL: How can I get out? I'm going crazy all this dodging about.

FRANK: Come and live with me. If you're ready to leave.

VAL: With the girls?

FRANK: With or without.

VAL: He'll never let me. He'll have them off me.

FRANK: Please do. (FRANK *kisses* VAL.)

VAL: I suppose I go home now. Unpack. (*She gets the* CHILDREN *and they go.*)

## SCENE FOUR

VAL *and* DEB.

VAL: You're to be a good girl, Deb, and look after Shona. Mummy will come and see you all the time. You can come and see Mummy and Frank. Mummy loves you very much. Daddy loves you very much. I'll only be down the road.

DEB: I want to go on the train.

VAL: We will go on the train sometime. We can't go now. Mummy's got to go and live with Frank because I love him. You be a good girl and look after Shona. Daddy's going to look after you. And Nan's going to look after you. Daddy loves you very much. I'll come and see you all the time.

DEB: I want new colours.

VAL: You've still got your old ones, haven't you. Lucky we didn't go away, you've still got all your things.

DEB: I want new colours.

VAL: I'll get you some new colours. Mummy's sorry. Love you very much. Look after Shona.

## SCENE FIVE

VAL *and* FRANK *dance together. Old-fashioned, formal, romantic, happy.*

## SCENE SIX

ANGELA *and* BECKY, *her stepdaughter, fifteen.* BECKY *is standing still.* ANGELA *has a cup of very hot water.*

ANGELA: You shouldn't let me treat you like this, Becky.

BECKY: Can I sit down now, Angela?

ANGELA: No, because you asked. Drink it standing up. And you didn't call me mum.

BECKY: You're not, that's why.

ANGELA: Wouldn't want to be the mother of a filthy little cow like you. Pity you didn't die with her. Your dad wishes you'd died with her. Now drink it quick. (BECKY *takes the cup and drops it. She goes to pick it up.*) Now look. Don't you dare pick it up. That's your trick is it, so I'll let you move? I'll have to punish you for breaking a cup. Why do you push me?

BECKY: Too hot. (ANGELA *fills another cup from a kettle.*)

ANGELA: It's meant to be hot. What you made of, girl? Ice cream? Going to melt in a bit of hot? I'll tell your dad what a bad girl you are if he phones up tonight and then he won't love you. He'll go off in his lorry one day and not come back and he'll send for me and he won't send for you. Say sorry and you needn't drink it. (BECKY *starts to drink it.*) Faster than that. Crybaby. Hurts, does it? Say sorry now. Sorry mummy. (BECKY *stands in silence.*) I'm not bothered. No one's going to come you know. No chance of anyone dropping in. We've got all afternoon and all evening and all night. We can do what we like so long as we get your dad's tea tomorrow.

BECKY: I'm going to tell him.

ANGELA: You tell him what you like and what won't I tell him about you.

BECKY: I'll tell someone. You'll be put in prison, you'll be burnt.

ANGELA: You can't tell because I'd kill you. You know that. Do you know that?

BECKY: Yes.

ANGELA: Do you?

BECKY: Yes.

ANGELA: Now why not say sorry and we'll have a biscuit and see what's on telly. You needn't say mummy, you can say, 'Sorry, Angela, I'm bad all through.' I don't want you driving me into a mood.

BECKY: Sorry, Angela, bad all through. (ANGELA *strokes Becky's hair then yanks it.*)

ANGELA: No stamina, have you? 'Sorry, Angela.' What you made of, girl?

# SCENE SEVEN

NELL *is hoeing her garden.* BECKY, DEB, SHONA *spying on her.*

DEB: Is she a man?

BECKY: No, she's a morphrodite.

DEB: What's that?

BECKY: A man and a woman both at once.

DEB: Can it have babies by itself?

BECKY: It has them with another morphrodite. Like snails. But she's never met one yet.

SHONA: Is she a witch?

BECKY: She eats little children, so watch out.

DEB: She talks to herself. That's spells.

BECKY: Angela says she makes trouble.

DEB: She goes in the gang with my mum.

BECKY: She makes trouble.

DEB: Let's get her wild.

BECKY: I hate her, don't you?

DEB: She makes me feel sick.

BECKY: Let's make her shout.

SHONA: Poo bum! Poo bum!

DEB: Shut up, Shona.

NELL: What you doing there?

BECKY: Watching you, so what?

NELL: Come out and watch me close up then.

DEB: Can I ask you something?

NELL: What?

DEB: Have you got — have you got — ?

NELL: What? (*They giggle.*) Well I don't know what you want. Want to help me with my garden? You can do some weeding.

BECKY: That's a funny hat.

NELL: That's a good old hat. It's a funny old hat.

SHONA: Poo bum.

NELL: You watch out, Shona, or you'll have a smack.

DEB: You hit my sister and I'll kill you.

BECKY: I'll kill you. Kill you with the hoe. You're horrible. (BECKY *takes the garden hoe and pokes it at* NELL.)

NELL: Watch what you're doing. Put it down.

DEB: Make her run. Give her a poke.

BECKY: Jump. Jump.

SHONA: Poo poo poo poo.

NELL: You stop that. (NELL *grabs* SHONA, *holds her in front of her, between herself and the hoe.*) Now you mind who you poke. (**SHONA** *screams and struggles.*) Give me my hoe and get on home.

**DEB:** You let her go.

**BECKY:** I'll have your foot. I'll have your eyes.

**NELL:** Right then, you stop in there like a little rabbit. (**NELL** *pushes* **SHONA** *into a rabbit hutch.*)

**SHONA:** Let me out.

**DEB:** Kill her.

**BECKY:** Let her out.

**NELL:** Give me that hoe first. Now shut up, Shona, or I'll have you for tea.

**DEB:** Kill her. (**BECKY** *screams and stabs at* **NELL**, *who ducks and gets her hat knocked off.*)

**NELL:** Now give me my hoe. (**BECKY** *gives her the hoe.*) Give me my hat. (**BECKY** *gives her the hat.*) And get out of my garden.

**DEB:** Shona.

**NELL:** What if I keep Shona an hour or two? Teach you a lesson.

**DEB:** Please let her go.

**SHONA:** Deb, get me out, I can't move, get me out.

**NELL:** Nasty, nasty children. What will you grow up like? Nasty. You should be entirely different. Everything. Everything. (**NELL** *lets* **SHONA** *out.*) You're the poo bum now, all rabbit business.

**SHONA:** Are you a witch?

**NELL:** No, I'm a princess. Now get out.

Girl's Song (**BECKY, DEB, SHONA**)

I want to be a nurse when I grow up
And I want to have children and get married.
But I don't think I'll leave the village when I grow up.

I'm never going to leave the village when I grow up even when I get married.
I think I'll stay in the village and be a nurse.

I want to be a hairdresser when I grow up or perhaps a teacher.
I don't really care if I get married or be a hairdresser.

I want to be a cook when I grow up.
If I couldn't be a cook I'd be a hairdresser.
But I don't really want to leave the village when I grow up.

I don't think much about what I want to be.
I don't mind housework.
I think I want to be a housewife until I think of another job.

When I grow up I'm going to be a nurse and if not a hairdresser.

I'm going to be a hairdresser when I grow up and if not a nurse.

# SCENE EIGHT

**MAY**, **VAL's** *mother, sixty, filling in a pools coupon.* **DEB** *and* **SHONA** *colouring.*

**MAY:** When the light comes down from behind the clouds it comes down like a ladder into the graveyards. And the dead people go up the light into heaven.

**SHONA:** Can you see them going up?

**MAY:** I never have. You look for them, my sugar. (*A long silence.*)

**DEB:** Sing something, nan.

**MAY:** I can't sing, my sugar. (*silence*)

**SHONA:** Go on, sing something.

**MAY:** I can't, I can't sing. (*silence*)

**SHONA:** Mum can sing.

**MAY:** Yes, she's got a nice voice, Val.

**DEB:** Sing something. (*Pause.* **MAY** *seems about to sing.*)

**MAY:** I can't sing, my sugar.

**DEB:** You're no good then, are you.

**MAY:** There's other things besides singing.

**DEB:** Like what?

(*Silence.* **VAL** *comes. They all go on with what they're doing.*)

VAL: Hello, mum. Hello, Deb. Oh Deb, hello. Shona, Shona. What are you drawing? Can't I look?

MAY: They're telling me off because I can't sing. You can sing them something since you're here.

VAL: You want me to sing you something, Deb?

DEB: No.

VAL: Shona? (*Pause.* VAL *starts to sing. She stops.*)

MAY: How long is this nonsense going to last?

VAL: Don't.

MAY: I'm ashamed of you.

VAL: Not in front.

MAY: What you after? Happiness? Got it have you? Bluebird of happiness? Got it have you? Bluebird? (*silence*) What you after?

DEB: Shut up.

VAL: Don't speak to your nan like that.

DEB: You shut up, / none of your business.

MAY: Don't speak to your mum like that. She's getting dreadful, Val. / You've only yourself to blame.

DEB: I'm not. You are. You're getting dreadful.

MAY: You see what I mean.

VAL: You're winding her up.

MAY: I'm winding her up? She was good as gold till you come in. / You better think what you're doing.

VAL: Don't start on me. Just because you had nothing.

MAY: Don't speak to me like that, / my girl, or it's out you go.

DEB: Don't speak to my mum.

VAL: I've not been here / five minutes.

DEB: Don't speak to my nan.

VAL: Shut up, Deb.

MAY: Don't speak to the child like that. (SHONA *screams and runs off. Silence.*) Don't go after her.

VAL: Don't you go after her.

MAY: Deb, you go and look after your sister.

DEB: No. (*pause*)

VAL: I'd better go after her.

DEB: Leave her alone.

MAY: Leave her alone a bit, best thing. (*silence*)

VAL: Never mind, Deb.

MAY: Get one thing straight. It's no trouble having them. They've always a place here.

VAL: I know that.

MAY: I'll stand by you. I stand by my children. (*silence*) I'd never have left you, Val.

VAL: Just don't.

MAY: I'd go through fire. What's stronger that that?

VAL: Just don't.

MAY: What's stronger? (*silence*)

DEB: I'll get Shona.

# SCENE NINE

MR. TEWSON *fifty-five and* MISS CADE *thirty-five, from the City.*

TEWSON: Suppose I was to die. I can claim fifty percent working farmer relief on my land value.

CADE: And thirty percent on the value of your working capital.

TEWSON: My son would still have a bill of—

CADE: Three hundred thousand pounds.

TEWSON: Which I don't have.

CADE: That's the position exactly.

TEWSON: It would mean selling a hundred and fifty acres.

CADE: That's what it would mean.

TEWSON: He could do that.

CADE: It's certainly an option.

TEWSON: Take a good few generations before the whole farm disappears. Eh?

CADE: Alternatively you can give land direct to the Inland Revenue. (*pause*) Alternatively.

TEWSON: I need to be bloody immortal. Then I'd never pay tax. You're bloody immortal, eh? City institutions are immortal.

CADE: The farmers who have sold to us are happy, Mr. Tewson.

TEWSON: Bloody driven to it. Don't have to like you as well. I've read about you, Miss Cade. Moguls.

CADE: The popular farming press unfortunately—

TEWSON: And tycoons. And barons.

CADE: The specialist journals take a longer view.

TEWSON: Who pushed the price of land up?

CADE: Not in fact the City.

TEWSON: I don't want these fields to be worth hundreds of thousands. More tax I have to pay.

CADE: We follow the market. The rise in prices is caused by government policies. Ever since the Health administration introduced rollover relief—

TEWSON: Same old fields. My great great grandfather, Miss Cade. (*pause*) I am a member of the Country Landowners Association. We have ears in the corridors of power. My family are landowners. If I sell to you I become a tenant on my grandfather's land. Our president appealed to us to keep our nerve.

CADE: With us, your grandson will farm his grandfather's acres. The same number of acres. More. You'll have the capital to reinvest. Land and machinery. (*pause*)

TEWSON: My family hold this land in trust for the nation.

CADE: We too have a sense of heritage. (*pause*)

TEWSON: Grandson, eh?

CADE: No reason why not.

TEWSON: When I say nation. You don't want to go too far in the public responsibility direction. You raise the spectre of nationalisation.

CADE: No danger of that. Think of us as yourself.

TEWSON: No problem getting a new tractor then.

CADE: I can leave the papers with you.

TEWSON: Cup of tea? Daresay Mrs. Tewson's made a cake. You want to watch the Transport and General Workers. The old agricultural union was no trouble. We'll have these buggers stopping the trains.

(**MISS CADE** *goes.* **TEWSON** *is following her. He is stopped by the sight of a woman working in the fields, a* **GHOST.**)

TEWSON: Good afternoon. Who's that? You're not one of Mrs. Hassett's girls.

GHOST: We are starving we will not stand this no longer. Rather than starve we are torment to set you on fire. You bloody farmers could not live if it was not for the poor, tis them that keep you bloody rascals alive, but there will be a slaughter made amongst you very soon. I should very well like to hang you the same as I hanged your beasts. You bloody rogue, I will light up a little fire for you the first opportunity I can make.

TEWSON: My father saw you. I didn't believe him.

GHOST: I been working in this field a hundred and fifty years. There ain't twenty in this parish but what hates you, bullhead.

TEWSON: Are you angry because I'm selling the farm?

GHOST: What difference will it make?

TEWSON: None, none, everything will go on the same.

GHOST: That's why I'm angry, bullhead.

TEWSON: I'm going.

GHOST: Get home then. I live in your house. I watch television with you. I stand beside your chair and watch the killings. I watch the food and I watch what makes people laugh. My baby died starving.

# SCENE TEN

*Women onion grading.* **SHIRLEY, NELL, ANGELA, ALICE.**

SHIRLEY: No Val today?

ANGELA: No time for onions.

NELL: Need the money though, won't she?

ALICE: Not surprised she don't come. You shouldn't be surprised.

SHIRLEY: What's that mean?

ALICE: Way you treat her.

SHIRLEY: What's that mean?

ALICE: Everyone's acting funny with her.

ANGELA: She's the one acting funny. Leave her own kiddies. If I had my own kiddies I wouldn't leave them.

ALICE: I know she's wicked but she's still my friend.

SHIRLEY: What you talking about wicked?

ALICE: It was sinners Jesus Christ come for so don't you judge.

SHIRLEY: Who said anything?

ALICE: Outside school yesterday, collecting time, no one said hello except me.

SHIRLEY: I wasn't there, was I. Expect me to shout from the other end of the street. Hello Val! Say hello now, shall I? Hello, Val! That'll cheer her up wherever she is. Altogether now, Hello—

ALICE: Never mind. You're all so—never mind.

NELL: Did I ever tell you about my grandfather?

SHIRLEY: When he was a boy and run away, that one?

NELL: I know you know, you'll have to hear it again.

ALICE: People are all miserable sinners. Miserable.

SHIRLEY: You want to tell Val, not us. Give her a fright.

ANGELA: This one of your dirty stories, Nell? Or one of your frightening ones?

SHIRLEY: It's funny.

NELL: He used to swear this really happened. When he was ten his mother died in childbirth, and his father soon got a woman in he said was a housekeeper, but she slept with him from the first night. My grandfather hated her and she hated him, and she'd send him to bed without any tea, and his father always took her side. So after a few months of this, early one morning when his father had gone to work but she wasn't up yet, he took some bread and some cold tea and he run off. He walked all day and it got real dark and he was frit as hell. There was no houses on the road, just an old green drove sometimes going off towards the coast, so he thought he'd have to sleep by the road. Then he sees a little light shining so he set off down the drove that led to it and he comes to an old stone house. So he knocks on the door and the woman comes, and she'd a candlestick in one hand and a big old copper stick in the other. But when she sees it's only a boy she says come in and she makes him sit by the fire and gives him a bowl of hot milk with some fat bacon in it and a hunk of brown bread. Then she says, 'Me and my husband are going out but you can sleep by the fire. But you must stay here in the kitchen,' she says, 'whatever you do, you mustn't go through that door,' and she points to the door at the back of the kitchen. Then her husband came and said that the pony trap was ready and he didn't look too pleased to see the boy but he didn't say nothing and off they went for their night out. So he sat by the fire and sat by the fire, and he thought I'll just take a look through that door. So he turned the handle but it was locked. And he saw a key lay on the dresser and he tried it and slowly opened the door, and then he wished he hadn't. There was a candle in the window which was the light he'd seen, and a long table, and on the table was a coffin with the lid off, and inside the coffin there was a body. And he was just going to shut the door and hurry back by the fire when the body in the coffin sat up and opened its eyes, and said, 'Who are you boy?' Oh he were petrified. But the body said, 'Don't be afraid, I'm not dead.' He said, 'Where have they gone?' meaning the woman and the husband. When he heard they were out he got out of the coffin and come in the kitchen and made some cocoa. Then he told my grandfather his missus had been having an affair with the chap from the next smallholding, and she was trying to get rid of him by putting rat poison in his food, and he'd fed it to some pigeons and they'd died. So what he'd done, he'd pretended to die, and she'd told the doctor he'd had a heart attack, and he'd been put in the coffin. And before that he'd sold the farm without telling the wife and had the money safe in the bank under another name. So he give my grandfather a screwdriver and said when the couple came home and screwed down the coffin, after they was in bed he was to unscrew it again. So he went back by the fire and pretended to be asleep, and he heard them screw up the coffin and laughing about how they'd got the old man's farm and kissing, and later he got the old fellow out and he were real glad because he said he wanted a pee so bad he could almost taste it. Then he got a large two tined pitchfork and a pickaxe handle and he said, 'Come on it's time to go.' My grandfather thought they were going to leave, but the old fellow crept upstairs, and gave the boy the candle and the pickaxe handle to carry, and he crept up and opened the door of the bedroom. There was the couple lying close together, completely naked and fast asleep. Then suddenly he raised the pitchfork and brung it down as hard as he could directly over their bare stomachs, so they were sort of stitched together. They screamed and screamed and he grabbed the pickaxe handle off of my grandfather and clubbed them on their heads till they lay still. Then he gets the man and takes him downstairs and puts him in the coffin and screws it up. He says, 'They'll bury him tomorrow and think it's me, and when they find her dead they'll know she was out drinking with her fellow and they'll think he killed her and done a bunk, so the police won't be looking for me,' he said, 'they'll be looking for him. And I'm going to start a new life in London or Australia, and if you talk about it I'll find you and slit your throat from ear to ear.' And he never did till he was so old he knew the old man must be dead, and even then he waited a good few years more, and I was the first person he ever told. The old fellow gave my grandfather a gold sovereign and told him to walk west and look for a job on a farm over that way, so he walked five days and slept five nights in barns, and got a job on a farm near Doncaster.

ANGELA: He never heard no more about it?

NELL: If it was in the paper he wouldn't know because he couldn't read. He never heard nothing about it, and his father never found him neither.

ALICE: You said it was funny, Shirley.

ANGELA: I don't reckon it's true.

SHIRLEY: Funny if it is true, eh Nell?

NELL: I believe it all right. Why not? There's harder things to believe than that. Makes me laugh.

# SCENE ELEVEN

SHIRLEY *working in the house. She goes from one job to another, ironing, mending, preparing dinner, minding a baby.* VAL *is there, not doing anything.* SHIRLEY *never stops throughout the scene.*

VAL: I made a cake Deb always likes and I had to throw half of it away. Frank and I don't like cake.

SHIRLEY: You're bound to miss them.

VAL: I do see them. (*silence*) It's right he should keep them. I see that. It's not his fault. He's a good father. It's better for them to stay in their own home. Frank's only got the one room. It makes sense. It's all for the best.

SHIRLEY: At harvest dad'd say, 'Come on, Shirley, you're marker.' Then if the shock fell over, 'Who's the marker?' I'd say, 'I'll go outside, let someone else be marker,' but he wouldn't let me. And leading the horse. 'What if he treads on my feet?' I never could work in front of a horse. Many's the time they'd bolt up the field. My mother wouldn't let me off. 'Just get on with it, Shirley.'

VAL: Can I help with something?

SHIRLEY: Thank you but I know how I like it. (*silence.*)

VAL: Is that Mary's baby?

SHIRLEY: No, it's Susan's.

VAL: You've so many grandchildren I lose track.

SHIRLEY: I'll be a great-grandmother next.

VAL: What, Sukey's never?

SHIRLEY: No, but she's sixteen now and I was a grandmother at thirty-two. (*silence*) Same thing when I went into service. I was fifteen and I hated it. They had me for a week's trial and I could have gone home at the end of it but I didn't want my mother to think she'd bred a gibber. Stayed my full year. (*silence*) I don't think she will somehow, Sukey. She's got green hair. Shocks her mother. Woken up, have we? (SHIRLEY *picks up the baby. Silence.*)

VAL: I can't remember what they look like.

SHIRLEY: You see them every other day.

VAL: I don't think I can have looked at them when I had them. I was busy with them all the time so I didn't look. Now when I meet them I really stare. But they're not the same.

SHIRLEY: You've too much time on your hands. You start thinking. Can't think

when you're working in the field can you? It's work work work, then you think, 'I wonder what the time is,' and it's dinnertime. Then you work again and you think, 'I wonder if it's time to go home,' and it is. Mind you, if I didn't need the money I wouldn't do any bugger out of a job.

VAL: Sukey's a freak round here but if she went to a city she wouldn't be, not so much. And I wouldn't.

SHIRLEY: You can take the baby off me if you want to do something. (VAL *takes the baby.*) We have to have something to talk about, Val, you mustn't mind if it's you. We'll soon stop. Same things people do in cities get done here, we're terrible here, you're the latest that's all. If it's what you want, get on with it. Frank left his wife two years ago and everyone's got used to that. What I can't be doing with is all this fuss you're making.

VAL: I can't hold the baby, it makes me cry. I'll do the ironing.

SHIRLEY: Give her here then. You don't want to be so soft. If you can't stop away from them, go back to them.

VAL: I can't leave Frank.

SHIRLEY: (*to the baby*) Nothing's perfect is it, my popper? There's a good girl.
(SHIRLEY's *husband* GEOFFREY, *sixty, comes in. By the end of the scene he has had the soup she prepared.*)

GEOFFREY: Dinner ready?

SHIRLEY: Just about.

VAL: Hello, Geoffrey.

GEOFFREY: Could do with some dinner.

SHIRLEY: Ent you got a civil tongue?

GEOFFREY: I don't hold you personally responsible, Val. You're a symptom of the times. Everything's changing, everything's going down. Strikes, militants, I see the Russians behind it. / All the boys want to do today

SHIRLEY: You expect too much Val. Till Susan was fifteen I never went out. Geoffrey wouldn't either, he wouldn't go to the pub without me. 'She's mine as much as yours', he say, I've

GEOFFREY: is drive their bikes and waste petrol. When we went to school we got beaten and when we got home we got beaten again. They don't want to work today.

SHIRLEY: as much right to stop in as what you have. (*pause*) Lived right out on the fen till ten years ago. You could stand at the door with your baby in your arms and not see a soul from one week's end to the next. / Delivery van come once a week. My sister come at Christmas.

GEOFFREY: Don't talk to me about unemployment. They've got four jobs. Doing other people out of jobs. Being a horseman was proper work, but all your Frank does is sit on a tractor. Sitting down's not work. Common market takes all the work. (*pause*) Only twenty in church on Sunday. Declining morals all round. Not like in the war. Those French sending rockets to the Argies, forgotten what we did for them I should think. / Common-market's a good thing for stopping wars.

SHIRLEY: I remember dad said to mum one Bank Holiday, 'Do you want go to out?' 'Yes please,' she said. 'Right,' he said, 'We'll go and pick groundsel.'

GEOFFREY: We had terrible times. If I had cracked tomatoes for my tea / I

SHIRLEY: It's easy living here like I do now.

GEOFFREY: thought I was lucky. So why shouldn't you have terrible times? Who are all these people / who come and live

SHIRLEY: Your biked be mud right up to the middle of the wheel.

GEOFFREY: here to have fun? I don't know anybody. Nobody does. Makes me wild. / My mother was glad she could

SHIRLEY: I'd think, 'If anything's after me it'll have to pedal.'

GEOFFREY: keep us alive, that's all. I'm growing Chinese radishes. I've never eaten Chinese food and I never will. Friend of mine grows Japanese radishes and takes them to Bradford, tries to sell them to the Pakis. Pakis don't want them. You want to pull yourself together, girl, that's what you want to do.

# SCENE TWELVE

*Women working down the field, stone picking. Bad weather.* SHIRLEY, VAL, ANGELA, BECKY, NELL.

SHIRLEY: (*sings*):
Who would true valour see
Let him come hither.
One here will constant be
Come wind come weather.
There's no discouragement
Shall make him once relent
His first avowed intent
To be a pilgrim.
(*It's hard singing in the wind. She's out of breath. No one joins in. A military plane flies over, very loud. Only* NELL *looks up. They go on working.* MR. TEWSON *comes out to watch.*)

NELL: Sod this.

ANGELA: Keep up, Beck. (*They reach the end of the field one by one and stop.*)

TEWSON: You're good workers, I'll say that for you.

NELL: Thank you very much.

TEWSON: Better workers than men. I've seen women working in my fields with icicles on their faces. I admire that.

SHIRLEY: Better than men all right.

NELL: Bloody fools, that's all.

ANGELA: What you crying for, Beck?

BECKY: I'm not.

SHIRLEY: Cold are you?

BECKY: No.

NELL: I am and so are you. What's going to makes us feel better? Sun going to come out? You going to top yourself, Tewson, like that farmer over Chatteris?

TEWSON: She's funny in the head, isn't she.

ANGELA: She likes a joke.

TEWSON: Better watch her tongue.

SHIRLEY: She's a good worker, Mr. Tewson, she don't do no harm.

NELL: Don't I though. Don't I do harm. I'll do you some harm one of these days, you old bugger.

ANGELA: What you made of, Becky?

SHIRLEY: You'll get used to it.

BECKY: I want to be a hairdresser.

TEWSON: That was a friend of mine you were speaking of. He found out he had six months to live. So he sold his orchards without telling anyone. Then before he started to suffer he took his life. Never said a word to his family. Carried it out alone, very bravely. I think that's a tragedy.

SHIRLEY: Well it is, yes.

TEWSON: Might clear up tonight. (TEWSON goes.)

NELL: Best hope if they all top themselves. Start with the queen and work down and I'll tell them when to stop. (VAL has only now finished her piece.)

SHIRLEY: All right, Val?

NELL: What's wrong with you?

VAL: Nothing.

NELL: Slows you up a lot for nothing.

VAL: It's like thick nothing. I can't get on. Makes my arms and legs heavy.

SHIRLEY: Still you're back with the kids, best thing. Just get on with it. (VAL starts working again.)

NELL: You think I'm the loony. Is she eating? Sleeping?

ANGELA: She wants to go to the doctor, get some valium. (She calls after VAL:) A man's not worth it, mate. Kids neither.

NELL: I'm not working in this.

SHIRLEY: Don't be soft.

NELL: It's more than rain, it's splinters. Come on, Becky, you've had enough.

BECKY: Can I stop, Angela? Please, mum, can I?

ANGELA: I've had enough myself. Can't work in this.

SHIRLEY: I can.

(NELL, ANGELA, BECKY move off. SHIRLEY starts working again. VAL works too, slower.)

# SCENE THIRTEEN

FRANK and VAL.

VAL: Frank.

FRANK: What?

VAL: I wanted to see you.

FRANK: Why? (silence) Coming back to me?

VAL: No.

FRANK: Then what? What? (silence) I don't want to see you, Val.

VAL: No.

FRANK: Stay with me tonight. (silence)

VAL: No.

FRANK: Please go away.

# SCENE FOURTEEN

Baptist women's meeting. MAVIS, MRS. FINCH, MARGARET. VAL and ALICE arrive. Happy, loving. Song: 'He's Our Lord.'

MRS. FINCH: God is doing wonderful things among us.

MAVIS: I hope you'll stay with us because we all love each other.

ALICE: She's a friend of mine. I brought her.

MAVIS: Alice is a beautiful friend to have. (They sing: 'Thank you Jesus.' ALICE puts her arm round VAL. MRS. FINCH comforts VAL too.)

MRS. FINCH: How lovely to be here again with all my sisters. And specially lovely to welcome new faces. We hope you will commit yourself to the Lord because with him you will have everything. And without him, nothing. This is not a perfect world and we can't be perfect in it. You know how we work cleaning our houses or weeding our gardens, but they're never perfect, there's always another job to start again. But our Lord Jesus is perfect, and in him we are made perfect. That doesn't mean I'm perfect. You know I'm not. I know you're not. But we've plunged ourselves body and soul in the water of God. Next Sunday Margaret will be baptised and she'll testify before the whole congregation. Tonight she's going to share with her loving sisters how she accepted the Lord into her life.

MARGARET: I thought I would be nervous but I'm not. Because Jesus is giving me strength to speak. I don't know where to begin because I've been unhappy as long as I can remember. My mother and father were unhappy too. I think my grandparents were unhappy. My father was a violent man. You'd hear my mother, you'd say, 'Are you all right, mum?' But that's a long time ago. I wasn't very lucky in my marriage. So after that I was on my own except I had my little girl. Some of you knew her. But for those of you who didn't, she couldn't see. I thought at first that was why she couldn't learn things but it turned out to be in her head as well. But I taught her to walk, they said she wouldn't but she did. She slept in my bed, she wouldn't let me turn away from her, she'd put her hand on my face. It was after she died I started drinking, which has been my great sin and brought misery to myself and those who love me. I betrayed them again and again by saying I would give it up, but the drink would have me hiding a little away. But my loving sisters in Christ stood by me. I thought if God wants me he'll give me a sign, because I couldn't believe he really would want someone as terrible as me. I thought if I hear two words today, one beginning with M for Margaret, my name, and one with J for Jesus, close together, then I'll know how close I am to him. And that very afternoon I was at Mavis's house and her

little boy was having his tea, and he said, 'More jam, mum.' So that was how close Jesus was to me, right inside my heart. That was when I decided to be baptised. But I slid back and had a drink again and next day I was in despair. I thought God can't want me, nobody can want me. And a thrush got into my kitchen. I thought if that bird can fly out, I can fly out of my pain. I stood there and watched, I didn't open another window, there was just the one window open. The poor bird beat and beat round the room, the tears were running down my face. And at last at last it found the window and went straight through into the air. I cried tears of joy because I knew Jesus would save me. / So I went to Malcom and said baptise me now because I'm ready. I want to give myself over completely to God so there's nothing else of me left, and then the pain will be gone and I'll be saved.

VAL: I want to go.

ALICE: What? Val?

VAL: I'm going. You needn't.

ALICE: Aren't you well?

VAL: I feel sick.

ALICE: I'm coming, I'm coming. (VAL and ALICE leave. They are outside alone. Night.)

ALICE: It's a powerful effect.

VAL: Yes.

ALICE: I'm glad I brought you, Val.

VAL: I hated it.

ALICE: What do you mean?

VAL: That poor woman.

ALICE: She's all right now, thank the Lord.

VAL: She just liked a drink. No wonder. Can't you understand her wanting a drink?

ALICE: Of course I can. So can Jesus. That's why he forgives her.

VAL: She thinks she's rubbish.

ALICE: We're all rubbish but Jesus still loves us so it's all right.

VAL: It was kind of you to bring me. I loved the singing. And everyone was so loving.

ALICE: Well then? That's it, isn't it? Better than we get every day, isn't it? How cold everyone is to each other? All the women there look after each other. I was dreadful after the miscarriage and they saved my life. Let Jesus help you, Val, because I know you're desperate. You need to plunge in. What else are you going to do? Poor Val. (ALICE *hugs* VAL.)

VAL: Can't you give me a hug without Jesus?

ALICE: Of course not, we love better in Jesus.

VAL: I'd rather take valium.

## SCENE FIFTEEN

VAL *and* FRANK.

VAL: I was frightened.

FRANK: When?

VAL: When I left you.

FRANK: I was frightened when you came back.

VAL: Are you now?

FRANK: Thought of killing myself after you'd gone. Lucky I didn't.

VAL: What are you frightened of?

FRANK: Going mad. Heights. Beauty.

VAL: Lucky we live in a flat country.

## SCENE SIXTEEN

IVY's *birthday.* IVY, *ninety,* MAY's *mother.* MAY, DEB, SHONA.

IVY: Sometimes I think I was never there. You can remember a thing because someone told you. When they were dredging the mud out of the leat. I can picture the gantry clear as a bell. But whether I was there or someone told me, I don't know. Am I ninety? Ninety is it? (*They sing 'Happy Birthday'.*\*) 'Are you the bloody union man?' he'd

\*Note: producers are hereby advised that "Happy Birthday" is a copyrighted song. A licence to produce FEN does not include rights to use this song. Permission should be secured from the owner of the copyright.

say to Jack. 'Are you the bloody union man?' And Jack'd say, 'Are you going to pay him, because if not I'll splash it all over.'

MAY: Kiss your greatnan, Shona.

IVY: Ever kill a mouse, Shona? Tuppence a score. How old are you?

SHIRLEY: Six.

IVY: I come home late from school on purpose so I wouldn't have to help mum with the beet. So I had to go without my tea and straight out to the field. 'You can have tea in the dark,' mum said, 'but you can't pick beet in the dark.' I were six then. Jack didn't wear shoes till he were fourteen. You could stick a pin in. Walked through the night to the union meeting. Fellow come round on his bike and made his speech in the empty street and everybody'd be in the house listening because they daren't go out because what old Tewson might say. 'Vote for the blues, boys,' he'd say and he'd give them money to drink. They'd pull off the blue ribbons behind the hedge. Still have the drink though. You'd close your eyes at night, it was time to open them in the morning. Jack'd be out in the yard at midnight. 'It's my tilley lamp and my wick,' I said, 'you owe me for that, Mr. Tewson.' Chased him with a besom. 'You join that union, Jack,' I said. Nothing I couldn't do then. Now my balance takes me and I go over backwards. There was five of us if you count my brother John that had his face bit off by the horse. 'Are you the bloody union man?' That quack who said he could cure cancer. Took the insides of sheep and said it was the cancer he got out. I didn't believe it but most of them did. Stoned the doctor's house when he drove him out. Welcomed him back with a brass band. Laudanum pills were a great thing for pain. Walk from Littleport to Wisbech in no time. Ninety is it? Old fellow lived next to us, he was a hundred. He'd come out on the bank and shout out to the undertaker lived on the other side, 'Jarvis, Jarvis, come and make my coffin.' 'Are you the bloody union man?' he'd say. 'Yes I am,' he'd say, 'and what about it?' They don't marry today with the same love. 'Jarvis, come and make my coffin.'

# SCENE SEVENTEEN

VAL *and* FRANK. *Outdoors. Night.*

FRANK: What you doing?

VAL: Can't sleep.

FRANK: Come back to bed. I can't sleep with you up.

VAL: I'm not too bad in the day, am I?

FRANK: Go back to them then.

VAL: Tried that.

FRANK: He'd have you back still.

VAL: Tried it already.

FRANK: If I went away it might be easier. We'd know it was for definite.

VAL: You could always come back. I'd come after you.

FRANK: I'd better kill myself hadn't I. Be out of your way then.

VAL: Don't be stupid.

FRANK: The girls are all right, you know.

VAL: I just want them. I can't help it. I just want them.

FRANK: I left my family.

VAL: Not for me.

FRANK: I didn't say it was for you. I said I manage.

VAL: I'm the one who should kill themself. I'm the one can't get used to how things are. I can't bear it either way, without them or without you.

FRANK: Try and get them off him again.

VAL: We've been over that. They're his just as much. Why should he lose everything? He's got the place. We've been over that.

FRANK: Let's go to bed. I'm cold.

VAL: One of us better die I think.

# SCENE EIGHTEEN

*Women playing darts in the pub.* SHIRLEY, NELL, ALICE, ANGELA. FRANK *alone is joined by* NELL.

NELL: How's Mr. Tewson then? (FRANK *doesn't answer.*) You're his right-hand man.

FRANK: I do my job.

NELL: I'm nobody's right hand. And proud of it. I'm their left foot more like. Two left feet.

FRANK: Bloody trouble-maker.

NELL: I just can't think like they do. I don't know why. I was brought up here like everyone else. My family thinks like everyone else. Why can't I? I've tried to. I've given up now. I see it all as rotten. What finished me off was my case. Acton's that closed down.

FRANK: Made trouble there.

NELL: I wanted what they owed me—ten years I'd topped their effing carrots. You all thought I was off the road. You'll never think I'm normal now. Thank God, eh. (NELL *goes to play darts.* ANGELA *joins* FRANK.)

ANGELA: All alone?

FRANK: Just having a pint.

ANGELA: How's Val?

FRANK: Fine.

ANGELA: Never thought you were the type.

FRANK: What type?

ANGELA: After the married women.

FRANK: I'm not.

ANGELA: I got married too soon you know. I think forty-five's a good age to get married. Before that you want a bit of fun. You having fun?

FRANK: No.

ANGELA: Maybe it's gone on too long.

FRANK: Should never have started.

ANGELA: You can always try again.

FRANK: Too late for that.

ANGELA: You've got no spirit, Frank. Nobody has round here. Flat and dull like the landscape. I am too. I want to live in the country.

FRANK: What's this then?

ANGELA: I like more scenery. The Lake District's got scenery. We went there on our honeymoon. He said we were going to live in the country. I wouldn't have come. Real country is romantic. Away from it all. Makes you feel better.

FRANK: This is real country. People work in it. You want a holiday.

ANGELA: I want more than two weeks. You wouldn't consider running away with me?

FRANK: I'm thinking of killing myself.

ANGELA: God, so am I, all the time. We'll never do it. We'll be two old dears of ninety in this pub and never even kissed each other. (ANGELA *goes back to darts.*)

NELL: Tell you something about Tewson. He's got a sticker in the back of his car, Buy British Beef. And what sort of car is it?

FRANK: Opel.

NELL: There, see?

FRANK: He's sold the farm, hasn't he? He's just a tenant himself. He had to, to get money for new equipment.

NELL: So who's boss? Who do you have a go at? Acton's was Ross, Ross is Imperial Foods, Imperial Foods is Imperial Tobacco, so where does that stop? He's your friend, I know that. Good to your brother, all that. Nice old fellow.

FRANK: That's right.

NELL: You don't think I'm crackers, do you?

FRANK: No.

NELL: I don't think you are neither. You cheer up anyway. Don't give them the satisfaction.

FRANK: I'm fine, thank you.

NELL: You never see a farmer on a bike.

# SCENE NINETEEN

ANGELA *and* BECKY. ANGELA *has an exercise book of* BECKY'S.

BECKY: It's private.

ANGELA: Nothing's private from me.

BECKY: Give it back.

ANGELA: Ashamed of it? I should think so. It's rubbish. And it's dirty. And it doesn't rhyme properly. Listen to this.

BECKY: No.

ANGELA: You're going to listen to this, Becky. You wrote it, you hear it. (*She reads:*)

When I'm dead and buried in the earth
Everyone will cry and be sorry then.
Nightingales will sing and wolves will howl.
I'll come back and frighten you to death.

Who? Me, I suppose. Me?

BECKY: No.

ANGELA: Who?

BECKY: Anyone.

ANGELA: Me, but you won't. You've got a horrible mind. (*She reads:*)

The saint was burnt alive
The crackling fat ran down.
Everyone ran to hear her scream
They thought it was a bad dream.

Eugh. Oh this is very touching. (*She reads:*)

Mother where are you sweet and dear?
Your lonely child is waiting here.

BECKY: No, no, shut up.

ANGELA: If you could see what's done to me
You'd come and get me out of here. /
My love for you is always true—

BECKY: Mother where are you sweet and dear?
Your lonely child is waiting here.
If you could see what's done to me
You'd come and get me out of here.
My love for you is always true
Mother mother sweet and dear.

ANGELA: You shut up, Becky. I never said you could. Becky I'm warning you. Just for that you've got to hear another one. Not a word. Now this is dirty. Wrote this in bed I expect (*She reads:*)

He pressed her with a passionate embrace
Tears ran down all over her face.
He put his hand upon her breast
Which gave her a sweet rest.
He put his hand upon her cunt
And put his cock up her.

That doesn't even rhyme, you filthy
child.

He made love to her all night long.
They listened to the birdsong.

What puts filth like that into your head?
What if I showed your dad?
BECKY: No.
ANGELA: Lucky I'm your friend.
BECKY: I'll never do another one.
ANGELA: I don't care. Hope you don't. You
should do one for Frank.
BECKY: I don't love Frank.
ANGELA: You love Frank, do you? I hadn't
guessed that.
BECKY: I don't. I said I don't. You do.
ANGELA: What? Watch out, Becky, don't get
me started. Make a poem about him dy-
ing.
BECKY: He's not dead?
ANGELA: He tried to. He took some pills, but
Val got the ambulance.
BECKY: When? When?
ANGELA: I'll make one.

Frank was miserable and wished he was
dead.
He had horrible thoughts in his head.
He took some pills to end his life.
Too bad he got saved by his silly wife.
Not his wife.
Now he's got to go on being alive
Like all the rest of us here who survive.
I stay alive so Frank may as well.
He won't go to heaven and he's already
in hell.
Poor Frank was never very cheerful
(*She stops, stuck for a rhyme.*)
BECKY: Except when he goes to the pub and
then he's beerful. (*They laugh.*)

ANGELA: Those pills must have made him
feel sick.
And wish he'd never followed his prick.
(*They laugh.*)
BECKY: That's quite good. (*silence*)
ANGELA: Becky, why do you like me? I don't
want you to like me. (*silence*)
BECKY: Poor Frank. Imagine.

# SCENE TWENTY

VAL *and* SHONA.

VAL: Shona. I hoped I'd see you.
SHONA: I've been to the shop for nan.
VAL: What did you get?
SHONA: Sliced loaf, pound of sausages, but-
terscotch Instant Whip, and a Marathon
for me and Deb, I'm going to cut it in
half. The warts have gone off my hands
because nan said get some meat and she
got some meat yesterday and it was liver
and it wasn't cooked yet but she cooked
it for tea but I didn't like it but I liked the
bacon. She cut off a bit and rubbed it on
my warts, Deb said Eugh. Then me and
Deb buried it in the garden near where
nan's dog's buried. There was one here
and one here and another one and some
more. I watched 'Top of the Pops' last
night and I saw Madness. Deb likes them
best but I don't.
VAL: What do you like?
SHONA: I don't like Bucks Fizz because
Mandy does. She's not my friend because I took the blue felt tip for doing
eskimos and Miss said use the wax ones
but I have to have felt tips so I got it and
Mandy says she won't choose me when
it's sides.
VAL: She'll probably have forgotten by tomorrow.
SHONA: Nan says you mustn't cut your
toenails on Sunday or the devil gets
you.
VAL: It's just a joke.

SHONA: My toenails don't need cutting because nan cut them already. What hangs on a tree and it's brown?

VAL: What?

SHONA: Des O'Conker. What's yellow and got red spots?

VAL: The sun with measles.

SHONA: Knock knock.

VAL: Who's there?

SHONA: A man without a hat on.

VAL: What?

SHONA: Why did the mouse run up the clock?

VAL: Why?

SHONA: To see what time it is.

VAL: Shona, when you grow up I hope you're happy.

SHONA: I'm going to be an eskimo. Mandy can't because she can't make an igloo. She can come on my sledge. Nan said to be quick.

VAL: Why does an elephant paint its toenails red?

SHONA: Footprints in the butter.

VAL: No, that's how you know it's been in the fridge.

SHONA: Why then?

VAL: So it can hide in a cherry tree.

SHONA: Deb knows that one. Nan doesn't. (SHONA *goes.*)

## SCENE TWENTY-ONE

VAL *and* FRANK.

VAL: I've got it all worked out. (VAL *pulls up her shirt.*) Look. I marked the place with a biro. That's where the knife has to go in. I can't do it to myself.

FRANK: I can't even kill a dog.

VAL: I've been feeling happy all day because I decided.

FRANK: You marked the place with a biro.

VAL: I know it's funny but I want it to work.

FRANK: It's ridiculous.

VAL: Just say you love me and put the knife in and hold me till it's over. (VAL *gives* FRANK *the knife.*)

FRANK: We don't have to do this. (*silence*)

VAL: Say you love me.

FRANK: You know that.

VAL: But say it.

FRANK: I nearly did it. I nearly killed you. (*He throws the knife down.*)

VAL: Do it. Do it.

FRANK: How can I?

VAL: Just do it. (*silence*)

FRANK: Are you cold? I'm shivering. Let's have a fire and some tea. Eh, Val? (FRANK *picks up an axe and is about to go out.*) Remember—

VAL: What?

FRANK: Early on. It wasn't going to be like this. (*silence*) Why do you—?

VAL: What?

FRANK: All right then. All right. (*He kills her with the axe. He puts her body in the wardrobe. He sits on the floor with his back against the wardrobe door. She comes in from the other side.*)

VAL: It's dark. I can see through you. No, you're better now.

FRANK: Does it go on?

VAL: There's so much happening. There's all those people and I know about them. There's a girl who died. I saw you put me in the wardrobe, I was up by the ceiling, I watched. I could have gone but I wanted to stay with you and I found myself coming back in. There's so many of them all at once. He drowned in the river carrying his torch and they saw the light shining up through the water. There's the girl again, a long time ago when they believed in boggarts. The boy died of measles in the first war. The girl, I'll try and tell you about her and keep the others out. A lot of children died that winter and she's still white and weak though it's nearly time to wake the spring—stand at the door at dawn and when you see a green mist rise from the fields you throw out bread and salt, and that gets the boggarts to make everything grow again. She's getting whiter and sillier and she wants the spring. She says maybe the green mist will make her strong. So every day they're waiting for the green mist. I can't keep them out. Her baby died starving. She died starving. Who? She says if the green mist don't come tomorrow she can't wait. 'If I could see spring again I wouldn't ask to live longer than one of the cowslips at the gate.' The mother says, 'Hush, the bog-garts'll hear you.' Next day, the green mist. It's sweet, can you smell it? Her mother carries her to the door. She throws out bread and salt. The earth is awake. Every day she's stronger, the cowslips are budding, she's running everywhere. She's so strange and beautiful they can hardly look. Is that all? A boy talks to her at the gate. He picks a cowslip without much noticing. 'Did you pick that?' She's a wrinkled white dead thing like the cowslip. There's so many, I can't keep them out. They're not all dead. There's someone crying in her sleep. It's Becky.

**FRANK:** I can hear her.

**VAL:** She's having a nightmare. She's running downstairs away from Angela. She's out on the road but she can't run fast enough. She's running on her hands and feet to go faster, she's swimming up the road, she's trying to fly but she can't get up because Angela's after her, and she gets to school and sits down at her desk. But the teacher's Angela. She comes nearer. But she knows how to wake herself up, she's done it before, she doesn't run away, she must hurl herself at Angela—jump! jump! and she's falling—but it's wrong, instead of waking up in bed she's falling into another dream and she's here. (**BECKY** *is there.*)

**BECKY:** I want to wake up.

**VAL:** It's my fault.

**BECKY:** I want to wake up. Angela beats me. She shuts me in the dark. She put a cigarette on my arm. She's here. (**ANGELA** *is there.*)

**ANGELA:** Becky, do you feel it? I don't, not yet. There's a pain somewhere. I can see so far and nothing's coming. I stand in a field and I'm not there. I have to make something happen. I can hurt you, can't I? You feel it, don't you? Let me burn you. I have to hurt you worse. I think I can feel something. It's my own pain. I must be here if it hurts.

**BECKY:** You can't, I won't, I'm not playing. You're not here. (**NELL** *crosses on stilts.*)

**NELL:** I was walking out on the fen. The sun spoke to me. It said, 'Turn back, turn back.' I said, 'I won't turn back for you or anyone.' (**NELL** *goes.* **SHIRLEY** *is ironing the field.*)

**SHIRLEY:** My grandmother told me her grandmother said when times were bad they'd mutilate the cattle. Go out in the night and cut a sheep's throat or ham-string a horse or stab a cow with a fork. They didn't take the sheep, they didn't want the meat. She stabbed a lamb. She slashed a foal. 'What for?' I said. They felt quieter after that. I cried for the hurt animals. I'd forgotten that. I'd forgotten what it was like to be unhappy. I don't want to.

**FRANK:** I've killed the only person I love.

**VAL:** It's what I wanted.

**FRANK:** You should have wanted something different.

**VAL:** My mother wanted to be a singer. That's why she'd never sing. (**MAY** *is there. She sings. That is, we hear, as if she were singing, a fragment of opera.*)

## SUMMARY

Roman playwrights popularized *tragicomedy*, a mixed dramatic form, which looked ahead to flexible writing conventions where serious plays with averted catastrophes became popular with Shakespeare and others in the seventeenth century. In modern times, tragicomedy, with its mixed moods and varied responses of happiness and unhappiness, anguish and despair, has found favor with playwrights concerned with representing the static, uneventful quality of our lives. In the twentieth century, our perspectives on the causes of human travail have changed. Luigi Pirandello pinpoints the bewildering contradictions in life; Samuel Beckett cites "accursed time"; others blame society or the captalist state. Our avant garde writers have introduced new forms (new ways of dramatizing) and new contents (new ways of perceiving) into the theatre of the mid-twentieth century. These fresh theatrical structures, as observed in Caryl Churchill's *Fen*, often serve a serious ethical and social purpose while they examine our laughter and anger as responses to the condition of being human.

The next chapter discusses the "well-made" writing of the modern theatre in which the certain hands of such skilled playwrights as Henrik Ibsen, George Bernard Shaw, and Lillian Hellman have lifted the mere crafting of entertaining plays into provocative studies of human behavior and modern society.

## NOTES

1. George Bernard Shaw, Preface to *Major Barbara* (New York: Dodd, Mead and Company, 1957): 203.

2. Martin Esslin, "New Form in the Theatre," *Reflections: Essays on Modern Theatre* (Garden City, N.Y.: Doubleday, 1969): 3–10.

3. Geraldine Cousin, "The Common Imagination and the Individual Voice: An Interview with Caryl Churchill," *New Theatre Quarterly*, 4 (February 1988): 6.

4. Geraldine Cousin, *Churchill The Playwright* (London: Methuen, 1989): 46–55.

# The Little Foxes

## LILLIAN HELLMAN

*Lillian Hellman (1905–1984) was born in New Orleans and educated in New York City where her family moved when she was five years old. Before graduating from New York University, she went to work in a publisher's office and began her career as a playreader, chiefly for theatrical producer Herman Shumlin. She began work on a play of her own (The Children's Hour) which Shumlin successfully produced and directed on Broadway in 1934. The play's lesbian themes shocked audiences. In 1939, she wrote the play that many consider her finest, The Little Foxes, which deals with the venality of her fictional Southern family, the Hubbards. Watch on the Rhine (1941), Another Part of the Forest (1946), The Autumn Garden (1951), and Toys in the Attic (1960) were Hellman's further contributions to American drama during a career that spanned 46 years.*

*As were many writers of her generation, including her long-time friend, novelist Dashiell Hammett, Hellman was caught up in the fifties in the investigations of the House Un-American Activities Committee (HUAC) into communist-inspired activities in the entertainment industry. In her testimony before the committee, Hellman made her famous pronouncement about not "cutting her conscience to fit this year's fashion."[4] She refused to name friends and associates who might have had Communist associations. Though exonerated, her career suffered and was only successfully reclaimed twenty years later in a series of memoirs: An Unfinished Woman (1969), Pentimento (1973), and Scoundrel Time (1976).*

*Lillian Hellman's reputation as a dramatist rests on a handful of tightly constructed plays skillfully depicting human perversity and evil. The destructive power of evil—its ability to corrode family relationships and nourish malignant public opinion through innuendo and rumor—is a common theme in her plays. Always a "moral writer," Hellman emphasizes human*

*imperfections and the consequences of evil in finely tuned melodramatic plays in which the strong triumph over the weak in spirit.*

## INTRODUCTION

*The Little Foxes*, which opened on Broadway on February 15, 1939, is generally considered Lillian Hellman's finest play, and actress Tallulah Bankhead's performance as Regina Giddens one of the most outstanding in Broadway history. The twin factors of Hellman's taut writing and the venomous role of Regina have combined to make *The Little Foxes* a popular classic of the American theatre.

The popularity of the play with audiences has lead critics to talk about its brilliant construction, deftness of plot, unexpected turns of fortune, and clever display of human venality. Hellman, by her own admission, set about to write the best play that she could to follow upon the controversial success of *The Children's Hour* and the failure of *Days to Come* (1936). Drawing upon a distant connection with her mother's wealthy relatives living in Demopolis, Alabama, at the turn of the century when the "machine came to the cotton" bringing along with it great wealth and social status to the waiting bourgeoisie, Hellman constructed a play that combined a social awareness of economic and racial conditions in the emerging "new" South of the 1890s. In *The Little Foxes*, Hellman simultaneously indicts and admires the fierce materialism and soulless scheming of the new captains of industry.

*The Little Foxes* is admirably well made. A spacious and elegant 1890's drawingroom is the setting for a display of familial hates, loves, and suspicions that mirror a larger power struggle among the Hubbard siblings, mixed with an American brand of business greed. Hellman drew upon the skeletons in her family closet and into the American past in the South that she had experienced as a child and studied as an adult. The Hubbard family is the centerpiece for a powerful drama of greed and venality that fascinates as it unfolds methodically and relentlessly.

In the first act we learn from servants Cal and Addie that the family is entertaining an important dinner guest from Chicago, and as they enter, we meet the Hubbards one by one. First Birdie, the naive aristocratic wife of Oscar Hubbard, followed by her brutish husband and oafish son, Leo. The central players follow: Regina, who commands the household; Benjamin Hubbard, the family's business tycoon; and their guest William Marshall. They toast their new business partnership of Hubbard Sons and Marshall, Cotton Mills, and to Southern cotton mills in general as the "Rembrandts of investments." Regina dreams of elegant parties in Chicago with no thought for her ill husband, Horace Giddens, who has been in a Baltimore hospital for five months. Regina, like her queenly name, is a commanding presence. She is self-centered, aggressive, and unencumbered by petty sympathies, and she clearly dominates the Hubbards. Only her brother Ben is in her class as a competitor.

With a Scribean precision, Hellman dispenses information in credible conversation, gradually, sparingly, moment by moment, filling in the portraits of the Hubbards as the action unfolds. At the end of the first act, it is clear that the Hubbards need Horace's cash to invest in the new cotton mill. Regina bargains for a larger percentage of the ownership to persuade Horace to come home. The power struggle momentarily shifts from Ben and Oscar to Regina who sends Alexandra to Baltimore to persuade Horace to return.

As the curtain comes down, the battle lines are drawn. Alexandra and Birdie, like the servants, are mere pawns in the game for wealth and power, and Oscar Hubbard is no match for his brother and sister. Hellman's Hubbards fascinate onlookers as they play from the strength of scheming intellect and heartless ambition to rule the earth. The title of the play was suggested by Dorothy Parker from the Biblical text of the *Song of Solomon* (II, 15): "Take us the foxes, the little foxes, that spoil the vines, for our vines have tender grapes." That the Hubbards, and all like them, spoil the earth with their materialism, greed, and just plain meanness is Hellman's message. Nevertheless, they are compelling as they maneuver without conscience or compassion to control the mill's ownership and the great wealth that it promises.

The second act injects the complication of Horace's delay in returning home (he and Alexandra stopped for the night in Mobile) and his refusal to become a partner in the Hubbard scheme to build cotton mills on the backs of poor blacks and whites. This reversal of Regina's expectations intensifies the situation, for time is a factor. The Hubbard share of the money must be in Chicago by week's end. We learn from Leo of an unexpected *secret:* Horace has $88,000 in Union Pacific bonds, in a safe deposit box in the bank where Leo works, that could be "borrowed," for Horace rarely checks the box. As Horace refuses to get rich by cheating poor people, and Oscar and Ben persuade Leo to steal the bonds, we are aware that Hellman is not writing a surface melodrama. Rather, she has hurled the audience into a den of Southern foxes who are fighting, quarreling, competing (as they have done at dinner every Friday night for a lifetime) for high stakes. They are true to themselves, true to their time, and true to their society. They reveal the worst in themselves, and their stark portraits achieve greater clarity outlined against those of Birdie, Alexandra, Addie, and Horace. In the final moments of this emotionally raw second act, Horace alerts us to their more devastating social damage: Their cheap wages, their use of the state's water resources, and their false promises of riches to the laborers will create another slave class for industry and great wealth for themselves.

The third act begins with a momentary lull in the storm as Alexandra, Birdie, and Horace have a quiet family moment together. Yet, the main action is not forgotten. The infamous safe deposit box rests beside Horace, who sets his own strategy in motion. He sends Cal to the bank to ask the director to bring Horace's attorney to the house in the evening. Next, Horace proposes to change his will, leaving Alexandra as his sole heir. Regina returns to learn from Horace that Leo has stolen the bonds and that Horace intends to let the brothers "borrow" the bonds from Regina as a loan. In his new will, Horace will leave only the bonds to his wife. Regina's fury exceeds the rage she displayed in the first act, revealing all of her suppressed feelings for her husband. Horace collapses under her brutal revelations. As he reaches for his medicine, he breaks the bottle and pleads with Regina to send for Addie. Regina does not move as he struggles to climb the stairs to get a second bottle. He collapses and only after he is very still does Regina call for Addie and Cal to send for the doctor.

As Ben and Oscar arrive, Leo forces them to listen to his story about Horace's discovery of the stolen bonds. Regina enters and confronts them with her knowledge of the theft and reveals to the wiley Ben that Horace intended to say that he had "loaned" them the bonds. Regina reminds them that they are safe as long as Horace is alive, but if he doesn't live, she will want seventy-five percent of the Hubbard's share of the mill in exchange for the bonds; otherwise she'll send them to jail. Their quarrel is interrupted by Alexandra's announcement that Horace is dead. Regina is triumphant in this reversal of

fortune and only momentarily shaken by Alexandra's incriminating question: "What was Papa doing on the staircase?" Ben is philosophical about Regina's victory, unlike Oscar and Leo who exit angrily. Ben knows that he has been bested for the moment, but he has a new perspective on their roles in history: "The century's turning, the world is open. Open for people like you and me. . . . There are hundreds of Hubbards sitting in rooms like this throughout the country. All their names aren't Hubbard, but they are all Hubbards and they will own this country some day. We'll get along." With this speech, Hellman puts the Hubbard story in a larger context. Like so many writers during the Depression years, Hellman deplored the evils of unrestrained free enterprise that forced society to live at the mercy of a few greedy men and women.

The battle is over, Regina has won, and the resolution resolves the minor conflict between mother and daughter. Alexandra announces that she will not go to Chicago with Regina but she will go away somewhere. Regina is surprised. As she turns to go up the stairs, she hesitates and asks Alexandra if she would like to sleep in her room tonight. Alexandra counters with: "Are you afraid, Mama?" If she is, Regina does not admit it and disappears into the bedroom alone. Alexandra is seen in the company of Addie as the curtain comes down.

*The Little Foxes* is a highly charged theatrical experience made more so by Hellman's careful ordering of characters and events in which each of the three acts has its emotional peaks, reversals of fortune, and anticipations of more scheming to come. What keeps the play from becoming a mechanical exercise in the manipulation of strongboxes, stolen bonds, spilled medicine, and death on a staircase is Hellman's understanding of human truths. The Hubbards did exist and do exist, they did and do conquer, as we reflect upon the modern financial wizards who have manipulated Wall Street with insider trading and the savings and loan industry for personal gain. We believe the Hubbards' financial and personal machinations because we know human nature and we know the history of our country. Regina, it is true, is a magnificent embodiment of perverse evil: cold, hard, determined, selfish, beautiful, larger than life, yet grounded to the life that made her. Genetic guidance, social conventions, and traditions of marriage and inheritance for women in the 1890s' South have created both a Regina and a Birdie. With Birdie, we observe the Southern aristocracy enslaved by the new breed of entrepreneurs that emerged following the Civil War. A pathetic figure, she merits our compassion and understanding. However, Regina is an admirable member of the tribe of Hubbard who has learned to fight for and to take what she wants without conscience, compassion, or hesitation. She is the new woman that Hellman introduced to audiences in 1939, and Regina has continued to be not loved but admired as a vivid stage portrait. Moreover, unlike the Scribean play, *The Little Foxes* is without its firm moralisms at the play's end. Hellman has provided no reward for virtue, no punishment for vice, the stock in trade for the well-made play and melodrama. Hellman has written an "honest" play without the trappings of the conventional moral ending. She has dared to depict unpleasant characters who suppress their humanity for personal gain and who exist at the play's end with some rewarded, some mildly scathed, but all prepared to fight again another day.

# The Little Foxes

*"Take us the foxes, the little foxes,*
*that spoil the vines; for our vines*
*have tender grapes."*

**CHARACTERS**

ADDIE
CAL
BIRDIE HUBBARD
OSCAR HUBBARD
LEO HUBBARD
REGINA GIDDENS
WILLIAM MARSHALL
BENJAMIN HUBBARD
ALEXANDRA GIDDENS
HORACE GIDDENS

*The scene of the play is the living room of the Giddens house in a small town in the South.*

ACT ONE:   The Spring of 1900, evening.
ACT TWO:   A week later, early morning.
ACT THREE:   Two weeks later, late afternoon

*There has been no attempt to write Southern dialect. It is to be understood that the accents are Southern.*

## ACT ONE

SCENE—*The living room of the Giddens house, in a small town in the deep South, the Spring of 1900. Upstage is a staircase leading to the second story. Upstage, right, are double doors to the dining room. When these doors are open we see a section of the dining room and the furniture. Upstage, left, is an entrance hall with a coat-rack and umbrella stand. There are large lace-curtained windows on the left wall. The room is lit by a center gas chandelier and painted china oil lamps on the tables. Against the wall is a large piano. Downstage, right, are a high couch, a large table, several chairs. Against the left back wall are a table and several chairs. Near the window there are a smaller couch and tables. The room is good-looking, the furniture expensive; but it reflects no particular taste. Everything is of the best and that is all.*

AT RISE: ADDIE, *a tall, nice-looking Negro woman of about fifty-five, is closing the windows. From behind the closed dining-room doors there is the sound of voices. After a second,* CAL, *a middle-aged Negro, comes in from the entrance hall carrying a tray with glasses and a bottle of port.* ADDIE *crosses, takes the tray from him, puts it on table, begins to arrange it.*

ADDIE (*Pointing to the bottle*):  You gone stark out of your head?

CAL:  No, smart lady, I ain't. Miss Regina told me to get out that bottle. (*Points to bottle.*) That very bottle for the mighty honored guest. When Miss Regina changes orders like that you can bet your dime she got her reason.

ADDIE (*Points to dining room*):  Go on. You'll be needed.

CAL:  Miss Zan she had two helpings frozen fruit cream and she tell that honored guest, she tell him that you make the best frozen fruit cream in all the South.

ADDIE (*Smiles, pleased*):  Did she? Well, see that Belle saves a little for her. She like it right before she go to bed. Save a few little cakes, too, she like—

(*The dining-room doors are opened and quickly closed again by* BIRDIE HUBBARD. BIRDIE *is a woman of about forty, with a pretty, well-bred, faded face. Her movements are usually nervous and timid, but now, as she comes running into the room, she is gay and excited.* CAL *turns to* BIRDIE.)

BIRDIE: Oh, Cal. (*Closes door.*) I want you to get one of the kitchen boys to run home for me. He's to look in my desk drawer and— (*To* ADDIE.) My, Addie. What a good supper! Just as good as good can be.

ADDIE: You look pretty this evening, Miss Birdie, and young.

BIRDIE (*Laughing*): Me, young? (*Turns back to* CAL.) Maybe you better find Simon and tell him to do it himself. He's to look in my desk, the left drawer, and bring my music album right away. Mr. Marshall is very anxious to see it because of his father and the opera in Chicago. (*To* ADDIE.) Mr. Marshall is such a polite man with his manners and very educated and cultured and I've told him all about how my mama and papa used to go to Europe for the music— (*Laughs. To* ADDIE.) Imagine going all the way to Europe just to listen to music. Wouldn't that be nice, Addie? Just to sit there and listen and— (*Turns and steps to* CAL.) *Left* drawer, Cal. Tell him that twice because he forgets. And tell him not to let any of the things drop out of the album and to bring it right in here when he comes back.

(*The dining-room doors are opened and quickly closed by* OSCAR HUBBARD. *He is a man in his late forties.*)

CAL: Yes'm. But Simon he won't get it right. But I'll tell him.

BIRDIE: Left drawer, Cal, and tell him to bring the blue book and—

OSCAR (*Sharply*): Birdie.

BIRDIE (*Turning nervously*): Oh, Oscar. I was just sending Simon for my music album.

OSCAR (*To* CAL): Never mind about the album. Miss Birdie has changed her mind.

BIRDIE: But, really, Oscar. Really I promised Mr. Marshall. I—

(CAL *looks at them, exits.*)

OSCAR: Why do you leave the dinner table and go running about like a child?

BIRDIE (*Trying to be gay*): But, Oscar, Mr. Marshall said most specially he *wanted* to see my album. I told him about the time Mama met Wagner, and Mrs. Wagner gave her the signed program and the big picture. Mr. Marshall wants to see that. Very, very much. We had such a nice talk and—

OSCAR (*Taking a step to her*): You have been chattering to him like a magpie. You haven't let him be for a second. I can't think he came South to be bored with you.

BIRDIE (*Quickly, hurt*): He wasn't bored. I don't believe he was bored. He's a very educated, cultured gentleman. (*Her voice rises.*) I just don't believe it. You always talk like that when I'm having a nice time.

OSCAR (*Turning to her, sharply*): You have had too much wine. Get yourself in hand now.

BIRDIE (*Drawing back, about to cry, shrilly*): What am I doing? I am not doing anything. What am I doing?

OSCAR (*Taking a step to her, tensely*): I said get yourself in hand. Stop acting like a fool.

BIRDIE (*Turns to him, quietly*): I don't believe he was bored. I just don't believe it. Some people like music and like to talk about it. That's all I was doing.

(LEO HUBBARD *comes hurrying through the dining-room door. He is a young man of twenty, with a weak kind of good looks.*)

LEO: Mama! Papa! They are coming in now.

OSCAR (*Softly*): Sit down, Birdie. Sit down now. (BIRDIE *sits down, bows her head as if to hide her face.*)

(*The dining-room doors are opened by* CAL.

*We see people beginning to rise from the table.* REGINA GIDDENS *comes in with* WILLIAM MARSHALL. REGINA *is a handsome woman of forty.* MARSHALL *is forty-five, pleasant-looking, self-possessed. Behind them comes* ALEXANDRA GIDDENS, *a very pretty, rather delicate-looking girl of seventeen. She is followed by* BENJAMIN HUBBARD, *fifty-five, with a large jovial face and the light graceful movements that one often finds in large men.*)

REGINA: Mr. Marshall, I think you're trying to console me. Chicago may be the noisiest, dirtiest city in the world but I should still prefer it to the sound of our horses and the smell of our azaleas. I should like crowds of people, and theatres, and lovely women—*Very* lovely women, Mr. Marshall?

MARSHALL (*Crossing to sofa*): In Chicago? Oh, I suppose so. But I can tell you this: I've never dined there with three *such* lovely ladies.
(ADDIE *begins to pass the port.*)

BEN: Our Southern women are well favored.

LEO (*Laughs*): But one must go to Mobile for the ladies, sir. Very elegant worldly ladies, too.

BEN (*Looks at him very deliberately*): Worldly, eh? *Worldly*, did you say?

OSCAR (*Hastily, to* LEO): Your uncle Ben means that worldliness is not a mark of beauty in any woman.

LEO (*quickly*): Of course, Uncle Ben. I didn't mean—

MARSHALL: Your port is excellent, Mrs. Giddens.

REGINA: Thank you, Mr. Marshall. We had been saving that bottle, hoping we could open it just for you.

ALEXANDRA (*As* ADDIE *comes to her with the tray*): Oh. May I *really*, Addie?

ADDIE: Better ask Mama.

ALEXANDRA: May I, Mama?

REGINA (*Nods, smiles*): In Mr. Marshall's honor.

ALEXANDRA (*Smiles*): Mr. Marshall, this will be the first taste of port I've ever had.
(ADDIE *serves* LEO.)

MARSHALL: No one ever had their first taste of a better port. (*He lifts his glass in a toast; she lifts hers; they both drink.*) Well, I suppose it is all true, Mrs. Giddens.

REGINA: What is true?

MARSHALL: That you Southerners occupy a unique position in America. You live better than the rest of us, you eat better, you drink better. I wonder you find time, or want to find time, to do business.

BEN: A great many Southerners don't.

MARSHALL: Do all of you live here together?

REGINA: Here with me? (*Laughs.*) Oh, no. My brother Ben lives next door. My brother Oscar and his family live in the next square.

BEN: But we are a very close family. We've always *wanted* it that way.

MARSHALL: That is very pleasant. Keeping your family together to share each other's lives. My family moves around too much. My children seem never to come home. Away at school in the winter; in the summer, Europe with their mother—

REGINA (*Eagerly*): Oh, yes. Even down here we read about Mrs. Marshall in the society pages.

MARSHALL: I dare say. She moves about a great deal. And all of you are part of the same business? Hubbard Sons?

BEN (*Motions to* OSCAR): Oscar and me. (*Motions to* REGINA.) My Sister's good husband is a banker.

MARSHALL (*Looks at* REGINA, surprised): Oh.

REGINA: I am so sorry that my husband isn't here to meet you. He's been very ill. He is at Johns Hopkins. But he will be home soon. We think he is getting better now.

LEO: I work for Uncle Horace. (REGINA *looks at him.*) I mean I work for Uncle Horace at his bank. I keep an eye on things while he's away.

REGINA (*Smiles*): Really, Leo?

BEN (*Looks at* LEO, *then to* MARSHALL): Modesty in the young is as excellent as it is rare. (*Looks at* LEO *again.*)

OSCAR (*To* LEO): Your uncle means that a young man should speak more modestly.

LEO (*Hastily, taking a step to* BEN): Oh, I didn't mean, sir—

MARSHALL: Oh, Mrs. Hubbard. Where's that Wagner autograph you promised to let me see? My train will be leaving soon and—

BIRDIE: The autograph? Oh. Well. Really, Mr. Marshall, I didn't mean to chatter so about it. Really I— (*Nervously, looking at* OSCAR.) You must excuse me. I didn't get it because, well, because I had—I—I had a little headache and—

OSCAR: My wife is a miserable victim of headaches.

REGINA (*Quickly*): Mr. Marshall said at supper that he would like you to play for him, Alexandra.

ALEXANDRA (*Who has been looking at* BIRDIE): It's not I who play well, sir. It's my aunt. She plays just wonderfully. She's my teacher. (*Rises. Eagerly.*) May, we play a duet? May we, Mama?

BIRDIE (*Taking* ALEXANDRA'S *hand*): Thank you, dear. But I have my headache now. I—

OSCAR (*Sharply*): Don't be stubborn, Birdie. Mr. Marshall wants you to play.

MARSHALL: Indeed I do. If your headache isn't—

BIRDIE (*Hesitates, then gets up, pleased*): But I'd like to, sir. Very much. (*She and* ALEXANDRA *go to the piano.*)

MARSHALL: It's very remarkable how you Southern aristocrats have kept together. Kept together and kept what belonged to you.

BEN: You misunderstand, sir. Southern aristocrats have *not* kept together and have *not* kept what belonged to them.

MARSHALL (*Laughs, indicates room*): You don't call this keeping what belongs to you?

BEN: But we are not aristocrats. (*Points to* BIRDIE *at the piano.*) Our brother's wife is the only one of us who belongs to the Southern aristocracy.

(BIRDIE *looks towards* BEN.)

MARSHALL (*Smiles*): My information is that you people have been here, and solidly here, for a long time.

OSCAR: And so we have. Since our great-grandfather.

BEN (*Smiles*): Who was *not* an aristocrat, like Birdie's.

MARSHALL (*A little sharply*): You make great distinctions.

BEN: Oh, they have been made for us. And maybe they are important distinctions. (*Leans forward, intimately.*) Now you take Birdie's family. When my great-grandfather came here they were the highest-tone plantation owners in this state.

LEO (*Steps to* MARSHALL. *Proudly*): My mother's grandfather was *governor* of the state before the war.

OSCAR: They owned the plantation, Lionnet. You may have heard of it, sir?

MARSHALL (*Laughs*): No, I've never heard of anything but brick houses on a lake, and cotton mills.

BEN: Lionnet in its day was the best cotton land in the South. It still brings us in a fair crop. (*Sits back.*) Ah, they were great days for those people—even when I can remember. They had the best of everything. (BIRDIE *turns to them.*) Cloth from Paris, trips to Europe, horses you can't raise any more, niggers to lift their fingers—

BIRDIE (*Suddenly*): We were good to our people. Everybody knew that. We were better to them than—

(MARSHALL *looks up at* BIRDIE.)

REGINA: Why, Birdie. You aren't playing.

BEN: But when the war comes these fine gentlemen ride off and leave the cotton, *and* the women, to rot.

BIRDIE: My father was killed in the war. He was a fine soldier, Mr. Marshall. A fine man.

REGINA: Oh, certainly, Birdie. A famous soldier.

BEN (*To* BIRDIE): But that isn't the tale I am telling Mr. Marshall. (*To* MARSHALL.) Well, sir, the war ends. (BIRDIE *goes back to piano.*) Lionnet is almost ruined, and the sons finish ruining it. And there were thousands like them. Why? (*Leans forward.*) Because the Southern aristocrat can adapt himself to nothing. Too high-tone to try.

MARSHALL: Sometimes it is difficult to learn new ways. (BIRDIE *and* ALEXANDRA *begin to play.* MARSHALL *leans forward, listening.*)

BEN: Perhaps, perhaps. (*He sees that* MARSHALL *is listening to the music. Irritated, he turns to* BIRDIE *and* ALEXANDRA *at the piano, then back to* MARSHALL.) You're right, Mr. Marshall. It is difficult to learn new ways. But maybe that's why it's profitable. *Our* grandfather and *our* father learned the new ways and learned how to make them pay. They work. (*Smiles nastily.*) *They* are in trade. Hubbard Sons, Merchandise. Others, Birdie's family, for example, look down on them. (*Settles back in chair.*) To make a long story short, Lionnet now belongs to *us.* (BIRDIE *stops playing.*) Twenty years ago we took over their land, their cotton, and their daughter.

(BIRDIE *rises and stands stiffly by the piano.* MARSHALL, *who has been watching her, rises.*)

MARSHALL: May I bring you a glass of port, Mrs. Hubbard?

BIRDIE (*Softly*): No, thank you, sir. You are most polite.

REGINA (*Sharply, to* BEN): You are boring Mr. Marshall with these ancient family tales.

BEN: I hope not. I hope not. I am trying to make an important point—(*Bows to* MARSHALL.) for our future business partner.

OSCAR (*To* MARSHALL): My brother always says that it's folks like us who have struggled and fought to bring to our land some of the prosperity of your land.

BEN: Some people call that patriotism.

REGINA (*Laughs gaily*): I hope you don't find my brothers too obvious, Mr. Marshall. I'm afraid they mean that this is the time for the ladies to leave the gentlemen to talk business.

MARSHALL (*Hastily*): Not at all. We settled everything this afternoon. (MARSHALL *looks at his watch.*) I have only a few minutes before I must leave for the train. (*Smiles at her.*) And I insist they be spent with you.

REGINA: *And* with another glass of port.

MARSHALL: Thank you.

BEN (*To* REGINA): My sister is right. (*To* MARSHALL.) I am a plain man and I am trying to say a plain thing. A man ain't only in business for what he can get out of it. It's got to give him something here. (*Puts hand to his breast.*) That's every bit as true for the nigger picking cotton for a silver quarter, as it is for you and me. (REGINA *gives* MARSHALL *a glass of port.*) If it don't give him something here, then he don't pick the cotton right. Money isn't all. Not by three shots.

MARSHALL: Really? Well, I always thought it was a great deal.

REGINA: And so did I, Mr. Marshall.

MARSHALL (*Leans forward. Pleasantly, but with meaning*): Now you don't have to convince me that you are the right people for the deal. I wouldn't be here if you hadn't convinced me six months ago. You want the mill here, and I want it here. It isn't my business to find out *why* you want it.

BEN: To bring the machine to the cotton, and not the cotton to the machine.

MARSHALL (*Amused*): You have a turn for neat phrases, Hubbard. Well, however grand your reasons are, mine are simple:

I want to make money and I believe I'll make it on you. (*As* BEN *starts to speak, he smiles.*) Mind you, I have no objections to more high-minded reasons. They are mighty valuable in business. It's fine to have partners who so closely follow the teachings of Christ. (*Gets up.*) And now I must leave for my train.

REGINA: I'm sorry you won't stay over with us, Mr. Marshall, but you'll come again. Any time you like.

BEN (*Motions to* LEO, *indicating the bottle*): Fill them up, boy, fill them up. (LEO *moves around filling the glasses as* BEN *speaks.*) Down here, sir, we have a strange custom. We drink the *last* drink for a toast. That's to prove that the Southerner is always still on his feet for the last drink. (*Picks up his glass.*) It was Henry Frick, your Mr. Henry Frick, who said, "Railroads are the Rembrandts of investments." Well, *I* say, "Southern cotton mills *will be* the Rembrandts of investment." So I give you the firm of Hubbard Sons and Marshall, Cotton Mills, and to it a long and prosperous life.

(*They all pick up their glasses.* MARSHALL *looks at them, amused. Then he, too, lifts his glass, smiles.*)

OSCAR: The children will drive you to the depot. Leo! Alexandra! You will drive Mr. Marshall down.

LEO (*Eagerly, looks at* BEN *who nods*): Yes, sir. (*To* MARSHALL.) Not often Uncle Ben lets *me* drive the horses. And a beautiful pair they are. (*Starts for hall.*) Come on, Zan.

ALEXANDRA: May I drive tonight, Uncle Ben, please? I'd like to and—

BEN (*Shakes his head, laughs*): In your evening clothes? Oh, no, my dear.

ALEXANDRA: But Leo always— (*Stops, exits quickly.*)

REGINA: I don't like to say good-bye to you, Mr. Marshall.

MARSHALL: Then we won't say good-bye. You have promised that you would come and let me show you Chicago. Do I have to make you promise again?

REGINA (*Looks at him as he presses her hand*): I promise again.

MARSHALL (*Touches her hand again, then moves to* BIRDIE): Good-bye, Mrs. Hubbard.

BIRDIE (*Shyly, with sweetness and dignity*): Good-bye, sir.

MARSHALL (*As he passes* REGINA): Remember.

REGINA: I will.

OSCAR: We'll see you to the carriage.

(MARSHALL *exits, followed by* BEN *and* OSCAR. *For a second* REGINA *and* BIRDIE *stand looking after them. Then* REGINA *throws up her arms, laughs happily.*)

REGINA: And there, Birdie, goes the man who has opened the door to our future.

BIRDIE (*Surprised at the unaccustomed friendliness*): What?

REGINA (*Turning to her*): *Our future.* Yours and mine, Ben's and Oscar's, the children— (*Looks at* BIRDIE'S *puzzled face, laughs.*) Our future! (*Gaily.*) You were charming at supper, Birdie. Mr. Marshall certainly thought so.

BIRDIE (*Pleased*): Why, Regina! Do you think he did?

REGINA: Can't you tell when you're being admired?

BIRDIE: Oscar said I bored Mr. Marshall. (*Then quietly.*) But he admired *you.* He told me so.

REGINA: What did he say?

BIRDIE: He said to me, "I hope your sister-in-law will come to Chicago. Chicago will be at her feet." He said the ladies would bow to your manners and the gentlemen to your looks.

REGINA: Did he? He seems a lonely man. Imagine being lonely with all that money. I don't think he likes his wife.

BIRDIE: Not like his wife? What a thing to say.

REGINA: She's away a great deal. He said that several times. And once he made fun of her being so social and high-tone. But that fits in all right. (*Sits back, arms on back of sofa, stretches.*) Her being social, I mean. She can introduce me. It won't take long with an introduction from her.

BIRDIE (*Bewildered*): Introduce you? In Chicago? You mean you really might go? Oh, Regina, you can't leave here. What about Horace?

REGINA: Don't look so scared about everything, Birdie. I'm going to live in Chicago. I've always wanted to. And now there'll be plenty of money to go with.

BIRDIE: But Horace won't be able to move around. You know what the doctor wrote.

REGINA: There'll be millions, Birdie, millions. You know what I've always said when people told me we were rich? I said I think you should either be a nigger or a millionaire. In between, like us, what for? (*Laughs. Looks at* BIRDIE.) But I'm not going away tomorrow, Birdie. There's plenty of time to worry about Horace when he comes home. If he ever decides to come home.

BIRDIE: Will we be going to Chicago? I mean, Oscar and Leo and me?

REGINA: You? I shouldn't think so. (*Laughs.*) Well, we must remember tonight. It's a very important night and we mustn't forget it. We shall plan all the things we'd like to have and then we'll really have them. Make a wish, Birdie, any wish. It's bound to come true now. (BEN *and* OSCAR *enter.*)

BIRDIE (*Laughs*): Well. Well, I don't know. Maybe. (REGINA *turns to look at* BEN.) Well, I guess I'd know right off what I wanted. (OSCAR *stands by the upper window, waves to the departing carriage.*)

REGINA (*Looks up at* BEN, *smiles. He smiles back at her.*) Well, you did it.

BEN: Looks like it might be we did.

REGINA (*Springs up, laughs*): Looks like it! Don't pretend. You're like a cat who's been licking the cream. (*Crosses to wine bottle.*) Now we must all have a drink to celebrate.

OSCAR: The children, Alexandra and Leo, make a very handsome couple, Regina. Marshall remarked himself what fine young folks they were. How well they looked together!

REGINA (*Sharply*): Yes. You said that before, Oscar.

BEN: Yes, sir. It's beginning to look as if the deal's all set. I may not be a subtle man—but—(*Turns to them. After a second.*) Now somebody ask me how I know the deal is set.

OSCAR: What do you mean, Ben?

BEN: You remember I told him that down here we drink the *last* drink for a toast?

OSCAR (*Thoughtfully*): Yes. I never heard that before.

BEN: Nobody's ever heard it before. God forgives those who invent what they need. I already had his signature. But we've all done business with men whose word over a glass is better than a bond. Anyway it don't hurt to have both.

OSCAR (*Turns to* REGINA): You understand what Ben means?

REGINA (*Smiles*): Yes, Oscar. I understand. I understood immediately.

BEN (*Looks at her admiringly*): Did you, Regina? Well, when he lifted his glass to drink, I closed my eyes and saw the bricks going into place.

REGINA: And *I* saw a lot more than that.

BEN: Slowly, slowly. As yet we have only our hopes.

REGINA: Birdie and I have just been planning what we want. I know what I want. What will you want, Ben?

BEN: Caution. Don't count the chickens. (*Leans back, laughs.*) Well, God would allow us a little daydreaming. Good for the soul when you've worked hard enough to deserve it. (*Pauses.*) I think I'll have a stable. For a long time I've had my good eyes on Carter's in Savannah. A rich man's pleasure, the sport of kings, why not the sport of Hubbards? Why not?

REGINA (*Smiles*): Why not? What will you have, Oscar?

OSCAR: I don't know. (*Thoughtfully.*) The pleasure of seeing the bricks grow will be enough for me.

BEN: Oh, of course. Our *greatest* pleasure will be to see the bricks grow. But we are all entitled to a little side indulgence.

OSCAR: Yes, I suppose so. Well, then, I think we might take a few trips here and there, eh, Birdie?

BIRDIE (*Surprised at being consulted*): Yes, Oscar. I'd like that.

OSCAR: We might even make a regular trip to Jekyll Island. I've heard the Cornelly place is for sale. We might think about buying it. Make a nice change. Do you good, Birdie, a change of climate. Fine shooting on Jekyll, the best.

BIRDIE: I'd like—

OSCAR (*Indulgently*): What would you like?

BIRDIE: *Two* things. Two things I'd like most.

REGINA: Two! I should like a thousand. You are modest, Birdie.

BIRDIE (*Warmly, delighted with the unexpected interest*): I should like to have Lionnet back. I know you own it now, but I'd like to see it fixed up again, the way Mama and Papa had it. Every year it used to get a nice coat of paint—Papa was very particular about the paint—and the lawn was so smooth all the way down to the river, with the trims of zinnias and red-feather plush. And the figs and blue little plums and the scuppernongs—(*Smiles. Turns to* REGINA.) The organ is still there and it wouldn't cost much to fix. We could have parties for Zan, the way Mama used to have for me.

BEN: That's a pretty picture, Birdie. Might be a most pleasant way to live. (*Dismissing* BIRDIE.) What do you want, Regina?

BIRDIE (*Very happily, not noticing that they are no longer listening to her*): I could have a cutting garden. Just where Mama's used to be. Oh, I do think we could be happier there. Papa used to say that *nobody* had ever lost their temper at Lionnet, and *nobody* ever would. Papa would never let anybody be nasty-spoken or mean. No, sir. He just didn't like it.

BEN: What do you want, Regina?

REGINA: I'm going to Chicago. And when I'm settled there and know the right people and the right things to buy—because I certainly don't know—I shall go to Paris and buy them. (*Laughs.*) I'm going to leave you and Oscar to count the bricks.

BIRDIE: Oscar. Please let me have Lionnet back.

OSCAR (*To* REGINA): You are serious about moving to Chicago?

BEN: She is going to see the great world and leave us in the little one. Well, we'll come and visit you and meet all the great and be proud to think you are our sister.

REGINA (*Gaily*): Certainly. And you won't even have to learn to be subtle, Ben. Stay as you are. You will be rich and the rich don't have to be subtle.

OSCAR: But what about Alexandra? She's seventeen. Old enough to be thinking about marrying.

BIRDIE: And, Oscar, I have one more wish. Just one more wish.

OSCAR (*Turns*): What is it, Birdie? What are you saying?

BIRDIE: I want you to stop shooting. I mean, so much. I don't like to see animals and birds killed just for the killing. You only throw them away—

BEN (*To* REGINA): It'll take a great deal of money to live as you're planning, Regina.

REGINA: Certainly. But there'll be plenty of money. You have estimated the profits very high.

BEN: I have—

BIRDIE (OSCAR *is looking at her furiously*): And you never let anybody else shoot, and the niggers need it so much to keep from starving. It's wicked to shoot food just because you like to shoot, when poor people need it so—

BEN (*Laughs*): I have estimated the profits very high—for myself.

REGINA: What did you say?

BIRDIE: I've always wanted to speak about it, Oscar.

OSCAR (*Slowly, carefully*): What are you chattering about?

BIRDIE (*Nervously*): I was talking about Lionnet and—and about your shooting—

OSCAR: You are exciting yourself.

REGINA (*To* BEN): I didn't hear you. There was so much talking.

OSCAR (*To* BIRDIE): You have been acting very childish, very excited, all evening.

BIRDIE: Regina asked me what I'd like.

REGINA: What did you say, Ben?

BIRDIE: Now that we'll be so rich everybody was saying what they would like, so *I* said what *I* would like, too.

BEN: I said— (*He is interrupted by* OSCAR.)

OSCAR (*To* BIRDIE): Very well. We've all heard you. That's enough now.

BEN: I am waiting. (*They stop.*) I am waiting for you to finish. You and Birdie. Four conversations are three too many. (BIRDIE *slowly sits down.* BEN *smiles, to* REGINA.) I said that I had, and I do, estimate the profits very high—for myself, and Oscar, of course.

REGINA (*Slowly*): And what does that mean? (BEN *shrugs, looks towards* OSCAR.)

OSCAR (*Looks at* BEN, *clears throat*): Well, Regina, it's like this. For forty-nine per cent Marshall will put up four hundred thousand dollars. For fifty-one per cent— (*Smiles archly.*) a controlling interest, mind you, we will put up two hundred and twenty-five thousand dollars besides offering him certain benefits that our (*Looks at* BEN.) local position allows us to manage. Ben means that two hundred and twenty-five thousand dollars is a lot of money.

REGINA: I know the terms and I know it's a lot of money.

BEN (*Nodding*): It is.

OSCAR: Ben means that we are ready with our two-thirds of the money. Your third, Horace's I mean, doesn't seem to be ready. (*Raises his hand as* REGINA *starts to speak.*) Ben has written to Horace, I have written, and you have written. He answers. But he never mentions this business. Yet we have explained it to him in great detail, and told him the urgency. Still he never mentions it. Ben has been very patient, Regina. Naturally, you are our sister and we want you to benefit from anything we do.

REGINA: And in addition to your concern for me, you do not want control to go out of the family. (*To* BEN.) That right, Ben?

BEN: That's cynical. (*Smiles.*) Cynicism is an unpleasant way of saying the truth.

OSCAR: No need to be cynical. We'd have no trouble raising the third share, the share that you want to take.

REGINA: I am sure you could get the third share, the share you were saving for me. But that would give you a strange partner. And strange partners sometimes want a great deal. (*Smiles unpleasantly.*) But perhaps it would be wise for you to find him.

OSCAR: Now, now. Nobody says we *want* to do that. We would like to have you in and you would like to come in.

REGINA: Yes. I certainly would.

BEN (*Laughs, puts up his hand*): But we haven't heard from Horace.

REGINA: I've given my word that Horace will put up the money. That should be enough.

BEN: Oh, it was enough. I took your word. But I've got to have more than your word now. The contracts will be signed this week, and Marshall will want to see our money soon after. Regina, Horace has been in Baltimore for five months. I know that you've written him to come home, and that he hasn't come.

OSCAR: It's beginning to look as if he doesn't want to come home.

REGINA: Of course he wants to come home. You can't move around with heart trouble at any moment you choose. You know what doctors are like once they get their hands on a case like this—

OSCAR: They can't very well keep him from answering letters, can they? (REGINA *turns to* BEN.) They couldn't keep him from arranging for the money if he wanted to—

REGINA: Has it occurred to you that Horace is also a good business man?

BEN: Certainly. He is a shrewd trader. Always has been. The bank is proof of that.

REGINA: Then, possibly, he may be keeping silent because he doesn't think he is getting enough for his money. (*Looks at* OSCAR.) Seventy-five thousand he has to put up. That's a lot of money, too.

OSCAR: Nonsense. He knows a good thing when he hears it. He knows that we can make *twice* the profit on cotton goods manufactured *here* than can be made in the North.

BEN: That isn't what Regina means. (*Smiles.*) May I interpret you, Regina? (*To* OSCAR.) Regina is saying that Horace wants *more* than a third of our share.

OSCAR: But he's only putting up a third of the money. You put up a third and you get a third. What else *could* he expect?

REGINA: Well, *I* don't know. I don't know about these things. It would seem that if you put up a third you should only get a third. But then again, there's no law about it, is there? I should think that if you knew your money was very badly needed, well, you just might say, I want more, I want a bigger share. You

boys have done that. I've heard you say so.

BEN (*After a pause, laughs*): So you believe he has deliberately held out? For a larger share? (*Leaning forward.*) Well, I *don't* believe it. But I *do* believe that's what *you* want. Am I right, Regina?

REGINA: Oh, I shouldn't like to be too definite. But I *could* say that I wouldn't like to persuade Horace unless he did get a larger share. I must look after his interests. It seems only natural—

OSCAR: And where would the larger share come from?

REGINA: I don't know. That's not my business. (*Giggles.*) But perhaps it could come off your share, Oscar.

(REGINA *and* BEN *laugh.*)

OSCAR (*Rises and wheels furiously on both of them as they laugh*): What kind of talk is this?

BEN: I haven't said a thing.

OSCAR (*To* REGINA): *You* are talking very big tonight.

REGINA (*Stops laughing*): Am I? Well, you should know me well enough to know that I wouldn't be asking for things I didn't think I could get.

OSCAR: Listen. I don't believe you can even get Horace to come home, much less get money from him or talk quite so big about what you want.

REGINA: Oh, I can get him home.

OSCAR: Then why haven't you?

REGINA: I thought I should fight his battles for him, before he came home. Horace is a very sick man. And even if *you* don't care how sick he is, I do.

BEN: Stop this foolish squabbling. How can you get him home?

REGINA: I will send Alexandra to Baltimore. She will ask him to come home. She will say that she *wants* him to come home, and that *I* want him to come home.

BIRDIE (*Suddenly*) Well, of course she wants him here, but he's sick and maybe he's happy where he is.

REGINA (*Ignores* BIRDIE, *to* BEN): You agree that he will come home if she asks him to, if she says that I miss him and want him—

BEN (*Looks at her, smiles*): I admire you, Regina. And I agree. That's settled now and— (*Starts to rise.*)

REGINA (*Quickly*): But before she brings him home, I want to know what he's going to get.

BEN: What do you want?

REGINA: Twice what you offered.

BEN: Well, you won't get it.

OSCAR (*To* REGINA): I think you've gone crazy.

REGINA: I don't want to fight, Ben—

BEN: I don't either. You won't get it. There isn't any chance of that. (*Roguishly.*) You're holding us up, and that's not pretty, Regina, not pretty. (*Holds up his hand as he sees she is about to speak.*) But we need you, and I don't want to fight. Here's what I'll do: I'll give Horace forty per cent, instead of the thirty-three and a third he really should get. I'll do that, provided he is home and his money is up within two weeks. How's that?

REGINA: All right.

OSCAR: I've asked before: where is this extra share coming from?

BEN (*Pleasantly*): From you. From your share.

OSCAR (*Furiously*): From me, is it? That's just fine and dandy. That's my reward. For thirty-five years I've worked my hands to the bone for you. For thirty-five years I've done all the things you didn't want to do. And this is what I—

BEN (*Turns slowly to look at* OSCAR. OSCAR *breaks off*): My, my. I am being attacked tonight on all sides. First by my sister, then by my brother. And I ain't a man who likes being attacked. I can't believe that God wants the strong to parade their strength, but I don't mind doing it if it's got to be done. (*Leans back in his chair.*) You ought to take these things bet-

ter, Oscar. I've made you money in the past. I'm going to make you more money now. You'll be a very rich man. What's the difference to any of us if a little more goes here, a little less goes there—it's all in the family. And it will stay in the family. I'll never marry. (ADDIE *enters, begins to gather the glasses from the table.* OSCAR *turns to* BEN.) So my money will go to Alexandra and Leo. They may even marry some day and— (ADDIE *looks at* BEN.)

BIRDIE (*Rising*): Marry—Zan and Leo—

OSCAR (*Carefully*): That would make a great difference in my feelings. If they married.

BEN: Yes, that's what I mean. Of course it would make a difference.

OSCAR (*Carefully*): Is that what *you* mean, Regina?

REGINA: Oh, it's too far away. Well talk about it in a few years.

OSCAR: I want to talk about it now.

BEN (*Nods*): Naturally.

REGINA: There's a lot of things to consider. They are first cousins, and—

OSCAR: That isn't unusual. Our grandmother and grandfather were first cousins.

REGINA (*Giggles*): And look at us.
    (BEN *giggles.*)

OSCAR (*Angrily*): You're both being very gay with my money.

BEN (*Sighs*): These quarrels. I dislike them so. (*Leans forward to* REGINA.) A marriage might be a very wise arrangement, for several reasons. And then, Oscar has given up something for you. You should try to manage something for him.

REGINA: I haven't said I was opposed to it. But Leo is a wild boy. There were those times when he took a little money from the bank and—

OSCAR: That's all past history—

REGINA: Oh, I know. And I know all young men are wild. I'm only mentioning it to show you that there are considerations—

BEN (*Irritated because she does not understand that he is trying to keep* OSCAR *quiet*): All right, so there are. But please assure Oscar that you will think about it very seriously.

REGINA (*Smiles, nods*): Very well. I assure Oscar that I will think about it seriously.

OSCAR (*Sharply*): That is not an answer.

REGINA (*Rises*): My, you're in a bad humor and you shall put me in one. I have said all that I am willing to say now. After all, Horace has to give his consent, too.

OSCAR: Horace will do what you tell him to.

REGINA: Yes, I think he will.

OSCAR: And I have your word that you will try to—

REGINA (*Patiently*): Yes, Oscar. You have my word that I will think about it. Now do leave me alone.

(*There is the sound of the front door being closed.*)

BIRDIE: I—Alexandra is only seventeen. She—

REGINA (*Calling*): Alexandra? Are you back?

ALEXANDRA: Yes, Mama.

LEO (*Comes into the room*): Mr. Marshall got off safe and sound. Weren't those fine clothes he had? You can always spot clothes made in a good place. Looks like maybe they were done in England. Lots of men in the North send all the way to England for their stuff.

BEN (*To* LEO): Were you careful driving the horses?

LEO: Oh, yes, sir. I was.

(ALEXANDRA *has come in on* BEN'S *question, hears the answer, looks angrily at* LEO.)

ALEXANDRA: It's a lovely night. You should have come, Aunt Birdie.

REGINA: Were you gracious to Mr. Marshall?

ALEXANDRA: I think so, Mama. I liked him.

REGINA: Good. And now I have great news for you. You are going to Baltimore in the morning to bring your father home.

ALEXANDRA (*Gasps, then delighted*): Me? Papa said I should come? That must mean— (*Turns to* ADDIE.) Addie, he must be well. Think of it, he'll be back home again. We'll bring him home.

REGINA: You are going alone, Alexandra.

ADDIE (ALEXANDRA *has turned in surprise*): Going alone? Going by herself? A child that age! Mr. Horace ain't going to like Zan traipsing up there by herself.

REGINA (*Sharply*): Go upstairs and lay out Alexandra's things.

ADDIE: He'd expect me to be along—

REGINA: I'll be up in a few minutes to tell you what to pack. (ADDIE *slowly begins to climb the steps. To* ALEXANDRA.) I should think you'd like going alone. At your age it certainly would have delighted me. You're a strange girl, Alexandra. Addie has babied you so much.

ALEXANDRA: I only thought it would be more fun if Addie and I went together.

BIRDIE (*Timidly*): Maybe I could go with her, Regina. I'd really like to.

REGINA: She is going alone. She is getting old enough to take some responsibilities.

OSCAR: She'd better learn now. She's almost old enough to get married. (*Jovially, to* LEO, *slapping him on shoulder.*) Eh, son?

LEO: Huh?

OSCAR (*Annoyed with* LEO *for not understanding*): Old enough to get married, you're thinking, eh?

LEO: Oh, yes, sir. (*Feebly.*) Lots of girls get married at Zan's age. Look at Mary Prester and Johanna and—

REGINA: Well, she's not getting married tomorrow. But she is going to Baltimore tomorrow, so let's talk about that. (*To* ALEXANDRA.) You'll be glad to have Papa home again.

ALEXANDRA: I wanted to go before, Mama. You remember that. But you said *you* couldn't go, and that *I* couldn't go alone.

REGINA:  I've changed my mind. (*Too casually.*) You're to tell Papa how much you missed him, and that he must come home now—for your sake. Tell him that you *need* him home.

ALEXANDRA:  Need him home? I don't understand.

REGINA:  There is nothing for you to understand. You are simply to say what I have told you.

BIRDIE (*Rises*):  He may be too sick. She couldn't do that—

ALEXANDRA:  Yes. He may be too sick to travel. I couldn't make him think he had to come home for me, if he is too sick to—

REGINA (*Looks at her, sharply, challengingly*):  You *couldn't* do what I tell you to do, Alexandra?

ALEXANDRA (*Quietly*):  No. I couldn't. If I thought it would hurt him.

REGINA (*After a second's silence, smiles pleasantly*):  But you are doing this for Papa's own good. (*Takes* ALEXANDRA'S *hand.*) You must let me be the judge of his condition. It's the best possible cure for him to come home and be taken care of here. He mustn't stay there any longer and listen to those alarmist doctors. You are doing this entirely for his sake. Tell your papa that I want him to come home, that I miss him very much.

ALEXANDRA (*Slowly*):  Yes, Mama.

REGINA (*To the others. Rises*):  I must go and start getting Alexandra ready now. Why don't you all go home?

BEN (*Rises*):  I'll attend to the railroad ticket. One of the boys will bring it over. Good night, everybody. Have a nice trip, Alexandra. The food on the train is very good. The celery is so crisp. Have a good time and act like a little lady. (*Exits.*)

REGINA:  Good night, Ben. Good night, Oscar— (*Playfully.*) Don't be so glum, Oscar. It makes you look as if you had chronic indigestion.

BIRDIE:  Good night, Regina.

REGINA:  Good night, Birdie. (*Exits upstairs.*)

OSCAR (*Starts for hall*):  Come along.

LEO (*To* ALEXANDRA):  Imagine your not wanting to go! What a little fool you are. Wish it were me. What I could do in a place like Baltimore!

ALEXANDRA (*Angrily, looking away from him*):  Mind your business. I can guess the kind of things *you* could do.

LEO (*Laughs*):  Oh, no, you couldn't. (*He exits.*)

REGINA (*Calling from the top of the stairs*):  Come on, Alexandra.

BIRDIE (*Quickly, softly*):  Zan.

ALEXANDRA:  I don't understand about my going, Aunt Birdie. (*Shrugs.*) But anyway, Papa will be home again. (*Pats* BIRDIE'S *arm.*) Don't worry about me. I can take care of myself. Really I can.

BIRDIE (*Shakes her head, softly*):  That's not what I'm worried about. Zan—

ALEXANDRA (*Comes close to her*):  What's the matter?

BIRDIE:  It's about Leo—

ALEXANDRA (*Whispering*):  He beat the horses. That's why we were late getting back. We had to wait until they cooled off. He always beats the horses as if—

BIRDIE (*Whispering frantically, holding* ALEXANDRA'S *hands*):  He's my son. My own son. But you are more to me—more to me than my own child. I love you more than anybody else—

ALEXANDRA:  Don't worry about the horses. I'm sorry I told you.

BIRDIE (*Her voice rising*):  *I am not worrying about the horses.* I am worrying about *you.* You are *not* going to marry Leo. I am not going to let them do that to you—

ALEXANDRA:  Marry? To Leo? (*Laughs.*) I wouldn't marry, Aunt Birdie. I've never even thought about it—

BIRDIE: But they have thought about it. (*Wildly.*) Zan, I couldn't stand to think about such a thing. You and— (OSCAR *has come into the doorway on* ALEXANDRA'S *speech. He is standing quietly, listening.*)

ALEXANDRA (*Laughs*): But I'm not going to marry. And I'm certainly not going to marry Leo.

BIRDIE: Don't you understand? They'll make you. They'll make you—

ALEXANDRA (*Takes* BIRDIE'S *hands, quietly, firmly*): That's foolish, Aunt Birdie. I'm grown now. Nobody can make me do anything.

BIRDIE: I just couldn't stand—

OSCAR (*Sharply*): Birdie. (BIRDIE *looks up, draws quickly away from* ALEXANDRA. *She stands rigid, frightened. Quietly.*) Birdie, get your hat and coat.

ADDIE (*Calls from upstairs*): Come on, baby. Your mama's waiting for you, and she ain't nobody to keep waiting.

ALEXANDRA: All right. (*Then softly, embracing* BIRDIE.) Good night, Aunt Birdie. (*As she passes* OSCAR.) Good night, Uncle Oscar. (BIRDIE *begins to move slowly towards the door as* ALEXANDRA *climbs the stairs.* ALEXANDRA *is almost out of view when* BIRDIE *reaches* OSCAR *in the doorway. As* BIRDIE *quickly attempts to pass him, he slaps her hard, across the face.* BIRDIE *cries out, puts her hand to her face. On the cry,* ALEXANDRA *turns, begins to run down the stairs.*) Aunt Birdie! What happened? What happened? I—

BIRDIE (*Softly, without turning*): Nothing, darling. Nothing happened. (*Quickly, as if anxious to keep* ALEXANDRA *from coming close.*) Now go to bed. (OSCAR *exits.*) Nothing happened. (*Turns to* ALEXANDRA *who is holding her hand.*) I only—I only twisted my ankle. (*She goes out.* ALEXANDRA *stands on the stairs looking after her as if she were puzzled and frightened.*)

*Curtain*

# ACT TWO

SCENE—*Same as Act One. A week later, morning.*

AT RISE: *The light comes from the open shutter of the right window; the other shutters are tightly closed.* ADDIE *is standing at the window, looking out. Near the dining-room doors are brooms, mops, rags, etc. After a second,* OSCAR *comes into the entrance hall, looks in the room, shivers, decides not to take his hat and coat off, comes into the room. At the sound of the door,* ADDIE *turns to see who has come in.*

ADDIE (*Without interest*): Oh, it's you, Mr. Oscar.

OSCAR: What is this? It's not night. What's the matter here? (*Shivers.*) Fine thing at this time of the morning. Blinds all closed. (ADDIE *begins to open shutters.*) Where's Miss Regina? It's cold in here.

ADDIE: Miss Regina ain't down yet.

OSCAR: She had any word?

ADDIE (*Wearily*): No, sir.

OSCAR: Wouldn't you think a girl that age could get on a train at one place and have sense enough to get off at another?

ADDIE: Something must have happened. If Zan say she was coming last night, she's coming last night. Unless something happened. Sure fire disgrace to let a baby like that go all that way alone to bring home a sick man without—

OSCAR: You do a lot of judging around here, Addie, eh? Judging of your white folks, I mean.

ADDIE (*Looks at him, sighs*): I'm tired. I been up all night watching for them.

REGINA (*Speaking from the upstairs hall*): Who's downstairs, Addie? (*She appears in a dressing gown, peers down from the landing.* ADDIE *picks up broom, dustpan and brush and exits.*) Oh, it's you, Oscar. What are you doing here so early? I haven't been down yet. I'm not finished dressing.

OSCAR (*Speaking up to her*): You had any word from them?

REGINA: No.

OSCAR: Then something certainly has happened. People don't just say they are arriving on Thursday night, and they haven't come by Friday morning.

REGINA: Oh, nothing has happened. Alexandra just hasn't got sense enough to send a message.

OSCAR: If nothing's happened, then why aren't they here?

REGINA: You asked me that ten times last night. My, you do fret so, Oscar. Anything might have happened. They may have missed connections in Atlanta, the train may have been delayed —oh, a hundred things could have kept them.

OSCAR: Where's Ben?

REGINA (*As she disappears upstairs*): Where should he be? At home, probably. Really, Oscar, I don't tuck him in his bed and I don't take him out of it. Have some coffee and don't worry so much.

OSCAR: Have some coffee? There isn't any coffee. (*Looks at his watch, shakes his head. After a second* CAL *enters with a large silver tray, coffee urn, small cups, newspaper.*) Oh, there you are. Is everything in this fancy house always late?

CAL (*Looks at him surprised*): You ain't out shooting this morning, Mr. Oscar?

OSCAR: First day I missed since I had my head cold. First day I missed in eight years.

CAL: Yes, sir. I bet you. Simon he say you had a mighty good day yesterday morning. That's what Simon say. (*Brings* OSCAR *coffee and newspaper.*)

OSCAR: Pretty good, pretty good.

CAL (*Laughs, slyly*): Bet you got enough bob-white and squirrel to give every nigger in town a Jesus-party. Most of 'em ain't had no meat since the cotton picking was over. Bet they'd give anything for a little piece of that meat—

OSCAR (*Turns his head to look at* CAL): Cal, if I catch a nigger in this town going shooting, you know what's going to happen. (LEO *enters.*)

CAL (*Hastily*): Yes, sir, Mr. Oscar. I didn't say nothing about nothing. It was Simon who told me and—Morning, Mr. Leo. You gentlemen having your breakfast with us here?

LEO: The boys in the bank don't know a thing. They haven't had any message. (CAL *waits for an answer, gets none, shrugs, moves to door, exits.*)

OSCAR (*Peers at* LEO): What you doing here, son?

LEO: You told me to find out if the boys at the bank had any message from Uncle Horace or Zan—

OSCAR: I told you if they had a message to bring it here. I told you that if they didn't have a message to stay at the bank and do your work.

LEO: Oh, I guess I misunderstood.

OSCAR: You didn't misunderstand. You just were looking for any excuse to take an hour off. (LEO *pours a cup of coffee.*) You got to stop that kind of thing. You got to start settling down. You going to be a married man one of these days.

LEO: Yes, sir.

OSCAR: You also got to stop with that woman in Mobile. (*As* LEO *is about to speak.*) You're young and I haven't got no objections to outside women. That is, I haven't got no objections so long as they don't interfere with serious things. Outside women are all right in their place, but *now* isn't their place. You got to realize that.

LEO (*Nods*): Yes, sir. I'll tell her. She'll act all right about it.

OSCAR: Also, you got to start working harder at the bank. You got to convince your Uncle Horace you going to make a fit husband for Alexandra.

LEO: What do you think has happened to them? Supposed to be here last night—

(*Laughs.*) Bet you Uncle Ben's mighty worried. Seventy-five thousand dollars worried.

OSCAR (*Smiles happily*): Ought to be worried. Damn well ought to be. First he don't answer the letters, then he don't come home— (*Giggles.*)

LEO: What will happen if Uncle Horace don't come home or don't—

OSCAR: Or don't put up the money? Oh, we'll get it from outside. Easy enough.

LEO (*Surprised*): But *you* don't want outsiders.

OSCAR: What do I care who gets my share? I been shaved already. Serve Ben right if he had to give away some of his.

LEO: Damn shame what they did to you.

OSCAR (*Looking up the stairs*): Don't talk so loud. Don't you worry. When I die, you'll have as much as the rest. You might have yours *and* Alexandra's. I'm not so easily licked.

LEO: I wasn't thinking of myself, Papa—

OSCAR: Well, you should be, you should be. It's every man's duty to think of himself.

LEO: You think Uncle Horace don't want to go in on this?

OSCAR (*Giggles*): That's my hunch. He hasn't showed any signs of loving it yet.

LEO (*Laughs*): But he hasn't listened to Aunt Regina yet, either. Oh, he'll go along. It's too good a thing. Why wouldn't he want to? He's got plenty and plenty to invest with. He don't even have to sell anything. Eighty-eight thousand worth of Union Pacific bonds sitting right in his safe deposit box. All he's got to do is open the box.

OSCAR (*After a pause. Looks at his watch*): Mighty late breakfast in this fancy house. Yes, he's had those bonds for fifteen years. Bought them when they were low and just locked them up.

LEO: Yeah. Just has to open the box and take them out. That's all. Easy as easy can be. (*Laughs.*) The things in that box! There's all those bonds, looking mighty fine. (OSCAR *slowly puts down his newspaper and turns to* LEO.) Then right next to them is a baby shoe of Zan's and a cheap old cameo on a string, and, *and*—nobody'd believe this—a piece of an old violin. Not even a whole violin. Just a piece of an old thing, a piece of a violin.

OSCAR (*Very softly, as if he were trying to control his voice*): A piece of a violin! What do you think of that!

LEO: Yes, sirree. A lot of other crazy things, too. A poem, I guess it is, signed with his mother's name, and two old schoolbooks with notes and— (LEO *catches* OSCAR'S *look. His voice trails off. He turns his head away.*)

OSCAR (*Very softly*): How do you know what's in the box, son?

LEO (*Stops, draws back, frightened, realizing what he has said*): Oh, well. Well, er. Well, one of the boys, sir. It was one of the boys at the bank. He took old Manders' keys. It was Joe Horns. He just up and took Manders' keys and, and—well, took the box out. (*Quickly.*) Then they all asked me if I wanted to see, too. So I looked a little, I guess, but then I made them close up the box quick and I told them never—

OSCAR (*Looks at him*): Joe Horns, you say? He opened it?

LEO: Yes, sir, yes, he did. My word of honor. (*Very nervously looking away.*) I suppose that don't excuse *me* for looking— (*Looking at* OSCAR.) but I did make him close it up and put the keys back in Manders' drawer—

OSCAR (*Leans forward, very softly*): Tell me the truth, Leo. I am not going to be angry with you. Did you open the box yourself?

LEO: *No, sir, I didn't.* I told you I didn't. No, I—

OSCAR (*Irritated, patient*): I am *not* going to be angry with you. (*Watching* LEO *carefully.*) Sometimes a young fellow deserves credit for looking round him to see what's going on. Sometimes that's a good sign in a fellow your age. (OSCAR *rises*.) Many great men have made their fortune with their eyes. Did you open the box?

LEO (*Very puzzled*): No. I—

OSCAR (*Moves to* LEO): Did you open the box? It may have been—well, it may have been a good thing if you had.

LEO (*After a long pause*): I opened it.

OSCAR (*Quickly*): Is that the truth? (LEO *nods*.) Does anybody else know that you opened it? Come, Leo, don't be afraid of speaking the truth to me.

LEO: No. Nobody knew. Nobody was in the bank when I did it. But—

OSCAR: Did your Uncle Horace ever know you opened it?

LEO (*Shakes his head*): He only looks in it once every six months when he cuts the coupons, and sometimes Manders even does that for him. Uncle Horace don't even have the keys. Manders keeps them for him. Imagine not looking at all that. You can bet if I had the bonds, I'd watch 'em like—

OSCAR: If you had them. (LEO *watches him*.) If you had them. Then you could have a share in the mill, you and me. A fine, big share, too. (*Pauses, shrugs*.) Well, a man can't be shot for wanting to see his son get on in the world, can he, boy?

LEO (*Looks up, begins to understand*): No, he can't. Natural enough. (*Laughs*.) But I haven't got the bonds and Uncle Horace has. And now he can just sit back and wait to be a millionaire.

OSCAR (*Innocently*): You think your Uncle Horace likes you well enough to lend you the bonds if he decides not to use them himself?

LEO: Papa, it must be that you haven't had your breakfast! (*Laughs loudly*) Lend me the bonds! My God—

OSCAR (*Disappointed*): No, I suppose not. Just a fancy of mine. A loan for three months, maybe four, easy enough for us to pay it back then. Anyway, this is only April— (*Slowly counting the months on his fingers*.) and if he doesn't look at them until Fall, he wouldn't even miss them out of the box.

LEO: That's it. He wouldn't even miss them. Ah, well—

OSCAR: No, sir. Wouldn't even miss them. How could he miss them if he never looks at them? (*Sighs as* LEO *stares at him*.) Well, here we are sitting around waiting for him to come home and invest his money in something he hasn't lifted his hand to get. But I can't help thinking he's acting strange. You laugh when I say he could lend you the bonds if he's not going to use them himself. But would it hurt him?

LEO (*Slowly looking at* OSCAR): No. No, it wouldn't.

OSCAR: People ought to help other people. But that's not always the way it happens. (BEN *enters, hangs his coat and hat in hall. Very carefully*.) And so sometimes you got to think of yourself. (*As* LEO *stares at him*, BEN *appears in the doorway*.) Morning, Ben.

BEN (*Coming in, carrying his newspaper*): Fine sunny morning. Any news from the runaways?

REGINA (*On the staircase*): There's no news or you would have heard it. Quite a convention so early in the morning, aren't you all? (*Goes to coffee urn*.)

OSCAR: You rising mighty late these days. Is that the way they do things in Chicago society?

BEN (*Looking at his paper*): Old Carter died up in Senateville. Eighty-one is a good time for us all, eh? What do you think has really happened to Horace, Regina?

REGINA: Nothing.

BEN (*Too casually*): You don't think maybe he never started from Baltimore and never intends to start?

REGINA (*Irritated*): Of course they've started. Didn't I have a letter from Alexandra? What is so strange about people arriving late? He has that cousin in Savannah he's so fond of. He may have stopped to see him. They'll be along today some time, very flattered that you and Oscar are so worried about them.

BEN: I'm a natural worrier. Especially when I am getting ready to close a business deal and one of my partners remains silent and invisible.

REGINA (*Laughs*): Oh, is that it? I thought you were worried about Horace's health.

OSCAR: Oh, that too. Who could help but worry? I'm worried. This is the first day I haven't shot since my head cold.

REGINA (*Starts towards dining room*): Then you haven't had your breakfast. Come along. (OSCAR and LEO *follow her*.)

BEN: Regina. (*She turns at dining-room door.*) That cousin of Horace's has been dead for years and, in any case, the train does not go through Savannah.

REGINA (*Laughs, continues into dining room, seats herself*): Did he die? You're always remembering about people dying. (BEN *rises*.) Now I intend to eat my breakfast in peace, and read my newspaper.

BEN (*Goes towards dining room as he talks*): This is second breakfast for me. My first was bad. Celia ain't the cook she used to be. Too old to have taste any more. If she hadn't belonged to Mama, I'd send her off to the country.

(OSCAR and LEO *start to eat*. BEN *seats himself*.)

LEO: Uncle Horace will have some tales to tell, I bet. Baltimore is a lively town.

REGINA (*To* CAL): The grits isn't hot enough. Take it back.

CAL: Oh, yes'm. (*Calling into kitchen as he exits*.) Grits didn't hold the heat. Grits didn't hold the heat.

LEO: When I was at school three of the boys and myself took a train once and went over to Baltimore. It was so big we thought we were in Europe. I was just a kid then—

REGINA: I find it very pleasant (ADDIE *enters*.) to have breakfast alone. I hate chattering before I've had something hot. (CAL *closes the dining-room doors*.) Do be still, Leo.

(ADDIE *comes into the room, begins gathering up the cups, carries them to the large tray. Outside there are the sounds of voices. Quickly* ADDIE *runs into the hall. A few seconds later she appears again in the doorway, her arm around the shoulders of* HORACE GIDDENS, *supporting him.* HORACE *is a tall man of about forty-five. He has been good looking, but now his face is tired and ill. He walks stiffly, as if it were an enormous effort, and carefully, as if he were unsure of his balance.* ADDIE *takes off his overcoat and hangs it on the hall tree. She then helps him to a chair*.)

HORACE: How are you, Addie? How have you been?

ADDIE: I'm all right, Mr. Horace. I've just been worried about you.

(ALEXANDRA *enters. She is flushed and excited, her hat awry, her face dirty. Her arms are full of packages, but she comes quickly to* ADDIE.)

ALEXANDRA: Now don't tell me how worried you were. We couldn't help it and there was no way to send a message.

ADDIE (*Begins to take packages from* ALEXANDRA): Yes, sir, I was mighty worried.

ALEXANDRA: We had to stop in Mobile over night. Papa— (*Looks at him.*) Papa didn't feel well. The trip was too much for him, and I made him stop and rest— (*As* ADDIE *takes the last package.*) No, don't take that. That's father's medicine. I'll hold it. It mustn't break. Now, about the stuff outside. Papa must have his wheel chair. I'll get that and the valises—

ADDIE (*Very happy, holding* ALEXANDRA'S *arms*): Since when you got to carry your own valises? Since when I ain't old enough to hold a bottle of medicine? (HORACE *coughs*.) You feel all right, Mr. Horace?

HORACE (*Nods*): Glad to be sitting down.

ALEXANDRA (*Opening package of medicine*): He doesn't feel all right. (ADDIE *looks at her, then at* HORACE.) He just says that. The trip was very hard on him, and now he must go right to bed.

ADDIE (*Looking at him carefully*): Them fancy doctors, they give you help?

HORACE: They did their best.

ALEXANDRA (*Has become conscious of the voices in the dining room*): I bet Mama was worried. I better tell her we're here now. (*She starts for door.*)

HORACE: Zan. (*She stops.*) Not for a minute, dear.

ALEXANDRA: Oh, Papa, you feel bad again. I knew you did. Do you want your medicine?

HORACE: No, I don't feel that way. I'm just tired, darling. Let me rest a little.

ALEXANDRA: Yes, but Mama will be mad if I don't tell her we're here.

ADDIE: They're all in there eating breakfast.

ALEXANDRA: Oh, are they all here? Why do they *always* have to be here? I was hoping Papa wouldn't have to see anybody, that it would be nice for him and quiet.

ADDIE: Then let your papa rest for a minute.

HORACE: Addie, I bet your coffee's as good as ever. They don't have such good coffee up North. (*Looks at the urn.*) Is it as good, Addie?

(ADDIE *starts for coffee urn.*)

ALEXANDRA: No. Dr. Reeves said not much coffee. Just now and then. I'm the nurse now, Addie.

ADDIE: You'd be a better one if you didn't look so dirty. Now go and take a bath, Miss Grown-up. Change your linens, get out a fresh dress and give your hair a good brushing—go on—

ALEXANDRA: Will you be all right, Papa?

ADDIE: Go on.

ALEXANDRA (*On stairs, talks as she goes up*): The pills Papa must take once every four hours. And the bottle only when—only if he feels very bad. Now don't move until I come back and don't talk much and remember about his medicine, Addie—

ADDIE: Ring for Belle and have her help you and then I'll make you a fresh breakfast.

ALEXANDRA (*As she disappears*): How's Aunt Birdie? Is she here?

ADDIE: It ain't right for you to have coffee? It will hurt you?

HORACE (*Slowly*): Nothing can make much difference now. Get me a cup, Addie. (*She looks at him, crosses to urn, pours a cup.*) Funny. They can't make coffee up North. (ADDIE *brings him a cup.*) They don't like red pepper, either. (*He takes the cup and gulps it greedily.*) God, that's good. You remember how I used to drink it? Ten, twelve cups a day. So strong it had to stain the cup. (*Then slowly.*) Addie, before I see anybody else, I want to know why Zan came to fetch me home. She's tried to tell me, but she doesn't seem to know herself.

ADDIE (*Turns away*): I don't know. All I know is big things are going on. Everybody going to be high-tone rich. Big rich. You too. All because smoke's going to start out of a building that ain't even up yet.

HORACE: I've heard about it.

ADDIE: And, er— (*Hesitates—steps to him.*) And—well, Zan, she going to marry Mr. Leo in a little while.

HORACE (*Looks at her, then very slowly*): What are you talking about?

ADDIE: That's right. That's the talk, God, help us.

HORACE (*Angrily*): What's the talk?

ADDIE: I'm telling you. There's going to be a wedding— (*Angrily turns away.*) Over my dead body there is.

HORACE (*After a second, quietly*): Go and tell them I'm home.

ADDIE (*Hesitates*): Now you ain't to get excited. You're to be in your bed—

HORACE: Go on, Addie. Go and say I'm back. (ADDIE *opens dining-room doors. He rises with difficulty, stands stiff, as if he were in pain, facing the dining room.*)

ADDIE: Miss Regina. They're home. They got here—

REGINA: Horace! (REGINA *quickly rises, runs into the room. Warmly.*) Horace! You've finally arrived. (*As she kisses him, the others come forward, all talking together.*)

BEN (*In doorway, carrying a napkin*): Well, sir, you had us all mighty worried. (*He steps forward. They shake hands.* ADDIE *exits.*)

OSCAR: You're a sight for sore eyes.

HORACE: Hello, Ben.

(LEO *enters, eating a biscuit.*)

OSCAR: And how you feel? Tip-top, I bet, because that's the way you're looking.

HORACE (*Coldly, irritated with* OSCAR'S *lie*): Hello, Oscar. Hello, Leo, how are you?

LEO (*Shaking hands*): I'm fine, sir. But a lot better now that you're back.

REGINA: Now sit down. What did happen to you and where's Alexandra? I am so excited about seeing you that I almost forgot about her.

HORACE: I didn't feel good, a little weak, I guess, and we stopped over night to rest. Zan's upstairs washing off the train dirt.

REGINA: Oh, I am so sorry the trip was hard on you. I didn't think that—

HORACE: Well, it's just as if I had never been away. All of you here—

BEN: Waiting to welcome you home.

(BIRDIE *bursts in. She is wearing a flannel kimono and her face is flushed and excited.*)

BIRDIE (*Runs to him, kisses him*): Horace!

HORACE: (*Warmly pressing her arm*): I was just wondering where you were, Birdie.

BIRDIE (*Excited*): Oh, I would have been here. I didn't know you were back until Simon said he saw the buggy. (*She draws back to look at him. Her face sobers.*) Oh, you don't look well, Horace. No, you don't.

REGINA (*Laughs*): Birdie, what a thing to say—

HORACE (*Looking at* OSCAR): Oscar thinks I look very well.

OSCAR (*Annoyed. Turns on* LEO): Don't stand there holding that biscuit in your hand.

LEO: Oh, well. I'll just finish my breakfast, Uncle Horace, and then I'll give you all the news about the bank— (*He exits into the dining room.*)

OSCAR: And what is that costume you have on?

BIRDIE (*Looking at* HORACE): Now that you're home, you'll feel better. Plenty of good rest and we'll take such fine care of you. (*Stops.*) But where is Zan? I missed her so much.

OSCAR: I asked you what is that strange costume you're parading around in?

BIRDIE (*Nervously, backing towards stairs*): Me? Oh! It's my wrapper. I was so excited about Horace I just rushed out of the house—

OSCAR: Did you come across the square dressed that way? My dear Birdie, I—

HORACE (*To* REGINA, *wearily*): Yes, it's just like old times.

REGINA (*Quickly to* OSCAR): Now, no fights. This is a holiday.

BIRDIE (*Runs quickly up the stairs*): Zan! Zannie!

OSCAR: Birdie! (*She stops.*)

BIRDIE: Oh. Tell Zan I'll be back in a little while. (*Whispers.*) Sorry, Oscar. (*Exits.*)

REGINA (*To* OSCAR *and* BEN): Why don't you go finish your breakfast and let Horace rest for a minute?

BEN (*Crossing to dining room with* OSCAR): Never leave a meal unfinished. There are too many poor people who need the food. Mighty glad to see you home, Horace. Fine to have you back. Fine to have you back.

OSCAR (*To* LEO *as* BEN *closes dining-room doors*): Your mother has gone crazy. Running around the streets like a woman—
(*The moment* REGINA *and* HORACE *are alone, they become awkward and self-conscious.*)

REGINA (*Laughs awkwardly*): Well. Here we are. It's been a long time. (HORACE *smiles.*) Five months. You know, Horace, I wanted to come and be with you in the hospital, but I didn't know where my duty was. Here, or with you. But you know how much I *wanted* to come.

HORACE: That's kind of you, Regina. There was no need to come.

REGINA: Oh, but there was. Five months lying there all by yourself, no kinfolks, no friends. Don't try to tell me you didn't have a bad time of it.

HORACE: I didn't have a bad time. (*As she shakes her head, he becomes insistent.*) No, I didn't, Regina. Oh, at first when I—when I heard the news about myself—but after I got used to that, I liked it there.

REGINA: You *liked* it? (*Coldly.*) Isn't that strange. You liked it so well you didn't want to come home?

HORACE: That's not the way to put it. (*Then, kindly, as he sees her turn her head away.*) But there I was and I got kind of used to it, kind of to like lying there and thinking. (*Smiles.*) I never had much time to think before. And time's become valuable to me.

REGINA: It sounds almost like a holiday.

HORACE (*Laughs*): It was, sort of. The first holiday I've had since I was a little kid.

REGINA: And here I was thinking you were in pain and—

HORACE (*Quietly*): I was in pain.

REGINA: And instead you were having a holiday! A holiday of thinking. Couldn't you have done that here?

HORACE: I wanted to do it before I came here. I was thinking about us.

REGINA: About us? About you and me? Thinking about you and me after all these years. (*Unpleasantly.*) You shall tell me everything you thought—some day.

HORACE (*There is silence for a minute*): Regina. (*She turns to him.*) Why did you send Zan to Baltimore?

REGINA: Why? Because I wanted you home. You can't make anything suspicious out of that, can you?

HORACE: I didn't mean to make anything suspicious about it. (*Hesitantly, taking her hand.*) Zan said you wanted me to come home. I was so pleased at that and touched, it made me feel good.

REGINA (*Taking away her hand, turns*): Touched that I should want you home?

HORACE (*Sighs*): I'm saying all the wrong things as usual. Let's try to get along better. There isn't so much more time. Regina, what's all this crazy talk I've been hearing about Zan and Leo? Zan and Leo marrying?

REGINA (*Turning to him, sharply*): Who gossips so much around here?

HORACE (*Shocked*) Regina!

REGINA (*Annoyed, anxious to quiet him*): It's some foolishness that Oscar thought up. I'll explain later. I have no intention of allowing any such arrangement. It was simply a way of keeping Oscar quiet in all this business I've been writing you about—

HORACE (*Carefully*): What has Zan to do with any business of Oscar's? Whatever it is, you had better put it out of Oscar's head immediately. You know what I think of Leo.

REGINA: But there's no need to talk about it now.

HORACE: There is no need to talk about it ever. Not as long as I live. (HORACE *stops, slowly turns to look at her.*) As long as I live. I've been in a hospital for five months. Yet since I've been here you have not once asked me about—about my health. (*Then gently.*) Well, I suppose they've written you. I can't live very long.

REGINA (*Coldly*): I've never understood why people have to talk about this kind of thing.

HORACE (*There is a silence. Then he looks up at her, his face cold*): You misunderstand. I don't intend to gossip about my sickness. I thought it was only fair to tell you. I was not asking for your sympathy.

REGINA (*Sharply, turns to him*): What do the doctors think caused your bad heart?

HORACE: What do you mean?

REGINA: They didn't think it possible, did they, that your fancy women may have—

HORACE (*Smiles unpleasantly*): Caused my heart to be bad? I don't think that's the best scientific theory. You don't catch heart trouble in bed.

REGINA (*Angrily*): I didn't think you did. I only thought you might catch a bad conscience—in bed, as you say.

HORACE: I didn't tell them about my bad conscience. Or about my fancy women. Nor did I tell them that my wife has not wanted me in bed with her for— (*Sharply.*) How long is it, Regina? (RE-GINA *turns to him.*) Ten years? Did you bring me home for this, to make me feel guilty again? That means you want something. But you'll not make me feel guilty any more. My "thinking" has made a difference.

REGINA: I see that it has. (*She looks towards dining-room door. Then comes to him, her manner warm and friendly.*) It's foolish for us to fight this way. I didn't mean to be unpleasant. I was stupid.

HORACE (*Wearily*): God knows I didn't either. I came home wanting so much not to fight, and then all of a sudden there we were. I got hurt and—

REGINA (*Hastily*): It's all my fault. I didn't ask about—about your illness because I

didn't want to remind you of it. Anyway I never believe doctors when they talk about— (*Brightly.*) when they talk like that.

HORACE (*Not looking at her*): Well, we'll try our best with each other. (*He rises.*)

REGINA (*Quickly*): I'll try. Honestly, I will. Horace, Horace, I know you're tired but, but—couldn't you stay down here a few minutes longer? I want Ben to tell you something.

HORACE: Tomorrow.

REGINA: I'd like to now. It's very important to me. It's very important to all of us. (*Gaily, as she moves toward dining room.*) Important to your beloved daughter. She'll be a very great heiress—

HORACE: Will she? That's nice.

REGINA (*Opens doors*): Ben, are you finished breakfast?

HORACE: Is this the mill business I've had so many letters about?

REGINA (*To* BEN): Horace would like to talk to you now.

HORACE: Horace would not like to talk to you now. I am very tired, Regina—

REGINA (*Comes to him*): Please. You've said we'll try our best with each other. I'll try. Really, I will. Please do this for me now. You will see what I've done while you've been away. How I watched your interests. (*Laughs gaily.*) And I've done very well too. But things can't be delayed any longer. Everything must be settled this week— (HORACE *sits down.* BEN *enters.* OSCAR *has stayed in the dining room, his head turned to watch them.* LEO *is pretending to read the newspaper.*) Now you must tell Horace all about it. Only be quick because he is very tired and must go to bed. (HORACE *is looking up at her. His face hardens as she speaks.*) But I think your news will be better for him than all the medicine in the world.

BEN (*Looking at* HORACE): It could wait. Horace may not feel like talking today.

REGINA: What an old faker you are! You know it can't wait. You know it must be finished this week. You've been just as anxious for Horace to get here as I've been.

BEN (*Very jovial*): I suppose I have been. And why not? Horace has done Hubbard Sons many a good turn. Why shouldn't I be anxious to help him now?

REGINA (*Laughs*): Help him! Help him when you need him, that's what you mean.

BEN: What a woman you married, Horace. (*Laughs awkwardly when* HORACE *does not answer.*) Well, then I'll make it quick. You know what I've been telling you for years. How I've always said that every one of us little Southern business men had great things—(*Extends his arm.*)—right beyond our finger tips. It's been my dream: my dream to make those fingers grow longer. I'm a lucky man, Horace, a lucky man. To dream and to live to get what you've dreamed of. That's *my* idea of a lucky man. (*Looks at his fingers as his arm drops slowly.*) For thirty years I've cried bring the cotton mills to the cotton. (HORACE *opens medicine bottle.*) Well, finally I got up nerve to go to Marshall Company in Chicago.

HORACE: I know all this. (*He takes the medicine.* REGINA *rises, steps to him.*)

BEN: Can I get you something?

HORACE: Some water, please.

REGINA (*Turns quickly*): Oh, I'm sorry. Let me. (*Brings him a glass of water. He drinks as they wait in silence.*) You feel all right now?

HORACE: Yes. You wrote me. I know all that. (OSCAR *enters from dining room.*)

REGINA (*Triumphantly*): But you don't know that in the last few days Ben has agreed to give us—you, I mean—a much larger share.

HORACE: Really? That's very generous of him.

BEN (*Laughs*): It wasn't so generous of me. It was smart of Regina.

REGINA (*As if she were signaling* HORACE): I explained to Ben that perhaps you hadn't answered his letters because you didn't think he was offering you enough, and that the time was getting short and you could guess how much he needed you—

HORACE (*Smiles at her, nods*): And I could guess that he wants to keep control in the family?

REGINA (*To* BEN, *triumphantly*): Exactly. (*To* HORACE.) So I did a little bargaining for you and convinced my brothers they weren't the only Hubbards who had a business sense.

HORACE: Did you have to convince them of that? How little people know about each other! (*Laughs.*) But you'll know better about Regina next time, eh, Ben? (BEN, REGINA, HORACE *laugh together.* OSCAR'S *face is angry.*) Now let's see. We're getting a bigger share. (*Looking at* OSCAR.) Who's getting less?

BEN: Oscar.

HORACE: Well, Oscar, you've grown very unselfish. What's happened to you? (LEO *enters from dining room.*)

BEN (*Quickly, before* OSCAR *can answer*): Oscar doesn't mind. Not worth fighting about now, eh, Oscar?

OSCAR (*Angrily*): I'll get mine in the end. You can be sure of that. I've got my son's future to think about.

HORACE (*Sharply*): Leo? Oh, I see. (*Puts his head back, laughs.* REGINA *looks at him nervously.*) I am beginning to see. Everybody will get theirs.

BEN: I knew you'd see it. Seventy-five thousand, and that seventy-five thousand will make you a million.

REGINA (*Steps to table, leaning forward*): It will, Horace, it will.

HORACE: I believe you. (*After a second.*) Now I can understand Oscar's self-sacrifice, but what did you have to promise Marshall Company besides the money you're putting up?

BEN: They wouldn't take promises. They wanted guarantees.

HORACE: Of what?

BEN (*Nods*): Water power. Free and plenty of it.

HORACE: You got them that, of course.

BEN: Cheap. You'd think the Governor of a great state would make his price a little higher. From pride, you know. (HORACE *smiles*. BEN *smiles*.) Cheap wages. "What do you mean by cheap wages?" I say to Marshall. "Less than Massachusetts," he says to me, "and that averages eight a week." "Eight a week! By God," I tell him, "*I'd* work for eight a week myself." Why, there ain't a mountain white or a town nigger but wouldn't give his right arm for three silver dollars every week, eh, Horace?

HORACE: Sure. And they'll take less than that when you get around to playing them off against each other. You can save a little money that way, Ben. (*Angrily.*) And make them hate each other just a little more than they do now.

REGINA: What's all this about?

BEN (*Laughs*): There'll be no trouble from anybody, white or black. Marshall said that to me. "What about strikes? That's all we've had in Massachusetts for the last three years." I say to him, "What's a strike? I never heard of one. Come South, Marshall. We got good folks and we don't stand for any fancy fooling."

HORACE: You're right. (*Slowly.*) Well, it looks like you made a good deal for yourselves, and for Marshall, too. (*To* BEN.) Your father used to say he made the thousands and you boys would make the millions. I think he was right. (*Rises.*)

REGINA (*They are all looking at* HORACE. *She laughs nervously*): Millions for *us*, too.

HORACE: Us? You and me? I don't think so. We've got enough money, Regina. We'll just sit by and watch the boys grow rich.

(*They watch* HORACE *tensely as he begins to move towards the staircase. He passes* LEO, *looks at him for a second*.) How's everything at the bank, Leo?

LEO: Fine, sir. Everything is fine.

HORACE: How are all the ladies in Mobile? (HORACE *turns to* REGINA, *sharply*.) Whatever made you think I'd let Zan marry—

REGINA: Do you mean that you are turning this down? Is it possible that's what you mean?

BEN: No, that's not what he means. Turning down a fortune. Horace is tired. He'd rather talk about it tomorrow—

REGINA: We can't keep putting it off this way. Oscar must be in Chicago by the end of the week with the money and contracts.

OSCAR (*Giggles, pleased*): Yes, sir. Got to be there end of the week. No sense going without the money.

REGINA (*Tensely*): I've waited long enough for your answer. I'm not going to wait any longer.

HORACE (*Very deliberately*): I'm very tired now, Regina.

BEN (*Hastily*): Now, Horace probably has his reasons. Things he'd like explained. Tomorrow will do. I can—

REGINA (*Turns to* BEN, *sharply*): I want to know his reasons now! (*Turns back to* HORACE.)

HORACE (*As he climbs the steps*): I don't know them all myself. Let's leave it at that.

REGINA: We shall not leave it at that! We have waited for you here like children. Waited for you to come home.

HORACE: So that you could invest my money. So this is why you wanted me home? Well, I had hoped— (*Quietly.*) If you are disappointed, Regina, I'm sorry. But I must do what I think best. We'll talk about it another day.

REGINA: We'll talk about it now. Just you and me.

HORACE (*Looks down at her. His voice is tense*): Please, Regina. It's been a hard trip. I don't feel well. Please leave me alone now.

REGINA (*Quietly*): I want to talk to you, Horace. I'm coming up. (*He looks at her for a minute, then moves on again out of sight. She begins to climb the stairs.*)

BEN (*Softly.* REGINA *turns to him as he speaks*): Sometimes it is better to wait for the sun to rise again. (*She does not answer.*) And sometimes, as our mother used to tell you, (REGINA *starts up stairs.*) it's unwise for a good-looking woman to frown. (BEN *rises, moves toward stairs.*) Softness and a smile do more to the heart of men— (*She disappears.* BEN *stands looking up the stairs. There is a long silence. Then, suddenly,* OSCAR *giggles.*)

OSCAR: Let us hope she'll change his mind. Let us hope. (*After a second* BEN *crosses to table, picks up his newspaper.* OSCAR *looks at* BEN. *The silence makes* LEO *uncomfortable.*)

LEO: The paper says twenty-seven cases of yellow fever in New Orleans. Guess the flood-waters caused it. (*Nobody pays attention.*) Thought they were building the levees high enough. Like the niggers always say: a man born of woman can't build nothing high enough for the Mississippi. (*Gets no answer. Gives an embarrassed laugh.*)

(*Upstairs there is the sound of voices. The voices are not loud, but* BEN, OSCAR, LEO *become conscious of them.* LEO *crosses to landing, looks up, listens.*)

OSCAR (*Pointing up*): Now just suppose she don't change his mind? Just suppose he keeps on refusing?

BEN (*Without conviction*): He's tired. It was a mistake to talk to him today. He's a sick man, but he isn't a crazy one.

OSCAR (*Giggles*): But just suppose he is crazy. What then?

BEN (*Puts down his paper, peers at* OSCAR): Then we'll go outside for the money. There's plenty who would give it.

OSCAR: And plenty who will want a lot for what they give. The ones who are rich enough to give will be smart enough to want. That means we'd be working for them, don't it, Ben?

BEN: You don't have to tell me the things I told you six months ago.

OSCAR: Oh, you're right not to worry. She'll change his mind. She always has. (*There is a silence. Suddenly* REGINA'S *voice becomes louder and sharper. All of them begin to listen now. Slowly* BEN *rises, goes to listen by the staircase.* OSCAR, *watching him, smiles. As they listen* REGINA'S *voice becomes very loud.* HORACE'S *voice is no longer heard.*) Maybe. But I don't believe it. I never did believe he was going in with us.

BEN (*Turning on him*): What the hell do you expect me to do?

OSCAR (*Mildly*): Nothing. You done your almighty best. Nobody could blame you if the whole thing just dripped away right through our fingers. You can't do a thing. But there may be something I could do for us. (OSCAR *rises.*) Or, I might better say, Leo could do for us. (BEN *stops, turns, looks at* OSCAR. LEO *is staring at* OSCAR.) Ain't that true, son? Ain't it true you might be able to help your own kinfolks?

LEO (*Nervously taking a step to him*): Papa, I—

BEN (*Slowly*): How would he help us, Oscar?

OSCAR: Leo's got a friend. Leo's friend owns eighty-eight thousand dollars in Union Pacific bonds. (BEN *turns to look at* LEO.) Leo's friend don't look at the bonds much—not for five or six months at a time.

BEN (*After a pause*): Union Pacific. Uh, huh. Let me understand. Leo's friend would—would lend him these bonds and he—

OSCAR (*Nods*): Would be kind enough to lend them to us.

BEN: Leo.

LEO (*Excited, comes to him*): Yes, sir?

BEN: When would your friend be wanting the bonds back?

LEO (*Very nervous*): I don't know. I—well, I—

OSCAR (*Sharply. Steps to him*): You told me he won't look at them until Fall—

LEO: Oh, that's right. But I—not till Fall. Uncle Horace never—

BEN (*Sharply*): Be still.

OSCAR (*Smiles at* LEO): Your uncle doesn't wish to know your friend's name.

LEO (*Starts to laugh*): That's a good one. Not know his name—

OSCAR: Shut up, Leo! (LEO *turns away slowly, moves to table.* BEN *turns to* OSCAR.) He won't look at them again until September. That gives us five months. Leo will return the bonds in three months. And we'll have no trouble raising the money once the mills are going up. Will Marshall accept bonds?

(BEN *stops to listen to sudden sharp voices from above. The voices are now very angry and very loud.*)

BEN (*Smiling*): Why not? Why not? (*Laughs.*) Good. We are lucky. We'll take the loan from Leo's friend—I think he will make a safer partner than our sister. (*Nods towards stairs. Turns to* LEO.) How soon can you get them?

LEO: Today. Right now. They're in the safe-deposit box and—

BEN (*Sharply*): I don't want to know where they are.

OSCAR (*Laughs*): We will keep it secret from you. (*Pats* BEN'S *arm.*)

BEN (*Smiles*): Good. Draw a check for our part. You can take the night train for Chicago. Well, Oscar (*Holds out his hand.*), good luck to us.

OSCAR: Leo will be taken care of?

LEO: I'm entitled to Uncle Horace's share. I'd enjoy being a partner—

BEN (*Turns to stare at him*): You would? You can go to hell, you little— (*Starts towards* LEO.)

OSCAR (*Nervously*): Now, now. He didn't mean that. I only want to be sure he'll get something out of all this.

BEN: Of course. We'll take care of him. We won't have any trouble about that. I'll see you at the store.

OSCAR (*Nods*): That's settled then. Come on, son. (*Starts for door.*)

LEO (*Puts out his hand*): I didn't mean just that. I was only going to say what a great day this was for me and— (BEN *ignores his hand.*)

BEN: Go on.

(LEO *looks at him, turns, follows* OSCAR *out.* BEN *stands where he is, thinking. Again the voices upstairs can be heard.* REGINA'S *voice is high and furious.* BEN *looks up, smiles, winces at the noise.*)

ALEXANDRA (*Upstairs*): Mama—Mama—don't . . . (*The noise of running footsteps is heard and* ALEXANDRA *comes running down the steps, speaking as she comes.*) Uncle Ben! Uncle Ben! Please go up. Please make Mama stop. Uncle Ben, he's sick, he's so sick. How can Mama talk to him like that—please, make her stop. She'll—

BEN: Alexandra, you have a tender heart.

ALEXANDRA (*Crying*): Go on up, Uncle Ben please— (*Suddenly the voices stop. A second later there is the sound of a door being slammed.*)

BEN: Now you see. Everything is over. Don't worry. (*He starts for the door.*) Alexandra, I want you to tell your mother how sorry I am that I had to leave. And don't worry so, my dear. Married folk frequently raise their voices, unfortunately. (*He starts to put on his hat and coat as* REGINA *appears on the stairs.*)

ALEXANDRA (*Furiously*): How can you treat Papa like this? He's sick. He's very sick. Don't you know that? I won't let you.

REGINA: Mind your business, Alexandra. (*To* BEN. *Her voice is cold and calm.*) How much longer can you wait for the money?

BEN (*Putting on his coat*): He has refused? My, that's too bad.

REGINA: He will change his mind. I'll find a way to make him. What's the longest you can wait now?

BEN: I could wait until next week. But I can't wait until next week. (*He giggles, pleased at the joke.*) I could but I can't. Could and can't. Well, I must go now. I'm very late—

REGINA (*Coming downstairs towards him*): You're not going. I want to talk to you.

BEN: I was about to give Alexandra a message for you. I wanted to tell you that Oscar is going to Chicago tonight, so we can't be here for our usual Friday supper.

REGINA (*Tensely*): Oscar is going to Chi— (*Softly.*) What do you mean?

BEN: Just that. Everything is settled. He's going on to deliver to Marshall—

REGINA (*Taking a step to him*): I demand to know what— You are lying. You are trying to scare me. *You haven't got the money.* How could you have it? You can't have— (BEN *laughs.*) You will wait until I—

(HORACE *comes into view on the landing.*)

BEN: You are getting out of hand. Since when do I take orders from you?

REGINA: Wait, you— (BEN *stops.*) How *can* he go to Chicago? Did a ghost arrive with the money? (BEN *starts for the hall.*) I don't believe you. Come back here. (RE-GINA *starts after him.*) Come back here, you— (*The door slams. She stops in the doorway, staring, her fists clenched. After a pause she turns slowly.*)

HORACE (*Very quietly*): It's a great day when you and Ben cross swords. I've been waiting for it for years.

ALEXANDRA: Papa, Papa, please go back! You will—

HORACE: And so they don't need you, and so you will not have your millions, after all.

REGINA (*Turns slowly*): You hate to see anybody live now, don't you? You hate to think that I'm going to be alive and have what I want.

HORACE: I should have known you'd think that was the reason.

REGINA: Because you're going to die and you know you're going to die.

ALEXANDRA (*Shrilly*): Mama! Don't— Don't listen, Papa. Just don't listen. Go away—

HORACE: Not to keep you from getting what you want. Not even partly that. (*Holding to the rail.*) I'm sick of you, sick of this house, sick of my life here. I'm sick of your brothers and their dirty tricks to make a dime. There must be better ways of getting rich than cheating niggers on a pound of bacon. Why should I give you the money? (*Very angrily.*) To pound the bones of this town to make dividends for you to spend? You wreck the town, you and your brothers, *you* wreck the town and live on it. Not me. Maybe it's easy for the dying to be honest. But it's not my fault I'm dying. (ADDIE *enters, stands at door quietly.*) I'll do no more harm now. I've done enough. I'll die my own way. And I'll do it without making the world any worse. I leave that to you.

REGINA (*Looks up at him slowly, calmly*): I hope you die. I hope you die soon. (*Smiles.*) I'll be waiting for you to die.

ALEXANDRA (*Shrieking*): Papa! Don't— Don't listen— Don't—

ADDIE: Come here, Zan. Come out of this room.

(ALEXANDRA *runs quickly to* ADDIE, *who holds her.* HORACE *turns slowly and starts upstairs.*)

*Curtain*

# ACT THREE

SCENE—*Same as Act One. Two weeks later. It is late afternoon, and it is raining.*

AT RISE: HORACE *is sitting near the window in a wheel chair. On the table next to him is a safe-deposit box, and a small bottle of medicine.* BIRDIE *and* ALEXANDRA *are playing the piano. On a chair is a large sewing basket.*

BIRDIE (*Counting for* ALEXANDRA): One and two and three and four. One and two and three and four. (*Nods—turns to* HORACE.) We once played together, Horace. Remember?

HORACE (*Has been looking out of the window*) What, Birdie?

BIRDIE: We played together. You and me.

ALEXANDRA: Papa used to play?

BIRDIE: Indeed he did. (ADDIE *appears at the door in a large kitchen apron. She is wiping her hands on a towel.*) He played the fiddle and very well, too.

ALEXANDRA (*Turns to smile at* HORACE): I never knew—

ADDIE: Where's your mama?

ALEXANDRA: Gone to Miss Safronia's to fit her dresses.

(ADDIE *nods, starts to exit.*)

HORACE: Addie.

ADDIE: Yes, Mr. Horace.

HORACE (*Speaks as if he had made a sudden decision*): Tell Cal to get on his things. I want him to go an errand.

(ADDIE *nods, exits.* HORACE *moves nervously in his chair, looks out of the window.*)

ALEXANDRA (*Who has been watching him*): It's too bad it's been raining all day, Papa. But you can go out in the yard tomorrow. Don't be restless.

HORACE: I'm not restless, darling.

BIRDIE: I remember so well the time we played together, your papa and me. It was the first time Oscar brought me here to supper. I had never seen all the Hubbards together before, and you know what a ninny I am and how shy. (*Turns to look at* HORACE.) You said you could play the fiddle and you'd be much obliged if I'd play with you. I was obliged to *you*, all right, all right. (*Laughs when he does not answer her.*) Horace, you haven't heard a word I've said.

HORACE: Birdie, when did Oscar get back from Chicago?

BIRDIE: Yesterday. Hasn't he been here yet?

ALEXANDRA (*Stops playing*): No. Neither has Uncle Ben since—since that day.

BIRDIE: Oh, I didn't know it was *that* bad. Oscar never tells me anything—

HORACE (*Smiles, nods*): The Hubbards have had their great quarrel. I knew it would come some day. (*Laughs.*) It came.

ALEXANDRA: It came. It certainly came all right.

BIRDIE (*Amazed*): But Oscar was in such a good humor when he got home, I didn't—

HORACE: Yes, I can understand that.

(ADDIE *enters carrying a large tray with glasses, a carafe of elderberry wine and a plate of cookies, which she puts on the table.*)

ALEXANDRA: Addie! A party! What for?

ADDIE: Nothing for. I had the fresh butter, so I made the cakes, and a little elderberry does the stomach good in the rain.

BIRDIE: Isn't this nice! A party just for us. Let's play party music, Zan.

(ALEXANDRA *begins to play a gay piece.*)

ADDIE (*To* HORACE, *wheeling his chair to center*): Come over here, Mr. Horace, and don't be thinking so much. A glass of elderberry will do more good.

(ALEXANDRA *reaches for a cake.* BIRDIE *pours herself a glass of wine.*)

ALEXANDRA: Good cakes, Addie. It's nice here. Just us. Be nice if it could always be this way.

BIRDIE (*Nods happily*): Quiet and restful.

ADDIE: Well, it won't be that way long. Little while now, even sitting here, you'll hear the red bricks going into place. The next day the smoke'll be pushing out the chimneys and by church time that Sunday every human born of woman will be living on chicken. That's how Mr. Ben's been telling the story.

**HORACE** (*Looks at her*): They believe it that way?

**ADDIE:** Believe it? They used to believing what Mr. Ben orders. There ain't been so much talk around here since Sherman's army didn't come near.

**HORACE** (*Softly*): They are fools.

**ADDIE** (*Nods, sits down with the sewing basket*): You ain't born in the South unless you're a fool.

**BIRDIE** (*Has drunk another glass of wine*): But we didn't play together after that night. Oscar said he didn't like me to play on the piano. (*Turns to* **ALEXANDRA**.) You know what he said that night?

**ALEXANDRA:** Who?

**BIRDIE:** Oscar. He said that music made him nervous. He said he just sat and waited for the next note. (**ALEXANDRA** *laughs.*) He wasn't poking fun. He meant it. Ah, well— (*She finishes her glass, shakes her head.* **HORACE** *looks at her, smiles.*) Your papa don't like to admit it, but he's been mighty kind to me all these years. (*Running the back of her hand along his sleeve.*) Often he'd step in when somebody said something and once— (*She stops, turns away, her face still.*) Once he stopped Oscar from— (*She stops, turns. Quickly.*) I'm sorry I said that. Why, here I am so happy and yet I think about bad things. (*Laughs nervously.*) That's not right, now, is it? (*She pours a drink.* **CAL** *appears in the door. He has on an old coat and is carrying a torn umbrella.*)

**ALEXANDRA:** Have a cake, Cal.

**CAL** (*Comes in, takes a cake*): Yes'm. You want me, Mr. Horace?

**HORACE:** What time is it, Cal?

**CAL:** 'Bout ten minutes before it's five.

**HORACE:** All right. Now you walk yourself down to the bank.

**CAL:** It'll be closed. Nobody'll be there but Mr. Manders, Mr. Joe Horns, Mr. Leo—

**HORACE:** Go in the back way. They'll be at the table, going over the day's business. (*Points to the deposit box.*) See that box?

**CAL** (*Nods*): Yes, sir.

**HORACE:** You tell Mr. Manders that Mr. Horace says he's much obliged to him for bringing the box, it arrived all right.

**CAL** (*Bewildered*): He know you got the box. He bring it himself Wednesday. I opened the door to him and he say, "Hello, Cal, coming on to summer weather."

**HORACE:** You say just what I tell you. Understand?

(**BIRDIE** *pours another drink, stands at table.*)

**CAL:** No, sir. I ain't going to say I understand. I'm going down and tell a man he give you something he already know he give you, and you say "understand."

**HORACE:** Now, Cal.

**CAL:** Yes, sir. I just going to say you obliged for the box coming all right. I ain't going to understand it, but I'm going to say it.

**HORACE:** And tell him I want him to come over here after supper, and to bring Mr. Sol Fowler with him.

**CAL** (*Nods*): He's to come after supper and bring Mr. Sol Fowler, your attorney-at-law, with him.

**HORACE** (*Smiles*): That's right. Just walk right in the back room and say your piece. (*Slowly.*) In front of everybody.

**CAL:** Yes, sir. (*Mumbles to himself as he exits.*)

**ALEXANDRA** (*Who has been watching* **HORACE**): Is anything the matter, Papa?

**HORACE:** Oh, no. Nothing.

**ADDIE:** Miss Birdie, that elderberry going to give you a headache spell.

**BIRDIE** (*Beginning to be drunk. Gaily*): Oh, I don't think so. I don't think it will.

**ALEXANDRA** (*As* **HORACE** *puts his hand to his throat*): Do you want your medicine, Papa?

**HORACE:** No, no. I'm all right, darling.

**BIRDIE:** Mama used to give me elderberry wine when I was a little girl. For hiccoughs. (*Laughs.*) You know, I don't think people get hiccoughs any more. Isn't that funny? (**BIRDIE** *laughs.* **HORACE** *and* **ALEXANDRA** *laugh.*) I used to get hiccoughs just when I shouldn't have.

**ADDIE** (*Nods*): And nobody gets growing pains no more. That is funny. Just as if there was some style in what you get. One year an ailment's stylish and the next year it ain't.

**BIRDIE** (*Turns*): I remember. It was my first big party, at Lionnet I mean, and I was so excited, and there I was with hiccoughs and Mama laughing. (*Softly. Looking at carafe.*) Mama always laughed. (*Picks up carafe.*) A big party, a lovely dress from Mr. Worth in Paris, France, and hiccoughs. (*Pours drink.*) My brother pounding me on the back and Mama with the elderberry bottle, laughing at me. Everybody was on their way to come, and I was such a ninny, hiccoughing away. (*Drinks.*) You know, that was the first day I ever saw Oscar Hubbard. The Ballongs were selling their horses and he was going there to buy. He passed and lifted his hat—we could see him from the window—and my brother, to tease Mama, said maybe we should have invited the Hubbards to the party. He said Mama didn't like them because they kept a store, and he said that was old-fashioned of her. (*Her face lights up.*) And then, and *then,* I saw Mama angry for the first time in my life. She said that wasn't the reason. She said she was old-fashioned, but not that way. She said she was old-fashioned enough not to like people who killed animals they couldn't use, and who made their money charging awful interest to poor, ignorant niggers and cheating them on what they bought. She was very angry, Mama was.

I had never seen her face like that. And then suddenly she laughed and said, "Look, I've frightened Birdie out of the hiccoughs." (*Her head drops. Then softly.*) And so she had. They were all gone. (*Moves to sofa, sits.*)

**ADDIE:** Yeah, they got mighty well off cheating niggers. Well, there are people who eat the earth and eat all the people on it like in the Bible with the locusts. Then there are people who stand around and watch them eat it. (*Softly.*) Sometimes I think it ain't right to stand and watch them do it.

**BIRDIE** (*Thoughtfully*): Like I say, if we could only go back to Lionnet. Everybody'd be better there. They'd be good and kind. I like people to be kind. (*Pours drink.*) Don't you, Horace; don't you like people to be kind?

**HORACE:** Yes, Birdie.

**BIRDIE** (*Very drunk now*): Yes, that was the first day I ever saw Oscar. Who would have thought— (*Quickly.*) You all want to know something? Well, I don't like Leo. My very own son, and I don't like him. (*Laughs, gaily.*) My, I guess I even like Oscar more.

**ALEXANDRA:** Why did you marry Uncle Oscar?

**ADDIE** (*Sharply*): That's no question for you to be asking.

**HORACE** (*Sharply*): Why not? She's heard enough around here to ask anything.

**ALEXANDRA:** Aunt Birdie, why did you marry Uncle Oscar?

**BIRDIE:** I don't know. I thought I liked him. He was kind to me and I thought it was because he liked me too. But that wasn't the reason— (*Wheels on* **ALEXANDRA**.) Ask why *he* married *me.* I can tell you that: He's told it to me often enough.

**ADDIE** (*Leaning forward*): Miss Birdie, don't—

**BIRDIE** (*Speaking very rapidly, tensely*): My family was good and the cotton on Lionnet's fields was better. Ben Hubbard wanted the cotton and (*Rises.*) Oscar Hubbard married it for him. He was kind to me, then. He used to smile at me. He hasn't smiled at me since. Everybody knew that's what he married me for. (**ADDIE** *rises.*) Everybody but me. Stupid, stupid me.

**ALEXANDRA** (*To* **HORACE**, *holding his hand, softly*): I see. (*Hesitates.*) Papa, I mean— when you feel better couldn't we go away? I mean, by ourselves. Couldn't we find a way to go—

**HORACE:** Yes, I know what you mean. We'll try to find a way. I promise you, darling.

**ADDIE** (*Moves to* **BIRDIE**): Rest a bit, Miss Birdie. You get talking like this you'll get a headache and—

**BIRDIE** (*Sharply, turning to her*): I've never had a headache in my life. (*Begins to cry hysterically.*) You know it as well as I do. (*Turns to* **ALEXANDRA**.) I never had a headache, Zan. That's a lie they tell for me. I drink. All by myself, in my own room, by myself, I drink. Then, when they want to hide it, they say, "Birdie's got a headache again"—

**ALEXANDRA** (*Comes to her quickly*): Aunt Birdie.

**BIRDIE** (*Turning away*): Even you won't like me now. You won't like me any more.

**ALEXANDRA:** I love you. I'll always love you.

**BIRDIE** (*Furiously*): Well, don't. Don't love me. Because in twenty years you'll just be like me. They'll do all the same things to you. (*Begins to laugh hysterically.*) You know what? In twenty-two years I haven't had a whole day of happiness. Oh, a little, like today with you and all. But never a single, whole day. I say to myself, if only I had one more *whole* day, then— (*The laugh stops.*) And that's the way you'll be. And you'll trail after them, just like me, hoping they won't be so mean that day or say something to make you feel so bad—only you'll be worse off because you haven't got my Mama to remember— (*Turns away, her head drops. She stands quietly, swaying a little, holding onto the sofa.* **ALEXANDRA** *leans down, puts her cheek on* **BIRDIE'S** *arm.*)

**ALEXANDRA** (*To* **BIRDIE**): I guess we were all trying to make a happy day. You know, we sit around and try to pretend nothing's happened. We try to pretend we are not here. We make believe we are just by ourselves, some place else, and it doesn't seem to work. (*Kisses* **BIRDIE'S** *hand.*) Come now, Aunt Birdie, I'll walk you home. You and me. (*She takes* **BIRDIE'S** *arm. They move slowly out.*)

**BIRDIE** (*Softly as they exit*): You and me.

**ADDIE** (*After a minute*): Well. First time I ever heard Miss Birdie say a word. (**HORACE** *looks at her.*) Maybe it's good for her. I'm just sorry Zan had to hear it. (**HORACE** *moves his head as if he were uncomfortable.*) You feel bad, don't you? (*He shrugs.*)

**HORACE:** So you didn't want Zan to hear? It would be nice to let her stay innocent, like Birdie at her age. Let her listen now. Let her see everything. How else is she going to know that she's got to get away? I'm trying to show her that. I'm trying, but I've only got a little time left. She can even hate me when I'm dead, if she'll only learn to hate and fear this.

**ADDIE:** Mr. Horace—

**HORACE:** Pretty soon there'll be nobody to help her but you.

**ADDIE** (*Crossing to him*): What can I do?

**HORACE:** Take her away.

**ADDIE:** How can I do that? Do you think they'd let me just go away with her?

**HORACE:** I'll fix it so they can't stop you when you're ready to go. You'll go, Addie?

**ADDIE** (*After a second, softly*): Yes, sir. I promise. (*He touches her arm, nods.*)

**HORACE** (*Quietly*): I'm going to have Sol Fowler make me a new will. They'll make trouble, but you make Zan stand firm and Fowler'll do the rest. Addie, I'd like to leave you something for yourself. I always wanted to.

ADDIE (*Laughs*): Don't you do that, Mr. Horace. A nigger woman in a white man's will! I'd never get it nohow.

HORACE: I know. But upstairs in the armoire drawer there's seventeen hundred dollar bills. It's money left from my trip. It's in an envelope with your name. It's for you.

ADDIE: Seventeen hundred dollar bills! My God, Mr. Horace, I won't know how to count up that high. (*Shyly.*) It's mighty kind and good of you. I don't know what to say for thanks—

CAL (*Appears in doorway*): I'm back. (*No answer.*) I'm back.

ADDIE: So we see.

HORACE: Well?

CAL: Nothing. I just went down and spoke my piece. Just like you told me. I say, "Mr. Horace he thank you mightily for the safe box arriving in good shape and he say you come right after supper to his house and bring Mr. Attorney-at-law Sol Fowler with you." Then I wipe my hands on my coat. Every time I ever told a lie in my whole life, I wipe my hands right after. Can't help doing it. Well, while I'm wiping my hands, Mr. Leo jump up and say to me, "What box? What you talking about?"

HORACE (*Smiles*): Did he?

CAL: And Mr. Leo say he got to leave a little early cause he got something to do. And then Mr. Manders say Mr. Leo should sit right down and finish up his work and stop acting like somebody made him Mr. President. So he sit down. Now, just like I told you, Mr. Manders was mighty surprised with the message because he knows right well he brought the box— (*Points to box, sighs.*) But he took it all right. Some men take everything easy and some do not.

HORACE (*Puts his head back, laughs*): Mr. Leo was telling the truth; he *has* got something to do. I hope Manders don't keep him too long. (*Outside there is the sound of voices.* CAL *exits.* ADDIE *crosses quickly to* HORACE, *puts basket on table, begins to wheel his chair towards the stairs. Sharply.*) No. Leave me where I am.

ADDIE: But that's Miss Regina coming back.

HORACE (*Nods, looking at door*): Go away, Addie.

ADDIE (*Hesitates*): Mr. Horace. Don't talk no more today. You don't feel well and it won't do no good—

HORACE (*As he hears footsteps in the hall*): Go on. (*She looks at him for a second, then picks up her sewing from table and exits as* REGINA *comes in from hall.* HORACE'S *chair is now so placed that he is in front of the table with the medicine.* REGINA *stands in the hall, shakes umbrella, stands it in the corner, takes off her cloak and throws it over the banister. She stares at* HORACE.)

REGINA (*As she takes off her gloves*): We had agreed that you were to stay in your part of this house and I in mine. This room is *my* part of the house. Please don't come down here again.

HORACE: I won't.

REGINA (*Crosses towards bell-cord*): I'll get Cal to take you upstairs.

HORACE (*Smiles*): Before you do I want to tell you that after all, we have invested our money in Hubbard Sons and Marshall, Cotton Manufacturers.

REGINA (*Stops, turns, stares at him*): What are you talking about? You haven't seen Ben— When did you change your mind?

HORACE: I didn't change my mind. *I* didn't invest the money. (*Smiles.*) It was invested for me.

REGINA (*Angrily*): What—?

HORACE: I had eighty-eight thousand dollars' worth of Union Pacific bonds in that safe-deposit box. They are not there now. Go and look. (*As she stares at him, he points to the box.*) Go and look, Regina. (*She crosses quickly to the box, opens it.*) Those bonds are as negotiable as money.

REGINA (*Turns back to him*): What kind of joke are you playing now? Is this for my benefit?

HORACE: I don't look in that box very often, but three days ago, on Wednesday it was, because I had made a decision—

REGINA: I want to know what you are talking about.

HORACE (*Sharply*): Don't interrupt me again. Because I had made a decision, I sent for the box. The bonds were gone. Eighty-eight thousand dollars gone. (*He smiles at her.*)

REGINA (*After a moment's silence, quietly*): Do you think I'm crazy enough to believe what you're saying?

HORACE (*Shrugs*): Believe anything you like.

REGINA (*Stares at him, slowly*): Where did they go to?

HORACE: They are in Chicago. With Mr. Marshall, I should guess.

REGINA: What did they do? Walk to Chicago? Have you really gone crazy?

HORACE: Leo took the bonds.

REGINA (*Turns sharply then speaks softly, without conviction*): I don't believe it.

HORACE (*Leans forward*): I wasn't there but I can guess what happened. This fine gentleman, to whom you were willing to marry your daughter, took the keys and opened the box. You remember that the day of the fight Oscar went to Chicago? Well, he went with my bonds that his son Leo had stolen for him. (*Pleasantly.*) And for Ben, of course, too.

REGINA (*Slowly, nods*): When did you find out the bonds were gone?

HORACE: Wednesday night.

REGINA: I thought that's what you said. Why have you waited three days to do

anything? (*Suddenly laughs.*) This *will* make a fine story.

HORACE (*Nods*): Couldn't it?

REGINA (*Still laughing*): A fine story to hold over their heads. How could they be such fools? (*Turns to him.*)

HORACE: But I'm not going to hold it over their heads.

REGINA (*The laugh stops*): What?

HORACE (*Turns his chair to face her*): I'm going to let them keep the bonds—as a loan from you. An eighty-eight-thousand-dollar loan; they should be grateful to you. They will be, I think.

REGINA (*Slowly, smiles*): I see. You are punishing me. But I won't let you punish me. If you won't do anything, I will. Now. (*She starts for door.*)

HORACE: You won't do anything. Because you can't. (REGINA *stops.*) It won't do you any good to make trouble because I shall simply say that I lent them the bonds.

REGINA (*Slowly*): You would do that?

HORACE: Yes. For once in your life I am tying your hands. There is nothing for you to do. (*There is silence. Then she sits down.*)

REGINA: I see. You are going to lend them the bonds and let them keep all the profit they make on them, and there is nothing I can do about it. Is that right?

HORACE: Yes.

REGINA (*Softly*): Why did you say that I was making this gift?

HORACE: I was coming to that. I am going to make a new will, Regina, leaving you eighty-eight thousand dollars in Union Pacific bonds. The rest will go to Zan. It's true that your brothers have borrowed your share for a little while. After my death I advise you to talk to Ben and Oscar. They won't admit anything and Ben, I think, will be smart enough to see that he's safe. Because I knew about the theft and said nothing. Nor will I say anything as long as I live. Is that clear to you?

REGINA (*Nods, softly, without looking at him*): You will not say anything as long as you live.

HORACE: That's right. And by that time they will probably have replaced your bonds, and then they'll belong to you and nobody but us will ever know what happened. (*Stops, smiles.*) They'll be around any minute to see what I am going to do. I took good care to see that word reached Leo. They'll be mighty relieved to know I'm going to do nothing and Ben will think it all a capital joke on you. And that will be the end of that. There's nothing you can do to them, nothing you can do to me.

REGINA: You hate me very much.

HORACE: No.

REGINA: Oh, I think you do. (*Puts her head back, sighs.*) Well, we haven't been very good together. Anyway, I don't hate you either. I have only contempt for you. I've always had.

HORACE: From the very first?

REGINA: I think so.

HORACE: I was in love with *you.* But why did *you* marry *me?*

REGINA: I was lonely when I was young.

HORACE: *You* were lonely?

REGINA: Not the way people usually mean. Lonely for all the things I wasn't going to get. Everybody in this house was so busy and there was so little place for what I wanted. I wanted the world. Then, and then— (*Smiles.*) Papa died and left the money to Ben and Oscar.

HORACE: And you married me?

REGINA: Yes, I thought— But I was wrong. You were a small-town clerk then. You haven't changed.

HORACE (*Nods, smiles*): And that wasn't what you wanted.

REGINA: No. No, it wasn't what I wanted. (*Pauses, leans back, pleasantly.*) It took me a little while to find out I had made a mistake. As for you—I don't know. It was almost as if I couldn't stand the kind of man you were— (*Smiles, softly.*) I used to lie there at night, praying you wouldn't come near—

HORACE: Really? It was as bad as that?

REGINA (*Nods*): Remember when I went to Doctor Sloan and I told you he said there was something the matter with me and that you shouldn't touch me any more?

HORACE: I remember.

REGINA: But you believed it. I couldn't understand that. I couldn't understand that anybody could be such a soft fool. That was when I began to despise you.

HORACE (*Puts his hand to his throat, looks at the bottle of medicine on table*): Why didn't you leave me?

REGINA: I told you I married you for something. It turned out it was only for this. (*Carefully.*) This wasn't what I wanted, but it was something. I never thought about it much but if I had (HORACE *puts his hand to his throat.*) I'd have known that you would die before I would. But I couldn't have known that you would get heart trouble so early and so bad. I'm lucky, Horace. I've always been lucky. (HORACE *turns slowly to the medicine.*) I'll be lucky again. (HORACE *looks at her. Then he puts his hand to his throat. Because he cannot reach the bottle he moves the chair closer. He reaches for the medicine, takes out the cork, picks up the spoon. The bottle slips and smashes on the table. He draws in his breath, gasps.*)

HORACE: Please. Tell Addie— The other bottle is upstairs. (REGINA *has not moved. She does not move now. He stares at her. Then, suddenly as if he understood, he raises his voice. It is a panic-stricken whisper, too small to be heard outside the room.*) Addie! Addie! Come— (*Stops as he hears the softness of his voice. He makes a sudden, furious spring from the chair to the stairs, taking the first few steps as if he were a desperate runner. On the fourth step he slips, gasps, grasps the rail, makes a great effort to reach the landing. When he reaches the landing, he is on his knees. His knees give way, he falls on the landing, out of view.* REGINA *has not turned during his climb up the stairs. Now she waits a second. Then she goes below the landing, speaks up.*)

REGINA: Horace. Horace. (*When there is no answer, she turns, calls.*) Addie! Cal! Come in here. (*She starts up the steps.* ADDIE *and* CAL *appear. Both run towards the stairs.*) He's had an attack. Come up here. (*They run up the steps quickly.*)

CAL: My God. Mr. Horace—

(*They cannot be seen now.*)

REGINA (*Her voice comes from the head of the stairs*): Be still, Cal. Bring him in here. (*Before the footsteps and the voices have completely died away,* ALEXANDRA *appears in the hall door, in her raincloak and hood. She comes into the room, begins to unfasten the cloak, suddenly looks around, sees the empty wheel chair, stares, begins to move swiftly as if to look in the dining room. At the same moment* ADDIE *runs down the stairs.* ALEXANDRA *turns and stares up at* ADDIE.)

ALEXANDRA: Addie! What?

ADDIE (*Takes* ALEXANDRA *by the shoulders*): I'm going for the doctor. Go upstairs. (ALEXANDRA *looks at her, then quickly breaks away and runs up the steps.* ADDIE *exits. The stage is empty for a minute. Then the front doorbell begins to ring. When there is no answer, it rings again. A second later* LEO *appears in the hall, talking as he comes in.*)

LEO (*Very nervous*): Hello. (*Irritably.*) Never saw any use ringing a bell when a door was open. If you are going to ring a bell, then somebody should answer it. (*Gets in the room, looks around, puzzled, listens, hears no sound.*) Aunt Regina. (*He moves around restlessly.*) Addie. (*Waits.*) Where the hell— (*Crosses to the bell cord, rings it impatiently, waits, gets no answer, calls.*) Cal! Cal! (CAL *appears on the stair landing.*)

CAL (*His voice is soft, shaken*): Mr. Leo. Miss Regina says you stop that screaming noise.

LEO (*Angrily*): Where is everybody?

CAL: Mr. Horace he got an attack. He's bad. Miss Regina says you stop that noise.

LEO: Uncle Horace— What— What happened? (CAL *starts down the stairs, shakes his head, begins to move swiftly off.* LEO *looks around wildly.*) But when— You seen Mr. Oscar or Mr. Ben? (CAL *shakes his head. Moves on.* LEO *grabs him by the arm.*) Answer me, will you?

CAL: No, I ain't seen 'em. I ain't got time to answer you. I got to get things. (CAL *runs off.*)

LEO: But what's the matter with him? When did this happen— (*Calling after* CAL.) You'd think Papa'd be some place where you could find him. I been chasing him all afternoon.

(OSCAR *and* BEN *come into the room, talking excitedly.*)

OSCAR: I hope it's not a bad attack.

BEN: It's the first one he's had since he came home.

LEO: Papa, I've been looking all over town for you and Uncle Ben—

BEN: Where is he?

OSCAR: Addie said it was sudden.

BEN (*To* LEO): Where is he? When did it happen?

LEO: Upstairs. Will you listen to me, please? I been looking for you for—

OSCAR (*To* BEN): You think we should go up? (BEN, *looking up the steps, shakes his head.*)

BEN: I don't know. I don't know.

OSCAR (*Shakes his head*): But he was all right—

LEO (*Yelling*): Will you listen to me?

OSCAR (*Sharply*): What is the matter with you?

LEO: I been trying to tell you. I been trying to find you for an hour—

OSCAR: Tell me what?

LEO: Uncle Horace knows about the bonds. He knows about them. He's had the box since Wednesday—

BEN (*Sharply*): Stop shouting! What the hell are you talking about?

LEO (*Furiously*): I'm telling you he knows about the bonds. Ain't that clear enough—

OSCAR (*Grabbing* LEO'S *arm*): You God-damn fool! Stop screaming!

BEN: Now what happened? Talk quietly.

LEO: You heard me. Uncle Horace knows about the bonds. He's known since Wednesday.

BEN (*After a second*): How do you know that?

LEO: Because Cal comes down to Manders and says the box came O.K. and—

OSCAR (*Trembling*): That might not mean a thing—

LEO (*Angrily*): No? It might not, huh? Then he says Manders should come here tonight and bring Sol Fowler with him. I guess that don't mean a thing either.

OSCAR (*To* BEN): Ben— What— Do you think he's seen the—

BEN (*Motions to the box*): There's the box. (*Both* OSCAR *and* LEO *turn sharply.* LEO *makes a leap to the box.*) You ass. Put it down. What are you going to do with it, eat it?

LEO: I'm going to— (*Starts.*)

BEN (*Furiously*): Put it down. Don't touch it again. Now sit down and shut up for a minute.

OSCAR: Since Wednesday. (*To* LEO.) You said he had it since Wednesday. Why didn't he say something— (*To* BEN.) I don't understand—

LEO (*Taking a step*): I can put it back. I can put it back before anybody knows.

BEN (*Who is standing at the table, softly*): He's had it since Wednesday. Yet he hasn't said a word to us.

OSCAR: *Why? Why?*

LEO: What's the difference why? He was getting ready to say plenty. He was going to say it to Fowler tonight—

OSCAR (*Angrily*): Be still. (*Turns to* BEN, *looks at him, waits.*)

BEN (*After a minute*): I don't believe that.

LEO (*Wildly*): *You* don't believe it? What do I care what *you* believe? I do the dirty work and then—

BEN (*Turning his head sharply to* LEO): I'm remembering that. I'm remembering that, Leo.

OSCAR: What do you mean?

LEO: You—

BEN (*To* OSCAR.): If you don't shut that little fool up, I'll show you what I mean. For some reason he knows, but he don't say a word.

OSCAR: Maybe he didn't know that *we*—

BEN (*Quickly*): That *Leo*— He's no fool. Does Manders know the bonds are missing?

LEO: How could I tell? I was half crazy. I don't think so. Because Manders seemed kind of puzzled and—

OSCAR: But we got to find out— (*He breaks off as* CAL *comes into the room carrying a kettle of hot water.*)

BEN: How is he, Cal?

CAL: I don't know, Mr. Ben. He was bad. (*Going towards stairs.*)

OSCAR: But when did it happen?

CAL (*Shrugs*): He wasn't feeling bad early. (ADDIE *comes in quickly from the hall.*) Then there he is next thing on the landing, fallen over, his eyes tight—

ADDIE (*To* CAL): Dr. Sloan's over at the Ballongs. Hitch the buggy and go get him. (*She takes the kettle and cloths from him, pushes him, runs up the stairs.*) Go on. (*She disappears.* CAL *exits.*)

BEN: Never seen Sloan anywhere when you need him.

OSCAR (*Softly*): Sounds bad.

LEO: He would have told *her* about it. Aunt Regina. He would have told his own wife—

BEN (*Turning to* LEO): Yes, he might have told her. But they weren't on such pretty terms and maybe he didn't. Maybe he didn't. (*Goes quickly to* LEO.) Now, listen to me. If she doesn't know, it may work out all right. If she does know, you're to say he lent you the bonds.

LEO: Lent them to me! Who's going to believe that?

BEN: Nobody.

OSCAR (*To* LEO): Don't you understand? It can't do no harm to say it—

LEO: Why should I say he lent them to me? Why not to you? (*Carefully.*) Why not to Uncle Ben?

BEN (*Smiles*): Just because he didn't lend them to me. Remember that.

LEO: But all he has to do is say he didn't lend them to me—

BEN (*Furiously*): But for some reason, he doesn't seem to be talking, does he? (*There are footsteps above. They all stand looking at the stairs.* REGINA *begins to come slowly down.*)

BEN: What happened?

REGINA: He's had a bad attack.

OSCAR: Too bad. I'm so sorry we weren't here when—when Horace needed us.

BEN: When *you* needed us.

REGINA (*Looks at him*): Yes.

BEN: How is he? Can we—can we go up?

REGINA (*Shakes her head*): He's not conscious.

OSCAR (*Pacing around*): It's that—it's that bad? Wouldn't you think Sloan could be found quickly, just once, just once?

REGINA: I don't think there is much for him to do.

BEN: Oh, don't talk like that. He's come through attacks before. He will now. (REGINA *sits down. After a second she speaks softly.*)

REGINA: Well. We haven't seen each other since the day of our fight.

BEN (*Tenderly*): That was nothing. Why, you and Oscar and I used to fight when we were kids.

OSCAR (*Hurriedly*): Don't you think we should go up? Is there anything we can do for Horace—

BEN: You don't feel well. Ah—

REGINA (*Without looking at them*): No, I don't. (*Slight pause.*) Horace told me about the bonds this afternoon. (*There is an immediate shocked silence.*)

LEO: The bonds. What do you mean? What bonds? What—

BEN (*Looks at him furiously. Then to* REGINA): The Union Pacific bonds? *Horace's* Union Pacific bonds?

REGINA: Yes.

OSCAR (*Steps to her, very nervously*). Well. Well what— what about them? What— what could he say?

REGINA: He said that Leo had stolen the bonds and given them to you.

OSCAR (*Aghast, very loudly*): That's ridiculous, Regina, absolutely—

LEO: I don't know what you're talking about. What would I— Why—

REGINA (*Wearily to* BEN): Isn't it enough that he stole them from me? Do I have to listen to this in the bargain?

OSCAR: You are talking—

LEO: I didn't steal anything. I don't know why—

REGINA (*To* BEN): Would you ask them to stop that, please? (*There is silence for a minute.* BEN *glowers at* OSCAR *and* LEO.)

BEN: Aren't we starting at the wrong end, Regina? What did Horace tell you?

REGINA (*Smiles at him*): He told me that Leo had stolen the bonds.

LEO: I didn't steal—

REGINA: Please. Let me finish. Then he told me that he was going to pretend that he had lent them to you (LEO *turns sharply to* REGINA, *then looks at* OSCAR, *then looks back at* REGINA.) as a present from me— to my brothers. He said there was nothing I could do about it. He said the rest of his money would go to Alexandra. That is all. (*There is a silence.* OSCAR *coughs,* LEO *smiles slyly.*)

LEO (*Taking a step to her*): I told you he had lent them— I could have told you—

REGINA (*Ignores him, smiles sadly at* BEN): So I'm very badly off, you see. (*Carefully.*) But Horace said there was nothing I could do about it as long as he was alive to say he had lent you the bonds.

BEN: You shouldn't feel that way. It can all be explained, all be adjusted. It isn't as bad—

REGINA: So you, at least, are willing to admit that the bonds were stolen?

BEN (OSCAR *laughs nervously*): I admit no such thing. It's possible that Horace made up that part of the story to tease you— (*Looks at her.*) Or perhaps to punish you. Punish you.

REGINA (*Sadly*): It's not a pleasant story. I feel bad, Ben, naturally. I hadn't thought—

BEN: Now you shall have the bonds safely back. That was the understanding, wasn't it, Oscar?

OSCAR: Yes.

REGINA: I'm glad to know that. (*Smiles.*) Ah, I had greater hopes—

BEN: Don't talk that way. That's foolish. (*Looks at his watch.*) I think we ought to drive out for Sloan ourselves. If we can't find him we'll go over to Senateville for Doctor Morris. And don't think I'm dismissing this other business. I'm not. We'll have it all out on a more appropriate day.

REGINA (*Looks up, quietly*): I don't think you had better go yet. I think you had better stay and sit down.

BEN: We'll be back with Sloan.

REGINA: Cal has gone for him. I don't want you to go.

BEN: Now don't worry and—

REGINA: You will come back in this room and sit down. I have something more to say.

BEN (*Turns, comes towards her*): Since when do I take orders from you?

REGINA (*Smiles*): You don't—yet. (*Sharply.*) Come back, Oscar. You too, Leo.

OSCAR (*Sure of himself, laughs*): My dear Regina—

BEN (*Softly, pats her hand*): Horace has already clipped your wings and very wittily. Do I have to clip them, too? (*Smiles at her.*) You'd get farther with a smile, Regina. I'm a soft man for a woman's smile.

REGINA: I'm smiling, Ben. I'm smiling because you are quite safe while Horace lives. But I don't think Horace will live. And if he doesn't live I shall want seventy-five per cent in exchange for the bonds.

BEN (*Steps back, whistles, laughs*): Greedy! What a greedy girl you are! You want so much of everything.

REGINA: Yes. And if I don't get what I want I am going to put all three of you in jail.

OSCAR (*Furiously*): You're mighty crazy. Having just admitted—

BEN: And on what evidence would you put Oscar and Leo in jail?

REGINA (*Laughs, gaily*): Oscar, listen to him. He's getting ready to swear that it was you and Leo! What do you say to that? (OSCAR *turns furiously towards* BEN.) Oh, don't be angry, Oscar. I'm going to see that he goes in with you.

BEN: Try anything you like, Regina. (*Sharply.*) And now we can stop all this and say good-bye to you. (ALEXANDRA *comes slowly down the steps.*) It's his money and he's obviously willing to let us borrow it. (*More pleasantly.*) Learn to make threats when you can carry them through. For how many years have I told you a good-looking woman gets more by being soft and appealing? Mama used to tell you that. (*Looks at his watch.*) Where the hell is Sloan? (*To* OSCAR.) Take the buggy and— (*As* BEN *turns to* OSCAR, *he sees* ALEXANDRA. *She walks stiffly. She goes slowly to the lower window, her head bent. They all turn to look at her.*)

OSCAR (*After a second, moving toward her*): What? Alexandra— (*She does not answer.*

*After a second,* **ADDIE** *comes slowly down the stairs, moving as if she were very tired. At foot of steps, she looks at* **ALEXANDRA,** *then turns and slowly crosses to door and exits.* **REGINA** *rises.* **BEN** *looks nervously at* **ALEXANDRA,** *at* **REGINA.)**

**OSCAR** (*As* **ADDIE** *passes him, irritably to* **ALEXANDRA**): Well, what is— (*Turns into room—sees* **ADDIE** *at foot of steps.*) — what's? (**BEN** *puts up a hand, shakes his head.*) My God, I didn't know—who could have known—I didn't know he was that sick. Well, well—I— (**REGINA** *stands quietly, her back to them.*)

**BEN** (*Softly, sincerely*): Seems like yesterday when he first came here.

**OSCAR** (*Sincerely, nervously*): Yes, that's true. (*Turns to* **BEN.**) The whole town loved him and respected him.

**ALEXANDRA** (*Turns*): Did you love him, Uncle Oscar?

**OSCAR:** Certainly, I— What a strange thing to ask! I—

**ALEXANDRA:** Did you love him, Uncle Ben?

**BEN** (*Simply*): He had—

**ALEXANDRA** (*Suddenly starts to laugh very loudly*): And you, Mama, did you love him, too?

**REGINA:** I know what you feel, Alexandra, but please try to control yourself.

**ALEXANDRA** (*Still laughing*): I'm trying, Mama. I'm trying very hard.

**BEN:** Grief makes some people laugh and some people cry. It's better to cry, Alexandra.

**ALEXANDRA** (*The laugh has stopped. Tensely moves toward* **REGINA**): What was Papa doing on the staircase?

(**BEN** *turns to look at* **ALEXANDRA.**)

**REGINA:** Please go and lie down, my dear. We all need time to get over shocks like this. (**ALEXANDRA** *does not move.* **REGINA'S** *voice becomes softer, more insistent.*) Please go, Alexandra.

**ALEXANDRA:** No, Mama. I'll wait. I've got to talk to you.

**REGINA:** Later. Go and rest now.

**ALEXANDRA** (*Quietly*): I'll wait, Mama. I've plenty of time.

**REGINA** (*Hesitates, stares, makes a half shrug, turns back to* **BEN**): As I was saying. Tomorrow morning I am going up to Judge Simmes. I shall tell him about Leo.

**BEN** (*Motioning toward* **ALEXANDRA**): Not in front of the child, Regina. I—

**REGINA** (*Turns to him. Sharply*): I didn't ask her to stay. Tomorrow morning I go to Judge Simmes—

**OSCAR:** And what proof? What proof of all this—

**REGINA** (*Turns sharply*): None. I won't need any. The bonds are missing and they are with Marshall. That will be enough. If it isn't, I'll add what's necessary.

**BEN:** I'm sure of that.

**REGINA** (*Turns to* **BEN**): You can be quite sure.

**OSCAR:** We'll deny—

**REGINA:** Deny your heads off. You couldn't find a jury that wouldn't weep for a woman whose brothers steal from her. And you couldn't find twelve men in this state you haven't cheated and hate you for it.

**OSCAR:** What kind of talk is this? You couldn't do anything like that! We're your own brothers. (*Points upstairs.*) How can you talk that way when upstairs not five minutes ago—

**REGINA** (*Slowly*): There are people who can never go back, who must finish what they start. I am one of those people, Oscar. (*After a slight pause.*) Where was I? (*Smiles at* **BEN.**) Well, they'll convict you. But I won't care much if they don't. (*Leans forward, pleasantly.*) Because by that time you'll be ruined. I shall also tell my story to Mr. Marshall, who likes me, I think, and who will not want to be involved in your scandal. A respectable firm like Marshall and Company. The deal would be off in an hour. (*Turns to* *them angrily.*) And you know it. Now I don't want to hear any more from any of you. *You'll do no more bargaining in this house.* I'll take my seventy-five per cent and well forget the story forever. That's one way of doing it, and the way I prefer. You know me well enough to know that I don't mind taking the other way.

BEN (*After a second, slowly*): None of us have ever known you well enough, Regina.

REGINA: You're getting old, Ben. Your tricks aren't as smart as they used to be. (*There is no answer. She waits, then smiles.*) All right. I take it that's settled and I get what I asked for.

OSCAR (*Furiously to* BEN): Are you going to let her do this—

BEN (*Turns to look at him, slowly*): You have a suggestion?

REGINA (*Puts her arms above her head, stretches, laughs*): No, he hasn't. All right. Now, Leo, I have forgotten that you ever saw the bonds. (*Archly, to* BEN *and* OSCAR.) And as long as you boys both behave yourselves, I've forgotten that we ever talked about them. You can draw up the necessary papers tomorrow. (BEN *laughs.* LEO *stares at him, starts for door. Exits.* OSCAR *moves towards door angrily.* REGINA *looks at* BEN, *nods, laughs with him. For a second,* OSCAR *stands in the door, looking back at them. Then he exits.*)

REGINA: You're a good loser, Ben. I like that.

BEN (*He picks up his coat, then turns to her*): Well, I say to myself, what's the good? You and I aren't like Oscar. We're not sour people. I think that comes from a good digestion. Then, too, one loses today and wins tomorrow. I say to myself, years of planning and I get what I want. Then I don't get it. But I'm not discouraged. The century's turning, the world is open. Open for people like you and me. Ready for us, waiting for us. After all this is just the beginning. There are hundreds of Hubbards sitting in rooms like this throughout the country. All their names aren't Hubbard, but they are all Hubbards and they will own this country some day. We'll get along.

REGINA (*Smiles*): I think so.

BEN: Then, too, I say to myself, things may change. (*Looks at* ALEXANDRA.) I agree with Alexandra. What is a man in a wheel chair doing on a staircase? I ask myself that.

REGINA (*Looks up at him*): And what do you answer?

BEN: I have no answer. But maybe some day I will. Maybe never, but maybe some day. (*Smiles. Pats her arm.*) When I do, I'll let you know. (*Goes towards hall.*)

REGINA: When you do, write me. I will be in Chicago. (*Gaily.*) Ah, Ben, if Papa had only left me his money.

BEN: I'll see you tomorrow.

REGINA: Oh, yes. Certainly. You'll be sort of working for me now.

BEN (*As he passes* ALEXANDRA, *smiles*): Alexandra, you're turning out to be a right interesting girl. (*Looks at* REGINA.) Well, good night all. (*He exits.*)

REGINA (*Sits quietly for a second, stretches, turns to look at* ALEXANDRA): What do you want to talk to me about, Alexandra?

ALEXANDRA (*Slowly*): I've changed my mind. I don't want to talk. There's nothing to talk about now.

REGINA: You're acting very strange. Not like yourself. You've had a bad shock today. I know that. And you loved Papa, but you must have expected this to come some day. You knew how sick he was.

ALEXANDRA: I knew. We all knew.

REGINA: It will be good for you to get away from here. Good for me, too. Time heals most wounds, Alexandra. You're young, you shall have all the things I wanted. I'll make the world for you the way I wanted it to be for me. (*Uncomfortably.*)

Don't sit there staring. You've been around Birdie so much you're getting just like her.

ALEXANDRA (*Nods*): Funny. That's what Aunt Birdie said today.

REGINA (*Nods*): Be good for you to get away from all this.

(ADDIE *enters.*)

ADDIE: Cal is back, Miss Regina. He says Dr. Sloan will be coming in a few minutes.

REGINA: We'll go in a few weeks. A few weeks! That means two or three Saturdays, two or three Sundays. (*Sighs.*) Well, I'm very tired. I shall go to bed. I don't want any supper. Put the lights out and lock up. (ADDIE *moves to the piano lamp, turns it out.*) You go to your room, Alexandra. Addie will bring you something hot. You look very tired. (*Rises. To* ADDIE.) Call me when Dr. Sloan gets here. I don't want to see anybody else. I don't want any condolence calls tonight. The whole town will be over.

ALEXANDRA: Mama, I'm not coming with you. I'm not going to Chicago.

REGINA (*Turns to her*): You're very upset, Alexandra.

ALEXANDRA (*Quietly*): I mean what I say. With all my heart.

REGINA: We'll talk about it tomorrow. The morning will make a difference.

ALEXANDRA: It won't make any difference. And there isn't anything to talk about. I am going away from you. Because I want to. Because I know Papa would want me to.

REGINA (*Puzzled, careful, polite*): You *know* your papa wanted you to go away from me?

ALEXANDRA: Yes.

REGINA (*Softly*): And if I say no?

ALEXANDRA (*Looks at her*): Say it, Mama, say it. And see what happens.

REGINA (*Softly, after a pause*): And if I make you stay?

ALEXANDRA: That would be foolish. It wouldn't work in the end.

REGINA: You're very serious about it, aren't you? (*Crosses to stairs.*) Well, you'll change your mind in a few days.

ALEXANDRA: You only change your mind when you want to. And I won't want to.

REGINA (*Going up the steps*): Alexandra, I've come to the end of my rope. Somewhere there has to be what I want, too. Life goes too fast. Do what you want; think what you want; go where you want. I'd like to keep you with me, but I won't make you stay. Too many people used to make me do too many things. No, I won't make you stay.

ALEXANDRA: You couldn't, Mama, because I want to leave here. As I've never wanted anything in my life before. Because now I understand what Papa was trying to tell me. (*Pause.*) All in one day: Addie said there were people who ate the earth and other people who stood around and watched them do it. And just now Uncle Ben said the same thing. Really, he said the same thing. (*Tensely.*) Well, tell him for me, Mama, I'm not going to stand around and watch you do it. Tell him I'll be fighting as hard as he'll be fighting (*Rises.*) some place where people don't just stand around and watch.

REGINA: Well, you have spirit, after all. I used to think you were all sugar water. We don't have to be bad friends. I don't want us to be bad friends, Alexandra. (*Starts, stops, turns to* ALEXANDRA.) Would you like to come and talk to me, Alexandra? Would you—would you like to sleep in my room tonight?

ALEXANDRA (*Takes a step towards her*): Are you afraid, Mama? (REGINA *does not answer. She moves slowly out of sight.* ADDIE *comes to* ALEXANDRA, *presses her arm.*)

*The Curtain Falls*

## SUMMARY

The modern play that is well made is a satisfying experience for audiences. It is a form in which the audience can depend on the certain hand of the playwright to orchestrate characters and events in an orderly progression from beginning to end, through crises and climaxes, to a satisfying conclusion. Like any formula writing (mystery and spy novels are good examples), there are certain conventions to be observed because they work; that is, they hold our interest and generate suspense and satisfactory endings. Secrets, delayed letters, mysterious strongboxes, unexpected visitors, and misunderstandings complicate lives and lead to resolutions. The best examples of well-made writing, as found in the plays of Henrik Ibsen, George Bernard Shaw, and Lillian Hellman, combined meticulous craftsmanship with serious social and psychological insights into contemporary life and lifted the Scribean formula beyond the realm of mere entertainment into provocative and entertaining studies of modern humanity.

The next chapters deal with the changing practices of playwrights to evolve new dramatic ways and means—drama's "special mirrors"—to respond to changing societies, political systems, and theatrical forms.

## NOTES

1. *Conversations with Lillian Hellman*, ed. Jackson R. Bryer (Jackson: University Press of Mississippi, 1986): 115.

2. Stephen S. Stanton, *Camille and Other Plays* (New York: Hill and Wang, 1957): vii–x.

3. Eugène Scribe, *Oeuvres Completes de Eugène Scribe*, ed. E. Dentu (Paris, 1874): I, xxiv.

4. Lillian Hellman, *Scoundrel Time* (Boston: Little, Brown, 1971): 93.

# PART THREE

# ELEMENTS OF DRAMA

other level, the hero's inner life, revealed in his soliloquies, retards the usual revenge journey which is ordinarily mean, violent, and swift. Hamlet discourses on certain troubling matters. His mother, with indecent haste, has married the brother of her late husband. According to canon law, she has, therefore, committed incest ("the incestuous sheets"), for in early Christian doctrine the relatives of a husband and wife were considered "as one flesh." The Polonius family introduces complications of sexual love and filial loyalty into his discourse. And, although the ghost tells Hamlet the story of the murder and demands revenge, Hamlet delays executing revenge to verify the ghost's evidence. According to theological notions of the day, a Christian knew that the appearance of a spirit in the shape of a person recently deceased might be evil and set upon condemning one's soul to perdition.

Hamlet's revenge gains ground as he proves his uncle's guilt. Rosencrantz and Guildenstern tell him about the players and he improvises his mousetrap: "The play's the thing/Wherein I'll catch the conscience of the King." The trap springs and Claudius reveals his guilt beyond any doubt; thus, Hamlet knows he has been visited by a true ghost, not a devil or figment of his melancholy imagination.

Thus far, Hamlet's journey has moved along the road to confirming Claudius' guilt while exploring the essence of human nature. At this point, Hamlet has one clear opportunity to take his revenge. He discovers Claudius at prayer; they are alone, but the opportunity for vengeance is unsuitable. Revenge demands hell fire for the culprit and Claudius, at prayer, "seems" to be in a state of grace which would cancel out his eternal damnation. So, Hamlet passes into his mother's chamber and there mistakenly kills Polonius.

Now, there are three avengers: Hamlet, Laertes, and Fortinbras. We must remember that Hamlet's cousin, Fortinbras, whose father was killed by Hamlet's own father in a civil war, is also seeking to avenge his parent's untimely death and to regain his own property rights lost in battle. Events now begin to accelerate. To neutralize (and terminate) Hamlet, Claudius sends him away to England with his death warrant carried by Rosencrantz and Guildenstern. Ophelia goes mad from the weight of her losses (father and lover) and drowns herself. Hamlet unexpectedly returns, having escaped one trap, only to face another: the duel with Laertes.

This time, Ophelia's "maimed funeral rites" delay the final catastrophe. Hamlet and Laertes confront one another over the open grave. But neither avenger has satisfaction. Osric, the fashionable courtier, with his surface manners and fine clothes, is used to lay out the final mousetrap—a duel between Hamlet and Laertes. Now calamity is whole when vengeances are consummated, all the guilty are punished in one bloody ending, and Fortinbras is vindicated as well.

Viewed as a traditional revenge tragedy intersected by the hero's meditations on the quintessence of the human condition, the twin arcs of Hamlet's episodic journey through revenge and self-understanding can be easily traced. However, *Hamlet* is one of the great tragedies of all times, rising above the overly simplistic revenge motif to comment on universal human problems: on fathers and children, on mothers and sons, on love and sex, on loss and grief, on guilt and innocence, on corruption and wholesomeness, on ingratitude and loyalty, on acting and deceit, on anguish and despair, on irony and fate. The great soliloquies, some of Shakespeare's finest writing, interrupt the vengeful journey to explore these universal and timeless issues.

As one of the great figures of western tragedy, Hamlet has proved to be the most difficult of Shakespeare's heroes to understand. He is intelligent, witty, sensitive, grief-stricken, angry, disillusioned, contemplative, and violent. He is called upon to redeem a world (an "unweeded garden") for which he feels alienation and disgust. G. Wilson Knight summarized the play as "the story of a 'sweet prince' wrenched from life and dedicated alone to death."[7] It is Hamlet's dedication to death that marks the stages of his progress in this episodic journey of body, mind, and soul from his confrontation with the ghost to his death in the dueling chamber.

# The Tragedy of Hamlet Prince of Denmark

**DRAMATIS PERSONAE**

**CLAUDIUS**  King of Denmark

**HAMLET**  son to the late, and nephew to the present, King

**POLONIUS**  Lord Chamberlain

**HORATIO**  friend to Hamlet

**LAERTES**  son to Polonius

**VOLTEMAND**
**CORNELIUS**
**ROSENCRANTZ**  } courtiers
**GUILDENSTERN**
**OSRIC**
**A GENTLEMAN**

**A PRIEST**

**MARCELLUS**  } officers
**BARNARDO**

**FRANCISCO**  a soldier

**REYNALDO**  servant to Polonius

**PLAYERS**

**TWO CLOWNS**  gravediggers

**FORTINBRAS**  Prince of Norway

**A NORWEGIAN CAPTAIN**

**ENGLISH AMBASSADORS**

**GERTRUDE, QUEEN OF DENMARK**  mother to Hamlet

**OPHELIA**  daughter to Polonius

**GHOST** of Hamlet's father

**LORDS, LADIES, OFFICERS, SOLDIERS, SAILORS, MESSENGERS, ATTENDANTS**

**SCENE:**
*Elsinore*

# ACT I

**SCENE I**
*A guard platform of the castle.*

*Enter* **BARNARDO** *and* **FRANCISCO**, *two sentinels.*

**BARNARDO**
Who's there?

**FRANCISCO**
Nay, answer me. Stand and unfold°¹ yourself.

**BARNARDO**                                                     5
Long live the King!°

**FRANCISCO**
Barnardo?

**BARNARDO**
He.                                                                    10

**FRANCISCO**
You come most carefully upon your hour.

**BARNARDO**
'Tis now struck twelve. Get thee to bed, Francisco.

**FRANCISCO**                                                   15
For this relief much thanks. 'Tis bitter cold,
And I am sick at heart.

**BARNARDO**
Have you had quiet guard?

**FRANCISCO**                                                   20
Not a mouse stirring.

**BARNARDO**
Well, good night.
If you do meet Horatio and Marcellus,
The rivals° of my watch, bid them make haste.        25

*Enter* **HORATIO** *and* **MARCELLUS**.

**FRANCISCO**
I think I hear them. Stand, ho! Who is there?

**HORATIO**
Friends to this ground.

---

¹The degree sign (°) indicates a footnote, which is keyed to the text by the line number. Text references are printed in **bold** type; the annotation follows in roman type.

**I.i. 4 unfold** disclose  **6 Long live the King** (perhaps a password, perhaps a greeting)  **25 rivals** partners

30 **MARCELLUS**
And liegemen to the Dane.°
**FRANCISCO**
Give you° good night.
**MARCELLUS**
35 O, farewell, honest soldier.
Who hath relieved you?
**FRANCISCO**
Barnardo hath my place.
Give you good night. *Exit* FRANCISCO.
40 **MARCELLUS**
Holla, Barnardo!
**BARNARDO**
Say—
What, is Horatio there?
45 **HORATIO**
A piece of him.
**BARNARDO**
Welcome, Horatio. Welcome, good Marcellus.
**MARCELLUS**
50 What, has this thing appeared again tonight?
**BARNARDO**
I have seen nothing.
**MARCELLUS**
Horatio says 'tis but our fantasy,
55 And will not let belief take hold of him
Touching this dreaded sight twice seen of us;
Therefore I have entreated him along
With us to watch the minutes of this night,
That, if again this apparition come,
60 He may approve° our eyes and speak to it.
**HORATIO**
Tush, tush, 'twill not appear.
**BARNARDO**
Sit down awhile,
65 And let us once again assail your ears,
That are so fortified against our story,
What we have two nights seen.
**HORATIO**
Well, sit we down,
70 And let us hear Barnardo speak of this.
**BARNARDO**
Last night of all,
When yond same star that's westward from the
pole°
75 Had made his course t' illume that part of heaven

Where now it burns, Marcellus and myself,
The bell then beating one—
*Enter* GHOST.
**MARCELLUS**
Peace, break thee off. Look where it comes again.
**BARNARDO**
In the same figure like the king that's dead. 80
**MARCELLUS**
Thou art a scholar; speak to it, Horatio.
**BARNARDO**
Looks 'a not like the king? Mark it, Horatio. 85
**HORATIO**
Most like: it harrows me with fear and wonder.
**BARNARDO**
It would be spoke to.
**MARCELLUS** 90
Speak to it, Horatio.
**HORATIO**
What art thou that usurp'st this time of night,
Together with that fair and warlike form
In which the majesty of buried Denmark° 95
Did sometimes march? By heaven I charge thee,
speak.
**MARCELLUS**
It is offended.
**BARNARDO** 100
See, it stalks away.
**HORATIO**
Stay! Speak, speak. I charge thee, speak.
*Exit* GHOST.
**MARCELLUS**
'Tis gone and will not answer. 105
**BARNARDO**
How now, Horatio? You tremble and look pale.
Is not this something more than fantasy?
What think you on't?
**HORATIO** 110
Before my God, I might not this believe
Without the sensible and true avouch°
Of mine own eyes.
**MARCELLUS**
Is it not like the King? 115
**HORATIO**
As thou art to thyself.
Such was the very armor he had on
When he the ambitious Norway° combated:

---

31 **liegemen to the Dane** loyal subjects to the King of
Denmark  33 **Give you** God give you  60 **approve** confirm
74 **pole** polestar

95 **buried Denmark** the buried King of Denmark  112
**sensible and true avouch** sensory and true proof  119
**Norway** King of Norway

120 So frowned he once, when, in an angry parle,°
He smote the sledded Polacks° on the ice.
'Tis strange.

**MARCELLUS**
Thus twice before, and jump° at this dead hour,
125 With martial stalk hath he gone by our watch.

**HORATIO**
In what particular thought to work I know not;
But, in the gross and scope° of my opinion,
This bodes some strange eruption to our state.

130 **MARCELLUS**
Good now, sit down, and tell me he that knows,
Why this same strict and most observant watch
So nightly toils the subject° of the land,
And why such daily cast of brazen cannon
135 And foreign mart° for implements of war,
Why such impress° of shipwrights, whose sore
  task
Does not divide the Sunday from the week,
What might be toward° that this sweaty haste
140 Doth make the night joint-laborer with the day?
Who is't that can inform me?

**HORATIO**
That can I.
At least the whisper goes so: our last king,
145 Whose image even but now appeared to us,
Was, as you know, by Fortinbras of Norway,
Thereto pricked on by a most emulate pride,
Dared to the combat; in which our valiant Hamlet
(For so this side of our known world esteemed
150   him)
Did slay this Fortinbras, who, by a sealed compact
Well ratified by law and heraldry,°
Did forfeit, with his life, all those his lands
Which he stood seized° of, to the conqueror;
155 Against the which a moiety competent°
Was gagèd° by our King, which had returned
To the inheritance of Fortinbras,
Had he been vanquisher, as, by the same comart°
And carriage of the article designed,°

His fell to Hamlet. Now, sir, young Fortinbras,   160
Of unimprovèd° mettle hot and full,
Hath in the skirts° of Norway here and there
Sharked up° a list of lawless resolutes,°
For food and diet, to some enterprise
That hath a stomach in't° which is no other,   165
As it doth well appear unto our state,
But to recover of us by strong hand
And terms compulsatory, those foresaid lands
So by his father lost; and this, I take it,
Is the main motive of our preparations,   170
The source of this our watch, and the chief head°
Of this posthaste and romage° in the land.

**BARNARDO**
I think it be no other but e'en so;
Well may it sort° that this portentous figure   175
Comes armèd through our watch so like the King
That was and is the question of these wars.

**HORATIO**
A mote it is to trouble the mind's eye:
In the most high and palmy state of Rome,   180
A little ere the mightiest Julius fell,
The graves stood tenantless, and the sheeted dead
Did squeak and gibber in the Roman streets;°
As stars with trains of fire and dews of blood,
Disasters° in the sun; and the moist star,°   185
Upon whose influence Neptune's empire stands,
Was sick almost to doomsday with eclipse.
And even the like precurse° of feared events,
As harbingers° preceding still° the fates
And prologue to the omen° coming on,   190
Have heaven and earth together demonstrated
Unto our climatures° and countrymen.
*Enter* **GHOST**.
But soft, behold, lo where it comes again!
I'll cross it,° though it blast me.—Stay, illusion.

---

120 **parle** parley 121 **sledded Polacks** Poles in sledges
124 **jump** just 128 **gross and scope** general drift 133 **toils
the subject** makes the subjects toil 135 **mart** trading 136
**impress** forced service 139 **toward** in preparation 152
**law and heraldry** heraldic law (governing the combat)
154 **seized** possessed 155 **moiety competent** equal portion 156 **gagèd** engaged, pledged 158 **comart** agreement
159 **carriage of the article designed** import of the agreement drawn up

161 **unimprovèd** untried 162 **skirts** borders 163
**Sharked up** collected indiscriminately (as a shark gulps its
prey) 163 **resolutes** desperadoes 165 **hath a stomach in't**
i.e., requires courage 171 **head** fountainhead, origin 172
**romage** bustle 175 **sort** befit 183 **Did squeak . . . Roman streets** (the break in the sense which follows this line
suggests that a line has dropped out) 185 **Disasters**
threatening signs 185 **moist star** moon 188 **precurse** pre-
cursor, foreshadowing 189 **harbingers** forerunners 189
**still** always 190 **omen** calamity 192 **climatures** regions
194 **cross it** (1) cross its path, confront it (2) make the sign
of the cross in front of it

*It spreads his° arms.*

195 If thou hast any sound or use of voice,
Speak to me.
If there be any good thing to be done
That may to thee do ease and grace to me,
Speak to me.
200 If thou art privy to thy country's fate,
Which happily° foreknowing may avoid,
O, speak!
Or if thou hast uphoarded in thy life
Extorted° treasure in the womb of earth,
205 For which, they say, you spirits oft walk in death,
*The cock crows.*
Speak of it. Stay and speak. Stop it, Marcellus.

          MARCELLUS
Shall I strike at it with my partisan°?

          HORATIO
210 Do, if it will not stand.

          BARNARDO
'Tis here.

          HORATIO
'Tis here.

215      MARCELLUS
'Tis gone.
*Exit* GHOST.
We do it wrong, being so majestical,
To offer it the show of violence,
For it is as the air, invulnerable,
220 And our vain blows malicious mockery.

          BARNARDO
It was about to speak when the cock crew.

          HORATIO
And then it started, like a guilty thing
225 Upon a fearful summons. I have heard,
The cock, that is the trumpet to the morn,
Doth with his lofty and shrill-sounding throat
Awake the god of day, and at his warning,
Whether in sea or fire, in earth or air,
230 Th' extravagant and erring° spirit hies
To his confine; and of the truth herein
This present object made probation.°

          MARCELLUS
It faded on the crowing of the cock.
Some say that ever 'gainst° that season comes     235
Wherein our Savior's birth is celebrated,
This bird of dawning singeth all night long,
And then, they say, no spirit dare stir abroad,
The nights are wholesome, then no planets strike,°
No fairy takes,° nor witch hath power to charm:     240
So hallowed and so gracious is that time.

          HORATIO
So have I heard and do in part believe it.
But look, the morn in russet mantle clad
Walks o'er the dew of yon high eastward hill.     245
Break we our watch up, and by my advice
Let us impart what we have seen tonight
Unto young Hamlet, for upon my life
This spirit, dumb to us, will speak to him.
Do you consent we shall acquaint him with it,     250
As needful in our loves, fitting our duty?

          MARCELLUS
Let's do't, I pray, and I this morning know
Where we shall find him most convenient.
*(Exeunt.)*

## SCENE II

*The castle.*

*Flourish.° Enter* CLAUDIUS, KING OF DENMARK,
GERTRUDE THE QUEEN, COUNCILORS, POLO-
NIUS *and his son* LAERTES, HAMLET, *cum aliis*° (*in-
cluding* VOLTEMAND *and* CORNELIUS).

          KING
Though yet of Hamlet our dear brother's death
The memory be green, and that it us befitted
To bear our hearts in grief, and our whole
          kingdom                                    5
To be contracted in one brow of woe,
Yet so far hath discretion fought with nature
That we with wisest sorrow think on him
Together with remembrance of ourselves.
Therefore our sometime sister,° now our Queen,    10
Th' imperial jointress° to this warlike state,

---

s.d. **his** i.e., its, the ghost's (though possibly what is meant
is that Horatio spreads his own arms, making a cross of
himself) 201 **happily** haply, perhaps 204 **Extorted** ill-
won 208 **partisan** pike (a long-handled weapon) 230 **extravagant and erring** out of bounds and wandering 232
**probation** proof

235 **'gainst** just before   239 **strike** exert an evil influence
240 **takes** bewitches   **I.ii.** s.d. **Flourish** fanfare of trumpets
s.d. **cum aliis** with others (Latin)   10 **our sometime sister**
my (the royal "we") former sister-in-law   11 **jointress** joint
tenant, partner

Have we, as 'twere, with a defeated joy,
With an auspicious° and a dropping eye,
With mirth in funeral, and with dirge in marriage,
15 In equal scale weighing delight and dole,
Taken to wife. Nor have we herein barred
Your better wisdoms, which have freely gone.
With this affair along. For all, our thanks.
Now follows that you know young Fortinbras,
20 Holding a weak supposal of our worth,
Or thinking by our late dear brother's death
Our state to be disjoint and out of frame,°
Colleaguèd with this dream of his advantage,°
He hath not failed to pester us with message,
25 Importing the surrender of those lands
Lost by his father, with all bands of law,
To our most valiant brother. So much for him.
Now for ourself and for this time of meeting.
Thus much the business is: we have here writ
30 To Norway, uncle of young Fortinbras—
Who, impotent and bedrid, scarcely hears
Of this his nephew's purpose—to suppress
His further gait° herein, in that the levies,
The lists, and full proportions° are all made
35 Out of his subject;° and we here dispatch
You, good Cornelius, and you, Voltemand,
For bearers of this greeting to old Norway,
Giving to you no further personal power
To business with the King, more than the scope
40 Of these delated articles° allow.
Farewell, and let your haste commend your duty.
    CORNELIUS, **VOLTEMAND**
In that, and all things, will we show our duty.
    KING
45 We doubt it nothing. Heartily farewell.
    *Exit* **VOLTEMAND** *and* **CORNELIUS.**
And now, Laertes, what's the news with you?
You told us of some suit. What is't, Laertes?
You cannot speak of reason to the Dane
And lose your voice.° What wouldst thou beg,
50     Laertes,
That shall not be my offer, not thy asking?
The head is not more native° to the heart,
The hand more instrumental to the mouth,

Than is the throne of Denmark to thy father.
What wouldst thou have, Laertes?                    55
    **LAERTES**
My dread lord,
Your leave and favor to return to France,
From whence, though willingly I came to
    Denmark                                        60
To show my duty in your coronation,
Yet now I must confess, that duty done,
My thoughts and wishes bend again toward
    France
And bow them to your gracious leave and pardon.  65
    KING
Have you your father's leave? What says
Polonius?
    **POLONIUS**
He hath, my lord, wrung from me my slow leave  70
By laborsome petition, and at last
Upon his will I sealed my hard consent.°
I do beseech you give him leave to go.
    KING
Take thy fair hour, Laertes. Time be thine,        75
And thy best graces spend it at thy will.
But now, my cousin° Hamlet, and my son—
    **HAMLET**
(*Aside*) A little more than kin, and less than kind!°
    KING                                          80
How is it that the clouds still hang on you?
    **HAMLET**
Not so, my lord. I am too much in the sun.°
    QUEEN
Good Hamlet, cast thy nighted color off,           85
And let thine eye look like a friend on Denmark.
Do not forever with thy vailèd° lids
Seek for thy noble father in the dust.
Thou knowist 'tis common; all that lives must die,
Passing through nature to eternity.                90
    **HAMLET**
Ay, madam, it is common.°
    QUEEN
If it be,
Why seems it so particular with thee?              95

13 **auspicious** joyful  22 **frame** order  23 **advantage** superiority  33 **gait** proceeding  34 **proportions** supplies for war  35 **Out of his subject** i.e., out of old Norway's subjects and realm  40 **delated articles** detailed documents  49 **lose your voice** waste your breath  52 **native** related

72 **Upon his . . . hard consent** to his desire I gave my reluctant consent  77 **cousin** kinsman  79 **kind** (pun on the meanings "kindly" and "natural"; though doubly related—**more than kin**—Hamlet asserts that he neither resembles Claudius in nature or feels kindly toward him)  83 **sun** sunshine of royal favor (with a pun on "son")  87 **vailèd** lowered  92 **common** (1) universal (2) vulgar

HAMLET

Seems, madam? Nay, it is. I know not "seems."
'Tis not alone my inky cloak, good mother,
Nor customary suits of solemn black,
100 Nor windy suspiration° of forced breath,
No, nor the fruitful river in the eye,
Nor the dejected havior of the visage,
Together with all forms, moods, shapes of grief,
That can denote me truly. These indeed seem,
105 For they are actions that a man might play,
But I have that within which passes show;
These but the trappings and the suits of woe.

KING

'Tis sweet and commendable in your nature,
110     Hamlet,
To give these mourning duties to your father,
But you must know your father lost a father,
That father lost, lost his, and the survivor bound
In filial obligation for some term
115 To do obsequious° sorrow. But to persever
In obstinate condolement° is a course
Of impious stubbornness. 'Tis unmanly grief.
It shows a will most incorrect to heaven,
A heart unfortified, a mind impatient,
120 An understanding simple and unschooled.
For what we know must be and is as common
As any the most vulgar° thing to sense,
Why should we in our peevish opposition
Take it to heart? Fie, 'tis a fault to heaven,
125 A fault against the dead, a fault to nature,
To reason most absurd, whose common theme
Is death of fathers, and who still hath cried,
From the first corse° till he that died today,
"This must be so." We pray you throw to earth
130 This unprevailing° woe, and think of us
As of a father, for let the world take note
You are the most immediate to our throne,
And with no less nobility of love
Than that which dearest father bears his son
135 Do I impart toward you. For your intent
In going back to school in Wittenberg,
It is most retrograde° to our desire,
And we beseech you, bend you° to remain
Here in the cheer and comfort of our eye,
140 Our chiefest courtier, cousin, and our son.

QUEEN

Let not thy mother lose her prayers, Hamlet.
I pray thee stay with us, go not to Wittenberg.

HAMLET

I shall in all my best obey you, madam.          145

KING

Why, 'tis a loving and a fair reply.
Be as ourself in Denmark. Madam, come.
This gentle and unforced accord of Hamlet
Sits smiling to my heart, in grace whereof          150
No jocund health that Denmark drinks today,
But the great cannon to the clouds shall tell,
And the King's rouse° the heaven shall bruit°
     again,
Respeaking earthly thunder. Come away.          155
*Flourish. Exeunt all but* HAMLET.

HAMLET

O that this too too sullied° flesh would melt,
Thaw, and resolve itself into a dew,
Or that the Everlasting had not fixed
His canon° 'gainst self-slaughter. O God, God,          160
How weary, stale, flat, and unprofitable
Seem to me all the uses of this world!
Fie on't, ah, fie, 'tis an unweeded garden
That grows to seed. Things rank and gross in
     nature          165
Possess it merely.° That it should come to this:
But two months dead, nay, not so much, not two,
So excellent a king, that was to this
Hyperion° to a satyr, so loving to my mother
That he might not beteem° the winds of heaven          170
Visit her face too roughly. Heaven and earth,
Must I remember? Why, she would hang on him
As if increase of appetite had grown
By what it fed on; and yet within a month—
Let me not think on't; frailty, thy name is          175
     woman—
A little month, or ere those shoes were old
With which she followed my poor father's body
Like Niobe,° all tears, why she, even she—
O God, a beast that wants discourse of reason°          180

---

153 **rouse** deep drink  153 **bruit** announce noisily  157 **sullied** (Q2 has **sallied,** here modernized to **sullied,** which makes sense and is therefore given; but the Folio reading, **solid,** which fits better with **melt,** is quite possibly correct) 160 **canon** law  166 **merely** entirely  169 **Hyperion** the sun god, a model of beauty  170 **beteem** allow  179 **Niobe** (a mother who wept profusely at the death of her children) 180 **wants discourse of reason** lacks reasoning power

---

100 **windy suspiration** heavy sighing  115 **obsequious** suitable to obsequies (funerals)  116 **condolement** mourning 122 **vulgar** common  128 **corse** corpse  130 **unprevailing** unavailing  137 **retrograde** contrary  138 **bend you** incline

Would have mourned longer—married with my
    uncle,
My father's brother, but no more like my father
Than I to Hercules. Within a month,
185 Ere yet the salt of most unrighteous tears
Had left the flushing° in her gallèd eyes,
She married. O, most wicked speed, to post°
With such dexterity to incestuous° sheets!
It is not, nor it cannot come to good.
190 But break my heart, for I must hold my tongue.
    *Enter* **HORATIO, MARCELLUS,** *and* **BARNARDO.**
        **HORATIO**
Hail to your lordship!
        **HAMLET**
I am glad to see you well.
195 Horatio—or I do forget myself.
        **HORATIO**
The same, my lord, and your poor servant ever.
        **HAMLET**
Sir, my good friend, I'll change° that name
200 with you.
And what make you from Wittenberg, Horatio?
Marcellus.
        **MARCELLUS**
My good lord!
205       **HAMLET**
I am very glad to see you. (*To* **BARNARDO**)
Good even, sir.
But what, in faith, make you from Wittenberg?
        **HORATIO**
210 A truant disposition, good my lord.
        **HAMLET**
I would not hear your enemy say so,
Nor shall you do my ear that violence
To make it truster° of your own report
215 Against yourself. I know you are no truant.
But what is your affair in Elsinore?
We'll teach you to drink deep ere you depart.
        **HORATIO**
My lord, I came to see your father's funeral.
220       **HAMLET**
I prithee do not mock me, fellow student.
I think it was to see my mother's wedding.
        **HORATIO**
Indeed, my lord, it followed hard upon.

        **HAMLET**        225
Thrift, thrift, Horatio. The funeral baked meats
Did coldly furnish forth the marriage tables.
Would I had met my dearest° foe in heaven
Or ever I had seen that day, Horatio!
My father, methinks I see my father.    230
        **HORATIO**
Where, my lord?
        **HAMLET**
In my mind's eye, Horatio.
        **HORATIO**    235
I saw him once. 'A° was a goodly king.
        **HAMLET**
'A was a man, take him for all in all,
I shall not look upon his like again.
        **HORATIO**    240
My lord, I think I saw him yesternight.
        **HAMLET**
Saw? Who?
        **HORATIO**
My lord, the King your father.    245
        **HAMLET**
The King my father?
        **HORATIO**
Season your admiration° for a while
With an attent ear till I may deliver    250
Upon the witness of these gentlemen
This marvel to you.
        **HAMLET**
For God's love let me hear!
        **HORATIO**    255
Two nights together had these gentlemen,
Marcellus and Barnardo, on their watch
In the dead waste and middle of the night
Been thus encountered. A figure like your father,
Armèd at point exactly, cap-a-pe,°    260
Appears before them, and with solemn march
Goes slow and stately by them. Thrice he walked
By their oppressed and fear-surprisèd eyes,
Within his truncheon's length,° whilst they,
    distilled°    265
Almost to jelly with the act° of fear,
Stand dumb and speak not to him. This to me
In dreadful° secrecy impart they did,
And I with them the third night kept the watch,

---

186 **left the flushing** stopped reddening  187 **post** hasten
188 **incestuous** (canon law considered marriage with a
deceased brother's widow to be incestuous)  199 **change**
exchange  214 **truster** believer

228 **dearest** most intensely felt  236 **'A** he  249 **Season
your admiration** control your wonder  260 **cap-a-pe** head
to foot  264 **truncheon's length** space of a short staff  265
**distilled** reduced  266 **act** action  268 **dreadful** terrified

270 Where, as they had delivered, both in time,
Form of the thing, each word made true and good,
The apparition comes. I knew your father.
These hands are not more like.
       **HAMLET**
275 But where was this?
       **MARCELLUS**
My lord, upon the platform where we watched.
       **HAMLET**
Did you not speak to it?
280       **HORATIO**
My lord, I did;
But answer made it none. Yet once methought
It lifted up it° head and did address
Itself to motion like as it would speak:
285 But even then the morning cock crew loud,
And at the sound it shrunk in haste away
And vanished from our sight.
       **HAMLET**
'Tis very strange.
290       **HORATIO**
As I do live, my honored lord, 'tis true,
And we did think it writ down in our duty
To let you know of it.
       **HAMLET**
295 Indeed, indeed, sirs, but this troubles me.
Hold you the watch tonight?
       **ALL**
We do, my lord.
       **HAMLET**
300 Armed, say you?
      **ALL**
Armed, my lord.
       **HAMLET**
From top to toe?
305       **ALL**
My lord, from head to foot.
       **HAMLET**
Then saw you not his face.
       **HORATIO**
310 O, yes, my lord. He wore his beaver° up.
       **HAMLET**
What, looked he frowningly?
       **HORATIO**
315 A countenance more in sorrow than in anger.
       **HAMLET**
Pale or red?

       **HORATIO**
Nay, very pale.
       **HAMLET**
And fixed his eyes upon you?       320
       **HORATIO**
Most constantly.
       **HAMLET**
I would I had been there.
       **HORATIO**       325
It would have much amazed you.
       **HAMLET**
Very like, very like. Stayed it long?
       **HORATIO**
While one with moderate haste might tell° a    330
   hundred.
       **BOTH**
Longer, longer.
       **HORATIO**
Not when I saw't.       335
       **HAMLET**
His beard was grizzled,° no?
       **HORATIO**
It was as I have seen it in his life,
A sable silvered.°       340
       **HAMLET**
I will watch tonight.
Perchance 'twill walk again.
       **HORATIO**
I warr'nt it will.       345
       **HAMLET**
If it assume my noble father's person,
I'll speak to it though hell itself should gape
And bid me hold my peace. I pray you all,
If you have hitherto concealed this sight,    350
Let it be tenable° in your silence still,
And whatsomever else shall hap tonight,
Give it an understanding but no tongue;
I will requite your loves. So fare you well.
Upon the platform 'twixt eleven and twelve    355
I'll visit you.
       **ALL**
Our duty to your honor.
       **HAMLET**
Your loves, as mine to you. Farewell.    360
*Exeunt* (*all but* **HAMLET**).
My father's spirit—in arms? All is not well.

---

283 **it** its  310 **beaver** visor, face guard

330 **tell** count  337 **grizzled** gray  340 **sable silvered** black mingled with white  351 **tenable** held

I doubt° some foul play. Would the night were
   come!
Till then sit still, my soul. Foul deeds will rise,
365 Though all the earth o'erwhelm them, to men's
   eyes.
*Exit.*

## SCENE III

*A room.*

*Enter* LAERTES *and* OPHELIA, *his sister.*

    LAERTES
My necessaries are embarked. Farewell.
And, sister, as the winds give benefit
And convoy° is assistant, do not sleep,
5 But let me hear from you.
    OPHELIA
Do you doubt that?
    LAERTES
For Hamlet, and the trifling of his favor,
10 Hold it a fashion and a toy° in blood,
A violet in the youth of primy° nature,
Forward,° not permanent, sweet, not lasting,
The perfume and suppliance° of a minute,
No more.
15    OPHELIA
No more but so?
    LAERTES
Think it no more.
For nature crescent° does not grow alone
20 In thews° and bulk, but as this temple° waxes,
The inward service of the mind and soul
Grows wide withal. Perhaps he loves you now,
And now no soil nor cautel° doth besmirch
The virtue of his will; but you must fear,
25 His greatness weighed,° his will is not his own.
For he himself is subject to his birth.
He may not, as unvalued° persons do,
Carve for himself; for on his choice depends
The safety and health of this whole state;
30 And therefore must his choice be circumscribed
Unto the voice and yielding of that body

Whereof he is the head. Then if he says he loves
   you,
It fits your wisdom so far to believe it
As he in his particular act and place                    35
May give his saying deed, which is no further
Than the main voice of Denmark goes withal.
Then weigh what loss your honor may sustain
If with too credent° ear you list his songs,
Or lose your heart, or your chaste treasure open       40
To his unmastered importunity.
Fear it, Ophelia, fear it, my dear sister,
And keep you in the rear of your affection,
Out of the shot and danger of desire.
The chariest maid is prodigal enough                   45
If she unmask her beauty to the moon.
Virtue itself scapes not calumnious strokes.
The canker° galls the infants of the spring
Too oft before their buttons° be disclosed,
And in the morn and liquid dew of youth                50
Contagious blastments are most imminent.
Be wary then; best safety lies in fear;
Youth to itself rebels, though none else near.
    OPHELIA
I shall the effect of this good lesson keep             55
As watchman to my heart, but, good my brother,
Do not, as some ungracious° pastors do,
Show me the steep and thorny way to heaven,
Whiles, like a puffed and reckless libertine,
Himself the primrose path of dalliance treads          60
And recks not his own rede.°
*Enter* POLONIUS.
    LAERTES
O, fear me not.
I stay too long. But here my father comes.
A double blessing is a double grace;                    65
Occasion smiles upon a second leave.
    POLONIUS
Yet here, Laertes? Aboard, aboard, for shame!
The wind sits in the shoulder of your sail,
And you are stayed for. There—my blessing with         70
   thee,
And these few precepts in thy memory
Look thou character.° Give thy thoughts no
   tongue,
Nor any unproportioned° thought his act.                75

---

362 **doubt** suspect  **I.iii. 4 convoy** conveyance  10 **toy** idle
fancy  11 **primy** springlike  12 **Forward** premature  13
**suppliance** diversion  19 **crescent** growing  20 **thews**
muscles and sinews  20 **temple** i.e., the body  23 **cautel**
deceit  25 **greatness weighed** high rank considered  27
**unvalued** of low rank

39 **credent** credulous  48 **canker** cankerworm  49 **buttons**
buds  57 **ungracious** lacking grace  61 **recks not his own
rede** does not heed his own advice  73 **character** inscribe
75 **unproportioned** unbalanced

Be thou familiar, but by no means vulgar.
Those friends thou hast, and their adoption tried,
Grapple them unto thy soul with hoops of steel,
But do not dull thy palm with entertainment
80 Of each new-hatched, unfledged courage.° Beware
Of entrance to a quarrel; but being in,
Bear't that th' opposèd may beware of thee.
Give every man thine ear, but few thy voice;
Take each man's censure,° but reserve thy
85   judgment.
Costly thy habit as thy purse can buy,
But not expressed in fancy; rich, not gaudy,
For the apparel oft proclaims the man,
And they in France of the best rank and station
90 Are of a most select and generous, chief in that.°
Neither a borrower nor a lender be,
For loan oft loses both itself and friend,
And borrowing dulleth edge of husbandry.°
This above all, to thine own self be true,
95 And it must follow, as the night the day,
Thou canst not then be false to any man.
Farewell. My blessing season this° in thee!

> **LAERTES**
Most humbly do I take my leave, my lord.

100 **POLONIUS**
The time invites you. Go, your servants tend.°

> **LAERTES**
Farewell, Ophelia, and remember well
What I have said to you.

105 **OPHELIA**
'Tis in my memory locked,
And you yourself shall keep the key of it.

> **LAERTES**
Farewell.

*Exit* LAERTES.

110 **POLONIUS**
What is't, Ophelia, he hath said to you?

> **OPHELIA**
So please you, something touching the Lord
Hamlet.

115 **POLONIUS**
Marry,° well bethought.
'Tis told me he hath very oft of late

Given private time to you, and you yourself
Have of your audience been most free and
   bounteous.                                        120
If it be so—as so 'tis put on me,
And that in way of caution—I must tell you
You do not understand yourself so clearly
As it behooves my daughter and your honor.
What is between you? Give me up the truth.         125

> **OPHELIA**
He hath, my lord, of late made many tenders°
Of his affection to me.

> **POLONIUS**
Affection pooh! You speak like a green girl,       130
Unsifted° in such perilous circumstance.
Do you believe his tenders, as you call them?

> **OPHELIA**
I do not know, my lord, what I should think.

> **POLONIUS**                                       135
Marry, I will teach you. Think yourself a baby
That you have ta'en these tenders for true pay
Which are not sterling. Tender yourself more
   dearly,
Or (not to crack the wind of the poor phrase)      140
Tend'ring it thus you'll tender me a fool.°

> **OPHELIA**
My lord, he hath importuned me with love
In honorable fashion.

> **POLONIUS**                                       145
Ay, fashion you may call it. Go to, go to.

> **OPHELIA**
And hath given countenance to his speech, my
   lord,
With almost all the holy vows of heaven.           150

> **POLONIUS**
Ay, springes to catch woodcocks.° I do know,
When the blood burns, how prodigal the soul
Lends the tongue vows. These blazes, daughter,
Giving more light than heat, extinct in both,      155
Even in their promise, as it is a-making,
You must not take for fire. From this time
Be something scanter of your maiden presence.

---

80 **courage** gallant youth  84 **censure** opinion  90 **Are of
. . . in that** show their fine taste and their gentlemanly
instincts more in that than in any other point of manners
(Kittredge)  93 **husbandry** thrift  97 **season this** make
fruitful this (advice)  101 **tend** attend  116 **Marry** (a light
oath, from "By the Virgin Mary")

127 **tenders** offers (in line 132 it has the same meaning, but
in line 137 Polonius speaks of **tenders** in the sense of
counters or chips: in line 141 **Tend'ring** means "holding,"
and tender means "give," "present")  131 **Unsifted** untried  141 **tender me a fool** (1) present me with a fool
(2) present me with a baby  152 **springes to catch woodcocks** snares to catch stupid birds

Set your entreatments° at a higher rate
160 Than a command to parley. For Lord Hamlet,
Believe so much in him that he is young,
And with a larger tether may he walk
Than may be given you. In few, Ophelia,
Do not believe his vows, for they are brokers,°
165 Not of that dye° which their investments° show,
But mere implorators° of unholy suits,
Breathing like sanctified and pious bonds,°
The better to beguile. This is for all:
I would not, in plain terms, from this time forth
170 Have you so slander° any moment leisure
As to give words or talk with the Lord Hamlet.
Look to't, I charge you. Come your ways.
          OPHELIA
I shall obey, my lord. (*Exeunt.*)

**SCENE IV**

*A guard platform.*

*Enter* **HAMLET**, **HORATIO**, *and* **MARCELLUS**.

          HAMLET
The air bites shrewdly;° it is very cold.
          HORATIO
It is a nipping and an eager° air.
5          HAMLET
What hour now?
          HORATIO
I think it lacks of twelve.
          MARCELLUS
10 No, it is struck.
          HORATIO
Indeed? I heard it not. It then draws near the
     season
Wherein the spirit held his wont to walk.
*A flourish of trumpets, and two pieces go off.*
15 What does this mean, my lord?
          HAMLET
The King doth wake° tonight and takes his rouse,°
Keeps wassail, and the swagg'ring upspring°
     reels,

And as he drains his draughts of Rhenish° down   20
The kettledrum and trumpet thus bray out
The triumph of his pledge.°
          HORATIO
Is it a custom?
          HAMLET                                        25
Ay, marry, is't,
But to my mind, though I am native here
And to the manner born, it is a custom
More honored in the breach than the observance.
This heavy-headed revel east and west          30
Makes us traduced and taxed of° other nations.
They clepe° us drunkards and with swinish
     phrase
Soil our addition,° and indeed it takes
From our achievements, though performed at      35
     height,
The pith and marrow of our attribute.°
So oft it chances in particular men
That for some vicious mole° of nature in them,
As in their birth, wherein they are not guilty,  40
(Since nature cannot choose his origin)
By the o'ergrowth of some complexion,°
Oft breaking down the pales° and forts of reason,
Or by some habit that too much o'erleavens°
The form of plausive° manners, that (these men,  45
Carrying, I say, the stamp of one defect,
Being nature's livery, or fortune's star°)
Their virtues else, be they as pure as grace,
As infinite as man may undergo,
Shall in the general censure° take corruption    50
From that particular fault. The dram of evil
Doth all the noble substance of a doubt,
To his own scandal.°
*Enter* **GHOST**.
          HORATIO
Look, my lord, it comes.                          55

20 **Rhenish** Rhine wine   22 **The triumph of his pledge** the
achievement (of drinking a wine cup in one draught) of his
toast   31 **taxed of** blamed by   32 **clepe** call   34 **addition**
reputation (literally, "title of honor")   37 **attribute** reputation   39 **mole** blemish   42 **complexion** natural disposition
43 **pales** enclosures   44 **o'er-leavens** mixes with, corrupts
45 **plausive** pleasing   47 **nature's livery, or fortune's star**
nature's equipment (i.e., "innate"), or a person's destiny
determined by the stars   50 **general censure** popular judgment   51–53 **The dram . . . own scandal** (though the drift
is clear, there is no agreement as to the exact meaning of
these lines)

159 **entreatments** interviews   164 **brokers** procurers   165
**dye** i.e., kind   165 **investments** garments   166 **implora-
tors** solicitors   167 **bonds** pledges   170 **slander** disgrace
**I.iv.** 2 **shrewdly** bitterly   4 **eager** sharp   17 **wake** hold a
revel by night   17 **takes his rouse** carouses   18 **upspring**
(a dance)

**HAMLET**
Angels and ministers of grace defend us!
Be thou a spirit of health° or goblin damned,
Bring with thee airs from heaven or blasts from
60      hell,
Be thy intents wicked or charitable,
Thou com'st in such a questionable° shape
That I will speak to thee. I'll call these Hamlet,
King, father, royal Dane. O, answer me!
65 Let me not burst in ignorance, but tell
Why thy canonized° bones, hearsèd in death,
Have burst their cerements,° why the sepulcher
Wherein we saw thee quietly interred
Hath oped his ponderous and marble jaws
70 To cast thee up again. What may this mean
That thou, dead corse, again in complete steel,
Revisits thus the glimpses of the moon,
Making night hideous, and we fools of nature
So horridly to shake our disposition°
75 With thoughts beyond the reaches of our souls?
Say, why is this? Wherefore? What should we do?
**GHOST** *beckons* **HAMLET.**
    **HORATIO**
It beckons you to go away with it,
As if it some impartment° did desire
80 To you alone.
    **MARCELLUS**
Look with what courteous action
It waves you to a more removèd ground.
But do not go with it.
85    **HORATIO**
No, by no means.
    **HAMLET**
It will not speak. Then I will follow it.
    **HORATIO**
90 Do not, my lord.
    **HAMLET**
Why, what should be the fear?
I do not set my life at a pin's fee,
And for my soul, what can it do to that,
95 Being a thing immortal as itself?
It waves me forth again. I'll follow it.
    **HORATIO**
What if it tempt you toward the flood, my lord,
Or to the dreadful summit of the cliff

That beetles° o'er his base into the sea,     100
And there assume some other horrible form,
Which might deprive your sovereignty of reason°
And draw you into madness? Think of it.
The very place puts toys° of desperation,
Without more motive, into every brain     105
'That looks so many fathoms to the sea
And hears it roar beneath.
    **HAMLET**
It waves me still.
Go on; I'll follow thee.     110
    **MARCELLUS**
You shall not go, my lord.
    **HAMLET**
Hold off your hands.
    **HORATIO**     115
Be ruled. You shall not go.
    **HAMLET**
My fate cries out
And makes each petty artere° in this body
As hardy as the Nemean lion's nerve.°     120
Still am I called! Unhand me, gentlemen.
By heaven, I'll make a ghost of him that lets° me!
I say, away! Go on. I'll follow thee.
*Exit* **GHOST,** *and* **HAMLET.**
    **HORATIO**
He waxes desperate with imagination.     125
    **MARCELLUS**
Let's follow. 'Tis not fit thus to obey him.
    **HORATIO**
Have after! To what issue will this come?
    **MARCELLUS**     130
Something is rotten in the state of Denmark.
    **HORATIO**
Heaven will direct it.
    **MARCELLUS**
Nay, let's follow him. (*Exeunt.*)     135

## SCENE V

*The battlements.*

*Enter* **GHOST,** *and* **HAMLET**

    **HAMLET**
Whither wilt thou lead me?
Speak; I'll go no further.

---

58 **spirit of health** good spirit   62 **questionable** (1) capable
of discourse (2) dubious   66 **canonized** buried according
to the canon or ordinance of the church   67 **cerements**
waxed linen shroud   74 **shake our disposition** disturb us
79 **impartment** communication

100 **beetles** juts out   102 **deprive your sovereignty of reason**
destroy the sovereignty of your reason   104 **toys** whims,
fancies   119 **artere** artery   120 **Nemean lion's nerve** sinews
of the mythical lion slain by Hercules   122 **lets** hinders

GHOST

5 Mark me.

HAMLET

I will.

GHOST

My hour is almost come,

10 When I to sulf'rous and tormenting flames

Must render up myself.

HAMLET

Alas, poor ghost.

GHOST

15 Pity me not, but lend thy serious hearing

To what I shall unfold.

HAMLET

Speak. I am bound to hear.

GHOST

20 So art thou to revenge, when thou shalt hear.

HAMLET

What?

GHOST

I am thy father's spirit,

25 Doomed for a certain term to walk the night,

And for the day confined to fast in fires,

Till the foul crimes° done in my days of nature

Are burnt and purged away. But that I am forbid

To tell the secrets of my prison house,

30 I could a tale unfold whose lightest word

Would harrow up thy soul, freeze thy young

blood,

Make thy two eyes like stars start from their

spheres,°

35 Thy knotted and combinèd locks to part,

And each particular hair to stand an end

Like quills upon the fearful porpentine.°

But this eternal blazon° must not be

To ears of flesh and blood. List, list, O, list!

40 If thou didst ever thy dear father love—

HAMLET

O God!

GHOST

45 Revenge his foul and most unnatural murder.

HAMLET

Murder?

GHOST

Murder most foul, as in the best it is,

But this most foul, strange, and unnatural.

HAMLET                                                           50

Haste me to know't, that I, with wings as swift

As meditation° or the thoughts of love,

May sweep to my revenge.

GHOST

I find thee apt,                                              55

And duller shouldst thou be than the fat weed

That roots itself in ease on Lethe wharf,°

Wouldst thou not stir in this. Now, Hamlet, hear.

'Tis given out that, sleeping in my orchard,

A serpent stung me. So the whole ear of Denmark  60

Is by a forgèd process° of my death

Rankly abused. But know, thou noble youth,

The serpent that did sting thy father's life

Now wears his crown.

HAMLET                                                           65

O my prophetic soul!

My uncle?

GHOST

Ay, that incestuous, that adulterate° beast,

With witchcraft of his wits, with traitorous gifts—  70

O wicked wit and gifts, that have the power

So to seduce!—won to his shameful lust

The will of my most seeming-virtuous queen.

O Hamlet, what a failing-off was there,

From me, whose love was of that dignity          75

That it went hand in hand even with the vow

I made to her in marriage, and to decline

Upon a wretch whose natural gifts were poor

To those of mine.

But virtue, as it never will be moved,            80

Though lewdness° court it in a shape of heaven,

So lust, though to a radiant angel linked,

Will sate itself in a celestial bed

And prey on garbage.

But soft, methinks I scent the morning air;       85

Brief let me be. Sleeping within my orchard,

My custom always of the afternoon,

Upon my secure° hour thy uncle stole

With juice of cursed hebona° in a vial,

And in the porches of my ears did pour            90

The leperous distillment, whose effect

Holds such an enmity with blood of man

That swift as quicksilver it courses through

The natural gates and alleys of the body,

---

I.v. 27 **crimes** sins  34 **spheres** (in Ptolemaic astronomy, each planet was fixed in a hollow transparent shell concentric with the earth)  37 **fearful porpentine** timid porcupine  38 **eternal blazon** revelation of eternity

52 **meditation** thought  57 **Lethe wharf** bank of the river of forgetfulness in Hades  61 **forgèd process** false account  69 **adulterate** adulterous  81 **lewdness** lust  88 **secure** unsuspecting  89 **hebona** a poisonous plant

95 And with a sudden vigor it doth posset°
And curd, like eager° droppings into milk,
The thin and wholesome blood. So did it mine,
And a most instant tetter° barked about
Most lazarlike° with vile and loathsome crust
100 All my smooth body.
Thus was I, sleeping, by a brother's hand
Of life, of crown, of queen at once dispatched,
Cut off even in the blossoms of my sin,
Unhouseled, disappointed, unaneled,°
105 No reck'ning made, but sent to my account
With all my imperfections on my head.
O, horrible! O, horrible! Most horrible!
If thou hast nature in thee, bear it not.
Let not the royal bed of Denmark be
110 A couch for luxury° and damnèd incest.
But howsomever thou pursues this act,
Taint not thy mind, nor let thy soul contrive
Against thy mother aught. Leave her to heaven
And to those thorns that in her bosom lodge
115 To prick and sting her. Fare thee well at once.
The glowworm shows the matin° to be near
And 'gins to pale his uneffectual fire.
Adieu, adieu, adieu. Remember me. (*Exit.*)

     HAMLET
120 O all you host of heaven! O earth! What else?
And shall I couple hell? O fie! Hold, hold, my
    heart,
And you, my sinews, grow not instant old,
But bear me stiffly up. Remember thee?
125 Ay, thou poor ghost, whiles memory holds a seat
In this distracted globe.° Remember thee?
Yea, from the table° of my memory
I'll wipe away all trivial fond° records,
All saws° of books, all forms, all pressures° past
130 That youth and observation copied there,
And thy commandment all alone shall live
Within the book and volume of my brain,
Unmixed with baser matter. Yes, by heaven!
O most pernicious woman!
135 O villain, villain, smiling, damnèd villain!
My tables—meet it is I set it down

That one may smile, and smile, and be a villain.
At least I am sure it may be so in Denmark.
    (*Writes.*)
So, uncle, there you are. Now to my word:
It is "Adieu, adieu, remember me." 140
I have sworn't.

     HORATIO *and* MARCELLUS
(*Within*) My lord, my lord!
*Enter* HORATIO *and* MARCELLUS.
     MARCELLUS
Lord Hamlet! 145
     HORATIO
Heavens secure him!
     HAMLET
So be it!
     MARCELLUS 150
Illo, ho, ho,° my lord!
     HAMLET
Hillo, ho, ho, boy! Come, bird, come.
     MARCELLUS
How is't, my noble lord? 155
     HORATIO
What news, my lord?
     HAMLET
O, wonderful!
     HORATIO 160
Good my lord, tell it.
     HAMLET
No, you will reveal it.
     HORATIO
Not I, my lord, by heaven. 165
     MARCELLUS
Nor I, my lord.
     HAMLET
How say you then? Would heart of man once
    think it? 170
But you'll be secret?
     BOTH
Ay, by heaven, my lord.
     HAMLET
There's never a villain dwelling in all Denmark 175
But he's an arrant knave.
     HORATIO
There needs no ghost, my lord, come from the
    grave
To tell us this. 180

---

95 **posset** curdle  96 **eager** acid  98 **tatter** scab  99 **lazar-
like** leperlike  104 **Unhouseled, disappointed, unaneled**
without the sacrament of communion, unabsolved, without extreme unction  110 **luxury** lust  116 **matin** morning
126 **globe** i.e., his head  127 **table** tablet, notebook  128 **fond**
foolish  129 **saws** maxims  129 **pressures** impressions

151 **Illo, ho, ho** (falconer's call to his hawk)

**HAMLET**

Why, right, you are in the right;
And so, without more circumstance° at all,
I hold it fit that we shake hands and part:
185 You, as your business and desire shall point you,
For every man hath business and desire
Such as it is, and for my own poor part,
Look you, I'll go pray.

**HORATIO**

190 These are but wild and whirling words, my lord.

**HAMLET**

I am sorry they offend you, heartily;
Yes, faith, heartily.

**HORATIO**

195 There's no offense, my lord.

**HAMLET**

Yes, by Saint Patrick, but there is, Horatio,
And much offense too. Touching this vision here,
It is an honest ghost,° that let me tell you.
For your desire to know what is between us,
200 O'ermaster't as you may. And now, good friends,
As you are friends, scholars, and soldiers,
Give me one poor request.

**HORATIO**

205 What is't, my lord? We will.

**HAMLET**

Never make known what you have seen tonight.

**BOTH**

My lord, we will not.

210 **HAMLET**

Nay, but swear't.

**HORATIO**

In faith,
My lord, not I.

215 **MARCELLUS**

Nor I, my lord—in faith.

**HAMLET**

Upon my sword.

**MARCELLUS**

220 We have sworn, my lord, already.

**HAMLET**

Indeed, upon my sword, indeed.

**GHOST** *cries under the stage.*

**GHOST**

Swear.

**HAMLET**                                                     225

Ha, ha, boy, sayist thou so? Art thou there,
    truepenny?°
Come on. You hear this fellow in the cellarage.
Consent to swear.

**HORATIO**                                                   230

Propose the oath, my lord.

**HAMLET**

Never to speak of this that you have seen.
Swear by my sword.

**GHOST**                                                     235

(*Beneath*) Swear.

**HAMLET**

*Hic et ubique?°* then we'll shift our ground;
Come hither, gentlemen,
And lay your hands again upon my sword.            240
Never to speak of this that you have heard.
Swear by my sword.

**GHOST**

(*Beneath*) Swear by his sword.

**HAMLET**                                                    245

Well said, old mole! Canst work i' th' earth so
    fast?
A worthy pioner!° Once more remove, good
    friends.

**HORATIO**                                                   250

O day and night, but this is wondrous strange!

**HAMLET**

And therefore as a stranger give it welcome
There are more things in heaven and earth,
    Horatio,                                                  255
Then are dreamt of in you, philosophy.
But come:
Here as before, never, so help you mercy,
How strange or odd some'er I bear myself
(As I perchance hereafter shall think meet        260
To put an antic disposition° on),
That you, at such times seeing me, never shall
With arms encumb'red° thus, or this headshake,
Or by pronouncing of some doubtful phrase,
As "Well, well, we know," or "We could, and if    265
    we would,"
Or "If we list to speak," or "There be, an if they
    might,"
Or such ambiguous giving out, to note

---

183 **circumstance** details  198 **honest ghost** i.e., not a de-
mon in his father's shape

227 **truepenny** honest fellow  238 **hic et ubique** here and
everywhere (Latin)  248 **pioner** digger of mines  261 **antic
dispostion** fantastic behavior  263 **encumb'rd** folded

270 That you know aught of me—this do swear,
So grace and mercy at your most need help you.
       **GHOST**
(*Beneath*) Swear. (*They swear.*)
       **HAMLET**
275 Rest, rest, perturbed spirit. So, gentlemen,
With all my love I do commend me° to you,
And what so poor a man as Hamlet is
May do t' express his love and friending to you,
God willing, shall not lack. Let us go in together,
280 And still your fingers on your lips, I pray.
The time is out of joint. O cursèd spite,
That ever I was born to set it right!
Nay, come, let's go together. (*Exeunt.*)

# ACT II

**SCENE I**

*A room.*

*Enter old* **POLONIUS**, *with his man* **REYNALDO.**

       **POLONIUS**
Give him this money and these notes, Reynaldo.
       **REYNALDO**
I will, my lord.
5      **POLONIUS**
You shall do marvell's° wisely, good Reynaldo,
Before you visit him, to make inquire
Of his behavior.
       **REYNALDO**
10 My lord, I did intend it.
       **POLONIUS**
Marry, well said, very well said. Look you sir,
Inquire me first what Danskers° are in Paris,
And how, and who, what means, and where they
15      keep,°
What company, at what expense; and finding
By this encompassment° and drift of question
That they do know my son, come you more nearer
Than your particular demands° will touch it.
20 Take you as 'twere some distant knowledge of
       him,
As thus, "I know his father and his friends,
And in part him," Do you mark this, Reynaldo?

       **REYNALDO**
Ay, very well, my lord.                                    25
       **POLONIUS**
"And in part him, but," you may say,
"not well,
But if't be he I mean, he's very wild,
Addicted so and so." And there put on him         30
What forgeries° you please; marry, none so rank
As may dishonor him—take heed of that—
But, sir, such wanton, wild, and usual slips
As are companions noted and most known
To youth and liberty.                                      35
       **REYNALDO**
As gaming, my lord.
       **POLONIUS**
Ay, or drinking, fencing, swearing, quarreling.
Drabbing.° You may go so far.                          40
       **REYNALDO**
My lord, that would dishonor him.
       **POLONIUS**
Faith, no, as you may season it in the charge.
You must not put another scandal on him,            45
That he is open to incontinency.°
That's not my meaning. But breathe his faults so
       quaintly°
That they may seem the taints of liberty,
The flash and outbreak of a fiery mind,              50
A savageness in unreclaimèd blood,
Of general assault.°
       **REYNALDO**
But, my good lord—
       **POLONIUS**                                           55
Wherefore should you do this?
       **REYNALDO**
Ay, my lord,
I would know that.
       **POLONIUS**                                           60
Marry, sir, here's my drift,
And I believe it is a fetch of warrant.°
You laying these slight sullies on my son
As 'twere a thing a little soiled i' th' working,
Mark you,                                                   65
Your party in converse, him you would sound,
Having ever seen in the prenominate crimes°

---

276 **commend me** entrust myself   **II.i.** 6. **marvell's** marvel-
ous(ly)  13 **Danskers** Danes  15 **keep** dwell  17 **encom-
passment** circling  19 **demands** questions

31 **forgeries** inventions  40 **Drabbing** wenching  46 **incontinency** habitual licentiousness  48 **quaintly** ingeni-
ously, delicately  52 **Of general assault** common to all
men  62 **fetch of warrant** justifiable device  67 **Having . . .
crimes** if he has ever seen in the aforementioned crimes

The youth you breathe of guilty, be assured
He closes with you in this consequence:°
70 "Good sir," or so, or "friend," or "gentleman"—
According to the phrase or the addition°
Of man and country—
    REYNALDO
Very good, my lord.
75   POLONIUS
And then, sir, does 'a° this—'a does—
What was I about to say? By the mass, I was about
to say something! Where did I leave?
    REYNALDO
80 At "closes in the consequence," at "friend
or so," and "gentleman."
    POLONIUS
At "closes in the consequence"—Ay, marry!
He closes thus: "I know the gentleman;
85 I saw him yesterday, or t'other day,
Or then, or then, with such or such, and, as you
      say,
There was 'a gaming, there o'ertook in's rouse,
There falling out at tennis"; or perchance,
90 "I saw him enter such a house of sale,"
Videlicet,° a brothel, or so forth.
See you now—
Your bait of falsehood take this carp of truth,
And thus do we of wisdom and of reach,°
95 With windlasses° and with assays of bias,°
By indirections find directions out.
So, by my former lecture and advice,
Shall you my son. You have me, have you not?
    REYNALDO
100 My lord, I have.
    POLONIUS
God bye ye, fare ye well.
    REYNALDO
Good my lord.
105   POLONIUS
Observe his inclination in yourself.°
    REYNALDO
I shall, my lord.
    POLONIUS
110 And let him ply his music.

REYNALDO
Well, my lord.
    POLONIUS
Farewell. (*Exit* REYNALDO.)
*Enter* OPHELIA.
How now, Ophelia, what's the matter?                    115
    OPHELIA
O my lord, my lord, I have been so affrighted!
    POLONIUS
With what, i' th' name of God?
    OPHELIA                    120
My lord, as I was sewing in my closet,°
Lord Hamlet, with his doublet all unbraced,°
No hat upon his head, his stockings fouled,
Ungartered, and down-gyvèd° to his ankle,
Pale as his shirt, his knees knocking each other,    125
And with a look so piteous in purport,°
As if he had been loosèd out of hell
To speak of horrors—he comes before me.
    POLONIUS
Mad for thy love?                    130
    OPHELIA
My lord, I do not know,
But truly I do fear it.
    POLONIUS
What said he?                    135
    OPHELIA
He took me by the wrist and held me hard;
Then goes he to the length of all his arm,
And with his other hand thus o'er his brow
He falls to such perusal of my face                    140
As 'a would draw it. Long stayed he so.
At last, a little shaking of mine arm,
And thrice his head thus waving up and down,
He raised a sigh so piteous and profound
As it did seem to shatter all his bulk                    145
And end his being. That done, he lets me go,
And, with his head over his shoulder turned,
He seemed to find his way without his eyes,
For out o' doors he went without their helps,
And to the last bended their light on me.                    150
    POLONIUS
Come, go with me. I will go seek the King.
This is the very ecstasy° of love,
Whose violent property fordoes° itself

69 **He closes . . . this consequence** he falls in with you in this conclusion  71 **addition** title  76 **'a** he  91 **Videlicet** namely  94 **reach** far-reaching awareness(?)  95 **windlasses** circuitous courses  95 **assays of bias** indirect attempts (metaphor from bowling; **bias** = curved course) 106 **in yourself** for yourself

121 **closet** private room  122 **doublet all unbraced** jacket entirely unlaced  124 **down-gyvèd** hanging down like fetters  126 **purport** expression  153 **ecstasy** madness  154 **property fordoes** quality destroys

155 And leads the will to desperate undertakings
As oft as any passions under heaven
That does afflict our natures. I am sorry.
What, have you given him any hard words of late?
    OPHELIA
160 No, my good lord; but as you did command,
I did repel his letters and denied
His access to me.
    POLONIUS
That hath made him mad.
165 I am sorry that with better heed and judgment
I had not quoted° him. I feared he did but trifle
And meant to wrack thee; but beshrew my
    jealousy.°
By heaven, it is as proper° to our age
170 To cast beyond ourselves° in our opinions
As it is common for the younger sort
To lack discretion. Come, go we to the King.
This must be known, which, being kept close,
    might move
175 More grief to hide than hate to utter love.°
Come. (*Exeunt.*)

## SCENE II

*The castle.*

*Flourish. Enter* KING *and* QUEEN, ROSEN-
CRANTZ, *and* GUILDENSTERN (*with others*).

    KING
Welcome, dear Rosencrantz and Guildenstern.
Moreover that° we much did long to see you,
The need we have to use you did provoke
5 Our hasty sending. Something have you heard
Of Hamlet's transformation: so call it,
Sith° nor th' exterior nor the inward man
Resembles that it was. What it should be,
More than his father's death, that thus hath put
10     him
So much from th' understanding of himself,
I cannot dream of. I entreat you both

That, being of so° young days brought up with
    him,
And sith so neighbored to his youth and havior,° 15
That you vouchsafe your rest° here in our court
Some little time, so by your companies
To draw him on to pleasures, and to gather
So much as from occasion you may glean,
Whether aught to us unknown afflicts him thus, 20
That opened° lies within our remedy.
    QUEEN
Good gentlemen, he hath much talked of you,
And sure I am, two men there is not living
To whom he more adheres. If it will please you 25
To show us so much gentry° and good will
As to expend your time with us awhile
For the supply and profit of our hope,
Your visitation shall receive such thanks
As fits a king's remembrance. 30
    ROSENCRANTZ
Both your Majesties
Might, by the sovereign power you have of us,
Put your dread pleasures more into command
Than to entreaty. 35
    GUILDENSTERN
But we both obey,
And here give up ourselves in the full bent°
To lay our service freely at your feet, 40
To be commanded.
    KING
Thanks, Rosencrantz and gentle Guildenstern.
    QUEEN
Thanks, Guildenstern and gentle Rosencrantz.
And I beseech you instantly to visit 45
My too much changèd son. Go, some of you,
And bring these gentlemen where Hamlet is.
    GUILDENSTERN
Heavens make our presence and our practices
Pleasant and helpful to him! 50
    QUEEN
Ay, amen!
*Exeunt* ROSENCRANTZ *and* GUILDENSTERN
    (*with some Attendants*).
*Enter* POLONIUS.

---

166 **quoted** noted  168 **beshrew my jealousy** curse on my suspicions  169 **proper** natural  170 **To cast beyond ourselves** to be overcalculating  172–75 **Come, go . . . utter love** (the general meaning is that while telling the King of Hamlet's love may anger the King, more grief would come from keeping it secret)  II.ii. 3 **Moreover that** beside the fact that  7 **Sith** since

13 **of so** from such  15 **youth and havior** behavior in his youth  16 **vouchsafe your rest** consent to remain  21 **opened** revealed  26 **gentry** courtesy  39 **in the full bent** entirely (the figure is of a bow bent to its capacity)

**POLONIUS**
Th' ambassadors from Norway, my good lord,
55 Are joyfully returned.
**KING**
Thou still° hast been the father of good news.
**POLONIUS**
Have I, my lord? Assure you, my good liege,
60 I hold my duty, as I hold my soul,
Both to my God and to my gracious king;
And I do think, or else this brain of mine
Hunts not the trail of policy so sure°
As it hath used to do, that I have found
65 The very cause of Hamlet's lunacy.
**KING**
O, speak of that! That do I long to hear.
**POLONIUS**
Give first admittance to th' ambassadors.
70 My news shall be the fruit to that great feast.
**KING**
Thyself do grace to them and bring them in.
(*Exit* **POLONIUS**.)
He tells me, my dear Gertrude, he hath found
The head and source of all your son's distemper.
75    **QUEEN**
I doubt° it is no other but the main,°
His father's death and our o'erhasty marriage.
**KING**
Well, we shall sift him.
*Enter* **POLONIUS, VOLTEMAND,** *and* **CORNELIUS.**
80 Welcome, my good friends.
Say, Voltemand, what from our brother Norway?
**VOLTEMAND**
Most fair return of greetings and desires.
Upon our first,° he sent out to suppress
85 His nephew's levies, which to him appeared
To be a preparation 'gainst the Polack;
But better looked into, he truly found
It was against your Highness, whereat grieved,
That so his sickness, age, and impotence
90 Was falsely borne in hand,° sends out arrests
On Fortinbras; which he, in brief, obeys,
Receives rebuke from Norway, and in fine,°
Makes vow before his uncle never more
To give th' assay° of arms against your Majesty.
95 Whereon old Norway, overcome with joy,

Gives him threescore thousand crowns in annual
    fee
And his commission to employ those soldiers,
So levied as before, against the Polack,
With an entreaty, herein further shown,        100
(*Gives a paper.*)
That it might please you to give quiet pass
Through your dominions for this enterprise,
On such regards of safety and allowance°
As therein are set down.
    **KING**                                 105
It likes us well;
And at our more considered time° we'll read,
Answer, and think upon this business.
Meantime, we thank you for your well-took labor.
Go to your rest; at night we'll feast together.   110
Most welcome home!
*Exeunt* **AMBASSADORS.**
**POLONIUS**
This business is well ended.
My liege and madam, to expostulate°
What majesty should be, what duty is,          115
Why day is day, night night, and time is time.
Were nothing but to waste night, day, and time.
Therefore, since brevity is the soul of wit,°
And tediousness the limbs and outward
    flourishes,                                 120
I will be brief. Your noble son is mad.
Mad call I it, for, to define true madness,
What is't but to be nothing else but mad?
But let that go.
    **QUEEN**                                  125
More matter, with less art.
    **POLONIUS**
Madam, I swear I use no art at all.
That he's mad, 'tis true: 'tis true 'tis pity,
And pity 'tis 'tis true—a foolish figure.°      130
But farewell it, for I will use no art.
Mad let us grant him then; and now remains
That we find out the cause of this effect,
Or rather say, the cause of this defect,
For this effect defective comes by cause.       135
Thus it remains, and the remainder thus.
Perpend.°
I have a daughter: have, while she is mine,

---

57 **still** always  63 **Hunts not . . . so sure** does not follow
clues of political doings with such sureness  76 **doubt** suspect  76 **main** principal point  84 **first** first audience  90
**borne in hand** deceived  92 **in fine** finally  94 **assay** trial

103 **regards of safety and allowance** i.e., conditions  107
**considered time** time proper for considering  114 **expos-
tulate** discuss  118 **wit** wisdom, understanding  130 **figure** figure of rhetoric  137 **Perpend** consider carefully

Who in her duty and obedience, mark,
140 Hath given me this. Now gather, and surmise.
(*Reads*) *the letter.*
"To the celestial, and my soul's idol, the most
beautified Ophelia"—
That's an ill phrase, a vile phrase; "beautified" is a
vile phrase. But you shall hear. Thus:
145 "In her excellent white bosom, these, &c."
       QUEEN
Came this from Hamlet to her?
       POLONIUS
Good madam, stay awhile. I will be faithful.
150 "Doubt thou the stars are fire,
Doubt that the sun doth move;
Doubt° truth to be a liar,
But never doubt I love.
O dear Ophelia, I am ill at these numbers.° I have
155 not art to reckon my groans; but that I love thee
best, O most best, believe it. Adieu.
Thine evermore, most dear lady, whilst this
machine° is to him, HAMLET."
This in obedience hath my daughter shown me,
160 And more above° hath his solicitings,
As they fell out by time, by means, and place,
All given to mine ear.
       KING
But how hath she
165 Received his love?
       POLONIUS
What do you think of me?
       KING
As of a man faithful and honorable.
170     POLONIUS
I would fain prove so. But what might you think,
When I had seen this hot love on the wing
(As I perceived it, I must tell you that,
Before my daughter told me), what might you,
175 Or my dear Majesty your Queen here, think,
If I had played the desk or table book,°
Or given my heart a winking,° mute and dumb,
Or looked upon this love with idle sight?
What might you think? No, I went round to work
180 And my young mistress thus I did bespeak:
"Lord Hamlet is a prince, out of thy star.°

This must not be." And then I prescripts gave her,
That she should lock herself from his resort,
Admit no messengers, receive no tokens.
Which done, she took the fruits of my advice,          185
And he, repellèd, a short tale to make,
Fell into a sadness, then into a fast,
Thence to a watch,° thence into a weakness,
Thence to a lightness,° and, by this declension,
Into the madness wherein now he raves,               190
And all we mourn for.
       KING
Do you think 'tis this?
       QUEEN
It may be, very like.                                 195
       POLONIUS
Hath there been such a time, I would fain know
       that,
That I have positively said "'Tis so,"
When it proved otherwise?                             200
       KING
Not that I know.
       POLONIUS
(*Pointing to his head and shoulder*) Take this from
       this, if this be otherwise.                    205
If circumstances lead me, I will find
Where truth is hid, though it were hid indeed
Within the center.°
       KING
How may we try it further?                            210
       POLONIUS
You know sometimes he walks four hours
       together
Here in the lobby.
       QUEEN                                          215
So he does indeed.
       POLONIUS
At such a time I'll loose my daughter to him.
Be you and I behind an arras° then.
Mark the encounter. If he love her not,              220
And be not from his reason fall'n thereon,
Let me be no assistant for a state
But keep a farm and carters.
       KING
We will try it.                                       225
*Enter* **HAMLET** *reading on a book.*

---

152 **Doubt** suspect   154 **ill at these numbers** unskilled in
verses   158 **machine** complex device (here, his body)   160
**more above** in addition   176 **played the desk or table
book** i.e., been a passive recipient of secrets   177 **winking**
closing of the eyes   181 **star** sphere

188 **watch** wakefulness   189 **lightness** mental derange-
ment   208 **center** center of the earth   219 **arras** tapestry
hanging in front of a wall

**QUEEN**
But look where sadly the poor wretch comes
   reading.
**POLONIUS**
230 Away, I do beseech you both, away.
*Exit* KING *and* QUEEN.
I'll board him presently.° O, give me leave.
How does my good Lord Hamlet?
   **HAMLET**
Well, God-a-mercy.
235   **POLONIUS**
Do you know me, my lord?
   **HAMLET**
Excellent well. You are a fishmonger.°
   **POLONIUS**
240 Not I, my lord.
   **HAMLET**
Then I would you were so honest a man.
   **POLONIUS**
Honest, my lord?
245   **HAMLET**
Ay, sir. To be honest, as this world goes, is to be
one man picked out of ten thousand.
   **POLONIUS**
That's very true, my lord.
250   **HAMLET**
For if the sun breed maggots in a dead dog, being
a good kissing carrion°—Have you a daughter?
   **POLONIUS**
I have, my lord.
255   **HAMLET**
Let her not walk i' th' sun. Conception° is a
blessing, but as your daughter may conceive,
friend, look to't.
   **POLONIUS**
260 (*Aside*) How say you by that? Still harping on my
daughter. Yet he knew me not at first. 'A said I
was a fishmonger. 'A is far gone, far gone. And
truly in my youth I suffered much extremity for
love, very near this. I'll speak to him
265 again.—What do you read, my lord?
   **HAMLET**
Words, words, words.

**POLONIUS**
What is the matter, my lord?
   **HAMLET**                                                                  270
Between who?
   **POLONIUS**
I mean the matter° that you read, my lord.
   **HAMLET**
Slanders, sir; for the satirical rogue says here that    275
old men have gray beards, that their faces are
wrinkled, their eyes purging thick amber and
plum-tree gum, and that they have a plentiful
lack of wit, together with most weak hams. All
which, sir, though I most powerfully and potently    280
believe, yet I hold it not honesty° to have it thus
set down; for you yourself, sir, should be old as I
am if, like a crab, you could go backward.
   **POLONIUS**
(*Aside*) Though this be madness, yet there is    285
method in't. Will you walk out of the air, my lord?
   **HAMLET**
Into my grave.
   **POLONIUS**
Indeed, that's out of the air. (*Aside*). How    290
pregnant° sometimes his replies are! A happiness°
that often madness hits on, which reason and
sanity could not so prosperously be delivered of. I
will leave him and suddenly contrive the means
of meeting between him and my daughter.—My    295
lord, I will take my leave of you.
   **HAMLET**
You cannot take from me anything that I will
more willingly part withal—except my life, except
my life, except my life.    300
*Enter* GUILDENSTERN *and* ROSENCRANTZ.
   **POLONIUS**
Fare you well, my lord.
   **HAMLET**
These tedious old fools!
   **POLONIUS**                                                              305
You go to seek the Lord Hamlet? There he is.
   **ROSENCRANTZ**
(*To* POLONIUS) God save you, sir!
*Exit* POLONIUS.
   **GUILDENSTERN**
My honored lord!    310

---

231 **board him presently** accost him at once  238 **fishmonger** dealer in fish (slang for a procurer)  252 **a good kissing
carrion** (perhaps the meaning is "a good piece of flesh to
kiss," but many editors emend good to god, taking the
word to refer to the sun)  256 **Conception** (1) understanding (2) becoming pregnant

273 **matter** (Polonius means "subject matter," but Hamlet
pretends to take the word in the sense of "quarrel")  281
**honesty** decency  291 **pregnant** meaningful  291 **happiness** apt turn of phrase

**ROSENCRANTZ**

My most dear lord!

**HAMLET**

My excellent good friends! How dost thou,
315 Guildenstern? Ah, Rosencrantz! Good lads, how
do you both?

**ROSENCRANTZ**

As the indifferent° children of the earth.

**GUILDENSTERN**

320 Happy in that we are not overhappy. On
Fortune's cap we are not the very button.

**HAMLET**

Nor the soles of her shoe?

**ROSENCRANTZ**

325 Neither, my lord.

**HAMLET**

Then you live about her waist, or in the middle of
her favors?

**GUILDENSTERN**

330 Faith, her privates° we.

**HAMLET**

In the secret parts of Fortune? O, most true! She is
a strumpet. What news?

**ROSENCRANTZ**

335 None, my lord, but that the world's grown honest.

**HAMLET**

Then is doomsday near. But your news is not
true. Let me question more in particular. What
have you, my good friends, deserved at the hands
340 of Fortune that she sends you to prison hither?

**GUILDENSTERN**

Prison, my lord?

**HAMLET**

Denmark's a prison.

345 **ROSENCRANTZ**

Then is the world one.

**HAMLET**

A goodly one, in which there are many confines,
wards,° and dungeons, Denmark being one o' th'
350 worst.

**ROSENCRANTZ**

We think not so, my lord.

**HAMLET**

Why, then 'tis none to you, for there is nothing
355 either good or bad but thinking makes it so. To
me it is a prison.

**ROSENCRANTZ**

Why then your ambition makes it one. 'Tis too
narrow for your mind.

**HAMLET** 360

O God, I could be bounded in a nutshell and
count myself a king of infinite space, were it not
that I have bad dreams.

**GUILDENSTERN**

Which dreams indeed are ambition, for the very 365
substance of the ambitious is merely the shadow
of a dream.

**HAMLET**

A dream itself is but a shadow.

**ROSENCRANTZ** 370

Truly, and I hold ambition of so airy and light a
quality that it is but a shadow's shadow.

**HAMLET**

Then are our beggars bodies, and our monarchs
and outstretched heroes the beggars' shadows.° 375
Shall we to th' court? For, by my fay,° I cannot
reason.

**BOTH**

We'll wait upon you.

**HAMLET** 380

No such matter. I will not sort you with the rest of
my servants, for, to speak to you like an honest
man, I am most dreadfully attended. But in the
beaten way of friendship, what make you at
Elsinore? 385

**ROSENCRANTZ**

To visit you, my lord; no other occasion.

**HAMLET**

Beggar that I am, I am even poor in thanks, but I
thank you; and sure, dear friends, my thanks are 390
too dear a halfpenny.° Were you not sent for? Is it
your own inclining? Is it a free visitation? Come,
come, deal justly with me. Come, come; nay,
speak.

**GUILDENSTERN** 395

What should we say, my lord?

**HAMLET**

Why anything—but to th' purpose. You were sent
for, and there is a kind of confession in your
looks, which your modesties have not craft 400

---

374–76 **Then are . . . beggars' shadows** i.e., by your logic,
beggars (lacking ambition) are substantial, and great men
are elongated shadows 376 **fay** faith 391 **too dear a
halfpenny** i.e., not worth a halfpenny

---

318 **indifferent** ordinary   330 **privates** ordinary men (with
a pun on "private parts")   349 **wards** cells

enough to color. I know the good King and
Queen have sent for you.

ROSENCRANTZ

To what end, my lord?

405   HAMLET

That you must teach me. But let me conjure you
by the rights of our fellowship, by the consonancy
of our youth, by the obligation of our
everpreserved love, and by what more dear a
410  better proposer can charge you withal, be even
and direct with me, whether you were sent for or
no.

ROSENCRANTZ

(*Aside to* GUILDENSTERN) What say you?

415   HAMLET

(*Aside*) Nay then, I have an eye of you.—If you
love me, hold not off.

GUILDENSTERN

My lord, we were sent for.

420   HAMLET

I will tell you why; so shall my anticipation
prevent your discovery,° and your secrecy to the
King and Queen molt no feather. I have of late,
but wherefore I know not, lost all my mirth,
425  forgone all custom of exercises; and indeed, it
goes so heavily with my disposition that this
goodly frame, the earth, seems to me a sterile
promontory; this most excellent canopy, the air,
look you, this brave o'erhanging firmament, this
430  majestical roof fretted° with golden fire: why, it
appeareth nothing to me but a foul and pestilent
congregation of vapors. What a piece of work is a
man, how noble in reason, how infinite in
faculties, in form and moving how express° and
435  admirable, in action how like an angel, in
apprehension how like a god: the beauty of the
world, the paragon of animals; and yet to me,
what is this quintessence of dust? Man delights
not me; nor woman neither, though by your
440  smiling you seem to say so.

ROSENCRANTZ

My lord, there was no such stuff in my thoughts.

HAMLET

Why did ye laugh then, when I said "Man
445  delights not me"?

ROSENCRANTZ

To think, my lord, if you delight not in man, what
lenten° entertainment the players shall receive
from you. We coted° them on the way, and hither
are they coming to offer you service.                          450

HAMLET

He that plays the king shall be welcome; his
Majesty shall have tribute of me; the adventurous
knight shall use his foil and target°; the lover shall
not sigh gratis; the humorous man° shall end his       455
part in peace; the clown shall make those laugh
whose lungs are tickle o' th' sere° and the lady
shall say her mind freely, or° the blank verse shall
halt° for't. What players are they?

ROSENCRANTZ                                                      460

Even those you were wont to take such delight in,
the tragedians of the city.

HAMLET

How chances it they travel? Their residence, both
in reputation and profit, was better both ways.          465

ROSENCRANTZ

I think their inhibition° comes by the means of the
late innovation.°

HAMLET

Do they hold the same estimation they did when I    470
was in the city? Are they so followed?

ROSENCRANTZ

No indeed, are they not.

HAMLET

How comes it? Do they grow rusty?                          475

ROSENCRANTZ

Nay, their endeavor keeps in the wonted pace,
but there is, sir, an eyrie° of children, little eyases,
that cry out on the top of question° and are most
tyrannically° clapped for't. These are now the       480
fashion, and so berattle the common stages° (so

---

448 **lenten** meager  449 **coted** overtook  454 **target** shield
455 **humorous man** i.e., eccentric man (among stock characters in dramas were men dominated by a "humor" or
odd trait)  457 **tickle o' th' sere** on hair trigger (**sere** = part
of the gunlock)  458 **or** else  459 **halt** limp  467 **inhibition**
hindrance  468 **innovation** (probably an allusion to the
companies of child actors that had become popular and
were offering serious competition to the adult actors)  478
**eyrie** nest  478–79 **eyases, that . . . of question** unfledged
hawks that cry shrilly above others in matters of debate
480 **tyrannically** violently  481 **berattle the common
stages** cry down the public theaters (with the adult acting
companies)

---

422 **prevent your discovery** forestall your disclosure  430
**fretted** adorned  434 **express** exact

they call them) that many wearing rapiers are
afraid of goosequills° and dare scarce come
thither.

485 **HAMLET**
What, are they children? Who maintains 'em?
How are they escoted?° Will they pursue the
quality° no longer than they can sing? Will they
not say afterwards, if they should grow
490 themselves to common players (as it is most like,
if their means are no better), their writers do them
wrong to make them exclaim against their own
succession?°

**ROSENCRANTZ**
495 Faith, there has been much to-do on both sides,
and the nation holds it no sin to tarre° them to
controversy. There was, for a while, no money bid
for argument° unless the poet and the player
went to cuffs in the question.

500 **HAMLET**
Is't possible?

**GUILDENSTERN**
O, there has been much throwing about of brains.

**HAMLET**
505 Do the boys carry it away?

**ROSENCRANTZ**
Ay, that they do, my lord—Hercules and his
load° too.

**HAMLET**
510 It is not very strange, for my uncle is King of
Denmark, and those that would make mouths at
him while my father lived give twenty, forty,
fifty, a hundred ducats apiece for his picture in
little. 'Sblood,° there is something in this more
515 than natural, if philosophy could find it out.
*A flourish.*

**GUILDENSTERN**
There are the players.

**HAMLET**
Gentlemen, you are welcome to Elsinore. Your
520 hands, come then. Th' appurtenance of welcome
is fashion and ceremony. Let me comply° with

you in this garb,° lest my extent° to the players
(which I tell you must show fairly outwards)
should more appear like entertainment than
yours. You are welcome. But my uncle-father and   525
aunt-mother are deceived.

**GUILDENSTERN**
In what, my dear lord?

**HAMLET**
I am but mad north-northwest:° when the wind is   530
southerly I know a hawk from a handsaw.°
*Enter* **POLONIUS**.

**POLONIUS**
Well be with you, gentlemen.

**HAMLET**
Hark you, Guildenstern, and you too; at each ear   535
a hearer. That great baby you see there is not yet
out of his swaddling clouts.

**ROSENCRANTZ**
Happily° he is the second time come to them, for
they say an old man is twice a child.   540

**HAMLET**
I will prophesy he comes to tell me of the players.
Mark it.—You say right, sir; a Monday morning,
'twas then indeed.

**POLONIUS**   545
My lord, I have news to tell you.

**HAMLET**
My lord, I have news to tell you. When Roscius°
was an actor in Rome—

**POLONIUS**   550
The actors are come hither, my lord.

**HAMLET**
Buzz, buzz.°

**POLONIUS**
Upon my honor—   555

**HAMLET**
Then came each actor on his ass—

**POLONIUS**
The best actors in the world, either for tragedy,
comedy, history, pastoral, pastoral-comical,   560
historical-pastoral, tragical-historical,

---

483 **goosequills** pens (of satirists who ridicule the public
theaters and their audiences)   487 **escoted** financially sup-
ported   488 **quality** profession of acting   493 **succession**
future   496 **tarre** incite   498 **argument** plot of a play   507–
08 **Hercules and his load** i.e., the whole world (with a
reference to the Globe Theatre, which had a sign that represented Hercules bearing the globe)   514 **'Sblood** by
God's blood   521 **comply** be courteous

522 **garb** outward show   522 **extent** behavior   530 **north-
northwest** i.e., on one point of the compass only   531
**hawk from a handsaw** (**hawk** can refer not only to a bird
but to a kind of pickax; **handsaw**—a carpenter's tool—may
involve a similar pun on "hernshaw," a heron)   539 **Happily** perhaps   548 **Roscius** (a famous Roman comic actor)
553 **Buzz, buzz** (an interjection, perhaps indicating that the
news is old)

tragical-comical-historical-pastoral; scene
individable,° or poem unlimited.° Seneca° cannot
be too heavy, nor Plautus° too light. For the law
565 of writ and the liberty,° these are the only men.

**HAMLET**

O Jeptha, judge of Israel,° what a treasure hadst
thou!

**POLONIUS**

570 What a treasure had he, my lord?

**HAMLET**

Why,
"One fair daughter, and no more,
The which he lovèd passing well."

575    **POLONIUS**

(*Aside*) Still on my daughter.

**HAMLET**

Am I not i' th' right, old Jeptha?

**POLONIUS**

580 If you call me Jeptha, my lord, I have a daughter
that I love passing well.

**HAMLET**

Nay, that follows not.

**POLONIUS**

585 What follows, then, my lord?

**HAMLET**

Why,
"As by lot, God wot,"
and then, you know,
590 "It came to pass, as most like it was."
The first row of the pious chanson° will show you
more, for look where my abridgment° comes.
*Enter the* **PLAYERS.**
You are welcome, masters, welcome, all. I am
glad to see thee well. Welcome, good friend. O,
595 old friend, why, thy face is valanced° since I saw
thee last. Comist thou to beard me in Denmark?
What, my young lady° and mistress? By'r Lady,

your ladyship is nearer to heaven than when I
saw you last by the altitude of a chopine.° Pray
God your voice, like a piece of uncurrent gold, be        600
not cracked within the ring.°—Masters, you are
all welcome. We'll e'en to't like French falconers,
fly at anything we see. We'll have a speech
straight. Come, give us a taste of your quality.
Come, a passionate speech.                               605

**PLAYER**

What speech, my good lord?

**HAMLET**

I heard thee speak me a speech once, but it was
never acted, or if it was, not above once, for the      610
play, I remember, pleased not the million; 'twas
caviary to the general,° but it was (as I received it,
and others, whose judgments in such matters
cried in the top of° mine) an excellent play, well
digested in the scenes, set down with as much         615
modesty as cunning.° I remember one said there
were no sallets° in the lines to make the matter
savory; nor no matter in the phrase that might
indict the author of affectation, but called it an
honest method, as wholesome as sweet, and by         620
very much more handsome than fine.° One
speech in't I chiefly loved. 'Twas Aeneas' tale to
Dido, and thereabout of it especially when he
speaks of Priam's slaughter. If it live in your
memory, begin at this line—let me see, let me see:   625

"The rugged Pyrrhus, like th' Hyrcanian
beast°—"

'Tis not so; it begins with Pyrrhus:

"The rugged Pyrrhus, he whose sable° arms,
Black as his purpose, did the night resemble         630
When he lay couchèd in th' ominous horse,°
Hath now this dread and black complexion
    smeared

---

563 **scene individable** plays observing the unities of time,
place, and action   563 **poem unlimited** plays not restricted
by the tenets of criticism   563 **Seneca** (Roman tragic
dramatist)   564 **Plautus** (Roman comic dramatist)   565 **For
the law of writ and the liberty** (perhaps "for sticking to the
text and for improvising"; perhaps "for classical plays and
for modern loosely written plays")   567 **Jeptha, judge of
Israel** (the title of a ballad on the Hebrew judge who sacrificed his daughter; see Judges 11)   591 **row of the pious
chanson** stanza of the scriptural song   592 **abridgment**
(1) i.e., entertainers, who abridge the time (2) interrupts
595 **valanced** fringed (with a beard)   597 **young lady** i.e.,
boy for female roles

599 **chopine** thick-soled shoe   600–01 **like a piece . . . the
ring** (a coin was unfit for legal tender if a crack extended
from the edge through the ring enclosing the monarch's
head. Hamlet, punning on *ring,* refers to the change of
voice that the boy actor will undergo)   612 **caviary to the
general** i.e., too choice for the multitude   614 **in the top of**
overtopping   616 **modesty as cunning** restraint as art   617
**sallets** salads, spicy jests   621 **more handsome than fine**
well-proportioned rather than ornamented   626–27 **Hyrcanian beast** i.e., tiger (Hyrcania was in Asia)   629 **sable**
black   631 **ominous horse** i.e., wooden horse at the siege of
Troy

With heraldry more dismal.° Head to foot
635 Now is he total gules, horridly tricked°
With blood of father, mothers, daughters, sons,
Baked and impasted° with the parching streets,
That lend a tyrannous and a damnèd light
To their lord's murder. Roasted in wrath and fire,
640 And thus o'ersizèd° with coagulate gore,
With eyes like carbuncles, the hellish Pyrrhus
Old grandsire Priam seeks."

So, proceed you.
POLONIUS
645 Fore God, my lord, well spoken, with good accent
and good discretion.
PLAYER
"Anon he finds him,
Striking too short at Greeks. His antique sword,
650 Rebellious to his arm, lies where it falls,
Repugnant to command.° Unequal matched,
Pyrrhus at Priam drives, in rage strikes wide,
But with the whiff and wind of his fell sword
Th' unnervèd father falls. Then senseless Ilium,°
655 Seeming to feel this blow, with flaming top
Stoops to his base,° and with a hideous crash
Takes prisoner Pyrrhus' ear. For lo, his sword,
Which was declining on the milky head
Of reverend Priam, seemed i' th' air to stick.
660 So as a painted tyrant° Pyrrhus stood,
And like a neutral to his will and matter°
Did nothing.
But as we often see, against° some storm,
A silence in the heavens, the rack° stand still,
665 The bold winds speechless, and the orb below
As hush as death, anon the dreadful thunder
Doth rend the region, so after Pyrrhus' pause,
A rousèd vengeance sets him new awork,
And never did the Cyclops' hammers fall
670 On Mars's armor, forged for proof eterne,°
With less remorse than Pyrrhus' bleeding sword
Now falls on Priam.
Out, out, thou strumpet Fortune! All you gods,
In general synod° take away her power,

Break all the spokes and fellies° from her wheel,    675
And bowl the round nave° down the hill of
heaven,
As low as to the fiends."
POLONIUS
This is too long.    680
HAMLET
It shall to the barber's, with your beard.— Prithee
say on. He's for a jig or a tale of bawdry, or he
sleeps. Say on; come to Hecuba.
PLAYER
"But who (ah woe!) had seen the mobled°    685
queen—"
HAMLET
"The mobled queen"?
POLONIUS
That's good. "Mobled queen" is good.    690
PLAYER
"Run barefoot up and down, threat'ning the
flames
With bisson rheum;° a clout° upon that head    695
Where late the diadem stood, and for a robe,
About her lank and all o'erteemèd° loins,
A blanket in the alarm of fear caught up—
Who this had seen, with tongue in venom steeped
'Gainst Fortune's state would treason have    700
pronounced.
But if the gods themselves did see her then,
When she saw Pyrrhus make malicious sport
In mincing with his sword her husband's limbs,
The instant burst of clamor that she made    705
(Unless things mortal move them not at all)
Would have made milch° the burning eyes of
heaven
And passion in the gods."

POLONIUS    710
Look, whe'r° he has not turned his color, and has
tears in's eyes. Prithee no more.
HAMLET
'Tis well. I'll have thee speak out the rest of this
soon. Good my lord, will you see the players well    715
bestowed?° Do you hear? Let them be well used,
for they are the abstract and brief chronicles of the

---

634 **dismal** ill-omened  635 **total gules, horridly tricked**
all red, horridly adorned  637 **impasted** encrusted  640
**o'ersizèd** smeared over  651 **Repugnant to command** dis-
obedient  654 **senseless Ilium** insensate Troy  656 **Stoops
to his base** collapses (**his** = its)  660 **painted tyrant** tyrant
in a picture  661 **matter** task  663 **against** just before  664
**rack** clouds  670 **proof eterne** eternal endurance  674
**synod** council

675 **fellies** rims  676 **nave** hub  686 **mobled** muffled  695
**bisson rheum** blinding tears  695 **clout** rag  697
**o'erteemèd** exhausted with childbearing  707 **milch** moist
(literally, "milk-giving")  711 **whe'r** whether  716 **bestowed** housed

time. After your death you were better have a bad
epitaph than their ill report while you live.

720 **POLONIUS**

My lord, I will use them according to their desert.

**HAMLET**

God's bodkin,° man, much better! Use every man
after his desert, and who shall scape whipping?
725 Use them after your own honor and dignity. The
less they deserve, the more merit is in your
bounty. Take them in.

**POLONIUS**

Come, sirs.

730 **HAMLET**

Follow him, friends. We'll hear a play tomorrow.
(*Aside to* **PLAYER**) Dost thou hear me, old friend?
Can you play *The Murder of Gonzago?*

**PLAYER**

735 Ay, my lord.

**HAMLET**

We'll ha't tomorrow night. You could for a need
study a speech of some dozen or sixteen lines
which I would set down and insert in't, could you
740 not?

**PLAYER**

Ay, my lord.

**HAMLET**

Very well. Follow that lord, and look you mock
745 him not. My good friends, I'll leave you till night.
You are welcome to Elsinore.

*Exeunt* **POLONIUS** *and* **PLAYERS**.

**ROSENCRANTZ**

Good my lord.

*Exeunt* (**ROSENCRANTZ** *and* **GUILDENSTERN**).

**HAMLET**

750 Ay, so, God bye to you.—Now I am alone.
O, what a rogue and peasant slave
am I!
Is it not monstrous that this player here,
But in a fiction, in a dream of passion,°
755 Could force his soul so to his own conceit°
That from her working all his visage wanned,
Tears in his eyes, distraction in his aspect,
A broken voice, and his whole function° suiting
With forms° to his conceit? And all for nothing!
760 For Hebuca!
What's Hecuba to him, or he to Hecuba,

That he should weep for her? What would he do
Had he the motive and the cue for passion
That I have? He would drown the stage with tears
And cleave the general ear with horrid speech,          765
Make mad the guilty and appall the free,°
Confound the ignorant, and amaze indeed
The very faculties of eyes and ears.
Yet I,
A dull and muddy-mettled° rascal, peak          770
Like john-a-dreams,° unpregnant of° my cause,
And can say nothing. No, not for a king,
Upon whose property and most dear life
A damned defeat was made. Am I a coward?
Who calls me villain? Breaks my pate across?          775
Plucks off my beard and blows it in my face?
Tweaks me by the nose? Gives me the lie i' th'
        throat
As deep as to the lungs? Who does me this?
Ha, 'swounds,° I should take it, for it cannot be          780
But I am pigeon-livered° and lack gall
To make oppression bitter, or ere this
I should ha' fatted all the region kites°
With this slave's offal. Bloody, bawdy villain!
Remorseless, treacherous, lecherous, kindless°          785
        villain!
O, vengeance!
Why, what an ass am I! This is most brave,°
That I, the son of a dear father murdered,
Prompted to my revenge by heaven and hell,          790
Must, like a whore, unpack my heart with words
And fall a-cursing like a very drab,°
A stallion!° Fie upon't, foh! About,° my brains.
Hum—
I have heard that guilty creatures sitting at a play          795
Have by the very cunning of the scene
Been struck so to the soul that presently°
They have proclaimed their malefactions.
For murder, though it have no tongue, will speak
With most miraculous organ. I'll have these players          800

---

766 **appall the free** terrify (make pale?) the guiltless  770
**muddy-mettled** weak-spirited  770–71 **peak/Like John-a-dreams** mope like a dreamer  771 **unpregnant of** unquickened by  780 **'swounds** by God's wounds  781 **pigeon-livered** gentle as a dove  783 **region kites** kites (scavenger birds) of the sky  785 **kindless** unnatural  788 **brave** fine  792 **drab** prostitute  793 **stallion** male prostitute (perhaps one should adopt the Folio reading, **scullion** = kitchen wench)  793 **About** to work  797 **presently** immediately

---

723 **God's bodkin** by God's little body  754 **dream of passion** imaginary emotion  755 **conceit** imagination  758 **function** action  759 **forms** bodily expressions

Play something like the murder of my father
Before mine uncle. I'll observe his looks,
I'll tent° him to the quick. If 'a do blench,°
I know my course. The spirit that I have seen
805 May be a devil, and the devil hath power
T' assume a pleasing shape, yea, and perhaps
Out of my weakness and my melancholy,
As he is very potent with such spirits,
Abuses me to damn me. I'll have grounds
810 More relative° than this. The play's the thing
Wherein I'll catch the conscience of the King.
(*Exit.*)

# ACT III

## SCENE I

*The castle.*

*Enter* KING *and* QUEEN, POLONIUS, OPHELIA,
ROSENCRANTZ, GUILDENSTERN, LORDS.
    KING
And can you by no drift of conference°
Get from him why he puts on this confusion,
Grating so harshly all his days of quiet
5 With turbulent and dangerous lunacy?
    ROSENCRANTZ
He does confess he feels himself distracted,
But from what cause 'a will by no means speak.
    GUILDENSTERN
10 Nor do we find him forward to be sounded,°
But with a crafty madness keeps aloof
When we would bring him on to some confession
Of his true state.
    QUEEN
15 Did he receive you well?
    ROSENCRANTZ
Most like a gentleman.
    GUILDENSTERN
But with much forcing of his disposition.°
20     ROSENCRANTZ
Niggard of question,° but of our demands
Most free in his reply.

803 **tent** probe  803 **blench** flinch  810 **relative** (probably
"pertinent," but possibly "able to be related plausibly")
**III.i.** 2 **drift of conference** management of conversation
10 **forward to be sounded** willing to be questioned  19
**forcing of his disposition** effort  21 **Niggard of question**
uninclined to talk

    QUEEN
Did you assay° him
To any pastime?                                              25
    ROSENCRANTZ
Madam, it so fell out that certain players
We o'erraught° on the way; of these we told him,
And there did seem in him a kind of joy
To hear of it. They are here about the court,      30
And, as I think, they have already order
This night to play before him.
    POLONIUS
'Tis most true,
And he beseeched me to entreat your Majesties    35
To hear and see the matter.
    KING
With all my heart, and it doth much content me
To hear him so inclined.
Good gentlemen, give him a further edge          40
And drive his purpose into these delights.
    ROSENCRANTZ
We shall, my lord.
*Exeunt* ROSENCRANTZ *and* GUILDENSTERN.
    KING
Sweet Gertrude, leave us too,                    45
For we have closely° sent for Hamlet hither,
That he, as 'twere by accident, may here
Affront° Ophelia.
Her father and myself (lawful espials°)
Will so bestow ourselves that, seeing unseen,    50
We may of their encounter frankly judge
And gather by him, as he is behaved,
If't be th' affliction of his love or no
That thus he suffers for.
    QUEEN
                                                 55
I shall obey you.
And for your part, Ophelia, I do wish
That your good beauties be the happy cause
Of Hamlet's wildness. So shall I hope your virtues
Will bring him to his wonted way again,          60
To both your honors.
    OPHELIA
Madam, I wish it may.
(*Exit* QUEEN.)
    POLONIUS
Ophelia, walk you here.—Gracious, so please you,  65
We will bestow ourselves. (*To* OPHELIA) Read on
   this book,

24 **assay** tempt  28 **o'erraught** overtook  46 **closely** secretly  48 **Affront** meet face to face  49 **espials** spies

That show of such an exercise may color°
Your loneliness. We are oft to blame in this,
70 'Tis too much proved, that with devotion's visage
And pious action we do sugar o'er
The devil himself.
　　　　KING
　　(*Aside*) O, 'tis too true.
75 How smart a lash that speech doth give my
　　　　conscience!
The harlot's cheek, beautied with plast'ring art,
Is not more ugly to the thing that helps it
Than is my deed to my most painted word.
80 O heavy burden!
　　　　POLONIUS
I hear him coming. Let's withdraw, my lord.
(*Exeunt* KING *and* POLONIUS.)
*Enter* HAMLET.
　　　　HAMLET
To be, or not to be: that is the question:
85 Whether 'tis nobler in the mind to suffer
The slings and arrows of outrageous fortune,
Or to take arms against a sea of troubles,
And by opposing end them. To die, to sleep—
No more—and by a sleep to say we end
90 The heartache, and the thousand natural shocks
That flesh is heir to! 'Tis a consummation
Devoutly to be wished. To die, to sleep—
To sleep—perchance to dream: ay, there's the
　　　　rub,°
95 For in that sleep of death what dreams may come
When we have shuffled off this mortal coil,°
Must give us pause. There's the respect°
That makes calamity of so long life:°
For who would bear the whips and scorns of time,
100 Th' oppressor's wrong, the proud man's
　　　　contumely,
The pangs of despised love, the law's delay,
The insolence of office, and the spurns
That patient merit of th' unworthy takes,
105 When he himself might his quietus° make
With a bare bodkin?° Who would fardels° bear,

To grunt and sweat under a weary life,
But that the dread of something after death,
The undiscovered country, from whose bourn°
No traveler returns, puzzles the will,                110
And makes us rather bear those ills we have,
Than fly to others that we know not of?
Thus conscience° does make cowards of us all,
And thus the native hue of resolution
Is sicklied o'er with the pale cast° of thought,     115
And enterprises of great pitch° and moment,
With this regard° their current turn awry,
And lose the name of action.—Soft you now,
The fair Ophelia!—Nymph, in thy orisons°
Be all my sins remembered.                           120
　　　　OPHELIA
Good my lord,
How does your honor for this many a day?
　　　　HAMLET
I humbly thank you; well, well, well.                125
　　　　OPHELIA
My lord, I have remembrances of yours
That I have longèd long to redeliver.
I pray you now, receive them.
　　　　HAMLET                                          130
No, not I,
I never gave you aught.
　　　　OPHELIA
My honored lord, you know right well you did,
And with them words of so sweet breath            135
　　　　composed
As made these things more rich. Their perfume
　　　　lost,
Take these again, for to the noble mind
Rich gifts wax poor when givers prove unkind.      140
There, my lord.
　　　　HAMLET
Ha, ha! Are you honest?°
　　　　OPHELIA
My lord?                                             145
　　　　HAMLET
Are you fair?
　　　　OPHELIA
What means your lordship?

---

68 **exercise may color** act of devotion may give a plausible
hue to (the book is one of devotion)  94 **rub** impediment
(obstruction to a bowler's ball)  96 **coil** (1) turmoil (2) a
ring of rope (here the flesh encircling the soul)  97 **respect**
consideration  98 **makes calamity of so long life**
(1) makes calamity so long-lived (2) makes living so long a
calamity  105 **quietus** full discharge (a legal term)  106
**bodkin** dagger  106 **fardels** burdens

109 **bourn** region  113 **conscience** self-consciousness, intro-
spection  115 **cast** color  116 **pitch** height (a term from
falconry)  117 **regard** consideration  119 **orisons** prayers
144 **Are you honest** (1) are you modest (2) are you chaste
(3) have you integrity

150     **HAMLET**
That if you be honest and fair, your honesty
should admit no discourse to your beauty.°
    **OPHELIA**
Could beauty, my lord, have better commerce
155 than with honesty?
    **HAMLET**
Ay, truly; for the power of beauty will sooner
transform honesty from what it is to a bawd° than
the force of honesty can translate beauty into his
160 likeness. This was sometime a paradox, but now
the time gives it proof. I did love you once.
    **OPHELIA**
Indeed, my lord, you made me believe so.
    **HAMLET**
165 You should not have believed me, for virtue
cannot so inoculate° our old stock but we shall
relish of it.° I loved you not.
    **OPHELIA**
I was the more deceived.
170     **HAMLET**
Get thee to a nunnery. Why wouldst thou be a
breeder of sinners? I am myself indifferent
honest,° but yet I could accuse me of such things
that it were better my mother had not borne me: I
175 am very proud, revengeful, ambitious, with more
offenses at my beck° than I have thoughts to put
them in, imagination to give them shape, or time
to act them in. What should such fellows as I do
crawling between earth and heaven? We are
180 arrant knaves all; believe none of us. Go thy ways
to a nunnery. Where's your father?
    **OPHELIA**
At home, my lord.
    **HAMLET**
185 Let the doors be shut upon him, that he may play
the fool nowhere but in's own house. Farewell.
    **OPHELIA**
O help him, you sweet heavens!
    **HAMLET**
190 If thou dost marry, I'll give thee this plague for
thy dowry: be thou as chaste as ice, as pure as
snow, thou shalt not escape calumny. Get thee to
a nunnery. Go, farewell. Or if thou wilt needs

marry, marry a fool, for wise men know well
enough what monsters° you make of them. To a   195
nunnery, go,° and quickly too. Farewell.
    **OPHELIA**
Heavenly powers, restore him!
    **HAMLET**
I have heard of your paintings, well enough.   200
God hath given you one face, and you make
yourselves another. You jig and amble, and you
lisp; you nickname God's creatures and make
your wantonness your ignorance.° Go to, I'll no
more on't; it hath made me mad. I say we will   205
have no moe° marriage. Those that are married
already—all but one—shall live. The rest shall
keep as they are. To a nunnery, go. (*Exit.*)
    **OPHELIA**
O what a noble mind is here o'erthrown!   210
The courtier's, soldier's, scholar's, eye, tongue,
    sword,
Th' expectancy and rose° of the fair state,
The glass of fashion, and the mold of form,°
Th' observed of all observers, quite, quite down!   215
And I, of ladies most deject and wretched,
That sucked the honey of his musicked vows,
Now see that noble and most sovereign reason
Like sweet bells jangled, out of time and harsh,
That unmatched form and feature of blown° youth   220
Blasted with ecstasy.° O, woe is me
T' have seen what I have seen, see what I see!
*Enter* **KING** *and* **POLONIUS**.
    **KING**
Love? His affections° do not that way tend,
Nor what he spake, though it lacked form a little,   225
Was not like madness. There's something in his
    soul
O'er which his melancholy sits on brood,
And I do doubt° the hatch and the disclose
Will be some danger; which for to prevent,   230
I have in quick determination
Thus set it down: he shall with speed to England
For the demand of our neglected tribute.
Haply the seas, and countries different,

---

151–52 **your honesty . . . to your beauty** your modesty
should permit no approach to your beauty  158 **bawd** procurer  166 **inoculate** graft  167 **relish of it** smack of it (our
old sinful nature)  172–73 **indifferent honest** moderately
virtuous  176 **beck** call

195 **monsters** horned beasts, cuckolds  203–04 **make your
wantonness your ignorance** excuse your wanton speech
by pretending ignorance  206 **moe** more  213 **expectancy
and rose** i.e., fair hope  214 **The glass . . . of form** the mirror of fashion, and the pattern of excellent behavior  220
**blown** blooming  221 **ecstasy** madness  224 **affections** in-
clinations  229 **doubt** fear

235 With variable objects, shall expel
This something-settled° matter in his heart,
Whereon his brains still beating puts him thus
From fashion of himself. What think you on't?

POLONIUS

240 It shall do well. But yet do I believe
The origin and commencement of his grief
Sprung from neglected love. How now, Ophelia?
You need not tell us what Lord Hamlet said;
We heard it all. My lord, do as you please,

245 But if you hold it fit, after the play,
Let his queen mother all alone entreat him
To show his grief. Let her be round° with him,
And I'll be placed, so please you, in the ear
Of all their conference. If she find him not,°

250 To England send him, or confine him where
Your wisdom best shall think.

KING

It shall be so.
Madness in great ones must not unwatched go.
*Exeunt.*

## SCENE II

*The castle.*

*Enter* HAMLET *and three of the* PLAYERS.

HAMLET

Speak the speech, I pray you, as I pronounced it
to you, trippingly on the tongue. But if you
mouth it, as many of our players do, I had as lief
5  the town crier spoke my lines. Nor do not saw the
air too much with your hand, thus, but use all
gently, for in the very torrent, tempest, and (as I
may say) whirlwind of your passion, you must
acquire and beget a temperance that may give it
10  smoothness. O, it offends me to the soul to hear a
robustious periwig-pated° fellow tear a passion to
tatters, to very rags, to split the ears of the
groundlings,° who for the most part are capable
of° nothing but inexplicable dumb shows° and

noise. I would have such a fellow whipped for  15
o'erdoing Termagant. It out-herods Herod.° Pray
you avoid it.

PLAYER

I warrant your honor.

HAMLET                                              20

Be not too tame neither, but let your own
discretion be your tutor. Suit the action to the
word, the word to the action, with this special
observance, that you o'erstep not the modesty of
nature. For anything so o'erdone is from° the      25
purpose of playing, whose end, both at the first
and now, was and is, to hold, as 'twere, the
mirror up to nature; to show virtue her own
feature, scorn her own image, and the very age
and body of the time his form and pressure.°       30
Now, this overdone, or come tardy off, though it
makes the unskillful laugh, cannot but make the
judicious grieve, the censure of the which one
must in your allowance o'erweigh a whole theater
of others. O, there be players that I have seen     935
play, and heard others praise, and that highly
(not to speak it profanely), that neither having th'
accent of Christians, nor the gait of Christian,
pagan, nor man, have so strutted and bellowed
that I have thought some of Nature's               40
journeymen° had made men, and not made them
well, they imitated humanity so abominably.

PLAYER

I hope we have reformed that indifferently° with
us, sir.                                            45

HAMLET

O, reform it altogether! And let those that play
your clowns speak no more than is set down for
them, for there be of them that will themselves
laugh, to set on some quantity of barren           50
spectators to laugh too, though in the meantime
some necessary question of the play be then to be
considered. That's villainous and shows a most
pitiful ambition in the fool that uses it. Go make
you ready.                                          55
*Exit* PLAYERS.
*Enter* POLONIUS, GUILDENSTERN, *and*
ROSENCRANTZ.

---

236 **something-settled** somewhat settled   247 **round** blunt
249 **find him not** does not find him out  **III.ii.** 11
**robustious periwig-pated** boisterous wig-headed 13
**groundlings** those who stood in the pit of the theater (the
poorest and presumably most ignorant of the audience)
13–14 **are capable of** are able to understand  14 **dumb
shows** (it had been the fashion for actors to preface plays
or parts of plays with silent mime)

16 **Termagant . . . Herod** (boisterous characters in the old
mystery plays)  25 **from** contrary to  30 **pressure** image,
impress  41 **journeymen** workers not yet masters of their
craft  44 **indifferently** tolerably

How now, my lord? Will the King hear this piece
of work?
    POLONIUS
And the Queen too, and that presently.
60    HAMLET
Bid the players make haste. (*Exit* POLONIUS.)
Will you two help to hasten them?
    ROSENCRANTZ
Ay, my lord. (*Exeunt they two.*)
65    HAMLET
What, ho, Horatio!
*Enter* HORATIO.
    HORATIO
Here, sweet lord, at your service.
    HAMLET
70 Horatio, thou art e'en as just a man
As e'er my conversation coped withal.°
    HORATIO
O, my dear lord——
    HAMLET
75 Nay, do not think I flatter.
For what advancement° may I hope from thee,
That no revenue hast but thy good spirits
To feed and clothe thee? Why should the poor be
    flattered?
80 No, let the candied° tongue lick absurd pomp,
And crook the pregnant° hinges of the knee
Where thrift° may follow fawning. Dost thou
    hear?
Since my dear soul was mistress of her choice
85 And could of men distinguish her election,
S' hath sealed thee° for herself, for thou hast been
As one, in suff'ring all, that suffers nothing,
A man that Fortune's buffets and rewards
Hast ta'en with equal thanks; and blest are those
90 Whose blood° and judgment are so well
    commeddled°
That they are not a pipe for Fortune's finger
To sound what stop she please. Give me that man
That is not passion's slave, and I will wear him
95 In my heart's core, ay, in my heart of heart,
As I do thee. Something too much of this—
There is a play tonight before the King.

One scene of it comes near the circumstance
Which I have told thee, of my father's death.
I prithee, when thou seest that act afoot,    100
Even with the very comment° of thy soul
Observe my uncle. If his occulted° guilt
Do not itself unkennel in one speech,
It is a damnèd ghost that we have seen,
And my imaginations are as foul    105
As Vulcan's stithy.° Give him heedful note,
For I mine eyes will rivet to his face,
And after we will both our judgments join
In censure of his seeming.°
HORATIO: Well, my lord.    110
If 'a steal aught the whilst this play is playing,
And scape detecting, I will pay the theft.
*Enter Trumpets and Kettledrums,* KING, QUEEN,
POLONIUS, OPHELIA, ROSENCRANTZ,
GUILDENSTERN, *and other Lords attendant with his
Guard carrying torches. Danish March. Sound a
Flourish.*
    HAMLET
They are coming to the play: I must be idle;° Get
you a place.    115
    KING
How fares our cousin Hamlet?
    HAMLET
Excellent, i' faith, of the chameleon's dish;° I eat
the air, promise-crammed; you cannot feed    120
capons so.
    KING
I have nothing with this answer, Hamlet; these
words are not mine.
    HAMLET    125
No, nor mine now.
(*To* POLONIUS) My lord, you played once i' th'
university, you say?
    POLONIUS
That did I, my lord, and was accounted a good    130
actor.
    HAMLET
What did you enact?
    POLONIUS
I did enact Julius Caesar. I was killed i' th'    135
Capitol; Brutus killed me.

---

71 **coped withal** met with  76 **advancement** promotion
80 **candied** sugared, flattering  81 **pregnant** (1) pliant
(2) full of promise of good fortune  82 **thrift** profit  86 **S'
hath sealed thee** she (the soul) has set a mark on you  90
**blood** passion  91 **commeddled** blended

101 **very comment** deepest wisdom  102 **occulted** hidden
106 **stithy** forge, smithy  109 **censure of his seeming** judgment on his looks  114 **be idle** play the fool  119 **the chameleon's dish** air (on which chameleons were thought to live)

HAMLET

It was a brute part of him to kill so capital a calf
there. By the players ready?

140     ROSENCRANTZ

Ay, my lord. They stay upon your patience.

QUEEN

Come hither, my dear Hamlet, sit by me.

HAMLET

145 No, good mother. Here's metal more attractive.°

POLONIUS

(*To the* **KING**) O ho! Do you mark that?

HAMLET

Lady, shall I lie in your lap? (*He lies at* **OPHELIA'S**
150 *feet.*)

OPHELIA

No, my lord.

HAMLET

I mean, my head upon your lap?

155     OPHELIA

Ay, my lord.

HAMLET

Do you think I meant country matters?°

OPHELIA

160 I think nothing, my lord.

HAMLET

That's a fair thought to lie between maids' legs.

OPHELIA

What is, my lord?

165     HAMLET

Nothing.

OPHELIA

You are merry, my lord.

HAMLET

170 Who, I?

OPHELIA

Ay, my lord.

HAMLET

O God, your only jig-maker!° What should a man
175 do but be merry? For look you how cheerfully my
mother looks, and my father died within's two
hours.

OPHELIA

Nay, 'tis twice two months, my lord.

HAMLET                                                                    180

So long? Nay then, let the devil wear black, for I'll
have a suit of sables.° O heavens! Die two months
ago, and not forgotten yet? Then there's hope a
great man's memory may outlive his life half a
year. But, by'r Lady, 'a must build churches then,      185
or else shall 'a suffer not thinking on, with the
hobbyhorse,° whose epitaph is "For O, for O, the
hobbyhorse is forgot!"

*The trumpets sound. Dumb show follows: Enter a*
*King and a Queen very lovingly, the Queen embracing*
*him, and he her. She kneels; and makes show of*
*protestation unto him. He takes her up, and declines*
*his head upon her neck. He lies him down upon a bank*
*of flowers. She, seeing him asleep, leaves him. Anon*
*come in another man: takes off his crown, kisses it,*
*pours poison in the sleeper's ears, and leaves him. The*
*Queen returns, finds the King dead, makes passionate*
*action. The poisoner, with some three or four, come in*
*again, seem to condole with her. The dead body is*
*carried away. The poisoner woos the Queen with gifts;*
*she seems harsh awhile, but in the end accepts love.*
*(Exeunt.)*

OPHELIA

What means this, my lord?                                           190

HAMLET

Marry, this is miching mallecho;° it means
mischief.

OPHELIA

Belike this show imports the argument° of the        195
play.

*Enter* **PROLOGUE**.

HAMLET

We shall know by this fellow. The players cannot
keep counsel; they'll tell all.

OPHELIA                                                                   200

Will 'a tell us what this show meant?

HAMLET

Ay, or any show that you will show him. Be not
you ashamed to show, he'll not shame to tell you
what it means.                                                         205

OPHELIA

You are naught,° you are naught; I'll mark the
play.

---

145 **attractive** magnetic  158 **country matters** rustic doings
(with a pun on the vulgar word for the pudendum)  174
**jig-maker** composer of songs and dances (often a Fool,
who performed them)

182 **sables** (pun on "black" and "luxurious furs")  187
**hobbyhorse** mock horse worn by a performer in the morris
dance  192 **miching mallecho** sneaking mischief  195 **argument** plot  207 **naught** wicked, improper

PROLOGUE

210 For us, and for our tragedy,
Here stooping to your clemency,
We beg your hearing patiently. (*Exit.*)

HAMLET

Is this a prologue, or the posy of a ring?°

215 OPHELIA

'Tis brief, my lord.

HAMLET

As a woman's love.

*Enter (two* PLAYERS *as*) *King and Queen.*

PLAYER KING

220 Full thirty times hath Phoebus' cart° gone round
Neptune's salt wash° and Tellus'° orbèd ground,
And thirty dozen moons with borrowed sheen
About the world have times twelve thirties been,
Since love our hearts, and Hymen did our hands,
225 Unite commutual in most sacred bands.

PLAYER QUEEN

So many journeys may the sun and moon
Make us again count o'er ere love be done!
But woe is me, you are so sick of late,
230 So far from cheer and from your former state,
That I distrust° you. Yet, though I distrust,
Discomfort you, my lord, it nothing must.
For women fear too much, even as they love,
And women's fear and love hold quantity,
235 In neither aught, or in extremity.°
Now what my love is, proof° hath made you
          know,
And as my love is sized, my fear is so.
Where love is great, the littlest doubts are fear;
240 Where little fears grow great, great love grows
          there.

PLAYER KING

Faith, I must leave thee, love, and shortly too;
My operant° powers their functions leave to do:
245 And thou shalt live in this fair world behind,
Honored, beloved, and haply one as kind
For husband shalt thou—

PLAYER QUEEN

O, confound the rest!
Such love must needs be treason in my breast.    250
In second husband let me be accurst!
None wed the second but who killed the first.

HAMLET

(*Aside*) That's wormwood.°

PLAYER QUEEN                                          255

The instances° that second marriage move°
Are base respects of thrift,° but none of love.
A second time I kill my husband dead
When second husband kisses me in bed.

PLAYER KING                                          260

I do believe you think what now you speak,
But what we do determine oft we break.
Purpose is but the slave to memory,
Of violent birth, but poor validity,°
Which now like fruit unripe sticks on the tree,  265
But fall unshaken when they mellow be.
Most necessary 'tis that we forget
To pay ourselves what to ourselves is debt.
What to ourselves in passion we propose,
The passion ending, doth the purpose lose.       270
The violence of either grief or joy
Their own enactures° with themselves destroy;
Where joy most revels, grief doth most lament;
Grief joys, joy grieves, on slender accident.
This world is not for aye, nor 'tis not strange   275
That even our loves should with our fortunes
          change,
For tis a question left us yet to prove,
Whether love lead fortune, or else fortune love.
The great man down, you mark his favorite flies;  280
The poor advanced makes friends of enemies;
And hitherto doth love on fortune tend,
For who not needs shall never lack a friend;
And who in want a hollow friend doth try,
Directly seasons him° his enemy.                  285
But, orderly to end where I begun,
Our wills and fates do so contrary run
That our devices still are overthrown;
Our thoughts are ours, their ends none of our
          own.                                      290
So think thou wilt no second husband wed,
But die thy thoughts when thy first lord is dead.

---

214 **posy of a ring** motto inscribed in a ring  220 **Phoebus'
cart** the sun's chariot  221 **Neptune's salt wash** the sea
221 **Tellus** Roman goddess of the earth  231 **distrust** am
anxious about  234–35 **And women's ... in extremity**
(perhaps the idea is that women's anxiety is great or little
in proportion to their love. The previous line, unrhymed,
may be a false start that Shakespeare neglected to delete)
236 **proof** experience  244 **operant** active

254 **wormwood** a bitter herb  256 **instances** motives  256
**move** induce  257 **respects of thrift** considerations of
profit  264 **validity** strength  272 **enactures** acts  285 **seasons him** ripens him into

**PLAYER QUEEN**

Nor earth to me give food, nor heaven light,
295 Sport and repose lock from me day and night,
To desperation turn my trust and hope,
An anchor's° cheer in prison be my scope,
Each opposite that blanks° the face of joy
Meet what I would have well, and it destroy:
300 Both here and hence pursue me lasting strife,
If, once a widow, ever I be wife!

**HAMLET**

If she should break it now!

**PLAYER KING**

305 'Tis deeply sworn. Sweet, leave me here awhile;
My spirits grow dull, and fain I would beguile
The tedious day with sleep.

**PLAYER QUEEN**

Sleep rock thy brain,
*(He) sleeps.*
310 And never come mischance between us twain!
*Exit.*

**HAMLET**

Madam, how like you this play?

**QUEEN**

The lady doth protest too much, methinks.

315 **HAMLET**

O, but she'll keep her word.

**KING**

Have you heard the argument?° Is there no
offense in't?

325 **HAMLET**

No, no, they do but jest, poison in jest; no offense
i' th' world.

**KING**

What do you call the play?

325 **HAMLET**

*The Mousetrap.* Marry, how? Tropically.° This play
is the image of a murder done in Vienna:
Gonzago is the Duke's name; his wife, Baptista.
You shall see anon. 'Tis a knavish piece of work,
330 but what of that? Your Majesty, and we that have
free° souls, it touches us not. Let the galled jade
winch;° our withers are unwrung.
*Enter* LUCIANUS.
This is one Lucianus, nephew to the King.

**OPHELIA**

You are as good as a chorus, my lord.                    335

**HAMLET**

I could interpret° between you and your love, if I
could see the puppets dallying.

**OPHELIA**

You are keen,° my lord, you are keen.                    340

**HAMLET**

It would cost you a groaning to take off mine
edge.

**OPHELIA**

Still better, and worse.                    345

**HAMLET**

So you mistake° your husbands.—Begin,
murderer. Leave thy damnable faces and begin.
Come, the croaking raven doth bellow for
revenge.                    350

**LUCIANUS**

Thoughts black, hands apt, drugs fit, and time
agreeing.
Confederate season,° else no creature seeing,
Thou mixture rank, of midnight weeds collected,    355
With Hecate's ban° thrice blasted, thrice infected,
Thy natural magic and dire property°
On wholesome life usurps immediately.
*Pours the poison in his ears.*

**HAMLET**

'A poisons him i' th' garden for his estate. His    360
name's Gonzago. The story is extant, and written
in very choice Italian. You shall see anon how the
murderer gets the love of Gonzago's wife.

**OPHELIA**

The King rises.                    365

**HAMLET**

What, frighted with false fire?°

**QUEEN**

How fares my lord?

**POLONIUS**                    370

Give o'er the play.

**KING**

Give me some light. Away!

---

297 **anchor's** anchorite's, hermit's  298 **opposite that
blanks** adverse thing that blanches  323 **argument** plot
326 **Tropically** figuratively (with a pun on "trap")  331 **free**
innocent  331–32 **galled jade winch** chafed horse wince

337 **interpret** (like a showman explaining the action of
puppets)  340 **keen** (1) sharp (2) sexually aroused  347
**mistake** err in taking  354 **Confederate season** the opportunity allied with me  356 **Hecate's ban** the curse of the
goddess of sorcery  357 **property** nature  367 **false fire**
blank discharge of firearms

POLONIUS

375 Lights, lights, lights!

*Exeunt all but* **HAMLET** *and* **HORATIO.**

HAMLET

Why, let the strucken deer go weep,

The hart ungallèd play:

For some must watch, while some must sleep;

380 Thus runs the world away.

Would not this, sir, and a forest of feathers°—if
the

rest of my fortunes turn Turk° with me—with two

Provincial roses° on my razed° shoes, get me a

385 fellowship in a cry° of players?

HORATIO

Half a share.

HAMLET

A whole one, I.

390 For thou dost know, O Damon dear,

This realm dismantled was

Of Jove himself, and now reigns here

A very, very—pajock.°

HORATIO

395 You might have rhymed.°

HAMLET

O good Horatio, I'll take the ghost's word for a
thousand pound. Didst perceive?

HORATIO

400 Very well, my lord.

HAMLET

Upon the talk of poisoning?

HORATIO

I did very well note him.

405 HAMLET

Ah ha! Come, some music! Come, the recorders!°

For if the King like not the comedy,

Why then, belike he likes it not, perdy.°

Come, some music!

*Enter* **ROSENCRANTZ** *and* **GUILDENSTERN.**

410 GUILDENSTERN

Good my lord, vouchsafe me a word with you.

HAMLET

Sir, a whole history.

GUILDENSTERN

The King, sir—  415

HAMLET

Ay, sir, what of him?

GUILDENSTERN

Is in his retirement marvelous distemp'red.

HAMLET  420

With drink, sir?

GUILDENSTERN

No, my lord, with choler.°

HAMLET

Your wisdom should show itself more richer to  425
signify this to the doctor, for for me to put him to
his purgation would perhaps plunge him into
more choler.

GUILDENSTERN

Good my lord, put your discourse into some  430
frame,° and start not so wildly from my affair.

HAMLET

I am tame, sir; pronounce.

GUILDENSTERN

The Queen, your mother, in most great affliction  435
of spirit hath sent me to you.

HAMLET

You are welcome.

GUILDENSTERN

Nay, good my lord, this courtesy is not of the  440
right breed. If it shall please you to make me a
wholesome answer, I will do your mother's
commandment: if not, your pardon and my
return shall be the end of my business.

HAMLET  445

Sir, I cannot.

ROSENCRANTZ

What, my lord?

HAMLET

Make you a wholesome° answer; my wit's  450
diseased. But, sir, such answer as I can make, you
shall command, or rather, as you say, my mother.
Therefore no more, but to the matter. My mother,
you say—

ROSENCRANTZ  455

Then thus she says: your behavior hath struck her
into amazement and admiration.°

---

381 **feathers** (plumes were sometimes part of a costume)
383 **turn Turk** i.e., go bad, treat me badly  384 **Provincial
roses** rosettes like the roses of Provence (?)  384 **razed**
ornamented with slashes  385 **cry** pack, company  393 **pajock** peacock  395 **You might have rhymed** i.e., rhymed
"was" with "ass"  406 **recorders** flutelike instruments
408 **perdy** by God (French : **par dieu**)

423 **choler** anger (but Hamlet pretends to take the word in
its sense of "biliousness")  431 **frame** order, control  450
**wholesome** sane  457 **admiration** wonder

HAMLET
O wonderful son, that can so astonish a mother!
460 But is there no sequel at the heels of this mother's
admiration? Impart.

ROSENCRANTZ
She desires to speak with you in her closet ere
you go to bed.

465 HAMLET
We shall obey, were she ten times our mother.
Have you any further trade with us?

ROSENCRANTZ
My lord, you once did love me.

470 HAMLET
And do still, by these pickers and stealers.°

ROSENCRANTZ
Good my lord, what is your cause of distemper?
You do surely bar the door upon your own
475 liberty, if you deny your griefs to your friend.

HAMLET
Sir, I lack advancement°

ROSENCRANTZ
How can that be, when you have the voice of the
480 King himself for your succession in Denmark?
*Enter the* **PLAYERS** *with recorders.*

HAMLET
Ay, sir, but "while the grass grows"—the
proverb° is something musty. O, the recorders.
Let me see one. To withdraw° with you—why do
485 you go about to recover the wind° of me as if you
would drive me into a toil?°

GUILDENSTERN
O my lord, if my duty be too bold, my love is too
unmannerly.°

490 HAMLET
I do not understand that. Will you play upon this
pipe?

GUILDENSTERN
My lord, I cannot.

495 HAMLET
I pray you.

GUILDENSTERN
Believe me, I cannot.

HAMLET
I beseech you.                                                          500

GUILDENSTERN
I know no touch of it, my lord.

HAMLET
It is as easy as lying. Govern these ventages° with
your fingers and thumb, give it breath with your      505
mouth, and it will discourse most eloquent music.
Look you, these are the stops.

GUILDENSTERN
But these cannot I command to any utt'rance of
harmony; I have not the skill.                               510

HAMLET
Why, look you now, how unworthy a thing you
make of me! You would play upon me; you
would seem to know my stops; you would pluck
out the heart of my mystery; you would sound       515
me from my lowest note to the top of my
compass;° and there is much music, excellent
voice, in this little organ,° yet cannot you make it
speak. 'Sblood, do you think I am easier to be
played on than a pipe? Call me what instrument      520
you will, though you can fret° me, you cannot
play upon me.
*Enter* **POLONIUS**.
God bless you, sir!

POLONIUS
My lord, the Queen would speak with you, and      525
presently.

HAMLET
Do you see yonder cloud that's almost in shape of
a camel?

POLONIUS
By th' mass and 'tis, like a camel indeed.            530

HAMLET
Methinks it is like a weasel.

POLONIUS
It is backed like a weasel.                                   535

HAMLET
Or like a whale.

POLONIUS
Very like a whale.

---

471 **pickers and stealers** i.e., hands (with reference to the
prayer; "Keep my hands from picking and stealing")  477
**advancement** promotion  483 **proverb** ("While the grass
groweth, the horse starveth")  484 **withdraw** speak in private  485 **recover the wind** get on the windward side (as
in hunting)  486 **toil** snare  488–89 **if my duty . . . too
unmannerly** i.e., if these questions seem rude, it is because my love for you leads me beyond good manners.

504 **ventages** vents, stops on a recorder  517 **compass**
range of voice  518 **organ** i.e., the recorder  521 **fret** vex
(with a pun alluding to the frets, or ridges, that guide the
fingering on some instruments)

540 **HAMLET**

Then I will come to my mother by and by. (*Aside*)
They fool me to the top of my bent.°—I will come
by and by.°

**POLONIUS**

545 I will say so. (*Exit.*)

**HAMLET**

"By and by" is easily said. Leave me, friends.
*Exeunt all but* **HAMLET.**
'Tis now the very witching time of night,
When churchyards yawn, and hell itself breathes
550     out
Contagion to this world. Now could I drink hot
        blood
And do such bitter business as the day
Would quake to look on. Soft, now to my mother.
555 O heart, lose not thy nature; let not ever
The soul of Nero° enter this firm bosom.
Let me be cruel, not unnatural;
I will speak daggers to her, but use none.
My tongue and soul in this be hypocrites:
560 How in my words somever she be shent,°
To give them seals° never, my soul, consent!(*Exit.*)

## SCENE III

*The castle.*

*Enter* **KING**, **ROSENCRANTZ**, *and* **GUILD-
ENSTERN**

**KING**

I like him not, nor stands it safe with us
To let his madness range. Therefore prepare you.
I your commission will forthwith dispatch,
And he to England shall along with you.
5 The terms° of our estate may not endure
Hazard so near's° as doth hourly grow
Out of his brows.

**GUILDENSTERN**

10 We will ourselves provide.
Most holy and religious fear it is
To keep those many many bodies safe
That live and feed upon your Majesty.

**ROSENCRANTZ**

The single and peculiar° life is bound                        15
With all the strength and armor of the mind
To keep itself from noyance,° but much more
That spirit upon whose weal depends and rests
The lives of many. The cess of majesty°
Dies not alone, but like a gulf° doth draw            20
What's near it with it; or it is a massy wheel
Fixed on the summit of the highest mount,
To whose huge spokes ten thousand lesser things
Are mortised and adjoined, which when it falls,
Each small annexment, petty consequence,              25
Attends° the boist'rous ruin. Never alone
Did the King sigh, but with a general groan.

**KING**

Arm° you, I pray you, to this speedy voyage,
For we will fetters put about this fear,               30
Which now goes too free-footed.

**ROSENCRANTZ**

We will haste us.
*Exeunt Gentlemen.*
*Enter* **POLONIUS.**

**POLONIUS**

My lord, he's going to his mother's closet.°          35
Behind the arras I'll convey myself
To hear the process.° I'll warrant she'll tax him
        home,°
And, as you said, and wisely was it said,
'Tis meet that some more audience than a mother,    40
Since nature makes them partial, should o'erhear
The speech of vantage.° Fare you well, my liege.
I'll call upon you ere you go to bed
And tell you what I know.

**KING**                                              45

Thanks, dear my lord.
*Exit* (**POLONIUS**).
O, my offense is rank, it smells to heaven;
It hath the primal eldest curse° upon't,
A brother's murder. Pray can I not,
Though inclination be as sharp as will.               50
My stronger guilt defeats my strong intent,
And like a man to double business bound

---

542 **They fool . . . my bent** they compel me to play the fool
to the limit of my capacity  543 **by and by** very soon  556
**Nero** (Roman emperor who had his mother murdered)
560 **shent** rebuked  561 **give them seals** confirm them
with deeds  **III.iii.** 6 **terms** conditions  7 **near's** near us

15 **peculiar** individual, private  17 **noyance** injury  19 **cess
of majesty** cessation (death) of a king  20 **gulf** whirlpool
26 **Attends** waits on, participates in  29 **Arm** prepare  35
**closet** private room  37 **process** proceedings  37–38 **tax
him home** censure him sharply  42 **of vantage** from an
advantageous place  48 **primal eldest curse** (curse of Cain,
who killed Abel)

I stand in pause where I shall first begin,
And both neglect. What if this cursèd hand
55 Were thicker than itself with brother's blood,
Is there not rain enough in the sweet heavens
To wash it white as snow? Whereto serves mercy
But to confront° the visage of offense?
And what's in prayer but this twofold force,
60 To be forestallèd ere we come to fall,
Or pardoned being down? Then I'll look up.
My fault is past. But, O, what form of prayer
Can serve my turn? "Forgive me my foul
    murder"?
65 That cannot be, since I am still possessed
Of those effects° for which I did the murder,
My crown, mine own ambition, and my queen.
May one be pardoned and retain th' offense?
In the corrupted currents of this world
70 Offense's gilded hand may shove by justice,
And oft 'tis seen the wicked prize itself
Buys out the law. But 'tis not so above.
There is no shuffling°; there the action lies
In his true nature, and we ourselves compelled,
75 Even to the teeth and forehead of our faults,
To give in evidence. What then? What rests?°
Try what repentance can. What can it not?
Yet what can it when one cannot repent?
O wretched state! O bosom black as death!
80 O limèd soul,° that struggling to be free
Art more engaged!° Help, angels! Make assay.°
Bow, stubborn knees, and, heart with strings of
    steel,
Be soft as sinews of the newborn babe.
85 All may be well. (*He kneels.*)
  *Enter* HAMLET.
    HAMLET
Now might I do it pat, now 'a is a-praying,
And now I'll do't. And so 'a goes to heaven,
And so am I revenged. That would be scanned.°
90 A villain kills my father, and for that
I, his sole son, do this same villain send
To heaven.
Why, this is hire and salary, not revenge.
'A took my father grossly, full of bread,°

With all his crimes broad blown,° as flush° as   95
  May;
And how his audit° stands, who knows save
  heaven?
But in our circumstance and course of thought,
'Tis heavy with him; and am I then revenged,   100
To take him in the purging of his soul,
When he is fit and seasoned for his passage?
No.
Up, sword, and know thou a more horrid hent.°
When he is drunk asleep, or in his rage,   105
Or in th' incestuous pleasure of his bed,
At game a-swearing, or about some act
That has no relish° of salvation in't—
Then trip him, that his heels may kick at heaven,
And that his soul may be as damned and black   110
As hell, whereto it goes. My mother stays.
This physic° but prolongs thy sickly days. (*Exit.*)
    KING
(*Rises*) My words fly up, my thoughts remain
  below.   115
Words without thoughts never to heaven
go.(*Exit.*)

## SCENE IV

*The Queen's closet.*

*Enter* (QUEEN) GERTRUDE *and* POLONIUS.

    POLONIUS
'A will come straight. Look you lay home° to him.
Tell him his pranks have been too broad° to bear
  with,
And that your Grace hath screened and stood   5
  between
Much heat and him. I'll silence me even here.
Pray you be round with him.
    HAMLET
(*Within*) Mother, Mother, Mother!   10
    QUEEN
I'll warrant you; fear me not.
Withdraw; I hear him coming.
  (POLONIUS *hides behind the arras.*)
*Enter* HAMLET.

---

58 **confront** oppose  66 **effects** things gained  73 **shuffling** trickery  76 **rests** remains  80 **limèd** caught (as with birdlime, a sticky substance spread on boughs to snare birds)  81 **engaged** ensnared  81 **assay** an attempt  89 **would be scanned** ought to be looked into  94 **bread** i.e., worldly gratification

95 **crimes broad blown** sins in full bloom  95 **flush** vigorous  97 **audit** account  104 **hent** grasp (here, occasion for seizing)  108 **relish** flavor  112 **physic** (Claudius' purgation by prayer, as Hamlet thinks in line 101)  III.iv. 2 **lay home** thrust (rebuke) him sharply  3 **broad** unrestrained

HAMLET

15 Now, Mother, what's the matter?

QUEEN

Hamlet, thou hast thy father much offended.

HAMLET

Mother, you have my father much offended.

20 QUEEN

Come, come, you answer with an idle° tongue.

HAMLET

Go, go, you question with a wicked tongue.

QUEEN

25 Why, how now, Hamlet?

HAMLET

What's the matter now?

QUEEN

Have you forgot me?

30 HAMLET

No, by the rood,° not so!
You are the Queen, your husband's brother's wife,
And, would it were not so, you are my mother.

QUEEN

35 Nay, then I'll set those to you that can speak.

HAMLET

Come, come, and sit you down. You shall not budge.
You go not till I set you up a glass°
40 Where you may see the inmost part of you!

QUEEN

What wilt thou do? Thou wilt not murder me?
Help, ho!

POLONIUS

45 (Behind) What, ho! Help!

HAMLET

(Draws) How now? A rat? Dead for a ducat, dead!
(Makes a pass through the arras and) kills POLONIUS.

POLONIUS

(Behind) O, I am slain!

50 QUEEN

O me, what hast thou done?

HAMLET

Nay, I know not. Is it the King?

QUEEN

55 O, what a rash and bloody deed is this!

HAMLET

A bloody deed—almost as bad, good Mother,
As kill a king, and marry with his brother.

QUEEN

60 As kill a king?

21 idle foolish   31 rood cross   39 glass mirror

HAMLET

Ay, lady, it was my word.
(Lifts up the arras and sees POLONIUS.)
Thou wretched, rash, intruding fool, farewell!
I took thee for thy better. Take thy fortune.
Thou find'st to be too busy is some danger.—          65
Leave wringing of your hands. Peace, sit you down
And let me wring your heart, for so I shall
If it be made of penetrable stuff,
If damnèd custom have not brazed° it so              70
That it be proof° and bulwark against sense.°

QUEEN

What have I done that thou dar'st wag thy tongue
In noise so rude against me?

HAMLET                                                75

Such an act
That blurs the grace and blush of modesty,
Calls virtue hypocrite, takes off the rose
From the fair forehead of an innocent love,
And sets a blister° there, makes marriage vows      80
As false as dicers' oaths. O, such a deed
As from the body of contraction° plucks
The very soul, and sweet religion makes
A rhapsody° of words! Heaven's face does glow
O'er this solidity and compound mass               85
With heated visage, as against the doom
Is thoughtsick at the act.°

QUEEN

Ay me, what act,
That roars so loud and thunders in the index?°     90

HAMLET

Look here upon this picture, and on this,
The counterfeit presentment° of two brothers.
See what a grace was seated on this brow:
Hyperion's curls, the front° of Jove himself,       95
An eye like Mars, to threaten and command,
A station° like the herald Mercury
New lighted on a heaven-kissing hill—
A combination and a form indeed
Where every god did seem to set his seal           100

70 brazed hardened like brass  71 proof armor  71 sense
feeling  80 sets a blister brands (as a harlot)  82 contraction marriage contract  84 rhapsody senseless string  84–
87 Heaven's face . . . the act i.e., the face of heaven blushes
over this earth (compounded of four elements), the face
hot, as if Judgment Day were near, and it is thoughtsick at
the act  90 index prologue  93 counterfeit presentment
represented image  95 front forehead  97 station bearing

To give the world assurance of a man.
This was your husband. Look you now what
    follows.
Here is your husband, like a mildewed ear
105 Blasting his wholesome brother. Have you eyes?
Could you on this fair mountain leave to feed,
And batten° on this moor? Ha! Have you eyes?
You cannot call it love, for at your age
The heyday° in the blood is tame, it's humble,
110 And waits upon the judgment, and what
    judgment
Would step from this to this? Sense° sure you
    have,
Else could you not have motion, but sure that
115    sense
Is apoplexed,° for madness would not err,
Nor sense to ecstasy° was neer so thralled
But it reserved some quantity of choice
To serve in such a difference. What devil was't
120 That thus hath cozened you at hoodman-blind?°
Eyes without feeling, feeling without sight,
Ears without hands or eyes, smelling sans° all,
Or but a sickly part of one true sense
Could not so mope.°
125 O shame, where is thy blush? Rebellious hell,
If thou canst mutine in a matron's bones,
To flaming youth let virtue be as wax
And melt in her own fire. Proclaim no shame
When the compulsive ardor° gives the charge,
130 Since frost itself as actively doth burn,
And reason panders will.°
        QUEEN
O Hamlet, speak no more.
Thou turn'st mine eyes into my very soul,
135 And there I see such black and grainèd° spots
As will not leave their tinct.°
        HAMLET
Nay, but to live
In the rank sweat of an enseamèd° bed,

Stewed in corruption, honeying and making love   140
Over the nasty sty—
        QUEEN
O, speak to me no more.
These words like daggers enter in my ears.
No more, sweet Hamlet.   145
        HAMLET
A murderer and a villain,
A slave that is not twentieth part the tithe°
Of your precedent lord, a vice° of kings,
A cutpurse of the empire and the rule,   150
That from a shelf the precious diadem stole
And put it in his pocket—
        QUEEN
No more.
*Enter* GHOST.
        HAMLET   155
A king of shreds and patches—
Save me and hover o'er me with your wings,
You heavenly guards! What would your gracious
    figure?
        QUEEN   160
Alas, he's mad.
        HAMLET
Do you not come your tardy son to chide,
That, lapsed in time and passion, lets go by
Th' important acting of your dread command?   165
O, say!
        GHOST
Do not forget. This visitation
Is but to whet thy almost blunted purpose.
But look, amazement on thy mother sits.   170
O, step between her and her fighting soul!
Conceit° in weakest bodies strongest works.
Speak to her, Hamlet.
        HAMLET
How is it with you, lady?   175
        QUEEN
Alas, how is't with you,
That you do bend your eye on vacancy,
And with th' incorporal° air do hold discourse?
Forth at your eyes your spirits wildly peep,   180
And as the sleeping soldiers in th' alarm
Your bedded hair° like life in excrements°

107 **batten** feed gluttonously  109 **heyday** excitement  112
**Sense** feeling  116 **apoplexed** paralyzed  117 **ecstasy**
madness  120 **cozened you at hoodman-blind** cheated
you at blindman's buff  122 **sans** without  124 **mope** be
stupid  129 **compulsive ardor** compelling passion  131 **reason panders will** reason acts as a procurer for desire  135
**grainèd** dye in grain (fast dyed)  136 **tinct** color  139 **en-
seamèd** (perhaps "soaked in grease," i.e., sweaty; perhaps
"much wrinkled")

148 **tithe** tenth part  149 **vice** (like the Vice, a fool and mis-
chief-maker in the old morality plays)  172 **Conceit** imagination  179 **incorporal** bodiless  182 **bedded hair** hairs
laid flat  182 **excrements** outgrowths (here, the hair)

Start up and stand an end.° O gentle son,
Upon the heat and flame of thy distemper
185 Sprinkle cool patience. Whereon do you look?
    HAMLET
On him, on him! Look you, how pale he glares!
His form and cause conjoined, preaching to
    stones,
190 Would make them capable.°—Do not look upon
    me,
Lest with this piteous action you convert
My stern effects.° Then what I have to do
Will want true color; tears perchance for blood.
195     QUEEN
To whom do you speak this?
    HAMLET
Do you see nothing there?
    QUEEN
200 Nothing at all; yet all that is I see.
    HAMLET
Nor did you nothing hear?
    QUEEN
No, nothing but ourselves.
205     HAMLET
Why, look you there! Look how it steals away!
My father, in his habit° as he lived!
Look where he goes even now out at the portal!
*Exit* GHOST.
    QUEEN
210 This is the very coinage of your brain.
This bodiless creation ecstasy
Is very cunning in.
    HAMLET
Ecstasy?
215 My pulse as yours doth temperately keep time
And makes as healthful music. It is not madness
That I have uttered. Bring me to the test,
And I the matter will reword, which madness
Would gambol° from. Mother, for love of grace,
220 Lay not that flattering unction° to your soul,
That not your trespass but my madness speaks.
It will but skin and film the ulcerous place
Whiles rank corruption, mining° all within,
Infects unseen. Confess yourself to heaven,

Repent what's past, avoid what is to come, 225
And do not spread the compost° on the weeds
To make them ranker. Forgive me this my virtue.
For in the fatness of these pursy° times
Virtue itself of vice must pardon beg,
Yea, curb° and woo for leave to do him good. 230
    QUEEN
O Hamlet, thou hast cleft my heart in twain.
    HAMLET
O, throw away the worser part of it,
And live the purer with the other half. 235
Good night—but go not to my uncle's bed.
Assume a virtue, if you have it not.
That monster custom, who all sense doth eat,
Of habits devil, is angel yet in this,
That to the use° of actions fair and good 240
He likewise gives a frock or livery°
That aptly is put on. Refrain tonight,
And that shall lend a kind of easiness
To the next abstinence; the next more easy;
For use almost can change the stamp of nature, 245
And either° the devil, or throw him out
With wondrous potency. Once more, good night,
And when you are desirous to be blest,
I'll blessing beg of you.—For this same lord,
I do repent; but heaven hath pleased it so, 250
To punish me with this, and this with me,
That I must be their° scourge and minister.
I will bestow° him and will answer well
The death I gave him. So again, good night.
I must be cruel only to be kind. 255
Thus bad begins, and worse remains behind.
One word more, good lady.
    QUEEN
What shall I do?
    HAMLET 260
Not this, by no means, that I bid you do:
Let the bloat King tempt you again to bed,
Pinch wanton on your cheek, call you his mouse,
And let him, for a pair of reechy° kisses,

---

183 **an end** on end  190 **capable** receptive  192–93 **convert/My stern effects** divert my stern deeds  207 **habit** garment (Q1, though a "bad" quarto, is probably correct in saying that at line 156 the ghost enters "in his nightgown," i.e., dressing gown)  **219 gambol** start away  **220 unction** ointment  **223 mining** undermining

226 **compost** fertilizing substance  228 **pursy** bloated  230 **curb** bow low  240 **use** practice  241 **livery** characteristic garment (punning on "habits" in line 239)  246 **either** (probably a word is missing after **either;** among suggestions are "master," "curb," and "house;" but possibly **either** is a verb meaning "make easier")  252 **their** i.e., the heavens'  253 **bestow** stow, lodge  264 **reechy** foul (literally "smoky")

265 Or paddling in your neck with his damned
        fingers,
    Make you to ravel° all this matter out,
    That I essentially am not in madness,
    But mad in craft. 'Twere good you let him know,
270 For who that's but a queen, fair, sober, wise,
    Would from a paddock,° from a bat, a gib,°
    Such dear concernings hide? Who would do so?
    No, in despite of sense and secrecy,
    Unpeg the basket on the house's top,
275 Let the birds fly, and like the famous ape,
    To try conclusions,° in the basket creep
    And break your own neck down.
        QUEEN
    Be thou assured, if words be made of breath,
280 And breath of life, I have no life to breathe
    What thou hast said to me.
        HAMLET
    I must to England; you know that?
        QUEEN
285 Alack,
    I had forgot. 'Tis so concluded on.
        HAMLET
    There's letters sealed, and my two school fellows
    Whom I will trust as I will adders fanged,
290 They bear the mandate° they must sweep my way
    And marshal me to knavery. Let it work;
    For 'tis the sport to have the enginer
    Hoist with his own petar,° and 't shall go hard
    But I will delve one yard below their mines
295 And blow them at the moon. O, 'tis most sweet
    When in one line two crafts° directly meet.
    This man shall set me packing:
    I'll lug the guts into the neighbor room.
    Mother, good night. Indeed, this counselor
300 Is now most still, most secret, and most grave,
    Who was in life a foolish prating knave.
    Come, sir, to draw toward an end with you.
    Good night, Mother.

(*Exit the* QUEEN. *Then*) *exit* HAMLET, *tugging in*
POLONIUS.

## ACT IV

**SCENE I**

*The castle.*

*Enter* KING *and* QUEEN, *with* ROSENCRANTZ
*and* GUILDENSTERN.

        KING
    There's matter in these sighs. These profound
    heaves
    You must translate; 'tis fit we understand them.
    Where is your son?                              5
        QUEEN
    Bestow this place on us a little while.
    (*Exeunt* ROSENCRANTZ *and* GUILDENSTERN.)
    Ah, mine own lord, what have I seen tonight!
        KING
    What, Gertrude? How does Hamlet?              10
        QUEEN
    Mad as the sea and wind when both contend
    Which is the mightier. In his lawless fit,
    Behind the arras hearing something stir,
    Whips out his rapier, cries, "A rat, a rat!"    15
    And in this brainish apprehension° kills
    The unseen good old man.
    KING:  O heavy deed!
    It had been so with us, had we been there.
    His liberty is full of threats to all,           20
    To you yourself, to us, to every one.
    Alas, how shall this bloody deed be answered?
    It will be laid to us, whose providence°
    Should have kept short, restrained, and out of
        haunt°                                       25
    This mad young man. But so much was our love
    We would not understand what was most fit,
    But, like the owner of a foul disease,
    To keep it from divulging, let it feed
    Even on the pith of life. Where is he gone?     30
        QUEEN
    To draw apart the body he hath killed;
    O'er whom his very madness, like some ore
    Among a mineral° of metals base,
    Shows itself pure. 'A weeps for what is done.   35

---

267 **ravel** unravel, reveal   271 **paddock** toad   271 **gib** tom-
cat   276 **To try conclusions** to make experiments   290
**mandate** command   293 **petar** bomb   296 **crafts** (1) boats
(2) acts of guile, crafty schemes

IV.i.   16 **brainish apprehension** mad imagination   23
**providence** foresight   24–25 **out of haunt** away from association with others   33–34 **ore/Among a mineral** vein of
gold in a mine

KING
O Gertrude, come away!
The sun no sooner shall the mountains touch
But we will ship him hence, and this vile deed
40 We must with all our majesty and skill
Both countenance and excuse. Ho, Guildenstern!
*Enter* **ROSENCRANTZ** *and* **GUILDENSTERN**.
Friends both, go join you with some further aid:
Hamlet in madness hath Polonius slain,
And from his mother's closet hath he dragged
45     him.
Go seek him out; speak fair, and bring the body
Into the chapel. I pray you haste in this.
*Exeunt* **ROSENCRANTZ** *and* **GUILDENSTERN**.
Come, Gertrude, we'll call up our wisest friends
And let them know both what we mean to do
50 And what's untimely done . . .°
Whose whisper o'er the world's diameter,
As level as the cannon to his blank°
Transports his poisoned shot, may miss our name
And hit the woundless° air. O, come away!
55 My soul is full of discord and dismay. (*Exeunt*.)


## SCENE II

*The castle.*

*Enter* **HAMLET**.

HAMLET
Safely stowed.
**GENTLEMEN:** (*Within*) Hamlet! Lord Hamlet!
    HAMLET
5 But soft, what noise? Who calls on Hamlet? O,
here they come.
*Enter* **ROSENCRANTZ** *and* **GUILDENSTERN**.
    ROSENCRANTZ
What have you done, my lord, with the dead
body?
10     HAMLET
Compounded it with dust, whereto 'tis kin.
    ROSENCRANTZ
Tell us where 'tis, that we may take it thence
And bear it to the chapel.
15     HAMLET
Do not believe it.

    ROSENCRANTZ
Believe what?
    HAMLET
That I can keep your counsel and not mine own. 20
Besides, to be demanded of° a sponge, what
replication° should be made by the son of a king?
    ROSENCRANTZ
Take you me for a sponge, my lord?
    HAMLET 25
Ay, sir, that soaks up the King's countenance,° his
rewards, his authorities. But such officers do the
King best service in the end. He keeps them, like
an ape, in the corner of his jaw, first mouthed, to
be last swallowed. When he needs what you have 30
gleaned, it is but squeezing you and, sponge, you
shall be dry again.
    ROSENCRANTZ
I understand you not, my lord.
    HAMLET 35
I am glad of it: a knavish speech sleeps in a
foolish ear.
    ROSENCRANTZ
My lord, you must tell us where the body is and
go with us to the King. 40
    HAMLET
The body is with the King, but the King is not
with the body. The King is a thing——
    GUILDENSTERN
A thing, my lord? 45
    HAMLET
Of nothing. Bring me to him.
Hide fox, and all after.° (*Exeunt*.)


## SCENE III

*The castle.*

*Enter* **KING** *and two or three.*

    KING
I have sent to seek him and to find the body:
How dangerous is it that this man goes loose!
Yet must not we put the strong law on him:
He's loved of the distracted° multitude, 5
Who like not in their judgment, but their eyes,

---

50 **done . . .** (evidently something has dropped out of the
text. Capell's conjecture, "So, haply slander," is usually
printed) 52 **blank** white center of a target 54 **woundless**
invulnerable

**IV.ii.** 21 **demanded of** questioned by 22 **replication** reply
26 **countenance** favor 48 **Hide fox, and all after** (a cry in
a game such as hide-and-seek; Hamlet runs from the stage)
**IV.iii.** 5 **distracted** bewildered, senseless

And where 'tis so, th' offender's scourge is
     weighed,
But never the offense. To bear° all smooth and
10     even,
This sudden sending him away must seem
Deliberate pause.° Diseases desperate grown
By desperate appliance are relieved,
Or not at all.
*Enter* **ROSENCRANTZ**, (**GUILDENSTERN**,) *and all
the rest.*
15  How now? What hath befall'n?
     **ROSENCRANTZ**
Where the dead body is bestowed, my lord,
We cannot get from him.
     **KING**
20  But where is he?
     **ROSENCRANTZ**
Without, my lord; guarded, to know your
pleasure.
     **KING**
25  Bring him before us.
     **ROSENCRANTZ**
Ho! Bring in the lord.
*They enter.*
     **KING**
Now, Hamlet, where's Polonius?
30     **HAMLET**
At supper.
     **KING**
At supper? Where?
     **HAMLET**
35  Not where he eats, but where 'a is eaten. A certain
convocation of politic° worms are e'en at him.
Your worm is your only emperor for diet. We fat
all creatures else to fat us, and we fat ourselves
for maggots. Your fat king and your lean beggar
40  is but variable service°—two dishes, but to one
table. That's the end.
     **KING**
Alas, alas!
     **HAMLET**
45  A man may fish with the worm that hath eat of a
king, and eat of the fish that hath fed of that
worm.
     **KING**
What dost thou mean by this?

     **HAMLET**                                        50
Nothing but to show you how a king may go a
progress° through the guts of a beggar.
     **KING**
Where is Polonius?
     **HAMLET**                                        55
In heaven. Send thither to see. If your messenger
find him not there, seek him i' th' other place
yourself. But if indeed you find him not within
this month, you shall nose him as you go up the
stairs into the lobby.                                  60
     **KING**
(*To* **ATTENDANTS**) *Go seek him there.*
     **HAMLET**
'A will stay till you come.
(*Exeunt* **ATTENDANTS**.)
     **KING**                                          65
Hamlet, this deed, for thine especial safety,
Which we do tender° as we dearly grieve
For that which thou hast done, must send thee
     hence
With fiery quickness. Therefore prepare thyself.       70
The bark is ready and the wind at help,
Th' associates tend,° and everything is bent
For England.
     **HAMLET**
For England?                                           75
     **KING**
Ay, Hamlet.
     **HAMLET**
Good.
     **KING**                                          80
So is it, if thou knew'st our purposes.
     **HAMLET**
I see a cherub° that sees them. But come, for
England! Farewell, dear Mother.
     **KING**                                          85
Thy loving father, Hamlet.
     **HAMLET**
My mother—father and mother is man and wife,
man and wife is one flesh, and so, my mother.
Come, for England! (*Exit*)                            90
     **KING**
Follow him at foot;° tempt him with speed aboard.
Delay it not; I'll have him hence tonight.
Away! For everything is sealed and done

---

9 **bear** carry out   12 **pause** planning   36 **politic** statesman-
like, shrewd   40 **variable service** different courses

52 **progress** royal journey   67 **tender** hold dear   72 **tend**
wait   83 **cherub** angel of knowledge   92 **at foot** closely

95 That else leans° on th' affair. Pray you make haste.
(*Exeunt all but the* **KING**.)
And, England, if my love thou hold'st at aught—
As my great power thereof may give thee sense,
Since yet thy cicatrice° looks raw and red
After the Danish sword, and thy free awe°
100 Pays homage to us—thou mayst not coldly set
Our sovereign process,° which imports at full
By letters congruing to that effect
The present° death of Hamlet. Do it, England,
For like the hectic° in my blood he rages,
105 And thou must cure me. Till I know 'tis done,
Howe'er my haps,° my joys were ne'er begun.
(*Exit*.)

**SCENE IV**

*A plain in Denmark.*

*Enter* **FORTINBRAS** *with his Army over the stage.*

**FORTINBRAS**
Go, Captain, from me greet the Danish king.
Tell him that by his license Fortinbras
Craves the conveyance of° a promised march
5 Over his kingdom. You know the rendezvous.
If that his Majesty would aught with us,
We shall express our duty in his eye;°
And let him know so.
**CAPTAIN**
10 I will do't, my lord.
**FORTINBRAS**
Go softly° on.
(*Exeunt all but the* **CAPTAIN**.)
*Enter* **HAMLET, ROSENCRANTZ, &C.**
**HAMLET**
Good sir, whose powers° are these?
15 **CAPTAIN**
They are of Norway, sir.
**HAMLET**
How purposed, sir, I pray you?
**CAPTAIN**
20 Against some part of Poland.

**HAMLET**
Who commands them, sir?
**CAPTAIN**
The nephew to old Norway, Fortinbras.
**HAMLET**                                                     25
Goes it against the main° of Poland, sir,
Or for some frontier?
**CAPTAIN**
Truly to speak, and with no addition,°
We go to gain a little patch of ground                        30
That hath in it no profit but the name.
To pay five ducats, five, I would not farm it,
Nor will it yield to Norway or the Pole
A ranker° rate, should it be sold in fee.°
**HAMLET**                                                     35
Why, then the Polack never will defend it.
**CAPTAIN**
Yes, it is already garrisoned.
**HAMLET**
Two thousand souls and twenty thousand ducats   40
Will not debate° the question of this straw.
This is th' imposthume° of much wealth and
    peace,
That inward breaks, and shows no cause without
Why the man dies. I humbly thank you, sir.      45
**CAPTAIN**
God bye you, sir. (*Exit*.)
**ROSENCRANTZ**: Will't please you go, my lord?
**HAMLET**
I'll be with you straight. Go a little before.   50
(*Exeunt all but* **HAMLET**.)
How all occasions do inform against me
And spur my dull revenge! What is a man,
If his chief good and market° of his time
Be but to sleep and feed? A beast, no more.
Sure he that made us with such large discourse,°  55
Looking before and after, gave us not
That capability and godlike reason
To fust° in us unused. Now, whether it be
Bestial oblivion,° or some craven scruple
Of thinking too precisely on th' event°—          60
A thought which, quartered, hath but one part
    wisdom

95 **leans** depends  98 **cicatrice** scar  99 **free awe** uncompelled submission  100–01 **coldly set/Our sovereign process** regard slightly our royal command  103 **present** instant  104 **hectic** fever  105 **haps** chances, fortunes  IV.iv. 4 **conveyance of** escort for  7 **in his eye** before his eyes (i.e., in his presence)  12 **softly** slowly  14 **powers** forces

26 **main** main part  29 **with no addition** plainly  34 **ranker** higher  34 **in fee** outright  41 **debate** settle  42 **imposthume** abscess, ulcer  53 **market** profit  55 **discourse** understanding  58 **fust** grow moldy  59 **oblivion** forgetfulness  60 **event** outcome

And ever three parts coward—I do not know
Why yet I live to say, "This thing's to do,"
65 Sith I have cause, and will, and strength, and
      means
To do't. Examples gross° as earth exhort me.
Witness this army of such mass and charge,°
Led by a delicate and tender prince,
70 Whose spirit, with divine ambition puffed,
Makes mouths at the invisible event,°
Exposing what is mortal and unsure
To all that fortune, death, and danger dare,
Even for an eggshell. Rightly to be great
75 Is not° to stir without great argument,°
But greatly° to find quarrel in a straw
When honor's at the stake. How stand I then,
That have a father killed, a mother stained,
Excitements° of my reason and my blood,
80 And let all sleep, while to my shame I see
The imminent death of twenty thousand men
That for a fantasy and trick of fame°
Go to their graves like beds, fight for a plot
Whereon the numbers cannot try the cause,
85 Which is not tomb enough and continent°
To hide the slain? O, from this time forth,
My thoughts be bloody, or be nothing worth!
(*Exit.*)


## SCENE V

*The castle.*

*Enter* **HORATIO,** **(QUEEN) GERTRUDE,** *and a*
**GENTLEMAN.**

    **QUEEN**
I will not speak with her.
    **GENTLEMAN**
She is importunate, indeed distract.
5 Her mood will needs be pitied.
    **QUEEN**
What would she have?
    **GENTLEMAN**
She speaks much of her father, says she hears

There's tricks i' th' world, and hems, and beats  10
  her heart,
Spurns enviously at straws,° speaks things in
  doubt°
That carry but half sense. Her speech is nothing,
Yet the unshapèd use of it doth move             15
The hearers to collection;° they yawn° at it,
And botch the words up fit to their own thoughts,
Which, as her winks and nods and gestures yield
  them
Indeed would make one think there might be       20
  thought,
Though nothing sure, yet much unhappily.
    **HORATIO**
'Twere good she were spoken with, for she may
  strew
Dangerous conjectures in ill-breeding minds.     25
    **QUEEN**
Let her come in. (*Exit* **GENTLEMAN.**)
(*Aside*) To my sick soul (as sin's true nature is)
Each toy seems prologue to some great amiss;°    30
So full of artless jealousy° is guilt
It spills° itself in fearing to be spilt.
*Enter* **OPHELIA** (*distracted.*)
    **OPHELIA**
Where is the beauteous majesty of Denmark?
    **QUEEN**                                    35
How now, Ophelia?
    **OPHELIA**
(*She sings.*) How should I your truelove know
From another one?
By his cockle hat° and staff                      40
And his sandal shoon.°
    **QUEEN**
Alas, sweet lady, what imports this song?
    **OPHELIA**
Say you? Nay, pray you mark.                      45
He is dead and gone, lady, (*Song*)
He is dead and gone;
At his head a grass-green turf,

67 **gross** large, obvious 68 **charge** expense 71 **Makes mouths at the invisible event** makes scornful faces (is contemptuous of) the unseen outcome 75 **not** (the sense seems to require "not not") 75 **argument** reason 76 **greatly** i.e., nobly 79 **Excitements** incentives 82 **fantasy and trick of fame** illusion and trifle of reputation 85 **continent** receptacle, container

**IV.v. 12 Spurns enviously at straws** objects spitefully to insignificant matters 12–13 **in doubt** uncertainly 15–16 **Yet the . . . to collection** i.e., yet the formless manner of it moves her listeners to gather up some sort of meaning 16 **yawn** gape (?) 30 **amiss** misfortune 31 **artless jealousy** crude suspicion 32 **spills** destroys 40 **cockle hat** (a cockleshell on the hat was the sign of a pilgrim who had journeyed to shrines overseas. The association of lovers and pilgrims was a common one) 41 **shoon** shoes

At his heels a stone.
50 O, ho!
QUEEN
Nay, but Ophelia—
OPHELIA
Pray you mark.
55 (*Sings.*) White his shroud as the mountain snow—
*Enter* KING.
QUEEN
Alas, look here, my lord.
OPHELIA
Larded° all with sweet flowers (*Song*)
60 Which bewept to the grave did not go
With truelove showers.
KING
How do you, pretty lady?
OPHELIA
65 Well, God dild° you! They say the owl was a
baker's daughter.° Lord, we know what we are,
but know not what we may be. God be at your
table!
KING
70 Conceit° upon her father.
OPHELIA
Pray let's have no words of this, but when they
ask you what it means, say you this:
Tomorrow is Saint Valentine's day.° (*Song*)
75 All in the morning betime,
And I a maid at your window,
To be your Valentine.
Then up he rose and donned his clothes
And dupped° the chamber door,
80 Let in the maid, that out a maid
Never departed more.
KING
Pretty Ophelia.
OPHELIA
85 Indeed, la, without an oath, I'll make an end on't:
(*Sings.*) By Gis° and by Saint Charity,
Alack, and fie for shame!
Young men will do't if they come to't,
By Cock,° they are to blame.

Quoth she, "Before you tumbled me, 90
You promised me to wed."
He answers:
"So would I 'a' done, by yonder sun,
An thou hadst not come to my bed."
KING 95
How long hath she been thus?
OPHELIA
I hope all will be well. We must be patient, but I
cannot choose but weep to think they would lay
him i' th' cold ground. My brother shall know of 100
it; and so I thank you for your good counsel.
Come, my coach! Good night, ladies, good night.
Sweet ladies, good night, good night. (*Exit.*)
KING
Follow her close; give her good watch, I pray you. 105
(*Exit* HORATIO.)
O, this is the poison of deep grief, it springs
All from her father's death—and now behold!
O Gertrude, Gertrude,
When sorrows come, they come not single spies,
But in battalions: first, her father slain; 110
Next, your son gone, and he most violent author
Of his own just remove; the people muddied,°
Thick and unwholesome in their thoughts and
     whispers
For good Polonius' death, and we have done but 115
     greenly°
In huggermugger° to inter him; poor Ophelia
Divided from herself and her fair judgment,
Without the which we are pictures or mere beasts;
Last, and as much containing as all these, 120
Her brother is in secret come from France,
Feeds on his wonder,° keeps himself in clouds,
And wants not buzzers° to infect his ear
With pestilent speeches of his father's death,
Wherein necessity, of matter beggared,° 125
Will nothing stick° our person to arraign
In ear and ear. O my dear Gertrude, this,
Like to a murd'ring piece,° in many places
Gives me superfluous death. (*A noise within.*)
*Enter a* MESSENGER.
QUEEN 130
Alack, what noise is this?

59 **Larded** decorated 65 **dild** yield, i.e., reward 66
**baker's daughter** (an allusion to a tale of a baker's daughter who begrudged bread to Christ and was turned into an
owl) 70 **Conceit** brooding 74 **Saint Valentine's day** Feb.
14 (the notion was that a bachelor would become the true
love of the first girl he saw on this day) 79 **dupped**
opened (did up) 86 **Gis** (contraction of "Jesus") 89 **Cock**
(1) God (2) phallus

112 **muddied** muddled 116 **greenly** foolishly 117 **hug-
germugger** secret haste 122 **wonder** suspicion 123
**wants not buzzers** does not lack talebearers 125 **of matter
beggared** unprovided with facts 126 **Will nothing stick**
will not hesitate 128 **murd'ring piece** (a cannon that shot
a kind of shrapnel)

**KING**
Attend, where are my Switzers?° Let them guard
    the door.
135 What is the matter?
    **MESSENGER**
Save yourself, my lord.
The'ocean, overpeering of his list,°
Eats not the flats with more impiteous haste
140 Than young Laertes, in a riotous head,°
O'erbears your officers. The rabble call him lord,
And, as the world were now but to begin,
Antiquity forgot, custom not known,
The ratifiers and props of every word,
145 They cry, "Choose we! Laertes shall be king!"
Caps, hands, and tongues applaud it to the clouds,
"Laertes shall be king! Laertes king!" *A noise*
    *within.*
    **QUEEN**
150 How cheerfully on the false trail they cry!
O, this is counter,° you false Danish dogs!
*Enter* **LAERTES** *with others.*
    **KING**
The doors are broke.
    **LAERTES**
155 Where is this king?—Sirs, stand you all without.
    **ALL**
No, let's come in.
    **LAERTES**
I pray you give me leave.
160    **ALL**
We will, we will.
    **LAERTES**
I thank you. Keep the door.
(*Exeunt his* **FOLLOWERS**.) O thou vile King,
165 Give me my father.
    **QUEEN**
Calmly, good Laertes.
    **LAERTES**
That drop of blood that's calm proclaims me
170    bastard,
Cries cuckold° to my father, brands the harlot
Even here between the chaste unsmirchèd brow
Of my true mother.
    **KING**
175 What is the cause, Laertes,
That thy rebellion looks so giantlike?

Let him go, Gertrude. Do not fear° our person.
There's such divinity doth hedge a king
That treason can but peep to° what it would,
Acts little of his will. Tell me, Laertes,              180
Why thou art thus incensed. Let him go, Gertrude.
Speak, man.
    **LAERTES**
Where is my father?
    **KING**                                             185
Dead.
    **QUEEN**
But not by him.
    **KING**
Let him demand his fill.                                 190
    **LAERTES**
How came he dead? I'll not be juggled with.
To hell allegiance, vows to the blackest devil,
Conscience and grace to the profoundest pit!           195
I dare damnation. To this point I stand,
That both the worlds I give to negligence,°
Let come what comes, only I'll be revenged
Most throughly for my father.
    **KING**
Who shall stay you?                                     200
    **LAERTES**
My will, not all the world's.
And for my means, I'll husband them° so well
They shall go far with little.
    **KING**                                             205
Good Laertes,
If you desire to know the certainty
Of your dear father, is't writ in your revenge
That swoopstake° you will draw both friend and
    foe,                                                210
Winner and loser?
    **LAERTES**
None but his enemies.
    **KING**
Will you know them then?                                215
    **LAERTES**
To his good friends thus wide I'll ope my arms
And like the kind life-rend'ring pelican°,
Repast° them with my blood.

133 **Switzers** Swiss guards   138 **list** shore   140 **in a riotous
head** with a rebellious force   151 **counter** (a hound runs
counter when he follows the scent backward from the
prey)   171 **cuckold** man whose wife is unfaithful

177 **fear** fear for   179 **peep to** i.e., look at from a distance
197 **That both . . . to negligence** i.e., I care not what may
happen (to me) in this world or the next   203 **husband
them** use them economically   209 **swoopstake** in a clean
sweep   218 **pelican** (thought to feed its young with its own
blood)   219 **Repast** feed

220 **KING**
Why, now you speak
Like a good child and a true gentleman.
That I am guiltless of your father's death,
And am most sensibly° in grief for it,
225 It shall as level to your judgment 'pear
As day does to your eye.
*A noise within: "Let her come in."*
    **LAERTES**
How now? What noise is that?
*Enter OPHELIA.*
230 O heat, dry up my brains; tears seven times salt
Burn out the sense and virtue° of mine eye!
By heaven, thy madness shall be paid with weight
Till our scale turn the beam.° O rose of May,
Dear maid, kind sister, sweet Ophelia!
235 O heavens, is't possible a young maid's wits
Should be as mortal as an old man's life?
Nature is fine° in love, and where 'tis fine,
It sends some precious instance° of itself
After the thing it loves.
240 **OPHELIA**
They bore him barefaced on the bier (*Song*)
Hey non nony, nony, hey nony
And in his grave rained many a tear—
Fare you well, my dove!
245 **LAERTES**
Hadst thou thy wits, and didst persuade revenge,
It could not move thus.
    **OPHELIA**
You must sing "A-down a-down, and you call
250 him a-down-a." O, how the wheel° becomes it! It
is the false steward, that stole his master's
daughter.
    **LAERTES**
This nothing's more than matter.°
255 **OPHELIA**
There's rosemary, that's for remembrance. Pray
you, love, remember. And there is pansies, that's
for thoughts.
    **LAERTES**
260 A document° in madness,
thoughts and remembrance fitted.

**OPHELIA**
There's fennel° for you, and columbines. There's
rue for you, and here's some for me. We may call
it herb of grace o' Sundays. O, you must wear 265
your rue with a difference. There's a daisy. I
would give you some violets, but they withered
all when my father died. They say 'a made a good
end.
(*Sings*) For bonny sweet Robin is all my joy. 270
    **LAERTES**
Thought and affliction, passion, hell itself, She
turns to favor° and to prettiness.
    **OPHELIA**
And will 'a not come again? 275
And will 'a not come again?
No, no, he is dead,
Go to the deathbed,
He never will come again.
His beard was as white as snow, 280
All flaxen was his poll.°
He is gone, he is gone,
And we cast away moan.
God 'a' mercy on his soul!
And of all Christian souls, I pray God. God bye 285
    you.
(*Exit.*)
    **LAERTES**
Do you see this, O God?
    **KING**
Laertes, I must commune with your grief, 290
Or you deny me right. Go but apart,
Make choice of whom your wisest friends you
    will,
And they shall hear and judge 'twixt you and me.
If by direct or by collateral° hand 295
They find us touched,° we will our kingdom give,
Our crown, our life, and all that we call ours,
To you in satisfaction; but if not,
Be you content to lend your patience to us,
And we shall jointly labor with your soul 300
To give it due content.

263 **fennel** (the distribution of flowers in the ensuing lines has symbolic meaning, but the meaning is disputed. Perhaps **fennel**, flattery; **columbines**, cuckoldry; **rue**, sorrow for Ophelia and repentance for the Queen; **daisy**, dissembling; **violets**, faithfulness. For other interpretations, see J. W. Lever in *Review of English Studies*, New Series 3 [1952], pp. 123–29) 273 **favor** charm, beauty 281 **All flaxen was his poll** white as flax was his head 295 **collateral** indirect 296 **touched** implicated

224 **sensibly** acutely 231 **virtue** power 233 **turn the beam** weigh down the bar (of the balance) 237 **fine** refined, delicate 238 **instance** sample 250 **wheel** (of uncertain meaning, but probably a turn or dance of Ophelia's, rather than Fortune's wheel) 254 **This nothing's more than matter** this nonsense has more meaning than matters of consequence 260 **document** lesson

LAERTES
Let this be so.
His means of death, his obscure funeral—
305 No trophy, sword, nor hatchment° o'er his bones,
No noble rite nor formal ostentation°—
Cry to be heard, as 'twere from heaven to earth,
That I must call't in question.
KING
310 So you shall;
And where th' offense is, let the great ax fall.
I pray you go with me. (*Exeunt.*)

**SCENE VI**

*The castle.*

*Enter* HORATIO *and* OTHERS.

HORATIO
What are they that would speak with me?
GENTLEMAN
Seafaring men, sir. They say they have letters for
5 you.
HORATIO
Let them come in. (*Exit* ATTENDANT.) I do not
know from what part of the world I should be
greeted, if not from Lord Hamlet.
10 SAILOR
God bless you, sir.
HORATIO
Let Him bless thee too.
SAILOR
15 'A shall, sir, an't please Him. There's a letter for
you, sir—it came from th' ambassador that was
bound for England—if your name be Horatio, as I
am let to know it is.
HORATIO
20 (*Reads the letter.*) "Horatio, when thou shalt have
overlooked° this, give these fellows some means
to the King. They have letters for him. Ere we
were two days old at sea, a pirate of very warlike
appointment° gave us chase. Finding ourselves
25 too slow of sail, we put on a compelled valor, and
in the grapple I boarded them. On the instant
they got clear of our ship; so I alone became their
prisoner. They have dealt with me like thieves of
mercy, but they knew what they did: I am to do a

good turn for them. Let the King have the letters I   30
have sent, and repair thou to me with as much
speed as thou wouldest fly death. I have words to
speak in thine ear will make thee dumb; yet are
they much too light for the bore° of the matter.
These good fellows will bring thee where I am.     35
Rosencrantz and Guildenstern hold their course
for England. Of them I have much to tell thee.
Farewell. He that thou knowest thine, HAMLET."
Come, I will give you way for these your letters,
And do't the speedier that you may direct me        40
To him from whom you brought them. (*Exeunt.*)

**SCENE VII**

*The castle.*

*Enter* KING *and* LAERTES.

KING
Now must your conscience my acquittance seal,
And you must put me in your heart for friend,
Sith you have heard, and with a knowing ear,
That he which hath your noble father slain           5
Pursued my life.
LAERTES
It well appears. But tell me
Why you proceeded not against these feats
10 So criminal and so capital° in nature,
As by your safety, greatness, wisdom, all things
else,
You mainly° were stirred up.
KING
O, for two special reasons,                          15
Which may to you perhaps seem much
unsinewed,°
But yet to me they're strong. The Queen his
mother
Lives almost by his looks, and for myself—           20
My virtue or my plague, be it either which—
She is so conjunctive° to my life and soul,
That, as the star moves not but in his sphere,
I could not but by her. The other motive
Why to a public count° I might not go                25
Is the great love the general gender° bear him,
Who, dipping all his faults in their affection,

---

305 **hatchment** tablet bearing the coat of arms of the dead
306 **ostentation** ceremony   **IV.vi.** 21 **overlooked** surveyed
24 **appointment** equipment

34 **bore** caliber (here, "importance")   **IV.vii.** 10 **capital** deserving death 13 **mainly** powerfully 17 **unsinewed** weak  22 **conjunctive** closely united  25 **count** reckoning 26 **general gender** common people

Would, like the spring that turneth wood to
    stone,°
30 Convert his gyves° to graces; so that my arrows,
Too slightly timbered° for so loud a wind,
Would have reverted to my bow again,
And not where I had aimed them.

    LAERTES
35 And so have I a noble father lost,
A sister driven into desp'rate terms,°
Whose worth, if praises may go back again,°
Stood challenger on mount of all the age
For her perfections. But my revenge will come.

40     KING
Break not your sleeps for that. You must not think
That we are made of stuff so flat and dull
That we can let our beard be shook with danger,
And think it pastime. You shortly shall hear more.
45 I loved your father, and we love ourself,
And that, I hope, will teach you to imagine—
*Enter a* **MESSENGER** *with letters.*
How now? What news?

    MESSENGER
Letters, my lord, from Hamlet:
50 These to your Majesty; this to the Queen.

    KING
From Hamlet? Who brought them?

    MESSENGER
Sailors, my lord, they say; I saw them not.
55 They were given me by Claudio; he received them
Of him that brought them.

    KING
Laertes, you shall hear them.—
Leave us. (*Exit* **MESSENGER**.)
60 (*Reads.*) "High and mighty, you shall know I am
set naked° on your kingdom. Tomorrow shall I
beg leave to see your kingly eyes; when I shall
(first asking your pardon thereunto) recount the
occasion of my sudden and more strange return.
65 HAMLET."
What should this mean? Are all the rest come
    back?
Or is it some abuse,° and no such thing?

    LAERTES
70 Know you the hand?

    KING
'Tis Hamlet's character.° "Naked"!
And in a postscript here, he says "alone."
Can you devise° me?

    LAERTES
75 I am lost in it, my lord. But let him come.
It warms the very sickness in my heart
That I shall live and tell him to his teeth,
"Thus didst thou."

    KING
80 If it be so, Laertes
(As how should it be so? How otherwise?),
Will you be ruled by me?

    LAERTES
Ay, my lord,
85 So you will not o'errule me to a peace.

    KING
To thine own peace. If he be now returned,
As checking at° his voyage, and that he means
No more to undertake it, I will work him
90 To an exploit now ripe in my device,
Under the which he shall not choose but fall;
And for his death no wind of blame shall breathe,
But even his mother shall uncharge the practice°
And call it accident.
95

    LAERTES
My lord, I will be ruled;
The rather if you could devise it so
That I might be the organ.

    KING
100 It falls right.
You have been talked of since your travel much,
And that in Hamlet's hearing, for a quality
Wherein they say you shine. Your sum of parts
Did not together pluck such envy from him
105
As did that one, and that, in my regard,
Of the unworthiest siege.°

    LAERTES
What part is that, my lord?

    KING
110
A very riband in the cap of youth,
Yet needful too, for youth no less becomes
The light and careless livery that it wears
Than settled age his sables and his weeds,°

---

28–29 **spring that turneth wood to stone** (a spring in
Shakespeare's county was so charged with lime that it
would petrify wood placed in it) 30 **gyves** fetters 31 **tim-
bered** shafted 36 **terms** conditions 37 **go back again** revert
to what is past 61 **naked** destitute 68 **abuse** deception

72 **character** handwriting 74 **devise** advise 89 **checking
at** turning away from (a term in falconry) 94 **uncharge the
practice** not charge the device with treachery 107 **siege**
rank 114 **sables and his weeds** i.e., sober attire

115 Importing health and graveness. Two months
     since
  Here was a gentleman of Normandy.
  I have seen myself, and served against, the French,
  And they can° well on horseback, but this gallant
120 Had witchcraft in't. He grew unto his seat,
  And to such wondrous doing brought his horse
  As had he been incorpsed and deminatured
  With the brave beast. So far he topped my thought
  That I, in forgery° of shapes and tricks,
125 Come short of what he did.
      LAERTES
  A Norman was't?
      KING
  A Norman.
130     LAERTES
  Upon my life, Lamord.
      KING
  The very same.
      LAERTES
135 I know him well. He is the brooch° indeed
  And gem of all the nation.
      KING
  He made confession° of you,
  And gave you such a masterly report,
140 For art and exercise in your defense,
  And for your rapier most especial,
  That he cried out 'twould be a sight indeed
  If one could match you. The scrimers° of their
     nation
145 He swore had neither motion, guard, nor eye,
  If you opposed them. Sir, this report of his
  Did Hamlet so envenom with his envy
  That he could nothing do but wish and beg
  Your sudden coming o'er to play with you.
150 Now, out of this——
      LAERTES
  What out of this, my lord?
      KING
  Laertes, was your father dear to you?
155 Or are you like the painting of a sorrow,
  A face without a heart?
      LAERTES
  Why ask you this?
      KING
160 Not that I think you did not love your father,
  But that I know love is begun by time,

And that I see, in passages of proof,°
Time qualifies° the spark and fire of it.
There lives within the very flame of love
A kind of wick or snuff° that will abate it,                165
And nothing is at a like goodness still,°
For goodness, growing to a plurisy,°
Dies in his own too-much. That we would do
We should do when we would, for this "would"
    changes,                                          170
And hath abatements and delays as many
As there are tongues, are hands, are accidents,
And then this "should" is like a spendthrift sigh,°
That hurts by easing. But to the quick° of th'
    ulcer—                                            175
Hamlet comes back; what would you undertake
To show yourself in deed your father's son
More than in words?
      LAERTES
To cut his throat i' th' church!                           180
      KING
No place indeed should murder sanctuarize;°
Revenge should have no bounds. But, good
    Laertes,
Will you do this? Keep close within your chamber. 185
Hamlet returned shall know you are come home.
We'll put on those° shall praise your excellence
And set a double varnish on the fame
The Frenchman gave you, bring you in fine°
    together                                          190
And wager on your heads. He, being remiss,
Most generous, and free from all contriving,
Will not peruse the foils, so that with ease,
Or with a little shuffling, you may choose
A sword unbated,° and, in a pass of practice,°      195
Requite him for your father.
      LAERTES
I will do't,
And for that purpose I'll anoint my sword.
I bought an unction of a mountebank,°               200
So mortal that, but dip a knife in it,

---

162 **passages of proof** proved cases   163 **qualifies** diminishes   165 **snuff** residue of burnt wick (which dims the light)   166 **still** always   167 **plurisy** fullness, excess   173 **spendthrift sigh** (sighing provides ease, but because it was thought to thin the blood and so shorten life it was spendthrift)   174 **quick** sensitive flesh   182 **sanctuarize** protect   187 **We'll put on those** we'll incite persons who   189 **in fine** finally   195 **unbated** not blunted   195 **pass of practice** treacherous thrust   200 **mountebank** quack

119 **can** do   124 **forgery** invention   135 **brooch** ornament
138 **confession** report   143 **scrimers** fencers

Where it draws blood, no cataplasm° so rare,
Collected from all simples° that have virtue°
Under the moon, can save the thing
205 from death
That is but scratched withal. I'll touch my point
With this contagion, that, if I gall him slightly,
It may be death.
      KING
210 Let's further think of this,
Weigh what convenience both of time and means
May fit us to our shape.° If this should fail,
And that our drift look through° our bad
      performance,
215 'Twere better not assayed. Therefore this project
Should have a back or second, that might hold
If this did blast in proof.° Soft, let me see.
We'll make a solemn wager on your cunnings—
I ha't!
220 When in your motion you are hot and dry—
As make your bouts more violent to that end—
And that he calls for drink, I'll have prepared him
A chalice for the nonce,° whereon but sipping,
If he by chance escape your venomed stuck,°
225 Our purpose may hold there.—But stay, what
      noise?
    *Enter* QUEEN.
      QUEEN
One woe doth tread upon another's heel.
So fast they follow. Your sister's drowned,
230     Laertes.
      LAERTES
Drowned! O, where?
      QUEEN
There is a willow grows askant° the brook,
235 That shows his hoar° leaves in the glassy stream:
Therewith° fantastic garlands did she make
Of crowflowers, nettles, daisies, and long purples,
That liberal° shepherds give a grosser name,
But our cold maids do dead men's fingers call
240     them.
There on the pendent boughs her crownet° weeds
Clamb'ring to hang, an envious sliver° broke,

202 **cataplasm** poultice 203 **simples** medicinal herbs 203 **virtue** power (to heal) 212 **shape** role 213 **drift look through** purpose show through 217 **blast in proof** burst (fail) in performance 223 **nonce** occasion 224 **stuck** thrust 234 **askant** aslant 235 **hoar** silver-gray 236 **Therewith** i.e., with willow twigs 238 **liberal** free-spoken, coarse-mouthed 241 **crownet** coronet 242 **envious sliver** malicious branch

When down her weedy trophies and herself
Fell in the weeping brook. Her clothes spread
    wide,           245
And mermaidlike awhile they bore her up,
Which time she chanted snatches of old lauds,°
As one incapable° of her own distress,
Or like a creature native and indued°
Unto that element. But long it could not be    250
Till that her garments, heavy with their drink,
Pulled the poor wretch from her melodious lay
To muddy death.
      LAERTES
Alas, then she is drowned?           255
      QUEEN
Drowned, drowned.
      LAERTES
Too much of water hast thou, poor Ophelia,
And therefore I forbid my tears; but yet      260
It is our trick;° nature her custom holds,
Let shame say what it will: when these are gone,
The woman° will be out. Adieu, my lord.
I have a speech o' fire, that fain would blaze,
But that this folly drowns it.(*Exit.*)    265
      KING
Let's follow, Gertrude.
How much I had to do to calm his rage!
Now fear I this will give it start again;
Therefore let's follow. (*Exeunt.*)    270

# ACT V

## SCENE I

*A churchyard.*

*Enter* TWO CLOWNS°.

      CLOWN
Is she to be buried in Christian burial when she
willfully seeks her own salvation?
      OTHER
I tell thee she is. Therefore make her grave    5
straight.° The crowner° hath sate on her, and
finds it Christian burial.

247 **lauds** hymns 248 **incapable** unaware 249 **indued** in harmony with 261 **trick** trait, way 263 **woman** i.e., womanly part of me **V.i.** s.d. **Clowns** rustics 6 **straight** straightway 6 **crowner** coroner

**CLOWN**

How can that be, unless she drowned herself in
10 her own defense?

**OTHER**

Why, 'tis found so.

**CLOWN**

It must be *se offendendo;*° it cannot be else. For here
15 lies the point: if I drown myself wittingly, it
argues an act, and an act hath three branches— it
is to act, to do, to perform. Argal,° she drowned
herself wittingly.

**OTHER**

20 Nay, but hear you, Goodman Delver.

**CLOWN**

Give me leave. Here lies the water—good. Here
stands the man—good. If the man go to this water
and drown himself, it is, will he nill he,° he goes;
25 mark you that. But if the water come to him and
drown him, he drowns not himself. Argal, he that
is not guilty of his own death, shortens not his
own life.

**OTHER**

30 But is this law?

**CLOWN**

Ay marry, is't—crowner's quest° law.

**OTHER**

Will you ha' the truth on't? If this had not been a
35 gentlewoman, she should have been buried out o'
Christian burial.

**CLOWN**

Why, there thou say'st. And the more pity that
great folk should have count'nance° in this world
40 to drown or hang themselves more than their
even-Christen.° Come, my spade. There is no
ancient gentlemen but gard'ners, ditchers, and
gravemakers. They hold up° Adam's profession.

**OTHER**

45 Was he a gentleman?

**CLOWN**

'A was the first ever bore arms.°

**OTHER**

Why, he had none.

**CLOWN**

50 What, art a heathen? How dost thou understand
the Scripture? The Scripture says Adam digged.
Could he dig without arms? I'll put another
question to thee. If thou answerest me not to the
purpose, confess thyself—
55

**OTHER**

Go to.

**CLOWN**

What is he that builds stronger than either the
mason, the shipwright, or the carpenter?
60

**OTHER**

The gallowsmaker, for that frame outlives a
thousand tenants.

**CLOWN**

I like thy wit well, in good faith. The gallows does  65
well. But how does it well? It does well to those
that do ill. Now thou dost ill to say the gallows is
built stronger than the church. Argal, the gallows
may do well to thee. To't again, come.

**OTHER**
70

Who builds stronger than a mason, a shipwright,
or a carpenter?

**CLOWN**

Ay, tell me that, and unyoke.°

**OTHER**
75

Marry, now I can tell.

**CLOWN**

To't.

**OTHER**

Mass,° I cannot tell.
80

*Enter* **HAMLET** *and* **HORATIO** *afar off.*

**CLOWN**

Cudgel thy brains no more about it, for your dull
ass will not mend his pace with beating. And
when you are asked this question next, say "a
gravemaker" The houses he makes lasts till  85
doomsday. Go, get thee in, and fetch me a stoup°
of liquor.

(*Exit* **OTHER CLOWN.**)

In youth when I did love, did love, (*Song*)
Methought it was very sweet
To contract—O—the time for—a—my behove,°  90
O, methought there—a—was nothing—a—meet.

**HAMLET**

Has this fellow no feeling of his business? 'A
sings in gravemaking.

---

14 **se offendendo** (blunder for *se defendendo,* a legal term
meaning "in self-defense")  17 **Argal** (blunder for Latin
*ergo,* "therefore")  24 **will he nill he** will he or will he
not (whether he will or will not)  32 **quest** inquest  39
**count'nance** privilege  41 **even-Christen** fellow Christian
43 **hold up** keep up  47 **bore arms** had a coat of arms
(the sign of a gentleman)

74 **unyoke** i.e., stop work for the day  80 **Mass** by the mass
86 **stoup** tankard  90 **behove** advantage

95 **HORATIO**
Custom hath made it in him a property of
easiness.°
**HAMLET**
'Tis e'en so. The hand of little employment hath
100 the daintier sense.°
**CLOWN**
But age with his stealing steps (*Song*)
Hath clawed me in his clutch,
And hath shipped me into the land,
105 As if I had never been such.
(*Throws up a skull.*)
**HAMLET**
That skull had a tongue in it, and could sing once.
How the knave jowls° it to the ground, as if
'twere Cain's jawbone, that did the first murder!
110 This might be the pate of a politician, which this
ass now o'erreaches,° one that would circumvent
God, might it not?
**HORATIO**
It might, my lord.
115 **HAMLET**
Or, of a courtier, which could say "Good morrow,
sweet lord! How dost thou, sweet lord?" This
might be my Lord Such-a-one, that praised my
Lord Such-a-one's horse when 'a went to beg it,
120 might it not?
**HORATIO**
Ay, my lord.
**HAMLET**
Why, e'en so, and now my Lady Worm's,
125 chapless,° and knocked about the mazzard° with
a sexton's spade. Here's fine revolution, an we
had the trick to see't. Did these bones cost no
more the breeding but to play at loggets° with
them? Mine ache to think on't.
130 **CLOWN**
A pickax and a spade, a spade, (*Song*)
For and a shrouding sheet;
O, a pit of clay for to be made
For such a guest is meet.
(*Throws up another skull.*)

**HAMLET** 135
There's another. Why may not that be the skull of
a lawyer? Where be his quiddities° now, his
quillities,° his cases, his tenures,° and his tricks?
Why does he suffer this mad knave now to knock
him about the sconce° with a dirty shovel, and 140
will not tell him of his action of battery? Hum!
This fellow might be in's time a great buyer of
land, with his statutes, his recognizances, his
fines,° his double vouchers, his recoveries. Is this
the fine° of his fines, and the recovery of his 145
recoveries, to have his fine pate full of fine dirt?
Will his vouchers vouch him no more of his
purchases, and double ones too, than the length
and breadth of a pair of indentures?° The very
conveyances° of his lands will scarcely lie in this 150
box, and must th' inheritor himself have no more,
ha?
**HORATIO**
Not a jot more, my lord.
**HAMLET** 155
Is not parchment made of sheepskins?
**HORATIO:** Ay, my lord, and of calveskins too.
**HAMLET**
They are sheep and calves which seek out
assurance° in that. I will speak to this fellow. 160
Whose grave's this, sirrah?
**CLOWN**
Mine, sir.
(*Sings.*) O, a pit of clay for to be made 165
For such a guest is meet.
**HAMLET**
I think it be thine indeed, for thou liest in't.
**CLOWN**
You lie out on't, sir, and therefore 'tis not yours. 170
For my part, I do not lie in't, yet it is mine.
**HAMLET**
Thou dost lie in't, to be in't and say it is thine. 'Tis
for the dead, not for the quick;° therefore, thou liest.

137 **quiddities** subtle arguments (from Latin **quidditas,**
"whatness") 138 **quillities** fine distinctions 138 **tenures**
legal means of holding land 140 **sconce** head 143–44 **his
statutes, his recognizances, his fines** his documents giving a creditor control of a debtor's land, his bonds of
surety, his documents changing an entailed estate into fee
simple (unrestricted ownership) 145 **fine** end 149 **indentures** contracts 150 **conveyances** legal documents for
the transference of land 160 **assurance** safety 174 **quick**
living

96–97 **in him a property of easiness** easy for him  99–100
**hath the daintier sense** is more sensitive (because it is
not calloused) 108 **jowls** hurls 111 **o'erreaches** (1) reaches
over (2) has the advantage over  125 **chapless** lacking the
lower jaw 125 **mazzard** head 128 **loggets** (a game in
which small pieces of wood were thrown at an object)

175     **CLOWN**
'Tis a quick lie, sir; 'twill away again from me to
you.
    **HAMLET**
What man dost thou dig it for?
180     **CLOWN**
For no man, sir.
    **HAMLET**
What woman then?
    **CLOWN**
185 For none neither.
    **HAMLET**
Who is to be buried in't?
    **CLOWN**
One that was a woman, sir: but, rest her soul,
190 she's dead.
    **HAMLET**
How absolute° the knave is! We must speak by
the card,° or equivocation° will undo us. By the
Lord, Horatio, this three years I have took note of
195 it, the age is grown so picked° that the toe of the
peasant comes so near the heel of the courtier he
galls his kibe.° How long hast thou been a
gravemaker?
    **CLOWN**
200 Of all the days i' th' year, I came to't that day that
our last king Hamlet overcame Fortinbras.
    **HAMLET**
How long is that since?
    **CLOWN**
205 Cannot you tell that? Every fool can tell that. It
was that very day that young Hamlet was born—
he that is mad, and sent into England.
    **HAMLET**
Ay, marry, why was he sent into England?
210     **CLOWN**
Why, because 'a was mad. 'A shall recover his
wits there; or, if 'a do not, 'tis no great matter
there.
    **HAMLET**
215 Why?
    **CLOWN**
'Twill not be seen in him there. There the men are
as mad as he.
    **HAMLET**
220 How came he mad?

    **CLOWN**
Very strangely, they say.
    **HAMLET**
How strangely?
    **CLOWN**     225
Faith, e'en with losing his wits.
    **HAMLET**
Upon what ground?
    **CLOWN**
Why, here in Denmark. I have been sexton here,   230
man and boy, thirty years.
    **HAMLET**
How long will a man lie i' th' earth ere he rot?
    **CLOWN**
Faith, if 'a be not rotten before 'a die (as we have   235
many pocky corses° nowadays that will scarce
hold the laying in), 'a will last you some eight
year or nine year. A tanner will last you nine year.
    **HAMLET**
Why he, more than another?   240
    **CLOWN**
Why, sir, his hide is so tanned with his trade that
'a will keep out water a great while, and your
water is a sore decayer of your whoreson dead
body. Here's a skull now hath lien you i' th' earth   245
three and twenty years.
    **HAMLET**
Whose was it?
    **CLOWN**
A whoreson mad fellow's it was. Whose do you   250
think it was?
    **HAMLET**
Nay, I know not.
    **CLOWN**
A pestilence on him for a mad rogue! 'A poured a   255
flagon of Rhenish on my head once. This same
skull, sir, was, sir, Yorick's skull, the King's jester.
    **HAMLET**
This?
    **CLOWN**   260
E'en that.
    **HAMLET**
Let me see. (*Takes the skull.*) Alas, poor Yorick! I
knew him, Horatio, a fellow of infinite jest, of
most excellent fancy. He hath borne me on his   265
back a thousand times. And now how abhorred in

---

192 **absolute** positive, decided   192–93 **by the card** by the
compass card, i.e., exactly   193 **equivocation** ambiguity
195 **picked** refined   197 **kibe** sore on the back of the heel

236 **pocky corses** bodies of persons who had been infected
with the pox (syphilis)

my imagination it is! My gorge rises at it. Here
hung those lips that I have kissed I know not how
oft. Where be your gibes now? Your gambols,
270 your songs, your flashes of merriment that were
wont to set the table on a roar? Not one now to
mock your own grinning? Quite chapfall'n°?
Now get you to my lady's chamber, and tell her,
let her paint an inch thick, to this favor° she must
275 come. Make her laugh at that. Prithee, Horatio,
tell me one thing.

HORATIO
What's that, my lord?

HAMLET
280 Dost thou think Alexander looked o' this fashion
i' th' earth?

HORATIO
E'en so.

HAMLET
285 And smelt so? Pah! (*Puts down the skull.*)

HORATIO
E'en so, my lord.

HAMLET
To what base uses we may return, Horatio! Why
290 may not imagination trace the noble dust of
Alexander till 'a find it stopping a bunghole?

HORATIO
'Twere to consider too curiously,° to consider so.

HAMLET
295 No, faith, not a jot, but to follow him thither with
modesty enough,° and likelihood to lead it; as
thus: Alexander died, Alexander was buried,
Alexander returneth to dust; the dust is earth; of
earth we make loam; and why of that loam
300 whereto he was converted might they not stop a
beer barrel?
Imperious Caesar, dead and turned to clay,
Might stop a hole to keep the wind away.
O, that that earth which kept the world in awe
305 Should patch a wall t' expel the winter's flaw!°
But soft, but soft awhile! Here comes the King.
*Enter* KING, QUEEN, LAERTES, *and a coffin, with*
LORDS *attendant (and a* DOCTOR *of Divinity).*
The Queen, the courtiers. Who is this they follow?
And with such maimèd° rites? This doth betoken
The corse they follow did with desp'rate hand

Fordo it° own life. 'Twas of some estate.° 310
Couch° we awhile, and mark. (*Retires with*
HORATIO.)

LAERTES
What ceremony else?

HAMLET
That is Laertes, 315
A very noble youth. Mark.

LAERTES
What ceremony else?

DOCTOR
Her obsequies have been as far enlarged 320
As we have warranty. Her death was doubtful,°
And, but that great command o'ersways the order,
She should in ground unsanctified been lodged
Till the last trumpet. For charitable prayers,
Shards,° flints, and pebbles should be thrown on 325
her.
Yet here she is allowed her virgin crants,°
Her maiden strewments,° and the bringing home
Of bell and burial.

LAERTES 330
Must there no more be done?

DOCTOR
No more be done.
We should profane the service of the dead
To sing a requiem and such rest to her 335
As to peace-parted souls.

LAERTES
Lay her i' th' earth,
And from her fair and unpolluted flesh
May violets spring! I tell thee, churlish priest, 340
A minist'ring angel shall my sister be
When thou liest howling!

HAMLET
What, the fair Ophelia?

QUEEN 345
Sweets to the sweet! Farewell.
(*Scatters flowers.*)
I hoped thou shouldst have been my Hamlet's
wife.
I thought thy bride bed to have decked, sweet
maid, 350
And not have strewed thy grave.

272 **chapfall'n** (1) down in the mouth (2) jawless 274 **favor** facial appearance 293 **curiously** minutely 295–296 **with modesty enough** without exaggeration 305 **flaw** gust 308 **maimèd** incomplete

310 **Fordo it** destroy its 310 **estate** high rank 311 **Couch** hide 321 **doubtful** suspicious 325 **Shards** broken pieces of pottery 327 **crants** garlands 328 **strewments** i.e., of flowers

**LAERTES**

O, treble woe

Fall ten times treble on that cursèd head

355 Whose wicked deed thy most ingenious sense°

Deprived thee of! Hold off the earth awhile,

Till I have caught her once more in mine arms.

(*Leaps in the grave.*)

Now pile your dust upon the quick and dead

Till of this flat a mountain you have made

360 T'o'ertop old Pelion° or the skyish head

Of blue Olympus.

**HAMLET**

(*Coming forward*) What is he whose grief

Bears such an emphasis, whose phrase of sorrow

365 Conjures the wand'ring stars,° and makes them

stand

Like wonder-wounded hearers? This is I,

Hamlet the Dane.

**LAERTES**

370 The devil take thy soul! (*Grapples with him.*)°

**HAMLET**

Thou pray'st not well.

I prithee take thy fingers from my throat,

For, though I am not splenitive° and rash,

375 Yet have I in me something dangerous,

Which let thy wisdom fear. Hold off thy hand.

**KING**

Pluck them asunder.

**QUEEN**

380 Hamlet, Hamlet!

**ALL**

Gentlemen!

**HORATIO**

Good my lord, be quiet.

(*Attendants part them.*)

**HAMLET**                                                               385

Why, I will fight with him upon this theme

Until my eyelids will no longer wag.

**QUEEN**

O my son, what theme?

**HAMLET**                                                               390

I loved Ophelia. Forty thousand brothers

Could not with all their quantity of love

Make up my sum. What wilt thou do for her?

**KING**

O, he is mad, Laertes.                                                   395

**QUEEN**

For love of God forbear him.

**HAMLET:** 'Swounds, show me what thou't do.

Woo't weep? Woo't fight? Woo't fast? Woo't tear

thyself?                                                                 400

Woo't drink up eisel?° Eat a crocodile?

I'll do't. Dost thou come here to whine?

To outface me with leaping in her grave?

Be buried quick with her, and so will I.

And if thou prate of mountains, let them throw         405

Millions of acres on us, till our ground,

Singeing his pate against the burning zone,°

Make Ossa like a wart! Nay, an thou'lt mouth,

I'll rant as well as thou.

**QUEEN**                                                                410

This is mere madness;

And thus a while the fit will work on him.

Anon, as patient as the female dove

When that her golden couplets are disclosed,°

His silence will sit drooping.                                           415

**HAMLET**

Hear you, sir.

What is the reason that you use me thus?

I loved you ever. But it is no matter.

Let Hercules himself do what he may,                                     420

The cat will mew, and dog will have his day.

**KING**

I pray thee, good Horatio, wait upon him.

*Exit* **HAMLET** *and* **HORATIO**.

(*To* **LAERTES**) Strengthen your patience

in our last night's speech.                                              425

We'll put the matter to the present push.°

Good Gertrude, set some watch over your son.

355 **most ingenious sense** finely endowed mind  360 **Pe-lion** (according to classical legend, giants in their fight with the gods sought to reach heaven by piling Mount Pelion and Mount Ossa on Mount Olympus)  365 **wand'ring stars** planets  370 s.d. **Grapples with him** (Q1, a bad quarto, presumably reporting a version that toured, has a previous direction saying "Hamlet leaps in after Laertes." Possibly he does so, somewhat hysterically. But such a direction—absent from the two good texts, Q2 and F—makes Hamlet the aggressor, somewhat contradicting his next speech. Perhaps Laertes leaps out of the grave to attack Hamlet)  374 **splenitive** fiery (the spleen was thought to be the seat of anger)

401 **eisel** vinegar  407 **burning zone** sun's orbit  414 **golden couplets are disclosed** (the dove lays two eggs, and the newly hatched [disclosed] young are covered with golden down)  426 **present push** immediate test

This grave shall have a living° monument.
An hour of quiet shortly shall we see;
430 Till then in patience our proceeding be. (*Exeunt.*)

## SCENE II

*The castle.*

*Enter* HAMLET *and* HORATIO.

HAMLET
So much for this, sir; now shall you see the other.
You do remember all the circumstance?

HORATIO
5 Remember it, my lord!

HAMLET
Sir, in my heart there was a kind of fighting
That would not let me sleep. Methought I lay
Worse than the mutines in the bilboes.° Rashly
10 (And praised be rashness for it) let us know,
Our indiscretion sometime serves us well
When our deep plots do pall,° and that should
learn us
There's a divinity that shapes our ends,
15 Rough-hew them how we will.

HORATIO
That is most certain.

HAMLET
Up from my cabin,
20 My sea gown scarfed about me, in the dark
Groped I to find out them, had my desire,
Fingered° their packet, and in fine° withdrew
To mine own room again, making so bold,
My fears forgetting manners, to unseal
25 Their grand commission; where I found,
Horatio—
Ah, royal knavery!—an exact command,
Larded° with many several sorts of reasons,
Importing Denmark's health, and England's too,
30 With, ho, such bugs and goblins in my life,°
That on the supervise,° no leisure bated,°
No, not to stay the grinding of the ax,
My head should be struck off.

HORATIO
Is't possible? 35

HAMLET
Here's the commission; read it at more leisure.
But wilt thou hear now how I did proceed?

HORATIO
I beseech you. 40

HAMLET
Being thus benetted round with villains,
Or° I could make a prologue to my brains,
They had begun the play. I sat me down,
Devised a new commission, wrote it fair. 45
I once did hold it, as our statists° do,
A baseness to write fair,° and labored much
How to forget that learning, but, sir, now
It did me yeoman's service. Wilt thou know
Th' effect° of what I wrote? 50

HORATIO
Ay, good my lord.

HAMLET
An earnest conjuration from the King,
As England was his faithful tributary, 55
As love between them like the palm might
flourish,
As peace should still her wheaten garland wear
And stand a comma° 'tween their amities,
And many suchlike as's of great charge,° 60
That on the view and knowing of these contents,
Without debatement further, more or less,
He should those bearers put to sudden death,
Not shriving° time allowed.

HORATIO
How was this sealed? 65

HAMLET
Why, even in that was heaven ordinant.°
I had my father's signet in my purse,
Which was the model° of that Danish seal, 70
Folded the writ up in the form of th' other,
Subscribed it, gave't th' impression, placed it
safely,
The changeling never known. Now, the next day
Was our sea fight, and what to this was sequent 75
Thou knowest already.

---

428 **living** lasting (with perhaps also a reference to the plot against Hamlet's life) **V.ii. 9 mutines in the bilboes** mutineers in fetters 12 **pall** fail 22 **Fingered** stole 22 **in fine** finally 28 **Larded** enriched 30 **such bugs and goblins in my life** such bugbears and imagined terrors if I were allowed to live 31 **supervise** reading 31 **leisure bated** delay allowed

43 **Or** ere 46 **statists** statesmen 47 **fair** clearly 50 **effect** purport 59 **comma** link 60 **great charge** (1) serious exhortation (2) heavy burden (punning on **as's** and "asses") 64 **shriving** absolution 68 **ordinant** ruling 70 **model** counterpart

**HORATIO**
So Guildenstern and Rosencrantz go to't.
**HAMLET**
80 Why, man, they did make love to this
    employment.
They are not near my conscience; their defeat
Does by their own insinuation° grow.
'Tis dangerous when the baser nature comes
85 Between the pass° and fell° incensèd points
Of mighty opposites.
**HORATIO**
Why, what a king is this!
**HAMLET**
90 Does it not, think thee, stand me now upon°—
He that hath killed my king, and whored my
    mother,
Popped in between th' election° and my hopes,
Thrown out his angle° for my proper life,°
95 And with such coz'nage°—is't not perfect
    conscience
To quit° him with this arm? And is't not to be
    damned
To let this canker of our nature come
100 In further evil?
**HORATIO**
It must be shortly known to him from England
What is the issue of the business there.
**HAMLET**
It will be short; the interim's mine,
105 And a man's life's no more than to say "one."
But I am very sorry, good Horatio,
That to Laertes I forgot myself,
For by the image of my cause I see
The portraiture of his. I'll court his favors.
110 But sure the bravery° of his grief did put me
Into a tow'ring passion.
**HORATIO**
Peace, who comes here?
*Enter young* **OSRIC**, *a courtier.*
**OSRIC**
115 Your lordship is right welcome back to Denmark.
**HAMLET**
I humbly thank you, sir. (*Aside to* **HORATIO**) Dost
    know this waterfly?

**HORATIO**
(*Aside to* **HAMLET**) No, my good lord.     120
**HAMLET**
(*Aside to* **HORATIO**) Thy state is the more
gracious, for 'tis a vice to know him. He hath
much land, and fertile. Let a beast be lord of
beasts, and his crib shall stand at the king's mess.°   125
'Tis a chough,° but, as I say, spacious° in the
possession of dirt.
**OSRIC**
Sweet lord, if your lordship were at leisure, I
should impart a thing to you from his Majesty.   130
**HAMLET**
I will receive it, sir, with all diligence of spirit.
Put your bonnet to his right use. 'Tis for the
head.
**OSRIC**                                            135
I thank your lordship, it is very hot.
**HAMLET**
No, believe me, 'tis very cold; the wind is
northerly.
**OSRIC**                                            140
It is indifferent cold, my lord, indeed.
**HAMLET**
But yet methinks it is very sultry and hot for my
complexion.°
**OSRIC**                                            145
Exceedingly, my lord; it is very sultry, as 'twere
—I cannot tell how. But, my lord, his Majesty
bade me signify to you that 'a has laid a great
wager on your head. Sir, this is the matter—
**HAMLET**                                           150
I beseech you remember.
(**HAMLET** *moves him to put on his hat.*)
**OSRIC**
Nay, good my lord; for my ease, in good faith. Sir,
here is newly come to court Laertes—believe me,
an absolute gentleman, full of most excellent       155
differences,° of very soft society and great
showing. Indeed, to speak feelingly° of him, he is
the card° or calendar of gentry; for you shall find
in him the continent° of what part a gentleman
would see.                                           160

---

83 **insinuation** meddling  85 **pass** thrust  85 **fell** cruel  90
**stand me now upon** become incumbent upon me  93 **election** (the Danish monarchy was elective)  94 **angle** fishing
line  94 **my proper life** my own life  95 **coz'nage** trickery
97 **quit** pay back  110 **bravery** bravado

125 **mess** table  126 **chough** jackdaw (here, chatterer)  126
**spacious** well of  144 **complexion** temperament  156 **differences** distinguishing characteristics  157 **feelingly**
justly  158 **card** chart  159 **continent** summary

HAMLET

Sir, his definement° suffers no perdition° in you,
though, I know, to divide him inventorially
would dozy° th' arithmetic of memory, and yet
165 but yaw neither in respect of his quick sail.° But,
in the verity of extolment, I take him to be a soul
of great article,° and his infusion° of such dearth
and rareness as, to make true diction° of him, his
semblable° is his mirror, and who else would
170 trace him, his umbrage,° nothing more.

OSRIC

Your lordship speaks most infallibly of him.

HAMLET

The concernancy,° sir? Why do we wrap the
175 gentleman in our more rawer breath?

OSRIC

Sir?

HORATIO

Is't not possible to understand in another tongue?
180 You will to't,° sir, really.

HAMLET

What imports the nomination of this gentleman?

OSRIC

Of Laertes?

185 HORATIO

(*Aside to* **HAMLET**) His purse is empty already.
All's golden words are spent.

HAMLET

Of him, sir.

190 OSRIC

I know you are not ignorant——

HAMLET

I would you did, sir; yet, in faith, if you did, it
would not much approve° me. Well, sir?

195 OSRIC

You are not ignorant of what excellence Laertes
is——

HAMLET

I dare not confess that, lest I should compare with
200 him in excellence; but to know a man well were to
know himself.

OSRIC

I mean, sir, for his weapon; but in the imputation°
laid on him by them, in his meed° he's
unfellowed.                                                        205

HAMLET

What's his weapon?

OSRIC

Rapier and dagger.

HAMLET                                                              210

That's two of his weapons—but well.

OSRIC

The King, sir, hath wagered with him six Barbary
horses, against the which he has impawned,° as I
take it, six French rapiers and poniards, with their    215
assigns,° as girdle, hangers,° and so. Three of the
carriages,° in faith, are very dear to fancy, very
responsive° to the hilts, most delicate carriages,
and of very liberal conceit.°

HAMLET                                                              220

What call you the carriages?

HORATIO

(*Aside to* **HAMLET**) I knew you must be edified by
the margent° ere you had done.

OSRIC                                                               225

The carriages, sir, are the hangers.

HAMLET

The phrase would be more germane to the matter
if we could carry a cannon by our sides. I would it
might be hangers till then. But on! Six Barbary      230
horses against six French swords, their assigns,
and three liberal-conceited carriages—that's the
French bet against the Danish. Why is this all
impawned, as you call it?

OSRIC                                                               235

The King, sir, hath laid, sir, that in a dozen passes
between yourself and him he shall not exceed you
three hits; he hath laid on twelve for nine, and it
would come to immediate trial if your lordship
would vouchsafe the answer.                                       240

HAMLET

How if I answer no?

---

162 **definement** description  162 **perdition** loss  164 **dozy**
dizzy  164–65 **and yet . . . quick sail** i.e., and yet only stag-
ger despite all (**yaw neither**) in trying to overtake his
virtues  167 **article** (literally, "item," but here perhaps
"traits" or "importance")  167 **infusion** essential quality
168 **diction** description  169 **semblable** likeness  170 **umbrage** shadow  174 **concernancy** meaning  180 **will to't**
will get there  194 **approve** commend

203 **imputation** reputation  204 **meed** merit  214 **impawned** wagered  216 **assigns** accompaniments  216
**hangers** straps hanging the sword to the belt  217 **carriages** (an affected word for hangers)  218 **responsive** corresponding  219 **liberal conceit** elaborate design  224
**margent** i.e., marginal (explanatory) comment

OSRIC
I mean, my lord, the opposition of your person in
245 trial.

HAMLET
Sir, I will walk here in the hall. If it please his
Majesty, it is the breathing time of day with me.°
Let the foils be brought, the gentleman willing,
250 and the King hold his purpose. I will win for him
an I can; if not, I will gain nothing but my shame
and the odd hits.

OSRIC
Shall I deliver you e'en so?

255 HAMLET
To this effect, sir, after what flourish your nature
will.

OSRIC
I commend my duty to your lordship.

260 HAMLET
Yours, yours. (*Exit* OSRIC.) He does well to
commend it himself; there are no tongues else
for's turn.

HORATIO
265 This lapwing° runs away with the shell on his
head.

HAMLET
'A did comply, sir, with his dug° before 'a sucked
it. Thus he, and many more of the same breed that
270 I know the drossy age dotes on, only got the tune
of the time and, out of an habit of encounter,° a
kind of yeasty° collection, which carries them
through and through the most fanned and
winnowed opinions; and do but blow them to
275 their trial, the bubbles are out.°

*Enter a* LORD.

LORD
My lord, his Ma'esty commended him to you by
young Osric, who brings back to him that you
attend him in the hall. He sends to know if your
280 pleasure hold to play with Laertes, or that you
will take longer time.

HAMLET
I am constant to my purposes; they follow the
King's pleasure. If his fitness speaks, mine is
ready; now or whensoever, provided I be so able    285
as now.

LORD
The King and Queen and all are coming down.

HAMLET
In happy time.    290

LORD
The Queen desires you to use some gentle
entertainment° to Laertes before you fall to play.

HAMLET
She well instructs me. (*Exit* LORD.)    295

HORATIO
You will lose this wager, my lord.

HAMLET
I do not think so. Since he went into France I have
been in continual practice. I shall win at the odds.    300
But thou wouldst not think how ill all's here
about my heart. But it is no matter.

HORATIO
Nay, good my lord——

HAMLET    305
It is but foolery, but it is such a kind of
gaingiving° as would perhaps trouble a woman.

HORATIO
If your mind dislike anything, obey it. I will
forestall their repair hither and say you are not fit.    310

HAMLET
Not a whit, we defy augury. There is special
providence in the fall of a sparrow.° If it be now,
'tis not to come; if it be not to come, it will be
now; if it be not now, yet it will come. The    315
readiness is all. Since no man of aught he leaves
knows, what is't to leave betimes?° Let be.
*A table prepared.* (*Enter*) TRUMPETS, DRUMS, *and*
OFFICERS *with cushions;* KING, QUEEN, (OSRIC,)
*and all the* STATE, (*with*) *foils, daggers, (and stoups of
wine borne in); and* LAERTES.

KING
Come, Hamlet, come, and take this hand from me.
(*The* KING *puts* LAERTES' *hand into* HAMLET'S.)

248 **breathing time of day with me** time when I take
exercise 265 **lapwing** (the new-hatched lapwing was
thought to run around with half its shell on its head) 268
**'A did comply, sir, with his dug** he was ceremoniously
polite to his mother's breast 271 **out of an habit of encounter** out of his own superficial way of meeting and
conversing with people 272 **yeasty** frothy 275 **the bubbles are out** i.e., they are blown away (the reference is to
the "yeasty collection")

292–93 **to use some gentle entertainment** to be courteous
307 **gaingiving** misgiving 313 **the fall of a sparrow** (cf.
Matthew 10:29 "Are not two sparrows sold for a farthing?
and one of them shall not fall on the ground without your
Father") 317 **betimes** early

**HAMLET**

320 Give me your pardon, sir. I have done you wrong,
But pardon't, as you are a gentleman.
This presence° knows, and you must needs have heard,
325 How I am punished with a sore distraction.
What I have done
That might your nature, honor, and exception°
Roughly awake, I here proclaim was madness.
Was't Hamlet wronged Laertes? Never Hamlet.
330 If Hamlet from himself be ta'en away,
And when he's not himself does wrong Laertes,
Then Hamlet does it not, Hamlet denies it.
Who does it then? His madness. If't be so,
Hamlet is of the faction° that is wronged;
335 His madness is poor Hamlet's enemy.
Sir, in this audience,
Let my disclaiming from a purposed evil
Free me so far in your most generous thoughts
That I have shot my arrow o'er the house
340 And hurt my brother.

**LAERTES**

I am satisfied in nature,
Whose motive in this case should stir me most
345 To my revenge. But in my terms of honor
I stand aloof, and will no reconcilement
Till by some elder masters of known honor
I have a voice and precedent° of peace
To keep my name ungored. But till that time
350 I do receive your offered love like love,
And will not wrong it.

**HAMLET**

I embrace it freely,
And will this brother's wager frankly play.
355 Give us the foils. Come on.

**LAERTES**

Come, one for me.

**HAMLET**

I'll be your foil,° Laertes. In mine ignorance
360 Your skill shall, like a star i' th' darkest night,
Stick fiery off° indeed.

**LAERTES**

You mock me, sir.

**HAMLET**

No, by this hand.                                                           365

**KING**

Give me the foils, young Osric. Cousin Hamlet,
You know the wager?

**HAMLET**

Very well, my lord.                                                         370
Your grace has laid the odds o' th' weaker side.

**KING**

I do not fear it, I have seen you both;
But since he is bettered,° we have therefore odds.

**LAERTES**                                                                 375

This is too heavy; let me see another.

**HAMLET**

This likes me well. These foils have all a length?
*Prepare to play.*

**OSRIC**

Ay, my good lord.                                                           380

**KING**

Set me the stoups of wine upon that table.
If Hamlet give the first or second hit,
Or quit° in answer of the third exchange,
Let all the battlements their ordnance fire.                                385
The King shall drink to Hamlet's better breath,
And in the cup an union° shall be throw
Richer than that which four successive kings
In Denmark's crown have worn. Give me the cups,                             390
And let the kettle° to the trumpet speak,
The trumpet to the cannoneer without,
The cannons to the heavens, the heaven to earth,
"Now the King drinks to Hamlet." Come, begin.
*Trumpets the while.*
And you, the judges, bear a wary eye.                                       395

**HAMLET**

Come on, sir.

**LAERTES**

Come, my lord. *They play.*

**HAMLET**                                                                  400

One.

**LAERTES**

No.

**HAMLET**

Judgment?                                                                   405

**OSRIC**

A hit, a very palpable hit.
*Drum, trumpets, and shot. Flourish; a piece goes off.*

---

323 **presence** royal assembly  327 **exception** disapproval
334 **faction** party, side  348 **voice and precedent** authoritative opinion justified by precedent  359 **foil** (1) blunt sword (2) background (of metallic leaf) for a jewel  361 **Stick fiery off** stand out brilliantly

374 **bettered** has improved (in France)  384 **quit** repay, hit back  387 **union** pearl  391 **kettle** kettledrum

**LAERTES**

Well, again.

410  **KING**

Stay, give me drink. Hamlet, this pearl is thine.
Here's to thy health. Give him the cup.

**HAMLET**

I'll play this bout first; set it by awhile.

415  Come. (*They play.*) Another hit. What say you?

**LAERTES**

A touch, a touch; I do confess't.

**KING**

Our son shall win.

420  **QUEEN**

He's fat,° and scant of breath.
Here, Hamlet, take my napkin, rub thy brows.
The Queen carouses to thy fortune, Hamlet.

**HAMLET**

425  Good madam!

**KING**

Gertrude, do not drink.

**QUEEN**

I will, my lord; I pray you pardon me. (*Drinks.*)

430  **KING**

(*Aside*) It is the poisoned cup; it is too late.

**HAMLET**

I dare not drink yet, madam—by and by.

**QUEEN**

435  Come, let me wipe thy face.

**LAERTES**

My lord, I'll hit him now.

**KING**

I do not think't.

440  **LAERTES**

(*Aside*) And yet it is almost against my conscience.

**HAMLET**

Come for the third, Laertes. You do but dally.
I pray you pass with your best violence;

445  I am sure you make a wanton° of me.

**LAERTES**

Say you so? Come on. (*They*) *play.*

**OSRIC**

Nothing neither way.

450  **LAERTES**

Have at you now!
*In scuffling they change rapiers, (and both are
wounded).*

**KING**

Part them. They are incensed.

**HAMLET**

Nay, come—again! (*The* **QUEEN** *falls.*)          455

**OSRIC**

Look to the Queen there, ho!

**HORATIO**

'They bleed on both sides. How is it, my lord?

**OSRIC**                                           460

How is't, Laertes?

**LAERTES**

Why, as a woodcock to mine own springe,° Osric.
I am justly killed with mine own treachery.

**HAMLET**                                          465

How does the Queen?

**KING**

She sounds° to see them bleed.

**QUEEN**

No, no, the drink, the drink! O my dear Hamlet!     470
The drink, the drink! I am poisoned. (*Dies.*)

**HAMLET**

O villainy! Ho! Let the door be locked.
Treachery! Seek it out. (**LAERTES** *falls.*)

**LAERTES**                                         475

It is here, Hamlet. Hamlet, thou art slain;
No medicine in the world can do thee good.
In thee there is not half an hour's life.
The treacherous instrument is in thy hand,
Unbated and envenomed. The foul practice°        480
Hath turned itself on me. Lo, here I lie,
Never to rise again. Thy mother's poisoned.
I can no more. The King, the King's to blame.

**HAMLET**

The point envenomed too?                            485
Then, venom, to thy work. *Hurts the* **KING**.

**ALL**

Treason! Treason!

**KING**

O, yet defend me, friends. I am but hurt.           490

**HAMLET**

Here, thou incestuous, murd'rous, damnèd
Dane,
Drink off his potion. Is thy union here?
Follow my mother. **KING** *dies.*                  495

**LAERTES**

He is justly served.
It is a poison tempered° by himself.

---

421 **fat** (1) sweaty (2) out of training  445 **wanton** spoiled
child

463 **springe** snare  468 **sounds** swoons  480 **practice** deception  498 **tempered** mixed

Exchange forgiveness with me, noble Hamlet.
500 Mine and my father's death come not upon thee,
Nor thine on me! (*Dies.*)
　　　HAMLET
Heaven make thee free of it! I follow thee.
I am dead, Horatio. Wretched Queen, adieu!
505 You that look pale and tremble at this chance,
That are but mutes°, or audience to this act,
Had I but time (as this fell sergeant,° Death,
Is strict in his arrest) O, I could tell you—
But let it be. Horatio, I am dead;
510 Thou livest; report me and my cause aright
To the unsatisfied.°
　　　HORATIO
Never believe it.
I am more an antique Roman° than a Dane.
515 Here's yet some liquor left.
　　　HAMLET
As th' art a man,
Give me the cup. Let go. By heaven, I'll ha't!
O God, Horatio, what a wounded name,
520 Things standing thus unknown, shall live behind
　　　me!
If thou didst ever hold me in thy heart,
Absent thee from felicity° awhile,
And in this harsh world draw thy breath in pain,
525 To tell my story. *A march afar off.* (*Exit* OSRIC.)
What warlike noise is this?
*Enter* OSRIC.
　　　OSRIC
Young Fortinbras, with conquest come from
　　　Poland,
530 To th' ambassadors of England gives
This warlike volley.
　　　HAMLET
O, I die, Horatio!
The potent poison quite o'ercrows° my spirit.
535 I cannot live to hear the news from England,
But I do prophesy th' election lights
On Fortinbras. He has my dying voice.
So tell him, with th' occurrents,° more and less,
Which have solicited°—the rest is silence. (*Dies.*)

　　　HORATIO                                                         540
Now cracks a noble heart. Good night, sweet
　　　Prince,
And flights of angels sing thee to thy rest.
(*March within.*)
Why does the drum come hither?
*Enter* FORTINBRAS, *with the* AMBASSADORS *with*
DRUM, COLORS, *and* ATTENDANTS.
　　　FORTINBRAS                                                      545
Where is this sight?
　　　HORATIO
What is it you would see?
If aught of woe or wonder, cease your search.
　　　FORTINBRAS                                                      550
This quarry° cries on havoc.° O proud Death,
What feast is toward° in thine eternal cell
That thou so many princes at a shot
So bloodily hast struck?
　　　AMBASSADOR                                                      555
The sight is dismal;
And our affairs from England come too late.
The ears are senseless that should give us hearing
To tell him his commandment is fulfilled,
That Rosencrantz and Guildenstern are dead.       560
Where should we have our thanks?
　　　HORATIO
Not from his° mouth,
Had it th' ability of life to thank you.
He never gave commandment for their death.        565
But since, so jump° upon this bloody question,
You from the Polack wars, and you from England,
Are here arrived, give order that these bodies
High on a stage° be placèd to the view,
And let me speak to th' yet unknowing world        570
How these things came about. So shall you hear
Of carnal, bloody, and unnatural acts,
Of accidental judgments, casual° slaughters,
Of deaths put on by cunning and forced cause,
And, in this upshot, purposes mistook              575
Fall'n on th' inventors' heads. All this can I
Truly deliver.
　　　FORTINBRAS
Let us haste to hear it,
And call the noblest to the audience.              580
For me, with sorrow I embrace my fortune.

---

506 **mutes** performers who have no words to speak  507
**fell sergeant** dread sheriff's officer  511 **unsatisfied** uninformed  514 **antique Roman** (with reference to the old
Roman fashion of suicide)  523 **felicity** i.e., the felicity of
death  534 **o'ercrows** overpowers (as a triumphant cock
crows over its weak opponent)  538 **occurrents** occur-
rences  539 **solicited** incited

551 **quarry** heap of slain bodies  551 **cries on havoc** proclaims general slaughter  552 **toward** in preparation  563
**his** (Claudius')  566 **jump** precisely  569 **stage** platform
573 **casual** not humanly planned, chance

I have some rights of memory° in this kingdom,
Which now to claim my vantage doth invite me.
    **HORATIO**
585 Of that I shall have also cause to speak,
And from his mouth whose voice will draw on°
    more.
But let this same be presently performed,
Even while men's minds are wild, lest more
590     mischance
On° plots and errors happen.
    **FORTINBRAS**
Let four captains
Bear Hamlet like a soldier to the stage,
595 For he was likely, had he been put on,°
To have proved most royal; and for his passage°
The soldiers' music and the rite of war
Speak loudly for him.
Take up the bodies. Such a sight as this
600 Becomes the field,° but here shows much amiss.
Go, bid the soldiers shoot.
*Exeunt marching; after the which a peal of ordnance
are shot off.*
        FINIS

582 **rights of memory** remembered claims  586 **voice will
draw on** vote will influence  591 **On** on top of  595 **put on**
advanced (to the throne)  596 **passage** death  600 **field**
battlefield

## SUMMARY

A play's structure is largely shaped by two factors: how the writer perceives human experience and by established writing conventions he or she may adopt, reject, or alter in the creation of a play. A play's structure is also influenced in large measure by society and by the theatre conventions of the time. Sophocles' methods of organizing human activities in *Oedipus the King* reflect not only the writer's vision of humanity's relation to the universe but also his vision of the plays mirroring its theatre and times. The controlled, orderly development of Oedipus' unrelenting quest for truth reflects a moral philosophy grounded in cause and effect;

that is, all acts have predictable consequences. Moreover, the conventions of the fifth-century Greek theatre required that the principal episodes be separated by choral odes, and that the episodes include the messenger's report, the arias of suffering, and confrontations between hero and others. Climactic (classical) structure takes its name from the ever-contracting circle of the hero's choices which leads quickly to discovery and resolution.

In contrast, Elizabethan playwrights developed an expanding progression of events as a variation on the medieval idea of "life as a journey" between birth and death. Like the Greeks, they also perceived an orderly world whose theatre was a mirror held up to a divinely appointed universe. Mirroring a cosmic order, episodic structure is expansive, encompassing many characters, events, locations, and years. It conforms to a kind of fluid staging where any and all can happen—from shipwrecks to battles to love scenes. There are leaps in time, gaps between events, and variety in characters and circumstances. Action becomes journey in the present, not confrontation with the past.

Playwrights of modern realism, like Henrik Ibsen and August Strindberg, adhered largely to the older compressed play structure to demonstrate the causes and effects of heredity and environment on individuals and societies. Climactic play structure continues to be popular among writers for our commercial theatre because of its compressed action and limited characters.

However, in its self-conscious departure from the past, our modern age has also evolved eclectic forms to mirror its disjunctions: epic (for episodic), situational (for absurd), and reflexive (for postmodern). Each term describes a particular vision of the world which structures time, space, and situations that both mirror and comment upon the writer's understanding of the human condition.

## NOTES

1. Bertolt Brecht, "A Short Organon for the Theatre," *Brecht on Theatre: The Development of an Aesthetic,* trans. and ed. John Willett (New York: Hill and Wang, 1964): 204.

2. Suzanne K. Langer, *Feeling and Form: A Theory of Art* (New York: Charles Scribner's Sons, 1953): 307.

3. For my understanding of climactic and episodic play structure, I am indebted to Bernard Beckerman's fine discussion in *Dynamics of Dramas: Theory and Method of Analysis* (New York: Alfred A. Knopf, 1970): 186–209.

4. Eugene Ionesco, *Notes and Counter Notes: Writings on the Theatre,* trans. Donald Watson (New York: Grove Press, 1964): 257.

5. Martin Esslin, "The Theatre of the Absurd," *Theatre in the Twentieth Century,* ed. Robert W. Corrigan (New York: Grove Press, 1963): 233.

6. Esslin 244.

7. G. Wilson Knight, *The Wheel of Fire: Interpretations of Shakespearean Tragedy* (New York: Meridian Books, 1957): 46.

# The Glass Menagerie

## TENNESSEE WILLIAMS

*Tennessee Williams (1911–1983) was born Thomas Lanier Williams in Columbus, Mississippi, the son of a traveling salesman and an Episcopalian minister's daughter. The family, including siblings Rose Isabel and Walter Dakin, moved to St. Louis in 1918 where Williams grew up. He was educated at Missouri University, Washington University (St. Louis), and later at the University of Iowa where he received his B.A. degree.*

*In 1939, Story magazine published his short story, "The Field of Blue Children," the first work to appear under the name "Tennessee" Williams, which was probably a nickname given to him in college because of his southern accent. Earlier that year, he won a Group Theatre prize with* American Blues *(one-acts) and attracted the interest of New York agent Audrey Wood, who represented him for the next thirty-two years.*

*In 1945* The Glass Menagerie *marked Williams' first major success and established him as an important American playwright. Two years later with the resounding Broadway success of* A Streetcar Named Desire, *Williams was acclaimed as the "new" Eugene O'Neill. Other major plays followed:* Summer and Smoke *(1948),* The Rose Tattoo *(1951),* Camino Real *(1953),* Cat on a Hot Tin Roof *(1955),* Sweet Bird of Youth *(1959), and* The Night of the Iguana *(1961). Though his later plays, such as* Small Craft Warnings *(1972) and* Vieux Carré *(1977), failed to please critics, he continued to write until his death. Williams is our preeminent American playwright, having added at least five major plays to the modern repertory along with some of the great dramatic roles: Amanda Wingfield, Blanche DuBois, Stanley Kowalski, Alma Winemiller, Serafina Delle Rose, Big Daddy Pollitt, and Alexandra del Lago.*

## INTRODUCTION

*The Glass Menagerie*, written in 1944 and originally titled *The Gentleman Caller*, is one of the great plays of the American theatre whose central characters—Amanda, Tom, and Laura—are emotionally and economically maimed individuals. In the play's action, they became powerful images of human alienation and despair. The play's events trace, in seven scenes, Tom's memories of his family in the 1930s through the crisis leading up to his escape from his stultifying home and job. The Wingfield family is physically isolated in a St. Louis tenement building. (Their apartment faces on an alleyway and is entered by a fire escape.) The father, whose photograph hangs on the living room wall, abandoned his wife and two children long ago. As Tom says of his father, "He was a telephone man who fell in love with long distances. . . ."

Williams' characters are a blend of self-absorbing needs and desperate courage. His "menagerie" is comprised of the oppressed, the fragile, and the needful. Amanda Wingfield reincarnates pride, pretensions, disappointment, perseverance, and desperation. She clings to her illusions of a more gentle life in the Mississippi Delta and of the exhilaration of receiving seventeen gentlemen callers in one youthful day. Her daughter Laura, physically impaired from a childhood illness, has retreated in young adulthood into her own fantasy world. Like a piece from her glass animal collection from which the play takes its title, Laura is too fragile to come into contact with the harsh realities of a world where her need for love, companionship, and self-esteem are unlikely to be fulfilled. Tom, who carries the playwright's name, escapes his life of boredom by going to movies night after night. He finally chooses the merchant marine over his life of domestic entrapment.

The fourth character is the "gentleman caller" who brings the reality of the outside world into their lives. In one brief evening, he introduces hope, warmth, sympathy, companionship, and finally disillusionment into their lives. He is a "nice, ordinary, young man" who comes to dinner at Tom's invitation urged on by his mother to provide an eligible suitor for his sister. However, the outsider becomes the playwright's catalyst for demonstrating to his hero-narrator the gap between what is and what ought to be. Williams described the dinner guest as "the long-delayed but always expected something we live for." After the gentleman caller departs, nothing will ever again be the same for the Wingfield family. While Amanda keeps up the pretense that there will be others, Laura and Tom can no longer sustain their illusions about the life their mother imagines is just around the corner for them: success and marriage. Tom escapes to freedom, though not from his guilt for abandoning his family; and the candles, which illuminate the real world of unpaid electric bills, are forever snuffed out in Laura's life as she retreats further from reality into a world inhabited by glass replicas of animals which can be fondled and loved, but can never wound or frighten.

Williams called this play about human desperation and courage a "memory" play. Tom, the poet-narrator, exists both without and within the play. In seven scenes, he narrates his memories of another time, place, occasion, and family. Dressed as a merchant seaman, a sign of his apartness, he sets the

beginning scene: "I am the narrator of the play, and also a character in it." As narrator, he controls time past and present. The drama is enriched by the imaginative freedom of the narrator to choose scenes, seemingly at will, and to tell his story of illusion and despair. By using the device of a narrator, the harsh reality of the Wingfield family's impoverished existence is softened and blurred because they are, in one sense, creatures of Tom's imagination. In the same way, Amanda and Laura's illusions soften and blur their perceptions of reality. To one, southern gentility and mores are the operable way of life; to the other, isolation in daydreams provides refuge from a frightening world.

To enhance the slightly unreal presentation of the play's world, Williams originally called for such expressionistic staging devices as the use of projections or "legends" to label scenes (these were omitted from the original production) and the use of a scrim ("the transparent fourth wall of the building") to ascend out of sight of the audience after the opening scene and to descend again during Tom's final speech. The scrim was to remind audiences that the play was the invention of a dramatic character and should be viewed as events projected from memory and distanced by time.

However, the social and psychological dimensions of the characters are wholly clear (and realistic) in Williams' exploration of the "beauty and meaning in the confusion of living." Tom Wingfield is oppressed by the suffocating realities of his daily life at the warehouse and in his mother's home. Amanda desperately sets herself the task of marrying Laura off in an act both selfish and cruel. Laura, shy and handicapped, retreats from her mother's ambitions into an imaginative world of glass animals whose fragility and uniqueness replicate her own. In the end, both siblings escape the dangerous world of burning human needs; only their strategies differ. Moreover, the fact that the Wingfield home is entered by a fire escape is no accidental poetic image. In scene seven, Tom exits the smoldering embers of his mother's and sister's desperation.

The story as told by Tom-the-poet is likewise *his* glass menagerie. The images from his past are fragile, distorted by memory and vulnerable to time. They even have names: Amanda, Laura, Tom. As Williams says of him, he is "a poet with a job in a warehouse. His nature is not remorseless, but to escape from a trap he has to act without pity." But, in telling the story from afar, Tom makes an effort to explain and ameliorate his sense of guilt for abandoning, like his father before him, his familial responsibilities in the name of peace and freedom.

Williams' characters, such as we find in *The Glass Menagerie*, carry a knowledge that pain and defeat await them both in the real and in the imagined world. For them, there is no escape from life's anguish and loneliness. Nevertheless, Williams celebrates courage and compassion in his maimed and anguished characters. Despite her selfishness, Amanda has tried to help her children; despite her infirmity, Laura has tried to adjust to the world outside; despite his frustrations, Tom has attempted to be a responsible son and brother. They have consistently failed. The knowledge of their failure and of their courage to go on despite failure is Williams' celebration of humanity's endurance and quiet nobility.

# The Glass Menagerie

*Nobody, not even the rain, has such small hands.*
—e. e. cummings

**SCENE**

*An Alley in St. Louis*

 *Part I. Preparation for a Gentleman Caller.*
 *Part II. The Gentleman Calls.*
 *Time: Now and the Past.*

**THE CHARACTERS**

**AMANDA WINGFIELD** (*the mother*) A little woman of great but confused vitality clinging frantically to another time and place. Her characterization must be carefully created, not copied from type. She is not paranoiac, but her life is paranoia. There is much to admire in Amanda, and as much to love and pity as there is to laugh at. Certainly she has endurance and a kind of heroism, and though her foolishness makes her unwittingly cruel at times, there is tenderness in her slight person.

**LAURA WINGFIELD** (*her daughter*) Amanda, having failed to establish contact with reality, continues to live vitally in her illusions, but Laura's situation is even graver. A childhood illness has left her crippled, one leg slightly shorter than the other, and held in a brace. This defect need not be more than suggested on the stage. Stemming from this, Laura's separation increases till she is like a piece of her own glass collection, too exquisitely fragile to move from the shelf.

**TOM WINGFIELD** (*her son*) And the narrator of the play. A poet with a job in a warehouse. His nature is not remorseless, but to escape from a trap he has to act without pity.

**JIM O'CONNOR** (*the gentleman caller*) A nice, ordinary, young man.

## SCENE ONE

*The Wingfield apartment is in the rear of the building, one of those vast hive-like conglomerations of cellular living-units that flower as warty growths in overcrowded urban centers of lower middle-class population and are symptomatic of the impulse of this largest and fundamentally enslaved section of American society to avoid fluidity and differentiation and to exist and function as one interfused mass of automatism.*

*The apartment faces an alley and is entered by a fire escape, a structure whose name is a touch of accidental poetic truth, for all of these huge buildings are always burning with the slow and implacable fires of human desperation. The fire escape is part of what we see—that is, the landing of it and steps descending from it.*

*The scene is memory and is therefore nonrealistic. Memory takes a lot of poetic license. It omits some details; others are exaggerated, according to the emotional value of the articles it touches, for memory is seated predominantly in the heart. The interior is therefore rather dim and poetic.*

*At the rise of the curtain, the audience is faced with the dark, grim rear wall of the Wingfield tenement. This building is flanked on both sides by dark, narrow alleys which run into murky canyons of tangled clotheslines, garbage cans, and the sinister latticework of neighboring fire escapes. It is up and down these side alleys that exterior entrances and exits are made during the play. At the end of* **TOM'S** *opening commentary, the dark tenement wall slowly becomes* *transparent and reveals the interior of the ground-floor Wingfield apartment.*

*Nearest the audience is the living room, which also serves as a sleeping room for* LAURA, *the sofa unfolding to make her bed. Just beyond, separated from the living room by a wide arch or second proscenium with transparent faded portieres (or second curtain), is the dining room. In an old-fashioned whatnot in the living room are seen scores of transparent glass animals. A blown-up photograph of the father hangs on the wall of the living room, to the left of the archway. It is the face of a very handsome young man in a doughboy's First World War cap. He is gallantly smiling, ineluctably smiling, as if to say "I will be smiling forever."*

*Also hanging on the wall, near the photograph, are a typewriter keyboard chart and a Gregg shorthand diagram. An upright typewriter on a small table stands beneath the charts.*

*The audience hears and sees the opening scene in the dining room through both the transparent fourth wall of the building and the transparent gauze portieres of the dining-room arch. It is during this revealing scene that the fourth wall slowly ascends, out of sight. This transparent exterior wall is not brought down again until the very end of the play, during Tom's final speech.*

*The narrator is an undisguised convention of the play. He takes whatever license with dramatic convention is convenient to his purposes.*

TOM *enters, dressed as a merchant sailor, and strolls across to the fire escape. There he stops and lights a cigarette. He addresses the audience.*

TOM:  Yes, I have tricks in my pocket, I have things up my sleeve. But I am the opposite of a stage magician. He gives you illusion that has the appearance of truth. I give you truth in the pleasant disguise of illusion.

To begin with, I turn back time. I reverse it to that quaint period, the thirties, when the huge middle class of America was matriculating in a school for the blind. Their eyes had failed them, or they had failed their eyes, and so they were having their fingers pressed forcibly down on the fiery Braille alphabet of a dissolving economy.

In Spain there was revolution. Here there was only shouting and confusion. In Spain there was Guernica. Here there were disturbances of labor, sometimes pretty violent, in otherwise peaceful cities such as Chicago, Cleveland, Saint Louis . . .

This is the social background of the play.

*Music begins to play.*

The play is memory. Being a memory play, it is dimly lighted, it is sentimental, it is not realistic. In memory everything seems to happen to music. That explains the fiddle in the wings.

I am the narrator of the play, and also a character in it. The other characters are my mother, Amanda, my sister, Laura, and a gentleman caller who appears in the final scenes. He is the most realistic character in the play, being an emissary from a world of reality that we were somehow set apart from. But since I have a poet's weakness for symbols, I am using this character also as a symbol; he is the long-delayed but always expected something that we live for. There is a fifth character in the play who doesn't appear except in this larger-than-life-size photograph over the mantel. This is our father who left us a long time ago. He was a telephone man who fell in love with long distances; he gave up his job with the telephone company and skipped the light fantastic out of town . . .

The last we heard of him was a picture postcard from Mazatlan, on the Pacific coast of Mexico, containing a message of two words: "Hello—Goodbye!" and no address.

I think the rest of the play will explain itself . . .

AMANDA'S *voice becomes audible through the portieres.*

*Legend on screen: "Ou sont les neiges."*

TOM *divides the portieres and enters the dining room.* AMANDA *and* LAURA *are seated at a drop-leaf table. Eating is indicated by gestures without food or utensils.* AMANDA *faces the audience.* TOM *and* LAURA *are seated in profile. The interior has lit up softly and through the scrim we see* AMANDA *and* LAURA *seated at the table.*

AMANDA (*calling*): Tom?

TOM: Yes, Mother.

AMANDA: We can't say grace until you come to the table!

TOM: Coming, Mother. (*He bows slightly and withdraws, reappearing a few moments later in his place at the table.*)

AMANDA (*to her son*): Honey, don't *push* with your *fingers.* If you have to push with something, the thing to push with is a crust of bread. And chew—chew! Animals have secretions in their stomachs which enable them to digest food without mastication, but human beings are supposed to chew their food before they swallow it down. Eat food leisurely, son, and really enjoy it. A well-cooked meal has lots of delicate flavors that have to be held in the mouth for appreciation. So chew your food and give your salivary glands a chance to function!

TOM *deliberately lays his imaginary fork down and pushes his chair back from the table.*

TOM: I haven't enjoyed one bite of this dinner because of your constant directions on how to eat it. It's you that make me rush through meals with your hawklike attention to every bite I take. Sickening—spoils my appetite—all this discussion of—animals' secretion—salivary glands—mastication!

AMANDA (*lightly*): Temperament like a Metropolitan star!

TOM *rises and walks toward the living room.* You're not excused from the table.

TOM: I'm getting a cigarette.

AMANDA: You smoke too much.

LAURA *rises.*

LAURA: I'll bring in the blanc mange.

TOM *remains standing with his cigarette by the portieres.*

AMANDA (*rising*): No, sister, no, sister—you be the lady this time and I'll be the darky.

LAURA: I'm already up.

AMANDA: Resume your seat, little sister—I want you to stay fresh and pretty—for gentlemen callers!

LAURA (*sitting down*): I'm not expecting any gentlemen callers.

AMANDA (*crossing out to the kitchenette, airily*): Sometimes they come when they are least expected! Why, I remember one Sunday afternoon in Blue Mountain—

*She enters the kitchenette.*

TOM: I know what's coming!

LAURA: Yes. But let her tell it.

TOM: Again?

LAURA: She loves to tell it.

AMANDA *returns with a bowl of dessert.*

AMANDA: One Sunday afternoon in Blue Mountain—your mother received—*seventeen!*—gentlemen callers! Why, sometimes there weren't chairs enough to accommodate them all. We had to send the nigger over to bring in folding chairs from the parish house.

TOM (*remaining at the portieres*): How did you entertain those gentlemen callers?

AMANDA: I understood the art of conversation!

TOM: I bet you could talk.

AMANDA: Girls in those days *knew* how to talk, I can tell you.

TOM: Yes?

*Image on screen: Amanda as a girl on a porch, greeting callers.*

AMANDA: They knew how to entertain their gentlemen callers. It wasn't enough for a girl to be possessed of a pretty face and a graceful figure—although I wasn't slighted in either respect. She also needed to have a nimble wit and a tongue to meet all occasions.

TOM: What did you talk about?

AMANDA: Things of importance going on in the world! Never anything coarse or common or vulgar.

*She addresses* TOM *as though he were seated in the vacant chair at the table though he remains by the portieres. He plays this scene as though reading from a script.*

My callers were gentlemen—all! Among my callers were some of the most prominent young planters of the Mississippi Delta—planters and sons of planters!

TOM *motions for music and a spot of light on* AMANDA. *Her eyes lift, her face glows, her voice becomes rich and elegiac.*

*Screen legend: "Ou sont les neiges d'antan?"*

There was young Champ Laughlin who later became vice-president of the Delta Planters Bank. Hadley Stevenson who was drowned in Moon Lake and left his widow one hundred and fifty thousand in Government bonds. There were the Cutrere brothers, Wesley and Bates. Bates was one of my bright particular beaux! He got in a quarrel with that wild Wainwright boy. They shot it out on the floor of Moon Lake Casino. Bates was shot through the stomach. Died in the ambulance on his way to Memphis. His widow was also well provided-for, came into eight or ten thousand acres, that's all. She married him on the rebound—never loved her—carried my picture on him the night he died! And there was that boy that every girl in the Delta had set her cap for! That beautiful, brilliant young Fitzhugh boy from Greene County!

TOM: What did he leave his widow?

AMANDA: He never married! Gracious, you talk as though all of my old admirers had turned up their toes to the daisies!

TOM: Isn't this the first you've mentioned that still survives?

AMANDA: That Fitzhugh boy went North and made a fortune—came to be known as the Wolf of Wall Street! He had the Midas touch, whatever he touched turned to gold! And I could have been Mrs. Duncan J. Fitzhugh, mind you! But—I picked your *father!*

LAURA (*rising*): Mother, let me clear the table.

AMANDA: No, dear, you go in front and study your typewriter chart. Or practice your shorthand a little. Stay fresh and pretty!—It's almost time for our gentlemen callers to start arriving. (*She flounces girlishly toward the kitchenette*) How many do you suppose we're going to entertain this afternoon?

TOM *throws down the paper and jumps up with a groan.*

LAURA (*alone in the dining room*): I don't believe we're going to receive any, Mother.

AMANDA (*reappearing airily*): What? No one —not one? You must be joking!

LAURA *nervously echoes her laugh. She slips in a fugitive manner through the half-open portieres and draws them gently behind her. A shaft of very clear light is thrown on her face against the faded tapestry of the curtains. Faintly the music of "The Glass Menagerie" is heard as she continues, lightly:*

Not one gentleman caller? It can't be true! There must be a flood, there must have been a tornado!

LAURA: It isn't a flood, it's not a tornado, Mother. I'm just not popular like you were in Blue Mountain. . . .

TOM *utters another groan.* LAURA *glances at him with a faint, apologetic smile. Her voice catches a little:*

Mother's afraid I'm going to be an old maid.

*The scene dims out with the "Glass Menagerie" music.*

# SCENE TWO

*On the dark stage the screen is lighted with the image of blue roses. Gradually* LAURA'S *figure becomes apparent and the screen goes out. The music subsides.*

    LAURA *is seated in the delicate ivory chair at the small clawfoot table. She wears a dress of soft violet material for a kimono—her hair is tied back from her forehead with a ribbon. She is washing and polishing her collection of glass.* AMANDA *appears on the fire escape steps. At the sound of her ascent,* LAURA *catches her breath, thrusts the bowl of ornaments away, and seats herself stiffly before the diagram of the typewriter keyboard as though it held her spellbound. Something has happened to* AMANDA. *It is written in her face as she climbs to the landing: a look that is grim and hopeless and a little absurd. She has on one of those cheap or imitation velvety-looking cloth coats with imitation fur collar. Her hat is five or six years old, one of those dreadful cloche hats that were worn in the late Twenties, and she is clutching an enormous black patent-leather pocketbook with nickel clasps and initials. This is her full-dress outfit, the one she usually wears to the D.A.R. Before entering she looks through the door. She purses her lips, opens her eyes very wide, rolls them upward and shakes her head. Then she slowly lets herself in the door. Seeing her mother's expression* LAURA *touches her lips with a nervous gesture.*

LAURA: Hello, Mother, I was—(*She makes a nervous gesture toward the chart on the wall.* AMANDA *leans against the shut door and stares at* LAURA *with a martyred look.*)

AMANDA: Deception? Deception? (*She slowly removes her hat and gloves, continuing the sweet suffering stare. She lets the hat and gloves fall on the floor—a bit of acting.*)

LAURA (*shakily*): How was the D.A.R. meeting?

    AMANDA *slowly opens her purse and removes a dainty white handkerchief which she shakes out delicately and delicately touches to her lips and nostrils.*

Didn't you go to the D.A.R. meeting, Mother?

AMANDA (*faintly, almost inaudibly*): —No.— No. (*then more forcibly:*) I did not have the strength—to go to the D.A.R. In fact, I did not have the courage! I wanted to find a hole in the ground and hide myself in it forever! (*She crosses slowly to the wall and removes the diagram of the typewriter keyboard. She holds it in front of her for a second, staring at it sweetly and sorrowfully—then bites her lips and tears it in two pieces.*)

LAURA (*faintly*): Why did you do that, Mother?

    AMANDA *repeats the same procedure with the chart of the Gregg Alphabet.*

Why are you—

AMANDA: Why? Why? How old are you, Laura?

LAURA: Mother, you know my age.

AMANDA: I thought that you were an adult; it seems that I was mistaken. (*She crosses slowly to the sofa and sinks down and stares at* LAURA.)

LAURA: Please don't stare at me, Mother.

    AMANDA *closes her eyes and lowers her head. There is a ten-second pause.*

AMANDA: What are we going to do, what is going to become of us, what is the future? *There is another pause.*

LAURA: Has something happened, Mother?

    AMANDA *draws a long breath, takes out the handkerchief again, goes through the dabbing process.*

Mother, has—something happened?

AMANDA: I'll be all right in a minute, I'm just bewildered—(*She hesitates.*)—by life. . . .

LAURA: Mother, I wish that you would tell me what's happened!

AMANDA: As you know, I was supposed to be inducted into my office at the D.A.R. this afternoon.

*Screen image: A swarm of typewriters.*

But I stopped off at Rubicam's Business College to speak to your teachers about your having a cold and ask them what progress they thought you were making down there.

LAURA: Oh. . . .

AMANDA: I went to the typing instructor and introduced myself as your mother. She didn't know who you were. "Wingfield," she said, "We don't have any such student enrolled at the school!"

I assured her she did, that you had been going to classes since early in January.

"I wonder," she said, "If you could be talking about that terribly shy little girl who dropped out of school after only a few days' attendance?"

"No," I said, "Laura, my daughter, has been going to school every day for the past six weeks!"

"Excuse me," she said. She took the attendance book out and there was your name, unmistakably printed, and all the dates you were absent until they decided that you had dropped out of school.

I still said, "No, there must have been some mistake! There must have been some mix-up in the records!"

And she said, "No—I remember her perfectly now. Her hands shook so that she couldn't hit the right keys! The first time we gave a speed test, she broke down completely—was sick at the stomach and almost had to be carried into the wash room! After that morning she never showed up any more. We phoned the house but never got any answer"— While I was working at Famous-Barr, I suppose, demonstrating those—

*She indicates a brassiere with her hands.*

Oh! I felt so weak I could barely keep on my feet! I had to sit down while they got me a glass of water! Fifty dollars' tuition, all of our plans—my hopes and ambitions for you—just gone up the spout, just gone up the spout like that.

LAURA *draws a long breath and gets awkwardly to her feet. She crosses to the Victrola and winds it up.*

What are you doing?

LAURA: Oh! (*She releases the handle and returns to her seat.*)

AMANDA: Laura, where have you been going when you've gone out pretending that you were going to business college?

LAURA: I've just been going out walking.

AMANDA: That's not true.

LAURA: It is. I just went walking.

AMANDA: Walking? Walking? In winter? Deliberately courting pneumonia in that light coat? Where did you walk to, Laura?

LAURA: All sorts of places—mostly in the park.

AMANDA: Even after you'd started catching that cold?

LAURA: It was the lesser of two evils, Mother. *Screen image:* Winter scene in a park. I couldn't go back there. I—threw up—on the floor!

AMANDA: From half past seven till after five every day you mean to tell me you walked around in the park, because you wanted to make me think that you were still going to Rubicam's Business College?

LAURA: It wasn't as bad as it sounds. I went inside places to get warmed up.

AMANDA: Inside where?

LAURA: I went in the art museum and the bird houses at the Zoo. I visited the penguins every day! Sometimes I did without lunch and went to the movies. Lately I've been spending most of my afternoons in the Jewel Box, that big glass house where they raise the tropical flowers.

AMANDA: You did all this to deceive me, just for deception? (LAURA *looks down.*) Why?

LAURA: Mother, when you're disappointed, you get that awful suffering look on your face, like the picture of Jesus' mother in the museum!

AMANDA: Hush!

LAURA:  I couldn't face it.

*There is a pause. A whisper of strings is heard. Legend on screen: "The Crust of Humility."*

AMANDA (*hopelessly fingering the huge pocketbook*):  So what are we going to do the rest of our lives? Stay home and watch the parades go by? Amuse ourselves with the glass menagerie, darling? Eternally play those worn-out phonograph records your father left as a painful reminder of him? We won't have a business career—we've given that up because it gave us nervous indigestion! (*She laughs wearily.*) What is there left but dependency all our lives? I know so well what becomes of unmarried women who aren't prepared to occupy a position. I've seen such pitiful cases in the South—barely tolerated spinsters living upon the grudging patronage of sister's husband or brother's wife!—stuck away in some little mousetrap of a room—encouraged by one in-law to visit another—little birdlike women without any nest—eating the crust of humility all their life! Is that the future that we've mapped out for ourselves? I swear it's the only alternative I can think of! (*She pauses.*) It isn't a very pleasant alternative, is it? (*She pauses again.*) Of course—some girls do marry.

LAURA *twists her hands nervously.*

Haven't you ever liked some boy?

LAURA:  Yes. I liked one once. (*She rises.*) I came across his picture a while ago.

AMANDA (*with some interest*):  He gave you his picture?

LAURA:  No, it's in the yearbook.

AMANDA (*disappointed*):  Oh—a high school boy.

*Screen image:* Jim as the high school hero bearing a silver cup.

LAURA:  Yes. His name was Jim. (*She lifts the heavy annual from the claw-foot table.*) Here he is in *The Pirates of Penzance.*

AMANDA (*absently*):  The what?

LAURA:  The operetta the senior class put on. He had a wonderful voice and we sat across the aisle from each other Mondays, Wednesdays and Fridays in the Aud. Here he is with the silver cup for debating! See his grin?

AMANDA (*absently*):  He must have had a jolly disposition.

LAURA:  He used to call me—Blue Roses.

*Screen image:* Blue roses.

AMANDA:  Why did he call you such a name as that?

LAURA:  When I had that attack of pleurosis—he asked me what was the matter when I came back. I said pleurosis—he thought that I said Blue Roses! So that's what he always called me after that. Whenever he saw me, he'd holler, "Hello, Blue Roses!" I didn't care for the girl that he went out with. Emily Meisenbach. Emily was the best-dressed girl at Soldan. She never struck me, though, as being sincere. . . . It says in the Personal Section—they're engaged. That's—six years ago! They must be married by now.

AMANDA:  Girls that aren't cut out for business careers usually wind up married to some nice man. (*She gets up with a spark of revival.*) Sister, that's what you'll do!

LAURA *utters a startled, doubtful laugh. She reaches quickly for a piece of glass.*

LAURA:  But, Mother—

AMANDA:  Yes? (*She goes over to the photograph.*)

LAURA (*in a tone of frightened apology*):  I'm—crippled!

AMANDA:  Nonsense! Laura, I've told you never, never to use that word. Why, you're not crippled, you just have a little defect—hardly noticeable, even! When people have some slight disadvantage like that, they cultivate other things to make up for it—develop charm—and vivacity—and—*charm!* That's all you have to do! (*She turns again to the photograph.*)

One thing your father had *plenty of*—was charm!
*The scene fades out with music.*

# SCENE THREE

*Legend on screen: "After the fiasco—"*
TOM *speaks from the fire escape landing.*

TOM:  After the fiasco at Rubicam's Business College, the idea of getting a gentleman caller for Laura began to play a more and more important part in Mother's calculations. It became an obsession. Like some archetype of the universal unconscious, the image of the gentleman caller haunted our small apartment. . . .
*Screen image: A young man at the door of a house with flowers.*
An evening at home rarely passed without some allusion to this image, this specter, this hope. . . . Even when he wasn't mentioned, his presence hung in Mother's preoccupied look and in my sister's frightened, apologetic manner— hung like a sentence passed upon the Wingfields!
Mother was a woman of action as well as words. She began to take logical steps in the planned direction. Late that winter and in the early spring—realizing that extra money would be needed to properly feather the nest and plume the bird—she conducted a vigorous campaign on the telephone, roping in subscribers to one of those magazines for matrons called *The Homemaker's Companion*, the type of journal that features the serialized sublimations of ladies of letters who think in terms of delicate cup-like breasts, slim, tapering waists, rich, creamy thighs, eyes like wood smoke in autumn, fingers that soothe and caress like strains of music, bodies as powerful as Etruscan sculpture.
*Screen image: The cover of a glamor magazine.*

AMANDA *enters with the telephone on a long extension cord. She is spotlighted in the dim stage.*
AMANDA:  Ida Scott? This is Amanda Wingfield! We *missed* you at the D.A.R. last Monday! I said to myself: She's probably suffering with that sinus condition! How is that sinus condition?
Horrors! Heaven have mercy!—You're a Christian martyr, yes, that's what you are, a Christian martyr!
Well, I just now happened to notice that your subscription to the `Companion's` about to expire! Yes, it expires with the next issue, honey!—just when that wonderful new serial by Bessie Mae Hopper is getting off to such an exciting start. Oh, honey, it's something that you can't miss! You remember how *Gone with the Wind* took everybody by storm? You simply couldn't go out if you hadn't read it. All everybody *talked* was Scarlett O'Hara. Well, this is a book that critics already compare to *Gone with the Wind*. It's the *Gone with the Wind* of the post-World-War generation!—What?—Burning?—Oh, honey, don't let them burn, go take a look in the oven and I'll hold the wire! Heavens—I think she's hung up!
*The scene dims out.*
*Legend on screen: "You think I'm in love with Continental Shoemakers?"*
*Before the lights come up again, the violent voices of* TOM *and* AMANDA *are heard. They are quarreling behind the portieres. In front of them stands* LAURA *with clenched hands and panicky expression. A clear pool of light is on her figure throughout this scene.*
TOM:  What in Christ's name am I—
AMANDA (*shrilly*):  Don't you use that—
TOM:  —supposed to do!
AMANDA:  —expression! Not in my—
TOM:  Ohhh!
AMANDA:  —presence! Have you gone out of your senses?
TOM:  I have, that's true, *driven* out!

AMANDA: What is the matter with you, you —big—big—IDIOT!

TOM: Look!—I've got no thing, no single thing—

AMANDA: Lower your voice!

TOM: —in my life here that I can call my OWN! Everything is—

AMANDA: Stop that shouting!

TOM: Yesterday you confiscated my books! You had the nerve to—

AMANDA: I took that horrible novel back to the library—yes! That hideous book by that insane Mr. Lawrence.

*TOM laughs wildly.*

I cannot control the output of diseased minds or people who cater to them—

*TOM laughs still more wildly.*

BUT I WON'T ALLOW SUCH FILTH BROUGHT INTO MY HOUSE! No, no, no, no, no!

TOM: House, house! Who pays rent on it, who makes a slave of himself to—

AMANDA (*fairly screeching*): Don't you DARE to—

TOM: No, no, I mustn't say things! *I've* got to just—

AMANDA: Let me tell you—

TOM: I don't want to hear any more!

*He tears the portieres open. The dining-room area is lit with a turgid smoky red glow. Now we see AMANDA; her hair is in metal curlers and she is wearing a very old bathrobe, much too large for her slight figure, a relic of the faithless Mr. Wingfield. The upright typewriter now stands on the drop-leaf table, along with a wild disarray of manuscripts. The quarrel was probably precipitated by AMANDA'S interruption of TOM'S creative labor. A chair lies overthrown on the floor. Their gesticulating shadows are cast on the ceiling by the fiery glow.*

AMANDA: You *will* hear more, you—

TOM: No, I won't hear more, I'm going out!

AMANDA: You come right back in—

TOM: Out, out, out! Because I'm—

AMANDA: Come back here, Tom Wingfield! I'm not through talking to you!

TOM: Oh, go—

LAURA (*desperately*): —Tom!

AMANDA: You're going to listen, and no more insolence from you! I'm at the end of my patience!

*He comes back toward her.*

TOM: What do you think I'm at? Aren't I supposed to have any patience to reach the end of, Mother? I know, I know. It seems unimportant to you, what I'm *doing*—what I *want* to do—having a little *difference* between them! You don't think that—

AMANDA: I think you've been doing things that you're ashamed of. That's why you act like this. I don't believe that you go every night to the movies. Nobody goes to the movies night after night. Nobody in their right minds goes to the movies as often as you pretend to. People don't go to the movies at nearly midnight, and movies don't let out at two A.M. Come in stumbling. Muttering to yourself like a maniac! You get three hours' sleep and then go to work. Oh, I can picture the way you're doing down there. Moping, doping, because you're in no condition.

TOM (*wildly*): No, I'm in no condition!

AMANDA: What right have you got to jeopardize your job? Jeopardize the security of us all? How do you think we'd manage if you were—

TOM: Listen! You think I'm crazy about the *warehouse*? (*He bends fiercely toward her slight figure.*) You think I'm in love with the Continental Shoemakers? You think I want to spend fifty-five *years* down there in that—*celotex interior!* with—*fluorescent—tubes!* Look! I'd rather somebody picked up a crowbar and battered out my brains—than go back mornings! I *go!* Every time you come in yelling that God-damn "*Rise and Shine!*" "*Rise and Shine!*" I say to myself, "How *lucky dead* people are!" But I get up. I *go!* For sixty-five dollars a month I give up all that I dream of doing and being *ever*! And you say self—*self's* all I ever think of. Why, listen, if self is what I thought of, Mother, I'd be where he is—GONE! (*He points to his father's picture.*) As far as the system of transportation reaches! (*He starts past her. She grabs his arm.*) Don't grab at me, Mother!

AMANDA:  Where are you going?

TOM:  I'm going to the *movies*!

AMANDA:  I don't believe that lie!

TOM *crouches toward her, overtowering her tiny figure. She backs away, gasping.*

TOM:  I'm going to opium dens! Yes, opium dens, dens of vice and criminals' hangouts, Mother. I've joined the Hogan Gang, I'm a hired assassin, I carry a tommy gun in a violin case! I run a string of cat houses in the Valley! They call me Killer, Killer Wingfield, I'm leading a double-life, a simple, honest warehouse worker by day, by night a dynamic *czar* of the *underworld*, Mother. I go to gambling casinos, I spin away fortunes on the roulette table! I wear a patch over one eye and a false mustache, sometimes I put on green whiskers. On those occasions they call me—*El Diablo!* Oh, I could tell you many things to make you sleepless! My enemies plan to dynamite this place. They're going to blow us all sky-high some night! I'll be glad, very happy, and so will you! You'll go up, up on a broomstick, over Blue Mountain with seventeen gentlemen callers! You ugly—babbling old—witch. . . .

*He goes through a series of violent, clumsy movements, seizing his overcoat, lunging to the door, pulling it fiercely open. The women watch him, aghast. His arm catches in the sleeve of the coat as he struggles to pull it on. For a moment he is pinioned by the bulky garment. With an outraged groan he tears the coat off again, splitting the shoulder of it, and hurls it across the room. It strikes against the shelf of* LAURA'S *glass collection,*

*and there is a tinkle of shattering glass.* LAURA *cries out as if wounded.*

*Music.*

*Screen legend: "The Glass Menagerie."*

LAURA (*shrilly*): My glass!—menagerie. . . . (*She covers her face and turns away.*)

But AMANDA *is still stunned and stupefied by the "ugly witch" so that she barely notices this occurrence. Now she recovers her speech.*

AMANDA (*in an awful voice*):  I won't speak to you—until you apologize!

*She crosses through the portieres and draws them together behind her.* TOM *is left with* LAURA. LAURA *clings weakly to the mantel with her face averted.* TOM *stares at her stupidly for a moment. Then he crosses to the shelf. He drops awkwardly on his knees to collect the fallen glass, glancing at* LAURA *as if he would speak but couldn't.*

*"The Glass Menagerie" music steals in as the scene dims out.*

# SCENE FOUR

*The interior of the apartment is dark. There is a faint light in the alley. A deep-voiced bell in a church is tolling the hour of five.*

TOM *appears at the top of the alley. After each solemn boom of the bell in the tower, he shakes a little noisemaker or rattle as if to express the tiny spasm of man in contrast to the sustained power and dignity of the Almighty. This and the unsteadiness of his advance make it evident that he has been drinking. As he climbs the few steps to the fire escape landing light steals up inside.* LAURA *appears in the front room in a nightdresss. She notices that* TOM'S *bed is empty.* TOM *fishes in his pockets for his door key, removing a motley assortment of articles in the search, including a shower of movie ticket stubs and an empty bottle. At last he finds the key, but just as he is about to insert it, it slips from his fingers. He strikes a match and crouches below the door.*

TOM (*bitterly*): One  crack—and  it  falls through!

LAURA *opens the door.*

LAURA: Tom! Tom, what are you doing?

TOM: Looking for a door key.

LAURA: Where have you been all this time?

TOM: I have been to the movies.

LAURA: All this time at the movies?

TOM: There was a very long program. There was a Garbo picture and a Mickey Mouse and a travelogue and a newsreel and a preview of coming attractions. And there was an organ solo and a collection for the Milk Fund—simultaneously—which ended up in a terrible fight between a fat lady and an usher!

LAURA (innocently): Did you have to stay through everything?

TOM: Of course! And, oh, I forgot! There was a big stage show! The headliner on this stage show was Malvolio the Magician. He performed wonderful tricks, many of them, such as pouring water back and forth between pitchers. First it turned to wine and then it turned to beer and then it turned to whisky. I know it was whisky it finally turned into because he needed somebody to come up out of the audience to help him, and I came up —both shows! It was Kentucky Straight Bourbon. A very generous fellow, he gave souvenirs. (He pulls from his back pocket a shimmering rainbow-colored scarf.) He gave me this. This is his magic scarf. You can have it, Laura. You wave it over a canary cage and you get a bowl of goldfish. You wave it over the goldfish bowl and they fly away canaries.... But the wonderfullest trick of all was the coffin trick. We nailed him into a coffin and he got out of the coffin without removing one nail. (He has come inside.) There is a trick that would come in handy for me— get me out of this two-by-four situation! (He flops onto the bed and starts removing his shoes.)

LAURA: Tom—shhh!

TOM: What're you shushing me for?

LAURA: You'll wake up Mother.

TOM: Goody, goody! Pay 'er back for all those "Rise an' Shines." (He lies down, groaning.) You know it don't take much intelligence to get yourself into a nailed-up coffin, Laura. But who in hell ever got himself out of one without removing one nail?

As if in answer, the father's grinning photograph lights up. The scene dims out. Immediately following, the church bell is heard striking six. At the sixth stroke the alarm clock goes off in AMANDA'S room, and after a few moments we hear her calling: "Rise and Shine! Rise and Shine! LAURA, go tell your brother to rise and shine!"

TOM (sitting up slowly): I'll rise—but I won't shine.

The light increases.

AMANDA: Laura, tell your brother his coffee is ready.

LAURA slips into the front room.

LAURA: Tom!—It's nearly seven. Don't make Mother nervous.

He stares at her stupidly.

(beseechingly:) Tom, speak to Mother this morning. Make up with her, apologize, speak to her!

TOM: She won't to me. It's her that started not speaking.

LAURA: If you just say you're sorry she'll start speaking.

TOM: Her not speaking—is that such a tragedy?

LAURA: Please—please!

AMANDA (calling from the kitchenette): Laura, are you going to do what I asked you to do, or do I have to get dressed and go out myself?

LAURA: Going, going—soon as I get on my coat!

She pulls on a shapeless felt hat with a nervous, jerky movement, pleadingly glancing at TOM. She rushes awkwardly for her coat. The coat is one of AMANDA'S, inaccurately made-over, the sleeves too short for LAURA. Butter and what else?

AMANDA (*entering from the kitchenette*): Just butter. Tell them to charge it.

LAURA: Mother, they make such faces when I do that.

AMANDA: Sticks and stones can break our bones, but the expression on Mr. Garfinkel's face won't harm us! Tell your brother his coffee is getting cold.

LAURA (*at the door*): Do what I asked you, will you, will you, Tom?

*He looks sullenly away.*

AMANDA: Laura, go now or just don't go at all!

LAURA (*rushing out*): Going—going!

*A second later she cries out.* TOM *springs up and crosses to the door.* TOM *opens the door.*

TOM: Laura?

LAURA: I'm all right. I slipped, but I'm all right.

AMANDA (*peering anxiously after her*): If anyone breaks a leg on those fire-escape steps, the landlord ought to be sued for every cent he possesses! (*She shuts the door. Now she remembers she isn't speaking to* TOM *and returns to the other room.*) *As* TOM *comes listlessly for his coffee, she turns her back to him and stands rigidly facing the window on the gloomy gray vault of the areaway. Its light on her face with its aged but childish features is cruelly sharp, satirical as a Daumier print. The music of "Ave Maria," is heard softly.*

TOM *glances sheepishly but sullenly at her averted figure and slumps at the table. The coffee is scalding hot; he sips it and gasps and spits it back in the cup. At his gasp,* AMANDA *catches her breath and half turns. Then she catches herself and turns back to the window.* TOM *blows on his coffee, glancing sidewise at his mother. She clears her throat.* TOM *clears his. He starts to rise, sinks back down again, scratches his head, clears his throat again.* AMANDA *coughs.* TOM *raises his cup in both hands to blow on it, his eyes staring over the rim of it at his mother for several moments. Then he slowly sets the cup down and awkwardly and hesitantly rises from the chair.*

TOM (*hoarsely*): Mother. I—I apologize, Mother.

AMANDA *draws a quick, shuddering breath. Her face works grotesquely. She breaks into childlike tears.*

I'm sorry for what I said, for everything that I said, I didn't mean it.

AMANDA (*sobbingly*): My devotion has made me a witch and so I make myself hateful to my children!

TOM: *No*, you *don't*.

AMANDA: I worry so much, don't sleep, it makes me nervous!

TOM (*gently*): I understand that.

AMANDA: I've had to put up a solitary battle all these years. But you're my right-hand bower! Don't fall down, don't fail!

TOM (*gently*): I try, Mother.

AMANDA (*with great enthusiasm*): Try and you will *succeed!* (*The notion makes her breathless.*) Why, you—you're just *full* of natural endowments! Both of my children —they're *unusual* children! Don't you think I know it? I'm so—*proud!* Happy and—feel I've—so much to be thankful for but—promise me one thing, son!

TOM: What, Mother?

AMANDA: Promise, son, you'll—never be a drunkard!

TOM (*turns to her grinning*): I will never be a drunkard, Mother.

AMANDA: That's what frightened me so, that you'd be drinking! Eat a bowl of Purina!

TOM: Just coffee, Mother.

AMANDA: Shredded wheat biscuit?

TOM: No. No, Mother, just coffee.

AMANDA: You can't put in a day's work on an empty stomach. You've got ten minutes—don't gulp! Drinking too-hot liquids makes cancer of the stomach. . . . Put cream in.

TOM: No, thank you.

AMANDA: To cool it.

TOM: No! No, thank you, I want it black.

AMANDA: I know, but it's not good for you. We have to do all that we can to build ourselves up. In these trying times we live in, all that we have to cling to is—each other.... That's why it's so important to—Tom, I—I sent out your sister so I could discuss something with you. If you hadn't spoken I would have spoken to you. (*She sits down.*)

TOM (*gently*): What is it, Mother, that you want to discuss?

AMANDA: *Laura!*

> TOM *puts his cup down slowly.*
> *Legend on screen: "Laura." Music: "The Glass Menagerie."*

TOM: —Oh.—Laura ...

AMANDA (*touching his's sleeve*): You know how Laura is. So quiet but—still water runs deep! She notices things and I think she—broods about them.

> TOM *looks up.*

A few days ago I came in and she was crying.

TOM: What about?

AMANDA: You.

TOM: Me?

AMANDA: She has an idea that you're not happy here.

TOM: What gave her that idea?

AMANDA: What gives her any idea? However, you do act strangely. I—I'm not criticizing, understand *that!* I know your ambitions do not lie in the warehouse, that like everybody in the whole wide world—you've had to—make sacrifices, but—Tom—Tom—life's not easy, it calls for—Spartan endurance! There's so many things in my heart that I cannot describe to you! I've never told you but I—*loved* your father....

TOM (*gently*): I know that, Mother.

AMANDA: And you—when I see you taking after his ways! Staying out late—and—well, you *had* been drinking the night you were in that—terrifying condition!

Laura says that you hate the apartment and that you go out nights to get away from it! Is that true, Tom?

TOM: No. You say there's so much in your heart that you can't describe to me. That's true of me, too. There's so much in my heart that I can't describe to you! So let's respect each other's—

AMANDA: But, why—*why*, Tom—are you always so *restless?* Where do you *go* to, nights?

TOM: I—go to the movies.

AMANDA: Why do you go to the movies so much, Tom?

TOM: I go to the movies because—I like adventure. Adventure is something I don't have much of at work, so I go to the movies.

AMANDA: But, Tom, you go to the movies *entirely* too *much!*

TOM: I like a lot of adventure.

> AMANDA *looks baffled, then hurt. As the familiar inquisition resumes,* TOM *becomes hard and impatient again.* AMANDA *slips back into her querulous attitude toward him. Image on screen: A sailing vessel with Jolly Roger.*

AMANDA: Most young men find adventure in their careers.

TOM: Then most young men are not employed in a warehouse.

AMANDA: The world is full of young men employed in warehouses and offices and factories.

TOM: Do all of them find adventure in their careers?

AMANDA: They do or they do without it! Not everybody has a craze for adventure.

TOM: Man is by instinct a lover, a hunter, a fighter, and none of those instincts are given much play at the warehouse!

AMANDA: Man is by instinct! Don't quote instinct to me! Instinct is something that people have got away from! It belongs to animals! Christian adults don't want it!

TOM: What do Christian adults want, then, Mother?

AMANDA: Superior things! Things of the mind and the spirit! Only animals have to satisfy instincts! Surely your aims are somewhat higher than theirs! Than monkeys—pigs—

TOM: I reckon they're not.

AMANDA: You're joking. However, that isn't what I wanted to discuss.

TOM (*rising*): I haven't much time.

AMANDA (*pushing his shoulders*): Sit down.

TOM: You want me to punch in red at the warehouse, Mother?

AMANDA: You have five minutes. I want to talk about Laura.

*Screen legend: "Plans and Provisions."*

TOM: All right! What about Laura?

AMANDA: We have to be making some plans and provisions for her. She's older than you, two years, and nothing has happened. She just drifts along doing nothing. It frightens me terribly how she just drifts along.

TOM: I guess she's the type that people call home girls.

AMANDA: There's no such type, and if there is, it's a pity! That is unless the home is hers, with a husband!

TOM: What?

AMANDA: Oh, I can see the handwriting on the wall as plain as I see the nose in front of my face! It's terrifying! More and more you remind me of your father! He was out all hours without explanation!— Then *left*! Goodbye! And me with the bag to hold. I saw that letter you got from the Merchant Marine. I know what you're dreaming of. I'm not standing here blindfolded. (*She pauses.*) Very well, then. Then *do* it! But not till there's somebody to take your place.

TOM: What do you mean?

AMANDA: I mean that as soon as Laura has got somebody to take care of her, married, a home of her own, independent—

why, then you'll be free to go wherever you please, on land, on sea, whichever way the wind blows you! But until that time you've got to look out for your sister. I don't say me because I'm old and don't matter! I say for your sister because she's young and dependent.

I put her in business college—a dismal failure! Frightened her so it made her sick at the stomach. I took her over to the Young People's League at the church. Another fiasco. She spoke to nobody, nobody spoke to her. Now all she does is fool with those pieces of glass and play those worn-out records. What kind of a life is that for a girl to lead?

TOM: What can I do about it?

AMANDA: Overcome selfishness! Self, self, self is all that you ever think of!

TOM *springs up and crosses to get his coat. It is ugly and bulky. He pulls on a cap with earmuffs.*

Where is your muffler? Put your wool muffler on!

*He snatches it angrily from the closet, tosses it around his neck and pulls both ends tight.*

Tom! I haven't said what I had in mind to ask you.

TOM: I'm too late to—

AMANDA (*catching his arm—very importunately; then shyly*): Down at the warehouse, aren't there some—nice young men?

TOM: No!

AMANDA: There *must* be—some . . .

TOM: Mother—(*He gestures.*)

AMANDA: Find out one that's clean-living— doesn't drink and ask him out for sister!

TOM: What?

AMANDA: For *sister*! To *meet*! Get *acquainted*!

TOM (*stamping to the door*): Oh, my go-osh!

AMANDA: Will you?

*He opens the door. She says, imploringly:*

Will you?

(*He starts down the fire escape.*)

Will you? Will you, dear?

TOM (*calling back*):  Yes!

AMANDA *closes the door hesitantly and with a troubled but faintly hopeful expression.*
*Screen image:* The cover of a glamor magazine.
*The spotlight picks up* AMANDA *at the phone.*

AMANDA:  Ella Cartwright? This is Amanda Wingfield! How are you, honey? How is that kidney condition?

*There is a five-second pause.*

Horrors!

*There is another pause.*

You're a Christian martyr, yes, honey, that's what you are, a Christian martyr! Well, I just now happened to notice in my little red book that your subscription to the *Companion* has just run out! I knew that you wouldn't want to miss out on the wonderful serial starting in this new issue. It's by Bessie Mae Hopper, the first thing she's written since *Honeymoon for Three.* Wasn't that a strange and interesting story? Well, this one is even lovelier, I believe. It has a sophisticated society background. It's all about the horsey set on Long Island!

*The light fades out.*

# SCENE FIVE

*Legend on the screen:* "Annunciation."
*Music is heard as the light slowly comes on.*

It is early dusk of a spring evening. Supper has just been finished in the Wingfield apartment. AMANDA *and* LAURA, *in light-colored dresses, are removing dishes from the table in the dining room, which is shadowy, their movements formalized almost as a dance or ritual, their moving forms as pale and silent as moths.* TOM, *in white shirt and trousers, rises from the table and crosses toward the fire escape.*

AMANDA (*as he passes her*):  Son, will you do me a favor?

TOM:  What?

AMANDA:  Comb your hair! You look so pretty when your hair is combed!

TOM *slouches on the sofa with the evening paper. Its enormous headline reads:* "Franco Triumphs."

There is only one respect in which I would like you to emulate your father.

TOM:  What respect is that?

AMANDA:  The care he always took of his appearance. He never allowed himself to look untidy.

*He throws down the paper and crosses to the fire escape.*

Where are you going?

TOM:  I'm going out to smoke.

AMANDA:  You smoke too much. A pack a day at fifteen cents a pack. How much would that amount to in a month? Thirty times fifteen is how much, Tom? Figure it out and you will be astounded at what you could save. Enough to give you a night-school course in accounting at Washington U.! Just think what a wonderful thing that would be for you, son!

TOM *is unmoved by the thought.*

TOM:  I'd rather smoke. (*He steps out on the landing, letting the screen door slam.*)

AMANDA (*sharply*):  I know! That's the tragedy of it. . . .

(*Alone, she turns to look at her husband's picture.*)

*Dance music:* "The World Is Waiting for the Sunrise!"

TOM (*to the audience*):  Across the alley from us was the Paradise Dance Hall. On evenings in spring the windows and doors were open and the music came outdoors. Sometimes the lights were turned out except for a large glass sphere that hung from the ceiling. It would turn slowly about and filter the dusk with delicate rainbow colors. Then the orchestra played a waltz or a tango, something that had a slow and sensuous rhythm. Couples would come outside, to the relative privacy of the alley. You could see them kissing behind ash pits and telephone poles. This was the compensation for lives that passed like mine, without any change or adventure. Adventure and change were imminent in this year. They were waiting around the corner for all these kids. Suspended in the mist over Berchtesgaden, caught in the folds of Chamberlain's umbrella. In Spain there was Guernica! But here there was only hot swing music and liquor, dance halls, bars, and movies, and sex that hung in the gloom like a chandelier and flooded the world with brief, deceptive rainbows. . . . All the world was waiting for bombardments!

AMANDA *turns from the picture and comes outside.*

AMANDA (*sighing*): A fire escape landing's a poor excuse for a porch. (*She spreads a newspaper on a step and sits down, gracefully and demurely as if she were settling into a swing on a Mississippi veranda.*) What are you looking at?

TOM: The moon.

AMANDA: Is there a moon this evening?

TOM: It's rising over Garfinkel's Delicatessen.

AMANDA: So it is! A little silver slipper of a moon. Have you made a wish on it yet?

TOM: Um-hum.

AMANDA: What did you wish for?

TOM: That's a secret.

AMANDA: A secret, huh? Well, I won't tell mine either. I will be just as mysterious as you.

TOM: I bet I can guess what yours is.

AMANDA: Is my head so transparent?

TOM: You're not a sphinx.

AMANDA: No, I don't have secrets. I'll tell you what I wished for on the moon. Success and happiness for my precious children! I wish for that whenever there's a moon, and when there isn't a moon, I wish for it, too.

TOM: I thought perhaps you wished for a gentleman caller.

AMANDA: Why do you say that?

TOM: Don't you remember asking me to fetch one?

AMANDA: I remember suggesting that it would be nice for your sister if you brought home some nice young man from the warehouse. I think that I've made that suggestion more than once.

TOM: Yes, you have made it repeatedly.

AMANDA: Well?

TOM: We are going to have one.

AMANDA: *What?*

TOM: A gentleman caller!
*The annunciation is celebrated with music.*
AMANDA *rises.*
*Image on screen: A caller with a bouquet.*

AMANDA: You mean you have asked some nice young man to come over?

TOM: Yep. I've asked him to dinner.

AMANDA: You really did?

TOM: I did!

AMANDA: You did, and did he—*accept?*

TOM: He did!

AMANDA: Well, well—well, well! That's—lovely!

TOM: I thought that you would be pleased.

AMANDA: It's definite then?

TOM: Very definite.

AMANDA: Soon?

TOM: Very soon.

AMANDA: For heaven's sake, stop putting on and tell me some things, will you?

TOM: What things do you want me to tell you?

AMANDA: *Naturally* I would like to know when he's *coming!*

TOM: He's coming tomorrow.

AMANDA: *Tomorrow?*

TOM: Yep. Tomorrow.

AMANDA: But, Tom!

TOM: Yes, Mother?

AMANDA: Tomorrow gives me no time!

TOM: Time for what?

AMANDA: Preparations! Why didn't you phone me at once, as soon as you asked him, the minute that he accepted? Then, don't you see, I could have been getting ready!

TOM: You don't have to make any fuss.

AMANDA: Oh, Tom, Tom, Tom, of course I have to make a fuss! I want things nice, not sloppy! Not thrown together. I'll certainly have to do some fast thinking, won't I?

TOM: I don't see why you have to think at all.

AMANDA: You just don't know. We can't have a gentleman caller in a pigsty! All my wedding silver has to be polished, the monogrammed table linen ought to be laundered! The windows have to be washed and fresh curtains put up. And how about clothes? We have to *wear* something, don't we?

TOM: Mother, this boy is no one to make a fuss over!

AMANDA: Do you realize he's the first young man we've introduced to your sister? It's terrible, dreadful, disgraceful that poor little sister has never received a single gentleman caller! Tom, come inside! (*She opens the screen door.*)

TOM: What for?

AMANDA: I want to ask you some things.

TOM: If you're going to make such a fuss, I'll call it off, I'll tell him not to come!

AMANDA: You certainly won't do anything of the kind. Nothing offends people worse than broken engagements. It simply means I'll have to work like a Turk! We won't be brilliant, but we will pass inspection. Come on inside.

TOM *follows her inside, groaning.*
Sit down.

TOM: Any particular place you would like me to sit?

AMANDA: Thank heavens I've got that new sofa! I'm also making payments on a floor lamp I'll have sent out! And put the chintz covers on, they'll brighten things up! Of course I'd hoped to have these walls re-papered. . . . What is the young man's name?

TOM: His name is O'Connor.

AMANDA: That, of course, means fish—tomorrow is Friday! I'll have that salmon loaf—with Durkee's dressing! What does he do? He works at the warehouse?

TOM: Of course! How else would I—

AMANDA: Tom, he—doesn't drink?

TOM: Why do you ask me that?

AMANDA: Your father *did!*

TOM: Don't get started on that!

AMANDA: He *does* drink, then?

TOM: Not that I know of!

AMANDA: Make sure, be certain! The last thing I want for my daughter's a boy who drinks!

TOM: Aren't you being a little bit premature? Mr. O'Connor has not yet appeared on the scene!

AMANDA: But will tomorrow. To meet your sister, and what do I know about his character? Nothing! Old maids are better off than wives of drunkards!

TOM: Oh, my God!

AMANDA: Be still!

TOM (*leaning forward to whisper*): Lots of fellows meet girls whom they don't marry!

AMANDA: Oh, talk sensibly, Tom—and don't be sarcastic!
*She has gotten a hairbrush.*

TOM: What are you doing?

AMANDA: I'm brushing that cowlick down! (*She attacks his hair with the brush.*) What is this young man's position at the warehouse?

TOM (*submitting grimly to the brush and the interrogation*): This young man's position is that of a shipping clerk, Mother.

AMANDA: Sounds to me like a fairly responsible job, the sort of a job *you* would be in if you just had more *get-up.* What is his salary? Have you any idea?

TOM: I would judge it to be approximately eighty-five dollars a month.

AMANDA: Well—not princely, but—

TOM: Twenty more than I make.

AMANDA: Yes, how well I know! But for a family man, eighty-five dollars a month is not much more than you can just get by on. . . .

TOM: Yes, but Mr. O'Connor is not a family man.

AMANDA: He might be, mightn't he? Some time in the future?

TOM: I see. Plans and provisions.

AMANDA: You are the only young man that I know of who ignores the fact that the future becomes the present, the present the past, and the past turns into everlasting regret if you don't plan for it!

TOM: I will think that over and see what I can make of it.

AMANDA: Don't be supercilious with your mother! Tell me some more about this— what do you call him?

TOM: James D. O'Connor. The D. is for Delaney.

AMANDA: Irish on *both* sides! *Gracious!* And doesn't drink?

TOM: Shall I call him up and ask him right this minute?

AMANDA: The only way to find out about those things is to make discreet inquiries at the proper moment. When I was a girl in Blue Mountain and it was suspected that a young man drank, the girl whose attentions he had been receiving, if any girl *was*, would sometimes speak to the minister of his church, or rather her father would if her father was living, and sort of feel him out on the young man's character. That is the way such things are discreetly handled to keep a young woman from making a tragic mistake!

TOM: Then how did you happen to make a tragic mistake?

AMANDA: That innocent look of your father's had everyone fooled! He *smiled*— the world was *enchanted!* No girl can do worse than put herself at the mercy of a handsome appearance! I hope that Mr. O'Connor is not too good-looking.

TOM: No, he's not too good-looking. He's covered with freckles and hasn't too much of a nose.

AMANDA: He's not right-down homely, though?

TOM: Not right-down homely. Just medium homely, I'd say.

AMANDA: Character's what to look for in a man.

TOM: That's what I've always said, Mother.

AMANDA: You've never said anything of the kind and I suspect you would never give it a thought.

TOM: Don't be so suspicious of me.

AMANDA: At least I hope he's the type that's up and coming.

TOM: I think he really goes in for self-improvement.

AMANDA: What reason have you to think so?

TOM: He goes to night school.

AMANDA (*beaming*): Splendid! What does he do, I mean study?

TOM: Radio engineering and public speaking!

AMANDA: Then he has visions of being advanced in the world! Any young man who studies public speaking is aiming to have an executive job some day! And radio engineering? A thing for the future! Both of these facts are very illuminating. Those are the sort of things that a mother should know concerning any young man who comes to call on her daughter. Seriously or—not.

TOM: One little warning. He doesn't know about Laura. I didn't let on that we had dark ulterior motives. I just said, why don't you come and have dinner with us? He said okay and that was the whole conversation.

AMANDA: I bet it was! You're eloquent as an oyster. However, he'll know about Laura when he gets here. When he sees how lovely and sweet and pretty she is, he'll thank his lucky stars he was asked to dinner.

TOM: Mother, you mustn't expect too much of Laura.

AMANDA: What do you mean?

TOM: Laura seems all those things to you and me because she's ours and we love her. We don't even notice she's crippled any more.

AMANDA: Don't say crippled! You know that I never allow that word to be used!

TOM: But face facts, Mother. She is and—that's not all—

AMANDA: What do you mean "not all"?

TOM: Laura is very different from other girls.

AMANDA: I think the difference is all to her advantage.

TOM: Not quite all—in the eyes of others—strangers—she's terribly shy and lives in a world of her own and those things make her seem a little peculiar to people outside the house.

AMANDA: Don't say peculiar.

TOM: Face the facts. She is.

*The dance hall music changes to a tango that has a minor and somewhat ominous tone.*

AMANDA: In what way is she peculiar—may I ask?

TOM (*gently*): She lives in a world of her own—a world of little glass ornaments, Mother. . . .

*He gets up.* AMANDA *remains holding the brush, looking at him, troubled.*

She plays old phonograph records and—that's about all—

(*He glances at himself in the mirror and crosses to the door.*)

AMANDA (*sharply*): Where are you going?

TOM: I'm going to the movies. (*He goes out the screen door.*)

AMANDA: Not to the movies, every night to the movies! (*She follows quickly to the screen door.*) I don't believe you always go to the movies!

*He is gone.* AMANDA *looks worriedly after him for a moment. Then vitality and optimism return and she turns from the door,*

*crossing to the portieres.*

Laura! Laura!

LAURA *answers from the kitchenette.*

LAURA: Yes, Mother.

AMANDA: Let those dishes go and come in front!

LAURA *appears with a dish towel.* AMANDA *speaks to her gaily.*

Laura, come here and make a wish on the moon!

*Screen image: The Moon.*

LAURA (*entering*): Moon—moon?

AMANDA: A little silver slipper of a moon. Look over your left shoulder, Laura, and make a wish!

LAURA *looks faintly puzzled as if called out of sleep.* AMANDA *seizes her shoulders and turns her at an angle by the door.*

Now! Now, darling, *wish!*

LAURA: What shall I wish for, Mother?

AMANDA (*her voice trembling and her eyes suddenly filling with tears*): Happiness! Good fortune!

*The sound of the violin rises and the stage dims out.*

# SCENE SIX

*The light comes up on the fire escape landing.*

TOM *is leaning against the grill, smoking.*

*Screen image: The high school hero.*

TOM: And so the following evening I brought Jim home to dinner. I had known Jim slightly in high school. In high school Jim was a hero. He had tremendous Irish good nature and vitality with the scrubbed and polished look of white chinaware. He seemed to move in a continual spotlight. He was a star in basketball, captain of the debating club, president of the senior class and the glee club and he sang the male lead in the annual light operas. He was always running or bounding, never just walking. He seemed always at the point of defeating the law of gravity. He was shooting with such velocity through his adolescence that you would logically expect him to arrive at nothing short of the White House by the time he was thirty. But Jim apparently ran into more interference after his graduation from Soldan. His speed had definitely slowed. Six years after he left high school he was holding a job that wasn't much better than mine.

*Screen image:* The Clerk.

He was the only one at the warehouse with whom I was on friendly terms. I was valuable to him as someone who could remember his former glory, who had seen him win basketball games and the silver cup in debating. He knew of my secret practice of retiring to a cabinet of the washroom to work on poems when business was slack in the warehouse. He called me Shakespeare. And while the other boys in the warehouse regarded me with suspicious hostility, Jim took a humorous attitude toward me. Gradually his attitude affected the others, their hostility wore off and they also began to smile at me as people smile at an oddly fashioned dog who trots across their path at some distance.

I knew that Jim and Laura had known each other at Soldan, and I had heard Laura speak admiringly of his voice. I didn't know if Jim remembered her or not. In high school Laura had been as unobtrusive as Jim had been astonishing. If he did remember Laura, it was not as my sister, for when I asked him to dinner, he grinned and said, "You know, Shakespeare, I never thought of you as having folks!"

He was about to discover that I did. . . .

*Legend on screen:* "The accent of a coming foot."

*The light dims out on* **TOM** *and comes up in the Wingfield living room—a delicate lemony light. It is about five on a Friday evening*

*of late spring which comes "scattering poems in the sky."*

**AMANDA** *has worked like a Turk in preparation for the gentleman caller. The results are astonishing. The new floor lamp with its rose silk shade is in place, a colored paper lantern conceals the broken light fixture in the ceiling, new billowing white curtains are at the windows, chintz covers are on the chairs and sofa, a pair of new sofa pillows make their initial appearance. Open boxes and tissue paper are scattered on the floor.*

**LAURA** *stands in the middle of the room with lifted arms while* **AMANDA** *crouches before her, adjusting the hem of a new dress, devout and ritualistic. The dress is colored and designed by memory. The arrangement of* **LAURA'S** *hair is changed; it is softer and more becoming. A fragile, unearthly prettiness has come out in* **LAURA**: *she is like a piece of translucent glass touched by light, given a momentary radiance, not actual, not lasting.*

**AMANDA** (*impatiently*): Why are you trembling?

**LAURA:** Mother, you've made me so nervous!

**AMANDA:** How have I made you nervous?

**LAURA:** By all this fuss! You make it seem so important!

**AMANDA:** I don't understand you, Laura. You couldn't be satisfied with just sitting home, and yet whenever I try to arrange something for you, you seem to resist it. (*She gets up.*) Now take a look at yourself. No, wait! Wait just a moment—I have an idea!

**LAURA:** What is it now?

**AMANDA** *produces two powder puffs which she wraps in handkerchiefs and stuffs in* **LAURA'S** *bosom.*

**LAURA:** Mother, what are you doing?

**AMANDA:** They call them "Gay Deceivers"!

**LAURA:** I won't wear them!

**AMANDA:** You will!

**LAURA:** Why should I?

AMANDA: Because, to be painfully honest, your chest is flat.

LAURA: You make it seem like we were setting a trap.

AMANDA: All pretty girls are a trap, a pretty trap, and men expect them to be.

*Legend on screen: "A pretty trap."*

Now look at yourself, young lady. This is the prettiest you will ever be! (*She stands back to admire Laura.*) I've got to fix myself now! You're going to be surprised by your mother's appearance!

AMANDA *crosses through the portieres, humming gaily.* LAURA *moves slowly to the long mirror and stares solemnly at herself. A wind blows the white curtains inward in a slow, graceful motion and with a faint, sorrowful sighing.*

AMANDA (*from somewhere behind the portieres*): It isn't dark enough yet.

LAURA *turns slowly before the mirror with a troubled look.*

*Legend on screen: "This is my sister: Celebrate her with strings!" Music plays.*

AMANDA (*laughing, still not visible*): I'm going to show you something. I'm going to make a spectacular appearance!

LAURA: What is it, Mother?

AMANDA: Possess your soul in patience—you will see! Something I've resurrected from that old trunk! Styles haven't changed so terribly much after all.... (*She parts the portieres.*) Now just look at your mother! (*She wears a girlish frock of yellowed voile with a blue silk sash. She carries a bunch of jonquils—the legend of her youth is nearly revived. Now she speaks feverishly:*) This is the dress in which I led the cotillion. Won the cakewalk twice at Sunset Hill, wore one Spring to the Governor's Ball in Jackson! See how I sashayed around the ballroom, Laura? (*She raises her skirt and does a mincing step around the room.*) I wore it on Sundays for my gentlemen callers! I had it on the day I met your father.... I had malaria fever all that Spring. The change of climate from East Tennessee to the Delta—weakened resistance. I had a little temperature all the time—not enough to be serious—just enough to make me restless and giddy! Invitations poured in—parties all over the Delta! "Stay in bed," said Mother, "you have a fever!"—but I just wouldn't. I took quinine but kept on going, going! Evenings, dances! Afternoons, long, long rides! Picnics—lovely! So lovely, that country in May—all lacy with dogwood, literally flooded with jonquils! That was the spring I had the craze for jonquils. Jonquils became an absolute obsession. Mother said, "Honey, there's no more room for jonquils." And still I kept on bringing in more jonquils. Whenever, wherever I saw them, I'd say, "Stop! Stop! I see jonquils!" I made the young men help me gather the jonquils! It was a joke, Amanda and her jonquils. Finally there were no more vases to hold them, every available space was filled with jonquils. No vases to hold them? All right, I'll hold them myself! And then I—(*She stops in front of the picture. Music plays.*) met your father! Malaria fever and jonquils and then—this—boy.... (*She switches on the rose-colored lamp.*) I hope they get here before it starts to rain. (*She crosses the room and places the jonquils in a bowl on the table.*) I gave your brother a little extra change so he and Mr. O'Connor could take the service car home.

LAURA (*with an altered look*): What did you say his name was?

AMANDA: O'Connor.

LAURA: What is his first name?

AMANDA: I don't remember. Oh, yes, I do. It was—Jim!

LAURA *sways slightly and catches hold of a chair.*

*Legend on screen: "Not Jim!"*

LAURA (*faintly*): Not—Jim!

AMANDA: Yes, that was it, it was Jim! I've never known a Jim that wasn't nice!
*The music becomes ominous.*

LAURA: Are you sure his name is Jim O'Connor?

AMANDA: Yes. Why?

LAURA: Is he the one that Tom used to know in high school?

AMANDA: He didn't say so. I think he just got to know him at the warehouse.

LAURA: There was a Jim O'Connor we both knew in high school—(*then, with effort*) If that is the one that Tom is bringing to dinner—you'll have to excuse me, I won't come to the table.

AMANDA: What sort of nonsense is this?

LAURA: You asked me once if I'd ever liked a boy. Don't you remember I showed you this boy's picture?

AMANDA: You mean the boy you showed me in the yearbook?

LAURA: Yes, that boy.

AMANDA: Laura, Laura, were you in love with that boy?

LAURA: I don't know, Mother. All I know is I couldn't sit at the table if it was him!

AMANDA: It won't be him! It isn't the least bit likely. But whether it is or not, you will come to the table. You will not be excused.

LAURA: I'll have to be, Mother.

AMANDA: I don't intend to humor your silliness, Laura. I've had too much from you and your brother, both! So just sit down and compose yourself till they come. Tom has forgotten his key so you'll have to let them in, when they arrive.

LAURA (*panicky*): Oh, Mother—*you* answer the door!

AMANDA (*lightly*): I'll be in the kitchen—busy!

LAURA: Oh, Mother, please answer the door, don't make me do it!

AMANDA (*crossing into the kitchenette*): I've got to fix the dressing for the salmon.

Fuss, fuss—silliness!–over a gentleman caller!
*The door swings shut.* LAURA *is left alone.*
*Legend on screen: "Terror!"*
*She utters a low moan and turns off the lamp—sits stiffly on the edge of the sofa, knotting her fingers together.*
*Legend on screen: "The Opening of a Door!"*
TOM *and* JIM *appear on the fire escape steps and climb to the landing. Hearing their approach,* LAURA *rises with a panicky gesture. She retreats to the portieres. The doorbell rings.* LAURA *catches her breath and touches her throat. Low drums sound.*

AMANDA (*calling*): Laura, sweetheart! The door!
LAURA *stares at it without moving.*

JIM: I think we just beat the rain.

TOM: Uh-huh. (*He rings again, nervously. Jim whistles and fishes for a cigarette.*)

AMANDA (*very, very gaily*): Laura, that is your brother and Mr. O'Connor! Will you let them in, darling?
LAURA *crosses toward the kitchenette door.*

LAURA (*breathlessly*): Mother—you go to the door!
AMANDA *steps out of the kitchenette and stares furiously at* LAURA. *She points imperiously at the door.*

LAURA: Please, please!

AMANDA (*in a fierce whisper*): What is the matter with you, you silly thing?

LAURA (*desperately*): Please, you answer it, *please!*

AMANDA: I told you I wasn't going to humor you, Laura. Why have you chosen this moment to lose your mind?

LAURA: Please, please, please, you go!

AMANDA: You'll have to go to the door because I can't!

LAURA (*despairingly*): I can't either!

AMANDA: *Why?*

LAURA: I'm *sick!*

AMANDA: I'm sick, too—of your nonsense! Why can't you and your brother be normal people? Fantastic whims and behavior!

**TOM** *gives a long ring.*

Preposterous goings on! Can you give me one reason—(*She calls out lyrically.*) *Coming! just one second!*—why you should be afraid to open a door? Now you answer it, Laura!

**LAURA:** Oh, oh, oh. . . . (*She returns through the portieres, darts to the Victrola, winds it frantically and turns it on.*)

**AMANDA:** Laura Wingfield, you march right to that door!

**LAURA:** *Yes—yes, Mother!*

*A faraway, scratchy rendition of "Dardanella" softens the air and gives her strength to move through it. She slips to the door and draws it cautiously open.* **TOM** *enters with the caller,* **JIM O'CONNOR.**

**TOM:** Laura, this is Jim. Jim, this is my sister, Laura.

**JIM** (*stepping inside*): I didn't know that Shakespeare had a sister!

**LAURA** (*retreating, stiff and trembling, from the door*): How—how do you do?

**JIM** (*heartily, extending his hand*): Okay!

*LAURA touches it hesitantly with hers.*

**JIM:** Your hand's *cold*, Laura!

**LAURA:** Yes, well—I've been playing the Victrola. . . .

**JIM:** Must have been playing classical music on it! You ought to play a little hot swing music to warm you up!

**LAURA:** Excuse me—I haven't finished playing the Victrola. . . . (*She turns awkwardly and hurries into the front room. She pauses a second by the Victrola. Then she catches her breath and darts through the portieres like a frightened deer.*)

**JIM** (*grinning*): What was the matter?

**TOM:** Oh—with Laura? Laura is—terribly shy.

**JIM:** Shy, huh? It's unusual to meet a shy girl nowadays. I don't believe you ever mentioned you had a sister.

**TOM:** Well, now you know. I have one. Here is the *Post Dispatch.* You want a piece of it?

**JIM:** Uh-huh.

**TOM:** What piece? The comics?

**JIM:** Sports! (*He glances at it.*) Ole Dizzy Dean is on his bad behavior.

**TOM** (*uninterested*): Yeah? (*He lights a cigarette and goes over to the fire-escape door.*)

**JIM:** Where are *you* going?

**TOM:** I'm going out on the terrace.

**JIM** (*going after him*): You know, Shakespeare—I'm going to sell you a bill of goods!

**TOM:** What goods?

**JIM:** A course I'm taking.

**TOM:** Huh?

**JIM:** In public speaking! You and me, we're not the warehouse type.

**TOM:** Thanks—that's good news. But what has public speaking got to do with it?

**JIM:** It fits you for—executive positions!

**TOM:** Awww.

**JIM:** I tell you it's done a helluva lot for me.

*Image on screen:* Executive at his desk.

**TOM:** In what respect?

**JIM:** In every! Ask yourself what is the difference between you an' me and men in the office down front? Brains?—No!—Ability?—No! Then what? Just one little thing—

**TOM:** What is that one little thing?

**JIM:** Primarily it amounts to—social poise! Being able to square up to people and hold your own on any social level!

**AMANDA** (*from the kitchenette*): Tom?

**TOM:** Yes, Mother?

**AMANDA:** Is that you and Mr. O'Connor?

**TOM:** Yes, Mother.

**AMANDA:** Well, you just make yourselves comfortable in there.

**TOM:** Yes, Mother.

**AMANDA:** Ask Mr. O'Connor if he would like to wash his hands.

**JIM:** Aw, no—no–thank you–I took care of that at the warehouse. Tom—

TOM: Yes?

JIM: Mr. Mendoza was speaking to me about you.

TOM: Favorably?

JIM: What do you think?

TOM: Well—

JIM: You're going to be out of a job if you don't wake up.

TOM: I am waking up—

JIM: You show no signs.

TOM: The signs are interior.

*Image on screen:* The sailing vessel with the Jolly Roger again.

TOM: I'm planning to change. (*He leans over the fire-escape rail, speaking with quiet exhilaration. The incandescent marquees and signs of the first-run movie houses light his face from across the alley. He looks like a voyager.*) I'm right at the point of committing myself to a future that doesn't include the warehouse and Mr. Mendoza or even a night-school course in public speaking.

JIM: What are you gassing about?

TOM: I'm tired of the movies.

JIM: Movies!

TOM: Yes, movies! Look at them—(*a wave toward the marvels of Grand Avenue*) All of those glamorous people—having adventures—hogging it all, gobbling the whole thing up! You know what happens? People go to the *movies* instead of *moving!* Hollywood characters are supposed to have all the adventures for everybody in America, while everybody in America sits in a dark room and watches them have them! Yes, until there's a war. That's when adventure becomes available to the masses! *Everyone's* dish, not only Gable's! Then the people in the dark room come out of the dark room to have some adventures themselves—goody, goody! It's our turn now, to go to the South Sea Island—to make a safari—to be exotic, far-off! But I'm not patient. I don't want to wait till then. I'm tired of the movies and I am *about* to *move!*

JIM (*incredulously*): Move?

TOM: Yes.

JIM: When?

TOM: Soon!

JIM: Where? Where?

*The music seems to answer the question, while* TOM *thinks it over. He searches in his pockets.*

TOM: I'm starting to boil inside. I know I seem dreamy, but inside—well, I'm boiling! Whenever I pick up a shoe, I shudder a little thinking how short life is and what I am doing! Whatever that means, I know it doesn't mean shoes—except as something to wear on a traveler's feet! (*He finds what he has been searching for in his pockets and holds out a paper to Jim.*) Look—

JIM: What?

TOM: I'm a member.

JIM (*reading*): The Union of Merchant Seamen.

TOM: I paid my dues this month, instead of the light bill.

JIM: You will regret it when they turn the lights off.

TOM: I won't be here.

JIM: How about your mother?

TOM: I'm like my father. The bastard son of a bastard! Did you notice how he's grinning in his picture in there? And he's been absent going on sixteen years!

JIM: You're just talking, you drip. How does your mother feel about it?

TOM: Shhh! Here comes Mother! Mother is not acquainted with my plans!

AMANDA (*coming through the portieres*): Where are you all?

TOM: On the terrace, Mother.

*They start inside. She advances to them.* TOM *is distinctly shocked at her appearance. Even* JIM *blinks a little. He is making his first contact with girlish Southern vivacity and in spite of the night-school course in public speaking is somewhat thrown off the beam by the unexpected outlay of social charm. Certain responses are attempted by* JIM *but are swept aside by* AMANDA'S *gay laughter and chatter.* TOM *is embarrassed but after the first shock* JIM *reacts very warmly. He grins and chuckles, is altogether won over.*

*Image on screen: Amanda as a girl.*

AMANDA (*coyly smiling, shaking her girlish ringlets*): Well, well, well, so this is Mr. O'Connor. Introductions entirely unnecessary. I've heard so much about you from my boy. I finally said to him, Tom—good gracious!–why don't you bring this paragon to supper? I'd like to meet this nice young man at the warehouse!—instead of just hearing him sing your praises so much! I don't know why my son is so stand-offish—that's not Southern behavior!

Let's sit down and—I think we could stand a little more air in here! Tom, leave the door open. I felt a nice fresh breeze a moment ago. Where has it gone to? Mmm, so warm already! And not quite summer, even. We're going to burn up when summer really gets started. However, we're having—we're having a very light supper. I think light things are better fo' this time of year. The same as light clothes are. Light clothes an' light food are what warm weather calls fo'. You know our blood gets so thick during th' winter—it takes a while fo' us to *adjust* ou'selves!—when the season changes. . . . It's come so quick this year. I wasn't prepared. All of a sudden—heavens! Already summer! I ran to the trunk an' pulled out this light dress—terribly old! Historical almost! But feels so good—so good an' co-ol, y' know. . . .

TOM: Mother—

AMANDA: Yes, honey?

TOM: How about—supper?

AMANDA: Honey, you go ask Sister if supper is ready! You know that Sister is in full charge of supper! Tell her you hungry boys are waiting for it. (*to* JIM) Have you met Laura?

JIM: She—

AMANDA: Let you in? Oh, good, you've met already! It's rare for a girl as sweet an' pretty as Laura to be domestic! But Laura is, thank heavens, not only pretty but also very domestic. I'm not at all. I never was a bit. I never could make a thing but angel-food cake. Well, in the South we had so many servants. Gone, gone, gone. All vestige of gracious living! Gone completely! I wasn't prepared for what the future brought me. All of my gentlemen callers were sons of planters and so of course I assumed that I would be married to one and raise my family on a large piece of land with plenty of servants. But man proposes—and woman accepts the proposal! To vary that old, old saying a little bit—I married no planter! I married a man who worked for the telephone company! That gallantly smiling gentleman over there! (*She points to the picture.*) A telephone man who—fell in love with long-distance! Now he travels and I don't even know where! But what am I going on for about my—tribulations? Tell me yours—I hope you don't have any! Tom?

TOM (*returning*): Yes, Mother?

AMANDA: Is supper nearly ready?

TOM: It looks to me like supper is on the table.

AMANDA: Let me look—(*She rises prettily and looks through the portieres.*) Oh, lovely! But where is Sister?

TOM: Laura is not feeling well and she says that she thinks she'd better not come to the table.

AMANDA: What? Nonsense! Laura? Oh, Laura!

LAURA (*from the kitchenette, faintly*): Yes, Mother.

AMANDA:  You really must come to the table. We won't be seated until you come to the table! Come in, Mr. O'Connor. You sit over there, and I'll. . . . Laura? Laura Wingfield! You're keeping us waiting, honey! We can't say grace until you come to the table!

*The kitchenette door is pushed weakly open and* LAURA *comes in. She is obviously quite faint, her lips trembling, her eyes wide and staring. She moves unsteadily toward the table.*

*Screen legend: "Terror!"*

*Outside a summer storm is coming on abruptly. The white curtains billow inward at the windows and there is a sorrowful murmur from the deep blue dusk.*

LAURA *suddenly stumbles; she catches at a chair with a faint moan.*

TOM:  Laura!

AMANDA:  Laura!

*There is a clap of thunder.*

*Screen legend: "Ah!"*

(*despairingly*) Why, Laura, you *are* ill, darling! Tom, help your sister into the living room, dear! Sit in the living room, Laura—rest on the sofa. Well! (*to* JIM *as* TOM *helps his sister to the sofa in the living room*) Standing over the hot stove made her ill! I told her that it was just too warm this evening, but—

TOM *comes back to the table.*

Is Laura all right now?

TOM:  Yes.

AMANDA:  What *is* that? Rain? A nice cool rain has come up! (*She gives* JIM *a frightened look.*) I think we may—have grace—now . . .

(TOM *looks at her stupidly.*) Tom, honey—you say grace!

TOM:  Oh . . . "For these and all thy mercies—"

*They bow their heads,* AMANDA *stealing a nervous glance at* JIM. *In the living room*

LAURA, *stretched on the sofa, clenches her hand to her lips, to hold back a shuddering sob.*

God's Holy Name be praised—

*The scene dims out.*

# SCENE SEVEN

*It is half an hour later. Dinner is just being finished in the dining room.* LAURA *is still huddled upon the sofa, her feet drawn under her, her head resting on a pale blue pillow, her eyes wide and mysteriously watchful. The new floor lamp with its shade of rose-colored silk gives a soft, becoming light to her face, bringing out the fragile, unearthly prettiness which usually escapes attention. From outside there is a steady murmur of rain, but it is slackening and soon stops; the air outside becomes pale and luminous as the moon breaks through the clouds. A moment after the curtain rises, the lights in both rooms flicker and go out.*

JIM:  Hey, there, Mr. Light Bulb!

AMANDA *laughs nervously.*

*Legend on screen: "Suspension of a public service."*

AMANDA:  Where was Moses when the lights went out? Ha-ha. Do you know the answer to that one, Mr. O'Connor?

JIM:  No, Ma'am, what's the answer?

AMANDA:  In the dark!

JIM *laughs appreciatively.*

Everybody sit still. I'll light the candles. Isn't it lucky we have them on the table? Where's a match? Which of you gentlemen can provide a match?

JIM:  Here.

AMANDA:  Thank you, Sir.

JIM:  Not at all, Ma'am!

AMANDA (*as she lights the candles*):  I guess the fuse has burnt out. Mr. O'Connor, can you tell a burnt-out fuse? I know I can't and Tom is a total loss when it comes to mechanics.

*They rise from the table and go into the kitchenette, from where their voices are heard.*

Oh, be careful you don't bump into something. We don't want our gentleman caller to break his neck. Now wouldn't that be a fine howdy-do?

JIM: Ha-ha! Where is the fuse-box?

AMANDA: Right here next to the stove. Can you see anything?

JIM: Just a minute.

AMANDA: Isn't electricity a mysterious thing? Wasn't it Benjamin Franklin who tied a key to a kite? We live in such a mysterious universe, don't we? Some people say that science clears up all the mysteries for us. In my opinion it only creates more! Have you found it yet?

JIM: No, Ma'am. All these fuses look okay to me.

AMANDA: Tom!

TOM: Yes, Mother?

AMANDA: That light bill I gave you several days ago. The one I told you we got the notices about?

*Legend on screen: "Ha!"*

TOM: Oh—yeah.

AMANDA: You didn't neglect to pay it by any chance?

TOM: Why, I—

AMANDA: Didn't! I might have known it!

JIM: Shakespeare probably wrote a poem on that light bill, Mrs. Wingfield.

AMANDA: I might have known better than to trust him with it! There's such a high price for negligence in this world!

JIM: Maybe the poem will win a ten-dollar prize.

AMANDA: We'll just have to spend the remainder of the evening in the nineteenth century, before Mr. Edison made the Mazda lamp!

JIM: Candlelight is my favorite kind of light.

AMANDA: That shows you're romantic! But that's no excuse for Tom. Well, we got through dinner. Very considerate of them to let us get through dinner before they plunged us into everlasting darkness, wasn't it, Mr. O'Connor?

JIM: Ha-ha!

AMANDA: Tom, as a penalty for your carelessness you can help me with the dishes.

JIM: Let me give you a hand.

AMANDA: Indeed you will not!

JIM: I ought to be good for something.

AMANDA: Good for something? (*Her tone is rhapsodic.*) *You?* Why, Mr. O'Connor, nobody, *nobody's* given me this much entertainment in years—as you have!

JIM: Aw, now, Mrs. Wingfield!

AMANDA: I'm not exaggerating, not one bit! But Sister is all by her lonesome. You go keep her company in the parlor! I'll give you this lovely old candelabrum that used to be on the altar at the Church of the Heavenly Rest. It was melted a little out of shape when the church burnt down. Lightning struck it one spring. Gypsy Jones was holding a revival at the time and he intimated that the church was destroyed because the Episcopalians gave card parties.

JIM: Ha-ha.

AMANDA: And how about you coaxing Sister to drink a little wine? I think it would be good for her! Can you carry both at once?

JIM: Sure. I'm Superman!

AMANDA: Now, Thomas, get into this apron!

JIM *comes into the dining room, carrying the candelabrum, its candles lighted, in one hand and a glass of wine in the other. The door of the kitchenette swings closed on* AMANDA'S *gay laughter; the flickering light approaches the portieres.* LAURA *sits up nervously as* JIM *enters. She can hardly speak from the almost intolerable strain of being alone with a stranger.*

*Screen legend: "I don't suppose you remember me at all!"*

*At first, before* JIM'S *warmth overcomes her paralyzing shyness,* LAURA'S *voice is thin and breathless, as though she had just run up a steep flight of stairs.* JIM'S *attitude is gently humorous. While the incident is apparently unimportant, it is to* LAURA *the climax of her secret life.*

JIM:  Hello there, Laura.

LAURA (*faintly*):  Hello.

*She clears her throat.*

JIM:  How are you feeling now? Better?

LAURA:  Yes. Yes, thank you.

JIM:  This is for you. A little dandelion wine. (*He extends the glass toward her with extravagant gallantry.*)

LAURA:  Thank you.

JIM:  Drink it—but don't get drunk!

*He laughs heartily.* LAURA *takes the glass uncertainly; she laughs shyly.*

Where shall I set the candles?

LAURA:  Oh—oh, anywhere . . .

JIM:  How about here on the floor? Any objections?

LAURA:  No.

JIM:  I'll spread a newspaper under to catch the drippings. I like to sit on the floor. Mind if I do?

LAURA:  Oh, no.

JIM:  Give me a pillow!

LAURA:  What?

JIM:  A pillow?

LAURA:  Oh . . . (*She hands him one quickly.*)

JIM:  How about you? Don't you like to sit on the floor?

LAURA:  Oh—yes.

JIM:  Why don't you, then?

LAURA:  I—will.

JIM:  Take a pillow!

LAURA *does. She sits on the floor on the other side of the candelabrum.* JIM *crosses his legs and smiles engagingly at her.* I can't hardly see you sitting way over there.

LAURA:  I can—see you.

JIM:  I know, but that's not fair, I'm in the limelight.

LAURA *moves her pillow closer.*

Good! Now I can see you! Comfortable?

LAURA:  Yes.

JIM:  So am I. Comfortable as a cow! Will you have some gum?

LAURA:  No, thank you.

JIM:  I think that I will indulge, with your permission. (*He musingly unwraps a stick of gum and holds it up.*) Think of the fortune made by the guy that invented the first piece of chewing gum. Amazing, huh? The Wrigley Building is one of the sights of Chicago—I saw it when I went up to the Century of Progress. Did you take in the Century of Progress?

LAURA:  No, I didn't.

JIM:  Well, it was quite a wonderful exposition. What impressed me most was the Hall of Science. Gives you an idea of what the future will be in America, even more wonderful than the present time is! (*There is a pause.* JIM *smiles at her.*) Your brother tells me you're shy. Is that right, Laura?

LAURA:  I—don't know.

JIM:  I judge you to be an old-fashioned type of girl. Well, I think that's a pretty good type to be. Hope you don't think I'm being too personal—do you?

LAURA (*hastily, out of embarrassment*):  I believe I will take a piece of gum, if you—don't mind. (*clearing her throat*) Mr. O'Connor, have you—kept up with your singing?

JIM:  Singing? Me?

LAURA:  Yes. I remember what a beautiful voice you had.

JIM:  When did you hear me sing?

LAURA *does not answer, and in the long pause which follows a man's voice is heard singing offstage.*

VOICE:
O blow, ye winds, heigh-ho,
A-roving I will go!
    I'm off to my love
    With a boxing glove—
Ten thousand miles away!

JIM:  You say you've heard me sing?

LAURA:  Oh, yes! Yes, very often . . . I—don't suppose—you remember me—at all?

JIM (*smiling doubtfully*): You know I have an idea I've seen you before. I had that idea soon as you opened the door. It seemed almost like I was about to remember your name. But the name that I started to call you—wasn't a name! And so I stopped myself before I said it.

LAURA: Wasn't it—Blue Roses?

JIM (*springing up, grinning*): Blue Roses! My gosh, yes—Blue Roses! That's what I had on my tongue when you opened the door! Isn't it funny what tricks your memory plays? I didn't connect you with high school somehow or other. But that's where it was; it was high school. I didn't even know you were Shakespeare's sister! Gosh, I'm sorry.

LAURA: I didn't expect you to. You—barely knew me!

JIM: But we did have a speaking acquaintance, huh?

LAURA: Yes, we—spoke to each other.

JIM: When did you recognize me?

LAURA: Oh, right away!

JIM: Soon as I came in the door?

LAURA: When I heard your name I thought it was probably you. I knew that Tom used to know you a little in high school. So when you came in the door—well, then I was—sure.

JIM: Why didn't you *say* something, then?

LAURA (*breathlessly*): I didn't know what to say, I was—too surprised!

JIM: For goodness' sakes! You know, this sure is funny!

LAURA: Yes! Yes, isn't it, though . . .

JIM: Didn't we have a class in something together?

LAURA: Yes, we did.

JIM: What class was that?

LAURA: It was—singing—chorus!

JIM: Aw!

LAURA: I sat across the aisle from you in the Aud.

JIM: Aw.

LAURA: Mondays, Wednesdays, and Fridays.

JIM: Now I remember—you always came in late.

LAURA: Yes, it was so hard for me, getting upstairs. I had that brace on my leg—it clumped so loud!

JIM: I never heard any clumping.

LAURA (*wincing at the recollection*): To me it sounded like—thunder!

JIM: Well, well, well, I never even noticed.

LAURA: And everybody was seated before I came in. I had to walk in front of all those people. My seat was in the back row. I had to go clumping all the way up the aisle with everyone watching!

JIM: You shouldn't have been self-conscious.

LAURA: I know, but I was. It was always such a relief when the singing started.

JIM: Aw, yes, I've placed you now! I used to call you Blue Roses. How is it that I got started calling you that?

LAURA: I was out of school a little while with pleurosis. When I came back you asked me what was the matter. I said I had pleurosis—you thought I said *Blue Roses*. That's what you always called me after that!

JIM: I hope you didn't mind.

LAURA: Oh, no—I liked it. You see, I wasn't acquainted with many—people. . . .

JIM: As I remember you sort of stuck by yourself.

LAURA: I—I—never have much luck at—making friends.

JIM: I don't see why you wouldn't.

LAURA: Well, I—started out badly.

JIM: You mean being—

LAURA: Yes, it sort of—stood between me—

JIM: You shouldn't have let it!

LAURA: I know, but it did, and—

JIM: You were shy with people!

LAURA: I tried not to be but never could—

JIM: Overcome it?

LAURA: No, I—I never could!

JIM: I guess being shy is something you have to work out of kind of gradually.

LAURA (*sorrowfully*): Yes—I guess it—

JIM: Takes time!

LAURA: Yes—

JIM: People are not so dreadful when you know them. That's what you have to remember! And everybody has problems, not just you, but practically everybody has got some problems. You think of yourself as having the only problems, as being the only one who is disappointed. But just look around you and you will see lots of people as disappointed as you are. For instance, I hoped when I was going to high school that I would be further along at this time, six years later, that I am now. You remember that wonderful write-up I had in *The Torch*?

LAURA: Yes! (*She rises and crosses to the table.*)

JIM: It said I was bound to succeed in anything I went into!

LAURA *returns with the high school yearbook.*

Holy Jeez! *The Torch!*

*He accepts it reverently. They smile across the book with mutual wonder.* LAURA *crouches beside him and they begin to turn the pages.* LAURA'S *shyness is dissolving in his warmth.*

LAURA: Here you are in *The Pirates of Penzance!*

JIM (*wistfully*): I sang the baritone lead in that operetta.

LAURA (*raptly*): So—beautifully!

JIM (*protesting*): Aw—

LAURA: Yes, yes—beautifully—beautifully!

JIM: You heard me?

LAURA: All three times!

JIM: No!

LAURA: Yes!

JIM: All three performances?

LAURA (*looking down*): Yes.

JIM: Why?

LAURA: I—wanted to ask you to—autograph my program.

*She takes the program from the back of the yearbook and shows it to him.*

JIM: Why didn't you ask me to?

LAURA: You were always surrounded by your own friends so much that I never had a chance to.

JIM: You should have just—

LAURA: Well, I—thought you might think I was—

JIM: Thought I might think you was—what?

LAURA: Oh—

JIM (*with a reflective relish*): I was beleaguered by females in those days.

LAURA: You were terribly popular!

JIM: Yeah—

LAURA: You had such a—friendly way—

JIM: I was spoiled in high school.

LAURA: Everybody—liked you!

JIM: Including you?

LAURA: I—yes, I—did, too—(*She gently closes the book in her lap.*)

JIM: Well, well, well! Give me that program, Laura.

*She hands it to him. He signs it with a flourish.*

There you are—better late than never!

LAURA: Oh, I—what a—surprise!

JIM: My signature isn't worth very much right now. But some day—maybe—it will increase in value! Being disappointed is one thing and being discouraged is something else. I am disappointed but I am not discouraged. I'm twenty-three years old. How old are you?

LAURA: I'll be twenty-four in June.

JIM: That's not old age!

LAURA: No, but—

JIM: You finished high school?

LAURA (*with difficulty*): I didn't go back.

JIM: You mean you dropped out?

LAURA: I made bad grades in my final examinations. (*She rises and replaces the book and the program on the table. Her voice is strained.*) How is—Emily Meisenbach getting along?

JIM: Oh, that kraut-head!

LAURA: Why do you call her that?

JIM: That's what she was.

LAURA: You're not still—going with her?

JIM: I never see her.

LAURA: It said in the "Personal" section that you were—engaged!

JIM: I know, but I wasn't impressed by that—propaganda!

LAURA: It wasn't—the truth?

JIM: Only in Emily's optimistic opinion!

LAURA: Oh—

*Legend: "What have you done since high school?"*

JIM *lights a cigarette and leans indolently back on his elbows smiling at* LAURA *with a warmth and charm which lights her inwardly with altar candles. She remains by the table, picks up a piece from the glass menagerie collection, and turns it in her hands to cover her tumult.*

JIM (*after several reflective puffs on his cigarette*): What have you done since high school?

*She seems not to hear him.*

Huh?

LAURA *looks up.*

I said what have you done since high school, Laura?

LAURA: Nothing much.

JIM: You must have been doing something these six long years.

LAURA: Yes.

JIM: Well, then, such as what?

LAURA: I took a business course at business college—

JIM: How did that work out?

LAURA: Well, not very—well—I had to drop out, it gave me—indigestion—

JIM *laughs gently.*

JIM: What are you doing now?

LAURA: I don't do anything—much. Oh, please don't think I sit around doing nothing! My glass collection takes up a good deal of time. Glass is something you have to take good care of.

JIM: What did you say—about glass?

LAURA: Collection I said—I have one—(*She clears her throat and turns away again, acutely shy.*)

JIM (*abruptly*): You know what I judge to be the trouble with you? Inferiority complex! Know what that is? That's what they call it when someone low-rates himself! I understand it because I had it, too. Although my case was not so aggravated as yours seems to be. I had it until I took up public speaking, developed my voice, and learned that I had an aptitude for science. Before that time I never thought of myself as being outstanding in any way whatsoever! Now I've never made a regular study of it, but I have a friend who says I can analyze people better than doctors that make a profession of it. I don't claim that to be necessarily true, but I can sure guess a person's psychology, Laura! (*He takes out his gum.*) Excuse me, Laura. I always take it out when the flavor is gone. I'll use this scrap of paper to wrap it in. I know how it is to get it stuck on a shoe. (*He wraps the gum in paper and puts it in his pocket.*) Yep— that's what I judge to be your principal trouble. A lack of confidence in yourself as a person. You don't have the proper amount of faith in yourself. I'm basing that fact on a number of your remarks and also on certain observations I've made. For instance that clumping you thought was so awful in high school. You say that you even dreaded to walk into class. You see what you did? You dropped out of school, you gave up an education because of a clump, which as far as I know was practically non-existent! A little physical defect is what you have. Hardly noticeable even! Magnified thousands of times by imagination! You know what my strong advice to you is? Think of yourself as *superior* in some way!

LAURA: In what way would I think?

JIM:  Why, man alive, Laura! Just look about you a little. What do you see? A world full of common people! All of 'em born and all of 'em going to die! Which of them has one-tenth of your good points! Or mine! Or anyone else's, as far as that goes—gosh! Everybody excels in some one thing. Some in many! (*He unconsciously glances at himself in the mirror.*) All you've got to do is discover in *what!* Take me, for instance. (*He adjusts his tie at the mirror.*) My interest happens to lie in electro-dynamics. I'm taking a course in radio engineering at night school, Laura, on top of a fairly responsible job at the warehouse. I'm taking that course and studying public speaking.

LAURA:  Ohhhh.

JIM:  Because I believe in the future of television! (*turning his back to her.*) I wish to be ready to go up right along with it. Therefore I'm planning to get in on the ground floor. In fact I've already made the right connections and all that remains is for the industry itself to get under way! Full steam—(*His eyes are starry.*) Knowledge—Zzzzzp! *Money*—Zzzzzzp!—*Power!* That's the cycle democracy is built on!
*His attitude is convincingly dynamic.* LAURA *stares at him, even her shyness eclipsed in her absolute wonder. He suddenly grins.*
I guess you think I think a lot of myself!

LAURA:  No—o-o-o, I—

JIM:  Now how about you? Isn't there something you take more interest in than anything else?

LAURA:  Well, I do—as I said—have my—glass collection—
*A peal of girlish laughter rings from the kitchenette.*

JIM:  I'm not right sure I know what you're talking about. What kind of glass is it?

LAURA:  Little articles of it, they're ornaments mostly! Most of them are little animals made out of glass, the tiniest little animals in the world. Mother calls them a glass menagerie! Here's an example of one, if you'd like to see it! This one is one of the oldest. It's nearly thirteen.
*Music:* "The Glass Menagerie."
*He stretches out his hand.*
Oh, be careful—if you breathe, it breaks!

JIM:  I'd better not take it. I'm pretty clumsy with things.

LAURA:  Go on, I trust you with him! (*She places the piece in his palm.*) There now—you're holding him gently! Hold him over the light, he loves the light! You see how the light shines through him?

JIM:  It sure does shine!

LAURA:  I shouldn't be partial, but he is my favorite one.

JIM:  What kind of a thing is this one supposed to be?

LAURA:  Haven't you noticed the single horn on his forehead?

JIM:  A unicorn, huh?

LAURA:  Mmmm-hmmm!

JIM:  Unicorns—aren't they extinct in the modern world?

LAURA:  I know!

JIM:  Poor little fellow, he must feel sort of lonesome.

LAURA (*smiling*):  Well, if he does, he doesn't complain about it. He stays on a shelf with some horses that don't have horns and all of them seem to get along nicely together.

JIM:  How do you know?

LAURA (*lightly*):  I haven't heard any arguments among them!

JIM (*grinning*):  No arguments, huh? Well, that's a pretty good sign! Where shall I set him?

LAURA:  Put him on the table. They all like a change of scenery once in a while!

JIM:  Well, well, well, well—(*He places the glass piece on the table, then raises his arms and stretches.*) Look how big my shadow is when I stretch!

LAURA:  Oh, oh, yes—it stretches across the ceiling!

JIM (*crossing to the door*):  I think it's stopped raining. (*He opens the fire-escape door and the background music changes to a dance tune.*) Where does the music come from?

LAURA:  From the Paradise Dance Hall across the alley.

JIM:  How about cutting the rug a little, Miss Wingfield?

LAURA:  Oh, I—

JIM:  Or is your program filled up? Let me have a look at it. (*He grasps an imaginary card.*) Why, every dance is taken! I'll just have to scratch some out.
*Waltz music: "La Golondrina."*
Ahhh, a waltz! (*He executes some sweeping turns by himself, then holds his arms toward* LAURA.)

LAURA (*breathlessly*):  I—can't dance!

JIM:  There you go, that inferiority stuff!

LAURA:  I've never danced in my life!

JIM:  Come on, try!

LAURA:  Oh, but I'd step on you!

JIM:  I'm not made out of glass.

LAURA:  How—how—how do we start?

JIM:  Just leave it to me. You hold your arms out a little.

LAURA:  Like this?

JIM (*taking her in his arms*):  A little bit higher. Right. Now don't tighten up, that's the main thing about it—relax.

LAURA (*laughing breathlessly*):  It's hard not to.

JIM:  Okay.

LAURA:  I'm afraid you can't budge me.

JIM:  What do you bet I can't? (*He swings her into motion.*)

LAURA:  Goodness, yes, you can!

JIM:  Let yourself go, now, Laura, just let yourself go.

LAURA:  I'm—

JIM:  Come on!

LAURA:  —trying!

JIM:  Not so stiff—easy does it!

LAURA:  I know but I'm—

JIM:  Loosen th' backbone! There now, that's a lot better.

LAURA:  Am I?

JIM:  Lots, lots better! (*He moves her about the room in a clumsy waltz.*)

LAURA:  Oh, my!

JIM:  Ha-ha!

LAURA:  Oh, my goodness!

JIM:  Ha-ha-ha!
*They suddenly bump into the table, and the glass piece on it falls to the floor.* JIM *stops the dance.*
*What did we hit on?*

LAURA:  Table.

JIM:  Did something fall off it? I think—

LAURA:  Yes.

JIM:  I hope that it wasn't the little glass horse with the horn!

LAURA:  Yes. (*She stoops to pick it up.*)

JIM:  Aw, aw, aw. Is it broken?

LAURA:  Now it is just like all the other horses.

JIM:  It's lost its—

LAURA:  Horn! It doesn't matter. Maybe it's a blessing in disguise.

JIM:  You'll never forgive me. I bet that that was your favorite piece of glass.

LAURA:  I don't have favorites much. It's no tragedy, Freckles. Glass breaks so easily. No matter how careful you are. The traffic jars the shelves and things fall off them.

JIM:  Still I'm awfully sorry that I was the cause.

LAURA (*smiling*):  I'll just imagine he had an operation. The horn was removed to make him feel less—freakish!
*They both laugh.*
Now he will feel more at home with the other horses, the ones that don't have horns. . . .

JIM:  Ha-ha, that's very funny! (*Suddenly he is serious.*) I'm glad to see that you have a sense of humor. You know—you're—well—very different! Surprisingly different from anyone else I know! (*His voice becomes soft and hesitant with a genuine feeling.*) Do you mind me telling you that?

LAURA *is abashed beyond speech.*

I mean it in a nice way—

LAURA *nods shyly, looking away.*

You make me feel sort of—I don't know how to put it! I'm usually pretty good at expressing things, but—this is something that I don't know how to say!

LAURA *touches her throat and clears it— turns the broken unicorn in her hands. His voice becomes softer.*

Has anyone ever told you that you were pretty?

*There is a pause, and the music rises slightly.* LAURA *looks up slowly, with wonder, and shakes her head.*

Well, you are! In a very different way from anyone else. And all the nicer because of the difference, too.

*His voice becomes low and husky.* LAURA *turns away, nearly faint with the novelty of her emotions.*

I wish that you were my sister. I'd teach you to have some confidence in yourself. The different people are not like other people, but being different is nothing to be ashamed of. Because other people are not such wonderful people. They're one hundred times one thousand. You're one times one! They walk all over the earth. You just stay here. They're common as— weeds, but—you—well, you're—*Blue Roses!*

*Image on screen:* Blue Roses.

*The music changes.*

LAURA: But blue is wrong for—roses. . . .

JIM: It's right for you! You're—pretty!

LAURA: In what respect am I pretty?

JIM: In all respects—believe me! Your eyes—your hair—are pretty! Your hands are pretty! (*He catches hold of her hand.*) You think I'm making this up because I'm invited to dinner and have to be nice. Oh, I could do that! I could put on an act for you, Laura, and say lots of things without being very sincere. But this time I am. I'm talking to you sincerely. I hap-

pened to notice you had this inferiority complex that keeps you from feeling comfortable with people. Somebody needs to build your confidence up and make you proud instead of shy and turning away and—blushing. Somebody— ought to—*kiss you, Laura!*

*His hand slips slowly up her arm to her shoulder as the music swells tumultuously. He suddenly turns her about and kisses her on the lips. When he releases her,* LAURA *sinks on the sofa with a bright, dazed look.* JIM *backs away and fishes in his pocket for a cigarette.*

*Legend on screen:* "A souvenir.

Stumblejohn!

*He lights the cigarette, avoiding her look. There is a peal of girlish laughter from* AMANDA *in the kitchenette.* LAURA *slowly raises and opens her hand. It still contains the little broken glass animal. She looks at it with a tender, bewildered expression.*

Stumblejohn! I shouldn't have done that—that was way off the beam. You don't smoke, do you?

*She looks up, smiling, not hearing the question. He sits beside her rather gingerly. She looks at him speechlessly—waiting. He coughs decorously and moves a little farther aside as he considers the situation and senses her feelings, dimly, with perturbation. He speaks gently.*

Would you—care for a—mint?

*She doesn't seem to hear him but her look grows brighter even.*

Peppermint? Life Saver? My pocket's a regular drugstore—wherever I go. . . . (*He pops a mint in his mouth. Then he gulps and decides to make a clean breast of it. He speaks slowly and gingerly.*) Laura, you know, if I had a sister like you, I'd do the same thing as Tom. I'd bring out fellows and—introduce her to them. The right type of boys—of a type to—appreciate her. Only—well—he made a mistake about me. Maybe I've got no call to be saying this. That may not have been the idea in having me over. But what if it was? There's nothing wrong about that. The only trouble is that in my case—I'm not in a situation to—do the right thing. I can't take down your number and say I'll phone. I can't call up next week and—ask for a date. I thought I had better explain the situation in case you—misunderstood it and—I hurt your feelings. . . .

*There is a pause. Slowly, very slowly,* LAURA'S *look changes, her eyes returning slowly from his to the glass figure in her palm.* AMANDA *utters another gay laugh in the kitchenette.*

LAURA (*faintly*): You—won't—call again?

JIM: No, Laura, I can't. (*He rises from the sofa.*) As I was just explaining, I've—got strings on me. Laura, I've—been going steady! I go out all the time with a girl named Betty. She's a home-girl like you, and Catholic, and Irish, and in a great many ways we—get along fine. I met her last summer on a moonlight boat trip up the river to Alton, on the *Majestic.* Well— right away from the start it was—love! *Legend:* Love!

LAURA *sways slightly forward and grips the arm of the sofa. He fails to notice, now enrapt in his own comfortable being.*

Being in love has made a new man of me! *Leaning stiffly forward, clutching the arm of the sofa,* LAURA *struggles visibly with her storm. But* JIM *is oblivious; she is a long way off.*

The power of love is really pretty tremendous! Love is something that— changes the whole world, Laura!

*The storm abates a little and* LAURA *leans back. He notices her again.*

It happened that Betty's aunt took sick, she got a wire and had to go to Centralia. So Tom—when he asked me to dinner—I naturally just accepted the invitation, not knowing that you—that he—that I— (*He stops awkwardly.*)

Huh—I'm a stumblejohn!

*He flops back on the sofa. The holy candles on the altar of* LAURA'S *face have been snuffed out. There is a look of almost infinite desolation.* JIM *glances at her uneasily.*

I wish that you would—say something.

*She bites her lip which was trembling and then bravely smiles. She opens her hand again on the broken glass figure. Then she gently takes his hand and raises it level with her own. She carefully places the unicorn in the palm of his hand, then pushes his fingers closed upon it.*

What are you—doing that for? You want me to have him? Laura?

*She nods.*

What for?

LAURA: A—souvenir. . . .

*She rises unsteadily and crouches beside the Victrola to wind it up.*

*Legend on screen:* "Things have a way of turning out so badly!" *Or image:* "Gentleman caller waving goodbye—gaily."

*At this moment* AMANDA *rushes brightly back into the living room. She bears a pitcher of fruit punch in an old-fashioned cut-glass pitcher, and a plate of macaroons. The plate has a gold border and poppies painted on it.*

AMANDA: Well, well, well! Isn't the air delightful after the shower? I've made you children a little liquid refreshment.

(*She turns gaily to* JIM.) Jim, do you know that song about lemonade?

"Lemonade, lemonade
made in the shade and stirred with a spade—
Good enough for any old maid!"

JIM (*uneasily*): Ha-ha! No—I never heard it.

AMANDA: Why, Laura! You look so serious!

JIM: We were having a serious conversation.

AMANDA: Good! Now you're better acquainted!

JIM (*uncertainly*): Ha-ha! Yes.

AMANDA: You modern young people are much more serious-minded than my generation. I was so gay as a girl!

JIM: You haven't changed, Mrs. Wingfield.

AMANDA: Tonight I'm rejuvenated! The gaiety of the occasion, Mr. O'Connor! (*she tosses her head with a peal of laughter, spilling some lemonade.*) Oooo! I'm baptizing myself!

JIM: Here—let me—

AMANDA (*setting the pitcher down*): There now. I discovered we had some maraschino cherries. I dumped them in, juice and all!

JIM: You shouldn't have gone to that trouble, Mrs. Wingfield.

AMANDA: Trouble, trouble? Why, it was loads of fun! Didn't you hear me cutting up in the kitchen? I bet your ears were burning! I told Tom how outdone with him I was for keeping you to himself so long a time! He should have brought you over much, much sooner! Well, now that you've found your way, I want you to be a very frequent caller! Not just occasional but all the time. Oh, we're going to have a lot of gay times together! I see them coming! Mmm, just breathe that air! So fresh, and the moon's so pretty! I'll skip back out—I know where my place is when young folks are having a—serious conversation!

JIM: Oh, don't go out, Mrs. Wingfield. The fact of the matter is I've got to be going.

AMANDA: Going, now? You're joking! Why, it's only the shank of the evening, Mr. O'Connor!

JIM: Well, you know how it is.

AMANDA: You mean you're a young workingman and have to keep workingmen's hours. We'll let you off early tonight. But only on the condition that next time you stay later. What's the best night for you? Isn't Saturday night the best night for you workingmen?

JIM: I have a couple of time-clocks to punch, Mrs. Wingfield. One at morning, another one at night!

AMANDA: My, but you *are* ambitious! You work at night, too?

JIM: No, Ma'am, not work but—Betty!
*He crosses deliberately to pick up his hat. The band at the Paradise Dance Hall goes into a tender waltz.*

AMANDA: Betty? Betty? Who's—Betty!
*There is an ominous cracking sound in the sky.*

JIM: Oh, just a girl. The girl I go steady with!
*He smiles charmingly. The sky falls.*
*Legend:* "The Sky Falls."

AMANDA (*a long-drawn exhalation*): Ohhhh . . . Is it a serious romance, Mr. O'Connor?

JIM: We're going to be married the second Sunday in June.

AMANDA: Ohhhh—how nice! Tom didn't mention that you were engaged to be married.

JIM: The cat's not out of the bag at the warehouse yet. You know how they are. They call you Romeo and stuff like that. (*He stops at the oval mirror to put on his hat. He carefully shapes the brim and the crown to give a discreetly dashing effect.*) It's been a wonderful evening, Mrs. Wingfield. I guess this is what they mean by Southern hospitality.

AMANDA: It really wasn't anything at all.

JIM: I hope it don't seem like I'm rushing off. But I promised Betty I'd pick her up at the Wabash depot, an' by the time I get my jalopy down there her train'll be in. Some women are pretty upset if you keep 'em waiting.

AMANDA: Yes, I know—the tyranny of women! (*She extends her hand.*) Goodbye, Mr. O'Connor. I wish you luck—and happiness—and success! All three of them, and so does Laura! Don't you, Laura?

LAURA: Yes!

JIM (*taking* LAURA'S *hand*): Goodbye, Laura. I'm certainly going to treasure that souvenir. And don't you forget the good advice I gave you. (*He raises his voice to a cheery shout.*) So long, Shakespeare! Thanks again, ladies. Good night!
*He grins and ducks jauntily out. Still bravely grimacing,* AMANDA *closes the door on the*

*gentleman caller. Then she turns back to the room with a puzzled expression. She and* LAURA *don't dare to face each other.* LAURA *crouches beside the Victrola to wind it.*

AMANDA (*faintly*): Things have a way of turning out so badly. I don't believe that I would play the Victrola. Well, well—well! Our gentleman caller was engaged to be married! (*She raises her voice.*) Tom!

TOM (*from the kitchenette*): Yes, Mother?

AMANDA: Come in here a minute. I want to tell you something awfully funny.

TOM (*entering with a macaroon and a glass of the lemonade*): Has the gentleman caller gotten away already?

AMANDA: The gentleman caller has made an early departure. What a wonderful joke you played on us!

TOM: How do you mean?

AMANDA: You didn't mention that he was engaged to be married.

TOM: Jim? Engaged?

AMANDA: That's what he just informed us.

TOM: I'll be jiggered! I didn't know about that.

AMANDA: That seems very peculiar.

TOM: What's peculiar about it?

AMANDA: Didn't you call him your best friend down at the warehouse?

TOM: He is, but how did I know?

AMANDA: It seems extremely peculiar that you wouldn't know your best friend was going to be married!

TOM: The warehouse is where I work, not where I know things about people!

AMANDA: You don't know things anywhere! You live in a dream; you manufacture illusions!

*He crosses to the door.*

Where are you going?

TOM: I'm going to the movies.

AMANDA: That's right, now that you've had us make such fools of ourselves. The effort, the preparations, all the expense! The new floor lamp, the rug, the clothes

for Laura! All for what? To entertain some other girl's fiancé! Go to the movies, go! Don't think about us, a mother deserted, an unmarried sister who's crippled and has no job! Don't let anything interfere with your selfish pleasure! Just go, go, go—to the movies!

TOM: All right, I will! The more you shout about my selfishness to me the quicker I'll go, and I won't go to the movies!

AMANDA: Go, then! Go to the moon—you selfish dreamer!

TOM *smashes his glass on the floor. He plunges out on the fire escape, slamming the door.* LAURA *screams in fright. The dance-hall music becomes louder.* TOM *stands on the fire escape, gripping the rail. The moon breaks through the storm clouds, illuminating his face.*

*Legend on screen:* "And so goodbye. . . ."

TOM'S *closing speech is timed with what is happening inside the house. We see, as though through soundproof glass, that* AMANDA *appears to be making a comforting speech to* LAURA, *who is huddled upon the sofa. Now that we cannot hear the mother's speech, her silliness is gone and she has dignity and tragic beauty.* LAURA'S *hair hides her face until, at the end of the speech, she lifts her head to smile at her mother.* AMANDA'S *gestures are slow and graceful, almost dancelike, as she comforts her daughter. At the end of her speech she glances a moment at the father's picture—then withdraws through the portieres. At the close of* TOM'S *speech,* LAURA *blows out the candles, ending the play.*

TOM: I didn't go to the moon, I went much further—for time is the longest distance between two places. Not long after that I was fired for writing a poem on the lid of a shoe-box. I left Saint Louis. I descended the steps of this fire escape for a last time and followed, from then on, in my father's footsteps, attempting to find in motion what was lost in space. I traveled around a great deal. The cities swept about me like dead leaves, leaves that were brightly colored but torn away from the branches. I would have stopped, but I was pursued by something. It always came upon me unawares, taking me altogether by surprise. Perhaps it was a familiar bit of music. Perhaps it was only a piece of transparent glass. Perhaps I am walking along a street at night, in some strange city, before I have found companions. I pass the lighted window of a shop where perfume is sold. The window is filled with pieces of colored glass, tiny transparent bottles in delicate colors, like bits of a shattered rainbow. Then all at once my sister touches my shoulder. I turn around and look into her eyes. Oh, Laura, Laura, I tried to leave you behind me, but I am more faithful than I intended to be! I reach for a cigarette, I cross the street, I run into the movies or a bar, I buy a drink, I speak to the nearest stranger—anything that can blow your candles out!

**LAURA** *bends over the candles.*

For nowadays the world is lit by lightning! Blow out your candles, Laura— and so goodbye. . . .

*She blows the candles out.*

## PRODUCTION NOTES (PLAYWRIGHT'S)

Being a "memory play," *The Glass Menagerie* can be presented with unusual freedom of convention. Because of its considerably delicate or tenuous material, atmospheric touches and subtleties of direction play a particularly important part. Expressionism and all other unconventional techniques in drama have only one valid aim, and that is a closer approach to truth. When a play employs unconventional techniques, it is not, or

certainly shouldn't be, trying to escape its responsibility of dealing with reality, or interpreting experience, but is actually or should be attempting to find a closer approach, a more penetrating and vivid expression of things as they are. The straight realistic play with its genuine Frigidaire and authentic ice-cubes, its characters who speak exactly as its audience speaks, corresponds to the academic landscape and has the same virtue of a photographic likeness. Everyone should know nowadays the unimportance of the photographic in art: that truth, life, or reality is an organic thing which the poetic imagination can represent or suggest, in essence, only through transformation, through changing into other forms than those which were merely present in appearance.

These remarks are not meant as a preface only to this particular play. They have to do with a conception of a new, plastic theatre which must take the place of the exhausted theatre of realistic conventions if the theatre is to resume vitality as a part of our culture.

THE SCREEN DEVICE:  There is *only one important difference between the original and the acting version of the play* and that is the *omission* in the latter of the device that I tentatively included in my *original* script. This device was the use of a screen on which were projected magic-lantern slides bearing images or titles. I do not regret the omission of this device from the original Broadway production. The extraordinary power of Miss Taylor's* performance made it suitable to have the utmost simplicity in the physical production. But I think it may be interesting to some readers to see how this device was conceived. So I am putting it into the published manuscript. These images and leg-

---

*Actress Laurette Taylor created the role of Amanda Wingfield.

ends, projected from behind, were cast on a section of wall between the front-room and dining-room areas, which should be indistinguishable from the rest when not in use.

The purpose of this will probably be apparent. It is to give accent to certain values in each scene. Each scene contains a particular point (or several) which is structurally the most important. In an episodic play, such as this, the basic structure or narrative line may be obscured from the audience; the effect may seem fragmentary rather than architectural. This may not be the fault of the play so much as a lack of attention in the audience. The legend or image upon the screen will strengthen the effect of what is merely allusion in the writing and allow the primary point to be made more simply and lightly than if the entire responsibility were on the spoken lines. Aside from this structural value, I think the screen will have a definite emotional appeal, less definable but just as important. An imaginative producer or director may invent many other uses for this device than those indicated in the present script. In fact the possibilities of the device seem much larger to me than the instance of this play can possibly utilize.

THE MUSIC: Another extra-literary accent in this play is provided by the use of music. A single recurring tune, "The Glass Menagerie," is used to give emotional emphasis to suitable passages. This tune is like circus music, not when you are on the grounds or in the immediate vicinity of the parade, but when you are at some distance and very likely thinking of something else. It seems under those circumstances to continue almost interminably and it weaves in and out of your preoccupied consciousness; then it is the lightest, most delicate music in the world and perhaps the saddest. It expresses the surface vivacity of life with the underlying strain of immutable and inexpressible sorrow. When you look at a piece of delicately spun glass you think of two things: how beautiful it is and how easily it can be broken. Both of those ideas should be woven into the recurring tune, which dips in and out of the play as if it were carried on a wind that changes. It serves as a thread of connection and allusion between the narrator with his separate point in time and space and the subject of his story. Between each episode it returns as reference to the emotion, nostalgia, which is the first condition of the play. It is primarily Laura's music and therefore comes out most clearly when the play focuses upon her and the lovely fragility of glass which is her image.

THE LIGHTING: The lighting in the play is not realistic. In keeping with the atmosphere of memory, the stage is dim. Shafts of light are focused on selected areas or actors, sometimes in contradistinction to what is the apparent center. For instance, in the quarrel scene between Tom and Amanda, in which Laura has no active part, the clearest pool of light is on her figure. This is also true of the supper scene, when her silent figure on the sofa should remain the visual center. The light upon Laura should be distinct from the others, having a peculiar pristine clarity such as light used in early religious portraits of female saints or madonnas. A certain correspondence to light in religious paintings, such as El Greco's,* where the figures are radiant in atmosphere that is relatively dusky, could be effectively used throughout the play. (It will also permit a more effective use of the screen.) A free, imaginative use of light can be of enormous value in giving a mobile, plastic quality to plays of a more or less static nature.

*Tennessee Williams*

---

*A seventeenth-century Spanish painter.

## SUMMARY

Drama's characters, like the novel's, are fictional. However, they differ from those found in the novel because they are created to be given life by actors. At all times there are two levels of humanity at work in drama's characters. One level involves the story's characters as individualized forms of motives and actions in special circumstances. The second concerns dramatic characters as images of humanity having the potential to be given life by actors.

Drama's characters can be understood, first, as general types of humanity by observing gender, age, profession, clothing, manners, gestures, and speech. Second, since characters are also individualized images of humanity, we must carefully assess what they say and what they do to understand their particular habits, motives, and acts. As we said, drama's action springs from character. After all, in the old way of thinking about drama as an imitation of an action or of human events, those doing the imitating are characters, or reflected human beings. They may be as complex as Hamlet, as vulnerable as Laura Wingfield, or as conniving as Joseph Surface. Yet, their speech, gestures, and actions determine who they are and what their acts mean in the special circumstances devised by the playwright.

Over the centuries, drama's central characters have changed from royalty to commoners—from kings and princes to traveling salesmen and blue-collar workers. The change of social class and universal deeds is a result of changing intellectual and social thought. Since the mid-eighteenth century, new subjects, social classes, milieus, events, and commentaries have been introduced into plays, bringing about significant changes in the types and circumstances of those human beings represented in drama. Topics of heredity, environment, economics, and the unconscious have replaced older notions of cosmic forces and mysterious fates at work in our lives. As subject matter is reduced so, too, is a character's stature. Consequently, we argue in modern times for the dignity and worthiness of ordinary individuals in an effort to define a new kind of heroism for the modern world.

Since 1950, avant garde writers have placed their representative characters in an absurd world devoid of purpose and meaning. A recognizable humanity—individuals like those we encounter in our everyday lives—is exchanged for mechanical characters whose struggles are senseless, futile, and oppressive. The loss of a coherent unity of character and purpose is concomitant with the loss of coherent plots and meaningful actions. The postmodernists, rejecting the absurdist paradigms of senselessness and purposelessness, have dissolved the ego which we can still discover in Samuel Beckett's character May in *Footfalls*. In postmodernist texts, a recognizable humanity is replaced by masks and images through which writers can speak of the contradictions of social history. An example of this contradiction is the terrorist who destroys people and societies in an apocalyptic vision of preservation.

However, avant garde writers remain in the minority, and fully dimensional characters like those created by Tennessee Williams are representative of the mainstream approach to creating (or "fleshing out") dramatic character. The Wingfield family— Amanda, Tom, Laura—is Williams' articulation of the beauty, pain, vulnerability, and desperation to be found in the confusion of living. In Williams' dramatic world, as in the plays of other mainstream contemporary playwrights, character is still defined by situation, motives, feelings, gestures, actions, and words. Our next discussion deals with an understanding of the playwright's lan-guage—the verbal text—which differs re-markably from the language of poetry and the novel.

## NOTES

1. R. C. Lewis, "A Playwright Named Tennessee," *The New York Times Magazine* 7 Dec. 1947: 67.
2. Martin Esslin, *The Field of Drama: How Signs of Drama Create Meaning on Stage & Screen* (New York: Methuen, 1987): 84–85.
3. Francis Fergusson, *The Idea of a Theater: A Study of Ten Plays The Art of Drama in Changing Perspectives* (New Jersey: Princeton University Press, 1968): 255.
4. Arthur Miller, "Tragedy and the Common Man," *The New York Times* 27 Feb. 1949: II, 1, 3.
5. Eugene Ionesco, *Notes and Counter Notes: Writings on the Theatre*, trans. Donald Watson (New York: Grove Press, 1964): 257.
6. August Strindberg, "Preface to *Miss Julie*" in *Six Plays of Strindberg*, trans. Elizabeth Sprigge (Garden City, N.Y.: Doubleday & Company, 1955): 65.
7. August Strindberg, "Author's Note to A *Dream Play*," in *Six Plays by Strindberg*, trans. Elizabeth Sprigge (Garden City, N.Y.: Doubleday & Company, 1955): 193.
8. Ionesco 163.
9. Heiner Müller, "19 Answers," *Hamletmachine and Other Texts for the Stage*, ed. and trans. Carl Weber (New York: Performing Arts Journal Publications, 1984): 138.

# CHAPTER 9

# Understanding Language

Brian Cousins as Yasha in Arena Stage's production of *The Cherry Orchard*, directed by Lucian Pintilie. (*Photo by George deVincent, courtesy of Arena Stage, Washington, D.C.*)

POLONIUS: *What do you read, my lord?*
HAMLET: *Words, words, words.*

—William Shakespeare

## THE VERBAL TEXT

The language of a play is most often thought of as *words* that appear on the printed page as dialogue the actor makes into living speech (or speech acts) exchanged between characters. Martin Esslin called the play's dialogue the "verbal text."[1] In fact, the verbal text is more than dialogue, for it designates the spoken and the unspoken, the verbal and the nonverbal, the sounds and silences, the signs and symbols, of human communication.

George Steiner defined *drama* as "language under such high pressure of feeling that the words carry a necessary and immediate connotation of gesture."[2] Drama's words convey feelings and gestures; they can be active and reactive. The opening dialogue of Shakespeare's *Hamlet* is keenly active as two guards challenge one another on the battlements at midnight:

BERNARDO: Who's there?
FRANCISCO: Nay, answer me.
Stand and unfold yourself. (1.1)

Having seen a ghostly figure while guarding the castle at Elsinore, the soldiers are cautious and frightened. Bernardo's question ("Who's there?") challenges Francisco, demanding identification. Francisco behaves likewise. He is frightened and demands to be answered ("Nay, answer me."). In modern speech he is saying to Bernardo, "No, *you* identify yourself to *me!*" Each soldier is actively using language to challenge the identity of the other in a threatening situation. They want information and their words also convey the menacing use of their weapons.

In contrast to the aggressive dialogue of the guards in *Hamlet*, Anton Chekhov's dialogue in *The Cherry Orchard*, written in 1903, is reactive or mainly passive responses to people and situations. The opening moments of *The Cherry Orchard* reveal in the predawn light two individuals who have waited all night for the arrival of the estate's owner and her entourage from Paris. The servant Dooniasha with candle in hand awakens Lopakhin, a rich merchant, with the news that the train has arrived at the station. In their first lines of dialogue, the characters "react" to place, time, and situation—the fact of the train's arrival, the family's imminent appearance, the time of day, and their night's vigil.

LOPAKHIN: The train's arrived, thank God. What time is it?
DOONIASHA: It's nearly two. (*Blows out the candle.*) It's light already.
LOPAKHIN: How late was the train then? Two hours at least. (*Yawns and stretches.*) How stupid I am! What a fool I've made of myself! Came here on purpose to go to the station and meet them—and then overslept! . . . Dropped off to sleep in the chair. Annoying . . . I wish you'd woken me up.
DOONIASHA: I thought you'd gone. (*Listens.*) Sounds as if they're coming. (1)

## LANGUAGE AS ORGANIZATION

The language of a play organizes our perceptions of the elements of drama, such as action, plot, character, and meaning. It is enhanced by sounds, silences, gestures, lighting, costume, scenery, movement, and music. Unlike our random conversations in restaurants and coffee shops, the playwright's language is written to be spoken by actors on stage before audiences. Therefore, the playwright's use of language is highly selective and purposeful. All speech in drama produces meaning on several levels, as it does in real life. First, the language of the play is the playwright's means of providing background information, of developing plot and action, and of expressing the characters' conscious thoughts and feelings. Second, it conveys the characters' subconscious feelings in latent or hidden meanings embedded in words and/or gestures. Chekhov's use of language is often deceptive, for his characters frequently avoid or hide their true feelings.

In reading a Chekhov play, we have to be especially careful to distinguish between what a character *does* and what that same character *says*. Chekhov did not intend to confuse readers and audiences, but he believed there were contradictions between our words and our actions. He believed that while people went about their daily routines of eating, drinking, working, and amusing themselves, their lives were taking shape and they were being made happy or unhappy. For example, in *The Cherry Orchard*, Lopakhin contemplates proposing marriage to Varia, Madame Ranyevskaia's adopted daughter; the couple talks around the subject with restrained emotions while routinely packing to leave the estate, but Lopakhin exits without proposing and they go their separate ways forever.

Unlike conversations in real life, the playwright uses certain accepted conventions to convey a character's interior thoughts. Shakespeare's poetic dialogue allows Hamlet to express his feelings and thoughts in blank verse (unrhymed iambic pentameter), often in some of the most eloquent soliloquies found in the English language. Many of Shakespeare's lines and phrases have become a part of a commonplace vocabulary. For example,

To be, or not to be—that is the question.

The play's the thing. . . .

—Frailty, thy name is woman!

Thus conscience does make cowards of us all. . . .

These are lines from the great soliloquies where Hamlet, alone on stage, speaks his thoughts aloud for audiences to overhear his internal debates and subsequent decisions.

As a soliloquy demonstrates, drama's language is highly selective, often complex, and charged with verbal nuance and gesture. It is a vehicle for characters to speak aloud thoughts, choices, and motives. It also involves implied meanings and assumptions relating to historical time and place, such as the assumed "majesty of kings" among Shakespeare's characters. It is language designed to be given life in the theatre by actors as characters. Its purpose is to express ideas, feelings, attitudes, intentions, and, finally, the meaning of the play's completed action. This is why we say a play's language is selective and purposeful and highly unlike our random daily conversations.

It is true that the words we use to communicate to the world around us also accomplish many of the same things as stage language: We express ideas, attitudes, feelings, and intentions. We also surround ourselves in daily life with music; we "dress" for special occasions like weddings, rock concerts, or job interviews; and we invent scenarios to get us through such awkward periods as meeting strangers, dealing with irate parents, or impressing VIPs. However, there is an important difference between a play's language, constructed to be spoken by an actor in the theatre, and everyday conversation. The playwright selects the language (verbal and nonverbal) that appears on the text's printed page and the actor controls the living quality of the playwright's words. By avoiding the randomness of everyday conversation, stage language shapes the play's action, directs the plot, and controls the characters' experiences in action, plot, and resolution.

While a play's language is carefully arranged by the playwright, there are also other theatrical influences on the verbal text. Directors, actors, and designers—through the use of movement, costumes, scenery, lighting, and sound—collaborate with the playwright to create a meaningful pattern of communication.

As we study the various possibilities of drama's language, we become attuned to its verbal and nonverbal characteristics. Let us begin with the stage directions (the *didascalia*) the reader of a modern text encounters on the printed page at the outset. Next, let us consider verbal and nonverbal elements, including sounds, subtext, and stage properties. All types of stage language are found in the final printed text which is approved by the playwright before publication in an effort to preserve the ephemeral qualities of the text-as-performance.

## STAGE DIRECTIONS

Before the printing machine and a general readership for plays, stage directions (if they existed at all) were used solely by theatre personnel. In modern editions of *Hamlet*, we find such abbreviated directions as *"A flourish" "Exeunt," "Aside," "Dies,"* and *"Exit Ghost."* It is assumed these directions were added later to Shakespeare's original promptbook by playwright or players. Since the first folio, or first collection of Shakespeare's complete works, was printed in 1623, twenty-three years after the first performance of *Hamlet* and seven years after Shakespeare's death, the validity of the "directions" as Shakespeare's are further suspect. Nevertheless, by modern standards, they are sparse.

Modern stage directions are included at the beginning of each act and provide information about how the playwright imagined details of the three-dimensional stage space, that is, Hedda Gabler's drawing room or Amanda Wingfield's tenement apartment. Stage directions are largely for the reader's information, for audiences experience the play's environment visually and aurally. Stage directions include facts about geography, season of the year, time of day or night, weather conditions, decor, dress, mood, stage properties, music cues, and general impressions of place or environment. The modern reader has the advantage of knowing how Chekhov visualized the opening scene of *The Cherry Orchard*, for he described in detail the room where the family will arrive with the dawn and where the cherry orchard can be seen in the background.

> *A room which used to be the children's bedroom and is still referred to as the "nursery." There are several doors: one of them leads into* ANIA'S *room. It is early morning: the sun is just coming up. The windows of the room are shut, but through them the cherry trees can be seen in blossom. It is May, but in the orchard there is morning frost.* (1)

On the other hand, Shakespeare and his contemporaries did not have the advantage of sophisticated print technology, Nor were they very interested in the specifics of environment as a factor that shapes human events. Their writing tradition was to place all indications of time, place, weather, and mood in the dialogue of minor characters who usually began the play. They provided the background information and also captured the audience's attention preparatory to the entrance of the principals. In the jargon of the theatre, these are "weather lines." Within eleven lines of the beginning of *Hamlet*, the two guards have given us a sense of place ("castle battlements"), time ("'Tis now struck twelve"), weather ("'Tis bitter cold"), mood ("I am sick at heart"), and what's happening ("not a mouse stirring").

In play analysis, stage directions must not be ignored, for they provide crucial information and raise questions to be answered as action and plot develop. For example, why are the guards in *Hamlet* uneasy and relieved to report that not a "mouse is stirring"? We learn shortly about the ghost's appearance and then follow all the complicated events associated with the ghost's reappearance to Hamlet. In Shakespeare's plays, stage directions are chiefly embedded in dialogue. In Chekhov's plays, written 300 years later, the directions are separated from the dialogue and often prefatory to the action. In *The Cherry Orchard*, we learn in the initial stage directions that the cherry trees are in blossom and are part of the play's scenic background. As the play's complications unfold, choices about these trees and the land where they are located will determine the future of the Ranyevskaia estate.

## VERBAL LANGUAGE

As we look at the page of a play, we are aware of *words* as key elements for making things happen in the theatre. Language or dialogue on a printed page has the potential for bringing human presence and activity onto the stage. Words spoken by actors convey plot, action, character, emotions, relationships, ideas, motives, sounds, and commentary. Words also individualize characters by giving them speech patterns, regional dialects, and vocabularies special to social classes and to professions.

In modern language theory, words are at once signs and symbols. As signs, words can create a picture of an object (called an *icon*), such as a throne or a sword. Othello uses words as iconic signs when he says to his opponents, "Keep up your bright *swords*, for the dew will rust them" (1.2). A second type is the *index* sign (the gesture), such as an actor's pointing to a person or object. In *Hamlet*, Claudius literally gestures for "lights" (torches and candles) to end the mockery of the play-within-the-play and to cast away the shadows of his crime. The third type is the *symbol* which is more familiar to us as readers of literature. Symbols have multiple meanings, depending on their dramatic or literary contexts. Symbols differ from signs in that they have complex connections to their referents. The poet Robert Frost wrote of the "road not taken." As a poetic symbol, Frost's "road" is not simply a pathway through the woods that divided in two directions, forcing the individual to choose between them. Frost's "two roads that diverged in a yellow wood" are symbols for any choice in life between two alternatives which appear, at the time, equally attractive, but which in later years will have made a significant difference on the kinds of life experiences one has had. Like Frost's road, symbols have ranged over the centuries from national flags (for nations), roses (for love), doves (for peace), night (for death), to stars (for permanency), and so on. In the theatre, unlike in poetry, symbols can be both verbal and nonverbal. The cherry orchard itself is a complex symbol. The orchard is a symbol of tradition and beauty, but it is also an object of much debate regarding how to save the estate and a way of life. Chekhov also used symbolic sounds to enhance a play's meaning. The sound of a snapped string midway in *The Cherry Orchard* becomes an aural symbol of the pain and loss to come at the play's end.

Signs and symbols create the rich texture of dramatic language. The reader must catch all nuances of verbal and nonverbal meaning. For example, Chekhov titled his play *The Cherry Orchard*; play titles always carry a large burden of a playwright's intentions. The orchard, as symbol, is variously interpreted as the passing of the old way of life in provincial Russia, circa 1900, and the coming of a new social order. Through the four acts of the play, the orchard symbolizes the many ways Chekhov's characters deal with or fail to deal with life's demands. In the final stage direction as the orchard is destroyed, it becomes a symbol of change: the passing of a way of life and the start of a new and different world.

## NONVERBAL LANGUAGE

In addition to words—the verbal text—the theatre's language communicates to us through many other means: the actors' presence, sounds, lighting effects, movement, silences, gestures, activity, inactivity, color, music, songs, costumes, scenic devices, stage properties, and film projections or images. During a performance, the stage is filled with the simultaneous aspects of the play's theatrical life which goes beyond the verbal text. In stage directions, the playwright indicates sounds, silences, colors, activities, and so on. It remains, however, for the theatre's collaborators to make nonverbal language effective on stage. In *The Cherry Orchard*, the sound of the snapped string and the thud of an ax against a tree at the play's end are nonverbal means of communicating the destruction of the family's treasure and their way of life. The final stage direction in *The Cherry Orchard* is one of the most renown in the history of western drama.

> (*A distant sound is heard, coming as if out of the sky, like the sound of a string snapping, slowly and sadly dying away. Silence ensues, broken only by the sound of an axe striking a tree in the orchard far away.*) (4)

In imagining such a powerful and symbolic moment, the playwright knows that without the skills of the theatre's sound designer, the aural effect will not have its full symbolic meaning and theatrical impact. The reader's job is more difficult than the audience's.

What the audience experiences, we must imagine based wholly upon the verbal text, that is, upon the words we read, not the sounds we actually hear.

## SOUNDS AND SILENCES

The end of *The Cherry Orchard* demonstrates how sounds are some of the theatre's most powerful nonverbal language and, consequently, some of the writer's most effective tools. Shakespeare used trumpets to announce the entrance of the court in *Hamlet* and thunder machines to simulate the storms in *Macbeth* and *King Lear*, for example. With modern sound technology, almost any effect is possible—from passing trains to marching bands to the fading sound of a snapped string. As readers, we have to recreate these sounds in the mind's ear just as we visualize the play's action in the mind's eye. The task is not easy. Sounds are sometimes alternated with silences, words with pauses, activity with inactivity. Readers must be attuned to the absence of words and be prepared to understand pauses and silences just as we comprehend the meaning of a character's words and actions. The last scene of *The Cherry Orchard* shows how Chekhov juxtaposed sounds with silences to achieve another level of meaning. In the family's hurried departure from the estate that has been sold at auction, Feers, the elderly valet, has been forgotten and left behind. His final speech is placed between stage directions calling for offstage sounds of doors being locked and carriages driving away and the distant sound of a breaking string which fades away to silence before the sound of the ax is heard striking a tree in the orchard.

Discovering that he has been forgotten, Feers talks to himself in fragmented dialogue punctuated by frequent pauses. These pauses, or brief silences, indicate the winding down of a single life and also of a way of life. The fact that he is alone, locked in the house, sick and dying, tells us more vividly than any narration that "life has passed him by." At the end of *The Cherry Orchard*, we hear and see a world in transition.

## SUBTEXT

The notion of *subtext* is a post-Chekhovian concept used by actors, directors, and critics in the modern theatre to identify a character's inner thoughts, feelings, and intentions not explicitly expressed in dialogue. In performance, the subtext—the inner life of a character—is supplied by the actor. In playwriting, subtext—the inner life of the work and its implied meanings—is an outgrowth of characters avoiding directness. In imitation of "real life," modern playwrights create characters who rarely say simply and directly what they truly mean because people in real life often avoid being too direct for many reasons: out of politeness, shyness, subterfuge, boredom, or style. Moreover, people rarely reveal their personal problems to one another, but rather camouflage their anxieties with verbal trivia. In the proposal scene (4) in *The Cherry Orchard*, Varia and Lopakhin, rather than confront their feelings, talk about luggage, weather, jobs, distances, train schedules, but not about marriage. *The Cherry Orchard* illustrates how broken speech, the irrelevant remark, or the avoided topic can allude to passion, to dreams, and to lost hopes. In contrast, Shakespeare wrote Hamlet's soliloquies to *reveal* the inner content of the prince's thoughts and feelings.

Subtext is underlying, unspoken thoughts, emotions, and implications separate from spoken words (dialogue). As in life, the meaning of the words spoken in drama, especially in modern times, is usually charged with latent or hidden meanings. What is going on between characters is ultimately derived from the given situation. In Chekhov's play, the family waits to learn from Lopakhin and Gayev the outcome of the estate's auction (3). Upon their return, the two men are reluctant to share their information and feelings. Gayev hides his distress over the loss of the estate behind complaints of hunger and fatigue. Lopakhin, who has bought the estate, tries to suppress his joy (the son of a serf now owns the estate!) and to delay the inevitable announcement which will bring pain to the family.

Finally, subtext is a collaboration between writer and actor that reveals the character's inner life, but the collaboration begins with the verbal text. As readers, we seek out clues to inner feelings and responses in language and stage directions. For example, Madame Ranyevskaia's spendthrift nature is underscored when she gives a beggar a gold coin, choosing it over a silver piece when, as Varia says, "There's nothing in the house for people to eat, and you gave him a gold piece" (2). The gesture is grand and typical of an individual who has for years borrowed and spent with no thought for the inevitable day of reckoning.

In modern writing, characters usually retain deep feelings and thoughts but either avoid talking about them or lack the vocabulary to articulate their painful thoughts and feelings. Hence, we must be aware of the gap between the expressed and the unexpressed that contributes to the inner life of the play.

## STAGE PROPERTIES

From earliest times, playwrights have made use of large and small movable objects in the theatre to enliven audience interest, to aid the actor's work, to further the storyline, and to resolve the play's ending. Greek playwrights used a cranelike device (the *mechane*) to lower and raise gods and humans into the playing space, wagons (the *ekkyklema*) for displaying the dead, and perhaps even chariots for spectacular entrances. The Elizabethans used set pieces, costumes, and properties, such as thrones, cages, beds, crowns, swords, and skulls, to enhance the telling of the story. These objects were also introduced into the verbal text and used by the characters. One of the most famous instances is the use of a skull in the gravedigger's scene in *Hamlet* (5.1). The gravedigger's act of tossing up a skull from the grave he is preparing to receive Ophelia's body results in Hamlet's meditation on the impermanency of life and the famous "Alas, poor Yorick!" speech. The skull's presence in the actor's hand rivets the audience's attention to the subject of death and mortality. The skull, as a stage property, adds to the rich language of the theatre as both an iconic sign of death and a symbol of mortality.

By the nineteenth century, stage language was influenced by the new "realism" and by a theatre technology unknown in Shakespeare's day. The concern for stage realism resulted in reproducing speech, dress, and behavior appropriate to a character's socioeconomic background and psychological makeup. To enhance the illusion of a candid representation on stage of everyday reality (as the audience would understand or recognize it) and to maintain language's symbolic ambiguity and richness, playwrights made use of "real" objects, such as furniture, table lamps, books, pistols, stoves, keys, and family portraits, appropriate to the stage environment and action. They endowed ordinary objects logically found in the environment with symbolic meanings. In some realistic plays, for example, table lamps and sunlight glimpsed through windows became symbols of "throwing light on a subject," or of a character's new understanding.

In *Hedda Gabler*, written in 1890 at the height of stage realism as a new writing and performance style, Henrik Ibsen used personal and decorative objects found in the Tesman home as symbols of the neurotic and destructive forces at work within his heroine. For example, Hedda's dueling pistols inherited from her father, General Gabler, and the wood-burning stove are part of the drawing room decor. The pistols and the stove are at once ordinary and symbolic objects. The pistols can be discharged and the stove presumably has fire in it, but both are symbolic of Hedda's destructive nature fueled by her boredom, jealousy, and neurotic inability to adapt to the proscribed gender role of her day—housewife and mother. As symbols of her destructiveness, the dueling pistols are associated with the former life style of General Gabler's daughter, now the scholarly George Tesman's wife, and are part of her personal possessions kept in the drawing room. One pistol plays a part in Eilif Lovborg's accidental death and the other in Hedda's suicide. The stove is used by Hedda in a jealous rage to burn her former lover's manuscript and destroy his life's work.

In *The Cherry Orchard*, Varia, Madame Ranyevskaia's adopted daughter, housekeeper, and general factotum, wears the household keys fastened to her belt at all times. They complete her costume, but are literal signs of her authority and responsibility in the household. When Lopakhin announces that he has bought the estate at auction, Varia removes the keys from her belt and without comment throws them on the drawing room floor at Lopakhin's feet (3). The keys are familiar objects, but Varia's gesture with them makes an eloquent statement about the change of the estate's ownership, the material loss and gain, and the psychological pain and pleasure of those involved in the transfer of ownership. In terms of stage realism, the keys are ordinary signs of the character's social status and symbolic of the family's ownership of the estate. As they are cast down, they symbolize the family's change of fortune.

In *Buried Child*, a contemporary play, Sam Shepard used more bizarre, though equally real, objects to compound the play's nonverbal effects in his portrait of modern family life. Carrots are sliced up on stage by Shelly with malicious energy, symbolizing the castration of the American male; the father's head is brutally shaved, signifying his loss of authority; and a baby's skeleton is retrieved from its burial place in the back yard and brought on stage as both sign and symbol of the betrayal, guilt, and violence in the family's history.

Stage properties are powerful nonverbal means (both signs and symbols) of enhancing the play's visual impact, of endowing the stage picture with ordinary yet richly ambiguous objects, and of reinforcing the play's meaning. They are three-dimensional elements of the theatre's language.

# The Cherry Orchard

## ANTON CHEKHOV

*Anton Pavlovich Chekhov (1860–1904) was born in southern Russia, the grandson of a serf and the son of a grocer. He studied medicine at Moscow University but never practiced regularly because of ill health and literary interests. During his student years, he wrote short stories to earn money and was soon accepted into literary circles. He began his playwriting career in the 1880s with one-act farces,* The Marriage Proposal *and* The Bear. The Sea Gull, *written in 1896, was his first full-length play to capture the serious attention of theatre managers, but it was a colossal failure when produced in St. Petersburg. Two years later, it was a brilliant success with the new Moscow Art Theatre and established his reputation as a major playwright.*

*Chekhov's career was defined by his association with the Moscow Art Theatre between 1898 and 1904. He redefined stage realism by writing plays without direct, purposive action which chronicled the lives of rural Russians. Director Constantin Stanislavsky's methods of interpreting the inner truth of Chekhov's characters and the mood of his plays resulted in one of the great theatrical collaborations.*

*During his last years, Chekhov lived in Yalta, where he had gone for his health, and made occasional trips to Moscow to see his plays. He married the Moscow Art Theatre's leading actress, Olga Knipper, for whom he had written parts in his last three plays. He died of tuberculosis at a German spa in 1904 and was buried in Moscow.*

*During his short career, Chekhov wrote four masterpieces of modern stage realism:* The Sea Gull, Uncle Vanya, The Three Sisters, *and* The Cherry Orchard.

## INTRODUCTION

Anton Chekhov wrote plays that chronicled the lives of ordinary people in rural Russia at the turn of the century. In doing so, he created a new type of realistic dramaturgy distinguished by understated plots and disjointed dialogue that mirrored the stagnant lives of provincial gentry, doctors, writers, tutors, servants, hangers-on, merchants, and government officials. He depicted them as going about their daily routines of working, eating, drinking, talking, reading, falling in and out of love, and playing cards and billiards while their lives were subtly altered for better or for worse. Banal conversation and unspectacular lives are the fabric of Chekhov's art. The dramatic action of a Chekhov play is contained within the inconsequential and habitual routines of living and surviving.

Of his different writing style, Chekhov said:

> *After all, in real life, people don't spend every moment in shooting one another, hanging themselves, or making declarations of love. They do not spend all their time saying clever things. They are more occupied with eating, drinking, flirting, and saying stupidities, and these are the things which ought to be shown on the stage. . . . People eat their dinner, just eat their dinner, and all the time their happiness is taking form, or their lives are being destroyed.[3]*

Chekhov's approach to writing for the theatre in the 1890s set a standard and style that continue to influence playwrights today. *The Cherry Orchard*, which many consider his masterpiece, conveys the perfection of Chekhov's unique dramaturgy: Seemingly purposeless activities and aimless dialogue gradually reveal the lives of rural Russians living on the estates owned by their families for centuries. For example, Madame Ranyevskaia returns to her estate after some years in Paris only to find that it has been mortgaged to pay her debts and is to be sold at auction. Half-hearted attempts are made by her relatives to collect money owed her by a neighboring landowner, but he is also in financial straits. For a time, they rely on an uncertain legacy from a wealthy relative, or a rich marriage for the daughter Ania. As the head of the family, Madame Ranyevskaia seems incapable of coping with her financial situation and the looming reality of the loss of the estate at auction. The only realistic proposal for saving the estate comes from Lopakhin, a wealthy merchant whose father was a serf on the estate. In the first act, Lopakhin suggests cutting down the famous cherry orchard (for it no longer produces income) and dividing the land into acreage for summer cottages to create a modern-day "subdivision." The family rejects the idea of destroying such beauty and tradition, but they have no plan of action.

Chekhov contains the action of the play —loss and gain—within a realistic framework of the family's arrival and departure. Their arrival at the beginning and their departure at the end are realistic means of bringing disparate people together to demonstrate their hopes and dreams among the most ordinary activities, such as eating, drinking, playing billiards, talking, and daydreaming. However, in *The Cherry Orchard*, time passes and the characters do nothing to take control of their lives (and to save the estate). Things are put off until "tomorrow" and unrealistic strategies are discussed. In the meantime, the play is climaxed by the sale of the estate (which takes place off stage and whose outcome is reported). Chekhov's aim was to divert attention away from the "big" theatrical moments of nineteenth-century melodrama (suicides, murders, duels, auctions) and to examine the reactions of recognizable characters to how their lives are being shaped by events over which they have exercised little, if any, control. His concept of stage realism was to define the play's environment, make use of indirect action and dialogue, and present characters whose happiness or unhappiness grows out of inconsequential events. Chekhov avoided large "stage" moments of confrontation and physical action. For Chekhov, ordinary moments more accurately reflected the day-to-day reality of our lives rather than sordid murders, ghosts, battles, and so on. To universalize his statement about what it is to experience lives of commonplace routines, disappointments, and habituation, Chekhov added to indirect action and understated dialogue, such nonverbal sound effects as the distant "breaking string," to remind us that time passes, lives take shape, and people are made happy or unhappy as their worlds change.

# The Cherry Orchard

## A COMEDY IN FOUR ACTS

**CHARACTERS IN THE PLAY**

**RANYEVSKAIA**, Liubov Andryeevna (Liuba), a landowner

**ANIA** (Anichka), her daughter, aged 17

**VARIA** (Varvara Mihailovna), her adopted daughter, aged 24

**GAYEV**, Leonid Andryeevich (Lionia), brother of Mme Ranyevskaia

**LOPAKHIN**, Yermolai Aleksyeevich, a businessman

**TROFIMOV**, Piotr Serghyeevich (Pyetia), a student

**SIMEONOV-PISHCHIK**, Boris Borisovich, a landowner

**CHARLOTTA IVANOVNA**, a German governess

**YEPIHODOV**, Semion Pantelyeevich, a clerk on Ranyevskaia's estate

**DOONIASHA** (Avdotyia Fiodorovna), a parlourmaid

**FEERS** (Feers Nikolayevich), a man-servant, aged 87

**YASHA**, a young man-servant

**A TRAMP**

**STATION-MASTER**

**POST-OFFICE CLERK**

**GUESTS, SERVANTS**

*The action takes place on the estate of Mme. Ranyevskaia.*

## ACT ONE

*A room which used to be the children's bedroom and is still referred to as the 'nursery'. There are several doors: one of them leads into* ANIA'S *room.*

*It is early morning: the sun is just coming up. The windows of the room are shut, but through them the cherry trees can be seen in blossom. It is May, but in the orchard there is morning frost.*

*Enter* DOONIASHA, *carrying a candle, and* LOPAKHIN *with a book in his hand.*

**LOPAKHIN:** The train's arrived, thank God. What time is it?

**DOONIASHA:** It's nearly two. (*Blows out the candle.*) It's light already.

**LOPAKHIN:** How late was the train then? Two hours at least. (*Yawns and stretches.*) How stupid I am! What a fool I've made of myself! Came here on purpose to go to the station and meet them—and then overslept! . . . Dropped off to sleep in the chair. Annoying . . . I wish you'd woken me up.

**DOONIASHA:** I thought you'd gone. (*Listens.*) Sounds as if they're coming.

**LOPAKHIN** (*also listens*): No. . . . They'll have to get their luggage out, and all that. . . . (*Pause.*) Liubov Andryeevna has been abroad for five years, I don't know what she's like now. . . . She used to be a good soul. An easy-going, simple kind of person. I remember when I was a boy of about fifteen, my father—he had a small shop in the village then—hit me in the face and made my nose bleed. . . . We had come to the manor for something or other, and he'd been drinking, I remember it as if it happened yesterday: Liubov Andryeevna—she was still young and slender then—brought me in and took me to the washstand in this very room, the nursery it was then. 'Don't cry, little peasant,' she said, 'it'll be better before you're old enough to get married'. . . . (*Pause.*) 'Little peasant'. . . . She was right enough, my father was a peasant. Yet here I am—all dressed up in a white waistcoat and brown shoes. . . . But you can't make a silk purse out of a sow's ear. I am rich, I've got a lot of money, but anyone can see I'm just a peasant, anyone who takes the trouble to think about me and look under my skin. (*Turning over pages in the book.*) I've been reading this book, and I haven't understood a word of it. I fell asleep reading it. (*Pause.*)

DOONIASHA: The dogs didn't sleep all night: they know their masters are coming.

LOPAKHIN: What's the matter, Dooniasha?

DOONIASHA: My hands are trembling. I feel as if I'm going to faint.

LOPAKHIN: You're too refined and sensitive, Dooniasha. You dress yourself up like a lady, and you do your hair like one, too. That won't do, you know. You must remember your place.

*Enter* YEPIHODOV *with a bunch of flowers; he wears a jacket and brightly polished high boots which squeak loudly; as he comes in, he drops the flowers.*

YEPIHODOV (*picks up the flowers*): The gardener sent these. He says they're to go in the dining-room. (*Hands the flowers to* DOONIASHA.)

LOPAKHIN: And bring me some kvass.

DOONIASHA: Very well.

YEPIHODOV: There's a frost outside, three degrees of it, and the cherry trees are covered with bloom. I can't approve of this climate of ours, you know. (*Sighs.*) No, I can't. It doesn't contribute to—to things, I mean. And do you know, Yermolai Aleksyeevich, I bought myself a pair of boots the day before yesterday, and they squeak so terribly . . . well, I

mean to say, it's utterly impossible, you know . . . What can I put on them?

LOPAKHIN: Oh, leave me alone. You make me tired.

YEPIHODOV: Every day something or other unpleasant happens to me. But I don't complain; I'm accustomed to it, I even laugh at it.

*Enter* DOONIASHA; *she serves* LOPAKHIN *with kvass.*

I'll leave you now. (*Bumps into a chair which falls over.*)

You see! (*Triumphantly.*) You can see for yourself what it is, I mean to say . . . so to speak. . . . It's simply extraordinary! (*Goes out.*)

DOONIASHA: I want to tell you a secret, Yermolai Aleksyeevich. Yepihodov proposed to me.

LOPAKHIN: Ah!

DOONIASHA: I don't know what to do. . . . He's a quiet man, but sometimes he gets talking, and then you can't understand anything he says. It sounds nice, it sounds very moving, but you just can't understand it. I think I like him a little, and he's madly in love with me. He's an unlucky sort of person, something unpleasant seems to happen to him every day. That's why they tease him and call him 'two-and-twenty misfortunes'.

LOPAKHIN: (*listens*). I think I can hear them coming. . . .

DOONIASHA: Coming! . . . Oh, dear! I don't know what's the matter with me. . . . I feel cold all over.

LOPAKHIN: Yes, they really are coming! Let's go and meet them at the door. I wonder if she'll recognize me? We haven't met for five years.

DOONIASHA (*agitated*): I'm going to faint. . . . Oh, I'm fainting! . . .

*The sound of two coaches driving up to the house is heard.* LOPAKHIN *and* DOONIASHA *go out quickly. The stage is empty. Then there are sounds of people arriving in the adjoining room.* FEERS, *leaning on a stick, crosses the stage hurriedly: he has been to the station to meet Liubov Andryeevna. He is dressed in an old-fashioned livery coat and a top hat and is muttering to himself, though it is impossible to make out what he is saying. The noises off stage become louder. A voice says: 'Let's go through here'. Enter* LIUBOV ANDRYEEVNA, ANIA *and* CHARLOTTA IVANOVNA, *leading a small dog, all in travelling clothes,* VARIA, *wearing an overcoat and a kerchief over her head,* GAYEV, SIMEONOV-PISHCHIK, LOPAKHIN, DOONIASHA, *carrying a bundle and an umbrella, and other servants with luggage.*

ANIA: Let's go through here. You remember what room this is, Mamma?

LIUBOV ANDRYEEVNA (*joyfully, through her tears*): The nursery!

VARIA: How cold it is! My hands are quite numb. (*To* LIUBOV ANDRYEEVNA.) Your rooms are just as you left them, Mamma dear, the white one, and the mauve one.

LIUBOV ANDRYEEVNA: The nursery, my dear, my beautiful room! . . . I used to sleep here when I was little. . . . (*Cries.*) And now I feel as if I were little again. . . . (*She kisses her brother, then* VARIA, *then her brother again.*) And Varia is just the same as ever, looking like a nun. I recognized Dooniasha, too. (*Kisses* DOONIASHA.)

GAYEV: The train was two hours late. Just think of it! What efficiency!

CHARLOTTA (*to* PISHCHIK): My dog actually eats nuts.

PISHCHIK (*astonished*): Fancy that!
*They all go out except* ANIA *and* DOONIASHA.

DOONIASHA: We've waited and waited for you. . . . (*Helps* ANIA *to take off her hat and coat.*)

ANIA: I haven't slept for four nights. . . . I'm frozen.

DOONIASHA: You went away during Lent and it was snowing and freezing then, but now it's spring-time. Darling! (*She laughs and kisses her.*) I could hardly bear waiting for you, my pet, my precious. . . . But I must tell you at once, I can't wait a minute longer. . . .

ANIA (*without enthusiasm*): What is it this time? . . .

DOONIASHA: Yepihodov, the clerk, proposed to me just after Easter.

ANIA: You never talk about anything else. . . . (*Tidies her hair.*) I've lost all my hairpins. . . . (*She is very tired and can hardly keep on her feet.*)

DOONIASHA: I really don't know what to think. He loves me . . . he does love me so!

ANIA (*looking through the door into her room, tenderly*): My own room, my own windows, just as if I had never been away! I'm home again! Tomorrow I'm going to get up and run straight into the garden! Oh, if only I could go to bed and sleep now! I couldn't sleep all the way back, I was so worried.

DOONIASHA: Piotr Serghyeevich arrived the day before yesterday.

ANIA (*joyfully*): Pyetia!

DOONIASHA: He's sleeping in the bathhouse, and living there, too. 'I wouldn't like to inconvenience them,' he said. (*Looks at her watch.*) I ought to wake him up, but Varvara Mihailovna told me not to. 'Don't you wake him,' she said.
*Enter* VARIA *with a bunch of keys at her waist.*

VARIA: Dooniasha, make some coffee, quick! Mamma is asking for coffee.

DOONIASHA: It'll be ready in a moment. (*Goes out.*)

VARIA: Thank God, you've arrived. You're home again. (*Embracing her.*) My darling's come back! My precious!

ANIA: If you only knew the things I had to put up with!

VARIA: I can just imagine it.

ANIA: I left just before Easter: it was cold then. Charlotta never stopped talking, never left off doing her silly conjuring tricks all the way. Why did you make me take Charlotta?

VARIA: But how could you go alone, darling? At seventeen!

ANIA: When we arrived in Paris it was cold and snowing. My French was awful. Mamma was living on the fifth floor, and when I got there she had visitors. There were some French ladies there and an old priest with a little book, and the room was full of cigarette smoke, so untidy and uncomfortable. Suddenly I felt so sorry for Mamma, so sorry, that I took her head between my hands, and just couldn't let it go.... Afterwards Mamma cried and was very sweet to me.

VARIA (*tearfully*): I can hardly bear listening to you. . . .

ANIA: She had already sold her villa near Mentone, and she had nothing left, positively nothing. And I hadn't any money left either, not a penny: I had hardly enough to get to Paris. And Mamma couldn't grasp that! In station restaurants she would order the most expensive dishes and tip the waiters a rouble each. Charlotta was just the same. And Yasha expected a full-course dinner for himself: it was simply dreadful. You know, Yasha is Mamma's valet, we brought him with us.

VARIA: Yes, I've seen the wretch.

ANIA: Well, how are things going? Have we paid the interest?

VARIA: Far from it.

ANIA: Oh dear! Oh dear!

VARIA: The estate will be up for sale in August.

ANIA: Oh dear!

LOPAKHIN (*puts his head through the door and bleats*): Me-e-e. . . . (*Disappears.*)

VARIA (*tearfully*): I'd like to give him this. . . . (*Clenches her fist.*)

ANIA (*her arms round* VARIA, *dropping her voice*): Varia, has he proposed to you?

VARIA *shakes her head.*

But he loves you. . . . Why don't you talk it over with him, what are you waiting for?

VARIA: I don't believe anything will come of it. He's too busy, he's no time to think of me. . . . He takes no notice of me at all. I'd rather he didn't come, it makes me miserable to see him. Everyone's talking of our wedding, everyone's congratulating me, but in fact there's nothing in it, it's all a kind of dream. (*In a changed tone of voice.*) You've got a new broach, a bee, isn't it?

ANIA (*sadly*): Mamma bought it for me. (*She goes into her room and now speaks gaily, like a child.*) You know, I went up in a balloon in Paris!

VARIA: My darling's home again! My precious girl!

(DOONIASHA *returns with a coffee-pot and prepares coffee.*)

VARIA (*standing by* ANIA'S *door*): You know, dearest, as I go about the house doing my odd jobs, I'm always dreaming and dreaming. If only we could marry you to some rich man, I feel my mind would be at ease. I'd go away then, first to a hermitage, then on to Kiev, to Moscow . . . walking from one holy place to another. I'd go on and on. Oh, what a beautiful life!

ANIA: The birds are singing in the garden. What time is it?

VARIA: It must be gone two. Time you went to bed, darling. (*Goes into* ANIA'S *room.*) A beautiful life!

*Enter* YASHA, *carrying a travelling rug and a small bag.*

YASHA (*crossing the stage, in an affectedly genteel voice*): May I go through here?

DOONIASHA: I can hardly recognize you, Yasha. You've changed so abroad.

YASHA: Hm! And who are you?

DOONIASHA: When you left here, I was no bigger than this. . . . (*Shows her height from the floor with her hand.*) I'm Dooni-asha, Fiodor Kosoyedov's daughter. You can't remember!

YASHA: Hm! Quite a little peach! (*Looks round, puts his arms round her; she cries out and drops a saucer.* YASHA *goes out quickly.*)

VARIA (*in the doorway, crossly*): What's going on here?

DOONIASHA (*tearfully*): I've broken a saucer.

VARIA: That's a good omen.

ANIA (*coming out of her room*): We ought to warn Mamma that Pyetia is here.

VARIA: I gave orders not to wake him.

ANIA (*pensively*): It was six years ago that father died, and then, only a month after that, little brother Grisha was drowned in the river. He was only seven, such a pretty little boy! Mamma couldn't bear it and went away...she never looked back. (*Shivers.*) How well I understand her! If she only knew how I understand her! (*Pause.*) And, of course, Pyetia Trofi-mov was Grisha's tutor, he might remind her....

*Enter* FEERS, *wearing a jacket and a white waistcoat.*

FEERS (*goes to the coffee-pot, preoccupied*): Madam will have her coffee here. (*Puts on white gloves.*) Is the coffee ready? (*To* DOONIASHA, *severely.*) What about the cream?

DOONIASHA: Oh, my goodness! (*Goes out quickly.*)

FEERS (*fussing around the coffee-pot*): The girl's daft... (*Mutters.*) From Paris.... The master used to go to Paris years ago. ... Used to go by coach.... (*Laughs.*)

VARIA: Feers, what are you laughing at?

FEERS: What can I get you, Madam? (*Happily.*) The mistress is home again! Home at last! I don't mind if I die now.... (*Weeps with joy.*)

*Enter* LIUBOV ANDRYEEVNA, LOPAKHIN, GAYEV *and* SIMEONOV-PISHCHIK, *the last wearing a long peasant coat of finely-woven cloth and wide trousers tucked inside high*

boots. GAYEV, *as he comes in, moves his arms and body as if he were playing billiards.*

LIUBOV ANDRYEEVNA: How does it go now? Let me think. . . . I pot the red. . . . I go in off into the middle pocket!

GAYEV: I pot into the corner pocket ... Years ago you and I slept in this room, little brother and sister together; and now I'm fifty-one, strange as it may seem.

LOPAKHIN: Yes, time flies.

GAYEV: What?

LOPAKHIN: Time flies, I say.

GAYEV: This place smells of patchouli. . . .

ANIA: I think I'll go to bed. Good-night, Mamma. (*Kisses her.*)

LIUBOV ANDRYEEVNA: My precious child! (*Kisses her hands.*) You're glad to be home, aren't you? I still feel dazed.

ANIA: Good-night, Uncle.

GAYEV (*kisses her face and hands*): God bless you! How like your mother you are! (*To his sister.*) You looked exactly like her at her age, Liuba.

ANIA *shakes hands with* LOPAKHIN *and* PISHCHIK, *goes out and shuts the door after her.*

LIUBOV ANDRYEEVNA: She's very tired.

PISHCHIK: It's a long journey.

VARIA (*to* LOPAKHIN *and* PISHCHIK): Well, gentlemen? It's past two, time to break up the party.

LIUBOV ANDRYEEVNA (*laughs*): You're just the same, Varia. (*Draws* VARIA *to her and kisses her.*) Let me have some coffee, then we'll all go. (FEERS *places a cushion under her feet.*) Thank you, my dear. I've got into the habit of drinking coffee. I drink it day and night. Thank you, my dear old friend. (*Kisses* FEERS.)

VARIA: I'd better see if all the luggage is there. (*Goes out.*)

LIUBOV ANDRYEEVNA: Is it really me sitting here? (*Laughs.*) I feel like dancing and flinging my arms about. (*Hides her face in her hands.*) What if I'm just dreaming? God, how I love my own country! I love it so much, I could hardly see it from the train, I was crying all the time. (*Through tears.*) However, I must drink my coffee. Thank you, Feers, thank you, my dear old friend. I am so glad I found you still alive.

FEERS: The day before yesterday.

GAYEV: He doesn't hear very well.

LOPAKHIN: I've got to leave for Kharkov soon after four. What a nuisance! I'd like to have a good look at you, to have a talk. . . . You look as lovely as ever.

PISHCHIK (*breathing heavily*): She looks prettier. In her Parisian clothes . . . enough to turn anybody's head!

LOPAKHIN: Your brother here—Leonid Andryeevich—says that I'm a country bumpkin, a tight-fisted peasant, but I don't take any notice of that. Let him say what he likes. The only thing I want is for you to have faith in me as you did before. Merciful God! My father was your father's serf, and your grandfather's, too, but you did so much for me in the past that I forget everything and love you as if you were my own sister . . . more than my own sister.

LIUBOV ANDRYEEVNA: I just can't sit still, I simply can't! (*She jumps up and walks about the room in great agitation.*) This happiness is too much for me. You can laugh at me, I'm foolish. . . . My dear bookcase! (*Kisses bookcase.*) My own little table!

GAYEV: You know, old Nanny died while you were away.

LIUBOV ANDRYEEVNA (*Sits down and drinks coffee*): Yes, I know. May the Kingdom of Heaven be hers. They wrote to tell me.

GAYEV: Anastasiy died, too. Petrooshka Kosoy has left me and is working for the police in town. (*Takes a box of boiled sweets from his pocket and puts one in his mouth.*)

PISHCHIK: My daughter, Dashenka, sends her greetings to you.

LOPAKHIN: I feel I'd like to tell you something nice, something jolly. (*Glances at his watch.*) I'll have to go in a moment, there's no time to talk. However, I could tell you in a few words. You know, of course, that your cherry orchard is going to be sold to pay your debts. The auction is to take place on the twenty-second of August, but there's no need for you to worry. You can sleep in peace, my dear; there's a way out. This is my plan, please listen carefully. Your estate is only twenty miles from town, and the railway line is not far away. Now, if your cherry orchard and the land along the river are divided into plots and leased out for summer residences you'll have a yearly income of at least twenty-five thousand roubles.

GAYEV: But what nonsense!

LIUBOV ANDRYEEVNA: I don't quite understand you, Yermolai Aleksyeevich.

LOPAKHIN: You'll charge the tenants at least twenty-five roubles a year for a plot of one acre, and if you advertise now, I'm prepared to stake any amount you like that you won't have a spot of land unoccupied by the autumn: it will be snatched up. In fact, I really feel I must congratulate you, you're saved after all! It's a marvellous situation and the river's deep enough for bathing. But, of course, the place will have to be cleaned up, put in order. For instance, all the old outbuildings will have to be pulled down, as well as this house which is no good to anybody. The old cherry orchard should be cut down, too.

LIUBOV ANDRYEEVNA: Cut down? My dear man, forgive me, you don't seem to understand. If there's one thing interesting, one thing really outstanding in the whole county, it's our cherry orchard.

LOPAKHIN: The only outstanding thing about this orchard is that it's very large. It only produces a crop every other year, and then there's nobody to buy it.

GAYEV: This orchard is actually mentioned in the Encyclopaedia.

LOPAKHIN (*glancing at his watch*): If you can't think clearly about it, or come to a decision, the cherry orchard and the whole estate as well will be sold by auction. You must decide! There's no other way out, I assure you. There's no other way.

FEERS: In the old days, forty or fifty years ago, the cherries were dried, preserved, marinaded, made into jam, and sometimes . . .

GAYEV: Be quiet, Feers.

FEERS: And sometimes, whole cartloads of dried cherries were sent to Moscow and Kharkov. The money they fetched! And the dried cherries in those days were soft, juicy, sweet, tasty. . . . They knew how to do it then . . . they had a recipe. . . .

LIUBOV ANDRYEEVNA: And where is that recipe now?

FEERS: Forgotten. No one can remember it.

PISHCHIK (*to* LIUBOV ANDRYEEVNA): What was it like in Paris? Did you eat frogs?

LIUBOV ANDRYEEVNA: I ate crocodiles.

PISHCHIK: Fancy that!

LOPAKHIN: Up to just recently there were only gentry and peasants living in the country, but now there are all these summer residents. All the towns, even quite small ones, are surrounded with villas. And probably in the course of the next twenty years or so, these people will multiply tremendously. At present they merely drink tea on the verandah, but they might start cultivating their plots of land, and then your cherry orchard would be gay with life and wealth and luxury. . . .

GAYEV (*indignantly*): What nonsense!
*Enter* VARIA *and* YASHA.

VARIA: Here are two telegrams for you, Mamma dear. (*Picks out a key and unlocks an old bookcase with a jingling noise.*) Here they are.

LIUBOV ANDRYEEVNA: They are from Paris. (*Tears them up without reading them.*) I've finished with Paris.

GAYEV: Do you know, Liuba, how old this bookcase is? A week ago I pulled out the bottom drawer, and I found some figures burnt in the wood. It was made exactly a hundred years ago. What do you think of that, eh? We ought to celebrate its anniversary. An inanimate object, true, but still—a bookcase!

PISHCHIK (*astonished*): A hundred years! Fancy that!

GAYEV: Yes. . . . This is a valuable piece of furniture. (*Feeling round the bookcase with his hands.*) My dear, venerable bookcase! I salute you! For more than a hundred years you have devoted yourself to the highest ideals of goodness and justice. For a hundred years you have never failed to fill us with an urge to useful work; several generations of our family have had their courage sustained and their faith in a better future fortified by your silent call; you have fostered in us the ideal of public good and social consciousness. *Pause.*

LOPAKHIN: Yes. . . .

LIUBOV ANDRYEEVNA: You're just the same, Lionia.

GAYEV (*slightly embarrassed*): I pot into the corner pocket! I pot into the middle pocket! . . .

LOPAKHIN (*glances at his watch*): Well, it's time for me to be going.

YASHA (*brings medicine to* LIUBOV ANDRYEEVNA): Would you care to take your pills now?

PISHCHIK: Don't take medicines, my dear . . . they don't do you any good . . . or harm either. Let me have them. (*Takes the box from her, pours the pills into the palm of his hand, blows on them, puts them all into his mouth and takes a drink of kvass.*) There!

LIUBOV ANDRYEEVNA (*alarmed*): But you're mad!

PISHCHIK: I've taken all the pills.

LOPAKHIN: What a digestion!
*All laugh.*

FEERS: His honour came to see us in Holy Week, and ate half-a-bucketful of salt cucumbers. (*Mutters.*)

LIUBOV ANDRYEEVNA: What is it he's saying?

VARIA: He's been muttering for the last three years. We're accustomed to it.

YASHA: It's his age. . . .

> CHARLOTTA IVANOVNA, *very thin and tightly laced in a white dress, with a lorgnette at her waist, passes across the stage.*

LOPAKHIN: Forgive me, Charlotta Ivanovna, I haven't yet had time to say how d'you do to you. (*Tries to kiss her hand.*)

CHARLOTTA (*withdrawing her hand*): If you were permitted to kiss a lady's hand, you'd want to kiss her elbow next, and then her shoulder.

LOPAKHIN: I'm unlucky today.

> *All laugh.*

Charlotta Ivanovna, do a trick for us.

CHARLOTTA: There's no need to, now. I want to go to bed. (*Goes out.*)

LOPAKHIN: I'll see you in three weeks' time. (*Kisses* LIUBOV ANDRYEEVNA'S *hand.*) Meanwhile, good-bye. Time to go. (*To* GAYEV.) Au revoir. (*Embraces* PISHCHIK.) Au revoir. (*Shakes hands with* VARIA, *then with* FEERS *and* YASHA.) I don't want to go, really. (*To* LIUBOV ANDRYEEVNA.) If you think over this question of country villas and come to a decision, let me know, and I'll get you a loan of fifty thousand or more. Think it over seriously.

VARIA (*crossly*): Will you ever go away?

LOPAKHIN: I'm going, I'm going. (*Goes out.*)

GAYEV: What a boor! I beg your pardon. . . . Varia's going to marry him, he's Varia's precious fiancé.

VARIA: Place don't say anything uncalled for, Uncle dear.

LIUBOV ANDRYEEVNA: Well, Varia, I shall be very glad. He's a good man.

PISHCHIK: He's a man . . . let's admit it . . . a most admirable fellow. . . . My Dashenka says so, too . . . she says all sorts of things. . . . (*He drops asleep and snores, but wakes up again at once.*) Incidentally, my dear, will you lend me two hundred and forty roubles? I've got to pay the interest on the mortgage tomorrow. . . .

VARIA (*in alarm*): We haven't got it, we really haven't!

LIUBOV ANDRYEEVNA: It's quite true, I have nothing.

PISHCHIK: It'll turn up. (*Laughs.*) I never lose hope. Sometimes I think everything's lost, I'm ruined, and then—lo and behold!—a railway line is built through my land, and they pay me for it! Something or other is sure to happen, tomorrow, if not today. Perhaps Dashenka will win two hundred thousand roubles. She's got a lottery ticket.

LIUBOV ANDRYEEVNA: I've finished my coffee; now I can go and rest.

FEERS (*brushing* GAYEV, *admonishing him*): You've put on the wrong pair of trousers again! What am I to do with you?

VARIA (*in a low voice*): Ania's asleep. (*Quietly opens a window.*) The sun has risen, it's warmer already. Look, Mamma dear, how wonderful the trees are! Heavens, what lovely air! The starlings are singing!

GAYEV (*opens another window*): The orchard is all white. You haven't forgotten, Liuba? How straight this long avenue is— quite straight, just like a ribbon that's been stretched taut. It glitters on moonlit nights. Do you remember? You haven't forgotten?

LIUBOV ANDRYEEVNA (*looks through the window at the orchard*): Oh, my childhood, my innocent childhood! I used to sleep in this nursery; I used to look on to the orchard from here, and I woke up happy every morning. In those days the orchard was just as it is now, nothing has changed. (*Laughs happily.*) All, all white! Oh, my orchard! After the dark, stormy autumn and the cold winter, you are young and joyous again; the angels have not forsaken you! If only this burden could be taken from me, if only I could forget my past!

GAYEV: Yes, and now the orchard is going to be sold to pay our debts, strange as it seems. . . .

LIUBOV ANDRYEEVNA: Look, there's Mother walking through the orchard . . . in a white dress! (*Laughs happily.*) It is her!

GAYEV: Where?

VARIA: Bless you, Mamma dear!

LIUBOV ANDRYEEVNA: It's no one, I only imagined it. Over there, you see, on the right, by the turning to the summer house there's a small white tree and it's bending over . . . it looks like a woman. *Enter* TROFIMOV. *He is dressed in a shabby student's uniform, and wears glasses.*

LIUBOV ANDRYEEVNA: What a wonderful orchard! Masses of white blossom, the blue sky. . . .

TROFIMOV: Liubov Andryeevna! (*She turns to him.*) I'll just make my bow and go at once. (*Kisses her hand warmly.*) I was told to wait until the morning, but it was too much for my patience.

LIUBOV ANDRYEEVNA *looks at him, puzzled.*

VARIA (*through tears*): This is Pyetia Trofimov.

TROFIMOV: Pyetia Trofimov, I used to be tutor to your Grisha. Have I really changed so much?

LIUBOV ANDRYEEVNA *puts her arms round him and weeps quietly.*

GAYEV (*embarrassed*): Now, now, Liuba. . . .

VARIA (*weeps*): Didn't I tell you to wait until tomorrow, Pyetia?

LIUBOV ANDRYEEVNA: My Grisha . . . my little boy . . . Grisha . . . my son . . .

VARIA: There's nothing for it, Mamma darling. It was God's will.

TROFIMOV (*gently, with emotion*): Don't, don't . . .

LIUBOV ANDRYEEVNA (*quietly weeping*): My little boy was lost . . . drowned . . . . What for? What for, my friend? (*More quietly.*) Ania's asleep there, and here I am, shouting and making a scene. Well, Pyetia? How is it you've lost your good looks? Why have you aged so?

TROFIMOV: A peasant woman in the train called me 'that moth-eaten gent'.

LIUBOV ANDRYEEVNA: In those days you were quite a boy, a nice young student, and now your hair is thin, you wear glasses. . . . Are you still a student? (*Walks to the door.*)

TROFIMOV: I expect I shall be a student to the end of my days.

LIUBOV ANDRYEEVNA (*kisses her brother, then* VARIA): Well, go to bed now. You have aged, too, Leonid.

PISHCHIK (*following her*): So you're going to bed now? Och, my gout! I'd better stay the night here. And tomorrow morning, Liubov Andryeevna, my dear, I'd like to borrow those two hundred and forty roubles.

GAYEV: How the fellow keeps at it!

PISHCHIK: Two hundred and forty roubles. . . . You see, I've got to pay the interest on the mortgage.

LIUBOV ANDRYEEVNA: I have no money, my dear.

PISHCHIK: I'll pay you back, my dear lady. It's a trifling amount, after all.

LIUBOV ANDRYEEVNA: Very well, then. Leonid will give you the money. You give him the money, Leonid.

GAYEV: I'll be delighted; anything he wants, of course!

LIUBOV ANDRYEEVNA: What else can we do? He needs it. He'll pay it back.

LIUBOV ANDRYEEVNA, TROFIMOV, PISHCHIK *and* FEERS *go out,* GAYEV, VARIA *and* YASHA *remain.*

GAYEV: My sister hasn't lost her habit of throwing money away. (*To* YASHA.) Out of the way, my man, you smell of the kitchen.

YASHA (*with a sneer*):  I see you're just the same as you used to be, Leonid Andryeevich.

GAYEV:  What's that? (*To* VARIA.) What did he say?

VARIA (*to* YASHA):  Your mother's come from the village, she's been sitting in the servants' hall since yesterday, wanting to see you.

YASHA:  I wish she'd leave me alone!

VARIA:  You . . . aren't you ashamed of yourself?

YASHA:  It's quite unnecessary. She could have come tomorrow. (YASHA *goes out.*)

VARIA:  Dear Mamma is just the same as she used to be, she hasn't changed a bit. If she had her own way, she'd give away everything.

GAYEV:  Yes. . . . You know, if a lot of cures are suggested for a disease, it means that the disease is incurable. I've been thinking and puzzling my brains, and I've thought of plenty of ways out, plenty—which means there aren't any. It would be a good thing if somebody left us some money, or if we married off our Ania to some very rich man, or if one of us went to Yaroslavl and tried our luck with the old aunt, the Countess. You know she's very rich.

VARIA (*weeping*):  If only God would help us.

GAYEV:  Do stop blubbering! The Countess is very rich, but she doesn't like us. . . . First, because my sister married a solicitor, and not a nobleman. . . .

ANIA *appears in the doorway.*

She married a man who wasn't of noble birth . . . and then you can't say her behaviour's been exactly virtuous. She's a good, kind, lovable person, and I'm very fond of her, but whatever extenuating circumstances you may think of, you must admit that she's a bit easy-going morally. You can sense it in every movement. . . .

VARIA (*in a whisper*):  Ania's standing in the doorway.

GAYEV:  What? (*A pause.*) Funny thing, something's got into my right eye. . . . I can't see properly. And on Thursday, when I was at the District Court. . . .

ANIA *comes in.*

VARIA:  Well, why aren't you asleep, Ania?

ANIA:  I can't get to sleep. I just can't.

GAYEV:  My dear little girl! (*Kisses* ANIA'S *face and hands.*) My dear child! (*Through tears.*) You're not just a niece to me, you're an angel, you're everything to me. Please believe me, believe . . .

ANIA:  I believe you, Uncle. Everyone loves you, respects you . . . but, dear Uncle, you oughtn't to talk, you ought to try to keep quiet. What was that you were saying just now about my mother, about your own sister? Why were you saying it?

GAYEV:  Yes, yes! (*He takes her hand and puts it over his face.*) You're quite right, it's dreadful! My God! My God! And the speech I made today in front of the bookcase . . . so foolish! And it was only after I'd finished that I realized it was foolish.

VARIA:  It's true, Uncle dear, you ought to try to keep quiet. Just keep quiet, that's all.

ANIA:  If you keep quiet, you'll be happier in yourself.

GAYEV:  I'll be quiet. (*Kisses* ANIA'S *and* VARIA'S *hands.*) I'll be quiet. But I must tell you something important. Last Thursday I went to the District Court, and I got talking with some friends, and from what they said it looks as if it might be possible to get a loan on promissory notes, in order to pay the interest to the bank.

VARIA:  If only God would help us!

GAYEV:  I'll go there again on Tuesday and have another talk. (*To* VARIA.) Don't keep crying. (*To* ANIA.) Your Mother's going to have a talk with Lopakhin: he won't refuse her, of course. And after you've had a rest, you will go to Yaroslavl, to see the Countess, your grandmother. And so we'll approach the matter from three angles, and—the thing's done! We shall pay the interest, I'm sure of it. (*He puts a sweet into his mouth.*) I swear on my honour, on anything you like, that the estate will not be sold! (*Excited.*) I'll stake my happiness! Here's my hand, you can call me a good-for-nothing liar if I allow the auction to take place. I swear on my soul!

ANIA (*calmer, with an air of happiness*): How good you are, Uncle, and how sensible! (*Puts her arms round him.*) I feel calmer now. I feel so calm and happy.

*Enter* FEERS.

FEERS (*reproachfully*): Leonid Andryeevich, aren't you ashamed of yourself? When are you going to bed?

GAYEV: Presently, presently. You go away, Feers. I don't need your help. Well, children dear, bye-bye now. . . . All the news tomorrow, you must go to bed now. (*Kisses* ANIA *and* VARIA.) You know, I'm a man of the 'eighties. People don't think much of that period, but all the same, I can say that I've suffered quite a lot in the course of my life for my convictions. It's not for nothing that the peasants love me. You have to know the peasants! You have to know from which side . . .

ANIA: You're starting it again, Uncle!

VARIA: You'd better keep quiet, Uncle dear.

FEERS (*sternly*): Leonid Andryeevich!

GAYEV: Coming, coming! Go to bed! In off the cushion! I pot the white! . . . (*Goes out;* FEERS *hobbles after him.*)

ANIA: My mind is at rest now. I don't really feel like going to Yaroslavl, I don't like Grandmamma; but still, I'm not worrying. I'm grateful to Uncle. (*She sits down.*)

VARIA: I must get some sleep. I'm going. Oh, by the way, while you were away something unpleasant happened here. You know, there are only a few old servants living in the servants' quarters: just Yefemooshka, Polia, Yevstignei and Karp.

Well, they let some tramps sleep there, and I didn't say anything about it. But some time afterwards I heard some gossip; people said I had ordered them to be fed on nothing but dried peas. Because I was mean, you see. . . . Yevstignei was at the bottom of it all. 'Well,' I said to myself, 'if that's how the matter stands, just you wait!' So I sent for Yevstignei. (*Yawns.*) In he comes. 'What's all this, Yevstignei,' I said to him, 'idiot that you are.' . . . (*She walks up to* ANIA.) Anichka! (*A pause.*) She's asleep! . . . (*Takes her arm*) Come to bed! Come! (*Leads her away.*) My darling's fallen asleep! Come. . . .

*They go towards the door. The sound of a shepherd's pipe is heard from far away, beyond the orchard.* TROFIMOV *crosses the stage, but, seeing* VARIA *and* ANIA, *stops.*

VARIA: Sh-sh! She's asleep . . . asleep . . . Come, my dear.

ANIA (*softly, half-asleep*): I'm so tired. . . . I can hear bells tinkling all the time. . . . Uncle . . . dear . . . Mamma and Uncle. . . .

VARIA: Come, darling, come. . . . (*They go into* ANIA'S *room.*)

TROFIMOV (*deeply moved*): Ania . . . my one bright star! My spring flower!

CURTAIN

# ACT TWO

*An old wayside shrine in the open country; it leans slightly to one side and has evidently been long abandoned. Beside it there are a well, an old seat and a number of large stones which apparently served as gravestones in the past. A road leads to* GAYEV'S *estate. On one side and some distance away is a row of dark poplars, and it is there that the cherry orchard begins. Further away is seen a line of telegraph poles, and beyond them, on the horizon, the vague outlines of a large town, visible only in very good, clear weather.*

*The sun is about to set.* CHARLOTTA, YASHA *and* DOONIASHA *are sitting on the seat;* YEPIHODOV *is standing near by, playing a gui-*

*tar; all look pensive.* **CHARLOTTA** *is wearing a man's old peaked cap; she has taken a shot-gun off her shoulder and is adjusting a buckle on the strap.*

**CHARLOTTA** (*thoughtfully*): I don't know how old I am. I haven't got a proper identity card, you see . . . and I keep on imagining I'm still quite young. When I was little, father and mother used to tour the fairs and give performances—very good ones they were, too. And I used to jump the *salto-mortale* and do all sorts of other tricks. When Papa and Mamma died, a German lady took me into her house and began to give me lessons. So then I grew up and became a governess. But where I come from and who I am, I don't know. Who my parents were—perhaps they weren't properly married—I don't know. (*She takes a cucumber from her pocket and begins to eat it.*) I don't know anything. (*Pause.*) I'm longing to talk to someone, but there isn't anyone. I haven't anyone . . . .

**YEPIHODOV** (*plays the guitar and sings*): 'What care I for the noisy world? . . . What are friends and foes to me?' How pleasant it is to play the mandoline!

**DOONIASHA:** That's a guitar, not a mandoline. (*She looks at herself in a hand mirror and powders her face.*)

**YEPIHODOV:** To a man that's crazy with love this is a mandoline. (*Sings quietly.*) 'If only my heart might be warmed by the ardour of love requited.' . . .
  **YASHA** *joins in.*

**CHARLOTTA:** How dreadful their singing is! . . . Ach! It is like the jackals.

**DOONIASHA** (*to* **YASHA**): You are lucky to have been abroad!

**YASHA:** Of course I am. I'm bound to agree with you there. (*Yawns, then lights a cigar.*)

**YEPIHODOV:** Stands to reason. Abroad everything's been in full swing. . . . I mean to say, everything's been going on for ever so long.

**YASHA:** Obviously.

**YEPIHODOV:** Personally, I'm a cultured sort of fellow, I read all sorts of extraordinary books, you know, but somehow I can't seem to make out where I'm going, what it is I really want, I mean to say—to live or to shoot myself, so to speak. All the same, I always carry a revolver on me. Here it is. (*Shows the revolver.*)

**CHARLOTTA:** I have finished. Now I'm going. (*Slips the strap of the gun over her shoulder.*) Yes, you are a very clever man, Yepihodov, and rather frightening, too; the women must fall madly in love with you! Brrr! (*Walks off.*) All these clever people are so stupid, I have no one to talk to. I am so lonely, always so lonely, no one belongs to me, and . . . and who I am, what I exist for, nobody knows. . . . (*Goes out leisurely.*)

**YEPIHODOV:** Candidly speaking, and I do want to keep strictly to the point, by the way, but I feel I simply must explain that Fate, so to speak, treats me absolutely without mercy, just like a storm treats a small ship, as it were. I mean to say, supposing I'm wrong, for instance, then why should I wake up this morning and suddenly see a simply colossal spider sitting on my chest? like this. . . . (*Makes a gesture with both hands.*) Or supposing I pick up a jug to have a drink of kvass, there's sure to be something frightful inside it, such as a cockroach. (*Pause.*) Have you read Buckle? (*Pause.*) May I trouble you for a word, Avdotya Fiodorovna?

**DOONIASHA:** All right, carry on.

**YEPIHODOV:** I'd very much like to speak to you alone. (*Sighs.*)

**DOONIASHA** (*embarrassed*): Very well then . . . only will you bring me my little cape first. . . . It's hanging beside the wardrobe. It's rather chilly here. . . .

**YEPIHODOV:** Very well, I'll bring it. . . . Now I know what to do with my revolver. (*Picks up his guitar and goes, twanging it.*)

YASHA: Two-and-twenty misfortunes! He's a stupid fellow, between you and me. (*Yawns.*)

DOONIASHA: I hope to God he won't shoot himself. (*Pause.*) I've got sort of anxious, worrying all the time. I came to live here with the Master and Mistress when I was still a little girl you see. Now I've got out of the way of living a simple life, and my hands are as white ... as white as a young lady's. I've grown sensitive and delicate, just as if I was one of the nobility; I'm afraid of everything. ... Just afraid. If you deceive me, Yasha, I don't know what will happen to my nerves.

YASHA (*kisses her*): Little peach! Mind you, a girl ought to keep herself in hand, you know. Personally I dislike it more than anything if a girl doesn't behave herself.

DOONIASHA: I love you so much, so much! You're educated, you can reason about everything.

*Pause.*

YASHA (*yawns*): Y-yes. ... To my way of thinking, it's like this: if a girl loves somebody, it means she's immoral. (*Pause.*) It's nice to smoke a cigar in the open air. ... (*Listens.*) Someone's coming this way. Our ladies and gentlemen. ... (DOONIASHA *impulsively puts her arms round him.*) Go home now, as if you'd been down to the river bathing; go by this path, or you'll meet them, and they might think I've been keeping company with you. I couldn't stand that.

DOONIASHA (*coughing softly*): My head's aching from that cigar. ... (*Goes out.*)

YASHA *remains sitting by the shrine. Enter* LIUBOV ANDRYEEVNA, GAYEV *and* LOPAKHIN.

LOPAKHIN: We must decide once and for all: time won't wait. After all, my question's quite a simple one. Do you consent to lease your land for villas, or don't you? You can answer in one word: yes or no? Just one word!

LIUBOV ANDRYEEVNA: Who's been smoking such abominable cigars here? (*Sits down.*)

GAYEV: How very convenient it is having a railway here. (*Sits down.*) Here we are—we've been up to town for lunch and we're back home already. I pot the red into the middle pocket! I'd like to go indoors now and have just one game. ...

LIUBOV ANDRYEEVNA: You've plenty of time.

LOPAKHIN: Just one word! (*Beseechingly.*) Do give me an answer!

GAYEV (*yawns*): What do you say?

LIUBOV ANDRYEEVNA (*looking into her purse*): Yesterday I had a lot of money, but today there's hardly any left. My poor Varia is feeding everyone on milk soups to economize; the old servants in the kitchen get nothing but dried peas to eat, and here I am, spending money senselessly, I don't know why. ... (*She drops the purse, scattering gold coins.*) Now I've scattered it all over the place. ... (*Annoyed.*)

YASHA: Allow me, Madam, I'll pick them up in a minute. (*Gathers up the money.*)

LIUBOV ANDRYEEVNA: Thank you, Yasha. ... Why did I go out to lunch? It was quite vile, that restaurant of yours, with its beastly music; and the table-cloths smelt of soap, too. ... Need one drink so much, Lionia? Need one eat so much? And talk so much? Today at the restaurant you talked too much again, and it was all so pointless. About the seventies, about the decadents. And who to? Fancy talking about the decadents to the restaurant waiters!

LOPAKHIN: Yes, fancy.

GAYEV (*waving his hand*): I'm hopeless, I know. (*To* YASHA, *with irritation.*) Why are you always buzzing about in front of me?

YASHA (*laughs*): I can never hear you talk without laughing.

GAYEV (*to his sister*):  Either he goes, or I do. . . .

LIUBOV ANDRYEEVNA:  Go away, Yasha, go along.

YASHA (*hands the purse to* LIUBOV ANDRYEEVNA):  I'll go now. (*He can hardly restrain his laughter.*) This very minute. . . . (*Goes out.*)

LOPAKHIN:  You know, that wealthy fellow Deriganov, he's intending to buy your estate. They say he's coming to the auction himself.

LIUBOV ANDRYEEVNA:  Where did you hear that?

LOPAKHIN:  They were saying so in town.

GAYEV:  Our Aunt in Yaroslavl promised to send us money but when and how much it will be we don't know.

LOPAKHIN:  How much will she send you? A hundred thousand? Two hundred?

LIUBOV ANDRYEEVNA:  Well, hardly. . . . Ten or twelve thousand, perhaps. We'll be thankful for that much.

LOPAKHIN:  You must forgive me for saying it, but really I've never met such feckless, unbusiness-like, queer people as you are. You are told in plain language that your estate is up for sale, and you simply don't seem to understand it.

LIUBOV ANDRYEEVNA:  But what are we to do? Tell us, what?

LOPAKHIN:  I keep on telling you. Every day I tell you the same thing. You must lease the cherry orchard and the land for villas, and you must do it now, as soon as possible. The auction is going to be held almost at once. Please do try to understand! Once you definitely decide to have the villas, you'll be able to borrow as much money as you like, and then you'll be out of the wood.

LIUBOV ANDRYEEVNA:  Villas and summer visitors! Forgive me, but it's so vulgar.

GAYEV:  I absolutely agree with you.

LOPAKHIN:  Honestly, I feel I shall burst into tears, or shriek, or fall down and faint. I simply can't stand it. You've literally worn me out. (*To* GAYEV.) An old woman, that's what you are!

GAYEV:  What's that?

LOPAKHIN:  An old woman!

LIUBOV ANDRYEEVNA (*alarmed*):  No, don't go, do stay, my dear. Please stay! Perhaps we could think of something.

LOPAKHIN:  It hardly seems worth trying.

LIUBOV ANDRYEEVNA:  Don't go, please! Somehow it's more cheerful with you here. (*Pause.*) I keep expecting something dreadful to happen . . . as if the house were going to fall down on us.

GAYEV (*in deep thought*):  I cannon off the cushions! I pot into the middle pocket. . . .

LIUBOV ANDRYEEVNA:  We've sinned too much. . . .

LOPAKHIN:  Sinned, indeed! What were your sins?

GAYEV (*puts a sweet into his mouth*):  They say I've eaten up my whole fortune in sweets. (*Laughs.*)

LIUBOV ANDRYEEVNA:  Oh, my sins! Look at the way I've always squandered money, continually. It was sheer madness. And then I got married to a man who only knew how to get into debt. Champagne killed him—he was a terrific drinker— and then, worse luck I fell in love with someone else. We had an affair, and just at that very time—it was my first punishment, a blow straight to my heart—my little boy was drowned here, in this river . . . and then I went abroad. I went away for good, and never meant to return, I never meant to see the river again . . . I just shut my eyes and ran away in a frenzy of grief, but *he* . . . he followed me. It was so cruel and brutal of him! I bought a villa near Mentone because he fell ill there, you see, and for three years I never had any rest, day or night. He was a sick man, he quite wore me out; my soul seemed to dry right up. Then, last year when the villa had to be sold to pay the debts, I went to Paris, and there he robbed me and left me; he went away and lived with another woman. . . . I tried to poison myself . . . It was all so foolish, so shameful! And then suddenly I felt an urge to come back to Russia, to my own country and my little girl. . . . (*Wipes away her tears.*) Oh, Lord, Lord, be merciful, forgive me my sins! Don't punish me any more! (*Takes a telegram out of her pocket.*) I had this from Paris today. He's asking my forgiveness, begging me to return. . . . (*Tears up the telegram.*) Sounds like music somewhere. (*Listens.*)

GAYEV: That's our famous Jewish band. Do you remember, four violins, a flute and a contrabass?

LIUBOV ANDRYEEVNA: Is that still in existence? It would be nice to get them to come to the house one day, and we could have a little dance.

LOPAKHIN (*listens*): I can't hear anything. . . . (*Sings quietly.*) 'And the Germans, if you pay, will turn Russian into Frenchman, so they say.' . . . (*Laughs.*) I saw such a good play at the theatre yesterday. Very amusing.

LIUBOV ANDRYEEVNA: I'm sure it wasn't at all amusing. Instead of going to see plays, you should take a good look at yourself. Just think what a drab kind of life you lead, what a lot of nonsense you talk!

LOPAKHIN: It's perfectly true. Yes, I admit it, we lead an idiotic existence. . . . (*Pause.*) My Dad was a peasant, a blockhead, he didn't understand anything, and he didn't teach me anything, but just beat me when he was drunk, and always with a stick at that. As a matter of fact, I'm just as much of a fool and a half-wit myself. No one taught me anything, my writing is awful, I'm ashamed even to show it to people: it's just like a pig's.

LIUBOV ANDRYEEVNA: You ought to get married, my friend.

LOPAKHIN: Yes. . . . That's true.

LIUBOV ANDRYEEVNA: You ought to marry our Varia. She's a nice girl.

LOPAKHIN: Yes.

LIUBOV ANDRYEEVNA: She comes from the common folk, and she's a hard-working girl: she can work the whole day without stopping. But the main thing is that she loves you, and you've been attracted by her for a long time yourself.

LOPAKHIN: Well. . . . I'm quite willing. . . . She's a nice girl.
*Pause.*

GAYEV: I've been offered a job at the bank. Six thousand a year. Have you heard?

LIUBOV ANDRYEEVNA: Indeed I have. You'd better stay where you are.
*Enter* FEERS *with an overcoat.*

FEERS (*to* GAYEV): Will you please put it on, Sir, it's so chilly.

GAYEV (*Puts on the overcoat*): You *are* a nuisance.

FEERS: Tut, tut! You went off this morning and never told me you were going. (*Looks him over.*)

LIUBOV ANDRYEEVNA: How you've aged, Feers!

FEERS: What can I get you, Madam?

LOPAKHIN: They say, you've aged a lot.

FEERS: I've been alive a long time. They were going to marry me off before your Dad was born. (*Laughs.*) And when Freedom was granted to the people, I'd already been made a chief valet. I wouldn't take my Freedom then, I stayed with the Master and Mistress. . . . (*Pause.*) I remember everyone was glad at the time, but what they were glad about, no one knew.

LOPAKHIN: Oh, yes, it was a good life all right! At least, people got flogged!

FEERS (*not having heard him*): Rather! The peasants belonged to the gentry, and the gentry belonged to the peasants; but now everything's separate, and you can't understand anything.

GAYEV: Be quiet, Feers. Tomorrow I must go to town. I was promised an introduction to some general or other who'll lend us some money on a promissory note.

LOPAKHIN: Nothing will come of that. And you won't be able to pay the interest, anyway.

LIUBOV ANDRYEEVNA: He's talking through his hat. There aren't any generals.

*Enter* TROFIMOV, ANIA *and* VARIA.

GAYEV: Here come the children.

ANIA: There's Mamma.

LIUBOV ANDRYEEVNA: Come here, my dears. My dear children. . . . (*Embraces* ANIA *and* VARIA.) If you both only knew how much I love you! Sit down beside me, here.

*All sit down.*

LOPAKHIN: Our 'eternal student' is always with the young ladies.

TROFIMOV: It's none of your business, anyway.

LOPAKHIN: He'll soon be fifty, yet he's still a student.

TROFIMOV: I wish you'd drop your idiotic jokes.

LOPAKHIN: But why are you getting annoyed? You *are* a queer chap!

TROFIMOV: Why do you keep pestering me?

LOPAKHIN (*laughs*): Just let me ask you one question: what do you make of me?

TROFIMOV: My opinion of you, Yermolai Aleksyeevich, is simply this: you're a wealthy man, and before long you'll be a millionaire; and in so far as a wild beast is necessary because it devours everything in its path and so converts one kind of matter into another, you are necessary also.

*Everybody laughs.*

VARIA: You'd better tell us about the planets, Pyetia.

LIUBOV ANDRYEEVNA: No, let's continue what we were talking about yesterday.

TROFIMOV: What were we talking about?

GAYEV: About pride.

TROFIMOV: We talked a lot yesterday, but we didn't agree on anything. The proud man, in the sense you understand him, has something mystical about him. Maybe you're right in a way, but if we try to think it out simply, without being too far-fetched about it, the question arises—why should he be proud? Where's the sense in being proud when you consider that Man, as a species, is not very well constructed physiologically, and, in the vast majority of cases is coarse, stupid, and profoundly unhappy, too? We ought to stop all this self-admiration. We ought to—just work.

GAYEV: You'll die just the same, whatever you do.

TROFIMOV: Who knows? And anyway, what does it mean—to die? It may be that Man is possessed of a hundred senses, and only the five that are known to us perish in death, while the remaining ninety-five live on afterwards.

LIUBOV ANDRYEEVNA: How clever you are, Pyetia!

LOPAKHIN (*ironically*): Oh, awfully clever!

TROFIMOV: Humanity is perpetually advancing, always seeking to perfect its own powers. One day all the things that are beyond our grasp at present are going to fall within our reach, only to achieve this we've got to work with all our might, to help the people who are seeking after truth. Here, in Russia, very few people have started to work, so far. Nearly all the members of the intelligentsia that I know care for nothing, do nothing and are still incapable of work. They call themselves 'intelligentsia', but they still talk contemptuously to their servants, they treat the peasants as if they were animals, they study without achieving anything, they don't read anything serious, they just do nothing. As for science, they only talk about it, and they don't understand much about art either. They all look very grave and go about with grim expressions on their faces, and they only discuss important matters and philosophize. Yet all the time anyone can see that our work-people are abominably fed and have to sleep without proper beds, thirty to forty to a room, with bed-bugs, bad smells, damp, and immorality everywhere. It's perfectly obvious that all our nice-sounding talk is intended only to mislead ourselves and others. Tell me then, where are the crèches which we're always talking about, where are the reading rooms? We only write about them in novels, but actually there just aren't any. There's nothing but dirt, bestiality, Asiatic customs. . . . I'm afraid of these deadly serious faces, I don't like them; I'm afraid of serious talk. It would be better for us just to keep quiet.

LOPAKHIN: Well, let me tell you that *I'm* up soon after four every morning, and I work from morning till night. I always have money in hand, my own and other people's, and I have plenty of opportunities to learn what the people around me are like. You only have to start on a job of work to realize how few honest, decent people there are about. Sometimes, when I can't sleep, I start brooding over it. The Lord God has given us vast forests, immense fields, wide horizons; surely we ought to be giants, living in such a country as this. . . .

LIUBOV ANDRYEEVNA: Whatever do you want giants for? They're all right in fairytales, otherwise they're just terrifying.

YEPIHODOV *crosses the stage in the background, playing his guitar.*

LIUBOV ANDRYEEVNA (*pensively*): There goes Yepihodov. . . .

ANIA (*pensively*): There goes Yepihodov. . . .

GAYEV: The sun's gone down, ladies and gentlemen.

TROFIMOV: Yes.

GAYEV (*in a subdued voice, as if reciting a poem*): Oh, glorious Nature, shining with eternal light, so beautiful, yet so indifferent to our fate . . . you, whom we call Mother, uniting in yourself both Life and Death, you live and you destroy. . . .

VARIA (*imploringly*): Uncle, dear!

ANIA: You're starting again, Uncle!

TROFIMOV: You'd better screw back off the red into the middle pocket.

GAYEV: I'll keep quiet, I'll keep quiet.

*They all sit deep in thought; the silence is only broken by the subdued muttering of* FEERS. *Suddenly a distant sound is heard, coming as if out of the sky, like the sound of a string snapping, slowly and sadly dying away.*

LIUBOV ANDRYEEVNA: What was that?

LOPAKHIN: I don't know. Somewhere a long way off a lift cable in one of the mines must have broken. But it must be somewhere very far away.

GAYEV: Or perhaps it was some bird . . . a heron, perhaps.

TROFIMOV: Or an owl. . . .

LIUBOV ANDRYEEVNA (*shudders*): It sounded unpleasant, somehow. . . .

*A pause.*

FEERS: It was the same before the misfortune: the owl hooted and the samovar kept singing.

GAYEV: What misfortune?

FEERS: Before they gave us Freedom.

*A pause.*

LIUBOV ANDRYEEVNA: Come along, my friends! Let us go home, it's getting dark. (*To* ANIA.) You've got tears in your eyes. What is it, my little one? (*Embraces her.*)

ANIA: Never mind, Mamma. It's nothing.

TROFIMOV: Someone's coming.

*Enter* A TRAMP *in a white battered peaked cap and an overcoat; he is slightly tipsy.*

THE TRAMP: Excuse me, can I get straight to the station through here?

GAYEV: You can. Follow the road.

THE TRAMP: I'm greatly obliged to you, Sir. (*Coughs.*) Lovely weather today. (*Recites.*) 'Oh, my brother, my suffering brother!... Come to mother Volga, whose groans....' (*To* VARIA.) Mademoiselle, may a starving Russian citizen trouble you for a few coppers?

VARIA *cries out, frightened.*

LOPAKHIN (*angrily*): Really, there's a limit to everything!

LIUBOV ANDRYEEVNA (*at a loss what to do*): Take this . . . here you are. (*Searches in her purse.*) I have no silver.... Never mind, here's a gold one....

THE TRAMP: I'm deeply grateful to you! (*Goes off.*)

*Laughter.*

VARIA (*frightened*): I'm going.... I'm going. ... Oh, Mamma dear, you know there's no food in the house, and you gave him all that!

LIUBOV ANDRYEEVNA: Well, what can you do with a fool like me? I'll give you all I've got when we get home. Yermolai Aleksyeevich, you'll lend me some more, won't you?

LOPAKHIN: Certainly I will.

LIUBOV ANDRYEEVNA: Let's go on now, it's time. By the way, Varia, we almost fixed up your marriage just now. I congratulate you.

VARIA (*through her tears*): It's no laughing matter, Mamma!

LOPAKHIN: Go to a nunnery, Ohmelia! . . .

GAYEV: Look how my hands are trembling: I haven't played billiards for a long time.

LOPAKHIN: Ohmelia, oh nymph, remember me in thy orisons!

LIUBOV ANDRYEEVNA: Come along, everybody. It's almost supper time.

VARIA: That man scared me so. My heart keeps thumping.

LOPAKHIN: My friends, just one word, please just one word: on the twenty-second of August the cherry orchard is going to be sold. Just consider that! Just think. . . .

*All go out, except* TROFIMOV *and* ANIA.

ANIA (*laughs*): Thank the tramp for this! He frightened Varia, now we are alone.

TROFIMOV: Varia's afraid—afraid we might suddenly fall in love with each other—so she follows us about all day long. She's so narrow-minded, she can't grasp that we are above falling in love. To rid ourselves of all that's petty and unreal, all that prevents us from being happy and free, that's the whole aim and meaning of our life. Forward! Let's march on irresistibly towards that bright star over there, shining in the distance! Forward! Don't fall behind, friends!

ANIA (*raising her hands*): How well you talk! (*A pause.*) It's wonderful here today.

TROFIMOV: Yes, the weather's marvellous.

ANIA: What have you done to me, Pyetia? Why is it that I don't love the cherry orchard as I used to? I used to love it so dearly, it seemed to me that there wasn't a better place in all the world than our orchard.

TROFIMOV: The whole of Russia is our orchard. The earth is great and beautiful and there are many, many wonderful places on it. (*A pause.*) Just think, Ania: your grandfather, your great grandfather and all your forefathers were serf owners—they owned living souls. Don't you see human beings gazing at you from every cherry tree in your orchard, from every leaf and every tree-trunk, don't you hear voices? . . . They owned living souls—and it has perverted you all, those who came before you, and you who are living now, so that your mother, your uncle and even you yourself no longer realize that you're living in debt, at other people's expense, at the expense of people you don't admit further than the kitchen. We are at least two hundred years behind the times; we still have no real background, no clear attitude to our past, we just philosophize and complain of depression, or drink vodka. Yet it's perfectly clear that to begin to live in the present, we must first atone for our past and be finished with it, and we can only atone for it by suffering, by extraordinary, unceasing exertion. You must understand this, Ania.

ANIA: The house we live in hasn't really been ours for a long time. I'll leave it, I give you my word.

TROFIMOV: Leave it, and if you have any keys to it, throw them down a well. Be free like the wind.

ANIA (*in rapture*): How well you put it!

TROFIMOV: You must believe me, Ania, you must. I'm not thirty yet, I'm young, and I'm still a student, but I've suffered so much already. As soon as the winter comes, I get half-starved, and ill, and worried, poor as a beggar, and there's hardly anywhere I haven't been to, where I haven't been driven to by Fate. And yet, always, every moment of the day and night my soul has been filled with such marvellous hopes and visions. I can see happiness, Ania, I can see it coming. . . .

ANIA (*pensively*): The moon's coming up.

YEPIHODOV *can be heard playing his guitar, the same melancholy tune as before. The moon rises. Somewhere in the vicinity of the poplars* VARIA *is looking for* ANIA *and calling:* 'Ania! Where are you?'

TROFIMOV: Yes, the moon is rising. (*A pause.*) There it is—happiness—it's coming nearer and nearer, I seem to hear its footsteps. And if we don't see it, if we don't know when it comes, what does it matter? Other people will see it!

VARIA'S VOICE: Ania! Where are you?

TROFIMOV: That Varia again! (*Angrily.*) It's disgusting!

ANIA: Well? Let us go to the river. It's nice there.

TROFIMOV: Let's go.

TROFIMOV and ANIA *go out.*

VARIA'S VOICE: Ania! Ania!

CURTAIN

# ACT THREE

*The drawing-room of the Ranyevskaia's house. Adjoining the drawing-room at the back, and connected to it by an archway, is the ballroom. A Jewish band, the same that was mentioned in Act II, is heard playing in the hall. It is evening; the candles in a chandelier are alight. In the ballroom a party is dancing the Grand-Rond,* SIMEONOV-PISHCHIK *is heard to call out:* 'Promenade à une paire!', *then all come into the drawing-room.* PISHCHIK *and* CHARLOTTA IVANOVNA *form the leading couple, then come* TROFIMOV *and* LIUBOV ANDRYEEVNA, ANIA *with a post-office clerk,* VARIA *with the station-master, and so on.* VARIA *cries quietly and wipes away her tears as she dances.* DOONIASHA *is in the last couple. They walk across the drawing-room.* PISHCHIK *shouts:* 'Grand rond balancez!' *and* 'Les cavaliers à genoux et remerciez vos dames!'

FEERS, *wearing a tail-coat, crosses the room with soda-water on a tray.* PISHCHIK *and* TROFIMOV *re-enter the drawing-room.*

PISHCHIK: I've got this high blood-pressure—I've had a stroke twice already, you know—and it makes dancing difficult; but if you're one of a pack, as the saying goes, you've got to wag your tail, whether you bark or not. Actually I'm as strong as a horse. My dear father—he liked his little joke, God bless him—he used to say that the ancient family of Simeonov-Pishchik was descended from the very same horse that Caligula sat in the Senate. (*Sits down.*) But the trouble is, we've no money. A hungry dog can only think about food. . . . (*Falls asleep and snores, but wakes up almost at once.*) Just like myself—I can't think of anything but money. . . .

TROFIMOV: It's quite true, there *is* something horsy about your build.

PISHCHIK: Oh, well, the horse is a good animal, you can sell a horse. . . .

*From the adjoining room comes the sound of someone playing billiards.* VARIA *appears in the ballroom, under the arch.*

TROFIMOV (*teasing her*): Madame Lopakhin! Madame Lopakhin!

VARIA (*angrily*): The 'moth-eaten gent'!

TROFIMOV: Yes, I am a moth-eaten gent, and I'm proud of it.

VARIA (*brooding bitterly*): So now we've hired a band—but how are we going to pay for it? (*Goes out.*)

TROFIMOV (*to* PISHCHIK): If all the energy you've wasted in the course of a life-time looking for money to pay interest on your debts—if all that energy had been used for something else, you'd probably have turned the world upside down by now.

PISHCHIK: The philosopher Nietzsche, the greatest, the most famous—a man of the highest intellect, in fact—says it's justifiable to forge bank-notes.

TROFIMOV: Have you read Nietzsche then?

PISHCHIK: Well, no. . . . Dashenka told me. But just now I'm in such a frightful position that I wouldn't mind forging a few bank-notes. The day after tomorrow I've got to pay three hundred and ten roubles. I've borrowed one hundred and thirty already. . . . (*Feels in his pockets with alarm.*) The money's gone! I've lost the money. (*Tearfully.*) Where's the money? (*With an expression of joy.*) Here it is, inside the lining! The shock's made me sweat! . . .

*Enter* LIUBOV ANDRYEEVNA *and* CHARLOTTA.

LIUBOV ANDRYEEVNA (*singing 'Lezghinka'[1] under her breath*): Why is Leonid so late? What's he doing in town? (*To* DOONIASHA.) Dooniasha, offer the musicians some tea.

TROFIMOV: I suppose the auction didn't take place.

LIUBOV ANDRYEEVNA: The band came at the wrong time, and the party started at the wrong time. . . . Well . . . never mind. . . . (*Sits down and sings quietly.*)

CHARLOTTA (*hands a pack of cards to* PISHCHIK): Here's a pack of cards—think of any card, now.

PISHCHIK: I've thought of one.

CHARLOTTA: Now shuffle the pack. That's right. Now give it to me, my good Monsieur Pishchik. *Ein, zwei, drei!* Now look for it. There it is, in your breast pocket.

PISHCHIK (*takes the card out of his breast-pocket*): The eight of spades, absolutely right! (*In astonishment.*) Fancy that!

CHARLOTTA (*holding the pack of cards on the palm of her hand, to* TROFIMOV): Tell me quickly, which card is on top?

TROFIMOV: Well. . . . Let us say, the queen of spades.

CHARLOTTA: Here it is! (*She claps her hand over the pack of cards, which disappears.*) What fine weather we're having today! (*A woman's voice, apparently coming from beneath the floor, answers her: 'Oh yes, Madam, the weather's perfectly marvellous!'*)

CHARLOTTA (*addressing the voice*): How charming you are, quite delightful!

VOICE: And I like you very much also Madam.

STATION-MASTER (*applauding*): Madame ventriloquist, well done!

PISHCHIK (*astonished*): Fancy that! Charlotta Ivanovna, how fascinating you are! I'm quite in love with you!

[1]A popular dance tune.

CHARLOTTA (*shrugging her shoulders*): In love? Do you know how to love? *Guter Mensch, aber schlechter Musikant.*

TROFIMOV (*slaps* PISHCHIK *on the shoulder*): A regular old horse!

CHARLOTTA: Attention please! Here's just one more trick. (*She takes a rug from a chair.*) Now I'm offering this very nice rug for sale.... (*Shakes it out.*) Would anyone like to buy it?

PISHCHIK (*astonished*): Just fancy!

CHARLOTTA: *Ein, zwei, drei!* (*She lifts up the rug and discloses* ANIA *standing behind it;* ANIA *drops a curtsey, runs to her mother, gives her a hug, then runs back into the ballroom. Everyone is delighted.*)

LOPAKHIN (*clapping*): Bravo, bravo!

CHARLOTTA: Just once more. *Ein, zwei, drei!* (*Lifts the rug; behind it stands* VARIA, *who bows.*)

PISHCHIK (*astonished*): Fancy that!

CHARLOTTA: Finished! (*She throws the rug over* PISHCHIK, *curtseys and runs off to the ballroom.*)

PISHCHIK (*hurries after her*): The little rascal! ... Have you ever seen anything like it ... have you ever.... (*Goes out.*)

LIUBOV ANDRYEEVNA: Still no Leonid. I can't understand what he's doing all this time in town. In any case, everything must be over by now, either the estate's been sold or the auction never took place. Why must he keep us in ignorance so long?

VARIA (*trying to comfort her*): Uncle bought it, dear Uncle, I'm sure he did.

TROFIMOV (*sarcastically*): Oh yes?

VARIA: Grandmamma sent him power of attorney to buy the estate in her name, and transfer the mortgage to her. She's done it for Ania's sake.... God will help us, I'm sure of it—Uncle will buy the estate.

LIUBOV ANDRYEEVNA: Grandmamma sent us fifteen thousand roubles to buy the estate in her name—she doesn't trust us,

you see—but the money wouldn't even pay the interest. (*She covers her face with her hands.*) Today my fate is being decided, my fate....

TROFIMOV (*to* VARIA, *teasingly*): Madame Lopakhin!

VARIA (*crossly*): The eternal student! Why, you've been thrown out of the University twice already!

LIUBOV ANDRYEEVNA: Why get so cross, Varia? He does tease you about Lopakhin, but what's the harm? If you feel inclined to, why don't you marry Lopakhin: he's a nice, interesting fellow. Of course, if you don't feel like it, don't. No one's trying to force you, darling.

VARIA: I do take it very seriously, Mamma dear ... and I want to be frank with you about it ... he's a nice man and I like him.

LIUBOV ANDRYEEVNA: Then marry him. What are you waiting for? I can't understand you.

VARIA: Mamma darling, I can't propose to him myself, can I? It's two years now since everyone started talking to me about him, and everyone is still doing it, but he either says nothing, or else he just talks in a sort of bantering way. I understand what's the matter. He's getting rich, he's occupied with his business, and he's no time for me. If only I had some money, just a little, even a hundred roubles, then I'd have left everything and gone away, the farther the better. I'd have gone into a convent.

TROFIMOV: A beautiful life!

VARIA (*to* TROFIMOV): Of course, a student like you has to be clever! (*Softly and tearfully.*) How plain you've become, Pyetia, how much older you look! (*To* LIUBOV ANDRYEEVNA, *her tearfulness gone.*) The only thing I can't bear, Mamma dear, is to be without work. I must be doing something all the time.

*Enter* YASHA.

**YASHA** (*with difficulty restraining his laughter*): Yepihodov's broken a billiard cue! . . . (*Goes out.*)

**VARIA:** But why is Yepihodov here? Who allowed him to play billiards? I can't understand these people. . . . (*Goes out.*)

**LIUBOV ANDRYEEVNA:** Don't tease her, Pyetia. Don't you see she's upset already?

**TROFIMOV:** She's too much of a busy-body, she will poke her nose into other people's affairs. She wouldn't leave us alone the whole summer, neither Ania, nor me. She was afraid we might fall in love with each other. Why should she mind? Besides, I didn't show any sign of it. I'm too far removed from such trivialities. We are above love!

**LIUBOV ANDRYEEVNA:** And I suppose I'm below love. (*In great agitation.*) Why isn't Leonid back? I only want to know whether the estate's sold or not. Such a calamity seems so incredible that somehow I don't even know what to think, I feel quite lost. Honestly, I feel I could shriek out loud this very moment. . . . I shall be doing something silly. Help me, Pyetia. Say something, speak!

**TROFIMOV:** Isn't it all the same whether the estate's sold today or not? It's finished and done with long ago, there's no turning back, the bridges are burnt. You must keep calm, my dear; you mustn't deceive yourself, for once in your life you must look the truth straight in the face.

**LIUBOV ANDRYEEVNA:** What truth? *You* can see where the truth is and where it isn't, but I seem to have lost my power of vision, I don't see anything. You're able to solve all your problems in a resolute way—but, tell me, my dear boy, isn't that because you're young, because you're not old enough yet to have suffered on account of your problems. You look ahead so boldly—but isn't that because life is still hidden from your young eyes, so that you're not able to foresee anything dreadful, or expect it? You've a more courageous and honest and serious nature than we have, but do consider our position carefully, do be generous—even if only a little bit—and spare me. I was born here, you know, my father and mother lived here, and my grandfather, too, and I love this house—I can't conceive life without the cherry orchard, and if it really has to be sold, then sell me with it. . . . (*Embraces* **TROFIMOV,** *kisses him on the forehead.*) You know, my son was drowned here. . . . (*Weeps.*) Have pity on me, my dear, dear friend.

**TROFIMOV:** You know that I sympathize with you with all my heart.

**LIUBOV ANDRYEEVNA:** But you must say it differently . . . differently. (*Takes out a handkerchief; a telegram falls on to the floor.*) There's such a weight on my mind today, you can't imagine. This place is too noisy, my very soul seems to shudder with every sound, and I'm trembling all over—yet I can't go to my room for fear of being alone and quiet. . . . Don't blame me, Pyetia. . . . I love you as if you were my own child. I would willingly let Ania marry you, honestly I would, but, my dear boy, you must study, you must finish your course. You don't do anything, Fate seems to drive you from one place to another—such a strange thing. . . . Isn't it? Isn't it? And you should do something about your beard, make it grow somehow. . . . (*Laughs.*) You are a funny boy!

**TROFIMOV** (*picks up the telegram*): I don't want to be a dandy.

**LIUBOV ANDRYEEVNA:** That telegram's from Paris. I get one everyday. . . . Yesterday and today. That savage is ill again, and things are going badly with him. . . . He wants me to forgive him, implores me to return, and, really, I do feel I ought to go to Paris and stay near him for a bit. You're looking very stern, Pyetia, but what's to be done, my dear boy, what am I to do? He's ill, and lonely, and unhappy, and who's there to take care of him, to prevent him from making a fool of himself, and give him his medicine at the proper time? And anyway, why should I hide it, or keep quiet about it? I love him, of course I love him. I do, I do. . . . It's a millstone round my neck, and I'm going to the bottom with it—but I love him and I can't live without him. (*She presses* TROFIMOV'S *hand.*) Don't think badly of me; Pyetia, don't speak, don't say anything. . . .

TROFIMOV (*with strong emotion*): Please— please forgive my frankness, but that man's been robbing you!

LIUBOV ANDRYEEVNA: No, no, no, you mustn't talk like that. . . . (*Puts her hands over her ears.*)

TROFIMOV: He's a cad, you're the only one who doesn't know it! He's a petty-minded cad, a worthless . . .

LIUBOV ANDRYEEVNA (*angry, but in control of herself*): You're twenty-six or twenty-seven years old, but you're still like a schoolboy in a prep school!

TROFIMOV: Never mind me!

LIUBOV ANDRYEEVNA: You ought to be a man, at your age you ought to understand people who are in love. And you ought to be able to love . . . to fall in love! (*Angrily.*) Yes, yes! And you're not 'pure', but you just make a fad of purity, you're a ridiculous crank, a freak. . . .

TROFIMOV (*horrified*): What is she saying?

LIUBOV ANDRYEEVNA: 'I'm above love!' You're not above love, you're daft, as our Feers would say. Not to have a mistress at your age! . . .

TROFIMOV (*horrified*): This is dreadful! What's she saying? (*Walks quickly towards the ballroom, his head between his hands.*) This is dreadful. . . . I can't, I'm

going. . . . (*Goes out, but returns at once.*) Everything's finished between us! (*Goes out through the door into the hall.*)

LIUBOV ANDRYEEVNA (*calls after him*): Pyetia, wait! You funny fellow, I was joking! Pyetia!

*From the hall comes the sound of someone running quickly upstairs; then falling down with a crash. There are shrieks from* ANIA *and* VARIA, *followed by laughter.*

What's happened?

ANIA *runs in.*

ANIA (*laughing*): Pyetia's fallen downstairs. (*Runs out.*)

LIUBOV ANDRYEEVNA: What a queer fellow he is!

*The* STATION-MASTER *stands in the middle of the ballroom and begins to recite 'The Sinner' by Alexyei Tolstoy. The others listen, but he has hardly had time to recite more than a few lines when the sound of a waltz reaches them from the hall, and the recitation breaks off. Everyone dances. Enter from the hall:* TROFIMOV, ANIA, VARIA.

LIUBOV ANDRYEEVNA: Now, Pyetia . . . there, my dear boy . . . I ask your forgiveness . . . let's dance. . . . (*She dances with* PYETIA.)

ANIA *and* VARIA *dance.*

*Enter* FEERS, *then* YASHA. FEERS *stands his walking stick by the side door.* YASHA *looks at the dancers from the drawing-room.*

YASHA: How goes it, Grandad?

FEERS: I'm not too well. . . . We used to have generals, barons, and admirals dancing at our balls, but now we send for the post-office clerk and the station-master, and even they don't come too willingly. I seem to have grown so weak somehow. . . . My old master, that's the mistress's grandfather, used to give everyone powdered sealing wax for medicine, whatever the illness was. I've been taking it every day for the last twenty years, or perhaps even longer. Maybe that's why I'm still alive.

YASHA: How you weary me, Grandad! (*Yawns.*) I wish you'd go away and die soon.

FEERS: Eh, you! . . . You're daft. . . . (*Mutters.*) TROFIMOV *and* LIUBOV ANDRYEEVNA *dance in the ballroom, then in the drawing-room.*

LIUBOV ANDRYEEVNA: Thank you. I'd like to sit down for a bit. (*Sits down.*) I'm tired. *Enter* ANIA.

ANIA (*agitated*): A man in the kitchen was saying just now that the cherry orchard was sold today.

LIUBOV ANDRYEEVNA: Sold? Who to?

ANIA: He didn't say. He's gone. (*She dances with* TROFIMOV; *both go to the ballroom.*)

YASHA: There was some old man there, gossiping away. A stranger.

FEERS: And Leonid Andryeevich's not back, yet, he's still not back. He's only got his light overcoat on—his 'between-seasons' coat—and he might easily catch a cold. These youngsters!

LIUBOV ANDRYEEVNA: I feel as though I'm going to die. Yasha, go and find out who bought it.

YASHA: But the old man's been gone a long time. (*Laughs.*)

LIUBOV ANDRYEEVNA (*With a touch of annoyance*): Well, what are you laughing at? What are you so happy about?

YASHA: Yepihodov's such a comic chap—a stupid fellow. Two-and-twenty misfortunes!

LIUBOV ANDRYEEVNA: Feers, if the estate is sold, where will you go?

FEERS: I'll go wherever you order me to.

LIUBOV ANDRYEEVNA: Why are you looking like that? Are you ill? You should go to bed, you know . . .

FEERS: Yes. . . . (*With a faint smile.*) If I went to bed, who'd wait on the guests, who'd keep things going? There's no one in the house but me.

YASHA (*to* LIUBOV ANDRYEEVNA): Liubov Andryeevna! I want to ask you for something, please! If you go to Paris again, do me a favour and take me with you. It's quite impossible for me to stay here. (*Looking round, in a subdued voice.*) There's no need for me to say it: you can see it for yourself—the people are uneducated, and they're immoral, too. Besides, it's so boring, and the food they give you in the kitchen is abominable. Then this Feers keeps on walking around and muttering all sorts of silly things. Take me with you, please do!

*Enter* PISHCHIK.

PISHCHIK: Allow me to ask you for a dance, beautiful lady. . . . (LIUBOV ANDRYEEVNA *gets up to dance.*) I'll have that hundred and eighty roubles from you all the same, my charmer . . . . Yes, I will. . . . (*Dances.*) Just one hundred and eighty roubles, that's all . . . .

*They go into the ballroom.*

YASHA (*sings quietly*): 'Will you understand the agitation of my soul? . . . '

*In the ballroom a woman in check trousers and a grey top hat starts jumping in the air and throwing her arms about; there are shouts of: 'Bravo, Charlotta Ivanovna!'*

DOONIASHA (*stops to powder her face*): The young mistress ordered me to dance: there are so many gentlemen and only a few ladies; but I get so dizzy from dancing, and my heart beats too fast. Feers Nikolayevich, the post-office clerk told me something just now that quite took my breath away.

*The music stops.*

FEERS: What did he tell you?

DOONIASHA: You are like a flower, he said.

YASHA (*yawns*): What ignorance! . . . (*Goes out.*)

DOONIASHA: Like a flower. . . . I'm so sensitive, I love it when people say nice things to me.

FEERS: You'll get your head turned all right.

*Enter* YEPIHODOV.

YEPIHODOV: Avdotyia Fiodorovna, you don't seem to want to look at me . . . as if

I were some sort of insect. (*Sighs.*) What a life!

**DOONIASHA:** What is it you want?

**YEPIHODOV:** Perhaps you may be right, no doubt. (*Sighs.*) But, of course, if one looks at it from a certain point of view—if I may so express myself—forgive my frankness—you've driven me into such a state.... I know what my fate is; every day some misfortune's sure to happen to me, but I've been so long accustomed to it, that I look at life with a smile. You gave me your word, and though I . . .

**DOONIASHA:** Please, please, let's have a talk later, but now leave me alone. I feel in a kind of dream just now. (*Plays with her fan.*)

**YEPIHODOV:** Some misfortune or other happens to me every day, and yet—if I may so express myself—I only smile, I even laugh.

*VARIA enters from the ballroom.*

**VARIA:** Haven't you gone yet, Semion? What an ill-mannered fellow you are, really! (*To* **DOONIASHA**.) You'd better go, Dooniasha. (*To* **YEPIHODOV**.) First you go and play billiards and break a cue, and now you're walking about the drawing-room, like a visitor.

**YEPIHODOV:** Permit me to inform you that you can't start imposing penalties on me.

**VARIA:** I'm not imposing penalties, I'm merely telling you. All you do is to walk from one place to another, instead of getting on with your work. We keep a clerk, but what for no one knows.

**YEPIHODOV** (*offended*): Whether I work, walk about, eat or play billiards, the only people who are entitled to judge my actions are those who are older than me and know what they're talking about.

**VARIA:** You dare say that to me? (*Flying into a temper.*) You dare to say that? You're suggesting I don't know what I'm talking about? Get out of here! This very minute!

**YEPIHODOV** (*cowed*): I wish you'd express yourself more delicately.

**VARIA** (*beside herself*): Get out this minute! Out!

*He goes go the door, she follows him.*

Two-and-twenty misfortunes! I don't want any more of you here! I don't want ever to set eyes on you again!

**YEPIHODOV** *goes out; his voice is heard from outside the door: 'I'll complain about you.'*

Ah, you're coming back, are you? (*She seizes the stick which* **FEERS** *left by the door.*) Come along, come along . . . I'll show you! Ah, you're coming back . . . are you? There, I'll give it to you. . . . (*Swings the stick, and at that moment* **LOPAKHIN** *enters.*)

**LOPAKHIN** (*whom the stick did not, in fact, touch*): Thank you very much!

**VARIA** (*angry and sarcastic*): I beg your pardon!

**LOPAKHIN:** Don't mention it. Thanks for a pleasant surprise.

**VARIA:** It's not worth thanking me for. (*Goes to the side, then looks round and says gently.*) I haven't hurt you, have I?

**LOPAKHIN:** No, not at all. . . . There's a huge bump coming up, though.

**VOICES IN THE BALLROOM:** Lopakhin's arrived! Yermolai Aleksyeevich!

**PISHCHIK:** Look here, you can see him, you can hear him! . . . (*Embraces* **LOPAKHIN**.) You smell of cognac, my dear fellow, my bonny boy! We're making merry here, too.

*Enter* **LIUBOV ANDRYEEVNA**.

**LIUBOV ANDRYEEVNA:** It's you, Yermolai Aleksyeevich? Why have you been so long? Where is Leonid?

**LOPAKHIN:** Leonid Andryeevich returned with me, he's coming along.

**LIUBOV ANDRYEEVNA** (*agitated*): Well, what happened? Was there an auction? Speak, tell me!

**LOPAKHIN** (*embarrassed, fearing to betray his joy*): The auction was over by four

o'clock. . . . We missed our train and had to wait until half-past nine. (*With a deep sigh.*) Ugh! My head's going round. . . .
*Enter* GAYEV; *he carries some parcels in his right hand and wipes away his tears with his left.*

LIUBOV ANDRYEEVNA: Lionia, what happened? Well, Lionia? (*Impatiently, with tears.*) Tell me quickly, for God's sake! . . .

GAYEV (*does not reply, but waves his hand at her. To* FEERS, *weeping*): Here, take this . . . it's some anchovies and Kerch herrings. . . . I've had nothing to eat all day. . . . What I've been through!
*Through the open door leading to the billiard room comes the sound of billiard balls in play and* YASHA'S *voice saying: 'Seven and eighteen'.* GAYEV'S *expression changes and he stops crying.*
I'm dreadfully tired. Come, Feers, I want to change. (*Goes out through the ballroom,* FEERS *following.*)

PISHCHIK: What happened at the auction? Come, do tell us!

LIUBOV ANDRYEEVNA: Has the cherry orchard been sold?

LOPAKHIN: It has.

LIUBOV ANDRYEEVNA: Who bought it?

LOPAKHIN: I did.
*A pause.*

LIUBOV ANDRYEEVNA *is overcome; only the fact that she is standing beside a table and a chair prevents her from falling.* VARIA *takes a bundle of keys off her belt, throws them on the floor in the middle of the drawing-room and walks out.*
Yes, I bought it. Wait a moment, ladies and gentlemen, do, please. I don't feel quite clear in my head, I hardly know how to talk. . . . (*Laughs.*) When we got to the auction, Deriganov was there already. Of course, Leonid Andryeevich only had fifteen thousand roubles, and Deriganov at once bid thirty over and above the mortgage. I could see how things were going, so I muscled in and

offered forty. He bid forty-five, I bid fifty-five; he kept on adding five thousand each time and I added ten thousand each time. Well, it finished at last—I bid ninety thousand over and above the mortgage, and I got the property. Yes, the cherry orchard's mine now! Mine! (*Laughs.*) My God! the cherry orchard's mine! Come on, tell me I'm drunk, tell me I'm out of my mind, say I've imagined all this. . . . (*Stamps his foot.*) Don't laugh at me! If only my father and grandfather could rise from their graves and see everything that's happened. . . . how their Yermolai, their much-beaten, half-literate Yermolai, the lad that used to run about with bare feet in the winter . . . how he's bought this estate, the most beautiful place on God's earth! Yes, I've bought the very estate where my father and grandfather were serfs, where they weren't even admitted to the kitchen! I must be asleep, I must be dreaming, I only think it's true . . . it's all just my imagination, my imagination's been wandering. . . . (*Picks up the keys, smiling tenderly.*) She threw these down because she wanted to show she's not mistress here any more. (*Jingles the keys.*) Well, never mind. (*The band is heard tuning up.*) Hi! you musicians, come on now, play something, I want some music! Now then, all of you, just you wait and see Yermolai Lopakhin take an axe to the cherry orchard, just you see the trees come crashing down! We're going to build a whole lot of new villas, and our children and great-grandchildren are going to see a new living world growing up here. . . . Come on there, let's have some music!
*The band plays.* LIUBOV ANDRYEEVNA *has sunk into a chair and is crying bitterly.* (*Reproachfully.*) Why didn't you listen to me before, why didn't you? My poor, dear lady, you can't undo it now. (*With great emotion.*) Oh, if only we could be done

with all this, if only we could alter this distorted unhappy life somehow!

**PISHCHIK** (*taking his arm, in a subdued voice*): She's crying. Come into the ballroom, leave her alone.... Come along.... (*Takes his arm and leads him away to the ballroom.*)

**LOPAKHIN:** Never mind! Come on, band, play up, play up! Everything must be just as *I* wish it now. (*Ironically.*) Here comes the new landowner, here comes the owner of the cherry orchard! (*He pushes a small table accidentally and nearly knocks over some candle-sticks.*) Never mind, I can pay for everything! (*Goes out with* **PISHCHIK.**)

*No one remains in the ballroom or drawing-room save* **LIUBOV ANDRYEEVNA,** *who sits hunched up in a chair, crying bitterly. The band continues playing quietly.* **ANIA** *and* **TROFIMOV** *enter quickly;* **ANIA** *goes up to her mother and kneels beside her,* **TROFIMOV** *remains standing by the entrance to the ballroom.*

**ANIA:** Mamma!... Mamma, you're crying? Dear, kind, sweet Mamma, my darling precious, how I love you! God bless you, Mamma! The cherry orchard's sold, it's quite true, there isn't any cherry orchard any more, it's true... but don't cry, Mamma, you still have your life ahead of you, you still have your dear, innocent heart. You must come away with me, darling, we must get away from here! We'll plant a new orchard, even more splendid than this one—and when you see it, you'll understand everything, your heart will be filled with happiness, like the sun in the evening; and then you'll smile again, Mamma! Come with me, darling, do come!...

CURTAIN

# ACT FOUR

*The same setting as for Act I. There are no pictures on the walls or curtains at the windows;* *only a few remaining pieces of furniture are piled up in a corner, as if for sale. There is an oppressive sense of emptiness. At the back of the stage, beside the door, suitcases and other pieces of luggage have been piled together as if ready for a journey. The voices of* **VARIA** *and* **ANIA** *can be heard through the door on the left, which is open.* **LOPAKHIN** *stands waiting;* **YASHA** *is holding a tray laden with glasses of champagne. In the hall* **YEPIHODOV** *is tying up a large box. From somewhere behind the scenes comes the low hum of voices: the peasants have called to say good-bye.* **GAYEV'S** *voice is heard; saying: 'Thank you, friends, thank you.'*

**YASHA:** The villagers have come to say good-bye. In my view, Yermolai Aleksyeevich, they're kind-hearted folk, but they haven't much understanding.

*The hum subsides.* **LIUBOV ANDRYEEVNA** *and* **GAYEV** *enter from the hall;* **LIUBOV ANDRYEEVNA** *is not crying but her face is pale and tremulous. She seems unable to speak.*

**GAYEV:** You gave them your purse, Liuba. You shouldn't have done that. You really shouldn't.

**LIUBOV ANDRYEEVNA:** I couldn't help myself, I couldn't help myself!

*Both go out.*

**LOPAKHIN** (*calls after them through the door*): Have some champagne, please do, please! Just one little glass before you go. I didn't think of bringing any from town, and I could only get one bottle at the station. Do have some, please. (*A pause.*) Won't you have any, ladies and gentlemen? (*Walks away from the door.*) If I'd known, I wouldn't have brought any.... Then I won't have any either.

*YASHA carefully puts the tray on a chair.*

You have a drink, Yasha, if nobody else will.

**YASHA:** Here's to the travellers! And here's to you staying behind. (*Drinks.*) This champagne isn't the real thing, I can tell you.

**LOPAKHIN:** Eight roubles a bottle. (*A pause.*) It's devilishly cold here.

**YASHA:** The stoves weren't lit today. It doesn't matter as we're going. (*Laughs.*)

**LOPAKHIN:** Why are you laughing?

**YASHA:** Because I'm feeling glad.

**LOPAKHIN:** October's here, but it's still sunny and calm, as if it were summer. Good building weather. (*Looks at his watch, then at the door.*) Ladies and gentlemen, don't forget there are only forty-six minutes before the train's due to leave. That means we must start in twenty minutes. Hurry up.

*TROFIMOV, wearing an overcoat, comes in from outdoors.*

**TROFIMOV:** I think it's time to start. The horses are at the door. God knows where my goloshes are, they've disappeared. (*Calls through the door.*) Ania, my goloshes aren't here; I can't find them.

**LOPAKHIN:** And I must be off to Kharkov. I'll travel with you on the same train. I shall stay the whole winter in Kharkov: I've hung around here too long, and it's torture having no work to do. I can't be without work: I just don't know what to do with my hands; they feel limp and strange, as if they didn't belong to me.

**TROFIMOV:** We'll soon be gone, then you can start your useful labours again.

**LOPAKHIN:** Have a little drink, do.

**TROFIMOV:** No, thanks.

**LOPAKHIN:** You're going to Moscow, then?

**TROFIMOV:** Yes, I'll see them off to town, and then, tomorrow I'm off to Moscow.

**LOPAKHIN:** Well, well. . . . I expect the professors are holding up their lectures, waiting for your arrival!

**TROFIMOV:** That's none of your business.

**LOPAKHIN:** How many years have you been studying at the university?

**TROFIMOV:** I wish you'd think up something new, that's old and stale. (*Looks for his goloshes.*) Incidentally, as we're not likely to meet again, I'd like to give you a bit of advice, by way of a farewell: stop throwing your arms about! Try to get rid of that habit of making wide, sweeping gestures. Yes, and all this talk, too, about building villas, these calculations about summer residents that are going to turn into smallholders, these forecasts—they're all sweeping gestures, too. . . . When all's said and done, I like you, despite everything. You've a fine, sensitive soul. . . .

**LOPAKHIN** (*embraces him*): Good-bye, my friend. Thank you for everything. I can let you have some money for your journey, if you need it.

**TROFIMOV:** Whatever for? I don't want it.

**LOPAKHIN:** But you haven't any!

**TROFIMOV:** Yes, I have, thank you. I've just had some for a translation. Here it is, in my pocket. (*Anxiously.*) But I can't see my goloshes anywhere.

**VARIA** (*from the other room*): Take your beastly things! (*She throws a pair of rubber goloshes into the room.*)

**TROFIMOV:** But why are you angry, Varia? Hm . . . but these aren't my goloshes!

**LOPAKHIN:** I had a thousand acres of poppy sown last spring, and now I've just made forty thousand net profit on it. And when they were in bloom, what a picture it was! What I want to say is that I've made the forty thousand, and now I'm offering to lend you money because I'm in a position to do it. Why are you so stuck up? I'm a peasant . . . I've no manners.

**TROFIMOV:** Your father was a peasant, mine had a chemist's shop. But there's nothing in that.

**LOPAKHIN** *takes out his wallet.*

Leave it alone, leave it alone. . . . Even if you offered me two hundred thousand, I wouldn't take it. I'm a free man. And all that you value so highly and hold so dear, you rich men—and beggars, too, for that matter—none of it has the slightest power over me—it's all just so much fluff blowing about in the air. I'm strong, I'm proud, I can do without you, I can pass you by. Humanity is advancing towards the highest truth, the greatest happiness that it is possible to achieve on earth, and I am in the van!

LOPAKHIN: Will you get there?

TROFIMOV: Yes. (*A pause.*) I'll get there myself, or show others the way to get there. *The sound of an axe striking a tree is heard in the distance.*

LOPAKHIN: Well, good-bye, my friend, it's time to go. We show off in front of one another, and in the meantime life is slipping by. When I work for long hours on end, without taking any time off, I feel happier in my mind and I even imagine I know why I exist. But how many people there are in Russia, my friend, who exist to no purpose whatever! Well, never mind, perhaps it's no matter. They say, Leonid Andryeevich has taken a post at the bank, at six thousand a year. I don't expect he'll stick to it: he's too lazy. . . .

ANIA (*in the doorway*): Mamma asks you not to cut the orchard down until she's left.

TROFIMOV: I should say not! Haven't you got any tact? (*Goes out through the hall.*)

LOPAKHIN: All right, all right. . . . These people! (*Follows* TROFIMOV.)

ANIA: Has Feers been taken to hospital?

YASHA: I told them to take him this morning. He's gone, I think.

ANIA (*to* YEPIHODOV, *who passes through the ballroom*): Semion Pantelyeevich, will you please find out whether Feers has been taken to hospital?

YASHA (*offended*): I told Yegor this morning. Need you ask ten times?

YEPIHODOV: This superannuated Feers—candidly speaking, I mean—he's beyond repair, he ought to go and join his ancestors. As for me, I can only envy him. (*He places a suitcase on top of a cardboard hat-box and squashes it.*) There you are, you see! . . . I might have known it! (*Goes out.*)

YASHA (*sardonically*): Two-and-twenty misfortunes!

VARIA (*from behind the door*): Has Feers been taken to the hospital?

ANIA: Yes.

VARIA: Why haven't they taken the letter to the doctor, then?

ANIA: I'll send someone after them with it. . . . (*Goes out.*)

VARIA (*from adjoining room*): Where's Yasha? Tell him, his mother is here and wants to say good-bye to him.

YASHA (*waves his hand*): She makes me lose patience with her.
*While the foregoing action has been taking place,* DOONIASHA *has been fussing with the luggage; now that* YASHA *is alone, she comes up to him.*

DOONIASHA: If only you'd look at me once, Yasha! You're going . . . you're leaving me behind! . . . (*She cries and throws her arms round his neck.*)

YASHA: What's the point of crying? (*Drinks champagne.*) In a week's time I'll be in Paris again. Tomorrow we'll get into an express train—and off we'll go—we shall just disappear! I can hardly believe it. Vive la France! This place doesn't suit me, I can't live here—there's nothing going on. I've seen enough of all this ignorance. I've had enough of it. (*Drinks.*) What are you crying for? Behave like a respectable girl, then there won't be any need to cry.

DOONIASHA (*looking into a hand-mirror and powdering her nose*): Write to me from Paris, won't you? You know that I've loved you, Yasha. I've loved you so much! I've got a soft heart, Yasha!

YASHA: Someone's coming. (*Pretends to be busy with a suitcase, singing quietly to himself*)
*Enter* LIUBOV ANDRYEEVNA, GAYEV, ANIA *and* CHARLOTTA IVANOVNA.

GAYEV: We ought to be going. There isn't much time left. (*Looks at* YASHA.) Who's smelling of herring here?

LIUBOV ANDRYEEVNA: In ten minutes we ought to be getting into the carriage.... (*Glances round the room.*) Good-bye, dear house, old grandfather house. Winter will pass, spring will come again, and then you won't be here any more, you'll be pulled down. How much these walls have seen! (*Kisses her daughter ardently.*) My little treasure, you look simply radiant, your eyes are shining like diamonds. Are you glad? Very glad?

ANIA: Yes, very. Our new life is just beginning, Mamma!

GAYEV (*brightly*): So it is indeed, everything's all right now. Before the cherry orchard was sold everybody was worried and upset, but as soon as it was all settled finally and once for all, everybody calmed down, and felt quite cheerful, in fact.... I'm an employee of a bank now, a financier.... I pot the red ... and you, Liuba, you're looking better, too, when all's said and done. There's no doubt about it.

LIUBOV ANDRYEEVNA: Yes, my nerves are better, it's true.
*Someone helps her on with her hat and coat.*
I'm sleeping better, too. Take my things out, Yasha, it's time. (*To* ANIA.) My little girl, we'll soon be seeing each other again. I'm going to Paris—I shall live there on the money which your Grandmamma in Yaroslavl sent us to buy the estate—God bless Grandmamma!—and that money won't last long either.

ANIA: You'll come back soon, Mamma ... quite soon, won't you? I shall study and pass my exams at the high school and then I'll work and help you. We'll read all sorts of books together, Mamma ... won't we? (*She kisses her mother's hands.*) We'll read during the long autumn evenings, we'll read lots of books, and a new, wonderful world will open up before us.... (*Dreamily.*) Mamma, come back....

LIUBOV ANDRYEEVNA: I'll come back, my precious. (*Embraces her.*)
*Enter* LOPAKHIN. CHARLOTTA *quickly sings to herself.*

GAYEV: Happy Charlotta! She's singing.

CHARLOTTA (*picks up a bundle that looks like a baby in swaddling clothes.*): Bye-bye, little baby. (*A sound like a baby crying is heard.*) Be quiet, my sweet, be a good little boy. (*The 'crying' continues.*) My heart goes out to you, baby! (*Throws the bundle down.*) Are you going to find me another job, please? I can't do without one.

LOPAKHIN: We'll find you one, Charlotta Ivanovna, don't worry.

GAYEV: Everybody's leaving us, Varia's going away ... we've suddenly become unwanted.

CHARLOTTA: I haven't got anywhere to live in town. I shall have to go. (*Hums.*) Oh, well, never mind.
*Enter* PISHCHIK.

LOPAKHIN: What a phenomenon!

PISHCHIK (*out of breath*): Och, let me get my breath.... I'm worn out.... My good friends.... Give me some water....

GAYEV: I suppose you've come to borrow money? I'd better go.... Excuse me.... (*Goes out.*)

PISHCHIK: I've not been to see you for a long time ... my beautiful lady.... (*To* LOPAKHIN.) So you're here ... I'm glad to see you ... you're a man of great intelligence ... here ... take this.... (*Hands money to* LOPAKHIN.) Four hundred roubles.... I still owe you eight hundred and forty....

LOPAKHIN (*shrugs his shoulders, bewildered*): It's like a dream .... Where did you get it from?

PISHCHIK: Wait a moment.... I'm so hot.... A most extraordinary thing happened. Some English people came to see me and discovered a sort of white clay on my land. . . . (*To* LIUBOV ANDRYEEVNA.) Here's four hundred for you also my dear . . . enchantress. . . . (*Hands her the money.*) You'll get the rest later on. (*Takes a drink of water.*) Just now a young fellow in the train was telling me that some great philosopher or other . . . advises people to jump off roofs. You just jump off, he says, and that settles the whole problem. (*As though astonished at what he has just said.*) Fancy that! More water, please.

LOPAKHIN: Who were these Englishmen?

PISHCHIK: I let the land with the clay to them for twenty-four years. . . . And now you must excuse me, I'm in a hurry. I've got to get along as quickly as I can. I'm going to Znoikov's, then to Kardamonov's. . . . I owe money to all of them (*Drinks.*) Good health to you all. I'll call again on Thursday. . . .

LIUBOV ANDRYEEVNA: We're just on the point of moving to town, and tomorrow I'm going abroad.

PISHCHIK: What's that? (*In agitation.*) What are you going to town for? I see now . . . this furniture and the suitcases. . . . Well, never mind. (*Tearfully.*) Never mind. . . . These Englishmen, you know, they're men of the greatest intelligence. . . . Never mind. . . . I wish you every happiness, God be with you. Never mind, everything comes to an end eventually. (*Kisses* LIUBOV ANDRYEEVNA'S *hand.*) And when you hear that my end has come, just think of—a horse, and say: 'There used to be fellow like that once . . . Simeonov-Pishchik his name was—God be with him!' Wonderful weather we're having. Yes. . . . (*Goes out, overcome with embarrassment, but returns at once and stands in the doorway.*) Dashenka sent greetings to you. (*Goes out.*)

LIUBOV ANDRYEEVNA: Well, we can go now. I'm leaving with two worries on my mind. One is Feers—he's sick, you know. (*Glances at her watch.*) We have another five minutes or so. . . .

ANIA: Mamma, Feers has been taken to hospital already. Yasha sent him this morning.

LIUBOV ANDRYEEVNA: The other is Varia. She's been accustomed to getting up early and working, and now, without work, she's like a fish out of water. She's got so thin and pale, and she cries a lot, poor thing. (*A pause.*) You know very well, Yermolai Aleksyeevich, that I'd been hoping to get her married to you . . . and everything seemed to show that you meant to marry her, too. (*Whispers to* ANIA, *who nods to* CHARLOTTA, *and they both go out.*) She loves you, and you must be fond of her, too . . . and I just don't know, I just don't know why you seem to keep away from each other. I don't understand it.

LOPAKHIN: Neither do I myself, I must confess. It's all so strange somehow. . . . If there's still time, I'm ready even now. . . . Let's settle it at once—and get it over! Without you here, I don't feel I shall ever propose to her.

LIUBOV ANDRYEEVNA: That's an excellent idea! You'll hardly need more than a minute, that's all. I'll call her at once.

LOPAKHIN: There's champagne here, too, quite suitable for the occasion. (*Takes a look at the glasses.*) But they're empty, someone's drunk it up. (YASHA *coughs.*) I should have said lapped it up.

LIUBOV ANDRYEEVNA (*With animation*): I'm so glad. We'll go outside. Yasha, allez! I'll call her. . . . (*Through the door.*) Varia, come here a moment, leave what you're doing for a minute! Varia! (*Goes out with* YASHA.)

LOPAKHIN (*glancing at his watch*): Yes. . . . (*A pause.*)

*Suppressed laughter and whispering is heard from behind the door, and finally* VARIA *comes in and starts examining the luggage. After some time she says:*

VARIA: It's strange, I just can't find . . .

LOPAKHIN: What are you looking for?

VARIA: I packed the things myself, yet I can't remember. . . .

*A pause.*

LOPAKHIN: Where are you going to now, Varvara Mihailovna?

VARIA: I? To the Rogulins. I've agreed to look after the house for them . . . to be their housekeeper, or something.

LOPAKHIN: That's at Yashnevo, isn't it? About seventy miles from here. (*A pause.*) So this is the end of life in this house. . . .

VARIA (*examining the luggage*): But where could it be? Or perhaps I've packed it in the trunk? . . . Yes, life in this house has come to an end . . . there won't be any more. . . .

LOPAKHIN: And I'm going to Kharkov presently. . . . On the next train. I've got a lot to do there. And I'm leaving Yepihodov here. . . . I've engaged him.

VARIA: Well! . . .

LOPAKHIN: Do you remember, last year about this time it was snowing already, but now it's quite still and sunny. It's rather cold, though. . . . About three degrees of frost.

VARIA: I haven't looked. (*A pause.*) Besides, our thermometer's broken. . . . (*A pause.*) *A voice is heard from outside the door: 'Yermolai Aleksyeevich!'*

LOPAKHIN (*as if he had long been expecting it*): Coming this moment! (*Goes out quickly.*) VARIA, *sitting on the floor, with her head on the bundle of clothes, sobs softly. The door opens,* LIUBOV ANDRYEEVNA *enters quietly.*

LIUBOV ANDRYEEVNA: Well? (*A pause.*) We must go.

VARIA (*stops crying and wipes her eyes*): Yes, it's time, Mamma dear. I'll just be able to get to the Rogulins today, if only we don't miss the train.

LIUBOV ANDRYEEVNA (*calls through the door*): Ania, put your coat on.

*Enter* ANIA, *followed by* GAYEV *and* CHARLOTTA IVANOVNA. GAYEV *wears a heavy overcoat with a hood. Servants and coachmen come into the room.* YEPIHODOV *fusses with the luggage.*

Now we can start on our journey!

ANIA (*joyfully*): Yes, our journey!

GAYEV: My friends, my dear, kind friends! Now as I leave this house for ever, how can I remain silent, how can I refrain from expressing to you, as a last farewell, the feelings which now overwhelm me. . . .

ANIA (*imploringly*): Uncle!

VARIA: Uncle, dear, please don't!

GAYEV (*downcast*): I pot the red and follow through. . . . I'll keep quiet.

*Enter* TROFIMOV, *then* LOPAKHIN.

TROFIMOV: Well, ladies and gentlemen, it's time to go.

LOPAKHIN: Yepihodov, my coat!

LIUBOV ANDRYEEVNA: I'll just sit down for one little minute more. I feel as if I'd never seen the walls and ceilings of this house before, and now I look at them with such longing and affection. . . .

GAYEV: I remember when I was six years old—it was Holy Trinity day—I was sitting on this window-still, looking at Father—he was just going to church. . . .

LIUBOV ANDRYEEVNA: Have they taken out all the luggage?

LOPAKHIN: It looks as if they have. (*To* YEPIHODOV, *as he puts on his coat.*) See that everything's all right, Yepihodov.

YEPIHODOV (*in a husky voice*): Don't worry, Yermolai Aleksyeevich!

LOPAKHIN: What are you talking like that for?

YEPIHODOV: I've just had a drink of water, I must have swallowed something.

YASHA (*with contempt*): What ignorance!

LIUBOV ANDRYEEVNA: When we leave here there won't be a soul in the place. . . .

**LOPAKHIN:** Until the spring.

**VARIA** (*pulls an umbrella from a bundle of clothes;* **LOPAKHIN** *pretends to be frightened that she is going to strike him*): Now, why ... why are you doing that? ... I never thought of ...

**TROFIMOV:** Ladies and gentlemen, come, let's get into the carriage. It's high time. The train will be in soon.

**VARIA:** Pyetia, here they are, your goloshes, beside the suitcase. (*Tearfully.*) And how dirty and worn-out they are! ...

**TROFIMOV** (*puts them on*): Come along, ladies and gentlemen!

**GAYEV** (*greatly embarrassed, afraid of breaking into tears*): The train, the station. ... In off into the middle pocket. ...

**LIUBOV ANDRYEEVNA:** Let us go!

**LOPAKHIN:** Is everyone here? No one left behind? (*Locks the door on the left.*) There are some things put away there, it had better be locked up. Come along!

**ANIA:** Good-bye, old house! Good-bye, old life!

**TROFIMOV:** Greetings to the new life! ... (*Goes out with* **ANIA**.)

**VARIA** *glances round the room and goes out slowly.* **YASHA** *and* **CHARLOTTA**, *with her little dog, follow.*

**LOPAKHIN:** And so, until the spring. Come along, ladies and gentlemen. ... Au revoir! (*Goes out.*)

**LIUBOV ANDRYEEVNA** *and* **GAYEV** *are left alone. They seem to have been waiting for this moment, and now they embrace each other and sob quietly, with restraint, so as not to be heard.*

**GAYEV** (*with despair in his voice*): Sister, my sister. ...

**LIUBOV ANDRYEEVNA:** Oh my darling, my precious, my beautiful orchard! My life, my youth, my happiness ... good-bye! ... Good-bye!

**ANIA'S VOICE** (*gaily*): Mamma! ...

**TROFIMOV'S VOICE** (*gaily and excitedly*): Ah-oo! ...

**LIUBOV ANDRYEEVNA:** For the last time—to look at these walls, these windows. ... Mother used to love walking up and down this room. ...

**GAYEV:** Sister, my sister! ...

**ANIA'S VOICE:** Mamma!

**TROFIMOV'S VOICE:** Ah-oo!

**LIUBOV ANDRYEEVNA:** We're coming. ... (*Both go out.*)

*The stage is empty. The sound of doors being locked is heard, then of carriages driving off. It grows quiet. The stillness is broken by the dull thuds of an axe on a tree. They sound forlorn and sad.*

*There is a sound of footsteps and from the door on the right* **FEERS** *appears. He is dressed, as usual, in a coat and white waistcoat, and is wearing slippers. He looks ill.*

**FEERS** (*walks up to the middle door and tries the handle*): Locked. They've gone. ... (*Sits down on a sofa.*) They forgot about me. Never mind. ... I'll sit here for a bit. I don't suppose Leonid Andryeevich put on his fur coat, I expect he's gone in his light one. ... (*Sighs, preoccupied.*) I didn't see to it. ... These youngsters! ... (*Mutters something unintelligible.*) My life's gone as if I'd never lived. ... (*Lies down.*) I'll lie down a bit. You haven't got any strength left, nothing's left, nothing. ... Oh, you ... you're daft! ... (*Lies motionless.*)

*A distant sound is heard, coming as if out of the sky, like the sound of a string snapping, slowly and sadly dying away. Silence ensues, broken only by the sound of an axe striking a tree in the orchard far away.*

CURTAIN

## SUMMARY

Language in the theatre is often deceptive because it is multifaceted and written to be spoken, not read. The playwright puts words on a page and creates the "verbal text" which is intended to be acted before an audience.

This verbal text—the dialogue or spoken text—is taken by the playwright's collaborators—directors, actors, designers—and transferred into a living reality in time and space for the length of the performance.

Language in the theatre is complex. It is not merely the spoken word written by the playwright as dialogue, though when we read a play we tend to equate theatre language with words and words with the playwright's text and meaning. Playwrights do not communicate images, energy, and meaning through words alone. The language of a play involves communication among characters and with audiences, including highly complex systems of words, signs, symbols, sounds, and silences. In some instances, characters use language not to reveal information so much as to conceal their feelings and intentions. In addition, the theatre's technology, depending on the historical period, enters into the communication system between the theatre's artists and audiences.

Playwrights and critics have spoken about the uniqueness of language written for the theatre and how it differs from the language of poetry and fiction. The key to the success of a playwright's words or dialogue is *performability*. The words of the drama must have the potential for action, gesture, feeling, sound, and aliveness. The actor fills the character's words, actions, gestures, and intentions with a living presence.

In the next chapter we consider the playwright's *scenography,* a term first applied to theatrical designers with artistic control over all design elements, including scenery, lighting, costumes, and sound. Playwrights have their own kind of scenography which applies to the play's geography (both literal and psychological), its interior or exterior environment (or both), and to the symbolic and philosophical meaning of the dramatic landscape as it relates to universal truths about humankind.

## NOTES

1. Martin Esslin, *The Field of Drama: How the Signs of Drama Create Meaning on Stage & Screen* (New York: Methuen, 1987): 82.
2. George Steiner, *The Death of Tragedy* (New York: Oxford University Press, 1963): 275.

3. Maurice Valency, *The Breaking String: The Plays of Anton Chekhov* (New York: Oxford University Press, 1966): 249.

# On The Verge or
# The Geography of Yearning

❦

## Eric Overmyer

*Eric Overmyer (1951— ), born in Boulder, Colorado, emerged on the American scene in the 1980s as playwright in residence at Center Stage in Baltimore, Maryland. His award-winning plays include* The Heliotrope Bouquet by Scott Joplin and Louis Chauvin, In Perpetuity Throughout the Universe, On The Verge or The Geography of Yearning, Native Speech, *and* In a Pig's Valise. *For the La Jolla Playhouse in California he collaborated on* Don Quixote *and for the Manhattan Theatre Club in New York City,* Mid Vida Loca Tropicana. *He is a recipient of playwriting grants from the McKnight Foundation, the National Endowment for the Arts, the Rockefeller Foundation, and the New York Foundation for the Arts. He has taught playwriting at the Yale Drama School where* On The Verge or The Geography of Yearning *was produced by the Yale Repertory Theatre in the 1991–92 season.*

## INTRODUCTION

*On The Verge or The Geography of Yearning* was first produced at Center Stage, Baltimore, on January 5, 1985. The twenty-two scenes take us through a wilderness of time travel covering almost seven decades. Overmyer's scenography is identified variously as jungles and mountains of "Terra Incognita" to that remote outpost of 1955 America—"Nicky Paradise's Bar and Grill." Unencumbered by the scenic demands of stage naturalism, Overmyer's travellers journey in an almost empty space (the bare stage itself becomes a metaphor for "terra incognito"), through a continuum of space, time, history, geography, feminism, fashion, and language. One of the characters says as an inadvertent key to the audience's relationship to Overmyer's scenographic method, "My imagination seems to sculpt the landscape."

As in Brechtian staging, each scene is introduced by a scene title at the start, and by an actor speaking her newly contrived journal entry directly to the audience at the close. These devices frame the scene and prepare for the one to follow. The core of each scene engages some aspect of the play's true concern, called by the playwright "the quality of yearning, courage, and imagination."[4]

Primarily through language, Overmyer brings nineteenth-century values and contradictions face to face with mid-twentieth-century culture. The play is a celebration of words exploring a vast and colorful word-palette for a variety of meanings as well as contextural ironies. Overmyer's delightful word games include free association (a novel called *Herzog*), versification ("This is my bridge, baby, and I'm the Troll/To slip on over you gotta pay the toll"), anachronisms (Cool Whip in 1888), malapropisms ("I am delicious! I mean delirious."), and colloquialisms ("daft duo"). Moreover, he juxtaposes formal, polite speech of educated Victorian women with our modern social, political, commercial, and technological jargon and vulgarisms. On one level, the play is about the debasement of language through neologisms and slogans. As one of the women says, "I have seen the future. It is slang."

Act One is set in the distant Victorian colonial past, on the verge of the modern world. Our three explorers experience the geography of African jungles and Tibetan mountains as they move forward into a future of 1955 America filled with the detritus of "I Like Ike" campaign buttons, Cool Whip, whirlpools, go-go boots, and hoola hoops. Fanny, the mid-westerner, and Alex, the apostle of the future, are satisfied with their discovery of the "future" in 1955 at the Paradise Bar and Grill. Alex says, "We have found the future and it is now." Mary, the studious anthropologist, is not satisfied and yearns for new mysteries and explorations. "I am on the verge," she repeats, as she exits a final time into the future with intuitions of such new discoveries as revolving credit, mood elevators, and meltdowns.

The human yearning for mystery, discovery, and new experience is depicted in Overmyer's play with minimal scenic devices and with a profusion of language. *On The Verge or The Geography of Yearning* is about language as the defining element of cultural experience. The polite multisyllabic language of the Victorian era where the women explore uncharted continents is exchanged for the quick rhythms and monosyllabic words of modern America, circa 1955. The hip language, fast foods, rapid transportation, and instant gratifications of the second act stand in contrast to the more personalized experiences of the former age. Mary, the anthropologist and Overmyer's heroine, has the courage to move beyond the Eisenhower era into the remaining uncharted continents of "quarks and quasars"—where the unknown reaches of space are as vast for the modern explorer as the African continent was for the likes of Stanley and Livingstone.

# On The Verge or
# The Geography of Yearning

The play begins in 1888.
In Terra Incognita.

*Perhaps the imagination is on the verge
of recovering its rights.*

André Breton
(paraphrased by Eric Overmyer)

FANNY

MARY

ALEXANDRA

GROVER, ALPHONSE, THE GORGE TROLL, THE
    YETI, GUS, MADAME NHU, MR. COFFEE,
    and NICKY PARADISE

All three ladies are *adventurers.*

ALPHONSE, GROVER, et al., are played by a
single actor.

The ladies are American, and speak a good
19th-century American speech—not British,
nor mid-Atlantic.

The ladies are in full Victorian trekking
dress, plus practical accessories—pith helmets, etc.

The titles and journal entries separate each
scene. The titles of each scene should be conveyed visually, or aurally, by slide, sign, or
recording. The titles are essential, and *must*
be used.

The Journal Entries are done to the audience
as direct address. They are not being written
in the moment, but have been composed previously, and are now being shared.

# ACT ONE

**(1) ON THE VERGE**
(*The ladies are in a hot, white light.*)
**MARY:** Day One. Landfall.
**FANNY:** Beach.
**MARY:** Island or continent?
**ALEX:** Isthmus or archipelago?
**FANNY:** Beach. Narrow ribbon. Cliff face.
    Sheer. Beyond—?
**ALEX:** Up and over—?
**FANNY:** Unbearable anticipation.
**MARY:** Mysterious interior.
    (*They sigh.*)
**MARY:** We have reached our embarcadero.
**ALEX:** Into the unknown.
**MARY:** 1888. The last undiscovered, unex-
    plored—bit.
**ALEX:** Of globe.
**FANNY:** The sudden force of circumstance.
**ALEX:** An inheritance.
**MARY:** Money and time. Time and money.
**FANNY:** Grover said—
**MARY:** A mandate from the Boston Geo—
**FANNY:** "Go!"
**ALEX:** We find ourselves—
**FANNY:** Up against it—in the Antipodes—

MARY: Latitude 15 degrees south—

FANNY: Of the Equator.

MARY: Longitude 125 degrees west—

FANNY: Of Greenwich.

ALEX: Somewhere east of Australia, and west of Peru.

MARY: Tropics.

FANNY: Should be good anchovy fishing.

MARY: Poised.

FANNY: On the brink.

ALEX: On the beach.

MARY: On the verge.

ALEX: Set to trek.

MARY: Trekking in *Terra Incognita!*
(*They clasp hands.*)

MARY, ALEX, AND FANNY: Terra Incognita!
(MARY *comes down to do her journal entry.*)

    MARY: Before I began my travels in the uncharted reaches of the world, an avuncular colleague took me aside. "I have heard your peregrinations are impelled, in part, by scientific curiosity," he said. "Allow me to offer you some sage counsel. Always take measurements, young lady. And always take them from the adult male." (*Beat*) Sound advice.

### (2) TAKING STOCK—OR—ON SARTORIAL CUSTOM, CIVIL AND SAVAGE

MARY: I have always traveled solo hitherto.

FANNY: As have I.

ALEX: As have I.

MARY: Occasionally encountering a sister sojourner on a trek—

FANNY: Pausing briefly for the pro forma cuppa—

ALEX: And then going our separate ways, alone.

MARY: By "alone", you mean of course in the company of dozens of native bearers, beaters, porters, sherpas, and guides.

FANNY: We agreed. No porters.

ALEX: (*Sighs*) No sherpas.

FANNY: You carry what you collect.
(*They begin to do inventory.*)

MARY: Machetes. Three.

FANNY: Umbrellas. A brace.

ALEX: Rope. Some yards.

FANNY: A gross of hand-tinted picture postcards.

MARY: By your own hand, Fanny?

FANNY: I had them fabricated. I anticipate they will not be readily available en route.

ALEX: Imaginative preconceptions of Terra Incognita, Fanny?

FANNY: Preconceptions? Precisely.

ALEX: Are you clairvoyant, Fanny?

FANNY: Look. Generic scenes of general interest. Generic fauna. Generic jungle. Generic bush.

MARY: They will complement our cartography, which is highly speculative and totally fanciful. Ink pens. Journals, hand-sewn and leather-bound.

FANNY: Hand me my toothbrush, won't you?

MARY: Peacock feathers. Beads. Colored glass. Patent medicines. Specimen bags. Lanterns. Butterfly nets. Cello. Ocarina. Mandolin. Rock-climbing apparatus. *Sherry*. A Persian carpet of modest dimension. Parasols. Mosquito netting. Mineral water. Canteens. Water colors. Sketching canvas. Canopy clips. Bamboo staves. Quartz knives. Iodine. Shepherd's pie. Barley sugar. Lemon drops.

FANNY: Pith helmets.
(*She distributes them. They don them ceremoniously, and in unison.*)

MARY: We're not short of pith—that's sure.
(FANNY *pulls out a rhinestoned tiara and blonde wig.*)

FANNY: Whenever I must palaver with pasha or poobah, I don this tonsorial getup. And lay out a formal tea. It never fails to impress.

MARY: I don't wonder.

FANNY: It stands to reason. Savages are naked. For the most part.

ALEX: I for one am impressed. I've a Kodak!
(*She rummages.*)

MARY: No, really?

FANNY: Where did you get it?

ALEX: Friends in high places.

FANNY: Show.

(ALEX *shows.*)

FANNY: Is that it? That little box?

ALEX: The film, it's called, captures the image.

FANNY: Oh?

ALEX: Like honey. Insects in amber. Silver nitrate. I have no way of printing the images. That requires a laboratory. Which would have meant porters.

FANNY: We agreed.

ALEX: We did. Fanny—

(FANNY *models tiara and wig.* ALEX *Kodaks her.*)

FANNY: You won't see what you've Kodaked?

ALEX: Not until we return home.

FANNY: How do you know that it works?

ALEX: You just trust. You "click". You store. You protect. You wait.

FANNY: You hope and pray.

ALEX: You trust. Transport. Guard with your very life. Years of deserts, mountains, pagan tribesmen and inclement weather. Back in civilization, you hand over your nascent images. Have they survived the travails of the trek? Breathless, you await the results of the chemical revelation. With a little luck—voila! Kodaks! Lovely momentoes. And, best of all, incontrovertible proof for posterity. Documentation.

MARY: I wouldn't trust 'em. Misleading. The natives say they steal your spirit.

ALEX: Funny word, native.

MARY: A Kodak is no more the thing itself than an etching. Flat. A shadow. Physical specimens are what counts. Hides, horns, and bobtails.

FANNY: We agreed. No porters.

ALEX: Your natives are mistaken. An unseen moment that would have vanished without a trace is brought to light. The spirit is not stolen. It is illuminated.

MARY: Mysticism.

ALEX: Science.

MARY: That's not science, dear. That's engineering. No, Alexandra, we must have something the Boston Geo can lay hands on.

FANNY: You carry what you collect.

MARY: Physical evidence. Not impressions. Not imagery. Not emotion. Objectivity. Not poetry, m'dears. Not romance. You know what I'm saying.

ALEX AND FANNY: Mmmmmmmmmmmmmmmm.

MARY: Shall we saddle up?

(*Something in the sand catches* ALEX'S *eye. She uncovers it.*)

ALEX: A glint in the sand.

FANNY: Hooper do!

MARY: An artifact! So soon! This is lucky!

ALEX: Qu'est ce que c'est?

(*She picks up a metal button and hands it to* MARY.)

ALEX: Gloss this.

MARY: Metallic button. Writing. Oh, this is lucky. Latin letters. What a surprise. I'd have thought runes.

FANNY: I'd have thought glyphs. Can you make it out?

MARY: Not English.

FANNY: Phonetically.

MARY: (*puzzles it out.*) "Hec—kwhod—ont".

FANNY: There's a question mark after it. It's a question.

(*They try various pronunciations and inquisitive inflections.*)

ALL: "Hec—kwhod—ont"? "Hec—kwhod—ont"? "Hec—kwhod—ont"?

FANNY: Pity it's not English.

ALEX: You didn't expect English, did you, Fanny?

MARY: It would not have surprised me. English is everywhere.

FANNY: A good thing, too.

MARY: Is it? English is the vehicle, and its engine is Empire.

FANNY: Stuff.

ALEX: Perhaps we'll find a translator.

MARY: The first of many mysteries!

(ALEX *does her journal entry.*)

ALEX: I have seen wonders in the Himalayas. Magic. Mystery. In Ladakh, it was a quotidian trick for the lamas to raise their body temperatures by mere mental exertion. Sheer dint of will. They would sleep all night in snowbanks. At dawn, they would douse themselves in freezing streams. Then, ice-blue and on the verge of extinction, they would sit lotus and meditate ferociously. Instantly, steam would sizzle off them in clouds, rising past their furrowed brows. In an hour, their robes would be dry as toast—and neatly pressed. (*Beat*)

In the blue shadow of Crystal Mountain, I watched a Bon shaman wrap himself in his black cape, fold himself thrice, become a giant origami crow, flap flap flap his wings, rise into the sky, and fly across the saffron moon. (*Beat*)

In Lhasa, on the bone-white hill of the Potala, before the lunar congregation of Buddhist alchemists, I saw the Dalai Lama himself transmute great buckets of gold coins. (*Beat*)

Into yak butter.

## (3) UP AND OVER

(*The ladies saddle up.*)

MARY: Let us trek.

FANNY: Mary! Alexandra!

ALEX: Ladies! To the wall!

(*They trek.*)

FANNY: Look behind us.

MARY: Is something gaining?

FANNY: In the sand.

ALEX: Ooooo!

MARY: Our footprints.

FANNY: Making our mark.

(*They continue trekking.*)

MARY: (*A deep inhalation*) Salt air always brings out the metaphysician in me.

FANNY: I always leave Grover in Terre Haute. The Antipodes are not the sort of place one should bring a man.

(*They reach the cliff face.* FANNY *eyeballs it.*)

FANNY: Steep.

MARY: Daunting.

FANNY: Truculent.

MARY: Vertiginous.

ALEX: Child's cake.

(*They prepare their ropes.*)

ALEX: Surely you will both agree trousers would be far more practical for scaling this promontory.

MARY: Alexandra, the civilizing Mission of Woman is to reduce the amount of masculinity in the world. Not add to it by wearing trousers. The wearing of trousers—by women—leads inexorably to riding astride a horse. Instead of the modest sidesaddle.

FANNY: And encourages the use of the bicycle. Which for women can never by proper.

ALEX: I happen to be a "wheel enthusiast". And I have often worn trousers—out of sight of civilized settlement, to be sure—whilst wheeling. Or riding horseback. *Astride.* Far more comfortable and sensible than sidesaddle.

FANNY: What can one say?

ALEX: Out of sight of sedentary eyes, I whip off my skirt, under which I have worn sturdy trousers, and am set for practical traveling.

FANNY: Alexandra, are you wearing trousers at this moment?

ALEX: Trousers, ladies, are the future!

MARY: Yes, I am constantly told by armchair travelers that I must wear trousers in the jungle, and leave my skirt at home.

FANNY: Men can be soooo trying.

ALEX: Ladies, I am not advocating trousers for general usage. Or polite society. But there are times one simply must—bite the bullet!

MARY: I pay no heed, and have often had cause to celebrate my independence. One evening in Malaya near dusk, I fell ten feet into a man-eating tiger trap.

Found myself nestled on a cathedral of punji sticks. If I had been wearing trousers, I would have been pierced to the core, and done for.

FANNY: A petticoat is the only thing for punji sticks. A good stiff petticoat is worth its weight in gold. (*Snorts*) Trousers in the tropics!

ALEX: Oh, jungles. In the Himalayas, trousers are de rigueur. Allons!

(ALEX *leads the way. They scale the cliff. Jungle light. Jungle sounds. Dazzled, they survey the surround.*)

ALEX: A jeweled jungle!

(FANNY *comes down to do her journal entry.*)

FANNY: I introduced croquet to the headhunters of the headwaters of the Putamayo. The sport of kings. They loved it. Simply adored the game. Of course, I insisted they use only regulation wooden balls. I would accept no substitutes. The rascals were always batting their latest trophies about. I was strict. They respected me for that.

## (4) THE MYSTERIOUS INTERIOR

ALEX: Terra Incognita!

FANNY: Ooooo. Hooper do!

MARY: The mysterious interior.

ALEX: Fantastic! A jeweled jungle! I am extruded! I mean ecstatic. Not extruded.

MARY: Ladies, shall we bushwhack?

(*They step forward and bushwhack.*)

FANNY: Some years back, while on assignment in the Amazon River Basin, for my favorite tabloid, *True Trek*, my arch nemesis on *The Globetrotteress* reported I had got myself up in male haberdashery.

MARY: Did you sue?

FANNY: Grover sued. I would have had the wretch horse-whipped.

MARY: I would sooner saunter across the Sahara sans sandals than don trousers. An umbrella comes in handy. In the jungle.

ALEX: Jungle is not my metier.

MARY: We know. Fanny, what thousand and one uses do you find for your umbrella?

FANNY: Prodding the suddenly faint of heart. Marine soundings. Poking hippopotamii. And whacking the recalcitrant croc. Thwack! The Mighty Silurian!

ALEX: What is a Mighty Silurian?

MARY: So Fanny's lurid tabloids call the crocodile.

ALEX: (*Working out a lyric*) Umbrella. Hmmm. Chum. Fella. Drum. Fun. Swa—swa—swa—swa—Swoon! Ta—ta—ta—Typhoon! La la—tropical fever has got me in its mighty thrall.

(*A sudden downpour. The ladies blossom their umbrellas.*)

FANNY: No, dear. There's no protection from a tropical downpour.

ALEX: None?

FANNY: It must be endured.

ALEX: Jungle jungle, what a foreboding—

(*The rain stops.*)

ALEX: —what a mystery. A jeweled jungle!

FANNY: It'll do. Puts one in mind of the great cloud forest of the Orinoco.

MARY: Not annoying! Not annoying at all! (*With great resolve*) Ladies—shall we whack the bush?

(*They start forward, whacking the bush.*)

FANNY: Ah, the familiar chop chop swack swack. Takes me back. The cloud forest of the Orinoco. Now there is a jungle, ladies. Spiders the size of flapjacks! They flop on you out of the trees! You have to get 'em on the fly! Cut 'em in half in mid-air! Thwack! Spider blood splatters!—hello, what's this? Mysteries underfoot.

(FANNY *finds something: An old-fashioned egg beater, slightly rusty. She holds it various ways, rotors it, giggles.*)

FANNY: What do you think it could be?

MARY: A fan. For this glaze of tropical heat.

FANNY: (*Rotors*) Does not generate the slightest breeze.

MARY: A talisman.

FANNY: Totem.

MARY: Amulet.

FANNY: Taboo. Alexandra?

(*She hands it to* ALEX, *who turns it beaters-down, and rotors it with resolve.*)

ALEX: Marsupial's unicycle. (*Hands it to* FANNY *who puts it in her belt, like a six-shooter.*)

JOURNAL ENTRY:

MARY: The bane of my many travels in the tropics is a bland, mucilagenous paste called manioc, made from the forlorn and despicable cassava, a tuber of dubious provenance. A vile concoction, manioc tastes, in the best of recipes, like a bottom of a budgie's cage—and is more suited for masonry than human consumption. Manioc is the quintessential native chop, occurring circumglobularly in the tropics. For those with a taste for prussic acid, manioc may be just your cup of tea.

## (5) NATIVE CHOP

(*The ladies are bushwhacking. Jungle noises all about.*)

ALEX: I am delicious! I mean delirious. Not delicious.

MARY: Ladies! Shall we whack the bush?

(*They start off.* ALEX *pricks herself on a thorn.*)

ALEX: Ow! Ligament, juicy Nordic, quiz!

FANNY: Marvelous strange oaths, Alexandra.

ALEX: These spikey stickers are a bother. Itch! Lasso pork liquor!

MARY: The bush has its logic.

ALEX: Fine. The glacier is my milieu. Give me an ice face, a mountain of howling wind or stone, or an impassable crevasse. Below zero, I'm in my element. Why can't a jungle be more like a park?

FANNY: Regulated undergrowth?

ALEX: Why not? A little order.

MARY: A jungle has its order, of course.

ALEX: Tips for lady travelers? Or just brushing up on your next address to the Boston Geo?

MARY: Don't snip, or snipe. Dear.

FANNY: When I was last at the Explorer's Club, I had the most extraordinary meal. It was written up in *True Trek*.

ALEX: Please, Fanny, not one of those stories.

MARY: This jungle is not so awful. As jungles go, this jungle is not annoying.

ALEX: It is nothing but. It is one annoyance after another.

MARY: It is dry. A dry jungle is a mercy.

ALEX: Mary, it is soggy. It is saturated. I have fungi growing on my corset stays.

MARY: Comparatively dry. As jungles go, this one is almost arid. Oh, I have waded through swamps for hours on end, emerging at last with a frill of leeches around my neck like an astrakhan collar.

ALEX: There are no astrakhan leeches in the Himalayas. No spikey swamp stickers, no mighty Silurians—

MARY: But there are abominable snowmen. I've read Fanny's tabloids.

FANNY: Abominable snowman was on the menu when I was last at the Explorers' Club. But I suspect it was yak. They pride themselves on their Native Chop. I always have something outlandish. Thinking about the Explorers' Club whets my appetite. We must stop for refreshment. (*She puts down her pack and rummages, preparing a snack.*) On my last visit, we had buffalo hump, glacé bees' knees, and armadillo knuckles. Which I for one never suspected armadillos had. Followed by muckleshoots, sweet and sour zebra, wolverine surprise, porcupine quills à la Louis quatorze, locust liqueur, and the celebrated moose mousse. I hear not a good year for gnu, I said. I'd skip the snake salad, if I were you, my companion replied, and the candied cats' eyes aren't worth a penny postcard home. We both agreed to eschew the jellied viscera.

ALEX: Fanny, you make the gorge rise.

FANNY: The Explorers are famous for their grubs. Their motto: Grubs from around the globe! And there are always the usual boyish sallies about mighty good grub. Ho ho. Sheer bravado. The explorers are always throwing up in their top hats at the end of an evening.

MARY: I regret I have never had the pleasure.

FANNY: The grand art of Native Chop is quite impossible to recreate in the effete precincts of civilization.

MARY: Native Chop, in my experience, is inevitably manioc.

FANNY: Always and forever, world without end. Have you ever had manioc fritters?

MARY: No.

FANNY: Not bad. Not good—but not bad.

ALEX: I am famous.

FANNY: Date bread?

MARY: Please.

ALEX: I mean famished. Not famous.

MARY: (*Takes date bread.*) Thank you. This is scrumptious, Fanny.

FANNY: Alex—

ALEX: Thank you. Mmmm, lovely.

MARY: Super, Fanny. Puts manioc to shame.

FANNY: High praise.

MARY: Ubiquitous manioc. We won't escape it. Mark my words. (*Shudders*) Native Chop.

FANNY: This is not Africa, Mary. This is Terra Incognita. Cream cheese?

ALEX: I don't believe I've ever. What is it?

FANNY: Not cream and not cheese, but it's thick and rich and comes in tins.

ALEX: Thick and rich? Like Mrs. Butterworth!

MARY: Who is Mrs. Butterworth?
(*Pause*)

ALEX: Oh. (*Beat*) I don't know.

MARY: I'll hazard some. Looks harmless. Spread it on my date bread. Thank you. Has the same consistency as manioc.

FANNY: Mary!

ALEX: What a treat! Is it new?

FANNY: Invented in Chicago, I believe. Well, everything is. Take the ice cream sandwich.

ALEX: I've never had one. This is rather nice. Where did you get it? Friends in high places? Will it keep?

FANNY: We must devour it immediately. You know, I don't remember packing it. Or buying it for that matter. I didn't make it. I made the date bread.
(*Pause*)

MARY: Another slice, Fanny.

FANNY: You know, only a few days on, and I am desperate for a bath.

MARY: I concur. What is life without a loofah? Look!
(*They peer ahead.*)

ALEX: He's wearing a uniform.

FANNY: What power? Whose sphere of influence is this plateau?

MARY: This is Terra Incognita! A New World. Sans spheres.

FANNY: Manifest Destiny and the American Way are not spheres.

ALEX: (*To herself*) Rhomboids of influence, trapezoids of destiny.

FANNY: We are emissaries, Alexandra, of the good will and benignity of President McKinley. Cleveland. Taft. Whoever is president now. You know. One of those Ohio politicians. Muttonchops.

ALEX: Can you name the Vice-President?

FANNY: Not if my life depended on it.

ALEX: Nor I.

MARY: Perhaps he traded for it.

FANNY: The Vice-Presidency? Of course he traded for it. He's a Democrat. Well? Isn't he?

MARY: No, the native. Perhaps he traded for the uniform.

ALEX: Shall we palaver? He sees us. (*She waves.*)

MARY: I once traded twelve calico blouses to the Masai. Empress sleeves.

ALEX: What did you trade them for?

MARY: My life. White knuckles and chewed nails, dear.

ALEX: (*Dreamily*) The Masai. Sigh.

MARY: When worn by a brawny warrior with nothing—but red paint—and a necklace of leopard tails—(*Beat*) a calico blouse—(*Beat*) is really quite—(*Beat*) fetching.

ALEX: I should think so.

FANNY: I once encountered the Masai. I said: Wow! Wow! Wow!

ALEX: And how did they reply?

MARY: He's approaching.

FANNY: They seemed to like that. Let's set tea. I'll change.

(FANNY *goes off to change.* MARY *and* ALEX *watch the native's approach, as they prepare for tea.*)

ALEX: Funny word, native. Assuming he is a native. Everyone is a native of somewhere, when you think about it. So I guess he must be a native at that. Where are you a native, Mary?

MARY: I haven't a thing to wear. I wish I could wash. Oh, what is life without a loofah!

JOURNAL ENTRY:

MARY: In Kuala Lumpur, the seraglio of the Sultan was—a honeycomb. It was as many-chambered as the heart of the tribe. I recall the cavernous steam rooms on cold evenings, full of echoing voices and escarpments of mist. The inlaid geometric gold-leaf calligraphy. The rattan sofas. The acres of tile the color of sky. And a sponge conjured from the exoskeleton of an indigenous fruit. The loofah. Loofah—

**(6) HIGH TEA—OR, MANY PARTS ARE EDIBLE**

(*The ladies have set tea.* FANNY *has donned not only her wig and tiara, but an elaborate rhinestoned gown. Their guest,* ALPHONSE, *wears an impeccable German airman's uniform, and speaks with an extravagant German accent.*)

ALEX: Loofah. Loofah. Now there's a word to conjure with! Powerful juju.

FANNY: More date bread?

ALPHONSE: Oh zank you zo much.

FANNY: Another cup of tea?

ALPHONSE: No, zank you. Mein kidneys are floatingk. Heh heh.

ALEX: Are you a native?

ALPHONSE: Zorry?

ALEX: You don't mind my asking.

ALPHONSE: Nein.

MARY: If you don't mind my saying so, Mr. Bismark—

ALPHONSE: Please. Call me Alphonse.

MARY: Alphonse. If you don't mind my saying so, you sound a trifle German.

ALPHONSE: Alsace-Lorraine.

ALEX: Fascinating.

FANNY: How do you happen to find yourself here?

MARY: Is Alsace-Lorraine French or German these days?

ALPHONSE: Gut qvestion. Geography iz deztiny, ladies!

ALEX: Oh, that's good! I'll make a note of it.

MARY: Alphonse, sprechen sie Deutsch, s'il vous plait?

ALPHONSE: Nein. I never haf been dere.

FANNY: How do you happen to find yourself in this country, did you say?

ALPHONSE: I am a native.

ALEX: This is not Alsace-Lorraine—am I wrong?

ALPHONSE: I never haf been dere. I haf not der foggiest notion vich vay Alsace-Lorraine iz. Schtraight up in der air, vy not, eh?

MARY: Forgive me, but I don't follow.

ALPHONSE: He vas! Him. Not me. No! No! No! No eat! No eat! No eat Alphonse! No eat Alphonse! I am warning you! I am schtringy! No eat Alphonse! Aaaaaiii-ieeeeeeeeeeeee!

(*A stricken pause.*)

FANNY: I no savvy, as they say out west in Indian Territory. What is this fellow's problem?

MARY: He is not Alphonse from Alsace-Lorraine.

ALPHONSE: No vay, José. I'm from right here at home. Dat vas him. Alphonse. Der von I ate. His uniform, his accent. His syntax. Zide effects. Occupational hazard. Hoppens everytime I eat schomevon.

FANNY: Oh, goodness.

ALPHONSE: I should schtick to date bread. Delicious. (*He has another slice.*)

ALEX: He's a cannibal.

FANNY: Now that's really native chop.

MARY: Nothing to be alarmed about. Cannibals are perfectly rational human beings.

FANNY: You are a liberal, Mary.

MARY: I am an anthropologist. I traveled extensively amongst the Indigos. Cannibals—but lively. Anthropophagii tend to be sluggish, you know. I found them no bother to me at all. Of course, you had to keep them from eating your porters. Frequent head counts were the order of the day. There are two sorts of folks in the world. The sort you drink with, and the sort you eat with. Cannibals you drink with.

ALPHONSE: Ja! I am a Free Mason! (*Pause*) Or, radder, that little rascal Alphonse vas a Free Mason. Egxcuze me, ladies, I am, at der moment, a little confuzed. Too zoon after zupper.

MARY: A Free Mason. What else do you know about your—about Alphonse.

ALPHONSE: He vas a pilot.

FANNY: A riverboat?

ALPHONSE: Nein, nein, nein. He flew. May I have some more of zis date bread, pliz? Und creamcheese? Good schtuff, zis creamcheese.

MARY: You were saying, Alphonse?

ALPHONSE: I vas sayingk, I vas sayingk, ja, um, I vas, he vas, ve vas, whoever ve vas now, ve vere a pilot. Of a flyingk machine.

FANNY: Nonsense.

ALPHONSE: Ja, you betcha. Heavier dan der air. A dirigible.

MARY: A dirigible.

ALPHONSE: Ja. Dirigible.

FANNY: A dirigible.

ALEX: Dirigible.

ALPHONSE: Dirigible, ja, dirigible.

MARY: What is a dirigible? Alphonse?

ALEX: What a succulent word! Dirigible, dirigible, dirigible. Dirigible. Dirigible.

MARY: Alex!

ALEX: Up your old dirigible. Give us your huddled dirigibles, yearning to breathe free. Have a dirigible on me, big fella. One mint dirigible to go.

(*A pause.* ALPHONSE *regards* ALEX *askance.*)

ALPHONSE: Vell, it's a balloon.

MARY: Hot air?

ALPHONSE: Inert gazz.

ALEX: Inelegible dirigible. Illegible dirigible. Incorrigible dirigible. Gerbil in a dirigible! I'll wager it's one of those words which has no true rhyme in English. Of course, it's not an English word, is it?

FANNY: You must explain your obsession with rhyme. It borders on the unhealthy. I've read that preoccupation with rhyme is one of the symptoms of incipient hysteria.

ALEX: Knackwurst!

MARY: What happened to the dirigible, Alphonse?

ALPHONSE: Schtill dere, as far as I know. You vant a look, cuties?

FANNY: You, sir, are growing impertinent.

ALPHONSE: Zay, dat's a nice vig you got dere. Mein zizter haz a vig like dat.

FANNY: Does she enjoy it?

ALPHONSE: She lofs it! A lot!

MARY: How do we locate your dirigible?

ALPHONSE: Follow der yellow brick road, shveeties.

MARY: Zorry? Ah—sorry?

ALPHONSE: Take der segund egxit. Vatch for der Burma Shave signs. Oh, buoy. I should never had taken dat exxtra schlice of date bread. Never eat on a full schtomach.

MARY: Alphonse—

ALPHONSE: Egxcuze me, ladies. Zank you for der chow. You must come to eat viz me shomeday. I make a mean manioc strudel.

ALEX: Manioc, my favorite.

FANNY: Have you ever had manioc fritters?

ALPHONSE: Ve vill haf to trade recipes.

MARY: Alphonse, couldn't you see your way clear to guide us to the dirigible? We'll pay wages.

ALPHONSE: Zorry. I am not vell. I haf to get zis Alphonse out of mein zyztem. Perhops ve meet again, mein blue angels. Vaya con Dios!

MARY: Auf wiedersehn.

ALPHONSE: (*He hands* FANNY *a bundle.*) A token of mein steam. Big juju. Love dat vig. (*He exits.*)

FANNY: His steam, indeed.

(*She unwraps it. It's another egg beater, a rather different model.* FANNY *hands it to* ALEX.)

FANNY: I've already got one.

ALEX: Thank you so much. I'll keep it with me always.

(*They rotor at one another and laugh.*)

MARY: A cannibal from Alsace-Lorraine. Will wonders never cease?

FANNY: Yes, Mary, there are two sorts of people in the world. There are cannibals—and there are lunch.

MARY: Fanny, you are a Social Darwinist.

ALEX: What do you suppose he meant by Burma Shave?

FANNY: I've been to Burma.

MARY: As have I.

ALEX: (*With sudden fierce conviction*) There are no cannibals in Tibet! No matter what the Red Chinese claim! (*Pause*)

MARY AND FANNY: What on Earth is a Red Chinese?

JOURNAL ENTRY:

MARY: By and large the company has been charming. As a confirmed-since-childhood solo sojourner, I am astonished. Perhaps I have overvalued the pleasures of solitude heretofore.

(*Takes a deep breath.*) I feel the rare air of Terra Incognita working its way upon me like acid on an old coin, the tarnish of the past dissolving in a solvent of iridescent light. I tingle. Objects shimmer on the horizon. At sunset, a tantalizing mist, a web, a membrane envelopes us.

## (7) EMBER TALES

(*Twilight descends. A campfire. The ladies are telling tales.*)

MARY: There is nothing so fascinating as fire.

FANNY: When I was sleeping in a rice paddy under a blood moon, near the Irriwaddy River Delta, I awoke to find myself surrounded. By a band of cut-throat dacoits. Thuggees. Brigands. Buccaneers. They wore turbans with rubies set in the brow, and bejeweled daggers. And they were led by a woman—a Bandit Queen! She was a devotee of Kali, the Goddess of Death!

ALEX: I am often asked about Tibetan cuisine. In Lamdo, I apprenticed myself to a sorcerer. My mentor had quarrelled with a rival shaman. A blood feud. One morning, Master Dzo baked two great cakes of ground millet. He baked them flat as platters and hard as wheels. When the cakes were cool, he spun them into the sky. Hurled them, as though they were discuses. They spun and spun, rising in the sky, sailing over the city until they searched out the stone hut of the second sorcerer. The cakes whirled like saw blades, swooped down, and sliced the hut in half. Battered it to crumbs. (*Beat*) I think that sums up Tibetan cuisine. It is not haute.

FANNY: While travelling in the Rockie Mountains some years back, I repelled a rabid drooling grizzly bear with a series of piercing yodels. (*She demonstrates: three bloodcurdling yodels.*)

MARY: That reminds me of my father, who was a famous pharmacist.

**ALEX:** Did your father yodel, Mary?

**MARY:** No. He invented a tonic for cataarh.

**ALEX:** After an hour, their robes would be dry as toast. And neatly pressed. Extraordinary visages. They would *concentrate*.

**FANNY:** I once encountered the Masai. I said—"Wow"!

**MARY:** Talking drums always bring out the Neolithic Man in me.

(*Pause*)

(**FANNY,** *reflecting on the Masai, silently mouthes a "Wow!" The ladies settle in for the night.*)

(**FANNY** *does her journal entry.*)

JOURNAL ENTRY:

**FANNY:** Dear Grover. We had lunch today—or was it yesterday—with the most amicable cannibal. He admired my wig. The tabloids will feast. I can hear *The Globetrotteress* licking her chops now. "Fanny's Cannibal—Discovers Maneating Balloonist in Darkest Antipodes—Boston Geo Views Claim Warily." The jaundice of yellow journalism. One more card in the catalogue my critics are fond of calling Fanny's Follies. (*Beat*) Terra Incognita exhilarates. Intoxicates. There is an hallucinatory spiciness to the air. We are in the grip of a communal fever dream. Alex mutters continually about the "Red Chinese", and Mary makes reference to an anthropological penny-dreadful entitled *The Naked and the Dead*. Myself, I dream about mysterious machinery, discover strange objects in my baggage, and strange phrases in my mouth: "Air-mail." "Blue-sky ventures." "So long."

**(8) AN APPARITION**

(*The ladies are sleeping around the fire.* **FANNY** *snores, a ferocious sound. A figure appears on the edge of the light:* **GROVER, FANNY's** *husband, a prosperous Mid-West broker. He is wearing a large black oval carved African mask. He listens* to **FANNY** *snore. Scratches his eyebrow. Growls softly.* **FANNY** *awakes with a start.*)

**FANNY:** What? Who? (*Looks closer. Mouthes a silent "Wow!" She gets up and approaches him.*) I have no calico blouses, but I will trade you cream cheese. It is not bad. Not manioc, but not bad.

(**GROVER** *chuckles.* **FANNY** *examines* **GROVER's** *suit and shoes.*)

**FANNY:** Are you or are you not Masai?

**GROVER:** I'm just your grizz-a-ly bear, Fanny. (*Taking off mask.*) What a snore, Fanny. You'll keep the leopards away.

**FANNY:** Grover!

**GROVER:** Don't be cross.

**FANNY:** Why shouldn't I be? Bother a body in the middle of the night. In the middle of the jungle.

**GROVER:** I came to give you a message.

**FANNY:** I'm all ears.

**GROVER:** Don't speculate on the future.

(*Pause*)

**FANNY:** Your mother warned me you were hermetic.

**GROVER:** I also wanted to say goodbye.

**FANNY:** Grover, we said goodbye. In Terre Haute. Some months ago. Are you staying dry?

**GROVER:** Dry as toast. Well, Fanny. I had something up my sleeve for Arbor Day next. It was—sorta special. Yikes. Well, Fanny. Goodnight.

**FANNY:** Goodnight, Grover. Are those new shoes?

**GROVER:** Don't forget to write.

**FANNY:** Do I ever?

**GROVER:** You are a faithful correspondent, Fanny. Goodbye.

(*He disappears.* **FANNY** *stares after him. Shivers a little.* **ALEX** *wakes, gets up, goes to* **FANNY,** *and taps her on the shoulder. She starts.*)

**FANNY:** Oh!

**ALEX:** Fanny—are you a somnambulist?

**FANNY:** What? Oh, I must be. Fancy that.

**ALEX:** Come back to the fire.

(ALEX *returns to the fire.*)

FANNY: I have had the most vivid dream.

(MARY *arises and does her Journal Entry.*)

MARY: At dawn and dusk, the essence of the jungle increases a hundredfold. The air becomes heavy with perfume. It throbs with unseen presence. A savage tapestry of squawks, cries, and caws presses upon one with an almost palpable pressure. A cacophonous echolalia—snarling, sinister menace—as though the sound of the jungle itself could tear one limb from limb.

## (9) FORT APACHE

(*Dawn breaks. Jungle noises. The ladies break camp. The ladies travel. Jungle noises all about.*
*The ladies are alert, cautious.*
*Suspenseful.*
*The jungle noises increase in ferocity. They become menacing.*
*The ladies draw and open their umbrellas. They form a defensive triangle, shoulder to shoulder.*
*The jungle noises attack, snarl, and snap.*
*The ladies fend off the jungle noises with their umbrellas, fencing and jabbing sharply.*
*The umbrellas blossom.*
*The ladies rotate across the stage, a vanquishing star, scattering the jungle noises, which howl and flee.*
*The ladies lower their umbrellas. They celebrate quietly.*)

ALEX: Funny word, native. Native. Native. (*She Kodaks an imaginary native.*) Image. Native. Imagenative. Imaginative. I am a native of the image. An indigine of the imagination. Gone native. Renegade. Commanchero.

## (10) IN THE JUNGLE—THE MIGHTY JUNGLE

(*The ladies bushwhack through a swamp.*)

ALEX: Ooo, ow, natter blast! Savage sour lichtenstein! Lactating minuet! This jungle exhausts me! Surely you must agree trousers would be far and away more practical for this primeval muck.

MARY: On the contrary, Alexandra. One evening near dusk, as we were negotiating the treacherous Black Quicksands of Baluchistan, I slipped off solid ground, and found myself sinking into infinite bog. Fortunately, my sturdy skirt ballooned around me, held its shape and kept me bouyant until assistance arrived. A few moments later, I lost half a dozen porters in the blink of an eye. Sucked under the sands, like that! Fooop! Poor men weren't wearing skirts.

ALEX: Ah! Look!

(*Sound of a croc.* FANNY *vanquishes it.*)

FANNY: The mighty Silurian! Thwack!

(*The ladies reach solid ground.*)

MARY: Time for a nose powder.

FANNY: I could do with a bit of a primp.

ALEX: I'll follow suit.

(*They pull beaded handbags from their packs, move some distance through the jungle, and freshen up.*)

MARY: In the Congo, I was known as Only Me.

ALEX: Only Me?

MARY: I would enter a village or burst into a clearing or emerge from the bush shouting, "it's only me, it's only me!"

FANNY: Immediately disarming the hostile natives, who naturally enough spoke English.

MARY: Dear Fanny. Tone of voice is everything.

FANNY: I was known as Bébé Bwana.

ALEX: Bébé?

FANNY: It's difficult to explain. Out of context.

MARY: I never got over being called "Sir."

ALEX: Nor I.

FANNY: Nor I.

MARY: Human once more.

FANNY: I am revivified.

ALEX: I am refurbished. I mean refreshed. Not refurbished. Ah! Feel that breeze, ladies!

(*The wind comes up. The ladies prepare for cold weather, donning scarves, goggles, etc.*)

JOURNAL ENTRY:

FANNY:  I felt as though I were a prisoner in a kaleidescope.

## (11) A PRISONER IN A KALEIDESCOPE

(*The wind comes up. They move across the stage. The wind whistles. They stop.*)

FANNY:  Alexandra. Here's your howling ice field.

ALEXANDRA:  My forte. Allons!

(*They cross the ice field in slow motion. The invisible rope between them breaks, and they begin twirling slowly over the ice, in different directions, away from one another, toward the edges, in silence. At the brink, they stop. Teeter. Freeze. Relax. They catch their breath.*)

MARY:  A narrow one—

ALEX:  Whoo whistle lug—

FANNY:  A scrape—

(*Relieved laughter. They make their way carefully to the center and one another.*)

MARY:  What happened, did the rope—

ALEX:  The rope—

FANNY:  It snapped, I felt it go—

ALEX:  Broke—

MARY:  Spinning like a gyro—

ALEX:  Spinning—

MARY:  Graceful, I was so—

FANNY:  So—

MARY:  Calm—

FANNY:  Calm, yes—

FANNY AND MARY:  Calm—

FANNY:  Eeerily calm—

ALEX:  Spinning toward the lip of the void—

MARY:  My mind clear—

ALEX:  Into the infinite cerulean—

MARY:  I thought of my father, the famous pharmacist—

ALEX:  Did your life, you know, flash before you?

MARY:  Too dizzy, my dear—

ALEX:  They say drowning sailors—

MARY:  No, just him.

FANNY:  I felt as though I were a prisoner in a kaleidescope.

ALEX:  Oh, Fanny, that's good.

MARY:  A book title. I'd make a note of it.

(FANNY *does. They sigh.*)

ALEX:  Whew, lacerated fingerbowl!

MARY:  Fingerbowl, indeed! Well said, Alex.

FANNY:  A scrape. A palpable scrape.

MARY:  Sheer luck, running into that ice wall.

FANNY:  Fortuitous.

ALEX:  I'm all over bruises in the morning.

(FANNY *is hit by a snowball.*)

FANNY:  Alexandra!

ALEX:  Yes?

FANNY:  High spirits need not always be accompanied by hi-jinks.

ALEX:  You always cast your eye upon me because I'm the youngest. But that missile came from over there.

(*They all look. A barrage of snowballs. They dodge.*)

MARY:  Oh, dear!

FANNY:  Watch yourselves! Oh, Alexandra!

(*Dodging,* ALEX *slips and pratfalls. The breath flies out of her.*)

ALEX:  Whomp!

MARY:  Are you all right?

(*A yeti appears at the stage edge. A silky mane from head-to-foot.*)

YETI:  (*Growls beast language*) ARRGGGGRRRACKAAACK!

MARY:  A silkie.

ALEX:  (*Picking herself up.*) Silkies are seals, silly. That's a yeti.

YETI:  (*Growls beast language*) LLLLLLLLUUUUUUUURRRRRAAAAAAAEEECCCCCKOOO!

ALEX:  Oh, yes you are!

YETI:  (*Growls beast language*) RASSRASSRASS!

ALEX:  Tibet teems with 'em, m'dears. Yes, Fanny's tabloids call them abominable snowmen.

FANNY:  He's not so abominable.

MARY:  He's rather adorable.

ALEX:  He's smallish, for a yeti.

MARY:  He's a baby yeti.

FANNY AND MARY:  He's sweet.

(*The ladies chick and coo and gush, luring the yeti closer. He retreats, terrified.*)

YETI: (*Growls beast language*) WHHHUUU-WHHHAAAASNARP! (*He vanishes.*)

MARY: Oh, dear. Frightened him off.

ALEX: The yeti is shy and elusive. Although his cry is often human, and tuneful. (*From offstage:*)

YETI: (*Growls beast language*) AIIIIYIIIIIII-YAIIIAIWHA!

FANNY: The little sasquatch has gone for more snowballs, no doubt. (*She is hit by a snowball.*) AHHHH!

MARY: Baby yeti may have yeti cronies. I think prudence dictates we move on. (*They hike downstage. Peer into a deep gorge.*)

ALEX: Ooo!

FANNY: Precipice.

MARY: Chilling.

ALEX: This gorge is so like the Himalayas!

MARY: There's a bridge. Vines and planks. Shall we risk it?

FANNY: By all means. (*ALEX takes three Andean breaths.*)

ALEX: Now—this (*Breath*) is (*Breath*) air (*Breath*) ladies!

JOURNAL ENTRY:

FANNY: An awful yawning chasm. An antedeluvian suspension.

## (12) NOT QUITE ROBERT LOWELL

(*The ladies are crossing a high gorge on a swaying, single-plank, vine-rope bridge.*)

MARY: "Mysticism and Mesmerism in Madagascar" was a paper I delivered to the Ladies Fetish and Taboo Society of Annapolis. It was a sensation. I followed that with "Tribadism in the Tropics"—which caused quite a stir. Rubbed several spectators the wrong way.

ALEX: What is "tribadism"?

FANNY: (*Knowing exactly what it is*) I'm sure I haven't the least notion.

ALEX: This gorge is so like the Himalayas.

FANNY: I am convinced that the modern craze for anthropology is actually a subterranean sexual inflamation, flimsily got up as scientific curiosity.

ALEX: I am hypnotized.

FANNY: An unhealthy obsession with rites—

ALEX: I mean homesick. Not hypnotized.

FANNY: Mating rites, puberty rites, rites of sacrifice, rites of passage, poly this and poly that and poly the other—

ALEX: Nacho frazzle asterisk! It is so delicious to be out of that leech-infested swelter. Look! (*They turn in the direction ALEX points.*) Oh! Dirigible!

MARY: Pilotless. Caroming off the canyon walls.

FANNY: The Flying Dutchman dirigible! What a story for *True Trek*! (*They have nearly completed their crossing. Their way is blocked by the GORGE TROLL, a young man in a leather jacket, blue jeans, t-shirt, and sideburns and greased-back hair.*)

TROLL:

What have we here but travelers three
Comin' cross the bridge to rap with me
In Xanadu said Ka-u-ba-la Khan
Hey there sweet things what's goin' on?
(*Pause*)

FANNY: Alex, I believe verse is your province.

ALEX: You speak English!

TROLL:

This ain't Swahili, I gotta confess
You hearin' more if you talkin' less

FANNY: Swahili seems mathematically more probable than English, my good man. Although I welcome its appearance in this obscure corner of the globe—even in your ghastly patois.

TROLL:

Castigate the way I talk—
I'll agitate the way you walk!
(*He sways the bridge.*)

ALL: Whoooooooo!

MARY: English is the language of Empire, Fanny.

FANNY: I do not wish to embroil us in a political discussion on *the lip of the void*, Mary. Don't you think we ought to seek Terra Firma?

**TROLL:**
> You may not dig my lingo but I'll settle
> your hash
> You wanna get by me gotta have some
> cash

**FANNY:** I don't believe I savvy.

**TROLL:**
> This is my bridge, baby, and I'm the Troll
> To step on over you gotta pay the toll.

**ALEX:** A troll's toll. How droll. He's good.
But not quite Robert Lowell.

**FANNY:** Alex.

**ALEX:** Whoever he is. Robert Lowell, I mean.

**FANNY:** This is extortion!

**TROLL:**
> You want sun sometimes you get rain
> instead
> If you can't hack it you shoulda stood in
> bed

**MARY:** When in Rome.
(*She pays. They cross off*)

**MARY:** Baksheesh! In Terra Incognita!

**TROLL:** Baksheesh-kabob, baby.

**ALEX:** What's it like, being a troll?

**TROLL:** Like?

**ALEX:** How do you find it?

**TROLL:** This is just my day job.

**FANNY:** You're not a born-to-the-bridge
troll?

**TROLL:** I'm an actor. I study.

**FANNY:** Where do you study?

**TROLL:** At the Studio.

**FANNY:** That seems reasonable. Have you
done Congreve?

**TROLL:** I don't think so.

**FANNY:** What have you done?

**TROLL:** C'mon, I've done it all. "Sense memory," "emotional recall," "private moment"—

**MARY:** These must be new plays from Terra
Incognita. Indigenous drama. How
would you characterize "Private Moment"?

**TROLL:** Intense.

**FANNY:** You aren't, by any chance, Mr. Coffee?

**TROLL:** Not the last time I looked. Hey, ladies. Costume drama—get over it. (*To*
**ALEX**) You I like. What about a spin on
my chopper?

**ALEX:** Some other time.

**TROLL:**
> Your loss, angel food.
> Ladies, take it light
> And everything will be all right.
(*He exits.*)

**ALEX:** Vaya con díos!
(*Sound of an enormous unmufflered motorcycle roaring off into the sunset.*)

**MARY:** I think we must presume English
to be the Lingua Franca of Terra Incognita.

**FANNY:** (*Snorts*) None dare call it English.

**MARY:** Did you fancy his lyrics, Alexandra?

**ALEX:** No. But I admired his dedication to
his art.

**MARY:** Irony is not one of your strong suits,
is it?

**ALEX:** What do you mean? I understand that
troll! Despite outward appearances, I am
an artist, not an intrepid polytopian.

**FANNY:** Oh, Alex, for goodness sakes, yes
you are. You're one of the original polytopians, don't dissemble.

**ALEX:** Well, yes, I am. High adventure and
stupefying risk are my metier. But, ladies—all this rigor and unimaginable
hardship, all this uninsurable danger, all
this adrenal giddiness, all this oxygen
debt and spartan discipline and rude hy-
giene—all this is mere prelude. A prologue to my brilliant career. I'm not
making a life out of all this tramping
about, you know. I shall shed my wanderlust like a damp poncho. And become a lyricist. Of popular songs.

**FANNY:** Victor Herbert quakes.

**MARY:** I wonder what that conveyance was?

**ALEX:** He called it a chopper.

**FANNY:** Loud.

**ALEX:** (*With sudden conviction*) The future is
loud!

JOURNAL ENTRY:

MARY: I feel a sea change coming over me. A disturbance of my very molecules. As though the chemical composition of my blood has been altered by breathing the rare air of Terra Incognita. I have begun to dream in a new language. My imagination seems to sculpt the landscape. Images flow between the inner and outer worlds, and I can no longer determine their point of origin. I have a growing premonition we are about to pierce the membrane.

## (13) PLOT THICKENER

*(The ladies have moved some distance from the bridge.)*

FANNY: I rather think that Troll is one of the elusive Mole People. The speculative literature on the Antipodes postulates the existence of a subterranean race. Oh, look—*(She has spied a bit of paper caught in a branch. She plucks it.)*

ALEX: Share, Fanny.

FANNY: A clipping. Folded thrice. From *The New York Times.*

MARY: Reputable. Trustworthy.

FANNY: The *Herald-Tribune,* pour moi. This sheds new light. Terra Incognita cannot be utterly benighted if one can get *The New York Times. (Studies clipping)* A Kodak of a man. Never heard of this fellow. Behind him an impressive array of snow mountains. His arms are spread—so: *(Imitates a man gesturing about the size of a large fish.)* The caption reads: President Nixon. Grand Tetons. June, 1972. Quote: "I had trout from the lake for dinner last night. They were so good I had them again for breakfast. I haven't had anything but cereal for breakfast since 1953." Endquote.
*(Pause)*

MARY: 1953? 1972?

ALEX: Printer's errors?

MARY: Two such errors in one tiny *Times'* item? Not credible.

FANNY: Dickensian character. Looks like something off the bottom of the sea bed. *(Pause)* President. President Nixon. President of what?

ALEX: Some eating club or other. Where men have breakfast, and compare their trophies.

MARY: No. The United States.

FANNY: How do you know?

MARY: I just know. Don't ask me how.

FANNY: I thought McKinley was President.

MARY: Garfield.

ALEX: Taft, you daft duo.

FANNY: Alexandra, the interjection of song lyrics into otherwise civilized conversation is strictly prohibited.

ALEX: Surely not President of the United States. How could a man who hasn't had an egg for breakfast in twenty years be President of the United States?

FANNY: You know, he rather resembles an orangutan in a dinner jacket.

MARY: I could do with some trout.

ALEX: The Grand Tetons are a lovely little range.

FANNY: Someday they will be preserved as a national park by Teddy Roosevelt.

MARY: Teddy Roosevelt?

ALEX: I've never heard of him.

FANNY: Oh, yes you have. Bully bear and San Juan Hill, and all that.

ALEX: No.

FANNY: His statue is in front of the Museum of Natural History.

MARY: In New York? No. It is not. Not when I was there last.

FANNY: Certainly not. That statue will not be erected until 1936.
*(Pause)*

ALEX: Do you know why there is evil in the world?

FANNY: Metaphysical speculation, Alexandra?

**MARY:** I don't think so. Do you?

**ALEX:** Yes, I do.

**FANNY:** You are so young.

**MARY:** Why is there evil in the world, Alexandra?

**ALEX:** To thicken the plot.

(*Pause*)

**FANNY:** I believe you are exactly right.

(**ALEX** *seizes the clipping.*)

**ALEX:** (*Happily*) This is plot thickener!

**MARY:** Yes!

**FANNY:** Yes! Ladies, we are in a strange new world.

**MARY:** Terra Incognita, by definition, could not be otherwise. I have a theory. One that explains the unknown objects. The strange words in our mouths. The references to persons unknown that spring to mind. Spring to mind. It is spring in our minds, ladies. A New World. Blossoming! Within and without! I believe, with each step, each chop of the machete, we are advancing through the wilderness of time as well as space. Chronology as well as geography. Not—as we usually do in savage lands, moving backward into the past, into pre-history—but forward, into the future! A New World, within and without! Beckoning!

(*Pause*)

**FANNY:** A new world! Within and without!

**ALEX:** It would explain the dirigible.

**FANNY:** The clipping from 1972.

**ALEX:** The Nixon.

**MARY:** Mrs. Butterworth. Burma Shave. Cream cheese.

**ALEX:** Robert Lowell. The troll.

**FANNY:** It would explain why, now, burning in my forebrain like a Mosaic tablet, is the copyright date for a novel entitled *Herzog.*

**MARY:** Something else is happening, obviously. Something even more astonishing. Not only are we advancing in time, not only are we encountering the future with every step—(*Beat*) Ladies, we are beginning to know the future! (*Beat*) It is entering into our consciousness. Like mustard gas. Whatever that is. Wait a moment. I'll tell you. (*She osmoses.*) Oh. Oh. Oh. Unfortunate simile. I withdraw it.

**ALEX:** We are absorbing the future! Through osmosis!

**FANNY:** As long as you're at it, osmos Red Chinese for us.

**ALEX:** Let me try. (*She osmoses.*) Something's coming in, yes, like a radio transmission. (*She holds up a hand.*) Don't ask. (*She osmoses.*) Hmmmm.

**FANNY:** Yes?

**ALEX:** Little Red Book. Great Leap Forward. Swimming the Yangtze River. Tractor Operas.

**FANNY:** Operas about tractors?

**ALEX:** Running dogs. And—(*Osmoses.*) They're friends of Nixon!

(*The ladies leap about excitedly.*)

**MARY:** Ladies, this is fantastic. I presume you are feeling—with me—slightly tremulous—a bit fluttery around the gills. Ladies, I don't know about you, but I am experiencing a definite, a palpable—yearning for the future!

**ALEX:** Oh, Mary! Yes! (*Osmoses a moment.*) Radio. Radio is. Oh. I can't believe that! Voices on the air, ladies! Sounds voodoo. You'll just have to osmose your own description.

(*Pause*)

**MARY:** We are imbued with the future.

(*Pause*)

**FANNY:** One doesn't have to like it.

(*Pause*)

**MARY:** Nostalgia for the future.

(*Pause*)

**ALEX:** I shall make my fortune in radio.

(*Pause*)

**MARY:** We shall go from year to year, as if we were going from tribe to tribe.

**ALEX:** Big fun!

(MARY *finds a button in the grass.*)

MARY: Look. Another button. Similar to the one we found our first day on the beach.

FANNY: "Hec—kwhod—ont"?

MARY: Once could be a fluke. Twice is a trend.

ALEX: What what what does the button read, Mary?

MARY: "I—Like—Ike".
(*Pause. Simultaneously*)

MARY, ALEX, AND FANNY: Who's Ike?
(*They laugh. Pause.*)

FANNY: I don't know about all of you, but I do have a sudden craving. A burning desire. Intense, painful longing. (*Beat*) For "Cool Whip."
(*Pause*)

ALEX AND MARY: Hmmmmmmm.
(*The ladies come downstage, grasp hands, and survey their prospects.*)

MARY: Ladies! Let us segue!
(*They disappear in a blaze of light.*)
Act Break

# ACT TWO

## (14) FANMAIL FROM THE FUTURE

(*The ladies are fording a stream, their skirts hiked up.*)

FANNY: Ladies, we are in a strange new world. Where life as we know it is, well, not as we know it.

MARY: Treacherous underfoot. Careful on the bank.

ALEX: You will agree that trousers are eminently more sensible for situations like these.

MARY: Not at all.

FANNY: They'd be drenched. Damp for days at this altitude.

ALEX: You roll them up! You roll them up! You roll them up!

FANNY: Alexandra, collect yourself!

MARY: For all our sakes.
(*They have reached the other side and unhike their skirts.*)

ALEX: You cannot resist the future! It is futile! You must embrace it with all your heart!

FANNY: Alexandra. One has to accept the future. One doesn't have to embrace it.

ALEX: Pendejo!

MARY: Ladies, we are on the frontier of the future.

FANNY: I have always been a pioneer.

MARY: We have been encountering residue from the future. Flotsam from many different moments.

FANNY: "Fanmail" from the future.

MARY: What is "fanmail", Fanny?

FANNY: (*Osmosing*) Mash notes. Autographed glossies. Secret decoder rings.

MARY: Multiple mysteries!
(*A pathway of light. Objects appear in the air before them: a dazzling array of toys and junk and gadgets and souvenirs and appliances and electronic wonders, everything from an acid-pink hula hoop to a silver laser video disc.*)
(*The ladies gasp, delighted.*)

FANNY: "Fallout" from the future!
(*They begin to examine the objects, oooing and murmuring and clucking.*)
(FANNY *tries to osmose an odd toy.*)

FANNY: "Tweezer"! No. "Yo-yo"! No. "Mr. Coffee"! No. My osmos is not quite right.
(ALEX *follows suit.*)

ALEX: "Slot machine." "Juke box." "Squirt gun." "Brass knuckles."
(FANNY *finds a magazine.*)

FANNY: A tabloid "*The National Review*". (*She puts it in her pack.*)

ALEX: "Ovaltine." "Bosco." "Double Bubble." "Velvee-eeta."

MARY: A rain forest of fossils from the future.

ALEX: Oh, look! A mini-dirigible! (*She reads the fine print on an inflatable banana.*) "Not to be used as a life preserver." Hmmmm.
(FANNY *peers into a side-view mirror from an automobile.*)

FANNY: "Objects in mirror may be closer than they appear"? Hmmmm. Well,

Mary, here is your physical evidence. What do you make of it?

MARY: Ladies. We have the artifacts—

(*They hold up their artifacts, including egg beaters and buttons.* FANNY *and* ALEX *have been wearing their egg beaters like pistols.*)

MARY: —we must find their historical moment. Let us camp tonight in this—orchard of the future. Tomorrow we shall enter fully the era that awaits us.

FANNY: I hope with all my heart I shall be able to have a bath. And find a post office.

(ALEX *points at* MARY'S *Ike button.*)

ALEX: Ladies, let us not forget. "Ike" is waiting.

(FANNY *and* ALEX *rotor at one another.*)

JOURNAL ENTRY:

MARY: We spent the night in the future. Around us swirled a silent storm of images, a star shower of light from a new world.

**(15) THE STARRY DEEP**

(*A starry night falls. The ladies pitch a gossamer canopy. They light lanterns. They write in their journals, each by her own light.*)

ALEX: Under a calliope of stars. Below the firmament. The glittering empyrean. The night above the dingle starry. (*Beat*) That's not mine. Damn this interference. (*Beat*) The vasty deep. The starry deep. (*Beat*) Under welkin.

MARY: Difficult to hack one's way through this thicket of voices from the future.

FANNY: Grover, my tender parsnip—shall I ever see you again?

MARY: Notes for a paper for the Boston Geo. I have tentatively dubbed this phenomenon we are experiencing—chronokinesis. (*Beat*) Fanny's tabloids will call it "time travel."

FANNY: Time travel is a tricky business, dear Grover. Beyond our ken.

MARY: Chronokinesis! Life membership in the Boston Geo. The Academy of Arts and Sciences. Honorary membership in the Royal Geo and Academie Française. Director of the Smithsonian. The first woman. The Nobel Prize in physics—

ALEX: My fellow polytopians are splendid and intrepid. Mary is excessively anecdotal, and Fanny scorns my lyrics.

FANNY: Mary and Alexandra are quite sweet, really. Appalling politics. Appalling. If we are detained in this country, I shall order them both a subscription to *The National Review*. I am quite certain you would adore *The National Review*, Grover. I do. It is the sole thing I've so far discovered in the future which reminds me of the nineteenth century.

ALEX: I foresee the day—it is exceedingly easy to foresee the day here—I foresee the day Fanny will eat her words. I shall secure an exclusive recording contract with a multinational conglomerate, and make consecutive gold records. (*Beat*) Note: meditate and osmose what those things are, exactly.

FANNY: The possibility exists that we shall not return, dear Grover. Certainly—in the northern hemisphere—one cannot simply go back and forth in time as one pleases. Time is not a revolving door. We have access to the future here. Do we have egress as well?

ALEX: We are beseiged by a barrage of fact. From here the future looks positively—

MARY: The future looks—

ALEX: The future looks positively—AMERICAN.

FANNY: Loud—

MARY: —invigorating. Quite promising, except, perhaps, for the theatre—which threatens to degenerate into imitations of anthropological kinship studies.

FANNY: We ought to be approaching a post office. Of course, it is a verity that the tropical post will forever be a sink of inefficiency, world without end.

ALEX: I expect to publish these memoirs with an insert of Kodak reproductions. I adore Kodaking.

FANNY: Can the post office deliver to you, in 1889, a letter from me—some decades later? I know they can do it the other way round. That's commonplace.

MARY: I for one am looking forward to meeting this "Ike." "Ike" "Ike" "Ike." "Iko Iko." "Willy and the hand jive."

FANNY: Beyond our ken, dear Grover. Trust you are staying dry. All my love. From Terra Incognita to Terra Haute. Fanny.
(As MARY and FANNY sleep, ALEX comes down and does her journal entry.)
ALEX: (Taking a deep breath) The rare air of the future. Breathe. Aspirate. Aspire. A—spire. (She takes another deep breath.) One of the ecstasies of hiking in the Himalayas was to crest a ridge, and suddenly confront the infinite surround. Mountains and rivers without end. Untouched. Glistening with possibility. We are climbing a spire of time. The topography of the future is coming into view. Unmapped and unnamed. Distant vistas shining. You must not shrink. You must embrace it with all your heart.

## (16) MANNA FROM HEAVEN—OR, AMONG THE JESUITS

(Dawn. The ladies stir, take down the gossamer canopy.)
FANNY: I slept not a wink.
MARY: Nor I.
ALEX: Nor I.
MARY: Fascinating as fire imagery. I long to learn more about "Willy and the Hand Jive."
FANNY: From what little I could fathom, the future seems a dubious prospect.
ALEX: (A sudden transmission) Beep!
FANNY: I beg your pardon.
ALEX: Wrong!
FANNY: Are you contradicting me, young lady?

(ALEX does cheerleader moves.)
ALEX: College bowl! State for twenty! The future is not a dubious prospect! The future is—just a bowl of cherries!
FANNY: Mary, we must locate a translator. Alexandra will soon be totally incomprehensible.
ALEX: Fanny, the future is now!
FANNY: Alexandra. (Sighs) I would elude the future, if I could.
ALEX: Fanny, you must embrace it with all your heart.
FANNY: Why? Why why why why why?
ALEX: Fanny, you sound like a broken record, a busy signal, a car alarm—
FANNY: Alexandra! (Beat) I must accept the future, Alexandra, as I accept the existence of cyclones and pit vipers and bad grammar. But you would have me embrace them?
ALEX: Yes!
FANNY: You would. Cyclones? Pit vipers? Bad grammar?
ALEX: In a way. Yes.
FANNY: You are a feckless child.
ALEX: And you, Fanny, you—are—so—so—so—SQUARE!
(Pause)
FANNY: I have seen the future. And it is slang.
(Pause)
MARY: It is uncommonly close this morning. I must put on a new face.
ALEX: I'll follow suit.
(MARY and ALEX exit.)
(FANNY takes out her letter to GROVER, which has grown into a small volume. She calms herself by writing.)
FANNY: Dearest Grover. Another addendum. As we home in on the future, I begin to feel curiously at ease, and happy. Content. We have been cantering along at a terrific clip. The future looms. (Pause. She opens a music box. It plays.) The future looms as steady and stable as a table top. I anticipate we shall find a year

which suits me perfectly, and settle in for a long refreshment. I shall have a bath. There will be a post office. Oh, dear Grover—I feel we are on the verge of something grand.

(*An elegant gentleman in a beautiful white suit—*MR. COFFEE—*appears at the end of the path.* FANNY *is quite taken with him.*)

MR. COFFEE: Good afternoon, Madame.

FANNY: Sir.

(*He moves to her. He takes two cigarettes from a silver case, lights them, and gives one to her.*)

FANNY: Thank you. (*A little giddy*) And I don't even smoke. (*A sultry dual inhalation*) Oooo. In my day, sir, a lady did not smoke tobacco.

MR. COFFEE: Modern times, Fanny, modern times.

FANNY: Too true.

MR. COFFEE: How are you finding your travels?

FANNY: Trying.

MR. COFFEE: Worth the candle?

FANNY: Without question. (*Beat*) Are you Mr. Coffee?

MR. COFFEE: I've been called worse.

FANNY: I've had a premonition about meeting you.

MR. COFFEE: I'm sure you have.

FANNY: You are not of this era.

MR. COFFEE: No. Not exclusively.

FANNY: Much too well spoken. Let me tell you, Mr. Coffee—language takes a beating in the future.

MR. COFFEE: And that goes double for diction. These things are cyclical, my dear. Do not despair. What goes around, comes around.

FANNY: Is that a local proverb?

MR. COFFEE: One of my favorites. An airmail letter?

FANNY: "Air-mail"? How funny. If you say so.

MR. COFFEE: (*Without looking*) Terre Haute, 1889. Airmail part of the way. Then Pony Express.

FANNY: (*Laughs*) Terre Haute is not Indian Territory, Mr. Coffee. This letter is a long-running serialization by now. I must mail it before the cost of postage becomes absolutely prohibitive.

MR. COFFEE: Preserve it for posterity. A fascinating memoir. You wouldn't want people to forget.

FANNY: Oh, no, it's much too long to copy. I suppose I could edit out the personal parts.

MR. COFFEE: If you venture on into the future, you'll eventually come across something called a xerox.

FANNY: Oh, zeeroxen, I've seen those in Greenland.

(*Pause*)

MR. COFFEE: There is no hope of Grover ever receiving your letter, Fanny.

FANNY: The postal system is worrisome, Mr. Coffee, but not yet hopeless.

(*Pause*)

(FANNY *understands.*)

FANNY: Do you know Grover?

MR. COFFEE: We've met.

FANNY: Recently?

MR. COFFEE: Seems like only yesterday. But I have no sense of time.

FANNY: How was he? Was he dry?

MR. COFFEE: Dry as toast. Frankly, he's been better. Bit of a cough. His wife was not unduly concerned.

FANNY: I'm his wife.

MR. COFFEE: His second wife. He had you declared legally dead, dear. Terre Haute Superior Court, 1910.

FANNY: That man.

MR. COFFEE: Remarried a few years later.

FANNY: He never minded being alone when we were married.

MR. COFFEE: The Great War made him anxious. And wealthy.

FANNY: I thought those were new shoes. He came to me, Mr. Coffee. In a dream. (*Beat*) He told me not to speculate on the future.

MR. COFFEE: In his own brokerish fashion, Grover was trying to say—so long.

FANNY: So long. So long. (*Beat*) When did you last see Grover, Mr. Coffee?

MR. COFFEE: Our one and only meeting. October, 1929.

(*Pause*)

FANNY: How—?

MR. COFFEE: He hurled himself off the top of a grain silo.

FANNY: Oh, dear.

MR. COFFEE: Part of a gentle rain of brokers who fell from heaven that autumn all over the country.

FANNY: I've been out of touch.

MR. COFFEE: Grover was speculating on the commodities market. Blue sky ventures. You know. Futures.

FANNY: Blue sky ventures. Did he miss me?

MR. COFFEE: Very much, once he realized you were never coming home from Terra Incognita. Less and less, over the years. He'd get a little misty on the seminal holidays. Christmas. Easter. Arbor Day. Each and every Arbor Day he'd have three or four peppermint schnapps, in your memory, and plant a bush in the back yard. (*Beat*) At heart, he wasn't surprised you never returned from Terra Incognita. He'd always suspected you'd disappear one day. Vanish without a trace.

FANNY: Yes. He was always rather taken aback whenever I walked through the front door. Well. Thank you, Mr. Coffee.

MR. COFFEE: My pleasure.

FANNY: Tell me, Mr. Coffee. Do you find it easy to foresee the future?

MR. COFFEE: I've never had any trouble.

FANNY: No. I don't suppose you would.

MR. COFFEE: But I confine myself to the basics.

FANNY: We will meet again, I trust.

MR. COFFEE: I feel certain of it.

FANNY: But not for many years.

MR. COFFEE: You never know. (*He takes her hand.*)

FANNY: I have been wanting to speak to you.

MR. COFFEE: Yes. Here I am, after all. (*Kisses her hand.*) A bien tot.

FANNY: Vaya con dios, Mr. Coffee.

MR. COFFEE: Charming. See you later. Alligator.

(*He exits. Passing* MARY *and* ALEX.)

MR. COFFEE: Ladies. (*He disappears.*)

MARY: Who on earth was that?

ALEX: (*Osmosing*) That was "Bebe Rebozo"!

FANNY: That was Mr. Coffee.

ALEX: Oh. Really. Sometimes this osmosing is wildly inaccurate.

MARY: The multiple possibilities of the future, dear. A man might be Mr. Coffee, or he might be Bebe Rebozo. What's his line?

FANNY: Prognostication. He had news. We're on the right track.

MARY: Splendid. Saddle up.

(ALEX *and* MARY *pick up their stuff and start off.*)

JOURNAL ENTRY:

FANNY: (FANNY, *after a moment, silently folds the letter, tucks it away, and closes the music box.*)

## (17) VINTAGE CRYSTAL

(*Moonlight. A beautiful unearthly snow begins to fall.*)

ALEX: What is that?

FANNY: Snow. Unless I miss my guess.

ALEX: Cold and wet on the tongue. Melts right off.

FANNY: Snow it is.

ALEX: Like no snow I've known before.

FANNY: A new snow. A strange snow. An unknown snow.

MARY: Lambent. Luminous.

ALEX: Snow from the moon, ladies!

FANNY: Yes!

MARY: Yes! Lunar snow is not annoying!

(ALEX *catches snow and tastes.*)

ALEX: Lunar snow is, despite its apparent immaturity, a vintage precipitate. Coarser and sweeter than Himalayan, it stands up to all but the most robust Karakoram. Fruitier than Rocky Mountain powder, and a touch more acidic than Vermont sludge, it is altogether full-bodied and elusive. This is a young snow but not a callow snow, and should be confronted early—like the finest Hindu Kush—before the blush is off the slush, and the bloom is gone.

**(18) WOODY'S ESSO**
(Music: "Rock Around the Clock" *playing on a radio. A gas pump and an Esso sign appear. Music fades out.*)

ALEX: Civilization.

MARY: The outskirts.

FANNY: How far our standards have fallen.

ALEX: If I were wearing trousers at this moment, I would change.

FANNY: (*An outburst*) You needn't suck up to me, Alexandra!

MARY: Fanny! Is that a vulgarity?
(*A pause*)

FANNY: I am sorry, Alexandra. I plead the future.

ALEX: I understand.

FANNY: You needn't mollify me, is what I meant. It seems to me that you were right.

ALEX: How nice. About what, dear Fanny?

FANNY: Trousers. Trousers trousers trousers. It seems clear to me that everyone in the future wears 'em. I am so glad I shan't live to see it. Of course, I am seeing it. I am so flummoxed. I wonder if we will remember all this when we return home.

MARY: If we return home.
(*A palanquin, with its shades drawn, rolls on. On it, a sign: The Dragon Lady, Fortunes Told, Palms Read, Charts, Crystal Ball, Tarot Cards, Etc.*)

MARY: I know what that is—

ALEX: A "hot rod."

MARY: A palanquin.

FANNY: Honestly, Alexandra, how quickly you've forgotten our own era.

MARY: Do you realize that palanquin is now an antique?

FANNY: So are we, my dear, so are we.

MARY: But what is it doing here? (*Indicates gas pump*) And what is that? And who is The Dragon Lady?

FANNY: Warrants investigation.
(*They start forward. A hand with long painted fingernails pulls back the shade suddenly, startling the ladies. It is MADAME NHU, who is wearing a beautiful if slightly ferocious half-mask. The eyes of the mask are Asian, the cheekbones high, and she wears a wig of long, jet-black hair. The effect is at once feminine and frightening. She looks them over. Her voice is low (not falsetto), and she speaks with a slight accent, both French and Asian.*)

MME. NHU: Come closer. Let me scrutinize you.
(*They approach cautiously. MME. NHU holds up a hand. They stop. After a moment, she begins to speak.*)

MME. NHU: Serious trouble will pass you by. Your mind is filled with new ideas—make use of them. He who does not accept cash when offered is no businessman. You are worrying about something that will never happen. Your talents will be recognized and suitably rewarded. You will never need to worry about a steady income. Soon you will be sitting on top of the world. The night life is for you. Praise your wife, even if it frightens her. You have an unusual equipment for success, be sure to use it properly. Be as soft as you can be and as hard as you have to be. Someone is speaking well of you. A new diet or exercise program can be unusually beneficial for you now. An unpleasant situation will soon be cleared to your satisfaction. Read more fine books and better magazines. Avoid fried foods, which angry up the blood. Let them eat barbecue!
(*A pause.*)
(*The ladies look at one another.*)

(MME. NHU *thrusts out a plate with three fortune cookies on it. They each take a cookie.*)

MME. NHU: Let me tell you secret. The future is now. (*She pulls the shade and disappears.*)

ALEX: That was an image.

MARY: An oracle.

FANNY: Inscrutable.

ALEX: What are these? (*Osmoses*) "Fortune cookies"!

MARY: No smell.

FANNY: No taste.

ALEX: Edible?

FANNY: Definitely not.

MARY: (*Breaks hers open.*) Inside—a scrap of paper.

ALEX: (*Likewise*) A message.

FANNY: (*Likewise*) Fanmail from some flounder.

(*They read their messages.*)

ALEX: You will become rich and famous.

FANNY: You will meet a tall dark stranger.

MARY: You will go on a long journey.

ALEX: This is exhilarating!

(*She approaches the palanquin, steps on an invisible rubber-tube gas station bell. It chimes: ding-dong, ding-dong.*)

(GUS, *a fresh-faced American teenager, appears, wearing a baseball cap and chewing gum. Boundless energy.*)

GUS: Hi! What'll it be? Hey! Wow! Gosh! Hello!

FANNY: Greetings, young man, from President McTaft.

GUS: Swell feathers and fancy duds! You ladies look kinda like Kitty! Golly! You goin' to the prom or what! Gosh!

ALEX: Kitty?

GUS: Didja watch *Gunsmoke* last night? Or *Cimarron City*?

ALEX: Kitty?

GUS: Kitty see she runs the saloon and she's in love with Marshall Dillon who's the sheriff but he'll never marry her cause he's a bachelor—see *Bachelor Father?*

FANNY: My dear boy, a bachelor father is a paradox. An oxymoron. A contradiction in terms.

ALEX: Ladies—the future.

FANNY: (*Snorts*) Bachelor father. Mary, you have found your niche. Your prurient interest in anthropological smut should stand you in good stead. Bachelor father.

MARY: Oh, Fanny. Let us introduce ourselves.

ALEX: I'm Alexandra. This is Mary—

MARY: Hello, young man.

ALEX: And this is Fanny.

GUS: Hi! Hi! Hi! I'm Gus!

ALEX: Good afternoon, Gus.

GUS: Great! Wow, you ladies are kooky, no offense.

ALEX: How nice of you to say so.

FANNY: Gus, we are so very pleased to meet you. You are the first person we have encountered in our travels with a reasonable accent and an acceptable demeanor.

GUS: Lucky for me, huh? You ladies broke down somewhere? I don't see your eggbeater. Say, who do you like in the Series? The Dodgers or the Yanks?

(*Pause. Finally,* ALEX *smiles sweetly and says judiciously:*)

ALEX: Whom do you like?

GUS: I like the Dodgers.

ALEX: Then so do I.

GUS: Great!

MARY: Gus, dear, tell us about the palanquin.

ALEX: About the Dragon Lady.

MARY: A lady of ferocious aspect.

GUS: Madame Nhu.

ALEX: Madame Who?

GUS: Madame Nhu. She rents a parking space from Woody.

MARY: How did Madame Nhu and her palanquin happen to land here?

GUS: Just showed up one day. Out of the blue.

FANNY: Gus, dear, what year is it?

GUS: You don't know?! Come off it.

ALEX: We do not know. Honestly. It's hard to explain.

GUS: 1955. Everybody knows that.

ALEX: We don't.

GUS: Gee, I'm sorry. I'd give you a calendar—(*Blushes*) but they're not for girls. (*Beat*) Hey, you guys are kidding me. Huh? Huh? Come on, lay off. Just 'cause I'm a teenager.

MARY: What's a teenager?

FANNY: What's an Esso?

GUS: Esso is service, parts and dependability. So you're tourists, huh? I thought you had to be, I woulda remembered *you*.

MARY: Travelers, not tourists.

ALEX: Polytopians. Travelers to many lands.

FANNY: Charting the unknown.

MARY: Geography, cartography, ethnology, and the natural sciences.

GUS: Great. I could use a vacation myself. You need anything? Soda, gum, roadmaps, oil? Chiclets?

ALEX: I would like a "Chiclet", please.

GUS: Take two, they're small.

(GUS *gives* ALEX *some Chiclets. She examines them, pops them into her mouth, and chews.*)

GUS: Where you ladies from?

MARY: We are traveling through time, Gus.

GUS: You dames are some kidders. No? You mean it? You're on the level? Wow! Like you're from another time?! Another dimension?! PARALLEL UNIVERSE?! Wait'll I tell my Dad! I saw this show— (*Beat as he looks them over.*) Wow, so this is how they dress in history! Gee! Do you wanna come to my social studies class? So, do you believe in UFOs?

ALEX: Chiclets are sweet and tough, like dried manioc.

FANNY: Ah, Gus. We are looking for someone. Perhaps you know him.

ALEX: Ike.

MARY: Perhaps you've heard of him.

GUS: Ike who?

ALEX: We do not know his surname.

MARY: We found his name on this button.

GUS: Nicky might know. He knows everybody.

(MARY *hands* GUS *the button.*)

GUS: Ho ho.

FANNY: You know this Ike.

GUS: Yeah, sure I know this Ike. Hangs out at the station. Wants to be a grease monkey in his spare time. I'm showing him the ropes. You guys. Whatta buncha kidders.

ALEX: You don't know him?

GUS: My dad voted for him. Come on. What are ya, gonna vote for that other clown, the Chicago egghead? "I Like Ike." Great.

ALEX: Do you like Ike, Gus?

GUS: My dad likes him! I betcha Nicky knows this Ike. 'Sides, you wanna stay there while you're in Peligrosa, doncha? Hold on, let me draw you a map. (*He disappears.*)

ALEX: Mary! Fanny! Facts!

FANNY: Chronological and geographical. We are in Peligrosa!

MARY: In the vicinity of 1955!

ALEX: Perhaps 1955 is the apotheosis of the future!

FANNY: This Ike must be a local Poobah!

ALEX: We shall palaver.

(GUS *reappears, with a map.*)

GUS: Okay, dokey, here's directions to Nicky's.

MARY: Is it far?

GUS: Just a hop skip and a jump. We're giving these away with a full tank. But for you guys—it's on the house.

(GUS *hands* MARY *an egg beater of yet a third design.*)

MARY: Marvelous! A matched set!

ALEX: Ladies! Whip them out!

(FANNY *and* ALEX *whip out their egg beaters. They all rotor and laugh. From this point on, the* LADIES *always wear their egg-beaters.*)

GUS: You collect 'em?!? I'd give you green stamps, but Woody'd kill me if—

FANNY: Gus, dear, does this Nicky fellow have a bath?

GUS: Nicky's—are you kidding? Does he have a bath? Are you kidding? He's got everything! He'll probably put you up. Wait'll you see the set-up at Nicky's. You are gonna flip!

FANNY: Hooper do! (*She grabs the map.*) Gus, my undying devotion. Ladies—dog my heels.

ALEX: Adieu, Gus.

GUS: See you later, alligator.

MARY: Thank you, Gus. Perhaps we'll pass this way again.

GUS: After awhile, crocodile.

MARY: Ah, Gus! The Mighty Silurian!

GUS: Whatever you say, lady. Give Nicky some skin for me.

MARY: Whatever you say, Gus.
(GUS *exits.*)
(*Traveling music throbs: The theme from* Peter Gunn. *The ladies travel. They reach a spot, and huddle around a map.*)

MARY: X marks the spot.
(Peter Gunn *fades away.*)

ALEX: Have we misread it?

FANNY: Impossible. But perhaps we've passed it.

ALEX: My eyes were peeled.

FANNY: In time. Perhaps we've passed it in time. Perhaps it was here once. But now it's gone.

MARY: I think not. I have an unshakable conviction we have come to the center of 1955.

ALEX: Smack dab in the middle.

MARY: Well said, Alex.

FANNY: If the map's right, and the time's right, where the devil is this Nicky fellow? I'll horsewhip anyone who stands between me and a hot bath.

ALEX: I broke up a knife fight with a whip once. Oh, yes I did. Two sherpas were vying for a place by the fire.
(*Strains of Big Band music.*)

MARY: Do you hear that music?

FANNY: A mynah bird escaped from a cocktail lounge.

ALEX: Fanny, you redefine pessimism. What is a "cocktail lounge"?

FANNY: Osmose it yourself.

ALEX: (*Osmosing*) "Happy Hour"!
(*A loud burst of Big Band music.*)

MARY: Ladies—I believe we're on the verge!
(*All three ladies do journal entry in unison.*)

ALEX, MARY, AND FANNY: We arrive in '55!

**(19) PARADISE '55**
(*Lights! A flashy sign, neon:* NICKY'S. *Some palm trees and streamers: A gaudy, prerevolutionary Havana-style nightclub.*)
(NICKY *rolls on with a piano and live mike. Does a splashy finish.*)

NICKY: Vaya! Vaya! Vaya! Con! Diós! Wo Wo Wo Wo Wo—yeaaaaaah! Pow!
(*The ladies applaud.*)

NICKY: You're too kind.
(*Checks them out.*)

NICKY: My my my my my my my. Holy cow. What have we here. Our humble joint. Nicky's Peligrosa Paradise Bar and Grill. Graced by style, beauty, pulchritude and wit. Hi, I'm Nicky Paradise. Welcome to paradise—where hospitality still means something.

ALEX: (*Instantly smitten*) O brave new world, that has such creatures in it!

FANNY: Alex, you are a terrible plagiarist.

MARY: Instantly smitten.

NICKY: Make yourselves at home. (*His best smile*) Mi casa es su casa! (*Reprise—best smile*) My house is your house. Toss back a coupla stiff ones, grab a bite, cool out in the casino, catch a show, let your hair down, loosen your corsets—

MARY, FANNY, AND ALEX: Mr. Nicky!

NICKY: Please. Nicky.

ALEXANDRA: Alexandra Cafuffle.

FANNY: Mrs. Cranberry. You may call me Fanny.

NICKY: It would break my heart if I couldn't.

MARY: Mary Baltimore. From Boston.

NICKY: Such tropicana, such femminality. Overwhelmed, truly.
(*He dashes to the piano and plays and sings a phrase of "BAD BOY."*)

NICKY: "I'm just a bad boy-oy-oy-oy-oy-oy-oy-oy-oy-oy-oy—
All dressed up in fancy clothes
I am takin' the trouble
To blow all my bubbles away."

ALEX: Mr. Paradise!

NICKY: Nicky.

FANNY: Mr. Paradise—

NICKY: Nicky, Nicky, Nicky!

FANNY: Nicky, Nicky, Nicky. I hope you won't think me indelicate—

NICKY: Never.

FANNY: —but I simply must have a scrub immediately. Post haste. It's been eons. Can you arrange for me to have a bath?

NICKY: For you, Fanny—a whirlpool. (*He snaps his fingers and plays the piano. A light appears.*) Follow that light, Fanny. Don't be stingy with the bubbles. That's what they're there for.

FANNY: Bubbles. I won't ask. I'll just hold my nose and dive in. Ladies.
(*She exits.*)

NICKY *sings and plays after her:* "Vaya Con Diós My Darling/Vaya Con Diós My Love.")

MARY: Nicky's Peligrosa Paradise Bar and Grill?

NICKY: Be there or—(*Smiles his best smile*) be square.
(*MARY holds out her button.*)

MARY: Perhaps you can shed some light.

NICKY: Oh yeah. I like Ike. Who doesn't?

MARY: Who don't?

NICKY: Have it your way, Mary. I'm easy.

MARY: I like Ike. Heck, who don't?

NICKY: Hardly anybody.
(*MARY pulls out the original button she found on the beach.*)

MARY: Indeed. "Heckwhodon't?" Heck—who—don't. It's a companion button. I like Ike. Heck, who don't?

NICKY: You're sharp. Need a job?

ALEX: Brava, Mary! I love a good mystery, don't you?
(*MARY pins the buttons on ALEX.*)

MARY: Do you know him? Gus said you might.

ALEX: We would very much like to meet him.

MARY: He has become a point of some interest with us.

ALEX: Do you know this Ike?

NICKY: We're like this. Never vacations anywhere but Nicky's. He and Mamie are nuts about the joint. He's gonna make Nicky's a national monument.

ALEX: Is he in residence at present?

NICKY: Yeah, he's in back, smoking a cigar. I'll take you around.

ALEX: Oh, goody. I'll Kodak him for posterity!

NICKY: You'll like Ike. Everybody does. He's a likeable guy. Plays a fair round of golf. No duffer, Ike. You play?

MARY: The Scottish game? No. Speaking of games, am I correct in understanding that there is a gambling emporium on the premises?

NICKY: The casino. First rate. Slap a little blackjack, shoot some craps, spin the wheel, pull some slots, float a check. Whatever.

MARY: Gambling provides a fascinating study in cross-cultural comparisons. For instance, did you know that the Ute Indians of the American West are avid gamblers, and will wager their life's possessions on a single throw of the dice?

NICKY: No, I did not know that. Did you know that the Nevada looney bins are full of catatonic blue-haired ladies going like this? (*He demonstrates: catatonic slot-machine addicts plus sound effects.*)

**MARY:** No, I did not. Fascinating. I do not indulge, personally, of course, but with your permission, I should like to take notes.

(**NICKY** *hands her some chips.*)

**NICKY:** Have a ball, Mar'—knock yourself out.

(*He snaps his fingers, plays the piano. A light appears.*)

**MARY:** Not annoying! (*She follows the light. As she is about to exit, she turns;*) Ah, Nicky. Gus said to give you some of his skin.

**NICKY:** Thanks, doll.

(*She exits.* **NICKY** *plays, sings after her:* "There Goes My Baby/Movin' On Down the Line.")

(*He turns his attentions to* **ALEX**)

**NICKY:** Great kid, Gus.

**ALEX:** He drew us a map. That is how we located you.

**NICKY:** No, it's not.

**ALEX:** I beg your pardon.

**NICKY:** I said, that's not how you came to Nicky's, Al.

**ALEX:** Are you contradicting me?

**NICKY:** It wasn't a map that brought you to me, Al. It was—(*Best smile*) Kismet.

**ALEX:** I don't understand.

**NICKY:** You were destined to come to Nicky's.

**ALEX:** Perhaps you're right. I do have a positive feeling about 1955. It's—it's—it's—keen!

**NICKY:** I'm having a great year. So you stopped at Woody's. See the Dragon Lady?

**ALEX:** Madame Nhu?

**NICKY:** Madame Nhu. She's usually parked out front, filing her foot-long nails.

**ALEX:** Lovely palanquin.

**NICKY:** Isat what it is? I thought it was a chopped Chevy. Ike should be done with his cigar now. Want to meet him?

**ALEX:** Desperately.

(**NICKY** *snaps his fingers, plays the piano. A light.*)

**NICKY:** Second door on the right. Knock three times. If Mamie answers, come back. We'll do it later.

**ALEX:** At long last, Ike! I'm off to meet the Ike! Ta! Ike get a kick out of you! Ike, can't get you out of my mind!

**NICKY:** Hold your hula hoops! Al, you aren't, by any chance, a lyricist?

**ALEX:** How did you guess?

**NICKY:** I can spot talent! I could use a good word jockey. Meet me in the lounge later. We'll pen some tunes. I have a lucrative new contract to script some billboards for Burma Shave.

**ALEX:** Fantastic! I've been dying to know what Burma Shave is.

**NICKY:** Al, I told you. Kismet.

**ALEX:** Ike can't get no satisfaction!

(*She exits. As* **NICKY** *styles on the piano* **FANNY** *enters, resplendent and transformed in 50's cocktail dress and blonde wig, still wearing eggbeater.*)

**NICKY:** Holy smokes! I have not seen duds like that since High-School Confidential.

(*He sweeps* **FANNY** *off her feet.*)

**NICKY:** What do you say we trip the light fantastic?

(*They do a slow romantic dance to Duke Ellington's* Dual Highway, **NICKY** *showing* **FANNY** *some sharp moves.* **FANNY** *grows more confident with every step. By the end of the dance, they are falling in love. They finish the dance and go to the table.*)

**NICKY:** Fred and Ginger have nothing on us—nothing! (*Gets intimate.*) Say, do you remember those little Danny Boone hats with the wacky raccoon tails?

**FANNY:** I'm afraid not.

**NICKY:** They were a gas. How was the whirlpool?

(*After a sensuous pause,* **FANNY** *says:*)

**FANNY:** Wow—Wow—Wow! Captivating. All those little jets of water were—quite—mesmerizing. I feel light-headed. Swoozy all over. (*Beat*) Jacuzzi all over.

**NICKY:** I don't follow you.

FANNY: Your whirlpool is called a jacuzzi. Or will be.

NICKY: I like the sound of that. Jacuzz'.

FANNY: Your establishment is uncanny. A veritable pleasure dome.

NICKY: I like to think of it that way. (*She pulls out one of her postcards.*)

FANNY: It's just like my postcard.

NICKY: Hey! Where did you get this? These are sharp!

FANNY: I brought it with me. It's a postcard from the future. Of Nicky's. The view come true! Generic nightspot.

NICKY: Like I always say, Fanny—the future is now. I'm gonna put 'em in all the rooms with the Gideon Bibles.

FANNY: Mister Paradise—

NICKY: Hey, I'm gonna get cross wit' you—

FANNY: Nicky. Since we've been in the vicinity of 1955, there's something I've had a craving for—

NICKY: Please. Say no more. (*He prestidigitates a huge glass goblet and two spoons. As* FANNY *closes her eyes—*)

FANNY: I am agog with anticipation. (*He holds the goblet under her nose. She inhales deeply, with ecstasy, and slowly opens her eyes.*)

FANNY: Cool Whip!

NICKY: The Real McCoy. (*He hands her a spoon. They each dish out a spoonful of Cool Whip. They lock eyes. They lock arms, as though drinking champagne. They raise the spoons to their lips.*)

NICKY: Here's to you—Fanny. (*They clink spoons. They take a bite. A dazzled pause.*)

FANNY: Oh! good! (*Freeze. Music swells.* NICKY *and* FANNY *exit.*)

(ALEX *enters and does journal entry.*)

ALEX: (*Formally, still, a bit out of rhythm, and trying to snap her fingers, perhaps using* NICKY'S *Mike.*)
> On the go or at the beach
> After hours or safe at home

> For a cheek as smooth as a Georgia peach
> You need the shave that's like a poem—
> Burma Shave!

## (20) LATER THAT SAME EVENING

(ALEX *moves to the table and examines Cool Whip.*)

ALEX: (*Osmoses*) "Mo hair". No. "Jello mold". No. (*Tastes*) Noxema! Yes! Heaven!
(MARY *enters, to a swirl of music, tipsy and exhilarated.*)

MARY: I have experienced an epiphany in the casino. I beat the one-armed bandit, kid! As they say here in 1955. Look! (*She pours a cascade of nickels out of her helmet onto the table.*)

ALEX: Fantastic! I love the future!

MARY: And how did you do, Alexandra? Did you run the elusive Ike to ground? Tree him? Beard him in his lair?

ALEX: Mamie answered.

MARY: You'll collar him tomorrow. Quite a card, Ike. Una tarjeta, en español. Not many people know that.

ALEX: And how do you know that?

MARY: A bulletin from the future.

ALEX: What else does your bulletin tell you about Ike?
(MARY *osmoses.*)

MARY: He is a poobah of the first water. Golf clubs. Cardigan sweaters. (*Rubs her head.*) Cue ball.

ALEX: Cue ball?

MARY: (*With great dignity*)
> "He has got a cue ball head that is hard as lead—
> But he is all right with me.
> Wo wo."

ALEX: Mary.

MARY: It is extraordinary what blossoms in one's brain in this country. That is from something called—(*Osmoses*) "Rock and roll."

ALEX: "Rock and roll" . . . Whomp bop a lula a wombat too!

(*She then scats the guitar part to the Surfari's* WIPEOUT!, *doing 50's rock moves, and ending with a big finish.*)

ALEX: Wombat!

MARY: My. Osmosing the future is far more strenuous than navigating the upper reaches of the Congo.

ALEX: The January 1955 *Variety* magazine says rock and roll will be gone by June. Oh! What month are we?

MARY: I've no idea.

ALEX: I hope it's not June. I am dieting to rock and roll. I mean determined. Not dieting.

MARY: Hello, what's this? Manioc? (*She takes a spoonful of Cool Whip.*)

ALEX: Noxema.

MARY: Have you tried it?

ALEX: Mmm. The texture is indescribable.

MARY: (*Takes a big bite—savors*) Why, this is sheer heaven, Alexandra.

(FANNY *floats on, now in a tight evening dress, looking blowzy and wonderful; still wearing her eggbeater.*)

FANNY: More than sheer heaven, Mary. Paradise.

ALEX: You look the cat that swallowed the canary.

FANNY: We were dancing!

ALEX: Really.

FANNY: Nicky is a divine dancer.

ALEX: Have some Noxema.

FANNY: Cool Whip!

ALEX: Oh!

MARY: So this is Fanny's Cool Whip!

FANNY: Luscious, isn't it? I had the most extraordinary experience earlier this evening in a celestial contraption called a jacuzzi.

MARY: You should have seen the ecdysiastical "floor show" in the casino. The natives call it *Girls A Poppin'!* As fascinating as fire. From an anthropological point of view. Reminiscent of the vernal fertility rites in Sumatra, which always culminated in a riot of gymnastic—

FANNY: Mary, spare us your salacious anthropological details.

MARY: Remarkably supple. A cornucopia of concupiscence.

ALEX: Ladies—get a load of this! I am osmosing jingles like crazy! (*She licks a finger, presses it to her hip, makes a sizzling sound, and uses* NICKY's *mike.*)

    Okay, tiger, striped and brave
    A close clean scrape is what you crave
    To fashion's whim you are no slave
    You take if off—with Burma Shave!

FANNY: Wow! Wow! Wow!

ALEX: Jingles are the art form of the future!

FANNY: Why do they call it Burma Shave? What's it got to do with Burma?

MARY: I've been to Burma.

FANNY: As have I.

ALEX: The future is not dull!

FANNY: This is not the future, Alexandra. This is 1955.

MARY: Not annoying!

FANNY: Not bad! And that jacuzzi is really something.

(ALEX *dishes out a spoonful of Cool Whip. The others follow suit.*)

ALEX: To the future!

MARY: To us!

ALEX: To yetis and dirigibles—

FANNY: Jacuzzis—

MARY: To our adventures, many more!

ALEX: And here's to the elusive Ike!

(*They all clink spoons.*)

ALL: Cheers! Ike!

(*They all take a bite. A dazzled pause.*)

ALL: Oh, good!

(*Lights change.* FANNY *and* ALEX *exit.* MARY *comes downstage and does her Journal Entry.*)

MARY: The pleasures of Nicky's Peligrosa Paradise Bar and Grill were—philharmonic. I blossomed into—I almost blush to recall it—a bonafide voluptuary, sampling an assortment of what

were called, in the native parlance, 'lei-
sure-time activities'. Re-creation. The casino was an anthropologist's field day,
an anthology of human mis-demeanor.
It's fascinating as fire floorshow, *Girls-A-
Poppin'!*, held, I felt, the key to the culture, and was worth years of intense
scrutiny. Television proved an addictive,
if ultimately incomprehensible, hyp-
notic. And I thought the jacuzzi the
greatest piece of engineering since the
wheel. In short, I went, as the topical
lingo had it, on a "bender." (*Beat*)

   The Byzantine pleasures of Nicky's
intoxicate—but do not satiate. I flash and
yearn for adventures beyond the jacuzzi.

### (21) GO-GO BOOTS—OR,
### ROCK AND ROLL IS HERE TO STAY

(**FANNY** *and* **ALEX** *enter. It is some months later:*
**FANNY** *is wearing a sensible 50's sun dress and*
**ALEX** *is dressed in pedal pushers, carrying a surfboard.* **FANNY** *has a picnic basket and cooler. Both
wear eggbeaters.*)

**ALEX:** (*To* **FANNY**) I've yet to catch a glimpse
   of him. That Mamie guards him like a
   gryphon.

**FANNY:** Perhaps Ike is a yeti.

**ALEX:** Mary—look what I found! Surfboard!

**MARY:** What is the cultural application of a
   surfboard, Alexandra?

**ALEX:** Hang ten. Shoot the pipeline. Curl the
   Big Kahuna.

**MARY:** Whatever you say, Alex.

   (**FANNY** *pulls out a pair of white boots.*)

**FANNY:** Alexandra may have her surfboard,
   but I have my "go-go boots". A white
   ceremonial shoe. Worn while mashing
   potatoes, riding ponies, and palavering
   with the Watusi.

**MARY:** I've found a tile. (*She holds up a green
   tile.*)

**FANNY:** Terra cotta?

**MARY:** Congoleum.

**FANNY:** Congoleum. What's it got to do with
   the Congo?

**MARY:** I know not.

**FANNY:** I've been to the Congo.

**MARY:** As have I.

**ALEX:** Mary, you are the ginchiest. Hang in
   there.

**MARY:** I shall. I shall hang in there. I owe
   you a great debt, Alexandra.

**ALEX:** No prob, Mar'. No sweat. No skin off
   my nose.

**FANNY:** Alexandra. Only a moment in 1955,
   and already your language is beyond redemption.

**ALEX:** Loosen your living girdle, Fanny.

**MARY:** Ah, Alexandra, how are your jingles?

**ALEX:** I've given them up for rock and roll.

**FANNY:** A fleeting fad.

**ALEX:** Fanny, rock 'n roll is here to stay. So,
   when's the shindig?

**MARY:** Shingdig?

**FANNY:** I believe she means the authentic
   suburban charred meat festival you
   promised us.

**MARY:** Ah, yes. The bar-be-cue.

**ALEX:** Yes, what are we having—barbecued
   manioc?

**FANNY:** I am so excited. I haven't set foot
   outside the Paradise since our arrival.
   (**MARY** *picks up her pack, which is fully
   rigged out for trekking.*)

**FANNY:** Mary! Where on Earth is this picnic?
   You have enough gear for a trek.

**MARY:** I have discovered within myself a
   new world. A voluptuousness which as-
   tounds me with its magenta sunsets, its
   incarnadine passions, its indigo fevers,
   tropical storms, and throbbing scarlet
   heart. Having discovered my voluptu-
   ous inclination, I have no intention of
   leaving it unexplored. Ladies—the future beckons! Don't you see? What we all
   need is further adventures!

**ALEX:** Oh, Mary, yes!

**FANNY:** Might be nice. A few days trek. See
   something of the hinterlands.

**MARY:** I had in mind going on.

**ALEX:** Oh, I don't want to go back.

MARY: Not back. On.

FANNY: I adore 1955. It would break my heart, to leave. (*Beat*) I love this. The occasional barbecue. (*Beat*) Entre nous— we're engaged!

MARY *and* ALEX: Oh, Fanny!

FANNY: Thank you. We are very happy. The night Nicky popped the question, I was agog with anticipation. Yes I said yes yes oh yes I will my mountain flower as well you as another my flower of Andulusia and the pink and blue and yellow houses—(*Stops herself*) Goodness.

ALEX: What would Grover say?

FANNY: Ah, Grover, dear Grover, my tender parsnip. Grover will have apoplexy. You know, I can scarcely recall what Grover looks like. His face is fading from my memory like a hand-tinted picture postcard. I never told you. Grover passed on in 1929. Did away with himself, poor dear.

MARY: Poor Fanny. How do you know?

FANNY: Mr. Coffee told me. That man. Did you know he had me declared legally dead?

ALEX: No!

MARY: Well, three cheers for you, Fanny. (*Turns to* ALEX) Alex? There are new worlds out there. Where the air is rare.

ALEX: I have a date. I'm writing tunes with the Gorge Troll. We've got an offer from the House O' Hits. They want to buy our new number, *Mind Your Own Beeswax.* Then we're going for a spin on his chopper. Now that I know what a chopper is. (*Pause*)

MARY: It seems a shame to break up the team.

ALEX: You don't have to. (*Pause*)

MARY: Perhaps we are meant to be solo sojourners after all. (*Pause*)

FANNY: I'll go scout out a spot to fire up the briquets.

ALEX: I'll follow suit.

(*As they leave:*)

FANNY: Are you reading your subscription to *The National Review?*

ALEX: Troll and I are writing tunes. I haven't time for arcane political journals.

FANNY: Not arcane. Germane.

ALEX: That's not a true rhyme. But it's not bad.

FANNY: High praise.

(*They're gone.*)

(*Nicky's Peligrosa disappears as* MARY *comes downstage and does her Journal Entry.*)

MARY: My brain is full of exhilirating bulletins. On the horizon, a transcendent light flashes off the spires of the future. This New World is a garden. Splendors and wonders, marvels and mysteries. Miracles which top even Cool Whip.

**(22) THE GEOGRAPHY OF YEARNING**

(ALEX *enters, in motorcycle leathers.*)

ALEX: Nothing shall ever replace Cool Whip in my affections. So. You're really going?

MARY: Yes.

ALEX: Seems a shame.

MARY: I'm restless. Wanderlust. You know.

ALEX: I have a faint recollection. (*Beat*) I do feel a tug. But I belong here.

MARY: This is what you wanted. The show business.

ALEX: It's Kismet. Here in 1955 is my brilliant career. I am part of the entertainment industry.

MARY: Good for you.

ALEX: I am wanton.

MARY: Alex.

ALEX: I mean weepy. Not wanton.

(*They embrace.* FANNY *enters, dressed for bowling.*)

FANNY: You're still here. Thank goodness. Alexandra, what a get up.

(ALEX *shoots a look at* FANNY'S *own get-up.*)

MARY: Dear Fanny.

FANNY: I do have a bit of a hankering to hit the trail with you, old friend. But 1955 suits me. To a T-Bird. Nicky is such a—dancer.

MARY: Will you invite Ike to the wedding?

FANNY: Entre nous, he's Nicky's best man.

ALEX: Goody! I'll Polaroid him for posterity.

(NICKY *enters, also ready to bowl a few frames.*)

NICKY: Fan, you look sensational, doll. Al, I ran your latest lyric up the flagpole, and I saluted, sweetheart Mar'.

MARY: Nick'.

NICKY: And I used to think you had no sense of humor.

MARY: Live and learn.

NICKY: I sure will. So, what's the word, thunderbird?

MARY: Mr. Nicky, your emporium is most enticing. The sirens seduce.

NICKY: They really wail, don't they?

MARY: But I have strapped myself to the mast, and must sail on.

NICKY: When you gotta go, you gotta go. (*He hands her a container of Cool Whip.*) A little pick-me-up for the open road. You're not gonna find a lot of St. Bernard's with Cool Whip in their kegs. Happy trails.

MARY: Oh, Nicky. Congratulations.

NICKY: Fanny spilled the beans, huh?

MARY: I think so.

NICKY: Sorry you won't be here for the big day.

MARY: I shall be here in spirit.

NICKY: So long. Just remember the immortal words of Satchel Paige. Don't look back—something might be gaining on you.

MARY: Ah, the sage Satchel Paige. He also said, to keep the juices flowing, jangle around gently as you move.

NICKY: I'll keep it in mind.

MARY: Sound advice. I intend to follow it to the letter.

ALEX: Mary. Before you go. You must give us the lowdown on the future.

MARY: I've only had glimpses, mind you. Flashes. Bits of light.

(*She osmoses, uttering each new word as if it were being spoken for the very first time. Coining place names for a map of the New World:*)

MARY: Electric eyes. Automatic tellers. TV dinners. And that's just the beginning. Trailer parks. Mobile homes. Home economics.

O! Revolving credit! Spinoffs. Tax shelters, Subsidiary rights. Offshore banking. Venture capital. Residuals.

Non-dairy creamer. Non-profit foundations. No-fault insurance.

Pot stickers. Nehru jackets. Lava lamps. Day glo. Black light. The Peace Corps. Soul music. The Fab Four. Fern bars. Fondue. Free love. Romanian Cabernet Sauvignon.

Disposable income. Significant others. Mood elevators.

Mood rings. Mud wrestling. Super stars. Floating anchors. Guest hosts. Low riders. Slam dancing. Soft ware. Prime time. Time sharing. Word processors. Double speak. Hyper space. Holograms.

Aura cleansing. Angelic intervention. Pace makers. Walk mans. Synthesizers. Ghetto blasters. 45's. Saturday Night Specials.

Pulsars. Fiber optics. Remote control. Double think. Think tanks. The Domino Theory. The Third World. Boat people. Heavy water. Enhanced radiation. Silly Putty. Patty melts. Melt down. Ground zero.

Fellow travelers.

Windows of vulnerability.

(*Pause*)

FANNY: Fellow travelers, yes, yes, yes, yes, yes we are, yes!

ALEX: And vulnerable windows! Marvelous!

MARY: Ladies, what do you say we have one last rotor? Just—one for the road, as it were?

FANNY: Splendid idea.

(*Egg beaters appear.*)

**FANNY:** Ready?

**ALEX:** Set?

**MARY:** Rotor!

(*They rotor vigorously. A good long rotor and a good long laugh.*)

(*Finished,* **MARY** *steps downstage, whips off her long victorian skirt—*)

**ALEX:** Mary!

**FANNY:** Nicky, don't look!

(*—With a flourish. Underneath, she is wearing trousers.*)

**ALEX:** Brava, Mary!

**MARY:** I told you, Alexandra, I owe you a great deal.

**ALEX:** Intrepid trekking. Perhaps our paths will cross again, at some caravanserai of the future.

**MARY:** I feel certain of it. Our parabolas will intersect once more.

(*Sound of an enormous unmufflered motorcycle pulling up outside.*)

**ALEX:** That's Troll. Gotta go. Ciao.

**FANNY:** Catch you on the flip side.

(*She exits. Motorcycle roars off.*)

**MARY:** Mr. Nicky, thank you for everything.

(*She shakes his hand, and turns it into a hip handshake.*)

**NICKY:** Hey, hey, hey—

**MARY:** (*Gives him a wink*) Willy and the hand jive.

**NICKY:** You're hip, Mar'.

**MARY:** You, Nick', are impertinent. Give Gus some skin for me.

**NICKY:** So long.

**FANNY:** See you later, alligator. Au revoir, Bon voyage. Stay dry. Try to write. And look out for zeeroxen.

**MARY:** Goodbye, Fanny.

**FANNY:** Vaya con diós.

(**NICKY** *and* **FANNY** *exit.*)

(**MARY** *saddles up and comes downstage.*)

**MARY:** The splash of galaxies across the night sky always brings out the phenomenologist in me.

(*The stars come out.*)

**MARY:** Billions of new worlds, waiting to be discovered. Explored and illuminated. Within and without. The nautilus shell mimics the shape of the Milky Way. Quarks and quasars. My face is bathed in light from a vanished star. (*Beat*) I stand on the precipice. The air is rare. Bracing. Before me stretch dark distances. Clusters of light. What next? I have no idea. Many mysteries to come. I am on the verge.

(*She surveys the horizon and her prospects.*)

**MARY:** I have such a yearning for the future! It is boundless! (*She takes a deep breath.*) Not annoying. Not annoying at all!

(*She disappears in a blaze of light—*)

*End of play*

## SUMMARY

In this chapter we examined various ways ancient and modern playwrights indicated to readers the stage's visual support of the dramatic text. We referred to verbal notations of the stage's support as the playwright's scenography.

From earliest times, playwrights have used language to signal environmental factors: scene, space, time, weather, color, light, sound, furnishings, clothing. As readers, we study the dramatic text for clues whereby to imagine the "look" of the theatre space, what Patrice Pavis called "the stage's support." We think about the potential of these visual clues for psychological and philosophical meaning. Certainly, the theatre's performance conventions and technology influence the writer's approach to creating scenographic landscapes. For example, Elizabethan staging practices made possible an unimpeded flow of action with scene following scene from start to finish, taking place anywhere in this world or the next. In contrast, by the nineteenth century, the proscenium stage contained the action in a tight frame more appropriate to interior settings.

Throughout centuries, the playwright's "literary" scenography—so defined because these written directions, signs, symbols, and emblems are part of the dramatic text—has been labeled as "spectacle," "*mise en scène*," or "scenography." The writer's scenographic tools are found in descriptions of the play's geography, its interior and exterior landscapes, and the symbolic and philosophical meanings associated with visual signs and symbols unique to the theatre: settings, emblems, costumes, lighting, color, music, properties, and sound effects.

In a more complex way, the scenography of the written text is the playwright's detailed analogy to the virtual world as he or she perceives it for purposes of telling a story. It may be literal (a drawing room) as well as figurative (symbolic of a repressive society). Interior and exterior landscapes may be analogues for the inner emotional lives of the characters or the political instability of kingdoms. The landscapes of the dramatic text may use the stage cavity to display the writer's metaphysical concept of existence as an absurdist void. Or, the theatre may become the ultimate analogue for the writer who views life itself as pretense, or reality as performance. The meta-theatrical play that uses the stage-as-stage to present life's theatricality has as one of its goals an examination of the distinctions between art and life.

In the next chapters, we explore principal writing styles for the modern theatre—their roots, techniques, and subjects. Since realism has been the consistently dominant style of writing and performance for 150 years, we begin with discussions of modernism and stage realism.

## NOTES

1. Patrice Pavis, *Languages of the Stage: Essays on the Semiology of Theatre* (New York: Performing Arts Journal Publications, 1982): 145.
2. George R. Kernodle, *From Art to Theatre: Form and Convention in the Renaissance* (Chicago: University of Chicago Press, 1944): 145.
3. Richard Gilman, *The Making of Modern Drama: A Study of Buchner, Ibsen, Strindberg, Chekhov, Pi-* *randello, Brecht, Beckett, Handke* (New York: Farrar, Straus and Giroux, 1974): 157.
4. Eric Overmyer, *On The Verge or The Geography of Yearning* (New York: Broadway Publishing, Inc., 1990): 83.

# PART FOUR

# UNDERSTANDING MODERN WRITING STYLES

square inch left to put anything. I'll have to let it lie here, miss. (*Puts it on the piano.*)

MISS TESMAN: Well, Bertha dear, so now you have a new mistress. Heaven knows it nearly broke my heart to have to part with you.

BERTHA (*snivels*): What about me, Miss Juju? How do you suppose I felt? After all the happy years I've spent with you and Miss Rena?

MISS TESMAN: We must accept it bravely, Bertha. It was the only way. George needs you to take care of him. He could never manage without you. You've looked after him ever since he was a tiny boy.

BERTHA: Oh, but, Miss Juju, I can't help thinking about Miss Rena, lying there all helpless, poor dear. And that new girl! She'll never learn the proper way to handle an invalid.

MISS TESMAN: Oh, I'll manage to train her. I'll do most of the work myself, you know. You needn't worry about my poor sister, Bertha dear.

BERTHA: But, Miss Juju, there's another thing. I'm frightened madam may not find me suitable.

MISS TESMAN: Oh, nonsense, Bertha. There may be one or two little things to begin with—

BERTHA: She's a real lady. Wants everything just so.

MISS TESMAN: But of course she does! General Gabler's daughter! Think of what she was accustomed to when the general was alive. You remember how we used to see her out riding with her father? In that long black skirt? With the feather in her hat?

BERTHA: Oh, yes, miss. As if I could forget! But, Lord! I never dreamed I'd live to see a match between her and Master Georgie.

MISS TESMAN: Neither did I. By the way, Bertha, from now on you must stop calling him Master Georgie. You must say Dr. Tesman.

BERTHA: Yes, madam said something about that too. Last night—the moment they'd set foot inside the door. Is it true, then, miss?

MISS TESMAN: Indeed it is. Just fancy, Bertha, some foreigners have made him a doctor. It happened while they were away. I had no idea till he told me when they got off the boat.

BERTHA: Well, I suppose there's no limit to what he won't become. He's that clever. I never thought he'd go in for hospital work, though.

MISS TESMAN: No, he's not that kind of doctor. (*Nods impressively.*) In any case, you may soon have to address him by an even grander title.

BERTHA: You don't say! What might that be, miss?

MISS TESMAN (*smiles*): Ah! If you only knew! (*Moved.*) Dear God, if only poor Joachim could rise out of his grave and see what his little son has grown into! (*Looks round.*) But, Bertha, why have you done this? Taken the chintz covers off all the furniture!

BERTHA: Madam said I was to. Can't stand chintz covers on chairs, she said.

MISS TESMAN: But surely they're not going to use this room as a parlour?

BERTHA: So I gathered, miss. From what madam said. He didn't say anything. The Doctor.

GEORGE TESMAN *comes into the rear room from the right, humming, with an open, empty travelling-bag in his hand. He is about thirty-three, of medium height and youthful appearance, rather plump, with an open, round, contented face, and fair hair and beard. He wears spectacles, and is dressed in comfortable indoor clothes.*

MISS TESMAN: Good morning! Good morning, George!

TESMAN (*in open doorway*): Auntie Juju! Dear Auntie Juju! (*Comes forward and shakes her hand.*) You've come all the way out here! And so early! What?

MISS TESMAN: Well, I had to make sure you'd settled in comfortably.

TESMAN: But you can't have had a proper night's sleep.

MISS TESMAN: Oh, never mind that.

TESMAN: But you got home safely?

MISS TESMAN: Oh, yes. Judge Brack kindly saw me home.

TESMAN: We were so sorry we couldn't give you a lift. But you saw how it was—Hedda had so much luggage—and she insisted on having it all with her.

MISS TESMAN: Yes, I've never seen so much luggage.

BERTHA (*to* TESMAN): Shall I go and ask madam if there's anything I can lend her a hand with?

TESMAN: Er—thank you, Bertha, no, you needn't bother. She says if she wants you for anything she'll ring.

BERTHA (*over to right*): Oh. Very good.

TESMAN: Oh, Bertha—take this bag, will you?

BERTHA (*takes it*): I'll put it in the attic.
*She goes out into the hall.*

TESMAN: Just fancy, Auntie Juju, I filled that whole bag with notes for my book. You know, it's really incredible what I've managed to find rooting through those archives. By Jove! Wonderful old things no one even knew existed—

MISS TESMAN: I'm sure you didn't waste a single moment of your honeymoon, George dear.

TESMAN: No, I think I can truthfully claim that. But, Auntie Juju, do take your hat off. Here. Let me untie it for you. What?

MISS TESMAN (*as he does so*): Oh dear, oh dear! It's just as if you were still living at home with us.

TESMAN (*turns the hat in his hand and looks at it*): I say! What a splendid new hat!

MISS TESMAN: I bought it for Hedda's sake.

TESMAN: For Hedda's sake? What?

MISS TESMAN: So that Hedda needn't be ashamed of me, in case we ever go for a walk together.

TESMAN (*pats her cheek*): You still think of everything, don't you, Auntie Juju? (*Puts the hat down on a chair by the table.*) Come on, let's sit down here on the sofa. And have a little chat while we wait for Hedda.
*They sit. She puts her parasol in the corner of the sofa.*

MISS TESMAN (*clasps both his hands and looks at him*): Oh, George, it's so wonderful to have you back, and be able to see you with my own eyes again! Poor dear Joachim's own son!

TESMAN: What about me? It's wonderful for me to see you again, Auntie Juju. You've been a mother to me. And a father, too.

MISS TESMAN: You'll always keep a soft spot in your heart for your old aunties, won't you, George dear?

TESMAN: I suppose Auntie Rena's no better? What?

MISS TESMAN: Alas, no. I'm afraid she'll never get better, poor dear. She's lying there just as she has for all these years. Please God I may be allowed to keep her for a little longer. If I lost her I don't know what I'd do. Especially now I haven't you to look after.

TESMAN (*pats her on the back*): There, there, there!

MISS TESMAN (*with a sudden change of mood*): Oh, but, George, fancy you being a married man! And to think it's you who've won Hedda Gabler! The beautiful Hedda Gabler! Fancy! She was always so surrounded by admirers.

TESMAN (*hums a little and smiles contentedly*): Yes, I suppose there are quite a few people in this town who wouldn't mind being in my shoes. What?

MISS TESMAN: And what a honeymoon! Five months! Nearly six.

TESMAN: Well, I've done a lot of work, you know. All those archives to go through. And I've had to read lots of books.

MISS TESMAN: Yes, dear, of course. (*Lowers her voice confidentially.*) But tell me, George—haven't you any—any extra little piece of news to give me?

TESMAN: You mean, arising out of the honeymoon?

MISS TESMAN: Yes.

TESMAN: No, I don't think there's anything I didn't tell you in my letters. My doctorate, of course—but I told you about that last night, didn't I?

MISS TESMAN: Yes, yes, I didn't mean that kind of thing. I was just wondering—are you—are you expecting—?

TESMAN: Expecting what?

MISS TESMAN: Oh, come on, George, I'm your old aunt!

TESMAN: Well, actually—yes, I am expecting something.

MISS TESMAN: I knew it!

TESMAN: You'll be happy to learn that before very long I expect to become a—professor.

MISS TESMAN: Professor?

TESMAN: I think I may say that the matter has been decided. But, Auntie Juju, you know about this.

MISS TESMAN (*gives a little laugh*): Yes, of course. I'd forgotten. (*Changes her tone.*) But we were talking about your honeymoon. It must have cost a dreadful amount of money, George?

TESMAN: Oh well, you know, that big research grant I got helped a good deal.

MISS TESMAN: But how on earth did you manage to make it do for two?

TESMAN: Well, to tell the truth it was a bit tricky. What?

MISS TESMAN: Especially when one's travelling with a lady. A little bird tells me that makes things very much more expensive.

TESMAN: Well, yes, of course it does make things a little more expensive. But

Hedda has to do things in style, Auntie Juju. I mean, she has to. Anything less grand wouldn't have suited her.

MISS TESMAN: No, no, I suppose not. A honeymoon abroad seems to be the vogue nowadays. But tell me, have you had time to look round the house?

TESMAN: You bet. I've been up since the crack of dawn.

MISS TESMAN: Well, what do you think of it?

TESMAN: Splendid. Absolutely splendid. I'm only wondering what we're going to do with those two empty rooms between that little one and Hedda's bedroom.

MISS TESMAN (*laughs slyly*): Ah, George dear, I'm sure you'll manage to find some use for them—in time.

TESMAN: Yes, of course, Auntie Juju, how stupid of me. You're thinking of my books? What?

MISS TESMAN: Yes, yes, dear boy. I was thinking of your books.

TESMAN: You know, I'm so happy for Hedda's sake that we've managed to get this house. Before we became engaged she often used to say this was the only house in town she felt she could really bear to live in. It used to belong to Mrs. Falk—you know, the Prime Minister's widow.

MISS TESMAN: Fancy that! And what a stroke of luck it happened to come into the market. Just as you'd left on your honeymoon.

TESMAN: Yes, Auntie Juju, we've certainly had all the luck with us. What?

MISS TESMAN: But, George dear, the expense! It's going to make a dreadful hole in your pocket, all this.

TESMAN (*a little downcast*): Yes, I—I suppose it will, won't it?

MISS TESMAN: Oh, George, really!

TESMAN: How much do you think it'll cost? Roughly, I mean? What?

MISS TESMAN: I can't possibly say till I see the bills.

TESMAN: Well, luckily Judge Brack's managed to get it on very favourable terms. He wrote and told Hedda so.

MISS TESMAN: Don't you worry, George dear. Anyway, I've stood security for all the furniture and carpets.

TESMAN: Security? But dear, sweet Auntie Juju, how could you possibly stand security?

MISS TESMAN: I've arranged a mortgage on our annuity.

TESMAN (*jumps up*): What? On your annuity? And—Auntie Rena's?

MISS TESMAN: Yes. Well, I couldn't think of any other way.

TESMAN (*stands in front of her*): Auntie Juju, have you gone completely out of your mind? That annuity's all you and Auntie Rena have.

MISS TESMAN: All right, there's no need to get so excited about it. It's a pure formality, you know. Judge Brack told me so. He was so kind as to arrange it all for me. A pure formality; those were his very words.

TESMAN: I dare say. All the same—

MISS TESMAN: Anyway, you'll have a salary of your own now. And, good heavens, even if we did have to fork out a little— tighten our belts for a week or two— why, we'd be happy to do so for your sake.

TESMAN: Oh, Auntie Juju! Will you never stop sacrificing yourself for me?

MISS TESMAN (*gets up and puts her hands on his shoulders*): What else have I to live for but to smooth your road a little, my dear boy? You've never had any mother or father to turn to. And now at last we've achieved our goal. I won't deny we've had our little difficulties now and then. But now, thank the good Lord, George dear, all your worries are past.

TESMAN: Yes, it's wonderful really how everything's gone just right for me.

MISS TESMAN: Yes! And the enemies who tried to bar your way have been struck down. They have been made to bite the dust. The man who was your most dangerous rival has had the mightiest fall. And now he's lying there in the pit he dug for himself, poor misguided creature.

TESMAN: Have you heard any news of Eilert? Since I went away?

MISS TESMAN: Only that he's said to have published a new book.

TESMAN: What! Eilert Lœvborg? You mean—just recently? What?

MISS TESMAN: So they say. I don't imagine it can be of any value, do you? When your new book comes out, that'll be another story. What's it going to be about?

TESMAN: The domestic industries of Brabant in the Middle Ages.

MISS TESMAN: Oh, George! The things you know about!

TESMAN: Mind you, it may be some time before I actually get down to writing it. I've made these very extensive notes, and I've got to file and index them first.

MISS TESMAN: Ah, yes! Making notes; filing and indexing; you've always been wonderful at that. Poor dear Joachim was just the same.

TESMAN: I'm looking forward so much to getting down to that. Especially now I've a home of my own to work in.

MISS TESMAN: And above all, now that you have the girl you set your heart on, George dear.

TESMAN (*embraces her*): Oh, yes, Auntie Juju, yes! Hedda's the loveliest thing of all! (*Looks towards the doorway.*) I think I hear her coming. What?

HEDDA *enters the rear room from the left, and comes into the drawing-room. She is a woman of twenty-nine. Distinguished, aristocratic face and figure. Her complexion is pale and opalescent. Her eyes are steel-grey, with an expression of cold, calm serenity. Her hair is of a handsome auburn colour, but is not especially abundant. She is dressed in an elegant, somewhat loose-fitting morning gown.*

MISS TESMAN (*goes to greet her*): Good morning, Hedda dear! Good morning!

HEDDA (*holds out her hand*): Good morning, dear Miss Tesman. What an early hour to call. So kind of you.

MISS TESMAN (*seems somewhat embarrassed*): And has the young bride slept well in her new home?

HEDDA: Oh—thank you, yes. Passably well.

TESMAN (*laughs*): Passably? I say, Hedda, that's good! When I jumped out of bed, you were sleeping like a top.

HEDDA: Yes. Fortunately. One has to accustom oneself to anything new, Miss Tesman. It takes time. (*Looks left.*) Oh, that maid's left the french windows open. This room's flooded with sun.

MISS TESMAN (*goes towards the windows*): Oh—let me close them.

HEDDA: No, no, don't do that. Tesman dear, draw the curtains. This light's blinding me.

TESMAN (*at the windows*): Yes, yes, dear. There, Hedda, now you've got shade and fresh air.

HEDDA: This room needs fresh air. All these flowers—! But my dear Miss Tesman, won't you take a seat?

MISS TESMAN: No, really not, thank you. I just wanted to make sure you have everything you need. I must see about getting back home. My poor dear sister will be waiting for me.

TESMAN: Be sure to give her my love, won't you? Tell her I'll run over and see her later today.

MISS TESMAN: Oh yes, I'll tell her that. Oh, George—(*Fumbles in the pocket of her skirt.*) I almost forgot. I've brought something for you.

TESMAN: What's that, Auntie Juju? What?

MISS TESMAN (*pulls out a flat package wrapped in newspaper and gives it to him*): Open and see, dear boy.

TESMAN (*opens the package*): Good heavens! Auntie Juju, you've kept them! Hedda, this is really very touching. What?

HEDDA (*by the what-nots, on the right*): What is it, Tesman?

TESMAN: My old shoes! My slippers, Hedda!

HEDDA: Oh, them. I remember you kept talking about them on our honeymoon.

TESMAN: Yes, I missed them dreadfully. (*Goes over to her.*) Here, Hedda, take a look.

HEDDA (*goes away towards the stove*): Thanks, I won't bother.

TESMAN (*follows her*): Fancy, Hedda, Auntie Rena's embroidered them for me. Despite her being so ill. Oh, you can't imagine what memories they have for me.

HEDDA (*by the table*): Not for me.

MISS TESMAN: No, Hedda's right there, George.

TESMAN: Yes, but I thought since she's one of the family now—

HEDDA (*interrupts*): Tesman, we really can't go on keeping this maid.

MISS TESMAN: Not keep Bertha?

TESMAN: What makes you say that, dear? What?

HEDDA (*points*): Look at that! She's left her old hat lying on the chair.

TESMAN (*appalled, drops his slippers on the floor*): But, Hedda—!

HEDDA: Suppose someone came in and saw it?

TESMAN: But, Hedda—that's Auntie Juju's hat.

HEDDA: Oh?

MISS TESMAN (*picks up the hat*): Indeed it's mine. And it doesn't happen to be old, Hedda dear.

HEDDA: I didn't look at it very closely, Miss Tesman.

MISS TESMAN (*tying on the hat*): As a matter of fact, it's the first time I've worn it. As the good Lord is my witness.

TESMAN: It's very pretty, too. Really smart.

MISS TESMAN: Oh, I'm afraid it's nothing much really. (*Looks round.*) My parasol. Ah, there it is. (*Takes it.*) This is mine, too. (*Murmurs*) Not Bertha's.

TESMAN: A new hat and a new parasol! I say, Hedda, fancy that!

HEDDA: Very pretty and charming.

TESMAN: Yes, isn't it? What? But, Auntie Juju, take a good look at Hedda before you go. Isn't she pretty and charming?

MISS TESMAN: Dear boy, there's nothing new in that. Hedda's been a beauty ever since the day she was born. (*Nods and goes right.*)

TESMAN (*follows her*): Yes, but have you noticed how strong and healthy she's looking? And how she's filled out since we went away?

MISS TESMAN (*stops and turns*): Filled out?

HEDDA (*walks across the room*): Oh, can't we forget it?

TESMAN: Yes, Auntie Juju—you can't see it so clearly with that dress on. But I've good reason to know—

HEDDA (*by the french windows, impatiently*): You haven't good reason to know anything.

TESMAN: It must have been the mountain air up there in the Tyrol—

HEDDA (*curtly, interrupts him*): I'm exactly the same as when I went away.

TESMAN: You keep on saying so. But you're not. I'm right, aren't I, Auntie Juju?

MISS TESMAN (*has folded her hands and is gazing at her*): She's beautiful—beautiful. Hedda is beautiful. (*Goes over to HEDDA, takes her head between her hands, draws it down and kisses her hair.*) God bless and keep you, Hedda Tesman. For George's sake.

HEDDA (*frees herself politely*): Oh—let me go, please.

MISS TESMAN (*quietly, emotionally*): I shall come and see you both every day.

TESMAN: Yes, Auntie Juju, please do. What?

MISS TESMAN: Good-bye! Good-bye!

*She goes out into the hall.* TESMAN *follows her. The door remains open.* TESMAN *is heard sending his love to* AUNT RENA *and thanking* MISS TESMAN *for his slippers. Meanwhile* HEDDA *walks up and down the room, raising her arms and clenching her fists as though in desperation. Then she throws aside the curtains from the french windows and stands there, looking out. A few moments later* TESMAN *returns and closes the door behind him.*

TESMAN (*picks up his slippers from the floor*): What are you looking at Hedda?

HEDDA (*calm and controlled again*): Only the leaves. They're so golden and withered.

TESMAN (*wraps up the slippers and lays them on the table*): Well, we're in September now.

HEDDA (*restless again*): Yes. We're already into September.

TESMAN: Auntie Juju was behaving rather oddly, I thought, didn't you? Almost as though she was in church or something. I wonder what came over her. Any idea?

HEDDA: I hardly know her. Does she often act like that?

TESMAN: Not to the extent she did today.

HEDDA (*goes away from the french windows*): Do you think she was hurt by what I said about the hat?

TESMAN: Oh, I don't think so. A little at first, perhaps—

HEDDA: But what a thing to do, throw her hat down in someone's drawing-room. People don't do such things.

TESMAN: I'm sure Auntie Juju doesn't do it very often.

HEDDA: Oh well, I'll make it up with her.

TESMAN: Oh Hedda, would you?

HEDDA: When you see them this afternoon invite her to come out here this evening.

TESMAN: You bet I will! I say, there's another thing which would please her enormously.

HEDDA: Oh?

TESMAN: If you could bring yourself to call her Auntie Juju. For my sake, Hedda? What?

HEDDA: Oh no, really, Tesman, you mustn't ask me to do that. I've told you so once before. I'll try to call her Aunt Juliana. That's as far as I'll go.

TESMAN (after a moment): I say, Hedda, is anything wrong? What?

HEDDA: I'm just looking at my old piano. It doesn't really go with all this.

TESMAN: As soon as I start getting my salary we'll see about changing it.

HEDDA: No, no, don't let's change it. I don't want to part with it. We can move it into that little room and get another one to put in here.

TESMAN (a little downcast): Yes, we—might do that.

HEDDA (picks up the bunch of flowers from the piano): These flowers weren't here when we arrived last night.

TESMAN: I expect Auntie Juju brought them.

HEDDA: Here's a card. (Takes it out and reads.) 'Will come back later today.' Guess who it's from?

TESMAN: No idea. Who? What?

HEDDA: It says: 'Mrs. Elvsted.'

TESMAN: No, really? Mrs. Elvsted! She used to be Miss Rysing, didn't she?

HEDDA: Yes. She was the one with that irritating hair she was always showing off. I hear she used to be an old flame of yours.

TESMAN (laughs): That didn't last long. Anyway, that was before I got to know you, Hedda. By Jove, fancy her being in town!

HEDDA: Strange she should call. I only knew her at school.

TESMAN: Yes. I haven't seen her for—oh, heaven knows how long. I don't know how she manages to stick it out up there in the north. What?

HEDDA (thinks for a moment, then says suddenly): Tell me, Tesman, doesn't he live somewhere up in those parts? You know—Eilert Lœvborg?

TESMAN: Yes, that's right. So he does.

BERTHA enters from the hall.

BERTHA: She's here again, madam. The lady who came and left the flowers. (Points.) The ones you're holding.

HEDDA: Oh, is she? Well, show her in.

BERTHA opens the door for MRS. ELVSTED and goes out. MRS. ELVSTED is a delicately built woman with gentle, attractive features. Her eyes are light blue, large, and somewhat prominent, with a frightened, questioning expression. Her hair is extremely fair, almost flaxen, and is exceptionally wavy and abundant. She is two or three years younger than HEDDA. She is wearing a dark visiting dress, in good taste but not quite in the latest fashion.

HEDDA (goes cordially to greet her): Dear Mrs. Elvsted, good morning! How delightful to see you again after all this time!

MRS. ELVSTED (nervously, trying to control herself): Yes, it's many years since we met.

TESMAN: And since we met. What?

HEDDA: Thank you for your lovely flowers.

MRS. ELVSTED: I wanted to come yesterday afternoon. But they told me you were away—

TESMAN: You've only just arrived in town, then? What?

MRS. ELVSTED: I got here yesterday, around midday. Oh, I became almost desperate when I heard you weren't here.

HEDDA: Desperate? Why?

TESMAN: My dear Mrs. Rysing—Elvsted—

HEDDA: There's nothing wrong, I hope?

MRS. ELVSTED: Yes, there is. And I don't know anyone else here whom I can turn to.

HEDDA (puts the flowers down on the table): Come and sit with me on the sofa—

MRS. ELVSTED: Oh, I feel too restless to sit down.

HEDDA: You must. Come along, now.

*She pulls* MRS. ELVSTED *down on to the sofa and sits beside her.*

TESMAN: Well? Tell us. Mrs.—er—

HEDDA: Has something happened at home?

MRS. ELVSTED: Yes—that is, yes and no. Oh, I do hope you won't misunderstand me—

HEDDA: Then you'd better tell us the whole story, Mrs. Elvsted.

TESMAN: That's why you've come. What?

MRS. ELVSTED: Yes—yes, it is. Well, then— in case you don't already know—Eilert Lœvborg is in town.

HEDDA: Lœvborg here?

TESMAN: Eilert back in town? Fancy, Hedda, did you hear that?

HEDDA: Yes, of course I heard.

MRS. ELVSTED: He's been here a week. A whole week! In this city. Alone. With all those dreadful people—

HEDDA: But, my dear Mrs. Elvsted, what concern is he of yours?

MRS. ELVSTED (*gives her a frightened look and says quickly*): He's been tutoring the children.

HEDDA: Your children?

MRS. ELVSTED: My husband's. I have none.

HEDDA: Oh, you mean your stepchildren.

MRS. ELVSTED: Yes.

TESMAN (*gropingly*): But was he sufficiently—I don't know how to put it— sufficiently regular in his habits to be suited to such a post? What?

MRS. ELVSTED: For the past two to three years he has been living irreproachably.

TESMAN: You don't say! Hedda, do you hear that?

HEDDA: I hear.

MRS. ELVSTED: Quite irreproachably, I assure you. In every respect. All the same—in this big city—with money in his pockets—I'm so dreadfully frightened something may happen to him.

TESMAN: But why didn't he stay up there with you and your husband?

MRS. ELVSTED: Once his book had come out, he became restless.

TESMAN: Oh, yes—Auntie Juju said he's brought out a new book.

MRS. ELVSTED: Yes, a big new book about the history of civilization. A kind of general survey. It came out a fortnight ago. Everyone's been buying it and reading it—it's created a tremendous stir—

TESMAN: Has it really? It must be something he's dug up, then.

MRS. ELVSTED: You mean from the old days?

TESMAN: Yes.

MRS. ELVSTED: No, he's written it all since he came to live with us.

TESMAN: Well, that's splendid news, Hedda. Fancy that!

MRS. ELVSTED: Oh, yes! If only he can go on like this!

HEDDA: Have you met him since you came here?

MRS. ELVSTED: No, not yet. I had such dreadful difficulty finding his address. But this morning I managed to track him down at last.

HEDDA (*looks searchingly at her*): I must say I find it a little strange that your husband—hm—

MRS. ELVSTED (*starts nervously*): My husband! What do you mean?

HEDDA: That he should send you all the way here on an errand of this kind. I'm surprised he didn't come himself to keep an eye on his friend.

MRS. ELVSTED: Oh, no, no—my husband hasn't the time. Besides, I—er—wanted to do some shopping here.

HEDDA (*with a slight smile*): Ah. Well, that's different.

MRS. ELVSTED (*gets up quickly, restlessly*): Please, Mr. Tesman, I beg you—be kind to Eilert Lœvborg if he comes here. I'm sure he will. I mean, you used to be such good friends in the old days. And you're both studying the same subject, as far as

I can understand. You're in the same field, aren't you?

TESMAN: Well, we used to be, anyway.

MRS. ELVSTED: Yes—so I beg you earnestly, do please, please, keep an eye on him. Oh, Mr. Tesman, do promise me you will.

TESMAN: I shall be only too happy to do so, Mrs. Rysing.

HEDDA: Elvsted.

TESMAN: I'll do everything for Eilert that lies in my power. You can rely on that.

MRS. ELVSTED: Oh, how good and kind you are! (*Presses his hands.*) Thank you, thank you, thank you. (*Frightened.*) My husband's so fond of him, you see.

HEDDA (*gets up*): You'd better send him a note, Tesman. He may not come to you of his own accord.

TESMAN: Yes, that'd probably be the best plan, Hedda. What?

HEDDA: The sooner the better. Why not do it now?

MRS. ELVSTED (*pleadingly*): Oh yes, if only you would!

TESMAN: I'll do it this very moment. Do you have his address, Mrs.—er—Elvsted?

MRS. ELVSTED: Yes. (*Takes a small piece of paper from her pocket and gives it to him.*)

TESMAN: Good, good. Right, well, I'll go inside and—(*Looks round.*) Where are my slippers? Oh yes, here. (*Picks up the package and is about to go.*)

HEDDA: Try to sound friendly. Make it a nice long letter.

TESMAN: Right, I will.

MRS. ELVSTED: Please don't say anything about my having seen you.

TESMAN: Good heavens, no, of course not. What?

*He goes out through the rear room to the right.*

HEDDA (*goes over to* MRS. ELVSTED, *smiles, and says softly*): Well! Now we've killed two birds with one stone.

MRS. ELVSTED: What do you mean?

HEDDA: Didn't you realize I wanted to get him out of the room?

MRS. ELVSTED: So that he could write the letter?

HEDDA: And so that I could talk to you alone.

MRS. ELVSTED (*confused*): About this?

HEDDA: Yes, about this.

MRS. ELVSTED (*in alarm*): But there's nothing more to tell, Mrs. Tesman. Really there isn't.

HEDDA: Oh, yes, there is. There's a lot more. I can see that. Come along, let's sit down and have a little chat.

*She pushes* MRS. ELVSTED *down into the armchair by the stove and seats herself on one of the footstools.*

MRS. ELVSTED (*looks anxiously at her watch*): Really, Mrs. Tesman, I think I ought to be going now.

HEDDA: There's no hurry. Well? How are things at home?

MRS. ELVSTED: I'd rather not speak about that.

HEDDA: But, my dear, you can tell me. Good heavens, we were at school together.

MRS. ELVSTED: Yes, but you were a year senior to me. Oh, I used to be terribly frightened of you in those days.

HEDDA: Frightened of me?

MRS. ELVSTED: Yes, terribly frightened. Whenever you met me on the staircase you used to pull my hair.

HEDDA: No, did I?

MRS. ELVSTED: Yes. And once you said you'd burn it all off.

HEDDA: Oh, that was only in fun.

MRS. ELVSTED: Yes, but I was so silly in those days. And then afterwards—I mean, we've drifted so far apart. Our backgrounds were so different.

HEDDA: Well, now we must try to drift together again. Now listen. When we were at school we used to call each other by our Christian names—

MRS. ELVSTED: No, I'm sure you're mistaken.

HEDDA: I'm sure I'm not. I remember it quite clearly. Let's tell each other our secrets, as we used to in the old days. (*Moves closer on her footstool.*) There, now. (*Kisses her on the cheek.*) You must call me Hedda.

MRS. ELVSTED (*squeezes her hands and pats them*): Oh, you're so kind. I'm not used to people being so nice to me.

HEDDA: Now, now, now. And I shall call you Tora, the way I used to.

MRS. ELVSTED: My name is Thea.

HEDDA: Yes, of course. Of course. I meant Thea. (*Looks at her sympathetically.*) So you're not used to kindness, Thea? In your own home?

MRS. ELVSTED: Oh, if only I had a home! But I haven't. I've never had one.

HEDDA (*looks at her for a moment*): I thought that was it.

MRS. ELVSTED (*stares blankly and helplessly*): Yes—yes—yes.

HEDDA: I can't remember exactly, but didn't you first go to Mr. Elvsted as a housekeeper?

MRS. ELVSTED: Governess, actually. But his wife—at the time, I mean—she was an invalid, and had to spend most of her time in bed. So I had to look after the house, too.

HEDDA: But in the end, you became mistress of the house.

MRS. ELVSTED (*sadly*): Yes, I did.

HEDDA: Let me see. Roughly how long ago was that?

MRS. ELVSTED: When I got married, you mean?

HEDDA: Yes.

MRS. ELVSTED: About five years.

HEDDA: Yes; it must be about that.

MRS. ELVSTED: Oh, those five years! Especially the last two or three. Oh, Mrs. Tesman, if you only knew—!

HEDDA (*slaps her hand gently*): Mrs. Tesman? Oh, Thea!

MRS. ELVSTED: I'm sorry, I'll try to remember. Yes—if you had any idea—

HEDDA (*casually*): Eilert Lœvborg's been up there, too, for about three years, hasn't he?

MRS. ELVSTED (*looks at her uncertainly*): Eilert Lœvborg? Yes, he has.

HEDDA: Did you know him before? When you were here?

MRS. ELVSTED: No, not really. That is—I knew him by name, of course.

HEDDA: But up there, he used to visit you?

MRS. ELVSTED: Yes, he used to come and see us every day. To give the children lessons. I found I couldn't do that as well as manage the house.

HEDDA: I'm sure you couldn't. And your husband—? I suppose being a magistrate he has to away from home a good deal?

MRS. ELVSTED: Yes. You see, Mrs.—you see, Hedda, he has to cover the whole district.

HEDDA (*leans against the arm of* MRS. ELVSTED's *chair*): Poor, pretty little Thea! Now you must tell me the whole story. From beginning to end.

MRS. ELVSTED: Well—what do you want to know?

HEDDA: What kind of a man is your husband, Thea? I mean, as a person. Is he kind to you?

MRS. ELVSTED (*evasively*): I'm sure he does his best to be.

HEDDA: I only wonder if he isn't too old for you. There's more than twenty years between you, isn't there?

MRS. ELVSTED (*irritably*): Yes, there's that, too. Oh, there are so many things. We're different in every way. We've nothing in common. Nothing whatever.

HEDDA: But he loves you, surely? In his own way?

MRS. ELVSTED: Oh, I don't know. I think he just finds me useful. And then I don't cost much to keep. I'm cheap.

HEDDA: Now you're being stupid.

MRS. ELVSTED (*shakes her head*): It can't be any different. With him. He doesn't love anyone except himself. And perhaps the children—a little.

HEDDA: He must be fond of Eilert Lœvborg, Thea.

MRS. ELVSTED (*looks at her*): Eilert Lœvborg? What makes you think that?

HEDDA: Well, if he sends you all the way down here to look for him—(*Smiles almost imperceptibly.*) Besides, you said so yourself to Tesman.

MRS. ELVSTED (*with a nervous twitch*): Did I? Oh yes, I suppose I did. (*Impulsively, but keeping her voice low.*) Well, I might as well tell you the whole story. It's bound to come out sooner or later.

HEDDA: But, my dear Thea—?

MRS. ELVSTED: My husband had no idea I was coming here.

HEDDA: What? Your husband didn't know?

MRS. ELVSTED: No, of course not. As a matter of fact, he wasn't even there. He was away at the assizes. Oh, I couldn't stand it any longer, Hedda! I just couldn't. I'd be so dreadfully lonely up there now.

HEDDA: Go on.

MRS. ELVSTED: So I packed a few things. Secretly. And went.

HEDDA: Without telling anyone?

MRS. ELVSTED: Yes. I caught the train and came straight here.

HEDDA: But, my dear Thea! How brave of you!

MRS. ELVSTED (*gets up and walks across the room*): Well, what else could I do?

HEDDA: But what do you suppose your husband will say when you get back?

MRS. ELVSTED (*by the table, looks at her*): Back there? To him?

HEDDA: Yes. Surely—?

MRS. ELVSTED: I shall never go back to him.

HEDDA (*gets up and goes closer*): You mean you've left your home for good?

MRS. ELVSTED: Yes. I didn't see what else I could do.

HEDDA: But to do it so openly!

MRS. ELVSTED: Oh, it's no use trying to keep a thing like that secret.

HEDDA: But what do you suppose people will say?

MRS. ELVSTED: They can say what they like. (*Sits sadly, wearily on the sofa.*) I had to do it.

HEDDA (*after a short silence*): What do you intend to do now? How are you going to live?

MRS. ELVSTED: I don't know. I only know that I must live wherever Eilert Lœvborg is. If I am to go on living.

HEDDA (*moves a chair from the table, sits on it near* MRS. ELVSTED *and strokes her hands*): Tell me, Thea, how did this—friendship between you and Eilert Lœvborg begin?

MRS. ELVSTED: Oh, it came about gradually. I developed a kind of—power over him.

HEDDA: Oh?

MRS. ELVSTED: He gave up his old habits. Not because I asked him to. I'd never have dared to do that. I suppose he just noticed I didn't like that kind of thing. So he gave it up.

HEDDA (*hides a smile*): So you've made a new man of him! Clever little Thea!

MRS. ELVSTED: Yes—anyway, he says I have. And he's made a—sort of—real person of me. Taught me to think—and to understand all kinds of things.

HEDDA: Did he give you lessons, too?

MRS. ELVSTED: Not exactly lessons. But he talked to me. About—oh, you've no idea—so many things! And then he let me work with him. Oh, it was wonderful. I was so happy to be allowed to help him.

HEDDA: Did he allow you to help him?

MRS. ELVSTED: Yes. Whenever he wrote anything we always—did it together.

HEDDA: Like good friends?

MRS. ELVSTED (*eagerly*): Friends! Yes—why, Hedda that's exactly the word he used! Oh, I ought to feel so happy. But I can't. I don't know if it will last.

HEDDA: You don't seem very sure of him.

MRS. ELVSTED (*sadly*): Something stands between Eilert Loevborg and me. The shadow of another woman.

HEDDA: Who can that be?

MRS. ELVSTED: I don't know. Someone he used to be friendly with in—in the old days. Someone he's never been able to forget.

HEDDA: What has he told you about her?

MRS. ELVSTED: Oh, he only mentioned her once, casually.

HEDDA: Well! What did he say?

MRS. ELVSTED: He said when he left her she tried to shoot him with a pistol.

HEDDA (*cold, controlled*): What nonsense. People don't do such things. The kind of people we know.

MRS. ELVSTED: No. I think it must have been that red-haired singer he used to—

HEDDA: Ah yes, very probably.

MRS. ELVSTED: I remember they used to say she always carried a loaded pistol.

HEDDA: Well then, it must be her.

MRS. ELVSTED: But, Hedda, I hear she's come back, and is living here. Oh, I'm so desperate—!

HEDDA (*glances towards the rear room*): Ssh! Tesman's coming.(*Gets up and whispers.*) Thea, we mustn't breathe a word about this to anyone.

MRS. ELVSTED (*jumps up*): Oh, no, no! Please don't!

GEORGE TESMAN *appears from the right in the rear room with a letter in his hand, and comes into the drawing-room.*

TESMAN: Well, here's my little epistle all signed and sealed.

HEDDA: Good. I think Mrs. Elvsted wants to go now. Wait a moment—I'll see you as far as the garden gate.

TESMAN: Er—Hedda, do you think Bertha could deal with this?

HEDDA (*takes the letter*): I'll give her instructions.

BERTHA *enters from the hall.*

BERTHA: Judge Brack is here and asks if he may pay his respects to madam and the Doctor.

HEDDA: Yes, ask him to be so good as to come in. And—wait a moment—drop this letter in the post box.

BERTHA (*takes the letter*): Very good, madam. *She opens the door for* JUDGE BRACK, *and goes out.* JUDGE BRACK *is forty-five; rather short, but well built, and elastic in his movements. He has a roundish face with an aristocratic profile. His hair, cut short, is still almost black, and is carefully barbered. Eyes lively and humorous. Thick eyebrows. His moustache is also thick, and is trimmed square at the ends. He is wearing outdoor clothes which are elegant but a little too youthful for him. He has a monocle in one eye; now and then he lets it drop.*

BRACK (*hat in hand, bows*): May one presume to call so early?

HEDDA: One may presume.

TESMAN (*shakes his hand*): You're welcome here any time. Judge Brack—Mrs. Rysing.

HEDDA *sighs.*

BRACK (*bows*): Ah—charmed—

HEDDA (*looks at him and laughs*): What fun to be able to see you by daylight for once, Judge.

BRACK: Do I look—different?

HEDDA: Yes. A little younger, I think.

BRACK: Too kind.

TESMAN: Well, what do you think of Hedda? What? Doesn't she look well? Hasn't she filled out—?

HEDDA: Oh, do stop it. You ought to be thanking Judge Brack for all the inconvenience he's put himself to—

BRACK: Nonsense, it was a pleasure—

HEDDA: You're a loyal friend. But my other friend is pining to get away. Au revoir, Judge. I won't be a minute.

*Mutual salutations.* MRS. ELVSTED *and* HEDDA *go out through the hall.*

BRACK: Well, is your wife satisfied with everything?

TESMAN: Yes, we can't thank you enough. That is—we may have to shift one or two things around, she tells me. And we're short of one or two little items we'll have to purchase.

BRACK: Oh? Really?

TESMAN: But you mustn't worry your head about that. Hedda says she'll get what's needed. I say, why don't we sit down? What?

BRACK: Thanks, just for a moment. (*Sits at the table.*) There's something I'd like to talk to you about, my dear Tesman.

TESMAN: Oh? Ah yes, of course. (*Sits.*) After the feast comes the reckoning. What?

BRACK: Oh, never mind about the financial side—there's no hurry about that. Though I could wish we'd arranged things a little less palatially.

TESMAN: Good heavens, that'd never have done. Think of Hedda, my dear chap. You know her. I couldn't possibly ask her to live like a petty bourgeois.

BRACK: No, no—that's just the problem.

TESMAN: Anyway, it can't be long now before my nomination comes through.

BRACK: Well, you know, these things often take time.

TESMAN: Have you heard any more news? What?

BRACK: Nothing definite. (*Changing the subject*). Oh, by the way, I have one piece of news for you.

TESMAN: What?

BRACK: Your old friend Eilert Lœvborg is back in town.

TESMAN: I know that already.

BRACK: Oh? How did you hear that?

TESMAN: She told me. That lady who went out with Hedda.

BRACK: I see. What was her name? I didn't catch it.

TESMAN: Mrs. Elvsted.

BRACK: Oh, the magistrate's wife. Yes, Lœvborg's been living up near them, hasn't he?

TESMAN: I'm delighted to hear he's become a decent human being again.

BRACK: Yes, so they say.

TESMAN: I gather he's published a new book, too. What?

BRACK: Indeed he has.

TESMAN: I hear it's created rather a stir.

BRACK: Quite an unusual stir.

TESMAN: I say, isn't that splendid news! He's such a gifted chap—and I was afraid he'd gone to the dogs for good.

BRACK: Most people thought he had.

TESMAN: But I can't think what he'll do now. How on earth will he manage to make ends meet? What?

*As he speaks his last words* HEDDA *enters from the hall.*

HEDDA (*to* BRACK, *laughs slightly scornfully*): Tesman is always worrying about making ends meet.

TESMAN: We were talking about poor Eilert Lœvborg, Hedda dear.

HEDDA (*gives him a quick look*): Oh, were you? (*Sits in the armchair by the stove and asks casually.*) Is he in trouble?

TESMAN: Well, he must have run through his inheritance long ago by now. And he can't write a new book every year. What? So I'm wondering what's going to become of him.

BRACK: I may be able to enlighten you there.

TESMAN: Oh?

BRACK: You mustn't forget he has relatives who wield a good deal of influence.

TESMAN: Relatives? Oh, they've quite washed their hands of him, I'm afraid.

BRACK: They used to regard him as the hope of the family.

TESMAN: Used to, yes. But he's put an end to that.

HEDDA: Who knows? (*With a little smile.*) I hear the Elvsteds have made a new man of him.

BRACK: And then this book he's just published—

TESMAN: Well, let's hope they find something for him. I've just written him a note. Oh, by the way, Hedda, I asked him to come over and see us this evening.

BRACK: But, my dear chap, you're coming to me this evening. My bachelor party. You promised me last night when I met you at the boat.

HEDDA: Had you forgotten, Tesman?

TESMAN: Good heavens, yes, I'd quite forgotten.

BRACK: Anyway, you can be quite sure he won't turn up here.

TESMAN: Why do you think that? What?

BRACK (*a little unwillingly, gets up and rests his hands on the back of his chair*): My dear Tesman—and you, too, Mrs. Tesman— there's something I feel you ought to know.

TESMAN: Concerning Eilert?

BRACK: Concerning him and you.

TESMAN: Well, my dear judge, tell us please!

BRACK: You must be prepared for your nomination not to come through quite as quickly as you hope and expect.

TESMAN (*Jumps up uneasily*): Is anything wrong? What?

BRACK: There's a possibility that the appointment may be decided by competition—

TESMAN: Competition! Hedda, fancy that!

HEDDA (*leans further back in her chair*): Ah! How interesting!

TESMAN: But who else—? I say, you don't mean—?

BRACK: Exactly. By competition with Eilert Lœvborg.

TESMAN (*clasps his hands in alarm*): No, no, but this is inconceivable! It's absolutely impossible! What?

BRACK: Hm. We may find it'll happen, all the same.

TESMAN: No, but—Judge Brack, they couldn't be so inconsiderate towards me! (*Waves his arms.*) I mean, by Jove, I—I'm a married man! It was on the strength of this that Hedda and I *got* married! We've run up some pretty hefty debts. And borrowed money from Auntie Juju! I mean, good heavens, they practically promised me the appointment. What?

BRACK: Well, well, I'm sure you'll get it. But you'll have to go through a competition.

HEDDA (*motionless in her armchair*): How exciting, Tesman. It'll be a kind of duel, by Jove.

TESMAN: My dear Hedda, how can you take it so lightly?

HEDDA (*as before*): I'm not. I can't wait to see who's going to win.

BRACK: In any case, Mrs. Tesman, it's best you should know how things stand. I mean before you commit yourself to these little items I hear you're threatening to purchase.

HEDDA: I can't allow this to alter my plans.

BRACK: Indeed? Well, that's your business. Good-bye. (*To* TESMAN) I'll come and collect you on the way home from my afternoon walk.

TESMAN: Oh, yes, yes. I'm sorry. I'm all upside down just now.

HEDDA (*lying in her chair, holds out her hand*): Good-bye, Judge. See you this afternoon.

BRACK: Thank you. Good-bye, good-bye.

TESMAN (*sees him to the door*): Good-bye, my dear Judge. You will excuse me, won't you?

JUDGE BRACK *goes out through the hall.*

TESMAN (*pacing up and down*): Oh, Hedda! One oughtn't to go plunging off on wild adventures. What?

HEDDA (*looks at him and smiles*): Like you're doing?

TESMAN: Yes. I mean, there's no denying it, it was a pretty big adventure to go off and get married and set up house merely on expectation.

HEDDA: Perhaps you're right.

TESMAN: Well, anyway, we have our home, Hedda. My word, yes! The home we dreamed of. And set our hearts on. What?

HEDDA (*gets up slowly, wearily*): You agreed that we should enter society. And keep open house. That was the bargain.

TESMAN: Yes. Good heavens, I was looking forward to it all so much. To seeing you play hostess to a select circle! By Jove! What? Ah, well, for the time being we shall have to make do with each other's company, Hedda. Perhaps have Auntie Juju in now and then. Oh dear, this wasn't at all what you had in mind—

HEDDA: I won't be able to have a liveried footman. For a start.

TESMAN: Oh no, we couldn't possibly afford a footman.

HEDDA: And the bay mare you promised me—

TESMAN (*fearfully*): Bay mare!

HEDDA: I mustn't even think of that now.

TESMAN: Heaven forbid!

HEDDA (*walks across the room*): Ah, well. I still have one thing left to amuse myself with.

TESMAN (*joyfully*): Thank goodness for that. What's that, Hedda? What?

HEDDA (*in the open doorway, looks at him with concealed scorn*): My pistols, George darling.

TESMAN (*alarmed*): Pistols!

HEDDA (*her eyes cold*): General Gabler's pistols.

*She goes into the rear room and disappears.*

TESMAN (*runs to the doorway and calls after her*): For heaven's sake, Hedda dear, don't touch those things. They're dangerous. Hedda—please—for my sake! What?

# ACT TWO

*The same as in Act One, except that the piano has been removed and an elegant little writing-table, with a bookcase, stands in its place. By the sofa on the left a smaller table has been placed. Most of the flowers have been removed.* MRS. ELVSTED'S *bouquet stands on the larger table, downstage. It is afternoon.*

HEDDA, *dressed to receive callers, is alone in the room. She is standing by the open french windows, loading a revolver. The pair to it is lying in an open pistol-case on the writing-table.*

HEDDA (*looks down into the garden and calls*): Good afternoon, Judge.

BRACK (*in the distance, below*): Afternoon, Mrs. Tesman.

HEDDA (*raises the pistol and takes aim*): I'm going to shoot you, Judge Brack.

BRACK (*shouts from below*): No, no, no! Don't aim that thing at me!

HEDDA: This'll teach you to enter houses by the back door.

*She fires.*

BRACK (*below*): Have you gone completely out of your mind?

HEDDA: Oh dear! Did I hit you?

BRACK (*still outside*): Stop playing these silly tricks.

HEDDA: All right, Judge. Come along in.

JUDGE BRACK, *dressed for a bachelor party, enters through the french windows. He has a light overcoat on his arm.*

BRACK: For God's sake, haven't you stopped fooling around with those things yet? What are you trying to hit?

HEDDA: Oh, I was just shooting at the sky.

BRACK (*takes the pistol gently from her hand*): By your leave, ma'am. (*Looks at it.*) Ah, yes—I know this old friend well. (*Looks around.*) Where's the case? Oh, yes. (*Puts the pistol in the case and closes it.*) That's enough of that little game for today.

HEDDA: Well, what on earth *am* I to do?

BRACK: You haven't had any visitors?

HEDDA (*closes the french windows*): Not one. I suppose the best people are all still in the country.

BRACK: Your husband isn't home yet?

HEDDA (*locks the pistol-case away in a drawer of the writing-table*): No. The moment he'd finished eating he ran off to his aunties. He wasn't expecting you so early.

BRACK: Ah, why didn't I think of that? How stupid of me.

HEDDA (*turns her head and looks at him*): Why stupid?

BRACK: I'd have come a little sooner.

HEDDA (*walks across the room*): There'd have been no one to receive you. I've been in my room since lunch, dressing.

BRACK: You haven't a tiny crack in the door through which we might have negotiated?

HEDDA: You forgot to arrange one.

BRACK: Another stupidity.

HEDDA: Well, we'll have to sit down here. And wait. Tesman won't be back for some time.

BRACK: Sad. Well, I'll be patient.

HEDDA *sits on the corner of the sofa.* BRACK *puts his coat over the back of the nearest chair and seats himself, keeping his hat in his hand. Short pause. They look at each other.*

HEDDA: Well?

BRACK (*in the same tone of voice*): Well?

HEDDA: I asked first.

BRACK (*leans forward slightly*): Yes, well, now we can enjoy a nice, cosy little chat—Mrs. Hedda.

HEDDA (*leans further back in her chair*): It seems ages since we had a talk. I don't count last night or this morning.

BRACK: You mean: *à deux?*

HEDDA: Mm—yes. That's roughly what I meant.

BRACK: I've been longing so much for you to come home.

HEDDA: So have I.

BRACK: You? Really, Mrs. Hedda? And I thought you were having such a wonderful honeymoon.

HEDDA: Oh, yes. Wonderful!

BRACK: But your husband wrote such ecstatic letters.

HEDDA: He! Oh, yes! He thinks life has nothing better to offer than rooting around in libraries and copying old pieces of parchment, or whatever it is he does.

BRACK (*a little maliciously*): Well, that is his life. Most of it, anyway.

HEDDA: Yes, I know. Well, it's all right for him. But for me! Oh no, my dear Judge. I've been bored to death.

BRACK (*sympathetically*): Do you mean that? Seriously?

HEDDA: Yes. Can you imagine? Six whole months without ever meeting a single person who was one of us, and to whom I could talk about the kind of things we talk about.

BRACK: Yes, I can understand. I'd miss that, too.

HEDDA: That wasn't the worst, though.

BRACK: What was?

HEDDA: Having to spend every minute of one's life with—with the same person.

BRACK (*nods*): Yes. What a thought! Morning; noon; *and—*

HEDDA (*coldly*): As I said: every minute of one's life.

BRACK: I stand corrected. But dear Tesman is such a clever fellow, I should have thought one ought to be able—

HEDDA: Tesman is only interested in one thing, my dear Judge. His special subject.

BRACK: True.

HEDDA: And people who are only interested in one thing don't make the most amusing company. Not for long, anyway.

BRACK: Not even when they happen to be the person one loves?

HEDDA: Oh, don't use that sickly, stupid word.

BRACK (*starts*): But, Mrs. Hedda—!

HEDDA (*half laughing, half annoyed*): You just try it, Judge. Listening to the history of civilization morning, noon and—

BRACK (*corrects her*): Every minute of one's life.

HEDDA: All right. Oh, and those domestic industries of Brabant in the Middle Ages! That really is beyond the limit.

BRACK (*looks at her searchingly*): But, tell me—if you feel like this why on earth did you—? Hm—

HEDDA: Why on earth did I marry George Tesman?

BRACK: If you like to put it that way.

HEDDA: Do you think it so very strange?

BRACK: Yes—and no, Mrs. Hedda.

HEDDA: I'd danced myself tired, Judge. I felt my time was up—(*Gives a slight shudder.*) No, I mustn't say that. Or even think it.

BRACK: You've no rational cause to think it.

HEDDA: Oh—cause, cause—(*Looks searchingly at him.*) After all, George Tesman— well, I mean, he's a very respectable man.

BRACK: Very respectable, sound as a rock. No denying that.

HEDDA: And there's nothing exactly ridiculous about him. Is there?

BRACK: Ridiculous? N-no, I wouldn't say that.

HEDDA: Mm. He's very clever at collecting material and all that, isn't he? I mean, he may go quite far in time.

BRACK (*looks at her a little uncertainly*): I thought you believed, like everyone else, that he would become a very prominent man.

HEDDA (*looks tired*): Yes, I did. And when he came and begged me on his bended knees to be allowed to love and to cherish me, I didn't see why I shouldn't let him.

BRACK: No, well—if one looks at it like that—

HEDDA: It was more than my other admirers were prepared to do, Judge dear.

BRACK (*laughs*): Well, I can't answer for the others. As far as I myself am concerned, you know I've always had a considerable respect for the institution of marriage. As an institution.

HEDDA (*lightly*): Oh, I've never entertained any hopes of you.

BRACK: All I want is to have a circle of friends whom I can trust, whom I can help with advice or—or by any other means, and into whose houses I may come and go as a—trusted friend.

HEDDA: Of the husband?

BRACK (*bows*): Preferably, to be frank, of the wife. And of the husband too, of course. Yes, you know, this kind of triangle is a delightful arrangement for all parties concerned.

HEDDA: Yes, I often longed for a third person while I was away. Oh, those hours we spent alone in railway compartments—

BRACK: Fortunately your honeymoon is now over.

HEDDA (*shakes her head*): There's a long, long way still to go. I've only reached a stop on the line.

BRACK: Why not jump out and stretch your legs a little, Mrs. Hedda?

HEDDA: I'm not the jumping sort.

BRACK: Aren't you?

HEDDA: No. There's always someone around who—

BRACK (*laughs*): Who looks at one's legs?

HEDDA: Yes. Exactly.

BRACK: Well, but surely—

HEDDA (*with a gesture of rejection*): I don't like it. I'd rather stay where I am. Sitting in the compartment. *À deux.*

BRACK: But suppose a third person were to step into the compartment?

HEDDA: That would be different.

BRACK: A trusted friend—someone who understood—

HEDDA: And was lively and amusing—

BRACK: And interested in—more subjects than one—

HEDDA (*sighs audibly*): Yes, that'd be a relief.

BRACK (*hears the front door open and shut*): The triangle is completed.

HEDDA (*half under her breath*): And the train goes on.

GEORGE TESMAN, *in grey walking dress with a soft felt hat, enters from the hall. He has a number of paper-covered books under his arm and in his pockets.*

TESMAN (*goes over to the table by the corner sofa*): Phew! It's too hot to be lugging all this around. (*Puts the books down.*) I'm positively sweating, Hedda. Why, hullo, hullo! You here already, Judge? What? Bertha didn't tell me.

BRACK (*gets up*): I came in through the garden.

HEDDA: What are all those books you've got there?

TESMAN (*stands glancing through them*): Oh, some new publications dealing with my special subject. I had to buy them.

HEDDA: Your special subject?

BRACK: His special subject, Mrs. Tesman.

BRACK *and* HEDDA *exchange a smile.*

HEDDA: Haven't you collected enough material on your special subject?

TESMAN: My dear Hedda, one can never have too much. One must keep abreast of what other people are writing.

HEDDA: Yes. Of course.

TESMAN (*rooting among the books*): Look—I bought a copy of Eilert Lœvborg's new book, too. (*Holds it out to her.*) Perhaps you'd like to have a look at it, Hedda? What?

HEDDA: No, thank you. Er—yes, perhaps I will, later.

TESMAN: I glanced through it on my way home.

BRACK: What's your opinion—as a specialist on the subject?

TESMAN: I'm amazed how sound and balanced it is. He never used to write like that. (*Gathers his books together.*) Well, I must get down to these at once. I can hardly wait to cut the pages. Oh, I've got to change, too. (*To* BRACK) We don't have to be off just yet, do we? What?

BRACK: Heavens, no. We've plenty of time yet.

TESMAN: Good, I needn't hurry, then. (*Goes with his books, but stops and turns in the doorway.*) Oh, by the way, Hedda, Auntie Juju won't be coming to see you this evening.

HEDDA: Won't she? Oh—the hat, I suppose.

TESMAN: Good heavens, no. How could you think such a thing of Auntie Juju? Fancy—! No, Auntie Rena's very ill.

HEDDA: She always is.

TESMAN: Yes, but today she's been taken really bad.

HEDDA: Oh, then it's quite understandable that the other one should want to stay with her. Well, I shall have to swallow my disappointment.

TESMAN: You can't imagine how happy Auntie Juju was in spite of everything. At your looking so well after the honeymoon!

HEDDA (*half beneath her breath, as she rises*): Oh, these everlasting aunts!

TESMAN: What?

HEDDA (*goes over to the french windows*): Nothing.

TESMAN: Oh. All right. (*Goes into the rear room and out of sight.*)

BRACK: What was that about the hat?

HEDDA: Oh, something that happened with Miss Tesman this morning. She'd put her hat down on a chair. (*Looks at him and smiles.*) And I pretended to think it was the servant's.

BRACK (*shakes his head*): But, my dear Mrs. Hedda, how could you do such a thing? To that poor old lady?

HEDDA (*nervously, walking across the room*): Sometimes a mood like that hits me. And

I can't stop myself. (*Throws herself down in the armchair by the stove.*) Oh, I don't know how to explain it.

BRACK (*behind her chair*): You're not really happy. That's the answer.

HEDDA (*stares ahead of her*): Why on earth should I be happy? Can you give me a reason?

BRACK: Yes. For one thing you've got the home you always wanted.

HEDDA (*looks at him*): You really believe that story?

BRACK: You mean it isn't true?

HEDDA: Oh, yes, it's partly true.

BRACK: Well?

HEDDA: It's true I got Tesman to see me home from parties last summer—

BRACK: It was a pity my home lay in another direction.

HEDDA: Yes. Your interests lay in another direction, too.

BRACK (*laughs*): That's naughty of you, Mrs. Hedda. But to return to you and George—

HEDDA: Well, we walked past this house one evening. And poor Tesman was fidgeting in his boots trying to find something to talk about. I felt sorry for the great scholar—

BRACK (*smiles incredulously*): Did you? Hm.

HEDDA: Yes, honestly I did. Well, to help him out of his misery, I happened to say quite frivolously how much I'd love to live in this house.

BRACK: Was that all?

HEDDA: That evening, yes.

BRACK: But—afterwards?

HEDDA: Yes. My little frivolity had its consequences, my dear Judge.

BRACK: Our little frivolities do. Much too often, unfortunately.

HEDDA: Thank you. Well, it was our mutual admiration for the late Prime Minister's house that brought George Tesman and me together on common ground. So we got engaged, and we got married, and we went on our honeymoon, and—Ah

well, Judge, I've—made my bed and I must lie in it, I was about to say.

BRACK: How utterly fantastic! And you didn't really care in the least about the house?

HEDDA: God knows I didn't.

BRACK: Yes, but now that we've furnished it so beautifully for you?

HEDDA: Ugh—all the rooms smell of lavender and dried roses. But perhaps Auntie Juju brought that in.

BRACK (*laughs*): More likely the Prime Minister's widow, rest her soul.

HEDDA: Yes, it's got the odour of death about it. It reminds me of the flowers one has worn at a ball—the morning after. (*Clasps her hands behind her neck, leans back in the chair and looks up at him.*) Oh, my dear Judge, you've no idea how hideously bored I'm going to be out here.

BRACK: Couldn't you find some—occupation, Mrs. Hedda? Like your husband?

HEDDA: Occupation? That'd interest me?

BRACK: Well—preferably.

HEDDA: God knows what. I've often thought—(*Breaks off.*) No, that wouldn't work either.

BRACK: Who knows? Tell me about it.

HEDDA: I was thinking—if I could persuade Tesman to go into politics, for example.

BRACK (*laughs*): Tesman! No, honestly, I don't think he's quite cut out to be a politician.

HEDDA: Perhaps not. But if I could persuade him to have a go at it?

BRACK: What satisfaction would that give you? If he turned out to be no good? Why do you want to make him do that?

HEDDA: Because I'm bored. (*After a moment.*) You feel there's absolutely no possibility of Tesman becoming Prime Minister, then?

BRACK: Well, you know, Mrs. Hedda, for one thing he'd have to be pretty well off before he could become that.

HEDDA (*gets up impatiently*): There you are! (*Walks across the room.*) It's this wretched poverty that makes life so hateful. And ludicrous. Well, it is!

BRACK: I don't think that's the real cause.

HEDDA: What is, then?

BRACK: Nothing really exciting has ever happened to you.

HEDDA: Nothing serious, you mean?

BRACK: Call it that if you like. But now perhaps it may.

HEDDA (*tosses her head*): Oh, you're thinking of this competition for that wretched professorship? That's Tesman's affair. I'm not going to waste my time worrying about that.

BRACK: Very well, let's forget about that, then. But suppose you were to find yourself faced with what people call—to use the conventional phrase—the most solemn of human responsibilities? (*Smiles.*) A new responsibility, little Mrs. Hedda.

HEDDA (*angrily*): Be quiet! Nothing like that's going to happen.

BRACK (*warily*): We'll talk about it again in a year's time. If not earlier.

HEDDA (*curtly*): I've no leanings in that direction, Judge. I don't want any—responsibilities.

BRACK: But surely you must feel some inclination to make use of that—natural talent which every woman—

HEDDA (*over by the french windows*): Oh, be quiet, I say! I often think there's only one thing for which I have any natural talent.

BRACK (*goes closer*): And what is that, if I may be so bold as to ask?

HEDDA (*stands looking out*): For boring myself to death. Now you know. (*Turns, looks towards the rear room and laughs.*) Talking of boring, here comes the professor.

BRACK (*quietly, warningly*): Now, now, now, Mrs. Hedda!

GEORGE TESMAN, *in evening dress, with gloves and hat in his hand, enters through the rear room from the right.*

TESMAN: Hedda, hasn't any message come from Eilert? What?

HEDDA: No.

TESMAN: Ah, then we'll have him here presently. You wait and see.

BRACK: You really think he'll come?

TESMAN: Yes, I'm almost sure he will. What you were saying about him this morning is just gossip.

BRACK: Oh?

TESMAN: Yes, Auntie Juju said she didn't believe he'd ever dare to stand in my way again. Fancy that!

BRACK: Then everything in the garden's lovely.

TESMAN (*puts his hat, with his gloves in it, on a chair, right*): Yes, but you really must let me wait for him as long as possible.

BRACK: We've plenty of time. No one'll be turning up at my place before seven or half past.

TESMAN: Ah, then we can keep Hedda company a little longer. And see if he turns up. What?

HEDDA (*picks up* BRACK'S *coat and hat and carries them over to the corner sofa*): And if the worst comes to the worst, Mr. Lœvborg can sit here and talk to me.

BRACK (*offering to take his things from her*): No, please. What do you mean by 'if the worst comes to the worst'?

HEDDA: If he doesn't want to go with you and Tesman.

TESMAN (*looks doubtfully at her*): I say, Hedda, do you think it'll be all right for him to stay here with you? What? Remember Auntie Juju isn't coming.

HEDDA: Yes, but Mrs. Elvsted is. The three of us can have a cup of tea together.

TESMAN: Ah, that'll be all right.

BRACK (*smiles*): It's probably the safest solution as far as he's concerned.

HEDDA: Why?

BRACK: My dear Mrs. Tesman, you always say of my little bachelor parties that they

BRACK: Oh, I think honour and victory can be very splendid things—

TESMAN: Of course they can. Still—

HEDDA (*looks at* TESMAN, *with a cold smile*): You look as if you'd been hit by a thunderbolt.

TESMAN: Yes, I feel rather like it.

BRACK: There was a black cloud looming up, Mrs. Tesman. But it seems to have passed over.

HEDDA (*points towards the rear room*): Well, gentlemen, won't you go in and take a glass of cold punch?

BRACK (*glances at his watch*): One for the road. Yes, why not?

TESMAN: An admirable suggestion, Hedda. Admirable! Oh, I feel so relieved!

HEDDA: Won't you have one, too, Mr. Lœvborg?

LŒVBORG: No, thank you. I'd rather not.

BRACK: Great heavens, man, cold punch isn't poison. Take my word for it.

LŒVBORG: Not for everyone, perhaps.

HEDDA: I'll keep Mr. Lœvborg company while you drink.

TESMAN: Yes, Hedda dear, would you?

*He and* BRACK *go into the rear room, sit down, drink punch, smoke cigarettes and talk cheerfully during the following scene.* EILERT LŒVBORG *remains standing by the stove.* HEDDA *goes to the writing-table.*

HEDDA (*raising her voice slightly*): I've some photographs I'd like to show you, if you'd care to see them. Tesman and I visited the Tyrol on our way home.

*She comes back with an album, places it on the table by the sofa and sits in the upstage corner of the sofa.* EILERT LŒVBORG *comes towards her, stops, and looks at her. Then he takes a chair and sits down on her left, with his back towards the rear room.*

HEDDA (*opens the album*): You see these mountains, Mr. Lœvborg? That's the Ortler group. Tesman has written the name underneath. You see: 'The Ortler Group near Meran.'

LŒVBORG (*has not taken his eyes from her; says softly, slowly*): Hedda—Gabler!

HEDDA (*gives him a quick glance*): Ssh!

LŒVBORG (*repeats softly*): Hedda Gabler!

HEDDA (*looks at the album*): Yes, that used to be my name. When we first knew each other.

LŒVBORG: And from now on—for the rest of my life—I must teach myself never to say: Hedda Gabler.

HEDDA (*still turning the pages*): Yes, you must. You'd better start getting into practice. The sooner the better.

LŒVBORG: (*bitterly*): Hedda Gabler married? And to George Tesman!

HEDDA: Yes. Well—that's life.

LŒVBORG: Oh, Hedda, Hedda! How could you throw yourself away like that?

HEDDA (*looks sharply at him*): Stop it.

LŒVBORG: What do you mean?

TESMAN *comes in and goes towards the sofa.*

HEDDA (*hears him coming and says casually*): And this, Mr. Lœvborg, is the view from the Ampezzo valley. Look at those mountains. (*Glances affectionately up at* TESMAN.) What did you say those curious mountains were called, dear?

TESMAN: Let me have a look. Oh, those are the Dolomites.

HEDDA: Of course. Those are the Dolomites, Mr. Lœvborg.

TESMAN: Hedda, I just wanted to ask you, can't we bring some punch in here? A glass for you, anyway. What?

HEDDA: Thank you, yes. And a biscuit or two, perhaps.

TESMAN: You wouldn't like a cigarette?

HEDDA: No.

TESMAN: Right.

*He goes into the rear room and over to the right.* BRACK *is seated there, glancing occasionally at* HEDDA *and* LŒVBORG.

LŒVBORG (*softly, as before*): Answer me, Hedda. How could you do it?

HEDDA (*apparently absorbed in the album*): If you go on calling me Hedda I won't talk to you any more.

LŒVBORG: Mayn't I even when we're alone?

HEDDA: No. You can think it. But you mustn't say it.

LŒVBORG: Oh, I see. Because you love George Tesman.

HEDDA (*glances at him and smiles*): Love? Don't be funny.

LŒVBORG: You don't love him?

HEDDA: I don't intend to be unfaithful to him. That's not what I want.

LŒVBORG: Hedda—just tell me one thing—

HEDDA: Ssh!

*TESMAN enters from the rear room, carrying a tray.*

TESMAN: Here we are! Here come the refreshments.

*He puts the tray down on the table.*

HEDDA: Why didn't you ask the servant to bring it in?

TESMAN (*fills the glasses*): I like waiting on you, Hedda.

HEDDA: But you've filled both glasses. Mr. Lœvborg doesn't want to drink.

TESMAN: Yes, but Mrs. Elvsted'll be here soon.

HEDDA: Oh yes, that's true. Mrs. Elvsted—

TESMAN: Had you forgotten her? What?

HEDDA: We're so absorbed with these photographs. (*Shows him one.*) You remember this little village?

TESMAN: Oh, that one down by the Brenner Pass. We spent a night there—

HEDDA: Yes, and met all those amusing people.

TESMAN: Oh yes, it was there, wasn't it? By Jove, if only we could have had you with us, Eilert! Ah, well.

*He goes back into the other room and sits down with BRACK.*

LŒVBORG: Tell me one thing, Hedda.

HEDDA: Yes?

LŒVBORG: Didn't you love me either? Not—just a little?

HEDDA: Well now, I wonder? No, I think we were just good friends. (*Smiles.*) You certainly poured your heart out to me.

LŒVBORG: You begged me to.

HEDDA: Looking back on it, there was something beautiful and fascinating—and brave—about the way we told each other everything. That secret friendship no one else knew about.

LŒVBORG: Yes, Hedda, yes! Do you remember? How I used to come up to your father's house in the afternoon—and the General sat by the window and read his newspapers—with his back towards us—

HEDDA: And we sat on the sofa in the corner—

LŒVBORG: Always reading the same illustrated magazine—

HEDDA: We hadn't any photograph album.

LŒVBORG: Yes, Hedda. I regarded you as a kind of confessor. Told you things about myself which no one else knew about—then. Those days and nights of drinking and—oh, Hedda, what power did you have to make me confess such things?

HEDDA: Power? You think I had some power over you?

LŒVBORG: Yes—I don't know how else to explain it. And all those—oblique questions you asked me—

HEDDA: You knew what they meant.

LŒVBORG: But that you could sit there and ask me such questions! So unashamedly—

HEDDA: I thought you said they were oblique.

LŒVBORG: Yes, but you asked them so unashamedly. That you could question me about—about that kind of thing!

HEDDA: You answered willingly enough.

LŒVBORG: Yes—that's what I can't understand—looking back on it. But tell me,

Hedda—what you felt for me—wasn't that—love? When you asked me those questions and made me confess my sins to you, wasn't it because you wanted to wash me clean?

HEDDA: No, not exactly.

LŒVBORG: Why did you do it, then?

HEDDA: Do you find it so incredible that a young girl, given the chance in secret, should want to be allowed a glimpse into a forbidden world of whose existence she is supposed to be ignorant?

LŒVBORG: So that was it?

HEDDA: One reason. One reason—I think.

LŒVBORG: You didn't love me, then. You just wanted—knowledge. But if that was so, why did you break it off?

HEDDA: That was your fault.

LŒVBORG: It was you who put an end to it.

HEDDA: Yes, when I realized that our friendship was threatening to develop into something—something else. Shame on you, Eilert Lœvborg! How could you abuse the trust of your dearest friend?

LŒVBORG: (clenches his fist): Oh, why didn't you do it? Why didn't you shoot me dead? As you threatened to!

HEDDA: I was afraid. Of the scandal.

LŒVBORG: Yes, Hedda. You're a coward at heart.

HEDDA: A dreadful coward. (Changes her tone.) Luckily for you. Well, now you've found consolation with the Elvsteds.

LŒVBORG: I know what Thea's been telling you.

HEDDA: I dare say you told her about us.

LŒVBORG: Not a word. She's too silly to understand that kind of thing.

HEDDA: Silly?

LŒVBORG: She's silly about that kind of thing.

HEDDA: And I'm a coward. (Leans closer to him, without looking him in the eyes, and says quietly) But let me tell you something. Something you don't know.

LŒVBORG (tensely): Yes?

HEDDA: My failure to shoot you wasn't my worst act of cowardice that evening.

LŒVBORG (looks at her for a moment, realizes her meaning, and whispers passionately): Oh, Hedda! Hedda Gabler! Now I see what was behind those questions. Yes! It wasn't knowledge you wanted! It was life!

HEDDA (flashes a look at him and says quietly): Take care! Don't you delude yourself!
It has begun to grow dark. BERTHA, from outside, opens the door leading into the hall.

HEDDA (closes the album with a snap and cries, smiling): Ah, at last! Come in, Thea dear!
MRS. ELVSTED enters from the hall, in evening dress. The door is closed behind her.

HEDDA (on the sofa, stretches out her arms towards her): Thea darling, I thought you were never coming!
MRS. ELVSTED makes a slight bow to the gentlemen in the rear room as she passes the open doorway, and they to her. Then she goes to the table and holds out her hand to HEDDA. EILERT LŒVBORG has risen from his chair. He and MRS. ELVSTED nod silently to each other.

MRS. ELVSTED: Perhaps I ought to go in and say a few words to your husband?

HEDDA: Oh, there's no need. They're happy by themselves. They'll be going soon.

MRS. ELVSTED: Going?

HEDDA: Yes, they're off on a spree this evening.

MRS. ELVSTED (quickly, to LŒVBORG): You're not going with them?

LŒVBORG: No.

HEDDA: Mr. Lœvborg is staying here with us.

MRS. ELVSTED (takes a chair and is about to sit down beside him): Oh, how nice it is to be here!

HEDDA: No, Thea darling, not there. Come over here and sit beside me. I want to be in the middle.

MRS. ELVSTED: Yes, just as you wish.

*She goes round the table and sits on the sofa, on* HEDDA's *right.* LŒVBORG *sits down again in his chair.*

LŒVBORG (*after a short pause, to* HEDDA): Isn't she lovely to look at?

HEDDA (*strokes her hair gently*): Only to look at?

LŒVBORG: Yes. We're just good friends. We trust each other implicitly. We can talk to each other quite unashamedly.

HEDDA: No need to be oblique?

MRS. ELVSTED (*nestles close to* HEDDA *and says quietly*): Oh, Hedda, I'm so happy. Imagine—he says I've inspired him!

HEDDA (*looks at her with a smile*): Dear Thea! Does he really?

LŒVBORG: She has the courage of her convictions, Mrs. Tesman.

MRS. ELVSTED: I? Courage?

LŒVBORG: Absolute courage. Where friendship is concerned.

HEDDA: Yes. Courage. Yes. If only one had that—

LŒVBORG: Yes?

HEDDA: One might be able to live. In spite of everything. (*Changes her tone suddenly.*) Well, Thea darling, now you're going to drink a nice glass of cold punch.

MRS. ELVSTED: No thank you. I never drink anything like that.

HEDDA: Oh. You, Mr. Lœvborg?

LŒVBORG: Thank you, I don't either.

MRS. ELVSTED: No, he doesn't, either.

HEDDA (*looks into his eyes*): But if I want you to.

LŒVBORG: That doesn't make any difference.

HEDDA (*laughs*): Have I no power over you at all? Poor me!

LŒVBORG: Not where this is concerned.

HEDDA: Seriously, I think you should. For your own sake.

MRS. ELVSTED: Hedda!

LŒVBORG: Why?

HEDDA: Or perhaps I should say for other people's sake.

LŒVBORG: What do you mean?

HEDDA: People might think you didn't feel absolutely and unashamedly sure of yourself. In your heart of hearts.

MRS. ELVSTED (*quietly*): Oh, Hedda, no!

LŒVBORG: People can think what they like. For the present.

MRS. ELVSTED (*happily*): Yes, that's true.

HEDDA: I saw it so clearly in Judge Brack a few minutes ago.

LŒVBORG: Oh. What did you see?

HEDDA: He smiled so scornfully when he saw you were afraid to go in there and drink with them.

LŒVBORG: Afraid! I wanted to stay here and talk to you.

MRS. ELVSTED: That was only natural, Hedda.

HEDDA: But the Judge wasn't to know that. I saw him wink at Tesman when you showed you didn't dare to join their wretched little party.

LŒVBORG: Didn't dare! Are you saying I didn't dare?

HEDDA: I'm not saying so. But that was what Judge Brack thought.

LŒVBORG: Well, let him.

HEDDA: You're not going, then?

LŒVBORG: I'm staying with you and Thea.

MRS. ELVSTED: Yes, Hedda, of course he is.

HEDDA (*smiles, and nods approvingly to* LŒVBORG): Firm as a rock! A man of principle! That's how a man should be! (*Turns to* MRS. ELVSTED *and strokes her cheek.*) Didn't I tell you so this morning when you came here in such a panic—?

LŒVBORG (*starts*): Panic?

MRS. ELVSTED (*frightened*): Hedda! But—Hedda!

HEDDA: Well, now you can see for yourself. There's no earthly need for you to get scared to death just because—(*Stops.*)

Well! Let's all three cheer up and enjoy ourselves.

LŒVBORG: Mrs. Tesman, would you mind explaining to me what this is all about?

MRS. ELVSTED: Oh, my God, my God, Hedda, what are you saying? What are you doing?

HEDDA: Keep calm. That horrid Judge has his eye on you.

LŒVBORG: Scared to death, were you? For my sake?

MRS. ELVSTED (*quietly, trembling*): Oh, Hedda! You've made me so unhappy!

LŒVBORG (*looks coldly at her for a moment. His face is distorted*): So that was how much you trusted me.

MRS. ELVSTED: Eilert dear, please listen to me—

LŒVBORG (*takes one of the glasses of punch, raises it and says quietly, hoarsely*): Skoal, Thea!
*He empties the glass, puts it down and picks up one of the others.*

MRS. ELVSTED (*quietly*): Hedda, Hedda! Why did you want this to happen?

HEDDA: I—want it? Are you mad?

LŒVBORG: Skoal to you, too, Mrs. Tesman. Thanks for telling me the truth. Here's to the truth!
*He empties his glass and refills it.*

HEDDA (*puts her hand on his arm*): Steady. That's enough for now. Don't forget the party.

MRS. ELVSTED: No, no, no!

HEDDA: Ssh! They're looking at you.

LŒVBORG (*puts down his glass*): Thea, tell me the truth—

MRS. ELVSTED: Yes!

LŒVBORG: Did your husband know you were following me?

MRS. ELVSTED: Oh, Hedda!

LŒVBORG: Did you and he have an agreement that you should come here and keep an eye on me? Perhaps he gave you the idea? After all, he's a magistrate. I suppose he needed me back in his office. Or did he miss my companionship at the card-table?

MRS. ELVSTED (*quietly, sobbing*): Eilert, Eilert!

LŒVBORG (*seizes a glass and is about to fill it*): Let's drink to him, too.

HEDDA: No more now. Remember you're going to read your book to Tesman.

LŒVBORG (*calm again, puts down his glass*): That was silly of me, Thea. To take it like that, I mean. Don't be angry with me, my dear. You'll see—yes, and they'll see, too—that though I fell, I—1 have raised myself up again. With your help, Thea.

MRS. ELVSTED (*happily*): Oh, thank God!
BRACK *has meanwhile glanced at his watch. He and* TESMAN *get up and come into the drawing-room.*

BRACK (*takes his hat and overcoat*): Well, Mrs. Tesman, it's time for us to go.

HEDDA: Yes, I suppose it must be.

LŒVBORG (*gets up*): Time for me, too, Judge.

MRS. ELVSTED (*quietly, pleadingly*): Eilert, please don't!

HEDDA (*pinches her arm*): They can hear you.

MRS. ELVSTED (*gives a little cry*): Oh!

LŒVBORG (*to* BRACK): You were kind enough to ask me to join you.

BRACK: Are you coming?

LŒVBORG: If I may.

BRACK: Delighted.

LŒVBORG (*Puts the paper package in his pocket and says to* TESMAN): I'd like to show you one or two things before I send it off to the printer.

TESMAN: I say, that'll be fun. Fancy—! Oh, but, Hedda, how'll Mrs. Elvsted get home? What?

HEDDA: Oh, we'll manage somehow.

LŒVBORG (*glances over towards the ladies*): Mrs. Elvsted? I shall come back and collect her, naturally. (*Goes closer.*) About ten o'clock, Mrs. Tesman? Will that suit you?

HEDDA: Yes. That'll suit me admirably.

TESMAN: Good, that's settled. But you mustn't expect me back so early, Hedda.

HEDDA: Stay as long as you c—as long as you like, dear.

MRS. ELVSTED (*trying to hide her anxiety*): Well then, Mr. Lœvborg, I'll wait here till you come.

LŒVBORG (*his hat in his hand*): Pray do, Mrs. Elvsted.

BRACK: Well, gentlemen, now the party begins. I trust that, in the words of a certain fair lady, we shall enjoy good sport.

HEDDA: What a pity the fair lady can't be there, invisible.

BRACK: Why invisible?

HEDDA: So as to be able to hear some of your uncensored witticisms, your honour.

BRACK (*laughs*): Oh, I shouldn't advise the fair lady to do that.

TESMAN (*laughs, too*): I say, Hedda, that's good. What!

BRACK: Well, good night, ladies, good night!

LŒVBORG (*bows farewell*): About ten o'clock then.

BRACK, LŒVBORG *and* TESMAN *go out through the hall. As they do so,* BERTHA *enters from the rear room with a lighted lamp. She puts it on the drawing-room table, then goes out the way she came.*

MRS. ELVSTED (*has got up and is walking uneasily to and fro*): Oh, Hedda, Hedda! How is all this going to end?

HEDDA: At ten o'clock, then. He'll be here. I can see him. With a crown of vine leaves in his hair. Burning and unashamed!

MRS. ELVSTED: Oh, I do hope so!

HEDDA: Can't you see? Then he'll be himself again! He'll be a free man for the rest of his days!

MRS. ELVSTED: Please God you're right.

HEDDA: That's how he'll come! (*Gets up and goes closer.*) You can doubt him as much as you like. I believe in him! Now we'll see which of us—

MRS. ELVSTED: You're after something, Hedda.

HEDDA: Yes, I am. For once in my life I want to have the power to shape a man's destiny.

MRS. ELVSTED: Haven't you that power already?

HEDDA: No, I haven't. I've never had it.

MRS. ELVSTED: What about your husband?

HEDDA: Him! Oh, if you could only understand how poor I am. And you're allowed to be so rich, so rich! (*Clasps her passionately.*) I think I'll burn your hair off after all!

MRS. ELVSTED: Let me go! Let me go! You frighten me, Hedda!

BERTHA (*in the open doorway*): I've laid tea in the dining-room, madam.

HEDDA: Good, we're coming.

MRS. ELVSTED: No, no, no! I'd rather go home alone! Now—at once!

HEDDA: Rubbish! First you're going to have some tea, you little idiot. And then—at ten o'clock—Eilert Lœvborg will come. With a crown of vine leaves in his hair! *She drags* MRS. ELVSTED *almost forcibly towards the open doorway.*

# ACT THREE

*The same. The curtains are drawn across the open doorway, and also across the french windows. The lamp, half turned down, with a shade over it, is burning on the table. In the stove, the door of which is open, a fire has been burning, but it is now almost out.* MRS. ELVSTED, *wrapped in a large shawl and with her feet resting on a footstool, is sitting near the stove, huddled in the armchair.* HEDDA *is lying asleep on the sofa, fully dressed, with a blanket over her.*

MRS. ELVSTED (*after a pause, suddenly sits up in her chair and listens tensely. Then she sinks wearily back again and sighs.*): Not back yet! Oh, God! Oh, God! Not back yet!

BERTHA *tiptoes cautiously in from the hall. She has a letter in her hand.*

MRS. ELVSTED (*turns and whispers*): What is it? Has someone come?

BERTHA (*quietly*): Yes, a servant's just called with this letter.

MRS. ELVSTED (*quickly, holding out her hand*): A letter! Give it to me!

BERTHA: But it's for the Doctor, madam.

MRS. ELVSTED: Oh, I see.

BERTHA: Miss Tesman's maid brought it. I'll leave it here on the table.

MRS. ELVSTED: Yes, do.

BERTHA (*puts down the letter*): I'd better put the lamp out. It's starting to smoke.

MRS. ELVSTED: Yes, put it out. It'll soon be daylight.

BERTHA (*puts out the lamp*): It's daylight already, madam.

MRS. ELVSTED: Yes. Broad day. And not home yet.

BERTHA: Oh dear, I was afraid this would happen.

MRS. ELVSTED: Were you?

BERTHA: Yes. When I heard that a certain gentleman had returned to town, and saw him go off with them. I've heard all about him.

MRS. ELVSTED: Don't talk so loud. You'll wake your mistress.

BERTHA (*looks at the sofa and sighs*): Yes. Let her go on sleeping, poor dear. Shall I put some more wood on the fire?

MRS. ELVSTED: Thank you, don't bother on my account.

BERTHA: Very good.

*She goes quietly out through the hall.*

HEDDA (*wakes as the door closes and looks up*): What's that?

MRS. ELVSTED: It was only the maid.

HEDDA (*looks round*): What am I doing here? Oh, now I remember. (*Sits up on the sofa, stretches herself and rubs her eyes.*) What time is it, Thea?

MRS. ELVSTED: It's gone seven.

HEDDA: When did Tesman get back?

MRS. ELVSTED: He's not back yet.

HEDDA: Not home yet?

MRS. ELVSTED (*gets up*): No one's come.

HEDDA: And we sat up waiting for them till four o'clock.

MRS. ELVSTED: God! How I waited for him!

HEDDA (*yawns and says with her hand in front of her mouth*): Oh, dear. We might have saved ourselves the trouble.

MRS. ELVSTED: Did you manage to sleep?

HEDDA: Oh, yes. Quite well, I think. Didn't you get any?

MRS. ELVSTED: Not a wink. I couldn't, Hedda. I just couldn't.

HEDDA (*gets up and comes over to her*): Now, now, now. There's nothing to worry about. I know what's happened.

MRS. ELVSTED: What? Please tell me.

HEDDA: Well, obviously the party went on very late—

MRS. ELVSTED: Oh dear, I suppose it must have. But—

HEDDA: And Tesman didn't want to come home and wake us all up in the middle of the night. (*Laughs.*) Probably wasn't too keen to show his face either, after a spree like that.

MRS. ELVSTED: But where could he have gone?

HEDDA: I should think he's probably slept at his aunts'. They keep his old room for him.

MRS. ELVSTED: No, he can't be with them. A letter came for him just now from Miss Tesman. It's over there.

HEDDA: Oh? (*Looks at the envelope.*) Yes, it's Auntie Juju's handwriting. Well, he must still be at Judge Brack's, then. And Eilert Lœvborg is sitting there, reading to him. With a crown of vine leaves in his hair.

MRS. ELVSTED: Hedda, you're only saying that. You don't believe it.

HEDDA: Thea, you really are a little fool.

MRS. ELVSTED: Perhaps I am.

HEDDA: You look tired to death.

MRS. ELVSTED: Yes. I am tired to death.

HEDDA: Go to my room and lie down for a little. Do as I say, now; don't argue.

**MRS. ELVSTED:** No, no. I couldn't possibly sleep.

**HEDDA:** Of course you can.

**MRS. ELVSTED:** But your husband'll be home soon. And I must know at once—

**HEDDA:** I'll tell you when he comes.

**MRS. ELVSTED:** Promise me, Hedda?

**HEDDA:** Yes, don't worry. Go and get some sleep.

**MRS. ELVSTED:** Thank you. All right, I'll try. *She goes out through the rear room.* **HEDDA** *goes to the french windows and draws the curtains. Broad daylight floods into the room. She goes to the writing-table, takes a small hand-mirror from it and arranges her hair. Then she goes to the door leading into the hall and presses the bell. After a few moments,* **BERTHA** *enters.*

**BERTHA:** Did you want anything, madam?

**HEDDA:** Yes, put some more wood on the fire. I'm freezing.

**BERTHA:** Bless you, I'll soon have this room warmed up.

*(She rakes the embers together and puts a fresh piece of wood on them. Suddenly she stops and listens.)* There's someone at the front door, madam.

**HEDDA:** Well, go and open it. I'll see to the fire.

**BERTHA:** It'll burn up in a moment.

*She goes out through the hall.* **HEDDA** *kneels on the footstool and puts more wood in the stove. After a few seconds,* **GEORGE TESMAN** *enters from the hall. He looks tired, and rather worried. He tiptoes towards the open doorway and is about to slip through the curtains.*

**HEDDA** *(at the stove, without looking up):* Good morning.

**TESMAN** *(turns):* Hedda! *(Comes nearer.)* Good heavens, are you up already? What?

**HEDDA:** Yes, I got up very early this morning.

**TESMAN:** I was sure you'd still be sleeping. Fancy that!

**HEDDA:** Don't talk so loud. Mrs. Elvsted's asleep in my room.

**TESMAN:** Mrs. Elvsted? Has she stayed the night here?

**HEDDA:** Yes. No one came to escort her home.

**TESMAN:** Oh. No, I suppose not.

**HEDDA** *(closes the door of the stove and gets up):* Well. Was it fun?

**TESMAN:** Have you been anxious about me? What?

**HEDDA:** Not in the least. I asked if you'd had fun.

**TESMAN:** Oh yes, rather! Well, I thought, for once in a while—! The first part was the best; when Eilert read his book to me. We arrived over an hour too early—what about that, eh? Fancy—! Brack had a lot of things to see to, so Eilert read to me.

**HEDDA** *(sits at the right-hand side of the table):* Well? Tell me about it.

**TESMAN** *(sits on a footstool by the stove):* Honestly, Hedda, you've no idea what a book that's going to be. It's really one of the most remarkable things that's ever been written. By Jove!

**HEDDA:** Oh, never mind about the book—

**TESMAN:** I'm going to make a confession to you, Hedda. When he'd finished reading a sort of beastly feeling came over me.

**HEDDA:** Beastly feeling?

**TESMAN:** I found myself envying Eilert for being able to write like that. Imagine that, Hedda!

**HEDDA:** Yes. I can imagine.

**TESMAN:** What a tragedy that with all those gifts he should be so incorrigible.

**HEDDA:** You mean he's less afraid of life than most men?

**TESMAN:** Good heavens, no. He just doesn't know the meaning of the word moderation.

**HEDDA:** What happened afterwards?

**TESMAN:** Well, looking back on it, I suppose you might almost call it an orgy, Hedda.

**HEDDA:** Had he vine leaves in his hair?

TESMAN: Vine leaves? No, I didn't see any of them. He made a long, rambling oration in honour of the woman who'd inspired him to write this book. Yes, those were the words he used.

HEDDA: Did he name her?

TESMAN: No. But I suppose it must be Mrs. Elvsted. You wait and see!

HEDDA: Where did you leave him?

TESMAN: On the way home. We left in a bunch—the last of us, that is—and Brack came with us to get a little fresh air. Well, then, you see, we agreed we ought to see Eilert home. He'd had a drop too much.

HEDDA: You don't say?

TESMAN: But now comes the funny part, Hedda. Or I should really say the tragic part. Oh, I'm almost ashamed to tell you. For Eilert's sake, I mean—

HEDDA: Why, what happened?

TESMAN: Well, you see, as we were walking towards town I happened to drop behind for a minute. Only for a minute—er—you understand—

HEDDA: Yes, yes—?

TESMAN: Well then, when I ran on to catch them up, what do you think I found by the roadside. What?

HEDDA: How on earth should I know?

TESMAN: You mustn't tell anyone, Hedda. What? Promise me that—for Eilert's sake. (*Takes a package wrapped in paper from his coat pocket.*) Just fancy! I found this.

HEDDA: Isn't this the one he brought here yesterday?

TESMAN: Yes! The whole of that precious, irreplaceable manuscript! And he went and lost it! Didn't even notice! What about that? Tragic.

HEDDA: But why didn't you give it back to him?

TESMAN: I didn't dare to, in the state he was in.

HEDDA: Didn't you tell any of the others?

TESMAN: Good heavens, no. I didn't want to do that. For Eilert's sake, you understand.

HEDDA: Then no one else knows you have his manuscript?

TESMAN: No. And no one must be allowed to know.

HEDDA: Didn't it come up in the conversation later?

TESMAN: I didn't get a chance to talk to him any more. As soon as we got into the outskirts of town, he and one or two of the others gave us the slip. Disappeared, by Jove!

HEDDA: Oh? I suppose they took him home.

TESMAN: Yes, I imagine that was the idea. Brack left us, too.

HEDDA: And what have you been up to since then?

TESMAN: Well, I and one or two of the others—awfully jolly chaps, they were—went back to where one of them lived and had a cup of morning coffee. Morning-after-coffee—what? Ah, well. I'll just lie down for a bit and give Eilert time to sleep it off, poor chap, then I'll run over and give this back to him.

HEDDA (*holds out her hand for the package*): No, don't do that. Not just yet. Let me read it first.

TESMAN: Oh no, really, Hedda dear, honestly, I daren't do that.

HEDDA: Daren't?

TESMAN: No—imagine how desperate he'll be when he wakes up and finds his manuscript's missing. He hasn't any copy, you see. He told me so himself.

HEDDA: Can't a thing like that be rewritten?

TESMAN: Oh no, not possibly, I shouldn't think. I mean, the inspiration, you know—

HEDDA: Oh, yes, I'd forgotten that. (*Casually.*) By the way, there's a letter for you.

TESMAN: Is there? Fancy that!

HEDDA (*holds it out to him*): It came early this morning.

TESMAN: I say, it's from Auntie Juju! What on earth can it be? (*Puts the package on the other footstool, opens the letter, reads it and jumps up.*) Oh, Hedda! She says poor Auntie Rena's dying.

HEDDA: Well, we've been expecting that.

TESMAN: She says if I want to see her I must go quickly. I'll run over at once.

HEDDA (*hides a smile*): Run?

TESMAN: Hedda dear, I suppose you wouldn't like to come with me? What about that, eh?

HEDDA (*gets up and says wearily and with repulsion*): No, no, don't ask me to do anything like that. I can't bear illness or death. I loathe anything ugly.

TESMAN: Yes, yes. Of course. (*In a dither.*) My hat? My overcoat? Oh yes, in the hall. I do hope I won't get there too late, Hedda! What?

HEDDA: You'll be all right if you run.

BERTHA *enters from the hall.*

BERTHA: Judge Brack's outside and wants to know if he can come in.

TESMAN: At this hour? No, I can't possibly receive him now.

HEDDA: I can. (*To* BERTHA) Ask his honour to come in.

BERTHA *goes.*

HEDDA (*whispers quickly*): The manuscript, Tesman.

*She snatches it from the footstool.*

TESMAN: Yes, give it to me.

HEDDA: No, I'll look after it for now.

*She goes over to the writing-table and puts it in the bookcase.* TESMAN *stands dithering, unable to get his gloves on.* JUDGE BRACK *enters from the hall.*

HEDDA (*nods to him*): Well, you're an early bird.

BRACK: Yes, aren't I? (*To* TESMAN) Are you up and about, too?

TESMAN: Yes, I've got to go and see my aunts. Poor Auntie Rena's dying.

BRACK: Oh dear, is she? Then you mustn't let me detain you. At so tragic a—

TESMAN: Yes, I really must run. Good-bye! Good-bye!

*He runs out through the hall.*

HEDDA (*goes nearer*): You seem to have had excellent sport last night—Judge.

BRACK: Indeed yes, Mrs. Hedda. I haven't even had time to take my clothes off.

HEDDA: *You* haven't either?

BRACK: As you see. What's Tesman told you about last night's escapades?

HEDDA: Oh, only some boring story about having gone and drunk coffee somewhere.

BRACK: Yes, I've heard about that coffee-party. Eilert Lœvborg wasn't with them, I gather?

HEDDA: No, they took him home first.

BRACK: Did Tesman go with him?

HEDDA: No, one or two of the others, he said.

BRACK (*smiles*): George Tesman is a credulous man, Mrs. Hedda.

HEDDA: God knows. But—has something happened?

BRACK: Well, yes, I'm afraid it has.

HEDDA: I see. Sit down and tell me.

*She sits on the left of the table,* BRACK *at the long side of it, near her.*

HEDDA: Well?

BRACK: I had a special reason for keeping track of my guests last night. Or perhaps I should say some of my guests.

HEDDA: Including Eilert Lœvborg?

BRACK: I must confess—yes.

HEDDA: You're beginning to make me curious.

BRACK: Do you know where he and some of my other guests spent the latter half of last night, Mrs. Hedda?

HEDDA: Tell me. If it won't shock me.

BRACK: Oh, I don't think it'll shock you. They found themselves participating in an exceedingly animated *soirée*.

HEDDA: Of a sporting character?

BRACK: Of a highly sporting character.

HEDDA: Tell me more.

BRACK: Lœvborg had received an invitation in advance—as had the others. I knew all about that. But he had refused. As you know, he's become a new man.

HEDDA: Up at the Elvsteds', yes. But he went?

BRACK: Well, you see, Mrs. Hedda, last night at my house, unhappily, the spirit moved him.

HEDDA: Yes, I hear he became inspired.

BRACK: Somewhat violently inspired. And as a result, I suppose, his thoughts strayed. We men, alas, don't always stick to our principles as firmly as we should.

HEDDA: I'm sure you're an exception, Judge Brack. But go on about Lœvborg.

BRACK: Well, to cut a long story short, he ended up in the establishment of a certain Mademoiselle Danielle.

HEDDA: Mademoiselle Danielle?

BRACK: She was holding the *soirée*. For a selected circle of friends and admirers.

HEDDA: Has she got red hair?

BRACK: She has.

HEDDA: A singer of some kind?

BRACK: Yes—among other accomplishments. She's also a celebrated huntress—of men, Mrs. Hedda. I'm sure you've heard about her. Eilert Lœvborg used to be one of her most ardent patrons. In his salad days.

HEDDA: And how did all this end?

BRACK: Not entirely amicably, from all accounts. Mademoiselle Danielle began by receiving him with the utmost tenderness and ended by resorting to her fists.

HEDDA: Against Lœvborg?

BRACK: Yes. He accused her, or her friends, of having robbed him. He claimed his pocket-book had been stolen. Among other things. In short, he seems to have made a blood-thirsty scene.

HEDDA: And what did this lead to?

BRACK: It led to a general free-for-all, in which both sexes participated. Fortunately, in the end the police arrived.

HEDDA: The police, too?

BRACK: Yes. I'm afraid it may turn out to be rather an expensive joke for Master Eilert. Crazy fool!

HEDDA: Oh?

BRACK: Apparently he put up a very violent resistance. Hit one of the constables on the ear and tore his uniform. He had to accompany them to the police station.

HEDDA: Where did you learn all this?

BRACK: From the police.

HEDDA (*to herself*): So that's what happened. He didn't have a crown of vine leaves in his hair.

BRACK: Vine leaves, Mrs. Hedda?

HEDDA (*in her normal voice again*): But, tell me, Judge, why do you take such a close interest in Eilert Lœvborg?

BRACK: For one thing it'll hardly be a matter of complete indifference to me if it's revealed in court that he came there straight from my house.

HEDDA: Will it come to court?

BRACK: Of course. Well, I don't regard that as particularly serious. Still, I thought it my duty, as a friend of the family, to give you and your husband a full account of his nocturnal adventures.

HEDDA: Why?

BRACK: Because I've a shrewd suspicion that he's hoping to use you as a kind of screen.

HEDDA: What makes you think that?

BRACK: Oh, for heaven's sake, Mrs. Hedda, we're not blind. You wait and see. This Mrs. Elvsted won't be going back to her husband just yet.

HEDDA: Well, if there were anything between those two there are plenty of other places where they could meet.

BRACK: Not in anyone's home. From now on every respectable house will once again be closed to Eilert Lœvborg.

HEDDA: And mine should be, too, you mean?

BRACK: Yes. I confess I should find it more than irksome if this gentleman were to be granted unrestricted access to this house. If he were superfluously to intrude into—

HEDDA: The triangle?

BRACK: Precisely. For me it would be like losing a home.

HEDDA (*looks at him and smiles*): I see. You want to be the cock of the walk.

BRACK (*nods slowly and lowers his voice*): Yes, that is my aim. And I shall fight for it with—every weapon at my disposal.

HEDDA (*as her smile fades*): You're a dangerous man, aren't you? When you really want something.

BRACK: You think so?

HEDDA: Yes, I'm beginning to think so. I'm deeply thankful you haven't any kind of hold over me.

BRACK (*laughs equivocally*): Well, well, Mrs. Hedda—perhaps you're right. If I had, who knows what I might not think up?

HEDDA: Come, Judge Brack. That sounds almost like a threat.

BRACK (*gets up*): Heaven forbid! In the creation of a triangle—and its continuance—the question of compulsion should never arise.

HEDDA: Exactly what I was thinking.

BRACK: Well, I've said what I came to say. I must be getting back. Good-bye, Mrs. Hedda. (*Goes towards the french windows.*)

HEDDA (*gets up*): Are you going out through the garden?

BRACK: Yes, it's shorter.

HEDDA: Yes. And it's the back door, isn't it?

BRACK: I've nothing against back doors. They can be quite intriguing—sometimes.

HEDDA: When people fire pistols out of them, for example?

BRACK (*in the doorway, laughs*): Oh, people don't shoot tame cocks.

HEDDA (*laughs, too*): I suppose not. When they've only got one.

*They nod good-bye, laughing. He goes. She closes the french windows behind him, and stands for a moment, looking out pen-sively. Then she walks across the room and glances through the curtains in the open doorway. Goes to the writing-table, takes* LŒVBORG'S *package from the bookcase and is about to turn through the pages when* BERTHA *is heard remonstrating loudly in the hall.* HEDDA *turns and listens. She hastily puts the package back in the drawer, locks it and puts the key on the inkstand.* EILERT LŒVBORG, *with his overcoat on and his hat in his hand, throws the door open. He looks somewhat confused and excited.*

LŒVBORG (*shouts as he enters*): I must come in, I tell you! Let me pass!

*He closes the door, turns, sees* HEDDA, *controls himself immediately and bows.*

HEDDA (*at the writing table*): Well, Mr. Lœvborg, this is rather a late hour to be collecting Thea.

LŒVBORG: And an early hour to call on you. Please forgive me.

HEDDA: How do you know she's still here?

LŒVBORG: They told me at her lodgings that she has been out all night.

HEDDA (*goes to the table*): Did you notice anything about their behaviour when they told you?

LŒVBORG (*looks at her, puzzled*): Notice anything?

HEDDA: Did they sound as if they thought it—strange?

LŒVBORG (*suddenly understands*): Oh, I see what you mean. I'm dragging her down with me. No, as a matter of fact I didn't notice anything. I suppose Tesman isn't up yet?

HEDDA: No, I don't think so.

LŒVBORG: When did he get home?

HEDDA: Very late.

LŒVBORG: Did he tell you anything?

HEDDA: Yes. I gather you had a merry party at Judge Brack's last night.

LŒVBORG: He didn't tell you anything else?

HEDDA: I don't think so. I was so terribly sleepy—

MRS. ELVSTED *comes through the curtains in the open doorway.*

MRS. ELVSTED (*runs towards him*): Oh, Eilert! At last!

LŒVBORG: Yes—at last. And too late.

MRS. ELVSTED: What is too late?

LŒVBORG: Everything—now. I'm finished, Thea.

MRS. ELVSTED: Oh, no, no! Don't say that!

LŒVBORG: You'll say it yourself, when you've heard what I—

MRS. ELVSTED: I don't want to hear anything!

HEDDA: Perhaps you'd rather speak to her alone? I'd better go.

LŒVBORG: No, stay.

MRS. ELVSTED: But I don't want to hear anything, I tell you!

LŒVBORG: It's not about last night.

MRS. ELVSTED: Then what—?

LŒVBORG: I want to tell you that from now on we must stop seeing each other.

MRS. ELVSTED: Stop seeing each other!

HEDDA (*involuntarily*): I knew it!

LŒVBORG: I have no further use for you, Thea.

MRS. ELVSTED: You can stand there and say that! No further use for me! Surely I can go on helping you? We'll go on working together, won't we?

LŒVBORG: I don't intend to do any more work from now on.

MRS. ELVSTED (*desperately*): Then what use have I for my life?

LŒVBORG: You must try to live as if you had never known me.

MRS. ELVSTED: But I can't!

LŒVBORG: Try to, Thea. Go back home—

MRS. ELVSTED: Never! I want to be wherever you are! I won't let myself be driven away like this! I want to stay here—and be with you when the book comes out.

HEDDA (*whispers*): Ah, yes! The book!

LŒVBORG (*looks at her*): Our book; Thea's and mine. It belongs to both of us.

MRS. ELVSTED: Oh, yes! I feel that, too! And I've a right to be with you when it comes

into the world. I want to see people respect and honour you again. And the joy! The joy! I want to share it with you!

LŒVBORG: Thea—our book will never come into the world.

HEDDA: Ah!

MRS. ELVSTED: Not—?

LŒVBORG: It cannot. Ever.

MRS. ELVSTED: Eilert—what have you done with the manuscript?

HEDDA: Yes—the manuscript?

MRS. ELVSTED: Where is it?

LŒVBORG: Oh, Thea, please don't ask me that!

MRS. ELVSTED: Yes, yes—I must know. I've a right to know. Now!

LŒVBORG: The manuscript. Yes. I've torn it up.

MRS. ELVSTED (*screams*): No, no!

HEDDA (*involuntarily*): But that's not—!

LŒVBORG (*looks at her*): Not true, you think.

HEDDA (*controls herself*): Why—yes, of course it is, if you say so. It sounded so incredible—

LŒVBORG: It's true, nevertheless.

MRS. ELVSTED: Oh, my God, my God, Hedda—he's destroyed his own book!

LŒVBORG: I have destroyed my life. Why not my life's work, too?

MRS. ELVSTED: And you—did this last night?

LŒVBORG: Yes, Thea. I tore it into a thousand pieces. And scattered them out across the fjord. It's good, clean, salt water. Let it carry them away; let them drift in the current and the wind. And in a little while, they will sink. Deeper and deeper. As I shall, Thea.

MRS. ELVSTED: Do you know, Eilert—this book—all my life I shall feel as though you'd killed a little child.

LŒVBORG: You're right. It is like killing a child.

MRS. ELVSTED: But how could you? It was my child, too!

HEDDA (*almost inaudibly*): Oh—the child—!

MRS. ELVSTED (*breathes heavily*): It's all over, then. Well—I'll go now, Hedda.

HEDDA: You're not leaving town?

MRS. ELVSTED: I don't know what I'm going to do. I can't see anything except—darkness.

*She goes out through the hall.*

HEDDA (*waits a moment*): Aren't you going to escort her home, Mr. Lœvborg?

LŒVBORG: I? Through the streets? Do you want me to let people see her with me?

HEDDA: Of course, I don't know what else may have happened last night. But is it so utterly beyond redress?

LŒVBORG: It isn't just last night. It'll go on happening. I know it. But the curse of it is, I don't want to live that kind of life. I don't want to start all that again. She's broken my courage. I can't spit in the eyes of the world any longer.

HEDDA (*as though to herself*): That pretty little fool's been trying to shape a man's destiny. (*Looks at him.*) But how could you be so heartless towards her?

LŒVBORG: Don't call me heartless!

HEDDA: To go and destroy the one thing that's made her life worth living? You don't call that heartless?

LŒVBORG: Do you want to know the truth, Hedda?

HEDDA: The truth?

LŒVBORG: Promise me first—give me your word—that you'll never let Thea know about this.

HEDDA: I give you my word.

LŒVBORG: Good. Well, what I told her just now was a lie.

HEDDA: About the manuscript?

LŒVBORG: Yes. I didn't tear it up. Or throw it in the fjord.

HEDDA: You didn't? But where is it, then?

LŒVBORG: I destroyed it, all the same. I destroyed it, Hedda!

HEDDA: I don't understand.

LŒVBORG: Thea said that what I had done was like killing a child.

HEDDA: Yes. That's what she said.

LŒVBORG: But to kill a child isn't the worst thing a father can do to it.

HEDDA: What could be worse than that?

LŒVBORG: Hedda—suppose a man came home one morning, after a night of debauchery, and said to the mother of his child: 'Look here. I've been wandering round all night. I've been to—such-and-such a place and such-and-such a place. And I had our child with me. I took him to—these places. And I've lost him. Just—lost him. God knows where he is or whose hands he's fallen into.'

HEDDA: I see. But when all's said and done, this was only a book—

LŒVBORG: Thea's heart and soul were in that book. It was her whole life.

HEDDA: Yes, I understand.

LŒVBORG: Well, then you must also understand that she and I cannot possibly ever see each other again.

HEDDA: Where will you go?

LŒVBORG: Nowhere. I just want to put an end to it all. As soon as possible.

HEDDA (*takes a step towards him*): Eilert Lœvborg, listen to me. Do it—beautifully!

LŒVBORG: Beautifully? (*Smiles.*) With a crown of vine leaves in my hair? The way you used to dream of me—in the old days?

HEDDA: No. I don't believe in that crown any longer. But—do it beautifully, all the same. Just this once. Goodbye. You must go now. And don't come back.

LŒVBORG: Adieu, madame. Give my love to George Tesman. (*Turns to go.*)

HEDDA: Wait. I want to give you a souvenir to take with you.

*She goes over to the writing-table, opens the drawer and the pistol-case, and comes back to LŒVBORG with one of the pistols.*

LŒVBORG (*looks at her*): This? Is this the souvenir?

HEDDA (*nods slowly*): You recognize it? You looked down its barrel once.

LŒVBORG:  You should have used it then.

HEDDA:  Here! Use it now!

LŒVBORG (*puts the pistol in his breast pocket*):
Thank you.

HEDDA:  Do it beautifully, Eilert Lœvborg.
Only promise me that!

LŒVBORG:  Good-bye, Hedda Gabler.

*He goes out through the hall.* HEDDA *stands
by the door for a moment, listening. Then she
goes over to the writing-table, takes out the
package containing the manuscript, glances
inside it, pulls some of the pages half out and
looks at them. Then she takes it to the armchair by the stove and sits down with the
package in her lap. After a moment, she
opens the door of the stove; then she opens the
packet.*

HEDDA (*throws one of the pages into the stove
and whispers to herself*):  I'm burning your
child, Thea! You with your beautiful,
wavy hair! (*She throws a few more pages
into the stove.*) The child Eilert Lœvborg
gave you. (*Throws the rest of the manuscript in.*) I'm burning it! I'm burning
your child!

## ACT FOUR

*The same. It is evening. The drawing-room is in
darkness. The small room is illuminated by
the hanging lamp over the table. The curtains
are drawn across the french windows.*
HEDDA, *dressed in black, is walking up and
down in the darkened room. Then she goes
into the small room and crosses to the left. A
few chords are heard from the piano. She
comes back into the drawing-room.*

BERTHA *comes through the small room from
the right with a lighted lamp, which she
places on the table in front of the corner sofa
in the drawing-room. Her eyes are red with
crying, and she has black ribbons on her cap.
She goes quietly out, right.* HEDDA *goes over
to the french windows, draws the curtains
slightly to one side and looks out into the
darkness.*

*A few moments later,* MISS TESMAN *enters
from the hall. She is dressed in mourning,
with a black hat and veil.* HEDDA *goes to
meet her and holds out her hand.*

MISS TESMAN:  Well, Hedda, here I am in the
weeds of sorrow. My poor sister has
ended her struggles at last.

HEDDA:  I've already heard. Tesman sent me
a card.

MISS TESMAN:  Yes, he promised me he
would. But I thought, no, I must go and
break the news of death to Hedda myself—here, in the house of life.

HEDDA:  It's very kind of you.

MISS TESMAN:  Ah, Rena shouldn't have chosen a time like this to pass away. This is
no moment for Hedda's house to be a
place of mourning.

HEDDA (*changing the subject*):  She died
peacefully, Miss Tesman?

MISS TESMAN:  Oh, it was quite beautiful!
The end came so calmly. And she was so
happy at being able to see George once
again. And say good-bye to him. Hasn't
he come home yet?

HEDDA:  No. He wrote that I mustn't expect
him too soon. But please sit down.

MISS TESMAN:  No, thank you, Hedda dear—
bless you. I'd like to. But I've so little
time. I must dress her and lay her out as
well as I can. She shall go to her grave
looking really beautiful.

HEDDA:  Can't I help with anything?

MISS TESMAN:  Why, you mustn't think of
such a thing! Hedda Tesman mustn't let
her hands be soiled by contact with
death. Or her thoughts. Not at this time.

HEDDA:  One can't always control one's
thoughts.

MISS TESMAN (*continues*):  Ah, well, that's
life. Now we must start to sew poor
Rena's shroud. There'll be sewing to be
done in this house, too, before long, I
shouldn't wonder. But not for a shroud,
praise God.

GEORGE TESMAN *enters from the hall.*

HEDDA: You've come at last! Thank heavens!

TESMAN: Are you here, Auntie Juju? With Hedda? Fancy that!

MISS TESMAN: I was just on the point of leaving, dear boy. Well, have you done everything you promised me?

TESMAN: No, I'm afraid I forgot half of it. I'll have to run over again tomorrow. My head's in a complete whirl today. I can't collect my thoughts.

MISS TESMAN: But, George dear, you mustn't take it like this.

TESMAN: Oh? Well—er—how should I?

MISS TESMAN: You must be happy in your grief. Happy for what's happened. As I am.

TESMAN: Oh, yes, yes. You're thinking of Aunt Rena.

HEDDA: It'll be lonely for you now, Miss Tesman.

MISS TESMAN: For the first few days, yes. But it won't last long, I hope. Poor dear Rena's little room isn't going to stay empty.

TESMAN: Oh? Whom are you going to move in there? What?

MISS TESMAN: Oh, there's always some poor invalid who needs care and attention.

HEDDA: Do you really want another cross like that to bear?

MISS TESMAN: Cross! God forgive you, child. It's been no cross for me.

HEDDA: But now—if a complete stranger comes to live with you—?

MISS TESMAN: Oh, one soon makes friends with invalids. And I need so much to have someone to live for. Like you, my dear. Well, I expect there'll soon be work in this house too for an old aunt, praise God!

HEDDA: Oh—please!

TESMAN: My word, yes! What a splendid time the three of us could have together if—

HEDDA: If?

TESMAN (*uneasily*): Oh, never mind. It'll all work out. Let's hope so—what?

MISS TESMAN: Yes, yes. Well, I'm sure you two would like to be alone. (*Smiles.*) Perhaps Hedda may have something to tell you, George. Good-bye. I must go home to Rena. (*Turns to the door.*) Dear God, how strange! Now Rena is with me and with poor dear Joachim.

TESMAN: Why, yes, Auntie Juju! What?

MISS TESMAN *goes out through the hall.*

HEDDA (*follows* TESMAN *coldly and searchingly with her eyes*): I really believe this death distresses you more than it does her.

TESMAN: Oh, it isn't just Auntie Rena. It's Eilert I'm so worried about.

HEDDA (*quickly*): Is there any news of him?

TESMAN: I ran over to see him this afternoon. I wanted to tell him his manuscript was in safe hands.

HEDDA: Oh? You didn't find him?

TESMAN: No, he wasn't at home. But later I met Mrs. Elvsted and she told me he'd been here early this morning.

HEDDA: Yes, just after you'd left.

TESMAN: It seems he said he'd torn the manuscript up. What?

HEDDA: Yes, he claimed to have done so.

TESMAN: You told him we had it, of course?

HEDDA: No. (*Quickly.*) Did you tell Mrs. Elvsted?

TESMAN: No. I didn't like to. But you ought to have told him. Think if he should go home and do something desperate! Give me the manuscript, Hedda. I'll run over to him with it right away. Where did you put it?

HEDDA (*cold and motionless, leaning against the armchair*): I haven't got it any longer.

TESMAN: Haven't got it? What on earth do you mean?

HEDDA: I've burned it.

TESMAN (*starts, terrified*): Burned it! Burned Eilert's manuscript!

HEDDA: Don't shout. The servant will hear you.

TESMAN: Burned it! But in heaven's name—! Oh, no, no, no! This is impossible!

HEDDA: Well, it's true.

TESMAN: But, Hedda, do you realize what you've done? That's appropriating lost property! It's against the law! By God! You ask Judge Brack and see if I'm not right.

HEDDA: You'd be well advised not to talk about it to Judge Brack or anyone else.

TESMAN: But how could you go and do such a dreadful thing? What on earth put the idea into your head? What came over you? Answer me! What?

HEDDA (*represses an almost imperceptible smile*): I did it for your sake, George.

TESMAN: For my sake?

HEDDA: When you came home this morning and described how he'd read this book to you—

TESMAN: Yes, yes?

HEDDA: You admitted you were jealous of him.

TESMAN: But, good heavens, I didn't mean it literally!

HEDDA: No matter. I couldn't bear the thought that anyone else should push you into the background.

TESMAN (*torn between doubt and joy*): Hedda—is this true? But—but—but I never realized you loved me like that! Fancy that!

HEDDA: Well, I suppose you'd better know. I'm going to have—(*Breaks off and says violently*) No, no—you better ask your Auntie Juju. She'll tell you.

TESMAN: Hedda! I think I understand what you mean. (*Clasps his hands.*) Good heavens, can it really be true? What?

HEDDA: Don't shout. The servant will hear you.

TESMAN (*laughing with joy*): The servant! I say, that's good! The servant! Why,

that's Bertha! I'll run out and tell her at once!

HEDDA (*clenches her hands in despair*): Oh, it's destroying me, all this—it's destroying me!

TESMAN: I say, Hedda, what's up? What?

HEDDA (*cold, controlled*): Oh, it's all so—absurd—George.

TESMAN: Absurd? That I'm so happy? But surely—? Ah, well—perhaps I won't say anything to Bertha.

HEDDA: No, do. She might as well know, too.

TESMAN: No, no, I won't tell her yet. But Auntie Juju—I must let her know! And you—you called me George! For the first time! Fancy that! Oh, it'll make Auntie Juju so happy, all this! So very happy!

HEDDA: Will she be happy when she hears I've burned Eilert Lœvborg's manuscript—for your sake?

TESMAN: No, I'd forgotten about that. Of course, no one must be allowed to know about the manuscript. But that you're burning with love for me, Hedda, I must certainly let Auntie Juju know that. I say, I wonder if young wives often feel like that towards their husbands? What?

HEDDA: You might ask Auntie Juju about that, too.

TESMAN: I will, as soon as I get the chance. (*Looks uneasy and thoughtful again.*) But I say, you know, that manuscript. Dreadful business. Poor Eilert!

MRS. ELVSTED, *dressed as on her first visit, with hat and overcoat, enters from the hall.*

MRS. ELVSTED (*greets them hastily and tremulously*): Oh, Hedda dear, do please forgive me for coming here again.

HEDDA: Why, Thea, what's happened?

TESMAN: Is it anything to do with Eilert Lœvborg? What?

MRS. ELVSTED: Yes—I'm so dreadfully afraid he may have met with an accident.

HEDDA (*grips her arm*): You think so?

TESMAN: But, good heavens, Mrs. Elvsted, what makes you think that?

MRS. ELVSTED: I heard them talking about him at the boarding-house, as I went in. Oh, there are the most terrible rumours being spread about him in town today.

TESMAN: Er—yes, I heard about them, too. But I can testify that he went straight home to bed. Fancy—!

HEDDA: Well—what did they say in the boarding-house?

MRS. ELVSTED: Oh, I couldn't find out anything. Either they didn't know, or else— They stopped talking when they saw me. And I didn't dare to ask.

TESMAN (*fidgets uneasily*): We must hope— we must hope you misheard them, Mrs. Elvsted.

MRS. ELVSTED: No, no, I'm sure it was him they were talking about. I heard them say something about a hospital—

TESMAN: Hospital!

HEDDA: Oh no, surely that's impossible!

MRS. ELVSTED: Oh, I became so afraid. So I went up to his rooms and asked to see him.

HEDDA: Do you think that was wise, Thea?

MRS. ELVSTED: Well, what else could I do? I couldn't bear the uncertainty any longer.

TESMAN: But *you* didn't manage to find him either? What?

MRS. ELVSTED: No. And they had no idea where he was. They said he hadn't been home since yesterday afternoon.

TESMAN: Since yesterday? Fancy that!

MRS. ELVSTED: I'm sure he must have met with an accident.

TESMAN: Hedda, I wonder if I ought to go into town and make one or two enquiries?

HEDDA: No, no, don't you get mixed up in this.

JUDGE BRACK *enters from the hall, hat in hand.* BERTHA, *who has opened the door for him, closes it. He looks serious and greets them silently.*

TESMAN: Hullo, my dear Judge. Fancy seeing you!

BRACK: I had to come and talk to you.

TESMAN: I can see Auntie Juju's told you the news.

BRACK: Yes, I've heard about that, too.

TESMAN: Tragic, isn't it?

BRACK: Well, my dear chap, that depends how you look at it.

TESMAN (*looks uncertainly at him*): Has something else happened?

BRACK: Yes.

HEDDA: Another tragedy?

BRACK: That also depends on how you look at it, Mrs. Tesman.

MRS. ELVSTED: Oh, it's something to do with Eilert Lœvborg!

BRACK (*looks at her for a moment*): How did you guess? Perhaps you've heard already—?

MRS. ELVSTED (*confused*): No, no, not at all— I—

TESMAN: For heaven's sake, tell us!

BRACK (*shrugs his shoulders*): Well, I'm afraid they've taken him to the hospital. He's dying.

MRS. ELVSTED (*screams*): Oh God, God!

TESMAN: The hospital! Dying!

HEDDA (*involuntarily*): So quickly!

MRS. ELVSTED (*weeping*): Oh, Hedda! And we parted enemies!

HEDDA (*whispers*): Thea—Thea!

MRS. ELVSTED (*ignoring her*): I must see him! I must see him before he dies!

BRACK: It's no use, Mrs. Elvsted. No one's allowed to see him now.

MRS. ELVSTED: But what's happened to him? You must tell me!

TESMAN: He hasn't tried to do anything to himself? What?

HEDDA: Yes, he has. I'm sure of it.

TESMAN: Hedda, how can you—?

BRACK (*who has not taken his eyes from her*): I'm afraid you've guessed correctly, Mrs. Tesman.

MRS. ELVSTED: How dreadful!

TESMAN: Attempted suicide! Fancy that!

HEDDA: Shot himself!

BRACK: Right again, Mrs. Tesman—

MRS. ELVSTED (*tries to compose herself*): When did this happen, Judge Brack?

BRACK: This afternoon. Between three and four.

TESMAN: But, good heavens—where? What?

BRACK (*a little hesitantly*): Where? Why, my dear chap, in his rooms, of course.

MRS. ELVSTED: No, that's impossible. I was there soon after six.

BRACK: Well, it must have been somewhere else, then. I don't know exactly. I only know that they found him. He's shot himself—through the breast.

MRS. ELVSTED: Oh, how horrible! That he should end like that!

HEDDA (*to* BRACK): Through the breast, you said?

BRACK: That is what I said.

HEDDA: Not through the head?

BRACK: Through the breast, Mrs. Tesman.

HEDDA: The breast. Yes; yes. That's good, too.

BRACK: Why, Mrs. Tesman?

HEDDA: Oh—no, I didn't mean anything.

TESMAN: And the wound's dangerous, you say? What?

BRACK: Mortal. He's probably already dead.

MRS. ELVSTED: Yes, yes—I feel it! It's all over. All over. Oh Hedda—!

TESMAN: But, tell me, how did you manage to learn all this?

BRACK (*curtly*): From the police. I spoke to one of them.

HEDDA (*loudly, clearly*): Thank God! At last!

TESMAN (*appalled*): For God's sake, Hedda, what are you saying?

HEDDA: I am saying there's beauty in what he has done.

BRACK: Hm—Mrs. Tesman—

TESMAN: Beauty! Oh, but I say!

MRS. ELVSTED: Hedda, how can you talk of beauty in connection with a thing like this?

HEDDA: Eilert Lœvborg has settled his account with life. He's had the courage to do what—what he had to do.

MRS. ELVSTED: No, that's not why it happened. He did it because he was mad.

TESMAN: He did it because he was desperate.

HEDDA: You're wrong! I know!

MRS. ELVSTED: He must have been mad. The same as when he tore up the manuscript.

BRACK (*starts*): Manuscript? Did he tear it up?

MRS. ELVSTED: Yes. Last night.

TESMAN (*whispers*): Oh, Hedda, we shall never be able to escape from this.

BRACK: Hm. Strange.

TESMAN (*wanders round the room*): To think of Eilert dying like that. And not leaving behind him the thing that would have made his name endure.

MRS. ELVSTED: If only it could be pieced together again!

TESMAN: Yes, yes, yes! If only it could! I'd give anything—

MRS. ELVSTED: Perhaps it can, Mr. Tesman.

TESMAN: What do you mean?

MRS. ELVSTED (*searches in the pocket of her dress*): Look. I kept the notes he dictated it from.

HEDDA (*takes a step nearer*): Ah!

TESMAN: You kept them, Mrs. Elvsted! What?

MRS. ELVSTED: Yes, here they are. I brought them with me when I left home. They've been in my pocket ever since.

TESMAN: Let me have a look.

MRS. ELVSTED (*hands him a wad of small sheets of paper*): They're in a terrible muddle. All mixed up.

TESMAN: I say, just fancy if we could sort them out! Perhaps if we work on them together—?

MRS. ELVSTED: Oh, yes! Let's try, anyway!

TESMAN: We'll manage it. We must! I shall dedicate my life to this.

HEDDA: *You*, George? Your life?

TESMAN: Yes—well, all the time I can spare. My book'll have to wait. Hedda, you do understand? What? I owe it to Eilert's memory.

HEDDA: Perhaps.

TESMAN: Well, my dear Mrs. Elvsted, you and I'll have to pool our brains. No use crying over spilt milk, what? We must try to approach this matter calmly.

MRS. ELVSTED: Yes, yes, Mr. Tesman. I'll do my best.

TESMAN: Well, come over here and let's start looking at these notes right away. Where shall we sit? Here? No, the other room. You'll excuse us, won't you, Judge? Come along with me, Mrs. Elvsted.

MRS. ELVSTED: Oh, God! If only we can manage to do it!

TESMAN and MRS. ELVSTED *go into the rear room. He takes off his hat and overcoat. They sit at the table beneath the hanging lamp and absorb themselves in the notes.* HEDDA *walks across to the stove and sits in the armchair. After a moment,* BRACK *goes over to her.*

HEDDA (*half aloud*): Oh, Judge! This act of Eilert Lœvborg's—doesn't it give one a sense of release!

BRACK: Release, Mrs. Hedda? Well, it's a release for him, of course—

HEDDA: Oh, I don't mean him—I mean me! The release of knowing that someone can do something really brave! Something beautiful!

BRACK (*smiles*): Hm—my dear Mrs. Hedda—

HEDDA: Oh, I know what you're going to say. You're a *bourgeois* at heart, too, just like—ah, well!

BRACK (*looks at her*): Eilert Lœvborg has meant more to you than you're willing to admit to yourself. Or am I wrong?

HEDDA: I'm not answering questions like that from you. I only know that Eilert Lœvborg has had the courage to live according to his own principles. And now, at last, he's done something big! Something beautiful! To have the courage and the will to rise from the feast of life so early!

BRACK: It distresses me deeply, Mrs. Hedda, but I'm afraid I must rob you of that charming illusion.

HEDDA: Illusion?

BRACK: You wouldn't have been allowed to keep it for long, anyway.

HEDDA: What do you mean?

BRACK: He didn't shoot himself on purpose.

HEDDA: Not on purpose?

BRACK: No. It didn't happen quite the way I told you.

HEDDA: Have you been hiding something? What is it?

BRACK: In order to spare poor Mrs. Elvsted's feelings, I permitted myself one or two small—equivocations.

HEDDA: What?

BRACK: To begin with, he is already dead.

HEDDA: He died at the hospital?

BRACK: Yes. Without regaining consciousness.

HEDDA: What else haven't you told us?

BRACK: The incident didn't take place at his lodgings.

HEDDA: Well, that's utterly unimportant.

BRACK: Not utterly. The fact is, you see, that Eilert Lœvborg was found shot in Mademoiselle Danielle's boudoir.

HEDDA (*almost jumps up, but instead sinks back in her chair*): That's impossible. He can't have been there today.

BRACK: He was there this afternoon. He went to ask for something he claimed they'd taken from him. Talked some crazy nonsense about a child which had got lost—

HEDDA: Oh! So that was the reason!

BRACK: I thought at first he might have been referring to his manuscript. But I hear he destroyed that himself. So he must have meant his pocket-book—I suppose.

HEDDA: Yes, I suppose so. So they found him there?

BRACK: Yes; there. With a discharged pistol in his breast pocket. The shot had wounded him mortally.

HEDDA: Yes. In the breast.

BRACK: No. In the—stomach. The—lower part—

HEDDA (*looks at him with an expression of repulsion*): That, too! Oh, why does everything I touch become mean and ludicrous? It's like a curse!

BRACK: There's something else, Mrs. Hedda. It's rather disagreeable, too.

HEDDA: What?

BRACK: The pistol he had on him—

HEDDA: Yes? What about it?

BRACK: He must have stolen it.

HEDDA (*jumps up*): Stolen it! That isn't true! He didn't!

BRACK: It's the only explanation. He must have stolen it. Ssh!

TESMAN *and* MRS. ELVSTED *have got up from the table in the rear room and come into the drawing-room.*

TESMAN (*his hands full of papers*): Hedda, I can't see properly under that lamp. Do you think—?

HEDDA: I am thinking.

TESMAN: Do you think we could possibly use your writing-table for a little? What?

HEDDA: Yes, of course. (*Quickly.*) No, wait! Let me tidy it up first.

TESMAN: Oh, don't you trouble about that. There's plenty of room.

HEDDA: No, no, let me tidy it up first, I say. I'll take these in and put them on the piano. Here.

*She pulls an object, covered with sheets of music, out from under the bookcase, puts some more sheets on top and carries it all into the rear room and away to the left.* TESMAN *puts his papers on the writing-table and moves the lamp over from the corner table. He and* MRS. ELVSTED *sit down and begin working again.* HEDDA *comes back.*

HEDDA (*behind* MRS. ELVSTED'S *chair, ruffles her hair gently*): Well, my pretty Thea. And how is work progressing on Eilert Lœvborg's memorial?

MRS. ELVSTED (*looks up at her, dejectedly*): Oh, it's going to be terribly difficult to get these into any order.

TESMAN: We've got to do it. We must! After all, putting other people's papers into order is rather my specialty, what?

HEDDA *goes over to the stove and sits on one of the footstools.* BRACK *stands over her, leaning against the armchair.*

HEDDA (*whispers*): What was that you were saying about the pistol?

BRACK (*softly*): I said he must have stolen it.

HEDDA: Why do you think that?

BRACK: Because any other explanation is unthinkable, Mrs. Hedda. Or ought to be.

HEDDA: I see.

BRACK (*looks at her for a moment*): Eilert Lœvborg was here this morning. Wasn't he?

HEDDA: Yes.

BRACK: Were you alone with him?

HEDDA: For a few moments.

BRACK: You didn't leave the room while he was here?

HEDDA: No.

BRACK: Think again. Are you sure you didn't go out for a moment?

HEDDA: Oh—yes, I might have gone into the hall. Just for a few seconds.

BRACK: And where was your pistol-case during this time?

HEDDA: I'd locked it in that—

BRACK: Er—Mrs. Hedda?

HEDDA: It was lying over there on my writing-table.

BRACK: Have you looked to see if both the pistols are still there?

HEDDA: No.

BRACK: You needn't bother. I saw the pistol Lœvborg had when they found him. I recognized it at once. From yesterday. And other occasions.

HEDDA: Have you got it?

BRACK:  No. The police have it.

HEDDA:  What will the police do with this pistol?

BRACK:  Try to trace the owner.

HEDDA:  Do you think they'll succeed?

BRACK (*leans down and whispers*):  No, Hedda Gabler. Not as long as I hold my tongue.

HEDDA (*looks nervously at him*):  And if you don't?

BRACK (*shrugs his shoulders*):  You could always say he'd stolen it.

HEDDA:  I'd rather die!

BRACK (*smiles*):  People say that. They never do it.

HEDDA (*not replying*):  And suppose the pistol wasn't stolen? And they trace the owner? What then?

BRACK:  There'll be a scandal, Hedda.

HEDDA:  A scandal!

BRACK:  Yes, a scandal. The thing you're so frightened of. You'll have to appear in court together with Mademoiselle Danielle. She'll have to explain how it all happened. Was it an accident, or was it—homicide? Was he about to take the pistol from his pocket to threaten her? And did it go off? Or did she snatch the pistol from his hand, shoot him and then put it back in his pocket? She might quite easily have done it. She's a resourceful lady, is Mademoiselle Danielle.

HEDDA:  But I have nothing to do with this repulsive business.

BRACK:  No. But you'll have to answer one question. Why did you give Eilert Lœvborg this pistol? And what conclusions will people draw when it is proved you did give it to him?

HEDDA (*bows her head*):  That's true. I hadn't thought of that.

BRACK:  Well, luckily there's no danger as long as I hold my tongue.

HEDDA (*looks up at him*):  In other words, I'm in your power, Judge. From now on, you've got your hold over me.

BRACK (*whispers, more slowly*):  Hedda, my dearest—believe me—I will not abuse my position.

HEDDA:  Nevertheless, I'm in your power. Dependent on your will, and your demands. Not free. Still not free! (*Rises passionately.*) No. I couldn't bear that. No.

BRACK (*looks half-derisively at her*):  Most people resign themselves to the inevitable, sooner or later.

HEDDA (*returns his gaze*):  Possibly they do. *She goes across to the writing-table.*

HEDDA (*represses an involuntary smile and says in* TESMAN's *voice*):  Well, George. Think you'll be able to manage? What?

TESMAN:  Heaven knows, dear. This is going to take months and months.

HEDDA (*in the same tone as before*):  Fancy that, by Jove! (*Runs her hands gently through* MRS. ELVSTED's *hair.*) Doesn't it feel strange, Thea? Here you are working away with Tesman just the way you used to work with Eilert Lœvborg.

MRS. ELVSTED:  Oh—if only I can inspire your husband, too!

HEDDA:  Oh, it'll come. In time.

TESMAN:  Yes—do you know, Hedda, I really think I'm beginning to feel a bit—well—that way. But you go back and talk to Judge Brack.

HEDDA:  Can't I be of use to you two in any way?

TESMAN:  No, none at all. (*Turns his head.*) You'll have to keep Hedda company from now on, Judge, and see she doesn't get bored. If you don't mind.

BRACK (*glances at* HEDDA):  It'll be a pleasure.

HEDDA:  Thank you. But I'm tired this evening. I think I'll lie down on the sofa in there for a little while.

TESMAN:  Yes, dear—do. What? HEDDA *goes into the rear room and draws the curtains behind her. Short pause. Suddenly she begins to play a frenzied dance melody on the piano.*

MRS. ELVSTED (*starts up from her chair*): Oh, what's that?

TESMAN (*runs to the doorway*): Hedda dear, please! Don't play dance music tonight! Think of Auntie Rena. And Eilert.

HEDDA (*puts her head through the curtains*): And Auntie Juju. And all the rest of them. From now on I'll be quiet.
*She closes the curtains behind her.*

TESMAN (*at the writing-table*): It distresses her to watch us doing this. I say, Mrs. Elvsted, I've an idea. Why don't you move in with Auntie Juju? I'll run over each evening, and we can sit and work there. What?

MRS. ELVSTED: Yes, that might be the best plan.

HEDDA (*from the rear room*): I can hear what you're saying, Tesman. But how shall I spend the evenings out here?

TESMAN (*looking through his papers*): Oh, I'm sure Judge Brack'll be kind enough to come over and keep you company. You won't mind my not being here, Judge?

BRACK (*in the armchair, calls gaily*): I'll be delighted, Mrs. Tesman. I'll be here every evening. We'll have great fun together, you and I.

HEDDA (*loud and clear*): Yes, that'll suit you, won't it, Judge? The only cock on the dunghill—
*A shot is heard from the rear room.* TESMAN, MRS. ELVSTED *and* JUDGE BRACK *start from their chairs.*

TESMAN: Oh, she's playing with those pistols again.
*He pulls the curtains aside and runs in.* MRS. ELVSTED *follows him.* HEDDA *is lying dead on the sofa. Confusion and shouting.* BERTHA *enters in alarm from the right.*

TESMAN (*screams to* BRACK): She's shot herself! Shot herself in the head! Fancy that!

BRACK (*half paralysed in the armchair*): But, good God! People don't do such things!

## SUMMARY

The term *modern* has been applied to art, architecture, and writing for at least 150 years. In dramatic theory and criticism, *modernism* became associated with the new wave of realistic writers in the mid-nineteenth century, followed by the naturalists, symbolists, and expressionists.

As a way of perceiving contradictions and disconnections in experience, *modernism* was frequently synonymous with realism as the dominant "new" mode of representing experience in plays and novels. As a way of thinking about contemporary experience, modernism was also embraced by other styles of artistic expression. In drama, the symbolists departed from observing and recording outward appearance. They attempted to show the deeper contradictions of life's subjectivity and mystery by emphasizing symbols, myths, and moods. Of the French symbolist dramatists, Maurice Maeterlinck (1862–1949) was perhaps the best known. In *The Intruder* and *The Blind*, written in 1890, Maeterlinck argued that *silences* evoked the mystery and pain of existence often obscured by the hurly-burly of nineteenth-century life.

At the turn of the century, especially in Germany, expressionism reaffirmed the modernist view by portraying the disharmony between inner truth and external reality. The expressionists demonstrated the gap between social and political conditions, which mechanized and distorted human experience, and humanity's attainment of happiness and contentment. Published in 1912, *The Beggar* by Reinhard Johannes Sorge (1892–1916) is considered the first expressionist play. It shows the struggles between old conventions and new values in the efforts of a visionary poet to achieve fulfillment in a materialistic and insensitive society. As artistic means of presenting the conflicts between society's materialism and individual ideals, the expressionists used scenic distortions of line, garish colors, and exaggerated shapes and movements. Their plays incorporated telegraphic speech and disjointed episodes to underscore human struggle and discord.

In summary, modernist writers in the middle of the last century set about to describe the chasm between past and present which resulted in people becoming alienated from their surroundings, from others, and from themselves. The chief paradigm was the dissolution of those connections between a sense of personal worth and the facts of experience. In the instance of *Hedda Gabler*, Henrik Ibsen perceived no reconciliation between Hedda's psychic tendency to dissolution and the social structures that limited her life and determined her circumstances. With the past as the chief villain responsible for the contradictions and ills of modern life, human alienation from self, others, and society emerges in the 1890s as a recurrent theme in modern literature.

Since modernism as a mode of understanding essentially emerges in the drama with realism as a new writing and performance style, the next chapter considers "modern realism"—its subjects and methods.

## NOTES

1. Joseph Wood Krutch, *"Modernism" in Modern Drama: A Definition and an Estimate* (Ithaca, N.Y: Cornell University Press, 1953): vii–ix.

2. Peter Szondi, *Theory of the Modern Drama*, trans. Michael Hays (Minneapolis: University of Minnesota Press, 1987): viii.

3. Szondi 7.

4. Richard Gilman, *The Making of Modern Drama: A Study of Buchner, Ibsen, Strindberg, Chekhov, Pirandello, Brecht, Beckett, Handke* (New York: Farrar, Straus and Giroux, 1974): 67.

birth, his race, his father, his poverty, his employer, his society, and by his intellectual and emotional limitations. As victimizer, he takes advantage of his brother, Gabriel, whose war injuries have reduced him to a mental defective with a "metal plate" in his head. Troy bought the family house with Gabriel's army check, though Gabriel is permitted to live with them whenever he chooses. In his relationship with his son, Troy repeats his earlier experience with his own father. He also allows Cory no freedom to grow or to express his individuality. Troy loves his wife, but asserts his own freedom in a relationship with another woman after eighteen years of stultifying as a "good husband." He justifies himself to Rose: "Its not easy for me to admit that I been standing in the same place for eighteen years" (2.1). Rose answers, "I gave eighteen years of my life to stand in the same spot with you . . . What about my life?" (2.1). Wilson uses Troy Maxson's ambiguous moral status to question the mechanics of patriarchy and to universalize both central character and theme.

As we have seen, the well-made play generates theatrical crises (see Chapter 6). In *Fences*, Troy refuses to sign the recruitment form for his son to play college football because of his own failed struggle as a black to become a baseball player; he confesses his adultery to Rose and tells her of his child to be born to another woman; Cory attacks his father for physically abusing his mother; and Gabriel performs a ritual dance in anticipation of Troy's funeral at the play's end. The strange, mad dance, accompanied by Gabriel's howling sounds, is eerie but life-affirming. As he finishes, the stage directions suggest that "the gates of heaven stand open as wide as God's closet" (2.5). The family's love, forgiveness, and understanding of Troy Maxson find their cultural symbolism in Gabriel's atavistic ritual.

*Fences* is set respectively in 1957 and in 1965 in an African-American urban neighborhood. The action takes place on the front porch and in the yard of an "ancient two-story brick house set back in a small alley." The small dirt yard (which is fenced in as the play progresses) has a single tree from which hangs a homemade baseball of rags. Troy's baseball bat leans against the tree. This is the play's highly realistic environment where family and friends come and go, take their meals, experience their crises, and generally live out their unspectacular, though emotion-filled, lives. However, the play's centerpiece is the normal generational conflict between father and son. Wilson views *Fences* as a recycling of Troy's relationship with his father in his treatment of Cory. "I was trying to get at why Troy made the choices he made," Wilson said in an interview, "how they have influenced his values and how he attempts to pass those along to his son." He continued:

> Each generation gives the succeeding generation what they think they need. One question in the play is, "Are the tools we are given sufficient to compete in a world that is different from the one our parents knew?" I think they are—it's just that we have to do different things with the tools. . . . Troy's flaw is that he does not recognize that the world was changing.[7]

Writing in a realistic tradition, Wilson converts the yard "fence" into the play's controlling metaphor. The fence is *tangible* ("real" wood for the fence is sawed and hammered), but it is also Wilson's metaphor for the cultural situation of African-Americans in the late fifties. Every person in the play, with the exception of Raynell, is fenced in or out by personal and/or societal strictures. When asked why Rose wants to fence in the yard in the first place, Troy's friend, Bono, says: "Some people build fences to keep people out . . . and some people build fences to keep people in" (2.1). The Maxson family experiences both alternatives. Society has conspired to keep them out of the mainstream of American life. For instance, Troy and Bono are "refuse workers"; they are permitted to lift garbage but not to drive the union trucks that carry the refuse. At the play's end, all of the members of the Maxson family are fenced in: in a church (Rose), in a penitentiary (Rose's stepson), in a mental hospital (Gabriel), in the Marines (Cory). Troy's daughter, Raynell, is the only potentially free person, for the winds of social change are starting to blow in the new and turbulent decade of the 1960s.

As a realistic writer, Wilson also takes his secondary metaphors (baseball and food) from the life-long interests and habits of Troy and Rose. Not unlike Arthur Miller's Willie Loman in *Death of a Salesman* (1949), Troy lives on lost dreams, explaining his philosophy of life with baseball jargon—a language immediate and meaningful to his philosophy of existence. For example, he announces, "Death ain't nothing but a fastball on the outside corner." Or, on his race, Troy says, ". . . you born with two strikes on you before you come to the plate." And, he warns

Cory at each point of conflict between them: "Don't you strike out. You living with a full count. Don't you strike out."

The texture and rhythms of Troy's language underscore the uniqueness and dynamics of his character. From Rose and Gabriel's associations with food, Wilson establishes the social organization of the Maxson family, and, by extension, African-American culture of the time. As part of the ritual of living, food interests Wilson as a sign and symbol of the economic systems and cultural differences between black and white Americans. The family meals emanate from Rose's kitchen: chicken, biscuits, coffee, meatloaf, lima beans, and corn bread. Even the maimed Gabriel tries to be self-sufficient as he collects fruit and vegetables to sell. These small family rituals, like Troy's swinging at the rag baseball and Rose's predictable meals, illuminate the manners and life style of the urban African-American in the late fifties. While the father-son conflict is a universal generational conflict, August Wilson portrays in *Fences* the daily rituals of African-Americans to make a statement about black culture in America and its unique difference from white culture.

# Fences

> When the sins of our fathers visit us
> We do not have to play host.
> We can banish them with forgiveness
> As God, in His Largeness and Laws.
> —August Wilson

## CHARACTERS

TROY MAXSON
JIM BONO   TROY's *friend*
ROSE   TROY's *wife*
LYONS   TROY's *oldest son by previous marriage*
GABRIEL   TROY's *brother*
CORY   TROY *and* ROSE's *son*
RAYNELL   TROY's *daughter*

## THE PLAY

*Near the turn of the century, the destitute of Europe sprang on the city with tenacious claws and an honest and solid dream. The city devoured them. They swelled its belly until it burst into a thousand furnaces and sewing machines, a thousand butcher shops and bakers' ovens, a thousand churches and hospitals and funeral parlors and moneylenders. The city grew. It nourished itself and offered each man a partnership limited only by his talent, his guile, and his willingness and capacity for hard work. For the immigrants of Europe, a dream dared and won true.*

*The descendants of African slaves were offered no such welcome or participation. They came from places called the Carolinas and the Virginias, Georgia, Alabama, Mississippi, and Tennessee. They came strong, eager, searching. The city rejected them and they fled and settled along the riverbanks and under bridges in shallow, ramshackle houses made of sticks and tarpaper. They collected rags and wood. They sold the use of their muscles and their bodies. They cleaned houses and washed clothes, they shined shoes, and in quiet desperation and vengeful pride, they stole, and lived in pursuit of their own dream. That they could breathe free, finally, and stand to meet life with the force of dignity and whatever eloquence the heart could call upon.*

*By 1957, the hard-won victories of the European immigrants had solidified the industrial might of America. War had been confronted and won with new energies that used loyalty and patriotism as its fuel. Life was rich, full, and flourishing. The Milwaukee Braves won the World Series, and the hot winds of change that would make the sixties a turbulent, racing, dangerous, and provocative decade had not yet begun to blow full.*

## SETTING

*The setting is the yard which fronts the only entrance to the* **MAXSON** *household, an ancient two-story brick house set back off a small alley in a big-city neighborhood. The entrance to the house is gained by two or three steps leading to a wooden porch badly in need of paint.*

*A relatively recent addition to the house and running its full width, the porch lacks congruence. It is a sturdy porch with a flat roof. One or two chairs of dubious value sit at one end where the kitchen window opens onto the porch. An old-fashioned icebox stands silent guard at the opposite end.*

*The yard is a small dirt yard, partially fenced, except for the last scene, with a wooden sawhorse, a pile of lumber, and other fence-building equipment set off to the side. Opposite is a tree from which hangs a ball made of rags. A baseball*

*bat leans against the tree. Two oil drums serve as
garbage receptacles and sit near the house at right
to complete the setting.*

# ACT ONE

### SCENE ONE

*It is 1957.* TROY *and* BONO *enter the yard, engaged in conversation.* TROY *is fifty-three years
old, a large man with thick, heavy hands; it is this
largeness that he strives to fill out and make an
accommodation with. Together with his blackness, his largeness informs his sensibilities and
the choices he has made in his life.*

*Of the two men,* BONO *is obviously the fol-
lower. His commitment to their friendship of
thirty-odd years is rooted in his admiration of*
TROY'S *honesty, capacity for hard work, and his
strength, which* BONO *seeks to emulate.*

*It is Friday night, payday, and the one night
of the week the two men engage in a ritual of
talk and drink.* TROY *is usually the most talkative and at times he can be crude and almost
vulgar, though he is capable of rising to profound
heights of expression. The men carry lunch buckets and wear or carry burlap aprons and are
dressed in clothes suitable to their jobs as garbage
collectors.*

BONO: Troy, you ought to stop that lying!

TROY: I ain't lying! The nigger had a watermelon this big.

(*He indicates with his hands.*)

Talking about . . . "What watermelon,
Mr. Rand?" I liked to fell out! "What
watermelon, Mr. Rand?" . . . And it sitting there big as life.

BONO: What did Mr. Rand say?

TROY: Ain't said nothing. Figure if the nigger too dumb to know he carrying a watermelon, he wasn't gonna get much
sense out of him. Trying to hide that
great big old watermelon under his coat.
Afraid to let the white man see him carry
it home.

BONO: I'm like you . . . I ain't got no time for
them kind of people.

TROY: Now what he look like getting mad
cause he see the man from the union
talking to Mr. Rand?

BONO: He come to me talking about . . .
"Maxson gonna get us fired." I told him
to get away from me with that. He
walked away from me calling you a
trouble-maker. What Mr. Rand say?

TROY: Ain't said nothing. He told me to go
down the Commissioner's office next
Friday. They called me down there to see
them.

BONO: Well, as long as you got your complaint filed, they can't fire you. That's
what one of them white fellows tell me.

TROY: I ain't worried about them firing me.
They gonna fire me cause I asked a question? That's all I did. I went to Mr. Rand
and asked him, "Why? Why you got the
white mens driving and the colored lifting?" Told him, "what's the matter,
don't I count? You think only white fellows got sense enough to drive a truck.
That ain't no paper job! Hell, anybody
can drive a truck. How come you got all
whites driving and the colored lifting?"
He told me "take it to the union." Well,
hell, that's what I done! Now they
wanna come up with this pack of lies.

BONO: I told Brownie if the man come and
ask him any questions . . . just tell the
truth! It ain't nothing but something
they done trumped up on you cause you
filed a complaint on them.

TROY: Brownie don't understand nothing.
All I want them to do is change the job
description. Give everybody a chance to
drive the truck. Brownie can't see that.
He ain't got that much sense.

BONO: How you figure he be making out
with that gal be up at Taylors' all the
time . . . that Alberta gal?

TROY: Same as you and me. Getting just as
much as we is. Which is to say nothing.

BONO: It is, huh? I figure you doing a little better than me . . . and I ain't saying what I'm doing.

TROY: Aw, nigger, look here . . . I know you. If you had got anywhere near that gal, twenty minutes later you be looking to tell somebody. And the first one you gonna tell . . . that you gonna want to brag to . . . is gonna be me.

BONO: I ain't saying that. I see where you be eyeing her.

TROY: I eye all the women. I don't miss nothing. Don't never let nobody tell you Troy Maxson don't eye the women.

BONO: You been doing more than eyeing her. You done bought her a drink or two.

TROY: Hell yeah, I bought her a drink! What that mean? I bought you one, too. What that mean cause I buy her a drink? I'm just being polite.

BONO: It's alright to buy her one drink. That's what you call being polite. But when you wanna be buying two or three . . . that's what you call eyeing her.

TROY: Look here, as long as you known me . . . you ever known me to chase after women?

BONO: Hell yeah! Long as I done known you. You forgetting I knew you when.

TROY: Naw, I'm talking about since I been married to Rose?

BONO: Oh, not since you been married to Rose. Now, that's the truth, there. I can say that.

TROY: Alright then! Case closed.

BONO: I see you be walking up around Alberta's house. You supposed to be at Taylors' and you be walking up around there.

TROY: What you watching where I'm walking for? I ain't watching after you.

BONO: I seen you walking around there more than once.

TROY: Hell, you liable to see me walking anywhere! That don't mean nothing cause you see me walking around there.

BONO: Where she come from anyway? She just kinda showed up one day.

TROY: Tallahassee. You can look at her and tell she one of them Florida gals. They got some big healthy women down there. Grow them right up out the ground. Got a little bit of Indian in her. Most of them niggers down in Florida got some Indian in them.

BONO: I don't know about that Indian part. But she damn sure big and healthy. Woman wear some big stockings. Got them great big old legs and hips as wide as the Mississippi River.

TROY: Legs don't mean nothing. You don't do nothing but push them out of the way. But them hips cushion the ride!

BONO: Troy, you ain't got no sense.

TROY: It's the truth! Like you riding on Goodyears!

ROSE *enters from the house. She is ten years younger than* TROY, *her devotion to him stems from her recognition of the possibilities of her life without him: a succession of abusive men and their babies, a life of partying and running the streets, the Church, or aloneness with its attendant pain and frustration. She recognizes* TROY'S *spirit as a fine and illuminating one and she either ignores or forgives his faults, only some of which she recognizes. Though she doesn't drink, her presence is an integral part of the Friday night rituals. She alternates between the porch and the kitchen, where supper preparations are under way.*

ROSE: What you all out here getting into?

TROY: What you worried about what we getting into for? This is men talk, woman.

ROSE: What I care what you all talking about? Bono, you gonna stay for supper?

BONO: No, I thank you, Rose. But Lucille say she cooking up a pot of pigfeet.

TROY: Pigfeet! Hell, I'm going home with you! Might even stay the night if you got some pigfeet. You got something in there to top them pigfeet, Rose?

ROSE: I'm cooking up some chicken. I got some chicken and collard greens.

TROY: Well, go on back in the house and let me and Bono finish what we was talking about. This is men talk. I got some talk for you later. You know what kind of talk I mean. You go on and powder it up.

ROSE: Troy Maxson, don't you start that now!

TROY: (Puts his arm around her.) Aw, woman . . . come here. Look here, Bono . . . when I met this woman . . . I got out that place, say, "Hitch up my pony, saddle up my mare . . . there's a woman out there for me somewhere. I looked here. Looked there. Saw Rose and latched on to her." I latched on to her and told her—I'm gonna tell you the truth—I told her, "Baby, I don't wanna marry, I just wanna be your man." Rose told me . . . tell him what you told me, Rose.

ROSE: I told him if he wasn't the marrying kind, then move out the way so the marrying kind could find me.

TROY: That's what she told me. "Nigger, you in my way. You blocking the view! Move out the way so I can find me a husband." I thought it over two or three days. Come back—

ROSE: Ain't no two or three days nothing. You was back the same night.

TROY: Come back, told her . . . "Okay, baby . . . but I'm gonna buy me a banty rooster and put him out there in the backyard . . . and when he see a stranger come, he'll flap his wings and crow . . . " Look here, Bono, I could watch the front door by myself . . . it was that back door I was worried about.

ROSE: Troy, you ought not talk like that. Troy ain't doing nothing but telling a lie.

TROY: Only thing is . . . when we first got married . . . forget the rooster . . . we ain't had no yard!

BONO: I hear you tell it. Me and Lucille was staying down there on Logan Street. Had two rooms with the outhouse in the back. I ain't mind the outhouse none. But when that goddamn wind blow through there in the winter . . . that's what I'm talking about! To this day I wonder why in the hell I ever stayed down there for six long years. But see, I didn't know I could do no better. I thought only white folks had inside toilets and things.

ROSE: There's a lot of people don't know they can do no better than they doing now. That's just something you got to learn. A lot of folks still shop at Bella's.

TROY: Ain't nothing wrong with shopping at Bella's. She got fresh food.

ROSE: I ain't said nothing about if she got fresh food. I'm talking about what she charge. She charge ten cents more than the A&P.

TROY: The A&P ain't never done nothing for me. I spends my money where I'm treated right. I go down to Bella, say, "I need a loaf of bread, I'll pay you Friday." She give it to me. What sense that make when I got money to go and spend it somewhere else and ignore the person who done right by me? That ain't in the Bible.

ROSE: We ain't talking about what's in the Bible. What sense it make to shop there when she overcharge?

TROY: You shop where you want to. I'll do my shopping where the people been good to me.

ROSE: Well, I don't think it's right for her to overcharge. That's all I was saying.

BONO: Look here . . . I got to get on. Lucille going to be raising all kind of hell.

TROY: Where you going, nigger? We ain't finished this pint. Come here, finish this pint.

BONO: Well, hell, I am . . . if you ever turn the bottle loose.

TROY: (Hands him the bottle.) The only thing I say about the A&P is I'm glad Cory got that job down there. Help him take care of his school clothes and things. Gabe done moved out and things getting tight around here. He got that job. . . .He can start to look out for himself.

ROSE: Cory done went and got recruited by a college football team.

TROY: I told that boy about that football stuff. The white man ain't gonna let him get nowhere with that football. I told him when he first come to me with it. Now you come telling me he done went and got more tied up in it. He ought to go and get recruited in how to fix cars or something where he can make a living.

ROSE: He ain't talking about making no living playing football. It's just something the boys in school do. They gonna send a recruiter by to talk to you. He'll tell you he ain't talking about making no living playing football. It's a honor to be recruited.

TROY: It ain't gonna get him nowhere. Bono'll tell you that.

BONO: If he be like you in the sports . . . he's gonna be alright. Ain't but two men ever played baseball as good as you. That's Babe Ruth and Josh Gibson. Them's the only two men ever hit more home runs than you.

TROY: What it ever get me? Ain't got a pot to piss in or a window to throw it out of.

ROSE: Times have changed since you was playing baseball, Troy. That was before the war. Times have changed a lot since then.

TROY: How in hell they done changed?

ROSE: They got lots of colored boys playing ball now. Baseball and football.

BONO: You right about that, Rose. Times have changed, Troy. You just come along too early.

TROY: There ought not never have been no time called too early! Now you take that fellow . . . what's that fellow they had playing right field for the Yankees back then? You know who I'm talking about,

Bono. Used to play right field for the Yankees.

ROSE: Selkirk?

TROY: Selkirk! That's it! Man batting .269, understand? .269. What kind of sense that make? I was hitting .432 with thirty-seven home runs! Man batting .269 and playing right field for the Yankees! I saw Josh Gibson's daughter yesterday. She walking around with raggedy shoes on her feet. Now I bet you Selkirk's daughter ain't walking around with raggedy shoes on her feet! I bet you that!

ROSE: They got a lot of colored baseball players now. Jackie Robinson was the first. Folks had to wait for Jackie Robinson.

TROY: I done seen a hundred niggers play baseball better than Jackie Robinson. Hell, I know some teams Jackie Robinson couldn't even make! What you talking about Jackie Robinson. Jackie Robinson wasn't nobody. I'm talking about if you could play ball then they ought to have let you play. Don't care what color you were. Come telling me I come along too early. If you could play . . . then they ought to have let you play.

TROY *takes a long drink from the bottle.*

ROSE: You gonna drink yourself to death. You don't need to be drinking like that.

TROY: Death ain't nothing. I done seen him. Done wrassled with him. You can't tell me nothing about death. Death ain't nothing but a fastball on the outside corner. And you know what I'll do to that! Lookee here, Bono . . . am I lying? You get one of them fastballs, about waist high, over the outside corner of the plate where you can get the meat of the bat on it . . . and good god! You can kiss it goodbye. Now, am I lying?

BONO: Naw, you telling the truth there. I seen you do it.

TROY: If I'm lying . . . that 450 feet worth of lying!

*Pause.*

That's all death is to me. A fastball on the outside corner.

ROSE: I don't know why you want to get on talking about death.

TROY: Ain't nothing wrong with talking about death. That's part of life. Everybody gonna die. You gonna die, I'm gonna die. Bono's gonna die. Hell, we all gonna die.

ROSE: But you ain't got to talk about it. I don't like to talk about it.

TROY: You the one brought it up. Me and Bono was talking about baseball . . . you tell me I'm gonna drink myself to death. Ain't that right, Bono? You know I don't drink this but one night out of the week. That's Friday night. I'm gonna drink just enough to where I can handle it. Then I cuts it loose. I leave it alone. So don't you worry about me drinking myself to death. 'Cause I ain't worried about Death. I done seen him. I drone wrestled with him.

Look here, Bono . . . I looked up one day and Death was marching straight at me. Like Soldiers on Parade! The Army of Death was marching straight at me. The middle of July, 1941. It got real cold just like it be winter. It seem like Death himself reached out and touched me on the shoulder. He touch me just like I touch you. I got cold as ice and Death standing there grinning at me.

ROSE: Troy, why don't you hush that talk.

TROY: I say . . . What you want, Mr. Death? You be wanting me? You done brought your army to be getting me? I looked him dead in the eye. I wasn't fearing nothing. I was ready to tangle. Just like I'm ready to tangle now. The Bible say be ever vigilant. That's why I don't get but so drunk. I got to keep watch.

ROSE: Troy was right down there in Mercy Hospital. You remember he had pneu-monia? Laying there with a fever talking plumb out of his head.

TROY: Death standing there staring at me . . . carrying that sickle in his hand. Finally he say, "You want bound over for another year?" See, just like that . . . "You want bound over for another year?" I told him, "Bound over hell! Let's settle this now!"

It seem like he kinda fell back when I said that, and all the cold went out of me. I reached down and grabbed that sickle and threw it just as far as I could throw it . . . and me and him commenced to wrestling.

We wrestled for three days and three nights. I can't say where I found the strength from. Every time it seemed like he was gonna get the best of me, I'd reach way down deep inside myself and find the strength to do him one better.

ROSE: Every time Troy tell that story he find different ways to tell it. Different things to make up about it.

TROY: I ain't making up nothing. I'm telling you the facts of what happened. I wrestled with Death for three days and three nights and I'm standing here to tell you about it.

*Pause.*

Alright. At the end of the third night we done weakened each other to where we can't hardly move. Death stood up, throwed on his robe . . . had him a white robe with a hood on it. He throwed on that robe and went off to look for his sickle. Say, "I'll be back." Just like that. "I'll be back." I told him, say, "Yeah, but . . . you gonna have to find me!" I wasn't no fool. I wasn't going looking for him. Death ain't nothing to play with. And I know he's gonna get me. I know I got to join his army . . . his camp followers. But as long as I keep my strength and see him coming . . . as long as I keep up my vigilance . . . he's gonna have to fight to get me. I ain't going easy.

BONO: Well, look here, since you got to keep up your vigilance . . . let me have the bottle.

TROY: Aw hell, I shouldn't have told you that part. I should have left out that part.

ROSE: Troy be talking that stuff and half the time don't even know what he be talking about.

TROY: Bono know me better than that.

BONO: That's right. I know you. I know you got some Uncle Remus in your blood. You got more stories than the devil got sinners.

TROY: Aw hell, I done seen him too! Done talked with the devil.

ROSE: Troy, don't nobody wanna be hearing all that stuff.

LYONS *enters the yard from the street. Thirty-four years old,* TROY'S *son by a previous marriage, he sports a neatly trimmed goatee, sport coat, white shirt, tieless and buttoned at the collar. Though he fancies himself a musician, he is more caught up in the rituals and "idea" of being a musician than in the actual practice of the music. He has come to borrow money from* TROY, *and while he knows he will be successful, he is uncertain as to what extent his lifestyle will be held up to scrutiny and ridicule.*

LYONS: Hey, Pop.

TROY: What you come "Hey, Popping" me for?

LYONS: How you doing, Rose?

*He kisses her.*

Mr. Bono. How you doing?

BONO: Hey, Lyons . . . how you been?

TROY: He must have been doing alright. I ain't seen him around here last week.

ROSE: Troy, leave your boy alone. He come by to see you and you wanna start all that nonsense.

TROY: I ain't bothering Lyons.

*Offers him the bottle.*

Here . . . get you a drink. We got an understanding. I know why he come by to see me and he know I know.

LYONS: Come on, Pop . . . I just stopped by to say hi . . . see how you was doing.

TROY: You ain't stopped by yesterday.

ROSE: You gonna stay for supper, Lyons? I got some chicken cooking in the oven.

LYONS: No, Rose . . . thanks. I was just in the neighborhood and thought I'd stop by for a minute.

TROY: You was in the neighborhood alright, nigger. You telling the truth there. You was in the neighborhood cause it's my payday.

LYONS: Well, hell, since you mentioned it . . . let me have ten dollars.

TROY: I'll be damned! I'll die and go to hell and play blackjack with the devil before I give you ten dollars.

BONO: That's what I wanna know about . . . that devil you done seen.

LYONS: What . . . Pop done seen the devil? You too much, Pops.

TROY: Yeah, I done seen him. Talked to him too!

ROSE: You ain't seen no devil. I done told you that man ain't had nothing to do with the devil. Anything you can't understand, you want to call it the devil.

TROY: Look here, Bono . . . I went down to see Hertzberger about some furniture. Got three rooms for two-ninety-eight. That what it say on the radio. "Three rooms . . . two-ninety-eight." Even made up a little song about it. Go down there . . . man tell me I can't get no credit. I'm working every day and can't get no credit. What to do? I got an empty house with some raggedy furniture in it. Cory ain't got no bed. He's sleeping on a pile of rags on the floor. Working every day and can't get no credit. Come back here—Rose'll tell you—madder than hell. Sit down . . . try to figure what I'm gonna do. Come a knock on the door. Ain't been living here but three days. Who know I'm here? Open the door ... devil standing there bigger than life. White fellow ... got on good clothes and everything. Standing there with a clipboard in his hand. I ain't had to say nothing. First words come out of his mouth was ... "I understand you need some furniture and can't get no credit." I liked to fell over. He say "I'll give you all the credit you want, but you got to pay the interest on it." I told him, "Give me three rooms worth and charge whatever you want." Next day a truck pulled up here and two men unloaded them three rooms. Man what drove the truck give me a book. Say send ten dollars, first of every month to the address in the book and everything will be alright. Say if I miss a payment the devil was coming back and it'll be hell to pay. That was fifteen years ago. To this day ... the first of the month I send my ten dollars, Rose'll tell you.

ROSE: Troy lying.

TROY: I ain't never seen that man since. Now you tell me who else that could have been but the devil? I ain't sold my soul or nothing like that, you understand. Naw, I wouldn't have truck with the devil about nothing like that. I got my furniture and pays my ten dollars the first of the month just like clockwork.

BONO: How long you say you been paying this ten dollars a month?

TROY: Fifteen years!

BONO: Hell, ain't you finished paying for it yet? How much the man done charged you.

TROY: Aw hell, I done paid for it. I done paid for it ten times over! The fact is I'm scared to stop paying it.

ROSE: Troy lying. We got that furniture from Mr. Glickman. He ain't paying no ten dollars a month to nobody.

TROY: Aw hell, woman. Bono know I ain't that big a fool.

LYONS: I was just getting ready to say ... I know where there's a bridge for sale.

TROY: Look here, I'll tell you this ... it don't matter to me if he was the devil. It don't matter if the devil give credit. Somebody has got to give it.

ROSE: It ought to matter. You going around talking about having truck with the devil ... God's the one you gonna have to answer to. He's the one gonna be at the Judgment.

LYONS: Yeah, well, look here, Pop ... let me have that ten dollars. I'll give it back to you. Bonnie got a job working at the hospital.

TROY: What I tell you, Bono? The only time I see this nigger is when he wants something. That's the only time I see him.

LYONS: Come on, Pop, Mr. Bono don't want to hear all that. Let me have the ten dollars. I told you Bonnie working.

TROY: What that mean to me? "Bonnie working." I don't care if she working. Go ask her for the ten dollars if she working. Talking about "Bonnie working." Why ain't you working?

LYONS: Aw, Pop, you know I can't find no decent job. Where am I gonna get a job at? You know I can't get no job.

TROY: I told you I know some people down there. I can get you on the rubbish if you want to work. I told you that the last time you came by here asking me for something.

LYONS: Naw, Pop ... thanks. That ain't for me. I don't wanna be carrying nobody's rubbish. I don't wanna be punching nobody's time clock.

TROY: What's the matter, you too good to carry people's rubbish? Where you think that ten dollars you talking about come from? I'm just supposed to haul people's rubbish and give my money to you cause you too lazy to work. You too lazy to work and wanna know why you ain't got what I got.

ROSE: What hospital Bonnie working at? Mercy?

LYONS: She's down at Passavant working in the laundry.

TROY: I ain't got nothing as it is. I give you that ten dollars and I got to eat beans the rest of the week. Naw . . . you ain't getting no ten dollars here.

LYONS: You ain't got to be eating no beans. I don't know why you wanna say that.

TROY: I ain't got no extra money. Gabe done moved over to Miss Pearl's paying her the rent and things done got tight around here. I can't afford to be giving you every payday.

LYONS: I ain't asked you to give me nothing. I asked you to loan me ten dollars. I know you got ten dollars.

TROY: Yeah, I got it. You know why I got it? Cause I don't throw my money away out there in the streets. You living the fast life . . . wanna be a musician . . . running around in them clubs and things . . . then, you learn to take care of yourself. You ain't gonna find me going and asking nobody for nothing. I done spent too many years without.

LYONS: You and me is two different people, Pop.

TROY: I done learned my mistake and learned to do what's right by it. You still trying to get something for nothing. Life don't owe you nothing. You owe it to yourself. Ask Bono. He'll tell you I'm right.

LYONS: You got your way of dealing with the world . . . I got mine. The only thing that matters to me is the music.

TROY: Yeah, I can see that! It don't matter how you gonna eat . . . where your next dollar is coming from. You telling the truth there.

LYONS: I know I got to eat. But I got to live too. I need something that gonna help

me to get out of the bed in the morning. Make me feel like I belong in the world. I don't bother nobody. I just stay with my music cause that's the only way I can find to live in the world. Otherwise there ain't no telling what I might do. Now I don't come criticizing you and how you live. I just come by to ask you for ten dollars. I don't wanna hear all that about how I live.

TROY: Boy, your mama did a hell of a job raising you.

LYONS: You can't change me, Pop. I'm thirty-four years old. If you wanted to change me, you should have been there when I was growing up. I come by to see you . . . ask for ten dollars and you want to talk about how I was raised. You don't know nothing about how I was raised.

ROSE: Let the boy have ten dollars, Troy.

TROY: (To LYONS.) What the hell you looking at me for? I ain't got no ten dollars. You know what I do with my money.
(To ROSE.)
Give him ten dollars if you want him to have it.

ROSE: I will. Just as soon as you turn it loose.

TROY: (Handing ROSE the money.) There it is. Seventy-six dollars and forty-two cents. You see this, Bono? Now, I ain't gonna get but six of that back.

ROSE: You ought to stop telling that lie. Here, Lyons.
She hands him the money.

LYONS: Thanks, Rose. Look . . . I got to run . . . I'll see you later.

TROY: Wait a minute. You gonna say, "thanks, Rose" and ain't gonna look to see where she got that ten dollars from? See how they do me, Bono?

LYONS: I know she got it from you, Pop. Thanks. I'll give it back to you.

TROY: There he go telling another lie. Time I see that ten dollars . . . he'll be owing me thirty more.

LYONS: See you, Mr. Bono.

BONO: Take care, Lyons!

LYONS: Thanks, Pop. I'll see you again.

LYONS *exits the yard.*

TROY: I don't know why he don't go and get him a decent job and take care of that woman he got.

BONO: He'll be alright, Troy. The boy is still young.

TROY: The *boy* is thirty-four years old.

ROSE: Let's not get off into all that.

BONO: Look here . . . I got to be going. I got to be getting on. Lucille gonna be waiting.

TROY: (*Puts his arm around* ROSE.) See this woman, Bono? I love this woman. I love this woman so much it hurts. I love her so much . . . I done run out of ways of loving her. So I got to go back to basics. Don't you come by my house Monday morning talking about time to go to work . . . 'cause I'm still gonna be stroking!

ROSE: Troy! Stop it now!

BONO: I ain't paying him no mind, Rose. That ain't nothing but gin-talk. Go on, Troy. I'll see you Monday.

TROY: Don't you come by my house, nigger! I done told you what I'm gonna be doing.

*The lights go down to black.*

## SCENE TWO

*The lights come up on* ROSE *hanging up clothes. She hums and sings softly to herself. It is the following morning.*

ROSE: (*Sings*) Jesus, be a fence all around me every day
　　　　Jesus, I want you to protect me as I
　　　　　　travel on my way.
　　　　Jesus, be a fence all around me every
　　　　　　day.

TROY *enters from the house*

ROSE (*continued*): Jesus, I want you to
　　　　　　protect me
　　　　As I travel on my way.

*To* TROY.

'Morning. You ready for breakfast? I can fix it soon as I finish hanging up these clothes?

TROY: I got the coffee on. That'll be alright. I'll just drink some of that this morning.

ROSE: That 651 hit yesterday. That's the second time this month. Miss Pearl hit for a dollar . . . seem like those that need the least always get lucky. Poor folks can't get nothing.

TROY: Them numbers don't know nobody. I don't know why you fool with them. You and Lyons both.

ROSE: It's something to do.

TROY: You ain't doing nothing but throwing your money away.

ROSE: Troy, you know I don't play foolishly. I just play a nickel here and a nickel there.

TROY: That's two nickels you done thrown away.

ROSE: Now I hit sometimes . . . that makes up for it. It always comes in handy when I do hit. I don't hear you complaining then.

TROY: I ain't complaining now. I just say it's foolish. Trying to guess out of six hundred ways which way the number gonna come. If I had all the money niggers, these Negroes, throw away on numbers for one week—just one week—I'd be a rich man.

ROSE: Well, you wishing and calling it foolish ain't gonna stop folks from playing numbers. That's one thing for sure. Besides . . . some good things come from playing numbers. Look where Pope done bought him that restaurant off of numbers.

TROY: I can't stand niggers like that. Man ain't had two dimes to rub together. He walking around with his shoes all run over bumming money for cigarettes. Alright. Got lucky there and hit the numbers . . .

ROSE: Troy, I know all about it.

TROY: Had good sense, I'll say that for him. He ain't throwed his money away. I seen niggers hit the numbers and go through two thousand dollars in four days. Man bought him that restaurant down there ... fixed it up real nice ... and then didn't want nobody to come in it! A Negro go in there and can't get no kind of service. I seen a white fellow come in there and order a bowl of stew. Pope picked all the meat out the pot for him. Man ain't had nothing but a bowl of meat! Negro come behind him and ain't got nothing but the potatoes and carrots. Talking about what numbers do for people, you picked a wrong example. Ain't done nothing but make a worser fool out of him than he was before.

ROSE: Troy, you ought to stop worrying about what happened at work yesterday.

TROY: I ain't worried. Just told me to be down there at the Commissioner's office on Friday. Everybody think they gonna fire me. I ain't worried about them firing me. You ain't got to worry about that. (*Pause.*)
Where's Cory? Cory in the house? (*Calls.*) Cory?

ROSE: He gone out.

TROY: Out, huh? He gone out 'cause he know I want him to help me with this fence. I know how he is. That boy scared of work.
GABRIEL *enters. He comes halfway down the alley and, hearing* TROY'S *voice, stops.*

TROY (*continues*): He ain't done a lick of work in his life.

ROSE: He had to go to football practice. Coach wanted them to get in a little extra practice before the season start.

TROY: I got his practice ... running out of here before he get his chores done.

ROSE: Troy, what is wrong with you this morning? Don't nothing set right with you. Go on back in there and go to bed ... get up on the other side.

TROY: Why something got to be wrong with me? I ain't said nothing wrong with me.

ROSE: You got something to say about everything. First it's the numbers ... then it's the way the man runs his restaurant ... then you done got on Cory. What's it gonna be next? Take a look up there and see if the weather suits you ... or is it gonna be how you gonna put up the fence with the clothes hanging in the yard.

TROY: You hit the nail on the head then.

ROSE: I know you like I know the back of my hand. Go on in there and get you some coffee ... see if that straighten you up. 'Cause you ain't right this morning.
TROY *starts into the house and sees* GABRIEL. GABRIEL *starts singing.* TROY'S *brother, he is seven years younger than* TROY. *Injured in World War II, he has a metal plate in his head. He carries an old trumpet tied around his waist and believes with every fiber of his being that he is the Archangel Gabriel. He carries a chipped basket with an assortment of discarded fruits and vegetables he has picked up in the strip district and which he attempts to sell.*

GABRIEL: (*Singing.*)
Yes, ma'am, I got plums
You ask me how I sell them
Oh ten cents apiece
Three for a quarter
Come and buy now
'Cause I'm here today
And tomorrow I'll be gone
GABRIEL *enters.*
Hey, Rose!

ROSE: How you doing, Gabe?

GABRIEL: There's Troy ... Hey, Troy!

TROY: Hey, Gabe.
*Exit into kitchen.*

ROSE: (*To* GABRIEL.) What you got there?

GABRIEL: You know what I got, Rose. I got fruits and vegetables.

ROSE: (*Looking in basket.*) Where's all these plums you talking about?

GABRIEL: I ain't got no plums today, Rose. I was just singing that. Have some tomorrow. Put me in a big order for plums. Have enough plums tomorrow for St. Peter and everybody.

TROY *re-enters from kitchen, crosses to steps. To* ROSE.

Troy's mad at me.

TROY: I ain't mad at you. What I got to be mad at you about? You ain't done nothing to me.

GABRIEL: I just moved over to Miss Pearl's to keep out from in your way. I ain't mean no harm by it.

TROY: Who said anything about that? I ain't said anything about that.

GABRIEL: You ain't mad at me, is you?

TROY: Naw . . . I ain't mad at you, Gabe. If I was mad at you I'd tell you about it.

GABRIEL: Got me two rooms. In the basement. Got my own door too. Wanna see my key?

*He holds up a key.*

That's my own key! Ain't nobody else got a key like that. That's my key! My two rooms!

TROY: Well, that's good, Gabe. You got your own key . . . that's good.

ROSE: You hungry, Gabe? I was just fixing to cook Troy his breakfast.

GABRIEL: I'll take some biscuits. You got some biscuits? Did you know when I was in heaven . . . every morning me and St. Peter would sit down by the gate and eat some big fat biscuits? Oh, yeah! We had us a good time. We'd sit there and eat us them biscuits and then St. Peter would go off to sleep and tell me to wake him up when it's time to open the gates for the judgment.

ROSE: Well, come on . . . I'll make up a batch of biscuits.

ROSE *exits into the house.*

GABRIEL: Troy . . . St. Peter got your name in the book. I seen it. It say . . . Troy Maxson. I say . . . I know him! He got the same name like what I got. That's my brother!

TROY: How many times you gonna tell me that, Gabe?

GABRIEL: Ain't got my name in the book. Don't have to have my name. I done died and went to heaven. He got your name though. One morning St. Peter was looking at his book . . . marking it up for the judgment . . . and he let me see your name. Got it in there under M. Got Rose's name . . . I ain't seen it like I seen yours . . . but I know it's in there. He got a great big book. Got everybody's name what was ever been born. That's what he told me. But I seen your name. Seen it with my own eyes.

TROY: Go on in the house there. Rose going to fix you something to eat.

GABRIEL: Oh, I ain't hungry. I done had breakfast with Aunt Jemimah. She come by and cooked me up a whole mess of flapjacks. Remember how we used to eat them flapjacks?

TROY: Go on in the house and get you something to eat now.

GABRIEL: I got to go sell my plums. I done sold some tomatoes. Got me two quarters. Wanna see?

*He shows* TROY *his quarters.*

I'm gonna save them and buy me a new horn so St. Peter can hear me when it's time to open the gates.

GABRIEL *stops suddenly. Listens.*

Hear that? That's the hellhounds. I got to chase them out of here. Go on get out of here! Get out!

GABRIEL *exits singing.*

Better get ready for the judgment
Better get ready for the judgment
My Lord is coming down

ROSE *enters from the house.*

TROY: He gone off somewhere.

GABRIEL: (*Offstage*)

Better get ready for the judgment
Better get ready for the judgment morning

Better get ready for the judgment
My God is coming down

ROSE: He ain't eating right. Miss Pearl say she can't get him to eat nothing.

TROY: What you want me to do about it, Rose? I done did everything I can for the man. I can't make him get well. Man got half his head blown away . . . what you expect?

ROSE: Seem like something ought to be done to help him.

TROY: Man don't bother nobody. He just mixed up from that metal plate he got in his head. Ain't no sense for him to go back into the hospital.

ROSE: Least he be eating right. They can help him take care of himself.

TROY: Don't nobody wanna be locked up, Rose. What you wanna lock him up for? Man go over there and fight the war . . . messin' around with them Japs, get half his head blown off . . . and they give him a lousy three thousand dollars. And I had to swoop down on that.

ROSE: Is you fixing to go into that again?

TROY: That's the only way I got a roof over my head . . . cause of that metal plate.

ROSE: Ain't no sense you blaming yourself for nothing. Gabe wasn't in no condition to manage that money. You done what was right by him. Can't nobody say you ain't done what was right by him. Look how long you took care of him . . . till he wanted to have his own place and moved over there with Miss Pearl.

TROY: That ain't what I'm saying, woman! I'm just stating the facts. If my brother didn't have that metal plate in his head . . . I wouldn't have a pot to piss in or a window to throw it out of. And I'm fifty-three years old. Now see if you can understand that!

TROY *gets up from the porch and starts to exit the yard.*

ROSE: Where you going off to? You been running out of here every Saturday for weeks. I thought you was gonna work on this fence?

TROY: I'm gonna walk down to Taylors'. Listen to the ball game. I'll be back in a bit. I'll work on it when I get back.

*He exits the yard. The lights go to black.*

## SCENE THREE

*The lights come up on the yard. It is four hours later.* ROSE *is taking down the clothes from the line.* CORY *enters carrying his football equipment.*

ROSE: Your daddy like to had a fit with you running out of here this morning without doing your chores.

CORY: I told you I had to go to practice.

ROSE: He say you were supposed to help him with this fence.

CORY: He been saying that the last four or five Saturdays, and then he don't never do nothing, but go down to Taylors'. Did you tell him about the recruiter?

ROSE: Yeah, I told him,

CORY: What he say?

ROSE: He ain't said nothing too much. You get in there and get started on your chores before he gets back. Go on and scrub down them steps before he gets back here hollering and carrying on.

CORY: I'm hungry. What you got to eat, Mama?

ROSE: Go on and get started on your chores. I got some meat loaf in there. Go on and make you a sandwich . . . and don't leave no mess in there.

CORY *exits into the house.* ROSE *continues to take down the clothes.* TROY *enters the yard and sneaks up and grabs her from behind.*

Troy! Go on, now. You liked to scared me to death. What was the score of the game? Lucille had me on the phone and I couldn't keep up with it.

TROY: What I care about the game? Come here, woman. (*He tries to kiss her.*)

**ROSE:** I thought you went down Taylors' to listen to the game. Go on, Troy! You supposed to be putting up this fence.

**TROY:** (*Attempting to kiss her again.*) I'll put it up when I finish with what is at hand.

**ROSE:** Go on, Troy. I ain't studying you.

**TROY:** (*Chasing after her.*) I'm studying you . . . fixing to do my homework!

**ROSE:** Troy, you better leave me alone.

**TROY:** Where's Cory? That boy brought his butt home yet?

**ROSE:** He's in the house doing his chores.

**TROY:** (*Calling.*) Cory! Get your butt out here, boy!

*ROSE exits into the house with the laundry. TROY goes over to the pile of wood, picks up a board, and starts sawing. CORY enters from the house.*

**TROY:** You just now coming in here from leaving this morning?

**CORY:** Yeah, I had to go to football practice.

**TROY:** Yeah, what?

**CORY:** Yessir.

**TROY:** I ain't but two seconds off you noway. The garbage sitting in there overflowing . . . you ain't done none of your chores . . . and you come in here talking about "Yeah."

**CORY:** I was just getting ready to do my chores now, Pop . . .

**TROY:** Your first chore is to help me with this fence on Saturday. Everything else come after that. Now get that saw and cut them boards.

*CORY takes the saw and begins cutting the boards. TROY continues working. There is a long pause.*

**CORY:** Hey, Pop . . . why don't you buy a TV?

**TROY:** What I want with a TV? What I want one of them for?

**CORY:** Everybody got one. Earl, Ba Bra . . . Jesse!

**TROY:** I ain't asked you who had one. I say what I want with one?

**CORY:** So you can watch it. They got lots of things on TV. Baseball games and everything. We could watch the World Series.

**TROY:** Yeah . . . and how much this TV cost?

**CORY:** I don't know. They got them on sale for around two hundred dollars.

**TROY:** Two hundred dollars, huh?

**CORY:** That ain't that much, Pop.

**TROY:** Naw, it's just two hundred dollars. See that roof you got over your head at night? Let me tell you something about that roof. It's been over ten years since that roof was last tarred. See now . . . the snow come this winter and sit up there on that roof like it is . . . and it's gonna seep inside. It's just gonna be a little bit . . . ain't gonna hardly notice it. Then the next thing you know, it's gonna be leaking all over the house. Then the wood rot from all that water and you gonna need a whole new roof. Now, how much you think it cost to get that roof tarred?

**CORY:** I don't know.

**TROY:** Two hundred and sixty-four dollars . . . cash money. While you thinking about a TV, I got to be thinking about the roof . . . and whatever else go wrong around here. Now if you had two hundred dollars, what would you do . . . fix the roof or buy a TV?

**CORY:** I'd buy a TV. Then when the roof started to leak . . . when it needed fixing . . . I'd fix it.

**TROY:** Where you gonna get the money from? You done spent it for a TV. You gonna sit up and watch the water run all over your brand new TV.

**CORY:** Aw, Pop. You got money. I know you do.

**TROY:** Where I got it at, huh?

**CORY:** You got it in the bank.

**TROY:** You wanna see my bankbook? You wanna see that seventy-three dollars and twenty-two cents I got sitting up in there?

CORY: You ain't got to pay for it all at one time. You can put a down payment on it and carry it on home with you.

TROY: Not me. I ain't gonna owe nobody nothing if I can help it. Miss a payment and they come and snatch it right out your house. Then what you got? Now, soon as I get two hundred dollars clear, then I'll buy a TV. Right now, as soon as I get two hundred and sixty-four dollars, I'm gonna have this roof tarred.

CORY: Aw . . . Pop!

TROY: You go on and get you two hundred dollars and buy one if ya want it. I got better things to do with my money.

CORY: I can't get no two hundred dollars. I ain't never seen two hundred dollars.

TROY: I'll tell you what . . . you get you a hundred dollars and I'll put the other hundred with it.

CORY: Alright, I'm gonna show you.

TROY: You gonna show me how you can cut them boards right now.

CORY *begins to cut the boards. There is a long pause.*

CORY: The Pirates won today. That makes five in a row.

TROY: I ain't thinking about the Pirates. Got an all-white team. Got that boy . . . that Puerto Rican boy . . . Clemente. Don't even half-play him. That boy could be something if they give him a chance. Play him one day and sit him on the bench the next.

CORY: He gets a lot of chances to play.

TROY: I'm talking about playing regular. Playing every day so you can get your timing. That's what I'm talking about.

CORY: They got some white guys on the team that don't play every day. You can't play everybody at the same time.

TROY: If they got a white fellow sitting on the bench . . . you can bet your last dollar he can't play! The colored guy got to be twice as good before he get on the team.

That's why I don't want you to get all tied up in them sports. Man on the team and what it get him? They got colored on the team and don't use them. Same as not having them. All them teams the same.

CORY: The Braves got Hank Aaron and Wes Covington. Hank Aaron hit two home runs today. That makes forty-three.

TROY: Hank Aaron ain't nobody. That's what you supposed to do. That's how you supposed to play the game. Ain't nothing to it. It's just a matter of timing . . . getting the right follow-through. Hell, I can hit forty-three home runs right now!

CORY: Not off no major-league pitching, you couldn't.

TROY: We had better pitching in the Negro leagues. I hit seven home runs off of Satchel Paige. You can't get no better than that!

CORY: Sandy Koufax. He's leading the league in strikeouts.

TROY: I ain't thinking of no Sandy Koufax.

CORY: You got Warren Spahn and Lew Burdette. I bet you couldn't hit no home runs off of Warren Spahn.

TROY: I'm through with it now. You go on and cut them boards.

(*Pause.*)

Your mama tell me you done got recruited by a college football team? Is that right?

CORY: Yeah. Coach Zellman say the recruiter gonna be coming by to talk to you. Get you to sign the permission papers.

TROY: I thought you supposed to be working down there at the A&P. Ain't you suppose to be working down there after school?

CORY: Mr. Stawicki say he gonna hold my job for me until after the football season. Say starting next week I can work weekends.

TROY: I thought we had an understanding about this football stuff? You suppose to keep up with your chores and hold that job down at the A&P. Ain't been around here all day on a Saturday. Ain't none of your chores done . . . and now you telling me you done quit your job.

CORY: I'm gonna be working weekends.

TROY: You damn right you are! And ain't no need for nobody coming around here to talk to me about signing nothing.

CORY: Hey, Pop . . . you can't do that. He's coming all the way from North Carolina.

TROY: I don't care where he coming from. The white man ain't gonna let you get nowhere with that football noway. You go on and get your book-learning so you can work yourself up in that A&P or learn how to fix cars or build houses or something, get you a trade. That way you have something can't nobody take away from you. You go on and learn how to put your hands to some good use. Besides hauling people's garbage.

CORY: I get good grades, Pop. That's why the recruiter wants to talk with you. You got to keep up your grades to get recruited. This way I'll be going to college. I'll get a chance . . .

TROY: First you gonna get your butt down there to the A&P and get your job back.

CORY: Mr. Stawicki done already hired somebody else 'cause I told him I was playing football.

TROY: You a bigger fool than I thought . . . to let somebody take away your job so you can play some football. Where you gonna get your money to take out your girlfriend and whatnot? What kind of foolishness is that to let somebody take away your job?

CORY: I'm still gonna be working weekends.

TROY: Naw . . . naw. You getting your butt out of here and finding you another job.

CORY: Come on, Pop! I got to practice. I can't work after school and play football too.

The team needs me. That's what Coach Zellman say . . .

TROY: I don't care what nobody else say. I'm the boss . . . you understand? I'm the boss around here. I do the only saying what counts.

CORY: Come on, Pop!

TROY: I asked you . . . did you understand?

CORY: Yeah . . .

TROY: What?!

CORY: Yessir.

TROY: You go on down there to that A&P and see if you can get your job back. If you can't do both . . . then you quit the football team. You've got to take the crookeds with the straights.

CORY: Yessir.

(Pause.)

Can I ask you a question?

TROY: What the hell you wanna ask me? Mr. Stawicki the one you got the questions for.

CORY: How come you ain't never liked me?

TROY: Liked you? Who the hell say I got to like you? What law is there say I got to like you? Wanna stand up in my face and ask a damn fool-ass question like that. Talking about liking somebody. Come here, boy, when I talk to you.

CORY comes over to where TROY is working. He stands slouched over and TROY shoves him on his shoulder.

Straighten up, goddammit! I asked you a question . . . what law is there say I got to like you?

CORY: None.

TROY: Well, alright then! Don't you eat every day?

(Pause.)

Answer me when I talk to you! Don't you eat every day?

CORY: Yeah.

TROY: Nigger, as long as you in my house, you put that sir on the end of it when you talk to me!

CORY: Yes . . . sir.

TROY: You eat every day.

CORY: Yessir!

TROY: Got a roof over your head.

CORY: Yessir!

TROY: Got clothes on your back.

CORY: Yessir.

TROY: Why you think that is?

CORY: Cause of you.

TROY: Aw, hell I know it's 'cause of me . . . but why do you think that is?

CORY: (*Hesitant.*) Cause you like me.

TROY: Like you? I go out of here every morning . . . bust my butt . . . putting up with them crackers every day . . . cause I like you? You about the biggest fool I ever saw.

(*Pause.*)

It's my job. It's my responsibility! You understand that? A man got to take care of his family. You live in my house . . . sleep you behind on my bedclothes . . . fill you belly up with my food . . . cause you my son. You my flesh and blood. Not 'cause I like you! Cause it's my duty to take care of you. I owe a responsibility to you!

Let's get this straight right here . . . before it go along any further . . . I ain't got to like you. Mr. Rand don't give me my money come payday cause he likes me. He gives me cause he owe me. I done give you everything I had to give you. I gave you your life! Me and your mama worked that out between us. And liking your black ass wasn't part of the bargain. Don't you try and go through life worrying about if somebody like you or not. You best be making sure they doing right by you. You understand what I'm saying, boy?

CORY: Yessir.

TROY: Then get the hell out of my face, and get on down to that A&P.

ROSE *has been standing behind the screen door for much of the scene. She enters as* CORY *exits.*

ROSE: Why don't you let the boy go ahead and play football, Troy? Ain't no harm in that. He's just trying to be like you with the sports.

TROY: I don't want him to be like me! I want him to move as far away from my life as he can get. You the only decent thing that ever happened to me. I wish him that. But I don't wish him a thing else from my life. I decided seventeen years ago that boy wasn't getting involved in no sports. Not after what they did to me in the sports.

ROSE: Troy, why don't you admit you was too old to play in the major leagues? For once . . . why don't you admit that?

TROY: What do you mean too old? Don't come telling me I was too old. I just wasn't the right color. Hell, I'm fifty-three years old and can do better than Selkirk's .269 right now!

ROSE: How's was you gonna play ball when you were over forty? Sometimes I can't get no sense out of you.

TROY: I got good sense, woman. I got sense enough not to let my boy get hurt over playing no sports. You been mothering that boy too much. Worried about if people like him.

ROSE: Everything that boy do . . . he do for you. He wants you to say "Good job, son." That's all.

TROY: Rose, I ain't got time for that. He's alive. He's healthy. He's got to make his own way. I made mine. Ain't nobody gonna hold his hand when he get out there in that world.

ROSE: Times have changed from when you was young, Troy. People change. The world's changing around you and you can't even see it.

TROY: (*Slow, methodical.*) Woman . . . I do the best I can do. I come in here every Friday. I carry a sack of potatoes and a bucket of lard. You all line up at the door with your hands out. I give you the lint

from my pockets. I give you my sweat
and my blood. I ain't got no tears. I done
spent them. We go upstairs in that room
at night . . . and I fall down on you and
try to blast a hole into forever. I get up
Monday morning . . . find my lunch on
the table. I go out. Make my way. Find
my strength to carry me through to the
next Friday.
(*Pause.*)
That's all I got, Rose. That's all I got to
give. I can't give nothing else.
TROY *exits into the house. The lights go
down to black.*

**SCENE FOUR**

*It is Friday. Two weeks later.* CORY *starts out of
the house with his football equipment. The phone
rings.*

CORY: (*Calling.*) I got it!
   *He answers the phone and stands in the
   screen door talking.*
   Hello? Hey, Jesse. Naw . . . I was just get-
   ting ready to leave now.
ROSE: (*Calling.*) Cory!
CORY: I told you, man, them spikes is all tore
   up. You can use them if you want, but
   they ain't no good. Earl got some spikes.
ROSE: (*Calling.*) Cory!
CORY: (*Calling to* ROSE.) Mam? I'm talking to
   Jesse.
   (*Into phone.*)
   When she say that? (*Pause.*) Aw, you ly-
   ing, man. I'm gonna tell her you said that.
ROSE: (*Calling.*) Cory, don't you go no-
   where!
CORY: I got to go to the game, Ma!
   (*Into the phone.*)
   Yeah, hey, look, I'll talk to you later.
   Yeah, I'll meet you over Earl's house.
   Later. Bye, Ma.
   CORY *exits the house and starts out the yard.*
ROSE: Cory, where you going off to? You got
   that stuff all pulled out and thrown all
   over your room.

CORY: (*In the yard.*) I was looking for my
   spikes. Jesse wanted to borrow my spikes.
ROSE: Get up there and get that cleaned up
   before your daddy get back in here.
CORY: I got to go to the game! I'll clean it up
   *when I get back.*
   CORY *exits.*
ROSE: That's all he need to do is see that
   room all messed up.
   ROSE *exits into the house.* TROY *and* BONO
   *enter the yard.* TROY *is dressed in clothes
   other than his work clothes.*
BONO: He told him the same thing he told
   you. Take it to the union.
TROY: Brownie ain't got that much sense.
   Man wasn't thinking about nothing. He
   wait until I confront them on it . . . then
   he wanna come crying seniority.
   (*Calls.*)
   Hey, Rose!
BONO: I wish I could have seen Mr. Rand's
   face when he told you.
TROY: He couldn't get it out of his mouth!
   Liked to bit his tongue! When they called
   me down there to the Commissioner's
   office . . . he thought they was gonna fire
   me. Like everybody else.
BONO: I didn't think they was gonna fire
   you. I thought they was gonna put you
   on the warning paper.
TROY: Hey, Rose!
   (*To* BONO.)
   Yeah, Mr. Rand like to bit his tongue.
   TROY *breaks the seal on the bottle, takes a
   drink, and hands it to* BONO.
BONO: I see you run right down to Taylors'
   and told that Alberta gal.
TROY: (*Calling.*) Hey Rose! (*To* BONO.) I told
   everybody. Hey, Rose! I went down
   there to cash my check.
ROSE: (*Entering from the house.*) Hush all that
   hollering, man! I know you out here.
   What they say down there at the Com-
   missioner's office?
TROY: You supposed to come when I call
   you, woman. Bono'll tell you that.

(*To* BONO.)

Don't Lucille come when you call her?

ROSE:  Man, hush your mouth. I ain't no dog . . . talk about "come when you call me."

TROY:  (*Puts his arm around* ROSE.) You hear this, Bono? I had me an old dog used to get uppity like that. You say, "C'mere, Blue!" . . . and he just lay there and look at you. End up getting a stick and chasing him away trying to make him come.

ROSE:  I ain't studying you and your dog. I remember you used to sing that old song.

TROY:  (*He sings.*) Hear it ring! Hear it ring! I had a dog his name was Blue.

ROSE:  Don't nobody wanna hear you sing that old song.

TROY:  (*Sings.*) You know Blue was mighty true.

ROSE:  Used to have Cory running around here singing that song.

BONO:  Hell, I remember that song myself.

TROY:  (*Sings.*) You know Blue was a good old dog.

Blue treed a possum in a hollow log.

That was my daddy's song. My daddy made up that song.

ROSE:  I don't care who made it up. Don't nobody wanna hear you sing it.

TROY:  (*Makes a song like calling a dog.*) Come here, woman.

ROSE:  You come in here carrying on, I reckon they ain't fired you. What they say down there at the Commissioner's office?

TROY:  Look here, Rose . . . Mr. Rand called me into his office today when I got back from talking to them people down there . . . it come from up top . . . he called me in and told me they was making me a driver.

ROSE:  Troy, you kidding!

TROY:  No I ain't. Ask Bono.

ROSE:  Well, that's great, Troy. Now you don't have to hassle them people no more.

LYONS *enters from the street.*

TROY:  Aw hell, I wasn't looking to see you today. I thought you was in jail. Got it all over the front page of the *Courier* about them raiding Sefus' place . . . where you be hanging out with all them thugs.

LYONS:  Hey, Pop . . . that ain't got nothing to do with me. I don't go down there gambling. I go down there to sit in with the band. I ain't got nothing to do with the gambling part. They got some good music down there.

TROY:  They got some rogues . . . is what they got.

LYONS:  How you been, Mr. Bono? Hi, Rose.

BONO:  I see where you playing down at the Crawford Grill tonight.

ROSE:  How come you ain't brought Bonnie like I told you. You should have brought Bonnie with you, she ain't been over in a month of Sundays.

LYONS:  I was just in the neighborhood . . . thought I'd stop by.

TROY:  Here he come . . .

BONO:  Your daddy got a promotion on the rubbish. He's gonna be the first colored driver. Ain't got to do nothing but sit up there and read the paper like them white fellows.

LYONS:  Hey, Pop . . . if you knew how to read you'd be alright.

BONO:  Naw . . . naw . . . you mean if the nigger knew how to *drive* he'd be all right. Been fighting with them people about driving and ain't even got a license. Mr. Rand know you ain't got no driver's license?

TROY:  Driving ain't nothing. All you do is point the truck where you want it to go. Driving ain't nothing.

BONO:  Do Mr. Rand know you ain't got no driver's license? That's what I'm talking about. I ain't asked if driving was easy. I asked if Mr. Rand know you ain't got no driver's license.

TROY:  He ain't got to know. The man ain't got to know my business. Time he find out, I have two or three driver's licenses.

LYONS: (*Going into his pocket.*) Say, look here, Pop . . .

TROY: I knew it was coming. Didn't I tell you, Bono? I know what kind of "Look here, Pop" that was. The nigger fixing to ask me for some money. It's Friday night. It's my payday. All them rogues down there on the avenue . . . the ones that ain't in jail . . . and Lyons is hopping in his shoes to get down there with them.

LYONS: See, Pop . . . if you give somebody else a chance to talk sometime, you'd see that I was fixing to pay you back your ten dollars like I told you. Here . . . I told you I'd pay you when Bonnie got paid.

TROY: Naw . . . you go ahead and keep that ten dollars. Put it in the bank. The next time you feel like you wanna come by here and ask me for something . . . you go on down there and get that.

LYONS: Here's your ten dollars, Pop. I told you I don't want you to give me nothing. I just wanted to borrow ten dollars.

TROY: Naw . . . you go on and keep that for the next time you want to ask me.

LYONS: Come on, Pop . . . here go your ten dollars.

ROSE: Why don't you go on and let the boy pay you back, Troy?

LYONS: Here you go, Rose. If you don't take it I'm gonna have to hear about it for the next six months.
*He hands her the money.*

ROSE: You can hand yours over here too, Troy.

TROY: You see this, Bono. You see how they do me.

BONO: Yeah, Lucille do me the same way.
**GABRIEL** *is heard singing offstage. He enters.*

GABRIEL: Better get ready for the Judgment! Better get ready for . . . Hey! . . . Hey! . . . There's Troy's boy!

LYONS: How you doing, Uncle Gabe?

GABRIEL: Lyons . . . The King of the Jungle! Rose . . . hey, Rose. Got a flower for you.
*He takes a rose from his pocket.*
Picked it myself. That's the same rose like you is!

ROSE: That's right nice of you, Gabe.

LYONS: What you been doing, Uncle Gabe?

GABRIEL: Oh, I been chasing hellhounds and waiting on the time to tell St. Peter to open the gates.

LYONS: You been chasing hellhounds, huh? Well . . . you doing the right thing, Uncle Gabe. Somebody got to chase them.

GABRIEL: Oh, yeah . . . I know it. The devil's strong. The devil ain't no pushover. Hellhounds snipping at everybody's heels. But I got my trumpet waiting on the judgment time.

LYONS: Waiting on the Battle of Armageddon, huh?

GABRIEL: Ain't gonna be too much of a battle when God get to waving that Judgment sword. But the people's gonna have a hell of a time trying to get into heaven if them gates ain't open.

LYONS: (*Putting his arm around* GABRIEL.) You hear this, Pop. Uncle Gabe, you alright!

GABRIEL: (*Laughing with* LYONS.) Lyons! King of the Jungle.

ROSE: You gonna stay for supper, Gabe. Want me to fix you a plate?

GABRIEL: I'll take a sandwich, Rose. Don't want no plate. Just wanna eat with my hands. I'll take a sandwich.

ROSE: How about you, Lyons? You staying? Got some short ribs cooking.

LYONS: Naw, I won't eat nothing till after we finished playing.
(*Pause.*)
You ought to come down and listen to me play, Pop.

TROY: I don't like that Chinese music. All that noise.

ROSE: Go on in the house and wash up, Gabe . . . I'll fix you a sandwich.

GABRIEL: (*To* LYONS, *as he exits.*) Troy's mad at me.

LYONS: What you mad at Uncle Gabe for, Pop.

ROSE: He thinks Troy's mad at him cause he moved over to Miss Pearl's.

TROY: I ain't mad at the man. He can live where he want to live at.

LYONS: What he move over there for? Miss Pearl don't like nobody.

ROSE: She don't mind him none. She treats him real nice. She just don't allow all that singing.

TROY: She don't mind that rent he be paying . . . that's what she don't mind.

ROSE: Troy, I ain't going through that with you no more. He's over there cause he want to have his own place. He can come and go as he please.

TROY: Hell, he could come and go as he please here. I wasn't stopping him. I ain't put no rules on him.

ROSE: It ain't the same thing, Troy. And you know it.

GABRIEL *comes to the door.*

Now, that's the last I wanna hear about that. I don't wanna hear nothing else about Gabe and Miss Pearl. And next week . . .

GABRIEL: I'm ready for my sandwich, Rose.

ROSE: And next week . . . when that recruiter come from that school . . . I want you to sign that paper and go on and let Cory play football. Then that'll be the last I have to hear about that.

TROY: (*To* ROSE *as she exits into the house.*) I ain't thinking about Cory nothing.

LYONS: What . . . Cory got recruited? What school he going to?

TROY: That boy walking around here smelling his piss . . . thinking he's grown. Thinking he's gonna do what he want, irrespective of what I say. Look here, Bono . . . I left the Commissioner's office and went down to the A&P . . . that boy ain't working down there. He lying to

me. Telling me he ̶̶̶̶ telling me he working̶̶̶ ing me he working af̶̶̶ Stawicki tell me he ain't there at all!

LYONS: Cory just growing u̶ ̶s just busting at the seams trying to fill out your shoes.

TROY: I don't care what he's doing. When he get to the point where he wanna disobey me . . . then it's time for him to move on. Bono'll tell you that. I bet he ain't never disobeyed his daddy without paying the consequences.

BONO: I ain't never had a chance. My daddy came on through . . . but I ain't never knew him to see him . . . or what he had on his mind or where he went. Just moving on through. Searching out the New Land. That's what the old folks used to call it. See a fellow moving around from place to place . . . woman to woman . . . called it searching out the New Land. I can't say if he ever found it. I come along, didn't want no kids. Didn't know if I was gonna be in one place long enough to fix on them right as their daddy. I figured I was going searching too. As it turned out I been hooked up with Lucille near about as long as your daddy been with Rose. Going on sixteen years.

TROY: Sometimes I wish I hadn't known my daddy. He ain't cared nothing about no kids. A kid to him wasn't nothing. All he wanted was for you to learn how to walk so he could start you to working. When it come time for eating . . . he ate first. If there was anything left over, that's what you got. Man would sit down and eat two chickens and give you the wing.

LYONS: You ought to stop that, Pop. Everybody feed their kids. No matter how hard times is . . . everybody care about their kids. Make sure they have something to eat.

TROY: The only thing my daddy cared about was getting them bales of cotton in to Mr. Lubin. That's the only thing that mattered to him. Sometimes I used to wonder why he was living. Wonder why the devil hadn't come and got him. "Get them bales of cotton in to Mr. Lubin" and find out he owe him money . . .

LYONS: He should have just went on and left when he saw he couldn't get nowhere. That's what I would have done.

TROY: How he gonna leave with eleven kids? And where he gonna go? He ain't knew how to do nothing but farm. No, he was trapped and I think he knew it. But I'll say this for him . . . he felt a responsibility toward us. Maybe he ain't treated us the way I felt he should have . . . but without that responsibility he could have walked off and left us . . . made his own way.

BONO: A lot of them did. Back in those days what you talking about . . . they walk out their front door and just take on down one road or another and keep on walking.

LYONS: There you go! That's what I'm talking about.

BONO: Just keep on walking till you come to something else. Ain't you never heard of nobody having the walking blues? Well, that's what you call it when you just take off like that.

TROY: My daddy ain't had them walking blues! What you talking about? He stayed right there with his family. But he was just as evil as he could be. My mama couldn't stand him. Couldn't stand that evilness. She run off when I was about eight. She sneaked off one night after he had gone to sleep. Told me she was coming back for me. I ain't never seen her no more. All his women run off and left him. He wasn't good for nobody.

When my turn come to head out, I was fourteen and got to sniffing around Joe Canewell's daughter. Had us an old mule we called Greyboy. My daddy sent me out to do some plowing and I tied up Greyboy and went to fooling around with Joe Canewell's daughter. We done found us a nice little spot, got real cozy with each other. She about thirteen and we done figured we was grown anyway . . . so we down there enjoying ourselves . . . ain't thinking about nothing. We didn't know Greyboy had got loose and wandered back to the house and my daddy was looking for me. We down there by the creek enjoying ourselves when my daddy come up on us. Surprised us. He had them leather straps off the mule and commenced to whupping me like there was no tomorrow. I jumped up, mad and embarrassed. I was scared of my daddy. When he commenced to whupping on me . . . quite naturally I run to get out of the way.
(*Pause.*)
Now I thought he was mad cause I ain't done my work. But I see where he was chasing me off so he could have the gal for himself. When I see what the matter of it was, I lost all fear of my daddy. Right there is where I become a man . . . at fourteen years of age.
(*Pause.*)
Now it was my turn to run him off. I picked up them same reins that he had used on me. I picked up them reins and commenced to whupping on him. The gal jumped up and run off . . . and when my daddy turned to face me, I could see why the devil had never come to get him . . . cause he was the devil himself. I don't know what happened. When I woke up, I was laying right there by the creek, and Blue . . . this old dog we had . . . was licking my face. I thought I was blind. I couldn't see nothing. Both my eyes were swollen shut. I layed there and cried. I didn't know what I was gonna

do. The only thing I knew was the time had come for me to leave my daddy's house. And right there the world suddenly got big. And it was a long time before I could cut it down to where I could handle it.

Part of that cutting down was when I got to the place where I could feel him kicking in my blood and knew that the only thing that separated us was the matter of a few years.

GABRIEL *enters from the house with a sandwich.*

LYONS: What you got there, Uncle Gabe?

GABRIEL: Got me a ham sandwich. Rose gave me a ham sandwich.

TROY: I don't know what happened to him. I done lost touch with everybody except Gabriel. But I hope he's dead. I hope he found some peace.

LYONS: That's a heavy story, Pop. I didn't know you left home when you was fourteen.

TROY: And didn't know nothing. The only part of the world I knew was the forty-two acres of Mr. Lubin's land. That's all I knew about life.

LYONS: Fourteen's kinda young to be out on your own. (*Phone rings.*) I don't even think I was ready to be out on my own at fourteen. I don't know what I would have done.

TROY: I got up from the creek and walked on down to Mobile. I was through with farming. Figured I could do better in the city. So I walked the two hundred miles to Mobile.

LYONS: Wait a minute . . . you ain't walked no two hundred miles, Pop. Ain't nobody gonna walk no two hundred miles. You talking about some walking there.

BONO: That's the only way you got anywhere back in them days.

LYONS: Shhh. Damn if I wouldn't have hitched a ride with somebody!

TROY: Who you gonna hitch it with? They ain't had no cars and things like they got now. We talking about 1918.

ROSE: (*Entering.*) What you all out here getting into?

TROY: (*To* ROSE.) I'm telling Lyons how good he got it. He don't know nothing about this I'm talking.

ROSE: Lyons, that was Bonnie on the phone. She say you supposed to pick her up.

LYONS: Yeah, okay, Rose.

TROY: I walked on down to Mobile and hitched up with some of them fellows that was heading this way. Got up here and found out . . . not only couldn't you get a job . . . you couldn't find no place to live. I thought I was in freedom. Shhh. Colored folks living down there on the riverbanks in whatever kind of shelter they could find for themselves. Right down there under the Brady Street Bridge. Living in shacks made of sticks and tarpaper. Messed around there and went from bad to worse. Started stealing. First it was food. Then I figured, hell, if I steal money I can buy me some food. Buy me some shoes too! One thing led to another. Met your mama. I was young and anxious to be a man. Met your mama and had you. What I do that for? Now I got to worry about feeding you and her. Got to steal three times as much. Went out one day looking for somebody to rob . . . that's what I was, a robber. I'll tell you the truth. I'm ashamed of it today. But it's the truth. Went to rob this fellow . . . pulled out my knife . . . and he pulled out a gun. Shot me in the chest. It felt just like somebody had taken a hot branding iron and laid it on me. When he shot me I jumped at him with my knife. They told me I killed him and they put me in the penitentiary and locked me up for fifteen years. That's where I met Bono. That's where I learned how to play baseball. Got out that place and your mama had taken you and went on to make life without me. Fifteen years was a long time for her to wait. But that fifteen years cured me of that robbing stuff. Rose'll tell you. She asked me when I met her if I had gotten all that foolishness out of my system. And I told her, "Baby, it's you and baseball all what count with me." You hear me, Bono? I meant it too. She say, "Which one comes first?" I told her, "Baby, ain't no doubt it's baseball . . . but you stick and get old with me and we'll both outlive this baseball." Am I right, Rose? And it's true.

ROSE: Man, hush your mouth. You ain't said no such thing. Talking about, "Baby, you know you'll always be number one with me." That's what you was talking.

TROY: You hear that, Bono. That's why I love her.

BONO: Rose'll keep you straight. You get off the track, she'll straighten you up.

ROSE: Lyons, you better get on up and get Bonnie. She waiting on you.

LYONS: (Gets up to go.) Hey, Pop, why don't you come on down to the Grill and hear me play?

TROY: I ain't going down there. I'm too old to be sitting around in them clubs.

BONO: You got to be good to play down at the Grill.

LYONS: Come on, Pop . . .

TROY: I got to get up in the morning.

LYONS: You ain't got to stay long.

TROY: Naw, I'm gonna get my supper and go on to bed.

LYONS: Well, I got to go. I'll see you again.

TROY: Don't you come around my house on my payday.

ROSE: Pick up the phone and let somebody know you coming. And bring Bonnie with you. You know I'm always glad to see her.

LYONS: Yeah, I'll do that, Rose. You take care now. See you, Pop. See you, Mr. Bono. See you, Uncle Gabe.

GABRIEL: Lyons! King of the Jungle!
LYONS exits.

TROY: Is supper ready, woman? Me and you got some business to take care of. I'm gonna tear it up too.

ROSE: Troy, I done told you now!

TROY: (Puts his arm around BONO.) Aw hell, woman . . . this is Bono. Bono like family. I done known this nigger since . . . how long I done know you?

BONO: It's been a long time.

TROY: I done known this nigger since Skippy was a pup. Me and him done been through some times.

BONO: You sure right about that.

TROY: Hell, I done know him longer than I known you. And we still standing shoulder to shoulder. Hey, look here, Bono . . . a man can't ask for no more than that. Drinks to him.
I love you, nigger.

BONO: Hell, I love you too . . . but I got to get home see my woman. You got yours in hand. I got to go get mine.
BONO starts to exit as CORY enters the yard, dressed in his football uniform. He gives TROY a hard, uncompromising look.

CORY: What you do that for, Pop?
He throws his helmet down in the direction of TROY.

ROSE: What's the matter? Cory . . . what's the matter?

CORY: Papa done went up to the school and told Coach Zellman I can't play football no more. Wouldn't even let me play the game. Told him to tell the recruiter not to come.

ROSE: Troy . . .

TROY: What you Troying me for. Yeah, I did it. And the boy know why I did it.

CORY: Why you wanna do that to me? That was the one chance I had.

ROSE: Ain't nothing wrong with Cory playing football, Troy.

TROY: The boy lied to me. I told the nigger if he wanna play football . . . to keep up his chores and hold down that job at the A&P. That was the conditions. Stopped down there to see Mr. Stawicki . . .

CORY: I can't work after school during the football season, Pop! I tried to tell you that Mr. Stawicki's holding my job for me. You don't never want to listen to nobody. And then you wanna go and do this to me!

TROY: I ain't done nothing to you. You done it to yourself.

CORY: Just cause you didn't have a chance! You just scared I'm gonna be better than you, that's all.

TROY: Come here.

ROSE: Troy . . .

*CORY reluctantly crosses over to TROY.*

TROY: Alright! See. You done made a mistake.

CORY: I didn't even do nothing!

TROY: I'm gonna tell you what your mistake was. See . . . you swung at the ball and didn't hit it. That's strike one. See, you in the batter's box now. You swung and you missed. That's strike one. Don't you strike out!

*Lights fade to black.*

# ACT TWO

## SCENE ONE

*The following morning. CORY is at the tree hitting the ball with the bat. He tries to mimic TROY, but his swing is awkward, less sure. ROSE enters from the house.*

ROSE: Cory, I want you to help me with this cupboard.

CORY: I ain't quitting the team. I don't care what Poppa say.

ROSE: I'll talk to him when he gets back. He had to go see about your Uncle Gabe. The police done arrested him. Say he was disturbing the peace. He'll be back directly. Come on in here and help me clean out the top of this cupboard.

*CORY exits into the house. ROSE sees TROY and BONO coming down the alley.*

Troy . . . what they say down there?

TROY: Ain't said nothing. I give them fifty dollars and they let him go. I'll talk to you about it. Where's Cory?

ROSE: He's in there helping me clean out these cupboards.

TROY: Tell him to get his butt out here.

*TROY and BONO go over to the pile of wood. BONO picks up the saw and begins sawing.*

TROY: (*To* BONO.) All they want is the money. That makes six or seven times I done went down there and got him. See me coming they stick out their *hands.*

BONO: Yeah. I know what you mean. That's all they care about . . . that money. They don't care about what's right.
(*Pause.*)
Nigger, why you got to go and get some hard wood? You ain't doing nothing but building a little old fence. Get you some soft pine wood. That's all you need.

TROY: I know what I'm doing. This is outside wood. You put pine wood inside the house. Pine wood is inside wood. This here is outside wood. Now you tell me where the fence is gonna be?

BONO: You don't need this wood. You can put it up with pine wood and it'll stand as long as you gonna be here looking at it.

TROY: How you know how long I'm gonna be here, nigger? Hell, I might just live forever. Live longer than old man Horsely.

BONO: That's what Magee used to say.

TROY: Magee's a damn fool. Now you tell me who you ever heard of gonna pull their own teeth with a pair of rusty pliers.

BONO: The old folks . . . my granddaddy used to pull his teeth with pliers. They ain't had no dentists for the colored folks back then.

TROY: Get clean pliers! You understand? Clean pliers! Sterilize them! Besides we ain't living back then. All Magee had to do was walk over to Doc Goldblums.

BONO: I see where you and that Tallahassee gal . . . that Alberta . . . I see where you all done got tight.

TROY: What you mean "got tight"?

BONO: I see where you be laughing and joking with her all the time.

TROY: I laughs and jokes with all of them, Bono. You know me.

BONO: That ain't the kind of laughing and joking I'm talking about.

CORY *enters from the house.*

CORY: How you doing, Mr. Bono?

TROY: Cory? Get that saw from Bono and cut some wood. He talking about the wood's too hard to cut. Stand back there, Jim, and let that young boy show you how it's done.

BONO: He's sure welcome to it.

CORY *takes the saw and begins to cut the wood.*

Whew-e-e! Look at that. Big old strong boy. Look like Joe Louis. Hell, must be getting old the way I'm watching that boy whip through that wood.

CORY: I don't see why Mama want a fence around the yard noways.

TROY: Damn if I know either. What the hell she keeping out with it? She ain't got nothing nobody want.

BONO: Some people build fences to keep people out . . . and other people build fences to keep people in. Rose wants to hold on to you all. She loves you.

TROY: Hell, nigger, I don't need nobody to tell me my wife loves me, Cory . . . go on in the house and see if you can find that other saw.

CORY: Where's it at?

TROY: I said find it! Look for it till you find it!

CORY *exits into the house.*

What's that supposed to mean? Wanna keep us in?

BONO: Troy . . . I done known you seem like damn near my whole life. You and Rose both. I done know both of you all for a long time. I remember when you met Rose. When you was hitting them baseball out the park. A lot of them old gals was after you then. You had the pick of the litter. When you picked Rose, I was happy for you. That was the first time I knew you had any sense. I said . . . My man Troy knows what he's doing . . . I'm gonna follow this nigger . . . he might take me somewhere. I been following you too. I done learned a whole heap of things about life watching you. I done learned how to tell where the shit lies. How to tell it from the alfalfa. You done learned me a lot of things. You showed me how to not make the same mistakes . . . to take life as it comes along and keep putting one foot in front of the other. (*Pause.*)

Rose a good woman, Troy.

TROY: Hell, nigger, I know she a good woman. I been married to her for eighteen years. What you got on your mind, Bono?

BONO: I just say she a good woman. Just like I say anything. I ain't got to have nothing on my mind.

TROY: You just gonna say she a good woman and leave it hanging out there like that? Why you telling me she a good woman?

BONO: She loves you, Troy. Rose loves you.

TROY: You saying I don't measure up. That's what you trying to say. I don't measure up cause I'm seeing this other gal. I know what you trying to say.

BONO: I know what Rose means to you, Troy. I'm just trying to say I don't want to see you mess up.

TROY: Yeah, I appreciate that, Bono. If you was messing around on Lucille I'd be telling you the same thing.

BONO: Well, that's all I got to say. I just say that because I love you both.

TROY: Hell, you know me . . . I wasn't out there looking for nothing. You can't find a better woman than Rose. I know that. But seems like this woman just stuck onto me where I can't shake her loose. I done wrestled with it, tried to throw her off me . . . but she just stuck on tighter. Now she's stuck on for good.

BONO: You's in control . . . that's what you tell me all the time. You responsible for what you do.

TROY: I ain't ducking the responsibility of it. As long as it sets right in my heart . . . then I'm okay. Cause that's all I listen to. It'll tell me right from wrong every time. And I ain't talking about doing Rose no bad turn. I love Rose. She done carried me a long ways and I love and respect her for that.

BONO: I know you do. That's why I don't want to see you hurt her. But what you gonna do when she find out? What you got then? If you try and juggle both of them . . . sooner or later you gonna drop one of them. That's common sense.

TROY: Yeah, I hear what you saying, Bono. I been trying to figure a way to work it out.

BONO: Work it out right, Troy. I don't want to be getting all up between you and Rose's business . . . but work it so it come out right.

TROY: Aw hell, I get all up between you and Lucille's business. When you gonna get that woman that refrigerator she been wanting? Don't tell me you ain't got no money now. I know who your banker is. Mellon don't need that money bad as Lucille want that refrigerator. I'll tell you that.

BONO: Tell you what I'll do . . . when you finish building this fence for Rose . . . I'll buy Lucille that refrigerator.

TROY: You done stuck your foot in your mouth now!

TROY *grabs up a board and begins to saw.* BONO *starts to walk out the yard.*

Hey, nigger . . . where you going?

BONO: I'm going home. I know you don't expect me to help you now. I'm protecting my money. I wanna see you put that fence up by yourself. That's what I want to see. You'll be here another six months without me.

TROY: Nigger, you ain't right.

BONO: When it comes to my money . . . I'm right as fireworks on the Fourth of July.

TROY: Alright, we gonna see now. You better get out your bankbook.

BONO *exits, and* TROY *continues to work.* ROSE *enters from the house.*

ROSE: What they say down there? What's happening with Gabe?

TROY: I went down there and got him out. Cost me fifty dollars. Say he was disturbing the peace. Judge set up a hearing for him in three weeks. Say to show cause why he shouldn't be re-committed.

ROSE: What was he doing that cause them to arrest him?

TROY: Some kids was teasing him and he run them off home. Say he was howling and carrying on. Some folks seen him and called the police. That's all it was.

ROSE: Well, what's you say? What'd you tell the judge?

TROY: Told him I'd look after him. It didn't make no sense to recommit the man. He stuck out his big greasy palm and told me to give him fifty dollars and take him on home.

ROSE: Where's he at now? Where'd he go off to?

TROY: He's gone on about his business. He don't need nobody to hold his hand.

ROSE: Well, I don't know. Seem like that would be the best place for him if they did put him into the hospital. I know what you're gonna say. But that's what I think would be best.

TROY: The man done had his life ruined fighting for what? And they wanna take and lock him up. Let him be free. He don't bother nobody.

ROSE: Well, everybody got their own way of looking at it I guess. Come on and get your lunch. I got a bowl of lima beans and some cornbread in the oven. Come on get something to eat. Ain't no sense you fretting over Gabe.

ROSE *turns to go into the house.*

TROY: Rose . . . got something to tell you.

ROSE: Well, come on . . . wait till I get this food on the table.

TROY: Rose!

*She stops and turns around.*

I don't know how to say this.

(*Pause.*)

I can't explain it none. It just sort of grows on you till it gets out of hand. It starts out like a little bush . . . and the next thing you know it's a whole forest.

ROSE: Troy . . . what is you talking about?

TROY: I'm talking, woman, let me talk. I'm trying to find a way to tell you . . . I'm gonna be a daddy. I'm gonna be somebody's daddy.

ROSE: Troy . . . you're not telling me this? You're gonna be . . . what?

TROY: Rose . . . now . . . see . . .

ROSE: You telling me you gonna be somebody's daddy? You telling your *wife* this?

GABRIEL *enters from the street. He carries a rose in his hand.*

GABRIEL: Hey, Troy! Hey, Rose!

ROSE: I have to wait eighteen years to hear something like this.

GABRIEL: Hey, Rose . . . I got a flower for you. *He hands it to her.*

That's a rose. Same rose like you is.

ROSE: Thanks, Gabe.

GABRIEL: Troy, you ain't mad at me is you? Them bad mens come and put me away. You ain't mad at me is you?

TROY: Naw, Gabe, I ain't mad at you.

ROSE: Eighteen years and you wanna come with this.

GABRIEL: (*Takes a quarter out of his pocket.*) See what I got? Got a brand new quarter.

TROY: Rose . . . it's just . . .

ROSE: Ain't nothing you can say, Troy. Ain't no way of explaining that.

GABRIEL: Fellow that give me this quarter had a whole mess of them. I'm gonna keep this quarter till it stop shining.

ROSE: Gabe, go on in the house there. I got some watermelon in the frigidaire. Go on and get you a piece.

GABRIEL: Say, Rose . . . you know I was chasing hellhounds and them bad mens come and get me and take me away. Troy helped me. He come down there and told them they better let me go before he beat them up. Yeah, he did!

ROSE: You go on and get you a piece of watermelon, Gabe. Them bad mens is gone now.

GABRIEL: Okay, Rose . . . gonna get me some watermelon. The kind with the stripes on it.

GABRIEL *exits into the house.*

ROSE: Why, Troy? Why? After all these years to come dragging this in to me now. It don't make no sense at your age. I could have expected this ten or fifteen years ago, but not now.

TROY: Age ain't got nothing to do with it, Rose.

ROSE: I done tried to be everything a wife should be. Everything a wife could be. Been married eighteen years and I got to live to see the day you tell me you been seeing another woman and done fathered a child by her. And you know I ain't never wanted no half nothing in my family. My whole family is half. Everybody got different fathers and mothers . . . my two sisters and my brother. Can't hardly tell who's who. Can't never sit down and talk about Papa and Mama.

It's your papa and your mama and my papa and my mama . . .

TROY: Rose . . . stop it now.

ROSE: I ain't never wanted that for none of my children. And now you wanna drag your behind in here and tell me something like this.

TROY: You ought to know. It's time for you to know.

ROSE: Well, I don't want to know, goddamn it!

TROY: I can't just make it go away. It's done now. I can't wish the circumstance of the thing away.

ROSE: And you don't want to either. Maybe you want to wish me and my boy away. Maybe that's what you want? Well, you can't wish us away. I've got eighteen years of my life invested in you. You ought to have stayed upstairs in my bed where you belong.

TROY: Rose . . . now listen to me . . . we can get a handle on this thing. We can talk this out . . . come to an understanding.

ROSE: All of a sudden it's "we." Where was "we" at when you was down there rolling around with some god-forsaken woman? "We" should have come to an understanding before you started making a damn fool of yourself. You're a day late and a dollar short when it comes to an understanding with me.

TROY: It's just . . . She gives me a different idea . . . a different understanding about myself. I can step out of this house and get away from the pressures and problems . . . be a different man. I ain't got to wonder how I'm gonna pay the bills or get the roof fixed. I can just be a part of myself that I ain't never been.

ROSE: What I want to know . . . is do you plan to continue seeing her. That's all you can say to me.

TROY: I can sit up in her house and laugh. Do you understand what I'm saying. I can laugh out loud . . . and it feels good.

It reaches all the way down to the bottom of my shoes.

(Pause.)

Rose, I can't give that up.

ROSE: Maybe you ought to go on and stay down there with her . . . if she a better woman than me.

TROY: It ain't about nobody being a better woman or nothing. Rose, you ain't the blame. A man couldn't ask for no woman to be a better wife than you've been. I'm responsible for it. I done locked myself into a pattern trying to take care of you all that I forgot about myself.

ROSE: What the hell was I there for? That was my job, not somebody else's.

TROY: Rose, I done tried all my life to live decent . . . to live a clean . . . hard . . . useful life. I tried to be a good husband to you. In every way I knew how. Maybe I come into the world backwards, I don't know. But . . . you born with two strikes on you before you come to the plate. You got to guard it closely . . . always looking for the curve-ball on the inside corner. You can't afford to let none get past you. You can't afford a call strike. If you going down . . . you going down swinging. Everything lined up against you. What you gonna do. I fooled them, Rose. I bunted. When I found you and Cory and a halfway decent job . . . I was safe. Couldn't nothing touch me. I wasn't gonna strike out no more. I wasn't going back to the penitentiary. I wasn't gonna lay in the streets with a bottle of wine. I was safe. I had me a family. A job. I wasn't gonna get that last strike. I was on first looking for one of them boys to knock me in. To get me home.

ROSE: You should have stayed in my bed, Troy.

TROY: Then when I saw that gal . . . she firmed up my backbone. And I got think-

ing that if I tried . . . I just might be able
to steal second. Do you understand after
eighteen years I wanted to steal second.

ROSE: You should have held me tight. You
should have grabbed me and held on.

TROY: I stood on first base for eighteen years
and I thought . . . well, goddamn it . . .
go on for it!

ROSE: We're not talking about baseball!
We're talking about you going off to lay
in bed with another woman . . . and then
bring it home to me. That's what we're
talking about. We ain't talking about no
baseball.

TROY: Rose, you're not listening to me. I'm
trying the best way I can to explain it to
you. It's not easy for me to admit that I
been standing in the same place for
eighteen years.

ROSE: I been standing with you! I been right
here with you, Troy. I got a life too. I
gave eighteen years of my life to stand in
the same spot with you. Don't you
think I ever wanted other things?
Don't you think I had dreams and
hopes? What about my life? What
about me? Don't you think it ever
crossed my mind to want to know other
men? That I wanted to lay up somewhere and forget about my responsibilities? That I wanted someone to make me
laugh so I could feel good? You not the
only one who's got wants and needs.
But I held on to you, Troy. I took all my
feelings, my wants and needs, my
dreams . . . and I buried them inside you.
I planted a seed and watched and prayed
over it. I planted myself inside you and
waited to bloom. And it didn't take me
no eighteen years to find out the soil was
hard and rocky and it wasn't never
gonna bloom.

But I held on to you, Troy. I held you
tighter. You was my husband. I owed
you everything I had. Every part of me I

could find to give you. And upstairs in
that room . . . with the darkness falling
in on me . . . I gave everything I had to
try and erase the doubt that you wasn't
the finest man in the world. And wherever you was going . . . I wanted to be
there with you. Cause you was my husband. Cause that's the only way I was
gonna survive as your wife. You always
talking about what you give . . . and
what you don't have to give. But you
take too. You take . . . and don't even
know nobody's giving!

ROSE *turns to exit into the house;* TROY
*grabs her arm.*

TROY: You say I take and don't give!

ROSE: Troy! You're hurting me!

TROY: You say I take and don't give.

ROSE: Troy . . . you're hurting my arm! Let
go!

TROY: I done give you everything I got.
Don't you tell that lie on me.

ROSE: Troy!

TROY: Don't you tell that lie on me!

CORY *enters from the house.*

CORY: Mama!

ROSE: Troy. You're hurting me.

TROY: Don't you tell me about no taking and
giving.

CORY *comes up behind* TROY *and grabs him.*
TROY, *surprised, is thrown off balance just
as* CORY *throws a glancing blow that catches
him on the chest and knocks him down.* TROY
*is stunned, as is* CORY.

ROSE: Troy. Troy. No!

TROY *gets to his feet and starts at* CORY.
Troy . . . no. Please! Troy!

ROSE *pulls on* TROY *to hold him back.* TROY
*stops himself.*

TROY: (*To* CORY.) Alright. That's strike two.
You stay away from around me, boy.
Don't you strike out. You living with a
full count. Don't you strike out.

TROY *exits out the yard as the lights go
down.*

## SCENE TWO

*It is six months later, early afternoon.* **TROY** *enters from the house and starts to exit the yard.* **ROSE** *enters from the house.*

**ROSE:** Troy, I want to talk to you.

**TROY:** All of a sudden, after all this time, you want to talk to me, huh? You ain't wanted to talk to me for months. You ain't wanted to talk to me last night. You ain't wanted no part of me then. What you wanna talk to me about now?

**ROSE:** Tomorrow's Friday.

**TROY:** I know what day tomorrow is. You think I don't know tomorrow's Friday? My whole life I ain't done nothing but look to see Friday coming and you got to tell me it's Friday.

**ROSE:** I want to know if you're coming home.

**TROY:** I always come home, Rose. You know that. There ain't never been a night I ain't come home.

**ROSE:** That ain't what I mean . . . and you know it. I want to know if you're coming straight home after work.

**TROY:** I figure I'd cash my check . . . hang out at Taylors' with the boys . . . maybe play a game of checkers . . .

**ROSE:** Troy, I can't live like this. I won't live like this. You livin' on borrowed time with me. It's been going on six months now you ain't been coming home.

**TROY:** I be here every night. Every night of the year. That's 365 days.

**ROSE:** I want you to come home tomorrow after work.

**TROY:** Rose . . . I don't mess up my pay. You know that now. I take my pay and I give it to you. I don't have no money but what you give me back. I just want to have a little time to myself . . . a little time to enjoy life.

**ROSE:** What about me? When's my time to enjoy life?

**TROY:** I don't know what to tell you, Rose. I'm doing the best I can.

**ROSE:** You ain't been home from work but time enough to change your clothes and run out . . . and you wanna call that the best you can do?

**TROY:** I'm going over to the hospital to see Alberta. She went into the hospital this afternoon. Look like she might have the baby early. I won't be gone long.

**ROSE:** Well, you ought to know. They went over to Miss Pearl's and got Gabe today. She said you told them to go ahead and lock him up.

**TROY:** I ain't said no such thing. Whoever told you that is telling a lie. Pearl ain't doing nothing but telling a big fat lie.

**ROSE:** She ain't had to tell me. I read it on the papers.

**TROY:** I ain't told them nothing of the kind.

**ROSE:** I saw it right there on the papers.

**TROY:** What it say, huh?

**ROSE:** It said you told them to take him.

**TROY:** Then they screwed that up, just the way they screw up everything. I ain't worried about what they got on the paper.

**ROSE:** Say the government send part of his check to the hospital and the other part to you.

**TROY:** I ain't got nothing to do with that if that's the way it works. I ain't made up the rules about how it work.

**ROSE:** You did Gabe just like you did Cory. You wouldn't sign the paper for Cory . . . but you signed for Gabe. You signed that paper.

*The telephone is heard ringing inside the house.*

**TROY:** I told you I ain't signed nothing, woman! The only thing I signed was the release form. Hell, I can't read, I don't know what they had on that paper! I ain't signed nothing about sending Gabe away.

ROSE: I said send him to the hospital . . . you said let him be free . . . now you done went down there and signed him to the hospital for half his money. You went back on yourself, Troy. You gonna have to answer for that.

TROY: See now . . . you been over there talking to Miss Pearl. She done got mad cause she ain't getting Gabe's rent money. That's all it is. She's liable to say anything.

ROSE: Troy, I seen where you signed the paper.

TROY: You ain't seen nothing I signed. What she doing got papers on my brother anyway? Miss Pearl telling a big fat lie. And I'm gonna tell her about it too! You ain't seen nothing I signed. Say . . . you ain't seen nothing I signed.

ROSE *exits into the house to answer the telephone. Presently she returns.*

ROSE: Troy . . . that was the hospital. Alberta had the baby.

TROY: What she have? What is it?

ROSE: It's a girl.

TROY: I better get on down to the hospital to see her.

ROSE: Troy . . .

TROY: Rose . . . I got to go see her now. That's only right . . . what's the matter . . . the baby's alright, ain't it?

ROSE: Alberta died having the baby.

TROY: Died . . . you say she's dead? Alberta's dead?

ROSE: They said they done all they could. They couldn't do nothing for her.

TROY: The baby? How's the baby?

ROSE: They say it's healthy. I wonder who's gonna bury her.

TROY: She had a family, Rose. She wasn't living in the world by herself.

ROSE: I know she wasn't living in the world by herself.

TROY: Next thing you gonna want to know if she had any insurance.

ROSE: Troy, you ain't got to talk like that.

TROY: That's the first thing that jumped out of your mouth. "Who's gonna bury her?" Like I'm fixing to take on that task for myself.

ROSE: I am your wife. Don't push me away.

TROY: I ain't pushing nobody away. Just give me some space. That's all. Just give me some room to breathe.

ROSE *exits into the house.* TROY *walks about the yard.*

TROY: (*With a quiet rage that threatens to consume him.*) Alright . . . Mr. Death. See now . . . I'm gonna tell you what I'm gonna do. I'm gonna take and build me a fence around this yard. See? I'm gonna build me a fence around what belongs to me. And then I want you to stay on the other side. See? You stay over there until you're ready for me. Then you come on. Bring your army. Bring your sickle. Bring your wrestling clothes. I ain't gonna fall down on my vigilance this time. You ain't gonna sneak up on me no more. When you ready for me . . . when the top of your list say Troy Maxson . . . that's when you come around here. You come up and knock on the front door. Ain't nobody else got nothing to do with this. This is between you and me. Man to man. You stay on the other side of that fence until you are ready for me. Then you come up and knock on the front door. Anytime you want. I'll be ready for you. *The lights go down to black.*

### SCENE THREE

*The lights come up on the porch. It is late evening three days later.* ROSE *sits listening to the ball game waiting for* TROY. *The final out of the game is made and* ROSE *switches off the radio.* TROY *enters the yard carrying an infant wrapped in blankets. He stands back from the house and calls.*

ROSE *enters and stands on the porch. There is a long, awkward silence, the weight of which grows heavier with each passing second.*

TROY: Rose . . . I'm standing here with my daughter in my arms. She ain't but a wee bittie little old thing. She don't know nothing about grownups' business. She innocent . . . and she ain't got no mama.

ROSE: What you telling me for, Troy?

*She turns and exits into the house.*

TROY: Well . . . I guess we'll just sit out here on the porch.

*He sits down on the porch. There is an awkward indelicateness about the way he handles the baby. His largeness engulfs and seems to swallow it. He speaks loud enough for* ROSE *to hear.*

A man's got to do what's right for him. I ain't sorry for nothing I done. It felt right in my heart.

*To the baby.*

What you smiling at? Your daddy's a big man. Got these great big old hands. But sometimes he's scared. And right now your daddy's scared cause we sitting out here and ain't got no home. Oh, I been homeless before. I ain't had no little baby with me. But I been homeless. You just be out on the road by your lonesome and you see one of them trains coming and you just kinda go like this . . .

*He sings as a lullaby.*

Please, Mr. Engineer let a man ride the line
Please, Mr. Engineer let a man ride the line
I ain't got no ticket please let me ride the blinds

ROSE *enters from the house.* TROY *hearing her steps behind him, stands and faces her.*

She's my daughter, Rose. My own flesh and blood. I can't deny her no more than I can deny them boys.

*(Pause.)*

You and them boys is my family. You and them and this child is all I got in the world. So I guess what I'm saying is . . . I'd appreciate it if you'd help me take care of her.

ROSE: Okay, Troy . . . you're right. I'll take care of your baby for you . . . cause . . .

like you say . . . she's innocent . . . and you can't visit the sins of the father upon the child. A motherless child has got a hard time.

*She takes the baby from him.*

From right now . . . this child got a mother. But you a womanless man.

ROSE *turns and exits into the house with the baby. Lights go down to black.*

## SCENE FOUR

*It is two months later.* LYONS *enters from the street. He knocks on the door and calls.*

LYONS: Hey, Rose! *(Pause.)* Rose!

ROSE: *(From inside the house.)* Stop that yelling. You gonna wake up Raynell. I just got her to sleep.

LYONS: I just stopped by to pay Papa this twenty dollars I owe him. Where's Papa at?

ROSE: He should be here in a minute. I'm getting ready to go down to the church. Sit down and wait on him.

LYONS: I got to go pick up Bonnie over her mother's house.

ROSE: Well, sit it down there on the table. He'll get it.

LYONS: *(Enters the house and sets the money on the table.)* Tell Papa I said thanks. I'll see you again.

ROSE: Alright, Lyons. We'll see you.

LYONS *starts to exit as* CORY *enters.*

CORY: Hey, Lyons.

LYONS: What's happening, Cory. Say man, I'm sorry I missed your graduation. You know I had a gig and couldn't get away. Otherwise, I would have been there, man. So what you doing?

CORY: I'm trying to find a job.

LYONS: Yeah I know how that go, man. It's rough out here. Jobs are scarce.

CORY: Yeah, I know.

LYONS: Look here, I got to run. Talk to Papa . . . he know some people. He'll be able to help you get a job. Talk to him . . . see what he say.

CORY: Yeah . . . alright, Lyons.

LYONS: You take care. I'll talk to you soon. We'll find some time to talk.

*LYONS exits the yard. CORY wanders over to the tree, picks up the bat and assumes a batting stance. He studies an imaginary pitcher and swings. Dissatisfied with the result, he tries again. TROY enters. They eye each other for a beat. CORY puts the bat down and exits the yard. TROY starts into the house as ROSE exits with RAYNELL. She is carrying a cake.*

TROY: I'm coming in and everybody's going out.

ROSE: I'm taking this cake down to the church for the bakesale. Lyons was by to see you. He stopped by to pay you your twenty dollars. It's laying in there on the table.

TROY: (*Going into his pocket.*) Well . . . here go this money.

ROSE: Put it in there on the table, Troy. I'll get it.

TROY: What time you coming back?

ROSE: Ain't no use in you studying me. It don't matter what time I come back.

TROY: I just asked you a question, woman. What's the matter . . . can't I ask you a question?

ROSE: Troy, I don't want to go into it. Your dinner's in there on the stove. All you got to do is heat it up. And don't you be eating the rest of them cakes in there. I'm coming back for them. We having a bakesale at the church tomorrow.

*ROSE exits the yard. TROY sits down on the steps, takes a pint bottle from his pocket, opens it and drinks. He begins to sing.*

TROY:
Hear it ring! Hear it ring!
Had an old dog his name was Blue
You know Blue was mighty true
You know Blue was a good old dog

Blue trees a possum in a hollow log
You know from that he was a good old dog

*BONO enters the yard.*

BONO: Hey, Troy.

TROY: Hey, what's happening, Bono?

BONO: I just thought I'd stop by to see you.

TROY: What you stop by and see me for? You ain't stopped by in a month of Sundays. Hell, I must owe you money or something.

BONO: Since you got your promotion I can't keep up with you. Used to see you everyday. Now I don't even know what route you working.

TROY: They keep switching me around. Got me out in Greentree now . . . hauling white folk's garbage.

BONO: Greentree, huh? You lucky, at least you ain't got to be lifting them barrels. Damn if they ain't getting heavier. I'm gonna put in my two years and call it quits.

TROY: I'm thinking about retiring myself.

BONO: You got it easy. You can *drive* for another five years.

TROY: It ain't the same, Bono. It ain't like working the back of the truck. Ain't got nobody to talk to . . . feel like you working by yourself. Naw, I'm thinking about retiring. How's Lucille?

BONO: She alright. Her arthritis get to acting up on her sometime. Saw Rose on my way in. She going down to the church, huh?

TROY: Yeah, she took up going down there. All them preachers looking for somebody to fatten their pockets.
(*Pause.*)
Got some gin here.

BONO: Naw, thanks. I just stopped by to say hello.

TROY: Hell, nigger . . . you can take a drink. I ain't never known you to say no to a drink. You ain't got to work tomorrow.

BONO: I just stopped by. I'm fixing to go over to Skinner's. We got us a domino game going over his house every Friday.

TROY: Nigger, you can't play no dominoes. I used to whup you four games out of five.

BONO: Well, that learned me. I'm getting better.

TROY: Yeah? Well, that's alright.

BONO: Look here . . . I got to be getting on. Stop by sometime, huh?

TROY: Yeah, I'll do that, Bono. Lucille told Rose you bought her a new refrigerator.

BONO: Yeah, Rose told Lucille you had finally built your fence . . . so I figured we'd call it even.

TROY: I knew you would.

BONO: Yeah . . . okay. I'll be talking to you.

TROY: Yeah, take care, Bono. Good to see you. I'm gonna stop over.

BONO: Yeah. Okay, Troy.

BONO *exits.* TROY *drinks from the bottle.*

TROY:

Old Blue died and I dig his grave
Let him down with a golden chain
Every night when I hear old Blue bark
I know Blue treed a possum in Noah's Ark.

Hear it ring! Hear it ring!

CORY *enters the yard. They eye each other for a beat.* TROY *is sitting in the middle of the steps.* CORY *walks over.*

CORY: I got to get by.

TROY: Say what? What's you say?

CORY: You in my way. I got to get by.

TROY: You got to get by where? This is my house. Bought and paid for. In full. Took me fifteen years. And if you wanna go in my house and I'm sitting on the steps . . . you say excuse me. Like your mama taught you.

CORY: Come on, Pop . . . I got to get by.

CORY *starts to maneuver his way past* TROY. TROY *grabs his leg and shoves him back.*

TROY: You just gonna walk over top of me?

CORY: I live here too!

TROY: (*Advancing toward him.*) You just gonna walk over top of me in my own house?

CORY: I ain't scared of you.

TROY: I ain't asked if you was scared of me. I asked you if you was fixing to walk over top of me in my own house? That's the question. You ain't gonna say excuse me? You just gonna walk over top of me?

CORY: If you wanna put it like that.

TROY: How else am I gonna put it?

CORY: I was walking by you to go into the house cause you sitting on the steps drunk, singing to yourself. You can put it like that.

TROY: Without saying excuse me???

CORY *doesn't respond.*

I asked you a question. Without saying excuse me???

CORY: I ain't got to say excuse me to you. You don't count around here no more.

TROY: Oh, I see . . . I don't count around here no more. You ain't got to say excuse me to your daddy. All of a sudden you done got so grown that your daddy don't count around here no more . . . Around here in his own house and yard that he done paid for with the sweat of his brow. You done got so grown to where you gonna take over. You gonna take over my house. Is that right? You gonna wear my pants. You gonna go in there and stretch out on my bed. You ain't got to say excuse me cause I don't count around here no more. Is that right?

CORY: That's right. You always talking this dumb stuff. Now, why don't you just get out my way.

TROY: I guess you got someplace to sleep and something to put in your belly. You got that, huh? You got that? That's what you need. You got that, huh?

CORY: You don't know what I got. You ain't got to worry about what I got.

TROY: You right! You one hundred percent right! I done spent the last seventeen years worrying about what you got. Now it's your turn, see? I'll tell you what to do. You grown... we done established that. You a man. Now, let's see you act like one. Turn your behind around and walk out this yard. And when you get out there in the alley... you can forget about this house. See? Cause this is my house. You go on and be a man and get your own house. You can forget about this. 'Cause this is mine. You go on and get yours cause I'm through with doing for you.

CORY: You talking about what you did for me... what'd you ever give me?

TROY: Them feet and bones! That pumping heart, nigger! I gave you more than anybody else is ever gonna give you.

CORY: You ain't never gave me nothing! You ain't never done nothing but hold me back. Afraid I was gonna be better than you. All you ever did was try to make me scared of you. I used to tremble every time you called my name. Every time I heard your footsteps in the house. Wondering all the time... what's Papa gonna say if I do this?... What's he gonna say if I do that?... What's Papa gonna say if I turn on the radio? And Mama, too... she tries... but she's scared of you.

TROY: You leave your mama you of this. She ain't got nothing to do with this.

CORY: I don't know how she stand you... after what you did to her.

TROY: I told you to leave your Mama out of this!

*He advances toward* CORY.

CORY: What you gonna do... give me a whupping? You can't whup me no more. You're too old. You just an old man.

TROY: (*Shoves him on his shoulder.*) Nigger! That's what you are. You just another nigger on the street to me!

CORY: You crazy! You know that?

TROY: Go on now! You got the devil in you. Get on away from me!

CORY: You just a crazy old man... talking about I got the devil in me.

TROY: Yeah, I'm crazy! If you don't get on the other side of that yard... I'm gonna show you how crazy I am! Go on... get the hell out of my yard.

CORY: It ain't your yard. You took Uncle Gabe's money he got from the army to buy this house and then you put him out.

TROY: (TROY *advances on* CORY.) Get your black ass out of my yard!

TROY'S *advance backs* CORY *up against the tree.* CORY *grabs up the bat.*

CORY: I ain't going nowhere! Come on... put me out! I ain't scared of you.

TROY: That's my bat!

CORY: Come on!

TROY: Put my bat down!

CORY: Come on, put me out.

CORY *swings at* TROY, *who backs across the yard.*

What's the matter? You so bad... put me out!

TROY *advances toward* CORY.

CORY: (*Backing up.*) Come on! Come on!

TROY: You're gonna have to use it! You wanna draw that bat back on me... you're gonna have to use it.

CORY: Come on!... Come on!

CORY *swings the bat at* TROY *a second time. He misses.* TROY *continues to advance toward him.*

TROY: You're gonna have to kill me! You wanna draw that bat back on me. You're gonna have to kill me.

CORY, *backed up against the tree, can go no farther.* TROY *taunts him. He sticks out his head and offers him a target.*

Come on! Come on!

CORY *is unable to swing the bat.* TROY *grabs it.*

TROY: Then I'll show you.

CORY *and* TROY *struggle over the bat. The*

*struggle is fierce and fully engaged.* **TROY**
*ultimately is the stronger, and takes the bat
from* **CORY** *and stands over him ready to
swing. He stops himself*
Go on and get away from around my
house.

**CORY,** *stung by his defeat, picks himself up,
walks slowly out of the yard and up the alley.*

**CORY:** Tell Mama I'll be back for my things.

**TROY:** They'll be on the other side of that
fence.

**CORY** *exits.*

**TROY:** I can't taste nothing. Helluljah! I can't
taste nothing no more. (**TROY** *assumes a
batting posture and begins to taunt Death,
the fastball in the outside corner.*) Come on!
It's between you and me now! Come on!
Anytime you want! Come on! I be ready
for you . . . but I ain't gonna be easy.
*The lights go down on the scene.*

## SCENE FIVE

*The time is 1965. The lights come up in the yard.
It is the morning of* **TROY'S** *funeral. A funeral
plaque with a light hangs beside the door. There is
a small garden plot off to the side. There is noise
and activity in the house as* **ROSE,** **LYONS** *and*
**BONO** *have gathered. The door opens and* **RAY-
NELL,** *seven years old, enters dressed in a flannel
nightgown. She crosses to the garden and pokes
around with a stick.* **ROSE** *calls from the house.*

**ROSE:** Raynell!

**RAYNELL:** Mam?

**ROSE:** What you doing out there?

**RAYNELL:** Nothing.

   **ROSE** *comes to the door.*

**ROSE:** Girl, get in here and get dressed. What
you doing?

**RAYNELL:** Seeing if my garden growed.

**ROSE:** I told you it ain't gonna grow over-
night. You got to wait.

**RAYNELL:** It don't look like it never gonna
grow. Dag!

**ROSE:** I told you a watched pot never boils.
Get in here and get dressed.

**RAYNELL:** This ain't even no pot, Mama.

**ROSE:** You just have to give it a chance. It'll
grow. Now you come on and do what I
told you. We got to be getting ready.
This ain't no morning to be playing
around. You hear me?

**RAYNELL:** Yes, mam.

   **ROSE** *exits into the house.* **RAYNELL** *continues to poke at her garden with a stick.* **CORY**
   *enters. He is dressed in a Marine corporal's
   uniform, and carries a duffel bag. His posture is that of a military man, and his speech
   has a clipped sternness.*

**CORY:** (*To* **RAYNELL.**) Hi.
   (*Pause.*)
   I bet your name is Raynell.

**RAYNELL:** Uh huh.

**CORY:** Is your mama home?

   **RAYNELL** *runs up on the porch and calls
   through the screendoor.*

**RAYNELL:** Mama . . . there's some man out
here. Mama?

   **ROSE** *comes to the door.*

**ROSE:** Cory? Lord have mercy! Look here,
you all!

   **ROSE** *and* **CORY** *embrace in a tearful reunion
   as* **BONO** *and* **LYONS** *enter from the house
   dressed in funeral clothes.*

**BONO:** Aw, looka here . . .

**ROSE:** Done got all grown up!

**CORY:** Don't cry, Mama. What you crying
about?

**ROSE:** I'm just so glad you made it.

**CORY:** Hey Lyons. How you doing, Mr.
Bono.

   **LYONS** *goes to embrace* **CORY.**

**LYONS:** Look at you, man. Look at you.
Don't he look good, Rose. Got them Corporal stripes.

**ROSE:** What took you so long.

**CORY:** You know how the Marines are,
Mama. They got to get all their paper-
work straight before they let you do anything.

**ROSE:** Well, I'm sure glad you made it. They
let Lyons come. Your Uncle Gabe's still

in the hospital. They don't know if they gonna let him out or not. I just talked to them a little while ago.

LYONS: A Corporal in the United States Marines.

BONO: Your daddy knew you had it in you. He used to tell me all the time.

LYONS: Don't he look good, Mr. Bono?

BONO: Yeah, he remind me of Troy when I first met him.
(*Pause.*)
Say, Rose, Lucille's down at the church with the choir. I'm gonna go down and get the pallbearers lined up. I'll be back to get you all.

ROSE: Thanks, Jim.

CORY: See you, Mr. Bono.

LYONS: (*With his arm around* RAYNELL.) Cory . . . look at Raynell. Ain't she precious? She gonna break a whole lot of hearts.

ROSE: Raynell, come and say hello to your brother. This is your brother, Cory. You remember Cory.

RAYNELL: No, Mam.

CORY: She don't remember me, Mama.

ROSE: Well, we talk about you. She heard us talk about you.
(*To* RAYNELL.) This is your brother, Cory. Come on and say hello.

RAYNELL: Hi.

CORY: Hi. So you're Raynell. Mama told me a lot about you.

ROSE: You all come on into the house and let me fix you some breakfast. Keep up your strength.

CORY: I ain't hungry, Mama.

LYONS: You can fix me something, Rose. I'll be in there in a minute.

ROSE: Cory, you sure you don't want nothing. I know they ain't feeding you right.

CORY: No, Mama . . . thanks. I don't feel like eating. I'll get something later.

ROSE: Raynell . . . get on upstairs and get that dress on like I told you.
ROSE *and* RAYNELL *exit into the house.*

LYONS: So . . . I hear you thinking about getting married.

CORY: Yeah, I done found the right one, Lyons. It's about time.

LYONS: Me and Bonnie been split up about four years now. About the time Papa retired. I guess she just got tired of all them changes I was putting her through.
(*Pause.*)
I always knew you was gonna make something out yourself. Your head was always in the right direction. So . . . you gonna stay in . . . make it a career . . . put in your twenty years?

CORY: I don't know. I got six already, I think that's enough.

LYONS: Stick with Uncle Sam and retire early. Ain't nothing out here. I guess Rose told you what happened with me. They got me down the workhouse. I thought I was being slick cashing other people's checks.

CORY: How much time you doing?

LYONS: They give me three years. I got that beat now. I ain't got but nine more months. It ain't so bad. You learn to deal with it like anything else. You got to take the crookeds with the straights. That's what Papa used to say. He used to say that when he struck out. I seen him strike out three times in a row . . . and the next time up he hit the ball over the grandstand. Right out there in Homestead Field. He wasn't satisfied hitting in the seats . . . he want to hit it over everything! After the game he had two hundred people standing around waiting to shake his hand. You got to take the crookeds with the straights. Yeah, Papa was something else.

CORY: You still playing?

LYONS: Cory . . . you know I'm gonna do that. There's some fellows down there we got us a band . . . we gonna try and stay together when we get out . . . but yeah, I'm still playing. It still helps me to get out of bed in the morning. As long as it do that I'm gonna be right there playing and trying to make some sense out of it.

ROSE: (*Calling.*) Lyons, I got these eggs in the pan.

LYONS: Let me go on and get these eggs, man. Get ready to go bury Papa.

(*Pause.*)

How you doing? You doing alright?

CORY *nods.* LYONS *touches him on the shoulder and they share a moment of silent grief.* LYONS *exits into the house.* CORY *wanders about the yard.* RAYNELL *enters.*

RAYNELL: Hi.

CORY: Hi

RAYNELL: Did you used to sleep in my room?

CORY: Yeah . . . that used to be my room.

RAYNELL: That's what Papa call it. "Cory's room." It got your football in the closet.

ROSE *comes to the door.*

ROSE: Raynell, get in there and get them good shoes on.

RAYNELL: Mama, can't I wear these. Them other one hurt my feet.

ROSE: Well, they just gonna have to hurt your feet for a while. You ain't said they hurt your feet when you went down to the store and got them.

RAYNELL: They didn't hurt then. My feet done got bigger.

ROSE: Don't you give me no backtalk now. You get in there and get them shoes on.

RAYNELL *exits into the house.*

Ain't too much changed. He still got that piece of rag tied to that tree. He was out here swinging that bat. I was just ready to go back in the house. He swung that bat and bat and then just fell over. Seem like he swung it and stood there with this grin on his face . . . and then he just fell over. They carried him on down to the hospital but I knew there wasn't no need . . . why don't you come on in the house?

CORY: Mama . . . I got something to tell you. I don't know how to tell you this . . . but I've got to tell you . . . I'm not going to Papa's funeral.

ROSE: Boy, hush your mouth. That's your daddy you talking about. I don't want hear that kind of talk this morning. I done raised you to come to this? You standing there all healthy and grown talking about you ain't going to your daddy's funeral?

CORY: Mama . . . listen . . .

ROSE: I don't want to hear it, Cory. You just get that thought out of your head.

CORY: I can't drag Papa with me everywhere I go. I've got to say no to him. One time in my life I've got to say no.

ROSE: Don't nobody have to listen to nothing like that. I know you and your daddy ain't seen eye to eye, but I ain't got to listen to that kind of talk this morning. Whatever was between you and your daddy . . . the time has come to put it aside. Just take it and set it over there on the shelf and forget about it. Disrespecting your daddy ain't gonna make you a man, Cory. You got to find a way to come to that on your own. Not going to your daddy's funeral ain't gonna make you a man.

CORY: The whole time I was growing up . . . living in his house . . . Papa was like a shadow that followed you everywhere. It weighed on you and sunk into your flesh. It would wrap around you and lay there until you couldn't tell which one was you anymore. That shadow digging in your flesh. Trying to crawl in. Trying to live through you. Everywhere I looked, Troy Maxson was staring back at me . . . hiding under the bed . . . in the closet. I'm just saying I've got to find a way to get rid of that shadow, Mama.

ROSE: You just like him. You got him in you good.

CORY: Don't tell me that, Mama.

ROSE: You Troy Maxson all over again.

CORY: I don't want to be Troy Maxson. I want to be me.

ROSE: You can't be nobody but who you are, Cory. That shadow wasn't nothing but you growing into yourself. You either got to grow into it or cut it down to fit you. But that's all you got to make life with. That's all you got to measure yourself against that world out there. Your daddy wanted you to be everything he wasn't . . . and at the same time he tried to make you into everything he was. I don't know if he was right or wrong . . . but I do know he meant to do more good than he meant to do harm. He wasn't always right. Sometimes when he touched he bruised. And sometimes when he took me in his arms he cut. When I first met your daddy I thought . . . Here is a man I can lay down with and make a baby. That's the first thing I thought when I seen him. I was thirty years old and had done seen my share of men. But when he walked up to me and said, "I can dance a waltz that'll make you dizzy," I thought, Rose Lee, here is a man that you can open yourself up to and be filled to bursting. Here is a man that can fill all them empty spaces you been tipping around the edges of. One of them empty spaces was being somebody's mother.

I married your daddy and settled down to cooking his supper and keeping clean sheets on the bed. When your daddy walked through the house he was so big he filled it up. That was my first mistake. Not to make him leave some room for me. For my part in the matter. But at that time I wanted that. I wanted a house that I could sing in. And that's what your daddy gave me. I didn't know to keep up his strength I had to give up little pieces of mine. I did that. I took on his life as mine and mixed up the pieces so that you couldn't hardly tell which was which anymore. It was my choice. It was my life and I didn't have to live it like that. But that's what life offered me in the way of being a woman and I took it. I grabbed hold of it with both hands.

By the time Raynell came into the house, me and your daddy had done lost touch with one another. I didn't want to make my blessing off of nobody's misfortune . . . but I took on to Raynell like she was all them babies I had wanted and never had. *The phone rings.*

Like I'd been blessed to relive a part of my life. And if the Lord see fit to keep up my strength . . . I'm gonna do her just like your daddy did you . . . I'm gonna give her the best of what's in me.

RAYNELL: (*Entering, still with her old shoes.*) Mama . . . Reverend Tollivier on the phone.

ROSE *exits into the house.*

RAYNELL: Hi.

CORY: Hi.

RAYNELL: You in the Army or the Marines?

CORY: Marines.

RAYNELL: Papa said it was the Army. Did you know Blue?

CORY: Blue? Who's Blue?

RAYNELL: Papa's dog what he sing about all the time.

CORY: (*Singing.*) Hear it ring! Hear it ring!
I had a dog his name was Blue
You know Blue was mighty true
You know Blue was a good old dog
Blue treed a possum in a hollow log
You know from that he was a good old dog.
Hear it ring! Hear it ring!

RAYNELL *joins in singing.*

CORY AND RAYNELL: Blue treed a possum out on a limb
Blue looked at me and I looked at him
Grabbed that possum and put him in a sack

Blue stayed there till I came back
Old Blue's feets was big and round
Never allowed a possum to touch the ground.
Old Blue died and I dug his grave
I dug his grave with a silver spade
Let him down with a golden chain
And every night I call his name
Go on Blue, you good dog you
Go on Blue, you good dog you

**RAYNELL:** Blue laid down and died like a man
Blue laid down and died . . .

**BOTH:** Blue laid down and died like a man
Now he's treeing possums in the Promised Land
I'm gonna tell you this to let you know
Blue's gone where the good dogs go
When I hear old Blue bark
When I hear old Blue bark
Blue treed a possum in Noah's Ark
Blue treed a possum in Noah's Ark.
*ROSE comes to the screen door.*

**ROSE:** Cory, we gonna be ready to go in a minute.

**CORY:** (*To* RAYNELL.) You go on in the house and change them shoes like Mama told you so we can go to Papa's funeral.

**RAYNELL:** Okay, I'll be back.
*RAYNELL exits into the house. CORY gets up and crosses over to the tree. ROSE stands in the screen door watching him. GABRIEL enters from the alley.*

**GABRIEL:** (*Calling.*) Hey, Rose!

**ROSE:** Gabe?

**GABRIEL:** I'm here, Rose. Hey Rose, I'm here!
*ROSE enters from the house.*

**ROSE:** Lord . . . Look here, Lyons!

**LYONS:** See, I told you, Rose . . . I told you they'd let him come.

**CORY:** How you doing, Uncle Gabe?

**LYONS:** How you doing, Uncle Gabe?

**GABRIEL:** Hey, Rose. It's time. It's time to tell St. Peter to open the gates. Troy, you ready? You ready, Troy. I'm gonna tell St. Peter to open the gates. You get ready now.

**GABRIEL,** *with great fanfare, braces himself to blow. The trumpet is without a mouthpiece. He puts the end of it into his mouth and blows with great force, like a man who has been waiting some twenty-odd years for this single moment. No sound comes out of the trumpet. He braces himself and blows again with the same result. A third time he blows. There is a weight of impossible description that falls away and leaves him bare and exposed to a frightful realization. It is a trauma that a sane and normal mind would be unable to withstand. He begins to dance. A slow, strange dance, eerie and life-giving. A dance of atavistic signature and ritual.* **LYONS** *attempts to embrace him.* **GABRIEL** *pushes* **LYONS** *away. He begins to howl in what is an attempt at song, or perhaps a song turning back into itself in an attempt at speech. He finishes his dance and the gates of heaven stand open as wide as God's closet.*
That's the way that go!
BLACKOUT

## SUMMARY

As a principal writing and performance style for more than a century, *realism* implies a conception of dramatic reality different from that found in earlier works by Sophocles, Shakespeare, or Sheridan. Regardless of the times in which they live, all playwrights have their concepts of the "real" in human behavior and events, as we have seen in *Oedipus the King, Hamlet,* and *The School for Scandal.* The means of imitating that conception of reality changes with each writer and age. However, realism in the mind of its European pioneers in the 1860s implied a candid representation of the world around them. Along with their efforts to bring a new truth into the dramatic text (and hence onto the stage), came new subjects, characters, environments, language, and life styles taken from contemporary life. A new tragic hero, the somewhat ordinary individual, struggling for selfhood and dignity, emerged from living rooms, kitchens, flophouses, and streets to indict society. Early on, heredity and environment became the verifiable enemies of individual expression and freedom and the *causes célèbres* more so of the naturalists than the realists.

The realists tried to put on stage only what could be verified by observing ordinary life. The naturalistic movement, spearheaded by Emile Zola, was committed to presenting an even narrower view of reality by focusing on the sordid and squalid in contemporary life. The naturalists tried to show those powerful forces governing human lives over which we exercise little awareness or control. In their work, heredity and environment reached new pinnacles of importance. In trying to teach audiences a "social lesson," the naturalists drew characters and situations from social and economic types. Eventually, the loss of individuality in dramatic character and the repetition of sordid situations and themes lessened interest in their work.

The nineteenth-century realists rendered setting, character, and dialogue so close to actual life that audiences were convinced by the illusion of contemporary reality. Audiences responded to the familiar made both significant and universal. What seemed small, inconsequential, and overlooked became important and urgent. As a consequence, familiar events became dramatic fictions. The great realists, Ibsen, Strindberg, Shaw, and Chekhov, put their understanding of the world around them into dramatic form—often a variant of the well-made-play format—and held a dramatic magnifying glass up to commonplace realities.

Today, the goals of realistic writers have changed very little from those of their predecessors. Writing within the realistic tradition, Arthur Miller, David Mamet, Marsha Norman, and August Wilson construct verifiable worlds, exploring recognizable relationships, illuminating the social and the familial, and plunging beneath the surfaces of ordinary mid-twentieth-century life to arrive at the troubling relevances of human and social themes. The fact that realism holds a mirror up to humanity's insignificance and gives the ordinary and commonplace a new dimension is the source of its popular appeal.

Writing styles that *revolted* against the "illusion of the real" in the theatre span a period from the early 1900s to the present. These new experiments involved some of the most influential playwrights of our time, especially Bertolt Brecht and Samuel Beckett, whose plays are the subject of the next chapters.

## NOTES

1. Emile Zola, *Le Naturalism au Théâtre* in *Les Oeuvres Completes*, Vol. 42 (Paris: Francois Bernouard, 1927): 17.

2. Eric Bentley, *The Playwright as Thinker: A Study of Drama in Modern Times* (New York: Harcourt, Brace, Jovanovich, 1987): 4.

3. Joseph Wood Krutch, *"Modernism" in Modern Drama: A Definition and an Estimate* (Ithaca, N.Y.: Cornell University Press, 1953): 22

4. August Strindberg, "Preface" to *Miss Julie*, in *Six Plays of August Strindberg*, trans. Elizabeth Sprigge (New York: Doubleday & Company, 1955): 65–66.

5. Frederick Marker and Lise-Lone Marker, *The Scandinavian Theatre: A Short History* (Totowa, N. J.: Rowman and Littlefield, 1975): 154.

6. Zola 17.

7. August Wilson, "Interview," *In Their Own Words Contemporary American Playwrights: Interviews*, ed. David Savran (New York: Theatre Communications Group, 1988): 299.

ness of his age. In the 1930s what commended the subject of Galileo to Brecht was the analogy between the seventeenth-century scientist's underground activities against the authority of the Roman Catholic Church and those of the twentieth-century opponents to Hitler's Germany. In all instances, Brecht insisted that the play was neither an attack on the church nor the priesthood, but rather on reactionary authority in any age. In Galileo's time, science was a branch of theology. The church as the intellectual authority of the day was, therefore, the ultimate scientific, political, and spiritual court of appeal. Galileo's struggle in the name of intellectual freedom gives thinly disguised attention to present-day reactionary authorities of a totally secular kind.[2]

In the American version, written six years later as Brecht continued his exile in California, the nuclear age (the logical progression of Galileo's earlier discoveries) had dawned with all of its attendant horrors as new weapons of destruction. As Brecht was writing the first-draft version of his play in 1938–39, the German physicist Nils Bohr was making his discoveries in atomic theory that resulted in the splitting of the uranium atom; in 1945, as Brecht was working with Charles Laughton on a second script, the United States exhibited the atomic bomb's destructive possibilities on the Japanese cities of Hiroshima and Nagasaki. The playwright then faced the fact that the nuclear age was a product of the new science founded by Galileo at the beginning of the "scientific age" three hundred years prior. Brecht then set about to condemn Galileo as a traitor because the atomic bomb, in Brecht's view, had made the relationship between society and science into a matter of life and death for the human race.[3] In this second and darker version of the Galileo story, Brecht's admiration for his clever scientist is altered and Galileo is depicted as a gluttonous, self-serving, and unethical (if not "criminal") intellectual who

has betrayed humankind. In the second text, Brecht set about to demand not just freedom to research and teach, but a sense of social and moral responsibility toward humankind from the world's scientists. The point in 1947 was to demand from those who viewed scientific advances "as an end in itself," thus playing into the hands of those in power, a change and advancement of a utilitarian concept of science.[4] What Brecht has to say about his collaboration with Charles Laughton (and his thoughts on what the revised work has to say about modern science in 1945) is contained in a foreword to the German edition entitled "Building up a Part: Laughton's Galileo."

As a writer, Brecht used historical material—what he called *historification*—drawn from other times and places (ancient China in *The Caucasian Chalk Circle*, Germany's Thirty Years' War in *Mother Courage and Her Children*, the church-dominated Italy of the seventeenth century in *Galileo*) in order to get audiences to reflect upon oppressive social and political problems and events of the present time. Brecht argued that the theatre should not treat contemporary subjects in a direct way, but by putting similar events of the past on stage and by distancing us from immediate problems get us to see the parallels in history and to understand what actions should have been taken in the past (and were not), but can be undertaken in the present to correct social and political problems.

As an historical scientific figure, Galileo's life embraces a twofold responsibility: to the work to be achieved and then to humankind which the work serves. In his lecherous and gluttonous character, Brecht has at hand a genius whose most powerful instinct is curiosity and whose greatest sensual pleasure is the pleasure of discovery, whether of a well-cooked goose or of Jupiter's moons. To be able to indulge his appetites, Galileo is prepared to commit the basest acts: He cheats the Venetians by selling them the telescope he has not invented but merely reproduced from a traveller's description. He writes servile letters to the Medici prince whose tyrannies he despises. And, with the physical cowardice of the sensuous man, he recants his theories when merely shown the instruments of torture. In the earlier version of the play, Galileo's recantation was made to appear excusable as a deliberate and calculating act: By recanting he saved his life and gained the time to complete his treatise which was then smuggled out to the free world. Nevertheless, Brecht came increasingly to view the Galileos of the world as serving pure research devoid of ethical responsibility to humanity. In the Berlin text, he labels Galileo as a "social criminal, a complete rogue."[5] Galileo becomes a "criminal," in Brecht's harsher view of scientific progress, because by his cowardice he has established the tradition of the scientist's subservience to the state—the tradition that, according to Brecht, reached its culmination in the production of the atomic bomb for military purposes, which science put at the disposal of nonscientific people to serve their power politics.

## EPIC DEVICES

Brecht described his ideal theatre as using three key devices: *historification, epic,* and *alienation.* Brecht's theory of epic staging, as found in his writing, included progressive scenes to show the ascending or declining fortunes of the central figure, and no act divisions. In the epic style, each scene begins with titles, or legends, written on placards and other images suspended above the stage or projected on screens. For example, a sign—located above the stage and written in crude letters on a frame—depicts the changing time and places in Galileo's life. In pursuit of his researches and new patrons, he moves from Venice to Florence to Rome and back to Florence. Subsequent titles describe years, seasons, and Galileo's machinations, discoveries, and political fortunes. The scene titles are thematically consistent, describing Galileo in relation to three things: research, materialism, and authority.

> Eight long years with tongue in cheek
> Of what he knew he did not speak
> Then temptation grew too great
> And Galileo challenged fate. (8)

In the American version, sketches of Jupiter's moons, Leonardo da Vinci's technical drawings, and a Venetian warship were projected on screens to assist in the telling of the story.

The epic devices allow Brecht to express his political, sociological, and economic arguments, such as the connections between science and industry, individuals and governments, and the ultimate victimization of common humanity by both. Galileo vacillates between life's contradictions (an important point in Brecht's immersion in Marxist theory): the necessities of research and family, pure research and materialism, science and religion, profit and loss, hunger and gratification, and so on. In the downward spiral of Galileo's life (his isolation, poverty, poor health, and near blindness), Brecht offers a general judgment at the end of Scene 13 that Galileo failed his ethical responsibilities to humankind. Galileo explains to his former pupil:

> As a scientist I had an almost unique opportunity . . . I surrendered my knowledge to the powers that be, to use it, no, not *use* it, *abuse* it, as it suits their ends. I have betrayed my profession. Any man who does what I have done must not be tolerated in the ranks of science. (13)

Caught up in Galileo's plight and "heroic" passing of his forbidden writings to his pupil for future generations, few audiences have realized that this was the bitterest and most meaningful lesson of the play. Brecht's condemnation of his exemplar as hero and criminal is also an indictment of modern scientific-industrial-political power systems and those individuals in positions of influence.

What is clear in the epic style is that Brecht is concerned neither with biography nor the history of the seventeenth century, but with the historical and human problems of the twentieth century. The recantation scene (12) is the crisis scene of the play (all of the previous scenes have been arranged to build to this moment). The arrangement of the episodes permits us to interpret Galileo's behavior in recanting under pressure from the Inquisition. He has proved over and over again that he has only judged the powers of the world in so far as they were advantageous or detrimental to his researches. He has sacrificed his daughter's marriage (Scene 8), security for himself by rejecting the iron founder's offer of sanctuary (Scene 10), and his eyesight and reputation as a man of integrity (Scenes 12 and 13). In all things, though, Brecht's character is consistent. The inner makeup of Brecht's Galileo is determined by a hedonistic indulgence of life's pleasures and an excessive joy in experimentation and discovery. Nothing else matters, including the social importance of his discoveries. For this, Brecht increasingly condemns his scientist in the play's two later versions.

## I AM BECOME DEATH, THE DESTROYER OF WORLDS

The 1945–46 version of *Galileo* only slightly masks the theme of the relationship of scientific research to the most profound moral and social questions illuminated by the explosions on Hiroshima and Nagasaki. In the second text, Brecht has taken a bleak vision of "scientific progress," echoed in J. Robert Oppenheimer's famous cry—words from the Indian epic, the *Bhagavad Gita*—as he watched the first test explosion of an atomic weapon: "I am become death, the destroyer of worlds." By 1947, Brecht has a wholly negative view of Galileo whom he now regards as an "intellectual prostitute."[6] The recantation scene becomes thereby not an example of practical behavior but a clear case of the scientist allowing the powers that be to use him for their own nonhumanistic ends. What was frustrating for Brecht was that, despite his distancing devices, audiences refused to condemn the physicist before the Inquisition and secret efforts to preserve his writings elicited sympathy and highly emotional responses. Brecht concluded that "Technically, *Life of Galileo* is a great step backwards..." because he had been unable in his writing to distance the audience emotionally from Galileo's plight.[7] Brecht's concept of alienation (or distancing) is at work on two principal levels in the play: Galileo himself finds his world of 1600 to be unfamiliar, outdated, and in need of explanation. This fact accounts for the historical character's novelty, strangeness, and difference.[8] Audiences also sympathized with the character's strong lust for living, and, despite Brecht's many efforts to censor Galileo, they continued to applaud the scientist's struggles against reactionary authority.

Despite the epic devices, *Galileo* remained an old-fashioned play (almost classical) centered on the central figure's choices under pressure during which he has campaigned to change the world and has capitulated unheroically when faced with physical pain. Disillusioned by Galileo's recantation ("I, Galileo Galilei, Teacher of Mathematics and Physics, do hereby publicly renounce my teaching that the earth moves."), his student, Andrea Sarti, rejects his teacher with the famous line, "Unhappy is the land that breeds no heroes." Galileo replies, "Unhappy is the land that needs a hero." Galileo has not fulfilled the heroic role his pupils envisioned for him, for, in the horror of the moment, he has fallen victim to human frailty.

> GALILEO: They showed me the instruments.
> ANDREA: It was not a plan?
> GALILEO: It was not. (13)

Eric Bentley has called the play a tragicomedy of "heroic combat followed by unheroic capitulation." In the writing tradition of great tragicomic plays, he continued, there is in *Galileo* no noble contrition, no belated rebellion, but rather only undisguised self-loathing.[9] In explanation to Sarti at the play's end, Galileo says, "I have come to believe that I was never in real danger; for some years I was as strong as the authorities and I surrendered my knowledge to the powers that be" (Scene 13). In the new version, Galileo is given a long tirade of self-condemnation. Sarti is also placed in the wrong because he argues that "science has only one commandment: contribution." Galileo's retort is: "Then welcome to the gutter, dear colleague in science and brother in betrayal: I sold out, you are a buyer" (Scene 13).

In his theoretical writings, set down between 1948 and 1956, Brecht referred to his theatre and plays as "dialectical," further stressing the collision of conflicting ideas and social forces in his plays. The ultimate source of Brecht's dialectic in *Galileo* is the central figure of his corpulent and vociferous scientist whose greatness and enormous failure intrigued Brecht as a subject for epic theatre. The figure of the historical genius provided dialectical argument about the ultimate cost of scientific progress for humanity and the ethical responsibility to humankind of those individuals responsible for discoveries and inventions that have resulted not only in Chernobyl-like disasters but also in space exploration and detection of black holes in the universe.

The premiere of the English language version prepared jointly by Brecht and actor Charles Laughton, who played the lead and co-directed the play with Brecht (though the director of record was Joseph Losey), opened in Los Angeles at the Coronet Theatre on July 30, 1947. The production proceeded to Broadway following its successful California run, and opened at the Maxine Elliott Theatre on December 7, 1947 (the date on which the Japanese bombed Pearl Harbor six years earlier). By the time the played opened in New York, Brecht, following his appearance before the House Un-American Activities Committee in Washington, D.C., had returned to Europe. He had been subpoenaed to testify on the issue of Communist infiltration into the motion picture industry and played a role not unlike Galileo's before the Inquisition. Brecht prevaricated, entertained, and escaped to Europe, never to return to the United States.

*Galileo* is an important document as the last (if unfinished) aesthetic testament of Bertolt Brecht as a playwright and director. Unable to complete work on the Berliner Ensemble version of the text, he turned rehearsals over to Eric Engel and the play was produced in its third version on January 15, 1957, five months following Brecht's death.

# Galileo

## TRANSLATED BY CHARLES LAUGHTON

*It is my opinion that the earth is very noble and admirable*
*by reason of so many and so different alterations and generations*
*which are incessantly made therein.*

—Galileo Galilei

**CHARACTERS**
**GALILEO GALILEI**
**ANDREA SARTI,** *two actors: boy and man*
**MRS. SARTI**
**LUDOVICO MARSILI**
**PRIULI, THE CURATOR**
**SAGREDO,** *Galileo's friend*
**VIRGINIA GALILEI**
**TWO SENATORS**
**MATTI,** *an iron founder*
**PHILOSOPHER,** *later, Rector of the University*
**ELDERLY LADY**
**YOUNG LADY**
**FEDERZONI,** *assistant to Galileo*
**MATHEMATICIAN**
**LORD CHAMBERLAIN**
**FAT PRELATE**
**TWO SCHOLARS**
**TWO MONKS**
**INFURIATED MONK**
**OLD CARDINAL**
**ATTENDANT MONK**
**CHRISTOPHER CLAVIUS**
**LITTLE MONK**
**TWO SECRETARIES**
**CARDINAL BELLARMIN**
**CARDINAL BARBERINI**
**CARDINAL INQUISITOR**
**YOUNG GIRL**
**HER FRIEND**
**GIUSEPPE**
**STREET SINGER**
**HIS WIFE**

**REVELLER**
**A LOUD VOICE**
**INFORMER**
**TOWN CRIER**
**OFFICIAL**
**PEASANT**
**CUSTOMS OFFICER**
**BOY**
**SENATORS, OFFICIALS, PROFESSORS, LADIES, GUESTS, CHILDREN**

*There are two wordless roles: The Doge in scene 2 and Prince Cosmo de Medici in scene 4. The ballad of scene 9 is filled out by a pantomime: among the individuals in the pantomimic crowd are three extras (including the "King of Hungary"), Cobbler's Boy, Three Children, Peasant Woman, Monk, Rich Couple, Dwarf, Beggar, and Girl.*

## SCENE 1

*In the year sixteen hundred and nine*
*Science' light began to shine.*
*At Padua City in a modest house*
*Galileo Galilei set out to prove*
*The sun is still, the earth is on the move.*

(**GALILEO's** *scantily furnished study. Morning.* **GALILEO** *is washing himself. A barefooted boy,* **ANDREA,** *son of his housekeeper,* **MRS. SARTI,** *enters with a big astronomical model.*)

**GALILEO:** Where did you get that thing?
**ANDREA:** The coachman brought it.
**GALILEO:** Who sent it?

**ANDREA:** It said "From the Court of Naples" on the box.

**GALILEO:** I don't want their stupid presents. Illuminated manuscripts, a statue of Hercules the size of an elephant—they never send money.

**ANDREA:** But isn't this an astronomical instrument, Mr. Galilei?

**GALILEO:** That is an antique too. An expensive toy.

**ANDREA:** What's it for?

**GALILEO:** It's a map of the sky according to the wise men of ancient Greece. Bosh! We'll try and sell it to the university. They still teach it there.

**ANDREA:** How does it work, Mr. Galilei?

**GALILEO:** It's complicated.

**ANDREA:** I think I could understand it.

**GALILEO** (*interested*): Maybe. Let's begin at the beginning. Description!

**ANDREA:** There are metal rings, a lot of them.

**GALILEO:** How many?

**ANDREA:** Eight.

**GALILEO:** Correct. And?

**ANDREA:** There are words painted on the bands.

**GALILEO:** What words?

**ANDREA:** The names of stars.

**GALILEO:** Such as?

**ANDREA:** Here is a band with the sun on it and on the inside band is the moon.

**GALILEO:** Those metal bands represent crystal globes, eight of them.

**ANDREA:** Crystal?

**GALILEO:** Like huge soap bubbles one inside the other and the stars are supposed to be tacked on to them. Spin the band with the sun on it. (**ANDREA** *does.*) You see the fixed ball in the middle?

**ANDREA:** Yes.

**GALILEO:** That's the earth. For two thousand years man has chosen to believe that the sun and all the host of stars revolve about him. Well. The Pope, the Cardinals, the princes, the scholars, captains,

merchants, housewives, have pictured themselves squatting in the middle of an affair like that.

**ANDREA:** Locked up inside?

**GALILEO** (*triumphant*): Ah!

**ANDREA:** It's like a cage.

**GALILEO:** So you sensed that. (*Against the model.*) I like to think the ships began it.

**ANDREA:** Why?

**GALILEO:** They used to hug the coasts and then all of a sudden they left the coasts and spread over the oceans. A new age was coming. I was on to it years ago. I was a young man, in Siena. There was a group of masons arguing. They had to raise a block of granite. It was hot. To help matters, one of them wanted to try a new arrangement of ropes. After five minutes' discussion, out went a method which had been employed for a thousand years. The millennium of faith is ended, said I, this is the millennium of doubt. And we are pulling out of that contraption. The sayings of the wise men won't wash anymore. Everybody, at last, is getting nosy. I predict that in our time astronomy will become the gossip of the marketplace and the sons of fish-wives will pack the schools.

**ANDREA:** You're off again, Mr. Galilei. Give me the towel. (*He wipes some soap from Galilei's back.*)

**GALILEO:** By that time, with any luck, they will be learning that the earth rolls round the sun, and that their mothers, the captains, the scholars, the princes, and the Pope are rolling with it.

**ANDREA:** That turning-round-business is no good. I can see with my own eyes that the sun comes up in one place in the morning and goes down in a different place in the evening. It doesn't stand still, I can see it move.

**GALILEO:** You see nothing, all you do is gawk. Gawking is not seeing. (*He puts the*

*iron washstand in the middle of the room.)*
Now: that's the sun. Sit down. (ANDREA
*sits on a chair.* GALILEO *stands behind him.)*
Where is the sun, on your right or on
your left?

ANDREA: Left.

GALILEO: And how will it get to the right?

ANDREA: By your putting it there, of course.

GALILEO: Of course? (*He picks* ANDREA *up,
chair and all, and carries him round to the
other side of the washstand.) Now* where is
the sun?

ANDREA: On the right.

GALILEO: And did it move?

ANDREA: I did.

GALILEO: Wrong. Stupid! The chair moved.

ANDREA: But I was on it.

GALILEO: Of course. The chair is the earth,
and you're sitting on it.

(MRS. SARTI, *who has come in with a glass of
milk and a roll, has been watching.)*

MRS. SARTI: What are you doing with my
son, Mr. Galilei?

ANDREA: Now, mother, you don't understand.

MRS. SARTI: You understand, don't you?
Last night he tried to tell me that the
earth goes round the sun. You'll soon
have him saying that two times two is five.

GALILEO (*eating his breakfast*): Apparently we
are on the threshold of a new era, Mrs.
Sarti.

MRS. SARTI: Well, I hope we can pay the
milkman in this new era. A young gentleman is here to take private lessons and
he is well-dressed and don't you frighten
him away like you did the others. Wasting your time with Andrea! (*To* AN-
DREA.) How many times have I told you
not to wheedle free lessons out of Mr.
Galilei? (MRS. SARTI *goes.)*

GALILEO: So you thought enough of the
turning-round-business to tell your
mother about it.

ANDREA: Just to surprise her.

GALILEO: Andrea, I wouldn't talk about our
ideas outside.

ANDREA: Why not?

GALILEO: Certain of the authorities won't
like it.

ANDREA: Why not, if it's the truth?

GALILEO (*laughs*): Because we are like the
worms who are little and have dim
eyes and can hardly see the stars at
all, and the new astronomy is a
framework of guesses or very little
more—yet.

(MRS. SARTI *shows in* LUDOVICO MARSILI, *a
presentable young man.)*

GALILEO: This house is like a marketplace.
(*Pointing to the model.*) Move that out of
the way! Put it down there!

(LUDOVICO *does.)*

LUDOVICO: Good morning, sir. My name is
Ludovico Marsili.

GALILEO (*reading a letter of recommendation he
has brought*): You came by way of Holland and your family lives in the Campagna? Private lessons, thirty scudi a
month.

LUDOVICO: That's all right, of course, sir.

GALILEO: What is your subject?

LUDOVICO: Horses.

GALILEO: Aha.

LUDOVICO: I don't understand science, sir.

GALILEO: Aha.

LUDOVICO: They showed me an instrument
like that in Amsterdam. You'll pardon
me, sir, but it didn't make sense to me at
all.

GALILEO: It's out of date now.

(ANDREA *goes.)*

LUDOVICO: You'll have to be patient with
me, sir. Nothing in science makes sense
to me.

GALILEO: Aha.

LUDOVICO: I saw a brand new instrument°
in Amsterdam. A tube affair. "See things
five times as large as life!" It had two
lenses, one at each end, one lens bulged
and the other was like that. (*Gesture.*)
Any normal person would think that
different lenses cancel each other out.
They didn't! I just stood and looked a
fool.

GALILEO: I don't quite follow you. What
does one see enlarged?

LUDOVICO: Church steeples, pigeons, boats.
Anything at a distance.

GALILEO: Did you yourself—see things enlarged?

LUDOVICO: Yes, sir.

GALILEO: And the tube had two lenses? Was
it like this? (*He has been making a sketch.*)

(LUDOVICO *nods.*)

GALILEO: A recent invention?

LUDOVICO: It must be. They only started
peddling it on the streets a few days before I left Holland.

GALILEO (*starts to scribble calculations on the
sketch; almost friendly*): Why do you
bother your head with science? Why
don't you just breed horses?

(*Enter* MRS. SARTI. GALILEO *doesn't see her. She
listens to the following.*)

LUDOVICO: My mother is set on the idea that
science is necessary nowadays for conversation.

---

**brand new instrument:** The telescope was thought erro-
neously to have been invented by Hans Lippershey, who
made and sold telescopes in Middelburg, Netherlands, in
1608. When he applied for a patent, he was refused on the
grounds that the idea was widespread. Telescopes were
available for sale in Paris in 1609, then Germany, Italy,
and London in the same year. Galileo reinvented the
instrument by calculating the mathematical relationship
of the focal lengths of lenses. His versions were on the
order of ten times more powerful than those available,
and they also permitted the viewer to see things right
side up, which Lippershey's did not.

GALILEO: Aha. You'll find Latin or philosophy easier. (MRS. SARTI *catches his eye.*)
I'll see you on Tuesday afternoon.

LUDOVICO: I shall look forward to it, sir.

GALILEO: Good morning. (*He goes to the window and shouts into the street.*) Andrea!
Hey, Redhead, Redhead!

MRS. SARTI: The curator of the museum is
here to see you.

GALILEO: Don't look at me like that. I took
him, didn't I?

MRS. SARTI: I caught your eye in time.

GALILEO: Show the curator in.

(*She goes. He scribbles something on a new sheet
of paper. The* CURATOR *comes in.*)

CURATOR: Good morning, Mr. Galilei.

GALILEO: Lend me a scudo. (*He takes it and
goes to the window, wrapping the coin in the
paper on which he has been scribbling.*) Redhead, run to the spectacle-maker and
bring me two lenses; here are the meas-
urements. (*He throws the paper out of the
window. During the following scene*
GALILEO *studies his sketch of the lenses.*)

CURATOR: Mr. Galilei, I have come to return
your petition for an honorarium. Unfortunately I am unable to recommend your
request.

GALILEO: My good sir, how can I make ends
meet on five hundred scudi?

CURATOR: What about your private students?

GALILEO: If I spend all my time with students, when am I to study? My particular science is on the threshold of
important discoveries. (*He throws a
manuscript on the table.*) Here are my findings on the laws of failing bodies. That
should be worth two hundred scudi.

CURATOR: I am sure that any paper of yours
is of infinite worth, Mr. Galilei. . . .

GALILEO: I was limiting it to two hundred
scudi.

CURATOR (*cool*): Mr. Galilei, if you want
money and leisure, go to Florence. I have

no doubt Prince Cosmo de Medici will be glad to subsidize you, but eventually you will be forbidden to think—in the name of the Inquisition. (GALILEO *says nothing.*) Now let us not make a mountain out of a molehill. You are happy here in the Republic of Venice but you need money. Well, that's human, Mr. Galilei, may I suggest a simple solution? You remember that chart you made for the army to extract cube roots without any knowledge of mathematics? Now that was practical!

GALILEO: Bosh!

CURATOR: Don't say bosh about something that astounded the Chamber of Commerce. Our city elders are businessmen. Why don't you invent something useful that will bring them a little profit?

GALILEO (*playing with the sketch of the lenses; suddenly*): I see. Mr. Priuli, I may have something for you.

CURATOR: You don't say so.

GALILEO: It's not quite there yet, but . . .

CURATOR: You've never let me down yet, Galilei.

GALILEO: You are always an inspiration to me, Priuli.

CURATOR: You are a great man: a discontented man, but I've always said you are a great man.

GALILEO (*tartly*): My discontent, Priuli, is for the most part with myself. I am forty-six years of age and have achieved nothing which satisfies me.

CURATOR: I won't disturb you any further.

GALILEO: Thank you. Good morning.

CURATOR: Good morning. And thank you.

(*He goes.* GALILEO *sighs.* ANDREA *returns, bringing lenses.*)

ANDREA: One scudo was not enough. I had to leave my cap with him before he'd let me take them away.

GALILEO: We'll get it back someday. Give them to me. (*He takes the lenses over to the window, holding them in the relation they would have in a telescope.*)

ANDREA: What are those for?

GALILEO: Something for the senate. With any luck, they will rake in two hundred scudi. Take a look!

ANDREA: My, things look close! I can read the copper letters on the bell in the Campanile. And the washerwomen by the river, I can see their washboards!

GALILEO: Get out of the way. (*Looking through the lenses himself.*) Aha!

# SCENE 2

*No one's virtue is complete:*
*Great Galileo liked to eat.*
*You will not resent, we hope,*
*The truth about his telescope.*

(*The great arsenal of Venice, overlooking the harbor full of ships.* SENATORS *and* OFFICIALS *on one side,* GALILEO, *his daughter* VIRGINIA, *and his friend* SAGREDO *on the other side. They are dressed in formal, festive clothes.* VIRGINIA *is fourteen and charming. She carries a velvet cushion on which lies a brand new telescope. Behind* GALILEO *are some Artisans from the arsenal. There are onlookers,* LUDOVICO *amongst them.*)

CURATOR (*announcing*): Senators, Artisans of the Great Arsenal of Venice; Mr. Galileo Galilei, professor of mathematics at your University of Padua.

(GALILEO *steps forward and starts to speak.*)

GALILEO: Members of the High Senate! Gentlemen: I have great pleasure, as director of this institute, in presenting for your approval and acceptance an entirely new instrument originating from this our great arsenal of the Republic of Venice. As professor of mathematics at your University of Padua, your obedient servant has always counted it his privilege to offer you such discoveries and inventions as might prove lucrative to the manufacturers and merchants of our Venetian Republic. Thus, in all humility, I tender you this, my optical tube, or telescope, constructed, I assure you, on the most scientific and Christian principles, the product of seventeen years patient research at your University of Padua.

(**GALILEO** *steps back. The* **SENATORS** *applaud.*)

**SAGREDO** (*aside to* **GALILEO**): Now you will be able to pay your bills.

**GALILEO:** Yes. It will make money for them. But you realize that it is more than a money-making gadget?—I turned it on the moon last night . . .

**CURATOR** (*in his best chamber-of-commerce manner*): Gentlemen: Our Republic is to be congratulated not only because this new acquisition will be one more feather in the cap of Venetian culture . . . (*polite applause*) . . . not only because our own Mr. Galilei has generously handed this fresh product of his teeming brain entirely over to you, allowing you to manufacture as many of these highly salable articles as you please. . . .(*Considerable applause.*) But Gentlemen of the Senate, has it occurred to you that—with the help of this remarkable new instrument—the battle fleet of the enemy will be visible to us a full two hours before we are visible to him? (*Tremendous applause.*)

**GALILEO** (*aside to* **SAGREDO**): We have been held up three generations for lack of a thing like this. I want to go home.

**SAGREDO:** What about the moon?

**GALILEO:** Well, for one thing, it doesn't give off its own light.

**CURATOR** (*continuing his oration*): And now, Your Excellency, and Members of the Senate, Mr. Galilei entreats you to accept the instrument from the hands of his charming daughter Virginia.

(*Polite applause. He beckons to* **VIRGINIA** *who steps forward and presents the telescope to the* **DOGE.**)

**CURATOR** (*during this*): Mr. Galilei gives his invention entirely into your hands, Gentlemen, enjoining you to construct as many of these instruments as you may please.

(*More applause. The* **SENATORS** *gather round the telescope, examining it, and looking through it.*)

**GALILEO** (*aside to* **SAGREDO**): Do you know what the Milky Way is made of?

**SAGREDO:** No.

**GALILEO:** I do.

**CURATOR** (*interrupting*): Congratulations, Mr. Galilei. Your extra five hundred scudi a year are safe.

**GALILEO:** Pardon? What? Of course, the five hundred scudi! Yes!

(*A prosperous man is standing beside the* **CURATOR.**)

**CURATOR:** Mr. Galilei, Mr. Matti of Florence.

**MATTI:** You're opening new fields, Mr. Galilei. We could do with you at Florence.

**CURATOR:** Now, Mr. Matti, leave something to us poor Venetians.

**MATTI:** It is a pity that a great republic has to seek an excuse to pay its great men their right and proper dues.

**CURATOR:** Even a great man has to have an incentive. (*He joins the* **SENATORS** *at the telescope.*)

**MATTI:** I am an iron founder.

**GALILEO:** Iron founder!

**MATTI:** With factories at Pisa and Florence. I wanted to talk to you about a machine you designed for a friend of mine in Padua.

**GALILEO:** I'll put you on to someone to copy it for you, I am not going to have the time.—How are things in Florence?

(*They wander away.*)

**FIRST SENATOR** (*peering*): Extraordinary! They're having their lunch on that frigate. Lobsters! I'm hungry!

(*Laughter.*)

SECOND SENATOR: Oh, good heavens, look at her! I must tell my wife to stop bathing on the roof. When can I buy one of these things?

(*Laughter.* VIRGINIA *has spotted* LUDOVICO *among the onlookers and drags him to* GALILEO.)

VIRGINIA (*to* LUDOVICO): Did I do it nicely?

LUDOVICO: I thought so.

VIRGINIA: Here's Ludovico to congratulate you, father.

LUDOVICO (*embarrassed*): Congratulations, sir.

GALILEO: I improved it.

LUDOVICO: Yes, sir. I am beginning to understand science.

(GALILEO *is surrounded.*)

VIRGINIA: Isn't father a great man?

LUDOVICO: Yes.

VIRGINIA: Isn't that new thing father made pretty?

LUDOVICO: Yes, a pretty red. Where I saw it first it was covered in green.

VIRGINIA: What was?

LUDOVICO: Never mind. (*A short pause.*) Have you ever been to Holland?

(*They go. All Venice is congratulating* GALILEO, *who wants to go home.*)

# SCENE 3

*January ten, sixteen ten;*
*Galileo Galilei abolishes heaven.*

(GALILEO's *study at Padua. It is night.* GALILEO *and* SAGREDO *at a telescope.*)

SAGREDO (*softly*): The edge of the crescent is jagged. All along the dark part, near the shiny crescent, bright particles of light keep coming up, one after the other and growing larger and merging with the bright crescent.

GALILEO: How do you explain those spots of light?

SAGREDO: It can't be true . . .

GALILEO: Is *is* true: they are high mountains.

SAGREDO: On a star?

GALILEO: Yes. The shining particles are mountain peaks catching the first rays of the rising sun while the slopes of the mountains are still dark, and what you see is the sunlight moving down from the peaks into the valleys.

SAGREDO: But this gives the lie to all the astronomy that's been taught for the last two thousand years.

GALILEO: Yes. What you are seeing now has been seen by no other man beside myself.

SAGREDO: But the moon can't be an earth with mountains and valleys like our own any more than the earth can be a star.

GALILEO: The moon *is* an earth with mountains and valleys—and the earth *is* a star. As the moon appears to us, so we appear to the moon. From the moon, the earth looks sometimes like a crescent, sometimes like a half-globe, sometimes a full globe, and sometimes it is not visible at all.

SAGREDO: Galileo, this is frightening.

(*An urgent knocking on the door.*)

GALILEO: I've discovered something else, something even more astonishing.

(*More knocking.* GALILEO *opens the door and the* CURATOR *comes in.*)

CURATOR: There it is—your "miraculous optical tube." Do you know that this invention he so picturesquely termed "the fruit of seventeen years research" will be on sale tomorrow for two scudi apiece at every street corner in Venice? A shipload of them has just arrived from Holland.

SAGREDO: Oh, dear!

(GALILEO *turns his back and adjusts the telescope.*)

CURATOR: When I think of the poor gentlemen of the senate who believed they were getting an invention they could monopolize for their own profit. . . . Why, when they took their first look through the glass, it was only by the merest chance that they didn't see a peddler, seven times enlarged, selling tubes exactly like it at the corner of the street.

SAGREDO: Mr. Priuli, with the help of this instrument, Mr. Galilei has made discoveries that will revolutionize our concept of the universe.

CURATOR: Mr. Galilei provided the city with a first rate water pump and the irrigation works he designed function splendidly. How was I to expect this?

GALILEO (*still at the telescope*): Not so fast, Priuli. I may be on the track of a very large gadget. Certain of the stars appear to have regular movements. If there were a clock in the sky, it could be seen from anywhere. That might be useful for your shipowners.

CURATOR: I won't listen to you. I listened to you before, and as a reward for my friendship you have made me the laughingstock of the town. You can laugh— you got your money. But let me tell you this: you've destroyed my faith in a lot of things, Mr. Galilei. I'm disgusted with the world. That's all I have to say. (*He storms out.*)

GALILEO (*embarrassed*): Businessmen bore me, they suffer so. Did you see the frightened look in his eyes when he caught sight of a world not created solely for the purpose of doing business?

SAGREDO: Did you know that telescopes had been made in Holland?

GALILEO: I'd heard about it. But the one I made for the Senators was twice as good as any Dutchman's. Besides, I needed the money. How can I work, with the tax collector on the doorstep? And my poor daughter will never acquire a husband unless she has a dowry, she's not too bright. And I like to buy books—all kinds of books. Why not? And what

about my appetite? I don't think well unless I eat well. Can I help it if I get my best ideas over a good meal and a bottle of wine? They don't pay me as much as they pay the butcher's boy. If only I could have five years to do nothing but research! Come on. I am going to show you something else.

SAGREDO: I don't know that I want to look again.

GALILEO: This is one of the brighter nebulae of the Milky Way. What do you see?

SAGREDO: But it's made up of stars—countless stars.

GALILEO: Countless worlds.

SAGREDO (*hesitating*): What about the theory that the earth revolves round the sun? Have you run across anything about that?

GALILEO: No. But I noticed something on Tuesday that might prove a step towards even that. Where's Jupiter? There are four lesser stars near Jupiter. I happened on them on Monday but didn't take any particular note of their position. On Tuesday I looked again. I could have sworn they had moved. They have changed again. Tell me what you see.

SAGREDO: I only see three.

GALILEO: Where's the fourth? Let's get the charts and settle down to work.

(*They work and the lights dim. The lights go up again. It is near dawn.*)

GALILEO: The only place the fourth can be is round at the back of the larger star where we cannot see it. This means there are small stars revolving around a big star. Where are the crystal shells now that the stars are supposed to be fixed to?

SAGREDO: Jupiter can't be attached to anything: there are other stars revolving round it.

GALILEO: There is no support in the heavens. (SAGREDO *laughs awkwardly.*) Don't stand there looking at me as if it weren't true.

SAGREDO: I suppose it is true. I'm afraid.

GALILEO: Why?

SAGREDO: What do you think is going to happen to you for saying that there is another sun around which other earths revolve? And that there are only stars and no difference between earth and heaven? Where is God then?

GALILEO: What do you mean?

SAGREDO: God? Where is God?

GALILEO (*angrily*): Not there! Any more than he'd be here—if creatures from the moon came down to look for him!

SAGREDO: Then where is He?

GALILEO: I'm not a theologian: I'm a mathematician.

SAGREDO: You are a human being! (*Almost shouting.*) Where is God in your system of the universe?

GALILEO: Within ourselves. Or—nowhere.

SAGREDO: Ten years ago a man was burned at the stake for saying that.

GALILEO: Giordano Bruno° was an idiot: he spoke too soon. He would never have been condemned if he could have backed up what he said with proof.

SAGREDO (*incredulously*): Do you really believe proof will make any difference?

GALILEO: I believe in the human race. The only people that can't be reasoned with are the dead. Human beings are intelligent.

SAGREDO: Intelligent—or merely shrewd?

GALILEO: I know they call a donkey a horse when they want to sell it, and a horse a donkey when they want to buy it. But is that the whole story? Aren't they susceptible to truth as well? (*He fishes a small pebble out of his pocket.*) If anybody were

to drop a stone . . . (*drops the pebble*) . . . and tell them that it didn't fall, do you think they would keep quiet? The evidence of your own eyes is a very seductive thing. Sooner or later everybody must succumb to it.

SAGREDO: Galileo, I am helpless when you talk.

(*A church bell has been ringing for some time, calling people to Mass. Enter* VIRGINIA, *muffled up for Mass, carrying a candle, protected from the wind by a globe.*)

VIRGINIA: Oh, father, you promised to go to bed tonight, and it's five o'clock again.

GALILEO: Why are you up at this hour?

VIRGINIA: I'm going to Mass with Mrs. Sarti. Ludovico is going too. How was the night, father?

GALILEO: Bright.

VIRGINIA: What did you find through the tube?

GALILEO: Only some little specks by the side of a star. I must draw attention to them somehow. I think I'll name them after the Prince of Florence. Why not call them the Medicean planets? By the way, we may move to Florence. I've written to His Highness, asking if he can use me as Court Mathematician.

VIRGINIA: Oh, father, we'll be at the court!

SAGREDO (*amazed*): Galileo!

GALILEO: My dear Sagredo, I must have leisure. My only worry is that His Highness after all may not take me. I'm not accustomed to writing formal letters to great personages. Here, do you think this is the right sort of thing?

SAGREDO (*reads and quotes*): "Whose sole desire is to reside in Your Highness' presence—the rising sun of our great age." Cosmo de Medici is a boy of nine.

GALILEO: The only way a man like me can land a good job is by crawling on his stomach. Your father, my dear, is going to take his share of the pleasures of life in

---

**Giordano Bruno:** Bruno (1548–1600), one of the most distinguished Italian Renaissance thinkers, lectured in England, France, Germany, and other countries in Europe before being imprisoned for heresy by the Inquisition. After a period of confinement and a lengthy trial, he was burned at the stake. He believed, like Galileo, in the Copernican view of astronomy, which asserted that the earth rotated around the sun.

exchange for all his hard work, and about time too. I have no patience, Sagredo, with a man who doesn't use his brains to fill his belly. Run along to Mass now.

(VIRGINIA *goes.*)

SAGREDO: Galileo, do not go to Florence.

GALILEO: Why not?

SAGREDO: The monks are in power there.

GALILEO: Going to Mass is a small price to pay for a full belly. And there are many famous scholars at the court of Florence.

SAGREDO: Court monkeys.

GALILEO: I shall enjoy taking them by the scruff of the neck and making them look through the telescope.

SAGREDO: Galileo, you are traveling the road to disaster. You are suspicious and skeptical in science, but in politics you are as naive as your daughter! How can people in power leave a man at large who tells the truth, even if it be the truth about the distant stars? Can you see the Pope scribbling a note in his diary: "10th of January, 1610, Heaven abolished"? A moment ago, when you were at the telescope, I saw you tied to the stake, and when you said you believed in proof, I smelt burning flesh!

GALILEO: I am going to Florence.

*Before the next scene a curtain with the following legend on it is lowered:*

By setting the name of Medici in the sky, I am bestowing immortality upon the stars. I commend myself to you as your most faithful and devoted servant, whose sole desire is to reside in Your Highness' presence, the rising sun of our great age.

      —GALILEO GALILEI

# SCENE 4

(GALILEO's *house at Florence. Well-appointed.* GALILEO *is demonstrating his telescope to* PRINCE COSMO DE MEDICI, *a boy of nine, accompanied by his* LORD CHAMBERLAIN, LADIES *and* GENTLEMEN *of the Court, and an assortment of university* PROFESSORS. *With* GALILEO *are* ANDREA *and* FEDERZONI, *the new assistant (an old man).* MRS. SARTI *stands by. Before the scene opens the voice of the* PHILOSOPHER *can be heard.*)

VOICE OF THE PHILOSOPHER: Quaedam miracula universi. Orbes mystice canorae, arcus crystallini, circulatio corporum coelestium. Cyclorum epicyclorumque intoxicatio, integritas tabulae chordarum et architectura elata globorum coelestium.

GALILEO: Shall we speak in everyday language? My colleague Mr. Federzoni does not understand Latin.

PHILOSOPHER: Is it necessary that he should?

GALILEO: Yes.

PHILOSOPHER: Forgive me. I thought he was your mechanic.

ANDREA: Mr. Federzoni is a mechanic and a scholar.

PHILOSOPHER: Thank you, young man. If Mr. Federzoni insists . . .

GALILEO: I insist.

PHILOSOPHER: It will not be as clear, but it's your house. Your Highness . . . (*The* PRINCE *is ineffectually trying to establish contact with* ANDREA.) I was about to recall to Mr. Galilei some of the wonders of the universe as they are set down for us in the Divine Classics. (*The* LADIES *"ah."*) Remind him of the "mystically musical spheres, the crystal arches, the circulation of the heavenly bodies—"

ELDERLY LADY: Perfect poise!

PHILOSOPHER: "—the intoxication of the cycles and epicycles, the integrity of the tables of chords and the enraptured architecture of the celestial globes."

ELDERLY LADY: What diction!

PHILOSOPHER: May I pose the question: Why should we go out of our way to look for things that can only strike a discord in this ineffable harmony?

(*The* LADIES *applaud.*)

FEDERZONI: Take a look through here—you'll be interested.

ANDREA: Sit down here, please.

(*The* PROFESSORS *laugh.*)

MATHEMATICIAN: Mr. Galileo, nobody doubts that your brain child—or is it your adopted brain child?—is brilliantly contrived.

GALILEO: Your Highness, one can see the four stars as large as life, you know.

(*The* PRINCE *looks to the* ELDERLY LADY *for guidance.*)

MATHEMATICIAN: Ah. But has it occurred to you that an eyeglass through which one sees such phenomena might not be a too reliable eyeglass?

GALILEO: How is that?

MATHEMATICIAN: If one could be sure you would keep your temper, Mr. Galilei, I could suggest that what one sees in the eyeglass and what is in the heavens are two entirely different things.

GALILEO (*quietly*): You are suggesting fraud?

MATHEMATICIAN: No! How could I, in the presence of His Highness?

ELDERLY LADY: The gentlemen are just wondering if Your Highness' stars are really, really there!

(*Pause.*)

YOUNG LADY (*trying to be helpful*): Can one see the claws on the Great Bear?

GALILEO: And everything on Taurus the Bull.

FEDERZONI: Are you going to look through it or not?

MATHEMATICIAN: With the greatest of pleasure.

(*Pause. Nobody goes near the telescope. All of a sudden the boy* ANDREA *turns and marches pale and erect past them through the whole length of the room. The* GUESTS *follow with their eyes.*)

MRS. SARTI (*as he passes her*): What is the matter with you?

ANDREA (*shocked*): They are wicked.

PHILOSOPHER: Your Highness, it is a delicate matter and I had no intention of bringing it up, but Mr. Galilei was about to demonstrate the impossible. His new stars would have broken the outer crystal sphere—which we know of on the authority of Aristotle. I am sorry.

MATHEMATICIAN: The last word.

FEDERZONI: He had no telescope.

MATHEMATICIAN: Quite.

GALILEO (*keeping his temper*): "Truth is the daughter of Time, not of Authority." Gentlemen, the sum of our knowledge is pitiful. It has been my singular good fortune to find a new instrument which brings a small patch of the universe a little bit closer. It is at your disposal.

PHILOSOPHER: Where is all this leading?

GALILEO: Are we, as scholars, concerned with where the truth might lead us?

PHILOSOPHER: Mr. Galilei, the truth might lead us anywhere!

GALILEO: I can only beg you to look through my eyeglass.

MATHEMATICIAN (*wild*): If I understand Mr. Galilei correctly, he is asking us to discard the teachings of two thousand years.

GALILEO: For two thousand years we have been looking at the sky and didn't see the four moons of Jupiter, and there they were all the time. Why defend shaken teachings? You should be doing the shaking. (*The* PRINCE *is sleepy.*) Your Highness! My work in the Great Arsenal of Venice brought me in daily contact with sailors, carpenters, and so on. These men are unread. They depend on the evidence of their senses. But they taught me many new ways of doing things. The question is whether these gentlemen here want to be found out as fools by men who might not have had the advantages of a classical education but who are not afraid to use their eyes. I tell you that our dockyards are stirring with that same high curiosity which was the true glory of Ancient Greece.

(*Pause.*)

PHILOSOPHER: I have no doubt Mr. Galilei's theories will arouse the enthusiasm of the dockyards.

CHAMBERLAIN: Your Highness, I find to my amazement that this highly informative discussion has exceeded the time we had allowed for it. May I remind Your Highness that the State Ball begins in three-quarters of an hour?

(*The Court bows low.*)

ELDERLY LADY: We would really have liked to look through your eyeglass, Mr. Galilei, wouldn't we, Your Highness?

(*The PRINCE bows politely and is led to the door. GALILEO follows the PRINCE, CHAMBERLAIN, and LADIES towards the exit. The PROFESSORS remain at the telescope.*)

GALILEO (*almost servile*): All anybody has to do is look through the telescope, Your Highness.

(*MRS. SARTI takes a plate with candies to the PRINCE as he is walking out.*)

MRS. SARTI: A piece of homemade candy, Your Highness?

ELDERLY LADY: Not now. Thank you. It is too soon before His Highness' supper.

PHILOSOPHER: Wouldn't I like to take that thing to pieces.

MATHEMATICIAN: Ingenious contraption. It must be quite difficult to keep clean. (*He rubs the lens with his handkerchief and looks at the handkerchief*)

FEDERZONI: We did not paint the Medicean stars on the lens.

ELDERLY LADY (*to the PRINCE, who has whispered something to her*): No, no, no, there is nothing the matter with your stars!

CHAMBERLAIN (*across the stage to GALILEO*): His Highness will of course seek the opinion of the greatest living authority: Christopher Clavius, Chief Astronomer to the Papal College in Rome.

# SCENE 5

*Things take indeed a wondrous turn*
*When learned men do stoop to learn.*
*Clavius, we are pleased to say,*
*Upheld Galileo Galilei.*

(*A burst of laughter is heard and the curtains reveal a hall in the Collegium Romanum. HIGH CHURCHMEN, MONKS, and SCHOLARS standing about talking and laughing. GALILEO by himself in a corner.*)

FAT PRELATE (*shaking with laughter*): Hopeless! Hopeless! Hopeless! Will you tell me something people won't believe?

A SCHOLAR: Yes, that you don't love your stomach!

FAT PRELATE: They'd believe that. They only do not believe what's good for them. They doubt the devil, but fill them up with some fiddle-de-dee about the earth rolling like a marble in the gutter and they swallow it hook, line, and sinker. Sancta simplicitas!

(*He laughs until the tears run down his cheeks. The others laugh with him. A group has formed whose members boisterously begin to pretend they are standing on a rolling globe.*)

A MONK: It's rolling fast, I'm dizzy. May I hold on to you, Professor? (*He sways dizzily and clings to one of the scholars for support.*)

THE SCHOLAR: Old Mother Earth's been at the bottle again. Whoa!

MONK: Hey! Hey! We're slipping off! Help!

**SECOND SCHOLAR:** Look! There's Venus! Hold me, lads. Whee!

**SECOND MONK:** Don't, don't hurl us off on to the moon. There are nasty sharp mountain peaks on the moon, brethren!

**VARIOUSLY:** Hold tight! Hold tight! Don't look down! Hold tight! It'll make you giddy!

**FAT PRELATE:** And we cannot have giddy people in Holy Rome.

(*They rock with laughter. An* **INFURIATED MONK** *comes out from a large door at the rear holding a Bible in his hand and pointing out a page with his finger.*)

**INFURIATED MONK:** What does the Bible say—"Sun, stand thou still on Gideon and thou, moon, in the valley of Ajalon." Can the sun come to a standstill if it doesn't ever move? Does the Bible lie?

**FAT PRELATE:** How did Christopher Clavius, the greatest astronomer we have, get mixed up in an investigation of this kind?

**INFURIATED MONK:** He's in there with his eye glued to that diabolical instrument.

**FAT PRELATE** (*to* **GALILEO,** *who has been playing with his pebble and has dropped it*): Mr. Galilei, something dropped down.

**GALILEO:** Monsignor, are you sure it didn't drop up?

**INFURIATED MONK:** As astronomers we are aware that there are phenomena which are beyond us, but man can't expect to understand everything!

(*Enter a very old* **CARDINAL** *leaning on a* **MONK** *for support. Others move aside.*)

**OLD CARDINAL:** Aren't they out yet? Can't they reach a decision on that paltry matter? Christopher Clavius ought to know his astronomy after all these years. I am informed that Mr. Galilei transfers mankind from the center of the universe to somewhere on the outskirts. Mr. Galilei is therefore an enemy of mankind and

must be dealt with as such. Is it conceivable that God would trust this most precious fruit of His labor to a minor frolicking star? Would He have sent His Son to such a place? How can there be people with such twisted minds that they believe what they're told by the slave of a multiplication table?

**FAT PRELATE** (*quietly to* **CARDINAL**): The gentleman is over there.

**OLD CARDINAL:** So you are the man. You know my eyes are not what they were, but I can see you bear a striking resemblance to the man we burned. What was his name?

**MONK:** Your Eminence must avoid excitement the doctor said . . .

**OLD CARDINAL** (*disregarding him*): So you have degraded the earth despite the fact that you live by her and receive everything from her. I won't have it! I won't have it! I won't be a nobody on an inconsequential star briefly twirling hither and thither. I tread the earth, and the earth is firm beneath my feet, and there is no motion to the earth, and the earth is the center of all things, and I am the center of the earth, and the eye of the creator is upon me. About me revolve, affixed to their crystal shells, the lesser lights of the stars and the great light of the sun, created to give light upon me that God might see me—Man, God's greatest effort, the center of creation. "In the image of God created He him." Immortal . . . (*His strength fails him and he catches for the* **MONK** *for support.*)

**MONK:** You mustn't overtax your strength, Your Eminence.

(*At this moment the door at the rear opens and* **CHRISTOPHER CLAVIUS** *enters followed by his* **ASTRONOMERS.** *He strides hastily across the hall, looking neither to right nor left. As he goes by we hear him say—*)

CLAVIUS: He is right.

(*Deadly silence. All turn to* GALILEO.)

OLD CARDINAL: What is it? Have they reached a decision?

(*No one speaks.*)

MONK: It is time that Your Eminence went home.

(*The hall is emptying fast. One little* MONK *who had entered with* CLAVIUS *speaks to* GALILEO.)

LITTLE MONK: Mr. Galilei, I heard Father Clavius say: "Now it's for the theologians to set the heavens right again." You have won.

*Before the next scene a curtain with the following legend on it is lowered:*

> . . . As these new astronomical charts enable us to determine longitudes at sea and so make it possible to reach the new continents by the shortest routes, we would beseech Your Excellency to aid us in reaching Mr. Galilei, mathematician to the Court of Florence, who is now in Rome . . .
>
> —From a letter written by a member of the Genoa Chamber of Commerce and Navigation to the Papal Legation

# SCENE 6

*When Galileo was in Rome*
*A Cardinal asked him to his home*
*He wined and dined him as his guest*
*And only made one small request.*

(CARDINAL BELLARMIN's *house in Rome. Music is heard and the chatter of many guests.* TWO SECRETARIES *are at the rear of the stage at a desk.* GALILEO, *his daughter* VIRGINIA, *now twenty-one, and* LUDOVICO MARSILI, *who has become her fiancé, are just arriving. A few* GUESTS, *standing near the entrance with masks in their hands, nudge each other and are suddenly silent.* GALILEO *looks at them. They applaud him politely and bow.*)

VIRGINIA: O father! I'm so happy. I won't dance with anyone but you, Ludovico.

GALILEO (*to a* SECRETARY): I was to wait here for His Eminence.

FIRST SECRETARY: His Eminence will be with you in a few minutes.

VIRGINIA: Do I look proper?

LUDOVICO: You are showing some lace.

(GALILEO *puts his arms around their shoulders.*)

GALILEO (*quoting mischievously*): Fret not, daughter, if perchance
You attract a wanton glance.
The eyes that catch a trembling lace
Will guess the heartbeat's quickened pace.
Lovely woman still may be
Careless with felicity.

VIRGINIA (*to* GALILEO): Feel my heart.

GALILEO (*to* LUDOVICO): It's thumping.

VIRGINIA: I hope I always say the right thing.

LUDOVICO: She's afraid she's going to let us down.

VIRGINIA: Oh, I want to look beautiful.

GALILEO: You'd better. If you don't they'll start saying all over again that the earth doesn't turn.

LUDOVICO (*laughing*): It *doesn't* turn, sir.

(GALILEO *laughs.*)

GALILEO: Go and enjoy yourselves. (*He speaks to one of the* SECRETARIES.) A large fête?

FIRST SECRETARY: Two hundred and fifty guests, Mr. Galilei. We have represented here this evening most of the great families of Italy, the Orsinis, the Villanis, the Nuccolis, the Soldanieris, the Canes, the Lecchis, the Estensis, the Colombinis, the . . .

(VIRGINIA *comes running back.*)

VIRGINIA: Oh father, I didn't tell you: you're famous.

GALILEO: Why?

VIRGINIA: The hairdresser in the Via Vittorio kept four other ladies waiting and took me first. (*Exit.*)

GALILEO (*at the stairway, leaning over the well*): Rome!

(*Enter* CARDINAL BELLARMIN, *wearing the mask of a lamb, and* CARDINAL BARBERINI, *wearing the mask of a dove.*)

SECRETARIES: Their Eminences, Cardinals Bellarmin and Barberini.

(*The* CARDINALS *lower their masks.*)

GALILEO (*to* BELLARMIN): Your Eminence.

BELLARMIN: Mr. Galilei, Cardinal Barberini.

GALILEO: Your Eminence.

BARBERINI: So you are the father of that lovely child!

BELLARMIN: Who is inordinately proud of being her father's daughter.

(*They laugh.*)

BARBERINI (*points his finger at* GALILEO): "The sun riseth and setteth and returneth to its place," saith the Bible. What saith Galilei?

GALILEO: Appearances are notoriously deceptive, Your Eminence. Once when I was so high, I was standing on a ship that was pulling away from the shore and I shouted, "The shore is moving!" I know now that it was the ship which was moving.

BARBERINI (*laughs*): You can't catch that man. I tell you, Bellarmin, his moons around Jupiter are hard nuts to crack. Unfortunately for me I happened to glance at a few papers on astronomy once. It is harder to get rid of than the itch.

BELLARMIN: Let's move with the times. If it makes navigation easier for sailors to use new charts based on a new hypothesis let them have them. We only have to scotch doctrines that contradict Holy Writ.

(*He leans over the balustrade of the well and acknowledges various* GUESTS.)

BARBERINI: But Bellarmin, you haven't caught on to this fellow. The scriptures don't satisfy him. Copernicus does.

GALILEO: Copernicus? "He that withholdeth corn the people shall curse him." Book of Proverbs.

BARBERINI: "A prudent man concealeth knowledge." Also Book of Proverbs.

GALILEO: "Where no oxen are, the stable is clean, but much increase is by the strength of the ox."

BARBERINI: "He that ruleth his spirit is better than he that taketh a city."

GALILEO: "But a broken spirit drieth up the bones." (*Pause.*) "Doth not wisdom cry?"

BARBERINI: "Can one walk on hot coals and his feet not be scorched?"—Welcome to Rome, Friend Galileo. You recall the legend of our city's origin? Two small boys found sustenance and refuge with a she-wolf and from that day we have paid the price for the she-wolf's milk. But the place is not bad. We have everything for your pleasure—from a scholarly dispute with Bellarmin to ladies of high degree. Look at that woman flaunting herself. No? He wants a weighty discussion! All right! (*To* GALILEO.) You people speak in terms of circles and ellipses and regular velocities—simple movements that the human mind can grasp—very convenient—but suppose Almighty God had taken it into his head to make the stars move like that . . . (*he describes an irregular motion with his fingers through the air*) . . . then where would you be?

GALILEO: My good man—the Almighty would have endowed us with brains like that . . . (*repeats the movement*) . . . so that we could grasp the movements . . . (*repeats the movement*) . . . like that. I believe in the brain.

BARBERINI: I consider the brain inadequate. He doesn't answer. He is too polite to tell me he considers *my* brain inadequate. What is one to do with him? Butter wouldn't melt in his mouth. All he wants to do is to prove that God made a few boners in astronomy. God didn't study his astronomy hard enough before he composed Holy Writ. (*To the* SECRETARIES.) Don't take anything down. This is a scientific discussion among friends.

BELLARMIN (*to* GALILEO): Does it not appear more probable—even to you—that the Creator knows more about his work than the created?

GALILEO: In his blindness man is liable to misread not only the sky but also the Bible.

BELLARMIN: The interpretation of the Bible is a matter for the ministers of God. (GALILEO *remains silent.*) At last you are quiet. (*He gestures to the* SECRETARIES. *They start writing.*) Tonight the Holy Office has decided that the theory according to which the earth goes around the sun is foolish, absurd, and a heresy. I am charged, Mr. Galilei, with cautioning you to abandon these teachings. (*To the* FIRST SECRETARY.) Would you repeat that?

FIRST SECRETARY (*reading*): "His Eminence, Cardinal Bellarmin, to the aforesaid Galilei: The Holy Office has resolved that the theory according to which the earth goes around the sun is foolish, absurd, and a heresy. I am charged, Mr. Galilei, with cautioning you to abandon these teachings."

GALILEO (*rocking on his base*): But the facts!

BARBERINI (*consoling*): Your findings have been ratified by the Papal Observatory, Galilei. That should be most flattering to you . . .

BELLARMIN (*cutting in*): The Holy Office formulated the decree without going into details.

GALILEO (*to* BARBERINI): Do you realize, the future of all scientific research is . . .

BELLARMIN (*cutting in*): Completely assured, Mr. Galilei. It is not given to man to know the truth: it is granted to him to seek after the truth. Science is the legitimate and beloved daughter of the Church. She must have confidence in the Church.

GALILEO (*infuriated*): I would not try confidence by whistling her too often.

BARBERINI (*quickly*): Be careful what you're doing—you'll be throwing out the baby with the bath water, friend Galilei. (*Serious.*) We need you more than you need us.

BELLARMIN: Well, it is time we introduced our distinguished friend to our guests. The whole country talks of him!

BARBERINI: Let us replace our masks, Bellarmin. Poor Galilei hasn't got one.

(*He laughs. They take* GALILEO *out.*)

FIRST SECRETARY: Did you get his last sentence?

SECOND SECRETARY: Yes. Do you have what he said about believing in the brain?

(*Another cardinal—the* INQUISITOR—*enters.*)

INQUISITOR: Did the conference take place?

(*The* FIRST SECRETARY *hands him the papers and the* INQUISITOR *dismisses the* SECRETARIES. *They go. The* INQUISITOR *sits down and starts to read the transcription. Two or three* YOUNG LADIES *skitter across the stage; they see the* INQUISITOR *and curtsy as they go.*)

YOUNG GIRL: Who was that?

HER FRIEND: The Cardinal Inquisitor.

(*They giggle and go. Enter* VIRGINIA. *She curtsies as she goes. The* INQUISITOR *stops her.*)

INQUISITOR: Good evening, my child. Beautiful night. May I congratulate you on your betrothal? Your young man comes from a fine family. Are you staying with us here in Rome?

VIRGINIA: Not now, Your Eminence. I must go home to prepare for the wedding.

INQUISITOR: Ah. You are accompanying your father to Florence. That should please him. Science must be cold comfort in a home. Your youth and warmth will keep him down to earth. It is easy to get lost up there. (*He gestures to the sky.*)

VIRGINIA: He doesn't talk to me about the stars, Your Eminence.

INQUISITOR: No. (*He laughs.*) They don't eat fish in the fisherman's house. I can tell you something about astronomy. My child, it seems that God has blessed our modern astronomers with imaginations. It is quite alarming! Do you know that the earth—which we old fogies supposed to be so large—has shrunk to something no bigger than a walnut, and the new universe has grown so vast that prelates—and even cardinals—look like ants. Why, God Almighty might lose sight of a Pope! I wonder if I know your Father Confessor.

VIRGINIA: Father Christopherus, from Saint Ursula's at Florence, Your Eminence.

INQUISITOR: My dear child, your father will need you. Not so much now perhaps, but one of these days. You are pure, and there is strength in purity. Greatness is sometimes, indeed often, too heavy a burden for those to whom God has granted it. What man is so great that he has no place in a prayer? But I am keeping you, my dear. Your fiancé will be jealous of me, and I am afraid your father will never forgive me for holding forth on astronomy. Go to your dancing and remember me to Father Christopherus.

(VIRGINIA *kisses his ring and runs off. The* INQUISITOR *resumes his reading.*)

# SCENE 7

*Galileo, feeling grim,*
*A young monk came to visit him.*
*The monk was born of common folk.*
*It was of science that they spoke.*

(*Garden of the Florentine Ambassador in Rome. Distant hum of a great city.* GALILEO *and the* LITTLE MONK *of scene 5 are talking.*)

GALILEO: Let's hear it. That robe you're wearing gives you the right to say whatever you want to say. Let's hear it.

LITTLE MONK: I have studied physics, Mr. Galilei.

GALILEO: That might help us if it enabled you to admit that two and two are four.

LITTLE MONK: Mr. Galilei, I have spent four sleepless nights trying to reconcile the decree that I have read with the moons of Jupiter that I have seen. This morning I decided to come to see you after I had said Mass.

GALILEO: To tell me that Jupiter has no moons?

LITTLE MONK: No, I found out that I think the decree a wise decree. It has shocked me into realizing that free research has its dangers. I have had to decide to give up astronomy. However, I felt the impulse to confide in you some of the motives which have impelled even a passionate physicist to abandon his work.

GALILEO: Your motives are familiar to me.

LITTLE MONK: You mean, of course, the special powers invested in certain commissions of the Holy Office? But there is something else. I would like to talk to you about my family. I do not come from the great city. My parents are peasants in the Campagna, who know about the cultivation of the olive tree, and not much about anything else. Too often these days when I am trying to concentrate on tracking down the moons of Jupiter, I see my parents. I see them sitting by the fire with my sister, eating their curded cheese. I see the beams of the ceiling above them, which the smoke of centuries has blackened, and I can see the veins stand out on their toil-worn hands, and the little spoons in their hands. They scrape a living, and underlying their poverty there is a sort of order. There are routines. The routine of scrubbing the floors, the routine of the seasons in the olive orchard, the routine of paying taxes. The troubles that come to them are recurrent troubles. My father did not get his poor bent back all at once, but little by little, year by year, in the olive orchard; just as year after year, with unfailing regularity, childbirth has made my mother more and more sexless. They draw the strength they need to sweat with their loaded baskets up the stony paths, to bear children, even to eat, from the sight of the trees greening each year anew, from the reproachful face of the soil, which is never satisfied, and from the little church and Bible texts they hear there on Sunday. They have been told that God relies upon them and that the pageant of the world has been written around them that they may be tested in the important or unimportant parts handed out to them. How could they take it, were I to tell them that they are on a lump of stone ceaselessly spinning in empty space, circling around a second-rate star? What, then, would be the use of their patience, their acceptance of misery? What comfort, then, the Holy Scriptures, which have mercifully explained their crucifixion? The Holy Scriptures would then be proved full of mistakes. No, I see them begin to look frightened. I see them slowly put their spoons down on the table. They would feel cheated. "There is no eye watching over us, after all," they would say. "We have to start out on our own, at our time of life. Nobody has planned a part for us beyond this wretched one on a worthless star. There is no meaning in our misery. Hunger is just not having eaten. It is no test of strength. Effort is just stooping and carrying. It is not a virtue." Can you understand that I read into the decree of the Holy Office a noble motherly pity and a great goodness of the soul?

GALILEO (*embarrassed*): Hm, well at least you have found out that it is not a question of the satellites of Jupiter, but of the peasants of the Campagna! And don't try to break me down by the halo of beauty that radiates from old age. How does a pearl develop in an oyster? A jagged grain of sand makes its way into the oyster's shell and makes its life unbearable. The oyster exudes slime to cover the grain of sand and the slime eventually hardens into a pearl. The oyster nearly dies in the process. To hell with the pearl, give me the healthy oyster! And virtues are not exclusive to misery. If your parents were prosperous and happy, they might develop the virtues of happiness and prosperity. Today the virtues of exhaustion are caused by the exhausted land. For that my new water pumps could work more wonders than their ridiculous superhuman efforts. Be fruitful and multiply: for war will cut down the population, and our fields are barren! (*A pause.*) Shall I lie to your people?

LITTLE MONK: We must be silent from the highest of motives: the inward peace of less fortunate souls.

GALILEO: My dear man, as a bonus for not meddling with your parents' peace, the authorities are tendering me, on a silver platter, persecution-free, my share of the fat sweated from your parents, who, as you know, were made in God's image. Should I condone this decree, my motives might not be disinterested: easy life, no persecution, and so on.

**LITTLE MONK:** Mr. Galilei, I am a priest.

**GALILEO:** You are also a physicist. How can new machinery be evolved to domesticate the river water if we physicists are forbidden to study, discuss, and pool our findings about the greatest machinery of all, the machinery of the heavenly bodies? Can I reconcile my findings on the paths of falling bodies with the current belief in the tracks of witches on broom sticks? (*A pause.*) I am sorry—I shouldn't have said that.

**LITTLE MONK:** You don't think that the truth, if it is the truth, would make its way without us?

**GALILEO:** No! No! No! As much of the truth gets through as we push through. You talk about the Campagna peasants as if they were the moss on their huts. Naturally, if they don't get a move on and learn to think for themselves, the most efficient of irrigation systems cannot help them. I can see their divine patience, but where is their divine fury?

**LITTLE MONK** (*helpless*): They are old!

(**GALILEO** *stands for a moment, beaten; he cannot meet the* **LITTLE MONK**'s *eyes. He takes a manuscript from the table and throws it violently on the ground.*)

**LITTLE MONK:** What is that?

**GALILEO:** Here is writ what draws the ocean when it ebbs and flows. Let it lie there. Thou shalt not read. (**LITTLE MONK** *has picked up the manuscript.*) Already! An apple of the tree of knowledge, he can't wait, he wolfs it down. He will rot in hell for all eternity. Look at him, where are his manners?—Sometimes I think I would let them imprison me in a place a thousand feet beneath the earth where no light could reach me, if in exchange I could find out what stuff that is: "Light."

The bad thing is that, when I find something, I have to boast about it like a lover or a drunkard or a traitor. That is a hopeless vice and leads to the abyss. I wonder how long I shall be content to discuss it with my dog!

**LITTLE MONK** (*immersed in the manuscript*): I don't understand this sentence.

**GALILEO:** I'll explain it to you, I'll explain it to you.

(*They are sitting on the floor.*)

# SCENE 8

*Eight long years with tongue in cheek*
*Of what he knew he did not speak.*
*Then temptation grew 'too great*
*And Galileo challenged fate.*

(**GALILEO's** *house in Florence again. Galileo is supervising his Assistants* **ANDREA, FEDERZONI,** *and the* **LITTLE MONK** *who are about to prepare an experiment.* **MRS. SARTI** *and* **VIRGINIA** *are at a long table sewing bridal linen. There is a new telescope, larger than the old one. At the moment it is covered with a cloth.*)

**ANDREA** (*looking up a schedule*): Thursday. Afternoon. Floating bodies again. Ice, bowl of water, scales, and it says here an iron needle. Aristotle.

**VIRGINIA:** Ludovico likes to entertain. We must take care to be neat. His mother notices every stitch. She doesn't approve of father's books.

**MRS. SARTI:** That's all a thing of the past. He hasn't published a book for years.

**VIRGINIA:** That's true. Oh Sarti, it's fun sewing a trousseau.

**MRS. SARTI:** Virginia, I want to talk to you. You are very young, and you have no mother, and your father is putting those pieces of ice in water, and marriage is too serious a business to go into blind. Now you should go to see a real astronomer from the university and have him cast your horoscope so you know where you stand. (VIRGINIA *giggles*.) What's the matter?

VIRGINIA: I've been already.

MRS. SARTI: Tell Sarti.

VIRGINIA: I have to be careful for three months now because the sun is in Capricorn, but after that I get a favorable ascendant, and I can undertake a journey if I am careful of Uranus, as I'm a Scorpion.

MRS. SARTI: What about Ludovico?

VIRGINIA: He's a Leo, the astronomer said. Leos are sensual. (*Giggles*.)

(*There is a knock at the door, it opens. Enter the* RECTOR *of the University, the philosopher of scene 4, bringing a book*.)

RECTOR (*to* VIRGINIA): This is about the burning issue of the moment. He may want to glance over it. My faculty would appreciate his comments. No, don't disturb him now, my dear. Every minute one takes of your father's time is stolen from Italy. (*He goes*.)

VIRGINIA: Federzoni! The rector of the university brought this.

(FEDERZONI *takes it*.)

GALILEO: What's it about?

FEDERZONI (*spelling*): DE MACULIS IN SOLE.

ANDREA: Oh, it's on the sun spots!

(ANDREA *comes one side, and the* LITTLE MONK *the other, to look at the book*.)

ANDREA: A new one!

(FEDERZONI *resentfully puts the book into their hands and continues with the preparation of the experiment*.)

ANDREA: Listen to this dedication. (*Quotes*.) "To the greatest living authority on physics, Galileo Galilei."—I read Fabricius' paper the other day. Fabricius says the spots are clusters of planets between us and the sun.

LITTLE MONK: Doubtful.

GALILEO (*noncommittal*): Yes?

ANDREA: Paris and Prague hold that they are vapors from the sun. Federzoni doubts that.

FEDERZONI: Me? You leave me out. I said "hm," that was all. And don't discuss new things before me. I can't read the material, it's in Latin. (*He drops the scales and stands trembling with fury*.) Tell me, can I doubt anything?

(GALILEO *walks over and picks up the scales silently. Pause*.)

LITTLE MONK: There is happiness in doubting, I wonder why.

ANDREA: Aren't we going to take this up?

GALILEO: At the moment we are investigating floating bodies.

ANDREA: Mother has baskets full of letters from all over Europe asking his opinion.

FEDERZONI: The question is whether you can afford to remain silent.

GALILEO: I cannot afford to be smoked on a wood fire like a ham.

ANDREA (*surprised*): Ah. You think the sun spots may have something to do with that again? (GALILEO *does not answer*.)

ANDREA: Well, we stick to fiddling about with bits of ice in water. That can't hurt you.

GALILEO: Correct.—Our thesis!

ANDREA: All things that are lighter than water float, and all things that are heavier sink.

GALILEO: Aristotle says—

LITTLE MONK (*reading out of a book, translating*): "A broad and flat disk of ice, although heavier than water, still floats, because it is unable to divide the water."

GALILEO: Well. Now I push the ice below the surface. I take away the pressure of my hands. What happens?

(*Pause*.)

LITTLE MONK: It rises to the surface.

GALILEO: Correct. It seems to be able to divide the water as it's coming up, doesn't it?

LITTLE MONK: Could it be lighter than water after all?

GALILEO: Aha!

ANDREA: Then all things that are lighter than water float, and all things that are heavier sink. Q.e.d.°

GALILEO: Not at all. Hand me that iron needle. Heavier than water? (*They all nod.*) A piece of paper.
(*He places the needle on a piece of paper and floats it on the surface of the water. Pause.*) Do not be hasty with your conclusion. (*Pause.*) What happens?

FEDERZONI: The paper has sunk, the needle is floating.

VIRGINIA: What's the matter?

MRS. SARTI: Every time I hear them laugh it sends shivers down my spine.

(*There is a knocking at the outer door.*)

MRS. SARTI: Who's that at the door?

(*Enter LUDOVICO. VIRGINIA runs to him. They embrace.* LUDOVICO *is followed by a* SERVANT *with baggage.*)

MRS. SARTI: Well!

VIRGINIA: Oh! Why didn't you write that you were coming?

LUDOVICO: I decided on the spur of the moment. I was over inspecting our vineyards at Bucciole. I couldn't keep away.

GALILEO: Who's that?

LITTLE MONK: Miss Virginia's intended. What's the matter with your eyes?

---

**Q.e.d.:** In Latin, *quod erat demonstrandum,* "which was to be demonstrated," the usual ending on a logical examination using Aristotelian logic. The point is that it is not demonstrated; the experiment with the needle and the paper demonstrates the power of surface tension, which contradicts Andrea's earlier statement. Experimentation, in other words, is the final arbiter of what is true, not rules such as Andrea establishes.

GALILEO (*blinking*): Oh yes, it's Ludovico, so it is. Well! Sarti, get a jug of that Sicilian wine, the old kind. We celebrate.

(*Everybody sits down.* MRS. SARTI *has left, followed by Ludovico's* SERVANT.)

GALILEO: Well, Ludovico, old man. How are the horses?

LUDOVICO: The horses are fine.

GALILEO: Fine.

LUDOVICO: But those vineyards need a firm hand. (*To* VIRGINIA.) You look pale. Country life will suit you. Mother's planning on September.

VIRGINIA: I suppose I oughtn't, but stay here, I've got something to show you.

LUDOVICO: What?

VIRGINIA: Never mind. I won't be ten minutes. (*She runs out.*)

LUDOVICO: How's life these days, sir?

GALILEO: Dull.—How was the journey?

LUDOVICO: Dull.—Before I forget, mother sends her congratulations on your admirable tact over the latest rumblings of science.

GALILEO: Thank her from me.

LUDOVICO: Christopher Clavius had all Rome on its ears. He said he was afraid that the turning-around-business might crop up again on account of these spots on the sun.

ANDREA: Clavius is on the same track! (*To* LUDOVICO.) My mother's baskets are full of letters from all over Europe asking Mr. Galilei's opinion.

GALILEO: I am engaged in investigating the habits of floating bodies. Any harm in that?

(MRS. SARTI *reenters, followed by the* SERVANT. *They bring wine and glasses on a tray.*)

GALILEO (*hands out the wine*): What news from the Holy City, apart from the prospect of my sins?

LUDOVICO: The Holy Father is on his death bed. Hadn't you heard?

**LITTLE MONK:** My goodness! What about the succession?

**LUDOVICO:** All the talk is of Barberini.

**GALILEO:** Barberini?

**ANDREA:** Mr. Galilei knows Barberini.

**LITTLE MONK:** Cardinal Barberini is a mathematician.

**FEDERZONI:** A scientist in the chair of Peter!

(*Pause.*)

**GALILEO** (*cheering up enormously*): This means change. We might live to see the day, Federzoni, when we don't have to whisper that two and two are four. (*To* **LUDOVICO.**) I like this wine. Don't you, Ludovico?

**LUDOVICO:** I like it.

**GALILEO:** I know the hill where it is grown. The slope is steep and stony, the grape almost blue. I am fond of this wine.

**LUDOVICO:** Yes, sir.

**GALILEO:** There are shadows in this wine. It is almost sweet but just stops short.— Andrea, clear that stuff away, ice, bowl and needle.—I cherish the consolations of the flesh. I have no patience with cowards who call them weaknesses. I say there is a certain achievement in enjoying things.

(*The* **PUPILS** *get up and go to the experiment table.*)

**LITTLE MONK:** What are we to do?

**FEDERZONI:** He is starting on the sun.

(*They begin with clearing up.*)

**ANDREA** (*singing in a low voice*): The Bible proves the earth stands still,
The Pope, he swears with tears:
The earth stands still. To prove it so
He takes it by the ears.

**LUDOVICO:** What's the excitement?

**MRS. SARTI:** You're not going to start those hellish goings-on again, Mr. Galilei?

**ANDREA:** And gentlefolk, they say so too.
Each learned doctor proves,

(If you grease his palm): The earth stands still.
And yet—and yet it moves.

**GALILEO:** Barberini is in the ascendant, so your mother is uneasy, and you're sent to investigate me. Correct me if I am wrong, Ludovico. Clavius is right: These spots on the sun interest me.

**ANDREA:** We might find out that the sun also revolves. How would you like that, Ludovico?

**GALILEO:** Do you like my wine, Ludovico?

**LUDOVICO:** I told you I did, sir.

**GALILEO:** You really like it?

**LUDOVICO:** I like it.

**GALILEO:** Tell me, Ludovico, would you consider going so far as to accept a man's wine or his daughter without insisting that he drop his profession? I have no wish to intrude, but have the moons of Jupiter affected Virginia's bottom?

**MRS. SARTI:** That isn't funny, it's just vulgar. I am going for Virginia.

**LUDOVICO** (*keeps her back*): Marriages in families such as mine are not arranged on a basis of sexual attraction alone.

**GALILEO:** Did they keep you back from marrying my daughter for eight years because I was on probation?

**LUDOVICO:** My future wife must take her place in the family pew.

**GALILEO:** You mean, if the daughter of a bad man sat in your family pew, your peasants might stop paying the rent?

**LUDOVICO:** In a sort of way.

**GALILEO:** When I was your age, the only person I allowed to rap me on the knuckles was my girl.

**LUDOVICO:** My mother was assured that you had undertaken not to get mixed up in this turning-around-business again, sir.

**GALILEO:** We had a conservative Pope then.

**MRS. SARTI:** Had! His Holiness is not dead yet!

**GALILEO** (*with relish*): Pretty nearly.

MRS. SARTI: That man will weigh a chip of ice fifty times, but when it comes to something that's convenient, he believes it blindly. "Is His Holiness dead?"—"Pretty nearly!"

LUDOVICO: You will find, sir, if His Holiness passes away, the new Pope, whoever he turns out to be, will respect the convictions held by the solid families of the country.

GALILEO (*to* ANDREA): That remains to be seen.—Andrea, get out the screen. We'll throw the image of the sun on our screen to save our eyes.

LITTLE MONK: I thought you'd been working at it. Do you know when I guessed it? When you didn't recognize Mr. Marsili.

MRS. SARTI: If my son has to go to hell for sticking to you, that's my affair, but you have no right to trample on your daughter's happiness.

LUDOVICO (*to his* SERVANT): Giuseppe, take my baggage back to the coach, will you?

MRS. SARTI: This will kill her. (*She runs out, still clutching the jug.*)

LUDOVICO (*politely*): Mr. Galilei, if we Marsilis were to countenance teachings frowned on by the church, it would unsettle our peasants. Bear in mind: these poor people in their brute state get everything upside down. They are nothing but animals. They will never comprehend the finer points of astronomy. Why, two months ago a rumor went around, an apple had been found on a pear tree, and they left their work in the fields to discuss it.

GALILEO (*interested*): Did they?

LUDOVICO: I have seen the day when my poor mother has had to have a dog whipped before their eyes to remind them to keep their place. Oh, you may have seen the waving corn from the window of your comfortable coach. You have, no doubt, nibbled our olives, and absentmindedly eaten our cheese, but you can have no idea how much responsibility that sort of thing entails.

GALILEO: Young man, I do not eat my cheese absentmindedly. (*To* ANDREA.) Are we ready?

ANDREA: Yes, sir.

GALILEO (*leaves* LUDOVICO *and adjusts the mirror*): You would not confine your whippings to dogs to remind your peasants to keep their places, would you, Marsili?

LUDOVICO (*after a pause*): Mr. Galilei, you have a wonderful brain, it's a pity.

LITTLE MONK (*astonished*): He threatened you.

GALILEO: Yes. And he threatened you too. We might unsettle his peasants. Your sister, Fulganzio, who works the lever of the olive press, might laugh out loud if she heard the sun is not a gilded coat of arms but a lever too. The earth turns because the sun turns it.

ANDREA: That could interest his steward too and even his money lender—and the seaport towns . . .

FEDERZONI: None of them speak Latin.

GALILEO: I might write in plain language. The work we do is exacting. Who would go through the strain for less than the population at large!

LUDOVICO: I see you have made your decision. It was inevitable. You will always be a slave of your passions. Excuse me to Virginia, I think it's as well I don't see her now.

GALILEO: The dowry is at your disposal at any time.

LUDOVICO: Good afternoon. (*He goes followed by the* SERVANT.)

ANDREA: Exit Ludovico. To hell with all Marsilis, Villanis, Orsinis, Canes, Nuccolis, Soldanieris . . .

FEDERZONI: . . . who ordered the earth stand still because their castles might be shaken loose if it revolves . . .

LITTLE MONK: . . . and who only kiss the Pope's feet as long as he uses them to trample on the people. God made the physical world, God made the human brain. God will allow physics.

ANDREA: They will try to stop us.

GALILEO: Thus we enter the observation of these spots on the sun in which we are interested, at our own risk, not counting on protection from a problematical new Pope . . .

ANDREA: . . . but with great likelihood of dispelling Fabrizius' vapors, and the shadows of Paris and Prague, and of establishing the rotation of the sun . . .

GALILEO: . . . and with *some* likelihood of establishing the rotation of the sun. My intention is not to prove that I was right but to find out *whether* I was right. "Abandon hope all ye who enter—an observation." Before assuming these phenomena are spots, which would suit us, let us first set about proving that they are not—fried fish. We crawl by inches. What we find today we will wipe from the blackboard tomorrow and reject it— unless it shows up again the day after tomorrow. And if we find anything which would suit us, that thing we will eye with particular distrust. In fact, we will approach this observing of the sun with the implacable determination to prove that the earth stands still and only if hopelessly defeated in this pious undertaking can we allow ourselves to wonder if we may not have been right all the time: the earth revolves. Take the cloth off the telescope and turn it on the sun.

(*Quietly they start work. When the corruscating image of the sun is focused on the screen,* VIR-GINIA *enters hurriedly, her wedding dress on, her hair disheveled,* MRS. SARTI *with her, carrying her wedding veil. The two women realize what has happened.* VIRGINIA *faints.* ANDREA, LITTLE MONK, *and* GALILEO *rush to her.* FEDER-ZONI *continues working.*)

# SCENE 9

*On April Fool's Day, thirty two,*
*Of science there was much ado.*
*People had learned from Galilei:*
*They used his teaching in their way.*

(*Around the corner from the marketplace a* STREET SINGER *and his* WIFE, *who is costumed to represent the earth in a skeleton globe made of thin bands of brass, are holding the attention of a sprinkling of representative citizens, some in masquerade who were on their way to see the carnival procession. From the marketplace the noise of an impatient crowd.*)

BALLAD SINGER (*accompanied by his* WIFE *on the guitar*): When the Almighty made the universe
He made the earth and then he made the sun.
Then round the earth he bade the sun to turn—
That's in the Bible, Genesis, Chapter One.
And from that time all beings here below
Were in obedient circles meant to go:

Around the Pope the cardinals
Around the cardinals the bishops
Around the bishops the secretaries
Around the secretaries the aldermen
Around the aldermen the craftsmen
Around the craftsmen the servants
Around the servants the dogs, the chickens, and the beggars.

(*A conspicuous reveller—henceforth called the* SPINNER—*has slowly caught on and is exhibiting his idea of spinning around. He does not lose dignity, he faints with mock grace.*)

BALLAD SINGER: Up stood the learned Galileo
Glanced briefly at the sun
And said: "Almighty God was wrong
In Genesis, Chapter One!"

Now that was rash, my friends, it is no matter small
For heresy will spread today like foul diseases.

Change Holy Writ, forsooth? What will be left at all?

Why: each of us would say and do just what he pleases!

(*Three wretched* EXTRAS, *employed by the chamber of commerce, enter. Two of them, in ragged costumes, moodily bear a litter with a mock throne. The third sits on the throne. He wears sacking, a false beard, a prop crown, he carries a prop orb and sceptre, and around his chest the inscription* "THE KING OF HUNGARY." *The litter has a card with* "No. 4" *written on it. The litter bearers dump him down and listen to the* BALLAD SINGER.)

BALLAD SINGER: Good people, what will come to pass
If Galileo's teachings spread?
No altar boy will serve the Mass
No servant girl will make the bed.

Now that is grave, my friends, it is no matter small:
For independent spirit spreads like foul diseases!
(Yet life is sweet and man is weak and after all—
How nice it is, for a little change, to do just as one pleases!)

(*The* BALLAD SINGER *takes over the guitar. His* WIFE *dances around him, illustrating the motion of the earth. A* COBBLER'S BOY *with a pair of resplendent lacquered boots hung over his shoulder has been jumping up and down in mock excitement. There are three more children, dressed as grownups among the spectators, two together and a single one with mother. The* COBBLER'S BOY *takes the three* CHILDREN *in hand, forms a chain, and leads it, moving to the music, in and out among the spectators, "whipping" the chain so that the last child bumps into people. On the way past a* PEASANT WOMAN, *he steals an egg from her basket. She gestures to him to return it. As he passes her again he quietly breaks the egg over her head. The* KING OF HUNGARY *ceremoniously hands his orb to one of his bearers, marches*

*down with mock dignity, and chastises the* COBBLER'S BOY. *The parents remove the three* CHILDREN. *The unseemliness subsides.*)

BALLAD SINGER: The carpenters take wood and build
Their houses—not the church's pews.
And members of the cobblers' guild
Now boldly walk the streets—in shoes.
The tenant kicks the noble lord
Quite off the land he owned—like that!
The milk his wife once gave the priest
Now makes (at last!) her children fat.

Ts, ts, ts, ts, my friends, this is no matter small
For independent spirit spreads like foul diseases
People must keep their place, some down and some on top!
(Though it is nice, for a little change, to do just as one pleases!)

(*The* COBBLER'S BOY *has put on the lacquered boots he was carrying. He struts off. The* BALLAD SINGER *takes over the guitar again. His* WIFE *dances around him in increased tempo. A* MONK *has been standing near a rich* COUPLE, *who are in subdued costly clothes, without masks: shocked at the song, he now leaves. A* DWARF *in the costume of an astronomer turns his telescope on the departing* MONK, *thus drawing attention to the rich* COUPLE. *In imitation of the* COBBLER'S BOY, *the* SPINNER *forms a chain of grownups. They move to the music, in and out, and between the rich* COUPLE. *The* SPINNER *changes the* GENTLEMAN'S *bonnet for the ragged hat of a* BEGGAR. *The* GENTLEMAN *decides to take this in good part, and a* GIRL *is emboldened to take his dagger. The* GENTLEMAN *is miffed, throws the* BEGGAR'S *hat back. The* BEGGAR *discards the* GENTLEMAN'S *bonnet and drops it on the ground. The* KING OF HUNGARY *has walked from his throne, taken an egg from the* PEASANT WOMAN, *and paid for it. He now ceremoniously breaks it over the* GENTLEMAN'S *head as he is bending down to pick up his bonnet. The* GENTLEMAN *conducts the* LADY *away from the scene. The* KING OF HUNGARY, *about to resume his throne, finds one of the* CHILDREN *sitting on it. The* GENTLEMAN *returns to retrieve his dagger. Merriment. The* BALLAD SINGER *wanders off. This is part of his routine. His* WIFE *sings to the* SPINNER.)

WIFE:  Now speaking for myself I feel
    That I could also do with a change.
    You know, for me . . . (*Turning to a reveller*)
    . . . *you* have appeal
    Maybe tonight we could arrange . . .

(*The* DWARF-ASTRONOMER *has been amusing the people by focusing his telescope on her legs. The* BALLAD SINGER *has returned.*)

BALLAD SINGER:  No, no, no, no, no, stop,
    Galileo, stop!
    For independent spirit spreads like foul
    diseases
    People must keep their place, some
    down and some on top!
    (Though it is nice, for a little change, to
    do just as one pleases!)

(*The* SPECTATORS *stand embarrassed. A* GIRL *laughs loudly.*)

BALLAD SINGER AND HIS WIFE:  Good people
    who have trouble here below
    in serving cruel lords and gentle Jesus
    Who bids you turn the other cheek just
    so . . . (*With mimicry.*)
    While they prepare to strike the second
    blow:
    Obedience will never cure your woe
    So each of you wake up and do just as he
    pleases!

(*The* BALLAD SINGER *and his* WIFE *hurriedly start to try to sell pamphlets to the spectators.*)

BALLAD SINGER:  Read all about the earth go-
    ing round the sun, two centesemi only.
    As proved by the great Galileo. Two cen-
    tesemi only. Written by a local scholar.
    Understandable to one and all. Buy one
    for your friends, your children and your

aunty Rosa, two centesimi only. Abbreviated but complete. Fully illustrated
with pictures of the planets, including
Venus, two centesimi only.

(*During the speech of the* BALLAD SINGER *we hear the carnival procession approaching followed by laughter. A* REVELLER *rushes in.*)

REVELLER:  The procession!

(*The litter bearers speedily joggle out the* KING OF HUNGARY. *The* SPECTATORS *turn and look at the first float of the procession, which now makes its appearance. It bears a gigantic figure of* GALILEO, *holding in one hand an open Bible with the pages crossed out. The other hand points to the Bible, and the head mechanically turns from side to side as if to say "No! No!"*)

A LOUD VOICE:  Galileo, the Bible killer!

(*The laughter from the marketplace becomes uproarious. The* MONK *comes flying from the marketplace followed by delighted* CHILDREN.)

# SCENE 10

*The depths are hot, the heights are chill
The streets are loud, the court is still.*

(*Antechamber and staircase in the Medicean palace in Florence.* GALILEO, *with a book under his arm, waits with his* DAUGHTER *to be admitted to the presence of the* PRINCE.)

VIRGINIA:  They are a long time.
GALILEO:  Yes.
VIRGINIA:  Who is that funny-looking man?
    (*She indicates the* INFORMER *who has entered casually and seated himself in the background, taking no apparent notice of* GALILEO.)
GALILEO:  I don't know.
VIRGINIA:  It's not the first time I have seen
    him around. He gives me the creeps.
GALILEO:  Nonsense. We're in Florence, not
    among robbers in the mountains of Cor-
    sica.
VIRGINIA:  Here comes the Rector.

(*The* RECTOR *comes down the stairs.*)

GALILEO: Gaffone is a bore. He attaches himself to you.

(*The* RECTOR *passes, scarcely nodding.*)

GALILEO: My eyes are bad today. Did he acknowledge us?

VIRGINIA: Barely. (*Pause.*) What's in your book? Will they say it's heretical?

GALILEO: You hang around church too much. And getting up at dawn and scurrying to Mass is ruining your skin. You pray for me, don't you?

(*A* MAN *comes down the stairs.*)

VIRGINIA: Here's Mr. Matti. You designed a machine for his iron foundries.

MATTI: How were the squabs, Mr. Galilei? (*Low.*) My brother and I had a good laugh the other day. He picked up a racy pamphlet against the Bible somewhere. It quoted you.

GALILEO: The squabs, Matti, were wonderful, thank you again. Pamphlets I know nothing about. The Bible and Homer are my favorite reading.

MATTI: No necessity to be cautious with me, Mr. Galilei. I am on your side. I am not a man who knows about the motions of the stars, but you have championed the freedom to teach new things. Take that mechanical cultivator they have in Germany which you described to me. I can tell you, it will never be used in this country. The same circles that are hampering you now will forbid the physicians at Bologna to cut up corpses for research. Do you know, they have such things as money markets in Amsterdam and in London? Schools for business, too. Regular papers with news. Here we are not even free to make money. I have a stake in your career. They are against iron foundries because they say the gathering of so many workers in one place fosters immorality! If they ever try anything, Mr. Galilei, remember you have friends in all walks of life including an iron founder. Good luck to you. (*He goes.*)

GALILEO: Good man, but need he be so affectionate in public? His voice carries. They will always claim me as their spiritual leader particularly in places where it doesn't help me at all. I have written a book about the mechanics of the firmament, that is all. What they do or don't do with it is not my concern.

VIRGINIA (*loud*): If people only knew how you disagreed with those goings-on all over the country last All Fools day.

GALILEO: Yes. Offer honey to a bear, and lose your arm if the beast is hungry.

VIRGINIA (*low*): Did the prince ask you to come here today?

GALILEO: I sent word I was coming. He will want the book, he has paid for it. My health hasn't been any too good lately. I may accept Sagredo's invitation to stay with him in Padua for a few weeks.

VIRGINIA: You couldn't manage without your books.

GALILEO: Sagredo has an excellent library.

VIRGINIA: We haven't had this month's salary yet—

GALILEO: Yes. (*The* CARDINAL INQUISITOR *passes down the staircase. He bows deeply in answer to* GALILEO's *bow.*) What is he doing in Florence? If they try to do anything to me, the new Pope will meet them with an iron NO. And the Prince is my pupil, he would never have me extradited.

VIRGINIA: Psst. The Lord Chamberlain.

(*The* LORD CHAMBERLAIN *comes down the stairs.*)

LORD CHAMBERLAIN: His Highness had hoped to find time for you, Mr. Galilei. Unfortunately, he has to leave immediately to judge the parade at the Riding Academy. On what business did you wish to see His Highness?

GALILEO: I wanted to present my book to His Highness.

LORD CHAMBERLAIN: How are your eyes today?

GALILEO: So, so. With His Highness' permission, I am dedicating the book . . .

LORD CHAMBERLAIN: Your eyes are a matter of great concern to His Highness. Could it be that you have been looking too long and too often through your marvelous tube? (*He leaves without accepting the book.*)

VIRGINIA (*greatly agitated*): Father, I am afraid.

GALILEO: He didn't take the book, did he? (*Low and resolute.*) Keep a straight face. We are not going home, but to the house of the lens-grinder. There is a coach and horses in his backyard. Keep your eyes to the front, don't look back at that man.

(*They start. The* LORD CHAMBERLAIN *comes back.*)

LORD CHAMBERLAIN: Oh, Mr. Galilei! His Highness has just charged me to inform you that the Florentine Court is no longer in a position to oppose the request of the Holy Inquisition to interrogate you in Rome.

# SCENE 11

*The Pope*

(*A chamber in the Vatican. The Pope, Urban VIII—formerly* CARDINAL BARBERINI—*is giving audience to the* CARDINAL INQUISITOR. *The trampling and shuffling of many feet is heard throughout the scene from the adjoining corridors. During the scene the Pope is being robed for the conclave he is about to attend: at the beginning of the scene he is plainly* BARBERINI, *but as the scene proceeds he is more and more obscured by grandiose vestments.*)

POPE: No! No! No!

INQUISITOR (*referring to the owners of the shuffling feet*): Doctors of all chairs from the universities, representatives of the special orders of the church, representatives of the clergy as a whole who have come believing with childlike faith in the word of God as set forth in the scriptures, who have come to hear Your Holiness confirm their faith: and Your Holiness is really going to tell them that the Bible can no longer be regarded as the alphabet of truth?

POPE: I will not set myself up against the multiplication table. No!

INQUISITOR: Ah, that is what these people say, that it is the multiplication table. Their cry is, "The figures compel us," but where do these figures come from? Plainly they come from doubt. These men doubt everything. Can society stand on doubt and not on faith? "Thou art my master, but I doubt whether it is for the best." "This is my neighbor's house and my neighbor's wife, but why shouldn't they belong to me?" After the plague, after the new war, after the unparalleled disaster of the Reformation, your dwindling flock look to their shepherd, and now the mathematicians turn their tubes on the sky and announce to the world that you have not the best advice about the heavens either—up to now your only uncontested sphere of influence. This Galilei started meddling in machines at an early age. Now that men in ships are venturing on the great oceans—I am not against that of course—they are putting their faith in a brass bowl they call a compass and not in Almighty God.

POPE: This man is the greatest physicist of our time. He is the light of Italy, and not just any muddle-head.

INQUISITOR: Would we have had to arrest him otherwise? This bad man knows what he is doing, not writing his books in Latin, but in the jargon of the market-place.

POPE (*occupied with the shuffling feet*): That was not in the best of taste. (*A pause.*) These shuffling feet are making me nervous.

INQUISITOR: May they be more telling than my words, Your Holiness. Shall all these go from you with doubt in their hearts?

POPE: This man has friends. What about Versailles?° What about the Viennese court? They will call Holy Church a cesspool for defunct ideas. Keep your hands off him.

INQUISITOR: In practice it will never get far. He is a man of the flesh. He would soften at once.

POPE: He has more enjoyment in him than any man I ever saw. He loves eating and drinking and thinking. To excess. He indulges in thinking bouts! He cannot say no to an old wine or a new thought. (*Furious.*) I do not want a condemnation of physical facts. I do not want to hear battle cries: Church, church, church! Reason, reason, reason! (*Pause.*) These shuffling feet are intolerable. Has the whole world come to my door?

INQUISITOR: Not the whole world, Your Holiness. A select gathering of the faithful.

(*Pause.*)

POPE (*exhausted*): It is clearly understood: he is not to be tortured. (*Pause.*) At the very most, he may be shown the instruments.

INQUISITOR: That will be adequate, Your Holiness. Mr. Galilei understands machinery.

(*The eyes of* BARBERINI *look helplessly at the* CARDINAL INQUISITOR *from under the completely assembled panoply of Pope Urban VIII.*)

---

**Versailles:** This reference to the French court is an anachronism. The palace housing the court had not yet been built at Versailles. In Galileo's time, it was in Paris.

# SCENE 12

*June twenty-second, sixteen thirty-three,*
*A momentous date for you and me.*
*Of all the days that was the one*
*An age of reason could have begun.*

(*Again the garden of the Florentine Ambassador at Rome, where* GALILEO'S *assistants wait the news of the trial. The* LITTLE MONK *and* FEDERZONI *are attempting to concentrate on a game of chess.* VIRGINIA *kneels in a corner, praying and counting her beads.*)

LITTLE MONK: The Pope didn't even grant him an audience.

FEDERZONI: No more scientific discussions.

ANDREA: The "Discorsi" will never be finished. The sum of his findings. They will kill him.

FEDERZONI (*stealing a glance at him*): Do you really think so?

ANDREA: He will never recant.

(*Silence.*)

LITTLE MONK: You know when you lie awake at night how your mind fastens on to something irrelevant. Last night I kept thinking: if only they would let him take his little stone in with him, the appeal-to-reason-pebble that he always carries in his pocket.

FEDERZONI: In the room *they'll* take him to, he won't have a pocket.

ANDREA: But he will not recant.

LITTLE MONK: How can they beat the truth out of a man who gave his sight in order to see?

FEDERZONI: Maybe they can't.

(*Silence.*)

ANDREA (*speaking about* VIRGINIA): She is praying that he will recant.

FEDERZONI: Leave her alone. She doesn't know whether she's on her head or on her heels since they got hold of her. They brought her Father Confessor from Florence.

(*The* **INFORMER** *of scene 10 enters.*)

**INFORMER:** Mr. Galilei will be here soon. He may need a bed.

**FEDERZONI:** Have they let him out?

**INFORMER:** Mr. Galilei is expected to recant at five o'clock. The big bell of Saint Marcus will be rung and the complete text of his recantation publicly announced.

**ANDREA:** I don't believe it.

**INFORMER:** Mr. Galilei will be brought to the garden gate at the back of the house, to avoid the crowds collecting in the streets. (*He goes.*)

(*Silence.*)

**ANDREA:** The moon is an earth because the light of the moon is not her own. Jupiter is a fixed star, and four moons turn around Jupiter, therefore we are not shut in by crystal shells. The sun is the pivot of our world, therefore the earth is not the center. The earth moves, spinning about the sun. And he showed us. You can't make a man unsee what he has seen.

(*Silence.*)

**FEDERZONI:** Five o'clock is one minute.

(**VIRGINIA** *prays louder.*)

**ANDREA:** Listen all of you, they are murdering the truth.

(*He stops up his ears with his fingers. The two other pupils do the same.* **FEDERZONI** *goes over to the* **LITTLE MONK,** *and all of them stand absolutely still in cramped positions. Nothing happens. No bell sounds. After a silence, filled with the murmur of* **VIRGINIA'S** *prayers,* **FEDERZONI** *runs to the wall to look at the clock. He turns around, his expression changed. He shakes his head. They drop their hands.*)

**FEDERZONI:** No. No bell. It is three minutes after.

**LITTLE MONK:** He hasn't.

**ANDREA:** He held true. It is all right, it is all right.

**LITTLE MONK:** He did not recant.

**FEDERZONI:** No.

(*They embrace each other, they are delirious with joy.*)

**ANDREA:** So force cannot accomplish everything. What has been seen can't be unseen. Man is constant in the face of death.

**FEDERZONI:** June 22, 1633: dawn of the age of reason. I wouldn't have wanted to go on living if he had recanted.

**LITTLE MONK:** I didn't say anything, but I was in agony. Oh, ye of little faith!

**ANDREA:** I was sure.

**FEDERZONI:** It would have turned our morning to night.

**ANDREA:** It would have been as if the mountain had turned to water.

**LITTLE MONK** (*kneeling down, crying*): Oh God, I thank Thee.

**ANDREA:** Beaten humanity can lift its head. A man has stood up and said "no."

(*At this moment the bell of Saint Marcus begins to toll. They stand like statues.* **VIRGINIA** *stands up.*)

**VIRGINIA:** The bell of Saint Marcus. He is not damned.

(*From the street one hears the* **TOWN CRIER** *reading* **GALILEO'S** *recantation.*)

**TOWN CRIER:** I, Galileo Galilei, Teacher of Mathematics and Physics, do hereby publicly renounce my teaching that the earth moves. I foreswear this teaching with a sincere heart and unfeigned faith and detest and curse this and all other errors and heresies repugnant to the Holy Scriptures.

(*The lights dim; when they come up again the bell of Saint Marcus is petering out.* **VIRGINIA** *has gone but the* **SCHOLARS** *are still there waiting.*)

ANDREA (*loud*): The mountain did turn to water.

(GALILEO *has entered quietly and unnoticed. He is changed, almost unrecognizable. He has heard* ANDREA. *He waits some seconds by the door for somebody to greet him. Nobody does. They retreat from him. He goes slowly and, because of his bad sight, uncertainly, to the front of the stage where he finds a chair, and sits down.*)

ANDREA: I can't look at him. Tell him to go away.

FEDERZONI: Steady.

ANDREA (*hysterically*): He saved his big gut.

FEDERZONI: Get him a glass of water.

(*The* LITTLE MONK *fetches a glass of water for* ANDREA. *Nobody acknowledges the presence of* GALILEO, *who sits silently on his chair listening to the voice of the* TOWN CRIER, *now in another street.*)

ANDREA: I can walk. Just help me a bit.

(*They help him to the door.*)

ANDREA (*in the door*): "Unhappy is the land that breeds no hero."

GALILEO: No, Andrea: "Unhappy is the land that needs a hero."

*Before the next scene a curtain with the following legend on it is lowered:*

> You can plainly see that if a horse were to fall from a height of three or four feet, it could break its bones, whereas a dog would not suffer injury. The same applies to a cat from a height of as much as eight or ten feet, to a grasshopper from the top of a tower, and to an ant falling down from the moon. Nature could not allow a horse to become as big as twenty horses nor a giant as big as ten men, unless she were to change the proportions of all its members, particularly the bones. Thus the common assumption that great and small structures are equally tough is obviously wrong.
> —From the *Discorsi*

# SCENE 13

*1633–1642.*
*Galileo Galilei remains a prisoner of the Inquisition until his death.*

(*A country house near Florence. A large room simply furnished. There is a huge table, a leather chair, a globe of the world on a stand, and a narrow bed. A portion of the adjoining anteroom is visible, and the front door which opens into it.*)

(*An* OFFICIAL *of the Inquisition sits on guard in the anteroom.*)

(*In the large room,* GALILEO *is quietly experimenting with a bent wooden rail and a small ball of wood. He is still vigorous but almost blind.*)

(*After a while there is a knocking at the outside door. The* OFFICIAL *opens it to a* PEASANT *who brings a plucked goose.* VIRGINIA *comes from the kitchen. She is past forty.*)

PEASANT (*handing the goose to* VIRGINIA): I was told to deliver this here.

VIRGINIA: I didn't order a goose.

PEASANT: I was told to say it's from someone who was passing through.

(VIRGINIA *takes the goose, surprised. The* OFFICIAL *takes it from her and examines it suspiciously. Then, reassured, he hands it back to her. The* PEASANT *goes.* VIRGINIA *brings the goose in to* GALILEO.)

VIRGINIA: Somebody who was passing through sent you something.

GALILEO: What is it?

VIRGINIA: Can't you see it?

GALILEO: No. (*He walks over.*) A goose. Any name?

VIRGINIA: No.

GALILEO (*weighing the goose*): Solid.

VIRGINIA (*cautiously*): Will you eat the liver, if I have it cooked with a little apple?

GALILEO: I had my dinner. Are you under orders to finish me off with food?

VIRGINIA: It's not rich. And what is wrong with your eyes again? You should be able to see it.

GALILEO: You were standing in the light.

VIRGINIA: I was not.—You haven't been writing again?

GALILEO (*sneering*): What do you think?

(VIRGINIA *takes the goose out into the anteroom and speaks to the* OFFICIAL.)

VIRGINIA: You had better ask Monsignor Carpula to send the doctor. Father couldn't see this goose across the room.—Don't look at me like that. He has not been writing. He dictates everything to me, as you know.

OFFICIAL: Yes?

VIRGINIA: He abides by the rules. My father's repentance is sincere. I keep an eye on him. (*She hands him the goose.*) Tell the cook to fry the liver with an apple and an onion. (*She goes back into the large room.*) And you have no business to be doing that with those eyes of yours, father.

GALILEO: You may read me some Horace.

VIRGINIA: We should go on with your weekly letter to the Archbishop. Monsignor Carpula to whom we owe so much was all smiles the other day because the Archbishop had expressed his pleasure at your collaboration.

GALILEO: Where were we?

VIRGINIA (*sits down to take his dictation*): Paragraph four.

GALILEO: Read what you have.

VIRGINIA: "The position of the church in the matter of the unrest at Genoa. I agree with Cardinal Spoletti in the matter of the unrest among the Venetian ropemakers . . ."

GALILEO: Yes. (*Dictates.*) I agree with Cardinal Spoletti in the matter of the unrest among the Venetian ropemakers: it is better to distribute good nourishing food in the name of charity than to pay them more for their bellropes. It being surely better to strengthen their faith than to encourage their acquisitiveness. St. Paul says: Charity never faileth.—How is that?

VIRGINIA: It's beautiful, father.

GALILEO: It couldn't be taken as irony?

VIRGINIA: No. The Archbishop will like it. It's so practical.

GALILEO: I trust your judgment. Read it over slowly.

VIRGINIA: "The position of the Church in the matter of the unrest . . . "

(*There is a knocking at the outside door.* VIRGINIA *goes into the anteroom. The* OFFICIAL *opens the door. It is* ANDREA.)

ANDREA: Good evening. I am sorry to call so late, I'm on my way to Holland. I was asked to look him up. Can I go in?

VIRGINIA: I don't know whether he will see you. You never came.

ANDREA: Ask him.

(GALILEO *recognizes the voice. He sits motionless.* VIRGINIA *comes in to* GALILEO.)

GALILEO: Is that Andrea?

VIRGINIA: Yes. (*Pause.*) I will send him away.

GALILEO: Show him in.

(VIRGINIA *shows* ANDREA *in.* VIRGINIA *sits,* ANDREA *remains standing.*)

ANDREA (*cool*): Have you been keeping well, Mr. Galilei?

GALILEO: Sit down. What are you doing these days? What are you working on? I heard it was something about hydraulics in Milan.

ANDREA: As he knew I was passing through, Fabricius of Amsterdam asked me to visit you and inquire about your health.

(*Pause.*)

GALILEO: I am very well.

ANDREA (*formally*): I am glad I can report you are in good health.

GALILEO: Fabricius will be glad to hear it. And you might inform him that, on account of the depth of my repentance, I live in comparative comfort.

ANDREA: Yes, we understand that the church is more than pleased with you. Your complete acceptance has had its effect. Not one paper expounding a new thesis has made its appearance in Italy since your submission.

(*Pause.*)

GALILEO: Unfortunately there are countries not under the wing of the church. Would you not say the erroneous condemned theories are still taught—there?

ANDREA (*relentless*): Things are almost at a standstill.

GALILEO: Are they? (*Pause.*) Nothing from Descartes in Paris?

ANDREA: Yes. On receiving the news of your recantation, he shelved his treatise on the nature of light.

GALILEO: I sometimes worry about my assistants whom I led into error. Have they benefited by my example?

ANDREA: In order to work I have to go to Holland.

GALILEO: Yes.

ANDREA: Federzoni is grinding lenses again, back in some shop.

GALILEO: He can't read the books.

ANDREA: Fulganzio, our little monk, has abandoned research and is resting in peace in the church.

GALILEO: So. (*Pause.*) My superiors are looking forward to my spiritual recovery. I am progressing as well as can be expected.

VIRGINIA: You are doing well, father.

GALILEO: Virginia, leave the room.

(**VIRGINIA** *rises uncertainly and goes out.*)

VIRGINIA (*to the* OFFICIAL): He was his pupil, so now he is his enemy.—Help me in the kitchen.

(*She leaves the anteroom with the* OFFICIAL.)

ANDREA: May I go now, sir?

GALILEO: I do not know why you came, Sarti. To unsettle me? I have to be prudent.

ANDREA: I'll be on my way.

GALILEO: As it is, I have relapses. I completed the "Discorsi."

ANDREA: You completed what?

GALILEO: My "Discorsi."

ANDREA: How?

GALILEO: I am allowed pen and paper. My superiors are intelligent men. They know the habits of a lifetime cannot be broken abruptly. But they protect me from any unpleasant consequences: they lock my pages away as I dictate them. And I should know better than to risk my comfort. I wrote the "Discorsi" out again during the night. The manuscript is in the globe. My vanity has up to now prevented me from destroying it. If you consider taking it, you will shoulder the entire risk. You will say it was pirated from the original in the hands of the Holy Office.

(**ANDREA,** *as in a trance, has gone to the globe. He lifts the upper half and gets the book. He turns the pages as if wanting to devour them. In the background the opening sentences of the* Discorsi *appear:*

> *MY PURPOSE IS TO SET FORTH A VERY NEW SCIENCE DEALING WITH A VERY ANCIENT SUBJECT—MOTION. . . . AND I HAVE DISCOVERED BY EXPERIMENT SOME PROPERTIES OF IT WHICH ARE WORTH KNOWING. . . .)*

GALILEO: I had to employ my time somehow.

(*The text disappears.*)

ANDREA: Two new sciences! This will be the foundation stone of a new physics.

GALILEO: Yes. Put it under your coat.

ANDREA: And we thought you had deserted. (*In a low voice.*) Mr. Galilei, how

**GALILEO:** That would seem to have been proper. I taught you science and I decried the truth.

can I begin to express my shame. Mine has been the loudest voice against you.

**GALILEO:** That would seem to have been proper. I taught you science and I decried the truth.

**ANDREA:** Did you? I think not. Everything is changed!

**GALILEO:** What is changed?

**ANDREA:** You shielded the truth from the oppressor. Now I see! In your dealings with the Inquisition you used the same superb common sense you brought to physics.

**GALILEO:** Oh!

**ANDREA:** We lost our heads. With the crowd at the street corners we said: "He will die, he will never surrender!" You came back: "I surrendered but I am alive." We cried: "Your hands are stained!" You say: "Better stained than empty."

**GALILEO:** "Better stained than empty."—It sounds realistic. Sounds like me.

**ANDREA:** And I of all people should have known. I was twelve when you sold another man's telescope to the Venetian Senate, and saw you put it to immortal use. Your friends were baffled when you bowed to the Prince of Florence: Science gained a wider audience. You always laughed at heroics. "People who suffer bore me," you said. "Misfortunes are due mainly to miscalculations." And: "If there are obstacles, the shortest line between two points may be the crooked line."

**GALILEO:** It makes a picture.

**ANDREA:** And when you stooped to recant in 1633, I should have understood that you were again about your business.

**GALILEO:** My business being?

**ANDREA:** Science. The study of the properties of motion, mother of the machines which will themselves change the ugly face of the earth.

**GALILEO:** Aha!

**ANDREA:** You gained time to write a book that only you could write. Had you

burned at the stake in a blaze of glory they would have won.

**GALILEO:** They have won. And there is no such thing as a scientific work that only one man can write.

**ANDREA:** Then why did you recant, tell me that!

**GALILEO:** I recanted because I was afraid of physical pain.

**ANDREA:** No!

**GALILEO:** They showed me the instruments.

**ANDREA:** It was not a plan?

**GALILEO:** It was not.

(*Pause.*)

**ANDREA:** But you have contributed. Science has only one commandment: contribution. And you have contributed more than any man for a hundred years.

**GALILEO:** Have I? Then welcome to my gutter, dear colleague in science and brother in treason: I sold out, you are a buyer. The first sight of the book! His mouth watered and his scoldings were drowned. Blessed be our bargaining, whitewashing, death-fearing community!

**ANDREA:** The fear of death is human.

**GALILEO:** Even the church will teach you that to be weak is not human. It is just evil.

**ANDREA:** The church, yes! But science is not concerned with our weaknesses.

**GALILEO:** No? My dear Sarti, in spite of my present convictions, I may be able to give you a few pointers as to the concerns of your chosen profession.

(*Enter* VIRGINIA *with a platter.*)

In my spare time, I happen to have gone over this case. I have spare time.—Even a man who sells wool, however good he is at buying wool cheap and selling it dear, must be concerned with the standing of the wool trade. The practice of science would seem to call for valor. She trades in knowledge, which is the product of doubt. And this new art of doubt has enchanted the public. The plight of the multitude is old as the rocks, and is believed to be basic as the rocks. But now they have learned to doubt. They snatched the telescopes out of our hands and had them trained on their tormentors: prince, official, public moralist. The mechanism of the heavens was clearer, the mechanism of their courts was still murky. The battle to measure the heavens is won by doubt; by credulity the Roman housewife's battle for milk will always be lost. Word is passed down that this is of no concern to the scientist who is told he will only release such of his findings as do not disturb the peace, that is, the peace of mind of the well-to-do. Threats and bribes fill the air. Can the scientist hold out on the numbers?—For what reason do you labor? I take it the intent of science is to ease human existence. If you give way to coercion, science can be crippled, and your new machines may simply suggest new drudgeries. Should you then, in time, discover all there is to be discovered, your progress must then become a progress away from the bulk of humanity. The gulf might even grow so wide that the sound of your cheering at some new achievement would be echoed by a universal howl of horror.—As a scientist I had an almost unique opportunity. In my day astronomy emerged into the marketplace. At that particular time, had one man put up a fight, it could have had wide repercussions. I have come to believe that I was never in real danger; for some years I was as strong as the authorities, and I surrendered my knowledge to the powers that be, to use it, no, not *use* it, *abuse* it, as it suits their ends. I have betrayed my profession. Any man who does what I have done must not be tolerated in the ranks of science.

(**VIRGINIA,** *who has stood motionless, puts the platter on the table.*)

**VIRGINIA:** You are accepted in the ranks of the faithful, father.
**GALILEO** (*sees her*): Correct. (*He goes over to the table.*) I have to eat now.
**VIRGINIA:** We lock up at eight.
**ANDREA:** I am glad I came. (*He extends his hand.* **GALILEO** *ignores it and goes over to his meal.*)
**GALILEO** (*examining the plate; to* **ANDREA**): Somebody who knows me sent me a goose. I still enjoy eating.
**ANDREA:** And your opinion is now that the "new age" was an illusion?
**GALILEO:** Well.—This age of ours turned out to be a whore, spattered with blood. Maybe, new ages look like blood-spattered whores. Take care of yourself.
**ANDREA:** Yes. (*Unable to go.*) With reference to your evaluation of the author in question—I do not know the answer. But I cannot think that your savage analysis is the last word.
**GALILEO:** Thank you, sir.

(**OFFICIAL** *knocks at the door.*)

**VIRGINIA** (*showing* **ANDREA** *out*): I don't like visitors from the past, they excite him.

(*She lets him out. The* **OFFICIAL** *closes the iron door.* **VIRGINIA** *returns.*)

**GALILEO** (*eating*): Did you try and think who sent the goose?
**VIRGINIA:** Not Andrea.
**GALILEO:** Maybe not. I gave Redhead his first lesson; when he held out his hand, I had to remind myself he is teaching now.—How is the sky tonight?
**VIRGINIA** (*at the window*): Bright.

(**GALILEO** *continues eating.*)

# SCENE 14

*The great book o'er the border went
And, good folk, that was the end.*

*But we hope you'll keep in mind*
*You and I were left behind.*

(*Before a little Italian customs house early in the morning.* ANDREA *sits upon one of his traveling trunks at the barrier and reads* GALILEO'S *book. The window of a small house is still lit, and a big grotesque shadow, like an old witch and her cauldron, falls upon the house wall beyond. Barefoot* CHILDREN *in rags see it and point to the little house.*)

CHILDREN (*singing*): One, two, three, four, five, six,
Old Marina is a witch.
At night, on a broomstick she sits
And on the church steeple she spits.

CUSTOMS OFFICER (*to* ANDREA): Why are you making this journey?

ANDREA: I am a scholar.

CUSTOMS OFFICER (*to his* CLERK): Put down under "reason for leaving the country": Scholar. (*He points to the baggage.*) Books! Anything dangerous in these books?

ANDREA: What is dangerous?

CUSTOMS OFFICER: Religion. Politics.

ANDREA: These are nothing but mathematical formulas.

CUSTOMS OFFICER: What's that?

ANDREA: Figures.

CUSTOMS OFFICER: Oh, figures. No harm in figures. Just wait a minute, sir, we will soon have your papers stamped. (*He exits with* CLERK.)

(*Meanwhile, a little council of war among the* CHILDREN *has taken place.* ANDREA *quietly watches. One of the* BOYS, *pushed forward by the others, creeps up to the little house from which the shadow comes and takes the jug of milk on the doorstep.*)

ANDREA (*quietly*): What are you doing with that milk?

BOY (*stopping in mid-movement*): She is a witch.

(*The other* CHILDREN *run away behind the customs house. One of them shouts, "Run, Paolo!"*)

ANDREA: Hmm!—And because she is a witch she mustn't have milk. Is that the idea?

BOY: Yes.

ANDREA: And how do you know she is a witch?

BOY (*points to shadow on house wall*): Look!

ANDREA: Oh! I see.

BOY: And she rides on a broomstick at night—and she bewitches the coachman's horses. My cousin Luigi looked through the hole in the stable roof, that the snowstorm made, and heard the horses coughing something terrible.

ANDREA: Oh!—How big was the hole in the stable roof?

BOY: Luigi didn't tell. Why?

ANDREA: I was asking because maybe the horses got sick because it was cold in the stable. You had better ask Luigi how big that hole is.

BOY: You are not going to say Old Marina isn't a witch, because you can't.

ANDREA: No, I can't say she isn't a witch. I haven't looked into it. A man can't know about a thing he hasn't looked into, or can he?

BOY: No!—But THAT! (*He points to the shadow.*) She is stirring hell-broth.

ANDREA: Let's see. Do you want to take a look? I can lift you up.

BOY: You lift me to the window, mister! (*He takes a sling shot out of his pocket.*) I can really bash her from there.

ANDREA: Hadn't we better make sure she is a witch before we shoot? I'll hold that.

(*The* BOY *puts the milk jug down and follows him reluctantly to the window.* ANDREA *lifts the boy up so that he can look in.*)

ANDREA: What do you see?

BOY (*slowly*): Just an old girl cooking porridge.

ANDREA: Oh! Nothing to it then. Now look at her shadow, Paolo.

(*The* BOY *looks over his shoulder and back and compares the reality and the shadow.*)

BOY: The big thing is a soup ladle.

ANDREA: Ah! A ladle! You see, I would have taken it for a broomstick, but I haven't looked into the matter as you have, Paolo. Here is your sling.

CUSTOMS OFFICER (*returning with the* CLERK *and handing* ANDREA *his papers*): All present and correct. Good luck, sir.

(ANDREA *goes, reading* GALILEO's *book. The* CLERK *starts to bring his baggage after him. The barrier rises.* ANDREA *passes through, still reading the book. The* BOY *kicks over the milk jug.*)

BOY (*shouting after* ANDREA): She *is* a witch! She *is* a witch!

ANDREA: You saw with your own eyes: think it over!

(*The* BOY *joins the others. They sing.*)

One, two, three, four, five, six,
Old Marina is a witch.
At night, on a broomstick she sits
And on the church steeple she spits.

(*The* CUSTOMS OFFICERS *laugh.* ANDREA *goes.*)

## SUMMARY

The course of the modern European theatre was changed by the work of the German expressionists, Erwin Piscator and Bertolt Brecht. Their sphere of influence was exceptional. The expressionists brought the harsh politics of class struggle and capitalistic inequities onto the stage to demonstrate the dehumanizing plight of the average citizen caught up in the struggle for power and money. Along with Erwin Piscator, Brecht advocated the use of new technologies in the theatre to develop a kind of performance style (called *epic theatre*) that responded to the mechanized and accelerated routines of modern life. Brecht's serious reading of Karl Marx in the 1920s gave rise to Brecht's revolutionary postures toward the class struggle in politics and toward bourgeois "realism" in theatre. He went so far as to redefine Marx's concept of "alienation" as a mode of theatrical practice. In *Das Kapital*, Marx argued that the division of labor in modern industrial production created a separation (a distance) between the worker and the product. Workers, therefore, became dehumanized, mechanized, alienated from their work, the commodity, and society. Brecht's theatre sets out to "alienate" or "estrange" the audience from the seamless illusion of the realistic stage in order to train us to reflect upon and question the world, its politicians, its social and financial institutions.

Brecht's experiments with epic writing and staging resulted in both episodic and narrative plays, the aims of which were to show social and political contradictions at work in the world. His goal was to encourage audiences to learn from the lessons of history, such as the sad destinies of those perennial small-time profiteers, like Mother Courage, or the despised ends of those giant shapers of human destiny like Galileo Galilei.

Writing styles that *revolted* against the "illusion of the real" in the theatre span a period from the early 1900s to the present. New writing and staging experiments other than expressionism and epic theatre include a singular group of highly influential playwrights in France, England, and the United States called, collectively, *the theatre of the absurd*. Their plays, especially the work of Samuel Beckett and Eugene Ionesco, are the subject of the next chapter.

## NOTES

1. Eugene Ionesco, *Victims of Duty* (New York: Grove Press, 1958):119.

2. Bertolt Brecht, *Collected Plays Volume 5*, edited by Ralph Manheim and John Willett (New York: Vintage Books, 1972):216–217.

3. Ronald Hayman, *Brecht: A Biography* (New York: Oxford University Press, 1938): 296.

4. Eric Bentley, *The Brecht Commentaries* (London: Methuen, 1981): 190.

5. Martin Esslin, *Brecht: A Choice of Evils*, Fourth Edition (New York: Methuen, 1984): 234.

6. John Fuegi, *The Essential Brecht* (Los Angeles: Hennessey and Ingalls, 1972): 162.

7. Brecht 267.

8. Brecht 219.

9. Bentley 196.

Beckett's minimalist staging captures significant aspects of our humanness: crying, speaking, moving, walking, joking, waiting, remembering. The context is frustration, anxiety, dependency, habituation, and loss.

*Footfalls,* first performed at the Royal Court Theatre, London, in 1976, repeats Beckett's use of a darkened boxlike stage as a basic metaphor for the circumscribed life. May, some forty years old, carries on a dialogue in her mind ("revolving it all") with the disembodied voice of her dying or dead mother. It is never clear whether or not the dialogue takes place only in May's head, though we can hear the Mother's voice (*"from dark upstage"*) and May's spoken responses. The stage lights are concentrated on a strip of light on the floor over which May's feet are seen and her footsteps heard as she passes to and fro. May paces on a line parallel to the audience (a length of nine steps) left to right with a clearly audible tread. As she walks back and forth, she inquires how she can be of service to her mother "again." Their broken dialogue touches upon such topics as physical distress, illness, age, birth, disappointment, and memories.

Beckett's text is divided by lighting and sound effects into four segments. At the end of each segment, the stage directions require the lights to fade into darkness, steps to cease, and after a long pause, a chime to ring and lights to come up but with less intensity each time. The technique is to give audiences the sensation that time is passing—a life is being measured out by a succession of days filled with sameness, routine, starts and stops as day turns to night and back again to day for a lifetime.

The character, May, has grey hair and a grey wrap. She is first seen in dim light pacing out her measured steps: a visible metaphor for a half-lived life. This sequence occurs three times. Part four is the terminus: chime very faint, light even less; there is no trace of May. Then a fade out. In some 132 lines of dialogue, Beckett evokes a nearly silent life with no brightness, color, happiness, joy, or activity. May's pacing figure is barely visible in the dimness of an unfulfilled life. Behind the stage picture lies the sound of the Mother's voice reviewing their lives, presumably at the moment of her death, or possibly as May's memory of her voice. May's measured tread signifies her own predictable life of servitude, dependency, and distress. Her only protest against life has been, "This is not enough."

Beckett's rejection of movement, emotion, color, light, and complete sentences diminishes the character's presence and the actor's mobility. All the while a story is being told that reflects the incompleteness and destitution of two lives lived in habituation and dependency. Identity (except for May's name) and emotion are eliminated. The Mother's voice denies knowledge of why their lives seem unfulfilled. She refers to "it all"—the totality of their lives—some ten times until the figure and the voice, the visible and the invisible, disappear into the darkness of nonbeing. In the audience we are left with questions: What does it all mean? When did May's mother die? Is May's story autobiographical? Who is Amy (an anagram for May)? Why did May's mother have her so "late" in life? How old is May now? Why do May and Voice invent stories? Why does the illuminated stage grow smaller after each fade-out? Is *May* dead? Our questions about this drama, as about life, prove endless and go unanswered. What we perceive is a presence; what we hear are sounds of voices and footfalls; what we know, finally, is that human experience is composed of presence and absence. In the single figure of May pacing back and forth, Beckett slowly builds an image of life as sound in motion.

The aim of Beckett's minimalist art is to communicate an experience of existential totality. To do so, the dramatic text is reduced to a piece of monologue stripped of nonessentials like color, movement, music, and scenery. The authentic experience in the theatre for Beckett comes with the totality of being in its most concentrated form. For example, an aging woman pacing, split into perceiver and perceived, the speaker and the spoken to, but changing through time from moment to moment as she moves about. With death comes the only release from routine and disappointment.

The four segments of *Footfalls* summarize Beckett's vision of human experience: aging, dying, measuring; questions about birth ("Where it all began"); protests about insufficiencies ("not enough"); survival ("the semblance") and silence; memory ("revolving it all") and regret; dimness, darkness, and obliteration.

With economy of action and language, the playwright has sketched diminishing images of two lives whose resonances (footfalls and voices) are applicable to us all—being born, surviving mechanically, experiencing time, remembering others, questioning life's meaning, and experiencing loss. Like May's footfalls, we eventually become, with time, only dim echoes of our former selves. And then it is over.

# Footfalls

MAY (M), *dishevelled grey hair, worn grey wrap hiding feet, trailing.*

WOMAN'S VOICE (V) *from dark upstage.*

*Strip: downstage, parallel with front, length nine steps, width one metre, a little off centre audience right.*

$$L\frac{r\,l\,r\,l\,r\,l\,r\,l\,r}{l\,r\,l\,r\,l\,r\,l\,r\,l}R$$

*Pacing: starting with right foot (r) from right (R) to left (L), with left foot (l) from L to R.*
> *Turn: rightabout at L, leftabout at R.*
> *Steps: clearly audible rhythmic tread.*
> *Lighting: dim, strongest at floor level, less on body, least on head.*
> *Voices: both low and slow throughout.*
*Curtain. Stage in darkness. Faint single chime. Pause as echoes die. Fade up to dim on strip. Rest in darkness.* M *discovered pacing approaching L. Turns at L, paces three more lengths, halts facing front at R.*
> *Pause.*

M: Mother. (*Pause. No louder.*) Mother.
> *Pause.*
V: Yes, May.
M: Were you asleep?
V: Deep asleep. (*Pause.*) I heard you in my deep sleep. (*Pause.*) There is no sleep so deep I would not hear you there. (*Pause.* M *resumes pacing. Four lengths. After first length, synchronous with steps.*) . . . . . . . . . . . . . . . . . . . seven eight nine wheel . . . . . . . . seven eight nine wheel. (*Free.*) Will you not try to snatch a little sleep?
> M *halts facing front at R. Pause.*
M: Would you like me to inject you . . . again?

V: Yes, but it is too soon.
> *Pause.*
M: Would you like me to change your position . . . again?
V: Yes, but it is too soon.
> *Pause.*
M: Straighten your pillows? (*Pause.*) Change your drawsheet? (*Pause.*) Pass you the bedpan? (*Pause.*) The warming-pan? (*Pause.*) Dress your sores? (*Pause.*) Sponge you down? (*Pause.*) Moisten your poor lips? (*Pause.*) Pray with you? (*Pause.*) For you? (*Pause.*) Again.
> *Pause.*
V: Yes, but it is too soon.
> *Pause.* M *resumes pacing, after one length halts facing front at L. Pause.*
M: What age am I now?
V: And I? (*Pause. No louder.*) And I?
M: Ninety.
V: So much?
M: Eighty-nine, ninety.
V: I had you late. (*Pause.*) In life. (*Pause.*) Forgive me . . . again. (*Pause. No louder.*) Forgive me . . . again.
> *Pause.*
M: What age am I now?
V: In your forties.
M: So little?
V: I'm afraid so. (*Pause.* M *resumes pacing. After first turn at R.*) May. (*Pause. No louder.*) May.
M (*pacing*): Yes, Mother.
V: Will you never have done? (*Pause.*) Will you never have done . . . revolving it all?
M: (*halting*): It?

V: It all. (*Pause.*) In your poor mind. (*Pause.*) It all. (*Pause.*) It all.

*M resumes pacing. Five seconds. Fade out on strip. All in darkness. Steps cease.*

*Long pause.*

*Chime a little fainter. Pause for echoes. Fade up to a little less on strip. Rest in darkness.*

*M discovered facing front at R.*

*Pause.*

V: I walk here now. (*Pause.*) Rather I come and stand. (*Pause.*) At nightfall. (*Pause.*) She fancies she is alone. (*Pause.*) See how still she stands, how stark, with her face to the wall. (*Pause.*) How outwardly unmoved. (*Pause.*) She has not been out since girlhood. Not out since girlhood. (*Pause.*) Where is she, it may be asked. (*Pause.*) Why, in the old home, the same where she—(*Pause.*) The same where she began. (*Pause.*) Where it began. (*Pause.*) It all began. (*Pause.*) But this, this, when did this begin? (*Pause.*) When other girls of her age were out at . . . lacrosse she was already here. (*Pause.*) At this. (*Pause.*) The floor here, now bare, once was—(M *begins pacing. Steps a little slower.*) But let us watch her move, in silence. (M *paces. Towards end of second length.*) Watch how fast she wheels. (M *turns, paces. Synchronous with steps third length.*) Seven eight nine wheel. (M *turns at L, paces one more length, halts facing front at R.*) I say the floor here, now bare, this strip of floor, once was carpeted, a deep pile. Till one night, while still little more than a child, she called her mother and said, Mother, this is not enough. The mother: Not enough? May—the child's given name—May: Not enough. The mother: What do you mean, May, not enough, what can you possibly mean, May, not enough? May: I mean, Mother, that I must hear the feet, however faint they fall. The mother: The motion alone is not enough? May: No, Mother, the motion alone is not enough, I must hear the feet, however faint they fall. (*Pause.* M *resumes pacing. With pacing.*) Does she still sleep, it may be asked? Yes, some nights she does, in snatches, bows her poor head against the wall and snatches a little sleep. (*Pause.*) Still speak? Yes, some nights she does, when she fancies none can hear. (*Pause.*) Tells how it was. (*Pause.*) Tries to tell how it was. (*Pause.*) It all. (*Pause.*) It all.

*M continues pacing. Five seconds. Fade out on strip. All in darkness. Steps cease. Long pause.*

*Chime a little fainter still. Pause for echoes. Fade up to a little less still on strip.*

*Rest in darkness.* M *discovered facing front at R.*

*Pause.*

M: Sequel. (M *begins pacing, after two lengths halts facing front at R.*) Sequel. A little later, when she was quite forgotten, she began to—(*Pause.*) A little later, when as though she had never been, it never been, she began to walk. (*Pause.*) At nightfall. (*Pause.*) Slip out at nightfall and into the little church by the north door, always locked at that hour, and walk, up and down, up and down, His poor arm. (*Pause.*) Some nights she would halt, as one frozen by some shudder of the mind, and stand stark still till she could move again. But many also were the nights when she paced without pause, up and down, up and down, before vanishing the way she came. (*Pause.*) No sound. (*Pause.*) None at least to be heard. (*Pause.*) The semblance. (*Pause. Resumes pacing. Steps a little slower still. After two lengths halts facing front at R.*) The semblance. Faint, though by no means invisible, in a certain light. (*Pause.*) Given the right light. (*Pause.*) Grey rather than white, a pale shade of grey. (*Pause.*) Tattered. (*Pause.*) A tangle of tatters. (*Pause.*) A faint tangle of pale grey tatters. (*Pause.*) Watch it pass—

(*pause*)—watch her pass before the candelabrum how its flames, their light . . . like moon through passing . . . rack. (*Pause.*) Soon then after she was gone, as though never there, began to walk, up and down, up and down, that poor arm. (*Pause.*) At nightfall. (*Pause.*) That is to say, at certain seasons of the year, during Vespers. (*Pause.*) Necessarily. (*Pause. Resumes pacing. After one length halts facing front at L. Pause.*) Old Mrs. Winter, whom the reader will remember, old Mrs. Winter, one late autumn Sunday evening, on sitting down to supper with her daughter after worship, after a few half-hearted mouthfuls laid down her knife and fork and bowed her head. What is it, Mother, said the daughter, a most strange girl, though scarcely a girl any more . . . (*brokenly*) . . . dreadfully un— (*Pause. Normal voice.*) What is it, Mother, are you not feeling yourself? (*Pause.*) Mrs. W. did not at once reply. But finally, raising her head and fixing Amy—the daughter's given name, as the reader will remember—raising her head and fixing Amy full in the eye she said— (*pause*)—she murmured, fixing Amy full in the eye she murmured, Amy, did you observe anything . . . strange at Evensong? Amy: No, Mother, I did not. Mrs. W: Perhaps it was just my fancy. Amy: Just what exactly, Mother, did you perhaps fancy it was? (*Pause.*) Just what exactly, Mother, did you perhaps fancy this . . . strange thing was you observed? (*Pause.*) Mrs. W: You yourself observed nothing . . . strange? Amy: No, Mother, I myself did not, to put it mildly. Mrs. W: What do you mean, Amy, to put it mildly, what can you possibly mean, Amy, to put it mildly? Amy: I mean, Mother, that to say I observed nothing . . . strange is indeed to put it mildly. For I observed nothing of any kind, strange or otherwise. I saw nothing, heard nothing,

of any kind. I was not there. Mrs. W: Not there? Amy: Not there. Mrs. W: But I heard you respond. (*Pause.*) I heard you say Amen. (*Pause.*) How could you have responded if you were not there? (*Pause.*) How could you possibly have said Amen if, as you claim, you were not there? (*Pause.*) The love of God, and the fellowship of the Holy Ghost, be with us all, now, and for evermore. Amen. (*Pause.*) I heard you distinctly. (*Pause. Resumes pacing. After five steps halts without facing front. Long pause. Resumes pacing, halts facing front at R. Long pause.*) Amy. (*Pause. No louder.*) Amy. (*Pause.*) Yes, Mother. (*Pause.*) Will you never have done? (*Pause.*) Will you never have done . . . revolving it all? (*Pause.*) It? (*Pause.*) It all. (*Pause.*) In your poor mind. (*Pause.*) It all. (*Pause.*) It all.
*Pause. Fade out on strip. All in darkness. Pause.*
*Chime even a little fainter. Pause for echoes. Fade up to even a little less still on strip. No trace of May. Hold fifteen seconds. Fade out. Curtain.*

## SUMMARY

Our discussions of "recent writing styles have touched on two major stylistic movements, spanning seventy years of our century, that resulted in new subjects and dramatic forms for the modern theatre. The epic and absurdist movements represent special attitudes toward our life and times— one representing a socially constructive theatre and the other a theatre of basic existential situations.

Absurdist writers turned away from socioeconomic and political concerns in an apocalyptic vision of humanity caught up in a senseless, futile, and oppressive existence. They called their vision *absurd*. They pioneered a dramaturgy that did not debate or moralize issues, but rather *presented* an absurd universe by using concrete stage images and language emptied of meaning. For over thirty-five years, Samuel Beckett has been the leading spokesman for the theatrical absurd. His plays present the world as a terminal "void" and humanity's place in it as purposeless. We are born, we die, and in between we exist. Beckett's plays condense life's absurdness into remarkable images of existence in the void. In Beckett's minimalist art, the performance effectively becomes the play.

To analyze plays by Brecht and Beckett we must comprehend the *writer's vision* of modern society and the universe, along with the forms, conventions, and techniques used to convey their statements. More recently, the feminist movement has impacted on politics and art. Feminist playwrights have centered "woman" as drama's subject and evolved play forms representative of women's biologic cycles and domestic routines to comment on the condition of women (and men) in the modern industrial world. The new writing has had its impact on American, British, and French theatre of the 1980s. The next chapter examines this new writing and its perspectives on contemporary culture and society.

## NOTES

1. Martin Esslin, *The Theatre of the Absurd*, 3rd Edition (New York: Pelican Books, 1983): 23.

2. Eugene Ionesco, *Notes and Counter Notes: Writings on the Theatre*, trans. Donald Watson (New York: Grove Press, 1964): 257.

3. Albert Camus, *The Myth of Sisyphus and Other Essays* (New York: Vintage Books, 1955): 5.

rations for the breakfast meal and her habituated life as a servant. But, Olimpia's life has made her, like Orlando, also a tyrant over her domain. As a means of improving her condition in life she demands a "pressure cooker" and throws the silverware about and breaks cookware until she gets the money from Leticia. Moreover, she dictates at all times what the family will eat.

By the end of Scene 4, Fornes has established the contradictions within a partriarchical society: Orlando's will to power and control of his professional and domestic life; the treatment of the various classes of women as sexual objects and as slaves to domestic routines; the male tendency to violence as hunter, torturer, and rapist; and the various female responses to victimization. In contrast to the male role, the female-gendered activities include nurturing, serving, educating, feeding, housing, clothing, learning, and caring for the poor, the sick, and the well. As the scene fragments juxtapose the gender-related concerns, Fornes' social, sexual, and political ironies are revealed. With no clear gender-related distinctions, we view such activities as beating versus nurturing, brutalization versus selflessness, and torture versus caring. However, the essential question concerns the "conduct of life for both women and men." After surviving Orlando's beatings and sexual abuse, Nena raises the quintessential question about how to conduct herself in the face of unimaginable abuse: "I want to conduct each day of my life in the best possible way." She longs to value things, people, and pain. She continues, "And if someone should treat me unkindly, I should not blind myself with rage, but I should see them and receive them, since maybe they are in worse pain than me" (Scene 15).

The domestic unit in *The Conduct of Life* is a political microcosm for a tyrannical, male-dominated class system characterized by destructiveness, aggressiveness, and victimization. The system transforms women (and

also men) into creatures who are conditioned to engage in betrayal, aggression, and violence. Finally, after great psychological and physical abuse, Leticia betrays Orlando by taking a lover. When Orlando finds out (although Nena is his "kept" woman) and denigrates his wife in public, she takes a gun and kills him. Then, in a highly ambiguous gesture, Leticia places the gun in Nena's hand and says, "Please." Consistent with her victimization by life, Nena, in a "state of terror" and "numb acceptance," stares at the gun in her hand and then back at Leticia. This is how the play ends, thus avoiding closure, for there are at least two or more possible explanations for Leticia's action. Is she asking Nena to take the blame for Orlando's murder, or is she asking Nena to punish her, to end the life of another wounded creature? The ambiguity of the play's final moment and the lack of explicit resolution emphasize the continuing victimization of women (and men) by a patriarchal society.

In *The Conduct of Life*, the patriarchal death principle is enacted once again and handed on to another generation of women who are instinctively pacifistic and life-affirming. Fornes' play also asks when this social construct, which is oppressive to men and to women, will end.

In Fornes' world, women are conditioned and provoked to use "phallocentric" weapons, despite their instinctive dislike of violence, in life-denying acts. In Scene 2, Leticia rails against the killing of creatures, and by Scene 19 she has been provoked into shooting Orlando. However, in shifting the weapon to Nena she shows how victimization brutalizes the mind and spirit and creates other victims in an endless chain of tyranny. In *The Conduct of Life*, all classes and genders are swept up in the aggressive destructiveness of a violent, death-centered society where the essentials of life—food, clothing, shelter, safety, caring, loving—are swept away by oppression and cruelty.

# The Conduct of Life

## CHARACTERS

ORLANDO  An army lieutenant at the start of the play. A lieutenant commander soon after.

LETICIA  His wife, ten years his elder.

ALEJO  A lieutenant commander. Their friend.

NENA  A destitute girl of twelve.

OLIMPIA  A servant.

*A Latin American country. The present.*

*The floor is divided in four horizontal planes. Downstage is the livingroom, which is about ten feet deep. Center stage, eighteen inches high, is the diningroom, which is about ten feet deep. Further upstage, eighteen inches high, is a hallway which is about four feet deep. At each end of the hallway there is a door. The one to the right leads to the servants' quarters, the one to the left to the basement. Upstage, three feet lower than the hallway (same level as the livingroom), is the cellar, which is about sixteen feet deep. Most of the cellar is occupied by two platforms which are eight feet wide, eight feet deep, and three feet high. Upstage of the cellar are steps that lead up. Approximately ten feet above the cellar is another level, extending from the extreme left to the extreme right, which represents a warehouse. There is a door on the left of the warehouse. On the left and the right of the livingroom there are archways that lead to hallways or antechambers, the floors of these hallways are the same level as the diningroom. On the left and the right of the diningroom there is a second set of archways that lead to hallways or antechambers, the floors of which are the same level as the hallways. All along the edge of each level there is a step that leads to the next level. All floors and steps are*
black marble. *In the livingroom there are two chairs. One is to the left, next to a table with a telephone. The other is to the right. In the diningroom there are a large green marble table and three chairs. On the cellar floor there is a mattress to the right and a chair to the left. In the warehouse there is a table and a chair to the left, and a chair and some boxes and crates to the right.*

## SCENE 1

ORLANDO *is doing jumping-jacks in the upper left corner of the diningroom in the dark. A light, slowly, comes up on him. He wears military breeches held by suspenders, and riding boots. He does jumping-jacks as long as it can be endured. He stops, the center area starts to become visible. There is a chair upstage of the table. There is a linen towel on the left side of the table.* ORLANDO *dries his face with the towel and sits as he puts the towel around his neck.*

ORLANDO:  Thirty three and I'm still a lieutenant. In two years I'll receive a promotion or I'll leave the military. I promise I will not spend time feeling sorry for myself.—Instead I will study the situation and draw an effective plan of action. I must eliminate all obstacles.—I will make the acquaintance of people in high power. If I cannot achieve this on my own merit, I will marry a woman in high circles. Leticia must not be an obstacle.—Man must have an ideal, mine is to achieve maximum power. That is my destiny.—No other interest will deter me from this.—My sexual drive is detrimental to my ideals. I must no longer be overwhelmed by sexual passion or I will be degraded beyond hope of recovery. (*Lights fade to black.*)

# SCENE 2

ALEJO *sits to the right of the diningroom table.* ORLANDO *stands to* ALEJO'*s left. He is now a lieutenant commander. He wears an army tunic, breeches, and boots.* LETICIA *stands to the left. She wears a dress that suggests 1940s fashion.*

LETICIA: What! Me go hunting? Do you think I'm going to shoot a deer, the most beautiful animal in the world? Do you think I'm going to destroy a deer? On the contrary, I would run in the field and scream and wave my arms like a mad woman and try to scare them away so the hunters could not reach them. I'd run in front of the bullets and let the mad hunters kill me—stand in the way of the bullets—stop the bullets with my body. I don't see how anyone can shoot a deer.

ORLANDO: (*To* ALEJO.) Do you understand that? You, who are her friend, can you understand that? You don't think that is madness? She's mad. Tell her that— she'll think it's you who's mad. (*To* LETICIA.) Hunting is a sport! A skill! Don't talk about something you know nothing about. Must you have an opinion about every damn thing! Can't you keep your mouth shut when you don't know what you're talking about? (ORLANDO *exits right.*)

LETICIA: He told me that he didn't love me, and that his sole relationship to me was simply a marital one. What he means is that I am to keep this house, and he is to provide for it. That's what he said. That explains why he treats me the way he treats me. I never understood why he did, but now it's clear. He doesn't love me. I thought he loved me and that he stayed with me because he loved me and that's why I didn't understand his be-

havior. But now I know, because he told me that he sees me as a person who runs the house. I never understood that because I would have never—if he had said, "Would you marry me to run my house even if I don't love you," I would have never—I would have never believed what I was hearing. I would have never believed that these words were coming out of his mouth. Because I loved him. (ORLANDO *has entered.* LETICIA *sees him and exits left.* ORLANDO *enters and sits center.*)

ORLANDO: I didn't say any of that. I told her that she's not my heir. That's what I said. I told her that she's not in my will, and she will not receive a penny of my money if I die. That's what I said. I didn't say anything about running the house. I said she will not inherit a penny from me because I didn't want to be humiliated. She is capable of foolishness beyond anyone's imagination. Ask her what she would do if she were rich and could do anything she wants with her money. (LETICIA *enters.*)

LETICIA: I would distribute it among the poor.

ORLANDO: She has no respect for money.

LETICIA: That is not true. If I had money I would give it to those who need it. I know what money is, what money can do. It can feed people, it can put a roof over their heads. Money can do that. It can clothe them. What do you know about money? What does it mean to you? What do you do with money? Buy rifles? To shoot deer?

ORLANDO: You're foolish!—You're foolish! You're a foolish woman! (ORLANDO *exits. He speaks from offstage.*) Foolish. . . . Foolish. . . .

LETICIA: He has no respect for me. He is insensitive. He doesn't listen. You cannot reach him. He is deaf. He is an animal. Nothing touches him except sensuality.

He responds to food, to the flesh. To music sometimes, if it is romantic. To the moon. He is romantic but he is not aware of what you are feeling. I can't change him.—I'll tell you why I asked you to come. Because I want something from you.—I want you to educate me. I want to study. I want to study so I am not an ignorant person. I want to go to the university. I want to be knowledgeable. I'm tired of being ignored. I want to study political science. Is political science what diplomats study? Is that what it is? You have to teach me elemental things because I never finished grammar school. I would have to study a great deal. A great deal so I could enter the university. I would have to go through all the subjects. I would like to be a woman who speaks in a group and have others listen.

ALEJO: Why do you want to worry about any of that? What's the use? Do you think you can change anything? Do you think anyone can change anything?

LETICIA: Why not? (*Pause.*) Do you think I'm crazy?—He can't help it.—Do you think I'm crazy?—Because I love him? (*He looks away from her. Lights fade to black.*)

# SCENE 3

ORLANDO *enters the warehouse holding* NENA *close to him. She wears a gray over-large uniform. She is barefoot. She resists him. She is tearful and frightened. She pulls away and runs to the right wall. He follows her.*

ORLANDO: (*Softly.*) You called me a snake.

NENA: No, I didn't. (*He tries to reach her. She pushes his hands away from her.*) I was kidding.—I swear I was kidding.

*He grabs her and pushes her against the wall. He pushes his pelvis against her. He moves to the chair dragging her with him. She crawls to the left, pushes the table aside and stands behind it. He walks around the table. She goes under it. He grabs her foot and pulls her*

out toward the down-stage side. He opens his fly and pushes his pelvis against her. Lights fade to black.

# SCENE 4

OLIMPIA *is wiping crumbs off the diningroom table. She wears a plain gray uniform.* LETICIA *sits to the left of the table facing front. She wears a dressing gown. She writes in a notebook. There is some silverware on the table.* OLIMPIA *has a speech defect.*

LETICIA: Let's do this.

OLIMPIA: O.K. (*She continues wiping the table.*)

LETICIA: (*Still writing.*) What are you doing?

OLIMPIA: I'm doing what I always do.

LETICIA: Let's do this.

OLIMPIA: (*In a mumble.*) As soon as I finish doing this. You can't just ask me to do what you want me to do, and interrupt what I'm doing. I don't stop from the time I wake up in the morning to the time I go to sleep. You can't interrupt me whenever you want, not if you want me to get to the end of my work. I wake up at 5:30. I wash. I put on my clothes and make by bed. I go to the kitchen. I get the milk and the bread from outside and I put them on the counter. I open the icebox. I put one bottle in and take the butter out. I leave the other bottle on the counter. I shut the refrigerator door. I take the pan that I use for water and put water in it. I know how much. I put the pan on the stove, light the stove, cover it. I take the top off the milk and pour it in the milk pan except for a little. (*Indicating with her finger.*) Like this. For the cat. I put the pan on the stove, light the stove. I put coffee in the thing. I know how much. I light the oven and put bread in it. I come here, get the tablecloth and I lay it on the table. I shout "Breakfast." I get the napkins. I take the cups, the saucers, and the silver out and set the table. I go to the kitchen. I put the tray on the counter, put the butter on the tray. The water and the milk are getting hot. I pick up the cat's dish. I wash it. I pour the milk I left in the bottle in the milk dish. I put it on the floor for the cat. I shout "Breakfast." The water boils. I pour it in the thing. When the milk boils I turn off the gas and cover the milk. I get the bread from the oven. I slice it down the middle and butter it. Then I cut it in pieces (*indicating*) this big. I set a piece aside for me. I put the rest of the bread in the bread dish and shout "Breakfast." I pour the coffee in the coffee pot and the milk in the milk pitcher, except I leave (*indicating*) this much for me. I put them on the tray and bring them here. If you're not in the diningroom I call again. "Breakfast." I go to the kitchen, I fill the milk pan with water and let it soak. I pour my coffee, sit at the counter and eat my breakfast. I go upstairs to make your bed and clean your bathroom. I come down here to meet you and figure out what you want for lunch and dinner. And try to get you to think quickly so I can run to the market and get it bought before all the fresh stuff is bought up. Then, I start the day.

LETICIA:  So?

OLIMPIA:  So I need a steam pot.

LETICIA:  What is a steam pot?

OLIMPIA:  A pressure cooker.

LETICIA:  And you want a steam pot? Don't you have enough pots?

OLIMPIA:  No.

LETICIA:  Why do you want a steam pot?

OLIMPIA:  It cooks faster.

LETICIA:  How much is it?

OLIMPIA:  Expensive.

LETICIA:  How much?

OLIMPIA:  Twenty.

LETICIA:  Too expensive. (**OLIMPIA** *throws the silver on the floor.* **LETICIA** *turns her eyes up to the ceiling.*) Why do you want one more pot?

OLIMPIA:  I don't have a steam pot.

LETICIA:  A pressure cooker.

OLIMPIA:  A pressure cooker.

LETICIA:  You have too many pots. (**OLIMPIA** *goes to the kitchen and returns with an aluminum pan. She shows it to* **LETICIA**.)

OLIMPIA:  Look at this. (**LETICIA** *looks at it.*)

LETICIA:  What? (**OLIMPIA** *hits the pan against the back of a chair, breaking off a piece of the bottom.*)

OLIMPIA:  It's no good.

LETICIA:  All right! (*She takes money from her pocket and gives it to* **OLIMPIA**.) Here. Buy it!—What are we having for lunch?

OLIMPIA:  Fish.

LETICIA:  I don't like fish.—What else?

OLIMPIA:  Boiled plantains.

LETICIA:  Make something I like.

OLIMPIA:  Avocados. (**LETICIA** *gives a look of resentment to* **OLIMPIA**.)

LETICIA:  Why can't you make something I like?

OLIMPIA:  Avocados.

LETICIA:  Something that needs cooking.

OLIMPIA:  Bread pudding.

LETICIA:  And for dinner?

OLIMPIA:  Pot roast.

LETICIA:  What else?

OLIMPIA:  Rice.

LETICIA:  What else?

OLIMPIA:  Salad.

LETICIA:  What kind?

OLIMPIA:  Avocado.

LETICIA:  Again. (**OLIMPIA** *looks at* **LETICIA**.)

OLIMPIA:  You like avocados.

LETICIA:  Not again.—Tomatoes. (**OLIMPIA** *mumbles.*) What's wrong with tomatoes besides that you don't like them? (**OLIMPIA** *mumbles.*) Get some. (**OLIMPIA** *mumbles.*) What does that mean? (**OLIMPIA** *doesn't answer.*) Buy tomatoes.—What else?

OLIMPIA:  That's all.

LETICIA:  We need a green.

OLIMPIA:  Watercress.

LETICIA:  What else?

OLIMPIA:  Nothing.

LETICIA: For dessert.

OLIMPIA: Bread pudding.

LETICIA: Again.

OLIMPIA: Why not?

LETICIA: Make a flan.

OLIMPIA: No flan.

LETICIA: Why not?

OLIMPIA: No good.

LETICIA: Why no good!—Buy some fruit then.

OLIMPIA: What kind?

LETICIA: Pineapple. (OLIMPIA *shakes her head.*) Why not? (OLIMPIA *shakes her head.*) Mango.

OLIMPIA: No mango.

LETICIA: Buy some fruit! That's all. Don't forget bread. (LETICIA *hands* OLIMPIA *some bills.* OLIMPIA *holds it and waits for more.* LETICIA *hands her one more bill. Lights fade to black.*)

## SCENE 5

*The warehouse table is propped against the door. The chair on the left faces right. The door is pushed and the table falls to the floor.* ORLANDO *enters. He wears an undershirt with short sleeves, breeches with suspenders and boots. He looks around the room for* NENA. *Believing she has escaped, he becomes still and downcast. He turns to the door and stands there for a moment. He takes a few steps to the right and stands there for a moment staring fixedly. He hears a sound from behind the boxes, walks to them and takes a box off.* NENA *is there. Her head is covered with a blanket. He pulls the blanket off.* NENA *is motionless and staring into space. He looks at her for a while, then walks to the chair and sits facing right staring into space. A few moments pass. Lights fade to black.*

## SCENE 6

LETICIA *speaks on the telephone to* MONA.

LETICIA: Since they moved him to the new department he's different. (*Brief pause.*) He's distracted. I don't know where he goes in his mind. He doesn't listen to me. He worries. When I talk to him he doesn't listen. He's thinking about the job. He says he worries. What is there to worry about? Do you think there is anything to worry about? (*Brief pause.*) What meeting? (*Brief pause.*) Oh, sure. When is it? (*Brief pause.*) At what time? What do you mean I knew? No one told me.—I don't remember. Would you pick me up? (*Brief pause.*) At one? Isn't one early? (*Brief pause.*) Orlando may still be home at one. Sometimes he's here a little longer than usual. After lunch he sits and smokes. Don't you think one thirty will give us enough time? (*Brief pause.*) No. I can't leave while he's smoking . . . I'd rather not. I'd rather wait till he leaves. (*Brief pause.*) . . . One thirty, then. Thank you, Mona. (*Brief pause.*) See you then. Bye. (LETICIA *puts down the receiver and walks to stage right area.* ORLANDO'S *voice is heard offstage left. He and* ALEJO *enter halfway through the following speech.*)

ORLANDO: He made loud sounds not high-pitched like a horse. He sounded like a whale, like a wounded whale. He was pouring liquid from everywhere, his mouth, his nose, his eyes. He was not a horse but a sexual organ.—Helpless. A viscera.—Screaming. Making strange sounds. He collapsed on top of her. She wanted him off but he collapsed on top of her and stayed there on top of her. Like gum. He looked more like a whale than a horse. A seal. His muscles were soft. What does it feel like to be without shape like that. Without pride. She was indifferent. He stayed there for a while and then lifted himself off her and to the ground. (*Pause.*) He looked like a horse again.

LETICIA: Alejo, how are you? (ALEJO *kisses* LETICIA'S *hand.*)

ORLANDO: (*As he walks to the livingroom. He sits left facing front.*) Alejo is staying for dinner.

LETICIA: Would you like some coffee?

ALEJO: Yes, thank you.

LETICIA: Would you like some coffee, Orlando?

ORLANDO: Yes, thank you.

LETICIA: (*In a loud voice towards the kitchen.*) Olimpia . . .

OLIMPIA: What?

LETICIA: Coffee . . . (LETICIA *sits to the right of the table.* ALEJO *sits center.*)

ALEJO: Have you heard?

LETICIA: Yes, he's dead and I'm glad he's dead. An evil man. I knew he'd be killed. Who killed him?

ALEJO: Someone who knew him.

LETICIA: What is there to gain? So he's murdered. Someone else will do the job. Nothing will change. To destroy them all is to say we destroy us all.

ALEJO: Do you think we're all rotten?

LETICIA: Yes.

ORLANDO: A bad germ?

LETICIA: Yes.

ORLANDO: In our hearts?

LETICIA: Yes.—In our eyes.

ORLANDO: You're silly.

LETICIA: We're blind. We can't see beyond an arm's reach. We don't believe our life will last beyond the day. We only know what we have in our hand to put in our mouth, to put in our stomach, and to put in our pocket. We take care of our pocket, but not of our country. We take care of our stomachs but not of our hungry. We are primitive. We don't believe in the future. Each night when the sun goes down we think that's the end of life—so we have one last fling. We don't think we have a future. We don't think we have a country. Ask anybody, "Do you have a country?" They'll say, "Yes." Ask them, "What is your country?" They'll say, "My bed, my dinner plate." But, things can change. They can. I have changed. You have changed. He has changed.

ALEJO: Look at me. I used to be an idealist. Now I don't have any feeling for anything. I used to be strong, healthy, I looked at the future with hope.

LETICIA: Now you don't?

ALEJO: Now I don't. I know what viciousness is.

ORLANDO: What is viciousness?

ALEJO: You.

ORLANDO: Me?

ALEJO: The way you tortured Felo.

ORLANDO: I never tortured Felo.

ALEJO: You did.

ORLANDO: Boys play that way. You did too.

ALEJO: I didn't.

ORLANDO: He was repulsive to us.

ALEJO: I never hurt him.

ORLANDO: Well, you never stopped me.

ALEJO: I didn't know how to stop you. I didn't know anyone could behave the way you did. It frightened me. It changed me. I became hopeless. (ORLANDO *walks to the diningroom.*)

ORLANDO: You were always hopeless. (*He exits.* OLIMPIA *enters carrying three demitasse coffees on a tray. She places them on the table and exits.*)

ALEJO: I am sexually impotent. I have no feelings. Things pass through me which resemble feelings but I know they are not. I'm impotent.

LETICIA: Nonsense.

ALEJO: It's not nonsense. How can you say it's nonsense?—How can one live in a world that festers the way ours does and take any pleasure in life? (*Lights fade to black.*)

# SCENE 7

NENA *and* ORLANDO *stand against the wall in the warehouse. She is fully dressed. He is barebreasted. He pushes his pelvis against her gently. His lips touch her face as he speaks. The words are inaudible to the audience. On the table there is a tin plate with food and a tin cup with milk.*

ORLANDO: Look this way. I'm going to do something to you. (*She makes a move away from him.*) Don't do that. Don't move away. (*As he slides his hand along her side.*) I just want to put my hand here like this. (*He puts his lips on hers softly and speaks at the same time.*) Don't hold your lips so tight. Make them soft. Let them loose. So I can do this. (*She whimpers.*) Don't cry. I won't hurt you. This is all I'm going to do to you. Just hold your lips soft. Be nice. Be a nice girl. (*He pushes against her and reaches an orgasm. He remains motionless for a moment, then steps away from her still leaning his hand on the wall.*) Go eat. I brought you food. (*She goes to the table. He sits on the floor and watches her eat. She eats voraciously. She looks at the milk.*) Drink it. It's milk. It's good for you. (*She drinks the milk, the continues eating. Lights fade to black.*)

## SCENE 8

LETICIA *stands left of the diningroom table. She speaks words she has memorized.* OLIMPIA *sits to the left of the table. She holds a book close to her eyes. Her head moves from left to right along the written words as she mumbles the sound of imaginary words. She continues doing this through the rest of the scene.*

LETICIA: The impact of war is felt particularly in the economic realm. The destruction of property, private as well as public may paralyze the country. Foreign investment is virtually . . . (*To* OLIMPIA.) Is that right? (*Pause.*) Is that right!

OLIMPIA: Wait a moment. (*She continues mumbling and moving her head.*)

LETICIA: What for? (*Pause.*) You can't read. (*Pause.*) You can't read!

OLIMPIA: Wait a moment. (*She continues mumbling and moving her head.*)

LETICIA: (*Slapping the book off* OLIMPIA'S *hand.*) Why are you pretending you can read? (OLIMPIA *slaps* LETICIA'S *hands. They slap each other's hands. Lights fade to black.*)

## SCENE 9

ORLANDO *sits in the livingroom. He smokes. He faces front and is thoughtful.* LETICIA *and* OLIMPIA *are in the diningroom.* LETICIA *wears a hat and jacket. She tries to put a leather strap through the loops of a suitcase. There is a smaller piece of luggage on the floor.*

LETICIA: This strap is too wide. It doesn't fit through the loop. (ORLANDO *doesn't reply.*) Is this the right strap? Is this the strap that came with this suitacse? Did the strap that came with the suitcase break? If so, where is it? And when did it break? Why doesn't this strap fit the suitcase and how did it get here. Did you buy this strap, Orlando?

ORLANDO: I may have.

LETICIA: It doesn't fit.

ORLANDO: Hm.

LETICIA: It doesn't fit through the loops.

ORLANDO: Just strap it outside the loops. (LETICIA *stands.* OLIMPIA *tries to put the strap through the loop.*)

LETICIA: No. You're supposed to put it through the loops. That's what the loops are for. What happened to the other strap?

ORLANDO: It broke.

LETICIA: How?

ORLANDO: I used it for something.

LETICIA: What! (*He looks at her.*) You should have gotten me one that fit. What did you use it for?—Look at that.

OLIMPIA: Strap it outside the loops.

LETICIA: That wouldn't look right.

ORLANDO: (*Going to look at the suitcase.*) Why do you need the straps?

LETICIA: Because they come with it.

ORLANDO: You don't need them.

LETICIA: And travel like this?

ORLANDO: Use another suitcase.

LETICIA: What other suitcase. I don't have another. (ORLANDO *looks at his watch.*)

ORLANDO: You're going to miss your plane.

LETICIA: I'm not going. I'm not travelling like this.

ORLANDO: Go without it. I'll send it to you.

LETICIA: You'll get new luggage, repack it and send it to me?—All right. (*She starts to exit left.*) It's nice to travel light. (*Off stage.*) Do I have everything?—Come, Olimpia.

OLIMPIA *follows with the suitcases.* OR-LANDO *takes the larger suitcase from* OLIM-PIA. *She exits.* ORLANDO *goes up the hallway and exits through the left door. A moment later he enters holding* NENA *close to him. She is pale, dishevelled and has black circles around her eyes. She has a high fever and is almost unconscious. Her dress is torn and soiled. She is barefoot. He carries a new cotton dress on his arm. He takes her to the chair in the livingroom. He takes off the soiled dress and puts the new dress on her over a soiled slip.*

ORLANDO: That's nice. You look nice. (LETI-CIA'S *voice is heard. He hurriedly takes* NENA *out the door, closes it, and leans on it.*)

LETICIA: (*Off stage.*) It would take but a second. You run to the garage and get the little suitcase and I'll take out the things I need. (LETICIA *and* OLIMPIA *enter left.* OLIMPIA *exits right.*) Hurry. Hurry. It would take but a second. (*Seeing* OR-LANDO.) Orlando, I came back because I couldn't leave without anything at all. I came to get a few things because I have a smaller suitcase where I can take a few things. (*She puts the suitcase on the table, opens it and takes out the things she mentions.*) A pair of shoes . . . (OLIMPIA *enters right with a small suitcase.*)

OLIMPIA: Here.

| LETICIA: | OLIMPIA: |
|---|---|
| A nightgown, | A robe, |
| a robe, | a dress, |
| underwear, | a nightgown, |
| a dress, | underwear, |
| a sweater. | a sweater, |
| | a pair of shoes. |

LETICIA *closes the large suitcase.* OLIMPIA *closes the smaller suitcase.*

LETICIA: (*Starting to exit.*) Goodbye.

OLIMPIA: (*Following* LETICIA.) Goodbye.

ORLANDO: Goodbye. (*Lights fade to black.*)

# SCENE 10

NENA *is curled on the extreme right of the mattress.* ORLANDO *sits on the mattress using* NENA *as a back support.* ALEJO *sits on the chair. He holds a green paper on his hand.* OLIMPIA *sweeps the floor.*

ORLANDO: Tell them to check him. See if there's a scratch on him. There's not a scratch on that body. Why the fuss! Who was he and who's making a fuss? Why is he so important?

ALEJO: He was in deep. He knew names.

ORLANDO: I was never told that. But it wouldn't have mattered if they had because he died before I touched him.

ALEJO: You have to go to headquarters. They want you there.

ORLANDO: He came in screaming and he wouldn't stop. I had to wait for him to stop screaming before I could even pose a question to him. He wouldn't stop. I had put the poker to his neck to see if he would stop. Just to see if he would shut up. He just opened his eyes wide and started shaking and screamed even louder and fell over dead. Maybe he took something. I didn't do anything to him. If I didn't get anything from him it's because he died before I could get to him. He died of fear, not from anything I did to him. Tell them to do an autopsy. I'm telling you the truth. That's the truth. Why the fuss.

ALEJO: (*Starting to put the paper in his pocket.*) I'll tell them what you said.

ORLANDO: Let me see that. (ALEJO *takes it to him.* ORLANDO *looks at it and puts it back in* ALEJO's *hands.*) O.K. so it's a trap. So what side are you on? (*Pause.* ALEJO *says nothing.*) So what do they want? (*Pause.*) Who's going to question me? That's funny. That's very funny. They want to question me. They want to punch my eyes out? I knew something was wrong because they were getting nervous. Antonio was getting nervous. I went to him and I asked him if something was wrong. He said, no, nothing was wrong. But I could tell something was wrong. He looked at Velez and Velez looked back at him. They are stupid. They want to conceal something from me and they look at each other right in front of me, as if I'm blind, as if I can't tell that they are worried about something. As if there's something happening right in front of my nose but I'm blind and I can't see it. (*He grabs the paper from* ALEJO's *hand.*) You understand? (*He goes up the steps.*)

OLIMPIA: Like an alligator, big mouth and no brains. Lots of teeth but no brains. All tongue. (ORLANDO *enters through the left hallway door, and sits at the diningroom table.* ALEJO *enters a few moments later. He stands to the right.*)

ORLANDO: What kind of way is this to treat me?—After what I've done for them?— Is this a way to treat me?—I'll come up ... as soon as I can—I haven't been well.—O.K. I'll come up. I get depressed because things are bad and they are not going to improve. There's something malignant in the world. Destructiveness, aggressiveness.—Greed. People take what is not theirs. There is greed. I am

depressed, disillusioned ... with life ... with work ... family. I don't see hope. (*He sits. He speaks more to himself than to* ALEJO.) Some people get a cut in a finger and die. Because their veins are right next to their skin. There are people who, if you punch them in their stomach the skin around the stomach bursts and the bowels fall out. Other people, you cut them open and you don't see any veins. You can't find their intestines. There are people who don't even bleed. There are people who bleed like pigs. There are people who have the nerves right on their skins. You touch them and they scream. They have their vital organs close to the surface. You hit them and they burst an organ. I didn't even touch this one and he died. He died of fear. (*Lights fade to black.*)

# SCENE 11

NENA, ALEJO and OLIMPIA *sit cross-legged on the mattress in the basement.* NENA *sits right,* ALEJO *center,* OLIMPIA *left.* NENA *and* OLIMPIA *play pattycake.* ORLANDO *enters. He goes close to them.*

ORLANDO: What you you doing?

OLIMPIA: I'm playing with her.

ORLANDO: (*To* ALEJO.) What are you doing here? (ALEJO *looks at* ORLANDO *as a reply.* ORLANDO *speaks sarcastically.*) They're playing pattycake. (*He goes near* NENA.) So? (*Short pause.* NENA *giggles.*) Stop laughing! (NENA *is frightened.* OLIMPIA *holds her.*)

OLIMPIA: Why do you have to spoil everything. We were having a good time.

ORLANDO: Shut up! (NENA *whimpers.*) Stop whimpering. I can't stand your whimpering. I can't stand it. (*Timidly, she tries to speak words as she whimpers.*) Speak up. I can't hear you! She's crazy! Take her to the crazy house!

OLIMPIA: She's not crazy! She's a baby!

ORLANDO: She's not a baby! She's crazy! You think she's a baby? She's older than you think! How old do you think she is—Don't tell me that.

OLIMPIA: She's sick. Don't you see she's sick? Let her cry! (*To* NENA.) Cry!

ORLANDO: You drive me crazy too with your . . . (*He imitates her speech defect. She punches him repeatedly.*)

OLIMPIA: You drive me crazy! (*He pushes her off.*) You drive me crazy! You are a bastard! One day I'm going to kill you when you're asleep! I'm going to open you up and cut your entrails and feed them to the snakes. (*She tries to strangle him.*) I'm going to tear your heart out and feed it to the dogs! I'm going to cut your head open and have the cats eat your brain! (*Reaching for his fly.*) I'm going to cut your peepee and hang it on a tree and feed it to the birds!

ORLANDO: Get off me! I'm getting rid of you too! (*He starts to exit.*) I can't stand you!

OLIMPIA: Oh, yeah! I'm getting rid of you.

ORLANDO: I can't stand you!

OLIMPIA: I can't stand you!

ORLANDO: Meddler! (*To* ALEJO.) I can't stand you either.

OLIMPIA: (*Going to the stairs.*) Tell the boss! Tell her! She won't get rid of me! She'll get rid of you! What good are you! Tell her! (*She goes to* NENA.) Don't pay any attention to him. He's a coward.—You're pretty. (ORLANDO *enters through the hallway left door. He sits center at the dining-room table and leans his head on it.* LETICIA *enters. He turns to look at her.*)

LETICIA: You didn't send it. (*Lights fade to black.*)

## SCENE 12

LETICIA *sits next to the phone. She speaks to* MONA *in her mind.*

LETICIA: I walk through the house and I know where he's made love to her I think I hear his voice making love to her. Saying the same things he says to me, the same words.—(*There is a pause.*) There is someone here. He keeps someone here in the house. (*Pause.*) I don't dare look. (*Pause.*) No, there's nothing I can do. I can't do anything. (*She walks to the hallway. She hears footsteps. She moves rapidly to left and hides behind a pillar.* OLIMPIA *enters from right. She takes a few steps down the hallway. She carries a plate of food. She sees* LETICIA *and stops. She takes a few steps in various directions, then stops.*)

OLIMPIA: Here kitty, kitty. (LETICIA *walks to* OLIMPIA, *looks closely at the plate, then up at* OLIMPIA.)

LETICIA: What is it?

OLIMPIA: Food.

LETICIA: Who is it for? (OLIMPIA *turns her eyes away and doesn't answer.* LETICIA *decides to go to the cellar door. She stops halfway there.*) Who is it?

OLIMPIA: A cat. (LETICIA *opens the cellar door.*)

LETICIA: It's not a cat. I'm going down. (*She opens the door to the cellar and starts to go down.*) I want to see who is there.

ORLANDO: (*Offstage from the cellar.*) What is it you want? (*Lights fade to black.*)

## SCENE 13

ORLANDO *leans back on the chair in the basement. His legs are outstretched. His eyes are bloodshot and leery. His tunic is open.* NENA *is curled on the floor.* ORLANDO *speaks quietly. He is deeply absorbed.*

ORLANDO: What I do to you is out of love. Out of want. It's not what you think. I wish you didn't have to be hurt. I don't do it out of hatred. It is not out of rage. It is love. It is a quiet feeling. It's a pleasure. It is quiet and it pierces my insides in the most internal way. It is my most private self. And this I give to you.—Don't be afraid.—It is a desire to destroy and to see things destroyed and to see the inside of them.—It's my nature. I must hide this from others. But I don't feel remorse. I was born this way and I must have this.—I need love. I wish you did not feel hurt and recoil from me. (*Lights fade to black.*)

# SCENE 14

ORLANDO *sits to the right and* LETICIA *sits to the left of the table.*

LETICIA: Don't make her scream. (*There is a pause.*)

ORLANDO: You're crazy.

LETICIA: Don't I give you enough?

ORLANDO: (*He's calm.*) Don't start.

LETICIA: How long is she going to be here?

ORLANDO: Not long.

LETICIA: Don't make her cry. (*He looks at her.*) I can't stand it. (*Pause.*) Why do you make her scream?

ORLANDO: I don't make her scream.

LETICIA: She screams.

ORLANDO: I can't help it. (*Pause.*)

LETICIA: I tell you I can't stand it. I'm going to ask Mona to come and stay with me.

ORLANDO: No.

LETICIA: I want someone here with me.

ORLANDO: I don't want her here.

LETICIA: Why not?

ORLANDO: I don't.

LETICIA: I need someone here with me.

ORLANDO: Not now.

LETICIA: When?

ORLANDO: Soon enough.—She's going to stay here for a while. She's going to work for us. She'll be a servant here.

LETICIA: . . . No.

ORLANDO: She's going to be a servant here. (*Lights fade to black.*)

# SCENE 15

OLIMPIA *and* NENA *are sitting at the diningroom table. They are separating stones and other matter from dry beans.*

NENA: I used to clean beans when I was in the home. And also string beans. I also pressed clothes. The days were long. Some girls did hand sewing. They spent the day doing that. I didn't like it. When I did that, the day was even longer and there were times when I couldn't move even if I tried. And they said I couldn't go there anymore, that I had to stay in the yard. I didn't mind sitting in the yard looking at the birds. I went to the laundryroom and watched the women work. They let me go in and sit there. And they showed me how to press. I like to press because my mind wanders and I find satisfaction. I can iron all day. I like the way the wrinkles come out and things look nice. It's a miracle isn't it? I could earn a living pressing clothes. And I could find my grandpa and take care of him.

OLIMPIA: Where is your grandpa?

NENA: I don't know. (*They work a little in silence.*) He sleeps in the streets. Because he's too old to remember where he lives. He needs a person to take care of him. And I can take care of him. But I don't know where he is.—He doesn't know where I am.—He doesn't know who he is. He's too old. He doesn't know anything about himself. He only knows how to beg. And he knows that, only because he's hungry. He walks around and begs for food. He forgets to go home. He lives in the camp for the homeless and he has his own box. It's not an ugly box like the others. It is a real box. I used to live there with him. He took me with him when my mother died till they took me to the home. It is a big box. It's big enough for two. I could sleep in the front where it's cold. And he could sleep in the back where it's warmer. And he could lean on me. The floor is hard for him because he's skinny and it's hard on his poor bones. He could sleep on top of me if that would make him feel comfortable. I wouldn't mind. Except that he may pee on me because he pees in his pants. He doesn't know not to. He is incontinent. He can't hold it. His box was a little smelly. But that doesn't matter because I could clean it. All I would need is some soap. I could get plenty of water from the public faucet. And I could borrow a brush. You know how clean I could get it? As clean as new. You know what I would do? I would make holes in the floor so the pee would go down to the ground. And you know what else I would do?

OLIMPIA: What?

NENA: I would get straw and put it on the floor for him and for me and it would make it comfortable and clean and warm. How do you like that? Just as I did for my goat.

OLIMPIA: You have a goat?

NENA: . . . I did.

OLIMPIA: What happened to him?

NENA: He died. They killed him and ate him. Just like they did Christ.

OLIMPIA: Nobody ate Christ.

NENA: . . . I thought they did. My goat was eaten though.—In the home we had clean sheets. But that doesn't help. You can't sleep on clean sheets, not if there isn't someone watching over you while you sleep. And since my ma died there just wasn't anyone watching over me. Except you.—Aren't you? In the home they said guardian angels watch your sleep, but I didn't see any there. There weren't any. One day I heard my grandpa calling me and I went to look for him. And I didn't find him. I got tired and I slept in the street, and I was hungry and I was crying. And then he came to me and he spoke to me very softly so as not to scare me and he said he would give me something to eat and he said he would help me look for my grandpa.

And he put me in the back of his van . . . And he took me to a place. And he hurt me. I fought with him but I stopped fighting—because I couldn't fight anymore and he did things to me. And he locked me in. And sometimes he brought me food and sometimes he didn't. And he did things to me. And he beat me. And he hung me on the wall. And I got sick. And sometimes he brought me medicine. And then he said he had to take me somewhere. And he brought me here. And I am glad to be here because you are here. I only wish my grandpa were here too. He doesn't beat me so much anymore.

OLIMPIA: Why does he beat you? I hear him at night. He goes down the steps and I hear you cry. Why does he beat you?

NENA: Because I'm dirty.

OLIMPIA: You are not dirty.

NENA: I am. That's why he beats me. The dirt won't go away from inside me.—He comes downstairs when I'm sleeping and I hear him coming and it frightens me. And he takes the covers off me and I don't move because I'm frightened and because I feel cold and I think I'm going to die. And he puts his hand on me and he recites poetry. And he is almost naked. He wears a robe but he leaves it open and he feels himself as he recites. He touches himself and he touches his stomach and his breasts and his behind. He puts his fingers in my parts and he keeps reciting. Then he turns me on my stomach and puts himself inside me. And he says I belong to him. (*There is a pause.*) I want to conduct each day of my life in the best possible way. I should value the things I have. And I should value all those who are near me. And I should value the kindness that others bestow upon me. And if someone should treat me unkindly, I should not blind myself with rage, but I should see them and receive them, since maybe they are in worse pain than me. (*Lights fade to black.*)

# SCENE 16

LETICIA *speaks on the telephone with* MONA. *She speaks rapidly.*

LETICIA: He is violent. He has become more so. I sense it. I feel it in him.—I understand his thoughts. I know what he thinks.—I raised him. I practically did. He was a boy when I met him. I saw him grow. I was the first woman he loved. That's how young he was. I have to look after him, make sure he doesn't get into trouble. He's not wise. He's trusting. They are changing him.—He tortures people. I know he does. He tells me he doesn't but I know he does. I know it. How could I not. Sometimes he comes from headquarters and his hands are shaking. Why should he shake? What do they do there?—He should transfer. Why do that? He says he doesn't do it himself. That the officers don't do it. He says that people are not being tortured. That that is questionable.—Everybody knows it. How could he not know it when everybody knows it. Sometimes you see blood in the streets. Haven't you seen it? Why do they leave the bodies in the streets,—how evil, to frighten people? They tear their fingernails off and their poor hands are bloody and destroyed. And they mangle their genitals and expose them and they tear their eyes out and you can see the empty eyesockets in the skull. How awful, Mona. He musn't do it. I don't care if I don't have anything! What's money! I don't need a house as big as this! He's doing it for money! What other reason could he have! What other reason could he have!! He shouldn't do it. I cannot look at him

without thinking of it. He's doing it. I know he's doing it.—Shhhh! I hear steps. I'll call you later. Bye, Mona. I'll talk to you. (*She hangs up the receiver. Lights fade to black.*)

# SCENE 17

*The livingroom.* OLIMPIA *sits to the right,* NENA *to the left.*

OLIMPIA: I don't wear high heels because they hurt my feet. I used to have a pair but they hurt my feet and also (*Pointing to her calf*) here in my legs. So I don't wear them anymore even if they were pretty. Did you ever wear high heels? (NENA *shakes her head.*) Do you have ingrown nails? (NENA *looks at her questioningly.*) Nails that grow twisted into the flesh. (NENA *shakes her head.*) I don't either. Do you have sugar in the blood? (NENA *shakes her head.*) My mother had sugar in the blood and that's what she died of but she lived to be eighty six which is very old even if she had many things wrong with her. She had glaucoma and high blood pressure. (LETICIA *enters and sits center at the table.* NENA *starts to get up.* OLIMPIA *signals her to be still.* LETICIA *is not concerned with them.*)
LETICIA: So, what are you talking about?
OLIMPIA: Ingrown nails. (NENA *turns to* LETICIA *to make sure she may remain seated there.* LETICIA *is involved with her own thoughts.* NENA *turns front. Lights fade to black.*)

# SCENE 18

ORLANDO *is sleeping on the diningroom table. The telephone rings. He speaks as someone having a nightmare.*

ORLANDO: Ah! Ah! Ah! Get off me! Get off! I said get off! (LETICIA *enters.*)

LETICIA: (*Going to him.*) Orlando! What's the matter! What are you doing here!

ORLANDO: Get off me! Ah! Ah! Ah! Get off me!

LETICIA: Why are you sleeping here! On the table. (*Holding him close to her.*) Wake up.

ORLANDO: Let go of me. (*He slaps her hands as she tries to reach him.*) Get away from me. (*He goes to the floor on his knees and staggers to the telephone.*) Yes. Yes. it's me.—You did?—So?—It's true then.—What's the name?—Yes, sure.—Thanks.—Sure. (*He hangs up the receiver. He turns to look at* LETICIA. *Lights fade to black.*)

# SCENE 19

*Two chairs are placed side by side facing front in the center of the living room.* LETICIA *sits on the right.* ORLANDO *stands on the down left corner.* NENA *sits to the left of the dining room table facing front. She covers her face.* OLIMPIA *stands behind her, holding* NENA *and leaning her head on her.*

ORLANDO: Talk.

LETICIA: I can't talk like this.

ORLANDO: Why not?

LETICIA: In front of everyone.

ORLANDO: Why not?

LETICIA: It is personal. I don't need the whole world to know.

ORLANDO: Why not?

LETICIA: Because it's private. My life is private.

ORLANDO: Are you ashamed?

LETICIA: Yes, I am ashamed!

ORLANDO: What of...? What of...?—I want you to tell us—about your lover.

LETICIA: I don't have a lover. (*He grabs her by the hair.* OLIMPIA *holds on to* NENA *and hides her face.* NENA *covers her face.*)

ORLANDO: You have a lover.

LETICIA: That's a lie.

ORLANDO: (*Moving closer to her.*) It's not a lie. (*To* LETICIA.) Come on tell us. (*He pulls harder.*) What's his name? (*She emits a sound of pain. He pulls harder, leans toward her and speaks in a low tone.*) What's his name?

LETICIA: Albertico. (*He takes a moment to release her.*)

ORLANDO: Tell us about it. (*There is silence. He pulls her hair.*)

LETICIA: All right. (*He releases her.*)

ORLANDO: What's his name?

LETICIA: Albertico.

ORLANDO: Go on. (*Pause.*) Sit up! (*She does.*) Albertico what?

LETICIA: Estevez. (ORLANDO *sits next to her.*)

ORLANDO: Go on. (*Silence.*) Where did you first meet him?

LETICIA: At ... I ...

ORLANDO: (*He grabs her by the hair.*) In my office.

LETICIA: Yes.

ORLANDO: Don't lie.—When?

LETICIA: You know when.

ORLANDO: When! (*Silence.*) How did you meet him?

LETICIA: You introduced him to me. (*He lets her go.*)

ORLANDO: What else? (*Silence.*) Who is he!

LETICIA: He's a lieutenant.

ORLANDO: (*He stands.*) When did you meet with him?

LETICIA: Last week.

ORLANDO: When!

LETICIA: Last week.

ORLANDO: When!

LETICIA: Last week. I said last week.

ORLANDO: Where did you meet him?

LETICIA: ... In a house of rendezvous ...

ORLANDO: How did you arrange it?

LETICIA: ... I wrote to him ... I

ORLANDO: Did he approach you?

LETICIA: No.

ORLANDO: Did he!

LETICIA: No.

ORLANDO: (*He grabs her hair again.*) He did! How!

LETICIA: *I* approached him.

ORLANDO: How!

LETICIA: (*Aggressively.*) I looked at him! I looked at him! I looked at him! (*He lets her go.*)

ORLANDO: When did you look at him?

LETICIA: Please stop . . . !

ORLANDO: Where! When!

LETICIA: In your office!

ORLANDO: When?

LETICIA: I asked him to meet me!

ORLANDO: What did he say?

LETICIA: (*Aggressively.*) He walked away. He walked away! He walked away! I asked him to meet me.

ORLANDO: What was he like?

LETICIA: . . . Oh . . .

ORLANDO: Was he tender? Was he tender to you!

*She doesn't answer. He puts his hand inside her blouse. She lets out an excruciating scream. He lets her go and walks to the right of the diningroom. She goes to the telephone table, opens the drawer, takes a gun and shoots* ORLANDO. ORLANDO *falls dead.* NENA *runs to downstage of the table.* LETICIA *is disconcerted, then puts the revolver in* NENA's *hand and steps away from her.*

LETICIA: Please . . .

*NENA is in a state of terror and numb acceptance. She looks at the gun. Then, up. The lights fade.*

## SUMMARY

The feminist movement, which emerged in the 1970s, impacted on polities and art in the United States and western Europe. Examining the gender-biased "image of woman" in patriarchal cultures, feminist playwrights have militantly and didactically centered "woman" as drama's subject and evolved play forms analogous to women's biological cycles, sexual experiences, domestic routines. In general, their subjects are the alienation and repression of women throughout history. A playwright, like Maria Irene Fornes, who confronts the contemporary social-conditioning and abusive behavior of women *and* men has been both embraced by the feminists and rejected by them. Fornes herself rejects the categorizing of her work. She has remarked that to read *The Conduct of Life* as being about the subjugation of Latin American women is to limit the scope of the work. She has said of her writing that if her expression is "honest," it is "inevitable that it will often speak in a feminine way," but that she has never set about to write in a particular manner or about a particular subject.[5]

Fornes' work underscores the misunderstandings and contradictions inherent in feminist writing today. Women artists write from their personal perspectives which may or may not be philosophical and political observations about the role of women in western society. Since the women's movement is over twenty years old, certain assumptions are brought to their work by readers and audiences; that is, women as subjects are expected to be shown in traditional or nontraditional roles, or in roles of subservience, subjugation, or dominance to illustrate certain themes. However, the feminine voice entering the mainstream of theatre today introduces a woman's perspective, unexpected agendas, and new dramatic forms. By enlarging the parameters of western drama, feminist writing is reaching beyond narrow categories and bringing a different sensibility to examine human choices.

One vital new direction of *modernist* writing in the last decade of the twentieth century is the theatrical work that addresses issues of cultural diversity in a western Eurocentric society such as the United States. *Multiculturalism* and *interculturalism* are labels used to describe the rich diversity of American society and the fractures that appear at the seams of cultural hegemony as well. An unusually large number of playwrights and performance artists have emerged on the American scene in the last two decades. They address their ethnic identities and cultural differences and make art out of some of the most timely social and political issues of the new era in American politics.

## NOTES

1. Maria Irene Fornes, "Creative Danger," *American Theatre*, 2, No. 5 (Sept. 1985): 13, 15.
2. Sue-Ellen Case, *Feminism and Theatre* (New York: Methuen, 1988): 5–27.
3. Case 114–115.
4. Fornes 13, 15.
5. Fornes 13, 15.

now transformed by the Castro revolution, during which an uncle remained behind and committed suicide, inform the family's expressions of regret and loss. The mother of the bride, Sonia, longs for the untroubled innocence of her adolescence:

> Why can't life be like it was? Like my coming-out party. When my father introduced me to our society in my white dress.

Her practical sister, Miriam, puts the memory in a harsher perspective: "Sonia, they threw the parties to give us away . . . perfect merchandising."

*Broken Eggs* is a play that examines the collisions of two cultures and the reactions of three generations involved in the collision. The contradictions, fears, ambivalences, misunderstandings, social disturbances, and mixed messages are played out against the age-old rituals of marriage. As family traditions, religion, politics, and opiates collide with the "Anglo" culture, we gain insight into the cultural fractures that disrupt lives and change patterns of behavior. To assuage their sense of displacement, loss, and failure to belong, the older men turn to alcohol, the younger to cocaine; the older women to Valium, the younger to sex. All have experiences of struggling to survive in a strange land where they do not speak the language and fail to understand their unhappiness.

*Broken Eggs* is a comedy of family values tested against an alien culture and found to be strong and enduring. Despite the anger, unhappiness, confusion, and emotional chaos, the family, although somewhat frayed, survives intact. Each member has his or her own story of the pain of survival in a world where they have been thrust into exile by political revolution and forced to adapt. Old ways survive ("A Catholic does not get a divorce.") and new strategies emerge ("A valium—that's the only certain thing. It reassures you."). The generational struggle for identity, empowerment, and self-expression takes different forms but the play's overriding sentiment is that ethnic qualities and pride survive the collision of cultures and each generation derives its unique strength in its own way by retaining roots in memories, dreams, and daily rituals.

As an example of the intercultural text, *Broken Eggs* sets forth the dysfunction of an Hispanic family forced to relocate to Southern California as an outcome of the Cuban revolution. Of the three generations, the grandparents and the parents have retained their language and Hispanic traditions while they have experienced the painful sense of dislocation and separation. The children of Sonia and Osvaldo have willingly assimilated the new "Anglo" culture along with its metaphors ("You look better than Elizabeth Taylor in *Father of the Bride*."), drugs (cocaine), and acceptance of crossing ethnic lines (marrying into the Jewish family). The breaking eggs of the play's title are the three generations (parents and children) whose roots have been severed by the enforced exchange of cultures. Most affected are the middle-aged family members—Sonia, her ex-husband Osvaldo, and his sister Miriam. They have "cracked" under the strain of loss and difference. Their memories of white beaches and an innocent way of life protected by wealth and social status (all lost in the transition) are in contrast to the realities of their day-to-day existence in Southern California, where to accomplish the simplest tasks such as shopping at a supermarket or asking street directions of a policemen resulted in humiliation and estrangement. The family unit has been further severed by divorce (their Roman Catholicism did not deter the divorce in the new culture nor prevent Osvaldo from marrying his Argentinian mistress). The children, born in California, have wholly assimilated into the life styles of the culture into which they were born: Oscar flaunts his homosexuality, the unmarried Mimi is pregnant, and Lizette marries into another ethnic tradition.

The divorced parents, Sonia and Osvaldo, are at the center of Machado's intercultural story, for they exhibit the fragility and sharp edges of people existing in limbo—holding on to the past and watching helplessly the erosion of their lives in the present. They are trapped between remembrances of their past lives in Cuba before the revolution and their present dislocations in California. Machado presents a comedic analysis of the collision of cultures. The grandparents are forever separate from the new culture by inherited rituals and customs; the grandchildren have connected; but the middle-aged parents are suspended between two cultures. Their pain and fragile accommodations are the material of Machado's intercultural art.

# Broken Eggs

CHARACTERS

**SONIA MARQUEZ HERNANDEZ,** a Cuban woman

**LIZETTE,** Sonia's daughter, nineteen years old

**MIMI,** Sonia's daughter

**OSCAR,** Sonia's son

**MANUELA RIPOLL,** Sonia's mother

**OSVALDO MARQUEZ,** Sonia's ex-husband

**MIRIAM MARQUEZ,** Osvaldo's sister

**ALFREDO MARQUEZ,** Osvaldo's and Miriam's father

TIME

*A hot January day, 1979.*

PLACE

*A country club in Woodland Hills, California, a suburb of Los Angeles.*

## ACT ONE

*A waiting room off the main ballroom of a country club in Woodland Hills, California, a suburb of Los Angeles. The room is decorated for a wedding. Up center, sliding glass doors leading to the outside; stage right, a hallway leading to the dressing room; stage left, an archway containing the main entrance to the room and a hallway leading to the ballroom. A telephone booth in one corner. Two round tables, one set with coffee service and the other for the cake.*

*In the dark, we hear Mimi whistling the wedding march. As the lights come up, Lizette is practicing walking down the aisle. Mimi is drinking a Tab and watching Lizette. They are both dressed in casual clothes.*

**MIMI:** I never thought that any of us would get married, after all—

**LIZETTE:** Pretend you come from a happy home.

**MIMI:** We were the audience to one of the worst in the history of the arrangement.

**LIZETTE:** Well, I'm going to pretend that Mom and Dad are together for today.

**MIMI:** That's going to be hard to do if that mustached bitch, whore, cunt, Argentinian Nazi shows up to your wedding.

**LIZETTE:** Daddy promised me that his new wife had no wish to be here. She's not going to interfere.

**MIMI** *starts to gag.*

Mimi, why are you doing this.

**MIMI:** The whole family is going to be here.

**LIZETTE:** They're our family. Don't vomit again, Mimi, my wedding.

**MANUELA** (*Offstage*): Why didn't the bakery deliver it?

**MIMI:** Oh, no!

**LIZETTE:** Oh my God.

**MIMI** *and* **LIZETTE** *run to the offstage dressing room.*

**MANUELA** (*Offstage*): Who ever heard of getting up at 6 A.M.?

**SONIA** (*Offstage*): Mama, please—

**MANUELA** *and* **SONIA** *enter.* **SONIA** *is carrying two large cake boxes.* **MANUELA** *carries a third cake box.*

**MANUELA:** Well, why didn't they?

**SONIA:** Because the Cuban bakery only delivers in downtown L. A. They don't come out this far.

**MANUELA** *and* **SONIA** *start to assemble the cake.*

MANUELA: Then Osvaldo should have picked it up.

SONIA: It was my idea.

MANUELA: He should still pick it up, he's the man.

SONIA: He wanted to get a cake from this place, with frosting on it. But I wanted a cake to be covered with meringue, like mine.

MANUELA: You let your husband get away with everything.

SONIA: I didn't let him have a mistress.

MANUELA: Silly girl, she ended up being his wife!

SONIA: That won't last forever.

MANUELA: You were better off with a mistress. Now, you're the mistress.

SONIA: Please, help me set up the cake. . . . Osvaldo thought we should serve the cake on paper plates. I said no. There's nothing worse than paper plates. They only charge a dime a plate for the real ones and twenty dollars for the person who cuts it. I never saw a paper plate till I came to the USA.

MANUELA: She used witchcraft to take your husband away, and you did nothing.

SONIA: I will.

MANUELA: Then put powder in his drinks, like the witch lady told you to do.

SONIA: I won't need magic to get him back, Mama, don't put powders in his drink. It'll give him indigestion.

MANUELA: Don't worry.

SONIA: Swear to me. On my father's grave. *The cake is now assembled.*

MANUELA: I swear by the Virgin Mary, Saint Teresa my patron saint and all the saints, that I will not put anything into your husband's food . . . as long as his slut does not show up. Here. (*She hands* SONIA *a little bottle*)

SONIA: No.

MANUELA: In case you need it.

SONIA: I won't.

MANUELA: You might want it later. It also gives you diarrhea for at least three months. For love, you kiss the bottle, and thank the Virgin Mary. For diarrhea, you do the sign of the cross twice.

SONIA: All right.

MANUELA: If your father was alive, he'd shoot him for you.

SONIA: That's true.

MANUELA: Help me roll the cake out.

SONIA: No. They'll do it. They're getting the room ready now. They don't want us in there. We wait here—the groom's family across the way.

MANUELA: The Jews?

SONIA: The Rifkins. Then we make our entrance.

MANUELA: I see.

SONIA (*Looks at cake*): Perfect. Sugary and white . . . pure.

MANUELA: Beautiful.

SONIA: I'm getting nervous.

MANUELA: It's your daughter's wedding. A very big day in a mother's life, believe me.

SONIA: Yes, a wedding is a big day.

MANUELA: The day you got married your father told me, "We are too far away from our little girl." I said to him, "But, Oscar, we live only a mile away" He said, "You know that empty acre on the street where she lives now?" I said "Yes" He said, "I bought it and we are building another house there, then we can still be near our little girl."

SONIA: He loved me.

MANUELA: Worshipped you.

SONIA: I worshipped him. He'll be proud.

MANUELA: Where's your ex-husband, he's late.

LIZETTE *enters and makes herself a cup of coffee.* SONIA *helps her.*

SONIA: So how do you feel, Lizette, my big girl?

LIZETTE: I'm shaking.

MANUELA: That's good. You should be scared.

LIZETTE: Why, Grandma?

MANUELA: You look dark, did you sit out in the sun again?

LIZETTE: Yes, I wanted to get a tan.

MANUELA: Men don't like that, Lizette.

LIZETTE: How do you know?

SONIA: Mama, people like tans in America.

MANUELA: Men like women with white skin.

LIZETTE: That's a lie. They don't.

MANUELA: Don't talk back to me like that.

SONIA: No fights today, please, no fights. Lizette, tell her you're sorry. I'm nervous. I don't want to get a migraine, I want to enjoy today.

LIZETTE: Give me a kiss, Grandma.
*They kiss.*
Everything looks so good.

SONIA: It should—eight thousand dollars.

MANUELA: We spent more on your wedding and that was twenty-nine years ago. He should spend money on his daughter.

SONIA: He tries. He's just weak.

MANUELA: Don't defend him.

SONIA: I'm not.

MANUELA: Hate him. Curse him.

SONIA: I love him.

MANUELA: Sonia! Control yourself.

LIZETTE: He's probably scared to see everybody.

MANUELA: Good, the bastard.
LIZETTE *exits to dressing room.*

SONIA: Did I do a good job? Are you pleased by how it looks? (*She looks at the corsages and boutonnieres on a table*) Purples, pinks and white ribbons . . . tulle. Mama, Alfredo, Pedro. . . . No, not Pedro's . . . Oscar's. . . . He just looks like Pedro. Pedro! He got lost. He lost himself and then we lost him.

MANUELA: Sonia!

SONIA: I'll pin yours on, Mama.

MANUELA: Later, it'll wilt if you pin it now.

MIRIAM *enters. She is wearing a beige suit and a string of pearls.*

SONIA: Miriam, you're here on time. Thank you, Miriam.

MIRIAM: Sonia, look. (*Points at pearls*) They don't match. That means expensive. I bought them for the wedding.

MANUELA: Miriam, how pretty you look!

MIRIAM: Do you think the Jews will approve?

MANUELA: They're very nice, the Rifkins. They don't act Jewish. Lizette told me they put up a Christmas tree but what for I said to her?

MIRIAM: To fit in?

MANUELA: Why? Have you seen your brother?

MIRIAM: He picked us up last night from the airport.

MANUELA: Did he say anything to you?

MIRIAM: Yes, how old he's getting. . . . That's all he talks about.

MANUELA: Where's your husband?

MIRIAM: He couldn't come: business.

MANUELA: That's a mistake.

MIRIAM: I'm glad I got away.

MANUELA: But is he glad to be rid of you?

SONIA: Mama, go and see if Lizette needs help, please.

MANUELA: All right. Keep your husband happy, that's the lesson to learn from all this. Keep them happy. Let them have whatever they want. . . . Look at Sonia. (*She exits to dressing room*)

SONIA: Thank God for a moment of silence. Osvaldo this, Osvaldo that. Powder. Curse him. Poisons, shit . . .

MIRIAM: Are you all right? That faggot brother of mine is not worth one more tear: coward, mongoloid, retarded creep.

SONIA: Does he took happy to you?

MIRIAM: No.

SONIA: He looks sad?

MIRIAM: He always looked sad. Now he looks old and sad.

SONIA: Fear?

MIRIAM: Doesn't the Argentinian make him feel brave?

SONIA: He'll be mine again. He'll remember what it was like before the revolution. Alfredo and you being here will remind him of that. He'll remember our wedding—how perfect it was; how everything was right . . . the party, the limo, walking through the rose garden late at night, sleeping in the terrace room. I'm so hot I feel like I have a fever.

MIRIAM: "My darling children, do not go near the water, the sharks will eat you up." That's the lesson we were taught.

SONIA: Today I am going to show Osvaldo who's in control. Be nice to him today.

MIRIAM: He left you three months after your father died. He went because he knew you had no defense. He went off with that twenty-nine-year-old wetback. You know, we *had* to come here, but they *want* to come here. And you still want him back?

SONIA: If he apologizes, yes.

MIRIAM: Don't hold your breath. He lets everyone go. Pedro needed him—

SONIA: Don't accuse him of that, he just forgot.

MIRIAM: What? How could he forget. Pedro was our brother.

SONIA: He got so busy here working, that he forgot, he couldn't help him anyway. He was here, Pedro stayed in Cuba, you were in Miami, and I don't think anyone should blame anyone about that. No one was to blame!

MIRIAM: Oh, I'm having an attack . . . (*She shows* SONIA *her hands*) See how I'm shaking? It's like having a seizure. Where's water?

SONIA *gets her a glass of water. She takes two valium.*

You take one, too.

SONIA: No. Thank you.

MIMI *enters, goes to the pay phone, dials.*

MIRIAM: A valium makes you feel like you are floating in a warm beach.

SONIA: Varadero?

MIRIAM: Varadero, the Gulf of Mexico, Santa Mariá del Mar. It's because of these little pieces of magic that I escaped from the path. I did not follow the steps of my brothers and end up an alcoholic.

SONIA: Osvaldo never drank a lot.

MIRIAM: You forget.

SONIA: Well, drinking was not the problem.

MANUELA (*Entering*): I made Mimi call the brothel to see why your husband's late.

MIRIAM: Where's Lizette?

MANUELA: Down the hall. It says "Dressing Room."

MIRIAM: I got five hundred dollars, brand-new bills. (*She exits*)

SONIA: The world I grew up in is out of style; will we see it again, Mama?

MIMI (*Comes out of the phone booth*): She answered. She said "Yes?" I said "Where's my father?" She said "Gone." I said "Already!" She said "I'm getting ready for. . . ." I said "For what? Your funeral?" She hung up on me. She sounded stoned.

MANUELA: Sonia, someday it will be reality again, I promise.

MIMI: What?

SONIA: Cuba. Cuba will be a reality.

MIMI: It was and is a myth. Your life there is mythical.

MANUELA: That's not true. Her life was perfect. In the mornings, after she was married, Oscar would get up at six-thirty and send one of his bus drivers ten miles to buy bread from her favorite bakery, to buy bread for his little married girl.

SONIA: At around nine, I would wake up and walk out the door through the yard to the edge of the rose garden and call, "Papa, my bread."

MANUELA: The maid would run over, cross the street and hand her two pieces of hot buttered bread . . .

SONIA: I'd stick my hand through the gate and she'd hand me the bread. I'd walk back—into my mother-in-law's kitchen, and my coffee and milk would be waiting for me.

MIMI: Did you read the paper?

SONIA: The papers? I don't think so.

MIMI: Did you think about the world?

SONIA: No. I'd just watch your father sleep and eat my breakfast.

MANUELA: Every morning, "Papa, my bread." (*She goes to the outside doors and stays there, staring out*)

MIMI: You will never see it again. Even if you do go back, you will seem out of place; it will never be the same.

SONIA: No? You never saw it.

MIMI: And I will never see it.

SONIA: Never say never!

MIMI: What do you mean "Never say never"?!

SONIA: Never say never. Never is not real. It is a meaningless word. Always is a word that means something. Everything will happen always. The things that you feared and made your hands shake with horror, and you thought "not to me," will happen always.

MIMI: Stop it!

SONIA: I have thoughts, ideas. Just because I don't speak English well doesn't mean that I don't have feelings. A voice—a voice that thinks, a mind that talks.

MIMI: I didn't say that.

SONIA: So never say never, dear. Be ready for anything. Don't die being afraid. Don't, my darling.

MIMI: So simple.

MIRIAM *enters.*

SONIA: Yes, very simple, darling.

MIRIAM: What was simple?

SONIA: Life, when we were young.

MIRIAM: A little embarrassing, a little dishonest, but without real care; that's true. A few weeks ago I read an ad. It said "Liberate Cuba through the power of Voodoo." There was a picture of Fidel's head with three pins stuck through his temples.

MANUELA: They should stick pins in his penis.

SONIA: Mama! (*She laughs*)

MANUELA: Bastard.

MIRIAM: The idea was that if thousands of people bought the product, there would be a great curse that would surely kill him—all that for only $11.99. Twelve dollars would be all that was needed to overthrow the curse of our past.

LIZETTE *enters wearing a robe.*

MANUELA: We should try everything, anything.

LIZETTE: Today is my wedding, it is really happening in an hour, here, in Woodland Hills, California, Los Angeles. The United States of America, 1979. No Cuba today please, no Cuba today.

SONIA: Sorry.

MIMI: You want all the attention.

SONIA: Your wedding is going to be perfect. We are going to win this time.

LIZETTE: Win what?

MANUELA: The battle.

MIRIAM: "Honest woman" versus the "whore."

MIMI: But who's the "honest woman" and who's the "whore"?

MANUELA: Whores can be easily identified—they steal husbands.

MIRIAM: They're from Argentina.

SONIA: They say "yes" to everything. The good ones say "no."

LIZETTE: And we're the good ones.

SONIA: Yes. I am happy today. You are the bride, the wedding decorations came out perfect and we are having a party. Oo, oo, oo, oo, oo . . . *uh.*

*The women all start doing the conga in a circle. They sing.* OSVALDO *enters.*

Join the line.

LIZETTE: In back of me, Daddy.

MIRIAM: In front of me, Osvaldo.

*They dance.* **MIRIAM** *gooses* **OSVALDO.**

**OSVALDO:** First I kiss my daughter— (*He kisses* **LIZETTE**) then my other little girl— (*He kisses* **MIMI**) then my sister—
*He and* **MIRIAM** *blow each other a kiss.*
—then my wife. (He kisses **SONIA**)

**SONIA:** Your ex-wife.

**OSVALDO:** My daughter's mother.

**SONIA:** That's right.

> **MIRIAM** *lights a cigarette and goes outside.*

**MIMI:** We were together once, family: my mom, my dad, my big sister, my big brother. We ate breakfast and dinner together and drove down to Florida on our vacations, looked at pictures of Cuba together.

**SONIA:** And laughed, right?

**MIMI:** And then Papa gave us up.

**OSVALDO:** I never gave you up.

**MIMI:** To satisfy his urge.

**MANUELA:** Stop right now.

**OSVALDO:** Don't ever talk like that again.

**SONIA:** Isn't it true?

**OSVALDO:** It's more complex than that.

**SONIA:** More complex—how? No, stop.

**LIZETTE:** Please stop.

**MANUELA:** Don't fight.

**MIMI:** You see, Daddy, I understand you.

**OSVALDO:** You don't.

**MIMI:** I try.

**OSVALDO:** So do I.

**MIMI:** You don't.

**OSVALDO:** I'm going outside.

**LIZETTE:** Come, sit with me.

**SONIA:** You have to start getting dressed.

**LIZETTE:** Thank you for making *me* happy.

**OSVALDO:** I try.

> **LIZETTE** *and* **OSVALDO** *exit to dressing room.*

**SONIA:** Mimi, no more today. Please, no more.

**MIMI:** When you're born the third child, the marriage is already half apart, and being born into a family that's half over, half apart, is a disturbing thing to live with.

**SONIA:** Where did you read that?

**MIMI:** I didn't read it. It's my opinion. Based on my experience, of my life.

**SONIA:** We were never half apart.

**MIMI:** No, but that's what it felt like.

**MANUELA:** It's unheard of. It's unbelievable—

**MIMI:** What is she talking about now?

**MANUELA:** A Catholic does not get a divorce. They have a mistress and a wife but no divorce, a man does not leave everything.

**SONIA** (*To* **MIMI**): As difficult as it might be for you to understand, we were together, and a family when you were born. I wanted, we wanted, to have you. We had just gotten to the U.S., Lizette was ten months old. Your father had gotten his job as an accountant. We lived behind a hamburger stand between two furniture stores, away from everything we knew, afraid of everything around us. We were alone, no one spoke Spanish. Half of the people thought we were Communist, the other half traitors to a great cause; three thousand miles away from our real lives. But I wanted you and we believed in each other more than ever before. We were all we had.

**MIMI:** I wish it would have always stayed like that.

**SONIA:** So do I.

**MANUELA:** In Cuba, not in California, we want our Cuba back.

**MIMI:** It's too late for that, Grandma.

**MANUELA:** No.

**MIMI:** They like their government.

**MANUELA:** Who?

**MIMI:** The people who live there like socialism.

**MANUELA:** No. Who told you that?

**MIMI:** He's still in power, isn't he?

**MANUELA:** Because he oppresses them. He has the guns, Fidel has the bullets. Not the people. He runs the concentration camps. He has Russia behind him. China. We have nothing behind us. My cousins are starving there.

MIMI: At least they know who they are.

MANUELA: You don't? Well, I'll tell you. You're Manuela Sonia Marquez Hernandez. A Cuban girl. Don't forget what I just told you.

MIMI: No, Grandma. I'm Manuela Sonia Marquez, better known as Mimi Markwez. I was born in Canoga Park. I'm a first-generation white Hispanic American.

MANUELA: No you're not. You're a Cuban girl. Memorize what I just told you.

*LIZETTE and OSVALDO enter. LIZETTE is in her bra and slip.*

LIZETTE: My dress, Mama, help me, time to dress.

SONIA: The bride is finally ready, Mama, help me dress her in her wedding dress. Miriam, Mimi, she's going to put on her wedding dress.

*MIRIAM enters.*

MANUELA: You're going to look beautiful.

SONIA: And happy, right, dear?

LIZETTE: I'm happy. This is a happy day, like they tell you in church, your baptism, your first communion and your wedding. Come on, Mimi.

*All the women except SONIA exit to the dressing room.*

SONIA: That's how I felt. I felt just like her.

OSVALDO: When, Sonia?

SONIA: Twenty-nine years ago.

*SONIA exits to the dressing room. OSVALDO goes to the bar and pours himself a double of J&B. ALFREDO enters.*

ALFREDO: You the guard?

OSVALDO: No.

ALFREDO: Drinking so early in the morning.

OSVALDO: My nerves, Daddy.

ALFREDO: Nervous, you made your bed, lie in it.

OSVALDO: I do. I do lie in it.

ALFREDO: So don't complain.

OSVALDO: I'm just nervous, little Lizette is a woman now.

ALFREDO: You're lucky.

OSVALDO: Why?

ALFREDO: She turned out to be decent.

OSVALDO: Why wouldn't she?

ALFREDO: In America it's hard to keep girls decent, especially after what you did.

OSVALDO: I never deserted them.

ALFREDO: But divorce, you're an idiot. Why get married twice, once is enough. You can always have one on the side and keep your wife. But to marry your mistress is stupid, crazy and foolish. It's not done, son. It's not decent.

OSVALDO: And you know a lot about decency?!

ALFREDO: I stayed married.

OSVALDO: Daddy, she loved me. I loved her. We couldn't be away from each other. She left her husband.

ALFREDO: She wanted your money.

OSVALDO: What money?

ALFREDO: To a little immigrant you're Rockefeller.

OSVALDO: Women only wanted you for your money.

ALFREDO: I know. And I knew how to use my position.

OSVALDO: She loves me.

ALFREDO: Good, she loves you—you should have taken her out dancing. Not married her.

OSVALDO: I did what I wanted to do, that's all.

ALFREDO: You did what your mistress wanted you to do. That is all.

OSVALDO: I wanted to marry her. That's why I did it. I just didn't do what my family thought I was supposed to do.

ALFREDO: You're still a silly boy. (*Looking at wedding decorations and cake*) Well, very nice. Sonia still has taste.

OSVALDO: Yes, she does.

ALFREDO: When she was young I was always impressed by the way she dressed, by the way she looked, how she spoke. The way she treated my servants, my guests.

OSVALDO: She was very well brought up.

ALFREDO: Now your new one is common, right?

OSVALDO: She loves me. Respect her, please.

ALFREDO: So did Sonia. The only thing the new one had to offer is that she groans a little louder and played with your thing a little longer, right?

OSVALDO: That's not true.

ALFREDO: Boring you after five years?

OSVALDO: . . . A little.

ALFREDO: Then why?

*LIZETTE enters. She is dressed in her bride's dress.*

LIZETTE: I'm ready for my photographs, Bride and Father.

OSVALDO: You took better than Elizabeth Taylor in *Father of the Bride.*

ALFREDO: Sweetheart, you look beautiful.

LIZETTE: Thank you. He took pictures of Mama dressing me, putting on my veil. Now he wants pictures of you and me— then Mama, you and me—then Grandpa, you and me and Miriam—then Mama and me and Grandma—then with Mimi, et cetera, et cetera, et cetera, et cetera; all the combinations that make up my family.

OSVALDO: Are you excited?

LIZETTE: Yes, I am. And nervous, Daddy, I'm so excited and nervous.

SONIA *(Enters)*: Time for the pictures. Mimi will call me when she needs me again.

OSVALDO: Do I look handsome?

ALFREDO: Look at this place, beautiful, Sonia, a beautiful job. (*He gives* SONIA *a little kiss*)

SONIA: Thank you.

ALFREDO: She knows how to throw parties. Hmmm, Osvaldo, with taste. With class.

OSVALDO: With class.

SONIA: Osvaldo, come here a moment. Pin my corsage.

OSVALDO *goes over to the table with the corsages on it.*

I bought myself a purple orchid. It goes with the dress. I bought your wife the one with the two white gardenias. I figured she'd be wearing white, trying to compete with the bride. She's so young and pure, hmmm . . . (*She laughs*)

OSVALDO: She's not coming.

SONIA: It was a joke; I was making a little joke. I can joke about it now. Laugh. Did you dream about me again last night?

OSVALDO: Shh. Not in front of Lizette.

SONIA: I want to.

OSVALDO: We spent too much money on this, don't you think?

SONIA: No, I don't. I could have used more. Mama said they spent twice as much on our wedding.

OSVALDO: Did you tell them the exact number of people that RSVP'd so that we don't have to pay money for extra food?

SONIA: Lizette did, I can't communicate with them, my English—

OSVALDO: Your English is fine. I don't want to spend extra money.

SONIA: How much did you spend on your last wedding?

OSVALDO: She paid for it, she saved her money. She works, you know. She wanted a fancy wedding. I already had one. A sixteen-thousand-dollar one, according to your mother.

SONIA: Didn't *she*? Or was she not married to the guy she left for you?

OSVALDO: She was married. She doesn't live with people.

SONIA: Fool. When you got near fifty you turned into a fool; a silly, stupid, idiotic fool.

LIZETTE: No fights today.

OSVALDO *and* LIZETTE *start to exit.*

SONIA: I'm sorry. I swear, no fights . . . Osvaldo . . .

OSVALDO: Yes?

SONIA: You look debonair.

OSVALDO: Thank you, Sonia.

ALFREDO: Don't let it go to your head.

OSVALDO: You look magnifique.

SONIA: Thank you, Osvaldo.

LIZETTE *and* OSVALDO *exit to the ballroom.*

ALFREDO: Don't let it go to your head.

SONIA: He's insecure, about his looks.

ALFREDO: I tried to talk some sense into my son.

SONIA: Today we'll be dancing every dance together, in front of everybody. And I'll be the wife again. Divorces don't really count for Catholics. We're family, him and me.

ALFREDO: When you married him and moved in with us, I always thought you were like brother and sister.

SONIA: No, lovers. Stop teasing me. He's my only friend.

ALFREDO: Even now?

SONIA: Always, Alfredo, forever.

MIRIAM (*Enters from the ballroom*): Sonia, your turn for more snapshots—Father, Mother and Bride.

SONIA: She's happy, don't you think?

MIRIAM: The bride is in heaven.

SONIA: Excuse me, Alfredo, if you want breakfast, ask the waiter.

SONIA *exits.* MIRIAM *sits down.* ALFREDO *looks at the coffee and sits down.*

ALFREDO: Go get me a cup of coffee.

MIRIAM: No. Call the waiter, he'll get it for you.

ALFREDO: You do it for me.

MIRIAM: No.

ALFREDO: When did you stop talking to waiters?

MIRIAM: When I started talking to the gardener.

ALFREDO: What a sense of humor! What wit! What a girl, my daughter.

MIRIAM: Ruthless, like her dad.

ALFREDO: Exactly like me; you need to conquer. Go! Make sure it's hot!

MIRIAM *pours the coffee.*

If I were your husband I'd punish you every night: no money for you, no vacations, no cars, no credit cards, no pills, no maid. The way you exhibit yourself in your "see-through blouses" with no bras, and your skimpy bikinis.

MIRIAM (*Teasing* ALFREDO): Ooooh!

ALFREDO: How many horns did you put on his head?

MIRIAM: It excites him.

ALFREDO: That's not true.

MIRIAM: He feels lucky when he gets me, that I did not wither like all the other girls from my class, from our country, with their backward ways. Sugar, Daddy?

ALFREDO: Two lumps. No, three, and plenty of milk.

MIRIAM: There's only cream.

ALFREDO: Yes, cream is fine.

MIRIAM: Here, Daddy.

ALFREDO (*Takes one sip and puts coffee down*): What a vile taste American coffee has.

MIRIAM: I'm used to it, less caffeine.

ALFREDO: You did keep in shape.

MIMI *enters from the ballroom in her bridesmaid's gown.*

MIRIAM: So did you. Greed and lust keep us in shape.

MIMI: Grandpa, your turn. Both sets of grandparents, the Cubans and the Jews, the bride and the groom.

ALFREDO: How do I look, sweetheart?

MIMI: Dandy, Grandpa, dandy.

ALFREDO *exits.*

Who do you lust after?

MIRIAM: Your father.

MIMI: Your own brother?!

MIRIAM: I was joking—your father's too old now. Your brother, maybe.

MIMI: You are wild.

MIRIAM: If I would have been born in this country, to be a young girl in this country, without eyes staring at you all the time. To have freedom. I would never have gotten married. I wanted to be a tightrope walker in the circus . . . that's what I would have wanted.

MIMI: I never feel free.

MIRIAM: Do you get to go to a dance alone?

MIMI: Naturally.

MIRIAM: Then you have more freedom than I ever did.

MIMI: How awful for you.

MIRIAM: It made you choke, you felt strangled.

MIMI: What did you do?

MIRIAM: I found revenge.

MIMI: How?

MIRIAM: I'll tell you about it, one day, when there's more time.

MIMI: Can I ask you a question? Something that I wonder about? Did Uncle Pedro kill himself, was it suicide? Did Grandpa have mistresses?

MIRIAM: How do you know?

MIMI: Information slips out in the middle of a fight.

MIRIAM: He drank himself to death.

MIMI: Oh, I thought he did it violently.

MIRIAM: And your grandpa had a whole whorehouse full of wives.

MIMI *and* MIRIAM *laugh.*

MIMI: I'm like Grandpa. I'm pregnant . . .

MIRIAM: Don't kid me.

MIMI: Aunt Miriam, I am.

MIRIAM: Oh God.

MIMI: What are you doing?

MIRIAM: I need this. (*She takes a valium*) Don't you use a pill?

MIMI: With my mother.

MIRIAM: I don't understand.

MIMI: She'd kill me.

MIRIAM: True. Why did you do it?

MIMI: Freedom.

MIRIAM: Stupidity.

MIMI: Will you help me?

OSCAR *enters.*

MIRIAM: My God, a movie star.

OSCAR: No, just your nephew, Oscar.

MIRIAM: Your hair is combed. You cut your fingernails?

OSCAR: Better than that, a manicure. You two look sexy today.

MIRIAM: Thank you. She's not a virgin . . .

OSCAR: So?

MIMI: I'm pregnant—

MIRIAM: Don't tell him.

OSCAR: Oh, Mimi.

MIRIAM: What are you going to do?

OSCAR: Pretend she didn't say it. Poor Mimi.

MIMI: You're no saint.

OSCAR: I'm not pregnant.

MIMI: Not because you haven't tried.

OSCAR: Oh, I love *you.*

MANUELA *enters.*

MIRIAM: You better not talk.

MANUELA: You're here. Good.

MIMI: If you tell her, I'll tell her you're a fruit.

OSCAR: I don't care.

MIMI: Swear.

OSCAR: I swear.

MANUELA: You look beautiful. Here, sit on my lap.

OSCAR *sits on* MANUELA's *lap.*

MIRIAM: He'll get wrinkled.

MIMI: This is revolting.

MANUELA: I promised your mother that we will be polite.

MIMI: The slut is not coming.

OSCAR: Good. A curse on Argentina.

MANUELA: Oscar, if you ever see her, it is your duty to kick her in the ass. But be good to your father today. It's not his fault. We all know that your father is a decent man. We all know that she got control of him with as they say "powders."

MIMI: I think they call it "blowing."

MANUELA: Blowing? She blowed-up his ego, is that what you think?

MIMI: Right.

MANUELA: No. You are wrong. She did it with drugs. But your mother wants you not to fight with your father. She wants him back.

OSCAR: I'll have to react however I feel.

MANUELA: Your mother is weak and she cannot take another emotional scene. And these Jewish people that Lizette is marrying would never understand about witchcraft, after all they don't even believe in Christ.

OSCAR: I can't promise anything.

MANUELA: Today will be a happy day. Lizette is marrying a nice boy, he's buying her a house. And your mother has a plan.

OSCAR: Right . . .

MANUELA: Right, Miriam?

MIRIAM: You're right. But if I ever see that Argentinian.

MANUELA: You're going to be a good girl, right, Mimi?

MIMI: I'll do whatever the team decides.

OSCAR: Spoken like a true American.

SONIA (Enters): You made it in time for the pictures, thank God.

OSCAR: Do I have to pose with Dad?

SONIA: No fights.

OSCAR: All right. But I'm standing next to you.

SONIA: Thank you. Miriam, Mama, they want more pictures with you. And in ten minutes "The Family Portrait."

MIMI: That'll be a sight.

MANUELA: Is my hair all right?

SONIA: Yes. Here, put on your corsage.

MANUELA: Thank you.

MIRIAM: And for me?

SONIA: The gardenias.

    MIRIAM and MANUELA exit.

You took neat, Oscar. Thank God. The photographer suggested a family portrait, the entire family. He said it will be something we will cherish forever.

OSCAR: Why?

    OSVALDO enters.

SONIA: Well, the family portrait will be a record, proof that we were really a family. That we really existed, Oscar. Oscar, my father's name.

OSCAR: I'm glad you named me after him and not Osvaldo.

SONIA: At first I thought of naming you after your father, but then I thought, "That's so old-fashioned, it's 1951, time for something new."

OSCAR: Good for you.

MIMI: What a sign of liberation.

OSVALDO: Oh?!

OSCAR: So . . . continue, Mama.

SONIA: You like the story?

OSCAR: Yes.

SONIA: You, Mimi?

MIMI: Fascinating.

SONIA: Well, and since your grandpa has no son, I named you after him.

OSCAR: I bet he liked that.

SONIA: It made him very happy. I keep thinking he'll show up today. He'll walk in soon, my father. "Papa, do you like it?" And he would say . . .

MIMI: "We have to get back to Cuba."

OSCAR: "We have to fight!"

MIMI: "Where papayas grow as large as watermelons and guayabas and mangoes grow on trees. How could anyone starve in a place like that?"

OSVALDO: Then someone took it all away.

OSCAR: He had everything. He had pride, honor—

OSVALDO: True but someone took it away.

OSCAR: That doesn't matter.

OSVALDO: Well, it does, he lost.

SONIA: You loved him, I know you did, everyone did.

OSVALDO: Yes, right, I did.

OSCAR: He fought and he knew what he believed in. He knew what his life was about.

OSVALDO: Maybe that's why he wanted to die.

SONIA: No, just a stroke.

    Pause.

OSCAR: Daddy, do you like my suit?

OSVALDO: Well, it's really a sports coat and pants.

OSCAR: It's linen.

OSVALDO: It'll wrinkle.

OSCAR: I wanted to look nice.

SONIA: It does.

OSVALDO: It doesn't matter.

OSCAR: No, I don't suppose it really does.

**OSVALDO:** It means nothing.

**OSCAR:** What means something, Daddy?

**OSVALDO:** Columns that add up, neatly. Formulas where the answer is always guaranteed!

**OSCAR:** Guarantees mean something?!

**OSVALDO:** The answer. That's what means something.

**OSCAR:** Then I have a meaningless life.

**OSVALDO:** Stop it.

**OSCAR:** I never found any answers.

**OSVALDO:** Stop your melodrama.

**OSCAR:** I'm going to pretend you didn't say that. I'm twenty-eight years old and I refuse to get involved with you in the emotional ways that you used to abuse our relationship.

**MIMI:** Time for a Cuba Libre. (*She exits*)

**OSVALDO:** How much did that piece of dialogue cost me?

**OSCAR:** Let's stop.

**OSVALDO:** From which quack did you get that from?

**OSCAR:** From the one that told me you were in the closet.

**OSVALDO:** What closet?

> **SONIA** *goes to check if anyone's listening.*

**OSCAR:** It's an expression they have in America for men who are afraid, no, they question, no, who fears that he wants to suck cock.

> **OSVALDO** *slaps* **OSCAR.**

**OSVALDO:** Control yourself, learn to control your tongue!

**OSCAR:** Did that one hit home?

**OSVALDO:** Spoiled brat.

**OSCAR:** Takes one to know one. God, I despise you.

**OSVALDO:** I'm ashamed of you, you're such a nervous wreck, all those doctors, all the money I spend.

**OSCAR:** Thanks, Daddy, I had such a fine example of Manhood from you.

**OSVALDO:** Bum!

**OSCAR:** Fool.

**SONIA:** No psychology today! You're both the same, you're both so selfish, think of Lizette, her fiancé's family, what if they hear this. Quiet!

**OSCAR:** Leave us alone.

**SONIA:** No. I belong in this argument too, I'm the mother and the wife.

**OSCAR:** The ex-wife, Mama.

**SONIA:** No, in this particular triangle, the wife.

**OSCAR** (*To* **SONIA**): Your life is a failure.

**OSVALDO:** Because of you.

**SONIA:** Don't say that, Osvaldo. He's our son.

**OSVALDO:** He's just like you.

**SONIA:** What do you mean by that?!

**OSVALDO:** An emotional wreck.

**OSCAR:** That's better than being emotionally dead.

**OSVALDO:** I hate him.

**SONIA:** No. Osvaldo, how dare you! (*She cries*)

**OSCAR:** See what you've made, turned her into?!

**OSVALDO:** It's because of you.

**SONIA:** I refuse to be the cause of this fight, today we're having a wedding, so both of you smile.

**OSVALDO:** You're right, Sonia, I'm sorry.

**OSCAR:** God.

**SONIA:** I'm going to be with Lizette. You two control yourselves.

**OSCAR** (*Whispers*): Faggot.

> **SONIA** *exits.*

Sissy.

**OSVALDO:** I bet you know all about that?!

**OSCAR:** Yes, want to hear about it?

> **ALFREDO** *enters.*

**OSVALDO:** Not in front of your grandfather.

**OSCAR:** There's no way to talk to you, you petty bastard. (*He starts to cry*)

**OSVALDO:** Exactly like her, crying.

**OSCAR** (*Stops crying*): Because we were both unfortunate enough to have to know you in an intimate way.

**OSVALDO:** Other people don't feel that way.

OSCAR: That's because they're made of ice. A lot of Nazis in Argentina.

OSVALDO: Your sister needs me today. I'm going to make sure she's happy. Men don't cry. Now stop it. (*He exits*)

OSCAR: Right.

ALFREDO: Be careful.

OSCAR: About what?

ALFREDO: You show too much. Be on your guard.

OSCAR: So what?

ALFREDO: You let him see too much of you.

OSCAR: He's my father.

ALFREDO: He's a man first, my son second, your father third.

OSCAR: That's how he feels? He told you that? Did he?!

ALFREDO: Be a little more like me. And a little less like your other grandfather. He's dead. I'm still alive.

OSCAR: He was ill. It wasn't his fault.

ALFREDO: He was a fool.

OSCAR: No. That's not true.

ALFREDO: He was foolish. He trusted mankind. Money made him flabby. He thought if you gave a starving man a plate of food, he thanks you. He didn't know that he also resents you, he also waits. No one wants to beg for food, it's humiliating.

OSCAR: Of course no one wants to.

ALFREDO: So they wait. And when they regain their strength, they stab you in the back.

OSCAR: How can you think that's true?!

ALFREDO: We are the proof of my theory—Cubans. He did it to us—Fidel, our neighbors, everybody. So never feed a hungry man.

OSCAR: You don't really believe that.

MIMI (*Enters*): The picture, Grandpa. Oscar, the family portrait!

ALFREDO: I'm on my way. Comb your hair. Fix your tie. Your suit is already wrinkled.

OSCAR: Real linen does that.

ALFREDO *exits with* MIMI. OSCAR *takes out a bottle of cocaine—the kind that premeasures a hit. He goes outside but leaves the entrance door open. He snorts.*

Ah, breakfast.

OSCAR *snorts again.* OSVALDO *enters but does not see* OSCAR. *He goes straight to the bar, comes back with a drink—a J&B double—and gulps it down. He looks at the corsages. We hear* OSCAR *sniffing coke.*

OSVALDO (*To himself*): White, compete with the bride . . . very funny, Sonia.

SONIA (*Enters*): Osvaldo, we are waiting for you. The family portrait, come.

OSVALDO: No, I can't face them.

SONIA: Don't be silly.

OSVALDO: They love you. They hate me, my sister, my father, my children, they all hate me.

SONIA: They don't. No one hates their own family. It's a sin to hate people in your immediate family.

OSVALDO: They always hated me. Till I was seventeen I thought—

SONIA: That they had found you in a trash can, I know, Osvaldo. We need a record, a family portrait. The last one was taken at Oscar's seventh birthday. It's time for a new one.

OSVALDO: You don't need me.

SONIA: It wouldn't be one without you.

OSVALDO: For who?

SONIA: For everybody. Be brave. Take my hand. I won't bite.

OSVALDO *holds her hand.*

After all, I'm the mother and you are the father of the bride.

OSCAR (*Sticks his head in*): The Argentinian just drove up.

OSVALDO: Liar.

OSCAR: She looks drunk.

OSVALDO: Liar.

OSCAR: What do they drink in Argentina?

SONIA: Behave!

*A car starts honking.*

OSCAR: Sounds like your car.

OSVALDO: How dare she. How can she humiliate me. How can she disobey me.

SONIA: Oscar, go out and say your father is posing with his past family. Tell her that after the portrait is taken, she can come in.

OSCAR: But she has to sit in the back.

SONIA: No, I'm going to be polite. That's what I was taught.

OSVALDO: Go and tell her.

OSCAR: Remember, Mama, I did it for you. (*He exits*)

OSVALDO: Thank you. Hold my hand.

SONIA: Kiss me.

OSVALDO: Here?

SONIA: Yes, today I'm the mother and the wife.

OSVALDO *and* SONIA *kiss.*

OSVALDO: You did a good job.

SONIA: You do like it?

OSVALDO: I mean with our daughters. They're good girls . . . like their mother.

SONIA: They have a good father.

OSVALDO: That's true.

OSVALDO *and* SONIA *exit,* OSCAR *reenters.*

OSCAR: The family portrait? This family. . . . My family. The Father, Jesus Christ his only son and the Holy Ghost (*Crossing himself*) . . . why the *fuck* did you send me to this family.

*Blackout.*

END OF ACT ONE

# ACT TWO

*Afternoon. Offstage, the band is playing "Snow," an Argentinian folksong, and a woman is singing.* MIRIAM *is in the phone booth.* MIMI *is looking at the bridal bouquet and pulling it apart.* SONIA *enters eating cake.*

WOMAN'S VOICE (*Singing offstage*):
Don't sing brother, don't sing,
I hear Moscow is covered with snow.

And the wolves run away out of hunger.
Don't sing 'cause Olga's not coming.

Even if the sun shines again.
Even if the snow falls again.
Even if the sun shines again.
Even if the snow falls again.

Walking to Siberia tomorrow, oh,
Out goes the caravan,
Who knows if the sun
Will light our march of horror.

While in Moscow, my Olga, perhaps,
To another, her love she surrenders.
Don't sing brothers, don't sing.
For God's sake, oh God, no.

United by chains to the steppes
A thousand leagues we'll go walking.
Walking to Siberia, no.
Don't sing, I am filled with pain.
And Moscow is covered with snow.
And the snow has entered my soul.
Moscow now covered with snow.
And the snow has entered my soul.

SONIA: It's insult to injury an Argentinian song about going to Siberia, Russia. Moscow is covered with snow . . . what do Argentinians know about Moscow? I wish she'd go to Siberia tomorrow. (*To* MIMI) They are walking a thousand leagues to their exile . . . I took a plane ride ninety-nine miles, a forty-five-minute excursion to my doom.

MIRIAM (*To phone*): No, shit no! Liars.

SONIA: Don't sing, Sonia . . . (*She sings*) 'cause Moscow is covered with snow, right, Mimi?

MIMI: Right.

SONIA: When I first got here this place looked to me like a farm town. Are you happy, dear?

MIMI: I don't think so.

SONIA: No, say yes!

MIMI: Yes.

SONIA: That's good.

MIMI: Ciao!

MIMI *runs to the bathroom to puke.* OS-VALDO *enters.*

SONIA: So, you had to play a song for her?

OSVALDO: She told the band she wanted to sing it. But it's the only Argentinian song they know.

SONIA: Good for the band! Remember when we thought Fidel was going to send us to Russia, to Moscow? Siberia, Siberia, this place is like Siberia!

OSVALDO: It's too warm to be Siberia. (*He kisses* SONIA *passionately*) It was a beautiful ceremony. (*He kisses her again*)

SONIA: Dance with me. Tell them to play a danzón.

OSVALDO: Let's dance in here.

SONIA: She'll get angry? It's our daughter's wedding.

OSVALDO: She's my wife.

SONIA: I was first.

OSVALDO: You're both my wife.

OSVALDO *and* SONIA *dance.*

SONIA: Before my sixteenth birthday your family moved to Cojimar . . . your cousin brought you to the club.

OSVALDO: You were singing a Rita Hayworth song called "Put the Blame on . . . Me"?

SONIA: No, "Mame" . . . I was imitating her . . . did I look ridiculous?

OSVALDO: No!

SONIA (*Starts to do Rita's number, substituting "Cuban" for "Frisco"*):
Put the blame on Mame, boys
Put the blame on Mame
One night she started to shim and shake
That began the Cuban quake
So-o-o, put the blame on Mame, boys
Put the blame on Mame . . .

OSVALDO: You look sexy.

SONIA: I let you kiss me, then you became part of the club.

OSVALDO: On your seventeenth birthday I married you.

SONIA: Well, I kissed you.

OSVALDO: Was I the only one?

SONIA: Yes.

OSVALDO: And by your eighteenth birthday we had Oscar. I should go back to the party. She'll start looking for me.

SONIA: Tell her to relax. Tell the band to stop playing that stupid song. I want to dance. I want more Cuban music.

OSVALDO: All right! What song?

SONIA: "Guantanamera."

OSVALDO: They might know "Babalú."

SONIA: That's an American song.

MANUELA *and* ALFREDO *enter, in the middle of a conversation.* OSVALDO *exits to the ballroom.* SONIA *goes outside.*

MANUELA: The trouble is Americans are weak . . . they don't know how to make decisions.

ALFREDO: At least they are happy—

MANUELA: Why?

ALFREDO: Money!

MANUELA: You had that in Cuba, Alfredo, but—

ALFREDO: Look at my son—he has an accounting firm—

MANUELA: He's only a partner.

ALFREDO: He has a Lincoln Continental, a classy car; two beautiful houses, with pools and—

MANUELA: Don't talk about the prostitute's house in front of me, Alfredo, please.

ALFREDO: Forgive me.

MANUELA: We knew how to make decisions, we—

ALFREDO: Of course.

MANUELA: Fight who you don't agree with, do not doubt that you are right, and if they use force, you use force, bullets if you have to. Only right and wrong, no middle, not like Americans always asking questions, always in the middle, always maybe. Sometimes I think those Democrats are Communists—

ALFREDO: No, Manuela, you see in demo—

MANUELA: Democracy, Communism, the two don't go together, at least the Russians know that much. They don't let people complain in Russia, but here, anybody can do anything.

*The band is playing "Guantanamera."*

At last some good music, no more of that Argentinian shit. (*She hums some of the song*)

**ALFREDO:** That's one of my favorite songs.

**MANUELA:** Yes, beautiful.

**ALFREDO:** May I have this dance?

**MANUELA:** Yes . . . but do I remember how?

**MIMI** (*Who has reentered*): It'll come back to you, Grandma.

> **MANUELA, ALFREDO** *and* **MIMI** *exit to the dance floor.* **MIRIAM** *is still sitting in the phone booth, smoking.* **SONIA** *enters.* **MIRIAM** *opens the phone-booth doors.*

**MIRIAM:** I just made a phone call to Cuba, and you can.

**SONIA:** They got you through?

**MIRIAM:** Yes. The overseas operator said, "Sometimes they answer, but only if they feel like it."

**SONIA:** Who did you call?

**MIRIAM:** My . . . our house. . . . I sometimes think that I live at the same time there as here. That I left a dual spirit there. When I go to a funeral I look through the windows as I drive and the landscapes I see are the streets outside the cemetery in Guanabacoa, not Miami. A while ago I looked out at the dance floor and I thought I was in the ballroom back home. That's why I had to call. I miss the floor, the windows, the air, the roof.

**SONIA:** The house is still standing, though, it is still there.

**MIRIAM:** But we are not.

**SONIA:** I saw a picture of it. It hasn't been painted in twenty years, we painted it last.

**MIRIAM:** Sonia, she said upstairs he's crying again.

**SONIA:** You're sending chills up my spine.

**MIRIAM:** Is it Pedro crying?

**SONIA:** No, she was trying to scare you. We have to hold on to it, to the way we remember it, painted.

**MIRIAM:** I think I heard Pedro screaming in the garden before she hung up.

**SONIA:** No, he's dead, he went to heaven.

**MIRIAM:** No, he's in hell. If there's a heaven he's in hell. Suicides go to hell. He was the only one that managed to remain, death keeps him there. Maybe the house filled with strangers is his hell.

**SONIA:** Why he did it I'll never understand. Maybe he had to die for us?

**MIRIAM:** No, he didn't do it for *me*.

**SONIA:** Maybe that's the way things are, maybe one of us had to die. Maybe there's an order to all these things.

**MIRIAM:** There's no order to things, don't you know that by now? It's chaos, only chaos.

> **MIMI** *enters.*

**SONIA:** No, there's a more important reason, that's why he did it.

**MIMI:** What?

**SONIA:** This conversation is not for your ears.

**MIMI:** Why not?

> **LIZETTE** *enters.*

**SONIA:** Because it isn't, that's all.

**LIZETTE:** Mama! Daddy started dancing with her and Oscar's whistling at them, whispering "Puta, putica."

**MIRIAM:** The Americans won't understand what they are saying.

**LIZETTE:** Americans know what "puta" means. My husband is embarrassed. Other people get divorces and don't act like this. Tell him he must stop. No name-calling in Spanish or in English. This is a bilingual state.

**MIMI:** No, Mama, don't do it.

**MIRIAM:** Mimi's right, let them do whatever they want.

**SONIA:** Right, why should I protect her?

**LIZETTE:** How about me? Who's going to protect me?

**SONIA:** Your husband.

**MIMI:** Tell him to tell them to stop, you've got your husband now, your own little family unit.

LIZETTE: Fuck off, Mimi. I'm begging you, Mama, please. Just take him to the side and tell him to leave her alone, to let her have a good time.

SONIA: To let her have a good time?!

MIMI: I'll take care of it. (*She yells out to the ballroom*) Hey you slut, Miss Argentina. Don't use my sister's wedding for your crap. Come in here and fight it out with us!

MIRIAM: Mimi, she's flipping the bird at you. She's gesturing fuck you.

MIMI: Fuck yourself!

LIZETTE: Mama! Stop her! Oh God—

MIRIAM (*Yells to the ballroom*): You're just a bitch, lady.

LIZETTE (*Starts to cry*): Oh, God, oh, God—

SONIA: In a little while everybody will forget about it—

LIZETTE: Oh God, Mama. Everybody's looking at us. They are so embarrassed. You let them ruin my wedding. You promised. I hate you. It's a fiasco. I hate you, Mimi.

SONIA: Sorry, promises are something nobody keeps, including me.

LIZETTE: You're such assholes.

SONIA: Everybody's got their faults, learn to live with it!

LIZETTE: You failed me.

MIMI: That was great, Aunt Miriam.

SONIA: I'm sorry.

MIRIAM: Thanks, Mimi, it was fun.

OSVALDO (*Enters*): How could you . . .

MIRIAM: Careful!

OSVALDO: Help me, Sonia.

SONIA: Osvaldo, I've put up with a lot.

OSVALDO: How about me? I want you and your children to apologize to her.

SONIA: No.

MIMI: Never.

MIRIAM: She should leave the party and let the rest of us have a good time. What the hell is she doing here?

OSVALDO: For my sake, Sonia.

SONIA: I'm sorry, I can't.

OSVALDO: What am I going to do?

SONIA: Who do you love, me?

OSVALDO: Yes.

SONIA: Who do you love, her?

OSVALDO: Yes.

SONIA: So full of contradictions, so confused. I'll go tell her that. He loves both of us, Cuba and Argentina!

OSVALDO: This is not the time to kid me, look at Lizette, she's upset.

LIZETTE: I'll never be able to talk to my mother-in-law again.

MIRIAM: It's your fault, Osvaldo. He never moved from the garden.

OSVALDO: Miriam?! Who never moved from the garden?

MIRIAM: Pedro. He never left the garden.

OSVALDO: None of us have.

MIRIAM: He stayed. He took a razor blade but remained locked forever in our family's garden.

OSVALDO: He was a coward.

MIRIAM: Maybe you are the coward, you keep running away.

OSVALDO: From what?

OSCAR (*Enters, trying not to laugh*): I'm sorry. I behaved badly.

OSVALDO: Tell me, Miriam, from what? (*He exits*)

OSCAR: Don't cry, Lizette, forgive me? Hmm?

LIZETTE: Oscar, now they're starting to fight about Cuba. I just want to cry. They're going to tell my husband, "Your wife is from a crazy family. Are you sure she's not mentally disturbed?"

MIMI: Are you sure you're not mentally disturbed?

MIMI *and* OSCAR *laugh.* OSVALDO *reenters.*

OSVALDO: What do I run away from that he faced?

MIRIAM: That we lost everything.

SONIA: Everything, no.

OSVALDO: You think I don't know that?

MIRIAM: Pedro knew. He became invisible but remains in silence, as proof.

OSVALDO: As proof of what?

SONIA: That we are not a very nice family? Is that what you are saying?

OSVALDO: He had nothing to do with us, he was an alcoholic.

SONIA: He killed himself because of our sins.

OSVALDO: No, Sonia, that was Christ, Pedro was a drunk, not a Christ figure.

MIRIAM: Because of our lies, Sonia.

OSVALDO: What lies?

MIRIAM: Why did you desert him? You, his brother, you were the only one he spoke to, the only one he needed.

OSVALDO: He made me sick.

MIRIAM: You were always together, you always spent your days together.

OSVALDO: He was an alcoholic.

MIRIAM: We were all alcoholics.

SONIA: I was never an alcoholic.

MIRIAM: He needed you.

OSVALDO: He was perverted.

MIRIAM: We were all perverted. That's why the new society got rid of us.

OSVALDO: Our mother is not perverted!

MIRIAM: No, just insane.

SONIA: No, she's an honest woman, now your father—

OSVALDO: My father was just selfish, he had too many mistresses.

SONIA: Fifteen.

OSCAR: Fifteen?

MIMI: All at once?

LIZETTE: Who gives a fuck? Everybody in this family is a—

MIRIAM: I'm the one that suffered from that, not you, Osvaldo. You take after Daddy so don't complain. Why did you let Pedro kill himself?

OSVALDO: He wanted too much from me.

MIRIAM: He needed you.

OSVALDO: He wanted my mind, he wanted my . . . , my . . . , he wanted everything.

MIRIAM: You're glad he did it?

OSVALDO: I was relieved.

MIRIAM: He knew too much, ha!

SONIA: Too much of what?

MIRIAM: The perversions.

SONIA: What perversions?

MIRIAM: Too much about his perversions, darling Sonia, you married a corrupted family, you really deserved better.

OSCAR: Uh-huh.

LIZETTE: I'm closing the door.

MANUELA and ALFREDO enter.

MANUELA: I'll never forget what he said.

ALFREDO: When?

MANUELA: In 1959, after the son-of-a-bitch's first speech, he said, "That boy is going to be trouble . . . he's full of Commie ideals."

ALFREDO: I must say I did not suspect it. I was so bored with Batista's bullshit I thought, a revolution, good. We'll get rid of the bums, the loafers, but instead, they got rid of us.

MANUELA: I hope he rots. Rot, Fidel Castro, die of cancer of the balls.

ALFREDO: Let's hope.

MANUELA: Then they came. And they took our businesses away, one by one. And we had to let them do it. They took over each of them, one after the other. It took the milicianos three days. I looked at Oscar while they did it, for him it was like they . . . for him, that was his life's work, he felt like . . .

OSCAR: Like they were plucking out his heart. Like they were sticking pins into his brain. Like they were having birds peck out his genitals. Like he was being betrayed.

MANUELA: Yes, that's it.

ALFREDO: I hate myself for helping them, bastards.

MANUELA: All he wanted after that was—

SONIA: To fight back.

OSCAR: Right.

MIRIAM: I still do. I still want to fight somebody!

SONIA: But he did fight back. Till the day he died, he never gave up. Right, Mama?

MANUELA: "We are in an emergency," that's how he put it, "an emergency."

MIRIAM: Daddy. Daddy, I am in an emergency now. I have taken six valiums and it's only noon.

ALFREDO: Why?

MIRIAM: Because I want to strangle you every time I look at you.

LIZETTE: Quiet, they're going to want an annulment.

MANUELA: My God, Miriam!

OSCAR: Who?

ALFREDO: Why?

MIRIAM: Why?!

LIZETTE: The Jews, they're a quiet people.

ALFREDO: Yes, Miriam, why?

MIRIAM: Why did you send your mistresses' daughters to my school?!

MANUELA: Miriam, not in front of the children.

ALFREDO: Because it was a good school.

MIRIAM: People in my class wouldn't talk to me because of you!

ALFREDO: Sorry.

OSCAR: Sorry? That's all you have to say to her?! That's the only answer you give?!

ALFREDO: I don't know, what else should I say?

OSCAR: Why did you not once congratulate me for finishing the university?! Why did you let me drink? Why did you let Pedro drink?

ALFREDO: I never noticed that you drank.

MIMI: Why did you leave my mother, and leave me . . . and never came to see me play volleyball?

OSVALDO: Leave me alone, I'm talking to my father.

MIMI: And who are you to me?

MANUELA: Good girl, good question.

OSVALDO: You? Why did you make your daughter think that the only person in the world who deserved her love was your husband?!

MANUELA: He was strong.

OSVALDO: He got drunk. He was a coward when he died.

OSCAR: No. That's not true.

MANUELA: He was a real man. What are you?

LIZETTE: You mean old hag, don't you ever talk to my dad again like—

SONIA: Don't you ever call your grandmother that. She's my mother!

LIZETTE: I'm going back to the wedding. (*She exits*)

OSCAR: Why did they kick us out?
*Silence.*

OSVALDO: We left. We wanted to leave.

OSCAR: No one asked me.

SONIA: We had to protect you from them.

MIRIAM: That's right.

OSVALDO: They wanted to brainwash you, to turn you into a Communist.

OSCAR: No one explained it to me. You told me I was coming here for the weekend.

OSVALDO: It was not up to you.

SONIA: You were just a child, it was up to us.

OSVALDO: That's right.

MIRIAM: And we made the right decision, believe me,

OSCAR: Miriam, why did you let me be locked out? That day in Miami, November, 1962. The day the guy from the Jehovah's Witnesses came to see you. And you took him to your room to discuss the end of the world.

MIRIAM: It was a joke. I was only twenty. I don't believe in God.

OSCAR: Well, you locked me out. And I sat outside and you laughed at me, and I sat there by a tree and I wanted to die. I wanted to kill myself at the age of ten. I wanted to beat my head against the tree, and I thought, "Please stop working, brain, even they locked me out, even my family, not just my country, my family too!" Bastards! Fidel was right. If I had a gun, I'd shoot you. I curse you, you shits. Who asked me?

OSVALDO: The revolution had nothing to do with you. You don't *really* remember it, and believe it or not, it did not happen just for you, Oscar.

**OSCAR:** Yeah, I didn't notice you damaged.

**OSVALDO:** I had to go to the market at age thirty-two and shop for the first time in my life.

**MIMI:** So what?

**OSCAR:** God.

**OSVALDO:** And I could not tell what fruit was ripe and what fruit was not ripe. I did not know how to figure that out. I cried at the Food King market in Canoga Park. Some people saw me. (*He cries*)

**OSCAR:** Big deal.

**OSVALDO** (*Stops crying*): And Sonia, you refused to come and help me! You made me go do it alone. And shopping is the wife's duty.

**SONIA:** I couldn't. I felt weak. I was pregnant with Mimi. I'm sorry, Osvaldo. (*To* **OSCAR**) I wanted you to live a noble life.

**OSCAR:** How?

**SONIA:** I don't know. I taught you not to put your elbows on the table. You had perfect eating habits . . .

**OSCAR:** What does that have to do with nobility?

**SONIA:** It shows you're not common. That's noble.

**OSCAR:** No, Mama, nobility—

**SONIA:** Yes.

**OSCAR:** No, nobility has to do with caring about the ugly things, seeing trash and loving it. It has to do with compassion, not table manners. It has to do with thought, not what people think about you.

**SONIA:** Stop picking on me.

**OSCAR:** I'm not picking on you.

**SONIA:** Everybody is always picking on me. I failed, I know I failed.

**OSCAR:** No, you just don't try. Why don't you try?

**SONIA:** Try what?

**OSCAR:** To do something.

**SONIA:** No.

**OSCAR:** Why?

**SONIA:** I'm not some whore that can go from guy to guy.

**OSVALDO:** Are you talking about my wife?

**OSCAR:** Try it.

**SONIA:** Don't insult me. Stop insulting me.

**OSCAR:** You need somebody.

**SONIA:** Stop it!

**OSVALDO:** Leave her alone.

> **OSVALDO** *grabs* **SONIA**. *They walk towards the ballroom, then stop. We hear the band playing "Que Sera, Sera."*

**MANUELA:** I think they're going to dance.

**MIRIAM:** I want to see the Argentinian's expression.

> **SONIA** *and* **OSVALDO** *are now dancing. The others watch.* **MIMI** *and* **OSCAR** *go into the phone booth to snort coke.*

**ALFREDO:** Leave all three of them alone. (*He goes outside to smoke a cigar*)

> **MIRIAM** *and* **MANUELA** *walk past* **SONIA** *and* **OSVALDO** *toward the ballroom.*

**MIRIAM:** Why are you dancing out in the hall . . . afraid of Argentina?

> **MIRIAM** *and* **MANUELA** *exit.*

**OSVALDO:** I'd like to take a big piece of wood and beat some sense into her . . . No, I want to beat her to death!

**SONIA:** She went too far . . . she lost control . . . she gets excited.

**OSVALDO:** They always lose control. Pedro thought there was no limit . . . that you did not have to stop anywhere . . . life was a whim. . . . But I knew that you have to stop yourself . . . that's being civilized, that's what makes us different than dogs . . . you can't have everything you feel you want . . .

**SONIA:** He was a tortured soul . . . and you loved him . . .

**OSVALDO:** My big brother. (*He starts to cry*)

**SONIA:** And you tried to help him . . .

**OSVALDO:** How?

**SONIA:** The only way you knew how, with affection.

**OSVALDO:** Affection?

SONIA: Yes, and that's decent.

OSVALDO: Maybe it is. Maybe I am.

> SONIA *and* OSVALDO *kiss. He takes her out to the dance floor. She smiles.* OSCAR *and* MIMI *come out of the phone booth.* OSCAR *continues to snort cocaine.*

OSCAR: He did it. Well, at least he had the balls to take her out and dance. She won. You see if you have a plan and follow it . . . (*Sniff, sniff*) ah, hurray for the American dream.

MIMI: It's pathetic. They're still dancing. Oh God help us, she believes anything he tells her.

OSCAR: She had to endure too many things.

MIMI: What, losing her maid?

OSCAR: They never tell her the truth.

MIMI: And you do? You tell her the truth? Well, I'm gonna tell her.

OSCAR: I think you should get an abortion.

MIMI: Why should I?

OSCAR: To protect her.

MIMI: Why should I protect her.

OSCAR: I don't know. Lie to her. Tell Dad.

MIMI: Never mind. Pour me some more champagne.

> LIZETTE *enters.*

I hope one of those horny Cubans just off the boat is ready to rock and roll.

LIZETTE: No more scenes, Mimi. Dad and Mom are enough.

> MIMI *toasts* LIZETTE *with champagne.*

MIMI: Arrivederci. (*She exits*)

LIZETTE: They're out there dancing like they were in love or something—

OSCAR: Maybe they are.

LIZETTE: Never, he's being polite and she's showing off. And the Argentinian is complaining to me. And I don't want any part of any of you.

OSCAR: You don't! You think your husband is going to take you away from all this. Does he know about the suicides, how they drink till they explode . . . the violence we live with, the razor blades, the guns, the hangings, the one woman in

our family who set herself on fire while her three kids watched?

ALFREDO (*Who has reentered*): We are just hot-blooded and passionate, that's all.

OSCAR: Grandpa told me a week before . . . "Oscar," he told me . . . "they'll tell you soon I'm in the hospital. That means that I'm on my way out . . . this life here is ridiculous."

ALFREDO: Oscar Hernandez was a fool. That's a fool's kind of suicide, that's what I told you.

OSCAR: A lot of drinks when your blood pressure is high is not a fool's kind of suicide, it's just suicide. Despair, that's always the story of people that get kicked out, that have to find refuge, you and me . . . us.

LIZETTE: No, you. Everybody dies on the day that they're supposed to. Forget about it.

OSCAR: How can I?

ALFREDO: You better teach yourself to.

OSCAR: How can I? Have you taught yourself? Tell me, why do you want to live? For what?

ALFREDO: Because of me . . . here or over there, I still need me!

OSCAR: You don't have any honor.

ALFREDO: Honor for what?

OSCAR: For our country.

ALFREDO: That little island? . . . Look, Oscar, when Columbus first found it there were Indians there, imagine, Indians. So we eliminated the Indians, burned all of them, cleaned up the place. . . . We needed somebody to do the Indians' work so we bought ourselves slaves . . . and then the Spaniards, that's us, and the slaves started to . . . well, you know.

OSCAR: I can only imagine.

ALFREDO: Well, then we started calling ourselves natives. Cubans.

LIZETTE: That's right, a name they made up!

ALFREDO: Right! And we became a nation . . .

OSCAR: A race.

ALFREDO: Yes. And then the U.S. came and liked it, and bought and cheated their way into this little place. They told us (*He imitates a Texan accent*) "Such a pretty place you have, a valuable piece of real estate. We will help you!" So, they bought us.

OSCAR: We should have eliminated them!

ALFREDO: Maybe. But, what we did . . . was sell it to them and fight against each other for decades, trying to have control of what was left of this pretty place, this valuable piece of real estate. And a bearded guy on a hill talked to us about liberty, and justice, and humanity and humility—and we bought his story. And he took everything away from everybody. And we were forced to end up here. So, we bought their real estate. Do you know how Miami was built?

LIZETTE: With sand that they shipped in from Cojimar! Right?

ALFREDO: That's right. And your other grandfather could not accept the fact that it was just real estate. So he got drunk when he knew he had high blood pressure. What a fool.

LIZETTE: He tells the truth, Oscar.

OSCAR: And Mama thinks it was her country. And someday she'd go back. And I hoped it was my country. What a laugh, huh?

LIZETTE: If you ever tell Mama this, it'll kill her.

OSCAR: Maybe it wouldn't.

LIZETTE: She can't deal with real life, believe me. I'm her daughter, I know what she's really like.

OSCAR: And you can deal with everything?

LIZETTE: Sure. I grew up here, I have a Jewish name now . . . Mrs. Rifkin, that's my name.

OSCAR: Well, Mrs. Rifkin, I'm jealous of you.

ALFREDO: Time for a dance. I haven't danced with the mother of the groom.

(*He exits*)

LIZETTE: Try to get away, Mrs. Rifkin!

OSCAR: And the new Mrs. Rifkin is running away. You got away.

LIZETTE: Don't be jealous, Oscar. It's still all back here. (*She points to her brain*)

OSVALDO (*Enters*): One o'clock, Lizette.

LIZETTE: One more dance.

OSCAR: Why do you have to leave so soon?

LIZETTE: It's another two thousand for the entire day.

OSCAR: God.

OSVALDO: God what?

OSCAR: You have no class.

SONIA (*Enters*): Osvaldo, I have to talk to you.

OSVALDO: Why?

SONIA: Please, just do me a favor. I have to talk to you.

LIZETTE: Want to dance?

OSCAR: All right.

LIZETTE *and* OSCAR *exit.*

OSVALDO: What do you want, Sonia? Tell me, sweetheart.

SONIA (*Hysterical*): Don't be angry at me, there's no more wedding cake, we've run out of wedding cake. There's no more, nothing, no more wedding cake.

OSVALDO: That's all right, we should start getting them out. Tell them to start passing out the packages of rice.

SONIA: No, some people are asking for wedding cake. What do we do? What?

OSVALDO: They've had plenty to eat, a great lunch, a salad, chicken cacciatore, a pastry, all they could drink, champagne, coffee. Tell them to pass out the rice, get this over with, and let's go home.

SONIA: At a wedding, wedding cake is something people expect. I can't embarrass the grooms family again. What do we do, what are you going to do?!

OSVALDO: Let's go up to people we know . . .

SONIA: Only Cubans!

OSVALDO: All right, let's go up to all the Cubans we know and ask them not to eat the cake. Then serve it to the Jews. The Cubans won't care.

SONIA: You do it, I can't. I can't face them.

OSVALDO: No, do it, with me, come on.

OSCAR *enters. He is about to eat a piece of cake.* SONIA *grabs it away from him.*

OSCAR: What are you doing?

SONIA: You can't eat it, there's not enough.

OSCAR: Why?

OSVALDO: Just do what your mother says. Please, let's go.

SONIA: You do it.

OSVALDO: You're not coming with me?

SONIA: No, I'm sorry. I can't, I'm too embarrassed.

OSVALDO *exits.*

OSCAR: Okay, give it back to me now.

SONIA: No, take it to that man over there.

OSCAR: Why should I?

SONIA: He didn't get any cake. I think the waiters stole one of the layers. You take it to him. I think his name is Mr. Cohen, the man who's looking at us.

OSCAR: All right. Who?

SONIA (*Points discreetly*): The bald man.

OSCAR: Great.

MANUELA *and* MIRIAM *enter.*

MANUELA: Oh my God; Jesus, Sonia. Osvaldo just told me that we are out of cake.

OSCAR: We are. (*He exits*)

MANUELA: We were winning.

SONIA: The stupid waiters cut the pieces too big, Mama.

MANUELA: Americans! This is one of the great follies of my life.

SONIA: Of course, Mama, this is worse than the revolution.

MANUELA *goes outside.*

MIRIAM: No, in the revolution people died.

SONIA: They really did, didn't they?

MIRIAM: Real blood was shed, real Cuban blood.

SONIA: I forget sometimes.

MIRIAM: Only when I'm calm, that's when I remember, when I'm waking up or when I'm half asleep . . . at those moments.

SONIA: Let's go out to the dance floor and dance like we did at the Tropicana.

LIZETTE (*Enters*): I ripped my wedding dress.

SONIA: Oh well, dear, it's only supposed to last one day. Maybe the next wedding you go to, Lizette, will be mine.

LIZETTE: Who did you find, Mama?

SONIA: Your father.

LIZETTE: Mama, Daddy can't afford another wife.

SONIA: I'm not another wife, Lizette.

LIZETTE: I hope you are right.

MIRIAM: Wait a minute. (*She gives* LIZETTE *five hundred dollars*) In case you decide you need something else when you are on your honeymoon.

LIZETTE: Another five hundred. I think we have three thousand dollars in cash.

LIZETTE *exits to the dressing room.* MIRIAM *lights two cigarettes. She gives one to* SONIA.

MIRIAM: Let's go. Remember when we thought Fidel looked sexy.

SONIA: Shh.

MIRIAM *and* SONIA *sashay off to the ballroom.* OSVALDO *and* ALFREDO *enter.* OSVALDO *is eating a big piece of cake.*

ALFREDO: All women are hysterical.

OSVALDO: I got out there, took the cake from the Cubans, who were outraged. A couple of them called me a Jew. I took it to the Jews and they were as happy as can be. I offered them the cake but nobody wanted any. She made me go through all that for nothing.

ALFREDO: They were being polite, Jews don't like to appear greedy.

OSVALDO (*Eats the cake*): Well, it's delicious.

ALFREDO: It's Cuban cake.

OSVALDO: The only thing that I like Cuban is the food.

ALFREDO: Then start acting like a man. You have one crying in the back and the other demanding in the front!

OSVALDO: I do.

ALFREDO: You don't have the energy to play it both ways.

OSVALDO: What are you talking about?

ALFREDO: Your wife . . . Sonia!

OSVALDO: She'll never change.

ALFREDO: Why should she?!

OSVALDO: To be acceptable.

ALFREDO *slaps* OSVALDO. MIMI *enters.*

MIMI: The rice, we have to hit her with the rice.

OSVALDO *and* ALFREDO, *glaring at each other, exit with* MIMI. LIZETTE *enters in her honeymoon outfit and goes outside. She sees* MANUELA. *They come back in.*

LIZETTE: Grandma, you've been in the sun!

MANUELA: I was taking a nap. You know when you get old you need rest.

LIZETTE: You were crying, Grandma. Don't.

MANUELA: We didn't have enough cake!

LIZETTE: Nothing turned out right, Grandma, that's the truth.

MANUELA: You're right. Oscar would have made sure that we had a good time. My husband would have spent more money. I would have been proud. Your mother would have been proud. You would have been proud.

LIZETTE: Grandma, aren't you proud of me?

MANUELA: Yes.

LIZETTE: Did you love each other?

MANUELA: Yes, dear, we did.

LIZETTE: And you never doubted it?

MANUELA: No, dear.

LIZETTE: I hope I can do it. Wish me luck, Grandma. I don't want to fail. I want to be happy.

MANUELA: I hope that you know how to fight. Everything will try to stop and corrupt your life. I hope your husband is successful and that you have enough children.

LIZETTE: And that I never regret my life.

MANUELA: That will be my prayer.

LIZETTE: That if anyone goes, it's me, that I'm the one that walks. That he'll be hooked on me forever.

MANUELA: That's right.

LIZETTE: Thank you.

MANUELA: A beautiful dress. I'll get the rice.

LIZETTE: No, we are sneaking out. I don't want rice all over my clothes. In ten minutes tell them we tricked them, that we got away.

MANUELA: Go. Don't be nervous. Tonight everything will be all right. Don't worry, have a nice vacation.

LIZETTE: It's eighty degrees in Hawaii, it's an island, like Cuba.

MANUELA: Cuba was more beautiful.

LIZETTE *exits.*

Then politicians got in the way.

LIZETTE (*Offstage*): Honey, we did it. Give me a kiss.

MANUELA *goes outside.*

ENTIRE CAST (*Offstage*): Ah! Uh-Uh! Nooooooooooo!

LIZETTE (*Offstage*): My God, rice, run!

SONIA *enters, covered with rice, followed by* OSVALDO.

OSVALDO: It was a beautiful wedding.

SONIA: You're coming home with me?

OSVALDO: I can't.

SONIA: Yes, come with me.

OSVALDO: Not tonight.

SONIA: When?

OSVALDO: Never. (*Pause*) Nothing is left between you and me.

SONIA: Nothing?

OSVALDO: Nothing.

SONIA: I'm not even your mistress?

OSVALDO: That's right. Revolutions create hell for all people involved.

SONIA: Don't do this. We belong together, we were thrown out. Discarded. We stayed together, Cubans, we are Cubans. Nothing really came between us.

OSVALDO: Something did for me.

MIMI *enters.*

SONIA: What about our family? What we swore to Christ?

OSVALDO: I don't believe in anything, not even Christ.

SONIA: And me?

OSVALDO: I have another wife, she's my wife now. I have another life.

SONIA: If I was my father, I'd kill you!

MIMI (*To* OSVALDO): Your wife is waiting in the car. (*To* SONIA) She told me to tell him.

OSVALDO: Sonia, I'm starting fresh. You should too.

SONIA: I should, yes, I should. (*She takes out the bottle that* MANUELA *gave her in Act One and makes the sign of the cross twice*)

OSVALDO: That's right. (*He starts to exit*)

SONIA: Wait. One last toast.

OSVALDO: To the bride?

SONIA: No, to us. (*She goes to the fountain to pour them champagne, and puts the potion into* OSVALDO's *drink*)

MIMI: Osvaldo?

OSVALDO: How dare you call me that!

MIMI: Okay, Daddy, is that better? This family is the only life I know. It exists for me.

OSVALDO: This is between your mother and me.

MIMI: No, listen, Daddy, the family is continuing. I'm going to make sure of that.

OSVALDO: How? Mimi, how?

MIMI: Never mind, Osvaldo.
*Sound of car horn.*

OSVALDO: She's honking the horn, hurry, Sonia!
SONIA *hands* OSVALDO *the drink.*

SONIA: Money, love and the time to enjoy it, for both of us!

OSVALDO: Thanks. (*He gulps down the drink and exits*)

MIMI: Osvaldo, you jerk. Bastard!

SONIA: Don't worry, Mimi, he's going to have diarrhea till sometime in March.

MIMI: Finally.

SONIA: Put the blame on me. I don't speak the right way. I don't know how to ask the right questions.

MIMI: That's not true, Mama.

SONIA: When I first got here . . . I got lost. I tried to ask an old man for directions. I could not find the right words to ask him the directions. He said to me, "What's wrong with you, lady, somebody give you a lobotomy?" I repeated that word over and over to myself, "lobotomy, lobo-tomy, lo-bo-to-meee!" I looked it up. It said an insertion into the brain, for relief, of tension. I remembered people who had been lobotomized, that their minds could not express anything, they could feel nothing. They looked numb, always resting, then I realized that the old man was right.

MIMI: No. Mama.

SONIA: So I decided never to communicate or deal with this country again. Mimi, I don't know how to go back to my country. He made me realize that to him, I looked like a freak. Then I thought, but I'm still me to Osvaldo, he's trapped too. He must feel the same way too. Put the blame on me.
MIRIAM *and* OSCAR *enter.*

MIMI: Aunt Miriam, tell me, how did you find revenge?

MIRIAM: Against what?

MIMI: Your father.

MIRIAM: Oh, when my mother and father got to America, I made them live with me. I support them. Now they are old and they are dependent on me for everything.

MIMI: It's not worth it, Aunt Miriam.

MIRIAM: Yes it is.

MIMI: Grandma, I'm in the car.

MIRIAM: It's revenge.

OSCAR (*Shows* MIRIAM *the coke bottle*): My revenge!

MIRIAM: Everyone in this family's got a drug.

MANUELA (*Enters*): Mimi is taking me home?

SONIA: Yes, Mama, she's waiting in the car—

**MANUELA:** You didn't do it right.

**SONIA:** I'm sorry, Mama . . . I did it the way I was taught.

**MANUELA** *kisses* **OSCAR** *goodbye and then exits.*

Why can't life be like it was? Like my coming-out party. When my father introduced me to our society in my white dress.

**MIRIAM:** Sonia, they threw the parties to give us away . . . perfect merchandising; Latin women dressed like American movies, doing Viennese waltzes. "Oh, beautiful stream, so clear and bright, a radiant dream we sing to you, by shores that . . . "

**SONIA:** I wonder what it would have been like if we would have stayed?

**MIRIAM:** They would have ridiculed us.

**SONIA:** We would have had a country.

**MIRIAM:** We didn't have a choice.

**OSCAR** *exits to the ballroom.*

**SONIA:** Miriam, Pedro took his life because of that.

**MIRIAM:** No. Pedro did it because of days like today—afternoons like this one: when you are around the people you belong with and you feel like you're choking and don't know why. (*She takes out valium*) I'll give you a piece of magic.

**SONIA:** How many?

**MIRIAM:** One . . . no, two. A valium—that's the only certain thing. It reassures you. It lets you look at the truth. That's why psychiatrists prescribe them.

**SONIA:** You guarantee me Varadero? I'll be floating in Varadero Beach?

**MIRIAM:** If you take three you get to Varadero, Cuba.

**MIRIAM** *and* **SONIA** *take the valium. From the offstage ballroom we hear* **OSCAR** *speaking over the microphone.*

**OSCAR** (*Sniff . . . sniff*): . . . One, two, three, testing, one, three, three, two, testing. Lenin or some Commie like that said that "you cannot make an omelet without

breaking a few eggs." Funny guy. Testing. All right, now from somewhere in the armpit of the world, a little tune my mother taught me. (*He sings "Isla"*)

In an island
Far away from here
I left the life I knew
Island of mine
Country of mine
Mine and only mine
Terraces and houses
Country do you remember
Do you remember
Remember me?

**MIRIAM** (*Takes cushions from chair and puts them on the floor*): I want to float down Key Biscayne back to Varadero. Varadero, please, please come.

**MIRIAM** *lies on the cushions.* **SONIA** *looks at her.*

**SONIA:** Why is he making so much noise?!

**MIRIAM:** Shhh. I'm already there . . . miles and miles into the beach and the water is up to my knees . . . I float. The little fish nibble at my feet. I kick them. I'm in. I'm inside the place where I'm supposed to be.

**OSCAR** (*Singing offstage*):
You were once my island
I left you all alone
I live without your houses
Beautiful houses
Houses remembered.

**SONIA:** Sonia is not coming back. Cojimar, Sonia will never be back.

**OSCAR** (*Singing offstage*):
Eran mías
You were only mine
Never forget me
Don't forget me
Mi amor.

**MIMI** (*Enters*): Mama, what's she doing?

**SONIA:** Relaxing.

**MIMI:** Want to dance, Mama?

**SONIA:** Us?

**MIMI:** Yes.

SONIA: Yes.

OSCAR (*Singing offstage*):
En una isla
Lejos de aquí
Dejé
La vida mía
Madre mía
Isla mía

MIMI: They're going to kick us out.

SONIA: That's all right, Mimi. I've been kicked out of better places.

OSCAR (*Singing offstage*): Te dejé.

SONIA *and* MIMI *begin to dance. Lights fade as we hear the end of the song.*

END OF PLAY

## SUMMARY

The intercultural text demonstrates the collision of cultures as writers from minority cultures explore the contradictions, ambivalences, and difficulties of the struggle to retain ethnic, sexual, and ideological separateness in worlds that discourage exclusiveness. Within the context of cultural diversity, efforts to combine the riches of various cultures into new artistic achievements are celebrated under the label *transcultural*. Robert Brustein argues in "A House Divided" that "transcultural blending may be the most fully acknowledged artistic development of our time."[4] Julie Taymor's *Juan Darien* blends Indonesian-style puppetry and Mayan masks with Elliot Goldenthal's liturgical music and a Uruguayan fable by Horacio Quiroga. David Henry Hwang's *M. Butterfly* combined the plot of Italian opera based on an American play (*Madame Butterfly*) with the tale of the seduction of a French diplomat by a Chinese spy, enacted on a modified Kabuki stage. All operate under the banner of multiculturalism. However, the *intercultural* text, as we have used the term here, identifies and explores the conflicts, explosions, and quakes existing at the fissures where cultures rub against one another. Conflict has been the basis of drama since its beginnings in Greek culture. The intercultural is the most recent source of dramatic conflict as the basis for new American plays. Interculturalism is a newly recognized source of dramatic and artistic achievement related to colliding cultures within a country that has always celebrated the obliteration of cultural differences into the melting pot of American democracy.

The chapter on postmodernism takes us further into a general examination of such terms as *modern* and *postmodern* in contemporary art and art criticism. These new critical perspectives also attempt to classify ways in which today's artists and writers self-consciously assert their "differentness" from older traditions and styles.

## NOTES

1. Richard Schechner, "An Intercultural Primer," *American Theatre*, 8.7 (October 1991): 28–31, 135–136.

2. Schechner 30.

3. Schechner 30.

4. Robert Brustein, "A House Divided," *American Theatre*, 8.7 (October 1991): 45–46, 140–142.

ROTTEN IN THIS AGE OF HOPE." The contradictions of "rottenness" and "hope" are more globally fierce than Shakespeare's line, "Something is rotten in the state of Denmark." In Part One ("Family Scrapbook"), the actor as Hamlet tells the story of betrayal, violence, murder, and adultery while standing against a background of the ruins of modern Europe. He begins with "I was Hamlet," and describes the ruin of statecraft and the butchering of a populace within the context of the funeral of Hamlet's father and the betrayal of Gertrude, the wife, and Polonius, the statesman. Denmark is their prison, but "the wall" growing between Hamlet and his friend Horatio is clearly the former Berlin Wall that divided a country, people, friends, and families. To further emphasize the doubling of experience, Hamlet acknowledges that Horatio is also an *actor:* "I knew you're an actor. I am too, I am playing Hamlet. . . ." In "Family Scrapbook," the context of the *Hamlet* story, characters, and tragedy collapse into a stream-of-consciousness monologue spoken by an actor-as-Hamlet. The content is overlapping images of the disintegration of western Europe into a whorehouse of betrayal, corruption, and death similar to the older play's Denmark.

Ophelia, who has a clock for a heart, is both suicide and prisoner turned "heartless" terrorist in Part Two ("The Europe of Women"). As "Ophelia," the actor becomes collective woman—that is, all suicides, all victims, all daughters, all terrorists, all mass murderers, all revolutionaries, all women. She exists in time (in Shakespeare's play) and in the timelessness of all womankind (in Müller's play).

Part Three is a "Scherzo" and takes place in the "university of the dead." This scene fragment displays, largely through grotesque images, the death or impotency of western thought. It is now corrupted into a ballet of the dead in academic regalia, a cabaret striptease, and the transformation of Hamlet into a drag queen. The final image is of a female acrobat with "breast cancer." "The breast cancer radiates like a sun." The challenge for the reader/spectator is to absorb this collage of images (the multiplex signals) and to experience visually the vast decline of western civilization from Müller's perspective.

In Part Four, the actor-as-Hamlet steps out of his antique role into the modern world of "petrified" hope in the fragment titled quixotically as "Pest in Buda" (an anagram for Budapest, or the failed Hungarian revolt of 1956). Like Ophelia and Hungary, Hamlet turns to violence, obliterating such ideological leaders as Karl Marx, Nikolai Vladimir Ulyanov Lenin, and Mao Tsetung. Here the actor playing Hamlet removes makeup and costume and rejects his traditional stage role. He says, "I'm not Hamlet. I don't take part any more. The old story is meaningless in modern Europe, a mere 'petrification of a hope.'" This monologue is essentially Heiner Müller's reconstructing of the old text to speak to another more complex time. As the actor says, "My drama, if it still would happen, would happen in the time of the uprising." He then describes what could be the Hungarian uprising or any modern civil revolt—the street fighting, the tanks, the executions, the wholesale slaughter. At the conclusion of this part, the actor tears apart a photograph of the playwright, puts back on his Hamlet costume, and severs the sculpted heads of Marx, Lenin, and Mao from their pedestals. The torn photograph and the severed heads present a frightful picture of political, artistic, and intellectual disintegration.

The text ends (Part 5) with the image of Ophelia, motionless in a wheelchair, wrapped as a mummy sunk in the "deep sea." She speaks as Electra, the deserted daughter of King Agamemnon from Greek legend and classical drama. Like Electra, she is transformed by social and political circumstances into a condition of hatred, rebellion, and death. Nothing has changed in 2500 years of western civilization. Ophelia/Electra/Ulrike Meinhoff's litany is unchanged in its anger and defiance of social forces and political conditions: "Long live hate and contempt, rebellion and death."

*Hamletmachine* defies our expectations of a "new" treatment of Shakespeare's text. Müller uses the stage, like Brecht, as a place for public discourse, not for private confession. He has said that "The political task of art today is precisely the mobilization of imagination."[5] He prefers drama to other forms because it enables him "to say one thing and say the contrary." An amazing instance of this balancing of opposites in *Hamletmachine* is the moment when an actor slowly tears a photograph of the playwright in half. The playwright is not, Hamlet-like, contemplating suicide; however, since Shakespeare's *Hamlet* is the pretext for Müller's theatrical fragments, we must contemplate this interpretive option. For Müller, the photograph is like western history and the dramatic text itself—divided, torn, fragmented.

In *Hamletmachine*, Müller takes a public stand on the absence of coherent ideology and effective leadership in modern Europe. The statement is made, however, through the use of dislocating and violent images and sounds, along with contradictory statements. Hamlet begins by saying, "I was Hamlet," but later says he was Macbeth; stagehands place a refrigerator and three television sets around the actor playing Hamlet, who fails to notice them; and Hamlet splits the heads of Marx, Lenin, and Mao with an ax.

In this theatre piece, Müller mobilizes our imaginations to embrace the contradictions of literature and history, to consider modern Europe's failures—political, social, and individual. It is a scene of dislocation where Ophelia becomes a terrorist, Hamlet a demolisher of ideologues, and the actor reflects upon the older play. He says, "I was Hamlet"; "I am Ophelia"; "I'm not Hamlet"; "This is Electra speaking." The actor in the theatre, the figure in history, and the individual in modern society exist as a collage in the "heart of darkness," without hope, ideals, or identity. The world is a place of dislocation, breeding hate, contempt, rebellion, and death.

# Hamletmachine

### Translated by Carl Weber

## 1 FAMILY SCRAPBOOK

I was Hamlet. I stood at the shore and talked with the surf BLABLA, the ruins of Europe in back of me. The bells tolled the state-funeral, murderer and widow a couple, the councillors goose-stepping behind the highranking carcass' coffin, bawling with badly paid grief WHO IS THE CORPSE IN THE HEARSE/ ABOUT WHOM THERE'S SUCH A HUE AND CRY/'TIS THE CORPSE OF A GREAT/ GIVER OF ALMS the lane formed by the populace, creation of his statecraft HE WAS A MAN HE TOOK THEM ALL FOR ALL. I stopped the funeral procession, I pried open the coffin with my sword, the blade broke, yet with the blunt reminder I succeeded, and I dispensed my dead procreator FLESH LIKES TO KEEP THE COMPANY OF FLESH among the bums around me. The mourning turned into rejoicing, the rejoicing into lipsmacking, on top of the empty coffin the murderer humped the widow LET ME HELP YOU UP, UNCLE, OPEN YOUR LEGS, MAMA. I laid down on the ground and listened to the world doing its turns in step with the putrefaction.

I'M GOOD HAMLET GI'ME A CAUSE FOR GRIEF*

*The lines with an asterisk are in English in the German text.

AH THE WHOLE GLOBE FOR A REAL SORROW*
RICHARD THE THIRD I THE PRINCE-KILLING KING*
OH MY PEOPLE WHAT HAVE I DONE UNTO THEE*
I'M LUGGING MY OVERWEIGHT BRAIN LIKE A HUNCHBACK
CLOWN NUMBER TWO IN THE SPRING OF COMMUNISM
SOMETHING IS ROTTEN IN THIS AGE OF HOPE*
LET'S DELVE IN EARTH AND BLOW HER AT THE MOON*

Here comes the ghost who made me, the ax still in his skull. Keep your hat on, I know you've got one hole too many. I would my mother had one less when you were still of flesh: I would have been spared myself. Women should be sewed up—a world without mothers. We could butcher each other in peace and quiet, and with some confidence, if life gets too long for us or our throats too tight for our screams. What do you want of me? Is one state-funeral not enough for you? You old sponger. Is there no blood on your shoes? What's your corpse to me? Be glad the handle is sticking out, maybe you'll go to heaven. What are you waiting for? All the cocks have been butchered. Tomorrow morning has been cancelled.

SHALL I
AS IS THE CUSTOM STICK A PIECE OF IRON INTO

THE NEAREST FLESH OR THE SECOND
BEST
TO LATCH UNTO IT SINCE THE WORLD
IS SPINNING
LORD BREAK MY NECK WHILE I'M FALL-
ING FROM AN
ALEHOUSE BENCH

Enters Horatio. Confidant of my thoughts so full of blood since the morning is curtained by the empty sky. YOU'LL BE TOO LATE MY FRIEND FOR YOUR PAYCHECK/NO PART FOR YOU IN THIS MY TRAGEDY. Horatio, do you know me? Are you my friend, Horatio? If you know me how can you be my friend? Do you want to play Polonius who wants to sleep with his daughter, the delightful Ophelia, here she enters right on cue, look how she shakes her ass, a tragic character. HoratioPolonius. I knew you're an actor. I am too, I'm playing Hamlet. Denmark is a prison, a wall is growing between the two of us. Look what's growing from that wall. Exit Polonius. My mother the bride. Her breasts a rosebed, her womb the snakepit. Have you forgotten your lines, Mama. I'll prompt you. WASH THE MURDER OFF YOUR FACE MY PRINCE/AND OFFER THE NEW DENMARK YOUR GLAD EYE. I'll change you back into a virgin mother, so your king will have a bloodwedding. A MOTHER'S WOMB IS NOT A ONE-WAY STREET. Now, I tie your hands on your back with your bridal veil since I'm sick of your embrace. Now, I tear the wedding dress. Now, I smear the shreds of the wedding dress with the dust my father turned into, and with the soiled shreds your face your belly your breasts. Now, I take you, my mother, in his, my father's invisible tracks. I stifle your scream with my lips. Do you recognize the fruit of your womb? Now go to your wedding, whore, in the broad Danish

sunlight which shines on the living and the dead. I want to cram the corpse down the latrine so the palace will choke in royal shit. Then let me eat your heart, Ophelia, which weeps my tears.

# 2 THE EUROPE OF WOMEN

*Enormous room.\* **OPHELIA**. Her heart is a clock.*

**OPHELIA (CHORUS/HAMLET):** I am Ophelia. The one the river didn't keep. The woman dangling from the rope. The woman with her arteries cut open. The woman with the overdose. SNOW ON HER LIPS. The woman with her head in the gas stove. Yesterday I stopped killing myself. I'm alone with my breasts my thighs my womb. I smash the tools of my captivity, the chair the table the bed. I destroy the battlefield that was my home. I fling open the doors so the wind gets in and the scream of the world. I smash the window. With my bleeding hands I tear the photos of the men I loved and who used me on the bed on the table on the chair on the ground. I set fire to my prison. I throw my clothes into the fire. I wrench the clock that was my heart out of my breast. I walk into the street clothed in my blood.

# 3 SCHERZO

*The university of the dead. Whispering and muttering. From their gravestones (lecterns), the dead philosophers throw their books at **HAMLET**. Gallery (ballet) of the dead women. The woman dangling from the rope. The woman with her arteries cut open, etc. . . . **HAMLET** views them with the attitude of a visitor in a museum (theatre). The dead women tear his clothes off his body.*

---

\*English-language productions could use the entire quote from Karl Marx: Introduction to *Critique of Hegel's Philosophy of Law.*

*Out of an up-ended coffin, labeled* HAMLET 1, *step* CLAUDIUS *and* OPHELIA, *the latter dressed and made up like a whore. Striptease by* OPHELIA.

OPHELIA: Do you want to eat my heart, Hamlet? *Laughs.*

HAMLET: *Face in his hands.* I want to be a woman.

HAMLET *dresses in* OPHELIA'S *clothes,* OPHELIA *puts the make-up of a whore on his face,* CLAUDIUS—*now* HAMLET'S *father— laughs without uttering a sound,* OPHELIA *blows* HAMLET *a kiss and steps with* CLAUDIUS/HAMLETFATHER *back into the coffin.* HAMLET *poses as a whore. An angel, his face at the back of his head:* HORATIO. *He dances with Hamlet.*

VOICE(S): *From the coffin.* What thou killed thou shalt love.

*The dance grows faster and wilder. Laughter from the coffin. On a swing, the madonna with breast cancer.* HORATIO *opens an umbrella, embraces* HAMLET. *They freeze under the umbrella, embracing. The breast cancer radiates like a sun.*

# 4 PEST IN BUDA/BATTLE FOR GREENLAND

*Space 2, as destroyed by* OPHELIA. *An empty armor, an ax stuck in the helmet.*

HAMLET:
The stove is smoking in quarrelsome October
A BAD COLD HE HAD OF IT JUST THE WORST TIME*
JUST THE WORST TIME OF THE YEAR FOR A REVOLUTION*
Cement in bloom walks through the slums
Doctor Zhivago weeps
For his wolves
SOMETIMES IN WINTER THEY CAME INTO THE VILLAGE
AND TORE APART A PEASANT
*He takes off make-up and costume.*

THE ACTOR PLAYING HAMLET: I'm not Hamlet. I don't take part any more. My words have nothing to tell me anymore. My thoughts suck the blood out of the images. My drama doesn't happen anymore. Behind me the set is put up. By people who aren't interested in my drama, for people to whom it means nothing. I'm not interested in it anymore either. I won't play along anymore. *Unnoticed by the actor playing* HAMLET, *stagehands place a refrigerator and three TV-sets on the stage. Humming of the refrigerator. Three TV-channels without sound.* The set is a monument. It presents a man who made history, enlarged a hundred times. The petrification of a hope. His name is interchangeable, the hope has not been fulfilled. The monument is toppled into the dust, razed by those who succeeded him in power three years after the state funeral of the hated and most honored leader. The stone is inhabited. In the spacy nostrils and auditory canals, in the creases of skin and uniform of the demolished monument, the poorer inhabitants of the capital are dwelling. After an appropriate period, the uprising follows the toppling of the monument. My drama, if it still would happen, would happen in the time of the uprising. The uprising starts with a stroll. Against the traffic rules, during the working hours. The street belongs to the pedestrians. Here and there, a car is turned over. Nightmare of a knife thrower: Slowly driving down a one-way street towards an irrevocable parking space surrounded by armed pedestrians. Policemen, if in the way, are swept to the curb. When the procession approaches the government district it is stopped by a police line. People form groups, speakers arise from them. On the balcony of a government building, a man in badly fitting mufti appears and begins to speak too. When the first stone hits him, he retreats behind the double doors of bullet-proof glass. The call for more freedom turns into the cry for the overthrow of the government. People begin to disarm the policemen, to storm two, three buildings, a prison a police precinct an office of the secret police, they string up a dozen henchmen of the rulers by their heels, the government brings in troops, tanks. My place, if my drama would still happen, would be on both sides of the front, between the frontlines, over and above them. I stand in the stench of the crowd and hurl stones at policemen soldiers tanks bullet-proof glass. I look through the double doors of bullet-proof glass at the crowd pressing forward and smell the sweat of my fear. Choking with nausea, I shake my fist at myself who stands behind the bullet-proof glass. Shaking with fear and contempt, I see myself in the crowd pressing forward, foaming at the mouth, shaking my fist at myself. I string up my uniformed flesh by my own heels. I am the soldier in the gun turret, my head is empty under the helmet, the stifled scream under the tracks. I am the typewriter. I tie the noose when the ringleaders are strung up, I pull the stool from under their feet, I break my own neck. I am my own prisoner. I feed my own data into the computers. My parts are the spittle and the spittoon the knife and the wound the fang and the throat the neck and the rope. I am the data bank. Bleeding in the crowd. Breathing again behind the double doors. Oozing wordslime in my soundproof blurb over and above the battle. My drama didn't happen. The script has been lost. The actors put their faces on the rack in the dressing room. In his box, the prompter is rotting. The stuffed corpses in the house don't stir a hand. I go home and kill the time, at one/with my undivided self.

*Television The daily nausea Nausea*
*Of prefabricated babble Of decreed cheerfulness*
*How do you spell GEMÜTLICHKEIT*
*Give us this day our daily murder*
*Since thine is nothingness Nausea*
*Of the lies which are believed*
*By the liars and nobody else*
*Nausea*
*Of the lies which are believed Nausea*
*Of the mugs of the manipulators marked*
*By their struggle for positions votes bank accounts*
*Nausea A chariot armed with scythes sparkling with punchlines*
*I walk through streets stores Faces*
*Scarred by the consumers battle Poverty*
*Without dignity Poverty without the dignity*
*Of the knife the knuckleduster the clenched fist*
*The humiliated bodies of women*
*Hope of generations*
*Stifled in blood cowardice stupidity*
*Laughter from dead bellies*
*Hail Coca Cola*
*A kingdom*
*For a murderer*
*I WAS MACBETH*
*THE KING HAD OFFERED HIS THIRD MISTRESS TO ME*
*I KNEW EVERY MOLE ON HER HIPS*
*RASKOLNIKOV CLOSE TO THE HEART UNDER THE ONLY COAT*
*THE AX FOR THE*
*ONLY*
*SKULL OF THE PAWNBROKER*
*In the solitude of airports*
*I breathe again I am*
*A privileged person My nausea*
*Is a privilege*

*Protected by torture
Barbed wire Prisons*

*Photograph of the author.*

I don't want to eat drink breathe love a woman a man a child an animal anymore. I don't want to die anymore. I don't want to kill anymore.

*Tearing of the author's photograph.*

I force open my sealed flesh. I want to dwell in my veins, in the marrow of my bones, in the maze of my skull. I retreat into my entrails. I take my seat in my shit, in my blood. Somewhere bodies are torn apart so I can dwell in my shit. Somewhere bodies are opened so I can be alone with my blood. My thoughts are lesions in my brain. My brain is a scar. I want to be a machine. Arms for grabbing Legs to walk on, no pain no thoughts.

*TV screens go black. Blood oozes from the refrigerator. Three naked women: Marx, Lenin, Mao. They speak simultaneously, each one in his own language, the text:*

THE MAIN POINT IS TO OVERTHROW ALL EXISTING CONDITIONS . . . *

The **ACTOR OF HAMLET** *puts on make-up and costume.*

HAMLET THE DANE PRINCE AND MAG-GOT'S FODDER
STUMBLING FROM HOLE TO HOLE TO-WARDS THE FINAL
HOLE LISTLESS IN HIS BACK THE GHOST THAT ONCE
MADE HIM GREEN LIKE OPHELIA'S FLESH IN CHILDBED
AND SHORTLY ERE THE THIRD COCK'S CROW A CLOWN
WILL TEAR THE FOOL'S CAP OFF THE PHILOSOPHER
A BLOATED BLOODHOUND'LL CRAWL INTO THE ARMOR

*He steps into the armor, splits with the ax the heads of Marx, Lenin, Mao. Snow. Ice Age.*

# 5 FIERCELY ENDURING MILLENIUMS IN THE FEARFUL ARMOR

*The deep sea.* **OPHELIA** *in a wheelchair. Fish, debris, dead bodies and limbs drift by.*

**OPHELIA:**

*While two men in white smocks wrap gauze around her and the wheelchair, from bottom to top.*

This is Electra speaking. In the heart of darkness. Under the sun of torture. To the capitals of the world. In the name of the victims. I eject all the sperm I have received. I turn the milk of my breasts into lethal poison. I take back the world I gave birth to. I choke between my thighs the world I gave birth to. I bury it in my womb. Down with the happiness of submission. Long live hate and contempt, rebellion and death. When she walks through your bedrooms carrying butcher knives you'll know the truth.

*The men exit.* **OPHELIA** *remains on stage, motionless in her white wrappings.*

END

## SUMMARY

*Modernism* and *postmodernism* are descriptive terms used to distinguish our differentness from the past in art, thought, and politics. In drama, *modernism* applies more to new ideas than to new forms. For example, Henrik Ibsen's treatment of the irrational in *Hedda Gabler* breaks with dramatic tradition wherein the irrational was unusual, illogical, and mad! In Ibsen's treatment, the irrational achieves a logic of its own. Hedda's actions are intelligible, although not wholly explainable, once we glimpse the dark inner recesses of the character's unresolved conflicts. They range from her gender role, her class, her upbringing, and her delayed marriage to her ambitions, fears, jealousies, and obsessions. The treatment in art of human irrationality sets apart the moderns from the ancients.

Postmodernism, as the word implies, follows modernism. The new movement is still being debated and defined as a reaction against modernism. In the theatre, postmodern texts are fragmented and imagistic. Rejecting such traditional elements of playwriting as plot, character, action, and dialogue, postmodern writers aim for an experience of contradiction and consciousness. Heiner Müller's concern with the failure of western political systems and industrial societies to free human imagination energizes his texts. He sees political ideologies as repressive forces, continuing to shape the dark side of human nature. His plays re-present a world of bizarre images, fragmented discourse, and contradictory figures. In *Hamletmachine*, the allusion to Shakespeare's tragedy is a mere touchstone to Müller's multiple images and meanings reflective of the contradictions and dissolutions of contemporary civilization.

One overriding feature of postmodern writing is its allusiveness (the quotations within quotations). Allusions (literary, political, historical, mythological) are at once poetic, playful, ironic, and anarchic. As such, they multiply words, sounds, and images. Hamlet is Shakespeare's Hamlet; he is also Müller's Hamlet; he is the actor's Hamlet as well. As a composite figure, the Hamlet of *Hamletmachine* ranges throughout literary and modern European history as conservative and liberal, government official and revolutionary, optimist and pessimist, intellectual and sensualist, protector and destroyer. The doubling and the contradictions are one way of presenting the complexities and indeterminancies of the postmodern world.

## NOTES

1. "19 Answers by Heiner Müller" in *Hamletmachine and Other Texts for the Stage*, ed. Carl Weber (New York: Performing Arts Journal Publications, 1984): 137.
2. Richard Schechner, *The End of Humanism: Writings on Performance* (New York: Performing Arts Journal Publications, 1982): 97.
3. Denis Donoghue, "The Promiscuous Cool of Postmodernism," *The New York Times Book Review*, 22 (June 1986): 1, 36.
4. Ihab Hassan, "The Question of Postmodernism," *Performing Arts Journal 16*, 6, No. 1 (1981): 30–37.
5. "19 Answers by Heiner Müller" 138.

# Afterword

We began this study of play analysis with traditional approaches to the creation of drama's plots, action, character, language, and scenography. We have also followed the evolution of drama's genres and minor forms. We ended with modern attitudes and techniques that inform new styles, structures, and viewpoints in theatrical writing.

We examined classical, modern, and contemporary texts, climactic and episodic forms, epic and absurdist styles, modern and postmodern viewpoints, feminist and intercultural perspectives. In all, we discovered similarity and dissimilarity, the familiar and the strange. We can conclude that trends in writing for the theatre proceed by leaps and starts rather than by continuous routes. Continuity exists side by side with discontinuity. One movement almost instantly spawns a countermovement, and then a counter-countermovement, and so on. Nevertheless, there is a common denominator among playwrights from all periods of dramatic writing. They have a *passion* for writing for the theatre, a *consciousness* of drama's importance to culture and society, and a *playful seriousness* in the making of plays.

To understand plays written in Western society for over 2500 years is to comprehend our dramatic heritage and to experience the changing image of our humanness from classical to postmodern times. Dramatic art holds the mirror up to nature, politics, culture, and society—to our hearts and minds. The many ways devised by playwrights to mold the dramatic mirror through history and cultures and changing societies has been the subject of this book.

# Documents on Drama and Theatre

## The Poetics

### ARISTOTLE
**Translated by S. H. Butcher**

*The history of dramatic criticism begins with Aristotle's fragmentary treatise, called* The Poetics *(written* circa 335–323 B.C)*, which looked back on a body of plays written by greater and lesser writers of classical Greece. Aristotle established critical concerns for the nature of drama as imitation and for tragedy and comedy as forms of writing for the theatre.*

### [ART AS IMITATION]

Epic poetry and Tragedy, Comedy also and Dithyrambic poetry, and the music of the flute and of the lyre in most of their forms, are all in their general conception modes of imitation. They differ, however, from one another in three respects, the medium, the objects, the manner or mode of imitation, being in each case distinct.

Since the objects of imitation are men in action, and these men must be either of a higher or a lower type (for moral character mainly answers to these divisions, goodness and badness being the distinguishing marks of moral differences), it follows that we must represent men either as better than in real life, or as worse, or as they are. It is the same in painting. Polygnotus depicted men as nobler than they are, Pauson as less noble, Dionysius drew them true to life.

. . . The same distinction marks off Tragedy from Comedy; for Comedy aims at representing men as worse, Tragedy as better than in actual life.

There is still a third difference—the manner in which each of these objects may be imitated. For the medium being the same, and the objects the same, the poet may imitate by *narration*—in which case he can either take another personality as Homer does, or speak in his own person, unchanged—or he may present all his characters as living and moving before us.

### [ORIGINS OF DRAMA]

These, then, as we said at the beginning, are the three differences which distinguish artistic imitation,—the medium, the objects, and the manner. So that from one point of view, Sophocles is an imitator of the same kind as Homer—for both imitate higher types of character; from another point of view, of the same kind as Aristophanes—for both imitate persons acting and doing. Hence, some say, the name of 'drama' is given to such poems, as representing action. For the same reason the Dorians claim the invention both of Tragedy and Comedy. The claim to Comedy is put forward by the Megarians,—not only by those of Greece proper, who allege that it originated under their democracy, but also by the Megarians of Sicily, for the poet Epicharmus, who is much earlier than Chionides and Magnes, belonged to that country. Tragedy too is claimed by certain Dorians of the Peloponnese. In each case they appeal to the evidence of language. The outlying villages, they say, are by them called κῶμαι, by the Athenians δῆμοι: and they assume that Comedians were so named not from κωμάζειν 'to revel,' but because they wandered from village to village (κατὰ κώμας) being excluded contemptuously from the city. They add also that the Dorian word for 'doing' is δρᾶυ, and the Athenian, πρμττειυ.

This may suffice as to the number and nature of the various modes of imitation.

Poetry in general seems to have sprung from two causes, each of them lying deep in our nature. First, the instinct of imitation is implanted in man from childhood, one difference between him and other animals being that he is the most imitative of living creatures, and through imitation learns his earliest lessons; and no less universal is the pleasure felt in things imitated. We have evidence of this in the facts of experience. Objects which in themselves we view with pain, we delight to contemplate when reproduced with minute fidelity: such as the forms of the most ignoble animals and of dead bodies. The cause of this again is, that to learn gives the liveliest pleasure, not only to philosophers but to men in general; whose capacity, however, of learning is more limited. Thus the reason why men enjoy seeing a likeness is, that in contemplating it they find themselves learning or inferring, and saying perhaps, 'Ah, that is he.' For if you happen not to have seen the original, the pleasure will be due not to the imitation as such, but to the execution, the colouring, or some such other cause.

Imitation, then, is one instinct of our nature. Next, there is the instinct for 'harmony' and rhythm, metres being manifestly sections of rhythm. Persons, therefore, starting with this natural gift developed by degrees their special aptitudes, till their rude improvisations gave birth to Poetry.

Poetry now diverged in two directions, according to the individual character of the writers. The graver spirits imitated noble actions, and the actions of good men. The more trivial sort imitated the actions of meaner persons, at first composing satires, as the former did hymns to the gods and the praises of famous men. A poem of the satirical kind cannot indeed be put down to any author earlier than Homer; though many such writers probably there were. But from Homer onward, instances can be cited,—his own Margites, for example, and other similar compositions. The appropriate metre was also here introduced; hence the measure is still called the iambic or lampooning measure, being that in which people lampooned one another. Thus the older poets were distinguished as writers of heroic or of lampooning verse.

As, in the serious style, Homer is preeminent among poets, for he alone combined dramatic form with excellence of imitation, so he too first laid down the main lines of Comedy, by dramatising the ludicrous instead of writing personal satire. His Margites bears the same relation to Comedy that the Iliad and Odyssey do to Tragedy. But when Tragedy and Comedy came to light, the two classes of poets still followed their natural bent: the lampooners became writers of Comedy, and the Epic poets were succeeded by Tragedians, since the drama was a larger and higher form of art. . . .

. . . Tragedy—as also Comedy—was at first mere improvisation. The one originated with the authors of the Dithyramb, the other with those of the phallic songs, which are still in use in many of our cities. Tragedy advanced by slow degrees; each new element that showed itself was in turn developed. Having passed through many changes, it found its natural form, and there it stopped.

Aeschylus first introduced a second actor; he diminished the importance of the Chorus, and assigned the leading part to the dialogue. Sophocles raised the number of actors to three, and added scene-painting. Moreover, it was not till late that the short plot was discarded for one of greater compass, and the grotesque diction of the earlier satyric form for the stately manner of Tragedy.

Comedy is, as we have said, an imitation of characters of a lower type,—not, however, in the full sense of the word bad, the Ludicrous being merely a subdivision of the ugly. It consists in some defect or ugliness which is not painful or destructive. To take an obvious example, the comic mask is ugly and distorted, but does not imply pain.

The successive changes through which Tragedy passed, and the authors of these changes, are well known, whereas Comedy has had no history, because it was not at first treated seriously. It was late before the Archon granted a comic chorus to a poet; the performers were till then voluntary. Comedy had already taken definite shape when comic poets, distinctively so called, are heard of. Who furnished it with masks, or prologues, or increased the number of actors,—these and other similar details remain unknown. As for the plot, it came originally from Sicily; but of Athenian writers Crates was the first who, abandoning the 'iambic' or lampooning form, generalised his themes and plots.

Epic poetry agrees with Tragedy in so far as it is an imitation in verse of characters of a higher type. They differ, in that Epic poetry admits but one kind of metre, and is narrative in form. They differ, again, in their length: for Tragedy endeavours, as far as possible, to confine itself to a single revolution of the sun, or but slightly to exceed this limit; whereas the Epic action has no limits of time. . . .

## [ELEMENTS OF TRAGEDY]

Tragedy, then, is an imitation of an action that is serious, complete, and of a certain magnitude; in language embellished with each kind of artistic ornament, the several kinds being found in separate parts of the play; in the form of action, not of narrative; through pity and fear effecting the proper purgation of these emotions. By 'language embellished,' I mean language into which rhythm, 'harmony,' and song enter. By 'the several kinds in separate parts,' I mean, that some parts are rendered through the medium of verse alone, others again with the aid of song.

Now as tragic imitation implies persons acting, it necessarily follows, in the first place, that Spectacular equipment will be a part of Tragedy. Next, Song and Diction, for these are the medium of imitation. By 'Diction' I mean the mere metrical arrangement of the words; as for 'Song,' it is a term whose sense every one understands.

Again, Tragedy is the imitation of an action; and an action implies personal agents, who necessarily possess certain distinctive qualities both of character and thought; for it is by these that we qualify actions themselves, and these—thought and character—are the two natural causes from which actions spring, and on actions again all success or failure depends. Hence, the Plot is the imitation of the action—for by plot I here mean the arrangement of the incidents. By Character I mean that in virtue of which we ascribe certain qualities to the agents. Thought is required wherever a statement is proved, or, it may be, a general truth enunciated. Every Tragedy, therefore, must have six parts, which parts determine its quality—namely, Plot, Character, Diction, Thought, Spectacle, Song. Two of the parts constitute the medium of imitation, one the manner, and three the objects of imitation. And these complete the list. These elements have been employed, we may say, by the poets to a man; in fact, every play contains Spectacular elements as well as Character, Plot, Diction, Song, and Thought.

But most important of all is the structure of the incidents. For Tragedy is an imitation, not of men, but of an action and of life, and life consists in action, and its end is a mode of action, not a quality. Now character determines men's qualities, but it is by their actions that they are happy or the reverse. Dramatic action, therefore, is not with a view to the representation of character: character comes in as subsidiary to the actions. Hence the incidents and the plot are the end of a tragedy; and the end is the chief thing of all. Again, without action there cannot be a tragedy; there may be without character. The tragedies of most of our modern poets fail in the rendering of character; and of poets in general this is often true. It is the same in painting; and here lies the difference between Zeuxis and Polygnotus. Polygnotus delineates character well: the style of Zeuxis is devoid of ethical quality. Again, if you string together a set of speeches expressive of character, and well finished in point of diction and thought, you will not produce the essential tragic effect nearly so well as with a play which, however deficient in these respects, yet has a plot and artistically constructed incidents. Besides which, the most powerful elements of emotional interest in Tragedy—Peripeteia or Reversal of the Situation and Recognition scenes—are parts of the plot. A further proof is, that novices in the art attain to finish of diction and precision of portraiture before they can construct the plot. It is the same with almost all the early poets.

The Plot, then, is the first principle, and, as it were, the soul of a tragedy: Character holds the second place. A similar fact is seen in painting. The most beautiful colours, laid on confusedly, will not give as much pleasure as the chalk outline of a portrait. Thus Tragedy is the imitation of an action, and of the agents mainly with a view to the action.

Third in order is Thought,—that is, the faculty of saying what is possible and pertinent in given circumstances. In the case of oratory, this is the function of the political art and of the art of rhetoric: and so indeed the older poets make their characters speak the language of civic life; the poets of our time, the language of the rhetoricians. Character is that which reveals moral purpose, showing what kind of things a man chooses or avoids. Speeches, therefore, which do not make this manifest, or in which the speaker does not choose or avoid anything whatever, are not expressive of character. Thought, on the other hand, is found where something is proved to be or not to be, or a general maxim is enunciated.

Fourth among the elements enumerated comes Diction; by which I mean, as has been already said, the expression of the meaning in words; and its essence is the same both in verse and prose.

Of the remaining elements Song holds the chief place among the embellishments.

The Spectacle has, indeed, an emotional attraction of its own, but, of all the parts, it is the least artistic, and connected least with the art of poetry. For the power of Tragedy, we may be sure, is felt even apart from representation and actors. Besides, the production of spectacular effects depends more on the art of the stage machinist than on that of the poet.

[ON PLOT OR FABLE]

These principles being established, let us now discuss the proper structure of the Plot, since this is the first and most important thing in Tragedy.

Now, according to our definition, Tragedy is an imitation of an action that is complete, and whole, and of a certain magnitude; for there may be a whole that is wanting in magnitude. A whole is that which has a beginning, a middle, and an end. A beginning is that which does not itself follow anything by causal necessity, but after which something naturally is or comes to be. An end, on the contrary, is that which itself naturally follows some other thing, either by necessity, or as a rule, but has nothing following it. A middle is that which follows something as some other thing follows it. A well constructed plot, therefore, must neither begin nor end at haphazard, but conform to these principles.

## [ON UNITY]

Unity of plot does not, as some persons think, consist in the unity of the hero. For infinitely various are the incidents in one man's life which cannot be reduced to unity; and so, too, there are many actions of one man out of which we cannot make one action. Hence the error, as it appears, of all poets who have composed a Heracleid, a Theseid, or other poems of the kind. They imagine that as Heracles was one man, the story of Heracles must also be a unity. But Homer, as in all else he is of surpassing merit, here too—whether from art or natural genius—seems to have happily discerned the truth. In composing the Odyssey he did not include all the adventures of Odysseus—such as his wound on Parnassus, or his feigned madness at the mustering of the host—incidents between which there was no necessary or probable connexion: but he made the Odyssey, and likewise the Iliad, to centre round an action that in our sense of the word is one. As therefore, in the other imitative arts, the imitation is one when the object imitated is one, so the plot, being an imitation of an action, must imitate one action and that a whole, the structural union of the parts being such that, if any one of them is displaced or removed, the whole will be disjointed and disturbed. For a thing whose presence or absence makes no visible difference, is not an organic part of the whole.

## [ON PROBABILITY]

It is, moreover, evident from what has been said, that it is not the function of the poet to relate what has happened, but what may happen,—what is possible according to the law of probability or necessity. The poet and the historian differ not by writing in verse or in prose. The work of Herodotus might be put into verse, and it would still be a species of history, with metre no less than without it. The true difference is that one relates what has happened, the other what may happen. Poetry, therefore, is a more philosophical and a higher thing than history: for poetry tends to express the universal, history the particular. By the universal I mean how a person of a certain type will on occasion speak or act, according to the law of probability or necessity. . . .

But again, Tragedy is an imitation not only of a complete action, but of events inspiring fear or pity. Such an effect is best produced when the events come on us by surprise; and the effect is heightened when, at the same time, they follow as cause and effect. The tragic wonder will then be greater than if they happened of themselves or by accident; for even coincidences are most striking when they have an air of design. We may instance the statue of Mitys at Argos, which fell upon his murderer while he was a spectator at a festival, and killed him. Such events seem not to be due to mere chance.

Plots, therefore, constructed on these principles are necessarily the best.

### [ON SIMPLE AND COMPLEX PLOTS]

Plots are either Simple or Complex, for the actions in real life, of which the plots are an imitation, obviously show a similar distinction. An action which is one and continuous in the sense above defined, I call Simple, when the change of fortune takes place without Reversal of the Situation and without Recognition.

A Complex action is one in which the change is accompanied by such Reversal, or by Recognition, or by both. These last should arise from the internal structure of the plot, so that what follows should be the necessary or probable result of the preceding action. It makes all the difference whether any given event is a case of *propter hoc* or *post hoc*.

Reversal of the Situation is a change by which the action veers round to its opposite, subject always to our rule of probability or necessity. Thus in the Oedipus, the messenger comes to cheer Oedipus and free him from his alarms about his mother, but by revealing who he is, he produces the opposite effect. . . .

Recognition, as the name indicates, is a change from ignorance to knowledge, producing love or hate between the persons destined by the poet for good or bad fortune, The best form of recognition is coincident with a Reversal of the Situation, as in the Oedipus. . . . But the recognition which is most intimately connected with the plot and action is, as we have said, the recognition of persons. This recognition, combined with Reversal, will produce either pity or fear; and actions producing these effects are those which, by our definition, Tragedy represents. Moreover, it is upon such situations that the issues of good or bad fortune will depend. Recognition, then, being between persons, it may happen that one person only is recog-

nised by the other—when the latter is already known—or it may be necessary that the recognition should be on both sides. Thus Iphigenia is revealed to Orestes by the sending of the letter; but another act of recognition is required to make Orestes known to Iphigenia.

Two parts, then, of the Plot—Reversal of the Situation and Recognition—turn upon surprises. A third part is the Scene of Suffering. The Scene of Suffering is a destructive or painful action, such as death on the stage, bodily agony, wounds and the like.

### [ON PITY AND FEAR]

A perfect tragedy should, as we have seen, be arranged not on the simple but on the complex plan. It should, moreover, imitate actions which excite pity and fear, this being the distinctive mark of tragic imitation. It follows plainly, in the first place, that the change of fortune presented must not be the spectacle of a virtuous man brought from prosperity to adversity: for this moves neither pity nor fear; it merely shocks us. Nor, again, that of a bad man passing from adversity to prosperity: for nothing can be more alien to the spirit of Tragedy; it possesses no single tragic quality; it neither satisfies the moral sense nor calls forth pity or fear. Nor, again, should the downfall of the utter villain be exhibited. A plot of this kind would, doubtless, satisfy the moral sense, but it would inspire neither pity nor fear; for pity is aroused by unmerited misfortune, fear by the misfortune of a man like ourselves. Such an event, therefore, will be neither pitiful nor terrible.

### [ON CHARACTER]

There remains, then, the character between these two extremes,—that of a man who is not eminently good and just, yet whose misfortune is brought about not by vice or depravity, but by some error or frailty. He must be one who is highly renowned and prosperous,—a personage like Oedipus, Thyestes, or other illustrious men of such families.

A well constructed plot should, therefore, be single in its issue, rather than double as some maintain. The change of fortune should be not from bad to good, but, reversely, from good to bad. It should come about as the result not of vice, but of some great error or frailty, in a character either such as we have described, or better rather than worse. . . .

Fear and pity may be aroused by spectacular means; but they may also result from the inner structure of the piece, which is the better way, and indicates a superior poet. For the plot ought to be so constructed that, even without the aid of the eye, he who hears the tale told will thrill with horror and melt to pity at what takes place. This is the impression we should receive from hearing the story of the Oedipus. . . .

## [CHORUS]

The Chorus too should be regarded as one of the actors; it should be an integral part of the whole, and share in the action, in the manner not of Euripides but of Sophocles. As for the later poets, their choral songs pertain as little to the subject of the piece as to that of any other tragedy. They are, therefore, sung as mere interludes,—a practice first begun by Agathon. . . .

# Theatre for Pleasure or
# Theatre for Instruction

## BERTOLT BRECHT

*Bertolt Brecht probably wrote this essay in 1936 but it remained unpublished until 1957. In it, Brecht differentiates between* epic theatre *and* dramatic theatre. *In his discussion, he touches upon such epic devices as alienation, narration, projections, mechanized stages, the spectator, entertainment and instruction.*

A few years back, anybody talking about the modern theatre meant the theatre in Moscow, New York and Berlin. He might have thrown in a mention of Jouvet's productions in Paris or Cochran's in London, or *The Dybbuk* as given by the Habima (which is to all intents and purposes part of the Russian theatre, since Vakhtangov was its director). But broadly speaking there were only three capitals so far as modern theatre was concerned.

Russian, American and German theatres differed widely from one another, but were alike in being modern, that is to say in introducing technical and artistic innovations. In a sense they even achieved a certain stylistic resemblance, probably because technology is international (not just that part which is directly applied to the stage but also that which influences it, the film for instance), and because large progressive cities in large industrial countries are involved. Among the older capitalist countries it is the Berlin theatre that seemed of late to be in the lead. For a period all that is common to the modern theatre received its strongest and (so far) maturest expression there.

The Berlin theatre's last phase was the so-called epic theatre, and it showed the modern theatre's trend of development in its purest form. Whatever was labelled 'Zeitstück' or 'Piscatorbühne' or 'Lehrstück' belongs to the epic theatre.

## THE EPIC THEATRE

Many people imagine that the term 'epic theatre' is self-contradictory, as the epic and dramatic ways of narrating a story are held, following Aristotle, to be basically distinct. The difference between the two forms was never thought simply to lie in the fact that the one is performed by living beings while the other operates via the written word; epic works such as those of Homer and the medieval singers were at the same time theatrical performances, while dramas like Goethe's *Faust* and Byron's *Manfred* are agreed to have been more effective as books. Thus even by Aristotle's definition the difference between the dramatic and epic forms was attributed to their different methods of construction, whose laws were dealt with by two different branches of aesthetics. The method of construction depended on the different way of presenting the work to the public, sometimes via the stage, sometimes through a book; and independently of that there was the 'dramatic element' in epic works and the 'epic element' in dramatic. The bourgeois novel in the last century developed much that was 'dramatic', by which was meant the strong centralization of the story, a momentum that drew the separate parts into a common relationship. A particular passion of utterance, a certain emphasis on the clash of forces are hallmarks of the 'dramatic'. The epic writer Döblin provided an excellent criterion when he said that with an epic work, as opposed to a dramatic, one can as it were take a pair of scissors and cut it into individual pieces, which remain fully capable of life.

This is no place to explain how the opposition of epic and dramatic lost its rigidity after having long been held to be irreconcilable. Let us just point out that the technical advances alone were enough to permit the stage to incorporate an element of narrative in its dramatic productions. The possibility of projections, the greater adaptability of the stage due to mechanization, the film, all completed the theatre's equipment, and did so at a point where the most important transactions between people could no longer be shown simply by personifying the motive forces or subjecting the characters to invisible metaphysical powers.

To make these transactions intelligible the environment in which the people lived had to be brought to bear in a big and 'significant' way.

This environment had of course been shown in the existing drama, but only as seen from the central figure's point of view, and not as an independent element. It was defined by the hero's reactions to it. It was seen as a storm can be seen when one sees the ships on a sheet of water unfolding their sails, and the sails filling out. In the epic theatre it was to appear standing on its own.

The stage began to tell a story. The narrator was no longer missing, along with the fourth wall. Not only did the background adopt an attitude to the events on the stage—by big screens recalling other simultaneous events elsewhere, by projecting documents which confirmed or contradicted what the characters said, by concrete and intelligible figures to accompany abstract conversations,

by figures and sentences to support mimed transactions whose sense was unclear—but the actors too refrained from going over wholly into their role, remaining detached from the character they were playing and clearly inviting criticism of him.

The spectator was no longer in any way allowed to submit to an experience uncritically (and without practical consequences) by means of simple empathy with the characters in a play. The production took the subject-matter and the incidents shown and put them through a process of alienation: the alienation that is necessary to all understanding. When something seems 'the most obvious thing in the world' it means that any attempt to understand the world has been given up.

What is 'natural' must have the force of what is startling. This is the only way to expose the laws of cause and effect. People's activity must simultaneously be so and be capable of being different.

It was all a great change.

The dramatic theatre's spectator says: Yes, I have felt like that too—Just like me—It's only natural—It'll never change—The sufferings of this man appal me, because they are inescapable—That's great art; it all seems the most obvious thing in the world—I weep when they weep, I laugh when they laugh.

The epic theatre's spectator says: I'd never have thought it—That's not the way—That's extraordinary, hardly believable—It's got to stop—The sufferings of this man appal me, because they are unnecessary—That's great art: nothing obvious in it—I laugh when they weep, I weep when they laugh.

## THE INSTRUCTIVE THEATRE

The stage began to be instructive.

Oil, inflation, war, social struggles, the family, religion, wheat, the meat market, all became subjects for theatrical representation. Choruses enlightened the spectator about facts unknown to him. Films showed a montage of events from all over the world. Projections added statistical material. And as the 'background' came to the front of the stage so people's activity was subjected to criticism. Right and wrong courses of action were shown. People were shown who knew what they were doing, and others who did not. The theatre became an affair for philosophers, but only for such philosophers as wished not just to explain the world but also to change it. So we had philosophy, and we had instruction. And where was the amusement in all that? Were they sending us back to school, teaching us to read and write? Were we supposed to pass exams, work for diplomas?

Generally there is felt to be a very sharp distinction between learning and amusing oneself. The first may be useful, but only the second is pleasant. So we have to defend the epic theatre against the suspicion that it is a highly disagreeable, humourless, indeed strenuous affair.

Well: all that can be said is that the contrast between learning and amusing oneself is not laid down by divine rule; it is not one that has always been and must continue to be.

Undoubtedly there is much that is tedious about the kind of learning familiar to us from school, from our professional training, etc. But it must be remembered under what conditions and to what end that takes place.

It is really a commercial transaction. Knowledge is just a commodity. It is acquired in order to be resold. All those who have grown out of going to school have to do their learning virtually in secret, for anyone who admits that he still has something to learn devalues himself as a man whose knowledge is inadequate. Moreover the usefulness of learning is very much limited by factors outside the learner's control. There is unemployment, for instance, against which no knowledge can protect one. There is the division of labour, which makes generalized knowledge unnecessary and impossible. Learning is often among the concerns of those whom no amount of concern will get any forwarder. There is not much knowledge that leads to power, but plenty of knowledge to which only power can lead.

Learning has a very different function for different social strata. There are strata who cannot imagine any improvement in conditions: they find the conditions good enough for them. Whatever happens to oil they will benefit from it. And: they feel the years beginning to tell. There can't be all that many years more. What is the point of learning a lot now? They have said their final word: a grunt. But there is also strata 'waiting their turn' who are discontented with conditions, have a vast interest in the practical side of learning, want at all costs to find out where they stand, and know that they are lost without learning; these are the best and keenest learners. Similar differences apply to countries and peoples. Thus the pleasure of learning depends on all sorts of things; but none the less there is such a thing as pleasurable learning, cheerful and militant learning.

If there were not such amusement to be had from learning the theatre's whole structure would unfit it for teaching.

Theatre remains theatre even when it is instructive theatre, and in so far as it is good theatre it will amuse.

## THEATRE AND KNOWLEDGE

But what has knowledge got to do with art? We know that knowledge can be amusing, but not everything that is amusing belongs in the theatre.

I have often been told, when pointing out the invaluable services that modern knowledge and science, if properly applied, can perform for art and specially for the theatre, that art and knowledge are two estimable but wholly distinct fields of human activity. This is a fearful truism, of course, and it is as well to agree quickly that, like most truisms, it is perfectly true. Art and science work in quite different ways: agreed. But, bad as it may sound, I have to admit that I cannot get along as an artist without the use of one or two sciences. This may well arouse serious doubts as to my artistic capacities. People are used to seeing poets as unique and slightly unnatural beings who reveal with a truly godlike assurance things that other people can only recognize after much sweat and toil. It is naturally distasteful to have to admit that one does not belong to this select band. All the same, it must be admitted. It must at the same time be made clear that the scientific occupations just confessed to are not pardonable side interests, pursued on days off after a good week's work. We all know how Goethe was interested in natural history, Schiller in history: as a kind of hobby, it is charitable to assume. I have no wish promptly to accuse these two of having needed these sciences for their poetic activity; I am not trying to shelter behind them; but I must say that I do need the sciences. I have to admit, however, that I look askance at all sorts of people who I know do not operate on the level of scientific understanding: that is to say, who sing as the birds sing, or as people imagine the birds to sing. I don't mean by that that I would reject a charming poem about the taste of fried fish or the delights of a boating party just because the writer had not studied gastronomy or navigation. But in my view the great and complicated things that go on in the world cannot be adequately recognized by people who do not use every possible aid to understanding.

Let us suppose that great passions or great events have to be shown which influence the fate of nations. The lust for power is nowadays held to be such a passion. Given that a poet 'feels' this lust and wants to have

someone strive for power, how is he to show the exceedingly complicated machinery within which the struggle for power nowadays takes place? If his hero is a politician, how do politics work? If he is a business man, how does business work? And yet there are writers who find business and politics nothing like so passionately interesting as the individual's lust for power. How are they to acquire the necessary knowledge? They are scarcely likely to learn enough by going round and keeping their eyes open, though even then it is more than they would get by just rolling their eyes in an exalted frenzy. The foundation of a paper like the *Völkishcer Beobachter* or a business like Standard Oil is a pretty complicated affair, and such things cannot be conveyed just like that. One important field for the playwright is psychology. It is taken for granted that a poet, if not an ordinary man, must be able without further instruction to discover the motives that lead a man to commit murder; he must be able to give a picture of a murderer's mental state 'from within himself'. It is taken for granted that one only has to look inside oneself in such a case; and then there's always one's imagination. . . . There are various reasons why I can no longer surrender to this agreeable hope of getting a result quite so simply. I can no longer find in myself all those motives which the press or scientific reports show to have been observed in people. Like the average judge when pronouncing sentence, I cannot without further ado conjure up an adequate picture of a murderer's mental state. Modern psychology, from psychoanalysis to behaviorism, acquaints me with facts that lead me to judge the case quite differently, especially if I bear in mind the findings of sociology and do not overlook economics and history. You will say: but that's getting complicated. I have to answer that it *is* complicated. Even if you let yourself be convinced, and agree with me that a large slice of literature is exceedingly primitive, you may still ask with profound concern: won't an evening in such a theatre be a most alarming affair? The answer to that is: no.

Whatever knowledge is embodied in a piece of poetic writing has to be wholly transmuted into poetry. Its utilization fulfills the very pleasure that the poetic element provokes. If it does not at the same time fulfill that which is fulfilled by the scientific element, none the less in an age of great discoveries and inventions one must have a certain inclination to penetrate deeper into things—a desire to make the world controllable—if one is to be sure of enjoying its poetry.

## IS THE EPIC THEATRE SOME KIND OF 'MORAL INSTITUTION'?

According to Friedrich Schiller the theatre is supposed to be a moral institution. In making this demand it hardly occurred to Schiller that by moralizing from the stage he might drive the audience out of the theatre. Audiences had no objection to moralizing in his day. It was only later that Friedrich Nietzsche attacked him for blowing a moral trumpet. To Nietzsche any concern with morality was a depressing affair; to Schiller it seemed thoroughly enjoyable. He knew of nothing that could give greater amusement and satisfaction than the propagation of ideas. The bourgeoisie was setting about forming the ideas of the nation.

Putting one's house in order, patting oneself on the back, submitting one's account, is something highly agreeable. But describing the collapse of one's house, having pains in the back, paying one's account, is indeed a depressing affair, and that was how Friedrich Nietzsche saw things a century later. He was poorly disposed towards morality, and thus towards the previous Friedrich too.

The epic theatre was likewise often objected to as moralizing too much. Yet in the epic theatre moral arguments only took second place. Its aim was less to moralize than to observe. That is to say it observed, and then the thick end of the wedge followed: the story's moral. Of course we cannot pretend that we started our observations out of a pure passion for observing and without any more practical motive, only to be completely staggered by their results. Undoubtedly there were some painful discrepancies in our environment, circumstances that were barely tolerable, and this not merely on account of moral considerations. It is not only moral considerations that make hunger, cold and oppression hard to bear. Similarly the object of our inquiries was not just to arouse moral objections to such circumstances (even though they could easily be felt—though not by all the audience alike; such objections were seldom for instance felt by those who profited by the circumstances in question) but to discover means for their elimination. We were not in fact speaking in the name of morality but in that of the victims. These truly are two distinct matters, for the victims are often told that they ought to be contented with their lot, for moral reasons. Moralists of this sort see man as existing for morality, not morality for man. At least it should be possible to gather from the above to what degree and in what sense the epic theatre is a moral institution.

## CAN EPIC THEATRE BE PLAYED ANYWHERE?

Stylistically speaking, there is nothing all that new about the epic theatre. Its expository character and is emphasis on virtuosity bring it close to the old Asiatic theatre. Didactic tendencies are to be found in the medieval mystery plays and the classical Spanish theatre, and also in the the theatre of the Jesuits.

These theatrical forms corresponded to particular trends of their time, and vanished with them. Similarly the modern epic theatre is linked with certain trends. It cannot by any means be practiced universally. Most of the great nations today are not disposed to use the theatre for ventilating their problems. London, Paris, Tokyo and Rome maintain their theatres for quite different purposes. Up to now favourable circumstances for an epic and didactic theatre have only been found in a few places and for a short period of time. In Berlin Fascism put a very definite stop to the development of such a theatre.

It demands not only a certain technological level but a powerful movement in society which is interested to see vital questions freely aired with a view to their solution, and can defend this interest against every contrary trend.

The epic theatre is the broadest and most far-reaching attempt at large-scale modern theatre, and it has all those immense difficulties to overcome that always confront the vital forces in the sphere of politics, philosophy, science and art.

['Vergnügungstheater oder Lehrtheater?', from *Schriften zum Theater*, 1957]

# Towards a New Poetic

## SUE-ELLEN CASE

*Sue-Ellen Case is Professor of English at the University of California at Riverside. She is author of* Feminism and Theatre *(1988) and* Performing Feminisms: Feminist Critical Theory and Theatre *(1990).*

## THE NEW POETICS

During the 1980s, feminist theory has risen to prominence both within the feminist movement and within the context of dominant theoretical practices. Many academic disciplines, such as sociology, anthropology and political science, as well as those concerned with art and literature, have begun to alter their theoretical and methodological approaches to accommodate the strategies of feminist theory. Likewise, the new theories of post-structuralism, Lacanian psychoanalysis, semiotics and reception theory have been radically altered by the feminist discoveries in these fields. By 1985, feminist theory had taken its place in the mainstream of the philosophical and critical applications of ideas. Within the feminist movement, theory occupies a more problematic position. Many feminists consider the pursuit of theory to be elitist. They perceive its specialised discourse as a linguistic class bias that is inaccessible to working-class women, women of colour and the broad spectrum of women who have not enjoyed the privilege of higher education. Moreover, theory is characterised as separate from practice, luring feminists away from working on the issues of socio-political oppression and isolating them in the male-dominated realm of abstract ideas, commonly known as the 'ivory tower'. For

this reason, it is useful to locate the project of feminist theory within the realm of political practice.

From within the theoretical project, it is crucial to remember that feminism began in the streets, with demonstrations against the oppression of women.[1] The commitment to change was taken up by women in all professions, including academics and critics. Women working in the field of education discovered not only that their professional positions were influenced by patriarchal prejudice, but also that their subject matter represented the sexist biases of the dominant culture. In preparing students to enter the market place, they realised they must change not only what they were thinking about, but also how they were thinking. Academics transformed the social issues of the movement into themes and methods for research and criticism. In theatre, feminists applied the social critique of the movement to both the organisation of theatre practice and the analytical perception of the art, mixing critical discoveries such as the sexualisation of women on stage, the omission of women's narratives, the paucity of strong roles for women and the invisibility of lesbians and women of colour on stage, with the economic issues of wage inequities, patriarchal hiring-practices and union representation. Feminist critics and historians began to reconstruct the history of women in theatre, using the goals of consciousness-raising groups and social activists: to make women visible, to find their voice, to recover the works that the dominant history suppressed and to explain the historical process of the suppression of women and its effect on their achievements. At the same time, critics used these political strategies to create new ways to read a play, to view a production and to deconstruct the canon of dramatic criticism.

Because raising the consciousness of women was from the start central to the social movement, and this in turn made it important to understand modes of perception, psychological factors and patterns of thought, a natural working alliance between artists, theorists, historians, critics and social activists was created. Artists created new roles for women to play in the laboratory of theatre, where the stage offered opportunities for women's narratives and dialogues largely denied in the history of the dominant culture. Feminist plays could stage a kind of utopian CR group, in which women could interact with a freedom of experience and expression not easily attained in their daily lives. Critics could aid in consciousness-raising by accurately identifying the psychological, cultural and educational controls on women's consciousness and suggesting alternative modes of perception. By the 1980s, the joint efforts of feminist activists, artists and intellectuals had created a basic vocabulary for feminism and a topography of its enterprise. The period of initial explorations was over.

Once the broad parameters of the feminist project had been discovered, the need for a more solid, theoretical base began to be perceived. The perception of the sexualisation of women's identities prompted investigations into the dominant psychological theories of sexual development. Feminist studies of Freudian theory illuminated the way in which sexist biases informed the practice of psychoanalysis as well as the general practice of therapy, which is derived from several Freudian assumptions. In France, Jacques Lacan created a revision of Freud, which adapted his theories to more contemporary discoveries. Soon feminists began publishing critiques of Lacan. At the same time, feminist cultural theorists began to deconstruct the dominant cultural codes that enforced the sexualisation of women in systems of representation, utilising the new discoveries in semiotics and reception theory to deconstruct the alliance between sign systems and the patriarchal order. In the arts, practitioners expressed a desire for an overview of their disparate works as well as a theoretical model for the alliance between aesthetics and the basic feminist analysis. For example, at the first National Women's Theatre Festival, in Santa Cruz in 1983, three of the oldest feminist theatres in the United States admitted that their broader analysis of women's oppressions had given way to plays about specific issues. In dwelling on specific problems, they felt that perhaps they were beginning to lose their sense of the basic overall feminist critique. All of these new critical projects began to embrace deeper, more theoretical issues as it was realised that the perception of images rests upon epistemology, the practice of dialogue rests upon the nature of discourse, and the forms of representation are determined by the dominant philosophical systems in the culture at large.

For theatre, the basic theoretical project for feminism could be termed a 'new poetics', borrowing the notion from Aristotle's *Poetics*. New feminist theory would abandon the traditional patriarchal values embedded in prior notions of form, practice and audience response in order to construct new critical models and methodologies for the drama that would accommodate the presence of women in the art, support their liberation from the cultural fictions of the female gender and deconstruct the valorisation of the male gender. In pursuit of these objectives, feminist dramatic theory would borrow freely: new discoveries about gender and culture from the disciplines of anthropology, sociology and political science; feminist strategies for reading texts from the new work in English studies; psychosemiotic analyses of performance and representation from recent film theory; new theories of the 'subject' from psychosemiotics, post-modern criticism and post-structuralism; and certain strategies from the project called 'deconstruction'. This 'new poetics' would deconstruct the traditional systems of representation and perception of women and posit women in the position of the subject.

For the reader who is unfamiliar with these new theories, an effective starting-point for the intersection of new theory with performance and feminist poetics may be found in the field of semiotics. Keir Elam, in his book *The Semiotics of Theatre and Drama*, defines semiotics as 'a science dedicated to the study of the production of meaning in society . . . its objects are thus at once the different sign systems and codes at work in society and the actual messages and texts produced thereby'.[2] Semiotics, when applied to theatre, explores how theatre communicates, or how theatre produces a meaning. The basic operatives in the production of meaning are the signifier (or sign) and the signified. The signifier is the ensemble of elements in a theatrical production that compose its meaning—the text, the actor, the stage space, the lights, the blocking, and so on. The signified is the meaning or message which is derived from this signifier by the 'collective consciousness' of the audience. So, for example, semiotics seeks to describe the way in which the set becomes a sign: how it signifies place, time, social milieu and mood. Semiotics also identifies and explores those elements of the actor's performance that signify character and objective to the audience.

Since the signified is produced by the recipient of the signifier, semiotics identifies several texts within a performance situation. The written text is only one of these and is not necessarily the definitive one. There is the text printed in a book and read as literature, the text the director reads preparing for rehearsal, the rehearsal text the actor uses, and the production text the audience receives as it watches the play. Semiotics proposes that each of these texts is different and discrete, retaining an equal status with the other ones and representing appropriate material for a critical response. The constitution of a performance text, separate but equal to the written one, implies new dimensions in the co-production of the text. The importance of the author's intent gives way to the conditions of production and the composition of the audience in determining the meaning of the theatrical event. This implies that there is no aesthetic closure around the text, separating it from the conditions of its production. The performance text is constituted by the location of the theatre, the price of the ticket, the attitude of the ushers and the response of the audience as well as by the written dialogue and stage directions.

This semiotic constitution of the performance text is useful to a feminist poetics. Because the composition of the audience is an element in the co-production of the play's meaning, the gender of the audience members is crucial in determining what the feminist play might mean. The practice of performing before all-women audiences excludes men from the co-production of the play's meaning. Within a patriarchal culture, this exclusion may provide the only way certain elements of women's experience can be signified within the 'collective consciousness' of the audience. The insistence upon an all-woman audience, then, becomes an essential part of the composition of the theatrical event, rather than a social statement of separatism or reverse sexism. Likewise, ticket prices, child care, the time of the performance and the location of the theatre also co-produce the performance text, positing the accessibility of the production to working-class women, single mothers or women of colour as part of the meaning of the play. The gender, class and colour of the audience replace the aesthetic traditions of form or the isolated conditions of the author's intent within the interpretative strategies of dramatic theory, firmly allying poetics with feminist politics.

Perhaps even more important is the notion of the cultural encoding of the sign (or signifier), the semiotic discovery that provides a radical alteration of poetic strategies of performance. This notion positions a feminist analysis at the very foundation of communication—in the sign itself. Cultural encoding is the imprint of ideology upon the sign—the set of values, beliefs and ways of seeing that control the connotations of the sign in the culture at large. The norms of the culture assign meaning to the sign, prescribing its resonances with their biases. For a feminist, this means that the dominant notions of gender, class and race compose the meaning of the text of a play, the stage pictures of its production and the audience reception of its meaning. By describing the cultural encoding in a sign, semiotics reveals the covert cultural beliefs embedded in communication. Thus, the elements of theatrical communication such as language or set pieces no longer appear to be objective, utilitarian or in any sense value-free. The author's or director's or actor's intent ceases to be perceived as a singular enterprise; in so far as it communicates, it works in alliance with the ideology or beliefs of the culture at large.

The notion of encoding shifts the political implications of a theatrical performance from the interpretative sphere of the critic to the signification process of the performance, thereby assigning political alliance to the aesthetic realm. For example, there are cultural encodings in casting-decisions. Juliet, in *Romeo and Juliet*, usually conforms to certain standards of beauty found in the present-day culture. These standards control her costuming and make-up in foregrounding her beauty for the audience. Since Shakespeare wrote the play with a boy actor in mind, the common casting of Juliet does not proceed from the text; rather, it is determined by the cultural encoding inscribed in the image of the female love object. Similarly, the common practice of casting blonde women in the roles of *ingénues*, and dark women in secondary and vamp roles, is not based on the demands of the text, but betrays cultural attitudes about the relative innocence, purity and desirability of certain racial features. The blonde hair and fair skin of the *ingénue* are encoded with these values. The casting of beautiful women in *ingénue* roles, or the rise of the beautiful stage star, participates in patriarchal prejudices that control the sign system of the representation of women on stage.

For feminists, these discoveries help to illuminate how the image of a woman on stage participates directly in the dominant ideology of gender. Social conventions about the female gender will be encoded in all signs for women. Inscribed in body language, signs of gender can determine the blocking of a scene, by assigning bolder movements to the men and more restricted movements to the women, or by creating poses and positions that exploit the role of woman as sexual object. Stage movement replicates the proxemics of the social order, capitalising upon the spatial relationships in the culture at large between women and the sites of power.[3]

Overall, feminist semiotics concentrates on the notion of 'woman as sign'. From this perspective, a live woman standing on the stage is not a biological or natural reality, but 'a fictional construct, a distillate from diverse but congruent discourses dominant in Western cultures'.[4] In other words, the conventions of the stage produce a meaning for the sign 'woman', which is based upon their cultural associations with the female gender.

Feminist semiotic theory has attempted to describe and deconstruct this sign for 'woman', in order to distinguish biology from culture and experience from ideology. Whereas formerly feminist criticism presumed to know what a woman is, but rejected certain images of women, this new perspective brings into question the entire notion of how one knows what the sign 'woman' means. At this point, the entire gender category 'woman' is under feminist semiotic deconstruction.

Given the assumption that stage and audience co-produce the performance text, the meaning of the sign 'woman' is also created by the audience. The way the viewer perceives the woman on stage constitutes another theoretical enterprise. In her book *Women and Film*,[5] E. Ann Kaplan characterises this enterprise as 'the male gaze'. Kaplan asserts that the sign 'woman' is constructed by and for the male gaze. In the realm of theatrical production, the gaze is owned by the male: the majority of playwrights, directors and producers are men. This triumvirate determines the nature of the theatrical gaze, deriving the sign for 'woman' from their perspective. In the realm of audience reception, the gaze is encoded with culturally determined components of male sexual desire, perceiving 'woman' as a sexual object. This analysis of the male gaze is informed by feminist psychosemiotics, a combination of post-Lacanian psychoanalysis, semiotics and feminism. The entire argument is too complex and too lengthy to be developed in full here, and the reader is referred to books on feminism, semiotics and film by Kaplan, Teresa de Lauretis and Kaja Silverman. However, because of the centrality of this argument to the new understanding of the representation of women, it is necessary to describe certain portions of it in order to suggest the way in which it might serve a feminist poetics of theatre. Since psychosemiotics was developed in film criti-

cism, it must be adapted somewhat if it is to be applied to an analysis of the stage. For instance, whereas in film the principal means of organising the gaze is the camera, a different set of dynamics applies in relation to the stage. Nevertheless, the cultural constitution of the male gaze is essential for most of the performing arts.

The concept of the male gaze asserts that representations of women are perceived as they are seen by men. Here, the term 'men' represents the male subject in capitalist patriarchy. A simple example of how everyone sees a play as a male would see it might be the way a play induces the audience to view the female roles through the eyes of the male characters. When the *ingénue* makes her entrance, the audience sees her as the male protagonist sees her. The blocking of her entrance, her costume and the lighting are designed to reveal that she is the object of his desire. In this way, the audience also perceives her as an object of desire, by identifying with his male gaze. This example illustrates one major cultural assumption—that the male is the subject of the dramatic action. What psychosemiotics establishes is the nature of his subjectivity. This requires the dominant cultural description of the psychological self found in Freud and Lacan. For feminists, Freud and Lacan provide the patriarchal determination of sexual development that explains both the psychosexual male subject and the way that he has come to represent the subject position for the culture at large.

Using Freudian principles, Lacan explains the psychosexual development of the subject in terms of his relationship to symbols. The use of symbols (implying all discourse) is a compensation for the early experience of undifferentiated self-satisfaction. For Lacan, culture intrudes upon libidinal pleasure from the moment the infant begins to identify bodily zones. In other words, in infancy the body feels pleasure anywhere and everywhere—it is the culture which imposes limited erotic zones. Once attuned to cultural laws, the child then perceives that there is something like a self, a discrete unit of identity (Lacan's 'mirror stage'). He trades his earlier, undefined realm of self-satisfaction for the desire to be a self. The self is actually a cultural ideal, alienating him from his libidinal pleasure. The organisation of selfhood then drives him into the symbolic order of the culture. Thus, the subject's participation in the world of symbols is always marked by an alienation from the satisfaction of libidinal desires and the resulting state of unfulfilled desire. For the purposes of analysing performance, this means that the creation of theatre itself springs from the condition of unfulfilled desire in the male subject. He has been denied any real satisfaction and establishes the stage as a site for his alienated, symbolic yearning for satisfaction. This drive towards art determines its system of representation and the nature of the way it produces desire in the viewer.

This entire process excludes women from the role of the subject, or the producer of symbolic expressions. Because it is tied to a cultural castration, both Freud and Lacan locate the symbolic order in relation to the phallus of the child and the cultural 'Law of the Father', situating the entire production of art within the patriarchal order of father and son. Within this order of male desire and castration, the only role for women is as objects of that desire. The result is that women become fixed in the position of object of the gaze, rather than as the subject directing it; women appear in order to be looked upon rather than to do the looking. In that sense, 'woman' is constituted as 'Other'. Concomitantly, she is invested with those qualities which the masculine gazer desires to construct as 'Other' than himself. Thus, women on stage never represent the subject position—their desire is not symbolised in patriarchal culture. Nor do the dynamics of their desire operate within the theatrical experience. The audience becomes the male subject, exiled in the system of theatrical representation and driven by unfulfilled desire. When the audience looks at a woman on stage, she is perceived as a possible site for the fulfilment of that desire, transformed into a kind of cultural courtesan. When pushed to its extremes, this psychosemiotic analysis accounts for the complicity between the stage and pornography.

For women, one of the results of this representation of woman as 'Other' in the male gaze is that she also becomes an 'Other' to herself. Within the patriarchal system of signs, women do not have the cultural mechanisms of meaning to construct themselves as the subject rather than as the object of performance. A wedge is created between the sign 'woman' and real women that insinuates alienation into the very participation of women in the system of theatrical representation or within the system of communication in the dominant culture. This alienation between actual women and the sign 'woman' has already been illustrated in the description of Caryl Churchill's *Cloud Nine*. Remember that in Act I, Betty, the wife, is played by a man in drag. Betty is everything men want her to be—the drag role foregrounds her gender as a fiction of the male gaze. There is no real woman under the requirements of costume, make-up and body language. At this point in history, it may be that any representation of 'woman' is tainted by the encoding of that sign within a patriarchal culture. For this reason, some feminist film-makers do not use women as objects of the camera's gaze. Women are represented only by the narrative voice-over, which locates all images on the screen within the female narrative, producing a female subject rather than object of the film.

As demonstrated above, both the study of woman as sign and the study of woman as object are deconstructive strategies that aid in exposing the patriarchal encodings in the dominant system of representation. Yet the potential for women to emerge as subjects rather than objects opens up a field of new possibilities for women in theatre and its system of representation. Constructing woman as subject is the future, liberating work of a feminist new poetics. But, before exploring this work, the term 'subject' needs definition. The subject is a linguistic or philosophical function that can be represented by the pronoun 'I'. The subject represents a point of view. The subject in semiotics is that which controls the field of signs. Moving away from the Cartesian premise 'I think therefore I am', new theories no longer perceive the subject as the discrete basis of experience. Rather, the subject is a position in terms of a linguistic field or an artistic device such as narrative. What had earlier been considered a 'self', a biological or natural entity, imbued with the sense of the 'personal', is now perceived as a cultural construction and a semiotic function. The subject is an intersection of cultural codes and practices.

For feminists, gender is the crucial encoding of the subject that has made it historically a position unavailable for women to inhabit. The traditional subject has been the male subject, with whom everyone must identify. Scanning the 'masterpieces' of the theatre, with their focus on the male subject, one can see that women are called upon to identify with Hamlet, Oedipus, Faust and other male characters imbued with specifically male psychosexual anxieties. The idea that these are 'universal' characters represses the gender inscription in the notion of the self. Yet the dominance of the self as male has taken its historical toll on women, as is evident from women writers who lived in male drag, took male pen names (such as George Sand) and consistently created male protagonists in their works, unable to imagine a woman in the role of the subject of a narrative. Freud's theory of the Oedipal crisis has served to enforce the notion of self as male self. Its dominance in Western thought has securely tied the understanding of sexual development to the male subject. Nancy Chodorow, in her book *Mothering*, dismantles this Freudian model. Illustrating the way in which the girl child has a different dynamic of sexuality and need in the family unit from that of the boy, Chodorow successfully defeats the notions of the Electra complex, derivative of the Oedipal one, and 'penis envy', shifting Freud's focus on the boy to a new focus on the girl.

Nevertheless, the long ascendancy of Freudian psychology universalised his gender-specific theories of development, placing the male in a central subject position and the female in a subordinate, derivative and envious position. Freud's gender-specific notions of psychological development are central to many of the operations of the theatre. For example, they provide the basis of Method acting. The psychological construction of character, using techniques adapted from Stanislavski, places the female actor within the range of systems that have oppressed her very representation on stage. The techniques for the inner construction of a character rely on Freudian principles, leading the female actor into that misogynistic view of female sexuality. In building such characters as Amanda in Tennessee Williams's *Glass Menagerie*, the female actor learns to be passive, weak and dependent in her sexual role, with a fragile inner life that reveals no sexual desire. If one compares this kind of character to Alan Strang in Peter Shaffer's *Equus*, for example, it is easy to see the Freudian blindness to female desire. In *Equus*, the young man's sexuality is blatant and aggressive giving the male actor a complex and active internal monologue. In his interactions with the psychiatrist, he holds a subject position of developing sexuality. Female characters, when they do have a complex psychological base, are usually frustrated and unfulfilled—

like the Electra on whom their complex is based, they wait for the male to take the subject position of action. Their desire is for him to act, they make no attempt to act for their own fulfillment. From Antigone to Blanche Dubois, the female actor works on the passive, broken sexual development of her characters, which isolates them from the social community rather than integrating them into it. From a feminist perspective, the Method techniques for building these characters lead the female actor into inaccurate analyses of female sexuality.

Other acting techniques, such as the playing of an objective and establishing a through-line, are also culturally inscribed models from the patriarchal culture. Gillian Hanna of the Monstrous Regiment refers to such linear modes as peculiar to male experience, and insists that her feminist troupe hopes to refute them: 'It's precisely a refusal to accept . . . that life is linear . . . which has to do with male experience. . . .They [men] are born into a world where they can map out life . . . it has to do with a career. It has to do with your work. . . . Now for a woman, life is not like that. It doesn't have that pattern. For a woman life and experience is broken-backed.'[6] Hanna points out that men build a career for life and proceed through school to work in their professions, while women interrupt those processes with child-bearing, child-rearing, and so on. Thus, 'for them life doesn't have that kind of linear overview that it seems to have for men. . . . I think we've been trying to reflect that fragmented experience in what we do.' In other words, objectives and through-lines might not be suitable acting techniques for representing women's experiences. For the female actor to understand a female character, the through-line might be a fallacious way to work. Nevertheless, such work is required by the texts the actors inherit.

Logically, the rejection of these acting techniques implies a rejection of the kind of plays they serve. Playwrights who have been influenced by psychoanalysis both personally and formally have constructed texts that reflect the Freudian perspective on male and female sexual behaviour. A feminist review of the sexuality of Blanche in Williams's *A Streetcar Named Desire*, of the mother in Eugene O'Neill's *Long Day's Journey into Night*, or of Rosalyn in Arthur Miller's *The Misfits* could reveal the ways in which these characters were drawn from Freudian biases. Likewise, as may be seen from the relationships between Blanche and Stanley in *Streetcar*, the mother and the father in *Long Day's Journey*, and the dancer Rosalyn and cowboy Gay in *The Misfits*, these texts portray women's sexuality as subordinate and derivative in relation to that of the leading male characters, reflecting the subject position of male sexuality within the Freudian-based theatrical domain. Even the formal characteristics of certain genres betray the same values. Realism, in its focus on the domestic sphere and the family unit, reifies the male as sexual subject and the female as the sexual 'Other'. The portrayal of female characters within the family unit—with their confinement to the domestic setting, their dependence on the husband, their often defeatist, determinist view of the opportunities for change—makes realism a 'prisonhouse of art' for women, both in their representation on stage and in the female actor's preparation and production of such roles.

An even deeper analysis which has recently emerged in the realm of feminist psychosemiotics suggests that the form of narrative itself is complicit with the psychocultural repression of women. The film critic Laura Mulvey puts it this way: 'Sadism demands a story, depends on making something happen, forcing a change in another person, a battle of will and strength, victory/defeat, all occurring in a linear time with a beginning and an end.'[7] Mulvey describes the relationship of protagonist and antagonist as sado-masochistic. In her book *Alice Doesn't*, Teresa de Lauretis takes this idea and pushes it to a feminist conclusion: within the typical narrative, the male is the one who makes something happen (the typical hero), who forces a change in another through a battle of wills. He is given the role of the sadist. In love stories, the defeated one is typically the female. Within the narrative structure, the female plays the masochist to the male sadist. Freud has also drawn the character of female sexuality as a masochistic one, locating female masochism in the natural development of the child. The popularity of such stories indicates the sado-masochistic nature of desire in the community at large. The reader or the audience member who gains pleasure from this narrative structure joins in the reification of male and female sexuality as a battle in which the female is defeated. Desire, which propels the story forward, is sadistic and encoded in terms of male and female genders. The structure of narrative as well as its broad appeal enacts this process in the culture.

*Portrait of Dora* (*Portrait de Dora*, 1976), a play written by French feminist Hélène Cixous, illustrates the feminist perspective on this psychocultural process. Cixous has long been recognised by the international feminist community as a leading theoretician, especially for her provocative article 'The Laugh of the Medusa', on women and writing.[8] Dora was the result of a collaboration with director and playwright Simone Benmussa and is a good example of feminist psychological theory at work on the stage. Reversing the Freudian mandate, Cixous chose to dramatise a case in which Freud was confronted with the sexual development of a female. His attempt to overlay her experiences with his gender-specific theories provides several levels of irony and shifts of perspective in the play. Cixous places a woman in the subject position, revealing Freud's distance from her as an active sexual

subject, his attempt to force her into her 'proper' passive, patriarchal position (as she lies on her back on his couch) and his mythologising of her experience. The irony peaks when Dora tries to articulate her attraction to another woman, Mrs K. Freud cannot accommodate this attraction within his theoretical framework. Without a penis, there can be no sex. Therefore, he translates her desire for another woman into a displacement of desire for her father. Freud imposes the Electra complex onto the girl's experience. Instead, the girl exhibits a desire for the mother, a concept also recently developed by Nancy Chodorow in *Mothering*.

Freud continues to misrepresent what Dora tells him, aligning himself with the other men in the play who want to manipulate the girl's sexual development for their own ends. By the end of the play, Dora has rejected all of their impositions, walking off the stage as an independent woman. The final lines suggest that it is Freud who made a transference onto the patient, rather than the traditional, inverse process. The loose frame of the action is the process of psychoanalysis between Freud and Dora, which permits the intrusion of dream, fantasy and memory into the play. On the formal level, the play abandons the conventions of realism. Past, present and fantasy mix freely on stage, with characters coming and going without traditional motivations or playing-moments. Scenes between Dora and Freud and scenes presenting characters from her past occur simultaneously. Sound-effects that convey elements of Dora's subconscious images intrude upon the dialogue. In spite of Freud, Dora becomes the subject of sexuality, fragmenting the elements of her character through the formal devices of the play. The stage becomes a playing site for Dora's internal images. In her introduction to the published version of the play, Benmussa, who helped to develop the play as well as direct it, describes the stage as analogous to the process of psychoanalysis:

> In 'stage work', just as in 'dream work', a situation, or a desire, is projected into space by a word or a gesture: stage work produces images. Stage is the reflecting surface of a dream, of a deferred dream. It is the meeting place of the desires which . . . both accumulate and cancel each other out as they succeed one another, change their medium, pass from word to gesture, and from image to body. . . . They concentrate a desire very powerfully, but they create around them a nebulous zone which allows the spectator to divine the other, distant, obscure, ever-widening circles in which other desires are lying in wait.[9]

Female desire is the subject, the leading character of this drama.

Benmussa also notes that this play requires something different from the actors. She wants 'to cut the explanatory scenes and retain only the symbols. . . . To leave the actors in danger, as if balancing on the words, balancing on the gestures that filled the gaps between the words; to make the staging more like choreography than like the kind of acting usually considered appropriate to psychological situations.' In other words, the representation of Dora's desire, of female desire, is not trapped within the sado-machochistic dynamics of traditional narrative, or within the traditional representation of such a character as Dora; here, female desire plays freely across the stage in sounds, characters, intersections of fantasy and reality, and even through the role entitled 'the Voice of the Play'. In this way, the form releases the expression of female desire from the snares of patriarchal narrative structures and traditional forms of representation that have repressed woman as subject. Cixous and Benmussa are on their way to creating a new kind of representation of women on stage, reversing the patriarchal order of desire determined by Freudian theories and the male gaze. If, as Benmussa asserts above, the spectator is drawn into this new 'nebulous zone',

perhaps the dramaturgical experience of the play operates within the new poetics.

Simone Benmussa is the most prominent woman director to have consistently developed this new psychosemiotic approach to the dramatisation of female desire. Her productions, based on the works of such women writers as Virginia Woolf and Nathalie Sarraute, have played in Paris, London and New York. Her play *The Singular Life of Albert Nobbs* has already been described in Chapter 5. There, its subject matter was treated as an example of the dramatisation of modes of production and a class analysis. Within the present context, the formal devices of the play illustrate her experimentation with the order of representation. While *Dora* represents the liberation of the desiring female subject, *Albert Nobbs* represents the repressive effects of patriarchal culture. Only women appear on stage in this play, from the maids to the concierge. The male characters are invisible, intervening only by voice-overs and mysteriously moving doors. The story of the play is told by the voice of George Moore, the author of the short story from which the play was derived. Moore's voice begins and ends the play, placing the lives of these women within the patriarchal frame of the male creator. By placing all the male characters off stage but making their voices central to the movement of the plot, Benmussa shows that Albert, the woman in drag, and the other women operate within the invisible frame of patriarchal culture, which creates the interactions among women, and even drag itself, from the outside. Within the patriarchal frame, the oppression of the women in the play is opposed to the distant, elite situation of the men. At the same time, the absence of men on stage shifts the dramatic focus to the lives of women and their experiences. Benmussa creates representations of women within the traditional forms of narrative and character development, but foregrounds the patriarchal foundations of such forms.

## WOMEN'S LANGUAGE AND FORM

The discoveries about the political nature of traditional forms raises the question, 'Is there a women's form—a feminine morphology?' If women are to be the subjects rather than the objects of cultural production, doesn't this cultural revolution necessitate a new form and perhaps even a new discourse for women? This question has produced a major debate within feminist critical theory. [Chapter 4] describes the interest of radical feminists in a new vocabulary and forms. Many feminist critics closer to the materialist position would argue that the notion of a feminine form merely reifies the traditional gender constructions of masculine and feminine—that any liberation for women in art would come from their freedom to create in any kind of formal context. Others, closer to the position of the new poetics, would argue that a reorganisation of theories of libidinal development and dramaturgical devices would create a new position for the female desiring subject that would change the way the field of signs is constructed. Lacan's new compound of the Oedipal crisis and the acquisition of symbols has become a major catalyst in feminist theories of women and cultural forms.

Cixous's essay 'The Laugh of the Medusa' is a central text in the call for a new form. Cixous relates the fact that there have been few women writers to the notion that, culturally, women's bodies have been assimilated by the patriarchal system of desire and representation. Cixous calls on women to reclaim their bodies and their writing, establishing a reciprocal relationship between the two:

> By writing her self, woman will return to the body which has been more than confiscated from her, which has been turned into the uncanny stranger on display—the ailing or dead figure, which so often turns out to be the nasty companion, the cause and location of inhibitions. Censor the body and you censor breath and speech at the same time. Write your self. Your body must be heard.[10]

Cixous then describes what this new women's language, written from her body, will be like. The writing will be heterogenous and far-ranging: 'Woman unthinks the unifying, regulating history that homogenizes and channels forces, herding contradictions into a single battlefield.' In some ways, Cixous's position resembles Mary Daly's radical-feminist notion of 'Spinsters'. It also resembles Gillian Hanna's characterisation of male plays, and the Monstrous Regiment's search for a new form proceeding from women's experiences. Hanna characterises the male dramatic form as 'a sweep of history, something broad and heavy.... the male playwright's sensitivity is often like an empire builder—it wants to consume the whole world and then spit it out again in its own image'.[11]

The term that emerges in many articles concerning a new, feminine morphology is contiguity'. This is an organisational device that feminists have discovered in both early and modern works by women. Luce Irigaray describes it as a 'nearness', creating a form 'constantly in the process of weaving itself ... embracing words and yet casting them off', concerned not with clarity, but with what is 'touched upon'.[12] Cixous calls it 'working the in-between', and Jane Gallop describes it as 'the register of touching, nearness, presence, immediacy, contact'.[13] It can be elliptical rather than illustrative, fragmentary rather than whole, ambiguous rather than clear, and interrupted rather than complete. This contiguity exists within the text and at its borders: the feminine form seems to be without a sense of formal closure—in fact, it operates as an anti-closure. Cixous describes it this way: 'Her language does not contain, it carries; it does not hold back, it makes possible', signifying 'the erotogeneity of the heterogeneous'.[14] Without closure, the sense of beginning, middle and end, or a central focus, it abandons the hierarchical organising-principles of traditional form that served to elide women from discourse.

Women can inhabit the realm of the outsider—in Lacan's system, the one who 'lacks the lack'—and create a new discourse and form that exhibit the field of female experience.

Within the study of the theatre, several versions of masculine and feminine morphology have taken hold. For example, some feminist critics have described the form of tragedy as a replication of the male sexual experience. Tragedy is composed of foreplay, excitation and ejaculation (catharsis). The broader organisation of plot—complication, crisis and resolution—is also tied to this phallic experience. The central focus in male forms is labelled phallocentric, reflecting the nature of the male's sexual physiology. A female form might embody her sexual mode, aligned with multiple orgasms, with no dramatic focus on ejaculation or necessity to build to a single climax. The contiguous organisation would replace this ejaculatory form. The feminist critic might analyze the plays of Adrienne Kennedy, women's performance-art pieces or witches' cyclic rituals using this notion.

The opponents of this kind of thinking point out that what begins to emerge in this idea of feminine morphology is the sense that the female gender is real, rather than an invention of the patriarchy. Moreover, gender has been biologised—the notions of the female body and the male body have been used to recreate the dominant cultural systems of representation. Instead, these opponents argue, it would be better to realise that 'One is not Born a Woman' (the title of Monique Wittig's influential antigender article). The concept of a feminine morphology retains the traditional inscription of gender onto cultural forms, merely inverting the value system. Critics such as Wittig argue that, by valorising the feminine, feminists will keep women in the ghetto of gender. Some theatre practitioners have also responded negatively to the notion of feminine form. They feel it means that, if they work in traditional forms, they are not feminists (or feminine), and that their work is discounted because of their preference for those forms, rather than seen as marking an advance for women in the field by making their professional work visible.

Feminist critics who prescribe a feminine form have been termed 'essentialists' by their opponents. This means that they ignore the economic and historical conditions that have determined the process of cultural gender inscription. They are termed essentialists to contrast them with materialists, who emphasise the economic and historical advantages of gender inscription for the elite class of men in the patriarchy. To associate this process with biology is to subscribe to biological determinism, ignoring the contradictions and processes of history, such as class and race. In other words, the proposed feminine morphology would fall within the category of radical-feminist thought and be fundamentally opposed to materialist feminism. Instead, materialist creators prefer to explore non-gendered roles, behaviour and texts (see, for example, the description of Zeig's, and Wittig's experiments in acting techniques, in Chapter 4 [in *Feminism and Theatre*]).

It seems, however, that certain gains can be realised from both sides of the issue. Perhaps these positions could be combined in some way, or, within a historical context, perceived as alternative theoretical strategies for specific political purposes. They need not operate as competing theories for a controlling position that subsumes practice and organises positions, much like the theoretical strategies operating in the 'Name of the Father'. Rather, they would appear as tactics to be employed when they were useful in either dismantling the patriarchal structure or aiding in the cultural revolution. Theory would then be in the service of specific politic maneuvers rather than rising to a transcendent position. Retaining theory in a dialectical partnership with practice is one way to alleviate the anxieties among feminists that it is elitist. If a theory does not assume a transcendent posture, it can be used for the politics of the moment, adapted by them, and repeatedly altered or forsaken in different historical and political situations. The feminist activist-theorist can employ any techniques, methods, theories or ways of social organising she wishes in confronting or creating the situations in which she operates.

The arguments for and against a feminine morphology produce different political effects in different situations. For example, a feminist critic working in a conservative academic environment might make use of a feminine morphology to contradict the patriarchal valorisation of realism or other traditional forms. When used as a provocation, this morphological notion could invoke a defence of the traditional codes, raising questions concerning the canon and the structure of dramatic interpretation within the parameters of an alternative, feminist tradition. Again, such a morphology might provide a way to push for a reevaluation of women's work in the theatre, both by demonstrating the existence of a distinctively feminine form and by exposing the bastions of male privilege in the arts as political defences against it. The feminist critic, then, would no longer be cast in the negative role of the gadfly, or in the role of one on the defensive against the *status quo*, but would appear as the proponent of a new theory and an alternative practice.

On the other hand, in dialogue with feminists who valorise the gender inscription in the feminine morphology, the same critic might utilise the materialist analysis of form. In this case, she could raise the issues of race and class which are so important to the understanding and reception of works by women of colour and working-class women, and which have such a strong bearing on their relationship to the theatre. Here she could note their absence from many avant-

garde formalist experiments, as well as the absence of a historical context. By employing alternative theories at different times, the feminist critic would still remain firmly within the operations of the feminist movement, which has no leaders, no central organisation and no 'party line'. Swinging from theory to opposing theory as described here would not be a kind of 'playful pluralism', but a guerrilla action designed to provoke and focus the feminist critique.

In the theatre, the new poetics offers the feminist a blend of activism and theoretical practice. With the deconstruction of the forms of representation, and dialogue and modes of perception characteristic of patriarchal culture, the stage can be prepared for the entrance of the female subject, whose voice, sexuality and image have yet to be dramatised within the dominant culture. At this point in history, psychosemiotic strategies may provide a new kind of revolution, for in the late twentieth century the mode of production which is central to the oppression of many peoples lies within the ghettoes of signs and codes. In the age of television, computer languages and communication satellites, the production of signs creates the sense of what a person is, rather than reflects it (in the traditional mimetic order). The mode of cultural production is reversed: signs create reality rather than reflect it. This condition means that artists and cultural theorists may be the activists and the revolutionaries. Modes of discourse and representation may replace the Molotov cocktail.

The feminist in theatre can create the laboratory in which the single most effective mode of repression—gender—can be exposed, dismantled and removed; the same laboratory may produce the representation of a subject who is liberated from the repressions of the past and capable of signalling a new age for both women and men.

## NOTES

1. Carolyn Allen, 'Feminism and Postmodernism', in Joseph Natoli (ed.), *Tracing Literary Theory* (forthcoming).

2. Keir Elam, *The Semiotics of Theatre and Drama* (London: Methuen, 1980) p. 1.

3. See Nancy Henley, *Body Politics* (Englewood Cliffs, NJ: Prentice-Hall, 1977).

4. Teresa de Lauretis, *Alice Doesn't: Feminism, Semiotics and Cinema* (Bloomington: Indiana University Press, 1984) p. 5.

5. E. Ann Kaplan, *Women and Film* (New York: Methuen, 1981) p. 23.

6. Gillian Hanna, 'Feminism and Theatre', *Theatre Papers*, 2nd ser., no. 8, p. 8.

7. Laura Mulvey, 'Visual Pleasure and Narrative Cinema', *Screen*, 16.3 (1975) p. 14.

8. Hélène Cixous, 'The Laugh of the Medusa', in Marks and de Courtivron, *New French Feminisms*, pp. 245–64.

9. Simone Benmussa, *Benmussa Directs* (London: John Calder, 1979) p. 9.

10. Cixous, 'The Laugh of the Medusa', in Marks and de Courtivron, *New French Feminisms*, p. 250.

11. Hanna, in *Theatre Papers*, 2nd ser., no. 8, p. 8.

12. Luce Irigaray, 'This Sex Which Is Not One', in Marks and de Courtivron, *New French Feminisms*, pp. 99–106.

13. Jane Gallop, *The Daughter's Seduction: Feminism and Psychoanalysis* (Ithaca, NY: Cornell University Press, 1982) p. 30.

14. Cixous, 'The Laugh of the Medusa', in Marks and de Courtivron, *New French Feminisms*, p. 252.

# List of Critical Terms

Absurd
Action
*Agon*
Alienation/*Verfremdung*
Allegory
*Anagnorisis*
Antagonist
*Antistrophe*
Aside
Avant garde

Blank verse
Box set

Catastrophe
Catharsis
Character
*Chiton*
Chorus
Climactic structure
Climax
Comedy
Comedy of manners
Comic vision
*Commedia dell'arte*
Complication
Conflict
Convention
*Coryphaeus*
*Coup de théâtre*

Decorum
Denouement
*Deus ex machina*
Dialogue
*Didascalia*
Dithyramb
Doubleness
Double plot
Drama

Dramatic illusion
Dramatic time
Dramaturg
Dramaturgy
Dumbshow

*Ekkyklema*
Emblem
Endings
Epic theatre
Epilogue
Episode
Episodic structure
*Exodos*
Exposition
Expressionism

Farce
Fourth wall
Framing devices

Genre

*Hamartia*
*Hubris/hybris*

Illusion
Image
Imitation
Index sign
Interculturalism
Irony

Language

*Mechane*
Melodrama
Metaphor
Meta-Scene
Meta-theatre

*Mimesis*
Minimalism
*Mise-en-scène*
Modernism
Monologue
Multiculturalism
Musical comedy

Narration
Neoclassicism
New Comedy

Ode
Old Comedy
*Orchestra*

*Parabasis*
Paradigm
*Parados*
Performance
*Peripeteia*
*Pièce à thèse*
*Pièce bien faite*
Play-within-the-play
Plot
Postmodernism
*Praxis*
Problem play
Prologue/*prologos*
Proscenium
Protagonist

Realism
Recognition
Reflexive structure
Resolution
Retrospective
Revenge play
Reversal

Satire
Scenography
Sentimental drama
Signs
Situation
*Skene*
Soliloquy
Spectacle
Stage business
Stage directions
Stage properties
*Stichomythia*
*Strophe*

Subplot
Subtext
Suspense
Suspension of disbelief
Symbol/Symbolism
Synthetic fragment

Tetralogy
Theatre of the Absurd
Theatricalism
Tiring house
Tragedy
Tragicomedy

Tragic paradox
Tragic vision
Trilogy
Transculturalism
Trope

Unities

Verbal text
Verisimilitude

Well-made play

# Selected Readings

ALTER, JEAN. "From Text to Performance." *Poetics Today*, 2.3 (1981).

ARONSON, ARNOLD. *The History and Theory of Environmental Scenography*. Ann Arbor: University of Michigan Press, 1981.

AUSTIN, GAYLE. *Feminist Theories for Dramatic Criticism*. Ann Arbor: University of Michigan Press, 1990.

AUSTIN, JOHN L. *How to Do Things with Words*. Cambridge, Mass.: Harvard University Press, 1962.

BAKHTIN, MIKHAIL. *The Dialogic Imagination: Four Essays*. Ed. Michael Holquist. Trans. Caryl Emerson. Austin: University of Texas Press, 1981.

BARLOW, JUDITH E., ed. *Plays by American Women 1900–1930*. New York: Applause Theatre Book Publishers, 1985.

BARZUN, JACQUES. *Darwin, Marx, Wagner: Critique of a Heritage*. Second Edition. Chicago: University of Chicago Press, 1981.

BECKERMAN, BERNARD. *Dynamics of Drama: Theory and Method of Analysis*. New York: Alfred A. Knopf, 1970.

BENNETT, BENJAMIN. *Theater as Problem: Modern Drama and Its Place in Literature*. Ithaca, NY: Cornell University Press, 1990.

BENTLEY, ERIC. *The Brecht Commentaries 1943–1980*. New York: Grove Press, 1981.

_____. *The Life of the Drama*. New York: Applause Theatre Books Pub., 1991.

_____. *The Pirandello Commentaries*. Evanston, Ill.: Northwestern University Press, 1986.

_____. *The Playwright as Thinker: A Study of Drama in Modern Times*. New York: Harcourt, Brace, 1987.

_____, ed. *The Theory of the Modern Stage: An Introduction to Modern Theatre and Drama*. Baltimore, Md.: Penguin, 1976.

BERMEL, ALBERT. *Farce: A History from Aristophanes to Woody Allen*. New York: Simon and Schuster, 1982.

BETSKO, KATHLEEN, and RACHEL KOENIG, eds. *Interviews With Contemporary Playwrights*. New York: Beech Tree Books, 1987.

*Between Worlds: Contemporary Asian-American Plays*. Ed. Misha Berson. New York: Theatre Communications Group, 1990.

BIGSBY, C. W. E. *A Critical Introduction to Twentieth-Century American Drama*. 3 Vols. Cambridge: University Press, 1982–85.

_____. ed. *Contemporary English Drama*. New York: Holmes & Meier, 1981.

BLAU, HERBERT. *Blooded Thought: Occasions of Theatre*. New York: Performing Arts Journal Publications, 1982.

_____. *The Eye of the Prey: Subversions of the Postmodern*. Bloomington: Indiana University Press, 1987.

_____. *Take Up the Bodies: Theater at the Vanishing Point*. Urbana: University of Illinois Press, 1987.

BRATER, ENOCH. *Beyond Minimalism*. New York: Oxford University Press, 1987.

_____, ed. *Feminine Focus: The New Women Playwrights*. New York: Oxford University Press, 1989.

BRECHT, BERTOLT. *Brecht on Theatre: The Development of an Aesthetic*. Ed. and trans. John Willett. New York: Hill and Wang, 1964.

BROOK, PETER. *The Empty Space*. New York: Atheneum, 1978.

BROOKS, CLEANTH, and ROBERT B. HEILMAN, *Understanding Drama*. New York: Henry Holt and Company, 1958.

BROWNSTEIN, OSCAR. *Strategies of Drama: The Experience of Form*. Westport, CT: Greenwood Press, 1991.

BUTCHER, S. H. *Aristotle's Theory of Poetry and Fine Art*. Fourth Ed. New York: Dover, 1955.

CARLSON, MARVIN. *Theories of the Theatre: A Historical and Critical Survey from the Greeks to the Present*. Ithaca, N.Y.: Cornell University Press, 1985.

CASE, SUE-ELLEN. *Feminism and Theatre.* New York: Methuen, 1987.

———. *Performing Feminisms: Feminist Critical Theory and Theatre.* Baltimore: Johns Hopkins University Press, 1990.

COHN, RUBY. *From Desire to Godot.* Berkeley: University of California Press, 1987.

COLE, DAVID. *The Theatrical Event: A Mythos, A Vocabulary, A Perspective.* Middletown, Conn.: Wesleyan University Press, 1975.

*Conversations with Tennessee Williams.* Ed. Albert J. Devlin. Jackson: University Press of Mississippi, 1986.

COUSIN, GERALDINE. *Churchill the Playwright.* London: Methuen, 1989.

DAVIS, JESSICA MILNER. *Farce.* London: Methuen, 1978.

DERRIDA, JACQUES. *Writing and Difference.* Trans. Alan Bass. Chicago: University of Chicago Press, 1978.

DI GAETANI, JOHN L. *A Search for Postmodern Theater: Interviews with Contemporary Playwrights.* Westport, CT: Greenwood Press, 1991.

DOLAN, JILL. *The Feminist Spectator as Critic.* Ann Arbor, Mich.: UMI Research Press, 1988.

DUKORE, BERNARD F. *Dramatic Theory and Criticism: Greeks to Grotowski.* New York: Holt, Rinehart & Winston, 1974.

DURRENMATT, FRIEDRICH. "Problems of the Theatre." Trans. Gerhard Neilhaus. *Tulane Drama Review* (1958): 3–26.

EAGLETON, TERRY. *Literary Theory: An Introduction.* Minneapolis: University of Minnesota Press, 1983.

ECO, UMBERTO. "Semiotics of Theatrical Performance." *The Drama Review* (1977): 107–17.

ELAM, KEIR. *The Semiotics of Theatre and Drama.* New York: Methuen, 1980.

ESSLIN, MARTIN. *The Field of Drama: How the Signs of Drama Create Meaning on Stage & Screen.* New York: Methuen, 1987.

———. *The Theatre of the Absurd.* Third Ed. New York: Penguin, 1968.

FERGUSSON, FRANCIS. *The Idea of a Theater: A Study of Ten Plays. The Art of Drama in Changing Perspective.* New Jersey: Princeton University Press, 1968.

FREUD, SIGMUND. *Jokes and Their Relation to the Unconscious.* Trans. James Strachey. London: Heinemann, 1960.

FRYE, NORTHROP. *The Anatomy of Criticism.* New Jersey: Princeton University Press, 1957.

GAY, PETER. *Freud: A Life for Our Time.* New York: W. W. Norton & Company, 1988.

GILMAN, RICHARD. *The Making of Modern Drama: A Study of Buchner, Ibsen, Strindberg, Chekhov, Pirandello, Brecht, Handke.* New York: Da Capo, 1987.

GOLDMAN, MICHAEL. *The Actor's Freedom: Toward a Theory of Drama.* New York: Viking, 1975.

HART, LYNDA. *Making a Spectacle: Feminist Essays on Contemporary Women's Theatre.* Ann Arbor, Mich.: University of Michigan Press, 1989.

HINCHLIFFE, ARNOLD P. *The Absurd.* London: Methuen, 1969.

HIRST, DAVID L. *Tragicomedy.* London: Methuen, 1984.

HOLROYD, MICHAEL. *Bernard Shaw.* 3 Vols. New York: Random House, 1988–1991.

HONZL, JINDRICH. "The Dynamics of the Sign in the Theatre." *Semiotics of Art.* Eds. L. Matejka and I. R. Titunik. Cambridge, Mass.: MIT Press, 1976, pp. 74–93.

HOY, CYRUS. *The Hyacinth Room: An Investigation into the Nature of Comedy, Tragedy and Tragicomedy.* London: Methuen, 1967.

HUGHES, LEO. *A Century of English Farce.* Princeton, N.J.: University Press, 1956.

*Interculturalism and Performance.* Eds. Bonnie Marranca and Gautam Dasgupta. Baltimore, Md.: Johns Hopkins University Press, 1991.

*International Dictionary of Theatre.* 3 Vols. Detroit, Mich.: St. James Press, 1992–1993.

"Interview with Caryl Churchill by Geraldine Cousin." *New Theatre Quarterly,* 4 (February 1988): 6.

IONESCO, EUGENE. *Notes and Counter Notes: Writings on the Theatre.* Trans. Donald Watson. New York: Grove Press, 1964.

JAMESON, FREDERIC. *Postmodernism, or, The Cultural Logic of Late Capitalism.* Durham, NC: Duke University Press, 1991.

JONES, ROBERT EDMOND. *The Dramatic Imagination: Reflections and Speculations on the Art of the Theatre.* New York: Methuen Theatre Arts Books, 1987.

KALB, JONATHAN. *Beckett in Performance.* New York: Cambridge University Press, 1989.

KARL, FREDERICK R. *Modern and Modernism: The Sovereignty of the Artist 1885–1925.* New York: Atheneum, 1985.

KERNODLE, GEORGE R. *From Art to Theatre: Form and Convention in the Renaissance.* Chicago: University of Chicago Press, 1944.

KOTT, JAN. *The Theatre of Essence and Other Essays.* Evanston, Ill.: Northwestern University Press, 1984.

KOWZAN, TADEUSZ. "The Sign in the Theatre." *Diogenes,* 61 (1968): 52–80.

KRUTCH, JOSEPH WOOD. *"Modernism" in Modern Drama: A Definition and an Estimate.* Ithaca, N.Y.: Cornell University Press, 1953.

LANGER, SUZANNE K. *Feeling and Form: A Theory of Art.* New York: Charles Scribner's Sons, 1953.

MCNAMARA, BROOKS. *Theatres, Spaces, Environments.* New York: Drama Book Specialists, 1975.

MAMET, DAVID. *Writing in Restaurants.* New York: Viking Penguin, 1986.

MILLER, ARTHUR. *Timebends: A Life.* New York: Grove Press, 1987.

MÜLLER, HEINER. *Hamletmachine and Other Texts for the Stage.* Ed. and trans. Carl Weber. New York: Performing Arts Journal Publications, 1984.

OSBORN, M. ELIZABETH, ed. *On New Ground: Contemporary Hispanic-American Plays.* New York: Theatre Communications Group, 1987.

PAVIS, PATRICE. *Languages of the Stage: Essays in the Semiology of Theatre.* New York: Performing Arts Journal Publications, 1982.

PIRANDELLO, LUIGI. *On Humor.* Trans. Antonio Illiano and Daniel P. Testa. Chapel Hill: University of North Carolina Press, 1974.

_____ . *Naked Masks: Five Plays.* Ed. Eric Bentley. New York: E. P. Dutton, 1957.

*Playwrights on Playwriting: The Meaning and Making of Modern Drama from Ibsen to Ionesco.* Ed. Toby Cole. New York: Hill and Wang, 1961.

POLLARD, ARTHUR. *Satire.* London: Methuen, 1970.

RANDALL, PHYLLIS R., ed. *Caryl Churchill: A Casebook.* New York: Garland, 1989.

RICCI, C. "The Art of Scenography." *The Art Bulletin,* 10 (1927–28): 231–257.

ROKEN, FREDDIE. *Theatrical Space in Ibsen, Chekhov and Strindberg: Public Forms of Privacy.* Ann Arbor, Mich.: UMI Research Press, 1986.

SAVRAN, DAVID, ed. *In Their Own Words: Contemporary American Playwrights: Interviews.* New York: Theatre Communications Group, 1988.

SCHECHNER, RICHARD. *The End of Humanism: Writing on Performance.* New York: Performing Arts Journal Publications, 1982.

SEARLE, JOHN R. *Speech Acts. An Essay in the Philosophy of Language.* New York: Cambridge University Press, 1970.

*Shattering the Myth: Plays by Hispanic Women.* Eds. Denise Chavey and Linda Macias Feyder. New York: Arte Publico Press, 1992.

SOGLUIZZO, A. RICHARD. *Luigi Pirandello, Director: The Playwright in the Theatre.* Metuchen, N.J.: Scarecrow, 1982.

SONTAG, SUSAN. *Against Interpretation and Other Essays.* New York: Farrar, Straus & Giroux, 1986.

STATES, BERT O. *Irony and Drama.* Ithaca, N.Y.: Cornell University Press, 1971.

_____ . *Great Reckonings in Little Rooms: On the Phenomenology of Theater.* Berkeley: University of California Press, 1985.

STYAN, JOHN L. *Chekhov in Performance: A Commentary of the Major Plays.* New York: Cambridge University Press, 1971.

_____ . *The Dark Comedy: The Development of Modern Comic Tragedy.* New York: Cambridge University Press, 1967.

_____ . *Drama, Stage and Audience.* New York: Cambridge University Press, 1975.

_____ . *Modern Drama in Theory and Practice I: Realism and Naturalism.* New York: Cambridge University Press, 1983.

SZONDI, PETER. *Theory of the Modern Drama.* Ed. Michael Hays. Minneapolis: University of Minnesota Press, 1987.

TAYLOR, JOHN RUSSELL. *The Rise and Fall of the Well-Made Play.* New York: Hill & Wang, 1967.

*Theatre in the Twentieth Century.* Ed. Robert W. Corrigan. New York: Grove Press, 1963.

TURNER, VICTOR. *Dramas, Field and Metaphors: Symbolic Action in Human Society.* Ithaca, N.Y.: Cornell University Press, 1974.

_____ . *From Ritual to Theatre, The Human Seriousness of Play.* New York: Performing Arts Journal Publications, 1982.

WANDOR, MICHELENE. *Carry on, Understudies: Theatre and Sexual Politics.* London: Routledge & Kegan Paul, 1986.

WILES, TIMOTHY J. *The Theater Event: Modern Theories of Performance.* Chicago, Ill.: University of Chicago Press, 1980.

WILLETT, JOHN, ed. and trans. *Brecht on Theatre: The Development of an Aesthetic.* New York: New Directions, 1964.

———. *The Theatre of Bertolt Brecht: A Study of Eight Aspects.* New York: New Directions, 1964.

*Women in American Theatre.* Eds. Helen Krich Chinory and Linda Walsh Jenkins. Second Ed. New York: Theatre Communications Group, 1990.

WORTHEN, W. B. *Modern Drama and the Rhetoric of Theater.* Berkeley: University of California Press, 1992.

WRIGHT, ELIZABETH. *Postmodern Brecht: A Re-Presentation.* London: Routledge, 1989.

# INDEX

**CREDITS** (*continued*)

*Oedipus the King* by Sophocles from *The Complete Greek Tragedies* (pp. 10–76). David Grene, Translator. Chicago: University of Chicago Press, 1954. Copyright © 1954 by the University of Chicago. Reprinted with permission.

*The Colored Museum,* copyright © 1985, 1987 by George C. Wolfe. Reprinted by permission of International Creative Management, Inc.

*Fen* by Caryl Churchill. Reprinted by permission of Casarotto Ramsay, Ltd.

*The Little Foxes* by Lillian Hellman. Copyright 1939 and renewed 1967 by Lillian Hellman. Reprinted by permission of Random House, Inc.

Play and footnotes from *The Tragedy of Hamlet* by William Shakespeare, edited by Edward Hubler. Copyright © 1963 by Edward Hubler. Copyright © 1963, 1987 by Sylvan Barnet. Reprinted by arrangement with NAL Penguin, Inc., New York, New York.

*The Glass Menagerie* by Tennessee Williams. Copyright © 1945 by Tennessee Williams and Edwina D. Williams and renewed 1973 by Tennessee Williams. Reprinted by permission of Random House, Inc.

*The Cherry Orchard* (pp. 331–398) from *Plays* by Anton Chekhov, translated by Elisaveta Fen, (Penguin Classics, 1954), copyright © Elisaveta Fen, 1951, 1954. Reprinted by permission of Penguin Books, Ltd.

*On The Verge or The Geography of Yearning* by Eric Overmyer. Copyright © 1985 by Eric Overmyer. Reprinted by permission of William Morris Agency, Inc. on behalf of the Author. First produced Off-Broadway in New York City by The Acting Company in 1987.

*Hedda Gabler* by Henrik Ibsen, translated by Michael Meyer. Reprinted by permission of Harold Ober Associates Incorporated. Copyright 1961, 1989 by Michael Meyer.

*Fences* by August Wilson. Copyright © 1986 by August Wilson. Reprinted by arrangement with NAL Penguin, Inc., New York, New York.

*Galileo* by Bertolt Brecht, translated by Charles Laughton from *The Modern Repertoire,* Series Two (pp. 425–76), edited by Eric Bentley, © 1952. Reprinted by permission of Indiana University Press.

*Footfalls* by Samuel Beckett. Copyright © 1974, 1975, 1976 by Samuel Beckett. Reprinted by permission of Grove Press, Inc.

*The Conduct of Life* by Maria Irene Fornes, from *Maria Irene Fornes: Plays.* PAJ Publications, New York, 1986. Copyright © 1986. Reprinted by permission of The Johns Hopkins University Press.

*Broken Eggs* © 1984 by Eduardo Machado.

*Hamletmachine* by Heiner Müller, from *Hamletmachine and Other Texts for the Stage,* (pp. 53–58), translated by Carl Weber. © Verlag der Autoren, D-Frankfurt am Main, representing Henschelverlag, Berlin/Germany. English translation copyright © 1984 by Carl Weber. Reprinted by permission of The Johns Hopkins University Press.

**Text Credits**

**p. 4:** Excerpt from *Pentimento: A Book of Portraits* (pp. 151–152) by Lillian Hellman. Copyright © 1973, by Lillian Hellman. Reprinted by permission of Little, Brown and Co. **p. 4:** Excerpt from *The Field of Drama: How the Signs of Drama Create Meaning on Stage and Screen* (p. 24) by Martin Esslin (London: Methuen, 1987) reprinted with the permission of Routledge, Inc. **p. 6:** From Kott, Jan, *The Theatre of Essence and Other Essays* (Evanston, IL: Northwestern University Press, 1984), p. 211. Used with permission. **p. 56:** From *Writing in Restaurants* by David Mamet. Copyright © 1986 by David Mamet. Used by permission of Viking Penguin, a division of Penguin Books USA Inc. **p. 181:** Excerpt from "New Form in the Theatre" in *Reflections: Essays on Modern Theatre* by Martin Esslin (Garden City, NY: Doubleday & Co., 1969), pp. 3–10. Reprinted by permission of Curtis Brown, Ltd. Copyright © 1968 by Martin Esslin. **p. 183:** Excerpt from an interview with Caryl Churchill, entitled "The Common Imagination and the Individual Voice," by Geraldine Cousin in *New Theatre Quarterly,* 4 (February 1988), page 6. Reprinted by permission. **p. 148:** Excerpt from *Three Boulevard Farces by Georges Feydeau,* translated and introduction by John Mortimer, copyright © 1985. Reprinted by permission of the Peters Fraser & Dunlop Group Ltd. **pp. 151, 153:** Excerpt from the article "A Jam Session With George C. Wolfe" by Janice Simpson in *TheatreWeek* (October 26, 1992). Copyright © 1992 *TheatreWeek.* **p. 208:** Excerpt from an audio cassette program "An Interview with Lillian Hellman" available from Jeffrey Norton Publishers, Guilford, Connecticut. Reproduced with permission. **p. 260:** Excerpt from *Brecht on Theatre: Development of an Aesthetic,* edited and translated by John Willett. Copyright © 1964 by John Willett. Reprinted by permission of Farrar, Straus, and Giroux, Inc. **p. 260:** Excerpt from *Feeling and Form: A Theory of Art Developed from Philosophy in a New Key* by Susanne K. Langer. Copyright 1953 Charles Scribner's Sons; copyright renewed © 1981 Susanne K. Langer. Reprinted with permission of Macmillan Publishing Company. **p. 338:** Excerpt from "A Playwright Named Tennessee" by R.C. Lewis, *The New York Times,* Dec. 7, 1947 (magazine). Copyright © 1947 by The New York Times Company. Reprinted with permission. **p. 342:** Excerpt